Parallel
and Distributed
Computation

Parallel and Distributed Computation

Numerical Methods

Dimitri P. Bertsekas
Massachusetts Institute of Technology

John N. Tsitsiklis
Massachusetts Institute of Technology

 PRENTICE HALL, *Englewood Cliffs, New Jersey 07632*

Library of Congress Cataloging-in-Publication Data

BERTSEKAS, DIMITRI P.
      Parallel and distributed computation: numerical methods.

      Bibliography: p.
      Includes index.
      1. Parallel processing (Electronic computers)
I. Tsitsiklis, John N.   II. Title.
QA76.5.B457   1989   004'.35   88-9874
ISBN   0-13-648700-9

Editorial/production supervision and
        interior design: John Fleming/Gertrude Szyferblatt
Cover design: Diane Saxe
Manufacturing buyer: Mary Noonan

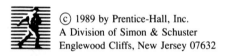
Printed in the United States of America
10   9   8   7   6   5   4   3   2   1

ISBN 0-13-648700-9

Prentice-Hall International (UK) Limited, *London*
Prentice-Hall of Australia Pty. Limited, *Sydney*
Prentice-Hall Canada, Inc., *Toronto*
Prentice-Hall Hispanoamericana, S.A., *Mexico*
Prentice-Hall of India Private Limited, *New Delhi*
Prentice-Hall of Japan, Inc., *Tokyo*
Simon & Schuster Asia Pte. Ltd., *Singapore*
Editora Prentice-Hall do Brasil, Ltda., *Rio de Janeiro*

To Joanna and Daphne

Contents

"If you were to boil your book down to a few words, what would be its message?"

Preface

Parallel and distributed computing systems offer the promise of a quantum leap in the computing power that can be brought to bear on many important problems. Whether and to what extent this promise can be fulfilled is still a matter of speculation, but several years of practical experience with both parallel computers and distributed data communication networks have brought about an understanding of the potential and limitations of parallel and distributed computation. The purpose of this book is to promote this understanding by focusing on algorithms that are naturally suited for large scale parallelization and that represent the best hope for solving problems which are much larger than those that can be solved at present.

Work on parallel and distributed computation spans several broad areas, such as the design of parallel machines, parallel programming languages, parallel algorithm development and analysis, and applications related issues. The focus of this book is on algorithms, and, even within this area, we restrict our attention primarily to numerical algorithms for solving systems of equations or optimization problems. Our choice of material is motivated by large problems for which it is essential to harness the power of massive parallelism, while keeping the communication overhead and delays within tolerable limits. Accordingly, we emphasize algorithms that admit a high degree of parallelization such as relaxation methods of the Jacobi and Gauss-Seidel type, and we address extensively issues of communication and synchronization. In particular, we discuss algorithms for interprocessor communication and we provide a comprehensive convergence analysis of asynchronous iterative methods.

The design of parallel algorithms can be pursued at several levels, and this explains to some extent the diversity of the literature on the subject. For example:

(a) One approach is to parallelize an existing serial algorithm, perhaps after modifications, or to develop a new and easier to parallelize algorithm, without being too specific about the implementation in particular types of machines. Here one might be concerned with the algorithm's convergence and rate of convergence (in either a synchronous or an asynchronous computing environment), and with the algorithm's potential for substantial speedup over its serial counterpart.

(b) A second approach is to focus on the details of implementation on a particular type of machine. The issues here are algorithmic correctness, as well as time and communication complexity of the implementation.

(c) In still another approach, the choice of the algorithm and the parallel machine are interdependent to the point where the design of one has a strong influence on the design of the other. A typical example is when a VLSI chip is designed to execute efficiently a special type of parallel algorithm.

We have mostly followed the first approach, concentrating on algorithmic analysis at a rather high level of abstraction. Our choice of algorithms, however, is such that in most cases, the methods of parallel implementation are either evident and straightforward, or else are covered by our broad discussion of parallel computation given in Chapter 1. We have not dealt with implementations in specific machines because types of machines are rapidly changing. Nonetheless, at several points, we have made reference to computations in regular architectures, such as mesh and hypercube, which are widely used. We carry out the analysis of various algorithms in considerable depth, guided by the belief that a thorough understanding of an algorithm is typically essential for its application to a challenging problem.

The book was developed through a course that we taught to graduate students at MIT. It is intended for use in graduate courses in engineering, computer science, operations research, and applied mathematics. We have assumed the equivalent of a first course in linear algebra and a grasp of advanced calculus and real analysis that most students are exposed to by the end of their undergraduate studies. Probabilistic notions beyond the theory of finite-state Markov chains are not needed with the exception of Section 7.8, which deals with stochastic gradient methods. We have not required any background in numerical analysis, graph algorithms, optimization, convexity, and duality, and we have consequently developed this material as needed in the main body of the text or the appendices. We note, however, that the mathematically mature reader who has some background in some of these fields is likely to benefit more from the book, and to gain deeper appreciation of the material.

The book can be used for several types of courses. One possibility is a course targeted on parallel algorithms, and intended for students who already have some knowledge of a subset of the fields of numerical analysis, graph theory, and optimization algorithms. Furthermore, such a course could have either a computer science flavor, by focusing on Chapters 1 and 8, and parts of Chapters 2, and 4 through 6, or alternatively a numerical computation flavor by focusing on Chapters 2, 3, and parts of Chapters 1 and 4 through 7. Another possibility is a general course on numerical methods with a strong bias towards parallelizable algorithms. The book lends itself for such a course because it develops economically a broad variety of self-contained basic material in considerable depth.

Chapter 1 contains an exposition of some generic issues that arise in a broad variety of parallel algorithms and are best addressed without specific reference to any particular algorithm. In particular, we discuss the scheduling of a set of processors for the parallel execution of a prescribed algorithm, some basic issues relating to interprocessor communication, and the effects of the communication penalty on the amount by which an algorithm can be speeded up. Special attention is paid to a few interesting architectures such as mesh and hypercube. We then consider issues of synchronization, and we contrast synchronous and asynchronous algorithms. In this chapter, we also introduce relaxation methods of the Gauss-Seidel and Jacobi type and some associated issues of parallelization, communication, and synchronization that are recurring themes throughout the book.

Chapter 2 deals with parallel algorithms for systems of linear equations and matrix inversion. It covers direct methods for general systems as well as systems with special structure, iterative methods, including their convergence analysis, and the conjugate gradient method.

Chapter 3 is devoted to iterative methods for nonlinear problems, such as finding fixed points of contraction mappings, unconstrained and constrained optimization, and variational inequalities. The convergence theory for such methods is developed in an economical way and emphasizes the case of Cartesian product constraint sets (in a primal and a dual setting), which lends itself naturally to parallelization and decomposition.

Chapter 4 deals with the shortest path problem and other, more general, dynamic programming problems. The dynamic programming algorithm can be viewed as a relaxation method and lends itself well for parallelization. We establish (and strengthen somewhat) the classical results for discounted and undiscounted Markovian decision problems, and we also discuss the associated parallel computation issues.

Chapter 5 is devoted to network flow problems. In the first four sections, we deal with the important class of linear problems, and we present some easily parallelizable algorithms, that are conceptually related to the Gauss-Seidel and Jacobi relaxation methods. We then discuss related algorithms for network problems with nonlinear convex cost. The methods of the first five sections can be viewed as relaxation methods applied in a space of dual (price) variables. In the last section we consider relaxation-like methods applied to nonlinear multicommodity flow problems in the primal space of flow variables.

The last three chapters deal with asynchronous algorithms in which each processor computes at its own pace, using intermediate results of other processors that are possibly outdated due to unpredictable communication delays. Among other topics, we develop asynchronous versions of all the major types of synchronous parallel algorithms that were discussed in previous chapters.

In Chapter 6, we introduce a general class of asynchronous iterative methods (called "totally asynchronous"), and we develop a general theorem for proving their convergence. This theorem is used repeatedly to establish the validity of a broad variety of asynchronous algorithms involving iteration mappings that are either monotone or contracting with respect to a weighted maximum norm. In particular, we show convergence of linear and nonlinear iterations involving weighted maximum norm contractions arising in the solution of systems of algebraic or differential equations, discounted dynamic programming, unconstrained and constrained optimization, and variational inequalities. We also discuss iterations involving monotone mappings arising in shortest path problems, undiscounted dynamic programming, and linear and nonlinear network flow problems.

In Chapter 7, we consider "partially asynchronous" algorithms in which some mild restrictions are placed on the amount of asynchronism present. We prove convergence of a variety of algorithms for fixed points of nonexpansive mappings, deterministic and stochastic optimization, Markov chains, load balancing in a computer network, and optimal routing in data networks.

Chapter 8 is similar in philosophy to Chapter 1 in that it deals with generic issues of parallel and distributed computation. It discusses the organization of an inherently asynchronous network of processors for the purpose of executing a general type of parallel algorithm. It addresses issues like termination detection, processor scheduling, methods for taking a "snapshot" of the global state of a computing system, synchronization via "rollback," and methods for maintaining communication with a center in the face of topological changes.

Many of our subjects can be covered independently of each other, thereby allowing the reader or an instructor to use material selectively to suit his/her needs. For example, the following groups of sections can be omitted without loss of continuity:

(a) Sections 2.1 to 2.3, that deal with direct methods for linear systems of equations.

(b) Sections 2.8, 4.2, 4.3, 7.3, 7.4, 7.7, and 7.8 that develop or use the theory of Markov chains.

(c) The material on decomposition methods based on duality in Section 3.4 and Subsection 3.5.7.

(d) The dynamic programming material of Sections 4.2 and 4.3.

(e) The material on linear network flow problems in Sections 5.1 to 5.4, and 6.5.

(f) Sections 5.6 and 7.6, dealing with nonlinear multicommodity network flow problems.

(g) The material on nonlinear network flow problems in Sections 5.5, 6.6, and Subsection 7.2.3.

Each major section contains several exercises that, for the most part, illustrate and supplement the theoretical developments of the text. They include algorithmic variations, convergence and complexity analysis, examples, and counterexamples. Some of the exercises are quite challenging, occasionally representing recent research. The serious reader will benefit a great deal from these exercises, which constitute one of the principal components of the text. Solutions of all the exercises are provided in a manual that will be available to instructors.

A substantial portion of our material has not been covered in other textbooks. This includes most of the last two sections of Chapter 1, much of the last two sections of Chapter 3, Sections 5.2 through 5.5, the entire Chapters 6 and 7, and most of Chapter 8. Some of the material presented was developed as the textbook was being written and has not yet been published elsewhere.

The literature on our subject is enormous, and our references are not comprehensive. We thus apologize in advance to the many authors whose work has not been cited. We have restricted ourselves to listing the sources that we have used, together with a selection of sources that contain material supplementing the text.

We are thankful to a number of individuals and institutions for their help. The inquisitive spirit of our students motivated us to think harder about many issues. We learned a great deal about distributed computation through our long association and collaboration with Bob Gallager and Pierre Humblet. We have appreciated our research collaboration with Michael Athans, David Castanon, Jon Eckstein, Eli Gafni, and Christos Papadimitriou, that produced some of the material included in the book. Tom Luo and Cuneyt Ozveren contributed research material that was incorporated in exercises. We are thankful for the helpful comments of a number of people, including Chee-Seng Chow, George Cybenko, Stratis Gallopoulos, George Hart, and Tom Richardson. Our greatest debt of gratitude to a single individual goes to Paul Tseng who worked closely with us on several of the topics presented, particularly the communication algorithms of Section 1.3, the network flow algorithms of Chapter 5, and the partially asynchronous algorithms of Section 7.2. In addition, Paul reviewed the entire manuscript, sharpened several proofs and results, and contributed much research in the form of exercises. We were fortunate to work at the Laboratory for Information and Decision Systems of M.I.T., which provided us with a stimulating research environment. Funding for our research was provided by the Army Research Office through the Center for Intelligent Control Systems, Bellcore Inc., the National Science Foundation, and the Office of Naval Research. The staff of Prentice Hall worked with efficiency and professionalism to produce the book under stringent time constraints.

1

Introduction

As we embark on the study of parallel and distributed numerical methods it is useful to reflect on their differences from their serial counterparts. There are several issues related to parallelization that do not arise in a serial context. A first issue is *task allocation*, that is, the breakdown of the total workload in smaller tasks assigned to different processors, and the proper sequencing of the tasks when some of them are interdependent and cannot be executed simultaneously. A second issue is the *communication* of interim computation results between the processors; our objective here is to carry out the communication efficiently, and to estimate its impact on performance. A third issue is the *synchronization* of the computations of different processors. In some methods, called *synchronous*, processors must wait at predetermined points for the completion of certain computations or for the arrival of certain data, and the mechanism used to enforce such synchronization may have an important effect on performance. In other methods, called *asynchronous*, there is no requirement for waiting at predetermined points, and the corresponding implications for the methods' validity must be assessed. Other issues relate to the development of appropriate performance measures for parallel methods, and the effects of the system's architecture on these performance measures.

Issues such as the above are important in a variety of contexts and are, therefore, most economically studied without reference to a specific numerical method. We address some of them in this introductory chapter, and we develop some results and methodological approaches that will be used throughout the book. Our analysis is not always fully rigorous because we do not always adhere to formal models of distributed computation. This helps us develop the main ideas in a more accessible and intuitive manner than it would be possible otherwise. At the same time our analysis is sufficiently detailed to provide the basis for more rigorous proofs where needed, and to convince most readers of the essential correctness of our results.

Section 1.1 contains a brief overview of some application domains and of the presently existing parallel computing systems. In Section 1.2, we consider a simple model of synchronous parallel computation, in which communication issues are ignored, and discuss the concepts of time complexity, speedup, and efficiency. We also discuss issues arising in the parallelization of iterative methods. In Section 1.3, we consider communication issues in parallel and distributed systems. Following a brief discussion of data link control and routing, we formulate some basic communication problems that arise frequently in the algorithms of subsequent chapters, and we provide optimal or nearly optimal algorithms for these problems. At the same time, we discuss the properties of some of the more popular processor interconnection networks. In Section 1.4, we consider methods for algorithm synchronization. We also introduce asynchronous algorithms, compare them informally with their synchronous counterparts, and provide a glimpse of some of their interesting convergence properties that will be the focal point of Chapters 6 and 7.

1.1 PARALLEL AND DISTRIBUTED ARCHITECTURES

Parallel and distributed computation is currently an area of intense research activity, motivated by a variety of factors. There has always been a need for the solution of very large computational problems, but it is only recently that technological advances have raised the possibility of massively parallel computation and have made the solution of such problems possible. Furthermore, the availability of powerful parallel computers is generating interest in new types of problems that were not addressed in the past. Accordingly, the development of parallel and distributed algorithms is guided by this interplay between old and new computational needs on the one hand, and technological progress on the other. To appreciate this effect, we briefly discuss some application areas and the types of computing systems that new technologies have made possible.

1.1.1 The Need for Parallel and Distributed Computation

We restrict attention to numerical computation, since this is the major application considered in this book. Symbolic computation and artificial intelligence applications have also played an important role in the development of the subject, but are outside our scope.

The original needs for fast computation have been in a number of contexts involving partial differential equations (PDEs), such as computational fluid dynamics and weather prediction, as well as in image processing, etc. In these applications, there is a large number of numerical computations to be performed. The desire to solve more and more complex problems has always been running ahead of the capabilities of the time, and has provided a driving force for the development of faster, and possibly parallel, computing machines. The above mentioned types of problems can be easily decomposed along a spatial dimension, and have therefore been prime candidates for parallelization, with a different computational unit (processor) assigned the task of manipulating the variables associated with a small region in space. Furthermore, in such problems, interactions between variables are local in nature, thus leading to the design of parallel computers consisting of a number of processors with nearest neighbor connections.

More recently, there has been increased interest in other types of large scale computation. Some examples are the analysis, simulation, and optimization of large scale interconnected systems, queueing systems being a noteworthy representative. Other examples relate to the solution of general systems of equations, mathematical programming, and optimization problems. A common property of such problems, as they arise in practice, is that they can be decomposed, but the subtasks obtained from such a decomposition tend to be fewer and more complex than those obtained in the context of partial differential equations. In particular, the regular and repetitive structure of PDEs is lost. Accordingly, one is led to use fewer and more powerful processors, coordinated through a more complex control mechanism.

In both of the above classes of applications, the main concerns are cost and speed: the hardware should not be prohibitively expensive, and the computation should terminate within an amount of time that is acceptable for the particular application.

A third area of application of parallel, or rather distributed, computation is in information acquisition, information extraction, and control, within geographically distributed systems. An example is a sensor network in which a set of geographically distributed sensors obtain information on the state of the environment and process it cooperatively. Another example is provided by data communication networks in which certain functions of the network (such as correct and timely routing of the messages traveling in the network) have to be controlled in a distributed manner, through the cooperation of the computers residing at the nodes of the network. In this context of distributed computation, the predominant issues are somewhat different from those discussed earlier. Besides cost and speed, there is a more fundamental concern: the distributed system should be able to operate correctly in the presence of limited, sometimes unreliable, communication capabilities, and often in the absence of a central control mechanism.

1.1.2 Parallel Computing Systems and their Classification

We discuss here how technology has responded to the computational needs just mentioned, and we provide a classification of existing systems. An important distinction is between *parallel* and *distributed* computing systems. Roughly speaking, parallel computing systems consist of several processors that are located within a small distance of each other. Their main purpose is to execute jointly a computational task and they have been designed with such a purpose in mind; communication between processors is reliable and predictable. Distributed computing systems are different in a number of

ways. Processors may be far apart, and interprocessor communication is more prob-
lematic. Communication delays may be unpredictable, and the communication links
themselves may be unreliable. Furthermore, the topology of a distributed system may
undergo changes while the system is operating, due to failures or repairs of communication links, as well as due to addition or removal of processors. Distributed computing
systems are usually loosely coupled; there is very little, if any, central coordination and
control. Each processor may be engaged in its own private activities while at the same
time cooperating with other processors in the context of some computational task. Often,
the cooperative computation in a distributed computing system is not the raison d'être
of the system; for example, a data network exists in order to service some data communication needs, and the distributed computation taking place in the network is only
a side activity supporting the main activity. For this reason, while the architecture of a
parallel system is typically under the control of a system's designer, the structure of some
distributed systems is dictated by exogenous considerations. Our subsequent discussion
in this section is geared toward parallel computing systems. A number of issues more
relevant to distributed systems will be touched upon in Sections 1.3 and 1.4. Still, there
is no clear dividing line between parallel and distributed systems: several algorithmic
issues are similar and we will often use the two terms interchangeably.

Traditional serial computers are characterized by the presence of a single locus
of control that determines the next instruction to be executed. The data to be operated
upon, during the execution of each instruction, are fetched from a global memory, one at
time. Thus, only one instruction is executed at a time, while the speed of memory access
and the speed of input–output devices can slow down the computation. Several methods
have been developed for alleviating these bottlenecks, cache memories and pipelining,
for example. The first supercomputers were developed on the basis of such advanced
computer architecture designs. By means of intelligent memory organization and use of
pipelining, supercomputers have been able to execute vector operations (e.g., addition of
two vectors) in time comparable to the time required for scalar operations (e.g., addition
of two numbers). Thus, as far as the user is concerned, supercomputers behave as if the
components of a vector are operated upon simultaneously. Nevertheless, there seem to
be some fundamental limitations to the speed of fast serial computers, notwithstanding
the fact that they are very costly.

Parallel computers have deviated from the above described model in a variety of
ways. The first such computers consisted of a one– or two–dimensional array of processors, with nearest neighbor interconnections. Such an interconnection pattern is very natural for spatially decomposable problems like PDEs and image processing. Furthermore,
there was a host computer overseeing and controlling the progress of the computation
by passing to the processors the instruction to be executed next.

Processor arrays are well suited for the applications for which they are designed,
but not necessarily for general purpose computation. Thus, more coarse–grained parallel
computers have been introduced, in which each processor has considerably more control
of its own computations, together with more computational power. Accordingly, the processors in such parallel computers are less tightly coupled. Such systems are sometimes
called *multiprocessors*, and they are designed so that they can flexibly support general
purpose computation.

Another line of development, resting on recent advances in very large scale integration (VLSI) technology, has led to closely coupled parallel computing systems (all computational elements are often placed on a single chip), designed for a special purpose, such as solving systems of linear equations with special structure, or performing fast Fourier transforms. Here the movement of data is very regular and the traditional notion of a stored program is not quite applicable; in effect, much of the program is encoded in the system hardware. *Systolic arrays* provide a prime example of such computing systems.

Still, the above discussion is too simple to accurately describe the wealth of parallel computers available today. For example, there are systems consisting of a large number of processors connected in some regular fashion, reminiscent of processor arrays, which are also capable of general purpose computation.

There are several parameters that can be used to describe or classify a parallel computer and we refer to these briefly.

(a) *Type and number of processors.* There are parallel computing systems with thousands of processors. Such systems are called *massively parallel*, and hold the greatest promise for significantly extending the range of practically solvable computational problems. A diametrically opposite option is *coarse–grained parallelism*, in which there is a small number of processors, say of the order of 10. In this case, each processor is usually fairly powerful, and the processors are loosely coupled, so that each processor may be performing a different type of task at any given time.

(b) *Presence or absence of a global control mechanism.* Parallel computers almost always have some central locus of control, but the question is one of degree: At what level of detail is the operation of the processors controlled? At one extreme, the global control mechanism is only used to load a program and the data to the processors, and each processor is allowed to work on its own thereafter. At the other extreme, the control mechanism is used to instruct each processor what to do at each step, as in the processor arrays mentioned earlier. Intermediate situations are also conceivable. A related popular classification along these lines distinguishes between SIMD (*Single Instruction Multiple Data*) and MIMD (*Multiple Instruction Multiple Data*) parallel computers, referring to the ability of different processors to execute different instructions at any given point in time.

(c) *Synchronous vs. asynchronous operation.* The distinction here refers to the presence or absence of a common global clock used to synchronize the operation of the different processors. Such synchronization is present in SIMD machines, by definition. Synchronous operation has some desirable properties: the behavior of the processors is much easier to control and algorithm design is considerably simplified. On the other hand, it may require some undesirable overhead and, in some contexts, synchronization may be just impossible. For example, it is quite hard to synchronize a data communication network and, even if this were feasible, it is questionable whether the associated overhead can be justified. Some related issues are discussed in Section 1.4. Finally, it should be noted that a parallel computing system operating asynchronously can simulate a synchronous system (see Section 1.4).

(d) *Processor interconnections.* A significant aspect of parallel computers is the mechanism by which processors exchange information. Generally speaking, there are two extreme alternatives known as *shared memory* and *message–passing* architectures, and a variety of hybrid designs lying in between. The first alternative uses a global shared memory that can be accessed by all processors. A processor can communicate to another by writing into the global memory, and then having the second processor read that same location in the memory. This solves the interprocessor communication problem, but introduces the problem of simultaneous accessing of different locations of the memory by several processors. A common approach for handling memory accesses is based on *switching systems,* such as the one depicted in Fig. 1.1.1. Naturally, the complexity of such switching systems has to increase with the number of processors; this is reflected in longer memory access times. On the other hand, under such an architecture, algorithm design is simplified, because, on a high level, the system behaves as if all processors were directly connected to each other.

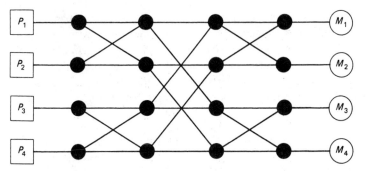

Figure 1.1.1   A switching system connecting processors P_i to memory elements M_i. Here the intermediate nodes correspond to switches. When a message reaches a switch, it can continue on either of the two outgoing links, depending on the destination and the routing algorithm being used. Notice that in this example, there are two alternative paths from each processor to each memory element, used to reduce the probability that two processors simultaneously attempt to utilize the same link. Such redundancy improves reliability, and provides some flexibility which reduces congestion.

In the second major approach, there is no shared memory, but rather each processor has its own *local memory.* (Of course, each processor may have its own local memory even if there is a shared memory.) Processors communicate through an *interconnection network* consisting of direct communication links joining certain pairs of processors, as shown in Fig. 1.1.2. Which processors are connected together is an important design choice. It would be best if all processors were directly connected to each other, but this is often not feasible: either there is an excessive number of links, which leads to increased cost, or the processors communicate through a shared bus, which leads to excessive delays when the number of processors is very large, due to the necessary bus contention.

There are also several possibilities for *hybrid* designs that combine certain features from the different approaches just described. Some examples are shown in Fig. 1.1.3, although several more combinations are possible.

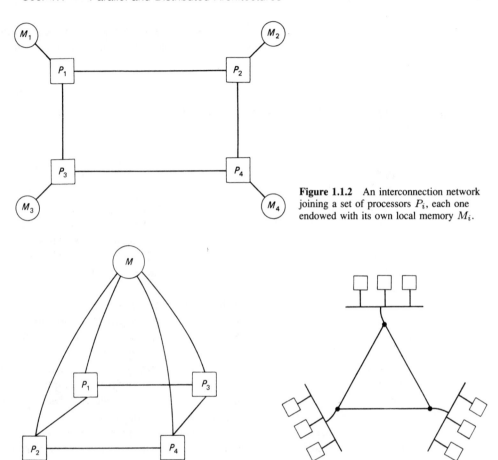

Figure 1.1.2 An interconnection network joining a set of processors P_i, each one endowed with its own local memory M_i.

(a)   (b)

Figure 1.1.3 Examples of hybrid designs: (a) coexistence of a shared memory and a point–to–point network; and (b) clusters of processors: a high speed bus serves for intracluster communication, and an interconnection network is used for intercluster communication.

When distant processors communicate through an interconnection network, there is usually a choice of several paths that can be used. Paths should be chosen so as to avoid underutilization of some at the expense of congestion of others. Furthermore, path selection has to be done locally, by processors that have only partial information on the congestion levels at distant parts of the network. How to do this best is the subject of the distributed routing problem. Routing in interconnection networks is briefly discussed in Subsection 1.3.3, and a particular formulation of the routing problem, relevant to data communication networks, is studied in Chapters 5 and 7.

The structure (topology) of interconnection networks is very important in both parallel and distributed computing systems, but there is an important difference. In parallel computers, the interconnection network is under the control of the designer and for this reason it is usually designed to be very regular, whereas in some distributed systems, like data communication networks, the topology of the network is predetermined and is usually irregular.

1.2 MODELS, COMPLEXITY MEASURES, AND SOME SIMPLE ALGORITHMS

1.2.1 Models

There is a variety of models of parallel and distributed computation, incorporating different assumptions on the computing power of each individual processor and on the interprocessor information transfer mechanism. For the applications considered in this book, formal models of parallel computation are not essential and we refer the reader to the literature for more detailed expositions (see the notes and sources at the end of the chapter).

Loosely stated, we shall assume that each processor is capable of executing certain basic instructions (such as the basic arithmetic operations, comparisons, branching instructions of the "if ... then" type, etc.), and that there is a mechanism through which processors may exchange information. Concerning the processors' computational power, it will be often assumed that each basic instruction requires one time unit. Concerning information exchange, we shall sometimes make the simplifying assumption that information transfers are instantaneous and cost–free. On other occasions, we shall assume that the processors communicate through a shared memory or by exchanging messages through an interconnection network. In the latter case, more specific assumptions on the delay incurred by messages as they travel through the network will be introduced as needed.

We postpone the discussion of communication issues for Section 1.3. We now describe in some detail a simple model that will be used to illustrate certain key aspects of parallel computation. This model is actually adequate for most of the synchronous algorithms considered in this book, as long as communication issues are ignored.

Representation of Parallel Algorithms by Directed Acyclic Graphs

A *directed acyclic graph* (*DAG*) is a directed graph that has no positive cycles, that is, no cycles consisting exclusively of forward arcs (see Appendix B). A DAG can be used to represent a parallel algorithm, as we proceed to show.

Let $G = (N, A)$ be a DAG, where $N = \{1, \ldots, |N|\}$ is the set of nodes, and A is the set of directed arcs. Each node represents an operation performed by an algorithm, and the arcs are used to represent data dependencies. In particular, an arc $(i, j) \in A$ indicates that the operation corresponding to node j uses the results of the operation corresponding to node i. An operation could be elementary (e.g., an arithmetic or a binary Boolean operation, as shown in Fig. 1.2.1), or it could be a high–level operation like the execution of a subroutine.

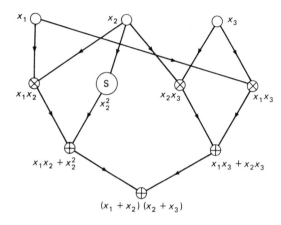

Figure 1.2.1 Representation of an algorithm for evaluating the arithmetic expression $(x_1 + x_2)(x_2 + x_3)$ by means of a DAG. The label at each node indicates the operation corresponding to that node. In particular, the label S stands for squaring.

We introduce some graph–theoretic terminology. We say that node $i \in N$ is a *predecessor* of node $j \in N$ if $(i, j) \in A$. The *in–degree* of node $i \in N$ is the number of predecessors of that node. The *out–degree* of node $i \in N$ is the number of nodes for which i is a predecessor. Nodes with in–degree zero are called *input* nodes and nodes with out–degree zero are called *output* nodes. We use N_0 to denote the set of nodes that are not input nodes. A *positive path* is a sequence $i_0, \ldots, i_K$ of nodes such that $(i_k, i_{k+1}) \in A$ for $k = 0, \ldots, K - 1$. The number K is called the *length* of the path. The *depth* of a DAG is defined as the largest length of the positive paths, and is denoted by D. It is seen that D is finite, as a consequence of acyclicity, and that a longest positive path must start at an input node and end at an output node. We assume throughout that G has at least one arc and therefore $D \geq 1$.

Let us denote by x_i the result of the operation corresponding to the ith node in the DAG. Then, the DAG can be viewed as a representation of functional dependencies of the form

$$x_i = f_i\Big(\{x_j \mid j \text{ is a predecessor of } i\}\Big).$$

Here f_i is a function describing the operation corresponding to the ith node. If i is an input node, then x_i does not depend on other variables and is viewed as an external input variable. Thus, the operation corresponding to an input node i essentially amounts to reading the value of the input variable x_i, and we will assume that this takes negligible time. For any node i that is not an input node (i.e., $i \in N_0$), we shall assume that the corresponding operation (that is, the evaluation of the function f_i) takes one time unit. This assumption is reasonable if each node represents an arithmetic operation. However, in more complicated numerical algorithms, the execution times corresponding to different nodes could be widely different. In that case, the assumption of unit time per operation may be considerably violated, with an attendant complication of the scheduling issues discussed below.

A DAG is only a partial representation of an algorithm. It specifies what operations are to be performed, on what operands, and imposes certain precedence constraints on the order that these operations are to be performed. To determine completely a parallel algorithm we have to specify which processor performs what operation and at what time. Let us assume that we have available a pool of p processors and that each processor is capable of performing any one of the desired operations. For any node i that is not an input node (i.e., $i \in N_0$), let P_i be the processor assigned the responsibility of performing the corresponding operation. Also, for $i \in N_0$, we let t_i be a positive integer variable specifying the time that the operation corresponding to node i is completed. No processors are assigned to input nodes, and we use the convention $t_i = 0$ for every input node i. There are two constraints that have to be imposed:

(a) A processor can perform at most one operation at a time. Thus, if $i \in N_0$, $j \in N_0$, $i \neq j$, and $t_i = t_j$, then $P_i \neq P_j$.

(b) If $(i, j) \in A$, then $t_j \geq t_i + 1$. This requirement reflects the fact that the operation corresponding to node j can only start after the operation corresponding to node i has been completed.

Once P_i and t_i have been fixed, subject to the above constraints, we say that the DAG has been *scheduled* for parallel execution, and we call the set $\{(i, P_i, t_i) \mid i \in N_0\}$ a *schedule*.

The above described setup could correspond to a variety of actual implementations. For example, processor P_i could store the result x_i of its operation in a shared memory from where it can be retrieved by other processors. Alternatively, in a message–passing implementation, processor P_i sends a message with the value of x_i to any processor P_j that needs this value [that is, $(i, j) \in A$]. In practice, a memory access or the transmission of a message may require some time and this has been neglected in our earlier discussion. For example, if a transmission of a message requires exactly τ time units, and if $(i, j) \in A$, then the constraint $t_j \geq t_i + 1$ should be modified to

$$t_j \geq t_i + 1, \qquad \text{if } P_i = P_j,$$

and

$$t_j \geq t_i + \tau + 1, \qquad \text{if } P_i \neq P_j.$$

In fact, even this requirement is rather crude, because the message delay τ may depend on the location of processors P_i and P_j in an interconnection network. In any case, memory access times and message delays are assumed to be negligible in this section and will be addressed in detail in Section 1.3.

1.2.2 Complexity Measures

We first define some notation that is used throughout the text. Let A be some subset of $\Re$ and let $f : A \mapsto \Re$ and $g : A \mapsto \Re$ be some functions. The notation $f(x) = O(g(x))$ [respectively, $f(x) = \Omega(g(x))$] means that there exists some positive constant

c and some x_0 such that for every $x \in A$ satisfying $x \geq x_0$, we have $|f(x)| \leq cg(x)$ [respectively, $f(x) \geq cg(x)$]. The notation $f(x) = \Theta\big(g(x)\big)$ means that both $f(x) = O\big(g(x)\big)$ and $f(x) = \Omega\big(g(x)\big)$ are true. We also use $\log x$ to denote the logarithm of x with base 2. Thus, $x = 2^{\log x}$ for every nonnegative real number x.

Complexity measures are intended to quantify the amount of computational resources utilized by a parallel algorithm. Some interesting complexity measures are the following:

(a) The number of processors

(b) The time until the algorithm terminates (time complexity)

(c) The number of messages transmitted in the course of the algorithm (communication complexity)

Complexity measures are often expressed as functions of the *size* of the problem being solved, informally defined as the number of inputs to the computation. (For example, in the problem of adding n integers, n is a natural measure of problem size.) If the problem size is held constant, it is still possible that the resources used depend on the actual values of the input variables. The usual approach in this case is to count the amount of resources required in the worst case over all possible choices of data corresponding to a given problem size.

There is a further subtlety in the definition of time complexity. It is conceivable that an algorithm has terminated, meaning that the desired outputs of the computation are available at some processors, but no individual processor is aware of this fact. In such a case, it is natural to count the additional time required for the processors to become aware of termination.

Time Complexity of Algorithms Specified by a DAG

In the case of parallel algorithms specified by a DAG, time complexity is easy to define precisely, as we proceed to show. Let $G = (N, A)$ be a DAG representing some parallel algorithm. Let $\{(i, P_i, t_i) \mid i \in N_0\}$ be a schedule for this DAG that uses p processors. The time spent by such a schedule is equal to $\max_{i \in N} t_i$. We define T_p as the minimum of $\max_{i \in N} t_i$, where the minimum is taken over all possible schedules that use p processors. We view T_p as the time complexity of the algorithm described by G. Note that T_p is a function of the number p of available processors.

We define

$$T_\infty = \min_{p \geq 1} T_p.$$

It is seen that T_p is a nonincreasing function of p, and is bounded below by 0. Since T_p is integer valued, there exists a minimal integer p^* such that $T_p = T_\infty$ for all $p \geq p^*$. We view T_∞ as the time complexity of the algorithm specified by G when a sufficiently large number of processors (at least p^*) is available.

We continue with a few observations. The quantity T_1 is the time needed for a serial execution of the algorithm under consideration. Evidently, T_1 is equal to the number of nodes in the DAG that are not input nodes. Another important fact is that T_∞ is equal to the depth of the DAG, which we proceed to prove.

Let $i_0, \ldots, i_K$ be a longest positive path in G. Then, node i_0 is an input node and K is equal to the depth D, by the definition of D. For any schedule, we have $t_{i_0} = 0$ and $t_{i_{k+1}} \geq t_{i_k} + 1$ (for $k = 0, \ldots, K - 1$), and it follows that $t_{i_K} \geq K = D$. We conclude that $T_\infty \geq D$. For the reverse inequality, we assign a different processor P_i to each node i and we let t_i be the number of arcs in a longest positive path from an input node to node i. (We set $t_i = 0$ if i is itself an input node.) If $(i, j) \in A$ then $t_j \geq t_i + 1$. This is because we can take a longest positive path from an input node to node i and append arc (i, j) to obtain a path to node j. It follows that we have a valid schedule and the corresponding time is $\max_i t_i = D$. Therefore, $T_\infty \leq D$, which proves that $T_\infty = D$.

For an arbitrary value of p, we have $T_1 \geq T_p \geq T_\infty$. The exact value of T_p is not easy to determine, in general. In fact the problem of computing T_p, given a particular DAG and a value of p, is a difficult combinatorial problem. This is not necessarily a concern because, as will be seen, there are some simple useful bounds for T_p.

Properties of T_p

Let us fix a DAG G. Our first result provides a fundamental limitation on the speed of a parallel algorithm.

Proposition 2.1. Suppose that for some output node i, there exists a positive path from every input node to i. Furthermore, suppose that the in–degree of each node is at most 2. Then,

$$T_\infty \geq \log n,$$

where n is the number of input nodes.

Proof. We say that a node j in the DAG depends on k inputs if there exist k input nodes and a positive path from each one of them to node j. (For completeness, we also say that an input node j depends on one input.) We prove, by induction on k, that $t_j \geq \log k$ for every node j depending on k inputs and for every schedule. The claim is clearly true if $k = 1$. Assume that the claim is true for every $k \leq k_0$ and consider a node j that depends on $k_0 + 1$ inputs. Since j can have at most two predecessors, it has a predecessor ℓ that depends on at least $\lceil (k_0 + 1)/2 \rceil$ inputs. Then, using the induction hypothesis,

$$t_j \geq t_\ell + 1 \geq \log \left\lceil \frac{k_0 + 1}{2} \right\rceil + 1 \geq \log(k_0 + 1),$$

and the induction is complete.   **Q.E.D.**

The next result expresses the fact that if the number of processors is reduced by a certain factor, then the execution time is increased by at most that factor.

Proposition 2.2.   If c is a positive integer and $q = cp$ then $T_p \leq cT_q$.

Proof. Consider a schedule which takes time T_q using q processors. At each stage, at most q operations are performed, and can be carried out in at most $q/p = c$ time units using p processors. We have thus obtained a schedule with p processors which takes at most cT_q time units.   **Q.E.D.**

Another useful result is the following:

Proposition 2.3.   For every p, we have

$$T_p < T_\infty + \frac{T_1}{p}.$$

Proof. Consider a schedule S for which the execution time is equal to T_∞ and, for every positive integer τ, let n_τ be the number of nodes i for which $t_i = \tau$. We define a new schedule S' that uses only p processors. The schedule S' proceeds in phases. At the τth phase, we perform the operations that were scheduled for time τ under the original schedule S. Given that there are p processors available, the τth phase can be completed in $\lceil n_\tau/p \rceil$ time units. Since T_p cannot be larger than the time required by schedule S', we obtain

$$T_p \leq \sum_{\tau=1}^{T_\infty} \left\lceil \frac{n_\tau}{p} \right\rceil < \sum_{\tau=1}^{T_\infty} \left(\frac{n_\tau}{p} + 1 \right) = \frac{T_1}{p} + T_\infty,$$

where we have used the fact that $\sum_{\tau=1}^{T_\infty} n_\tau$ is equal to T_1, the total number of nodes in the DAG that are not input nodes.   **Q.E.D.**

The following result is a corollary of Prop. 2.3.

Proposition 2.4.   (a) If $p \geq T_1/T_\infty$, then $T_p < 2T_\infty$. More generally, if $p = \Omega(T_1/T_\infty)$, then $T_p = O(T_\infty)$.
(b) If $p \leq T_1/T_\infty$, then

$$\frac{T_1}{p} \leq T_p < 2\frac{T_1}{p}.$$

More generally, if $p = O(T_1/T_\infty)$, then $T_p = \Theta(T_1/p)$.

Proof. (a) If $p \geq T_1/T_\infty$ [respectively, $p = \Omega(T_1/T_\infty)$], then $T_1/p \leq T_\infty$ [respectively, $T_1/p = O(T_\infty)$], and the result follows from Prop. 2.3.
(b) If $p \leq T_1/T_\infty$ [respectively, $p = O(T_1/T_\infty)$], then $T_\infty \leq T_1/p$ [respectively, $T_\infty = O(T_1/p)$], and Prop. 2.3 yields $T_p < 2T_1/p$ [respectively, $T_p = O(T_1/p)$]. Furthermore, Prop. 2.2 yields $T_1 \leq pT_p$, from which we obtain $T_p \geq T_1/p = \Omega(T_1/p)$. **Q.E.D.**

The last two results are of fundamental importance. They establish that although T_∞ is defined under the assumption of an unlimited number of processors, $\Omega(T_1/T_\infty)$ processors are actually sufficient to come within a constant factor of T_∞ [Prop. 2.4(a)]. Furthermore, a corresponding schedule is obtained by simply modifying an optimal schedule for the case of an unlimited number of processors (see the proof of Prop. 2.3), as opposed to solving a generally difficult scheduling problem. This suggests a methodology whereby we first develop a parallel algorithm as if an unlimited number of processors were available, and then adapt the algorithm to the available number of processors. The significance of Prop. 2.4(b) is that as long as $p = O(T_1/T_\infty)$, the availability of p processors allows us to speed up the computation by a factor proportional to p, which is the best possible. We thus see that for a number of processors nearly equal to T_1/T_∞, we obtain both optimal execution time and optimal speeding up of the computation (within constant factors).

Finding an Optimal DAG

It is seen that there can be several DAGs corresponding to different algorithms for the same computational problem (see Fig. 1.2.2). It may then be of interest to find a DAG for which T_p is minimized, where p is the number of available processors. Let us denote by T_p^* the value of T_p corresponding to such an optimal DAG and view it as the optimal parallel time, using p processors, for the computational problem under consideration. The value of T_p^* is a measure of the complexity of the problem, as opposed to T_p which is the complexity of a particular algorithm.

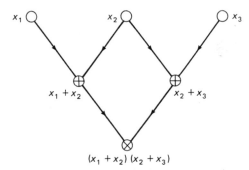

Figure 1.2.2   Another DAG representing an algorithm for evaluating the arithmetic expression $(x_1 + x_2)(x_2 + x_3)$. We have $T_1 = 3$ and $T_\infty = D = 2$. This should be contrasted with the DAG of Fig. 1.2.1 which solves the same computational problem and for which $T_1 = 7$ and $D = 3$. We conclude that the DAG given here represents a better parallel algorithm.

An explicit evaluation of T_p^* is usually very difficult. However, for several interesting classes of problems, there exist methods for constructing DAGs that come within a constant factor of the optimal. We do not pursue this issue any further and refer the reader to the notes and sources at the end of this chapter.

Speedup and Efficiency

We now assume that a particular model of parallel computation has been chosen. This could be the DAG model considered earlier, or any other model. Let us consider a computational problem parametrized by a variable n representing problem size. (In the DAG model, different problem sizes correspond to different numbers of input variables.

Thus, properly speaking, an algorithm is not specified by a single DAG, but rather by a family of DAGs, one for each problem size.) Time complexity is generally dependent on n, and we incorporate this dependence in our notation.

We describe a few concepts that are sometimes useful in comparing serial and parallel algorithms. Suppose that we have a parallel algorithm that uses p processors (p may depend on n), and that terminates in time $T_p(n)$. Let $T^*(n)$ be the optimal serial time to solve the same problem, that is, the time required by the best possible serial (uniprocessor) algorithm for this problem. The ratio

$$S_p(n) = \frac{T^*(n)}{T_p(n)}$$

is called the *speedup* of the algorithm, and describes the speed advantage of the parallel algorithm, compared to the best possible serial algorithm. The ratio

$$E_p(n) = \frac{S_p(n)}{p} = \frac{T^*(n)}{pT_p(n)}$$

is called the *efficiency* of the algorithm, and essentially measures the fraction of time that a typical processor is usefully employed. Ideally, $S_p(n) = p$ and $E_p(n) = 1$, in which case, the availability of p processors allows us to speed up the computation by a factor of p. For this to occur, the parallel algorithm should be such that no processor ever remains idle or does any unnecessary work. This ideal situation is practically unattainable. A more realistic objective is to aim at an efficiency that stays bounded away from zero, as n and p increase.

There is a difficulty with the above definitions because the optimal serial time $T^*(n)$ is unknown, even for seemingly simple computational problems like matrix multiplication. For this reason, $T^*(n)$ is sometimes defined differently. Some alternatives are the following:

(a) Let $T^*(n)$ be the time required by the best existing serial algorithm.

(b) Let $T^*(n)$ be the time required by a benchmark serial algorithm. For example, for multiplication of two dense $n \times n$ matrices, $\Theta(n^3)$ is a reasonable benchmark, even though there exist algorithms with substantially smaller time requirements [AHU74].

(c) Finally, we may let $T^*(n)$ be the time required by a single processor to execute the particular parallel algorithm being analyzed. (That is, we let a single processor simulate the operation of the p parallel processors.) With this choice of $T^*(n)$, efficiency relates to how well a particular algorithm has been parallelized, but provides no information on the absolute merits of the algorithm [in contrast with our earlier definitions of $T^*(n)$].

Notice that if $T^*(n)$ is defined as in (c), and if algorithms are specified by means of the DAG model, then $T^*(n)$ coincides with $T_1(n)$. In particular, if $p \leq O\big(T_1(n)/T_\infty(n)\big)$, then $T_p(n) = \Theta\big(T_1(n)/p\big)$ [Prop. 2.4(b)] and

$$E_p(n) = \frac{T_1(n)}{pT_p(n)} = \Theta(1).$$

This shows that if the number of processors is suitably small, then efficient parallel implementations are possible. Furthermore, if $p = \Theta\big(T_1(n)/T_\infty(n)\big)$, we also have $T_p(n) = \Theta\big(T_\infty(n)\big)$ [Prop. 2.4(a)] and we have a parallel implementation that is both efficient and has a time complexity within a constant factor from the optimum.

The above discussion suggests that efficiency of parallel implementation is not a concern, at least when an algorithm is specified by a DAG, and as long as communication issues are ignored. A more fundamental issue is whether the maximum attainable speedup $T_1(n)/T_\infty(n)$ can be made arbitrarily large, as n is increased. In certain applications, the required computations are quite unstructured, and there has been considerable debate on the range of achievable speedups in real world situations. The main difficulty is that some programs have some sections that are easily parallelizable, but also have some sections that are inherently sequential. When a large number of processors is available, the parallelizable sections are quickly executed, but the sequential sections lead to bottlenecks. This observation is known as *Amdahl's law* and can be quantified as follows: if a program consists of two sections, one that is inherently sequential and one that is fully parallelizable, and if the inherently sequential section consumes a fraction f of the total computation, then the speedup is limited by

$$S_p(n) \le \frac{1}{f + (1 - f)/p} \le \frac{1}{f}, \qquad \forall p.$$

On the other hand, there are numerous computational problems for which f decreases to zero as the size of the problem increases, and Amdahl's law is not a concern.

1.2.3 Examples: Vector and Matrix Computations

In this subsection, we consider some elementary but very common numerical computational tasks, present some simple parallel algorithms, and discuss their complexity and efficiency. All of the algorithms to be considered can be represented by DAGs and such representations will be occasionally employed. It is assumed that each addition or multiplication takes unit time and that processors are able to instantly exchange intermediate results. In practice, processors may be communicating through an interconnection network or through a shared memory and our analysis ignores the associated communication and memory access delays. Nevertheless, the algorithms considered here are simple enough so that they can be implemented in some architectures with negligible communication overhead. The communication aspects of such implementations will be discussed in Subsections 1.3.4 to 1.3.6.

Scalar Addition

The simplest computational task is the addition of n scalars. It is clear that the best serial algorithm requires $n - 1$ operations. Thus, $T^*(n) = n - 1$. We now present a parallel algorithm under the simplifying assumption that n is a power of 2. We partition the n scalars into $n/2$ disjoint pairs and we use $n/2$ different processors to add the two scalars in each pair. Thus, after one time unit, we are left with the task of adding only $n/2$ scalars. Continuing similarly, after $\log n$ stages, we are left with a single number and the computation terminates (see Fig. 1.2.3). This algorithm generalizes easily to the case where n is not a power of 2: the execution time becomes $\lceil \log n \rceil$ using $\lfloor n/2 \rfloor$ processors (see Fig. 1.2.3).

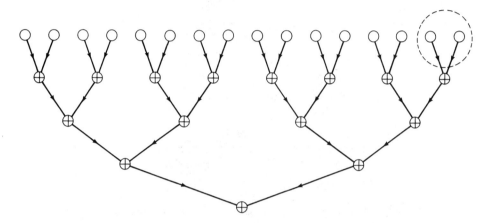

Figure 1.2.3   Parallel computation of the sum of 16 scalars. Eight processors are needed for the parallel additions at the first stage and a total of $4 = \log 16$ stages are needed. If the portion of the diagram enclosed in the dashed circle is removed, we obtain an algorithm for the parallel addition of 15 scalars. Notice that now only $7 = \lfloor 15/2 \rfloor$ processors are needed.

The efficiency of the above algorithm is

$$\frac{n-1}{\lfloor n/2 \rfloor \lceil \log n \rceil},$$

which goes to zero as n increases. An alternative parallel algorithm is obtained as follows (see Fig. 1.2.4). We assume for simplicity that $\log n$ is an integer, and that $n/\log n$ is an integer and a power of 2. We split the n numbers into $n/\log n$ groups of $\log n$ numbers each. We use $n/\log n$ processors and the ith processor adds the numbers in the ith group; this task takes time $\log n - 1$. We are then left with the task of adding $n/\log n$ numbers. This can be accomplished by our previous parallel algorithm in time $\log(n/\log n) \leq \log n$, using $n/(2\log n)$ processors. This two–phase algorithm requires time approximately equal to $2\log n$ (the speed is reduced by a factor of 2), but uses only $n/\log n$ processors and therefore its efficiency is approximately equal to $1/2$. Notice that we have chosen the number of processors p to be approximately equal to $T_1(n)/T_\infty(n)$. As discussed earlier, such a choice always leads to efficient algorithms. This example illustrates that with a small sacrifice in speed, efficiency can be substantially improved.

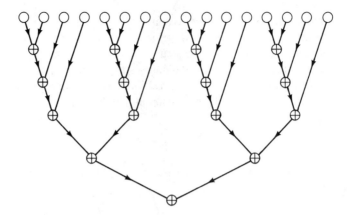

Figure 1.2.4   An alternative algorithm for the parallel addition of 16 scalars. Only four processors are used and the time requirements increase to 5 stages. Overall, however, there is an efficiency improvement over the algorithm of Fig. 1.2.3.

In fact, it will be seen later (Subsection 1.3.5) that decreasing the number of processors can also substantially decrease the communication requirements of an algorithm.

Inner Products

The inner product $\sum_{i=1}^{n} x_i y_i$ of two n–dimensional vectors can be computed in time $\lceil \log n \rceil + 1$ using n processors as follows: at the first step, each processor i computes the product $x_i y_i$ and then the $\lceil \log n \rceil$ time algorithm for scalar addition is used.

Matrix Addition and Multiplication

The sum of n matrices of dimensions $m \times m$ can be computed in time $\lceil \log n \rceil$ using $m^2 \lfloor n/2 \rfloor$ processors by letting a different group of $\lfloor n/2 \rfloor$ processors compute a different entry of the sum. Similarly, multiplication of two matrices of dimensions $m \times n$ and $n \times \ell$ consists of the evaluation of $m\ell$ inner products of n–dimensional vectors and can be therefore accomplished in time $\lceil \log n \rceil + 1$ using $nm\ell$ processors. In the case where $n = m = \ell$, the processor requirements become n^3. The corresponding number $T_1(n)$ of operations is $\Theta(n^3)$. In fact, there exist more economical algorithms for matrix multiplication in terms of processor requirements, or in terms of $T_1(n)$, but they are somewhat impractical and will not be considered here.

Powers of a Matrix

Suppose now that A is an $n \times n$ matrix and that we wish to compute A^k for some integer k. If k is a power of 2, this can be accomplished by repeated squaring: we first compute A^2; we then compute $A^2 A^2 = A^4$, etc. After $\log k$ stages, A^k is obtained. This procedure involves $\log k$ consecutive matrix multiplications and can be therefore carried out in time $\log k(\lceil \log n \rceil + 1)$ using n^3 processors. A simple modification of this procedure can be used to compute A^k in time $\Theta(\log k \cdot \log n)$ even if k is not a power of 2 (Exercise 2.4).

A consequence of the above discussion is that all the powers $A^2, \ldots, A^n$ of an $n \times n$ matrix can be computed in time $\Theta(\log^2 n)$ using n^4 processors by using a different group of n^3 processors for the computation of each power A^k. An alternative method for computing the powers $A^2, \ldots, A^n$, which avoids unnecessary duplication of computational effort, is shown in Fig. 1.2.5.

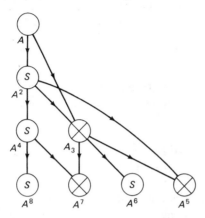

Figure 1.2.5 Parallel computation of the powers $A^2, \ldots, A^n$ of an $n \times n$ matrix A. A node with a label S represents a matrix squaring operation. At the first stage, A^2 is computed. At the second stage, A^3 and A^4 are computed by multiplying earlier computed matrices. More generally, at the kth stage, the matrices $A^{2^{k-1}+1}, \ldots, A^{2^k}$ are computed. Thus, $\Theta(\log n)$ stages suffice for the computation of $A^2, \ldots, A^n$. Each stage involves at most $\Theta(n)$ simultaneous matrix multiplications and can be carried out using n^4 processors in time $\Theta(\log n)$, leading to an overall time $\Theta(\log^2 n)$.

In the previously discussed algorithms, we have strived for the fastest possible execution times; such an approach often leads to excessive processor requirements and low efficiency. On the other hand, as discussed earlier, the same algorithms can be made efficient if the number of processors is chosen so that $p = O\big(T_1(n)/T_\infty(n)\big)$. For example, the product of two $n \times n$ matrices can be computed in time $\Theta(\log n)$ using $\Theta(n^3/\log n)$ processors, and the corresponding efficiency is $\Theta(1)$. If the number of processors is reduced even further, the execution time will be $\Theta\big(T_1(n)/p\big)$ [Prop. 2.4(b)]. Thus, two $n \times n$ matrices can be multiplied in time $\Theta(n)$ when n^2 processors are used, and in time $\Theta(n^2)$ when n processors are used.

1.2.4 Parallelization of Iterative Methods

Many interesting algorithms for the solution of systems of equations, optimization, and other problems have the structure

$$x(t+1) = f\big(x(t)\big), \qquad t = 0, 1, \ldots, \tag{2.1}$$

where each $x(t)$ is an n–dimensional vector, and f is some function from $\Re^n$ into itself. (Several examples will be seen in Chapters 2 and 3.) They are called *iterative* algorithms or, in certain contexts, *relaxation* methods. An alternative notation that is sometimes used in place of Eq. (2.1) is $x := f(x)$. Notice that if the sequence $\{x(t)\}$ generated by the above iteration converges to a limit x^*, and if the function f is continuous, then x^* is a *fixed point* of f, that is, it satisfies $x^* = f(x^*)$. A common special case arises when the function f is of the form $f(x) = Ax + b$, where A is a square matrix and b is a vector, in which case we are dealing with a *linear* iterative algorithm. In this subsection, we make some general observations on the possibilities for parallel execution of iterative algorithms. It should be mentioned here that the concept of time complexity is not quite relevant to algorithms of the form $x := f(x)$ unless a termination criterion is also specified.

Let $x_i(t)$ denote the ith component of $x(t)$ and let f_i denote the ith component of the function f. Then, we can write $x(t+1) = f\big(x(t)\big)$ as

$$x_i(t+1) = f_i\big(x_1(t), \ldots, x_n(t)\big), \qquad i = 1, \ldots, n. \tag{2.2}$$

The iterative algorithm $x := f(x)$ can be parallelized by letting each one of n processors update a different component of x according to Eq. (2.2). At each stage, the ith processor knows the value of all components of $x(t)$ on which f_i depends, computes the new value $x_i(t+1)$, and communicates it to other processors in order to start the next iteration.

The communication required for the execution of iteration (2.2) can be compactly described by means of a directed graph $G = (N, A)$, called the *dependency graph*. The set of nodes N is $\{1, \ldots, n\}$, corresponding to the components of x. For any two distinct nodes i and j, we let (i, j) be an arc of the dependency graph if and only if the function f_j depends on x_i, that is, if and only if processor i needs to communicate the values of $x_i(t)$ to processor j (see Fig. 1.2.6).

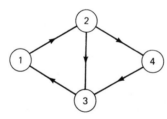

Figure 1.2.6 The dependency graph associated with an iteration of the form

$$x_1(t+1) = f_1\big(x_1(t), x_3(t)\big)$$
$$x_2(t+1) = f_2\big(x_1(t), x_2(t)\big)$$
$$x_3(t+1) = f_3\big(x_2(t), x_3(t), x_4(t)\big)$$
$$x_4(t+1) = f_4\big(x_2(t), x_4(t)\big).$$

Assuming that the iteration (2.1) is to be carried out only for $t = 0, 1, \ldots, T$, where T is some positive integer, the structure of the algorithm can be represented by means of a DAG. This DAG is essentially an "unfolding" in time of the above defined dependency graph (see Fig. 1.2.7).

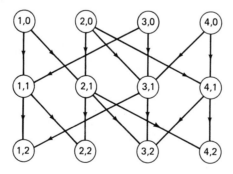

Figure 1.2.7 The DAG corresponding to two iterations when the function f has the dependency graph shown in Fig. 1.2.6. The nodes of the DAG are of the form (i, t), where $i \in \{1, \ldots, n\}$, and t is the iteration count. The arcs are of the form $\big((i, t), (j, t+1)\big)$, where (i, j) is an arc of the dependency graph or $i = j$.

Sometimes we may wish to employ a coarse–grained parallelization of the iteration $x := f(x)$. In particular, we decompose the vector space $\Re^n$ as a Cartesian product of lower dimensional subspaces $\Re^{n_j}$, $j = 1, \ldots, p$, where $\sum_{j=1}^{p} n_j = n$. Accordingly, any vector $x \in \Re^n$ is decomposed as $x = (x_1, \ldots, x_j, \ldots, x_p)$, where each x_j is itself an n_j–dimensional vector, called a *block–component* of x, or simply a component when no confusion can arise. Similarly, the iteration $x(t + 1) = f\big(x(t)\big)$ can be written as

$$x_j(t + 1) = f_j\big(x(t)\big), \qquad j = 1, \ldots, p, \tag{2.3}$$

where each f_j is a vector function mapping $\Re^n$ into $\Re^{n_j}$. We assign each one of p processors to update a different block–component according to Eq. (2.3), and the resulting parallel algorithm is said to be *block–parallelized*. A dependency graph $G = (N, A)$ can be again defined with $N = \{1, \ldots, p\}$ and $A = \{(i, j) \mid f_j \text{ depends on } x_i\}$. There are several reasons for being interested in block–parallelization. First, there may be too few processors available, so that we have to assign more than one component to each one of them. Second, certain scalar functions f_i may involve common computations, in which case it is natural to group them together. Finally, as will be discussed in Subsection 1.3.5, block–parallelization reduces the communication requirements of an algorithm.

In general, a parallelization that assigns the update of different components to different processors is meaningful when the computations involved in the update of each x_i are different, but could be wasteful otherwise. For example, suppose that each f_i is of the form

$$f_i(x_1, \ldots, x_n) = x_i + \left(\sum_{j=1}^{n} x_j^2 \right)^{1/2}.$$

In this example, it is clearly wasteful to let all processors simultaneously compute the value of $\left(\sum_{i=1}^{n} x_i^2 \right)^{1/2}$. This could be done by a single processor that subsequently communicates the result to the others. Even better, the processors could cooperate in the computation of this quantity, using, for example, the methods of Subsection 1.2.3. Nevertheless, in many cases, the evaluation of each f_i involves very little or no duplication of effort, and this is the situation in which we are mostly interested.

Gauss–Seidel Iterations

Iteration (2.2), in which all of the components of x are simultaneously updated, is sometimes called a *Jacobi*–type iteration. In an alternative form, the components of x are updated one at a time, and the most recently computed values of the other components are used. That is, Eq. (2.2) is changed to

$$x_i(t + 1) = f_i\Big(x_1(t + 1), \ldots, x_{i-1}(t + 1), x_i(t), \ldots, x_n(t)\Big), \qquad i = 1, \ldots, n. \tag{2.4}$$

The iteration (2.4) is called the *Gauss–Seidel algorithm based on the function f*. Gauss–Seidel algorithms are often preferable: they incorporate the newest available information, and for this reason, they sometimes converge faster than the corresponding Jacobi–type algorithms. (A result of this type will be proved in Section 2.6.)

From now on, we concentrate on a single Gauss–Seidel iteration (sometimes called a *sweep*), and investigate its parallelization potential. A Gauss–Seidel iteration may be completely non–parallelizable. For example, if every function f_i depends on all components x_j, then only one component can be updated at a time. On the other hand, when the dependency graph is sparse, it is possible that certain component updates can be performed in parallel. An example is shown in Fig. 1.2.8.

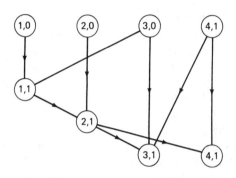

Figure 1.2.8 Illustration of the parallelization of Gauss–Seidel iterations. Let f be a function whose dependency graph is as in Fig. 1.2.6. The Gauss–Seidel algorithm based on f takes the form

$$x_1(t+1) = f_1\Big(x_1(t), x_3(t)\Big)$$

$$x_2(t+1) = f_2\Big(x_1(t+1), x_2(t)\Big)$$

$$x_3(t+1) = f_3\Big(x_2(t+1), x_3(t), x_4(t)\Big)$$

$$x_4(t+1) = f_4\Big(x_2(t+1), x_4(t)\Big).$$

The DAG shown illustrates the data dependencies in one iteration of the Gauss–Seidel algorithm. There are four updates to be performed, but the depth of the DAG is only 3. In particular, it is seen that x_3 and x_4 can be updated in parallel.

We notice that there are several alternative Gauss–Seidel algorithms corresponding to the same function f, because there is freedom in choosing the order in which the components are to be updated. For example, we might wish to update the components of x starting with x_n and proceeding backwards, with x_1 being updated last. Different updating orders, strictly speaking, correspond to different algorithms and the results produced are generally different. Nevertheless, in several applications, a Gauss–Seidel algorithm converges in the limit of a large number of iterations to the same value, irrespective of the updating order. As long as the speed of convergence corresponding to different updating orders is not drastically different, it is natural to choose an ordering for which the parallelism in each iteration is maximized (see Fig. 1.2.9).

We now develop a graph–theoretic formulation of the problem of finding an updating order that minimizes the parallel time needed for a sweep. Given the dependency graph $G = (N, A)$, a *coloring* of G, using K colors, is defined as a mapping $h : N \mapsto \{1, \ldots, K\}$ that assigns a "color" $k = h(i)$ to each node $i \in N$. The idea is that similarly colored variables will be updated in parallel. The following result shows that maximizing parallelism is equivalent to an "optimal coloring" problem.

Proposition 2.5.   The following are equivalent:

(i) There exists an ordering of the variables such that a sweep of the corresponding Gauss–Seidel algorithm can be performed in K parallel steps.

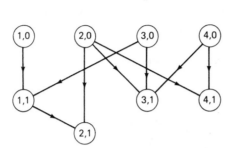

Figure 1.2.9 Illustration of the increase in parallelism when the updating order is changed. Here the function f is the same as in Figs. 1.2.6 to 1.2.8. We consider the following updating order:

$$x_1(t+1) = f_1\Big(x_1(t), x_3(t)\Big)$$
$$x_3(t+1) = f_3\Big(x_2(t), x_3(t), x_4(t)\Big)$$
$$x_4(t+1) = f_4\Big(x_2(t), x_4(t)\Big)$$
$$x_2(t+1) = f_2\Big(x_1(t+1), x_2(t)\Big).$$

The DAG shown illustrates the data dependencies in a typical iteration. Its depth is only 2. It is seen that a sweep can be executed in parallel in two time steps using two processors.

(ii) There exists a coloring of the dependency graph that uses K colors and with the property that there exists no positive cycle with all nodes on the cycle having the same color.

   Proof. We first show that (i) implies (ii). Consider an ordering of the variables with which a Gauss–Seidel iteration takes K parallel steps. We define $h(i)$, the color of node i, to be equal to k if the variable x_i is updated at the kth parallel stage. Consider a positive cycle $i_1, i_2, \ldots, i_m$, with $i_m = i_1$. Let us choose the node i_ℓ in the cycle $(1 \le \ell < m)$ that comes first in the assumed ordering. Since $i_{\ell+1}$ is ordered after i_ℓ, and since $(i_\ell, i_{\ell+1}) \in A$, the variable $x_{i_{\ell+1}}(t+1)$ depends on $x_{i_\ell}(t+1)$. It follows that x_{i_ℓ} and $x_{i_{\ell+1}}$ cannot be updated simultaneously and we have $h(i_\ell) \ne h(i_{\ell+1})$. This shows that in every positive cycle, there exist two nodes with different colors and (ii) has been proved.

   We now prove an auxiliary result. We show that if G is a directed acyclic graph, then its nodes can be ordered so that if $(i, j) \in A$, then j comes before i. The proof is as follows. For each node i, we let d_i be the largest possible number of arcs in a positive path that starts at i. (We let $d_i = 0$ if node i has no outgoing arcs.) It is seen that d_i is finite as a consequence of acyclicity. We then order the nodes in order of increasing values of d_i. (Ties among nodes with the same value of d_i are broken arbitrarily.) We see that if $(i, j) \in A$, then $d_i > d_j$. [This is because we can take a longest path starting from j and append the arc (i, j) to obtain an even longer path starting from i.] We conclude that j comes before i whenever $(i, j) \in A$, as desired.

   We now assume that (ii) holds. Let h be a coloring with K colors and with no positive cycle in which all nodes have the same color. For every color k, let G_k be the subgraph of G obtained by keeping only the nodes with color k and the arcs joining them. Each G_k is acyclic and, according to the result of the preceding paragraph, the nodes in G_k can be ordered so that j comes before i whenever $(i, j) \in A$. We order the nodes in G in order of increasing color; ties between nodes with the same color k are broken by using the ordering of the graph G_k. Consider the Gauss–Seidel iteration corresponding to this ordering. Let i and j be two distinct nodes with the same color k. If $(i, j) \notin A$ and $(j, i) \notin A$, then x_i and x_j can be clearly updated in parallel. The case where $(i, j) \in A$ and $(j, i) \in A$ is impossible because G_k is acyclic. If $(i, j) \in A$ and $(j, i) \notin A$, then j appears before i in the order we have constructed and therefore the computation of $x_j(t + 1)$ only requires the value of $x_i(t)$ and not the value of $x_i(t + 1)$. Finally, the case where $(j, i) \in A$ and $(i, j) \notin A$ is similar. We conclude that every x_i with the same color can be updated in parallel, thus proving (i).   **Q.E.D.**

For the dependency graph of Fig. 1.2.6 two colors suffice. In particular, we may let $h(1) = h(3) = h(4) = 1$ and $h(2) = 2$. Since every positive cycle goes through node 2, there exists no positive cycle with all nodes having the same color, as required. In particular, the subgraph G_1 in which only the nodes with color 1 are kept is acyclic. With d_i defined as in the proof of Prop. 2.5, we have $d_1 = 0$, $d_3 = 1$, and $d_4 = 2$. The ordering of the variables constructed in that proof is $(1, 3, 4, 2)$, and the corresponding Gauss–Seidel iteration is precisely the one shown in Fig. 1.2.9. According to Prop. 2.5, this ordering requires the least possible number of parallel stages per sweep, a fact that is easy to verify directly for this particular example.

Proposition 2.5 can be somewhat simplified in the case where the dependency graph has a certain symmetry property.

Proposition 2.6.   Suppose that $(i, j) \in A$ if and only if $(j, i) \in A$. Then, the following are equivalent:

(i) There exists an ordering of the variables such that a sweep of the corresponding Gauss–Seidel algorithm can be performed in K parallel steps.

(ii) There exists a coloring of the dependency graph that uses at most K colors and such that adjacent nodes have different colors [that is, if $(i, j) \in A$, then $h(i) \neq h(j)$].

Proof. It is sufficient to show that condition (ii) of this proposition is equivalent to condition (ii) of Prop. 2.5. Suppose that there exists a positive cycle with all the nodes on that cycle having the same color. Then there exist two adjacent nodes with the same color. Conversely, if $(i, j) \in A$, then $(j, i) \in A$ and the two arcs (i, j) and (j, i) form a positive cycle. Thus, if two neighboring nodes have the same color, there exists a positive cycle with all nodes on that cycle having the same color. This proves the equivalence of the two conditions and concludes the proof.   **Q.E.D.**

Unfortunately, the optimal coloring problems of Props. 2.5 and 2.6 are intractable (NP–complete): there is no known efficient algorithm for solving them, neither is it likely that an efficient algorithm will be found [GaJ79]. Nevertheless, problems arising in practice often have a special structure and a coloring with relatively few colors can sometimes be found by inspection. Some interesting cases are the following:

(a) Consider the undirected graph $\tilde{G}$ obtained by ignoring the orientation of the arcs of G. If $\tilde{G}$ is a tree, then two colors suffice: we choose an arbitrary node in the tree and we assign color 1 (respectively, 2) to all nodes in the graph that can be reached by traversing an even (respectively, odd) number of arcs.

(b) If every node in G has at most D neighbors, then $D + 1$ colors suffice. To see this, we color the nodes one by one. Assuming that the first i nodes have been colored, we consider node $i + 1$. Since we are using $D + 1$ colors, there is some color that can be used for node $i + 1$ while ensuring that it is colored differently from the already colored neighbors of $i + 1$.

When a coloring scheme is used for the parallel implementation of a Gauss–Seidel algorithm, it is wasteful to assign a different processor to each component of x, because each processor will be idle while variables of different colors are being updated. The obvious remedy is to use fewer processors, with each processor being assigned several variables with different associated colors.

Example 2.1.   *Red–Black Coloring of a Two–Dimensional Array*

In a variety of iterative algorithms of the form $x := f(x)$, employed for the numerical solution of partial differential equations or in image processing, each component of the vector x is associated with a particular point in a certain region of two–dimensional space. For example, let N be the set of all points $(i, j) \in \Re^2$, such that i and j are integers satisfying $0 \le i \le M$ and $0 \le j \le M$. Let x_{ij} be the component of the vector x corresponding to point (i, j). By connecting nearest neighbors, we form a graph $G = (N, A)$, as illustrated in Fig. 1.2.10. We view G as a directed graph, by making the arcs bidirectional, and we assume that it is the dependency graph associated to the iteration $x := f(x)$. Parallel execution of this iteration, in Jacobi fashion, is straightforward. We assign a different processor to each point (i, j). This processor is responsible for updating x_{ij} and, in order to do so, only needs to know the values of the components of x associated with neighboring points. Thus, it is most natural to assume that processors associated with neighboring points are joined by a direct communication link.

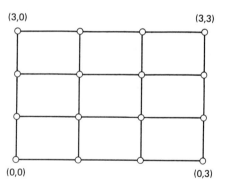

(3,0)   (3,3)

(0,0)   (0,3)

Figure 1.2.10 A common dependency graph associated with iterative algorithms arising in the solution of partial differential equations and in image processing.

Concerning the implementation of the associated Gauss–Seidel method, we notice that the graph of Fig. 1.2.10 can be colored using only two colors, as indicated in Fig. 1.2.11. If we were to assign one processor to each component x_{ij}, each processor would be idle half of the time. It is thus reasonable to assign two components with different corresponding colors to each processor. As shown in Fig. 1.2.11 this can be done while preserving the property that only nearest neighbors have to communicate to each other. In practice, the number of points involved is often large enough so that each processor is assigned more than two components of x. The coloring indicated in Fig. 1.2.11 is commonly known as *red–black* coloring and the associated Gauss–Seidel algorithm is known as *Gauss–Seidel with red–black ordering*.

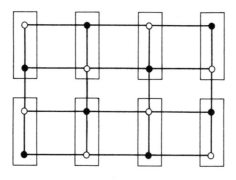

Figure 1.2.11 The nodes of the graph in Fig. 1.2.10 can be colored using two colors only. We can assign a pair of nodes with different colors to each processor and notice that only neighboring processors have to communicate.

EXERCISES

2.1. Formulate and prove a generalization of Prop. 2.1 under the assumption that the in–degree of each node is at most B, where B is some positive integer.

2.2. Prove Amdahl's law. How should $T^*(n)$ be defined for this law to hold?

2.3. (**Prefix Problem [LaF80].**)

    (a) Let $a_1, a_2, \ldots, a_n$ be given scalars. Provide an $O(\log n)$ time algorithm which uses $O(n)$ processors and evaluates all products of the form $\prod_{i=1}^{k} a_i$, where $k = 1, 2, \ldots, n$.

    (b) Generalize part (a) to provide an $O(\log n \cdot \log m)$ time algorithm for the case where each a_i is an $m \times m$ matrix.

    (c) Consider the vector difference equation

$$x(t + 1) = A(t)x(t) + u(t).$$

    Here, for $t = 0, 1, \ldots, n$, $x(t)$ and $u(t)$ are vectors in $\Re^m$, and $A(t)$ is an $m \times m$ matrix. Assume that $A(t)$, $u(t)$ are known for each t, and that $x(0)$ is also given. Use the result of part (b) to obtain an $O(\log n \cdot \log m)$ time parallel algorithm for computing $x(n)$.

2.4. Show how to compute the kth power of an $n \times n$ matrix in time $\Theta\big(\log k \cdot \log n\big)$ using n^3 processors, when k is not a power of 2.

2.5.   **(a)** Consider the scalar difference equation

$$x(t + 1) = a(t)x(t) + b(t)x(t - 1)$$

    and consider the problem of computing $x(n)$. The inputs of the computation are $x(-1)$, $x(0)$, $a(0), \ldots, a(n-1)$, $b(0), \ldots, b(n-1)$. Assuming that enough processors are available, find a parallel algorithm that takes time $\Theta(\log n)$. *Hint:* Write the difference equation in vector form and reduce the problem to the multiplication of n matrices of dimensions 2×2.

(b) Repeat part (a) with the only difference that $x(-1)$ is unknown but $x(n-1)$ is provided instead as an input to the computation, under the additional assumption that there exists a unique sequence $x(0), x(1), \ldots, x(n-1), x(n)$ satisfying the given initial and final conditions. *Hint:* Obtain a system of linear equations of the form

$$\begin{bmatrix} x(n) \\ x(n-1) \end{bmatrix} = D \begin{bmatrix} x(1) \\ x(0) \end{bmatrix},$$

where D is a 2×2 matrix that can be efficiently computed. Solve for $x(n)$ and $x(1)$.

2.6. Show that a polynomial $p(x) = a_n x^n + \cdots + a_1 x + a_0$ can be evaluated in parallel in time $\Theta(\log n)$. Here the inputs of the computation are the coefficients of the polynomial and the value of x.

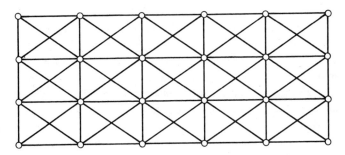

Figure 1.2.12   Dependency graph for nine-point discretizations (Exercise 2.7).

2.7. Consider the dependency graph G of Fig. 1.2.12, where all arcs are interpreted as being bidirectional. Such a dependency graph is obtained from so called "nine–point" discretizations of partial differential equations with two spatial variables [Ame77].

(a) Show that G cannot be colored with less than four colors.

(b) Find a coloring of G with four colors.

(c) Assuming that a mesh of processors is available (that is, a two–dimensional array of processors with nearest neighbor connections), show that we can assign four differently colored nodes to each processor in a way that the execution of the Gauss–Seidel algorithm requires only nearest neighbor communication.

1.3 COMMUNICATION ASPECTS OF PARALLEL AND DISTRIBUTED SYSTEMS

In many parallel and distributed algorithms and systems the time spent for interprocessor communication is a sizable fraction of the total time needed to solve a problem. In this case we say that the algorithm experiences substantial communication penalty or communication delays. We can think of the communication penalty as the ratio

$$CP = \frac{T_{TOTAL}}{T_{COMP}}, \tag{3.1}$$

where T_{TOTAL} is the time required by the algorithm to solve the given problem, and T_{COMP} is the corresponding time that can be attributed just to computation, that is, the time that would be required if all communication were instantaneous. This section is devoted to a discussion of a number of factors affecting the communication penalty.

To analyze communication issues, it is helpful to view the distributed computing system as a network of processors connected by communication links. Each processor uses its own local memory for storing some problem data and intermediate algorithmic results, and exchanges information with other processors in groups of bits called *packets* using the communication links of the network. The length of packets can be widely varying, ranging from a few tens of bits, to several thousands of bits. We assume that when a packet travels on a communication link, the bits of the packet are consecutively transmitted without interruption. A shared memory can also be viewed as a communication network, since each processor can send information to every other processor by storing it in the shared memory. This analogy can be extended to the case where the shared memory is organized in a hierarchy of memory sections, each, possibly, having a different access time for different processors. We will emphasize, however, a communication model based on direct processor–to–processor links, since such a model is somewhat easier to understand and analyze. We will also adopt a *store–and–forward* packet switching data communication model, whereby a packet that must travel over a route involving several processors, may have to wait at any one of these processors for some communication resource to become available before it gets transmitted to the next node. In some systems, it is possible that packets are divided and recombined at intermediate nodes on their routes, but we will not consider this possibility in our discussion. In another approach, called *circuit switching* (see [BeG87], [Sch87]), the communication resources needed for a packet's transfer are reserved via some mechanism before the packet's transfer begins. As a result the packet does not have to wait at any point along its route. Circuit switching is almost universally employed in telephone networks, but is seldom used in data networks or in parallel and distributed computing systems. It will not be considered further in this book.

Communication delays can be divided into four parts:

(a) *Communication processing time.* This is the time required to prepare information for transmission; for example, assembling information in packets, appending addressing and control information to the packets, selecting a link on which to transmit each packet, moving the packets to the appropriate buffers, etc.

(b) *Queueing time.* Once information is assembled into packets for transmission on some communication link, it must wait in a queue prior to the start of its transmission for a number of reasons. For example, the link may be temporarily unavailable because other information packets or system control packets are using it or are scheduled to use it ahead of the given packet; or because a contention resolution process is underway whereby the allocation of the link to several contending packets is being decided. Another reason is that it may be necessary to postpone the transmission of a packet to ensure the availability of needed resources (such as buffer space at its destination). In the case where the possibility of transmission errors is nonnegligible, the queueing time includes the time for the packet retransmissions needed to correct the errors. Queueing time is generally difficult to quantify precisely, but simplified models are often adequate to obtain valuable qualitative and quantitative conclusions.

(c) *Transmission time.* This is the time required for transmission of all the bits of the packet.

(d) *Propagation time.* This is the time between the end of transmission of the last bit of the packet at the transmitting processor, and the reception of the last bit of the packet at the receiving processor.

Depending on the given system and algorithm, one or more of the above times may be negligible. For example, in some cases the information is generated with sufficient regularity and the transmission resources are sufficiently plentiful so that there never is a need for queueing packets, whereas in other cases the physical distance between transmitter and receiver is so small that propagation delay is negligible.

For most systems, we can reasonably assume that the processing and propagation time on a given link is constant for all packets, and the transmission time is proportional to the number of bits (or length) of the packet. We thus arrive at the following formula for the delay of a packet in crossing a link:

$$D = P + RL + Q, \tag{3.2}$$

where P is the processing and propagation time, R is the transmission time required for a single bit, L is the length of the packet in bits, and Q is the queueing time. (We are using bits as the packet length unit, but any other unit that requires a fixed transmission time can be used.)

It is difficult to make general statements regarding the size of the various terms in the delay formula (3.2). In some systems, the transmission time RL is much larger than the processing and propagation time P, particularly when L includes a substantial number of overhead bits. In other cases, the reverse is true. In the great majority of presently existing systems, even when the packet does not contain much more than overhead, the sum $P + RL$ is much larger than the time required to execute an elementary numerical operation such as a floating point multiplication. This means that if a parallel algorithm requires transmission of a packet for every few numerical operations it performs, the communication time is likely to dominate its execution time.

Throughout this section we focus on packets as units of communication. It should be noted, however, that a packet is sometimes part of some "message" that makes sense only when received as a whole. A message may be segmented into several packets for transmission for a number of reasons, and it is then appropriate to focus on the delay of the entire message (from start of transmission of its first packet to the end of reception of its last packet). This complicates the situation because the message delay depends on how the message is segmented into packets, and on whether the transmission of the packets can be parallelized. For example, if a message is divided into n equal length packets that are transmitted over n equal delay, independent parallel communication paths, the message delay will be smaller by a factor n over the case where the entire message is transmitted over one of the paths. (This accounting assumes that the extra communication overhead when the message is segmented into several packets is negligible, and that the processing, propagation, and queueing delays are also negligible.)

Another possibility for parallelizing communication arises when a message is to be transmitted over a path of $k > 1$ links. If the message is segmented into n packets that are transmitted sequentially over the k–link path with a transmission time on each link equal to T per packet, the delay of the message will be $(n+k-1)T$ as compared with the delay of knT that will be required if the entire message is transmitted as a single packet. (This accounting neglects the effect of overhead, processing and propagation delays, and queueing, and assumes that a node must receive a packet in its entirety before relaying any portion of the packet to some other node.) The delay reduction is achieved by pipelining the transmission of the packets over the k links as shown in Fig. 1.3.1. It is seen that by making the packet size very small, the delay can be reduced by a factor nearly equal to the number of links of the path, to almost the time required to transmit the message over a single link. This motivates a special type of transmission method, sometimes called *cut–through transmission*, where a node can relay to another node any portion of a packet without waiting to receive the packet in its entirety. This amounts to segmenting the packet into many smaller packets to take advantage of the type of pipelining illustrated in Fig. 1.3.1. Naturally, this type of transmission method should be organized so that packets can be correctly put back together at their ultimate destination. We will not go into this subject further. We note also that the idea of pipelining of communication is applicable in other situations such as for example transmitting over a spanning tree (see Exercise 3.19).

Some of the most important factors that influence communication delays are the following:

(a) The algorithms used to control the communication network, mainly error control, routing, and flow control.

(b) The communication network topology, that is, the number, nature, and location of the communication links.

(c) The structure of the problem solved and the design of the algorithm to match this structure, including the degree of synchronization required by the algorithm.

The above factors are discussed in the subsequent subsections.

1.3.1 Communication Links

The precise method by which information is physically transmitted over a communication channel will not be important for us. It suffices for our purposes to view a communication

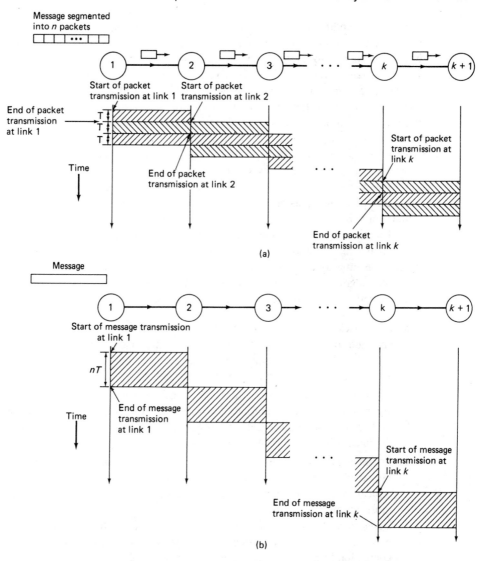

Figure 1.3.1 Segmentation of a message into packets to take advantage of pipelining over a path consisting of k communication links. In (a) the message is divided into n packets, each requiring T time units for transmission over a single link. The total time required is $(n + k - 1)T$. In (b) the message is transmitted as a whole on each link requiring nT time units on each link for a total of knT time units. (This accounting assumes that the overhead per packet and the processing, propagation, and queueing delays on all links are negligible.)

link as a *virtual bit pipe* along which bits travel, starting from one point referred to as the *transmitter* or the *origin*, and arriving at another point referred to as the *receiver* or the *destination*. There are several types of such pipes. One is the *synchronous* bit pipe, where the transmitter continuously sends bits at a fixed rate; packet bits if a packet is available for sending, and dummy bits otherwise. An example is a high speed point–to–point wire connection; this is the type of bit pipe that is the most common in parallel and distributed computing systems. A second type is the *intermittent synchronous* bit pipe, where the transmitter sends bits at a fixed rate when it has a packet to send, and sends nothing otherwise. An example is Ethernet, which is a local area network bus (see e.g. [BeG87]). Finally, a third type is the *asynchronous character* pipe, where packets are transmitted in groups of bits called *characters* (usually eight or nine bits some of which are used for synchronization); the bits within each character are sent at a fixed rate, but successive characters can be separated by variable delays, subject to a given minimum. A typical example involves low speed communication using personal computers, and/or dial up telephone lines. In all of these pipes, the physical representation of bits can take many different forms, using a variety of modulation and coding techniques that may include forward error correction; see [BeG87] and [Sta85].

The *capacity* of a communication link is the maximum rate at which bits can be transmitted over the corresponding bit pipe, and is equal to $1/R$, where R is the bit transmision time used in the delay equation (3.2). In the context of a given parallel or distributed algorithm, the transmission rate of bits that carry algorithm–related information is actually smaller due to a number of reasons:

(a) Each packet may carry overhead bits used for detecting the packet's start and end, and, possibly, for detecting errors in transmission (see the discussion of data link control in the next subsection); the effect of the overhead bits can usually be accounted for in the terms P or L of the delay formula (3.2).

(b) The link may be used in part to transmit packets that are unrelated to the distributed algorithm under consideration. For example, it may be necessary to transmit periodically some control packets needed to sustain the organizational structures of the underlying computing system.

(c) In some links the communication hardware may be time–shared between several virtual bit pipes, so each of these pipes can be used only part of the time. A typical example is when a processor can, at any one time, send a packet along at most one of several incident physical communication channels. Another example arises in multiaccess communication links, such as Ethernet and other local area networks, where a physical channel is shared among several virtual bit pipes on a contention basis. (Multiaccess channels and the algorithms that are used to control them will not be discussed in this book; see, e.g., [BeG87] and [Sta87].) When the physical communication hardware is shared between several communication links, the queueing time Q in the delay equation (3.2) is nonnegligible and must be taken into account. This complicates seriously the analysis of the communication penalty.

(d) Some scarce resource needed by the packets (such as, for example, buffer space at a subsequent destination) may be unavailable. Packets are then forced to wait for the resource to become available even though the communication link is available for transmission. Thus the rate of transmission of the packets is reduced to the rate at which the scarce resource becomes available. Algorithms that effect this type of rate reduction are called *flow control* algorithms. Flow control is discussed in many sources, e.g. [BeG87]. It will not be considered further in this book.

(e) In some communication links, there is a nonnegligible possibility that some bits are received differently than they were transmitted (e.g., a transmitted 0 is received as a 1), or are lost altogether (that is, their presence is not even detected). In such cases it is necessary to use a scheme that detects these malfunctions and retransmits the packets involved as many times as is necessary for ultimate correct reception. This lowers the rate at which information can be transmitted over the link, and simultaneously affects the queueing time Q in the delay formula (3.2), since a packet that is retransmitted may conceptually be viewed as waiting in queue up to the start of its first correct transmission.

Regardless of the nature of the corresponding virtual bit pipe, we would like to view a communication link as an *asynchronous packet pipe* that packets enter and exit after a delay D given by Eq. (3.2). The times of entry and exit, and the delay D need not exhibit any kind of deterministic regularity, but we would like to be able to assume that packets exit the pipe in the same order that they enter it, and that they are not altered in any way inside the pipe. This can be accomplished with the use of data link control algorithms that are discussed next.

1.3.2 Data Link Control

The two principal components of data link control (DLC) algorithms for virtual bit pipes are the mechanism of recognizing the start and end of packets (this is called *framing*), and the mechanism for *error detection and retransmission* of packets received in error. We assume throughout that packets arrive in the same order that they are sent, but that any one of them can get damaged in transmission or can get lost in the sense that its transmission may not be detected at the receiver.

We discuss framing briefly, and we refer to [BeG87] and [Sta85] for further description and analysis. A prerequisite for any framing technique, especially important for intermittent synchronous pipes and asynchronous character pipes, is a mechanism for recognizing the start of any bit stream following a period of idleness. This is a subject that relates to the design of the communication hardware, and will not be discussed further; see [Sta85]. One major framing technique is based on special bit sequences, called *flags*, that appear immediately before and after each packet. The receiver scans the incoming bit stream, and looks for a nonflag bit sequence following (or preceding) a flag to indicate the start (or end, respectively) of the packet. A technique known as *bit* or *character stuffing* is used to guard against the possibility that the flag sequence appears inside a packet; see [BeG87] and [Sta85]. A second major technique for framing is to encode, at the start of each packet, the number of bits of the packet (or to use a fixed packet length known to the receiver), allowing the receiver to distinguish the end of each packet. In this scheme a special resynchronization mechanism must be provided for the system to recover from a situation where a packet length is incorrectly received.

Error detection techniques are based on appending to the packets a sequence of extra bits, that are used to check for errors in transmission. An example of a primitive form of error detection is to form at the transmitter the modulo 2 sum of the bits of each packet, and add it to the end of the packet in the form of an extra bit (called the *parity check*). The receiver also forms the modulo 2 sum of the bits of the received packet, and compares it with the parity check. Assuming the parity check is received correctly, this method will detect all damaged packets with an odd number of bits in error, but will miss all damaged packets with an even number of bits in error. More sophisticated and reliable error detection techniques are based on adding, at the end of each packet, a bit sequence [called *cyclic redundancy check* (CRC) sequence] that is the remainder of the modulo 2 division of the polynomial having as coefficients the bits of the packet divided by a fixed polynomial having binary coefficients and called the *generator polynomial*. An example of a polynomial that is standard in data networks is $x^{16} + x^{15} + x^2 + 1$, in which case the CRC is 16 bits long. More generally, the length of the CRC is equal to the degree of the generator polynomial. The error detecting capability of the scheme typically increases with the length of the CRC sequence (see [Gal68] and [BeG87]). Note, however, that if there is a positive probability that any one bit can be received with error, there is no scheme that can guarantee foolproof protection against undetected errors. One must deal in practice with bit pipes where undetected errors are possible but very rare. Our subsequent discussion assumes that the error detection scheme used is infallible.

The typical method for correcting transmission errors is based on detecting which packets have been transmitted in error and retransmiting them as many times as is necessary for correct reception. In the simplest type of retransmission protocol, called *stop–and–wait*, the transmitter A sends a packet and the receiver B replies with a packet that contains either a positive acknowledgment (ACK) for a correct reception, or a negative acknowledgment (NAK) for an incorrect reception. If A receives a NAK, it retransmits the packet, and if it receives an ACK it transmits the next packet. It is interesting to note that the algorithm is distributed, since it involves two processors that do not share simultaneously the same information.

Despite its simplicity, the preceding algorithm involves considerable subtleties which illustrate some of the issues one has to deal with in implementing and justifying a distributed algorithm. The difficulty is that packets from A to B and from B to A can be delayed unpredictably in the communication channel, and they can also be lost. To guard against the possibility of a loss, it is necessary for A to take a timeout following the transmission of a packet, and retransmit the packet if it does not receive an ACK within a given period of time. On the other hand, it may be impossible to choose a timeout interval that is sufficiently small to ensure timely retransmission of lost packets, and is also sufficiently long to preclude retransmission of some packets that are merely delayed. Fig. 1.3.2 shows how this can lead to confusion at either A or B if the packets do not carry enough information to allow the unambiguous association of A to B packets with their corresponding acknowledgments. The remedy is to number sequentially the A to B packets, and to include on each acknowledgment packet the number of the A to B packet that is being acknowledged.

A final difficulty has to do with the fact that packet numbers can become arbitrarily large if transmission continues indefinitely, and can overflow any field with a finite

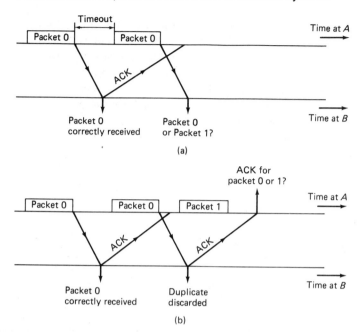

Figure 1.3.2   Illustration of the need to number both the A to B packets and the B to A packets in the stop–and–wait protocol. (a) Example of the confusion that can arise when packets from A to B are not numbered. The ACK for packet 0 is late to arrive, so A retransmits packet 0 after a timeout, but B cannot tell whether the second packet received is a duplicate of packet 0 or whether it is packet 1. (b) Example of the confusion that can arise when the B to A packets do not identify the packet that is being acknowledged. Here A cannot tell whether the second ACK is for packet 0 or for packet 1.

number of bits that will be provided for them. It turns out that it is sufficient to number packets modulo 2. An intuitive reason is that, at any given time, if there is a copy of packet i in the system (meaning that its transmission has started but its acknowledgment has not been received), there cannot simultaneously be a copy of packet $i + 2$ in the system, so that the former packet cannot be confused for the latter even though they carry the same modulo 2 sequence number. (All the copies of packet i are transmitted before all the copies of packet $i + 1$, so all the acknowledgments for copies of packet i are received before all the acknowledgments for copies of packet $i + 1$. Therefore, if a copy of packet i is in the system, then no acknowledgment for packet $i + 1$ must have been received, which implies that transmission of any copy of packet $i + 2$ cannot have started.)

The correctness of the preceding algorithm is intuitively rather obvious, but a rigorous proof requires a model of the combined state of A and B, as well as a prescription of how this state changes in response to all the possible packet receptions. The reader who tries to work out the details of this model (outlined in Exercise 3.1) may be surprised by the complexity and laboriousness of the argument needed to show rigorously the validity of a simple distributed algorithm such as the stop–and–wait protocol. This difficulty is symptomatic of the complicated nature of distributed algorithms involving several processors that exchange information along communication links. A detailed model of such a distributed algorithm requires that each processor be viewed as a system with an internal state that accepts as inputs packets received from other processors, and produces as outputs packets sent to other processors. The state changes in response to the input, and the output depends on the state and the input (see Fig. 1.3.3). While a serial algorithm consists of a single such system, a distributed algorithm consists of an interconnection of many such systems, yielding a composite system that can be quite complex to model, analyze, and implement.

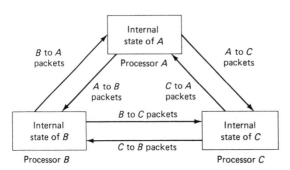

Figure 1.3.3 Representation of a distributed algorithm as an interconnection of subsystems, one per processor. Each subsystem/processor has an internal state that changes in response to packet receptions from other processors. A description of the distributed algorithm must include the rule by which the state of each processor changes, and the rule by which packets destined for other processors are generated.

The stop–and–wait protocol leads to long delays because a packet must wait in a queue until the reception of the acknowledgment of the previous packet. A more efficient scheme, which is widely used, is the *go–back–n algorithm*. The idea here is to allow sending as many as n packets following the last packet that has been acknowledged, while using timeouts to decide when to restransmit packets whose acknowledgment is late in coming. Thus, assuming that packet i is the highest numbered packet for which an acknowledgment packet has been received, the transmitter can send any of the packets $i + 1, i + 2, \ldots, i + n$. The receiver, however, acknowledges packets in order, that is, it does not acknowledge correct reception of packet $i + 1$ before it acknowledges correct reception of packet i. In fact, an acknowledgment packet indicates the next packet expected by the receiver, and thus simultaneously acknowledges all packets already received correctly. This algorithm yields, for $n = 1$, the stop–and–wait protocol, but avoids the long delays of that protocol by using $n > 1$. It is sufficient to number packets modulo m for any $m > n$. A rigorous proof, together with a description of other implementation details is given in [BeG87]. (For a heuristic argument, note that, at any given time, the number of consecutively numbered unacknowledged packets at the transmitter is at most n. Therefore, the range of possible packet numbers that are next expected at the receiver contains no more than $n + 1$ consecutive numbers. Hence, if $m > n$, packet number k and packet number $k + m$ cannot simultaneously be in this range, and there is no possibility of the receiver getting confused when packets are numbered modulo m.) The standard modulo number used for terrestrial communication links in data networks is $m = 8$.

We finally note that in some systems, where communication links are very reliable, an error detection and retransmission scheme is not used in order to save the associated overhead. On the other hand there are systems where, even with an infallible data link control scheme, some packets can get lost due to a failure of a node of the communication network. (Think of a packet that clears the DLC unit of an incoming link to a node, and waits to enter the DLC unit of an outgoing link of the node. If the node crashes while the packet is waiting, the packet will be lost.) In such cases, it may be necessary to provide an additional error detection and retransmission scheme at a network–wide level rather than at a link level; see [BeG87] and [Tan81]. Furthermore it is necessary to provide a mechanism, called a *topology broadcast algorithm*, for informing all nodes about node or link failures. Such algorithms are typically distributed, and are discussed in Section 8.5.

1.3.3 Routing

The routing algorithm in an interconnection network is the mechanism by which packets are guided to their destinations through the network. The main objective of the routing algorithm is to select paths of small total delay for each packet. If there were no queueing delays along any link, the path selection would be quite simple. From Eq. (3.2), the delay associated with every link (i, j) would be equal to $P_{ij} + R_{ij}L$, where P_{ij} and R_{ij} are the processing plus propagation time, and the transmission time per bit on link (i, j), respectively, and L is the number of bits of the given packet. The problem of minimum delay routing from an origin node to a destination node would then be reduced to the problem of finding a path connecting the two nodes with minimum sum of link delays; this problem, known as the *shortest path problem*, will be discussed in detail in Sections 4.1 and 6.4. Unfortunately this method for selecting routes is totally insensitive to a potentially large packet arrival rate at any one link. As a result, some links may receive an excessive amount of traffic, thereby invalidating the assumption of negligible queueing delay.

To alleviate systematic tendencies for data traffic to be concentrated on a few links, several forms of multiple–path and randomized routing have been suggested. The idea here is to use more than one path for every origin–destination node pair, and to select, more or less at random, one of these paths for each packet. In one such method a shortest path is determined for every origin–destination pair; however, a packet originating at node A and destined to node B is not routed on the A to B shortest path. Instead, an intermediate node D is randomly chosen, and the packet is first routed from A to D along the A to D shortest path, and then from D to the packet's destination B along the D to B shortest path. Choosing the intermediate node at random for each individual packet tends to avoid congestion on links that lie on the shortest paths of one or more origin–destination pairs with excessive traffic. The randomized routing method just described is easy to implement in many systems, and is supported by some interesting analysis for highly regular interconnection networks (see [VaB81], [Val82], [HaC87], and [MiC87]). It has the drawback that it delivers the packets from A to B out of order, since a different intermediate destination D may be chosen for two successive packets. Furthermore, by randomizing its routes, this method does not use any available knowledge of the traffic pattern associated with a given algorithm.

The possibility of multiple–path and randomized routing arises also in connection with a different context relating to storage limitations. In practice, one must deal with the fact that when the storage space of a node is full, the node cannot receive any packet along its incident links. Several approaches to cope with this problem include flow control methods (see [BeG87]), and/or acknowledgment and retransmission schemes, whereby a packet that cannot be received due to unavailability of buffer space is retransmitted following a suitable timeout. A different approach modifies the routing algorithm so that there is always available buffer space to store a received packet at each node [Hil85]. To understand this approach, let us assume that all links of the communication network can be used simultaneously and in both directions, and that each packet carries a destination address and requires unit transmission time on every link. We also assume that packets are transmitted in slots of unit time duration, and that slots are synchronized so that their start and end is simultaneous at all links. In a typical routing scheme, based on the shortest path routing method, each node, upon reception of a packet that is destined for a different node, uses table lookup to determine the next link on which the packet should be transmitted; we refer to this link as the *assigned link of the packet*. It is possible that more than one packet with the same assigned link is received by a node during a slot. We refer to this situation as a *packet collision*. If there is a packet collision in a given slot at a given node, and we insist that all the packets involved in the collision are routed through their assigned link, then at most one packet involved in the collision can be transmitted by the node in the subsequent slot, and the remaining packets must be stored by the node in a queue. This storage requirement can be eliminated by modifying the routing scheme so that all the packets involved in a collision at a given node during a given slot are transmitted in the next slot; one of them is transmitted on its assigned link, and the others are transmitted on some other links chosen at random from the set of links that are not assigned to any packet received in the previous slot. It can be seen that with this modification, at any node with d incident links, there can be at most d packets received in any one slot, and each of these packets will be transmitted along some link (not necessarily their assigned one) in the next slot. Therefore, there will be no queueing, and the storage space needed at the node is minimized. The price paid for this reduced storage requirement is that successive packets of the same origin–destination pair may be received out of order, and some packets may travel on long routes to their destinations; indeed, in this scheme, one may need to take precautions to ensure that a packet cannot travel on a cycle indefinitely.

An appropriate formulation of the minimum delay routing problem must take into account the queueing delays at the links, but, unfortunately, these delays cannot be easily quantified in general. There are, however, simplified models that represent queueing delay at a link as a function of the packet arrival rate at the link. Distributed optimal routing algorithms based on such models are discussed in Sections 5.6 and 7.6. They are useful in data network situations where there are many users sharing the network, with each user having a data rate that is small relative to the combined data rate of all users. In such networks, the packet arrival rate at a link is a meaningful quantity that can be measured as a time average over a suitable period of time; see [BeG87]. Unfortunately, in most computing systems, and for most algorithms, there is no meaningful notion of packet arrival rate at a link, in which case these simplified queueing models are not appropriate.

On the other hand, the networks of many parallel computing systems have some regular form, and the routing problem may be posed in connection with a given algorithm that generates packets in a regular and predictable pattern. It may then be possible to design a routing algorithm that is tailored to the system and the algorithm at hand. In the next subsection, we look at some possibilities along these lines.

1.3.4 Network Topologies

In many systems such as data networks, sensor networks, distributed databases, etc., geographical and other considerations usually lead to interconnection networks with irregular form. On the other hand, in systems whose principal function is numerical computation, the network typically exhibits some regularity, and is sometimes chosen with a particular application in mind. In this subsection we discuss some example networks, and we focus on their communication properties.

We will represent a communication network of processors as a graph $G = (N, A)$, also referred to, somewhat loosely, as a *topology*. The nodes of the graph correspond to the processors, and the presence of an (undirected) arc (i, j) indicates that there is a direct communication link that serves as an error free, asynchronous packet pipe between processor i and processor j in both directions. We assume that communication can take place simultaneously on all of the incident links of a node and in both directions. We also assume in each of the communication analyses of this subsection that, in the absence of queueing, the delays of all packets of equal length (i.e., with the same number of bits) are equal on all links. Unless the opposite is clearly implied by the context, we assume that the delay of each packet is one time unit on every link. A somewhat restrictive assumption that is implicit in our analysis of some communication algorithms is that these algorithms are simultaneously initiated at all processors. However, the qualitative conclusions of our discussion remain largely unchanged even if the preceding assumptions do not hold. We will often use the notation $O(\cdot)$, $\Omega(\cdot)$, and $\Theta(\cdot)$, introduced in Subsection 1.2.2 and in Appendix A.

Topologies are usually evaluated in terms of their suitability for some standard communication tasks. The following are some typical criteria:

(a) The *diameter* of the network, which is the maximum distance between any pair of nodes. Here the distance of a pair of nodes is the minimum number of links that have to be traversed to go from one node to the other. For a network of diameter r, the time for a packet to travel between two nodes is $O(r)$, assuming no queueing delays at the links.

(b) The *connectivity* of the network, which provides a measure of the number of "independent" paths connecting a pair of nodes. We can talk here about the node or the arc connectivity of the network, which is the minimum number of nodes (or arcs, respectively) that must be deleted before the network becomes disconnected. In some networks, a high connectivity is desirable for reliability purposes, so that communication can be maintained in the face of several link and node failures. Another important point is that if the network has arc connectivity k, then communication between any two nodes can be parallelized by making use of at least k paths with no pair of these paths having an arc in common (this follows from the max flow – min cut theorem [PaS82], and will not be proved here). Thus, a long message can be sent from node A to node B by splitting it into several packets, and by sending these packets in parallel on the arc–disjoint paths connecting A and B. In the absence of queueing delays and with negligible overhead and propagation time per packet, this reduces the communication time between any pair of nodes by a factor at least equal to the arc connectivity of the network. (However, the packets may arrive at the destination node in unpredictable order, so they may have to be put back in order to reconstruct the message. In some systems this may be undesirable because of the overhead involved, and possibly other reasons.) Note that the arc and node connectivity is bounded from above by the minimum value of the *degree* of a node defined as the number of incident arcs to the node.

(c) The *flexibility* provided in running efficiently a broad variety of algorithms. As an example, assuming that we have developed an algorithm that runs on a given network of processors represented by a graph $G' = (N', A')$, we may want to run the same algorithm on another network of processors represented by a graph $G = (N, A)$. This will be possible if G' can be imbedded into G in the sense that each node of G' can be mapped to a node of G in a way that the arcs of G' are associated with arcs of G, that is, if there exists a function $\sigma : N' \mapsto N$ such that $\sigma(i) \neq \sigma(j)$ if $i \neq j$ and $\big(\sigma(i), \sigma(j)\big) \in A$ for all $(i, j) \in A'$. In this case we say that G' can be *mapped* into G. The mapping problem also arises in another interesting context. Given a processor network with a fixed interconnection topology, an important issue is to divide a given computational task among the processors so that the communication penalty is kept at a minimum. Assume that the main task is divided into computational subtasks, and that each subtask will be assigned to a separate processor. Assume also that certain pairs (i, j) of subtasks interact, meaning that the execution of subtask i or j occasionally requires knowledge of certain values computed during execution of subtask j or i, respectively. It is then desirable to allocate subtasks to processors so that interacting subtasks are assigned to processors with a direct communication link. This problem can be formulated as a problem of mapping the graph $G' = (N', A')$ representing the subtask interactions into the graph $G = (N, A)$ representing the processor network. As an example, in executing the relaxation iteration

$$x_i(t + 1) = f_i\big(x_1(t), \ldots, x_n(t)\big), \qquad \forall\, i = 1, \ldots, n, \qquad (3.3)$$

discussed in Subsection 1.2.4, we want to be able to map the dependency graph (cf. Subsection 1.2.4) into the processor network. We thus see the advantages of a topology that is flexible, in the sense that many other topologies can be mapped into it.

(d) The *communication delay* required for some standard tasks that are important in many algorithms such as inner product computation, matrix–vector multiplication, etc. We describe a few such tasks.

Single Node and Multinode Broadcast: In the first communication task, we want to send the same packet from a given processor to every other processor (we call this a *single node broadcast*). In a generalized version of this problem, we want to do a single node broadcast simultaneously from all nodes (we call this a *multinode broadcast*). A typical example where a multinode broadcast is needed arises in relaxation iterations of the form (3.3). If we assume that there is a separate processor assigned to each variable, and that each function f_i in the right–hand side of Eq. (3.3) depends on all variables, then, at the end of an iteration, there is a need for every processor to send the value of its variable to every other processor, which is a multinode broadcast. A special case of this example arises in matrix–vector multiplication, and will be discussed in Example 3.1, and in Subsection 1.3.6.

Clearly, to solve the single node broadcast problem, it is sufficient to transmit the given node's packet along a *spanning tree rooted at the given node*, that is, a spanning tree of the network together with a direction on each link of the tree such that there is a unique positive path from the given node (called the *root*) to every other node. With an optimal choice of such a spanning tree, a single node broadcast takes $O(r)$ time, where r is the diameter of the network, as shown in Fig. 1.3.4(a). Note that if a long packet is involved in a single node broadcast, it can be segmented into smaller packets that can be transmitted sequentially along the spanning tree, thereby resulting in a potentially significant reduction of the broadcast time; this is similar to the pipelining effect that we discussed in connection with transmitting a long packet over a sequence of links (cf. Fig. 1.3.1). Suppose, in particular, that the packet requires one time unit for transmission on any link, and that it is segmented into m packets each requiring $1/m$ time units for transmission on any link (i.e., there is no extra communication overhead due to the segmentation). Then it can be seen that the time for the single node broadcast with a worst choice of the root node and an optimal choice of the spanning tree is reduced from r to $(r + m - 1)/m$ time units. For a more precise estimate that takes overhead into account, see Exercise 3.19.

To solve the multinode broadcast problem, we need to specify one spanning tree per root node. The difficulty here is that some links may belong to several spanning trees; this complicates the timing analysis, because several packets can arrive simultaneously at a node, and require transmission on the same link with a queueing delay resulting. This issue will be discussed later in the context of specific interconnection networks.

Single Node and Multinode Accumulation: There are two important communication problems that are dual to the single and multinode broadcasts, in the sense that the spanning tree(s) used to solve one problem can also be used to solve the dual in the same amount of communication time. In the first problem, called *single node accumulation*, we want to send to a given node a packet from every other node; we assume, however, that packets can be "combined" for transmission on any communication link, with a "combined" transmission time equal to the

SINGLE NODE BROADCAST   SINGLE NODE ACCUMULATION

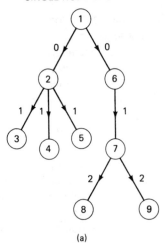
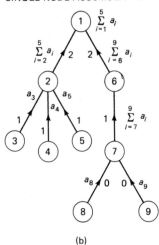

(a)   (b)

Figure 1.3.4   (a) A single node broadcast uses a tree that is rooted at a given node (which is node 1 in the figure). The time next to each link is the time at which transmission of the packet on the link begins. (b) A single node accumulation problem involving summation of n scalars $a_1, \ldots, a_n$ (one per processor) at the given node (which is node 1 in the figure). The time next to each link is the time at which transmission of the "combined" packet on the link begins, assuming that the time for scalar addition is negligible relative to the time required for packet transmission. The time for single node accumulation (or broadcast) is the maximum length of a path from a node to the root (or from the root to a node, respectively), counting each link as one unit. Thus, the single node accumulation and the single node broadcast take the same amount of time if a single packet in the latter problem corresponds to a scalar in the former problem.

transmission time of a single packet. This problem arises, for example, when we want to form at a given node a sum consisting of one term from each node as in an inner product calculation [see Fig. 1.3.4(b)]; we can view addition of scalars at a node as "combining" the corresponding packets into a single packet. The second problem, which is dual to a multinode broadcast, is called *multinode accumulation*, and involves a separate single node accumulation at each node. For example, it will be seen in Subsection 1.3.6 that a certain method for carrying out parallel matrix–vector multiplication involves a multinode accumulation.

It can be shown that a single node (or multinode) accumulation problem can be solved in the same time as a single node (respectively, multinode) broadcast problem. In particular, any single node (or multinode) accumulation algorithm can be viewed as a single node (or multinode, respectively) broadcast algorithm running in reverse time; the converse is also true. The process is illustrated in Fig. 1.3.4; the detailed mathematical proof is left for the reader.

Single Node Scatter, Single Node Gather, and Total Exchange: Another interesting communication problem is to send a packet from every node to every other node (here a node sends different packets to different nodes in contrast with the multinode broadcast problem where each node sends the same packet to every other node). We call this the *total exchange problem*, and we will see later that it arises frequently in connection with matrix computations. A related problem, called the *single node scatter* problem, involves sending a separate packet from a single node to every other node. A dual problem, called *single node gather* problem, involves collecting a packet at a given node from every other node. An algorithm that solves the single node scatter (or gather) problem consists of a schedule of packet transmissions on each link that properly takes queueing into account. By reversing this schedule as discussed in connection with the single node accumulation problem, it can be seen that for every algorithm that solves the single node scatter (or gather) problem, there is a corresponding algorithm that solves the single node gather (or scatter, respectively) problem, and takes the same amount of communication time.

Note that in a multinode broadcast, each node receives a different packet from every node, thereby solving the single node gather problem. Note also that the total exchange problem may be viewed as a multinode version of both a single node scatter and a single node gather problem, and also as a generalization of a multinode broadcast, whereby the packets sent by each node to different nodes are different. We conclude that the communication problems of the preceding discussion form a hierarchy in terms of difficulty, as illustrated in Fig. 1.3.5. An algorithm solving one problem in the hierarchy can also solve the next problem in the hierarchy in no additional time. In particular, a total exchange algorithm can also solve the multinode broadcast (accumulation) problem; a multinode broadcast (accumulation) algorithm can also solve the single node gather (scatter) problem; and a single node scatter (gather) algorithm can also solve the single node broadcast (accumulation) problem. Therefore, the communication requirements for these problems decrease in the order just given, regardless of the network being used.

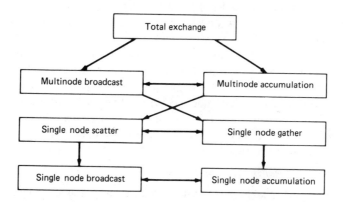

Figure 1.3.5 Hierarchy of basic communication problems in interconnection networks. A directed arc from problem A to problem B indicates that an algorithm that solves A can also solve B, and that the optimal time for solving A is not more than the optimal time for solving B. A horizontal bidirectional arc indicates a duality relation.

We now consider a number of specific topologies.

Complete Graph

Here there is a direct link between every pair of processors. Such a network can be implemented by means of a bus which is shared by all processors, or by means of some type of crossbar switch. Clearly this is an ideal network in terms of flexibility. Unfortunately, when the number of processors is very large, a crossbar switch becomes very costly, and a bus involves large queueing delays. Complete graphs, however, are frequently used to connect small numbers of processors in clusters in a hierarchical network, where the clusters are themselves connected via some other type of communication network.

Linear Processor Array

Here there are p processors/nodes numbered $1, 2, \ldots, p$, and there is a link $(i, i + 1)$ for every pair of successive processors [see Fig. 1.3.6(a)]. The diameter and connectivity properties of this network are the worst possible. Furthermore, one can map a linear array into most other networks of interest (all networks discussed in this section with the exception of trees). This means that the communication penalty for a given algorithm using a linear array can be no better than the corresponding penalty using most other networks. The time taken by an optimal single node broadcast algorithm depends on the origin node; at worst, it is $p - 1$ time units (assuming each packet transmission requires unit time), since the diameter of the linear array is $p - 1$. An optimal multinode broadcast algorithm takes the same amount of time thanks to the possibility of using all communication links in parallel [see Fig. 1.3.6(b)]. The time taken by an optimal single node scatter algorithm lies between the times taken by an optimal single node and an optimal multinode broadcast algorithm, and is therefore at worst $p - 1$ time units. In fact it can be shown that the time taken by an optimal single node broadcast algorithm as well as by an optimal single node scatter algorithm starting at node k is $\max\{k - 1, p - k\}$ time units (see Exercise 3.9). Finally, an optimal total exchange algorithm takes $\Theta(p^2)$ time. To see this, consider the link $(k, k + 1)$ that separates the array in two node subsets with k and $p - k$ nodes respectively. Since in a total exchange each node of one subset must send a packet to each node of the other subset, the link must carry $k(p - k)$ packet transmissions in each direction. Allowing for the worst possible link selection, we see that any total exchange algorithm takes at least $\max_k [k(p - k)]$ or (after some calculation) $\lceil (p^2 - 1)/4 \rceil$ time units. On the other hand, one way to solve the total exchange problem (not necessarily the fastest) is to solve sequentially p single node scatter problems, one for each of the p processors. Every one of these problems can be solved in no more than $p - 1$ time units, thereby showing that an optimal total exchange algorithm takes $\Theta(p^2)$ time.

Example 3.1.   *Matrix–Vector Multiplication*

Consider the problem of parallel multiplication of an $n \times n$ fully dense matrix with an n-dimensional vector, with subsequent communication of the result to all of the p processors of a linear array. We assume here that $n = pk$, where $k \geq 1$ is some integer, and that processor i knows the vector and the rows $(i - 1)k + 1$ to ik of the matrix, and calculates coordinates $(i - 1)k + 1$ to ik of the matrix–vector product. At the end of the calculation each processor

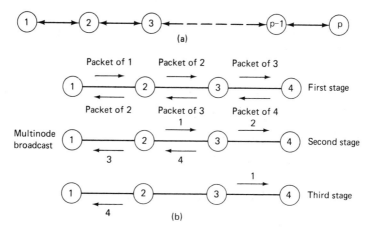

Figure 1.3.6 (a) Linear array with p processors. There is a bidirectional communication link $(i, i+1)$ for each $i = 1, 2, \ldots, p-1$. (b) A multinode broadcast in a linear array can be conducted in stages. At the first stage, each node sends to its neighbor(s) its own packet. Each node $i \in \{2, 3, \ldots, p-1\}$ that receives a packet from $i+1$ (or $i-1$) at some stage, relays this packet to $i-1$ (or $i+1$, respectively) at the next stage. Nodes 1 and p send a packet only at the first stage. Thus, at stage k, node i receives the packet of node $i-k$ (if $i > k$), and the packet of node $i+k$ (if $i \leq p-k$). The multinode broadcast is completed after $p-1$ stages. The figure illustrates this process for $p = 4$.

i sends these k coordinates to all other processors in a single packet. This is a multinode broadcast. Normalizing the length of a packet, we assume that each packet contains k data units and w units of overhead. We assume that the delay of each packet on each link is $\alpha(k + w)$, where α is some constant. (We neglect the processing and propagation delay; for the purposes of the subsequent calculation, it can be lumped into the overhead w.) The communication time using an optimal multinode broadcast algorithm is then $\Theta\big(p(k + w)\big)$, whereas the corresponding computation time is $\Theta(pk^2)$. We see, therefore, that for any given number of processors p, if $n = pk$ is sufficiently large, the time spent for communication is negligible relative to the time for computation. This phenomenon holds for many problems of interest (see Subsection 1.3.5), and is significant since it indicates that the communication penalty does not prevent the effective use of an increased number of processors in matrix–type problems as their dimension becomes larger. The appropriate number of processors used, however, should be chosen judiciously; it is not always advantageous to use as many processors as available. To see this, note that the computation time is $\Theta(nk)$ and the communication time is $\Theta\big(n(1 + w/k)\big)$. For many practical systems, the size of w is such that when k is small, the communication time becomes dominant.

Ring

This is a simple and common network that has the property that there is a path between any pair of processors even after any one communication link has failed. However, the number of links separating a pair of processors can be as large as $\lceil (p-1)/2 \rceil$, where p is the number of processors. It can be seen that all of the basic communication problems discussed earlier (single node and multinode broadcast, single node scatter, and total exchange) can be solved on a ring in a time that lies between the corresponding time on a linear array with the same number of nodes, and one–half that time (see Fig. 1.3.7 for the case of a multinode broadcast).

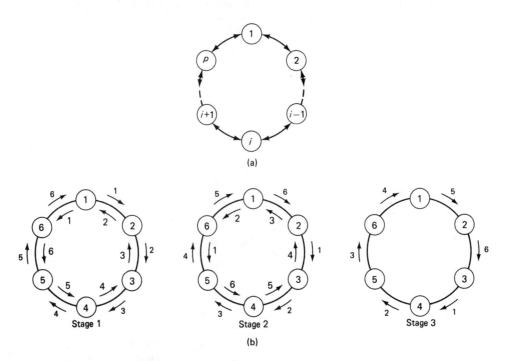

Figure 1.3.7 (a) A ring of p nodes having as links the pairs $(i, i+1)$ for $i = 1, 2, \ldots, p-1$, and $(p, 1)$. (b) A multinode broadcast on a ring with p nodes can be performed in $\lceil (p-1)/2 \rceil$ stages as follows: at stage 1, each node sends its own packet to its clockwise and counterclockwise neighbors. At stages $2, \ldots, \lceil (p-1)/2 \rceil$, each node sends to its clockwise neighbor the packet received from its counterclockwise neighbor at the previous stage; also, at stages $2, \ldots, \lceil (p-2)/2 \rceil$, each node sends to its counterclockwise neighbor the packet received from its clockwise neighbor at the previous stage. The figure illustrates this process for $p = 6$.

Tree

A tree network with p processors provides communication between every pair of processors with a minimal number of links ($p - 1$). One disadvantage of a tree is its low connectivity; the failure of any one of its links creates two subsets of processors that cannot communicate with each other. Furthermore, depending on the particular type of tree used, its diameter can be as large as $p - 1$ (note that the linear array is a special case of a tree). The star network has minimal diameter among tree topologies; however the central node of the star handles all the network traffic, and can become a bottleneck [see Fig. 1.3.8(a)]. It can be shown that the optimal time for a single node broadcast (or accumulation) and a single node gather (or scatter) on a tree with p processors is no more than $p - 1$ time units, whereas the optimal time for a multinode broadcast is

$p - 1$ time units (Exercises 3.2 and 3.9). The optimal time for a total exchange depends on the type of tree considered, and it is $O(p^2)$ based on the result for the single node gather problem stated earlier. An interesting type of tree is the *binary and balanced tree* described in Fig. 1.3.8(b). It can be seen that an optimal total exchange algorithm on a binary balanced tree takes $\Theta(p^2)$ time (Exercise 3.2).

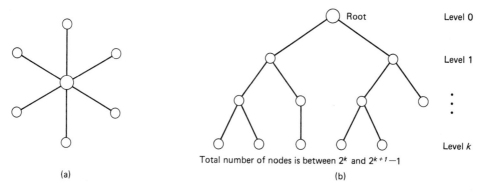

(a)   (b)

Figure 1.3.8   (a) A star network. (b) A binary balanced tree. Here there is a special node called the *root*. Each node i is connected to the root via a unique simple walk. The first node on this walk is called the *parent* of i. If j is the parent of i, then i is called a *child* of i. In a binary tree there can be at most two children for each node. A node with no children is said to be a *leaf* of the tree. A binary tree with p nodes is said to be balanced if the walk from each leaf node to the root contains either $\lceil \log(p+1) \rceil - 2$ or $\lceil \log(p+1) \rceil - 1$ links.

Mesh

Many large problems of interest are closely tied to the geometry of physical space. Mesh–connected processor arrays are often well suited for such problems. In a d–dimensional mesh the processors are arranged along the points of d–dimensional space that have integer coordinates, and there is a direct communication link between nearest neighbors. Using the graph formalism, the nodes of a d–dimensional mesh with n_i points along the ith dimension are the d–tuples $(x_1, \ldots, x_d)$ where each of the coordinates x_i, $i = 1, \ldots, d$, takes an integer value from 1 to n_i. The links are the pairs $\big((x_1, \ldots, x_d), (x'_1, \ldots, x'_d)\big)$ for which there exists some i such that $|x_i - x'_i| = 1$ and $x_j = x'_j$ for all $j \neq i$. The diameter of a mesh–connected network is $\sum_{i=1}^{d}(n_i - 1)$, which can be much smaller than the diameter of a ring and much larger than the diameter of a binary balanced tree with the same number of processors. A variation with smaller diameter is the *mesh network with wraparound* shown in Fig. 1.3.9.

Consider now the time needed to solve various communication problems on a d–dimensional mesh with p processors, which is *symmetric* in the sense that it has an equal number $(p^{1/d})$ of processors along each dimension. We assume that d is fixed and we estimate the communication time as a function of p. An optimal single node broadcast (or accumulation) algorithm takes $\Theta(p^{1/d})$ time, since the diameter is $d(p^{1/d} - 1)$. It is easily seen that a linear array with p nodes can be mapped into the symmetric mesh,

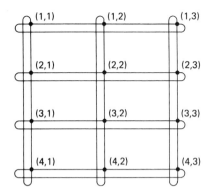
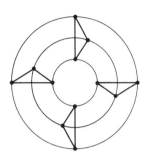

Figure 1.3.9 Meshes with wraparound. Here, in addition to the links of the ordinary mesh, we have the links $\big((x_1,\ldots,x_{i-1},1,x_{i+1},\ldots,x_d),(x_1,\ldots,x_{i-1},n_i,x_{i+1},\ldots,x_d)\big)$. The diameter is roughly half the diameter of the corresponding ordinary mesh.

and, therefore, the time taken by an optimal single node scatter (or gather) algorithm and by an optimal multinode broadcast (or accumulation) algorithm do not exceed the corresponding times for the linear array, which are $O(p)$. On the other hand, any single node scatter (and, *a fortiori*, multinode broadcast) algorithm takes $\Omega(p)$ time since $p-1$ packets are transmitted by the given node, and these packets must go over the incident links to the node, which are no more than $2d$. Therefore an optimal single node scatter (or gather) algorithm, and an optimal multinode broadcast (or accumulation) algorithm take $\Theta(p)$ time. Consider, finally, the total exchange problem. Exercise 3.6 gives a total exchange algorithm that takes $O(p^{(d+1)/d})$ time, and it turns out that any total exchange algorithm takes $\Omega(p^{(d+1)/d})$ time. To see this latter fact, assume for convenience that p is even and consider a $(d-1)$–dimensional plane that separates the mesh in two identical "halves" (a similar argument applies when p is odd). Each half contains $p/2$ processors, which must receive a total of $(p/2)^2$ packets from the $p/2$ processors of the other half. These packets must be transmitted over the $p^{(d-1)/d}$ communication links connecting the two halves requiring $\Omega(p^{(d+1)/d})$ time. Therefore, an optimal total exchange algorithm for a symmetric d–dimensional mesh takes $\Theta(p^{(d+1)/d})$ time.

Hypercube

Consider the set of all points in d–dimensional space with each coordinate equal to zero or one. These points may be thought of as the corners of a d–dimensional cube. We let these points correspond to processors, and we consider a communication link for every two points differing in a single coordinate. The resulting network is called a *hypercube* or *d–cube*. Fig. 1.3.10 shows a 3–cube and a 4–cube.

Formally, a d–cube is the d–dimensional mesh that has two processors in each dimension, that is, $n_i = 2$ for all i. To visualize better a d–cube, we assume that each processor has an identity number which is a binary string of length d (corresponding to the coordinates of a node of the d–cube). We can construct a hypercube of any dimension

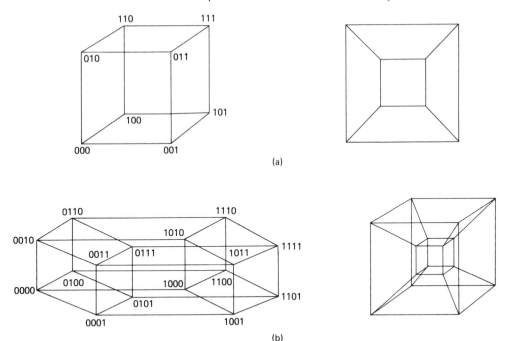

Figure 1.3.10 Two views of a 3–cube and a 4–cube. The cubes have been constructed by connecting the corresponding nodes of two identical lower–dimensional cubes. In the cubes on the left, a node belongs to the first lower–dimensional cube or the second depending on whether its identity has a leading 0 or a leading 1.

by connecting lower–dimensional cubes, starting with a 1–cube. In particular, we can start with two $(d-1)$–dimensional cubes and introduce a link connecting each pair of nodes with the same identity number. This constructs a d–cube with the identity number of each node obtained by adding a leading 0 or a leading 1 to its previous identity, depending on whether the node belongs to the first $(d-1)$–dimensional cube or the second (see Fig. 1.3.10).

The *Hamming distance* between two processors is the number of bits in which their identity numbers differ. Two processors are directly connected with a communication link if and only if their Hamming distance is unity, that is, if and only if their identity numbers differ in exactly one bit. The number of links on any path connecting two nodes cannot be less than the Hamming distance of the nodes. Furthermore, there is a path with a number of links that is equal to the Hamming distance. Such a path can be obtained by switching in sequence the bits in which the identity numbers of the two nodes differ (equivalently, by traversing the corresponding links of the hypercube). For example, in a 4–cube, to go from node (1101) to node (0110), we can first go to (0101), then to (0111), and finally to (0110). It follows that the diameter of a d–cube is d or $\log p$, where $p = 2^d$ is the number of processors.

Hypercube Mappings

The hypercube is a versatile architecture with many attractive features, some of which will be discussed in the sequel. We first illustrate the flexibility of the hypercube by showing how to map a ring and a mesh into it. Mapping a linear array of 2^d nodes into a hypercube amounts to constructing a sequence of 2^d distinct binary numbers with d bits each, with the property that successive numbers in the sequence differ in only one bit. Such sequences are called *Gray codes*, and have been studied extensively in coding theory [Ham86]. We can generate a particular type of Gray code, called a *reflected Gray code* (RGC), by a construction that is similar to the one used for constructing a d–cube from two $(d-1)$–cubes. This code has the property that the first and the last numbers in the sequence also differ in only one bit, so it provides a mapping of a ring with 2^d nodes into the hypercube. We start with the 1–bit Gray code sequence $\{0, 1\}$, and then insert a zero and a one in front of the two elements obtaining the two sequences $\{00, 01\}$ and $\{10, 11\}$. We then reverse the second sequence to obtain $\{11, 10\}$, and then concatenate the two sequences to obtain the 2–bit RGC

$$\{00, 01, 11, 10\}.$$

Generally, given a $(d-1)$–bit RGC

$$\{b_1, b_2, \ldots, b_p\},$$

where $p = 2^{d-1}$ and $b_1, \ldots, b_p$ are binary strings, the corresponding d–bit RGC is

$$\{0b_1, \ldots, 0b_p, 1b_p, \ldots, 1b_1\}.$$

As an example, the 3–bit and the 4–bit RGC, and the corresponding rings on the 3–cube and the 4–cube are shown in Fig. 1.3.11. The above construction maps a ring with 2^d nodes into the d–cube. It is also possible to map a ring of any even number of nodes p into a hypercube with $2^{\lceil \log p \rceil}$ nodes (see Exercise 3.4). It can be shown that every cycle in a hypercube has an even number of nodes (Exercise 3.4), so a ring with an odd number of nodes cannot be mapped into a hypercube.

The preceding recursive construction of the RGC sequence can be generalized in a way that will prove useful later. Let d_a and d_b be positive integers, and let $d = d_a + d_b$. Suppose that $\{a_1, a_2, \ldots, a_{p_a}\}$ and $\{b_1, b_2, \ldots, b_{p_b}\}$ are the d_a–bit and d_b–bit RGC sequences, where $p_a = 2^{d_a}$ and $p_b = 2^{d_b}$. Consider the $p_a \times p_b$ matrix of d–bit strings $\{a_i b_j \mid i = 1, 2, \ldots, p_a, \ j = 1, 2, \ldots, p_b\}$

$$\begin{bmatrix} a_1 b_1 & a_1 b_2 & \ldots & a_1 b_{p_b} \\ a_2 b_1 & a_2 b_2 & \ldots & a_2 b_{p_b} \\ \vdots & \vdots & \ddots & \vdots \\ a_{p_a} b_1 & a_{p_a} b_2 & \ldots & a_{p_a} b_{p_b} \end{bmatrix}.$$

119920

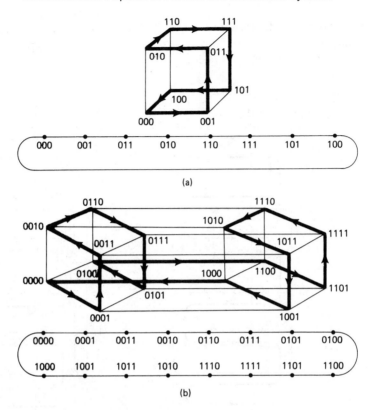

Figure 1.3.11   Reflected Gray code sequences, and the corresponding mappings of rings on (a) a 3–cube and (b) a 4–cube.

It can be proved that we can obtain the d–bit RGC sequence by sequentially traversing the rows of this matrix alternately from left to right, and from right to left, as shown:

$$
\begin{bmatrix}
a_1b_1 & \Longrightarrow & a_1b_2 & \Longrightarrow & \cdots & \Longrightarrow & a_1b_{p_b} \\
 & & & & & & \Downarrow \\
a_2b_1 & \Longleftarrow & a_2b_2 & \Longleftarrow & \cdots & \Longleftarrow & a_2b_{p_b} \\
\Downarrow & & & & & & \\
a_3b_1 & \Longrightarrow & a_3b_2 & \Longrightarrow & \cdots & \Longrightarrow & a_3b_{p_b} \\
 & & & & & & \Downarrow \\
\vdots & & \vdots & & \vdots & \ddots & \vdots \\
 & & & & & & \Downarrow \\
a_{p_a}b_1 & \Longleftarrow & a_{p_a}b_2 & \Longleftarrow & \cdots & \Longleftarrow & a_{p_a}b_{p_b}
\end{bmatrix}.
$$

An example is given in Fig. 1.3.12(a). A formal proof is obtained using the definition of the RGC sequence and induction on d, as illustrated in Fig. 1.3.12(b). The preceding construction also shows that the nodes of a d–cube can be arranged along a two–dimensional mesh with p_a and p_b nodes in the first and second dimensions, respectively. The (i, j)th element of the mesh, where $i = 1, 2, \ldots, p_a$ and $j = 1, 2, \ldots, p_b$, is the d–cube node with identity number $a_i b_j$. Each "row" (or "column") of the mesh corresponds to a hypercube with p_b (or p_a, respectively) nodes.

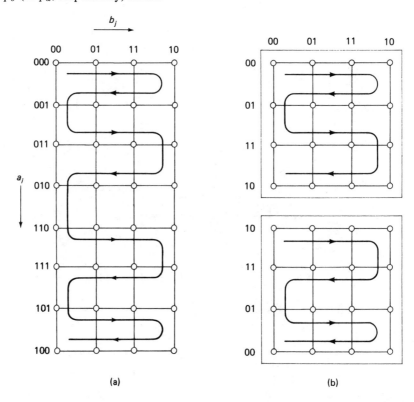

(a)   (b)

Figure 1.3.12 (a) Arrangement of the nodes of a 5–cube in a two-dimensional mesh with 8 rows and 4 columns. The 5-bit RGC sequence is obtained by starting at the mesh point $(000, 00)$, going right along the first row, then left along the second row, then right along the third row, etc., as indicated by the arrows. Each row corresponds to a 2–cube, and each column corresponds to a 3–cube. (b) Construction of the mapping of an 8×4 mesh (and the corresponding RGC) into a 5–cube, using two 4×4 meshes mapped into the 4–cube. The row numbering of the second mesh is first reversed as shown, and then the two meshes are joined, and a leading 0 or 1 is appended to the row number of the first or second mesh, respectively. This procedure can be generalized to prove by induction that the $(d_a + d_b)$–bit RGC sequence can be constructed from the d_a–bit and the d_b–bit RGC sequences, as stated in the text.

We can similarly obtain a general method for mapping a multidimensional mesh into a hypercube. Suppose we have a k–dimensional mesh with n_i points in the ith dimension, where $i = 1, \ldots, k$. We assume that $n_i = 2^{d_i}$, where d_i is some integer. Thus the number of mesh points is 2^d, where $d = d_1 + d_2 + \cdots + d_k$, and each mesh point can be denoted by $(x_1, x_2, \ldots, x_k)$, where x_i is an integer taking values from 1 to n_i. We map the mesh point $(x_1, x_2, \ldots, x_k)$ into the hypercube node with identity $s_1 s_2 \cdots s_k$, where s_i is the d_i–bit binary string which is the x_ith element of the d_i–bit RGC. Adjacent

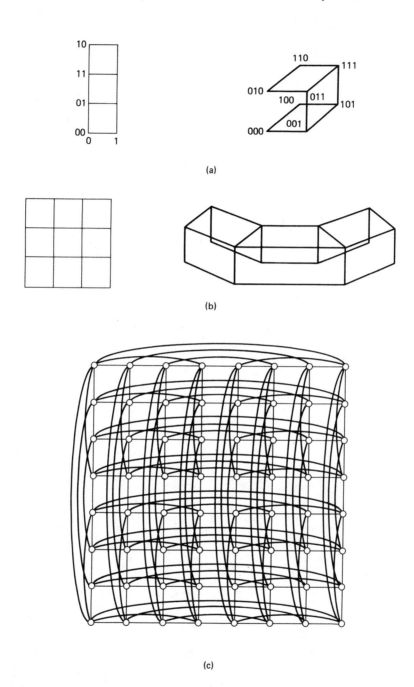

Figure 1.3.13 (a) Mapping a 2 × 4 mesh into a 3–cube. (b) Mapping a 4 × 4 mesh into a 4–cube. (c) A 6–cube arranged as an 8 × 8 mesh. Note that each row and each column of the mesh is a 3–cube.

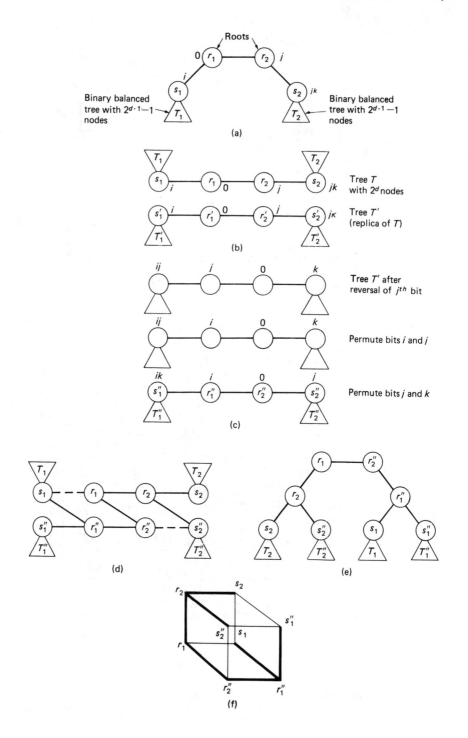

(a)

Binary balanced tree with $2^{d-1}-1$ nodes T_1

Binary balanced tree with $2^{d-1}-1$ nodes T_2

(b)

Tree T with 2^d nodes

Tree T' (replica of T)

(c)

Tree T' after reversal of jth bit

Permute bits i and j

Permute bits j and k

(d)

(e)

(f)

Figure 1.3.14 Recursive construction of a mapping of a two–rooted binary balanced tree into a hypercube. (a) A two–rooted binary tree with 2^d nodes mapped into a d–cube. Node r_1 is mapped into $(00\cdots0)$; nodes s_1 and r_2 are mapped into the d–cube nodes with the ith and jth bits set, respectively; node s_2 is mapped into the node with the jth and kth bits set. (b) Method for constructing a mapping of a two–rooted tree with 2^{d+1} nodes into the $(d+1)$–cube starting with two trees T and T', mapped into the d–cube. Three tranformations are applied sequentially to the node identity numbers of T', all of which yield mappings of T' into the d–cube. These are a reversal of the jth bit, a permutation of the ith and jth bits, and a permutation of the jth and kth bits [see part (c)]. The identity number for node r_2'' is now $(00\cdots0)$. The identities of nodes r_1'', and s_2'' differ from that of r_2'' in the ith and jth bit, respectively. The identity of node s_1'' differs from that of r_2'' in the ith and kth bits. A leading zero (one) is next appended to the identity number of each node of T (T', respectively, as transformed above). We now introduce the links (s_1, r_1''), (r_1, r_2''), (r_2, s_2'') as shown in part (d), thereby obtaining a mapping of the two–rooted tree shown in (e) into the $(d+1)$–cube. (f) Illustration of the mapping for $d = 2$.

nodes in the mesh differ by a unit in a single coordinate, say x_i, so the corresponding strings s_i are adjacent elements of the RGC sequence. Therefore, the corresponding nodes of the d–cube differ by a single bit in their identities, and must be adjacent. The desired mapping has thus been obtained. Fig. 1.3.13 illustrates the mapping for meshes in two dimensions. Note that a mesh with n_i points in the ith dimension can be mapped into a mesh with $2^{\lceil \log n_i \rceil}$ points in the ith dimension, and therefore can be mapped into a d–cube, where $d = \sum_{i=1}^{k} \lceil \log n_i \rceil$. Note also that because the first and the last elements of a RGC sequence differ in a single bit, the mapping just given can be used to map the corresponding mesh with wraparound (cf. Fig. 1.3.9) into the hypercube.

One can show that a complete binary tree, that is, a binary balanced tree with $2^d - 1$ nodes, cannot be mapped into a d–cube if $d \geq 3$ [BhI85]. On the other hand, a related tree of 2^d nodes, called a *two–rooted binary balanced tree*, can be mapped on the d–cube [BhI85]. This tree is obtained from a binary balanced tree by replacing the root node with two root nodes, each connected with the other and also connected with one binary balanced subtree as shown in Fig. 1.3.14. The construction of this mapping proceeds recursively using two trees each mapped into a d–cube to construct a tree mapped into the $(d+1)$–cube, starting with $d = 2$ (see Fig. 1.3.14). From the point of view of communication, we may consider the two root nodes, together with the link connecting them, as a single node that emulates the function of the (single) root of a binary balanced tree. Thus, using this mapping, it is possible to execute on a hypercube algorithms that are naturally suited for binary tree topologies.

Hypercube Communications

We now consider issues of communication. We first note that in contrast with tree topologies, the d–cube provides several "independent" paths between any pair of nodes (that is paths that do not share any links). The number of such paths is at most d, since there are d links incident to each node. It turns out that there are exactly d such paths (see Fig. 1.3.15). These paths, in addition, do not share any node other than the two end nodes, which shows that the node connectivity of the d–cube is d. If the identity numbers of the two end nodes differ by k bits, then k of the independent paths have k links, and the remaining $d - k$ paths have $k + 2$ links (see Fig. 1.3.15). This implies that simultaneous communication between two nodes of a hypercube along several paths can be done very efficiently.

Another property of the d–cube is that for each node i, there is a spanning tree rooted at i, and providing a path of d links or less from i to every node. Such a tree is constructed as shown in Fig. 1.3.16, and can be used for a single node broadcast from the root to all nodes that takes d time units. This is an improvement by a factor $(2^d - 1)/d$ over the corresponding time for the linear array with 2^d nodes. The same tree can be used to solve the dual problem of a single node accumulation in d time units. The two–rooted tree of Fig. 1.3.14 can also be used for the same purpose in place of the spanning tree of Fig. 1.3.16.

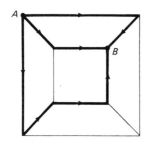

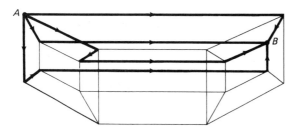

Figure 1.3.15 Construction of d independent paths connecting two nodes A and B of the d–cube with identity numbers differing in k bits [SaS88]. Without loss of generality, we assume that the first k bits of the identity numbers of A and B are different, and the remaining $d - k$ bits are the same.

We first construct k paths from A to B having k links each. The ith path is constructed as follows: start with the identity of A; reverse sequentially bit i through k; reverse sequentially bits 1 through $i - 1$.

We next construct $d - k$ paths from A to B having $k + 2$ links each. The ith path is constructed as follows: start with the identity of A; reverse the $(k + i)$th bit; reverse sequentially bits 1 through k; reverse again the $(k + i)$th bit.

It can be seen that all these paths do not share any node other than A and B, proving that the node connectivity of a d–cube is d. The figure illustrates the paths for a pair of nodes in the 3–cube and in the 4–cube.

Consider next the time needed for a multinode broadcast, whereby each processor sends a packet to every other processor. As in linear arrays, it is possible to exploit parallel communication on the links. In a d–cube, each node can receive at most d new packets simultaneously along its d incident links, and, since a separate packet is to be received from each of the $(2^d - 1)$ other nodes, we see that (assuming unit time for each packet transmission) any multinode broadcast algorithm takes at least $\lceil (2^d - 1)/d \rceil$ time. There are algorithms that attain this lower bound, and are therefore optimal. We construct such algorithms by means of a general procedure that generates multinode broadcast algorithms, starting from a single node broadcast algorithm and exploiting the symmetry of the network (see also Exercises 3.7 and 3.15).

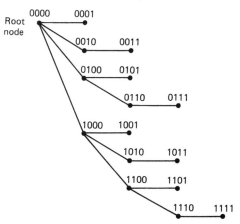

Figure 1.3.16 Spanning tree of a d–cube that is rooted at node $(00\cdots0)$, and provides a path of d links or less from the root node to every other node. The figure shows one possible construction for $d = 4$. The tree is constructed sequentially starting from the root by using the rule that the identities of the children of each node are obtained by reversing one of the zero bits of the identity of the parent that follow the rightmost unity bit. The leaf nodes are the ones that have one as the final bit in their identity. Using this tree, a single node broadcast from the root to all nodes, and a single node accumulation take $\Theta(d)$ communication time. The tree corresponding to an arbitrary root node with identity i can be obtained from the tree corresponding to the node with identity $(00\cdots0)$ by addition (mod 2) of the identity of each node on the tree with the identity of node i. [Here we use the fact that any two node identities x and y differ in exactly the same bits as $i \oplus x$ and $i \oplus y$, where $z \oplus w$ denotes the d-bit string obtained by performing modulo 2 addition of the kth bit of z and w for $k = 1, 2, \ldots, d$. Furthermore, we have $i \oplus (00\cdots0) = i$. As a result, if all identities j in the spanning tree shown are replaced by $i \oplus j$, all links shown will continue to be hypercube links and the resulting spanning tree will be rooted at the node with identity i.]

We represent an algorithm that broadcasts a packet from node $(00\cdots0)$ to all other nodes in m time units by a sequence of disjoint sets of directed links $A_1, A_2, \ldots, A_m$. Each A_i is the set of links on which transmission of the packet begins at time $i - 1$ and ends at time i. We impose on the sets A_i certain consistency requirements for accomplishing the single node broadcast. In particular, if S_i (E_i) is the set of identity numbers of the start (end, respectively) nodes of the links in A_i, we must have $S_1 = \{(00\cdots0)\}$, and $S_i \subset \{(00\cdots0)\} \cup \left(\cup_{k=1}^{i-1} E_k\right)$. Furthermore, every nonzero node identity must belong to some E_i. The set of all nodes together with the set of links $\left(\cup_{i=1}^{m} A_i\right)$ must form a subgraph which is a spanning tree [see Fig. 1.3.17(a)].

Consider now a d–bit string t representing the identity number of some node on the d–cube. For any node identity z, we denote by $t \oplus z$ the d–bit string obtained by performing modulo 2 addition of the jth bit of t and z for $j = 1, 2, \ldots, d$. It can be seen that an algorithm for broadcasting a packet from the node with identity t is specified by the sets

$$A_i(t) = \{(t \oplus x, t \oplus y) \mid (x, y) \in A_i\}, \qquad i = 1, 2, \ldots, m,$$

where $A_i(t)$ denotes the set of links on which transmission of the packet begins at time $i - 1$ and ends at time i. The proof of this is based on the fact that $t \oplus x$ and $t \oplus y$ differ in a particular bit if and only if x and y differ in the same bit, so $(t \oplus x, t \oplus y)$ is a link if and only if (x, y) is a link (see also Fig. 1.3.16).

We now describe a procedure for generating a multinode broadcast algorithm specified by the sets $A_i(t)$ for all possible values of i and t, starting from a single node broadcast algorithm specified by the sets $A_1, A_2, \ldots, A_m$. For any link (x, y), let $r_i(x, y)$ be the number of node identities t for which $(x, y) \in A_i(t)$, or, equivalently, $x = t \oplus w$

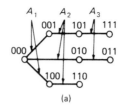

(a)

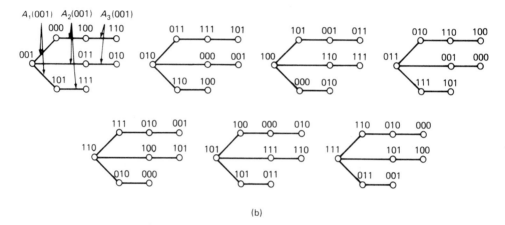

(b)

Figure 1.3.17   Generation of a multinode broadcast algorithm for the d–cube, starting from a single node broadcast algorithm. (a) The algorithm that broadcasts a packet from the node with identity $(00\cdots0)$ to all other nodes is specified by a sequence of sets of directed links $A_1, A_2, \ldots, A_m$. Each A_i is the set of links on which transmission begins at time $i-1$ and ends at time i. (b) A corresponding broadcast algorithm for each root node identity t is specified by the sets of links

$$A_i(t) = \{(t \oplus x, t \oplus y) \mid (x, y) \in A_i\},$$

where we denote by $t \oplus z$ the d–bit string obtained by performing modulo 2 addition of the jth bit of t and z for $j = 1, 2, \ldots, d$. The multinode broadcast algorithm is divided in m stages. Within stage i, the packet of each t is transmitted over the links in $A_i(t)$. Stage i takes time T_i. The figure shows the construction for an example where $d = 3$, $T_1 = 1$, $T_2 = 2$, $T_3 = 1$, and the multinode broadcast algorithm takes 4 time units. If the link $(000, 010)$ belonged to A_1 instead of A_2, the required time would be the optimal 3 time units.

and $y = t \oplus z$ for some link $(w, z) \in A_i$. For each of these node identities t, $A_i(t)$ specifies that there is a packet of t to be transmitted over link (x, y). It follows that for a fixed i, if transmission starts simultaneously in all the links of all the sets $A_i(t)$, then, allowing for queueing delays, the transmissions in all these links will be completed within time T_i given by

$$T_i = \max_{(x,y)} r_i(x, y).$$

Therefore, the total time taken by the multinode broadcast is at most $T_1 + T_2 + \cdots + T_m$. Thus efficient multinode broadcast algorithms can be obtained by choosing the sets $A_1, A_2, \ldots, A_m$ of the single node broadcast so that $T_1 + T_2 + \cdots + T_m$ is small. Figure

1.3.17(b) illustrates the sets $A_i(t)$ corresponding to all possible t and the times T_i for the case where $d = 3$. Note that $T_i = 1$ means that given any two links (x, y) and (x', y') of A_i, the bit in which x and y differ is not the same as the bit in which x' and y' differ. Thus, we have $T_2 > 1$ in Fig. 1.3.17 because the links $((000), (010))$ and $((100), (110))$ belong to A_2 but do not satisfy the preceding requirement. In Fig. 1.3.18 we give a method for selecting A_i so that $T_i = 1$ for all i, and the number of elements in each one of the sets $A_1, A_2, \ldots, A_{m-1}$ is d, while the number of elements in A_m is less than or equal to d. Since the total number of links in the spanning tree specified by $\cup_{i=1}^m A_i$ is $2^d - 1$, we conclude that $T_1 + T_2 + \cdots + T_m = m = \lceil (2^d - 1)/d \rceil$, and the corresponding multinode broadcast algorithm takes the optimal time $\lceil (2^d - 1)/d \rceil$.

An optimal single node scatter algorithm takes no more than the $\lceil (2^d - 1)/d \rceil$ time taken by an optimal multinode broadcast algorithm. Also, since $(2^d - 1)$ packets must be transmitted along the d incident links of the origin node, any single node scatter algorithm takes at least $\lceil (2^d - 1)/d \rceil$ time (assuming each packet requires unit time for transmission). It follows that $\lceil (2^d - 1)/d \rceil$ is the optimal time to solve the single node scatter problem and its dual, the single node gather problem. The sets of links $A_1, A_2, \ldots, A_m$ constructed in Fig. 1.3.18 can be used to define optimal scatter and gather algorithms for every processor. An alternative, based on a general method for constructing scatter and gather algorithms, is outlined in Exercise 3.9.

Consider next the total exchange problem, whereby each node transmits a separate packet to every other node. We can decompose the d–cube into two $(d - 1)$–cubes connected by 2^{d-1} links. We then see that $(2^{d-1})^2$ packets from each of the two cubes must be transmitted to the other cube over these 2^{d-1} links. Therefore, any total exchange algorithm cannot take less time than 2^{d-1} units. An algorithm that attains this lower bound within a factor of 2 is given in Fig. 1.3.19. We see, therefore, that an optimal total exchange algorithm takes $\Theta(2^d)$ communication time on the d–cube.

Table 3.1 compares the performance of a ring (or a linear array), a binary balanced tree, a symmetric mesh, and a hypercube for the basic communication problems discussed in this section.

TABLE 3.1 Solution times of optimal algorithms for the basic communication problems using a ring, a binary balanced tree, a d–dimensional symmetric mesh, and a hypercube with p processors. The times given for the ring hold also for a linear array.

Problem	Ring	Tree	Mesh	Hypercube
Single node broadcast **(or single node accumulation)**	$\Theta(p)$	$\Theta(\log p)$	$\Theta(p^{1/d})$	$\Theta(\log p)$
Single node scatter **(or single node gather)**	$\Theta(p)$	$\Theta(p)$	$\Theta(p)$	$\Theta(p/\log p)$
Multinode broadcast **(or multinode accumulation)**	$\Theta(p)$	$\Theta(p)$	$\Theta(p)$	$\Theta(p/\log p)$
Total exchange	$\Theta(p^2)$	$\Theta(p^2)$	$\Theta(p^{(d+1)/d})$	$\Theta(p)$

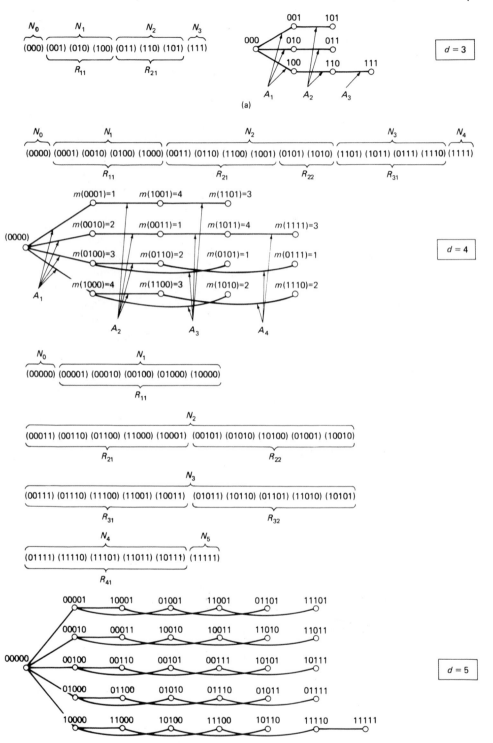

(a)

(c)

Figure 1.3.18 Construction of a multinode broadcast algorithm for a d–cube that takes $\lceil (2^d - 1)/d \rceil$ time. Let N_k, $k = 0, 1, \ldots, d$, be the set of node identities having k unity bits and $d - k$ zero bits. The number of elements in N_k is $\binom{d}{k} = d!/\big(k!\,(d - k)!\big)$. In particular, N_0 and N_d contain one element, the strings $(00 \cdots 0)$ and $(11 \cdots 1)$, respectively; the sets N_1 and N_{d-1} contain d elements; and for $2 \le k \le d - 2$ and $d \ge 5$, N_k contains at least $2d$ elements (when $d = 4$, the number of elements of N_2 is 6, as shown in the figure). We partition each set N_k, $k = 1, \ldots, d - 1$, into disjoint subsets $R_{k1}, \ldots, R_{kn_k}$ which are equivalence classes under a single bit rotation to the left, and we select R_{k1} to be the equivalence class of the element whose k rightmost bits are unity. Then we associate each node identity t with a distinct number $n(t) \in \{0, 1, 2, \ldots, 2^d - 1\}$ in the order

$$(00 \cdots 0)R_{11}R_{21} \cdots R_{2n_2} \cdots R_{k1} \cdots R_{kn_k} \cdots R_{(d-2)1} \cdots R_{(d-2)n_{d-2}}R_{(d-1)1}(11 \cdots 1)$$

[i.e., $n(00 \cdots 0) = 0$, $n(11 \cdots 1) = 2^d - 1$, and the other node identities are numbered consecutively in the above order between 1 and $2^d - 2$]. Let

$$m(t) = 1 + \big[(n(t) - 1)(\mathrm{mod}\ d) \big].$$

Thus the sequence of numbers $m(t)$ corresponding to the sequence of node identities $R_{11}R_{21} \ldots R_{(d-1)1}$ is $1, 2, \ldots, d, 1, 2, \ldots, d, 1, 2, \ldots$ (cf. the figure for the case $d = 4$). We specify the order of node identities within each set R_{kn} as follows: the first element t in each set R_{kn} is chosen so that the relation

the bit in position $m(t)$ from the right is a one   (*)

is satisfied, and the subsequent elements in R_{kn} are chosen so that each element is obtained by a single bit rotation to the left of the preceding element. Also, for the elements t of R_{k1}, we require that the bit in position $m(t) - 1$ [if $m(t) > 1$] or d [if $m(t) = 1$] from the right must be a zero. Then property (*) is satisfied for all elements of all sets R_{kn} (see the figure for the case $d = 4$). For $i = 1, 2, \ldots, \lceil (2^d - 1)/d \rceil - 1$, define

$$E_i = \{ t \mid (i - 1)d + 1 \le n(t) \le id \},$$

and for $i = 0$, and $i = m = \lceil (2^d - 1)/d \rceil$, define

$$E_0 = \{ (00 \cdots 0) \}, \qquad E_m = \{ t \mid (m - 1)d + 1 \le n(t) \le 2^d - 1 \}.$$

We define the set of links A_i as follows:

> For $i = 1, 2, \ldots, m$, each set A_i consists of the links that connect the node identities $t \in E_i$ with the corresponding node identities of $\cup_{k=0}^{i-1} E_k$ obtained from t by reversing the bit in position $m(t)$ [which is always a one by property (*)]. In particular, the node identities in each set R_{k1} are connected with corresponding node identities in $R_{(k-1)1}$, because, by construction, the bit in position $m(t)$ lies next to a zero for each node identity t in the set R_{k1}. There is an exception to the preceding construction in the case where $m(11 \cdots 1) = d$. The exception is that bit $d - 1$ of $(11 \cdots 1)$ (instead of bit d) is reversed to connect to $(101 \cdots 1)$ [which must be the last element of E_{m-1} because of the rule that the bit in position $m(t) - 1$ is a zero for all $t \in R_{(d-1)1}$ with $m(t) > 1$]; furthermore bit d (instead of bit $d - 1$) of the next to last element of E_m [which must be $(1101 \cdots 1)$] is reversed to connect to $(0101 \cdots 1)$. [Without this exception, $(11 \cdots 1)$ would be connected to $(011 \cdots 1)$, which is the first element of E_m and therefore does not belong to $\cup_{k=1}^{m-1} E_k$.]

To show that this definition of the sets A_i is legitimate, we need to verify that by reversing the specified bit of a node identity $t \in E_i$, we indeed obtain a node identity t' that belongs to $\cup_{k=1}^{i-1} E_k$, as opposed to E_i. [It cannot belong to E_k for $k > i$, because $n(t') < n(t)$.] In the case where $t = (11 \cdots 1)$, there is no difficulty if $m(11 \cdots 1) = d$ because of the way that this exceptional case was handled, while if $m(11 \cdots 1) < d$, it is seen that $(11 \cdots 1)$ is connected to the node $t' \in E_{m-1}$ for which $m(t') = m(11 \cdots 1) + 1$. In the case $t \ne (11 \cdots 1)$, it is sufficient to show that $n(t) - n(t') \ge d$. We consider two cases: a) If $t \in R_{kn}$ for some $n > 1$, then all of the d elements of R_{k1} are between t' and t, and the inequality $n(t) - n(t') \ge d$ follows. b) If $t \in R_{k1}$ then $t' \in R_{(k-1)1}$ and all of the elements of the sets $R_{(k-1)2}, \ldots, R_{(k-1)n_{k-1}}$ are between t' and t. There are $\binom{d}{k-1} - d$ such elements. If $2 < k < d$ and $d \ge 5$, it can be verified that $\binom{d}{k-1} - d \ge d$ and we are done. The cases $d = 3$ and $d = 4$ can be handled individually (see the figure). The cases $k = 1, 2$ create no difficulties because $R_{11} = E_1$, $R_{21} = E_2$. We finally notice that any two links in A_i correspond to reversals in different bit positions, so that $T_i = 1$ for all i.

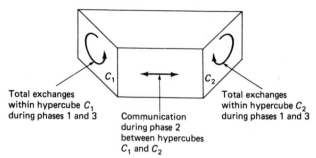

Total exchanges
within hypercube C_1
during phases 1 and 3

Communication
during phase 2
between hypercubes
C_1 and C_2

Total exchanges
within hypercube C_2
during phases 1 and 3

Figure 1.3.19   Recursive construction of a total exchange algorithm for the d–cube requiring time

$$T_d \leq 2^d - 1,$$

which is within a factor of 2 of the lower bound of 2^{d-1}. When $d = 1$, the obvious total exchange algorithm takes time $T_1 = 1$, so the above inequality holds for $d = 1$. Assuming we have a total exchange algorithm for the d–cube satisfying the inequality, we will construct a corresponding total exchange algorithm for the $(d+1)$–cube. Indeed let the $(d+1)$–cube be decomposed into two d–cubes denoted C_1 and C_2. The algorithm consists of three phases, the first two of which are carried out simultaneously. In the first phase, there is a total exchange within each of the cubes C_1 and C_2 (each node in C_1 exchanges its packets with the other nodes in C_1 and similarly for C_2). In the second phase, each node transmits to its counterpart node in the opposite d–cube all of the 2^d packets that are destined for the nodes of the opposite d–cube. In the third phase, there is a total exchange in each of the two d–cubes of the packets received in phase two. Phases 1 and 2 are carried out simultaneously. Since phase 1 is completed in time T_d, which is less than 2^d by the induction hypothesis, both phases 1 and 2 are completed by time 2^d. Phase 3 takes time T_d, and the entire algorithm takes time $T_{d+1} \leq T_d + 2^d \leq 2^{d+1} - 1$, where the last inequality follows from the induction hypothesis. The induction is complete.

Vector Shift on a Hypercube

We next consider a problem of redistributing data among the hypercube processors, which arises sometimes in connection with matrix computations. We mentioned earlier that a ring with 2^d nodes can be mapped into a d–cube, so that node i of the ring $(i = 0, \ldots, 2^d - 1)$ is mapped to the node whose identity is the $(i + 1)$st element of the d–bit RGC sequence. Let us number the nodes of a d–cube as $0, \ldots, 2^d - 1$ according to this mapping. Given some $m \in \{1, 2, 3, \ldots, 2^d - 1\}$, the problem is to send a packet from node i to node $(i + m)(\bmod\ 2^d)$, and to do this simultaneously for all nodes $i = 0, \ldots, 2^d - 1$. We call this the *generalized vector shift problem* because it arises when we have a 2^d–dimensional vector, which is distributed among the processors of a ring so that processor i holds coordinate i, and we want to shift the vector cyclically by m positions while preserving the property that processor i holds coordinate i. We will provide a generalized vector shift algorithm that takes $O(d)$ communication time. For this, we need an interesting class of ring mappings into the hypercube, which we now describe.

Consider the RGC sequence and the ring that it defines on the hypercube as just discussed. Let us define the *logical distance* of two nodes i and j to be the distance between i and j on the ring, and let us define the *physical distance* of i and j to be the minimal number of links that must be traversed on the d–cube to go from i to j (i.e., the Hamming distance of i and j). An important fact is that *two nodes at logical distance* 2^k, $k = 1, \ldots, d-1$, *are at physical distance 2*. The proof is given in Fig. 1.3.20, where it is also shown that for each $k = 0, 1, \ldots, d-1$, the nodes that are at logical distance 2^k from each other form a system of subrings called *subrings of level k*, and each subring has 2^{d-k} nodes. The subrings of level k can also be visualized from the mapping of the $2^{k-1} \times 2^{d-k+1}$ mesh on the d–cube given in Fig. 1.3.20. For $k > 0$, each subring consists of the elements of a column corresponding to either the even–numbered rows or the odd–numbered rows. Each node is on exactly one subring of level k for each k, and successive nodes on each subring are at a physical distance of 2 from each other if $k > 0$, and at a physical distance of 1 if $k = 0$; see Fig. 1.3.21. This shows that each

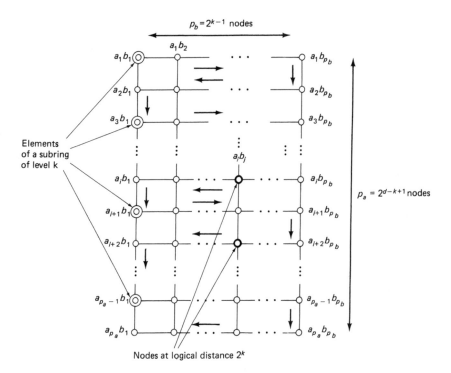

Figure 1.3.20 Proof that two nodes at logical distance 2^k are at physical distance 2 on the hypercube. Consider the mapping of the $p_a \times p_b$ mesh into a d–cube as shown, where $p_a = 2^{d-k+1}$ and $p_b = 2^{k-1}$. Then $\{a_1, a_2, \ldots, a_{p_a}\}$ is the $(d-k+1)$–bit RGC, and $\{b_1, b_2, \ldots, b_{p_b}\}$ is the $(k-1)$–bit RGC. The d–bit strings $a_i b_j$ ordered as in the figure are the elements of the d–bit RGC. Two nodes at logical distance 2^k have identity numbers of the form $a_i b_j$ and $a_{i+2} b_j$ as shown in the figure, and are, therefore, at physical distance 2.

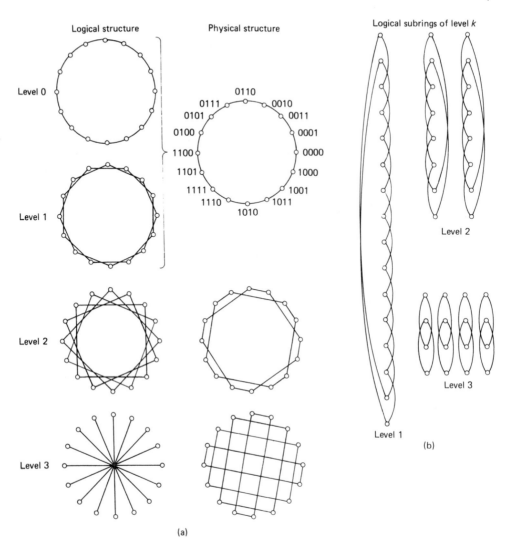

Figure 1.3.21   (a) Subrings of level $k = 0, 1, 2, 3$ on the 4–cube (from [McV87]). (b) The same subrings imbedded in the corresponding $2^{k-1} \times 2^{5-k}$ meshes for $k = 1, 2, 3$.

node i can send a packet to nodes $(i + 2^k)(\text{mod } 2^d)$ and $(i - 2^k)(\text{mod } 2^d)$ simultaneously with every other node over a path with two links if $k > 0$, or one link if $k = 0$.

An algorithm for solving the generalized vector shift problem is now clear. If $b_{d-1}b_{d-2} \cdots b_0$ is the binary representation of m, we move the packets successively on the subrings of the levels i that correspond to nonzero bits b_i. In particular, the packet of node i is sent to node $(i + m)(\text{mod } 2^d)$ by first sending it to node $(i + 1)(\text{mod } 2^d)$ on the zero level ring (if $b_0 = 1$), then to node $(i + b_0 + 2b_1)(\text{mod } 2^d)$ on a level 1 subring (if $b_1 = 1$), then to node $(i + b_0 + 2b_1 + 4b_2)(\text{mod } 2^d)$ on a level 2 subring (if $b_2 = 1$), etc.

The packet of node i traverses $b_0 + 2\sum_{k=1}^{d-1} b_k$ links, and travels simultaneously with the packet of every other node j. Thus, the algorithm takes $b_0 + 2\sum_{k=1}^{d-1} b_k$ time units, which is $O(d)$ as claimed earlier. This time, compared with the corresponding time when a ring of 2^d nodes is used for communication, is found much faster for $1 << m << 2^d - 1$. It turns out that the worst case communication time for the generalized vector shift problem can be reduced from $2d - 1$ to d via an algorithm that uses backward as well as forward shifts on the subrings (Exercise 3.12). For example, a shift of 7 can be effected by a shift on the level 0 subring (logical distance 1), followed by a shift on the level 1 subring (logical distance 2), followed by a shift on the level 2 subring (logical distance 4), requiring a total of 5 time units. Alternately, a shift of 7 can be effected by a shift on the level 3 subring (logical distance 8), followed by a backward shift on the level 0 subring (logical distance 1 backwards), for a total of 3 time units.

Communication Algorithms Using at Most One Link per Node

We next consider briefly the basic communication problems of this section under a potential restriction imposed by the transmission hardware of the interconnection network. We assume in particular that each processor can at any time transmit along at most one of its incident links. Among the algorithms considered so far, only the generalized vector shift algorithm on the d–cube satisfies this restriction.

It turns out that we can characterize the times taken by optimal algorithms for each of the basic communication problems of this section using a broad variety of interconnection networks, and subject to the constraint that each processor can transmit at most one packet at a time. The main results are collected in Table 3.2. To justify these results, suppose that $d(p)$ is the maximum degree of a node of a given type of interconnection network as a function of the number of processors p. Then, any communication algorithm where simultaneous transmission along all the incident links of a node is allowed can be emulated by an algorithm where transmission along only one incident link is allowed at the expense of a slowdown by a factor $d(p)$; in particular, the transmissions within each time unit of the former algorithm can be emulated by corresponding transmissions within $d(p)$ time units in the latter algorithm. It follows that for networks where $d(p)$ is independent of p, such as a ring, a binary balanced tree, and a symmetric mesh, the order of optimal time to solve a communication problem is the same when transmission along multiple incident links is allowed and when it is not. This justifies all entries of Table 3.2, with the exception of the entries for a hypercube where $d(p) = \log p$. For a hypercube, the preceding argument and the results of Table 3.1 show that any single node scatter, multinode broadcast, or total exchange algorithm takes time $O(p)$, $O(p)$, or $O(p \log p)$, respectively. The corresponding lower bounds are obtained by counting the total number of packets that must be transmitted in each problem, and by dividing by the number of nodes (see also Exercises 3.9 through 3.11). The estimate $\Theta(\log p)$ for a single node broadcast for a hypercube in Table 3.2 is shown by using the two–rooted tree mapping of Fig. 1.3.14. We finally note that the estimates of Table 3.2 can be established under the stronger requirement that each node can transmit at most one packet, and, simultaneously, *receive at most one packet* along its incident links. This can be done by modifying some of the algorithms given so that this stronger requirement is

TABLE 3.2 Solution times of optimal algorithms for the basic communication problems using a ring, a binary balanced tree, a d-dimensional symmetric mesh, and a hypercube with p processors, and assuming that a node can transmit along at most one incident link. The times given for the ring hold also for a linear array.

Problem	Ring	Tree	Mesh	Hypercube
Single node broadcast (**or single node accumulation**)	$\Theta(p)$	$\Theta(\log p)$	$\Theta(p^{1/d})$	$\Theta(\log p)$
Single node scatter (**or single node gather**)	$\Theta(p)$	$\Theta(p)$	$\Theta(p)$	$\Theta(p)$
Multinode broadcast (**or multinode accumulation**)	$\Theta(p)$	$\Theta(p)$	$\Theta(p)$	$\Theta(p)$
Total exchange	$\Theta(p^2)$	$\Theta(p^2)$	$\Theta(p^{(d+1)/d})$	$\Theta(p \log p)$

met, without affecting the corresponding order of solution time. The details are left for the reader (see also Exercises 3.9 through 3.11).

Optimal Algorithms

We have focused so far on the order of time taken by an optimal algorithm for a given type of communication problem and processor interconnection network. In every case, we obtained an algorithm that is optimal within a constant factor; that is, if T_a is the time required by the algorithm, there is a lower bound B on the number of time units required to solve the communication problem, and a scalar c (independent of the number of processors) such that

$$B \le T_a \le cB,$$

assuming that each packet transmission requires unit time. On several occasions, we gave exact values for B, T_a, and c. If, for a given algorithm, we have $c = 1$, then the algorithm attains the lower bound for the time to solve the communication problem, and is therefore optimal. Several algorithms given either in the main body of this section or in the exercises are optimal in this sense. Table 3.3 gives the results obtained for the d–cube in this subsection and in Exercises 3.9 through 3.11 for the case where simultaneous transmission along all incident links of a node is allowed and for the case where it is not. It is seen that we have obtained an optimal algorithm in all cases with the exception of a total exchange when simultaneous transmission along all incident links of a node is allowed.

Communication Bottlenecks of Interconnection Networks

We have examined so far in this section several communication problems for a variety of interconnection networks. In each case, we have been able to establish both a lower

TABLE 3.3 Bounds on the optimal times for solving the basic communication problems on a hypercube with p processors for the case where simultaneous transmission along all incident links of a processor is allowed, and for the case where it is not. We assume that each packet requires unit time for transmission on any link.

Problem	Simultaneous Transmission on All Incident Links Allowed		Simultaneous Transmission on Multiple Incident Links Not Allowed	
	Lower Bound	Upper Bound	Lower Bound	Upper Bound
Single node broadcast (or single node accumulation)	$\log p$	$\log p$	$\log p$	$\log p$
Single node scatter (or single node gather)	$\left\lceil \frac{p-1}{\log p} \right\rceil$	$\left\lceil \frac{p-1}{\log p} \right\rceil$	$p-1$	$p-1$
Multinode broadcast (or multinode accumulation)	$\left\lceil \frac{p-1}{\log p} \right\rceil$	$\left\lceil \frac{p-1}{\log p} \right\rceil$	$p-1$	$p-1$
Total exchange	$\frac{p}{2}$	$p-1$	$\frac{p}{2}\log p$	$\frac{p}{2}\log p$

bound on the order of time taken by an optimal algorithm and an algorithm that attains this lower bound. It is interesting to note that for a given communication problem, there is a particular characteristic, common to all interconnection networks examined, that determines the lower bound. We may view this characteristic as a *communication bottleneck* associated with the corresponding type of problem. Based on this viewpoint, we can obtain insight on the features of interconnection networks that make them desirable or undesirable for specific types of communication tasks, as we now explain.

In the following discussion we assume that all packet transmissions require one time unit, and that simultaneous transmission along all incident links of a node is allowed. Since the diameter of the network is equal to the time taken by an optimal single node broadcast algorithm with a worst choice of root node, we can view the diameter as the communication bottleneck for the single node broadcast problem (and, therefore, also for the single node accumulation problem).

Consider next the single node gather problem for a node with d incident links (i.e., a degree equal to d). If p is the number of processors, the node must receive $p-1$ packets over its d incident links, so $\lceil (p-1)/d \rceil$ is a lower bound on the solution time of any algorithm. This lower bound is tight for a hypercube, as shown earlier (Table 3.3), and is either tight or nearly tight for the other topologies examined in this section. We conclude that the minimum node degree in an interconnection network is a communication bottleneck for the single node gather (and, therefore, also for the single node scatter problem).

The reasoning used above for the single node gather problem applies also for the multinode accumulation problem, and it can be seen that the minimum node degree is a bottleneck for multinode accumulation (as well as for the multinode broadcast problem).

Consider, finally, the total exchange problem. For any partition of the node set N into two disjoint nonempty subsets N_1 and N_2, let L_{12} be the number of links connecting a node of N_1 with a node of N_2. The number of packets that will travel over these L_{12} links in any total exchange algorithm is at least $|N_1||N_2|$, where $|N_1|$ and $|N_2|$ are the number of nodes of N_1 and N_2, respectively. Therefore the corresponding solution time is bounded from below by

$$\max_{\text{All partitions }(N_1,N_2)} \left\{ \frac{|N_1||N_2|}{L_{12}} \right\}.$$

This number, called the *cross–section bound*, provides a tight underestimate of the order of time taken by an optimal total exchange algorithm for all the interconnection networks considered in this section, and may be viewed as a communication bottleneck for the total exchange problem. We note, however, that the cross–section bound is not valid when transmission along multiple incident links of a node is not allowed. An appropriate bound can be developed under these circumstances by lower bounding the number of link transmissions in any total exchange algorithm and dividing by the number of nodes. Such a lower bound is tight for the hypercube (see Exercise 3.10).

1.3.5 Concurrency and Communication Tradeoffs

We use the term *concurrency* as a broad measure of the number of processors that are, in some aggregate sense, simultaneously active in carrying out the computations of a given parallel algorithm. The degree of concurrency generally depends on the method by which the overall computation is broken down into smaller subtasks and is divided among the various processors for parallel execution. It is important for efficiency purposes that the computation time of parallel subtasks be relatively uniform across processors; otherwise, some processors will be idle waiting for others to finish their subtasks. This is known as *load balancing*. It is reasonable to conjecture that the number of packet exchanges used to coordinate the parallel subtasks increases with the number of subtasks, and that this is particularly true when the size of the subtasks is relatively uniform. It then follows that as the concurrency of an algorithm increases, the communication penalty for the algorithm also increases. Therefore, as we attempt to decrease the solution time of a given problem by using more and more processors, we must contend with increased communication penalty. This may place an upper bound on the size of problems of a given type that we can realistically solve even with an unlimited number of processors.

For a given problem, there are both general and problem–specific reasons why the communication penalty tends to increase with the number of processors. A first reason is the possibility of *pipelining of computation and communication*. If some of the computation results at a processor can be communicated to other processors while other results are still being computed, the communication penalty will be reduced. This type of pipelining is possible, for example, in relaxation iterations of the form

$$x_i(t+1) = f_i\big(x_1(t),\ldots,x_p(t)\big), \qquad i = 1,\ldots,p \tag{3.4}$$

(cf. the model considered in Subsection 1.2.4), where each x_i is a vector of dimension k that is assigned to a separate processor i and $n = pk$ is the dimension of the problem.

Pipelining of computation and communication is more pronounced when there is a large number of variables assigned to each processor; then the variables that have been already updated within an iteration can be made available to other processors while the updating of other variables is still pending. A second reason is that in many systems, a portion of each packet is used to carry overhead information. The length of this portion is usually fixed and independent of the total length of the packet. This means that there is a gain in efficiency when packets are long, since then the overhead per bit of data is diminished. It is clear that the length of the packets can be made longer if the number of variables updated by each processor using the relaxation iteration (3.4) is larger, since then the values of many variables can be transmitted to other processors as a single packet.

Even in the absence of overhead, and of pipelining of computation and communication, the communication penalty tends to be reduced as the dimension k of the component vectors x_i in the relaxation iteration (3.4) is increased. Suppose that processor i uses Eq. (3.4) to update the k–dimensional vector x_i, with knowledge of the other vectors x_j, $j \neq i$. Suppose also that the computation time for each update is $\Theta(nk)$ [as it will be for example when the function f_i in Eq. (3.4) is linear without any special sparsity structure]. After updating x_i, processor i must communicate the corresponding k variables to all other processors so that the next iteration can proceed. This can be done via a multinode broadcast, and if a linear array is used for this purpose, the optimal communication time is $\Theta(n)$, assuming that communication of k variables over a single link takes $\Theta(k)$ time. Thus, the ratio

$$\frac{T_{COMM}}{T_{COMP}} = \frac{\text{Communication time per iteration}}{\text{Computation time per iteration}}$$

is $\Theta(1/k)$, and the communication penalty becomes relatively insignificant as the number k of variables updated by each processor increases. The ratio T_{COMM}/T_{COMP} is independent of the problem dimension n; it only depends on k, that is, the size of the computation task per iteration for each processor.

A further observation from this analysis is that the speedup obtained through parallelization of the relaxation iteration (3.4) can be increased as the dimension n of the problem increases. In particular, the computation time per iteration on a serial machine is $\Theta(n^2)$ [it is $\Theta(nk)$ based on our earlier hypothesis and, for a serial machine, we have $p = 1$ and $k = n$], so the speedup using a linear array of p processors, each updating $k = n/p$ variables, becomes

$$\frac{\Theta(n^2)}{\Theta(n) + \Theta(nk)} = \Theta(p),$$

where the $\Theta(n)$ and $\Theta(nk)$ terms correspond to the communication time and the computation time, respectively.

We have thus reached the important conclusion that for relaxation iterations of the form (3.4), the communication penalty will not prevent the fruitful utilization of a large number of processors in parallel when the problem is large, even when a linear array (the "least powerful" network) is used for communication. What is needed, as the dimension of the problem increases, is a proportional increase of the number of processors p of the linear array that will keep the number k of variables per processor roughly constant at a level where the communication penalty is relatively small. Note also that when a hypercube is used in place of a linear array, the optimal multinode broadcast time is $\Theta\big((pk)/\log p\big)$, so the ratio T_{COMM}/T_{COMP} decreases from $\Theta(1/k)$ to $\Theta\big(1/(k\log p)\big)$. Therefore, as the dimension of the problem increases by a certain factor, the number of processors of the hypercube can be increased by a larger factor while keeping the communication penalty at a relatively insignificant level, and increasing the attainable speedup at a faster rate than with a linear array.

The preceding analysis does not assume any special structure for the iteration (3.4) other than the hypothesis that a single variable update takes $\Theta(n)$ time. In many other cases where there is special structure, the ratio T_{COMM}/T_{COMP} is also small for large k. An important example is associated with problems arising from discretization of two–dimensional physical space and with the so called *area–perimeter effect* (see Fig. 1.3.22). As shown in the figure, the number of variables that have to be communicated by a processor is $\Theta(\sqrt{k})$, and the time taken for communication on a mesh network or a hypercube is $\Theta(\sqrt{k})$. The time taken for each variable update is a constant, and the parallel computation time for each iteration is $\Theta(k)$. The ratio T_{COMM}/T_{COMP} is $\Theta(1/\sqrt{k})$. Figure 1.3.23 provides another example of a sparsity structure (block-tridiagonal) where the ratio T_{COMM}/T_{COMP} decreases quickly with k. Fig. 1.3.24 provides an unfavorable type of sparsity structure for matrix–vector multiplication, where T_{COMM}/T_{COMP} is relatively large.

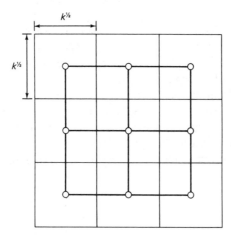

Figure 1.3.22 Structure arising from discretization of 2–dimensional space. Here the variables are partitioned in rectangles of physical space, and we assume that only neighboring variables interact (cf. the example in Subsection 1.2.4). Each rectangle contains k variables, and at the end of a relaxation iteration of the form (3.4), each rectangle must exchange $\Theta(\sqrt{k})$ variables with each of its neighboring rectangles. The communication time per relaxation iteration, using a mesh network for communication, is $\Theta(\sqrt{k})$, but the computation time is $\Theta(k)$.

The preceding discussion has focused on relaxation iterations of the form (3.4) which are important for the purposes of this book as they appear in the context of many algorithms. The conclusion is that with proper selection of the size of the computation task for each processor, the effects of communication can be minimized. Furthermore, as the size of the given problem increases without bound, the speedup can typically also

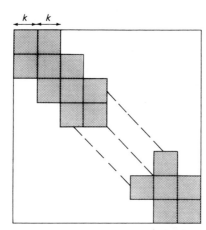

Figure 1.3.23 A block–tridiagonal sparsity structure for matrix–vector multiplication where the communication to computation time ratio is low when using a linear array for communication. Each block is assumed to be dense and to have k variables. Each relaxation iteration of the form (3.4) takes $\Theta(k)$ communication time (assuming a linear array is used), and $\Theta(k^2)$ computation time.

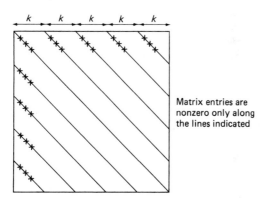

Matrix entries are nonzero only along the lines indicated

Figure 1.3.24 A matrix sparsity structure for matrix–vector multiplication where the communication to computation time ratio using a linear array of processors is relatively large. Here there are p processors, each computing $k = n/p$ successive coordinates of the product. The communication and the computation times are $\Theta(kp)$.

increase without bound by using an appropriate parallel machine. In other words, there is no *a priori* bound on the attainable speedup that is imposed by the communication requirements.

1.3.6 Examples of Matrix–Vector Calculations

In this subsection, we discuss some generic communication aspects of matrix calculations, and at the same time we illustrate some of the ideas of the previous subsections. We make the same assumptions as in Subsection 1.3.4 regarding the interconnection network of processors used. In particular, we assume that communication can take place simultaneously along all the incident links of a processor, and that in the absence of queueing, the delays of all packets of equal length are equal on all links.

Our principal examples are inner product formation and matrix–vector calculations such as

$$x(t+1) = Ax(t) + b, \qquad \forall\, t = 0, 1, \ldots, \tag{3.5}$$

which arise in iterative methods of the Jacobi and Gauss–Seidel types (Subsection 1.2.4 and Section 2.4). Similar situations arise also in the conjugate gradient method (Section 2.7), and more generally in cases where a sequence of matrix–vector and matrix–matrix multiplications, inner product formations, and vector additions are required with each calculation using the results of the preceding ones. Related examples also arise in other situations involving calculation of the minimum of a set of numbers instead of an inner product (see the material on shortest paths and dynamic programming in Chapter 4). An important characteristic of iterative calculations such as (3.5) is that following an iteration, it is necessary to store the results of the iteration [e.g., the vector $x(t+1)$ of Eq. (3.5)] at the appropriate processors as dictated by the needs of the next iteration. In our analysis, we will not account for the time taken for initial storage of the problem data [e.g., the matrix A, and the vectors b and $x(0)$ of Eq. (3.5)] at the appropriate processors. This additional time is negligible, assuming a large number of iterations are executed; otherwise, the following analysis can be easily modified to take it into account. This time can be reduced by pipelining the initial data input with the algorithmic computation and communication. Schemes that take advantage of this possibility are known as *systolic* algorithms, and are used for fast execution of highly specialized calculations on VLSI chips. Such algorithms are beyond the scope of this book (see [MeC80], [Kun82], [ADM82], and [Kun88]).

Inner Product

Assume that we have a network of p processors, and we want to form the inner product of two vectors a and b in $\Re^n$, where $n \geq p$. For simplicity, we assume that n is divisible by p, and we let $k = n/p$. It is then natural to store at each processor i the k coordinates of a and b numbered $(i-1)k + 1$ through ik, to form the partial inner product $c_i = \sum_{j=(i-1)k+1}^{ik} a_j b_j$, and then to accumulate the result using a spanning tree rooted at some node. We recognize this as a single node accumulation problem [cf. Fig. 1.3.4(b)]. The root node can send the final value of the inner product to all other nodes if needed; this is a single node broadcast problem. The following analysis can be generalized to account for this possibility without affecting the associated time estimates, but to simplify matters, we will assume that it is sufficient to obtain the inner product at the root node. An alternative to collecting the sum at a single node and then broadcasting it back to all nodes is given in Exercise 3.22 for the hypercube network.

Suppose that an addition and a multiplication take time α, and that transmission of a partial inner product along a link takes time β. Assume first that the processors are connected in a linear array. Then the optimal choice for the root node is a "middle" node that is at distance no more than $\lfloor p/2 \rfloor$ from every other node. The time to compute the inner product at the root node is then

$$k\alpha + (\alpha + \beta) \left\lfloor \frac{p}{2} \right\rfloor .$$

For a given dimension $n = pk$, this is written as

$$\frac{n\alpha}{p} + (\alpha + \beta)\left\lfloor \frac{p}{2} \right\rfloor. \tag{3.6}$$

We optimize approximately this expression over p by neglecting the fact that p is integer, thereby obtaining the approximate optimum value

$$p \approx \left(\frac{2\alpha n}{\alpha + \beta} \right)^{1/2}. \tag{3.7}$$

Thus, the optimal number of processors is substantially smaller than the maximum possible number n. In particular, when $\beta > (2n - 1)\alpha$, it is optimal to avoid the high communication cost associated with parallelism, and to use a single processor. This illustrates the tradeoff between concurrency and communication (cf. Subsection 1.3.5). From Eqs. (3.6) and (3.7) it is seen that the optimal parallel time to calculate the inner product grows with n as $n^{1/2}$ when the processors are connected in a linear array.

Assume now that a hypercube with p nodes is used to compute the inner product along the spanning tree of Fig. 1.3.16. Then it can be seen that the total time is

$$\frac{n\alpha}{p} + (\alpha + \beta)\log p,$$

and the optimal number of processors is given approximately by

$$p \approx \frac{\alpha n}{\alpha + \beta}. \tag{3.8}$$

The optimal parallel time to calculate the inner product grows with n as $\log n$, which is also the rate of growth when n processors are used and communication is assumed instantaneous (cf. Subsection 1.2.3). The optimal number of processors is much larger, and the time to solve the problem is much smaller, than with a linear array, reflecting the fact that communication on the hypercube is much more efficient. The performance gap between the two interconnection networks is narrowed when it is required to calculate several inner products simultaneously. Then a multinode accumulation is required in place of a single node accumulation. This takes little additional communication time on a linear array, but a lot more communication time on a hypercube (cf. the discussion of Subsection 1.3.4, and the following discussion on matrix–vector multiplication).

Matrix–Vector Multiplication

We next consider the parallel calculation of the matrix–vector product Ax on a network of p processors, where A is an $n \times n$ matrix, and x is an n–dimensional vector. We assume that n is divisible by p, and we denote $k = n/p$. There are two basic methods here, depending on whether A is distributed by rows or by columns among the processors.

(a) The *row storage method*, where processor i stores the k rows of A numbered $(i-1)k+1$ through ik as well as the vector x. Processor i then calculates the k coordinates numbered $(i-1)k+1$ through ik of the product Ax. We assume that the product Ax is to be used subsequently by all processors, so each node is required to transmit the updated values of these coordinates to all other nodes. This is a multinode broadcast problem.

(b) The *column storage method*, where processor i stores the k columns of A numbered $(i-1)k+1$ through ik, and the k coordinates of x numbered $(i-1)k+1$ through ik. Processor i then calculates the corresponding k terms in the sum that defines each coordinate of the product Ax. It is then necessary to accumulate the terms corresponding to the coordinates $(i-1)k+1$ through ik at node i. This is a multinode accumulation problem.

Note that converting a matrix from the row storage format to the column storage format requires solving a total exchange problem as defined in Subsection 1.3.4 [see also Exercise 3.10(d)].

There is an interesting duality relation between the times taken by the row and column storage methods, which is illustrated in Fig. 1.3.25. If the matrix A is fully dense, it can be seen that the two methods take comparable times regardless of the type of interconnection network used; they both involve an equal number of multiplications, and either a multinode broadcast or a multinode accumulation, which take equal time (except for the typically negligible time for a few additions) on any interconnection network. This conclusion extends to the case where the sparsity structure of A is the same as the sparsity structure of the transpose of A, for example, when A is symmetric. To see this, note that for each multiplication and addition performed in the case of the row storage method when A is used, there is a corresponding multiplication and addition for the column storage method when the transpose of A is used. Furthermore, if a node i must send a packet to node j in the case of the row storage method [i.e., the submatrix of A corresponding to rows $(j-1)k+1$ through jk and columns $(i-1)k+1$ through ik is nonzero], then node j must participate in the summation relating to the coordinates accumulated at node i in the column storage method when the transpose of A is used.

When A is not symmetric it may be difficult to determine which method is preferable without detailed knowledge of the sparsity structure of A and the interconnection network used. For an example where the row storage method takes more time than the column storage method, consider a matrix A with zero elements everywhere except along the first row and along the diagonal. Then, the row storage method requires a single node gather operation at node 1, whereas the column storage method requires a less time consuming single node accumulation at node 1. By using the transpose of the matrix just described we obtain an example where the row storage method takes less time than the column storage method. We finally note that when using the column storage method, each processor stores only a k–dimensional subvector of x, as opposed to storing the full vector x that is required in the row storage method. Thus the column storage method has an advantage in terms of memory requirements.

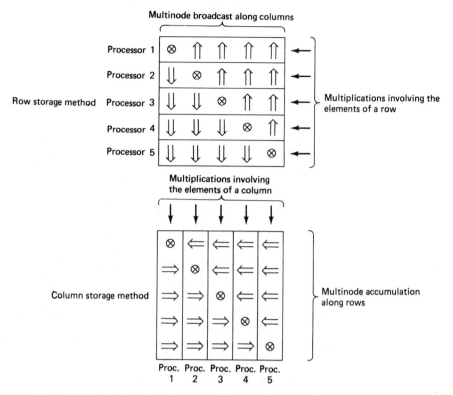

Figure 1.3.25 Duality of matrix–vector multiplication using the row storage and the column storage methods. In the row storage method, each processor performs multiplications involving the stored matrix rows, forms the corresponding coordinates of the product, and broadcasts these coordinates to the other processors. In the column storage method, each processor performs multiplications involving the stored matrix columns, and accumulates the corresponding coordinates of the product. All broadcasts (accumulations) are done in parallel by the processors, so a multinode broadcast (or accumulation, respectively) is required.

For a discussion of additional methods of matrix storage that can take advantage of sparsity structure, and corresponding timing analyses of matrix–vector calculations, we refer the reader to [McV87] and [FJL88].

Consider now the time to compute the product Ax using $p \leq n$ processors arranged in a linear array. We assume that the row storage method is used with each processor storing $k = n/p$ rows. Suppose that the time for an addition and a multiplication is α, and that the time to transmit a packet of k numbers over a link is $\beta + k\gamma$, where α, β, and γ are some positive constants. Suppose also that communication starts only after all computation is completed. Then the time for matrix–vector multiplication using a linear array is

$$\frac{\alpha n^2}{p} + (p-1)\left(\beta + \frac{n\gamma}{p}\right), \tag{3.9}$$

where the first term corresponds to the computation time, and the second term corresponds to the subsequent multinode broadcast needed to store the product Ax at all processors. The time (3.9) is optimized for

$$p \approx n \left(\frac{\alpha - \gamma/n}{\beta} \right)^{1/2},$$

which yields a roughly constant optimal number of rows per processor, $k = n/p \approx (\beta/\alpha)^{1/2}$, when n is large (cf. the discussion of Subsection 1.3.5). The total optimal time grows linearly with n. This is the same order of growth as when communication is instantaneous. Since the optimal multiplication time using any network into which a linear array can be mapped (such as a hypercube) cannot be more than the one using a linear array, and cannot be less than when communication is instantaneous, we conclude that for just about any interconnection network of interest, the time to form the product Ax using an optimally chosen number $p \leq n$ of processors grows linearly with n.

    We next consider the case where the number of available processors is larger than n. It was seen in Subsection 1.2.3 that when communication is instantaneous, the product Ax can be computed in $O(\log n)$ time using n^2 processors. We cannot achieve this bound when a linear array is used for communication, since it was seen earlier that the optimal time for an inner product of two n–dimensional vectors (an easier calculation than the matrix–vector product) grows as $n^{1/2}$. We can achieve the bound $O(\log n)$, however, by using a hypercube and the algorithm described in Fig. 1.3.26.

Matrix–Matrix Multiplication

We next discuss the problem of multiplying two $n \times n$ matrices. We assume first that a square mesh of n^2 processors is used. We also assume that the ijth element of each matrix is stored in processor (i, j), and the ijth element of the product must be eventually stored in the same processor (see Exercise 3.16 for the case of a different initial storage specification). Figure 1.3.27 gives an algorithm that takes $O(n)$ time. This is also the bound obtained when the product of two $n \times n$ matrices is formed in the usual way using n^2 processors with instantaneous communication. Note also that the kth power of an $n \times n$ matrix can be computed in time $O(n \log k)$ using a square mesh of n^2 processors with the ijth processor holding initially the ijth element of the matrix. This is done by successive squaring of the matrix if k is a power of 2. If k is not a power of 2, a similar procedure works in the same order of time; for example, to calculate A^{11}, we calculate successively A^2, A^4, A^8, $A^{10} = A^2 A^8$, and $A^{11} = A A^{10}$ (see the discussion of Subsection 1.2.3).

    We finally consider the matrix–matrix multiplication problem when n^3 processors are available. It was seen earlier that matrix–vector multiplication can be performed in time $O(\log n)$ using a hypercube of n^2 processors. The product of two $n \times n$ matrices A and B is the matrix having as columns the matrix–vector products $Ab_1, \ldots, Ab_n$, where $b_1, \ldots, b_n$ are the columns of B. These products can be computed in parallel using n^3 processors in time $O(\log n)$ (the same time as each one of them). One possible algorithm is formalized below.

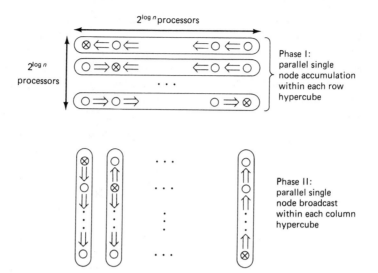

Figure 1.3.26   An $O(\log n)$ algorithm for multiplying an $n \times n$ matrix A with a vector $x \in \Re^n$ on a hypercube with n^2 processors, where n is a power of 2. We use the mapping of the $n \times n$ mesh into the hypercube under which each row and each column of the mesh is a hypercube with n nodes (cf. the construction described in Subsection 1.3.4 and illustrated in Fig. 1.3.12). Initially, processor (i, j) stores the ijth element of A and the jth coordinate of x, and at the end of the algorithm, it stores the jth coordinate of the product Ax. The algorithm consists of two phases, with each phase requiring $O(\log n)$ time. The first phase consists of a single node accumulation within each row, whereby the ith diagonal processor (i.e., the ith processor in the ith row) calculates the ith coordinate of Ax. The second phase consists of a single node broadcast within each column hypercube. Each processor in the jth column receives the jth coordinate of Ax accumulated in the first phase at the jth diagonal processor.

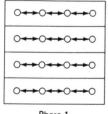

Phase 1

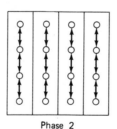

Phase 2

Figure 1.3.27   An $O(n)$ algorithm for multiplying two $n \times n$ matrices A and B with elements a_{ij} and b_{ij}, respectively, on an $n \times n$ mesh. Initially, processor (i, j) of the mesh holds elements a_{ij} and b_{ij}, and at the end of the algorithm, processor (i, j) will hold the ijth element $\sum_{m=1}^{n} a_{im}b_{mj}$ of the product AB.

The algorithm consists of three phases, each requiring $O(n)$ time. In the first phase, each processor (i, j) broadcasts a_{ij} to the processors in the ith row; these are n multinode broadcasts, one within each row, requiring $O(n)$ time. In the second phase, each processor (i, j) broadcasts b_{ij} to the processors in the jth column; these are n multinode broadcasts, one within each column, requiring $O(n)$ time. At the end of two phases, each processor (i, j) holds the values a_{im} and b_{mj} for $m = 1, 2, \ldots, n$, and can form the ijth element $\sum_{m=1}^{n} a_{im}b_{mj}$ of the product AB in time $O(n)$ (which is the third phase). Note that phases 1 and 2 can be done in parallel, assuming that simultaneous communication along all incident links is possible. Also, by appropriately interleaving additions, multiplications, and communications, the algorithm can be made more economical in terms of time and storage.

We assume that n is a power of 2, and that we have a hypercube of n^3 processors arranged in an $n \times n \times n$ array. Let a_{ij} and b_{ij} be the ijth elements of A and B, respectively, and let $c_{ik} = \sum_{j=1}^{n} a_{ij} b_{jk}$ be the ikth element of the product AB. We assume that each processor (i, j, k) initially holds the elements a_{ij} and b_{jk}, and we require that at the end of the algorithm, processor (i, j, k) holds the elements c_{ij} and c_{jk} of the product. Figure 1.3.28 gives a three–phase algorithm that performs the matrix multiplication in $O(\log n)$ time. A similar algorithm works in the same order of time for different initial and final storage specifications, taking advantage of the possibility

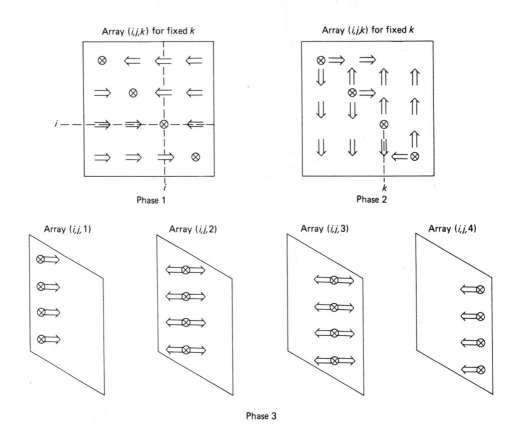

Figure 1.3.28   An $O(\log n)$ algorithm for multiplying two $n \times n$ matrices A and B with elements a_{ij} and b_{ij}, respectively, on an $n \times n \times n$ hypercube array. We assume that each processor (i, j, k) initially holds the elements a_{ij} and b_{jk}, and we require that at the end of the algorithm, processor (i, j, k) holds the ijth and jkth elements of the product. The algorithm consists of three phases, each requiring time $O(\log n)$. In the first phase, the ikth element of the product $c_{ik} = \sum_{j=1}^{n} a_{ij} b_{jk}$ is accumulated at processor (i, i, k) along the array (i, j, k), $j = 1, \ldots, n$. In the second phase, each processor (i, i, k) performs a single node broadcast of c_{ik} along the array (j, i, k), $j = 1, \ldots, n$, and also sends c_{ik} to processor (i, k, k). In the third phase, each processor (i, j, j) performs a single node broadcast of c_{ij} along the array (i, j, k), $k = 1, \ldots, n$.

of doing matrix transposition on a hypercube with n^3 processors in time $O(\log n)$ (see Exercise 3.18).

Consider now the calculation of A^k, where A is an $n \times n$ matrix and k is an integer. We can compute A^k by $O(\log k)$ multiplications of powers of A as discussed earlier. Thus, by using the preceding $O(\log n)$ matrix multiplication algorithm on a hypercube of n^3 processors, we can compute A^k in time $O\big((\log n)(\log k)\big)$. This is the same order of time as the one obtained in Subsection 1.2.3, where all communication was assumed instantaneous.

Table 3.4 summarizes some of the results of this subsection. The conclusion is that by using a suitable interconnection network such as a hypercube, we can perform some of the basic matrix calculations in the same order of time when there are communication delays as when communication is instantaneous. This is encouraging, but it does not imply that the communication penalty is negligible for these calculations; it only implies that the communication time grows with the problem dimension at a rate that is no larger than the rate of growth of the time needed exclusively for computations. For example, the communication time can be larger than the computation time by an arbitrary factor that is constant (independent of n), and still grow at the same rate as the computation time. Alternatively, in some algorithms, we can make the communication time negligible relative to the computation time (see the discussion in Subsection 1.3.5), but this requires a reduction of the number of processors used, and affects the attainable speedup in a different way.

TABLE 3.4 Upper bounds on the optimal times for matrix–vector calculations in $\Re^n$, and the corresponding interconnection networks with which these bounds can be achieved. These bounds are the same as those obtained for the same number of processors in Subsection 1.2.3, where communication was assumed instantaneous.

Problem	Time	Corresponding Topology
Inner Product	$O(\log n)$	Hypercube w/ $p = n$ processors
Matrix–Vector Multiplication	$O(n)$	Linear Array w/ $p = n$ processors
Matrix–Vector Multiplication	$O(\log n)$	Hypercube w/ $p = n^2$ processors
Matrix–Matrix Multiplication	$O(n)$	Mesh w/ $p = n^2$ processors
kth Power of a Matrix	$O(n \log k)$	Mesh w/ $p = n^2$ processors
Matrix–Matrix Multiplication	$O(\log n)$	Hypercube w/ $p = n^3$ processors
kth Power of a Matrix	$O\big((\log n)(\log k)\big)$	Hypercube w/ $p = n^3$ processors

EXERCISES

3.1. Use the following model to establish the validity of the stop–and–wait protocol between a transmitter A and a receiver B as outlined in Subsection 1.3.3 (with packets and acknowledgments numbered modulo 2). The rule for A is that if packet n [numbered $n(\mathrm{mod}\ 2)$] is the last packet transmitted by A at a given time, and if A started transmission of that packet at time t, then A will start retransmission of packet n at time $t + \Delta$ if no packet from B numbered $n(\mod 2)$ is received correctly in the interval $(t, t + \Delta)$, and it will start transmission of packet $n + 1$ upon receiving a packet from B numbered $n(\mod 2)$ (Δ here is some positive number denoting the timeout interval for A). The rule for B is that upon correct reception of a packet numbered k ($k = 0, 1$) it sends a packet numbered k to A. Furthermore, B stores in memory only the first correctly received packet numbered k ($k = 0, 1$) from every sequence of consecutive packets that are all numbered k. Assume that error detection is infallible, and that each packet is transmitted correctly after a finite time of tries. Assume also that at time $t = 0$, A starts sending packet 0, and there are no packets in transit in the communication channel between A and B in either direction. Show that the algorithm works correctly in the sense that all packets $0, 1, 2, \ldots$ sent by A are stored by B in the order sent, without errors, and only once. *Hint:* Let k_A (k_B) be the number (mod 2) of the last correctly received packet by A (B, respectively). Initially, $k_A = 1$, $k_B = 1$. Model how (k_A, k_B) changes in response to packet receptions.

3.2.   **(a)** [Top85] Consider a tree with p nodes. Show that an optimal multinode broadcast algorithm takes $p - 1$ time units. *Hint:* Use the following algorithm: at every time unit each processor i considers each of its incident links (i, j). If i has received a packet that it has neither sent already to j nor it has yet received from j, then i sends such a packet on link (i, j). If i does not have such a packet, it sends nothing on (i, j).

      (b) Show that the time taken by an optimal total exchange algorithm on a binary balanced tree is $\Theta(p^2)$. *Hint:* Count the number of packets that must go through the incident links of the root node and use part (a). For an upper bound, use part (a) or use the mapping of Fig. 1.3.29.

3.3. [SaS88] Let A and B be two adjacent nodes of a hypercube, and let S_A and S_B be the sets of nodes adjacent to A and B, respectively. Show that for every node $i \in S_A$, there exists a unique node $j \in S_B$ such that i is adjacent to j.

3.4. [SaS88]

      (a) Show that every cycle of a hypercube has an even number of nodes. *Hint:* Count the number of bit reversals as the cycle is traversed.

      (b) Show that a ring with an even number of nodes p ($4 \le p \le 2^d$) can be mapped into a d–cube, and that a ring with an odd number of nodes cannot be mapped into a hypercube. *Hint:* If p is even, imbed a ring with p nodes into a $2 \times 2^{d-1}$ mesh.

3.5. Number appropriately the nodes of the 4–cube in Fig. 1.3.13(b) in order to demonstrate that a 4×4 mesh with wraparound can be mapped into the 4–cube.

3.6. **(Total Exchange on a Mesh.)** Show inductively that an optimal total exchange algorithm takes $O(p^{(d+1)/d})$ time on a d–dimensional symmetric mesh with p processors by

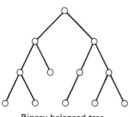

Binary balanced tree

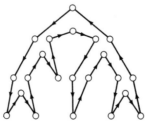

Unidirectional ring

Figure 1.3.29 Mapping a unidirectional ring into an undirected binary balanced tree.

showing that given a total exchange algorithm that takes $O\left(p^{d/(d-1)}\right)$ time on a $(d-1)$–dimensional symmetric mesh with p processors, there is a total exchange algorithm that takes $O\left(p^{(d+1)/d}\right)$ time on a d–dimensional symmetric mesh with p processors. *Hint:* Let the processors of the d–dimensional mesh be numbered $(x_1, x_2, \ldots, x_d)$, where $x_i = 1, \ldots, p^{1/d}$. In the first phase of the algorithm, perform in parallel $p^{1/d}$ total exchanges within each of the $p^{1/d}$ symmetric $(d-1)$–dimensional meshes obtained by fixing the value of x_1. In the second phase, perform in parallel $p^{(d-1)/d}$ total exchanges within each of the $p^{(d-1)/d}$ linear arrays obtained by fixing $x_2, x_3, \ldots, x_d$. Show that each phase takes $O(p^{(d+1)/d})$ time.

3.7. **(Multinode Broadcast for a Mesh with Wraparound, [Ozv87] and [Tse87].)** Consider an $n \times n$ mesh with wraparound, and assume that each packet transmission takes one time unit. Show that an optimal multinode broadcast algorithm takes $(n^2 - 1)/4$ time units if n is odd, and $n^2/4$ time units if n is even. *Hint:* For n odd, consider the spanning tree shown in Fig. 1.3.30 for broadcasting the packet of the middle node. For n even, consider first the spanning tree of Fig. 1.3.30 for the upper–left $(n-1) \times (n-1)$ portion of the mesh.

3.8. **(Two–Node Broadcast.)** Show that a two–node broadcast (a simultaneous single node broadcast from two distinct root nodes) can be performed on the d–cube in d time units. *Hint:* Split the d–cube into two halves each containing one of the root nodes.

3.9. **(Single Node Scatter Algorithms [Tse87].)** Consider an interconnection network G with p processors, a spanning tree T of G, and the problem of single node scatter from a node s of G.

   (a) Assume that transmission along at most one incident link of a processor is allowed. Show that a single node scatter from s takes $p-1$ time units using an optimal algorithm. *Hint:* Consider sending continuously packets from s along the spanning tree T, giving priority to the packets destined for nodes that are furthest away from s (break ties arbitrarily).

   (b) Assume that transmission along all the incident links of a processor is allowed. Let r be the number of neighbor nodes of s in the spanning tree T. Let T_i be the subtree of nodes that are connected with s via a simple walk that lies in T, and passes through the ith neighbor of s. Let N_i be the number of nodes in T_i. Construct an algorithm for single node scatter from s that uses links of T and takes $\max\{N_1, N_2, \ldots, N_r\}$ time units. *Hint:* Consider the following rule for s to send packets in each subtree: continuously send packets to distinct nodes in the subtree, giving priority to nodes furthest away from s (break ties arbitrarily).

   (c) Assume that transmission along all the incident links of a processor is allowed. Construct a spanning tree T for the d–cube such that the time $\max\{N_1, N_2, \ldots, N_r\}$ for the single node scatter is equal to the optimal time $\left\lceil (2^d - 1)/d \right\rceil$. *Hint:* Modify the construction of Fig. 1.3.18. Define R_{kn}, $n(t)$, and $m(t)$ as in Fig. 1.3.18, but choose the first element in each equivalence class R_{kn}, so that all nodes t with the same value of $m(t)$ belong to the same subtree. Do this by choosing the first element t in each R_{kn}, so that $m(t') = m(t)$, where t' is t with some unity bit of t changed to a zero, and the equivalence class of t' has d elements.

3.10. **(Total Exchange on the Hypercube [Tse87].)** Consider the total exchange problem in an interconnection network $G = (N, A)$, where transmission along at most one of the incident links of a node is allowed.

   (a) Define the *distance* from a node i to a node j to be the minimum number of arcs contained in walks that start at i and end at j. Suppose that G has a symmetry property, whereby the quantity

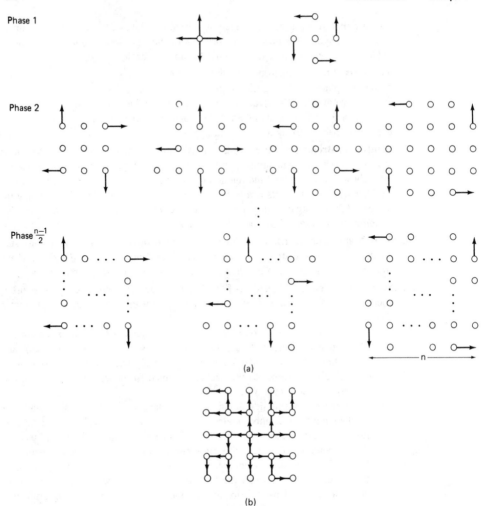

Figure 1.3.30 (a) Procedure to generate a spanning tree rooted at node $\big((n+1)/2, (n+1)/2\big)$ for a multinode broadcast algorithm in an $n \times n$ mesh with wraparound, where n is odd (cf. Exercise 3.7). The tree is generated by labeling nodes starting from the root node $\big((n+1)/2, (n+1)/2\big)$. The labeling procedure consists of $(n-1)/2$ phases. Phase k starts with a $(2k-1) \times (2k-1)$ mesh of labeled nodes and ends with a $(2k+1) \times (2k+1)$ mesh of labeled nodes. (b) Final spanning tree for a 5×5 mesh.

$$D(G) = \sum_{j \in N}(\text{Distance from } i \text{ to } j)$$

is the same for all nodes i. (Examples of networks that have this property are the hypercube and the mesh with wraparound.) Show that $D(G)$ is a lower bound for the time taken by any total exchange algorithm. *Hint:* In a total exchange, every node i must send a packet to every other node j. The number of packet transmissions before

j receives the packet is no less than the distance from i to j. Therefore, the total number of packet transmissions is at least

$$\sum_{i \in N} \sum_{j \in N} (\text{Distance from } i \text{ to } j) = pD(G),$$

where p is the number of processors. Since at most one packet transmission per processor is allowed at a time, the number of simultaneous packet transmissions can be at most p, thereby establishing the lower bound of $D(G)$ time units.

(b) For a d–cube show that $D(G) = d2^{d-1}$. *Hint:* There are exactly $\binom{d}{k} = d!/\big(k!\,(d-k)!\big)$ nodes that are at distance k from a given node, so

$$D(G) = \sum_{k=1}^{d} k \binom{d}{k} = d2^{d-1}.$$

(c) Modify the total exchange algorithm for the d–cube of Fig. 1.3.19 so that phases 1 and 2 are carried out sequentially rather than in parallel, and show inductively that it attains the lower bound of $d2^{d-1}$ time units.

(d) Verify that Fig. 1.3.31 correctly interprets the hypercube total exchange algorithms of Fig. 1.3.19 and (c) above as matrix transposition algorithms. Consider both the case where it is possible to use simultaneously all incident links of a node and the case where this is not possible. For $d = 4$, specify the time that the packet of each of the 16 processors reaches each of the other processors.

3.11. (**Broadcast Algorithms on the Hypercube [Tse87].**) Show that an optimal single node broadcast algorithm and an optimal multinode broadcast algorithm on the d–cube, under the restriction that each node can transmit at most one packet and simultaneously receive at most one packet at a time, take d and $(2^d - 1)$ time units, respectively. *Hint:* For a single node broadcast, d is a lower bound for the optimal time, since for every node, there is another node at distance d from it. Also, since in a multinode broadcast, each node receives $(2^d - 1)$ packets from the other nodes, $(2^d - 1)$ is a lower bound on the optimal time. To show that there are algorithms attaining these bounds, argue inductively. For $d = 1$, the obvious algorithms work. Assume that there are single node and multinode broadcast algorithms for the d–cube that take d and $(2^d - 1)$ time units, respectively. Consider a decomposition of the $(d+1)$–cube into two d–cubes. For a single node broadcast, send first the packet of the root node s to its counterpart s' in the opposite d–cube; then, perform a single node broadcast in parallel from s and s' within the corresponding d–cubes requiring d time units (by the induction hypothesis) for a total of $(d+1)$ time units. For a multinode broadcast, use the imbedding of a ring in a hypercube.

3.12. (**Optimal Generalized Vector Shift Algorithm [Ozv87].**) Show that there exists a generalized vector shift algorithm on the d–cube that takes no more than d time units. *Hint:* For $k = 1, 2, \ldots, d$, consider the set S_k of all integers $x(k)$ that can be generated by the recursion

$$x(t+1) = 2x(t) + u(t), \qquad \forall\, t = 0, 1, \ldots,$$

where $x(0) = 0$, and $u(t)$ can take the values -1, 0, or 1. Thus, S_k consists of all integers $x(k)$ of the form

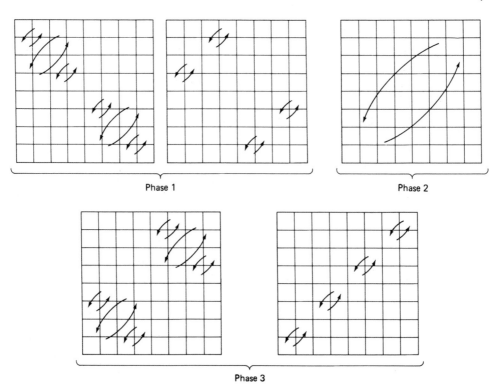

Figure 1.3.31 Interpretation of a total exchange algorithm for the 3–cube (cf. Fig. 1.3.19) as an 8×8 matrix transposition. Long arrows correspond to submatrix moves. The ith processor initially holds the ith row of the matrix, and at the end, it holds the ith column of the matrix. Assuming transmission along all the incident links of a node is allowed, phases 1 and 3 take 3 time units, phase 2 takes 4 time units, whereas phases 1 and 2 can be done in parallel.

$$x(k) = u(k-1) + 2u(k-2) + 2^2 u(k-3) + \cdots + 2^{k-1} u(0),$$

where $u(t)$ can take the values -1, 0, or 1. Show that S_k consists of all the integers in the interval $[-(2^k - 1), (2^k - 1)]$.

3.13. (The Butterfly.) The butterfly network consists of $(d+1)2^d$ processors, where d is some integer. The processors are arranged in $d+1$ rows and 2^d columns. The links are specified as shown in Fig. 1.3.32.

    (a) Show that if the processors of the top row and the corresponding incident links are removed, we obtain two identical butterflies of $d2^{d-1}$ processors.

    (b) Show that an optimal multinode broadcast algorithm on the butterfly takes $\Theta(d2^d)$ time.

3.14. (The Cube–Connected Cycles.) The cube–connected cycles network has $d2^d$ processors, where d is some integer. It is obtained from the d–cube by replacing each processor with a cycle of d processors, as illustrated in Fig. 1.3.33. In particular, each processor has an identity (i, j), where j is a d–bit binary string which is the corresponding d–cube processor identity, and i is an integer from 1 to d. There is a link between two processors with

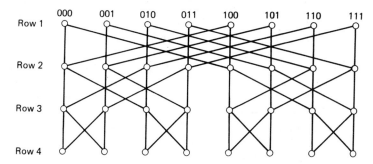

Figure 1.3.32 Illustration of the butterfly network consisting of $(d+1)2^d$ processors. The processors are arranged in $d+1$ rows and 2^d columns, where d is some integer. We label the rows consecutively as $1, 2, \ldots, d+1$, and we label the columns consecutively from 0 to $2^d - 1$ using the d-bit binary representation. Each processor n of row $i = 1, 2, \ldots, d$ is connected with two processors of row $i + 1$: the processor below it (same column), and the processor of the column whose label differs from that of the column of n in the ith bit from the left. The figure illustrates the case where $d = 3$.

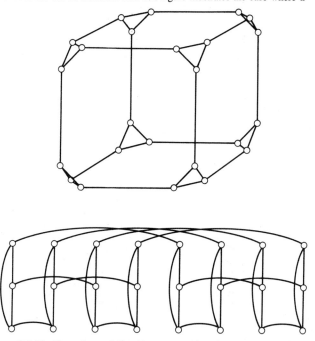

Figure 1.3.33 Two views of the cube–connected cycles network for $d = 3$.

identities (i, j) and (k, m) if and only if a) $i = k$ and j differs from m in the ith bit from the left or b) $j = m$ and $|i - k| = 1$ or $|i - k| = d - 1$. Derive the order of time taken by an optimal single node and multinode broadcast algorithm, and by an optimal total exchange algorithm.

3.15. **[Ozv87]** Modify the procedure given for hypercubes for generating multinode broadcast algorithms from single node broadcast algorithms so that it works for a ring and for a mesh with wraparound. *Hint:* Define the sets A_i as for a hypercube, and generate the sets $A_i(t)$ by using an appropriate operation in place of $\oplus$.

3.16. **(Matrix Multiplication.)** Given a square mesh of n^2 processors, show that multiplication of an $n \times n$ matrix A with the transpose of an $n \times n$ matrix B can be done in $O(n)$ time. We assume that the (i, j)th elements of A and B are stored in processor (i, j), and the (i, j)th element of the product AB' must be eventually stored in the same processor. *Hint:* Show that transposition of the matrix B can bo done in $O(n)$ time.

3.17. **(Matrix Transposition on the Hypercube [Tse87].)** Show that transposition of an $n \times n$ matrix can be done in $2 \log n$ time units on a hypercube of n^2 processors arranged as an $n \times n$ array (n is a power of 2 and each packet requires unit transmission time). We assume that the (i, j)th processor holds initially the (i, j)th element of the matrix, and must hold at the end of the algorithm the (j, i)th element of the matrix. *Hint:* Use the algorithm of Fig. 1.3.34.

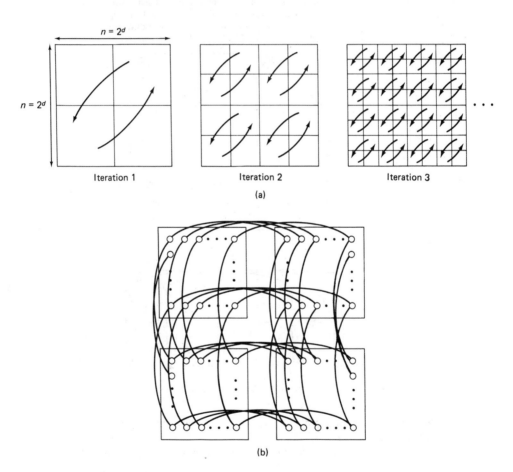

Figure 1.3.34 An algorithm for transposing an $n \times n$ matrix on an $n \times n$ hypercube array. Each of the iterations of (a) takes 2 time units using the links illustrated in (b).

3.18. (Matrix Transposition on the Hypercube.) This exercise considers algorithms for transposing 2–dimensional array data on a hypercube arranged as a 3–dimensional mesh array. Assume that n is a power of 2, and consider the hypercube with n^3 processors arranged in an $n \times n \times n$ array. Suppose that each processor (i, j, k) $(k = 1, \ldots, n)$ initially stores the (i, j)th element a_{ij} of a matrix A.

   (a) Show how the algorithm of Exercise 3.17 can be used to move a_{ij} to the processors (j, i, k) for $k = 1, \ldots, n$.

   (b) Construct an $O(\log n)$ time algorithm that for every (i, j), moves a_{ij} to the processors (i, k, j) for $k = 1, \ldots, n$.

3.19. (Pipelining of Computation and Communication in Single Node Broadcast.) Consider the problem of a single node broadcast of a packet in an interconnection network of n processors such that the maximum distance from every node to the root node is r. The packet can be divided in m packets, each requiring $(w + 1/m)$ time units for transmission on every link, where w represents the extra transmission time required for overhead. Show that it is possible to perform the single node broadcast in $(w + 1/m)(r + m - 1)$ time units, and that if $w > r - 1$, the optimal value of m is 1. Characterize the optimal value of m when $w \leq r - 1$.

3.20. Consider an iteration of the form

$$x := C'Cx + b,$$

where $x \in \Re^n$, $b \in \Re^n$, and C is an $m \times n$ matrix that has no special sparsity structure. This problem deals with parallelization of the iteration using n processors. Assume that each arithmetic operation takes one time unit and that each packet transmission takes d time units.

   (a) Assume that each processor i knows the entries of the ith column of C, and the ith coordinates x_i and b_i. Estimate the time needed per iteration for the two cases where the n processsors communicate via a hypercube and via a linear array.

   (b) Repeat part (a) for the case where the matrix product $C'C$ is given at the beginning of the algorithm, and processor i knows the entries of the ith row of $C'C$, the vector x, and the ith coordinate b_i.

   (c) Which implementation is better? (The answer may depend on the value of m.)

3.21. (Sparse Matrix–Vector Multiplication.) Consider forming the matrix–vector product Ax in $\Re^n$ using a hypercube of n processors. Initially, each processor stores the vector x and the ith row of A, and at the end, it must hold the product Ax. Assume that each arithmetic operation and each packet transmission take unit time. Show that if each row of A has no more than r nonzero elements, there is an algorithm that takes time $O\big(\max(n/\log n, r)\big)$. Provide a similar result for the case where each processor stores a column of A and the corresponding entry of x, and each column has no more than r nonzero elements.

3.22. (Addition of p Scalars on a Hypercube [DNS81].) Consider a hypercube with p processors, and suppose that each processor i holds a scalar a_i. We wish to calculate and store the sum $\sum_{i=1}^{p} a_i$ in each processor. Assume that transmission of a scalar over any link requires one time unit, and an addition requires negligible time. Consider the following algorithm: each processor i updates a scalar s_i at the end of each of $\log p$ stages. Initially, $s_i = a_i$. During the kth stage, each processor i transmits its current value s_i to the processor j whose identity number agrees with the one of i except for the kth bit from the left; processor j then adds the received value s_i to its current value s_j, and stores the result in place of s_j. Show that after $\log p$ time units, each processor holds the required sum. (This is faster by a factor of 2 over collecting the sum at a single processor along a spanning tree and broadcasting it back to all processors.)

3.23. **(Repeated Matrix–Vector Multiplication on a Hypercube [Tse88].)** Suppose that we have a hypercube with n^2 processors. Processor (i, j) stores the ijth element c_{ij} of an $n \times n$ matrix C and the jth coordinate x_j of a vector x.

    (a) Use the addition method of Exercise 3.22 in an algorithm that computes the jth coordinate of $C'Cx$ in $2 \log n$ time units. (Each transmission of a scalar over any link requires one time unit, and each multiplication and addition requires negligible time.)

    (b) Show that if C is symmetric, then the products $C^k x, k = 1, 2, \cdots, r$, where r is a positive integer, can be found in $r \log n$ time units.

3.24. **(Multinode Broadcast with Packets Combined [KVC88].)** Consider the multinode broadcast problem with the following difference: we assume that a node can combine any number k of packets and transmit them on any one link as a single packet in one time unit, rather than transmit them as k separate packets in k time units, as we assume in our standard model. Show that this problem can be solved by using a single node accumulation algorithm followed by a single node broadcast algorithm. In particular, an optimal algorithm for the problem takes at most $2d$ time units on a d–cube.

1.4 SYNCHRONIZATION ISSUES IN PARALLEL AND DISTRIBUTED ALGORITHMS

In any parallel or distributed algorithm, it is necessary to coordinate to some extent the activities of the different processors. This coordination is often implemented by dividing the algorithm in "phases". During each phase, every processor must execute a number of computations that depend on the results of the computations of other processors in previous phases; however, the timing of the computations at any one processor during a phase can be independent of the timing of computations at other processors within the same phase. In effect, within a phase, each processor does not interact with other processors as far as the given algorithm is concerned. All interaction takes place at the end of phases. We call such algorithms *synchronous*, and in this section, we compare them with other algorithms, called *asynchronous*, for which there is no notion of phases and the coordination of the computations of different processors is less strict. Throughout this section we emphasize the case of a message–passing system. Some of the ideas, however, are applicable, with proper interpretation, to shared memory systems.

1.4.1 Synchronous Algorithms

Suppose that a sequence of computations is divided into consecutive segments, called *phases* and numbered $1, 2, 3, \ldots$. The computations within each phase are divided among the n processors of a computing system. During a phase t, each processor i does some computations using the problem data, together with the information that it received from the other processors during the previous phases $1, 2, \ldots, t - 1$. Processor i then sends some information in the form of a message to each processor in a given subset $P(i, t) \subset \{1, 2, \ldots, n\}$, and the process is repeated at the next phase $t+1$. (The method by which a message is transmitted is not material in our discussion. In particular, a message can consist of several packets, in which case the time of reception of the message is the time of reception of the last packet.) An implicit assumption here is that the computations of different processors can be carried out "independently" within a phase, and that their relative timing is immaterial. This is necessary for the distributed algorithm to replicate the results of the original serial algorithm at the end of each phase. Note that in some cases, a processor may not know from which processors to expect a message during a phase, that is, a processor j may not know the set $\{i \mid j \in P(i, t)\}$.

As an example, consider the relaxation iteration

$$x_i(t + 1) = f_i\big(x_1(t), \ldots, x_n(t)\big), \qquad i = 1, \ldots, n, \tag{4.1}$$

discussed in Subsection 1.2.4, where variable x_i is updated by processor i. A corresponding distributed algorithm can be implemented by associating phases with the time instants t. The requirement here is that each processor i updates x_i using the relaxation iteration (4.1) and then sends a message with the updated value to all processors j for which x_i appears explicitly in the function f_j. Thus, the subset of processors $P(i, t)$ receiving a message from i during phase t is the set of all j for which (i, j) is an arc in the dependency graph discussed in Subsection 1.2.4.

Consider also the case where the relaxation iteration (4.1) is implemented in a shared memory machine. Here a processor sends a message to all processors simultaneously by writing it in the shared memory. Suppose that a processor will start a computation of a new phase only after all the messages of the previous phase have been written in the shared memory. Then, we have a special case of the preceding model, where

$$P(i, t) = \{1, 2, \ldots, n\},$$

and the reception of a message is simultaneous at all processors.

A distributed algorithm such as the one described above is said to be *synchronous*. It is mathematically equivalent to an algorithm governed by a global clock, that is, one for which the start of each phase is simultaneous for all processors, and the end of the message receptions is simultaneous for all messages. In order to implement a synchronous algorithm in an inherently asynchronous distributed system, we need a *synchronization mechanism*, i.e., an algorithm that is superimposed on the original and by which every processor can detect the end of each phase. Such an algorithm is called a *synchronizer*. In what follows in this section, we describe two approaches on which synchronizers are based, called *global synchronization* and *local synchronization*. A third approach, based on the idea of *rollback*, is discussed in Section 8.4, together with its application in simulation problems.

Global Synchronization

The idea here is to let each processor detect when all messages sent during a phase have been received, and only then to start the computation of the next phase. The conceptually simplest way for effecting global synchronization is through the use of *timeouts*. We assume that there is no global clock accessible by all processors, but instead, each processor can measure accurately the length of any time interval using a local clock. Suppose that there is a known upper bound T_p for the time required for each processor i to execute the computations of a phase, and for the associated messages sent by i to be received at their destinations. Suppose also that there is an (unknown) time interval of known length T_f during which all processors started the first phase. Then synchronization will be effected if each processor i starts the kth phase $k(T_p + T_f)$ time units after it started the first phase. Fig. 1.4.1 illustrates this process. The difficulty with this method is that the bounds T_p and T_f may be too conservative or unavailable.

Another approach is for every processor to send a *phase termination message* to every other processor once it knows that all of its own messages for a given phase have been received. We assume here that each message sent is acknowledged through a return message sent by the receiver to the transmitter, so each processor knows eventually that all the messages it sent during a phase have been received, at which time it can issue a phase termination message. Once a processor has sent its own phase termination message and has received the corresponding phase termination messages from all other processors, it can proceed with the computations of the next phase. In a shared memory system, this method is conceptually straightforward through the use of special variables that are accessible to all processors. There are a number of possible implementations (spin locks, semaphores, monitors; see [AHV85] and [Qui87]), which we will not discuss in detail. The basic conceptual idea is that the special variables should take at the right times particular values that indicate to the processors that a phase has ended, and it is therefore safe to proceed with the computations of the next phase.

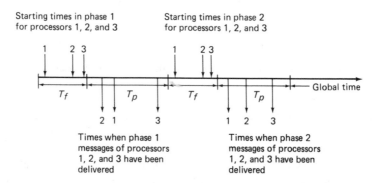

Figure 1.4.1 Implementation of global synchronization using timeouts. The starting times of the three processors for each phase are known to be within an interval of length T_f. For every processor, the time required for computation and message delivery within a phase is known to be no more than T_p. It is sufficient for each processor to start a new phase every $(T_f + T_p)$ time units.

In a message–passing system, global synchronization can be implemented by using a spanning tree and a special node designated as the root of the tree. The phase termination messages of the processors are collected at the root of the tree, starting from the leaves. Once the root has received the phase termination messages of all processors, it can send a phase initiation message to all other processors along the spanning tree, and each processor can begin a new phase upon reception of this message (see Fig. 1.4.2). It can be seen that this method essentially requires a single node accumulation followed by a single node broadcast (cf. Subsection 1.3.4). Therefore, the communication time for phase termination (subsequent to the time when acknowledgments for all processor messages in the phase have been received) is $\Theta(r)$, where r is the diameter of the network.

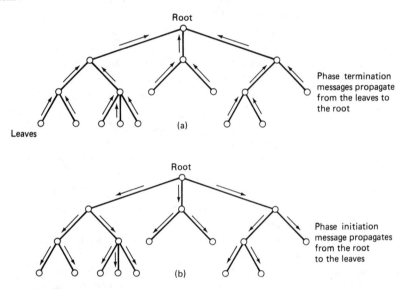

Figure 1.4.2 Global synchronization using a spanning tree, with a special node designated as the root of the tree. (a) Each node sends a phase termination message to its parent, when it has received acknowledgments for all the messages it sent during a phase, as well as phase termination messages from all its children. (b) The root, upon receiving a phase termination message from all its children, sends a phase initiation message to its children, who relay it to their children, and so on. Each node, upon receiving the phase initiation message, can start a new phase.

Local Synchronization

The main idea of this method is that if a processor knows which messages to expect in each phase, then it can start a new phase once it has received all these messages. In particular, processor j can start the computation of a new phase $t+1$ once it has received the messages of the previous phase t from all processors i in the set

$$\{i \mid j \in P(i,t)\}. \tag{4.2}$$

It is not necessary for a processor to know whether any other messages sent during phase t (including its own) have been received, so there is no need to waste time waiting for these receptions to be completed and to be confirmed. When processor j does not know the set (4.2) but instead knows a set S_j, where

$$S_j \supset \{i \mid j \in P(i,t)\}, \qquad \forall\, t,$$

the scheme can be modified so that all nodes $i \in S_j$ with $j \notin P(i,t)$ are required to send a "dummy" message to j during phase t. In this way, the situation is reduced to the case where the set (4.2) is known by j. Note, however, that with this modification, the local synchronization scheme may become undesirable if S_j contains many more elements than the set $\{i \mid j \in P(i,t)\}$.

When each processor j knows the set (4.2), it can be seen that the local synchronization method leads to no more communication penalty than any global synchronization method. Often, the communication penalty is considerably less. This is particularly so when the transmission time of messages on communication links is comparable to the time needed for computation in each phase, since, for global synchronization, additional messages may be required for acknowledgments, etc., as discussed earlier. Even without counting the time for acknowledgments, the difference between the execution times associated with the global and the local methods typically increases with the number of phases, due to the variability of the times for computation and message delivery by different processors within each phase. We demonstrate this phenomenon in the case where the times required by a processor to complete the delivery of messages associated with a phase are deterministic. For a related analysis when these times are random, independent, and exponentially distributed, see Exercise 4.1.

Let $T_{ij}(t)$ be the time required for processor i to do the computations of phase t and to deliver the corresponding message to processor $j \in P(i,t)$. To simplify notation, we assume that $i \in P(i,t)$, and we denote by $T_{ii}(t)$ the time required for i to do just the computations for phase t. Suppose that $P(i,t)$ and $T_{ij}(t)$ are known and independent of t [i.e., $P(i,t) = P_i$ and $T_{ij}(t) = T_{ij}$, for all t, i, and $j \in P_i$]. We will compare the local synchronization method with a global synchronization method, whereby a phase is considered completed as soon as every message of the phase has been delivered. We thus neglect any time needed for acknowledging the messages of the phase or for broadcasting the phase termination messages mentioned earlier. Assume that all processors start phase 1 simultaneously, and consider the times $L(k)$ and $G(k)$ required to complete k phases at all processors using the local and the global synchronization methods, respectively.

The time for a single phase using the global synchronization method is

$$G(1) = T_{max},$$

where

$$T_{max} = \max_{i=1,\dots,n,\ j \in P_i} T_{ij}.$$

Since each phase must be completed at all processors before a new phase can begin, we have

$$G(k) = kT_{max}. \tag{4.3}$$

To obtain the corresponding time for the local synchronization method, we define

$$C_{max} = \max_{Y} \frac{\sum_{(i,j) \in Y} T_{ij}}{|Y|},$$

where the maximum in the preceding definition is over all sequences Y of the form

$$\{(i_1, i_2), (i_2, i_3), \ldots, (i_m, i_1)\},$$

where $m = |Y| \geq 1$ and $i_{s+1} \in P_{i_s}$ for $s = 1, \ldots, m-1$, $i_1 \in P_{i_m}$. We form a directed graph having as node set

$$N = \{(t, i) \mid t = 1, \ldots, k+1, \ i = 1, \ldots, n\},$$

(see Fig. 1.4.3). There is an arc corresponding to each pair $((t, i), (t+1, j))$ where $t = 1, 2, \ldots, k$, and $j \in P_i$, and we view T_{ij} as the "length" of such an arc. Consider the set of all paths p starting at a node of the form $(1, i)$ and ending at a node of the form $(k+1, j)$. Let M_p be the length of path p, that is, the sum of the lengths of its arcs. Then, as seen from Fig. 1.4.3, $L(k)$ is the maximum of M_p over all paths p of the type just described, and for $k \geq n$, we have

$$L(k) \leq [k - (n-1)] C_{max} + (n-1)T_{max}. \tag{4.4}$$

Comparing Eqs. (4.3) and (4.4) we see that

$$G(k) - L(k) \geq [k - (n-1)] (T_{max} - C_{max}).$$

Thus, when

$$T_{max} - C_{max} > 0,$$

and k is large, the difference $G(k) - L(k)$ grows, in effect, proportionally with k. Note, however, that if the time required for message delivery is small relative to the time needed for the processors' computation during a phase, that is, $T_{ii} \simeq T_{ij}$ for all j, then the difference $T_{max} - C_{max}$ will be small or zero. (Take, for example, $n = 2$, $T_{11} = 2$, $T_{22} = 1$, and $T_{12} + T_{21} < 4$, in which case there is no difference in the communication penalty associated with the global and local synchronization methods.)

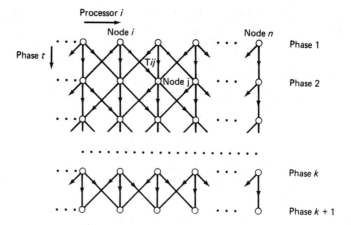

Figure 1.4.3 Estimating the time to complete k phases using the local synchronization method [cf. Eq. (4.4)]. We consider the acyclic graph with node set

$$N = \big\{(t, i) \mid t = 1, \ldots, k+1, \ i = 1, \ldots, n \big\},$$

and arcs $\big((t, i), (t+1, j)\big)$, where $t = 1, 2, \ldots, k$, and $j \in P_i$. In the example of the figure we have $P_1 = \{1, 2\}$, $P_n = \{n-1, n\}$, and $P_i = \{i-1, i, i+1\}$, for $i \neq 1, n$. We view T_{ij} as the length of such an arc. Since all the messages of the k phases must be received before the k phases can be completed, and each processor cannot begin a new phase without receiving the messages of the previous phase, the length of any path in this graph is less than or equal to $L(k)$. By induction on the number of phases k, it can be verified that $L(k)$ is equal to the length of some path. Therefore, $L(k)$ is equal to the length of a longest path. Let $\{(i_1, 1), (i_2, 2), \ldots, (i_{k+1}, k+1)\}$ be a longest path. Assume first that $i_m \neq i_{m+1}$ for all m. Consider the path $\{i_1, i_2, \ldots, i_{k+1}\}$ in the graph with set of nodes $\{1, \ldots, n\}$ and set of arcs $\{(i, j) \mid j \in P_i, \ j \neq i, \ i = 1, \ldots, n\}$. By using the Path Decomposition Theorem of Appendix B on this latter path, it is seen that the longest path can be broken down in two components:

(a) a (possibly empty) collection of subpaths of the form $\{(j_1, t), (j_2, t+1), \ldots, (j_m, t+m-1), (j_1, t+m)\}$, where $m > 1$, and $j_{s+1} \in P_{j_s}$ for $s = 1, \ldots, m-1$, $j_1 \in P_{j_m}$, corresponding to cycles obtained from the path $\{i_1, i_2, \ldots, i_{k+1}\}$;

(b) a set of at most $(n-1)$ additional arcs, corresponding to a simple path obtained from the path $\{i_1, i_2, \ldots, i_{k+1}\}$.

By bounding from above the lengths of the two components, we obtain the estimate (4.4). If $i_m = i_{m+1}$ for some m, the length of the arc $\big((i_m, m), (i_{m+1}, m+1)\big)$ is bounded above by C_{max}, and it is seen that Eq. (4.4) remains valid even in the presence of such arcs.

The preceding discussion suggests that the local synchronization method is usually superior to the global method in terms of communication penalty. On the other hand, there may be other factors, such as software complexity, that argue in favor of the global method, since this method is largely independent of the structure of the algorithm executed.

1.4.2 Asynchronous Algorithms and the Reduction of the Synchronization Penalty

The communication penalty, and the overall execution time of many algorithms, can often be substantially reduced by means of an asynchronous implementation. The analysis of asynchronous distributed algorithms is one of the focal points of this book, and in this subsection, we provide a preliminary and informal contrast with synchronous algorithms. A precise model of an asynchronous algorithm will be given later, but for the purposes of this section the following rough description will suffice.

Given a distributed algorithm, for each processor, there is a set of times at which the processor executes some computation, some other times at which the processor sends some messages to other processors, and yet some other times at which the processor receives messages from other processors. The algorithm is termed synchronous, in the sense of the preceding subsection, if it is mathematically equivalent to one for which the times of computation, message transmission, and message reception are fixed and given *a priori*. We say that the algorithm is asynchronous if these times (and, therefore, also the order of computations and message receptions at the processors) can vary widely in two different executions of the algorithm with an attendant effect on the results of the computation.

For another contrasting view, which is appropriate primarily for a message–passing system, we can think of a distributed algorithm as a collection of local algorithms. Each local algorithm is executed at a different processor and occasionally uses data generated by other local algorithms. In the simplest case of a synchronous algorithm, the timing of operations at each processor is completely determined and is enforced by using a global clock. A more complex type of synchronous algorithm is one in which the exact timing of operations at each local algorithm is not predetermined, but the local algorithms still have to wait at predetermined points for predetermined data to become available (cf. the discussion of local synchronization in the previous subsection). An example of an asynchronous algorithm is when local algorithms do not wait for predetermined data to become available; they keep on computing, trying to solve the given problem with whatever data happen to be available at the time.

The most extreme type of asynchronous algorithm is one that can tolerate changes in the problem data or in the distributed computing system, without restarting itself to some predetermined initial conditions. This situation arises principally in data networks, where the nodes and the communication links can fail or be repaired as various distributed algorithms that control the network are executed. In some networks, such as mobile packet radio networks, changes in the network topology can be frequent. In other networks, such changes may be infrequent, but the execution time of the algorithm considered may be so long that there is a nonnegligible probability of occurence of a topological change while the algorithm executes. For example, in general purpose data networks, some algorithms, such as the routing algorithm, are essentially always operating, so they must inevitably operate in the face of node and link failures. There are a number of difficulties here. First, one may have to keep all nodes informed of the link and node failures and repairs; this information can have a bearing on the distributed algorithm being executed. Doing so is not as easy as it may appear since failure information must be communicated over links that are themselves subject to failure; Fig. 1.4.4 provides an example. Second, a link or node failure that occurs while a distributed algorithm is executing on the data network will typically affect the algorithm. To cope with the situation, the algorithm should either be capable to adapt to the failure or it should be aborted and be restarted. Doing the latter may be nontrivial, since more failures can occur while the algorithm is being restarted. Such issues will be discussed in Chapter 8, where it will become evident that it is typically far simpler to restart asynchronous rather than synchronous algorithms, because asynchronous algorithms generally allow more flexibility in the choice of initial conditions.

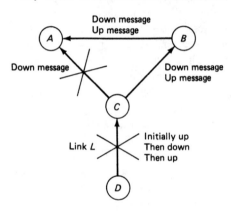

Figure 1.4.4 An example of the difficulties in communicating link failure information in a data network (from [BeG87]). Consider an algorithm that works as follows: whenever the status of a link changes, the end nodes of the link send this information to all their adjacent nodes, which in turn relay this information to their own adjacent nodes (if this information changes their view of the status of the link), etc. Here link L is initially up, then it goes down, and then up again. Suppose the down and up messages on links (C,B) and (B,A) travel faster than the down message travels on link (C,A). Also, suppose that link (C,A) goes down before the up message regarding link L travels on it.

Then the last message received by A asserts that link L is down while the link is actually up. The difficulty here is that link failures can cause old information to be perceived as new.

An important question is whether or not asynchronism helps to reduce the communication penalty and the overall solution time of a given algorithm. We discuss this next in the context of the Jacobi and Gauss–Seidel relaxation methods introduced in Subsection 1.2.4.

Asynchronous Relaxation Methods

Consider an n–processor system and an n–dimensional fixed point problem, whereby we want to find a vector $x = (x_1, x_2, \ldots, x_n)$ satisfying

$$x_i = f_i(x_1, x_2, \ldots, x_n), \qquad i = 1, 2, \ldots, n,$$

where f_i are given functions of n variables. Suppose that each processor i updates the variable x_i according to

$$x_i := f_i(x_1, x_2, \ldots, x_n), \qquad i = 1, 2, \ldots, n, \tag{4.5}$$

starting from a set of initial values for all variables. We will discuss in Chapters 2 and 3 several examples of updates of this type, and we will also consider more general types of updates.

A synchronous implementation of the algorithm requires that a processor i does not carry out its kth update without first receiving the results of the $(k-1)$st update from the processors whose variables appear in the function f_i. There is a certain inefficiency built into this requirement, which we call, somewhat loosely, the *synchronization penalty*. It is due to two factors:

(a) A processor i upon updating x_i must remain idle while waiting for messages to arrive from other processors (see Fig. 1.4.5). In particular, a slow communication channel slows the progress of the entire computation, as shown in Fig. 1.4.6(a).

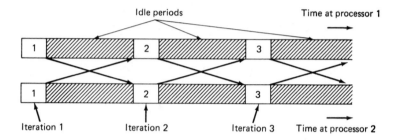

Figure 1.4.5 Illustration of the synchronization penalty due to long communication delays. Arrows indicate the times of message reception. Shaded areas indicate the idle periods when a processor is waiting for a message from the other processor.

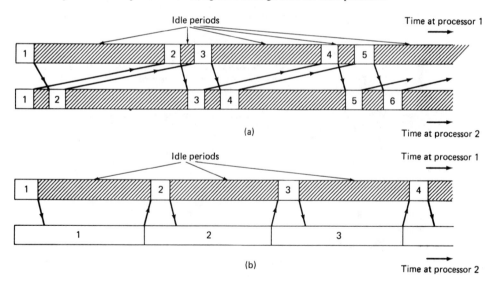

Figure 1.4.6 Illustration of the synchronization penalty due to a single slow communication channel [channel from 2 to 1 in (a)], and due to a single slow processor [second processor in (b)].

(b) Processors that are fast either because of high computing power or because of small workload per iteration, must wait for the slower processors to finish their iteration.

Thus the pace of the algorithm is dictated by the slowest processor, as shown in Fig. 1.4.6(b).

Note that the synchronization penalty contributes to the communication penalty in view of factor (a). It also contributes to a loss of efficiency when the computational load of each iteration is not well balanced among all processors in view of factor (b), and this can happen even if all communication is instantaneous.

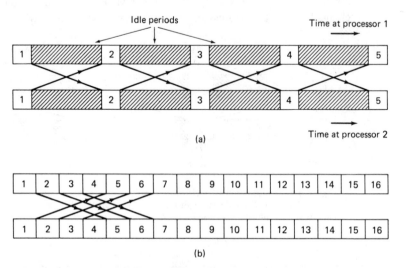

(a)

(b)

Figure 1.4.7 (a) Timing diagram for a synchronous algorithm. Arrows indicate the times of message reception. Shaded areas indicate the idle periods when the processor is waiting for a message from the other processor. Numbered areas indicate update periods at each processor. Idle periods are three times longer than computation periods in this example. (b) Timing diagram for an asynchronous algorithm. Arrows indicate the times of message reception. Numbered areas indicate update periods at each processor. The potential advantage of an asynchronous algorithm lies in the fact that it can execute more iterations per unit time because there is no waiting for message receptions, (three times more in this example). It is unclear, however, whether the additional iterations will accelerate convergence, since these iterations are based on out–of–date information.

In an asynchronous version of the preceding algorithm, there is much more flexibility regarding the use of the information received from other processors. What is required is that the kth update at processor i is carried out with knowledge of the results of *some* past update of every other processor, not necessarily the most recent update. Thus, for example, processor i may be executing its kth update using the results of the $(k + 10)$th update of some other processor j, while at the same time processor j may be executing its $(k + 100)$th update using the result of the $(k - 10)$th update of processor i. The speed of computation and communication can be different at different processors, and there can be substantial communication delays. Furthermore, these speeds and delays can vary unpredictably as the algorithm progresses. It is not even required that the communication links preserve the order of messages, so it is possible for a processor to use the kth update of some other processor at some time, and use the results of, say, the $(k-10)$th update of the same other processor at some later time. There is also flexibility regarding the initial conditions at each processor; the variables x_i available initially at different processors can differ, for the same i.

An asynchronous algorithm can potentially reduce the synchronization penalty caused by fast processors waiting for slow processors to complete their updates, and for slow communication channels to deliver messages (see Fig. 1.4.7). The reason is that processors can execute more iterations when they are not constrained to wait for the most recent results of the computation in other processors. There is a danger that iterations performed on the basis of outdated information will not be effective and may even be counterproductive. This issue will be considered in Chapters 6 and 7, where it will be seen that asynchronous iterative methods work only under certain conditions. When they do work, they typically reduce the synchronization penalty and result in faster problem solution. Their communication requirements, however, may exceed those of their synchronous counterparts. We provide a simple illustrative example. The conclusions from this example will be shown in more generality in Section 6.3.

Example 4.1.   *Convergence Rate Comparison of Synchronous and Asynchronous Methods*

Consider the two–dimensional fixed point problem

$$x = Ax,$$

where

$$A = \begin{bmatrix} a & b \\ b & a \end{bmatrix}.$$

The corresponding iteration is

$$x_1 := ax_1 + bx_2, \tag{4.6a}$$
$$x_2 := bx_1 + ax_2, \tag{4.6b}$$

where variables x_1 and x_2 are updated at processors 1 and 2, respectively, and are subsequently communicated to the other processor. Suppose that each update requires one unit of time, and the subsequent communication requires D units of time, where D is a positive integer. (The following conclusions depend crucially on the fact $D \geq 1$; see Exercise 4.2.) We consider a synchronous and an asynchronous algorithm operating as shown in Fig. 1.4.7.

In the synchronous algorithm, values of variables are received at times $t = D + 1, 2(D+1), \ldots$; variable updates are also initiated at these times, as well as at time $t = 0$, and variable updates are completed one time unit later. If $x_i(t)$, $i = 1, 2$, is the value available at processor i at an integer time t, we have

$$x_1(t+1) = ax_1(t-D) + bx_2(t-D), \tag{4.7a}$$
$$x_2(t+1) = bx_1(t-D) + ax_2(t-D), \tag{4.7b}$$

where

$$x_i(t) = x_i(0), \qquad -D \le t < 0, \quad i = 1, 2.$$

In the asynchronous algorithm, processor i updates variable x_i as many times as possible regardless of whether it has an up–to–date value of the variable of the other processor (cf. Fig. 1.4.7). Then $x_i(t)$ evolves for all t according to

$$x_1(t+1) = ax_1(t) + bx_2(t-D), \tag{4.8a}$$

$$x_2(t+1) = bx_1(t-D) + ax_2(t), \tag{4.8b}$$

where

$$x_i(t) = x_i(0), \qquad -D \le t < 0, \quad i = 1, 2.$$

We now want to compare the synchronous iteration (4.7) with the asynchronous iteration (4.8) for the same initial conditions $x_1(0)$ and $x_2(0)$. We first consider the issue of convergence. This subject will be discussed in detail in Chapters 2 and 6. It can be shown that if

$$|a| + |b| < 1,$$

the synchronous iteration (4.7) converges to the unique fixed point $x^* = (0,0)$ starting from arbitrary initial conditions; let $D = 0$ in the following argument that applies to the asynchronous version of the iteration.

For the matrix A considered, convergence of the asynchronous iteration (4.8) is also guaranteed if $|a|+|b| < 1$. We prove this with an argument that we will use in more generality in Section 6.2 to show convergence of asynchronous fixed point iterations under a broad set of assumptions. The key idea is that if for some $t' \ge 0$ and all t with $t' - D \le t \le t'$, the vector $x(t) = \big(x_1(t), x_2(t)\big)$ belongs to the l_∞–sphere of radius r

$$\big\{x \,\big|\, |x_1| \le r, |x_2| \le r\big\}, \tag{4.9}$$

then from Eq. (4.8) it follows that $x(t)$ will belong to the (smaller) l_∞–sphere of radius $(|a| + |b|)r$ for all $t \ge t' + 1$. Based on this fact, it follows that $x(t)$ will belong to the (even smaller) l_∞–sphere of radius $(|a| + |b|)^2 r$ for all $t \ge t' + D + 2$, and so on, proving convergence of $x(t)$ to the zero vector.

We next consider the rate of convergence of the synchronous iteration (4.7). We first observe that if $\rho > 0$ is such that

$$|a|\rho^{-D} + |b|\rho^{-D} \le \rho,$$

or, equivalently,

$$\big(|a| + |b|\big)^{1/(D+1)} \le \rho, \tag{4.10}$$

then the sequence generated by the synchronous iteration (4.7) satisfies

$$|x_i(t)| \leq C\rho^t, \qquad \forall \, t = 0, 1, \ldots, \tag{4.11}$$

where

$$C = \max\big\{|x_1(0)|, |x_2(0)|\big\}. \tag{4.12}$$

Indeed Eq. (4.11) holds for $t \leq 0$. Assume that it holds for all t up to some $\bar{t}$. Then, using Eqs. (4.10) and (4.11), we have

$$|x_1(\bar{t}+1)| \leq |a||x_1(\bar{t}-D)| + |b||x_2(\bar{t}-D)| \leq \big(|a|+|b|\big)C\rho^{\bar{t}-D} \leq C\rho^{\bar{t}+1},$$

and similarly $|x_2(\bar{t}+1)| \leq C\rho^{\bar{t}+1}$. Therefore, Eq. (4.11) holds for all $t \leq \bar{t}+1$ and the induction is complete. The smallest value of ρ for which Eq. (4.10), and hence also the rate of convergence estimate $|x_i(t)| \leq C\rho^t$, holds is

$$\rho_S = \big(|a|+|b|\big)^{1/(D+1)}. \tag{4.13}$$

A little thought shows also that there exist initial conditions for which the rate of convergence estimate $|x_i(t)| \leq C\rho^t$ fails to hold when $\rho < \rho_S$.

A nearly verbatim repetition of the preceding argument can be used to show that if

$$|a| + |b|\rho^{-D} \leq \rho, \tag{4.14}$$

then the sequence generated by the asynchronous iteration (4.8) satisfies the rate of convergence estimate $|x_i(t)| \leq C\rho^t$, with C given by Eq. (4.12). The smallest ρ satisfying Eq. (4.14), denoted by ρ_A, is the unique positive solution of the equation

$$|a| + |b|\rho^{-D} = \rho. \tag{4.15}$$

The construction of ρ_A and its relation with ρ_S are illustrated in Fig. 1.4.8. It can be seen that

$$\rho_A \leq \rho_S,$$

and the convergence rate estimate of the asynchronous iteration is better than the one of the synchronous version (see also Fig. 1.4.9). This indicates that the asynchronous iteration typically converges faster. Computational results support this hypothesis.

The preceding conclusions can be generalized as will be shown in Section 6.3. For example, the matrix A could be any $n \times n$ matrix with elements a_{ij} satisfying $\sum_{j=1}^{n} |a_{ij}| < 1$ for all i. Also, the updating and the communication delays need not be equal for all processors, communication channels, and iterations. It appears that variability of these delays favors the asynchronous over the synchronous algorithm, but this seems difficult to establish analytically.

Consider now the number of messages required to solve the problem to within a given $\epsilon > 0$. If for a given t and ρ, we have $|x_i(t)| \leq C\rho^t$, we obtain $|x_i(t)| \leq \epsilon$ if $C\rho^t \leq \epsilon$

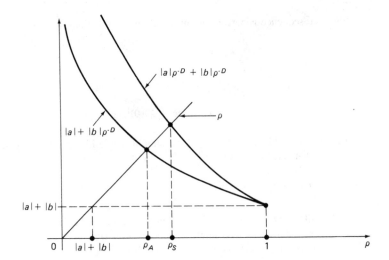

Figure 1.4.8   Construction of the convergence rate parameter ρ_A of the asynchronous iteration (4.8), and the corresponding parameter ρ_S for the synchronous iteration (4.7). We have $\rho_A < \rho_S$ except when $a = 0$ in which case $\rho_A = \rho_S$. For a given value of $|a| + |b|$, the ratio ρ_A/ρ_S is minimized when $|b| = 0$, in which case,

$$\frac{\rho_A}{\rho_S} = |a|^{D/(D+1)}.$$

More generally, as the strength of the coupling between the two variables x_1, and x_2 (i.e., the magnitude of $|b|$) decreases, the advantage of the asynchronous implementation in terms of rate of convergence increases.

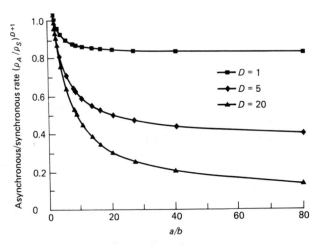

Figure 1.4.9   Plot of the value of $(\rho_A/\rho_S)^{(D+1)}$ for various values of the communication delay D, and the parameters a and b. In this example we have $|a| + |b| = 0.8$. The quantity $(\rho_A/\rho_S)^{(D+1)}$ is the ratio of error reduction factors per synchronous iteration ($D + 1$ time units), and tends to

$$\frac{|b|}{(1 - |a|)(|a| + |b|)}$$

as D increases to infinity.

or equivalently $t \geq |\log(\epsilon/C)|/|\log \rho|$. Therefore, if t_S and t_A are the times required to obtain $|x_i(t)| \leq \epsilon$, $i = 1, 2$, based on the convergence rate estimates for the synchronous and the asynchronous iterations, respectively, we obtain

$$\frac{t_S}{t_A} = \frac{|\log \rho_A|}{|\log \rho_S|} \geq 1.$$

The number m_S of message receptions per processor up to t_S for the synchronous iteration does not exceed $t_S/(D + 1)$, whereas the corresponding number m_A for the asynchronous iteration is t_A (cf. Fig. 1.4.7). Therefore, using Eq. (4.13) for ρ_S, we have

$$\frac{m_S}{m_A} \leq \frac{|\log \rho_A|}{(D + 1)|\log \rho_S|} = \frac{|\log \rho_A|}{|\log(|a| + |b|)|}.$$

From Fig. 1.4.8 we see that $|a| + |b| \leq \rho_A < 1$, so

$$\frac{m_S}{m_A} \leq 1.$$

The asynchronous algorithm requires more message transmissions because of the requirement of communication at the end of each variable update. An alternative asynchronous algorithm communicates the results every kth update, where $k \geq 2$ is some integer (but still updates every variable at each time unit). When $k = D + 1$ in the present example, the frequency of communication is the same as for the synchronous algorithm (4.7), and similar analysis as the one above (Exercise 4.3) shows that the asynchronous algorithm is guaranteed to solve the problem within any ϵ both faster and with fewer message transmissions than the synchronous version (but using a larger number of variable updates).

The conclusion in this example is that *asynchronism improves the convergence rate of iteration (4.6) but may increase the number of message transmissions.* In other words, *the communication penalty is reduced by asynchronous implementation at the expense of perhaps more frequent message exchange between processors.* This conclusion is consistent with other conclusions to be reached in related contexts. For example, in Section 6.4 we will see that the asynchronous Bellman–Ford algorithm takes no more time to solve a shortest path problem than the synchronous version, but may require many more message transmissions.

Note also that the tradeoff between execution time and number of message transmissions assumes that communication delays are not affected by the frequency of communication, that is, no queueing of messages occurs along communication links. With substantial queueing delays, an asynchronous algorithm can be much slower that its synchronous counterpart.

An important disadvantage of asynchronism is that it can destroy convergence properties that the algorithm may possess when executed synchronously. Indeed we will see (Section 6.3 and Chapter 7) that in some cases, it is necessary to place limitations on the size of communication delays to guarantee convergence. In all cases, the analysis of asynchronous algorithms is considerably more difficult than for their synchronous counterparts. We will also see that there are unifying themes in this analysis. In particular, it is possible to establish simultaneously the validity of important classes of asynchronous algorithms with widely varying character through the use of general and powerful convergence theorems and techniques (see Chapters 6 and 7).

Asynchronous algorithms can offer an additional advantage in relaxation methods, which can be understood by considering the Jacobi and the Gauss–Seidel methods for solving fixed point problems (cf. Subsection 1.2.4). The sequential form of the Jacobi method generates a sequence $x(t) = \big(x_1(t), x_2(t), \ldots, x_n(t)\big)$ according to

$$x_i(t+1) = f_i\big(x_1(t), x_2(t), \ldots, x_n(t)\big), \qquad i = 1, 2, \ldots, n$$

from a given set of initial values. The Gauss–Seidel method is similar, but uses the most recently generated values of the variables x_i in the update formulas. It takes the form

$$x_1(t+1) = f_1\big(x_1(t), x_2(t), \ldots, x_{n-1}(t), x_n(t)\big)$$
$$x_2(t+1) = f_2\big(x_1(t+1), x_2(t), \ldots, x_{n-1}(t), x_n(t)\big)$$
$$\cdots \qquad \cdots \qquad \cdots$$
$$x_n(t+1) = f_n\big(x_1(t+1), x_2(t+1), \ldots, x_{n-1}(t+1), x_n(t)\big).$$

The Jacobi method is better suited for distributed implementation; it is in effect equivalent to the synchronous distributed algorithm described earlier in connection with the update (4.5). The Gauss–Seidel method is not as well suited for parallel or distributed implementation. It is inherently sequential, although it can be parallelized to a substantial degree when the dependency graph is sparse; see Subsection 1.2.4. On the other hand the Gauss–Seidel method is frequently much faster than Jacobi; see Section 2.6. Generally speaking, convergence is typically accelerated if the updated values of the variables are incorporated into subsequent updates of other variables as quickly as possible. With some thought, it can be seen that in an asynchronous algorithm, updated values of variables can be incorporated into the computation faster than in a synchronous algorithm, as illustrated by Fig. 1.4.10. It is therefore plausible that an asynchronous algorithm can realize some of the speed advantage of Gauss–Seidel over Jacobi, without sacrificing any of the parallelism potential of Jacobi. This conjecture is supported only by limited computational experience at present.

EXERCISES

4.1. **[PaT87a]** Consider a synchronous algorithm operating in phases, and let $G(k)$ and $L(k)$ be the times required for all processors to complete k phases using the global and the local synchronization methods, respectively (cf. Subsection 1.4.1). Suppose that $P(i, t) = P_i$ for all i and t, and that the times $T_{ij}(t)$ required for processors i to send their messages to processors $j \in P_i$ are random, independent, and exponentially distributed with mean equal to 1. Assume that the number of elements in all the sets P_i is equal to some positive integer d. Show that

$$E\big[G(k)\big] = \Theta\big(k \log(nd)\big),$$

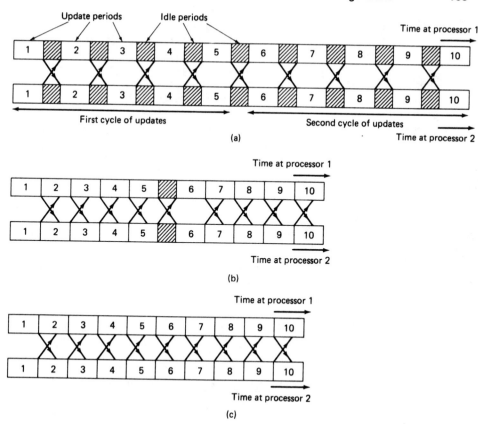

Figure 1.4.10 Illustration of the mechanism by which an asynchronous algorithm can realize the speed advantage of the Gauss–Seidel method over the Jacobi method. There are two processors solving a 10–variable problem and updating 5 variables each. The timing diagram in (a) is for a synchronous method that tries to incorporate new information as early as possible. This method has a large synchronization penalty. In the synchronous method of (b), the synchronization penalty is reduced through pipelining of computation and communication, but the updates of each processor are taken into account every five updates, thereby resulting in a Jacobi–like method. In the asynchronous method of (c), there is no synchronization penalty, while the result of each update is taken into account at the other processor after a delay of only one update. In this example, all updates take equal time. The synchronization penalty is exclusively due to communication delays. Unequal variable update times increase the synchronization penalty further.

whereas

$$E\bigl[L(k)\bigr] = \Theta(\log n + k \log d),$$

where $E[\cdot]$ denotes expectation. *Hint:* Use Props. D.1 and D.2 of Appendix D.

4.2. Consider the iteration (4.6) for the case where $|a| + |b| < 1$, $b \neq 0$, and the communication delay D is smaller than the time needed for an update. Show that for D sufficiently small, the synchronous algorithm has a better rate of convergence than the asynchronous algorithm.

4.3. Consider the iteration (4.6) for the case where $|a| + |b| < 1$, $a \neq 0$, let D be a positive integer and consider an asynchronous algorithm with limited communication that works as follows: values of variables are received at times $t = (D + 1), 2(D + 1), \ldots$ (just as in the synchronous version of Example 4.1), and variable updates are initiated at each time $t = 0, 1, \ldots$ and completed one time unit later (just as in the asynchronous version of Example 4.1). Thus, the update for variable x_1 and for $t = 0, (D + 1), 2(D + 1), \ldots$ has the form

$$x_1(t + 1) = ax_1(t) + bx_2(t - D),$$
$$x_1(t + 2) = ax_1(t + 1) + bx_2(t - D),$$

$$\cdots \qquad \cdots$$

$$x_1(t + D + 1) = ax_1(t + D) + bx_2(t - D).$$

Show that for all $i = 1, 2$ and t of the form $t = (D + 1), 2(D + 1), \ldots$, we have

$$|x_i(t - k)| \leq \max\{|x_1(0)|, |x_2(0)|\}\rho_S^{t-D}, \qquad \forall\, k = 0, 1, \ldots, D,$$

where $\rho_S = (|a| + |b|)^{1/(D+1)}$ is the synchronous convergence rate parameter of Example 4.1. Show also that the asynchronous algorithm is better than the synchronous algorithm both in terms of execution time and in terms of number of message transmissions.

NOTES AND SOURCES

There are several texts and surveys that describe parallel and distributed computing systems; see, for example, [HoJ81], [KuP81], [HwB84], [Hwa84], [Hoc85], and [Hwa87]. See [Sch80] and [Hil85] for integrated discussions of several aspects of some interesting computing systems. There have been a number of special issues on parallel and distributed computation in several journals, as well as a number of journals dealing exclusively with the subject. There is a number of textbooks dealing with parallel algorithms, see e.g., [HoJ81], [Sch84], [Akl85], [Qui87], and [FJL88]. See [MeC80], [KSS81], [Kun82], and [Kun88] for parallel computation using VLSI systems and systolic algorithms. Finally, different aspects of parallel computation are surveyed in [QuD84], [OLR85], [OrV85], [KiL86], and [Rib87].

1.1. Interconnection networks and switching systems are surveyed in [BrH83], [WuF84], and [IEE87]. The classification of parallel computers into SIMD and MIMD systems is from [Fly66].

1.2.1. The DAG model for parallel computation has been extensively used for arithmetic problems [BoM75], as well for problems involving Boolean variables.

In another class of models of parallel computation (known as PRAM models, Parallel Random Access Machine), each processor is modeled as a random access machine and processors communicate to each other through a shared memory. There are a few variations here depending on whether different processors are allowed to simultaneously read or write the same location in the shared memory. Some early references on this subject are [FoW78] and [Gol78]; see [OLR85] for a survey. For models of VLSI computation, see [Ull84].

1.2.2. Propositions 2.3 and 2.4 are from [Bre74]. The problem of finding a schedule that minimizes T_p has been thoroughly studied, see [Cof76] and [OLR85], for example. It can be efficiently solved when the number p of processors is 2 or when the DAG is a tree, but it is NP–complete in general.

The scheduling problem for the case where communication costs are taken into account has been considered in [PaY88]. In this context, it is sometimes preferable to let more than one processor perform the operation corresponding to some node, in order to avoid communication delays.

The construction of optimal or near–optimal parallel algorithms (that is, DAGs with close to minimal depth) for a given computational problem, has been well studied, particularly for the case of arithmetic problems (see e.g., [Bre74] and [MuP76]). See also [MiR85] for a method whereby a tree–like DAG is restructured on–line to obtain logarithmic depth.

Complexity measures for synchronous parallel computation have provided an interesting extension of the theory of computational complexity that had originated in the context of serial computation; see [OLR85]. Of particular interest here is the class NC, which is the class of problems that can be solved in time $O(\log^k n)$ using $O(n^k)$ processors, where k is some integer, and n is the size of the problem [Coo81]. This is sometimes described as the class of problems most amenable to massive parallelization.

1.2.3. Parallel algorithms have been developed for a variety of algebraic problems, such as polynomial evaluation ([MuP73] and [Mar73]), linear recurrences ([Kun76a] and [HyK77]), etc.

1.2.4. Proposition 2.6 is well known but Prop. 2.5 seems to be new. For further references on the application of coloring in the parallelization of Gauss–Seidel algorithms in the context of the numerical solution of partial differential equations see [OrV85]. The parallelization of iterations with a particular type of a regular structure is considered in [KMW67] and [RaK88].

1.3.1. Extensive discussions of communication network issues appear in a number of textbooks, such as [BeG87], [Hay84], [Sch87], [Sta85], and [Tan81].

1.3.2. For a view of the go–back–n DLC as a distributed algorithm and a corresponding analysis, see [BeG87].

1.3.3. Routing algorithms for data networks are discussed extensively in [BeG87]. For analysis of randomized routing algorithms in regular interconnection networks, see [VaB81], [Val82], [HaC87], and [MiC87].

1.3.4. The mapping problem for general architectures has been considered in [Bok81]. The problem of mapping various topologies on hypercubes is discussed in a number of sources including [BhI85], [SaS88], and [McV87]. Communication complexity analyses of various basic algorithms for hypercubes and other topologies can be found in [SaS85], [SaS86], and [McV87]. Our discussion is motivated by these references, and improves upon them in that it provides several new algorithms and problem complexity estimates. In particular, the multinode broadcast algorithm for a hypercube is new, and is the first that takes the minimal $\left(\lceil (2^d - 1)/d \rceil\right)$ number of steps (a related algorithm was given earlier in [Ozv87]; an $O(2^d/d)$ time algorithm was first derived in [SaS85]). The total exchange algorithms of Fig. 1.3.19 and Exercise 3.6 are new. Private communications by P. Tseng relating to this section have been very helpful.

1.3.5.   For a discussion of the concurrency and communication tradeoff in the context of matrix computations, see [GHN87].

1.3.6.   Matrix calculations on hypercubes are discussed extensively in [Joh87a], and [McV87]. Several matrix multiplication algorithms on a mesh and a hypercube are given in [DNS81].

1.4.1.   The complexity of a number of synchronization algorithms is analyzed in [Awe85]. Communication analyses of synchronized iterative methods are given in [DuB82]. The comparison between the local and the global synchronization methods is new.

1.4.2.   An early comparative discussion of synchronous and asynchronous algorithms is [Kun76b]. The convergence rate comparison between synchronous and asynchronous relaxation methods given in Example 4.1 is new; it will be generalized in Subsection 6.3.5.

PART 1
Synchronous Algorithms

2

Algorithms for Systems of Linear Equations and Matrix Inversion

Let A be an $n \times n$ real matrix, let b be a vector in $\Re^n$, and consider the system of linear equations

$$Ax = b,$$

where x is an unknown vector to be determined. There is a variety of methods for solving this system, usually classified as *direct* and *iterative*. Direct methods find the exact solution with a finite number of operations, typically of the order of n^3. Iterative methods do not obtain an exact solution of $Ax = b$ in finite time, but they converge to a solution asymptotically. Nevertheless, iterative methods often yield a solution, within acceptable precision, after a relatively small number of iterations, in which case they are preferred to direct methods. This is usually the case when n is very large, for example, when the system $Ax = b$ arises from discretization of a linear partial differential equation, and in many other applications. Iterative methods may also have smaller storage requirements than direct methods, when the matrix A is sparse. A more general problem is the computation of the inverse A^{-1} of A, which can also be solved by either direct or iterative methods.

In this chapter, we study parallel algorithms for solving the system $Ax = b$ and for matrix inversion. Some of these algorithms are just parallel implementations of traditional serial algorithms, whereas others are more recent, developed with the purpose of better exploiting parallelism. Furthermore, some of these algorithms are of purely theoretical interest, whereas others are widely used in practice. We discuss concepts of complexity and efficiency in the context of direct methods. These concepts are not quite applicable to iterative methods, which do not terminate in finite time. A more appropriate measure for such algorithms is their speed of convergence to the solution. Typical iterative methods converge *geometrically*, or *at the rate of a geometric progression*. This means that the sequence of vectors $\{x(t)\}$ generated by an iterative algorithm has the property $\|x(t) - x^*\| \leq c\rho^t$, where x^* is the solution of the system $Ax = b$, c is a positive constant, ρ is a positive constant smaller than 1, and $\|\cdot\|$ is a vector norm. The smaller the value of ρ, the faster is the convergence of the algorithm.

Throughout this chapter, a synchronous model of computation is assumed. Furthermore, we often assume an idealized model in which any two processors may communicate instantaneously via an interconnection network or a shared memory. In effect, communication costs are excluded from such an analysis. However, at several points, we pause to indicate how some of the more practical algorithms may be implemented on specific architectures with small or negligible communication penalty.

In Section 2.1, we present parallel direct algorithms for the case where the matrix A has a special structure; in particular, A is assumed to be triangular or tridiagonal. In Section 2.2, we present some classical direct methods for solving the system $Ax = b$ for the case of a general matrix A, and describe their parallel implementation. In Section 2.3, we present a very fast direct parallel algorithm for inverting a square matrix. This algorithm is of theoretical interest but is impractical due to excessive processor requirements and poor numerical stability. In Section 2.4, we present a few classical iterative methods for solving the system $Ax = b$, and in Section 2.5, we comment on their parallel implementation, including an example arising in the numerical solution of partial differential equations and a brief discussion of multigrid algorithms. In Section 2.6, we develop the machinery for the convergence analysis of iterative methods. While these results are classical and fairly old, some of the tools introduced here will be used in the much harder convergence proofs of asynchronous iterative algorithms (Chapters 6 and 7). In Section 2.7, we present the conjugate gradient method and comment on its parallelization. In Section 2.8, we study iterative algorithms for the computation of the invariant distribution of a finite state Markov chain. Finally, in Section 2.9, we present a very fast, Newton–like iterative algorithm for matrix inversion.

2.1 PARALLEL ALGORITHMS FOR LINEAR SYSTEMS WITH SPECIAL STRUCTURE

2.1.1 Triangular Matrices and Back Substitution

Let A be a lower triangular square matrix of dimensions $n \times n$, that is, $a_{ij} = 0$ for $i < j$. Our objective is to compute A^{-1}, assuming that A is invertible; equivalently, we assume that $a_{ii} \neq 0$ for all i. We first consider the case where $a_{ii} = 1$ for all i, and we subsequently generalize. We write $A = I - L$, where L is strictly lower triangular, that is, its elements ℓ_{ij} satisfy $\ell_{ij} = 0$ for $i \leq j$. It is straightforward to verify that the ijth element of L^k is zero if $i - j < k$, so $L^n = 0$.

Lemma 1.1.   If $A = I - L$, where L is strictly lower triangular, then

$$A^{-1} = (I + L + L^2 + \cdots + L^{n-1}). \tag{1.1}$$

Proof. Let B be the right–hand side of Eq. (1.1). An easy calculation yields $B(I - L) = I - L^n = I$, because $L^n = 0$. This implies that $B = A^{-1}$.   **Q.E.D.**

Equation (1.1) leads to a straighforward algorithm for computing A^{-1}: compute, in parallel, $L^2, \ldots, L^{n-1}$, and then add the results. According to the discussion in Subsection 1.2.3, all of these operations can be performed in time $O(\log^2 n)$ using n^4 processors, excluding communication costs. This algorithm, although very simple, uses an excessive number of processors. A more efficient algorithm is obtained using the following lemma.

Lemma 1.2.   If $A = I - L$, where L is strictly lower triangular, then

$$A^{-1} = (I + L^{2^{\lceil \log n \rceil - 1}})(I + L^{2^{\lceil \log n \rceil - 2}}) \cdots (I + L^4)(I + L^2)(I + L). \tag{1.2}$$

Proof. Expand the product in the right–hand side of Eq. (1.2). Since $L^n = 0$, we are left with $I + L + L^2 + \cdots + L^{n-1}$, which is equal to A^{-1}, by Lemma 1.1.   **Q.E.D.**

Lemma 1.2 leads to the following algorithm. We compute, by successive squaring, $L^2, L^4, \ldots, L^{2^{\lceil \log n \rceil - 1}}$, we add the identity to each one of these matrices, and, finally, we carry out the multiplications in the right–hand side of Eq. (1.2). The addition of the identity can be carried out in one time unit. The other steps consist of $O(\log n)$ successive matrix multiplications and can be carried out, with n^3 processors, in time $O(\log^2 n)$, excluding communication costs (Subsection 1.2.3).

Suppose now that the assumption $a_{ii} = 1$ fails. We define a diagonal matrix D, such that $d_{ii} = a_{ii}$ for each i, and notice that $D^{-1}A$ is triangular and has unit diagonal elements. Thus, we may first transform A to $D^{-1}A$ (this takes a single time unit using n^2 processors), invert $D^{-1}A$ to obtain $A^{-1}D$ (using the preceding algorithm), and finally right–multiply the result by D^{-1} (this takes a single time unit using n^2 processors) to recover A^{-1}. Therefore, the time required by the algorithm remains $O(\log^2 n)$ using n^3 processors.

We now present a different method, of the "divide–and–conquer" type, whose performance is comparable to that of the preceding algorithm (the assumption $a_{ii} = 1$ is no longer needed). We partition the A matrix into blocks:

$$A = \begin{bmatrix} A_1 & 0 \\ A_2 & A_3 \end{bmatrix},$$

where A_1 is of size $\lceil n/2 \rceil \times \lceil n/2 \rceil$. Notice that A_1 and A_3 are lower triangular. Moreover, it is easily shown that

$$A^{-1} = \begin{bmatrix} A_1^{-1} & 0 \\ -A_3^{-1}A_2A_1^{-1} & A_3^{-1} \end{bmatrix},$$

(multiply the above expressions for A and A^{-1} and verify that the product is the identity). Based on the above decomposition, we obtain the following algorithm. Given an $n \times n$ triangular matrix A:

1. If $n = 1$, then obtain A^{-1} in the obvious way.
2. If $n > 1$, then partition A as indicated above and do the following:
   (a) Invert (concurrently) A_1 and A_3. (Since A_1 and A_3 are lower triangular, they can be inverted by using the same algorithm.)
   (b) Multiply A_3^{-1} with A_2 to obtain $A_3^{-1}A_2$.
   (c) Right–multiply the result of (b) by A_1^{-1}.

Notice that steps (b) and (c) take $O(\log n)$ time using n^3 processors. Thus, if $T(n)$ denotes the time required by the algorithm for inverting a matrix of dimensions $n \times n$, we have $T(n) = T(\lceil n/2 \rceil) + O(\log n)$, which yields $T(n) = O(\log^2 n)$ using n^3 processors, excluding communication costs.

The methods presented so far do not simplify when one is faced with the presumably easier task of solving a system $Ax = b$. Furthermore, if communication overhead is properly taken into account, the time requirements can be much larger than $O(\log^2 n)$ for certain processor architectures. For this reason, and in view of their large processor requirements, these algorithms are theoretically interesting but impractical. We now describe a practical method for solving $Ax = b$, called *back substitution*, which is obtained by parallelizing the natural sequential algorithm for this problem.

Under the assumption that A is lower triangular, the ith equation of the system $Ax = b$ is

$$a_{i1}x_1 + a_{i2}x_2 + \cdots + a_{ii}x_i = b_i. \tag{1.3}$$

The following parallel version of the back substitution algorithm employs n processors. Suppose that at the beginning of the ith stage, the values of the variables $x_1, \ldots, x_{i-1}$ and of the expressions $a_{j1}x_1 + \cdots + a_{j,i-1}x_{i-1}$ for each $j \geq i$, are available. Then the ith processor evaluates x_i by solving Eq. (1.3):

$$x_i = \frac{1}{a_{ii}}\left(b_i - a_{i1}x_1 - \cdots - a_{i,i-1}x_{i-1}\right).$$

Finally, each processor j, with $j \geq i + 1$, evaluates the expression $a_{j1}x_1 + \cdots + a_{ji}x_i$ by adding $a_{ji}x_i$ to the previously available expression $a_{j1}x_1 + \cdots + a_{j,i-1}x_{i-1}$. The algorithm terminates at the end of the nth stage, when all variables $x_1, \ldots, x_n$ have been computed. Clearly, the parallel time required for each stage is constant. Therefore, the total time required by this version of back substitution is $O(n)$ using n processors and excluding communication costs.

We now compare the efficiencies of the algorithms presented so far. We recall that the efficiency of a parallel algorithm is defined (Subsection 1.2.2) to be equal to $T^*(n)/(pT_p(n))$, where n is a measure of problem size, p is the number of processors, $T_p(n)$ is the time spent by a parallel algorithm that uses p processors, and $T^*(n)$ is the time required by the fastest sequential algorithm (or by a benchmark sequential algorithm). Notice that any sequential algorithm needs $\Omega(n^2)$ time units to solve the problem $Ax = b$: the reason is that the solution depends on $\Omega(n^2)$ numbers, the entries of A. Furthermore, the back substitution algorithm, if serially implemented, takes $O(n^2)$ time. We therefore have $T^*(n) = \Theta(n^2)$. We then see that the efficiency of the first methods of this subsection is $O(1/(n \log^2 n))$, as opposed to the efficiency of back substitution, which is $\Theta(1)$. Back substitution is slower, but the other methods need an excessive number of processors, which is disproportionately large when compared with the additional speedup that these excess processors are providing. In practice, parallel back substitution is universally used, not only for its higher efficiency, but also because of its modest communication requirements, which will be analyzed shortly.

Back substitution can also be used for computing the inverse of a triangular matrix A as follows. Since $AA^{-1} = I$, we see that the ith column x^i of A^{-1} satisfies $Ax^i = e^i$, where e^i is the ith unit vector. Thus, A^{-1} is obtained by solving n systems of equations, and parallel back substitution can be used for each one. These systems can be solved simultaneously [$O(n)$ time using n^2 processors], or one at a time [$O(n^2)$ time using n processors].

We now turn to the implementation of back substitution on special architectures. It is natural to consider a linear array of n processors, whereby the ith processor is given the entries in the ith row of A and the ith component of the vector b. As shown in Fig. 2.1.1, it is possible, by pipelining the communication and interleaving it with the computation, to obtain $O(n)$ execution time. Thus, the communication penalty can only increase the execution time by a constant factor. If this constant factor is large, the impact of the communication penalty can be reduced by using fewer processors and assigning to each one several rows of the matrix A. (See Subsection 1.3.5 for the general effects of reduced numbers of processors on the communication penalty.) Finally, if a hypercube architecture is to be used instead, the communication penalty can only be smaller, since a linear array can be imbedded in a hypercube (Subsection 1.3.4).

There is also an alternative implementation of back substitution in which the ith processor is given the entries in the ith column of A. The issues are somewhat similar as in the previous implementation and the time requirements are again $O(n)$ using n processors (see Fig. 2.1.2).

2.1.2 Tridiagonal Systems and Odd–Even Reduction

We consider a system of equations $Ax = b$, where A is tridiagonal, that is, $a_{ij} = 0$ if $|i - j| > 1$. Such a system is of the form:

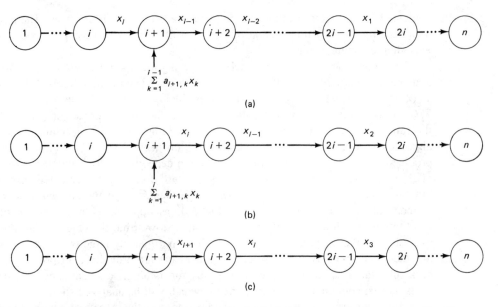

Figure 2.1.1 Implementation of back substitution in a linear array of n processors. The ith processor knows b_i and the entries of the ith row of A. The value of each x_i is transmitted to the right as soon as it is available and communication of such values is pipelined. (a) Snapshot of the algorithm as soon as x_i is computed. At this point, processor $i + 1$ has already received $x_1, \ldots, x_{i-1}$ and has evaluated the sum $\sum_{k=1}^{i-1} a_{i+1,k} x_k$. (b) Once x_i is received by processor $i + 1$, it is forwarded to the right and the sum $\sum_{k=1}^{i} a_{i+1,k} x_k$ is evaluated. Then, x_{i+1} is computed using Eq. (1.3). (c) The value of x_{i+1} is transmitted to processor $i + 2$. The time between the evaluation of two successive components x_i and x_{i+1} is $O(1)$, and the total time of the algorithm is proportional to n.

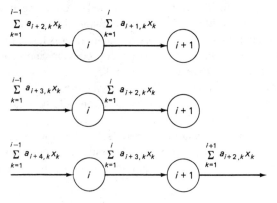

Figure 2.1.2 Alternative implementation of back substitution in a linear array of n processors. The ith processor knows b_i and the entries of the ith column of A. In (a), the value of x_i has just been computed by processor i. As soon as processor $i + 1$ receives $\sum_{k=1}^{i} a_{i+1,k} x_k$, it computes x_{i+1}. Then, processor $i + 1$ receives the value of $\sum_{k=1}^{i} a_{i+2,k} x_k$, as in (b), adds to it the value of $a_{i+2,i+1} x_{i+1}$, and transmits the sum $\sum_{k=1}^{i+1} a_{i+2,k} x_k$ to processor $i + 2$, as in (c). A detailed timing analysis shows that the total execution time is proportional to n.

$$g_1 x_1 + h_1 x_2 = b_1, \tag{1.4}$$

$$f_i x_{i-1} + g_i x_i + h_i x_{i+1} = b_i, \quad i = 2, 3, \ldots, n-1, \tag{1.5}$$

$$f_n x_{n-1} + g_n x_n = b_n. \tag{1.6}$$

Here, g_i are the diagonal elements of A and f_i (respectively, h_i) are the entries of A below (respectively, above) the diagonal. There are several methods for solving such a system and most of them are easily parallelizable. We describe here a representative one that is called *odd–even reduction*.

The basic idea is that if $g_i \neq 0$, we can solve Eq. (1.5) for x_i in terms of x_{i-1} and x_{i+1}. If we do this for every odd integer i and then substitute the expression for x_i into the remaining equations, we are left with a system of equations involving only the variables x_i, with i even. The resulting system of equations is again tridiagonal and has about half as many variables. The same procedure is then applied recursively.

We now describe the algorithm in more detail. To simplify the equations, we use the convention $x_0 = x_{n+1} = 0$, which makes Eq. (1.5) valid for $i = 1$ and $i = n$. We solve Eq. (1.5) for x_i and obtain

$$x_i = \frac{1}{g_i} \left(b_i - f_i x_{i-1} - h_i x_{i+1} \right). \tag{1.7}$$

We use Eq. (1.7), with i replaced by $i - 1$ and $i + 1$, to eliminate x_{i-1} and x_{i+1} from Eq. (1.5). This yields

$$\frac{f_i}{g_{i-1}} \left(b_{i-1} - f_{i-1} x_{i-2} - h_{i-1} x_i \right) + g_i x_i + \frac{h_i}{g_{i+1}} \left(b_{i+1} - f_{i+1} x_i - h_{i+1} x_{i+2} \right) = b_i,$$

which simplifies to

$$-\left(\frac{f_i f_{i-1}}{g_{i-1}} \right) x_{i-2} + \left(g_i - \frac{h_{i-1} f_i}{g_{i-1}} - \frac{h_i f_{i+1}}{g_{i+1}} \right) x_i - \left(\frac{h_i h_{i+1}}{g_{i+1}} \right) x_{i+2}$$
$$= b_i - \frac{f_i}{g_{i-1}} b_{i-1} - \frac{h_i}{g_{i+1}} b_{i+1}. \tag{1.8}$$

Consider Eq. (1.8) for each even index i, $1 \leq i \leq n$. It is a system in the variables $x_2, \ldots, x_{2\lfloor n/2 \rfloor}$, and it is clearly a tridiagonal system. We then use the same procedure, recursively, to obtain a smaller system, until we are left with a single equation in a single variable, which we solve directly. We then proceed backwards to obtain the values of the eliminated variables (see Fig. 2.1.3). Exercise 1.2 suggests a modification with which the backward evaluation of eliminated variables is not needed and the time of the algorithm is cut by a factor of two, approximately.

The algorithm breaks down if at some stage a division by zero is attempted [see Eq. (1.8)]. This may occur even if the original matrix A is nonsingular and has nonzero diagonal entries. In practice, this happens somewhat rarely and odd–even reduction is often used, although there are no theoretical guarantees.

For a timing analysis of the algorithm, notice that at each stage, the number of variables is reduced approximately by half. Thus, after $\Theta(\log n)$ stages, all but one of the variables are eliminated. At each stage, we need to compute the coefficients of the

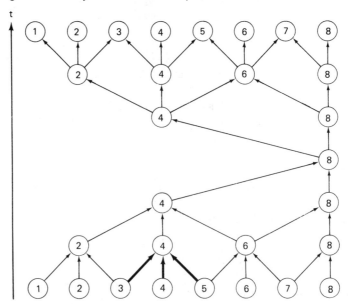

Figure 2.1.3 Illustration of odd–even reduction for $n = 8$. At the first stage, the variables x_1, x_3, x_5, and x_7 are eliminated using Eq. (1.7) to obtain a system of equations of the form of Eq. (1.8) involving x_2, x_4, x_6, and x_8. At the second stage, x_2 and x_6 are eliminated. Then x_4 is eliminated, which yields a single equation involving x_8. Once x_8 is evaluated, the remaining variables can be evaluated by following the reverse steps. For example, once x_2, x_4, x_6, and x_8 are evaluated, the values of x_1, x_3, x_5, and x_7 are readily obtained from Eq. (1.7). The arcs in this diagram indicate data dependencies. For example, the coefficients f_4', g_4', h_4', and b_4' of the equation $f_4' x_2 + g_4' x_4 + h_4' x_6 = b_4'$ obtained after the first reduction depend on f_i, g_i, h_i, and b_i for $i = 3, 4, 5$ [cf. Eq. (1.8)]. This fact is indicated by the thicker lines in the figure.

reduced system. It is immediate from Eq. (1.8) that this may be accomplished in four time units using $O(n)$ processors. A similar comment applies to the back substitution phase, during which the previously eliminated variables are evaluated. It follows that the overall algorithm can be implemented in $O(\log n)$ time using $O(n)$ processors. It is not hard to see that the total number of operations in this algorithm is only $O(n)$, because the computational requirements of each stage are about half of the requirements of the preceding stage. This implies that there exists a sequential algorithm that runs in $O(n)$ time. Furthermore, this is optimal because any sequential algorithm needs $\Omega(n)$ time just to read the input. We thus have $T^*(n) = \Theta(n)$ and we can conclude that the efficiency of the above described parallel implementation of the odd–even reduction algorithm is $\Theta(1/\log n)$. A more efficient implementation is suggested in Exercise 1.3.

We now study the implementation of odd–even reduction on parallel architectures with special interconnection topologies. Consider first a linear array of n processors and assume that each processor knows the entries of the ith row of the matrix A and the ith entry of b, and is responsible for eventually computing the value of x_i. The first stage of the computation [evaluation of the coefficients in Eq. (1.8)] is easily accomplished with $O(1)$ communication, because the ith processor (for i even) only needs to know the values of the coefficients possessed by neighboring processors. However, after k reductions, we are left with a system in the variables x_i, where i is an integer multiple of 2^k, and this implies that processor $i2^k$ has to communicate with processor $(i+1)2^k$. (This is evident from Fig. 2.1.3.) In particular, at the last reduction step, the communication overhead is $\Omega(n)$. It follows that the parallel execution time is $\Omega(n)$, which is at least as bad as for the serial algorithm. In fact, this conclusion could be reached more easily from the observation that the value of x_1 depends on data possessed by processors at $\Theta(n)$ distance away, and therefore the parallel execution time has to be $\Omega(n)$.

Consider next a linear array of p processors ($p < n$), each one in charge of n/p successive variables (assuming that n/p is an integer). During the first $N = \lfloor \log(n/p) \rfloor$ stages of the algorithm, most computations are local to each processor, the total number of arithmetic operations executed by each processor during these N stages is $O(n/p)$, and only a small amount of communication between neighboring processors is needed. After the Nth stage, we are left with a tridiagonal system in $O(p)$ variables. This system can be solved by transmitting its coefficients to a single processor, which solves it and broadcasts the results back to the p processors. This can be done with $O(p)$ time spent for communication and $O(p)$ time spent for computation. We conclude that the total time is $O(n/p) + O(p)$. By optimizing with respect to p, we obtain $p = \Theta(n^{1/2})$ and an $O(n^{1/2})$ total execution time, which is better than the $O(n)$ serial time but worse than the $O(\log n)$ time obtained assuming all communication is instantaneous.

We finally consider a hypercube architecture with n processors. Let a linear array of processors be imbedded in the hypercube, according to a reflected Gray code (Subsection 1.3.4). We use the terminology of Subsection 1.3.4: the *logical distance* of two processors is their distance as elements of the linear array, and their *physical distance* is their distance when all of the hypercube arcs are available. We found that a linear array is inappropriate because processors $i2^k$ and $(i + 1)2^k$ need to communicate at the kth stage. Let us now recall from Subsection 1.3.4 that, with a reflected Gray code imbedding, processors at logical distance 2^k, $k > 0$, have a physical distance equal to 2 and, furthermore, all pairs of processors of the form $\left(i2^k, (i + 1)2^k\right)$, $i = 1, 2, \ldots$, can communicate to each other, simultaneously, in two time units. It follows that each stage of the odd–even reduction algorithm can be accomplished with only $O(1)$ time spent for communication, thereby maintaining the total execution time at $O(\log n)$ using n processors. In practice, the communication requirements per stage may be dominant when compared to the computation requirements per stage, even though both are $O(1)$. It may then be appropriate to use a number of processors smaller than n, which reduces the associated communication penalty, as discussed in Subsection 1.3.5.

We close by pointing out that the odd–even reduction algorithm can also be applied to the solution of *block–tridiagonal* systems of equations. Such systems have the structure of Eqs. (1.4) to (1.6), except that each x_i is now a vector of dimension k and each f_i, g_i, and h_i is a matrix of dimensions $k \times k$. A key difference is that a term such as $1/g_{i-1}$ [see Eq. (1.8)] has to be interpreted as a matrix inverse. For this reason, each processor in a parallel implementation has to invert a $k \times k$ matrix at each stage. The computational requirements for each processor are now substantially larger [$O(k^3)$ per stage if the matrices g_i do not have any special structure], but the increase of the communication requirements is smaller [only $O(k^2)$ numbers need to be transmitted by each processor at each stage]. We conclude that the communication penalty is reduced as k increases.

EXERCISES

1.1. Consider the execution of parallel back substitution in a linear array of p processors, where $p < n$, and n/p is an integer. Suppose that each processor is given n/p consecutive rows of the matrix A, as well as the corresponding entries of the vector b. Assume that each message consists of a single real number and that all messages incur the same delay. Let $T(n, p)$ be the time spent by the algorithm, under the assumption that computation is instantaneous. Design the details of the algorithm so that $T(n, p)$ is made as small as possible and find an expression for $T(n, p)$.

1.2. **[HoJ81]** Modify the odd–even reduction algorithm so that at the end of the last stage of variable eliminations, the value of x_i is obtained for all i, thus avoiding the need for a backward substitution phase. Furthermore, this should be done with only n processors. *Hint:* With the algorithm of Fig. 2.1.3, the value of x_8 is obtained after the last elimination stage. Construct, for each i, a similar algorithm that produces the value of x_i, and run all those algorithms simultaneously.

1.3. Provide a parallel implementation of odd–even reduction that uses $O(n/\log n)$ processors and takes $O(\log n)$ time, neglecting communications costs.

2.2 PARALLEL DIRECT METHODS FOR GENERAL LINEAR EQUATIONS

Let A be a square matrix of size $n \times n$. Most direct methods for solving a system of linear equations of the form $Ax = b$ proceed by applying a set of simple transformations on both sides of the equation until the matrix A becomes triangular, and then solve the resulting system of equations by back substitution. These transformations consist of successively left–multiplying the matrix A by a sequence of matrices $M^{(1)}, \ldots, M^{(K)}$. The matrices $M^{(i)}$ are chosen with two objectives in mind: (a) multiplication of an arbitrary matrix by $M^{(i)}$ should have low computational requirements, and (b) the product $M^{(K)} M^{(K-1)} \cdots M^{(1)} A$ should be triangular. There are several ways of accomplishing this; two such methods, together with their parallel implementations, are discussed in this section.

Notice that the actual solution of the system $Ax = b$ is only a small step further from what was described above: in particular, while computing $M^{(K)} \cdots M^{(1)} A$, we may also compute the product $M^{(K)} \cdots M^{(1)} b$. Then, as long as each $M^{(i)}$ is invertible, the original system $Ax = b$ is equivalent to

$$(M^{(K)} \cdots M^{(1)} A)x = (M^{(K)} \cdots M^{(1)} b). \tag{2.1}$$

By construction, $M^{(K)} \cdots M^{(1)} A$ is triangular and the system (2.1) can be solved using back substitution in $O(n)$ time with n processors (Section 2.1).

If the inverse of A is desired, a similar procedure will do. While computing $M^{(K)} \cdots M^{(1)} A$, we also compute the product $M^{(K)} \cdots M^{(1)}$. Then, as long as each $M^{(i)}$ is invertible, A^{-1} can be computed using the equation

$$A^{-1} = \left(M^{(K)} \cdots M^{(1)} A\right)^{-1} \left(M^{(K)} \cdots M^{(1)}\right).$$

Since $M^{(K)} \cdots M^{(1)} A$ is triangular, it can be inverted using back substitution in $O(n)$ time using n^2 processors, or in $O(n^2)$ time using n processors. For these reasons, we will limit our further discussion to the task of triangularizing the matrix A.

2.2.1 Gaussian Elimination

Gaussian elimination is the classical procedure for solving linear equations whereby each variable, say the ith variable x_i, is expressed as a function of the variables $x_{i+1}, \ldots, x_n$ and is eliminated from the system. After $n - 1$ such steps, we are left with an equation in the single variable x_n, which is easily solved.

We now give a recursive definition of the algorithm. Let $C^{(0)} = A$ and $C^{(i)} = M^{(i)} \cdots M^{(1)} A$. Suppose that $C^{(i-1)}$ has been already computed for some i, $1 \leq i \leq n - 1$, and has the property that all subdiagonal entries of the jth column are zero for every j smaller than i. Equation (2.2) shows the structure of $C^{(i-1)}$, where an asterisk represents a generically nonzero entry:

$$C^{(i-1)} = \begin{bmatrix} * & \cdots & \cdots & \cdots & \cdots & * \\ 0 & \ddots & & & & \vdots \\ \vdots & \ddots & \ddots & & & \\ & & 0 & * & \cdots & * \\ \vdots & & \vdots & \vdots & & \\ 0 & \cdots & 0 & * & \cdots & * \end{bmatrix} \begin{matrix} \\ \\ \\ i \\ \\ \\ \end{matrix} \qquad (2.2)$$

(Notice that $C^{(0)}$ satisfies the above requirement, vacuously.) We now show how to determine a matrix $M^{(i)}$ so that $C^{(i)} = M^{(i)} C^{(i-1)}$ also has the desired property.

Let us assume for now that $C_{ii}^{(i-1)} \neq 0$. We let $M^{(i)} = I - N^{(i)}$, where $N^{(i)}$ is a matrix with the following structure:

$$
N^{(i)} = \begin{bmatrix}
0 & \cdots & \cdots & \cdots & \cdots & \cdots & 0 \\
0 & \ddots & & & & & \vdots \\
\vdots & \ddots & \ddots & & & & \\
& & 0 & 0 & \cdots & \cdots & 0 \\
& & \vdots & * & 0 & \cdots & 0 \\
\vdots & & \vdots & \vdots & \vdots & & \vdots \\
0 & \cdots & 0 & * & 0 & \cdots & 0
\end{bmatrix} \begin{matrix} \\ \\ \\ i \\ \\ \\ \\ \end{matrix}
$$

In particular, the nonzero entries of $N^{(i)}$ are given by $N_{ji}^{(i)} = C_{ji}^{(i-1)}/C_{ii}^{(i-1)}$, $j > i$. We verify that $C^{(i)} = \left(I - N^{(i)}\right)C^{(i-1)}$ has the desired property. Since the first $i - 1$ columns of $N^{(i)}$ are zero, it is seen that the first $i - 1$ columns of $C^{(i)}$ are the same as the corresponding columns of $C^{(i-1)}$. Consider now a subdiagonal entry of $C^{(i)}$ in the ith column, that is, an entry of the form $C_{ji}^{(i)}$, with $j > i$. Then,

$$
C_{ji}^{(i)} = C_{ji}^{(i-1)} - \frac{C_{ji}^{(i-1)}}{C_{ii}^{(i-1)}} C_{ii}^{(i-1)} = 0.
$$

We have thus completed an inductive proof that, with $M^{(i)}$ chosen as above, the matrices $C^{(i)}$ will be of the form of Eq. (2.2). In particular, $C^{(n-1)}$ is upper triangular, which was our stated goal.

Let us also note for future reference that the first i rows of $C^{(i)}$ and $C^{(i-1)}$ are equal and that for $j > i$, $k > i$, we have

$$
C_{jk}^{(i)} = C_{jk}^{(i-1)} - \sum_{\ell=1}^{n} N_{j\ell}^{(i)} C_{\ell k}^{(i-1)} = C_{jk}^{(i-1)} - N_{ji}^{(i)} C_{ik}^{(i-1)} = C_{jk}^{(i-1)} - \frac{C_{ji}^{(i-1)}}{C_{ii}^{(i-1)}} C_{ik}^{(i-1)}. \quad (2.3)
$$

The above method, called *Gaussian elimination without pivoting*, fails when $C_{ii}^{(i-1)}$ is zero. Even if $C_{ii}^{(i-1)}$ is nonzero but has a small magnitude, $M^{(i)}$ will have some very large entries and numerical problems are expected to arise. For this reason, Gaussian elimination without pivoting is used primarily when A is a symmetric matrix. In that case, it is known that $C_{ii}^{(i-1)}$ is never zero, nor do numerical problems arise, provided that A is invertible [GoV83].

For nonsymmetric problems, one may have to apply some kind of *pivoting*, that is, interchange two rows or two columns of $C^{(i-1)}$ so that the ith diagonal entry is nonzero and has, preferably, a large magnitude. The most common method, called *row pivoting*, works as follows: having computed $C^{(i-1)}$, find some $j^* \geq i$ such that

$$
|C_{j^* i}^{(i-1)}| = \max_{j \geq i} |C_{ji}^{(i-1)}|. \quad (2.4)
$$

Then, interchange rows i and j^* and proceed to compute $C^{(i)}$ as before.

The interchange of the ith and jth row of a matrix is equivalent to multiplication of that matrix, from the left, by the permutation matrix P^{ij}. (The entries of P^{ij} that are not shown are all zero.)

$$
P^{ij} = \begin{bmatrix}
1 & & & & & & & & \\
 & \ddots & & & & & & & \\
 & & 1 & & & & & & \\
 & & & 0 & \rule{1em}{0.4pt}1\rule{1em}{0.4pt} & & 1 & \rule{2em}{0.4pt} & \\
 & & & & 1 & \ddots & & & \\
 & & & & & 1 & & & \\
 & & & 1 & \rule{2em}{0.4pt} & & 0 & \rule{1em}{0.4pt}1\rule{1em}{0.4pt} & \\
 & & & & & & & \ddots & \\
 & & & & & & & & 1
\end{bmatrix}
\begin{matrix} \\ \\ \\ i \\ \\ \\ j \\ \\ \\ \end{matrix}
$$

In the context of the solution of linear systems, the right–hand side of the equation should be also multiplied by P^{ij}; this corresponds to interchanging the ith and jth entries of the vector in the right–hand side of the equation.

Gaussian elimination with row pivoting may suffer from poor numerical stability, but has been found to work well in practice [GoV83]. In particular, the maximum in Eq. (2.4) is always positive, except if the matrix A is singular, and therefore the method never breaks down unnecessarily (Exercise 2.1).

Let us point out here that the odd–even reduction algorithm for tridiagonal systems, presented in Subsection 2.1.2, can be viewed as a special case of Gaussian elimination, because odd–even reduction successively eliminates certain variables by expressing them as functions of the remaining variables. For general systems of equations, the variables can be eliminated only one at a time. However, the special structure of tridiagonal systems allows us to eliminate about half of the variables in a single step. Notice that in odd–even reduction, the variables are not eliminated in the usual order. For this reason, odd–even reduction is actually equivalent to Gaussian elimination performed on a matrix PAP', where P is an appropriate permutation matrix. In particular, P is such that it takes the odd–numbered rows and puts them on top; accordingly, the odd–numbered variables are the first to be eliminated. Notice also that odd–even reduction eliminates the variables according to a predetermined order. For this reason, it is equivalent to Gaussian elimination without pivoting. The case where odd–even reduction fails, due to an attempt to divide by zero, corresponds to the situation where pivoting is necessary. However, pivoting is undesirable in the solution of tridiagonal systems because it destroys the special structure of the system.

Parallel Implementations

We turn to the parallel implementation of the above methods. We first consider the case of no pivoting and do a preliminary analysis that ignores the communication penalty. By using the special structure of the matrix $M^{(i)}$, it follows that each entry of $C^{(i)}$ can be computed with just one multiplication, one division, and one subtraction [see Eq. (2.3)]. By using n^2 processors, this can be done for all entries of $C^{(i)}$ simultaneously, in three time units. Thus, the total parallel time to compute $C^{(n-1)}$ is approximately $3n$, using n^2 processors. With fewer processors, say n, the required time is $O(n^2)$. To determine the efficiency of parallel Gaussian elimination, we compare it against the $T^*(n) = \Theta(n^3)$ benchmark; although there exist sequential algorithms that need less than $O(n^3)$ time units, every practical algorithm, including the serial implementation of Gaussian elimination, needs $\Theta(n^3)$ time. We then see that the efficiency of parallel Gaussian elimination is $\Theta(1)$, for the cases where n^2 or n processors are used.

We now consider particular interconnection topologies and verify that the associated communication penalty is not excessive. In particular, Gaussian elimination without pivoting can be implemented on a square mesh of n^2 processors, with the total execution time remaining of the order of n. We associate each processor with a particular entry of the matrices being manipulated and the resulting movement of data is illustrated in Fig. 2.2.1. In order to keep the time requirements as small as $O(n)$, it is essential that messages communicated are appropriately pipelined, and that computations and communications are interleaved, meaning that the computations of stage $i + 1$ start before all messages sent during the ith stage are received; the details are left as an exercise (Exercise 2.2). Without such interleaving, the time requirements of the algorithm are $\Omega(n^2)$ [Saa86]. With the above mentioned interleaving, the time spent for communications is of the same order of magnitude as the time spent in arithmetic computations; in particular, if the time required for a single communication is substantially larger than the time required for a single computation, then the communication penalty can be significant and should be alleviated by using a smaller number of processors.

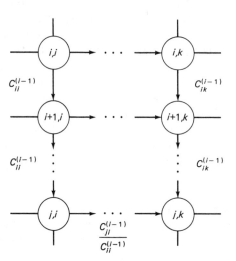

Figure 2.2.1   The movement of data in the execution of Gaussian elimination without pivoting in a mesh–connected architecture with n^2 processors. Suppose that the entries of $C^{(i-1)}$ have been computed. The value of $C_{ii}^{(i-1)}$ is propagated downward. Upon reception of this value, each processor (j, i), $j > i$, computes the ratio $C_{ji}^{(i-1)}/C_{ii}^{(i-1)}$ and transmits it to the processors to its right. In the meantime, the value of $C_{ik}^{(i-1)}$, for $k > i$, is propagated downward. Each processor (j, k), with $j > i$ and $k > i$, eventually receives $C_{ji}^{(i-1)}/C_{ii}^{(i-1)}$ and $C_{ik}^{(i-1)}$ and computes $C_{jk}^{(i)}$ according to Eq. (2.3). It is seen that a typical phase of the algorithm needs $\Theta(n)$ time for communication. Thus, if a new phase starts only after the previous one is completed, the algorithm needs $\Theta(n^2)$ time. On the other hand, by appropriately interleaving different phases, the execution time is reduced to $O(n)$.

On a hypercube architecture with $\Theta(n^2)$ processors, Gaussian elimination can be executed in $O(n)$ time because a mesh can be imbedded in a hypercube. Finally, a linear array of n processors can simulate an $n \times n$ mesh with a $O(n)$ reduction in speed; it follows that parallel Gaussian elimination can be executed in a linear array of n processors in $O(n^2)$ time.

The computational requirements of Gaussian elimination with pivoting are similar, except that at the beginning of a typical stage, we need to perform a comparison of $O(n)$ numbers and pick the largest [see Eq. (2.4)]. Let us neglect any communication costs for the time being. Under reasonable models of parallel computation in which a processor can compare two (but not more than two) numbers in unit time, we need $\Omega(\log n)$ time to compare n numbers no matter how many processors are available. (See e.g., Prop. 2.1 in Subsection 1.2.2.) For this reason, Gaussian elimination with pivoting takes $\Omega(n \log n)$ time when n^2 processors are available; the corresponding efficiency is $O(1/\log n)$, which decreases to zero as n increases. On the other hand, an $O(n \log n)$ parallelization is possible using only $O(n^2/\log n)$ processors, leading to $\Theta(1)$ efficiency. (See Prop. 2.4 in Subsection 1.2.2 and Exercise 2.4.) If n processors are available, then each stage takes $O(n)$ time, leading to a total execution time of $O(n^2)$. The efficiency is again $\Theta(1)$, similarly with Gaussian elimination without pivoting.

Pivoting is particularly undesirable when implementation in particular architectures is considered. For example, with an n^2–processor mesh–connected architecture, there is no implementation with $O(n \log n)$ running time (Exercise 2.3). On the other hand, $O(n \log n)$ time implementations are possible with a hypercube with $O(n^2)$ or even $O(n^2/\log n)$ processors (Exercise 2.4). Finally, if a linear array of n processors is used, with each processor associated with a particular column of the matrices being manipulated, then a row interchange does not lead to any data movement across processors, and the execution time remains $O(n^2)$, much as in Gaussian elimination without pivoting [ISS86].

Recall that the solution of a linear system of equations $Ax = b$ has a last phase during which a triangular system is solved, involving the upper triangular matrix produced at the last stage of the Gaussian elimination algorithm. We assume that back substitution will be used here. In a serial environment, back substitution needs $O(n^2)$ time which is negligible compared to the $O(n^3)$ time needed by Gaussian elimination. However, in a parallel environment, and if n^2 processors are used, the time devoted to back substitution is $O(n)$ (Subsection 2.1.1) and is comparable to the time needed for Gaussian elimination; thus, efficiency of implementation of back substitution becomes important. A related point concerns the case where a linear array of n processors is used and row pivoting is employed. If we employ an implementation of Gaussian elimination where the ith processor is associated to the ith column (as opposed to the ith row), we should also employ an implementation of back substitution where each processor knows a column of the triangular matrix produced by the Gaussian elimination algorithm. This is to avoid excessive movement of data between the Gaussian elimination phase and the back substitution phase.

The discussion in this subsection is summarized in Table 2.1.

TABLE 2.1   Bounds on the timing of Gaussian elimination for several architectures. The upper bounds are the same as those obtained for the same number of processors, if communication is assumed instantaneous.

Number of Processors	Architecture	Without Pivoting	With Pivoting
n^2	Hypercube	$O(n)$	$O(n \log n)$
n^2	Mesh	$O(n)$	$\Omega(n^{4/3})$
$n^2/\log n$	Hypercube	$O(n \log n)$	$O(n \log n)$
n	Hypercube	$O(n^2)$	$O(n^2)$
n	Linear Array	$O(n^2)$	$O(n^2)$

2.2.2 Triangularization Using Givens Rotations

We describe here an alternative method for triangularizing a square matrix. An important difference from Gaussian elimination is that the matrices $M^{(i)}$ are chosen to be orthogonal, that is, they have the property

$$\|M^{(i)}x\|_2 = \|x\|_2, \qquad \forall x \in \Re^n, \tag{2.5}$$

where $\| \cdot \|_2$ is the Euclidean norm. An equivalent definition of orthogonality is to require that $(M^{(i)})'M^{(i)} = I$. Orthogonal transformations are desirable in numerical analysis [GoV83] because they do not amplify the magnitude of past numerical errors.

Let C be a given matrix and suppose that its ith and jth rows have the property that there exists some $k \geq 1$ such that

$$C_{i\ell} = C_{j\ell} = 0, \qquad \forall \ell < k, \tag{2.6}$$

$$C_{jk} \neq 0, \tag{2.7}$$

that is, C has the structure

$$
C = \begin{bmatrix}
 & * & & & * & & \\
0 & \cdots & 0 & * & \cdots & * \\
 & & & & & & \\
0 & \cdots & 0 & * & \cdots & * \\
 & * & & \vdots & & *
\end{bmatrix}
\begin{matrix} \\ i \\ \\ j \\ \\ \end{matrix}
$$

$$k$$

where the entries that are not shown are generically nonzero. Consider now a matrix M of the form

$$M = \begin{bmatrix} 1 & & & & & & & & \\ & \ddots & & & & & & & \\ & & 1 & & & & & & \\ & & & c & \dfrac{1}{} & & s & & \\ & & & & & \ddots & & & \\ & & & & & 1 & & & \\ & & & s & \dfrac{1}{} & & -c & & \\ & & & & & & & \ddots & \\ & & & & & & & & 1 \end{bmatrix} \begin{matrix} \\ \\ \\ i \\ \\ \\ j \\ \\ \\ \end{matrix} \tag{2.8}$$

where all entries not shown are zero, and

$$c = \frac{C_{ik}}{\left(C_{ik}^2 + C_{jk}^2\right)^{1/2}}, \tag{2.9}$$

$$s = \frac{C_{jk}}{\left(C_{ik}^2 + C_{jk}^2\right)^{1/2}}. \tag{2.10}$$

Such a matrix M is called a Givens rotation. It is orthogonal (Exercise 2.5), and has the following properties:

(a) All rows of MC, other than the ith and the jth row, are the same as the corresponding rows of C.
(b) $[MC]_{i\ell} = [MC]_{j\ell} = 0$ for all ℓ such that $\ell < k$.
(c) $[MC]_{jk} = 0$.

Properties (a) and (b) are straightforward consequences of the structure of C and M. For property (c), notice that

$$[MC]_{jk} = \sum_{\ell=1}^{n} M_{j\ell}C_{\ell k} = \sum_{\ell=i,j} M_{j\ell}C_{\ell k} = M_{ji}C_{ik} + M_{jj}C_{jk} = sC_{ik} - cC_{jk} = 0.$$

We can use such Givens rotations to set the subdiagonal entries of a given matrix A to zero, one at a time, as follows. Suppose that, after a number of stages, we have obtained a matrix C. We then find some i, j, and k such that $k < j$ (that is, the jkth entry is below the diagonal) and such that the properties of Eqs. (2.6) and (2.7) are satisfied. We then choose M as described above. It follows that the jkth entry of MC is equal to zero; the rows, other than i and j, are not disturbed and the zeros in the first $k - 1$ entries of rows i and j are not destroyed. Since each such stage annihilates one more entry, this process must eventually stop. This happens if there exist no i, j, and k such that $k < j$ and such that Eqs. (2.6) and (2.7) hold. It is easily seen that this implies that we have obtained an upper triangular matrix.

We now discuss the parallel implementation of such an algorithm. Notice that a Givens rotation M affects only two rows. If two successive Givens rotations were to affect disjoint sets of rows, then these rotations could be applied simultaneously without changing the result. In fact, when n rows are available, up to $\lfloor n/2 \rfloor$ rotations can be applied simultaneously, as long as they operate on disjoint pairs of rows, and the result is the same as if they were applied sequentially. Although it is not possible to apply exactly $\lfloor n/2 \rfloor$ rotations at each time stage, one can come fairly close. We need here a systematic way of deciding which entries to annihilate at each stage. This is accomplished by means of a *schedule* that consists of two functions, $T(j, k)$ and $S(j, k)$, defined for $k < j$. The interpretation of these functions is the following: the jkth entry is annihilated at stage $T(j, k)$ by a Givens rotation operating on rows j and $S(j, k)$.

Any schedule has to satisfy two requirements:

(a) Concurrent rotations operate on different rows; mathematically, if $T(j, k) = T(j', k')$ and $(j, k) \neq (j', k')$, then the sets $\{j, S(j, k)\}$ and $\{j', S(j', k')\}$ are disjoint.

(b) If $T(j, k) = t$ and $S(j, k) = i$, then $T(j, \ell) < t$ and $T(i, \ell) < t$ for all $\ell < k$; this is to guarantee that Eq. (2.6) is satisfied at the time that the jkth entry is annihilated.

One particular schedule, illustrated in Fig. 2.2.2, is given by

$$T(j, k) = n - j + 2k - 1, \tag{2.11}$$

$$S(j, k) = j - 1. \tag{2.12}$$

We verify that this schedule has the desired properties. Suppose that $T(j, k) = T(j', k')$. Equation (2.11) yields $-j + 2k = -j' + 2k'$. If $j = j'$, then $k = k'$. If $j \neq j'$, then $j - j'$ is even and, in particular, $|j - j'| \geq 2$. Therefore, the sets $\{j, j - 1\}$ and $\{j', j' - 1\}$ are disjoint, which implies that the sets $\{j, S(j, k)\}$ and $\{j', S(j', k')\}$ are also disjoint, and property (a) is satisfied. For the second property, Eq. (2.11) shows that $T\big(S(j, k), \ell\big) = T(j - 1, \ell) = T(j, \ell) + 1 = n - j + 2\ell < n - j + 2k - 1 = T(j, k)$ for $\ell < k$.

We now estimate the number of stages required by the schedule of Eqs. (2.11) and (2.12). This is done by maximizing $T(j, k)$ over all j and k corresponding to subdiagonal entries. A little thought shows that the maximum is attained for $j = n$ and $k = n - 1$ and is equal to $2n - 3$. Thus, a total of $2n - 3$ parallel stages are sufficient. Concerning the computational requirements of each stage, ignoring communication costs, each Givens rotation can be performed using n processors in $O(1)$ time. This is because only $O(n)$ entries (two rows) are affected by each rotation, and the new value of each entry can be computed with a constant number of operations. Since we have up to $n/2$ simultaneous rotations at each stage, it follows that the computations at each stage can be performed in $O(1)$ time using n^2 processors. The total count for the entire algorithm is $O(n)$ time using n^2 processors. With n processors, the time requirement becomes $O(n^2)$. For either

$$
\begin{bmatrix}
* & & & & & & & \\
7 & * & & & & & & \\
6 & 8 & * & & & & & \\
5 & 7 & 9 & * & & & & \\
4 & 6 & 8 & 10 & * & & & \\
3 & 5 & 7 & 9 & 11 & * & & \\
2 & 4 & 6 & 8 & 10 & 12 & * & \\
1 & 3 & 5 & 7 & 9 & 11 & 13 & *
\end{bmatrix}
$$

Figure 2.2.2 The schedule of Eq. (2.11) for the case $n = 8$. The numbers indicate the stage at which the corresponding entry is annihilated.

case the efficiency is $\Theta(1)$ when compared with the benchmark $T^*(n) = \Theta(n^3)$ for serial algorithms.

We notice that the time requirements of the Givens rotation method are the same as for Gaussian elimination without pivoting when n^2 processors are used and communication costs are ignored; they are also the same as for Gaussian elimination with row pivoting when n processors are used. A more detailed analysis shows that Gaussian elimination is faster, by a small constant factor, when the same number of processors is used. This may be compensated by the better numerical properties of the Givens rotation method [GoV83].

As far as parallel implementation in special architectures is concerned, the algorithm can be implemented in a mesh of n^2 processors in time $O(n)$ [BBK84] and this implies that it can also be efficiently implemented in a hypercube of $O(n^2)$ processors [in $O(n)$ time] or a linear array of n processors [in $O(n^2)$ time]. The implementation in a mesh involves pipelining, and interleaving of computation and communication, and results in a very regular pattern for the movement of data. However, the details are somewhat tedious and the reader is referred to [BBK84].

EXERCISES

2.1. Show that if Gaussian elimination with row pivoting is used but the maximum in Eq. (2.4) is zero at some intermediate stage of the algorithm, then the matrix A is singular.

2.2. Show that Gaussian elimination without pivoting can be implemented in a mesh–connected architecture of n^2 processors in $O(n)$ time. *Hint:* See Fig. 2.2.1.

2.3. Consider a two–dimensional mesh–connected architecture. Assume that a processor cannot compare more than two numbers in unit time and that communication between neighboring processors takes unit time.

    (a) Show that the problem of computing the maximum of n numbers requires $\Omega(n^{1/3})$ time units regardless of the number of processors and even if each processor knows the values of all numbers to be compared.

    (b) Show that Gaussian elimination with row pivoting needs $\Omega(n^{4/3})$ time.

2.4. [**Cap87**] Show that Gaussian elimination with pivoting can be executed in a hypercube with $O(n^2/\log n)$ processors in time $O(n \log n)$. *Hint:* Arrange the processors as a $n \times (n/\log n)$ mesh. Assign to each processor $\Theta(\log n)$ entries of the same column. Show that the entries in each column can be compared in $O(\log n)$ time. Also, show that a row interchange, as well as any other communication required in a typical stage of the algorithm, takes $O(\log n)$ time.

2.5. Verify that the matrix M defined by Eqs. (2.8) to (2.10) is orthogonal.

2.6. Find a schedule for the algorithm based on Givens rotations for the case of an 8×8 matrix that needs fewer than 13 parallel stages. (Compare with Fig. 2.2.2.)

2.3 A FAST DIRECT MATRIX INVERSION ALGORITHM

All of the methods of Section 2.2 require time at least proportional to n for the solution of a system of n linear equations, and this raises the question whether a substantially faster algorithm is possible, assuming that an unlimited number of processors is available. While it was believed for some time that this was not possible, the algorithm in this section, due to Csanky [Csa76], produces the inverse of a square matrix in $O(\log^2 n)$ time. This algorithm is only of theoretical interest because it is prone to numerical problems and because it uses an excessive number (n^4) of processors. It is an open question whether there exist parallel matrix inversion algorithms whose time requirements are smaller than $O(\log^2 n)$. In fact, this problem is open even for the case of triangular matrices.

Given an $n \times n$ nonsingular matrix A, we consider the characteristic polynomial ϕ of A, defined by

$$\phi(\lambda) = \det(\lambda I - A) = \prod_{i=1}^{n}(\lambda - \lambda_i), \qquad (3.1)$$

where $\lambda_1, \ldots, \lambda_n$ are the eigenvalues of A. Let $c_1, \ldots, c_n$ be the coefficients of the characteristic polynomial, that is,

$$\phi(\lambda) = \lambda^n + c_1 \lambda^{n-1} + \cdots + c_{n-1} \lambda + c_n. \qquad (3.2)$$

By comparing Eqs. (3.1) and (3.2), we see that $c_n = (-1)^n \prod_{i=1}^{n} \lambda_i$; in particular, A is invertible if and only if $c_n \neq 0$, which we assume. The computation of A^{-1} uses the Cayley–Hamilton theorem (Prop. A.18 in Appendix A), which states that $\phi(A) = A^n + c_1 A^{n-1} + \cdots + c_{n-1} A + c_n I = 0$. Therefore, A^{-1} is given by

$$A^{-1} = -\frac{1}{c_n} \left(A^{n-1} + c_1 A^{n-2} + \cdots + c_{n-1} I \right). \qquad (3.3)$$

By using the discussion in Subsection 1.2.3, the matrices $A^2, \ldots, A^{n-1}$ can be all generated in time $O(\log^2 n)$ using n^4 processors. Therefore, it only remains to find a "fast" method for computing the coefficients of the characteristic polynomial.

We define the trace $\text{tr}(A)$ of a matrix A as the sum of its diagonal entries. The trace of a matrix is also equal to the sum of the eigenvalues (Prop. A.22 in Appendix A). We define $s_k = \sum_{i=1}^{n} \lambda_i^k$, where $\lambda_1, \ldots, \lambda_n$ are the eigenvalues of A. Since $\lambda_1^k, \ldots, \lambda_n^k$ are the eigenvalues of A^k [Prop. A.17(d) in Appendix A], it follows that $s_k = \text{tr}(A^k)$. In particular, the coefficients $s_1, \ldots, s_n$ can be computed by summing the diagonal entries of the matrices A^k. We now use a classical method, known as Leverrier's method [LeV40], that allows us to compute the coefficients of the characteristic polynomial in terms of $s_1, \ldots, s_n$.

Proposition 3.1.   The coefficients $c_1, \ldots, c_n$ and the coefficients $s_1, \ldots, s_n$ satisfy the following system of equations:

$$
\begin{bmatrix}
1 & 0 & \cdots & & \cdots & 0 \\
s_1 & 2 & 0 & & & \\
\vdots & \ddots & \ddots & \ddots & & \vdots \\
s_{k-1} & \cdots & s_1 & k & 0 & \vdots \\
\vdots & \ddots & & \ddots & \ddots & 0 \\
s_{n-1} & \cdots & s_{k-1} & \cdots & s_1 & n
\end{bmatrix}
\begin{bmatrix}
c_1 \\
\vdots \\
\vdots \\
\vdots \\
\vdots \\
c_n
\end{bmatrix}
= -
\begin{bmatrix}
s_1 \\
\vdots \\
\vdots \\
\vdots \\
\vdots \\
s_n
\end{bmatrix}.
\tag{3.4}
$$

Proof. The derivative of the characteristic polynomial is given by

$$
\frac{d\phi}{d\lambda}(\lambda) = n\lambda^{n-1} + c_1(n-1)\lambda^{n-2} + \cdots + c_{n-1}.
\tag{3.5}
$$

An alternative expression for $d\phi/d\lambda$ is obtained by differentiating both sides of Eq. (3.1). This yields

$$
\frac{d\phi}{d\lambda}(\lambda) = \frac{d}{d\lambda}\left[\prod_{i=1}^{n}(\lambda - \lambda_i)\right] = \sum_{i=1}^{n}\prod_{j\neq i}(\lambda - \lambda_i) = \sum_{i=1}^{n}\frac{\phi(\lambda)}{\lambda - \lambda_i}.
\tag{3.6}
$$

We now use the series expansion

$$
\frac{1}{\lambda - \lambda_i} = \frac{1}{\lambda(1 - \lambda_i/\lambda)} = \frac{1}{\lambda}\left(1 + \frac{\lambda_i}{\lambda} + \frac{\lambda_i^2}{\lambda^2} + \cdots\right),
\tag{3.7}
$$

which is valid for $|\lambda| > |\lambda_i|$. We use Eq. (3.7) in Eq. (3.6) to obtain

$$
\frac{d\phi}{d\lambda}(\lambda) = \frac{\phi(\lambda)}{\lambda}\sum_{i=1}^{n}\left(1 + \frac{\lambda_i}{\lambda} + \frac{\lambda_i^2}{\lambda^2} + \cdots\right)
$$
$$
= \left(\lambda^n + c_1\lambda^{n-1} + \cdots + c_n\right)\left(\frac{n}{\lambda} + \frac{s_1}{\lambda^2} + \frac{s_2}{\lambda^3} + \cdots\right),
\tag{3.8}
$$

where the last equality followed by changing the order of the summation and using the definition of s_k. The right–hand side of Eq. (3.8) is equal to the right–hand side of Eq. (3.5) for all values of λ satisfying $|\lambda| > |\lambda_i|$ and for all i. It follows that the coefficients of each power of λ must be the same in both expressions. By comparing the coefficients of λ^{n-k-1} for $k = 1, \ldots, n$, we obtain Eq. (3.4).   **Q.E.D.**

Notice that Eq. (3.4) is a lower triangular system of equations. Using the results of Section 2.1, we can solve for $c_1, \ldots, c_n$ in time $O(\log^2 n)$ using n^3 processors. We can now summarize the algorithm:

1. Compute A^k for $k = 2, \ldots, n$.
2. Compute s_k for $k = 1, \ldots, n$.
3. Solve the system (3.4) for $c_1, \ldots, c_n$.
4. Evaluate A^{-1} using Eq. (3.3).

Each one of these four steps can be executed in $O(\log^2 n)$ time using n^4 processors, and, therefore, this estimate is valid for the overall algorithm as well.

EXERCISES

3.1. (Cholesky factorization [Luo87]) Any symmetric positive definite matrix A can be expressed in the form $A = L'DL$, where L is a lower triangular matrix, and D is a diagonal matrix with positive diagonal entries. Devise a parallel algorithm that computes L and D in time $O(\log^3 n)$, where n is the size of the matrix A. *Hint:* Compute a square matrix X, of approximately half the size of A, such that

$$\begin{bmatrix} I & 0 \\ X & I \end{bmatrix} A \begin{bmatrix} I & X' \\ 0 & I \end{bmatrix} = \begin{bmatrix} B_1 & 0 \\ 0 & B_2 \end{bmatrix},$$

where B_1 and B_2 are some matrices, and proceed recursively.

2.4 CLASSICAL ITERATIVE METHODS FOR SYSTEMS OF LINEAR EQUATIONS

We present here a few classical iterative methods for solving linear equations. Such methods are widely used, especially for the solution of large problems such as those arising from the discretization of linear partial differential equations. For this reason, there is an extensive theory dealing with such methods, some of which is developed in Section 2.6.

Let A be an $n \times n$ matrix, let b be a vector in $\Re^n$, and consider the system of linear equations

$$Ax = b, \tag{4.1}$$

where x is an unknown vector to be determined. We assume that A is invertible, so that $Ax = b$ has a unique solution. We write the ith equation of the system $Ax = b$ as

$$\sum_{j=1}^{n} a_{ij}x_j = b_i, \tag{4.2}$$

where a_{ij} are the entries of A; also, x_j and b_i are the components of x and b, respectively. We assume that $a_{ii} \neq 0$ and solve for x_i to obtain

$$x_i = -\frac{1}{a_{ii}} \left[\sum_{j \neq i} a_{ij}x_j - b_i \right]. \tag{4.3}$$

If all components x_j, $j \neq i$, of the solution of $Ax = b$ are known, the remaining component x_i can be determined from Eq. (4.3). If instead some approximate estimates for the components x_j, $j \neq i$, are available, then we can use Eq. (4.3) to obtain an estimate of x_i. This can be done for each component of x simultaneously, leading to the following algorithm:

Jacobi algorithm.   Starting with some initial vector $x(0) \in \Re^n$, evaluate $x(t)$, $t = 1, 2, \ldots$, using the iteration

$$x_i(t + 1) = -\frac{1}{a_{ii}} \left[\sum_{j \neq i} a_{ij}x_j(t) - b_i \right]. \tag{4.4}$$

The Jacobi algorithm produces an infinite sequence $\{x(t)\}$ of elements of $\Re^n$. If this sequence converges to a limit x, then by taking the limit of both sides of Eq. (4.4) as t tends to infinity, we see that x satisfies Eq. (4.3) for each i, which is equivalent to x being a solution of $Ax = b$. Of course, it is possible that the algorithm diverges [$x(t)$ does not converge]; see Fig. 2.4.1. Conditions for convergence will be explored in Section 2.6.

In the above algorithm, each component of $x(t + 1)$ was evaluated based on Eq. (4.3) and the estimate $x(t)$ of the solution. If this algorithm is executed on a serial computer, by the time that $x_i(t + 1)$ is evaluated, we already have available some new estimates $x_j(t + 1)$ for the components of x with index j smaller than i. It may be preferable to employ these new estimates of x_j, $j < i$, when updating x_i. This leads to the following algorithm:

Gauss–Seidel algorithm.   Starting with some initial vector $x(0) \in \Re^n$, evaluate $x(t)$, $t = 1, 2, \ldots$, using the iteration

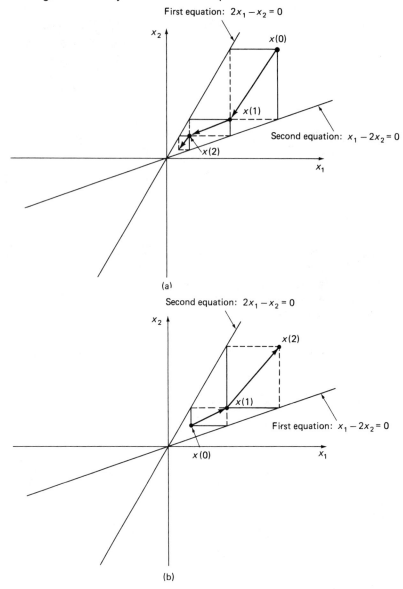

Figure 2.4.1 Illustration of the Jacobi algorithm for solving a system of linear equations. At each iteration, the ith equation is solved for the ith component with all other components fixed at their values at the start of the iteration. In (a), the Jacobi algorithm is applied to the system

$$\begin{bmatrix} 2 & -1 \\ -1 & 2 \end{bmatrix} \begin{bmatrix} x_1 \\ x_2 \end{bmatrix} = \begin{bmatrix} 0 \\ 0 \end{bmatrix}$$

and the iteration converges; in (b), the algorithm is applied to the equivalent system

$$\begin{bmatrix} -1 & 2 \\ 2 & -1 \end{bmatrix} \begin{bmatrix} x_1 \\ x_2 \end{bmatrix} = \begin{bmatrix} 0 \\ 0 \end{bmatrix}$$

in which the assignment of equations to components has been reversed, and the iteration diverges. In Section 2.6, it will be seen that convergence is enhanced if equations are assigned to components so that the diagonal elements a_{ii} are large (in absolute value) relative to the other coefficients a_{ij}, $i \neq j$.

$$x_i(t+1) = -\frac{1}{a_{ii}} \left[\sum_{j<i} a_{ij}x_j(t+1) + \sum_{j>i} a_{ij}x_j(t) - b_i \right]. \tag{4.5}$$

Figure 2.4.2 illustrates convergence and divergence of the algorithm. As discussed in Subsection 1.2.4, there are many different Gauss–Seidel algorithms for the same system of equations, depending on the particular order with which the variables are updated. In Eq. (4.5), we first update x_1, then x_2, etc. It is equally meaningful to start by updating x_n, then x_{n-1}, and proceed backwards, with x_1 being updated last. Any other order of updating is possible. Different orders of updating may produce substantially different results for the same system of equations.

A variation of the Jacobi and Gauss–Seidel methods is obtained if we use a nonzero scalar γ (called the *relaxation parameter*), and rewrite Eq. (4.3) in the equivalent form

$$x_i = (1-\gamma)x_i - \frac{\gamma}{a_{ii}} \left[\sum_{j\neq i} a_{ij}x_j - b_i \right], \tag{4.6}$$

thereby leading to the following algorithms:

Jacobi overrelaxation (JOR). Jacobi overrelaxation is similar to the Jacobi algorithm except that Eq. (4.4) is replaced by

$$x_i(t+1) = (1-\gamma)x_i(t) - \frac{\gamma}{a_{ii}} \left[\sum_{j\neq i}^n a_{ij}x_j(t) - b_i \right]. \tag{4.7}$$

In particular, if $0 < \gamma < 1$, the new value of x_i obtained from Eq. (4.7) is a convex combination of the old value of x_i and the new value of x_i that would have been obtained if the Jacobi iteration (4.4) was used. The next algorithm is a similar modification of the Gauss–Seidel algorithm.

Successive overrelaxation (SOR). Successive overrelaxation is the same as the Gauss–Seidel algorithm except that Eq. (4.5) is replaced by

$$x_i(t+1) = (1-\gamma)x_i(t) - \frac{\gamma}{a_{ii}} \left[\sum_{j<i} a_{ij}x_j(t+1) + \sum_{j>i} a_{ij}x_j(t) - b_i \right]. \tag{4.8}$$

Notice that the Jacobi and Gauss–Seidel algorithms are equivalent to the JOR and SOR algorithms, respectively, when $\gamma = 1$. The JOR and SOR algorithms are widely used because they often converge faster if γ is suitably chosen.

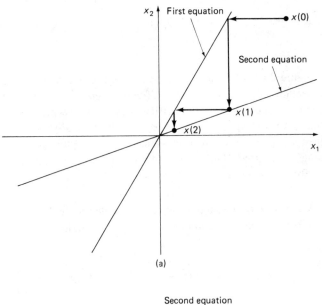

(a)

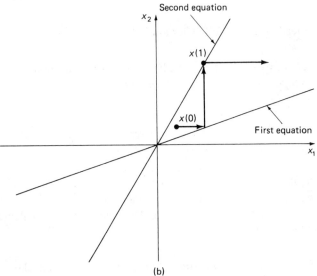

(b)

Figure 2.4.2   Illustration of convergence and divergence in the Gauss–Seidel algorithm for the same systems of equations as in Fig. 2.4.1.

Richardson's method.   Our next iterative method, which is sometimes called *Richardson's method* [HaY81], is obtained by rewriting the equation $Ax = b$ in the form $x = x - \gamma(Ax - b)$. The method is described by

$$x(t + 1) = x(t) - \gamma\left[Ax(t) - b\right],\tag{4.9}$$

where γ is a scalar relaxation parameter. A variant of Richardson's method is obtained if the iteration $x := x - \gamma(Ax - b)$ is executed in Gauss–Seidel fashion. This algorithm will be referred to as the RGS method and is described by the update equation

$$x_i(t + 1) = x_i(t) - \gamma \left[\sum_{j<i} a_{ij}x_j(t + 1) + \sum_{j\geq i} a_{ij}x_j(t) - b_i \right]. \qquad (4.10)$$

A more general class of algorithms is obtained by using an invertible matrix B to transform the equation $Ax = b$ to the equivalent equation

$$x = x - B(Ax - b) \qquad (4.11)$$

and then applying the iteration

$$x(t + 1) = x(t) - B\left[Ax(t) - b\right]. \qquad (4.12)$$

A Gauss–Seidel variant of this iteration is also possible.

The discussion following the presentation of the Jacobi algorithm applies to all of the other methods, and shows that the following is true.

Proposition 4.1.   If the sequence $\{x(t)\}$, generated by any of the above presented algorithms converges, then it converges to a solution of $Ax = b$.

2.5 PARALLEL IMPLEMENTATION OF CLASSICAL ITERATIVE METHODS

In this section, we comment on the parallelization of the iterative methods introduced in Section 2.4. Most of the computation in such methods consists of matrix–vector multiplications and the relevant facts have already been covered in Subsection 1.3.6. We concentrate on the case of message–passing architectures because the issues tend to be somewhat simpler for the case of shared memory systems. We discuss the case where the matrices involved are dense, as well as the sparse case, which is typical in problems originating from partial differential equations (Subsection 2.5.1). Finally, in Subsection 2.5.2, we describe multigrid methods and comment on their parallelizability.

The Jacobi, JOR, and Richardson's algorithms for the solution of the system $Ax = b$ are straightforward to implement in parallel since each iteration involves a matrix–vector multiplication. Suppose that there are n available processors, and that the ith processor is responsible for computing $x_i(t)$ at each iteration t. (The case where the number of processors is smaller than the number of variables is qualitatively similar and will be discussed shortly.) Suppose that the ith processor knows the entries of the ith row of A. (This is the row storage method of Subsection 1.3.6.) To compute $x_i(t + 1)$, processor

i has to know the values of $x_j(t)$ computed at the previous iteration by processors j for which $a_{ij} \neq 0$. If most of the entries of A are nonzero, it is easier to transmit x_j to all processors i, even if a_{ij} equals zero, because selective transmissions may introduce some unwarranted overhead. We are thus dealing with a multinode broadcast. As discussed in Subsection 1.3.4, the time to perform a multinode broadcast is $O(n)$ in a linear array or a mesh, and $O(n/\log n)$ in a hypercube. Given that each processor has to perform $\Theta(n)$ arithmetic operations at each stage (assuming that the matrix A has no special sparsity structure), the percentage of time spent on communications diminishes with n for a hypercube and remains constant for a linear array. In practice, this constant factor could be substantial and communication could dominate the execution time; in that case, there should be fewer processors, with more components assigned to each one, and the communication penalty can be made insignificant (Subsection 1.3.5).

In an alternative implementation, there are again n processors, with the ith processor in charge of the ith component x_i. However, we assume that the ith processor has access to the ith column of A, as opposed to the ith row of A. (This is the column storage method of Subsection 1.3.6.) Assuming that A is a fully dense matrix, the computation proceeds as follows. Each processor i evaluates $a_{ji}x_i$ for $j = 1, \ldots, n$. Then for each j, the quantities $a_{ji}x_i$ for $i = 1, \ldots, n$ are propagated to processor j, with partial sums formed along the way, which is a multinode accumulation. As discussed in Subsection 1.3.4, the time required for a multinode accumulation is equal to the time for a multinode broadcast, and we conclude that the communication requirements of the row and column storage methods are the same, for the dense case. Which of the two implementations is preferable may depend on fine details of a particular parallel computer.

We now consider the case where the matrix A is sparse. The sparsity structure of A determines a directed graph $G = (N, \mathcal{A})$, where $N = \{1, \ldots, n\}$ and the set of arcs $\mathcal{A}$ is the set $\{(i, j) \mid i \neq j \text{ and } a_{ji} \neq 0\}$ of all processor pairs (i, j) such that i needs to communicate to j. We recognize this as the dependency graph introduced in Subsection 1.2.4. Given a special architecture, efficient parallel implementations are obtained if the above dependency graph can be imbedded into the graph describing the interconnection topology. In that case, all communication takes place between neighboring processors and the communication penalty is minimal. An example will be shown in the next subsection. When such an imbedding cannot be found, the communication requirements of the row and column storage methods can be substantially different (see the discussion in Subsection 1.3.6), and this is an important difference from the dense case. There are also some alternative storage methods which are discussed in [McV87] and [FJL88].

We now consider the Gauss–Seidel, SOR, and RGS algorithms. These are not well suited for parallel implementation in general. To see this, consider the Gauss–Seidel algorithm and suppose that the matrix A is fully dense, that is, $a_{ij} \neq 0$ for all i and j. Then, for processor i to compute $x_i(t + 1)$, the value of $x_j(t + 1)$ is needed for every $j < i$. Hence, the algorithm is inherently sequential, because no two components of x can be updated simultaneously. This is quite unfortunate because SOR algorithms, with a suitable choice of γ, are often much faster [HaY81]. However, as discussed in Subsection 1.2.4, this difficulty may be often circumvented if the matrix A is sparse by employing a coloring scheme. This is always the case when the matrix A is obtained from discretization of a partial differential equation, and an example will be discussed in Subsection 2.5.1.

In practice, the number p of processors is often substantially smaller than the number n of variables. In this case, several variables can be assigned to each processor. All of the preceding discussion applies with minor modifications, and the communication penalty will typically be reduced under these circumstances, as discussed in Subsection 1.3.5.

A final point of interest concerns termination of iterative algorithms. Typical termination criteria used in practice evaluate an expression such as $\|Ax(t) - b\|$, where $\|\cdot\|$ is some norm, and terminate the algorithm if its value is small enough. Such testing for termination does not introduce any significant overhead in the case where A is dense. For example, suppose that $\|\cdot\|$ is the maximum norm $\|\cdot\|_\infty$. At each iteration, every processor computes the value of $\max_i |[Ax]_i - b_i|$, where i ranges over the indices of the variables assigned to that processor. These values can then be compared using a spanning tree, with each processor propagating toward the root of the tree the largest of its own value and the values it has received. Thus, termination detection requires a single node accumulation and adds little to the communication penalty when compared to the multinode broadcast or multinode accumulation involved in each iteration.

The considerations concerning termination detection are different when A is sparse and the variables have been assigned to the processors so that each iteration only requires nearest neighbor communication. Here the time spent on communications needed for executing one iteration is proportional to the number of variables assigned to each processor, whereas the communication time needed for termination testing is proportional to the diameter of the interconnection network. Consequently, unless the diameter is comparable or smaller than the number of variables assigned to each processor, it is meaningful to test for termination only once in a while. Alternatively, testing for termination could take place while the main algorithm continues with subsequent iterations. In the latter case, the value of $Ax - b$ used for the termination decision will be outdated by the time that this decision is made, but this typically does not have any particularly adverse consequences.

2.5.1 An Example: Poisson's Equation

As a prototype of a linear partial differential equation, we consider Poisson's equation on the unit square:

$$\frac{\partial^2 f}{\partial x^2}(x, y) + \frac{\partial^2 f}{\partial y^2}(x, y) = g(x, y), \qquad (x, y) \in [0, 1]^2, \qquad (5.1)$$

where $g : [0, 1]^2 \mapsto \Re$ is a known function. The objective is to find a function $f : [0, 1]^2 \mapsto \Re$ that satisfies Poisson's equation and has prescribed values on the boundary of the unit square. In order to solve this equation numerically, we consider the values of f only on a finite grid of points in the unit square. Let N be an integer larger than 2 and let

$$f_{i,j} = f\left(\frac{i}{N}, \frac{j}{N}\right), \qquad 0 \le i,j \le N,$$

$$g_{i,j} = g\left(\frac{i}{N}, \frac{j}{N}\right), \qquad 0 < i,j < N.$$

Assuming that f is sufficiently smooth and that Δ is a small scalar, we can use a central difference approximation for the second derivative of f (see Prop. A.33 in Appendix A) to obtain

$$\frac{\partial^2 f}{\partial x^2}(x,y) \approx \frac{1}{\Delta^2}\Big[f(x+\Delta,y) - 2f(x,y) + f(x-\Delta,y)\Big].$$

We use a similar approximation for $\partial^2 f/\partial y^2$, we let (x,y) be one of the grid points in the interior of the unit square, and we let $\Delta = 1/N$ to obtain

$$f_{i,j} = \frac{1}{4}\Big(f_{i+1,j} + f_{i-1,j} + f_{i,j+1} + f_{i,j-1}\Big) - \frac{1}{4N^2}g_{i,j}, \qquad 0 < i,j < N. \qquad (5.2)$$

This is a system of $(N-1)^2$ linear equations in $(N-1)^2$ unknowns, the unknowns being the values of f at the interior grid points. (Recall that the values of f on the boundary are given.) This system can be represented in the form $Ax = b$, where A is an $(N-1)^2 \times (N-1)^2$ matrix, x is a vector with the unknown values of $f_{i,j}$ at the interior grid points, and where b is a vector depending on $g_{i,j}$ and the known boundary values of f. Then, all of the methods of Section 2.4 become applicable. However, we do not need to write an explicit matrix representation in order to apply these methods; Eq. (5.2) already contains all the information needed. We notice that Eq. (5.2) expresses one variable in terms of the others, and we have one such equation for each variable. Thus, Eq. (5.2) has the same structure as Eq. (4.3) on which the iterative methods of the preceding section were based. Therefore, the updating equation of the JOR algorithm is

$$f_{i,j}(t+1) = (1-\gamma)f_{i,j}(t) + \frac{\gamma}{4}\Big[f_{i+1,j}(t) + f_{i-1,j}(t) + f_{i,j+1}(t) + f_{i,j-1}(t)\Big] - \frac{\gamma}{4N^2}g_{i,j},$$

$$0 < i,j < N.$$
$$(5.3)$$

If the right–hand side of Eq. (5.3) involves a boundary point, then the given boundary value is used. That is, we are setting $f_{i,j}(t) = f_{i,j}$ whenever i or j is equal to 0 or N.

    The parallel implementation of the JOR algorithm is straightforward. We assign a different processor to each interior grid point and notice that the processor responsible for updating $f_{i,j}$ can execute the iteration (5.3), provided that it knows the values of f at neighboring grid points, as computed at the previous iteration. Thus, the most natural parallel architecture is a mesh of $(N-1)^2$ processors such that neighboring processors correspond to neighboring grid points (see Fig. 2.5.1). At each stage of the algorithm, each processor transmits its most recently computed value of $f_{i,j}$ to its neighbors and then each processor uses the values received to update its own value according to Eq.

(5.3). In practice, the number of grid points is likely to exceed the number of processors, in which case it is meaningful to assign a block of adjacent grid points to each processor. Concurrency is reduced but the communication penalty is also reduced due to the area–perimeter effect discussed in Subsection 1.3.5.

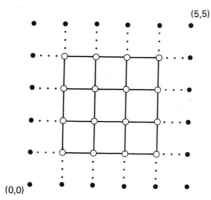

(5,5)

(0,0)

Figure 2.5.1 A 6 × 6 grid for the solution of Poisson's equation. A processor is assigned to each interior grid point and processors are connected as indicated. Furthermore, processors near the boundary need to know the boundary conditions for f at the points indicated by dashed lines. If the arcs are viewed as bidirectional, the graph of processors is also the dependency graph corresponding to the Jacobi and JOR algorithms.

We now turn to the parallel implementation of SOR. In the language of Subsection 1.2.4, this is the Gauss–Seidel algorithm based on the JOR iteration (5.3). The dependency graph of iteration (5.3) is shown in Fig. 2.5.1; it is identical to the dependency graph considered in Example 2.1 of Subsection 1.2.4, and the discussion in that subsection applies. In particular, this graph can be colored using two colors only. Furthermore, if each processor is assigned to two adjacent grid points, then a sweep (that is, an update of all components) takes the same time for either of the JOR and SOR algorithms. (In practice, each processor is often assigned several grid points and the time requirements of each iteration are again the same for JOR and SOR.) Generally, the SOR algorithm is preferred because it has a better rate of convergence [Var62].

Parallel implementations of SOR are also possible for more complicated discretizations of partial differential equations. For example, a so–called nine–point discretization gives rise to the dependency graph that was shown in Figure 1.2.12 of Subsection 1.2.4. According to Exercise 2.7 in that subsection, this dependency graph can be colored using four colors. It follows that if the number of grid points assigned to each processor is equal to 4 (or an integer multiple of 4), then the time for the execution of one iteration of SOR is the same as the time for one iteration of JOR.

We now recall from Subsection 1.3.4 that a mesh can be imbedded in a hypercube. It follows that the JOR and SOR algorithms for Poisson's equation can be implemented in a hypercube with communication taking place only between nearest neighbors. Thus, hypercubes are well suited for the numerical solution of partial differential equations.

2.5.2 Multigrid Methods

Multigrid methods are a special class of iterative algorithms for the numerical solution of partial differential equations. In these methods, a partial differential equation like Poisson's equation, is discretized for several choices of the grid spacings, and iterations take place on several such grids. The rationale behind such methods is that a fine grid is required to obtain an accurate solution, but iterations on coarser grids typically converge with fewer iterations. An appropriate combination of iterations on fine and coarse grids leads to the fastest known algorithms for the solution of certain types of partial differential equations. We will not be concerned here with the analytical aspects of such methods; the reader is referred to [Hac85]. We shall concentrate instead on their structure and on the data dependencies involved, and we shall explore the potential for their parallelization. For simplicity, we restrict our discussion to two–dimensional grids although the discussion generalizes to higher dimensions.

Let $G_0 = \{(i, j) \mid 1 \leq i, j \leq N\}$, where N is assumed to be a power of 2. We view G_0 as the finest grid. We also define coarser grids, $G_1, \ldots, G_D$, where D is an integer smaller than $\log N$, by letting

$$G_d = \left\{(i, j) \in G_0 \mid i \text{ and } j \text{ are integer multiples of } 2^d\right\}, \qquad d = 1, 2, \ldots, D,$$

(see Fig. 2.5.2). With each grid G_d and each $(i, j) \in G_d$, we associate a variable $x_{ij,d}$. A multigrid algorithm involves the following three types of computations:

(a) Relaxations on a given grid G_d. The next value of $x_{ij,d}$ is determined as a function of the values of its neighbors on the grid G_d. We assume that such relaxations take place only on a single grid at a time.

(b) Transfer to a finer grid (*interpolation*). The values of the finer grid variables $x_{ij,d-1}$ are computed in terms of the values of the coarser grid variables $x_{ij,d}$, according to some local rule. For example, $x_{ij,d-1}$ could be set equal to the average of the values of $x_{k\ell,d}$, where the average is taken over all $(k, \ell) \in G_d$ which are at a minimal distance from (i, j) (see Fig. 2.5.2).

(c) Transfer to a coarser grid (*projection*). The values of the coarser grid variables $x_{ij,d+1}$ are computed in terms of the values of the variables $x_{ij,d}$, according to some local rule. The simplest rule is to let $x_{ij,d+1} := x_{ij,d}$.

Suppose that we have N^2 processors available, and that the ijth processor is assigned the responsibility of computing the values of the variables $x_{ij,d}$ for every d such that $(i, j) \in G_d$. In order to execute the relaxation iterations on the finest grid efficiently, it is reasonable to use a two–dimensional mesh–connected array of processors. However, we notice that when relaxation iterations are executed on some coarser grid G_d, $d \neq 0$, then neighboring grid points on G_d correspond to distant processors on our mesh of processors and for this reason the mesh topology is unsuitable for multigrid methods.

Let us now consider a hypercube and suppose that a mesh of N^2 processors has been imbedded in a hypercube with N^2 nodes, using a reflected Gray code, as in Subsection 1.3.4. We recall certain key properties of this imbedding (see Fig. 2.5.3).

(a) For $j = 1, \ldots, N$, the jth "column" of the grid, which is the linear array $C_j = \{(i, j) \in G_0 \mid 1 \leq i \leq N\}$, is mapped to a smaller hypercube, with N nodes, contained in the original hypercube. The same is true for each "row" $R_i = \{(i, j) \in$

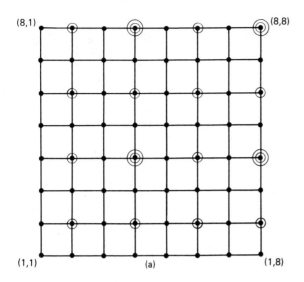

(8,1)   (8,8)

(1,1)   (a)   (1,8)

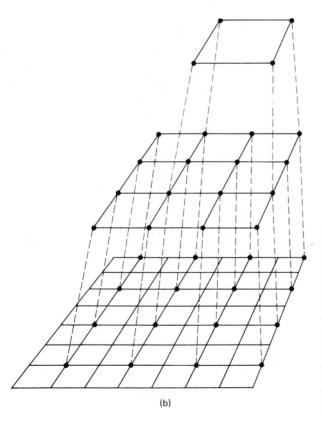

(b)

Figure 2.5.2 Two views of the different grids for the case $N = 8$. (a) Grid G_0 consists of all points in the diagram. Grid G_1 consists of the points marked with a circle and grid G_2 consists of the points marked with a double circle. In an interpolation step from G_1 to G_0, the value of $x_{33,0}$ could be set equal to the average of $x_{22,1}$, $x_{24,1}$, $x_{44,1}$, and $x_{42,1}$ associated with the closest grid points belonging to G_1. Similarly, the value of $x_{43,0}$ could be set to the average of $x_{44,1}$ and $x_{42,1}$. (b) Grids G_0, G_1, and G_2 are drawn separately. The dashed lines identify corresponding points in different grids.

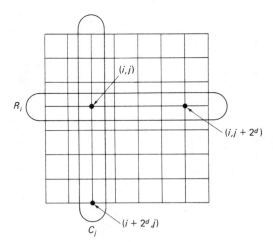

Figure 2.5.3 A mesh is imbedded into a hypercube so that each column C_j and each row R_i is imbedded in a smaller hypercube. The distance between points (i, j) and $(i + 2^d, j)$ [respectively, $(i, j + 2^d)$], when the arcs of the hypercube C_j (respectively, R_i) are used, is at most 2. Thus, any two processors that need to communicate during the relaxation iterations on grid G_d can do so within two time units. The hypercubes corresponding to each R_i and C_j do not share any arcs; also, concurrent communication within each R_i and each C_j is possible. It follows that all required communication can take place simultaneously for all $(i, j) \in G_d$.

$G_0 \mid 1 \leq j \leq n\}$. Furthermore, the mapping of each such column or row corresponds to a reflected Gray code. Finally, the subhypercubes to which each C_j and R_i is mapped do not share any arcs.

(b) Suppose that a linear array is mapped into a hypercube according to a reflected Gray code. Let the nodes be numbered according to their position in the linear array. Then, the physical distance of nodes i and $i + 2^d$ in the hypercube is equal to 1 if $d = 0$, and is equal to 2 if d is a positive integer. Furthermore, communication between nodes i and $i + 2^d$ of the linear array can take place simultaneously for all i, in two time units, using the "subrings of level d" (see Fig. 1.3.21 in Subsection 1.3.4).

It follows that the communication time per relaxation iteration is equal to at most 2, for every grid G_d. Similar reasoning shows that grid transfers can also be implemented in a hypercube using local communication only. We conclude that multigrid algorithms can be implemented on hypercubes so that the time devoted to communication is proportional to the computation time. In practice, several points of the finest grid could be assigned to each processor, and this reduces the communication penalty even further. As a most extreme case, if the number of grid points in the coarsest grid is equal to the number of processors, then most of the data dependencies involve variables residing inside the same processor and the communication penalty is rather small. In fact, in this case, it can be seen that there is no need for communication between distant processors even when a mesh–connected architecture is used.

We have assumed so far that relaxations take place in only one grid at a time. In an alternative method, called *concurrent multigrid*, relaxations are performed on several grids simultaneously. Hypercubes are again suitable for such methods, but the mapping problem is somewhat more involved [ChS86].

2.6 CONVERGENCE ANALYSIS OF CLASSICAL ITERATIVE METHODS

We have so far defined and discussed the parallel implementation of iterative methods for solving the system $Ax = b$, where A is an $n \times n$ invertible matrix. All of these methods have the property that if they converge, then they do so to the desired solution (Prop. 4.1). In this section, we derive conditions that guarantee convergence. The mathematical tools that we introduce here will also be of use in the analysis of asynchronous iterative algorithms in Chapters 6 and 7. Furthermore, the ideas of this section have natural generalizations to the contexts of nonlinear optimization and solution of systems of nonlinear equations (Chapter 3). We first develop a uniform representation of the different algorithms.

Let D be a diagonal matrix whose diagonal entries are equal to the corresponding diagonal entries of A, and let $B = A - D$, so that B is zero along the diagonal. Assuming that the diagonal entries of A are nonzero, the Jacobi algorithm can be written in matrix form as [cf. Eq. (4.4)]

$$x(t + 1) = -D^{-1}Bx(t) + D^{-1}b. \tag{6.1}$$

Similarly, one iteration of the JOR algorithm is described by

$$x(t + 1) = \left[(1 - \gamma)I - \gamma D^{-1}B \right] x(t) + \gamma D^{-1}b, \tag{6.2}$$

where I is the $n \times n$ identity matrix. To derive a similar matrix representation of the Gauss–Seidel and SOR algorithms, we decompose A as $A = L + D + U$, where L is strictly lower triangular, D is diagonal, and U is strictly upper triangular. Then, the SOR iteration (4.8) can be rewritten as

$$x(t + 1) = (1 - \gamma)x(t) - \gamma D^{-1}\left[Lx(t + 1) + Ux(t) - b \right],$$

which is equivalent to

$$x(t + 1) = \left(I + \gamma D^{-1}L \right)^{-1} \left[(1 - \gamma)I - \gamma D^{-1}U \right] x(t) + \gamma \left(I + \gamma D^{-1}L \right)^{-1} D^{-1}b. \tag{6.3}$$

Finally, Richardson's method is described by

$$x(t + 1) = (I - \gamma A)x(t) + \gamma b \tag{6.4}$$

and a representation resembling Eq. (6.3) is possible for the RGS algorithm of Eq. (4.10). Equations (6.1) to (6.4) can all be written in the form

$$x(t + 1) = Mx(t) + Gb, \tag{6.5}$$

where M and G are suitable matrices determined by A and the particular algorithm being used. (We call M the *iteration matrix* of an iterative algorithm.) Therefore, we only need to study the convergence of iteration (6.5). Let us assume that $I - M$ is invertible[†], so that there exists a unique x^* satisfying $x^* = Mx^* + Gb$, and let $y(t) = x(t) - x^*$. Then, $y(t+1) = My(t)$, which implies that $y(t) = M^t y(0)$ for every t. It is seen that the sequence $\{x(t)\}$ converges to x^* for all choices of $x(0)$ if and only if $y(t)$ converges to zero for all choices of $y(0)$. This happens if and only if M^t converges to zero, which is the case if and only if all of the eigenvalues of M have a magnitude smaller than 1, that is, if the *spectral radius* $\rho(M)$ is smaller than 1 (Def. A.9 and Prop. A.21 in Appendix A). We have thus proved the following fundamental result:

Proposition 6.1.   Assume that $I - M$ is invertible, let x^* satisfy $x^* = Mx^* + Gb$ and let $\{x(t)\}$ be the sequence generated by the iteration $x(t+1) = Mx(t) + Gb$. Then, $\lim_{t \to \infty} x(t) = x^*$ for all choices of $x(0)$ if and only if $\rho(M) < 1$.

Notice that the above condition for convergence refers only to the iteration matrix M and not to the vector b. We conclude that the iteration $x := Mx + Gb$ converges for all choices of b if and only if it converges for a particular choice of b, say $b = 0$.

Let us recall that the rate at which M^t converges to zero is basically governed by $\rho(M)$ (Prop. A.20 in Appendix A). For this reason, we will be comparing the rate of convergence of alternative iterative methods on the basis of the corresponding spectral radii.

Proposition 6.1 is the most general possible convergence result, but it is of limited use because the eigenvalues of M are rarely known exactly. Thus, more refined tools are called for. A very useful method for proving convergence of iterative methods consists of introducing a suitable distance function, or norm, and showing that each iteration reduces the distance of the current iterate from the desired point of convergence. For linear equations, the most useful norms are quadratic norms, like the Euclidean norm, and (weighted) maximum norms.

2.6.1 Background on Maximum Norms and Nonnegative Matrices

Let us recall some notation and a few facts from Appendix A. If w is a vector in $\Re^n$, the notations $w > 0$ and $w \geq 0$ indicate that all components of w are positive or nonnegative, respectively. Similarly, if A is a matrix, the notations $A > 0$ and $A \geq 0$ indicate that all entries of A are positive or nonnegative, respectively. For any two vectors w and v, the notation $w > v$ stands for $w - v > 0$. The notations $w < v$, $w \geq v$, $A > B$, etc. are to be interpreted accordingly. Given a vector w, we denote by $|w|$ the vector whose ith component equals $|w_i|$. Similarly, for any matrix A, we denote by $|A|$ the matrix whose entries are the absolute values of the entries of A. Given a vector $w > 0$, we define the weighted maximum norm $\|\cdot\|_\infty^w$ by $\|x\|_\infty^w = \max_i |x_i/w_i|$. In the special case

---

[†] In fact, for the algorithms introduced in Section 2.4, $I - M$ is guaranteed to be invertible, as long as A is invertible (Exercise 6.1).

where $w_i = 1$ for each i, we suppress the superscript w. Thus, $\|x\|_\infty = \max_i |x_i|$. The unit ball with respect to the norm $\|\cdot\|_\infty^w$, that is, the set of all x such that $\|x\|_\infty^w \le 1$ is actually a box rather than a sphere, as illustrated in Fig. 2.6.1.

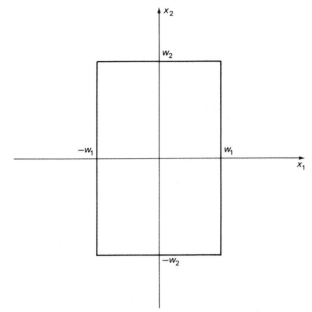

Figure 2.6.1   The unit ball $\left\{x \mid \|x\|_\infty^w \le 1\right\} = \left\{x \mid |x| \le w\right\}$ in the two–dimensional case.

The vector norm $\|\cdot\|_\infty^w$ induces a matrix norm, also denoted by $\|\cdot\|_\infty^w$, defined by

$$\|A\|_\infty^w = \max_{x \ne 0} \frac{\|Ax\|_\infty^w}{\|x\|_\infty^w},$$

where A is an $n \times n$ matrix. An alternative but equivalent definition of this norm is

$$\|A\|_\infty^w = \max_i \frac{1}{w_i} \sum_{j=1}^n |a_{ij}| w_j, \tag{6.6}$$

where a_{ij} are the entries of A [Prop. A.13(a) in Appendix A].

The following proposition lists a few useful facts. See Fig. 2.6.2 for an illustration of parts (b) and (d).

Proposition 6.2.   Let M and N be $n \times n$ matrices and let $w \in \Re^n$ be a positive vector.

(a) The matrix M is nonnegative ($M \ge 0$) if and only if it maps nonnegative vectors into nonnegative vectors.

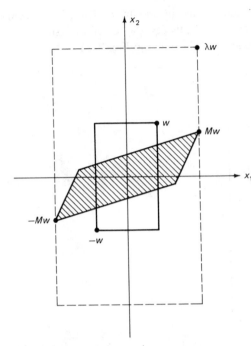

Figure 2.6.2 Illustration of the norm of a matrix $M \geq 0$. The shaded region is the image, under the mapping M, of the unit ball with respect to $\| \cdot \|_\infty^w$, that is, the set $\{Mx \mid \|x\|_\infty^w \leq 1\}$. The scalar λ is the smallest number such that $Mw \leq \lambda w$. In view of Prop. 6.2(d), we have $\lambda = \|M\|_\infty^w$.

(b) If $M \geq 0$, then $\|M\|_\infty^w = \|Mw\|_\infty^w$.

(c) We have $\| \, |M| \, \|_\infty^w = \|M\|_\infty^w$.

(d) Let $M \geq 0$. Then, for any scalar $\lambda > 0$, we have $\|M\|_\infty^w \leq \lambda$ if and only if $Mw \leq \lambda w$.

(e) We have $\rho(M) \leq \|M\|_\infty^w$.

(f) If $M \geq N \geq 0$, then $\|M\|_\infty^w \geq \|N\|_\infty^w$.

Proof.

(a) If $M \geq 0$ and $x \geq 0$, then it is obvious that $Mx \geq 0$. For the converse, suppose that the ijth entry of M is negative. Let x be the jth unit vector. Then the ith entry of Mx is negative.

(b) Using Eq. (6.6), we have

$$\|M\|_\infty^w = \max_i \frac{1}{w_i} \sum_{j=1}^n m_{ij} w_j = \max_i \frac{1}{w_i} [Mw]_i = \|Mw\|_\infty^w.$$

(c) This is an immediate consequence of Eq. (6.6).

(d) Using part (b), we have $\|M\|_\infty^w \leq \lambda$ if and only if $\|Mw\|_\infty^w \leq \lambda$, which is equivalent to $Mw \leq \lambda w$.

(e) This follows from the inequality $\rho(M) \leq \|M\|$, which holds for every induced norm $\| \cdot \|$ (Prop. A.20 in Appendix A).

(f) This is an immediate consequence of Eq. (6.6).   **Q.E.D.**

Showing that $\|M\|_\infty^w < 1$ is a simple method for proving that $\rho(M) < 1$, as long as the weighting vector w can be suitably chosen. However, this method is not universally applicable. In particular, there exist matrices M such that $\rho(M) < 1$, but for which there exists no $w > 0$ such that $\|M\|_\infty^w < 1$ (Exercise 6.2). Still, for nonnegative matrices, the property $\rho(M) < 1$ is equivalent to the existence of a positive vector w for which $\|M\|_\infty^w < 1$. This is a consequence of the Perron–Frobenius theorem, the most important result in the theory of nonnegative matrices, which will be presented and proved after a few definitions.

Given an $n \times n$ matrix M, with $n \geq 2$, we form a directed graph $G = (N, A)$, with nodes $N = \{1, \ldots, n\}$ and arcs $A = \{(i, j) \mid i \neq j \text{ and } m_{ij} \neq 0\}$, where m_{ij} is the ijth entry of M.

Definition 6.1.   An $n \times n$ matrix M, with $n \geq 2$, is called *irreducible* if for every $i, j \in N$ there exists a positive path in the above constructed graph G (i.e., a path with all arcs oriented as in the graph G) from i to j. For the case $n = 1$, M is called irreducible if its only element is nonzero.

An alternative and often useful characterization of irreducibility is the following:

Proposition 6.3.   An $n \times n$ matrix $M \geq 0$, with $n \geq 2$, is irreducible if and only if $(I + M)^{n-1} > 0$.

Proof. By using the definition of matrix multiplication, it is easy to check that for $i \neq j$, the ijth entry of $(I + M)^{n-1}$ is equal to the sum of positive multiples of all products of the form $\prod_{k=1}^{K-1} m_{i_k i_{k+1}}$, where $i_1 = i$, $i_K = j$, and $K \leq n$. Since $M \geq 0$, this sum is positive if and only if one of the summands is positive, which is the case if and only if there exists a positive path from i to j in the graph G associated with M. When $i = j$, the corresponding entry of $(I + M)^{n-1}$ is at least unity.   **Q.E.D.**

Proposition 6.4.   If an $n \times n$ matrix $M \geq 0$ is irreducible and if some nonnegative vector $x \geq 0$ satisfies $Mx = 0$, then $x = 0$.

Proof. The case $n = 1$ is trivial and we assume that $n \geq 2$. If all the entries of the jth column of M are equal to zero, then there is no path from any $i \neq j$ to j in the graph associated with M and therefore M is not irreducible. We conclude that every column of M has a nonzero entry and there exists a positive number a such that $\sum_{i=1}^n m_{ij} \geq a$ for each j. Suppose that $x \geq 0$ and $Mx = 0$. Then,

$$0 = \sum_{i=1}^{n}[Mx]_i = \sum_{i=1}^{n}\sum_{j=1}^{n}m_{ij}x_j = \sum_{j=1}^{n}x_j\sum_{i=1}^{n}m_{ij} \geq a\sum_{j=1}^{n}x_j.$$

Since $a > 0$, we conclude that $\sum_{j=1}^{n}x_j \leq 0$, and since $x \geq 0$, we obtain $x = 0$.
Q.E.D.

We now state and prove a few variants of the Perron–Frobenius theorem. The proof presented here uses the Brouwer Fixed Point Theorem [GuP74], whose proof is beyond the scope of this book. A longer proof that proceeds from first principles is outlined in Exercise 6.3.

Consider the unit simplex

$$S = \left\{x \in \Re^n \;\middle|\; x \geq 0 \text{ and } \sum_{i=1}^{n}x_i = 1\right\}.$$

Proposition 6.5.   (*Brouwer Fixed Point Theorem*) If $f : S \mapsto S$ is a continuous function, then there exists some $w \in S$ such that $f(w) = w$.

Proposition 6.6.   (*Perron–Frobenius Theorem*) Let M be an $n \times n$ nonnegative matrix.

(a) If M is irreducible, then $\rho(M)$ is an eigenvalue of M and there exists some $w > 0$ such that $Mw = \rho(M)w$. Furthermore, such a w is unique within a scalar multiple; that is, if some v also satisfies $Mv = \rho(M)v$, then $v = \alpha w$ for some scalar α. Finally, $\|M\|_\infty^w = \rho(M)$.

(b) $\rho(M)$ is an eigenvalue of M and there exists some $w \geq 0$, $w \neq 0$, such that $Mw = \rho(M)w$.

(c) For every $\epsilon > 0$, there exists some $w > 0$ such that $\rho(M) \leq \|M\|_\infty^w \leq \rho(M) + \epsilon$.

Proof. The case $n = 1$ is trivial and it will be assumed that $n \geq 2$.

(a) Let $M \geq 0$ be irreducible. We define a function $f : S \mapsto S$ with components

$$f_i(x) = \frac{[Mx]_i}{\sum_{j=1}^{n}[Mx]_j}, \qquad i = 1, \ldots, n.$$

Suppose that the denominator in the definition of f is equal to zero for some $x \in S$. Since $M \geq 0$ and $x \geq 0$, we conclude that $Mx = 0$. Then, Prop. 6.4 implies that $x = 0$, which contradicts the assumption $x \in S$. We conclude that the denominator is always nonzero and, therefore, f is well-defined and continuous on S. By Prop. 6.5, there exists some $w \in S$ such that $f(w) = w$. Let $\lambda = \sum_{i=1}^{n}[Mw]_i$. We have $\lambda > 0$ because otherwise $Mw = 0$, which would imply that $w = 0$. The equality $f(w) = w$ can be rewritten as $Mw = \lambda w$. In particular, λ is an eigenvalue of

M. We now have $(I + M)w = (1 + \lambda)w$ and $(I + M)^{n-1}w = (1 + \lambda)^{n-1}w$. By Prop. 6.3, $(I + M)^{n-1} > 0$, and since $w \geq 0$, $w \neq 0$, it is easily seen that $(I + M)^{n-1}w > 0$. This implies that $w > 0$.

We now show that $\lambda = \rho(M)$. Since λ is an eigenvalue of M, we obtain $\lambda \leq \rho(M)$. On the other hand, using the obvious fact $\|w\|_\infty^w = 1$ and Prop. 6.2(b), we obtain

$$\lambda = \|\lambda w\|_\infty^w = \|Mw\|_\infty^w = \|M\|_\infty^w \geq \rho(M),$$

where the last inequality is Prop. 6.2(e). The equality $\lambda = \rho(M)$ follows.

We now prove uniqueness of w. Suppose that a vector v satisfies $Mv = \rho(M)v$. If $v = 0$, then $v = \alpha w$, with $\alpha = 0$, and we are done. We now assume that $v \neq 0$ and we define $z = v/\|v\|_\infty^w$. Notice that $w \geq |z|$ and that $w_i = |z_i|$ for some i. By possibly replacing z by $-z$, we may and will assume that $w_i = z_i$ for some i. Either $z = w$, in which case v is a scalar multiple of w, or $z \neq w$, in which case we will obtain a contradiction. We have $M(w - z) = \rho(M)(w - z)$. Since M is irreducible, $(I + M)^{n-1} > 0$, and since $w - z \geq w - |z| \geq 0$ and $w \neq z$, we obtain $(I + M)^{n-1}(w - z) > 0$. On the other hand, $(I + M)^{n-1}(w - z) = \left(1 + \rho(M)\right)^{n-1}(w - z)$, whose ith component is equal to zero, by construction. This is a contradiction and proves the desired result.

(b) Let N_δ be an $n \times n$ matrix with all entries equal to δ, where δ is a positive scalar. Since $M + N_\delta$ is positive, it is irreducible and part (a) of the proposition applies. Thus, for each $\delta > 0$, there exists some $w_\delta > 0$ such that

$$(M + N_\delta)w_\delta = \rho(M + N_\delta)w_\delta. \tag{6.7}$$

Without any loss of generality, let us assume that each w_δ has been scaled so that its largest component is equal to 1. Then the set $\{w_\delta \mid \delta > 0\}$ is bounded. Since every bounded sequence in $\Re^n$ has a convergent subsequence (Prop. A.5 in Appendix A), it follows that there exists some vector w_0 and a sequence $\{\delta_k\}$ such that $\lim_{k \to \infty} \delta_k = 0$ and $\lim_{k \to \infty} w_{\delta_k} = w_0$. Since w_0 is the limit of positive vectors, it has to be nonnegative. By construction, $\|w_{\delta_k}\|_\infty = 1$ for each k, and since w_{δ_k} converges to w_0, it follows that $\|w_0\|_\infty = 1$; in particular, $w_0 \neq 0$.

We now take the limit of both sides of Eq. (6.7), as δ tends to zero along the sequence $\{\delta_k\}$. We see that Mw_{δ_k} converges to Mw_0; also $\|N_{\delta_k}w_{\delta_k}\|_\infty \leq n\delta_k\|w_{\delta_k}\|_\infty = n\delta_k$, which converges to zero. Thus, the left–hand side of Eq. (6.7) converges to Mw_0. We now use the fact that the spectral radius is a continuous function (Prop. A.19 in Appendix A) to conclude that $\rho(M + N_{\delta_k})$ converges to $\rho(M)$. Thus, the limit of the right–hand side of Eq. (6.7) is equal to $\rho(M)w_0$. This implies that $Mw_0 = \rho(M)w_0$ and proves part (b).

(c) The first inequality holds for every $w > 0$, by Prop. 6.2(e). Let $\delta > 0$ be small enough so that $\rho(M + N_\delta) \leq \rho(M) + \epsilon$, which is possible because of the continuity of the spectral radius. Let $w_\delta > 0$ be as in part (b). Then, using parts (f) and (b) of Prop. 6.2,

$$\|M\|_\infty^{w_\delta} \le \|M + N_\delta\|_\infty^{w_\delta} = \|(M + N_\delta)w_\delta\|_\infty^{w_\delta}$$
$$= \rho(M + N_\delta)\|w_\delta\|_\infty^{w_\delta} = \rho(M + N_\delta) \le \rho(M) + \epsilon.$$

Q.E.D.

Proposition 6.6(c) is illustrated by the following example. Let

$$M = \begin{bmatrix} 0 & 0 \\ 1 & 1 \end{bmatrix}.$$

The graph associated with this matrix is shown in Fig. 2.6.3 and we see that M is not irreducible. The characteristic polynomial of M is $\lambda(\lambda - 1)$ from which it follows that $\rho(M) = 1$. On the other hand, for any vector $w > 0$, we have $\|M\|_\infty^w = (w_1 + w_2)/w_2 > 1$. Thus, there does not exist any $w > 0$ such that $\|M\|_\infty^w = \rho(M)$. However, by taking w_1 arbitrarily small, $\|M\|_\infty^w$ comes arbitrarily close to $\rho(M)$, as predicted by Prop. 6.6(c).

Figure 2.6.3   The graph associated with the matrix

$$M = \begin{bmatrix} 0 & 0 \\ 1 & 1 \end{bmatrix}$$

which is not irreducible.

We now present a few useful consequences of the Perron-Frobenius theorem.

Corollary 6.1.   If M is a square nonnegative matrix then the following are equivalent:

   (i) $\rho(M) < 1$.
  (ii) There exists some $w > 0$ such that $\|M\|_\infty^w < 1$.
 (iii) There exist some $\lambda < 1$ and $w > 0$ such that $Mw \le \lambda w$.

Proof. Assume that (i) holds. Let $\epsilon > 0$ be small enough so that $\rho(M) + \epsilon < 1$. By using Prop. 6.6(c), there exists some $w > 0$ such that $\|M\|_\infty^w \le \rho(M) + \epsilon < 1$, which proves (ii). If (ii) holds, then, using the definition of $\|\cdot\|_\infty^w$, we obtain $Mw < w$, which proves (iii). Finally, if (iii) holds, then $\|M\|_\infty^w \le \lambda < 1$ and using Prop. 6.2(e), we obtain $\rho(M) < 1$, which proves (i) and concludes the proof.   **Q.E.D.**

Corollary 6.2.   Given any square matrix M, there exists some $w > 0$ such that $\|M\|_\infty^w < 1$ if and only if $\rho(|M|) < 1$.

Proof. By Prop. 6.2(c), we have $\|M\|_\infty^w = \big\| |M| \big\|_\infty^w$. The result follows from the equivalence of parts (i) and (ii) of Cor. 6.1 applied to the matrix $|M|$.   **Q.E.D.**

Corollary 6.3.   For any square matrix M, $\rho(M) \leq \rho(|M|)$.

Proof. By Prop. 6.6(c), for any $\epsilon > 0$, there exists some $w > 0$ such that

$$\rho(M) \leq \|M\|_\infty^w = \big\|\,|M|\,\big\|_\infty^w \leq \rho(|M|) + \epsilon.$$

Since ϵ was arbitrary, we can take the limit as ϵ decreases to zero to obtain the desired result.   **Q.E.D.**

2.6.2 Convergence Analysis Using Maximum Norms

We now use the Perron–Frobenius theorem and its corollaries to obtain sufficient conditions for convergence of iterative algorithms, and also to make a comparison between the Jacobi and the Gauss–Seidel methods.

Definition 6.2.   A square matrix A with entries a_{ij} is (row) *diagonally dominant* if

$$\sum_{j \neq i} |a_{ij}| < |a_{ii}|, \qquad \forall i.$$

Let A be a square row diagonally dominant matrix, and consider the iteration matrix M associated with the Jacobi algorithm for solving the equation $Ax = b$. Then, $|m_{ij}| = |a_{ij}|/|a_{ii}|$ for $j \neq i$, and $|m_{ii}| = 0$ [cf. Eq. (6.1)]. The assumption of diagonal dominance translates to the condition $\sum_{j=1}^n |m_{ij}| < 1$ for all i. Equivalently, $\|M\|_\infty < 1$ from which we conclude that $\rho(M) < 1$. We have thus proved the following.

Proposition 6.7.   If A is row diagonally dominant, then the Jacobi method for solving $Ax = b$ converges.

We continue with a general comparison of methods of the Jacobi and of the Gauss–Seidel type. Let us fix an $n \times n$ matrix M associated to an iteration $x := Mx + b$, where b is some fixed vector. Let $\hat{M}$ be the corresponding Gauss–Seidel iteration matrix, that is, the iteration matrix obtained if the components in the original iteration are updated one at a time. In particular, the matrix $\hat{M}$ satisfies

$$[\hat{M}x]_i = \sum_{j<i} m_{ij}[\hat{M}x]_j + \sum_{j\geq i} m_{ij}x_j, \qquad (6.8)$$

for every $x \in \Re^n$.

Proposition 6.8.   Suppose that $\rho(|M|) < 1$. Then, $\rho(\hat{M}) \leq \rho(|M|)$. (In particular, if $M \geq 0$ and the Jacobi–type iteration $x := Mx + b$ converges, then the corresponding Gauss–Seidel iteration also converges.)

Proof. Let us assume that $\rho(|M|) < 1$ and let us fix some $\epsilon > 0$ such that $\lambda = \rho(|M|) + \epsilon < 1$. Proposition 6.6(c) shows that there exists some $w > 0$ such that

$$\left\| \, |M|w \, \right\|_\infty^w = \left\| \, |M| \, \right\|_\infty^w \le \rho(|M|) + \epsilon = \lambda.$$

Therefore, $|M|w \le \lambda w$. Equivalently, for all i,

$$\sum_{j=1}^n |m_{ij}|w_j \le \lambda w_i.$$

Consider now some x such that $\|x\|_\infty^w = 1$ and let $y = \hat{M}x$. We will prove, by induction on i, that $|y_i| \le \lambda w_i$. Indeed, assuming that $|y_j| \le \lambda w_j$ for $j < i$, we obtain, from Eq. (6.8),

$$|y_i| \le \sum_{j<i} |m_{ij}| \cdot |y_j| + \sum_{j\ge i} |m_{ij}|w_j \le \sum_{j<i} |m_{ij}|w_j + \sum_{j\ge i} |m_{ij}|w_j \le \lambda w_i.$$

We conclude that $|\hat{M}x| \le \lambda w$ for every x satisfying $\|x\|_\infty^w = 1$. This implies that $\|\hat{M}\|_\infty^w \le \lambda$. Therefore, $\rho(\hat{M}) \le \lambda = \rho(|M|) + \epsilon$. Since this is true for every $\epsilon > 0$, the result follows.   **Q.E.D.**

We now focus on the solution of a system of equations $Ax = b$, where the entries of the A matrix satisfy $a_{ij} \le 0$ for all $i \ne j$, and $a_{ii} > 0$ for all i. The iteration matrix M_J associated with the Jacobi algorithm for solving such a system [cf. Eq. (4.4)] is given by $[M_J]_{ii} = 0$ and $[M_J]_{ij} = -a_{ij}/a_{ii}$ for $j \ne i$, and it follows that $M_J \ge 0$. Let M_{GS} be the iteration matrix for the Gauss–Seidel algorithm of Eq. (4.5). It is easily seen that $M_{GS} \ge 0$.

Proposition 6.9.   (*Stein–Rosenberg Theorem*) Under the above assumption on A, the following are true:

(a) If $\rho(M_J) < 1$, then $\rho(M_{GS}) \le \rho(M_J)$.

(b) If $\rho(M_J) \ge 1$, then $\rho(M_{GS}) \ge \rho(M_J)$.

Proof. Part (a) is simply a restatement of Prop. 6.8, because we have $|M_J| = M_J$. For part (b), start with some $w \ne 0$ such that $w \ge 0$ and $M_J w = \rho(M_J)w$, which exists because of Prop. 6.6(b). Let $y = M_{GS}w$. Proceeding as in the proof of Prop. 6.8, with the inequalities reversed, we obtain $y_i \ge \rho(M_J)w_i$ for each i. Therefore, $M_{GS}w = y \ge \rho(M_J)w$. Let $N = M_{GS}/\rho(M_J)$. Then, $Nw \ge w$ and $N^t w \ge w$, for all t. Since $w \ne 0$, it follows that N^t does not converge to zero, as t tends to infinity, and using Prop. A.21 in Appendix A, we have $\rho(N) \ge 1$. Thus, $\rho(M_{GS}) = \rho(M_J)\rho(N) \ge \rho(M_J)$, which concludes the proof.   **Q.E.D.**

Propositions 6.8 and 6.9 are useful because the iteration matrix M_J corresponding to the Jacobi method may be simpler to analyze when compared to the iteration matrix M_{GS} of the Gauss–Seidel method. Proposition 6.8 shows that, for the special case of nonnegative iteration matrices, if a Jacobi–type algorithm converges, then the corresponding Gauss–Seidel algorithm also converges, and its convergence rate is no worse than that of the Jacobi algorithm. This provides a justification for algorithms of the Gauss–Seidel type, that is, algorithms in which more recent data are used whenever available. Furthermore, notice that the proofs of Props. 6.8 and 6.9 remain valid when different updating orders of the components are considered. The implication is that iterative algorithms involving positive iteration matrices possess some intrinsic robustness with respect to the order of updates. This turns out to be a key element in the context of asynchronous algorithms, as will be seen in Chapter 6.

2.6.3 Convergence Analysis Using a Quadratic Cost Function

Quadratic cost functions are particularly useful in dealing with systems of equations $Ax = b$, where A is a symmetric positive definite matrix, which we are going to assume in this subsection (see Appendix A for a definition and properties of positive definite and symmetric matrices). Let us also recall that positive definite matrices are always invertible, so that the equation $Ax = b$ is guaranteed to have a unique solution. We will measure the progress of an algorithm by introducing the cost function $F(x) = \frac{1}{2}x'Ax - x'b$. Since A is positive definite, F is a strictly convex function [Prop. A.40(d) in Appendix A], and a vector x^* minimizes F if and only if $\nabla F(x^*) = 0$. We notice that $\nabla F(x) = Ax - b$, which shows that x^* is the solution of $Ax = b$ if and only if x^* minimizes F. (In particular, F has a unique minimum.)

We now interpret the Gauss–Seidel method in terms of the cost function F. Suppose that at some stage of the algorithm, we have a current vector x, and it is the turn of the ith component of x to be updated. Let $\bar{x}$ be the vector obtained after the update. Using the definition of the Gauss–Seidel method, we see that $\bar{x}$ is chosen so that the ith equation in the system $Ax = b$ is satisfied. Since the equations $Ax = b$ and $\nabla F(x) = 0$ are equivalent, it follows that $\bar{x}$ is chosen so that $\nabla_i F(\bar{x}) = 0$. Thus, the vector $\bar{x}$ is defined by the properties that all components except for the ith one are fixed and the ith component is chosen so as to satisfy $\nabla_i F(\bar{x}) = 0$. But this is equivalent to choosing $\bar{x}$ so as to minimize $F(y)$ over all y differing from x only along the ith coordinate. There are two distinct cases to be considered: either at the current point x we have $\nabla_i F(x) \neq 0$, in which case the update has nonzero size and $F(\bar{x}) < F(x)$; or $\nabla_i F(x) = 0$, x is not changed, and the value of F remains the same. In the latter case, one of two things will happen. Either a component j will be eventually found such that $\nabla_j F(x) \neq 0$ and a cost decrease will result; or $\nabla_j F(x) = 0$ for all j, in which case we are at a point at which $\nabla F(x) = 0$, that is, at a solution of $Ax = b$. To summarize, the Gauss–Seidel method proceeds by minimizing $F(x)$ successively along each coordinate, as illustrated in Fig. 2.6.4. By using this fact, it is not hard to show that $F(x)$ converges to the minimum of F (see Fig. 2.6.5). Accordingly, the vector x converges to the solution of $Ax = b$.

Let us now turn to the SOR method. As long as γ is positive, the direction of each update is the same as for the update that would be made by the Gauss–Seidel algorithm (starting from the same point), and the magnitude of the update is scaled by a factor of

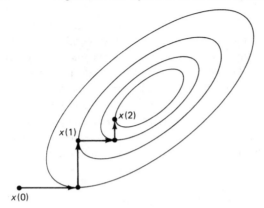

Figure 2.6.4 For a positive definite matrix A, the Gauss–Seidel method can be viewed as a coordinate descent method for minimizing the function $F(x) = \frac{1}{2}x'Ax - x'b$. The curves in this figure correspond to the level sets of F, that is, sets of points on which F is constant.

γ. It is then natural to look for the range of values of γ for which the cost does not increase. Since $F(x)$ is a quadratic function of x_i, the other coordinates being fixed, and since quadratic functions are symmetric around their minimizing point, it follows that (whenever the vector x is changed) we have a cost decrease if and only if $0 < \gamma < 2$. This discussion motivates the following result.

Proposition 6.10. Let A be symmetric and positive definite, and let x^* be the solution of $Ax = b$.

(a) If $\gamma \in (0, 2)$, then the sequence $\{x(t)\}$ generated by the SOR algorithm converges to x^*.

(b) If $\gamma \notin (0, 2)$, then for every choice of $x(0)$ different than x^*, the sequence generated by the SOR algorithm does not converge to x^*.

The proof of Prop. 6.10 consists of filling the gaps in the argument we provided above and is left as an exercise. Actually, part (a) of the proposition is a special case of Prop. 2.2 of Section 3.2, which covers the case of a general (not necessarily quadratic) cost function F.

Recall that the JOR method is the same as SOR except that all components are updated simultaneously. Since each component is updated by SOR in a direction that does not increase the cost, the same should be true for JOR, as long as $\gamma > 0$ is sufficiently small. Finally, Richardson's method is the same as JOR except that each component's update is not scaled by the factor $1/a_{ii}$. Thus, again each component is updated in a direction that does not increase the cost. This discussion motivates the following result. Its proof is omitted because it is a special case of the more general Prop. 2.1 of Section 3.2. However, the interested reader should have no difficulty in providing a proof.

Proposition 6.11. If A is symmetric and positive definite and if $\gamma > 0$ is sufficiently small, then the JOR and Richardson's algorithms converge to the solution of $Ax = b$.

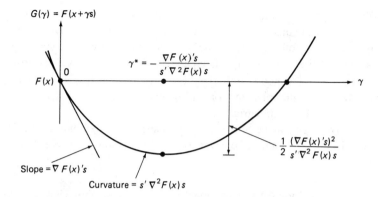

Figure 2.6.5 Illustration of cost reduction along a descent direction. Let A be a symmetric positive definite square matrix and consider a function F, given by $F(x) = \frac{1}{2}x'Ax$, along a direction s starting from the vector x. The function $G(\gamma) = F(x + \gamma s) = \frac{1}{2}(x + \gamma s)'A(x + \gamma s)$ of the stepsize is quadratic and is minimized at

$$\gamma^* = -\frac{\nabla F(x)'s}{s'\nabla^2 F(x)s} = -\frac{x'As}{s'As}.$$

The corresponding reduction is

$$F(x) - \min_{\gamma} F(x + \gamma s) = \frac{1}{2}\frac{\left(\nabla F(x)'s\right)^2}{s'\nabla^2 F(x)s}.$$

By using this figure, it can be shown that if $s^1, \ldots, s^n$ is a set of linearly independent directions and F is minimized at each iteration along one of these directions, and each of these directions is used infinitely often, then convergence to the unique minimizing vector of F is guaranteed. (The sequence $\{x(t)\}$ belongs to the bounded set $\{x \mid F(x) \leq F(x(0))\}$ and therefore has at least one limit point. The sequence of cost reductions must tend to zero, implying that the sequence of stepsizes tends to zero. Thus, every limit point x^* of the sequence $\{x(t)\}$ satisfies $\nabla F(x^*)'s^i = 0$ for $i = 1, \ldots, n$. Since $s^1, \ldots, s^n$ are linearly independent, we have $\nabla F(x^*) = 0$ and, therefore, $x^* = 0$.) If the direction vectors $s^1, \ldots, s^n$, are the unit vectors in $\Re^n$, we recover the Gauss–Seidel algorithm.

2.6.4 The Poisson Equation Revisited

We consider the system of equations

$$f_{i,j} = \frac{1}{4}\left(f_{i+1,j} + f_{i-1,j} + f_{i,j+1} + f_{i,j-1}\right) - \frac{1}{4N^2}g_{i,j}, \qquad 0 < i, j < N. \qquad (6.9)$$

obtained from the discretization of the Poisson equation on a square [cf. Eq. (5.2)]. We have one such equation for each variable $f_{i,j}$ corresponding to an interior grid point. These equations can be represented in the matrix form $Ax = b$ as follows. With every integer k such that $1 \leq k \leq (N-1)^2$, we associate a different interior grid point (i_k, j_k).

We arrange the unknowns $f_{i,j}$ in order of increasing k to form a vector f of unknowns. Then, the kth equation of the system $Ax = b$ is given by Eq. (6.9), with (i, j) replaced by (i_k, j_k). It follows that the matrix A has the following structure: (i) $a_{kk} = 1$ for each k, and (ii) if $k \neq \ell$, then $a_{k\ell}$ is equal to either $-\frac{1}{4}$ or it is equal to zero; in particular, it is equal to $-\frac{1}{4}$ if and only if $|i_k - i_\ell| + |j_k - j_\ell| = 1$, that is, if and only if (i_k, j_k) and (i_ℓ, j_ℓ) are neighboring interior grid points. It is clear that $a_{k\ell} = a_{\ell k}$ for every k, ℓ, and the matrix A is symmetric.

The eigenvalues of the iteration matrix corresponding to the Jacobi algorithm can be calculated explicitly; however, we prefer to show convergence using a quadratic cost function.

Proposition 6.12.   The matrix A constructed above is symmetric positive definite.

Proof. Symmetry has been already established. Using the discussion preceding the statement of the proposition, $f'Af$ is given by the following expression:

$$\sum_{i,j} \left[f_{i,j} \left(f_{i,j} - \frac{1}{4} \sum_{k,\ell} f_{k,\ell} \right) \right], \tag{6.10}$$

where the first summation is over all interior grid points and the second summation is over all (k, ℓ) that correspond to interior grid points neighboring with (i, j). By rearranging the terms in the expression (6.10), we can rewrite it as

$$\frac{1}{4} \sum_{(i,j),(k,\ell)} \left(f_{i,j}^2 + f_{k,\ell}^2 - 2f_{i,j}f_{k,\ell} \right) + \frac{1}{4} \sum_{(i,j)} f_{i,j}^2 \chi_{i,j}, \tag{6.11}$$

where the summation is over all pairs $\big((i, j), (k, \ell)\big)$ of neighboring interior grid points, and $\chi_{i,j}$ is the number of boundary points neighboring with (i, j). Using the fact $a^2 + b^2 - 2ab = (a - b)^2 \geq 0$, it follows that $f'Af \geq 0$ and therefore A is nonnegative definite. To prove positive definiteness, we assume that $f'Af = 0$, or, equivalently, that the expression (6.11) is equal to zero, and we will show that $f = 0$. If the expression (6.11) is equal to zero, it follows that $f_{i,j} = 0$ for all points (i, j) neighboring with the boundary, and $f_{i,j} = f_{k,\ell}$ for all pairs $\big((i, j), (k, \ell)\big)$ of neighboring points. This implies that $f_{i,j} = 0$ for every (i, j).   **Q.E.D.**

Since A is positive definite, the Gauss–Seidel algorithm converges by virtue of Prop. 6.10. We now notice that the diagonal elements of A are positive and the off-diagonal elements are less than or equal to zero. Consequently, Prop. 6.9 applies and shows that the Jacobi algorithm also converges. We have thus proved the following.

Proposition 6.13.   The Jacobi and Gauss–Seidel algorithms for solving the system (6.9) converge and the Gauss–Seidel algorithm converges faster, in the sense of Prop. 6.9.

Proposition 6.13 is one of the reasons for our interest in the parallel implementation of the Gauss–Seidel algorithm. In fact, in the present context, the equally efficiently parallelizable SOR algorithm is known to converge substantially faster than the Gauss–Seidel algorithm, when the relaxation parameter is suitably chosen ([Var62] and [HaY81]). The above discussion also extends to the numerical solution of more general classes of elliptic partial differential equations.

EXERCISES

6.1. Assuming that a square matrix A is invertible and has a nonzero diagonal, show that $I - M$ is invertible, where M is the iteration matrix defined by Eq. (6.5), corresponding to any one of the algorithms introduced in Section 2.4.

6.2. Find an example of a symmetric matrix M with no zero entries and such that $\rho(M) < 1$, but $\|M\|_\infty^w \geq 1$ for every positive vector w. *Hint:* The smallest possible example is of size 3×3.

6.3. This exercise leads to a proof of the Perron–Frobenius theorem (Prop. 6.6) that does not involve the Brouwer Fixed Point Theorem. Let M be an $n \times n$ irreducible nonnegative matrix. Our objective is to show that M has a positive eigenvector w.

Let $X = \{x \in \Re^n \mid x \geq 0, \ x \neq 0\}$. For every $x \in X$, let $r(x) = \sup\{\rho \mid Mx \geq \rho x\}$. Let $S = \{x \in X \mid \sum_{i=1}^n x_i = 1\}$. Let $\lambda = \sup\{r(x) \mid x \in X\}$.

 (a) Show that $\lambda > 0$. *Hint:* Let e be the vector in $\Re^n$ with all coordinates equal to 1; use the irreducibility of M to show that $Me > 0$ and conclude that $r(e) > 0$.

 (b) Show that $\lambda = \sup\{r(x) \mid x \in S\}$. *Hint:* Any vector in X can be scaled so that it belongs to S.

 (c) Let $Q = \{(I + M)^{n-1}x \mid x \in S\}$. Show that all elements of Q are positive vectors.

 (d) Show that $\lambda = \sup\{r(x) \mid x \in Q\}$. *Hint:* By definition, $\sup\{r(x) \mid x \in Q\} \leq \lambda$. For the reverse inequality, show that $r\big((I + M)^{n-1}x\big) \geq r(x)$ for $x \in S$, and use the result of (b).

 (e) Show that $r(\cdot)$ is a continuous function on Q. *Hint:* Show that

$$r(x) = \min_{1 \leq i \leq n} \left\{ \frac{1}{x_i} \sum_{j=1}^n m_{ij} x_j \right\}, \qquad x \in Q.$$

 (f) Show that there exists some $w \in Q$ such that $r(w) = \lambda$.

 (g) Let $z = Mw - \lambda w$. Show that $z = 0$, which proves that M has a positive eigenvector w. *Hint:* Use the definition of w to show that $z \geq 0$. If $z \neq 0$, then $(I+M)^{n-1}z > 0$, which shows that $M(I+M)^{n-1}w > \lambda(I+M)^{n-1}w$. Show that this contradicts the definition of λ.

6.4. Prove Prop. 6.10. *Hint:* For part (b) show that $F\big(x(t)\big) \geq F\big(x(0)\big)$ for all t.

6.5. Prove Prop. 6.11.

2.7 THE CONJUGATE GRADIENT METHOD

We consider a system $Ax = b$ of linear equations. It will be assumed throughout this section that A is an $n \times n$ symmetric and positive definite matrix. (If A is invertible but not symmetric, one may apply the methodology of this section to the system $A'Ax = A'b$.) Conjugate direction methods are motivated by a desire to accelerate the speed of convergence of the classical iterative methods for this particular class of problems. While they are guaranteed to find the solution after at most n iterations, they are best viewed as iterative methods, since usually fewer than n iterations are executed, particularly for large problems. These methods are in fact applicable to nonquadratic optimization problems as well. For such problems, they do not, in general, terminate after a finite number of iterations but still, when properly implemented, have attractive convergence and rate of convergence behavior.

For convenience, it will be assumed that $b = 0$. The modifications for the general case will be indicated later. The method is motivated in terms of the cost function

$$F(x) = \frac{1}{2}x'Ax.$$

This function is strictly convex, because of the positive definiteness of A [Prop. A.40(d) in Appendix A], and is minimized at $x = 0$, which is also the unique solution of the system $Ax = 0$.

An iteration of the method has the general form

$$x(t + 1) = x(t) + \gamma(t)s(t), \qquad t = 0, 1, \ldots, \tag{7.1}$$

where $s(t) \in \Re^n$ is a direction of update, and $\gamma(t)$ is a scalar stepsize defined by the line minimization

$$F\big(x(t) + \gamma(t)s(t)\big) = \min_{\gamma \in \Re} F\big(x(t) + \gamma s(t)\big). \tag{7.2}$$

The distinguishing feature of this method is the choice of the direction vectors $s(t)$; they are chosen so that they are mutually A–*conjugate*, that is, they have the property

$$s(t)'As(r) = 0, \qquad \text{if } t \neq r.$$

In what follows, we shall employ the notation

$$g(t) = Ax(t) = \nabla F\big(x(t)\big).$$

Some important consequences of conjugacy are the following.

Proposition 7.1. Suppose that $s(0), s(1), \ldots, s(t)$ are nonzero and mutually A–conjugate. Then:

(a) The vectors $s(0), s(1), \ldots, s(t)$ are linearly independent.

(b) We have

$$g(k+1)'s(i) = 0, \qquad \text{if } 0 \le i \le k \le t. \tag{7.3}$$

(c) For $k = 0, 1, \ldots, t+1$, the vector $x(k)$ minimizes F over the linear manifold

$$M_k = \left\{ x(0) + \alpha_0 s(0) + \cdots + \alpha_{k-1} s(k-1) \ \middle| \ \alpha_0, \ldots, \alpha_{k-1} \in \Re \right\}.$$

(d) The vectors $x(k)$ satisfy $F\big(x(k+1)\big) \le F\big(x(k)\big)$ for all $k \le t$.

Proof.

(a) Suppose the contrary. Then, there exists some $r \le t$ and some scalars $\alpha_0, \ldots, \alpha_{r-1}$ such that

$$s(r) = \sum_{i=0}^{r-1} \alpha_i s(i).$$

This implies that

$$s(r)'As(r) = \sum_{i=0}^{r-1} \alpha_i s(r)'As(i) = 0$$

which is impossible because $s(r) \ne 0$ and A is positive definite.

(b) By Eq. (7.2) and the chain rule, we have

$$0 = \frac{\partial}{\partial \gamma} F\big(x(k) + \gamma s(k)\big) \bigg|_{\gamma = \gamma(k)} = g(k+1)'s(k).$$

Thus, it only remains to prove Eq. (7.3) for $i < k$. We have for $i = 0, 1, \ldots, k-1$,

$$g(k+1)'s(i) = x(k+1)'As(i) = \left(x(i+1) + \sum_{j=i+1}^{k} \gamma(j)s(j) \right)' As(i)$$

$$= x(i+1)'As(i) = g(i+1)'s(i) = 0.$$

(c) It suffices to show that the partial derivatives

$$\frac{\partial F}{\partial \alpha_i}\big(x(0) + \alpha_0 s(0) + \cdots + \alpha_{k-1} s(k-1)\big),$$

evaluated at $\alpha_0 = \gamma(0), \ldots, \alpha_{k-1} = \gamma(k-1)$, are equal to zero for each $i \le k - 1$. This is equivalent to $g(k)'s(i) = 0$ for $i = 0, \ldots, k - 1$, which is true by part (b).

(d) Since $M_k \subset M_{k+1}$, the result follows from part (c).   **Q.E.D.**

2.7.1 Description of the Algorithm

We now describe the most important way of generating the conjugate directions $s(t)$. We start at some $x(0)$ and select $s(0) = -g(0) = -Ax(0)$. More generally, given the current vector $x(t)$, we evaluate the gradient $g(t) = Ax(t)$. If $g(t) = 0$, then $x(t) = 0$ and the algorithm terminates. Otherwise, a reasonable direction of update could be $s(t) = -g(t)$, which is a steepest descent direction [compare with Eq. (4.9) in Section 2.4; see also Section 3.2]. However, in general, this choice does not guarantee conjugacy. This suggests that we generate $s(t)$ according to the formula

$$s(t) = -g(t) + \sum_{i=0}^{t-1} c_i s(i), \tag{7.4}$$

where the coefficients c_i are chosen so that $s(t)$ is conjugate to $s(0), \ldots, s(t-1)$. Assuming that $s(0), \ldots, s(t-1)$ are already mutually conjugate, we need

$$0 = s(t)'As(j) = -g(t)'As(j) + \sum_{i=0}^{t-1} c_i s(i)'As(j) = -g(t)'As(j) + c_j s(j)'As(j),$$

$$j = 0, \ldots, t - 1,$$

which gives

$$c_j = \frac{g(t)'As(j)}{s(j)'As(j)}. \tag{7.5}$$

Notice that

$$g(j+1) - g(j) = A\big(x(j+1) - x(j)\big) = \gamma(j)As(j),$$

and Eq. (7.5) becomes

$$c_j = \frac{g(t)'\big(g(j+1) - g(j)\big)}{s(j)'\big(g(j+1) - g(j)\big)}. \tag{7.6}$$

(This step is legitimate provided that $\gamma(j) \ne 0$, and will be justified later.) Equation (7.4) shows that $g(j)$ is a linear combination of $s(0), \ldots, s(j)$, and, using Prop. 7.1(b), we obtain $g(t)'g(j) = 0$ for $j = 0, \ldots, t - 1$. We conclude that $c_j = 0$ if $j < t - 1$, and, from Eq. (7.4), the conjugate direction $s(t)$ is given as a linear combination of the gradient $g(t)$ and the previous conjugate direction $s(t-1)$, that is,

$$s(t) = -g(t) + \beta(t)s(t-1), \tag{7.7}$$

where

$$\beta(t) = \frac{g(t)'g(t)}{s(t-1)'\big(g(t) - g(t-1)\big)}. \tag{7.8}$$

An alternative expression for $\beta(t)$ is obtained by rewriting the denominator in Eq. (7.8) as

$$s(t-1)'\big(g(t) - g(t-1)\big) = \big(-g(t-1) + \beta(t-1)s(t-2)\big)'\big(g(t) - g(t-1)\big) = g(t-1)'g(t-1).$$

[In the last step, we have used Prop. 7.1(b), together with the fact that $g(t-1)$ is a linear combination of $s(0), \ldots, s(t-1)$.] This leads to

$$\beta(t) = \frac{g(t)'g(t)}{g(t-1)'g(t-1)}. \tag{7.9}$$

The next vector $x(t+1)$ is determined by $x(t+1) = x(t) + \gamma(t)s(t)$, where $\gamma(t)$ is defined by line minimization as in Eq. (7.2). A formula for $\gamma(t)$ is found by setting to zero the derivative (with respect to γ) of the function minimized in Eq. (7.2). Using the chain rule, we obtain

$$s(t)'A\big(x(t) + \gamma(t)s(t)\big) = 0,$$

which leads to

$$\gamma(t) = -\frac{s(t)'g(t)}{s(t)'As(t)}. \tag{7.10}$$

The conjugate direction method based on Eqs. (7.7), (7.9), and (7.10) is called the *conjugate gradient algorithm*. We will assume that the algorithm is terminated at the first time t such that $g(t) = 0$. We now show that the algorithm is well–defined, and, for this, we need to show that, until termination occurs, no division by zero is attempted in Eqs. (7.9) and (7.10). This is clearly true for Eq. (7.9). Concerning Eq. (7.10), since the matrix A is positive definite, the denominator will be equal to zero only if $s(t) = 0$. We therefore need to show that before termination [that is, if $g(0), \ldots, g(t)$ are nonzero], we have $s(t) \neq 0$. We proceed by induction. If $g(0) \neq 0$, then $s(0) \neq 0$. If $g(0), \ldots, g(t)$ are nonzero, we use the induction hypothesis that $s(t-1) \neq 0$ and we show that $s(t) \neq 0$. Indeed, if $s(t)$ were equal to zero, then $g(t)$ would be collinear with $s(t-1)$, because of Eq. (7.7). On the other hand, $g(t)$ is orthogonal to $s(t-1)$ [Prop. 7.1(b)] and, since $s(t-1) \neq 0$, we must have $g(t) = 0$, which is a contradiction.

We prove next that $\gamma(t)$ is nonzero unless the algorithm has terminated, which is needed to justify the step that led us from Eq. (7.5) to Eq. (7.6). In particular, we demonstrate that if $x(t) \neq 0$, then $\gamma(t) \neq 0$. For $t = 0$, we have $s(0) = -g(0)$. If

$x(0) \neq 0$ then $g(0) \neq 0$ and Eq. (7.10) shows that $\gamma(0) \neq 0$. Suppose now that $t \geq 1$, $x(t) \neq 0$, and $\gamma(t) = 0$. Equation (7.10) yields $s(t)'g(t) = 0$. We form the inner product of both sides of Eq. (7.7) with $g(t)$ to obtain

$$0 = s(t)'g(t) = -g(t)'g(t) + \beta(t)g(t)'s(t-1) = -g(t)'g(t),$$

where the last equality followed from Prop. 7.1(b). Thus, $g(t) = 0$, which contradicts our assumption that $x(t) \neq 0$.

We close this subsection by pointing out that Eqs. (7.7), (7.9), and (7.10) also define the conjugate gradient method for the case of a linear system $Ax = b$ when $b \neq 0$. The only difference is that $g(t)$ should be defined to be equal to $Ax(t) - b$. This can be demonstrated by repeating the previous arguments in terms of the cost function $F(x) = (1/2)(x - x^*)'A(x - x^*)$, where $x^* = A^{-1}b$.

2.7.2 Speed of Convergence

We now show that the conjugate gradient method terminates after at most n iterations, with $x(n) = 0$. Furthermore, the second part of the result to follow will lead us to interesting bounds on the speed of convergence when the number of iterations is smaller than n. For this purpose, it is convenient to introduce the linear manifold

$$H_k = \Big\{ x(0) + \alpha_1 A x(0) + \cdots + \alpha_k A^k x(0) \mid \alpha_1, \ldots, \alpha_k \in \Re \Big\}.$$

Proposition 7.2. For the conjugate gradient method, the following hold:

(a) The algorithm terminates after at most n steps; that is, there exists some $t \leq n$ such that $g(t) = 0$ and $x(t) = 0$.

(b) If $s(0), \ldots, s(t-1)$ are all nonzero, then $M_t = H_t$, where M_t is as in Prop. 7.1.

Proof.

(a) If the algorithm does not terminate after at most n steps, then $g(0), \ldots, g(n)$ are all nonzero, and, as shown earlier, the vectors $s(0), \ldots, s(n)$ are also nonzero and, therefore, linearly independent [Prop. 7.1(a)]. This is impossible since they belong to the n–dimensional vector space $\Re^n$. At termination we have $g(t) = 0$ and the equality $x(t) = 0$ follows because $g(t) = Ax(t)$ and A is nonsingular.

(b) Let $\bar{M}_t$ (respectively, $\bar{H}_t$) be the subspace of $\Re^n$ spanned by the collection of vectors $\{s(0), \ldots, s(t-1)\}$ [respectively, $\{Ax(0), \ldots, A^t x(0)\}$]. It is sufficient to show that $\bar{H}_t = \bar{M}_t$, and we proceed by induction. The result is true for $t = 1$ because $s(0) = -Ax(0)$. Suppose that $\bar{M}_{t-1} = \bar{H}_{t-1}$. Using Eq. (7.1), we see that $x(t-1) - x(0)$ is a linear combination of $s(0), \ldots, s(t-2)$ and therefore belongs to $\bar{M}_{t-1}$. Using the induction hypothesis, we obtain $x(t-1) - x(0) \in \bar{H}_{t-1}$. We then use the definition of $\bar{H}_t$ to see that $Ax(t-1) - Ax(0) \in \bar{H}_t$. Since $Ax(0) \in \bar{H}_t$, we conclude that $g(t-1) = -Ax(t-1) \in \bar{H}_t$. Furthermore, by the induction hypothesis, $s(t - 2) \in \bar{M}_{t-1} = \bar{H}_{t-1} \subset \bar{H}_t$. Equation (7.7) then implies that $s(t - 1) \in \bar{H}_t$. We conclude that $\bar{M}_t \subset \bar{H}_t$. It remains to show that $\bar{M}_t$ cannot be a proper subset of $\bar{H}_t$. This follows because the vectors $s(0), \ldots, s(t - 1)$ are linearly independent and the dimension of $\bar{M}_t$ is t, whereas the dimension of H_t cannot be more than t, since it is spanned by t vectors.   **Q.E.D.**

An important consequence of Props. 7.2(b) and 7.1(c) is that $x(t)$ minimizes $F(x)$ over the set H_t. By definition, H_t is the set of all vectors of the form $P(A)x(0)$, where P is a t–degree polynomial whose zero-th order term is equal to 1. Let $\mathcal{P}$ be the class of all such polynomials. We have

$$F\big(x(t)\big) \leq \frac{1}{2}x(0)' P(A)' AP(A)x(0), \qquad \forall P \in \mathcal{P}.$$

Let $A^{1/2}$ be a square root of A, as defined in Prop. A.27 in Appendix A. Since $A^{1/2}$ commutes with A, we obtain for every $P \in \mathcal{P}$,

$$F\big(x(t)\big) \leq \frac{1}{2}\Big(P(A)A^{1/2}x(0)\Big)'\Big(P(A)A^{1/2}x(0)\Big) = \frac{1}{2}\big\|P(A)A^{1/2}x(0)\big\|_2^2$$

$$\leq \frac{1}{2}\|P(A)\|_2^2 \cdot \|A^{1/2}x(0)\|_2^2 = \frac{1}{2}\|P(A)\|_2^2 \cdot \big(x(0)'Ax(0)\big) = \|P(A)\|_2^2 F\big(x(0)\big).$$

Let $\lambda_1, \ldots, \lambda_n$ be the eigenvalues of A. Then, the eigenvalues of $P(A)$ are equal to $P(\lambda_1), \ldots, P(\lambda_n)$ [this is proved similarly with Prop. A.17(d) in Appendix A]. Since A is symmetric, $P(A)$ is also symmetric and $\|P(A)\|_2$ is equal to the largest magnitude of the eigenvalues of $P(A)$ [Prop. A.24(a) in Appendix A]. We therefore conclude that

$$F\big(x(t)\big) \leq \max_{1 \leq i \leq n} \big(P(\lambda_i)\big)^2 F\big(x(0)\big), \qquad \forall P \in \mathcal{P}. \tag{7.11}$$

Inequality (7.11) provides an infinite class of bounds for $F\big(x(t)\big)$, parametrized by the polynomial $P(\cdot)$. If some prior knowledge on the location of the eigenvalues of A is available, interesting bounds are obtained by choosing the polynomial $P(\cdot)$ appropriately. As an example, assume that there exist some a and b, with $0 < a < b$, such that A has no eigenvalues smaller than a, and those eigenvalues that are larger than b take k distinct values. It can be shown (Exercise 7.1) that for every $x(0)$, the vector $x(k + 1)$ satisfies

$$F\big(x(k + 1)\big) \leq \left(\frac{b - a}{b + a}\right)^2 F\big(x(0)\big). \tag{7.12}$$

This shows that the method converges fast if most of the eigenvalues of A are clustered in a small interval and the remaining eigenvalues lie to the right of the interval. Another consequence is that if the eigenvalues of A take at most k distinct values, then the conjugate gradient method will find the minimum of F after at most k iterations. To see this, take the interval $[a, b]$ to be an arbitrarily small interval around the smallest eigenvalue of A.

2.7.3 Preconditioned Conjugate Gradient Method

This method is really the conjugate gradient method carried out in a new coordinate system. Let T be a symmetric invertible matrix and consider the system of equations $TATy = Tb$. If y solves the latter system, the vector $x = Ty$ vector solves the original system $Ax = b$. We will assume again that $b = 0$ and apply the conjugate gradient method to the system $TATy = 0$. [The same equations are valid even if $b \neq 0$, provided that $g(t)$ is defined to be equal to $Ax(t) - b$.] The method is described by [compare with Eqs. (7.1), (7.7), (7.9) and (7.10)]

$$y(t + 1) = y(t) + \gamma(t)\tilde{s}(t), \tag{7.13}$$

where $\tilde{s}(t)$ is generated by

$$\tilde{s}(0) = -TATy(0), \tag{7.14}$$

$$\tilde{s}(t) = -TATy(t) + \beta(t)\tilde{s}(t - 1), \qquad t = 1, 2, \ldots, \tag{7.15}$$

and where

$$\beta(t) = \frac{\left(TATy(t)\right)'\left(TATy(t)\right)}{\left(TATy(t - 1)\right)'\left(TATy(t - 1)\right)}, \tag{7.16}$$

$$\gamma(t) = -\frac{\tilde{s}(t)'TATy(t)}{\tilde{s}(t)'TAT\tilde{s}(t)}. \tag{7.17}$$

Setting $x(t) = Ty(t)$, $g(t) = Ax(t)$, $s(t) = T\tilde{s}(t)$ and, $H = T^2$, we obtain from Eqs. (7.13) to (7.17) the equivalent method

$$x(t + 1) = x(t) + \gamma(t)s(t),$$

$$s(0) = -Hg(0), \qquad s(t) = -Hg(t) + \beta(t)s(t - 1), \quad t = 1, 2, \ldots,$$

where

$$\beta(t) = \frac{g(t)'Hg(t)}{g(t - 1)'Hg(t - 1)}, \qquad \gamma(t) = -\frac{s(t)'g(t)}{s(t)'As(t)}.$$

Notice that the algorithm can be carried out without having to compute the matrix product TAT. Our earlier results guarantee that the algorithm converges in n iterations. Concerning the rate of convergence, inequality (7.11) is again applicable, except that the eigenvalues of $TAT = H^{1/2}AH^{1/2}$ are involved, replacing the eigenvalues of A.

For this reason, preconditioning may substantially enhance the speed of convergence, although finding a good choice of the scaling matrix H remains mostly an art.

2.7.4 Parallel Implementation

For simplicity, we only discuss the case of no preconditioning. Assuming that at the beginning of the tth iteration, $x(t)$, $s(t-1)$, and $g(t-1)'g(t-1)$ have already been computed, we need to evaluate the vectors $g(t) = Ax(t)$, the inner product $g(t)'g(t)$, determine $\beta(t)$ and $s(t)$ using Eqs. (7.9) and (7.7), then evaluate $As(t)$, and finally compute the inner products $s(t)'\big(As(t)\big)$, $s(t)'g(t)$, from which $\gamma(t)$ is determined [cf. Eq. (7.10)]. Neglecting vector additions and scalar–vector multiplications, the main computational requirements are two matrix–vector multiplications and three inner product computations. Furthermore, in all matrix–vector multiplications, the same matrix A is involved.

We only discuss the case of message–passing architectures. If n processors are available, it is natural to let the ith processor be in control of the ith component of the vectors of interest, that is, $x(t)$, $s(t)$, and $g(t)$. Inner products of such vectors are computed by letting the ith processor compute the product of the ith components and then accumulating partial sums along a tree of processors. This is a single node accumulation and takes time proportional to the diameter of the interconnection network. Then, the computed values of the inner products are broadcast to all processors. We now assume that each processor is given the entries in a different row of A. Then, a matrix–vector product like $Ax(t)$ may be computed by broadcasting the vector $x(t)$ (this is a multinode broadcast) and having the ith processor compute the inner product of x with the ith row of A. Alternatively, the ith processor could compute $[A]_{ji}x_i$ for each j, and these quantities could be propagated to each processor j, with partial sums formed along the way, as discussed in Subsection 1.3.6.[†] If fewer than n processors are available, the issues involved are the same except that there are more components, and more rows of the matrix A, assigned to each processor.

In the case where A is a sparse matrix, the multiplication of any vector by A may be performed more efficiently by using a special interconnection topology that exploits the sparsity structure of A. For example, if A arises from the discretization of a partial differential equation, a mesh–connected processor array is suitable, and the required matrix–vector multiplications can be executed in $O(1)$ time. Unfortunately, the speed of inner product computations is limited by the diameter of the interconnection network. For example, in an $n^{1/2} \times n^{1/2}$ mesh–connected array, $\Omega(n^{1/2})$ time units are required to evaluate an inner product $x'y$ when each component of x and y lies at a different processor. This creates a bottleneck that can be alleviated if there are some special hardware facilities (e.g., additional connections) allowing quick evaluation of inner products. Another option for reducing the communication penalty and increasing efficiency is to use fewer processors and to assign enough components to each processor

---

[†] Notice that there is no significant difference between row and column storage schemes for matrix–vector multiplication because the matrix A is symmetric.

so that the number of computations of each processor, per stage, is comparable to the diameter of the interconnection network. This constrains the number of processors that can be efficiently employed and limits the attainable speedup (Exercise 7.3).

EXERCISES

7.1. [Lue84] Prove inequality (7.12). *Hint:* Use the polynomial

$$P(\lambda) = \frac{2}{(a+b)\lambda_1 \cdots \lambda_k} \left(\frac{a+b}{2} - \lambda\right)(\lambda_1 - \lambda) \cdots (\lambda_k - \lambda),$$

where $\lambda_1, \ldots, \lambda_k$ are the values of the eigenvalues of A that are larger than b.

7.2. [Ber74] Let A be of the form

$$A = M + \sum_{i=1}^{k} v_i v_i',$$

where M is positive definite and symmetric and $v_1, \ldots, v_k$ are some vectors in $\Re^n$. Show that the preconditioned conjugate gradient method with $H = M^{-1}$ terminates in at most $k + 1$ steps.

7.3. Consider the discretized Poisson equation (Subsection 2.5.1) for a square domain with N grid points. Suppose that a two–dimensional mesh of p processors is used to execute the conjugate gradient algorithm, with each processor assigned N/p grid points in a square subdomain. Find the order of magnitude dependence of p on N that optimizes the execution time of each iteration. Assume that the time for one computation and the communication delay across any link are comparable.

7.4. Suppose that the conjugate gradient has not terminated at the kth iteration, that is, $x(k) \neq 0$. Show that $F\big(x(k+1)\big) < F\big(x(k)\big)$. [This strengthens Prop. 7.1(d).]

2.8 COMPUTATION OF THE INVARIANT DISTRIBUTION OF A MARKOV CHAIN

Markov chains are widely used as probabilistic models of stochastic systems, in queueing theory, for example. In applications, one often deals with Markov chains with very large state spaces, involving tens of thousands of states. It is often desired to compute the steady–state (invariant) probability distribution for such chains, and this is a computational task that calls for parallel computation. We present two variants of an easily parallelizable iterative algorithm.

Let P be the one–step transition probability matrix of a discrete–time homogeneous n–state Markov chain. The reader may wish to consult Appendix D for the relevant definitions. For the purposes of this section, we only need the following two properties of P:

$$P \geq 0, \tag{8.1}$$

$$\sum_{j=1}^{n} p_{ij} = 1. \tag{8.2}$$

Any matrix with these two properties is called a *stochastic* matrix.

A nonnegative row vector π^* whose components sum to 1, and that has the property $\pi^* = \pi^* P$ is called an *invariant distribution* of the Markov chain associated with P; the computation of such a vector π^* is the subject of this section.

Consider the following algorithm. We start with a row vector $\pi(0) \geq 0$ whose components add to 1, and we employ the iteration

$$\pi(t + 1) = \pi(t)P. \tag{8.3}$$

Equivalently,

$$\pi(t) = \pi(0)P^t, \qquad t \geq 0.$$

We present below some conditions under which this iteration converges to an invariant distribution π^*. We first recall some definitions from Appendix D.

Given an $n \times n$ stochastic matrix P, we form a directed graph $G = (N, A)$, where N is the set of states, and $A = \{(i, j) \mid p_{ij} > 0, \ i \neq j\}$, the set of arcs, is the set of all transitions that have positive probability. We say that P is *irreducible* if for every $i, j \in N$ there exists a positive path in the above graph from i to j, or if $n = 1$. Notice that this is the same definition as the one given in Section 2.6.

The stochastic matrix P is called *periodic* if there exists some $k > 1$ and some disjoint nonempty subsets $N_0, \ldots, N_{k-1}$ of the state space N such that if $i \in N_\ell$ and $p_{ij} > 0$, then $j \in N_{\ell+1 \pmod k}$. We say that P is *aperiodic* if it is not periodic. Finally, P is called *primitive* if there exists a positive integer t such that $P^t > 0$. Some examples are provided in Fig. 2.8.1.

Proposition 8.1.   A stochastic matrix P is primitive if and only if it is irreducible and aperiodic.

Proposition 8.1 is a well–known result in the theory of Markov chains [Var62]. We omit its proof because it will not be used. Instead, it will be assumed that we are dealing with a primitive matrix.

Proposition 8.2.   Let P be a stochastic matrix.

(a) The spectral radius $\rho(P)$ of P is equal to 1.

(b) If π is a row vector whose entries sum to 1, then the row vector πP has the same property.

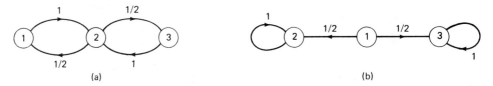

Figure 2.8.1   Some examples of Markov chains. For the Markov chain in (a), we have

$$P = \begin{bmatrix} 0 & 1 & 0 \\ 1/2 & 0 & 1/2 \\ 0 & 1 & 0 \end{bmatrix}$$

and it is easily seen that $P^t = P$ if $t > 0$ is odd, and

$$P^t = \begin{bmatrix} 1/2 & 0 & 1/2 \\ 0 & 1 & 0 \\ 1/2 & 0 & 1/2 \end{bmatrix}$$

if $t > 0$ is even. In particular, P^t does not converge. The matrix P is irreducible but neither primitive nor aperiodic. For the Markov chain in (b), we have

$$P^t = P = \begin{bmatrix} 0 & 1/2 & 1/2 \\ 0 & 1 & 0 \\ 0 & 0 & 1 \end{bmatrix}, \qquad \forall t \geq 1.$$

Notice that P is not irreducible but is aperiodic. The sequence $\{P^t\}$ converges, since it is constant, but the limits of different rows are different.

Proof.

(a) Let e be the column vector with all components equal to 1. From Eq. (8.2), we obtain $Pe = e$. Thus, 1 is an eigenvalue of P and $\rho(P) \geq 1$. On the other hand, $\rho(P) \leq \|P\|_\infty = 1$.

(b) We have

$$\sum_{i=1}^{n} [\pi P]_i = \sum_{i=1}^{n} \sum_{k=1}^{n} \pi_k p_{ki} = \sum_{k=1}^{n} \pi_k \sum_{i=1}^{n} p_{ki} = \sum_{k=1}^{n} \pi_k = 1.$$

Q.E.D.

Convergence of the iteration $\pi(t+1) = \pi(t)P$ is obtained from the following result. The examples in Fig. 2.8.1 illustrate the ways in which Prop. 8.3 fails to hold if P is not primitive.

Proposition 8.3.   Let P be a primitive stochastic matrix. Then:

(a) There exists a unique row vector π^* such that $\pi^* = \pi^* P$ and $\sum_{i=1}^{n} \pi_i^* = 1$. Furthermore, $\pi^* > 0$.

(b) The limit of P^t, as t tends to infinity, exists and is the matrix with all rows equal to π^*.

(c) If $\sum_{i=1}^{n} \pi_i(0) = 1$, then the iteration $\pi(t+1) = \pi(t)P$ converges to π^*.

Proof.

(a) Since P is primitive, it is irreducible. (This follows from the unproved Prop. 8.1, but is also a straightforward consequence of Prop. 6.3.) It then follows that P' is also irreducible. Since the eigenvalues of P' coincide with the eigenvalues of P [Prop. A.17(f) in Appendix A], we use Prop. 8.2(a) to obtain $\rho(P') = 1$. We then apply the Perron–Frobenius theorem (Prop. 6.6) to P' to assert the existence of a positive vector w such that $P'w = w$; equivalently, $w'P = w'$. The existence of π^* follows by normalizing w' so that its components sum to 1. Uniqueness follows from the uniqueness result in Prop. 6.6.

(b) Fix some $x \in \Re^n$. Let $M_t(x) = \max_i [P^t x]_i$ and $m_t(x) = \min_i [P^t x]_i$. The fact $\sum_{j=1}^{n} p_{ij} = 1$ and an easy induction show that $M_t(x)$ is nonincreasing and $m_t(x)$ is nondecreasing. They must therefore converge to some limits denoted by $M(x)$, $m(x)$.

Let T be such that $P^T > 0$, and let α be the smallest of the entries of P^T. Since the sum of the entries in each row of P^T is equal to 1 (Prop. D.3 in Appendix D), it is easily seen that

$$M_{t+T}(x) \le (1 - \alpha)M_t(x) + \alpha m_t(x),$$

and

$$m_{t+T}(x) \ge (1 - \alpha)m_t(x) + \alpha M_t(x).$$

Subtracting these two inequalities, we obtain

$$M_{t+T}(x) - m_{t+T}(x) \le (1 - 2\alpha)\big(M_t(x) - m_t(x)\big).$$

Taking the limit, as t tends to infinity, and using the positivity of α, we obtain $M(x) = m(x)$. It follows that $P^t x$ converges to $m(x)e$, where e is the vector with all components equal to 1. Let $e^1, \ldots, e^n$ be the unit vectors in $\Re^n$. Letting $x = e^1, \ldots, e^n$, we conclude that $P^t = P^t I = P^t[e^1 \ e^2 \ \ldots \ e^n]$ converges to $[m(e^1)e \ \ldots \ m(e^n)e]$, which is a matrix with all rows equal to the row vector $y = [m(e^1) \ldots m(e^n)]$. We now need to show that $y = \pi^*$. Since $Pe = e$, we have $P^t e = e$ for all t, and $\lim_{t \to \infty} P^t \left(\sum_{i=1}^n e^i \right) = \lim_{t \to \infty} P^t e = e$. Therefore, $\sum_{i=1}^n y_i = 1$. Finally, since $\lim_{t \to \infty} P^t = (\lim_{t \to \infty} P^t) P$, it follows that $y = yP$. Using the uniqueness result of part (a), we obtain $y = \pi^*$.

(c) By the result of part (b), all of the entries in the ith column of the limit of P^t are equal to π_i^*. It follows that the ith entry of $\pi(0)P^t$ converges to $\sum_{j=1}^n \pi_j(0)\pi_i^* = \pi_i^*$.   **Q.E.D.**

The iteration $\pi := \pi P$ admits a straightforward parallel implementation in which the ith processor is assigned the task of updating the ith component of the vector π and at each stage communicates its newly computed value to every other processor j such that $p_{ij} \neq 0$. This assumes that each processor j knows the entries in the jth column of P. A different implementation is obtained if each processor j knows the entries of the jth row of P; see the discussion in Subsection 1.3.6. An asynchronous version of this algorithm will be studied in Section 7.3.

We now consider a variant of the iteration $\pi := \pi P$. The new algorithm is almost the same except that one of the components of π, say the first one, is not iterated upon. Thus, the algorithm is described by

$$\pi_1(t+1) = \pi_1(t), \tag{8.4}$$

$$\pi_i(t+1) = \sum_{j=1}^n \pi_j(t)p_{ji}, \qquad i = 2, \dots, n. \tag{8.5}$$

The initialization of the algorithm is arbitrary, provided that $\pi_1(0) \neq 0$. In order to represent the algorithm in matrix form, we partition the matrix P as shown:

$$P = \begin{bmatrix} p_{11} & a \\ b & \tilde{P} \end{bmatrix}.$$

Here, a (respectively, b) is a row (respectively, column) vector of dimension $n-1$ and $\tilde{P}$ is the matrix of dimensions $(n-1) \times (n-1)$ obtained by deleting the first row and the first column of P. Let $\tilde{\pi}(t)$ be the row vector $(\pi_2(t), \dots, \pi_n(t))$. Then, Eq. (8.5) can be rewritten as

$$\tilde{\pi}(t+1) = \tilde{\pi}(t)\tilde{P} + \pi_1(0)a. \tag{8.6}$$

This iteration converges provided that $\rho(\tilde{P}) < 1$ (Prop. 6.1). The following result provides conditions for this to be the case and characterizes the limit of $\pi(t)$.

Proposition 8.4. Consider the directed graph associated with P, and assume that there exists a positive path from every state to state 1. Let $\{X(t) \mid t = 0, 1, \dots\}$ be a Markov chain whose one–step transition probabilities are given by P. Let T be a positive integer and let

$$\delta_T = \min_{i=2,\dots,n} \Pr\Big(\text{there exists some } \tau \le T \text{ such that } X(\tau) = 1 \ \Big| \ X(0) = i\Big). \quad (8.7)$$

(a) If T is chosen large enough, then $\delta_T > 0$.

(b) If $\delta_T > 0$, then

$$\rho(\tilde{P}) \le \left(\|\tilde{P}^T\|_\infty\right)^{1/T} \le (1 - \delta_T)^{1/T} < 1.$$

(c) The sequence $\{\pi(t)\}$ generated by Eqs. (8.4) and (8.5) converges to a vector π^* satisfying $\pi^* = \pi^* P$. If $\pi_1(0)$ is positive and $\pi(0) \ge 0$, then π^* is nonzero and all of its entries are nonnegative.

Proof.

(a) The positivity of δ_T is a straightforward consequence of the fact that for each $i \ne 1$, there exists a sequence of positive probability transitions leading from i to 1. We simply need to take T large enough so that for each $i \ne 1$, there exists at least one such path that uses no more than T arcs.

(b) Let

$$Q = \begin{bmatrix} 1 & 0 \\ b & \tilde{P} \end{bmatrix},$$

which is easily seen to be a stochastic matrix, and let $\{Y(t) \mid t = 0, 1, \dots\}$ be an associated Markov chain. We notice that $Y(t)$ has the same transition probabilities with $X(t)$ except that state 1 is an *absorbing* state: once $Y(t)$ becomes 1, it never changes. It follows that

$$\delta_T \le \Pr\Big(\text{there exists some } \tau \le T \text{ such that } Y(\tau) = 1 \big| Y(0) = i\Big) = [Q^T]_{i1},$$

$$i = 2, \dots, n. \quad (8.8)$$

We now notice that Q^T is of the form

$$Q^T = \begin{bmatrix} 1 & 0 \\ c & \tilde{P}^T \end{bmatrix}, \quad (8.9)$$

where c is an $(n - 1)$–dimensional column vector with all entries bounded below by δ_T. Since Q is a stochastic matrix, so is Q^T and each row sums to 1. It follows from Eq. (8.9) that the sum of the entries in any row of $\tilde{P}^T$ is bounded above by $1 - \delta_T$. Therefore, $\rho(\tilde{P}^T) \le \|\tilde{P}^T\|_\infty \le 1 - \delta_T$. The result follows because $\rho(\tilde{P}) = \left(\rho(\tilde{P}^T)\right)^{1/T}$.

(c) Since $\rho(\tilde{P}) < 1$, the system $\tilde{\pi} = \tilde{\pi}\tilde{P} + \pi_1(0)a$ has a unique solution $\tilde{\pi}$ and the sequence $\{\tilde{\pi}(t)\}$ converges to it. It follows that $\pi(t)$ converges to the vector $\pi^* = \big(\pi_1(0), \tilde{\pi}\big)$ and $\tilde{\pi}$ satisfies $\tilde{\pi} = \tilde{\pi}P + \pi_1(0)a$ [cf. Eq. (8.6)]. This shows that $\pi_i^* = [\pi^*P]_i$ for $i \neq 1$, and it remains to show that this equality also holds for $i = 1$. We have $\pi_j^* = \sum_{i=1}^n \pi_i^* p_{ij}$ for $j \neq 1$. Summing this equality for every $j \neq 1$, we obtain

$$\sum_{j=2}^n \pi_j^* = \sum_{j=2}^n \sum_{i=1}^n \pi_i^* p_{ij} = \sum_{i=1}^n \pi_i^*(1 - p_{i1})$$

which after cancellations yields $\pi_1^* = \sum_{i=1}^n \pi_i^* p_{i1} = [\pi^*P]_1$, as desired.

Suppose now that $\pi_1(0) > 0$. Then $\pi_1^* = \pi_1(0) > 0$. Also, if $\tilde{\pi}(0)$ is a nonnegative vector, it follows from Eq. (8.5) that $\tilde{\pi}(t)$ is nonnegative for every t, and the same conclusion obtains for π^*, since it is the limit of nonnegative vectors, which concludes the proof.   **Q.E.D.**

Notice that Prop. 8.4(b) provides us with an estimate of the convergence rate of the algorithm of Eqs. (8.4) and (8.5). Furthermore, the conditions for convergence are less stringent than those imposed in Prop. 8.3. For example, the Markov chain in Fig 2.8.1(a) satisfies the conditions of Prop. 8.4 but not those of Prop. 8.3. It should be pointed out that the components of the limit vector π^* do not, in general, add to 1. However, this may be remedied by multiplying the vector π^* obtained at termination of the algorithm, by a suitable scalar. The issues concerning the parallelization of the algorithm of Eqs. (8.4) and (8.5) are the same as for the algorithm of Eq. (8.3). Actually, this algorithm is also guaranteed to converge even if it is executed in a Gauss–Seidel fashion, without any deterioration of the convergence rate and with a potential improvement. This is because the iteration matrix $\tilde{P}$ is nonnegative, its spectral radius is less than 1, and Prop. 6.8 applies. This Gauss–Seidel algorithm is not always parallelizable, but in typical large scale Markov chains, the matrix P is very sparse and a coloring scheme can be applied (cf. Subsection 1.2.4). It will be seen in Section 6.3 that the algorithm of Eqs. (8.4) and (8.5) also converges when executed asynchronously.

EXERCISES

8.1. (**Power Method for the Eigenvalue Problem.**) The iteration $\pi := \pi P$ is a special case of a more general algorithm for finding an eigenvalue with largest magnitude of a given matrix A, together with an associated eigenvector. The algorithm is initialized with some $x(0) \neq 0$ and consists of the iteration

$$x(t + 1) = \frac{Ax(t)}{\|Ax(t)\|}, \tag{8.10}$$

where $\| \cdot \|$ is an arbitrary norm. Suppose that A has distinct eigenvalues $\lambda_1, \ldots, \lambda_n$ and corresponding nonzero eigenvectors $x^1, \ldots, x^n$. Suppose that $|\lambda_i| < |\lambda_1|$ for each $i \neq 1$ and that the iteration is initialized with some $x(0)$ that does not belong to the span of $x^2, \ldots, x^n$.

   (a) Show that the sequence $\{x(t)\}$ has a limit x satisfying $Ax = \lambda_1 x$. *Hint:* Use the Jordan form of the matrix A.

   (b) Show that iteration (8.3), with $\pi(0) \geq 0$ and $\sum_{i=1}^{n} \pi_i(0) = 1$, is of the form of Eq. (8.10), for a suitable choice of the norm $\| \cdot \|$.

8.2. This exercise and the next extend Prop. 8.3 to cover all cases where there is only one ergodic class (Appendix D) associated with the matrix P. Let P be an irreducible, but not necessarily primitive, stochastic matrix. Let α be some constant satisfying $0 < \alpha < 1$ and consider the matrix Q defined by $Q = (1 - \alpha)I + \alpha P$.

   (a) Show that Q is a primitive stochastic matrix. *Hint:* Use Prop. 6.3.

   (b) Show that there exists a row vector $\pi^* > 0$ satisfying $\pi^* P = \pi^*$, and, furthermore, such a vector is unique up to multiplication by a scalar. Suggest an algorithm for computing π^*.

8.3. Suppose that a stochastic matrix P has the structure

$$P = \begin{bmatrix} A & B \\ 0 & C \end{bmatrix},$$

where A, B, and C, are matrices of dimensions $n_1 \times n_1$, $n_1 \times (n-n_1)$, and $(n-n_1) \times (n-n_1)$, respectively. In particular, C is a stochastic matrix and we assume that it is also irreducible. We also assume that starting at any one of the first n_1 states, there is a positive probability that the state of the associated Markov chain becomes equal to one of the last $n - n_1$ states. Show that there exists a unique row vector $\pi^* \geq 0$ such that $\pi^* P = \pi^*$ and whose components sum to 1. *Hint:* To prove uniqueness, use the techique in the proof of Prop. 8.4 to show that $\rho(A) < 1$, conclude that the first n_1 components of π^* are equal to zero, and finally use the irreducibility of C.

8.4. Let P be an irreducible stochastic matrix and suppose that there exists some i such that $p_{ii} > 0$. Show that P is primitive.

2.9 FAST ITERATIVE MATRIX INVERSION

We consider here a method based on the classical Newton algorithm for iterative improvement of an approximate inverse of a square matrix A, assumed throughout to be invertible. This method is motivated by the desire for very small execution time $[O(\log^2 n)]$ without the drawbacks of the direct inversion algorithm of Section 2.3 (excessive number of processors and lack of numerical robustness). Small execution time rests on a distinctive property of Newton methods, *quadratic convergence*, that is, convergence at the same speed as the sequence $\{\rho^{2^t}\}$, where ρ is a positive constant smaller than 1. This is much faster than the geometric convergence rate $(\{\rho^t\})$ exhibited by the classical iterative methods analyzed in Section 2.6.

    Given a square matrix B of the same dimensions as A, we define a residual matrix $R(B) = I - BA$. Thus, $R(B)$ measures, in some sense, how far B is from being the inverse of A. Consider the following algorithm:

1. Start with some B_0 such that $\|I - B_0 A\|_2 < 1$.
2. Iteratively improve B_k by letting $B_{k+1} = (I + R(B_k))B_k = 2B_k - B_k A B_k$.

This iteration can be interpreted as Newton's method for solving the equation $X^{-1} - A = 0$ (see Exercise 9.1).

Some algebraic manipulation gives

$$R(B_{k+1}) = I - B_{k+1}A = I - (I + R(B_k))B_k A$$

$$= (I - B_k A) - R(B_k)B_k A = R(B_k)(I - B_k A) = (R(B_k))^2.$$

We therefore obtain $R(B_k) = (R(B_0))^{2^k}$. Using Prop. A.12(c) in Appendix A, we have

$$\|R(B_k)\|_2 = \left\|(R(B_0))^{2^k}\right\|_2 \leq \|R(B_0)\|_2^{2^k}. \tag{9.1}$$

Since we have assumed that $\|R(B_0)\| < 1$, the previous inequality shows that the norm of $R(B_k)$ converges very rapidly to zero; equivalently, B_k converges very rapidly to A^{-1}. So, the algorithm will be succesful provided that B_0 has been suitably chosen. The following choice of B_0 turns out to be convenient:

$$B_0 = \frac{A'}{\text{tr}(A'A)}, \tag{9.2}$$

where $\text{tr}(A'A)$, the *trace* of $A'A$, is defined as the sum of the diagonal entries of $A'A$. Other choices of B_0, some of them suitable in special cases, are given in Exercises 9.2 to 9.4.

For any nonsingular square matrix A, we let $\kappa(A) = \|A\|_2 \cdot \|A^{-1}\|_2$. This quantity is called the *condition number* of A and plays a prominent role in numerical analysis, as a measure of the difficulty of computing A^{-1} in the face of roundoff errors [GoV83]. Let $\lambda_1 \leq \lambda_2 \leq \cdots \leq \lambda_n$ be the eigenvalues of $A'A$. These eigenvalues are real and nonnegative because the matrix $A'A$ is symmetric nonnegative definite (Prop. A.26 in Appendix A). Furthermore, they are nonzero because A is assumed nonsingular. Another definition of the condition number is given by $\kappa(A) = (\lambda_n/\lambda_1)^{1/2}$. To see that the two definitions are equivalent, notice that $\lambda_n = \rho(A'A) = \|A'A\|_2 = \|A\|_2^2$ [Props. A.24(a) and A.25(d) in Appendix A], and that $1/\lambda_1 = \|(A'A)^{-1}\|_2 = \|A^{-1}(A^{-1})'\|_2 = \|A^{-1}\|_2^2$ [Props. A.25(f) and A.25(d) in Appendix A].

Proposition 9.1. If $B_0 = A'/\text{tr}(A'A)$, then $\|I - B_0 A\|_2 \leq 1 - 1/(n\kappa^2(A))$.

Proof. We have $\text{tr}(A'A) = \lambda_1 + \cdots + \lambda_n$ [Prop. A.22(a) in Appendix A]. It follows that the ith eigenvalue ρ_i of $I - B_0 A = I - A'A/\text{tr}(A'A)$ is equal to $1 - \lambda_i/(\lambda_1 + \cdots + \lambda_n)$. Since $\lambda_i \leq \lambda_1 + \cdots + \lambda_n$ for each i, we see that $\rho_i \geq 0$ for each i. Furthermore, since $\lambda_1 + \cdots + \lambda_n \leq n\lambda_n$, we obtain

$$\rho_i \le 1 - \frac{\lambda_i}{n\lambda_n} \le 1 - \frac{\lambda_1}{n\lambda_n} = 1 - \frac{1}{n\kappa^2(A)},$$

for each i. It follows that $\rho(I - B_0 A) = \max_i |\rho_i| \le 1 - 1/(n\kappa^2(A))$. The desired result follows because $I - B_0 A$ is symmetric and $\|I - B_0 A\|_2 = \rho(I - B_0 A)$ [Prop. A.24(a) in Appendix A].   **Q.E.D.**

The above proposition shows that if B_0 is chosen according to Eq. (9.2), then $\|I - B_0 A\|_2 < 1$. Furthermore, as long as the matrix A is not extremely ill–conditioned, $\|I - B_0 A\|_2$ is sufficiently smaller than 1 to lead to a practical algorithm. In particular, we have the following corollary of Prop. 9.1.

Corollary 9.1.   Suppose that $\kappa(A) \le n^d$ for some constant d, and let c be any positive integer. If $B_0 = A'/\text{tr}(A'A)$, then the matrix B_k produced after $k \ge (c + 2d + 1) \log n$ iterations of the algorithm satisfies

$$\|I - B_k A\|_2 \le 2^{-n^c}, \tag{9.3}$$

$$\|B_k - A^{-1}\|_2 \le 2^{-n^c} \frac{\kappa(A)}{\|A\|_2}. \tag{9.4}$$

Furthermore, such a B_k can be computed in parallel in time $O\big((c + d) \log^2 n\big)$ using n^3 processors.

Proof. The time and processor bounds are obvious, since each iteration involves two matrix multiplications, which can be performed in time $O(\log n)$, using n^3 processors (see Subsection 1.2.3). [The computation of $\text{tr}(A'A)$ is of no concern: it can be performed in time $O(\log n)$ using n^3 processors.]

Using Prop. 9.1 and Eq. (9.1),

$$\|I - B_k A\|_2 \le \left(1 - \frac{1}{n\kappa^2(A)}\right)^{n^{c+2d+1}} \le \left(1 - \frac{1}{n\kappa^2(A)}\right)^{(n\kappa^2(A))n^c} \le 2^{-n^c},$$

which proves Eq. (9.3). [The last inequality uses the bound $(1 - 1/\alpha)^\alpha \le 1/2$, for $\alpha \ge 2$.] Finally,

$$\|B_k - A^{-1}\|_2 = \|(B_k A - I)A^{-1}\|_2 \le \|I - B_k A\|_2 \cdot \|A^{-1}\|_2 = \|I - B_k A\|_2 \frac{\kappa(A)}{\|A\|_2},$$

which completes the proof.   **Q.E.D.**

Corollary 9.1 shows that, for all practical purposes, the computation time is a small multiple of $\log^2 n$. This is the same as for the direct algorithm of Section 2.3, except that only n^3 processors are used here as opposed to n^4 processors in Section 2.3. Furthermore, unlike the algorithm of Section 2.3, the present algorithm is robust with respect to numerical errors.

If fewer, say n, processors are available, a very accurate approximation of the inverse is obtained in $O(n^2 \log n)$ time steps. This is because the algorithm needs $O(\log n)$ stages and each stage can be executed in $O(n^2)$ time using n processors. This is somewhat slower than Gaussian elimination or the Givens rotation method (Section 2.2), which require $O(n^2)$ time with n processors.

The algorithm of this section can also be used for solving systems of linear equations: the solution of $Ax = b$ is found by first computing A^{-1} and then letting $x = A^{-1}b$. However, such a method may have certain drawbacks, especially if storage requirements are taken into account. In classical iterative methods (Section 2.4), we need to store the entries of the A matrix, together with the vector x on which we iterate, which is $O(n^2)$ storage. With the algorithm of this section, we need to store the A matrix and, at each stage, the current estimate of the inverse, which is again $O(n^2)$ storage. Suppose now that the A matrix is sparse. In a classical iterative method, only the nonzero entries of A need to be stored and storage requirements are drastically reduced. On the other hand, even if A is sparse, its inverse will not be sparse in general. Therefore, the approximate inverses B_k will not be sparse either. Consequently, with the algorithm of this section, sparsity does not reduce the storage requirements.

EXERCISES

9.1. (Newton Interpretation of the Iteration $B_{k+1} = 2B_k - B_k A B_k$.) Let $f : \Re^n \mapsto \Re^n$ be a continuously differentiable function. For every $x \in \Re^n$ and $d \in \Re^n$, we have

$$f(x + d) = f(x) + \nabla f(x)'d + h(x, d),$$

where h is some function with the property $\lim_{d \to 0} h(x, d)/\|d\| = 0$ for every $x \in \Re^n$, and $\| \cdot \|$ is an arbitrary vector norm (see Appendix A). We wish to solve the equation $f(x) = 0$. Starting from a current value of x, we ignore the term $h(x, d)$, approximate the function $f(x + d)$ by $f(x) + \nabla f(x)'d$, choose some d that sets the latter expression to zero, and let $x := x + d$. The equation $f(x) + \nabla f(x)'d = 0$ yields $d = -\left(\nabla f(x)'\right)^{-1} f(x)$ and the iteration becomes

$$x := x - \left(\nabla f(x)'\right)^{-1} f(x),$$

which is known as Newton's method. Let us now fix an $n \times n$ matrix A. For any invertible $n \times n$ matrix X, let $f(X) = A - X^{-1}$. Inverting A is equivalent to solving the equation $f(X) = 0$.

   (a) Show that $f(X + D) = A - X^{-1} + X^{-1}DX^{-1} + h(X, D)$, where the function h has the property $\lim_{D \to 0} h(X, D)/\|D\| = 0$ for every invertible matrix X, and $\| \cdot \|$ is an arbitrary matrix norm.
   Hint: Use the formula $(I - C)^{-1} = I + C + C^2 + \cdots$, which is valid for any matrix C of small enough norm.

(b) Choose a value of D that sets $f(X + D)$ to zero, while ignoring the term $h(X, D)$ of part (a).

(c) With D chosen as in (b), show that the iteration $X := X + D$ coincides with the iteration $X := 2X - XAX$.

9.2. [PaR85] Suppose that B_0 is chosen according to the formula

$$B_0 = \frac{A'}{\|A\|_\infty \cdot \|A\|_1},$$

as opposed to Eq. (9.2). Show that Prop. 9.1 remains valid. *Hint:* Use the inequalities $\|A\|_2^2 \le \|A\|_\infty \cdot \|A\|_1 \le n\|A\|_2^2$ (see Appendix A), and proceed as in Prop. 9.1.

9.3. [PaR85] Suppose that A is symmetric positive definite, and let

$$B_0 = \frac{I}{\|A\|_\infty}.$$

Show that $\|I - B_0 A\|_2 \le 1 - 1/\left(n^{1/2}\kappa(A)\right)$.

9.4. [PaR85] Suppose that the matrix A has the property

$$\left(1 - \frac{1}{n^c}\right)|a_{ii}| \ge \sum_{j \ne i}|a_{ij}|, \qquad \forall i,$$

and let B_0 be a diagonal matrix whose ith diagonal entry is equal to $1/a_{ii}$. Show that $\|I - B_0 A\|_\infty \le 1 - 1/n^c$.

NOTES AND SOURCES

Serial algorithms for matrix computations are the subject of [FaF63], [Hou64], [FoM67], [Ste73], and [GoV83]. For general surveys and discussion of parallel algorithms, see [Sam77], [Hel78], [Sam81], and [GHN87]. The survey paper [OrV85] focuses on parallel solution of partial differential equations but also provides an extensive discussion and list of references on parallel methods for linear equations.

2.1. The $O(\log^2 n)$ time algorithm for triangular matrix inversion based on Eq. (1.2) is from [Orc74] and [Hel74], and the "divide–and–conquer" algorithm is from [BoM75]. For other fast algorithms of this type, see [Hel78]. For a detailed discussion of the communication overhead of implementations of back substitution in a ring of processors, see [ISS86], which includes a comparison of the row and column storage schemes.

Odd–even reduction is due to [Hoc65] and its parallelization is discussed in [HoJ81]. See also [Hel76] for the block–tridiagonal case. Several parallel algorithms and discussions of communication issues can be found in [Sto75], [Hel78], [SaK77], [SaK78], [HoJ81], [GaV84], [Joh85a], and [Joh87b].

Other special structures that have been studied include banded systems ([Joh85b] and [SaS87]) and Toeplitz systems ([GrS81], [Bin84], and [GKK87]).

2.2.   See [GoV83] and [Hou64] for a detailed description and analysis of direct methods for general linear equations. The communication penalty of parallel matrix multiplication and inversion has been first considered in [Gen78], where an $\Omega(n)$ lower bound on the execution time for mesh–connected architectures is established.

A detailed timing analysis of parallel Gaussian elimination with $O(n)$ processors can be found in [LKK83] and processor scheduling for the case of sparse matrices is studied in [WiH80], in the absence of communication delays. The communication penalty is considered in [ISS86] for the case of a ring architecture, and a variety of lower bounds on the communication penalty is provided in [Saa86]. Other pivoting rules, different than the one given by Eq. (2.4), have also been considered ([Sam85a]) and some of them lead to efficient [$\Theta(n)$ time] implementations in mesh–connected architectures (see, e.g., [Sam81] and [GeK81]).

Parallel triangularization using Givens rotations, and the schedule of Eqs. (2.11) and (2.12), have been suggested in [SaK78]; see also [LKK83] for a detailed timing analysis for the case of $O(n)$ processors in the absence of communication delays. The reference [CoR86] contains a result showing that the schedule of Eqs. (2.11) and (2.12) is very close to being optimal, even though it can be somewhat improved (compare with Exercise 2.6). An implementation of the Givens method in a mesh of n^2 processors is given in [BBK84]. Implementations on systolic arrays are discussed in [Kun88].

Givens rotations are also used in a variety of other algorithms in which the objective is to set the entries of a matrix to zero, and most such algorithms admit efficient parallel implementations in mesh–connected, as well as in special purpose VLSI architectures [Kun88]. One important application area is in eigenvalue and singular value problems. Recent work on these problems includes [BrL85], [IpS85], [DoS87], and [LPS87].

2.3.   The algorithm of this section is from [Csa76]. Its processor requirements have been reduced in [PrS78]. An $O(\log^2 n)$ algorithm for Cholesky factorization (faster than the one in Exercise 3.1) is given in [Dat85].

2.4.   For further reading on iterative methods, see [Var62], [You71], and [HaY81].

2.5.   Parallel algorithms for linear PDEs are surveyed in [OrV85]. Algorithms and timing estimates for a particular parallel computer are considered in [Gal85]. See also [RAP87] for the effects of different partitionings of the problem domain and of different discretization methods.

For a precise description and convergence analyses of multigrid algorithms, see [Hac85]. Parallel implementations of multigrid algorithms have been discussed in [Bra81], [ChS85], [ChS86], and [McV87]. The implementation on a hypercube presented here is from [ChS86].

2.6.   There are several textbooks with comprehensive analyses of linear iterative methods and their convergence rate, such as [Var62] and [You71]. The Brouwer Fixed Point Theorem and the core of the proof the Perron–Frobenius theorem can be found in [GuP74]. The proof outlined in Exercise 6.3 is taken from [Var62], which provides several references on alternative proofs of this result; see also [Sen81].

2.7.   The conjugate gradient method is due to [HeS52]. For its properties when applied to nonlinear problems, see [Pol71]. For further readings for the linear case, see [FaF63] and [Lue84].

2.8.   For further readings on Markov chains and their steady state behavior, see [Ash] and [Ros83a]. The algorithm of Eqs. (8.4) and (8.5), and its Gauss–Seidel variant, appear to be new.

2.9.   The Newton method for matrix inversion is a classical algorithm, see [IsK66] and [Hou64]. The choice of B_0 in Prop. 9.1 is from [IsK66]. The use of this algorithm for parallel matrix inversion has been suggested in [Boj84a] and [PaR85]. Our complexity analysis is taken from [PaR85] which emphasizes the issue of appropriately choosing the initial matrix B_0.

3

Iterative Methods
for Nonlinear Problems

In this chapter, we consider iterative methods for the solution of a variety of nonlinear problems. Examples include:

(a) The solution of systems of nonlinear equations that arise in many types of modeling, simulation, and engineering design problems.

(b) Optimization problems, including linear programming, that arise in a broad variety of engineering design, economic modeling, and operations research applications.

(c) Variational inequalities that can be viewed as generalizations of both systems of equations and constrained optimization problems. Variational inequalities can also be used as models of saddle point and other problems arising in the theory of games, and as models for equilibrium studies in diverse fields ranging from economics to traffic engineering.

Nonlinear problems are typically solved by iterative methods, and the convergence analysis of these methods is one of the focal points of this chapter. We use two principal techniques. The first relies on the theory of contraction mappings, and the second is based on showing iterative reduction of the cost function of an underlying optimization problem. Throughout the chapter, we emphasize algorithms that are well suited for parallelization such as methods of the Jacobi and Gauss–Seidel relaxation type. For optimization problems, we discuss at length gradient projection methods and their scaled versions. We pay special attention to constraint sets that are Cartesian products and lend themselves to parallel calculations. We also develop some of the tools needed for the study of asynchronous parallel algorithms in Chapters 6 and 7.

An important aspect of convex constrained optimization problems is that they can be transformed into dual problems, which in many cases are easier to solve or are more amenable to parallel solution methods. Techniques based on duality, known as decomposition methods, have been widely used for the solution of large problems with special structure. These techniques are also particularly well suited for a parallel computing environment. We discuss a number of decomposition methods, and we delineate some problem structures that are well suited for their application.

In Section 3.1, we consider contraction mappings and associated fixed point problems and develop some broadly applicable tools. In Section 3.2, we study iterative algorithms for the solution of nonlinear optimization problems; these algorithms can be thought of as generalizations of the iterative methods for the solution of linear equations that were presented in Chapter 2. Then, in Section 3.3, we consider constrained optimization problems, with an emphasis on the problem of minimizing a cost function over a convex set. In Section 3.4, we discuss the use of duality transformations of optimization problems to enhance the parallelization of their solution. Finally, in Section 3.5, we consider algorithms for the solution of variational inequalities. Throughout, we comment on the potential for parallelization of the different methods.

3.1 CONTRACTION MAPPINGS

Several iterative algorithms can be written as

$$x(t+1) = T\big(x(t)\big), \qquad t = 0, 1, \ldots, \tag{1.1}$$

where T is a mapping from a subset X of $\Re^n$ into itself and has the property

$$\|T(x) - T(y)\| \le \alpha \|x - y\|, \qquad \forall x, y \in X. \tag{1.2}$$

Here $\| \cdot \|$ is some norm, and α is a constant belonging to $[0, 1)$. Such a mapping is called a *contraction mapping*, or simply a *contraction*, and iteration (1.1) is called a *contracting iteration*. The scalar α is called the *modulus* of T. A mapping $T : X \mapsto Y$, where $X, Y \subset \Re^n$, that satisfies Eq. (1.2), will also be called a contraction mapping, even if $X \ne Y$.

Let there be given a mapping $T : X \mapsto X$. Any vector $x^* \in X$ satisfying $T(x^*) = x^*$ is called a *fixed point* of T and the iteration $x := T(x)$ can be viewed as an algorithm for finding such a fixed point. The reason is that if the sequence $\{x(t)\}$ converges to some $x^* \in X$ and T is continuous at x^*, then x^* is a fixed point of T. We notice that contraction mappings are automatically continuous.

As an alternative to the contraction assumption (1.2), we will sometimes assume that a mapping $T : X \mapsto X$ has a fixed point $x^* \in X$ and the property

$$\|T(x) - x^*\| \leq \alpha \|x - x^*\|, \qquad \forall x \in X, \qquad (1.3)$$

where α, called the *modulus* of T, is again a constant belonging to $[0,1)$. Clearly, inequality (1.3) is weaker than the contraction condition (1.2). Any mapping T with the above properties will be called a *pseudocontraction* and the corresponding iteration $x := T(x)$ will be called a *pseudocontracting iteration*. (Pseudocontracting iterations will play an important role in the analysis of certain algorithms in Section 3.5.) Notice that the existence of a fixed point is part of the definition of a pseudocontraction and that a pseudocontraction is not necessarily continuous. Figure 3.1.1 shows an example of a contraction and a pseudocontraction.

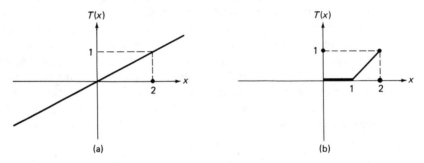

Figure 3.1.1 Illustration of a contraction and a pseudocontraction. (a) The mapping $T : \Re \mapsto \Re$ defined by $T(x) = x/2$ is a contraction with modulus $1/2$, and the iteration $x := T(x)$ converges to zero, which is a fixed point of T. (b) The mapping $T : [0,2] \mapsto [0,2]$ defined by $T(x) = \max\{0, x - 1\}$ is not a contraction since $|T(2) - T(1)| = 1$. On the other hand, it has a unique fixed point, equal to zero, and is a pseudocontraction because it is easily seen that $T(x) \leq x/2$ for every $x \in [0,2]$.

A mapping T could be a contraction (or a pseudocontraction) for some choice of the vector norm $\| \cdot \|$ and, at the same time, fail to be a contraction (respectively, a pseudocontraction) under a different choice of norm. Thus, the proper choice of a norm is critical. Some particularly interesting norms, for our purposes, are the weighted maximum norms. We have already seen an interesting class of mappings that are contractions with respect to a weighted maximum norm: Corollary 6.1 in Section 2.6 shows that a nonnegative matrix M has the property $\rho(M) < 1$ if and only if it is a contraction mapping with respect to some weighted maximum norm.

3.1.1 General Results

The following basic result shows that contraction mappings have a unique fixed point and the corresponding iteration $x := T(x)$ converges to it.

Proposition 1.1. (*Convergence of Contracting Iterations*) Suppose that $T : X \mapsto X$ is a contraction with modulus $\alpha \in [0,1)$ and that X is a closed subset of $\Re^n$. Then:

(a) (*Existence and Uniqueness of Fixed Points*) The mapping T has a unique fixed point $x^* \in X$.

(b) (*Geometric Convergence*) For every initial vector $x(0) \in X$, the sequence $\{x(t)\}$ generated by $x(t+1) = T\big(x(t)\big)$ converges to x^* geometrically. In particular,

$$\|x(t) - x^*\| \le \alpha^t \|x(0) - x^*\|, \qquad \forall t \ge 0.$$

Proof.

(a) Fix some $x(0) \in X$ and consider the sequence $\{x(t)\}$ generated by $x(t+1) = T\big(x(t)\big)$. We have, from inequality (1.2),

$$\|x(t+1) - x(t)\| \le \alpha \|x(t) - x(t-1)\|,$$

for all $t \ge 1$, which implies

$$\|x(t+1) - x(t)\| \le \alpha^t \|x(1) - x(0)\|, \qquad \forall t \ge 0.$$

It follows that for every $t \ge 0$ and $m \ge 1$, we have

$$\|x(t+m) - x(t)\| \le \sum_{i=1}^{m} \|x(t+i) - x(t+i-1)\|$$

$$\le \alpha^t (1 + \alpha + \cdots + \alpha^{m-1}) \|x(1) - x(0)\| \le \frac{\alpha^t}{1-\alpha} \|x(1) - x(0)\|.$$

Therefore, $\{x(t)\}$ is a Cauchy sequence and must converge to a limit x^* (Prop. A.5 in Appendix A). Furthermore, since X is closed, x^* belongs to X. We have for all $t \ge 1$,

$$\|T(x^*) - x^*\| \le \|T(x^*) - x(t)\| + \|x(t) - x^*\| \le \alpha \|x^* - x(t-1)\| + \|x(t) - x^*\|$$

and since $x(t)$ converges to x^*, we obtain $T(x^*) = x^*$. Therefore, the limit x^* of $x(t)$ is a fixed point of T. It is a unique fixed point because if y^* were another fixed point, we would have

$$\|x^* - y^*\| = \|T(x^*) - T(y^*)\| \le \alpha \|x^* - y^*\|$$

which implies that $x^* = y^*$.

(b) We have

$$\|x(t') - x^*\| = \big\|T\big(x(t'-1)\big) - T(x^*)\big\| \le \alpha \|x(t'-1) - x^*\|,$$

for all $t' \geq 1$, so by applying this relation successively for $t' = t, t - 1, \ldots, 1$, we obtain the desired result.   **Q.E.D.**

We now show that the convergence result of the above proposition remains valid for pseudocontractions as well.

Proposition 1.2.   (*Convergence of Pseudocontracting Iterations*) Suppose that $X \subset \Re^n$ and that the mapping $T : X \mapsto X$ is a pseudocontraction with a fixed point $x^* \in X$ and modulus $\alpha \in [0, 1)$. Then, T has no other fixed points and the sequence $\{x(t)\}$ generated by $x(t + 1) = T\big(x(t)\big)$ satisfies

$$\|x(t) - x^*\| \leq \alpha^t \|x(0) - x^*\|, \qquad \forall t \geq 0,$$

for every choice of the initial vector $x(0) \in X$. In particular, the sequence $\{x(t)\}$ converges to x^*.

Proof. Uniqueness of the fixed point follows as in the proof of Prop. 1.1. Now notice that the pseudocontraction condition (1.3) implies that

$$\|x(t) - x^*\| = \big\|T\big(x(t - 1)\big) - x^*\big\| \leq \alpha \|x(t - 1) - x^*\|,$$

for every $t \geq 1$, and the desired result follows by induction on t.   **Q.E.D.**

In order to apply a result such as Prop. 1.2, we often have to show that the mapping T has a fixed point. In some cases, an existence result is obtained from purely topological considerations. The following result, illustrated in Fig. 3.1.2, generalizes the Brouwer Fixed Point Theorem that was used in Section 2.6. Its proof is beyond the scope of this book (see e.g. [DuS63]).

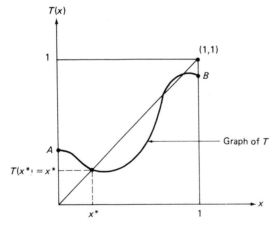

Figure 3.1.2 Illustration of the fixed point theorem (Prop. 1.3) for the case where T maps the unit interval $[0, 1]$ into itself. Here, point $A = \big(0, T(0)\big)$ lies on or above the diagonal of the unit square and point $B = \big(1, T(1)\big)$ lies on or below the diagonal. If T is continuous, its graph must cross the diagonal at some point (x^*, x^*) and such an x^* is a fixed point of T.

Proposition 1.3.   (*Leray–Schauder–Tychonoff Fixed Point Theorem*) If $X \subset \Re^n$ is nonempty, convex, and compact, and if $T : X \mapsto X$ is a continuous mapping, then there exists some $x^* \in X$ such that $T(x^*) = x^*$.

The iteration $x := T(x)$ can be implemented in parallel in the obvious manner (see Subsection 1.2.4). However, the parallelization can be wasteful if the mapping T is such that the updating of different components involves a substantial amount of common computations. This issue will be raised, in more specific contexts, in later sections. Efficient parallel implementations are often possible in the case where the set X is a Cartesian product of lower dimensional sets, which we study next.

3.1.2 Contractions Over Cartesian Product Sets

Throughout this subsection, we assume that $X = \prod_{i=1}^{m} X_i$, where each X_i is a nonempty subset of $\Re^{n_i}$, and where $n_1 + \cdots + n_m = n$. Accordingly, any vector $x \in X$ is decomposed as $x = (x_1, \ldots, x_m)$, with $x_i \in X_i$. We also assume that we are given a norm $\| \cdot \|_i$ on $\Re^{n_i}$ for each i, and that $\Re^n$ is endowed with the norm

$$\|x\| = \max_i \|x_i\|_i, \tag{1.4}$$

which we call a *block–maximum norm*.

Let $T : X \mapsto X$ be a contraction with modulus α, under the above introduced block–maximum norm. Such a mapping will be called a *block–contraction*. Let $T_i : X \mapsto X_i$ be the ith (block)–component of T, that is,

$$T(x) = \big(T_1(x), \ldots, T_m(x)\big).$$

Notice that

$$\|T_i(x) - T_i(y)\|_i \leq \max_j \|T_j(x) - T_j(y)\|_j = \|T(x) - T(y)\| \leq \alpha \|x - y\|, \qquad \forall x, y \in X, \forall i. \tag{1.5}$$

Gauss–Seidel Methods

Applying the mapping T, as in the iteration $x(t+1) = T\big(x(t)\big)$, corresponds to updating all components of x simultaneously. A Gauss–Seidel mode of implementation is also possible, whereby the block–components of x are updated one at a time. Due to the assumption that X is a Cartesian product, such a Gauss–Seidel iteration maps the set X into itself and the algorithm is well–defined. We now present a precise description and a proof of convergence of Gauss–Seidel iterations.

The mapping $\hat{T}_i : X \mapsto X$, corresponding to an update of the ith block–component only, is given by

$$\hat{T}_i(x) = \hat{T}_i(x_1, \ldots, x_m) = \big(x_1, \ldots, x_{i-1}, T_i(x), x_{i+1}, \ldots, x_m\big).$$

(The fact that $\hat{T}_i$ maps X into itself is a key consequence of the Cartesian product assumption.) Updating all the block–components of x, one at a time in increasing order, is equivalent to applying the mapping $S : X \mapsto X$, defined by

$$S = \hat{T}_m \circ \hat{T}_{m-1} \circ \cdots \circ \hat{T}_1,$$

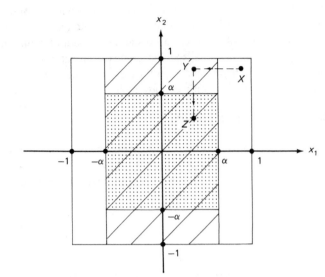

Figure 3.1.3 Illustration of Gauss–Seidel convergence for block–contracting iterations (cf. Prop. 1.4). Let $T : \Re^2 \mapsto \Re^2$ be a contraction, with respect to the maximum norm, with a fixed point $x^* = 0$ and modulus $\alpha < 1$. Consider one iteration of the Gauss–Seidel algorithm, starting from some x such that $\|x\|_\infty \le 1$. The update of the first component leads to the vector $y = \big(T_1(x), x_2\big)$ that belongs to the shaded region $[-\alpha, \alpha] \times [-1, 1]$. The update of the second component leads to the vector $z = S(x) = \big(y_1, T_2(y)\big) = \big(T_1(x), T_2\big(T_1(x), x_2\big)\big)$, which belongs to the dotted region $[-\alpha, \alpha] \times [-\alpha, \alpha]$. In particular, $\|z\|_\infty \le \alpha$.

where $\circ$ denotes composition. An equivalent definition of S is given by the equation

$$S_i(x) = T_i\big(S_1(x), \ldots, S_{i-1}(x), x_i, \ldots, x_m\big), \tag{1.6}$$

where $S_i : X \mapsto X_i$ is the ith block–component of S. It is seen that any fixed point of T is also a fixed point of S, and conversely. The mapping S will be called the *Gauss–Seidel mapping based on the mapping T* and the iteration $x(t+1) = S\big(x(t)\big)$ will be called the *Gauss–Seidel algorithm based on the mapping T*.

    Proposition 1.4.   (*Convergence of Gauss–Seidel Block-Contracting Iterations*) If $T : X \mapsto X$ is a block–contraction, then the Gauss–Seidel mapping S is also a block–contraction, with the same modulus as T. In particular, if X is closed, the sequence of vectors generated by the Gauss–Seidel algorithm based on the mapping T converges to the unique fixed point of T geometrically.

    Proof. We use the definition of S [Eq. (1.6)] and the block–contraction assumption [inequality (1.5), in particular] to obtain for every $x, y \in X$

$$\|S_i(x) - S_i(y)\|_i \le \alpha \max \left\{ \max_{j<i} \|S_j(x) - S_j(y)\|_j \,,\, \max_{j \ge i} \|x_j - y_j\|_j \right\}.$$

A simple induction on i yields $\|S_i(x) - S_i(y)\|_i \le \alpha \max_j \|x_j - y_j\|_j = \alpha \|x - y\|$ for all i. This proves that S is a block–contraction and the rest follows from the convergence result for contracting iterations (Prop. 1.1).   **Q.E.D.**

    Proposition 1.4 is illustrated in Fig. 3.1.3. The following result provides a generalization to the case of pseudocontractions.

Proposition 1.5.   (*Convergence of Gauss–Seidel Block-Pseudocontracting Itera-tions*) If a mapping $T : X \mapsto X$ has a fixed point x^* and is a pseudocontraction of modulus α with respect to a block–maximum norm $\| \cdot \|$, then the same is true for the Gauss–Seidel mapping S, that is,

$$\|S(x) - x^*\| \leq \alpha \|x - x^*\|, \qquad \forall x \in X.$$

In particular, the sequence generated by the Gauss–Seidel algorithm based on the mapping T converges to x^* geometrically.

Proof.   The proof of the inequality $\|S(x) - x^*\| \leq \alpha \|x - x^*\|$ is the same as for the case of block–contractions (Prop. 1.4), provided that we replace y by x^*. Convergence of the Gauss–Seidel algorithm follows from the convergence result for pseudocontracting iterations (Prop. 1.2), applied to the mapping S.   **Q.E.D.**

Component Solution Methods

We now investigate an alternative approach for finding a fixed point of T. We are looking for a solution of the system of equations $x = T(x)$. This system can be decomposed into m smaller systems of equations of the form

$$x_i = T_i(x_1, \ldots, x_m), \qquad i = 1, \ldots, m, \tag{1.7}$$

which have to be solved simultaneously. We will consider an algorithm that solves at each iteration the ith equation in the system (1.7) for x_i, while keeping the other components fixed. There is no established terminology for describing such an algorithm and we will be referring to it as the *component solution method*.

To be more specific, we let $R_i(x)$ be the set of all solutions of the ith equation in the system (1.7), defined by

$$R_i(x) = \Big\{ y_i \in X_i \ \Big| \ y_i = T_i(x_1, \ldots, x_{i-1}, y_i, x_{i+1}, \ldots, x_m) \Big\}. \tag{1.8}$$

The method proceeds as follows. Given a vector $x(t) \in X$, the ith block–component $x_i(t + 1)$ of the next vector is chosen to be a solution of the ith equation in the system (1.7), that is,

$$x_i(t + 1) \in R_i\big(x(t)\big).$$

The following result shows that $x_i(t + 1)$ is uniquely defined if T is a block–contraction.

Proposition 1.6.   Suppose that X is closed and that $T : X \mapsto X$ is a block–contraction. Then the set $R_i(x)$ has exactly one element for each i and for each $x \in X$.

Proof.   Fix some i and some $x \in X$, and consider the mapping $T_i^x : X_i \mapsto X_i$ defined by

$$T_i^x(y_i) = T_i(x_1, \ldots, x_{i-1}, y_i, x_{i+1}, \ldots, x_m). \tag{1.9}$$

Notice that $R_i(x)$ is, by definition, equal to the set of fixed points of T_i^x. By the block–contraction assumption [cf. inequality (1.5)], we have

$$\|T_i^x(y_i) - T_i^x(z_i)\|_i \leq \alpha \|y_i - z_i\|_i, \qquad \forall y_i, z_i \in X_i$$

and T_i^x is a contraction. The conclusion that $R_i(x)$ is a singleton follows from the existence and uniqueness result for fixed points of contraction mappings (Prop. 1.1). **Q.E.D.**

Assuming that each $R_i(x)$ is a singleton, we define a mapping $Q_i : X \mapsto X_i$ by letting $Q_i(x)$ be equal to the unique element of $R_i(x)$. We then define a mapping $Q : X \mapsto X$ by letting

$$Q(x) = \big(Q_1(x), \ldots, Q_m(x)\big)$$

(see Fig. 3.1.4). The component solution method is then described by

$$x(t+1) = Q\big(x(t)\big), \qquad t = 0, 1, \ldots. \tag{1.10}$$

In this iteration, all block–components of x are updated simultaneously. Alternatively, we could use the Gauss–Seidel algorithm based on the mapping Q, in which the block–components of x are updated one at a time (see Fig. 3.1.5). This will be called the *Gauss–Seidel component solution method.*

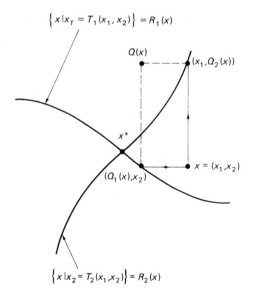

Figure 3.1.4 Illustration of the mapping Q used in the component solution method. Each curve is the set of points where the equation $x_1 = T_1(x_1, x_2)$ [respectively, $x_2 = T_2(x_1, x_2)$] is satisfied. At their intersection x^*, both equations are satisfied and x^* is a fixed point of T. The mapping Q_i corresponds to updating x_i so as to satisfy the ith equation while the other component is fixed.

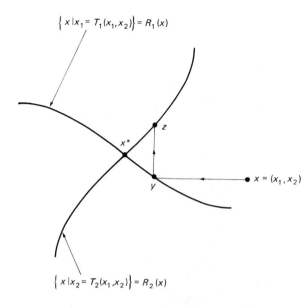

$\left\{ x \,|\, x_1 = T_1(x_1, x_2) \right\} = R_1(x)$

z

x^*

y

$x = (x_1, x_2)$

$\left\{ x \,|\, x_2 = T_2(x_1, x_2) \right\} = R_2(x)$

Figure 3.1.5 Illustration of the Gauss–Seidel component solution method. Starting from the vector $x = (x_1, x_2)$, an update of the first component leads to the point $y = \left(Q_1(x), x_2 \right)$ and an update of the second component leads to the point $z = \left(y_1, Q_2(y) \right) = \left(Q_1(x), Q_2\left(Q_1(x), x_2 \right) \right)$.

Convergence of the component solution method (1.10) and its Gauss–Seidel variant is obtained because Q inherits the contraction property of T, as shown next.

Proposition 1.7.   (*Convergence of Component Solution Methods for Block-Contractions*) If $T : X \mapsto X$ is a block–contraction, then Q is also a block–contraction with the same modulus as T. In particular, if X is closed, then the component solution method $x(t+1) = Q\left(x(t) \right)$, as well as the Gauss–Seidel algorithm based on Q, converge to the unique fixed point of T geometrically.

Proof. Let $x = (x_1, \ldots, x_m)$ and $y = (y_1, \ldots, y_m)$. By the definition of Q_i, we have $Q_i(x) \in R_i(x)$ and $Q_i(y) \in R_i(y)$. Therefore,

$$Q_i(x) = T_i\left(x_1, \ldots, x_{i-1}, Q_i(x), x_{i+1}, \ldots, x_m \right),$$

and

$$Q_i(y) = T_i\left(y_1, \ldots, y_{i-1}, Q_i(y), y_{i+1}, \ldots, y_m \right).$$

Using the block–contraction assumption for T [inequality (1.5)], we obtain

$$\|Q_i(x) - Q_i(y)\|_i \leq \alpha \max\left\{ \|Q_i(x) - Q_i(y)\|_i, \ \max_{j \neq i} \|x_j - y_j\|_j \right\}.$$

Since $\alpha < 1$, it follows that

$$\|Q_i(x) - Q_i(y)\|_i \le \alpha \max_{j \ne i} \|x_j - y_j\|_j \le \alpha \|x - y\|.$$

Since this is true for each i, we obtain $\|Q(x) - Q(y)\| \le \alpha \|x - y\|$, which shows that Q is also a block–contraction. Assuming that X is closed, Q has a unique fixed point x^*. The equation $x^* = Q(x^*)$ is equivalent to $\{x_i^*\} = R_i(x^*)$ for each i. Using the definition of $R_i(x^*)$, we conclude that $x^* = T(x^*)$ and x^* is the unique fixed point of T. The result follows because contracting iterations and their Gauss–Seidel variants are guaranteed to converge geometrically (Props. 1.1 and 1.4).   **Q.E.D.**

We now consider the case where T is a pseudocontraction with fixed point x^*. The major difference here is that there is no guarantee that the set $R_i(x)$ is a singleton; consequently, the mapping Q is not, in general, well-defined. In particular, $R_i(x)$ could be empty, in which case, the algorithm breaks down. It is also possible that $R_i(x)$ has many elements; in this case, our approach will be to assume that $Q_i(x)$ is chosen among the elements of $R_i(x)$ by means of some rule that we leave unspecified. The following result provides an easily verifiable condition for the sets $R_i(x)$ to be nonempty.

Proposition 1.8.   Suppose that the mapping $T : X \mapsto X$ is continuous and a pseudocontraction with respect to a block–maximum norm $\| \cdot \|$. If each set X_i is closed and convex, then the set $R_i(x)$ is nonempty for each i and for each $x \in X$.

Proof. Let x^* and α be the fixed point and the modulus of T, respectively. As in the proof of Prop. 1.6 we consider the mapping $T_i^x : X_i \mapsto X_i$, defined by

$$T_i^x(y_i) = T_i\big(x_1, \ldots, x_{i-1}, y_i, x_{i+1}, \ldots, x_m\big).$$

Fix some i and some $x \in X$. Consider the set

$$Y_i = \Big\{ y_i \;\Big|\; \|y_i - x_i^*\|_i \le \max_{j \ne i} \|x_j - x_j^*\|_j \Big\} \cap X_i.$$

Notice that for every $y_i \in Y_i$, we have

$$\|T_i^x(y_i) - x_i^*\|_i \le \alpha \max\Big\{ \|y_i - x_i^*\|_i, \; \max_{j \ne i} \|x_j - x_j^*\|_j \Big\} \le \max_{j \ne i} \|x_j - x_j^*\|_j,$$

which shows that $T_i^x(y_i) \in Y_i$. The set Y_i is closed and convex because it is the intersection of two closed and convex sets. Furthermore, Y_i is bounded and is therefore compact. Finally, T_i^x is continuous and the Leray–Schauder–Tychonoff Fixed Point Theorem (Prop. 1.3) shows that T_i^x has a fixed point. From the definition of T_i^x, such a fixed point is an element of $R_i(x)$.   **Q.E.D.**

The following result is an analog of Prop. 1.7.

Proposition 1.9.   (*Convergence of Component Solution Methods for Block-Pseudo-contractions*) Suppose that the mapping $T : X \mapsto X$ has a fixed point x^* and is a pseudocontraction with respect to a block–maximum norm $\| \cdot \|$. Suppose that for every i and $x \in X$, the set $R_i(x)$ is nonempty. Then, the mapping Q is also a pseudocontraction, with respect to the same norm, and x^* is its unique fixed point. In particular, the sequence $\{x(t)\}$ generated by the component solution method $x(t+1) = Q\big(x(t)\big)$, or by the Gauss–Seidel algorithm based on Q, converges to x^* geometrically.

Proof. Since $Q_i(x) \in R_i(x)$, we have

$$Q_i(x) = T_i\big(x_1, \ldots, x_{i-1}, Q_i(x), x_{i+1}, \ldots, x_m\big).$$

Using the pseudocontraction assumption on T, we obtain

$$\|Q_i(x) - x_i^*\|_i \leq \alpha \max \Big\{ \|Q_i(x) - x_i^*\|_i, \max_{j \neq i} \|x_j - x_j^*\|_j \Big\},$$

where $\alpha \in [0, 1)$ is the modulus of T. It follows that $\|Q(x) - x^*\| \leq \alpha \|x - x^*\|$ for every $x \in X$. In particular, x^* is the unique fixed point of Q and Q is a pseudocontraction. The desired conclusions follow from the convergence result for pseudocontracting iterations (Prop. 1.2) and their Gauss–Seidel variants (Prop. 1.5), applied to the mapping Q.   **Q.E.D.**

Results similar to those proved so far can also be obtained if T is a *monotone* mapping, that is, if T satisfies $T(x) \leq T(y)$ for every x, y such that $x \leq y$ (Exercise 1.4).

3.1.3 Some Useful Contraction Mappings

We assume again that $X \subset \Re^n$ and that X is decomposed as a Cartesian product of lower dimensional sets $X_i \subset \Re^{n_i}$, $i = 1, \ldots, m$. We consider a mapping $T : X \mapsto \Re^n$, whose ith block–component T_i is of the form

$$T_i(x) = x_i - \gamma G_i^{-1} f_i(x). \tag{1.11}$$

Here each f_i is a function from $\Re^n$ into $\Re^{n_i}$, γ is some scalar, and G_i is an invertible symmetric matrix of dimensions $n_i \times n_i$. Mappings of this form are very common in iterative methods for optimization and solution of systems of equations or variational inequalities, and they will keep recurring in subsequent sections of this chapter. We collect here certain sufficient conditions for such mappings to be block–contractions. These conditions will be invoked in later sections in order to establish the convergence of certain iterative methods.

The general nature of the conditions to be considered is best illustrated in the simple case where $X = \Re^n$ and $n_i = 1$, $G_i = 1$ for each i, and the mapping f has the form $f(x) = Ax$, where A is an $n \times n$ matrix. We then have

$$T(x) = x - \gamma Ax = (I - \gamma A)x,$$

which is reminiscent of iterative algorithms for linear equations [see Section 2.4, Eq. (4.9), for example]. The mapping T is a contraction with respect to the maximum norm $\|\cdot\|_\infty$ if and only if $\|I - \gamma A\|_\infty < 1$. From the formula for the maximum norm (Prop. A.13 in Appendix A), an equivalent condition is

$$\max_i \left\{ |1 - \gamma a_{ii}| + \sum_{j \neq i} |\gamma a_{ij}| \right\} < 1. \tag{1.12}$$

Assuming that γ is positive and small enough so that $\gamma |a_{ii}| \leq 1$ for each i, the expression in Eq. (1.12) is equal to

$$\max_i \left\{ 1 - \gamma a_{ii} + \gamma \sum_{j \neq i} |a_{ij}| \right\}.$$

It follows that for γ positive and small enough, the mapping T is a contraction if and only if $a_{ii} > 0$ and

$$\sum_{j \neq i} |a_{ij}| < a_{ii}, \qquad \forall i, \tag{1.13}$$

which is a diagonal dominance condition on A. Notice that if $f(x) = Ax$ then $\nabla_j f_i(x) = a_{ij}$. This suggests that the appropriate generalization of conditions (1.12) and (1.13) to the case of nonlinear functions f should be to replace a_{ij} by $\nabla_j f_i(x)$. Indeed, all of the conditions to be introduced in the sequel can be interpreted as diagonal dominance assumptions on the matrix ∇f of partial derivatives of f.

In the general case where the block–components of f have dimension $n_i \geq 1$, we use the notation $\nabla_j f_i(x)$ to denote the matrix of dimension $n_j \times n_i$ whose entries are the partial derivatives of the components of f_i with respect to the components of x_j. In particular, the kth column of $\nabla_j f_i(x)$ is the gradient vector of the kth component of f_i, when viewed as a function of x_j.

Since each $\nabla_j f_i(x)$ is a matrix rather than a scalar, a diagonal dominance condition on $\nabla f(x)$ should involve the norms of these matrices. The most suitable norms for such a purpose are induced matrix norms (see Appendix A) corresponding to the underlying vector norm on $\Re^n$. To be more specific, let $\|\cdot\|_i$ be an arbitrary norm on $\Re^{n_i}$, for each i, and let $\|\cdot\|$ be the corresponding block–maximum norm. With any matrix A of dimension $n_i \times n_j$, we associate the induced matrix norm

$$\|A\|_{ij} = \max_{x \neq 0} \frac{\|Ax\|_i}{\|x\|_j} = \max_{\|x\|_j = 1} \|Ax\|_i.$$

We are now ready to generalize the diagonal dominance conditions (1.12) and (1.13) to the case where f is nonlinear and the dimension n_i of each block–component is possibly larger than 1.

Proposition 1.10.   Suppose that X is convex. If $f : \Re^n \mapsto \Re^n$ is continuously differentiable and there exists a scalar $\alpha \in [0, 1)$ such that

$$\left\| I - \gamma G_i^{-1} \left(\nabla_i f_i(x) \right)' \right\|_{ii} + \sum_{j \neq i} \left\| \gamma G_i^{-1} \left(\nabla_j f_i(x) \right)' \right\|_{ij} \leq \alpha, \qquad \forall x \in X, \; \forall i, \quad (1.14)$$

then the mapping $T : X \mapsto \Re^n$ defined by $T_i(x) = x_i - \gamma G_i^{-1} f_i(x)$ is a contraction with respect to the block–maximum norm $\| \cdot \|$.

Proof.   We fix some i and $x, y \in X$, and we define a function $g_i : [0, 1] \mapsto \Re^{n_i}$ by

$$g_i(t) = tx_i + (1 - t)y_i - \gamma G_i^{-1} f_i \big(tx + (1 - t)y \big).$$

Notice that g_i is continuously differentiable. Let dg_i/dt be the n_i–dimensional vector consisting of the derivatives of the components of g_i. We then have

$$\|T_i(x) - T_i(y)\|_i = \|g_i(1) - g_i(0)\|_i = \left\| \int_0^1 \frac{dg_i(t)}{dt} \, dt \right\|_i$$

$$\leq \int_0^1 \left\| \frac{dg_i}{dt}(t) \right\|_i dt \leq \max_{t \in [0,1]} \left\| \frac{dg_i}{dt}(t) \right\|_i.$$

It, therefore, suffices to bound the norm of dg_i/dt. The chain rule yields

$$\left\| \frac{dg_i}{dt}(t) \right\|_i = \left\| x_i - y_i - \gamma G_i^{-1} \left(\nabla f_i \big(tx + (1 - t)y \big) \right)' (x - y) \right\|_i$$

$$= \left\| \left[I - \gamma G_i^{-1} \left(\nabla_i f_i \big(tx + (1 - t)y \big) \right)' \right] (x_i - y_i) \right.$$

$$\left. - \sum_{j \neq i} \gamma G_i^{-1} \left(\nabla_j f_i \big(tx + (1 - t)y \big) \right)' (x_j - y_j) \right\|_i$$

$$\leq \left\| I - \gamma G_i^{-1} \left(\nabla_i f_i \big(tx + (1 - t)y \big) \right)' \right\|_{ii} \cdot \|x_i - y_i\|_i$$

$$+ \sum_{j \neq i} \left\| \gamma G_i^{-1} \left(\nabla_j f_i \big(tx + (1 - t)y \big) \right)' \right\|_{ij} \cdot \|x_j - y_j\|_j$$

$$\leq \alpha \max_j \|x_j - y_j\|_j = \alpha \|x - y\|,$$

which establishes the contraction property. [We have used the assumption (1.14) with x replaced by $tx + (1 - t)y$; this vector belongs to X because X is assumed convex.] **Q.E.D.**

The condition (1.14) in the previous proposition is generally hard to verify. It is shown in the following that if $n_i = 1$ for each i, then this condition simplifies considerably and bears closer resemblance to the diagonal dominance condition (1.13).

Proposition 1.11. Assume the following:

(a) We have $n_i = 1$, for each i, the set X is convex, and the function $f : \Re^n \mapsto \Re^n$ is continuously differentiable.

(b) There exists a positive constant K such that

$$\nabla_i f_i(x) \leq K, \qquad \forall x \in X, \ \forall i.$$

(c) There exists some $\beta > 0$ such that

$$\sum_{j \neq i} |\nabla_j f_i(x)| \leq \nabla_i f_i(x) - \beta, \qquad \forall x \in X, \ \forall i, \tag{1.15}$$

Then, the mapping $T : X \mapsto \Re^n$ defined by $T(x) = x - \gamma f(x)$ is a contraction with respect to the maximum norm, provided that $0 < \gamma < 1/K$.

Proof. Under the assumption $0 < \gamma < 1/K$, we have

$$|1 - \gamma \nabla_i f_i(x)| + \gamma \sum_{j \neq i} |\nabla_j f_i(x)| = 1 - \gamma \left(\nabla_i f_i(x) - \sum_{j \neq i} |\nabla_j f_i(x)| \right) \leq 1 - \gamma \beta < 1, \tag{1.16}$$

which shows that inequality (1.14) holds. The result follows from Prop. 1.10.   **Q.E.D.**

A minor generalization of Prop. 1.11 is provided in Exercise 1.3.

The next two results are based on a particular choice of norms, namely weighted quadratic norms. For motivation purposes, let us temporarily consider the case where there is only one block–component and consider a mapping $T : X \mapsto \Re^n$ given by

$$T(x) = x - \gamma G^{-1} f(x), \qquad \forall x \in X, \tag{1.17}$$

where G is a symmetric positive definite matrix. The effect of G in Eq. (1.17) is to scale the direction in which x is changed when T is applied. Accordingly, it is reasonable to consider a norm that scales the components of x in a corresponding fashion. To this effect, we introduce the norm $\| \cdot \|_G$, defined by

$$\|x\|_G = \left(x'Gx \right)^{1/2}$$

and we look for conditions under which T is a contraction with respect to $\|\cdot\|_G$. An easy calculation yields

$$\|T(x) - T(y)\|_G^2 = \left((x-y) - \gamma G^{-1}\big(f(x) - f(y)\big)\right)' G\left((x-y) - \gamma G^{-1}\big(f(x) - f(y)\big)\right)$$

$$= \|x - y\|_G^2 + \gamma^2\big(f(x) - f(y)\big)' G^{-1}\big(f(x) - f(y)\big)$$

$$- 2\gamma\big(f(x) - f(y)\big)'(x - y).$$

If γ is chosen very small and the norm of $f(x) - f(y)$ is of the order of $\|x - y\|_G$, then the term involving γ^2 can be neglected. We then see that for T to be a contraction, it is sufficient to assume that γ is positive and small enough, and that

$$\big(f(x) - f(y)\big)'(x - y) \geq \alpha\|x - y\|_G^2, \qquad \forall x, y \in X, \tag{1.18}$$

where α is some positive constant. Inequality (1.18) is called a *strong monotonicity* condition and its significance will be explored further in Section 3.5. Let us simply notice here that if f is the linear function $f(x) = Ax$, then strong monotonicity is equivalent to the positive definiteness of A.

We now return to the general case where $X = \prod_{i=1}^m X_i \subset \prod_{i=1}^m \Re^{n_i}$, and where T is given by $T_i(x) = x_i - \gamma G_i^{-1} f_i(x)$ for each i. We assume that each matrix G_i is symmetric and positive definite. For each i, we define a norm $\|\cdot\|_i$ on $\Re^{n_i}$ by

$$\|x_i\|_i = \big(x'G_i x\big)^{1/2}.$$

These norms define a block–maximum norm $\|\cdot\|$ given by $\|x\| = \max_i \|x_i\|_i$. In keeping with the discussion in the preceding paragraph, we shall impose a bound on the magnitude of $f(x) - f(y)$ and a monotonicity condition similar to (1.18).

Proposition 1.12.   Suppose that each G_i is symmetric positive definite and let the norms $\|\cdot\|_i$ and $\|\cdot\|$ be as above. Suppose that there exist positive constants A_1, A_2, A_3, with $A_3 < A_2$, such that for each i and for each $x, y \in X$, we have

$$\|f_i(x) - f_i(y)\|_i \leq A_1 \|x - y\|, \tag{1.19}$$

and

$$\big(f_i(x) - f_i(y)\big)'(x_i - y_i) \geq A_2 \|x_i - y_i\|_i^2 - A_3\|x - y\|^2. \tag{1.20}$$

Then, provided that γ is positive and small enough, the mapping $T: X \mapsto \Re^n$, defined by $T_i(x) = x_i - \gamma G_i^{-1} f_i(x)$, is a contraction with respect to the block–maximum norm $\|\cdot\|$.

Proof. Let A_4 be a positive constant such that $x_i' G_i^{-1} x_i \leq A_4 x_i' G_i x_i$ for every $x_i \in \Re^{n_i}$. [The existence of such a constant follows from the positive definiteness of G_i; see Prop. A.28(c) in Appendix A.] Assuming that $0 < \gamma < 1/(2A_2)$, we have

$$
\begin{aligned}
\|T_i(x) - T_i(y)\|_i^2 = &\|x_i - y_i\|_i^2 + \gamma^2 \big(f_i(x) - f_i(y)\big)' G_i^{-1} \big(f_i(x) - f_i(y)\big) \\
&- 2\gamma \big(f_i(x) - f_i(y)\big)' (x_i - y_i) \\
\leq &\|x_i - y_i\|_i^2 + A_1^2 A_4 \gamma^2 \|x - y\|^2 - 2\gamma A_2 \|x_i - y_i\|_i^2 + 2\gamma A_3 \|x - y\|^2 \\
\leq &\Big(1 - 2\gamma A_2 + A_1^2 A_4 \gamma^2 + 2\gamma A_3\Big) \|x - y\|^2.
\end{aligned}
$$

If γ is also smaller than $2(A_2 - A_3)/(A_1^2 A_4)$, which is possible because $A_2 > A_3$, the expression $1 - 2\gamma A_2 + A_1^2 A_4 \gamma^2 + 2\gamma A_3$ is smaller than 1, which proves the result. **Q.E.D.**

We now simplify the conditions of Prop. 1.12, for the case where f is continuously differentiable. In the proof of our next result, we use the fact that if G_i is symmetric and positive definite, then the norm $\|x_i\|_i = (x_i' G_i x_i)^{1/2}$ is also equal to $\|G_i^{1/2} x_i\|_2$, where $G_i^{1/2}$ is a symmetric square root of G_i and $\|\cdot\|_2$ is the Euclidean norm (see Props. A.27 and A.28 in Appendix A).

Proposition 1.13. Assume the following:

(a) The set X is convex and the function $f : \Re^n \mapsto \Re^n$ is continuously differentiable.

(b) For each i, the matrix G_i is symmetric and positive definite.

(c) There exists a constant K such that $\|\nabla f(x)\|_2 \leq K$ for every $x \in X$.

(d) There exist some $\delta > 0$ and $\epsilon > 0$ such that $\nabla_i f_i(x)' - \delta G_i$ is nonnegative definite, for every i and $x \in X$, and such that

$$
\sum_{j \neq i} \Big\| G_j^{-1/2} \nabla_j f_i(x) G_i^{-1/2} \Big\|_2 \leq \delta(1 - \epsilon), \qquad \forall i, \ \forall x \in X. \tag{1.21}
$$

Then, provided that γ is positive and small enough, the mapping $T : X \mapsto \Re^n$, defined by $T_i(x) = x_i - \gamma G_i^{-1} f_i(x)$, is a contraction with respect to the block–maximum norm $\|x\| = \max_i (x_i' G_i x_i)^{1/2}$.

Proof. We shall verify that the assumptions of Prop. 1.12 are satisfied. Let us fix some i and some $x, y \in X$. We define a function $g : [0, 1] \mapsto \Re$ by

$$
g(t) = f_i \big(tx + (1 - t)y\big)' (x_i - y_i).
$$

The chain rule yields

$$\frac{dg}{dt}(t) = (x - y)'\nabla f_i\big(tx + (1 - t)y\big)(x_i - y_i).$$

Furthermore, the mean value theorem shows that there exists some $t_0 \in [0, 1]$ such that

$$g(1) - g(0) = \frac{dg}{dt}(t_0).$$

Let $z = t_0 x + (1 - t_0)y$ and note that z belongs to X because X is convex. We then have

$$\big(f_i(x) - f_i(y)\big)'(x_i - y_i) = g(1) - g(0) = \frac{dg}{dt}(t_0)$$

$$= (x - y)'\nabla f_i(z)(x_i - y_i)$$

$$= (x_i - y_i)'\nabla_i f_i(z)(x_i - y_i) + \sum_{j \neq i}(x_j - y_j)'\nabla_j f_i(z)(x_i - y_i)$$

$$\geq \delta\|x_i - y_i\|_i^2 + \sum_{j \neq i}(x_j - y_j)'G_j^{1/2}\left(G_j^{-1/2}\nabla_j f_i(z)G_i^{-1/2}\right)G_i^{1/2}(x_i - y_i)$$

$$\geq \delta\|x_i - y_i\|_i^2 - \sum_{j \neq i}\|G_j^{1/2}(x_j - y_j)\|_2 \cdot \|G_j^{-1/2}\nabla_j f_i(z)G_i^{-1/2}\|_2 \cdot \|G_i^{1/2}(x_i - y_i)\|_2$$

$$\geq \delta\|x_i - y_i\|_i^2 - \|x - y\|^2\sum_{j \neq i}\|G_j^{-1/2}\nabla_j f_i(z)G_i^{-1/2}\|_2$$

$$\geq \delta\|x_i - y_i\|_i^2 - \delta(1 - \epsilon)\|x - y\|^2,$$

where in the last two steps we used the definition of the norm $\|\cdot\|$ and inequality (1.21). This shows that condition (1.20) is satisfied with $A_2 = \delta$ and $A_3 = \delta(1 - \epsilon) < A_2$.

Condition (1.19) in Prop. 1.12 is a simple consequence of condition (c) and the mean value theorem. We conclude that Prop. 1.12 applies and shows that T is a contraction.   **Q.E.D.**

EXERCISES

1.1. Show that if $T : X \mapsto X$ is a contraction but X is not closed, then T need not have a fixed point.

1.2.   **(a)** Construct an example of a mapping T satisfying the assumptions of Prop. 1.8 and such that for some $x \in X$ and some i, the set $R_i(x)$ has more than one element.

　　(b) Construct an example to show that Prop. 1.8 is false without the assumption that X is convex.

    (c) Construct an example to show that Prop. 1.8 is false without the assumption that the mapping T is continuous.

1.3. Let a function $f : \Re^n \mapsto \Re^n$ satisfy the assumptions of Prop. 1.11 except that the condition (1.15) is replaced by

$$\sum_{j \neq i} w_j |\nabla_j f_i(x)| \leq w_i \nabla_i f_i(x) - \beta, \qquad \forall x \in X, \ \forall i,$$

where $w_1, \ldots, w_m$ are positive scalars. Show that for γ positive and small enough, the mapping T defined by $T(x) = x - \gamma f(x)$ is a contraction mapping with respect to a suitable norm.

1.4. (**Monotone Mappings.**) A mapping $T : \Re^n \mapsto \Re^n$ is called monotone if it satisfies $T(x) \leq T(y)$ for every $x, y \in \Re^n$ such that $x \leq y$. Suppose that T is monotone, continuous, has a unique fixed point x^*, and that there exist two vectors $y^*, z^* \in \Re^n$ such that $y^* \leq z^*$ and $T(y^*) \geq y^*$, $T(z^*) \leq z^*$. Let $H = \{x \mid y^* \leq x \leq z^*\}$.

    (a) Show that the sequence $\{x(t)\}$ generated by the iteration $x(t+1) = T\big(x(t)\big)$ converges to x^* if $x(0)$ is equal to either y^* or z^*. Furthermore, $x^* \in H$.

    (b) Show that the conclusion of part (a) remains valid for every $x(0) \in H$.

    (c) Show that the sequence of vectors generated by the Gauss–Seidel algorithm based on the mapping T converges to x^* for every initial vector $x(0)$ belonging to H.

    (d) We define $\hat{T}_i : \Re^n \mapsto \Re^n$ by

$$\hat{T}_i(x) = \hat{T}_i(x_1, \ldots, x_n) = \big(x_1, \ldots, x_{i-1}, T_i(x), x_{i+1}, \ldots, x_m\big). \qquad (1.22)$$

Consider the iteration $x(t+1) = \hat{T}_i\big(x(t)\big)$ and show that it converges to a finite vector for every $x(0) \in H$. *Hint:* This is essentially a one-dimensional iteration.

    (e) For any $x \in H$ and any i, let $Q_i(x)$ be the limit of $x_i(t)$, where $\{x(t)\}$ is the sequence generated by the iteration of part (d), initialized with $x(0) = x$. Show that the mapping $Q = (Q_1, \ldots, Q_n)$ is monotone on the set H. Construct an example showing that Q can be discontinuous.

    (f) Let Q be as in part (e). Show that the sequence generated by the iteration $x(t+1) = Q\big(x(t)\big)$ converges to x^* for every $x(0) \in H$, and that the same is true for the Gauss–Seidel algorithm based on Q.

3.2 UNCONSTRAINED OPTIMIZATION

In this section, we consider algorithms for minimizing a continuously differentiable cost function $F : \Re^n \mapsto \Re$. We have $\nabla F(x^*) = 0$ for every vector x^* that minimizes F (Prop. A.34 in Appendix A). In view of this fact, the minimization of F is related to the problem of solving the system $\nabla F(x) = 0$ of generally nonlinear equations. In fact, most iterative optimization algorithms are aimed at finding a solution of the equation $\nabla F(x) = 0$ without any guarantees that such a solution is a global minimizer of F. We will thus settle with this as our objective. In Chapter 2, we studied iterative algorithms for the solution of linear equations; the algorithms in this section can be viewed as their natural extensions to a nonlinear setting.

There are two main approaches for proving convergence of an algorithm for nonlinear optimization. In the *descent* approach, one shows that the value of the cost function keeps decreasing toward its minimal value. In an alternative approach, a suitable norm is introduced and one shows that the distance of the current iterate from a minimizing point decreases with each iteration. In what follows, both approaches will be considered.

3.2.1 The Main Algorithms

The algorithms to be presented can be motivated from the iterative algorithms for solving linear equations that were introduced in Section 2.4. Suppose that we are solving the linear system $Ax = b$, where A is a symmetric positive definite matrix. This is equivalent to minimizing a cost function F defined by $F(x) = \frac{1}{2}x'Ax - x'b$. In this context, $\nabla F(x) = Ax - b$ and $\nabla^2 F(x) = A$. We now recall the iterative algorithms introduced in Section 2.4 and the following generalizations suggest themselves:

Jacobi Algorithm. (Generalizing the JOR algorithm for linear equations):

$$x(t+1) = x(t) - \gamma \big[D\big(x(t)\big)\big]^{-1}\nabla F(x(t)), \qquad (2.1)$$

where γ is a positive stepsize, and where $D(x)$ is a diagonal matrix whose ith diagonal entry is $\nabla^2_{ii}F(x)$, assumed to be nonzero for each i.

Gauss-Seidel Algorithm. (Generalizing the SOR algorithm for linear equations):

$$x_i(t+1) = x_i(t) - \gamma\frac{\nabla_i F\big(z(i,t)\big)}{\nabla^2_{ii}F\big(z(i,t)\big)}, \qquad i = 1,\ldots,n, \qquad (2.2)$$

where $z(i,t) = \big(x_1(t+1),\ldots,x_{i-1}(t+1), x_i(t),\ldots,x_n(t)\big)$.

Gradient Algorithm. (Generalizing Richardson's algorithm for linear equations):

$$x(t+1) = x(t) - \gamma\nabla F\big(x(t)\big). \qquad (2.3)$$

A Gauss–Seidel variant of the gradient algorithm is obtained if Eq. (2.3) is replaced by

$$x_i(t+1) = x_i(t) - \gamma\nabla_i F\big(z(i,t)\big), \qquad i = 1,\ldots,n, \qquad (2.4)$$

where $z(i,t)$ is defined as in the Gauss–Seidel algorithm.

Given some $x \in \Re^n$ such that $\nabla F(x) \neq 0$, any vector $s \in \Re^n$ with the property $s'\nabla F(x) < 0$ is called a *descent direction*. The reason is that $s'\nabla F(x)$ is the directional derivative of F along the direction s and therefore, if γ is a sufficiently small positive constant, then $F(x + \gamma s) < F(x)$. Any algorithm that, given a current vector x satisfying $\nabla F(x) \neq 0$, updates x along a descent direction is called a *descent algorithm*. The gradient algorithm (2.3) is certainly a descent algorithm; in fact, it is often called the *steepest descent* algorithm because the direction of update is such that F tends to decrease as fast as possible, in the sense that $-\nabla F(x)/\|\nabla F(x)\|_2$ minimizes the directional derivative $s'\nabla F(x)$ over all directions s with $\|s\|_2 = 1$. The Gauss–Seidel variant (2.4) of the gradient algorithm is also a descent algorithm, and the same property holds for the Jacobi and Gauss–Seidel algorithms of Eqs. (2.1) and (2.2), respectively, under the assumption that $\nabla_{ii}^2 F(x) > 0$ for all $x \in \Re^n$. We can think of the Jacobi algorithm as a *scaled* version of the gradient algorithm, whereby the ith component of the update $-\gamma \nabla F(x(t))$ is scaled by a factor of $1/\nabla_{ii}^2 F(x(t))$. One can consider more general scaling methods and this leads to the following algorithm.

Scaled Gradient Algorithm.

$$x(t + 1) = x(t) - \gamma \big(D(t)\big)^{-1} \nabla F\big(x(t)\big), \tag{2.5}$$

where $D(t)$ is a scaling matrix. Quite often, $D(t)$ is chosen diagonal, which simplifies the task of inverting it. If $D(t)$ is indeed diagonal, its entries are positive, γ is positive, and $\nabla F\big(x(t)\big) \neq 0$, then it is seen that $\gamma \nabla F\big(x(t)\big)' \big(D(t)\big)^{-1} \nabla F\big(x(t)\big) > 0$ and the scaled gradient algorithm is a descent algorithm (see Fig. 3.2.1).

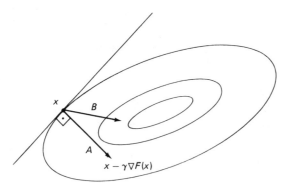

Figure 3.2.1 Descent directions of the gradient and the scaled gradient algorithms. The curves shown are sets of points where the value of F is constant. The vector A indicates the steepest descent direction. The vector B is another descent direction obtained by positive scaling of the components of A, as in the scaled gradient iteration $x := x - \gamma D^{-1} \nabla F(x)$, with D being diagonal and with positive diagonal entries. With proper scaling, the direction of B is preferable to that of A.

The parallel implementation of algorithms such as the Jacobi and gradient algorithms of Eqs. (2.1) and (2.3), respectively, is straightforward. We assign to the ith processor the task of updating the ith component of x. After each update, each processor communicates the newly computed value to those processors that require it. We notice that the ith processor has to know the current value of x_j only if $\nabla_i F$ or $\nabla_{ii}^2 F$ depends on x_j. For many large problems, $\nabla_i F$ and $\nabla_{ii}^2 F$ depend on only a few of the remaining components, the corresponding dependency graph is sparse, and the communication requirements of such algorithms are greatly reduced. The Gauss–Seidel algorithms of Eqs. (2.2) and (2.4) are generally unsuitable for parallel implementation except when the dependency graph is sparse, in which case, the coloring scheme discussed in Subsection 1.2.4 is applicable.

A related class of algorithms is obtained if instead of using a constant stepsize γ, we use a stepsize that leads to the largest possible reduction of the value of F. For example, in a modification of the gradient algorithm, we can let $x(t+1)$ be equal to $x(t) - \gamma(t)\nabla F\big(x(t)\big)$, where $\gamma(t)$ is the value of γ that minimizes $F\big(x(t) - \gamma\nabla F(x(t))\big)$ with respect to γ. Such algorithms often converge faster; on the other hand, the one–dimensional minimization that has to be carried out at each stage is not easily paral-lelizable in general. For this reason, in what follows, we concentrate attention to the case of a constant stepsize. We refer to the sources given at the end of the chapter for convergence analysis using other stepsize rules.

Newton and Approximate Newton Methods

Let us assume that F is twice continuously differentiable. An important method for nonlinear optimization is *Newton's algorithm*, described by the equation

$$x(t+1) = x(t) - \gamma\Big(\nabla^2 F\big(x(t)\big)\Big)^{-1}\nabla F\big(x(t)\big). \tag{2.6}$$

We notice that if $F(x) = \frac{1}{2}x'Ax - x'b$ and if $\gamma = 1$, then $x(t+1) = x(t) - A^{-1}\big(Ax(t) - b\big) = A^{-1}b$, which proves convergence in a single step. Accordingly, it can be shown that for nonquadratic problems, Newton's algorithm converges much faster (under certain assumptions) than the previously introduced algorithms, see e.g. [OrR70]. As an illustration of this fact, assume that F is twice continuously differentiable and has a local minimum x^* for which $\nabla^2 F(x^*)$ is positive definite. Suppose that we are given $x(t)$ which is close enough to x^* so that $\nabla^2 F\big(x(t)\big)$ is invertible. Let $x(t+1)$ be the vector generated by the Newton iteration (2.6) with $\gamma = 1$. We then have

$$x(t+1) - x^* = \big[\nabla^2 F\big(x(t)\big)\big]^{-1}\big[\nabla^2 F\big(x(t)\big)\big(x(t) - x^*\big) - \nabla F\big(x(t)\big)\big]$$

$$= \big[\nabla^2 F\big(x(t)\big)\big]^{-1}\int_0^1 \big[\nabla^2 F\big(x(t)\big) - \nabla^2 F\big(x^* + \xi\big(x(t) - x^*\big)\big)\big]\, d\xi\, \big(x(t) - x^*\big),$$

from which we obtain for any norm $\|\cdot\|$

$\|x(t+1) - x^*\|$

$$\leq \Big\|\big[\nabla^2 F\big(x(t)\big)\big]^{-1}\Big\| \cdot \Big(\int_0^1 \big\|\nabla^2 F\big(x(t)\big) - \nabla^2 F\big(x^* + \xi\big(x(t) - x^*\big)\big)\big\|\, d\xi\Big) \cdot \|x(t) - x^*\|.$$

Using the continuity of $\nabla^2 F(x)$, it follows that given any $\alpha \in (0,1)$ there exists some $\epsilon > 0$ such that

$$\|x(t+1) - x^*\| \leq \alpha\|x(t) - x^*\|,$$

for all $x(t)$ with $\|x(t) - x^*\| \leq \epsilon$. This is in contrast with the other algorithms we have been studying for which the preceding inequality cannot be proved for an arbitrarily small value of α, and establishes the faster convergence of Newton's algorithm. On the other hand, the Newton iteration (2.6) involves a matrix inverse that greatly amplifies the computational requirements per stage. The Jacobi algorithm (2.1) can be viewed as an approximation of Newton's algorithm in which the off–diagonal entries of the matrix $\nabla^2 F$ are ignored, thereby making the matrix inversion very easy. More generally, in scaled gradient algorithms of the form $x(t+1) = x(t) - \gamma \left(D(t) \right)^{-1} \nabla F\left(x(t) \right)$, it is usually desired to let $D(t)$ be an approximation of $\nabla^2 F\left(x(t) \right)$ that is easy to invert.

We now describe a related and frequently more practical class of algorithms, the *approximate Newton methods*, which are based on the Newton iteration (2.6) except that the inversion of the matrix $\nabla^2 F\left(x(t) \right)$ is not carried out to completion. Let

$$H = \nabla^2 F\left(x(t) \right)$$

and

$$g = \nabla F\left(x(t) \right).$$

Equation (2.6) becomes

$$x(t + 1) = x(t) + \gamma s, \tag{2.7}$$

where s is computed by solving the linear system $Hs = -g$. In an approximate Newton method, we employ an iterative algorithm for solving the system $Hs = -g$ and we terminate this algorithm after only a few iterations, before it converges. (Some common choices of iterative algorithms are the SOR method of Section 2.4 and the conjugate gradient method of Section 2.7, which, incidentally, are well–suited for parallelization.) This provides us with a direction vector $\hat{s}$ that is an approximation of s, and Eq. (2.7) is replaced by

$$x(t + 1) = x(t) + \gamma \hat{s}. \tag{2.8}$$

A remarkable fact is that the vector $\hat{s}$ is guaranteed, under certain assumptions, to be a direction of descent, which we proceed to demonstrate.

Suppose that $g \neq 0$ and that H is positive definite. (Conditions for H to be positive definite are provided by Prop. A.41 in Appendix A.) Furthermore, H is symmetric. Several iterative methods for solving the system $Hs = -g$ have the property that successive iterates reduce the value of the quadratic form $\frac{1}{2}s'Hs + g's$. This is the case, for example, for SOR (see the argument preceding Prop. 6.10 and Fig. 2.6.5, in Section 2.6) and for the conjugate gradient method (see Prop. 7.1 and Exercise 7.4 in Section 2.7). Therefore, if the iterative algorithm is initialized with $s = 0$ (or, more generally, with any s such that $\frac{1}{2}s'Hs \leq -g's$), the vector $\hat{s}$ produced after any finite number of iterations satisfies

$$\tfrac{1}{2}\hat{s}'H\hat{s} + g'\hat{s} < 0. \tag{2.9}$$

Since H is assumed positive definite, we obtain $g'\hat{s} < 0$, which shows that $\hat{s}$ is a direction of descent.

3.2.2 Convergence Analysis Using the Descent Approach

We now study the convergence of the previous algorithms using the descent approach. The proofs given will be generalized to the context of partially asynchronous algorithms in Chapter 7. The main line of argument is simple: we first show that each update reduces the value of the cost function by an amount that is bounded away from zero if the magnitude of the update is bounded away from zero. Given that the cost function is bounded below, it follows that the magnitude of the updates converges to zero. Then, one uses the formula for the updates to show that $\nabla F(x(t))$ must also converge to zero.

The following assumption on F will be used in most of the results of this section.

Assumption 2.1.

(a) There holds $F(x) \geq 0$ for every $x \in \Re^n$.

(b) *(Lipschitz Continuity of ∇F)* The function F is continuously differentiable and there exists a constant K such that

$$\|\nabla F(x) - \nabla F(y)\|_2 \leq K\|x - y\|_2, \qquad \forall x, y \in \Re^n.$$

A key consequence of Assumption 2.1 is provided by Prop. A.32 in Appendix A, which we repeat here for easier reference.

Lemma 2.1.   *(Descent Lemma)* If F satisfies the Lipschitz condition of Assumption 2.1(b), then

$$F(x + y) \leq F(x) + y'\nabla F(x) + \frac{K}{2}\|y\|_2^2, \qquad \forall x, y \in \Re^n.$$

The following convergence result covers a wide class of descent algorithms.

Proposition 2.1.   *(Convergence of Descent Algorithms)* Suppose that Assumption 2.1 holds and let K_1 and K_2 be positive constants. Consider the sequence $\{x(t)\}$ generated by an algorithm of the form

$$x(t + 1) = x(t) + \gamma s(t), \tag{2.10}$$

where $s(t)$ satisfies

$$\|s(t)\|_2 \geq K_1\|\nabla F(x(t))\|_2, \qquad \forall t, \tag{2.11}$$

and

$$s(t)'\nabla F\big(x(t)\big) \le -K_2 \|s(t)\|_2^2, \qquad \forall t. \tag{2.12}$$

If $0 < \gamma < 2K_2/K$, then

$$\lim_{t \to \infty} \nabla F\big(x(t)\big) = 0.$$

Proof. Using the Descent Lemma and the assumption (2.12), we obtain

$$F\big(x(t+1)\big) \le F\big(x(t)\big) + \gamma s(t)'\nabla F\big(x(t)\big) + \frac{K}{2}\gamma^2 \|s(t)\|_2^2$$

$$\le F\big(x(t)\big) - \gamma\left(K_2 - \frac{K\gamma}{2}\right)\|s(t)\|_2^2.$$

Let $\beta = \gamma(K_2 - K\gamma/2)$, which, by our assumptions on γ, is positive. We have one such inequality for every $t \ge 0$. Adding these inequalities and using the nonnegativity condition of Assumption 2.1(a), we obtain

$$0 \le F\big(x(t+1)\big) \le F\big(x(0)\big) - \beta \sum_{\tau=0}^{t} \|s(\tau)\|_2^2.$$

Since this inequality is true for all t, we obtain

$$\sum_{\tau=0}^{\infty} \|s(\tau)\|_2^2 \le \frac{1}{\beta}F\big(x(0)\big) < \infty.$$

This implies that $\lim_{t \to \infty} s(t) = 0$ and Eq. (2.11) shows that $\lim_{t \to \infty} \nabla F\big(x(t)\big) = 0$. **Q.E.D.**

Assumption 2.1 is stronger than necessary for Prop. 2.1 to hold. For example, instead of the nonnegativity condition on F, we could only assume that F is bounded below. The Lipschitz condition on ∇F can also be weakened somewhat (see Exercise 2.1). Besides Assumption 2.1, Prop. 2.1 involves two additional conditions, inequalities (2.11) and (2.12). Inequality (2.11) implies that $s(t) \ne 0$, and, therefore, $x(t+1) \ne x(t)$ whenever $\nabla F\big(x(t)\big) \ne 0$. Such a condition is necessary if the algorithm is to make any progress at all. Inequality (2.12) implies that the direction of update in Eq. (2.10) is a descent direction.

The conditions of Prop. 2.1 can be verified for a variety of algorithms, as we now show.

(a) For the gradient algorithm (2.4), we have $s(t) = -\nabla F\big(x(t)\big)$. Thus, $K_1 = K_2 = 1$, and we have convergence for $0 < \gamma < 2/K$.

(b) Consider the scaled gradient algorithm (2.5) for which $s(t) = -\big(D(t)\big)^{-1}\nabla F\big(x(t)\big)$. Assume that the sequence $\{D(t)\}$ is bounded and that for some $K_2 > 0$, the matrix $D(t) - K_2 I$ is nonnegative definite for each t. We then have

$$K_2\|s(t)\|_2^2 \le s(t)'D(t)s(t) = -s(t)'\nabla F\big(x(t)\big)$$

and inequality (2.12) is satisfied. Let $K_1 = 1/\sup_t \|D(t)\|_2$. We have $D(t)s(t) = -\nabla F\big(x(t)\big)$, which implies that $\|D(t)\|_2 \cdot \|s(t)\|_2 \ge \left\|\nabla F\big(x(t)\big)\right\|_2$. From the latter inequality, we obtain $\|s(t)\|_2 \ge K_1\left\|\nabla F\big(x(t)\big)\right\|_2$ and inequality (2.11) is satisfied.

(c) Assume that F is twice continuously differentiable and consider the Jacobi algorithm (2.1). This is a special case of the scaled gradient algorithm (2.5), with $D(t)$ diagonal. Assuming that $\nabla_{ii}^2 F(x)$ is bounded above by $1/K_1$ and below by K_2 for some positive constants K_1 and K_2, the discussion in (b) applies.

(d) Consider the approximate Newton method (2.8) and again let $g = \nabla F\big(x(t)\big)$ and $H = \nabla^2 F\big(x(t)\big)$. Whenever $g \ne 0$, we assume that $\hat{s}$ is chosen to satisfy $\frac{1}{2}\hat{s}'H\hat{s} + g'\hat{s} < 0$ [cf. Eq. (2.9)] and $\|\hat{s}\|_2 \ge K_1\|g\|_2$. Then, inequality (2.11) holds. We assume that F is twice continuously differentiable and that there exists a constant K_2 such that $\frac{1}{2}\nabla^2 F(x) - K_2 I$ is nonnegative definite for every x. We then have

$$-g'\hat{s} > \frac{1}{2}\hat{s}'H\hat{s} \ge K_2\|\hat{s}\|_2^2$$

and inequality (2.12) is also satisfied.

Convergence of algorithms of the Gauss–Seidel type can also be proved by an argument similar to that in Prop. 2.1.

Proposition 2.2.   (*Convergence of the Gauss–Seidel Algorithm*) Suppose that Assumption 2.1 holds and that F is twice differentiable. Assume that there exist constants $d_i, D_i > 0$ such that $0 < d_i \le \nabla_{ii}^2 F(x) \le D_i$ for all $x \in \Re^n$. If $0 < \gamma < 2d_i/D_i$ for all i, and if the sequence $\{x(t)\}$ is generated by the Gauss–Seidel algorithm (2.2), then $\lim_{t\to\infty} \nabla F(x(t)) = 0$.

Proof. Let $s^i(t)$ be a vector with all components equal to zero, except for the ith component, which is equal to $-\nabla_i F\big(z(i,t)\big)/\nabla_{ii}^2 F\big(z(i,t)\big)$. Notice that $z(i+1,t) = z(i,t) + \gamma s^i(t)$ for $1 \le i < n$ and $x(t+1) = z(n,t) + \gamma s^n(t)$. We use the Descent Lemma (Lemma 2.1), with the function F viewed as a function of the single variable x_i; we also use the bound $|\nabla_i F(x) - \nabla_i F(y)| \le D_i|x_i - y_i|$, which is valid for all x and y that differ only in the ith component. Then

$$F\big(z(i,t) + \gamma s^i(t)\big) \leq F\big(z(i,t)\big) + \gamma s^i(t)' \nabla F\big(z(i,t)\big) + \gamma^2 \frac{D_i}{2} \|s^i(t)\|_2^2$$

$$\leq F\big(z(i,t)\big) - \gamma d_i \|s^i(t)\|_2^2 + \gamma^2 \frac{D_i}{2} \|s^i(t)\|_2^2$$

$$= F\big(z(i,t)\big) - \gamma \left(d_i - \gamma \frac{D_i}{2}\right) \|s^i(t)\|_2^2.$$

With our assumption on γ, the quantity $\gamma(d_i - \gamma D_i/2)$ is positive. Thus, the steps in the proof of Prop. 2.1 remain valid and we conclude that

$$\sum_{t=0}^{\infty} \sum_{i=1}^{n} \|s^i(t)\|_2^2 < \infty.$$

Therefore, $\lim_{t\to\infty} s^i(t) = 0$ for all i, which implies that $\lim_{t\to\infty} \nabla_i F\big(z(i,t)\big) = 0$ and that $\lim_{t\to\infty} \big(z(i,t) - x(t)\big) = 0$. Using the Lipschitz continuity of ∇F [Assumption 2.1(b)], we obtain $\lim_{t\to\infty} \big(\nabla_i F\big(z(i,t)\big) - \nabla_i F\big(x(t)\big)\big) = 0$, from which we conclude that $\lim_{t\to\infty} \nabla_i F\big(x(t)\big) = 0$ for all i.   **Q.E.D.**

A similar result is possible for the Gauss–Seidel variant (2.4) of the gradient algorithm, but it is omitted. Notice that in the case of a quadratic cost function of the form $F(x) = \frac{1}{2}x'Ax - x'b$, we have $d_i = D_i = a_{ii}$ and the condition on γ becomes $0 < \gamma < 2$. Assuming that A is symmetric positive definite, F is minimized at the unique solution of the system $Ax = b$ and the Gauss–Seidel algorithm (2.2) coincides with the SOR method for linear equations. We conclude that Prop. 2.2 establishes the convergence of SOR for $0 < \gamma < 2$, which is Prop. 6.10(a) in Section 2.6. Similarly, Prop. 2.1 establishes the convergence of the JOR algorithm and of Richardson's method for solving the system $Ax = b$, when A is symmetric positive definite and γ is positive and small enough. This proves Prop. 6.11 in Section 2.6.

The preceding results say nothing about convergence of the sequence $\{x(t)\}$ and indeed there is nothing in our hypotheses that ensures boundedness of $x(t)$. On the other hand, the convergence of ∇F to zero and the continuity of ∇F imply that if x^* is a limit point of $x(t)$, then $\nabla F(x^*) = 0$.

3.2.3 The Case of a Convex Cost Function

The preceding results can be strengthened when F is a convex function (see Appendix A for a review of convexity notions). In particular, if F is convex and continuously differentiable, then any point x such that $\nabla F(x) = 0$ is guaranteed to be a global minimum of F [Prop. A.39(c) in Appendix A]. We then obtain the following result.

Proposition 2.3.   (*Convergence of Descent Methods in Convex Optimization*) Suppose that F is convex and satisfies Assumption 2.1, and that the sequence $\{x(t)\}$ is as in Prop. 2.1 or 2.2. If x^* is a limit point of the sequence $\{x(t)\}$, then x^* minimizes F.

The following result uses a more stringent assumption on the cost function F and leads to a bound on the convergence rate of the algorithms under consideration.

Proposition 2.4.   (*Geometric Convergence for Strongly Convex Problems*) Suppose, in addition to Assumption 2.1, that there exists some $\alpha > 0$ such that

$$\big(\nabla F(x) - \nabla F(y)\big)'(x - y) \geq \alpha \|x - y\|_2^2, \qquad \forall x, y \in \Re^n. \tag{2.13}$$

Then there exists a unique vector $x^* \in \Re^n$ that minimizes F. Furthermore, provided that γ is chosen positive and small enough, the sequence $\{x(t)\}$ generated by the gradient algorithm (2.3) converges to x^* geometrically.

Proof. Inequality (2.13) implies that the mapping $T : \Re^n \mapsto \Re^n$ defined by $T(x) = x - \gamma \nabla F(x)$ is a contraction with respect to the Euclidean norm $\| \cdot \|_2$, provided that γ is positive and sufficiently small. (Use Prop. 1.12 of Subsection 3.1.3, specialized to the case of a single block–component.) In particular, the mapping T has a unique fixed point x^* and the sequence generated by the gradient algorithm $x := T(x)$ converges to x^* geometrically. Such a fixed point satisfies $\nabla F(x^*) = 0$. Inequality (2.13) also implies that the function F is strictly convex (Prop. A.41 in Appendix A). It follows that x^* minimizes F [Prop. A.39(c) in Appendix A]. The strict convexity of F also implies that no other minimizing points of F exist [Prop. A.35(g) in Appendix A].   **Q.E.D.**

Any function F satisfying the condition (2.13) is called *strongly convex*. In the case where F is twice continuously differentiable, strong convexity is equivalent to positive definiteness of $\nabla^2 F(x)$, uniformly in x (Prop. A.41 in Appendix A). Intuitively, strong convexity amounts to assuming that the curvature of F is positive and bounded away from zero at every point. It should be also noticed that strong convexity of F is equivalent to strong monotonicity of ∇F (strong monotonicity was defined in Subsection 3.1.3). It turns out that under strong convexity, the Jacobi and Gauss–Seidel algorithms also converge to the optimal solution geometrically, but the proofs are omitted.

3.2.4 Nonlinear Algorithms

The algorithms considered so far are called *linearized* algorithms, because the update is a linear function of $\nabla F(x)$. This is in contrast to *nonlinear* or *coordinate descent* algorithms, which are based on a different idea. In the latter class of algorithms, we fix all of the components of x to some value, except for the ith component, and then we minimize $F(x)$ with respect to x_i. This procedure is repeated, leading to an iterative algorithm. There are two alternative implementations; in the first, called the *nonlinear Jacobi* algorithm, the minimizations with respect to the different components x_i are carried out simultaneously (see Fig. 3.2.2); in the second, called the *nonlinear Gauss–Seidel* algorithm, the minimizations are carried out successively for each component (see Fig. 3.2.3). Notice that each step involves the solution of one–dimensional minimization problems that are in many cases easy to solve with practically adequate precision.

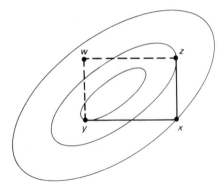

Figure 3.2.2 Illustration of an iteration of the nonlinear Jacobi algorithm. Given an initial vector x, we obtain the vectors y and z by minimizing along the first (respectively, second) coordinate. By combining the updates of both components, we obtain the new vector w.

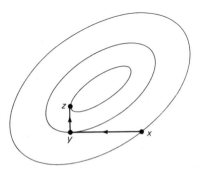

Figure 3.2.3 Illustration of an iteration of the nonlinear Gauss–Seidel algorithm. Given an initial vector x, we minimize with respect to the first coordinate to obtain the vector y, and then along the second coordinate to obtain the vector z.

Mathematically, the nonlinear Jacobi algorithm is described by the equation

$$x_i(t+1) = \arg\min_{x_i} F\Big(x_1(t), \ldots, x_{i-1}(t), x_i, x_{i+1}(t), \ldots, x_n(t)\Big) \qquad (2.14)$$

and the nonlinear Gauss–Seidel algorithm by the equation

$$x_i(t+1) = \arg\min_{x_i} F\Big(x_1(t+1), \ldots, x_{i-1}(t+1), x_i, x_{i+1}(t), \ldots, x_n(t)\Big). \qquad (2.15)$$

We are assuming here that a minimizing x_i always exists; if several minimizing x_i exist, $x_i(t+1)$ is chosen arbitrarily from the set of minimizing values.

Proposition 2.5. (*Convergence of the Nonlinear Gauss–Seidel Algorithm*) Suppose that $F : \Re^n \mapsto \Re$ is continuously differentiable and convex. Furthermore, suppose that for each i, F is a strictly convex function of x_i, when the values of the other components of x are held constant. Let $\{x(t)\}$ be the sequence generated by the nonlinear Gauss–Seidel algorithm, assumed to be well defined. Then, every limit point of $\{x(t)\}$ minimizes F over $\Re^n$.

The proof of Prop. 2.5 is omitted because it is a special case of a more general result to be proved later (Prop. 3.9 in Section 3.3). Let us just point out that Prop. 2.5

is derived using the descent approach for proving convergence. In particular, successive minimizations cannot increase the value of F. This shows that $F\big(x(t+1)\big) \leq F\big(x(t)\big)$ and implies the convergence of $F\big(x(t)\big)$ provided that F is bounded below. If F is not differentiable, the nonlinear Gauss–Seidel method can fail to converge to the minimum of F because it can stop at a nonoptimal "corner" point at which F is nondifferentiable and from which F cannot be reduced along any coordinate (Exercise 2.2). This difficulty will be encountered in the context of network flow problems in Chapter 5.

The proof just outlined fails altogether in the case of the nonlinear Jacobi algorithm; even though the minimization with respect to each coordinate cannot increase the value of F, the fact that these minimizations are carried out simultaneously allows the possibility that $F\big(x(t+1)\big) > F\big(x(t)\big)$. Convergence of the nonlinear Jacobi algorithm can be established using the results on contraction mappings of Section 3.1, under certain assumptions. We have, for example, the following result which is proved in more generality in the next section (Prop. 3.10).

Proposition 2.6.   (*Convergence of Nonlinear Algorithms under Contraction Assumptions*) Let $F : \Re^n \mapsto \Re$ be continuously differentiable, let γ be a positive scalar, and suppose that the mapping $T : \Re^n \mapsto \Re^n$, defined by $T(x) = x - \gamma \nabla F(x)$, is a contraction with respect to a weighted maximum norm. Then, there exists a unique vector x^* which minimizes F over $\Re^n$. Furthermore, the nonlinear Jacobi and Gauss–Seidel algorithms are well defined, that is, a minimizing x_i in Eqs. (2.14) and (2.15) always exists. Finally, the sequence $\{x(t)\}$ generated by either of these algorithms converges to x^* geometrically.

The contraction assumption of Prop. 2.6 is satisfied if the matrix $\nabla^2 F(x)$ satisfies a diagonal dominance condition [see Prop. 1.11 with the identification $f(x) = \nabla F(x)$]. A weaker condition is diagonal dominance with respect to some set of weights (see Exercise 1.3).

A different version of the nonlinear Gauss–Seidel algorithm is obtained if instead of minimizing with respect to a single component at a time, we decompose $\Re^n$ as a Cartesian product $\prod_{i=1}^m \Re^{n_i}$, and at each stage, we minimize with respect to the n_i–dimensional subvector x_i. Proposition 2.6 remains valid and such a Gauss–Seidel algorithm also converges, under a block–contraction assumption on the mapping $T(x) = x - \gamma \nabla F(x)$.

The machinery of contraction mappings of Section 3.1 could be also used to establish convergence of linearized algorithms. However, the results thus obtained are not any stronger than the results obtained using the descent approach.

EXERCISES

2.1. Suppose that the Lipschitz condition on ∇F of Assumption 2.1 is replaced by the following two conditions:

(i) For every bounded set $A \subset \Re^n$, there exists some constant K such that $\|\nabla F(x) - \nabla F(y)\|_2 \leq K\|x - y\|_2$ for all $x, y \in A$.

(ii) The set $\{x \mid F(x) \le c\}$ is bounded for every $c \in \Re$.

    (a) Show that condition (i) is always satisfied if F is twice continuously differentiable.

    (b) Show that Prop. 2.1 remains valid provided that the stepsize γ is allowed to depend on the choice of the initial vector $x(0)$. *Hint:* Choose a stepsize that guarantees that $x(t)$ stays within the set $\{x \mid F(x) \le F(x(0))\}$.

2.2. Show by means of an example that if F is continuous but not differentiable, then the nonlinear Jacobi and Gauss–Seidel algorithms can fail to converge to the minimum of F, even if F is strictly convex and has bounded level sets.

2.3. Suppose that F is quadratic of the form $F(x) = \frac{1}{2}x'Ax - b'x$, where A is an $n \times n$ positive definite symmetric matrix and $b \in \Re^n$ is given. Show that the Lipschitz condition $\|\nabla F(x) - \nabla F(y)\|_2 \le K\|x - y\|_2$ is satisfied with K equal to the maximal eigenvalue of A. Consider also the scaled gradient iteration $x(t+1) = x(t) - \gamma M^{-1}\nabla F(x(t))$, where M is positive definite and symmetric. Show that the method converges to $x^* = A^{-1}b$ if $\gamma \in (0, 2/\overline{K})$, where $\overline{K}$ is the maximum eigenvalue of $M^{-1/2}AM^{-1/2}$.

3.3 CONSTRAINED OPTIMIZATION

We consider in this section the problem of minimizing a cost function $F : \Re^n \mapsto \Re$ over a set $X \subset \Re^n$. Throughout, we assume that F is continuously differentiable and that X is nonempty, closed, and convex.

3.3.1 Optimality Conditions and the Projection Theorem

We start with a set of necessary and sufficient conditions for a vector $x \in X$ to be optimal.

    Proposition 3.1.   *(Optimality Conditions)*

(a) If a vector $x \in X$ minimizes F over X, then $(y - x)'\nabla F(x) \ge 0$ for every $y \in X$.

(b) If F is also convex on the set X, then the condition of part (a) is also sufficient for x to minimize F over X.

    Proof.

(a) Suppose that $(y - x)'\nabla F(x) < 0$ for some $y \in X$. Since this is the directional derivative of F along the direction of $y - x$, it follows that there exists some $\epsilon \in (0, 1)$ such that $F(x + \epsilon(y - x)) < F(x)$. Then, $x + \epsilon(y - x) \in X$, because X is convex, which proves that x does not minimize F over the set X.

(b) Suppose that $(y - x)'\nabla F(x) \ge 0$ holds for every $y \in X$. Then, using the convexity of F (Prop. A.39 in Appendix A), we obtain $F(y) \ge F(x) + (y - x)'\nabla F(x) \ge F(x)$ for every $y \in X$, and, therefore, x minimizes F over X. **Q.E.D.**

The linearized algorithms of Section 3.2 are not applicable to constrained optimization because, even if we start inside the feasible set X, an update can take us outside that set. A simple remedy is to project back to the set X whenever such a situation arises.

We use the notation $[x]^+$ to denote the orthogonal projection (with respect to the Euclidean norm) of a vector x onto the convex set X. In particular, $[x]^+$ is defined by

$$[x]^+ = \arg\min_{z \in X} \|z - x\|_2. \tag{3.1}$$

The following result ensures that $[x]^+$ is well defined and also provides some useful properties of the projection.

Proposition 3.2.   *(Projection Theorem)*

(a) For every $x \in \Re^n$, there exists a unique $z \in X$ that minimizes $\|z - x\|_2$ over all $z \in X$, and will be denoted by $[x]^+$.

(b) Given some $x \in \Re^n$, a vector $z \in X$ is equal to $[x]^+$ if and only if $(y - z)'(x - z) \leq 0$ for all $y \in X$.

(c) The mapping $f : \Re^n \mapsto X$ defined by $f(x) = [x]^+$ is continuous and nonexpansive, that is, $\|[x]^+ - [y]^+\|_2 \leq \|x - y\|_2$ for all $x, y \in \Re^n$.

Proof.

(a) Let x be fixed and let w be some element of X. Minimizing $\|x - z\|_2$ over all $z \in X$ is equivalent to minimizing the same function over all $z \in X$ such that $\|x - z\|_2 \leq \|x - w\|_2$, which is a compact set. Furthermore, the function g defined by $g(z) = \|z - x\|_2^2$ is continuous. Existence follows because a continuous function on a compact set always attains its minimum (Prop. A.8 in Appendix A).

To prove uniqueness, notice that the square of the Euclidean norm is a strictly convex function of its argument [Prop. A.40(d) in Appendix A]. Therefore, g is strictly convex and it follows that its minimum is attained at a unique point [Prop. A.35(g) in Appendix A].

(b) The vector $[x]^+$ is the minimizer of $g(z)$ over all $z \in X$. Notice that $\nabla g(z) = 2(z - x)$ and the result follows from the optimality conditions for constrained optimization problems (Prop. 3.1). (See Fig. 3.3.1 for an illustration of this result.)

(c) Let x and y be elements of $\Re^n$. From part (b), we have $\left(v - [x]^+\right)'\left(x - [x]^+\right) \leq 0$ for all $v \in X$. Since $[y]^+ \in X$, we obtain

$$\left([y]^+ - [x]^+\right)'\left(x - [x]^+\right) \leq 0.$$

Similarly,

$$\left([x]^+ - [y]^+\right)'\left(y - [y]^+\right) \leq 0.$$

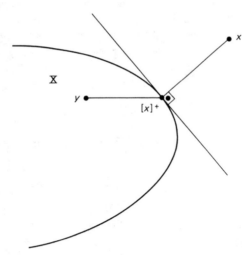

Figure 3.3.1 Illustration of the condition satisfied by the projection $[x]^+$. When the vector x is projected on the set X, the vector $x - [x]^+$ is normal to a plane supporting X at $[x]^+$. Each vector $y \in X$ lies on the other side of that plane, so the vectors $x - [x]^+$ and $y - [x]^+$ form an angle larger than or equal to 90 degrees or, equivalently, $\left(y - [x]^+\right)'\left(x - [x]^+\right) \le 0$.

Adding these two inequalities and rearranging, we obtain

$$\|[y]^+ - [x]^+\|_2^2 \le \left([y]^+ - [x]^+\right)'(y - x) \le \|[y]^+ - [x]^+\|_2 \cdot \|y - x\|_2,$$

which proves that $[\cdot]^+$ is nonexpansive and *a fortiori* continuous.   **Q.E.D.**

3.3.2 The Gradient Projection Algorithm

The gradient projection algorithm generalizes the gradient algorithm to the case where there are constraints, and is described by the equation

$$x(t + 1) = \left[x(t) - \gamma \nabla F\big(x(t)\big)\right]^+, \tag{3.2}$$

where γ is a positive stepsize (see Fig. 3.3.2). Let $T : X \mapsto X$ be the mapping that corresponds to one iteration of this algorithm, that is,

$$T(x) = \left[x - \gamma \nabla F(x)\right]^+.$$

For an equivalent definition of the mapping T, notice that $T(x)$ is the unique vector y that minimizes $\|y - x + \gamma \nabla F(x)\|_2^2$ over all $y \in X$. After expanding this quadratic function, discarding the term $\gamma^2 \|\nabla F(x)\|_2^2$, which does not depend on y, and dividing by 2γ, we conclude that $T(x)$ is the unique minimizer of

$$(y - x)' \nabla F(x) + \frac{1}{2\gamma} \|y - x\|_2^2, \tag{3.3}$$

over all $y \in X$.

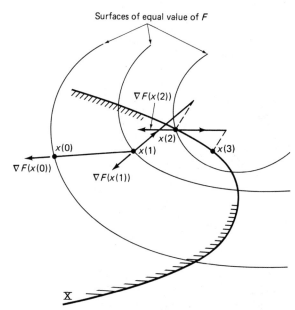

Figure 3.3.2 Illustration of a few iterations of the gradient projection method. Here $x(1) - \gamma \nabla F\big(x(1)\big)$ and $x(2) - \gamma \nabla F\big(x(2)\big)$ lie outside the feasible set X. These vectors are being projected on X in order to obtain $x(2)$ and $x(3)$, respectively.

We now study the convergence of the gradient projection algorithm under the same assumptions as in unconstrained optimization.

Assumption 3.1.

(a) There holds $F(x) \geq 0$ for all $x \in X$.

(b) (*Lipschitz Continuity of* ∇F) The function F is continuously differentiable and there exists a constant K such that

$$\|\nabla F(x) - \nabla F(y)\|_2 \leq K\|x - y\|_2, \qquad \forall x, y \in X. \tag{3.4}$$

The following result shows that for γ sufficiently small, each iteration of the gradient projection algorithm decreases the value of the cost function, unless a fixed point of the iteration mapping T has been reached.

Proposition 3.3.   (*Properties of the Gradient Projection Mapping*) If F satisfies the Lipschitz condition of Assumption 3.1(b), γ is positive, and $x \in X$, then:

(a) $F\big(T(x)\big) \leq F(x) - (1/\gamma - K/2)\|T(x) - x\|_2^2$.

(b) We have $T(x) = x$ if and only if $(y - x)'\nabla F(x) \geq 0$ for all $y \in X$. In particular, if F is convex on the set X, we have $T(x) = x$ if and only if x minimizes F over the set X.

(c) The mapping T is continuous.

$$\big(y - T(x)\big)'\big(x - \gamma \nabla F(x) - T(x)\big) \leq 0, \qquad \forall y \in X. \tag{3.5}$$

In particular, letting $y = x$, we obtain

$$\big(x - T(x)\big)'\big(x - \gamma \nabla F(x) - T(x)\big) \leq 0,$$

which yields $\gamma\big(T(x) - x\big)' \nabla F(x) \leq -\|T(x) - x\|_2^2$. Using the Descent Lemma (Lemma 2.1), we obtain

$$F\big(T(x)\big) \leq F(x) + \big(T(x) - x\big)' \nabla F(x) + \frac{K}{2}\|T(x) - x\|_2^2$$

$$\leq F(x) - \left(\frac{1}{\gamma} - \frac{K}{2}\right)\|T(x) - x\|_2^2,$$

which proves part (a).

  (b) By the Projection Theorem, the relation (3.5) can be used as the definition of $T(x)$. Thus, if $T(x) = x$, then $(y - x)'\gamma \nabla F(x) \geq 0$ for all $y \in X$. Conversely, if $(y - x)'\gamma \nabla F(x) \geq 0$ for every $y \in X$, then $(y - x)'(x - \gamma \nabla F(x) - x) \leq 0$, and we conclude that $x = T(x)$. In the convex case, the result follows from the optimality conditions for constrained optimization (Prop. 3.1).

  (c) Since F is continuously differentiable, the mapping $x \mapsto x - \gamma \nabla F(x)$ is continuous. Given that the projection mapping is also continuous [Prop. 3.2(c)], T is the composition of two continuous mappings and is therefore continuous.   **Q.E.D.**

From Prop. 3.3, the convergence of the gradient projection algorithm is straightforward to establish. Let $\{x(t)\}$ be the sequence of vectors generated by the algorithm. Assuming that $0 < \gamma < 2/K$, Prop. 3.3(a) shows that the sequence $\{F\big(x(t)\big)\}$ is nonincreasing, and if F is bounded below, this sequence converges, while $T\big(x(t)\big) - x(t)$ converges to zero. Let x^* be a limit point of the sequence $\{x(t)\}$ and let $\{x(t_k)\}$ be a subsequence converging to x^*. Then, $T\big(x(t_k)\big)$ also converges to x^* and the continuity of T implies that $T(x^*) = x^*$. Then, Prop. 3.3(b) shows that $(y - x^*)' \nabla F(x^*) \geq 0$, for all $y \in X$. We have thus proved the following.

    Proposition 3.4.   *(Convergence of the Gradient Projection Algorithm)* Suppose that F satisfies Assumption 3.1. If $0 < \gamma < 2/K$ and if x^* is a limit point of the sequence $\{x(t)\}$ generated by the gradient projection algorithm (3.2), then $(y - x^*)' \nabla F(x^*) \geq 0$ for all $y \in X$. In particular, if F is convex on the set X, then x^* minimizes F over the set X.

    Proposition 3.4 was proved by means of a descent argument. Using the general convergence properties of contracting iterations (Section 3.1), we can prove the following result, which provides us with a convergence rate estimate. The proof is omitted because it is almost identical to the proof of Prop. 2.4.

Proposition 3.5. (*Geometric Convergence for Strongly Convex Problems*) Suppose, in addition to Assumption 3.1, that there exists some $\alpha > 0$ such that

$$\left(\nabla F(x) - \nabla F(y)\right)'(x - y) \geq \alpha \|x - y\|_2^2, \qquad \forall x, y \in X.$$

Then, there exists a unique vector x^* that minimizes F over the set X. Furthermore, provided that γ is chosen positive and small enough, the sequence $\{x(t)\}$ generated by the gradient projection algorithm (3.2) converges to x^* geometrically.

3.3.3 Scaled Gradient Projection Algorithms

As in the case of unconstrained optimization, we may wish to scale the update direction $\nabla F\big(x(t)\big)$. We thus generalize the gradient projection algorithm (3.2) by letting

$$x(t + 1) = \left[x(t) - \gamma\big(M(t)\big)^{-1}\nabla F\big(x(t)\big)\right]^+, \tag{3.6}$$

where $M(t)$ is an invertible scaling matrix. Typically, $M(t)$ would be chosen to approximate the Hessian matrix $\nabla^2 F\big(x(t)\big)$. For example, in a projected Jacobi method, $M(t)$ would be diagonal, with its diagonal entries being equal to the diagonal entries of $\nabla^2 F\big(x(t)\big)$, thus generalizing the linearized Jacobi algorithm (2.1) of Section 3.2. However, the algorithm (3.6) fails, in general, to converge to a minimizing point, as illustrated in Fig. 3.3.3. For convergence to be obtained, the projection should be carried out with respect to a different coordinate system (equivalently, with respect to a different norm) determined by $M(t)$. (An alternative approach is discussed in Exercise 3.3.)

Let us temporarily assume that $M(t)$ is symmetric and positive definite. We consider the norm $\|\cdot\|_{M(t)}$ defined by

$$\|x\|_{M(t)} = \big(x'M(t)x\big)^{1/2}.$$

We then define $[x]^+_{M(t)}$ as the vector y that minimizes $\|y - x\|_{M(t)}$ over all $y \in X$, and we replace Eq. (3.6) by the iteration

$$x(t + 1) = \left[x(t) - \gamma\big(M(t)\big)^{-1}\nabla F\big(x(t)\big)\right]^+_{M(t)}. \tag{3.7}$$

As in the case of the unscaled gradient projection method, we can define $x(t + 1)$ as the solution of a quadratic programming problem [cf. the expression (3.3)]. In particular, it can be seen that

$$x(t + 1) = \arg\min_{y \in X} \left\{\frac{1}{2\gamma}\big(y - x(t)\big)'M(t)\big(y - x(t)\big) + \big(y - x(t)\big)'\nabla F\big(x(t)\big)\right\}. \tag{3.8}$$

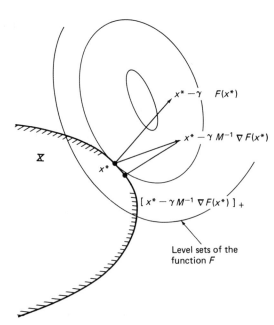

$x^* - \gamma \ F(x^*)$

$x^* - \gamma M^{-1} \nabla F(x^*)$

X

x^*

$[\, x^* - \gamma M^{-1} \nabla F(x^*) \,]_+$

Level sets of the
function F

Figure 3.3.3 Illustration of failure
of the algorithm $x(t+1) = \left[x(t) - \gamma M^{-1} \nabla F\big(x(t)\big) \right]^+$. Here, the
point x^* minimizes the convex function F
over the set X. However, the iteration
$x := [x - \gamma M^{-1} \nabla F(x)]^+$ does not have
x^* as a fixed point.

It is actually preferable to define $x(t+1)$ by means of the quadratic optimization in Eq. (3.8) rather than as a projection [cf. Eq. (3.7)], because the quadratic expression in Eq. (3.8) is well defined even if $M(t)$ is not an invertible matrix. (This provides some additional flexibility, which is sometimes useful. The algorithm that generates $x(t+1)$ according to Eq. (3.8) will be called the *scaled gradient projection* algorithm. For this algorithm to be well defined, we need to ensure that the minimum in Eq. (3.8) is attained at a unique element of X. The following auxiliary result provides sufficient conditions for this to be the case.

Proposition 3.6. Suppose that a matrix $M(t)$ is symmetric and satisfies the positivity condition

$$(x-y)'M(t)(x-y) \ge \alpha \|x-y\|_2^2, \qquad \forall x, y \in X, \tag{3.9}$$

where α is some positive constant. Then, the minimum in the quadratic programming problem of Eq. (3.8) is attained at a unique vector $y \in X$.

Proof. From inequality (3.9), it can be verified that the expression minimized in Eq. (3.8), viewed as a function of y, is a strictly convex function on the set X, which proves uniqueness. Furthermore, by inequality (3.9), this expression goes to infinity when $\|y\|_2$ goes to infinity. Therefore, the minimization can be restricted to a compact subset of X. Existence of a minimizing vector follows because a continuous function on a compact set attains its minimum (Weierstrass' theorem given as Prop. A.8 in Appendix A). **Q.E.D.**

The positivity condition (3.9) is satisfied if $M(t) - \alpha I$ is symmetric nonnegative definite. In that case, α is a lower bound for the smallest eigenvalue of $M(t)$. However, this is stronger than necessary. For example, if the set $\{x - y \mid x \in X, y \in X\}$ is contained in a proper subspace of $\Re^n$, then it is only the action of $M(t)$ on vectors in that subspace that matters. Roughly speaking, condition (3.9) states that the restriction of $M(t)$ on such a subspace is positive definite.

The following result generalizes Props. 3.2–3.4 to the case where scaling is used. The proof is similar to the proof of Props. 3.2–3.4 and is outlined in Exercise 3.2.

Proposition 3.7.   (*Properties and Convergence of the Scaled Projection Algorithm*) Let $\{M(t) \mid t = 0, 1, \ldots\}$ be a bounded sequence of $n \times n$ symmetric matrices and assume that for some $\alpha > 0$, each $M(t)$ satisfies the positivity condition (3.9). Let $F : \Re^n \mapsto \Re$ satisfy Assumption 3.1.

(a) For every $x \in \Re^n$, there exists a unique $y \in X$ that minimizes $(x - y)'M(t)(x - y)$ over the set X and will be denoted by $[x]^+_{M(t)}$, or $[x]^+_t$ for short.

(b) (*Scaled Projection Theorem*) Given some $x \in \Re^n$, a vector $z \in X$ is equal to $[x]^+_t$ if and only if $(y - z)'M(t)(x - z) \leq 0$ for all $y \in X$.

(c) There exists a constant A_1 such that

$$\left\| [x]^+_t - [y]^+_t \right\|_2 \leq A_1 \|x - y\|_2,$$

for every t and every $x, y \in \Re^n$.

(d) If $M(t)$ is also positive definite, then

$$\left([x]^+_t - [y]^+_t \right)' M(t) \left([x]^+_t - [y]^+_t \right) \leq (x - y)'M(t)(x - y), \qquad \forall x, y \in \Re^n.$$

Let $T_t : X \mapsto X$ be the mapping that corresponds to the tth iteration of the scaled gradient projection algorithm. That is, $x(t + 1) = T_t\big(x(t)\big)$, where $x(t + 1)$ is defined by the quadratic minimization in Eq. (3.8). We assume that γ is positive.

(e) We have $T_t(x) = x$ if and only if $(y - x)'\nabla F(x) \geq 0$ for every $y \in X$. In particular, if F is convex on the set X, we have $T_t(x) = x$ if and only if x minimizes F over the set X.

(f) There exists a constant A_2 such that

$$\|T_t(x) - T_t(y)\|_2 \leq A_2 \|x - y\|_2, \qquad \forall x, y \in X, \ \forall t.$$

(g) If γ is small enough, then there exists a positive constant A_3 such that $F\big(T_t(x)\big) \leq F(x) - A_3 \|T_t(x) - x\|^2_2$ for every $x \in X$ and every t.

(h) If γ is small enough, then any limit point x^* of the sequence $\{x(t)\}$ generated by the scaled gradient projection algorithm satisfies $(y - x^*)'\nabla F(x^*) \geq 0$ for every $y \in X$. If F is also convex on the set X then x^* minimizes F over the set X.

3.3.4 The Case of a Product Constraint Set: Parallel Implementations

The gradient projection algorithm is not, in general, amenable to parallel implementation. Even though the computation of $x - \gamma \nabla F(x)$ can be parallelized in the obvious manner, the computation of the projection is a nontrivial optimization problem involving all components of x. However, in the important special case where the set X is a box (i.e., $X = \prod_{i=1}^{n} [a_i, b_i]$ for some real numbers a_i, b_i), the projection of x on X is obtained by projecting the ith component of x on the interval $[a_i, b_i]$, which is straightforward and can be done independently for each component (see Fig. 3.3.4).

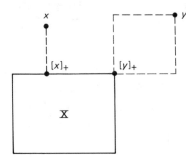

Figure 3.3.4 Illustration of the projection on a box. The ith component of the projection of a vector is the projection of its ith component.

More generally, suppose that the space R^n is represented as the Cartesian product of spaces $\Re^{n_i}$, where $n_1 + \cdots + n_m = n$, and that the constraint set X is a Cartesian product of sets X_i, where each X_i is a closed convex subset of $\Re^{n_i}$. Accordingly, we represent any vector $x \in \Re^n$ in the form $x = (x_1, \ldots, x_m)$, where each x_i is an element of R^{n_i}. It is easily seen that the projection of x on X is equal to the vector $([x_1]_1^+, \ldots, [x_m]_m^+)$, where $[x_i]_i^+$ is the projection of x_i onto X_i. The same discussion applies to the scaled gradient projection algorithm, provided that the scaling matrices $M(t)$ are block–diagonal. To see this, suppose that $M(t)$ is block–diagonal, the ith diagonal block $M_i(t)$ being of dimension $n_i \times n_i$. The quadratic expression minimized in Eq. (3.8) can be rewritten as

$$\sum_{i=1}^{m} \left[\frac{1}{2\gamma} \big(y_i - x_i(t)\big)' M_i(t) \big(y_i - x_i(t)\big) + \big(y_i - x_i(t)\big)' \nabla_i F\big(x(t)\big) \right]. \qquad (3.10)$$

Evidently, when X is a Cartesian product, minimizing the above quadratic expression over all $y \in X$ is equivalent to minimizing the ith summand over all $y_i \in X_i$ for each i. A parallel algorithm is then obtained because these minimizations can be carried out independently by different processors.

The assumption that X is a Cartesian product opens up the possibility for a Gauss–Seidel version of the gradient projection algorithm. We only discuss the case of identity scaling. The results are similar for the case of block–diagonal scaling, as long as the scaling matrices $M(t)$ satisfy the positivity condition (3.9).

The Gauss–Seidel algorithm (with identity scaling) is defined by the iteration

$$x_i(t+1) = \left[x_i(t) - \gamma \nabla_i F\big(z(i,t)\big) \right]_i^+, \tag{3.11}$$

where $z(i,t) = \big(x_1(t+1), \ldots, x_{i-1}(t+1), x_i(t), \ldots, x_m(t)\big)$, $1 \le i \le m$. To simplify notation in the following, we also let $z(m+1, t) = x(t+1)$.

Proposition 3.8. *(Convergence of the Gauss–Seidel Gradient Projection Algorithm)* If $F : \Re^n \mapsto \Re$ satisfies Assumption 3.1 and if γ is chosen positive and small enough, then any limit point x^* of the sequence $\{x(t)\}$ generated by the Gauss–Seidel algorithm (3.11) satisfies $(y - x^*)' \nabla F(x^*) \ge 0$ for all $y \in X$.

Proof. We apply Prop. 3.3(a) on the function F, viewed as a function of x_i alone, to conclude that if γ is sufficiently small, there exists some $A > 0$ such that

$$F\big(z(i+1, t)\big) \le F\big(z(i,t)\big) - A \big\| z(i+1, t) - z(i,t) \big\|_2^2, \qquad \forall t.$$

It follows that $F\big(x(t)\big)$ is nonincreasing and therefore converges. This implies that $z(i+1, t) - z(i,t)$ converges to zero for each i. In particular, $x(t+1) - x(t)$ converges to zero. Let x^* be a limit point of the sequence $\{x(t)\}$. Taking the limit in Eq. (3.11), along a sequence of times such that $x(t)$ converges to x^*, and using the continuity of ∇F and of the projection, we obtain $x_i^* = \left[x_i^* - \gamma \nabla_i F(x^*) \right]_i^+$ for all i. Thus, $x^* = \left[x^* - \gamma \nabla F(x^*) \right]^+$ and the result follows from Prop. 3.3(b).   **Q.E.D.**

3.3.5 Nonlinear Algorithms

Assuming that X is a Cartesian product, it is meaningful to consider the nonlinear Jacobi and Gauss–Seidel algorithms that are the natural extensions to the constrained case of the nonlinear algorithms introduced in Subsection 3.2.4. The *nonlinear Jacobi* algorithm is defined by

$$x_i(t+1) = \arg \min_{x_i \in X_i} F\Big(x_1(t), \ldots, x_{i-1}(t), x_i, x_{i+1}(t), \ldots, x_m(t)\Big), \tag{3.12}$$

and the *nonlinear Gauss–Seidel* algorithm is defined by

$$x_i(t+1) = \arg \min_{x_i \in X_i} F\Big(x_1(t+1), \ldots, x_{i-1}(t+1), x_i, x_{i+1}(t), \ldots, x_m(t)\Big). \tag{3.13}$$

Convergence of the nonlinear Gauss–Seidel algorithm can be established using the descent approach.

Proposition 3.9. *(Convergence of the Nonlinear Gauss–Seidel Algorithm)* Suppose that $F : \Re^n \mapsto \Re$ is continuously differentiable and convex on the set X. Furthermore, suppose that for each i, F is a strictly convex function of x_i, when the values of the other components of x are held constant. Let $\{x(t)\}$ be the sequence generated by the nonlinear Gauss–Seidel algorithm, assumed to be well defined. Then, every limit point of $\{x(t)\}$ minimizes F over X.

    Proof. Let

$$z^i(t) = \big(x_1(t+1), \ldots, x_i(t+1), x_{i+1}(t), \ldots, x_m(t)\big).$$

Using the definition (3.13) of the Gauss–Seidel iteration, we obtain

$$F\big(x(t)\big) \geq F\big(z^1(t)\big) \geq F\big(z^2(t)\big) \geq \cdots \geq F\big(z^{m-1}(t)\big) \geq F\big(x(t+1)\big), \qquad \forall t. \quad (3.14)$$

Let $x^* = \big(x_1^*, \ldots, x_m^*\big)$ be a limit point of the sequence $\{x(t)\}$. Notice that $x^* \in X$ because X is closed. Let $\{x(t_k)\}$ be a subsequence of $\{x(t)\}$ that converges to x^*. We notice from Eq. (3.14) that the sequence $\big\{F\big(x(t)\big)\big\}$ converges to either $-\infty$ or a finite real number. Using the convergence of $x(t_k)$ to x^* and the continuity of F, we see that $F\big(x(t_k)\big)$ converges to $F(x^*)$, and this implies that the entire sequence $\big\{F\big(x(t)\big)\big\}$ converges to $F(x^*)$. It now remains to show that x^* minimizes F over the set X.

    We first show that $x_1(t_k + 1) - x_1(t_k)$ converges to zero. Assume the contrary or, equivalently, that $z^1(t_k) - x(t_k)$ does not converge to zero. Let $\gamma(t_k) = \|z^1(t_k) - x(t_k)\|_2$. By possibly restricting to a subsequence of $\{t_k\}$, we may assume that there exists some $\gamma_0 > 0$ such that $\gamma(t_k) \geq \gamma_0$ for all k. Let $s^1(t_k) = \big(z^1(t_k) - x(t_k)\big)/\gamma(t_k)$. Thus, $z^1(t_k) = x(t_k) + \gamma(t_k)s^1(t_k)$, $\|s^1(t_k)\|_2 = 1$, and $s^1(t_k)$ differs from zero only along the first block–component. Notice that $s^1(t_k)$ belongs to a compact set and therefore has a limit point $\bar{s}^1$. By restricting to a further subsequence of $\{t_k\}$, we assume that $s^1(t_k)$ converges to $\bar{s}^1$.

    Let us fix some $\epsilon \in [0, 1]$. Notice that $0 \leq \epsilon\gamma_0 \leq \gamma(t_k)$. Therefore, $x(t_k) + \epsilon\gamma_0 s^1(t_k)$ lies on the segment joining $x(t_k)$ and $x(t_k) + \gamma(t_k)s^1(t_k) = z^1(t_k)$ and belongs to X because X is convex. Using the convexity of F, and the fact that $z^1(t_k)$ minimizes F over all x that differ from $x(t_k)$ along the first block–component, we obtain

$$F\big(z^1(t_k)\big) = F\big(x(t_k) + \gamma(t_k)s^1(t_k)\big) \leq F\big(x(t_k) + \epsilon\gamma_0 s^1(t_k)\big) \leq F\big(x(t_k)\big).$$

Since $F\big(x(t)\big)$ converges to $F(x^*)$, Eq. (3.14) shows that $F\big(z^1(t)\big)$ also converges to $F(x^*)$. We now take the limit as k tends to infinity, to obtain $F(x^*) \leq F\big(x^* + \epsilon\gamma_0\bar{s}^1\big) \leq F(x^*)$. We conclude that $F(x^*) = F\big(x^* + \epsilon\gamma_0\bar{s}^1\big)$, for every $\epsilon \in [0, 1]$. Since $\gamma_0\bar{s}^1 \neq 0$, this contradicts the strict convexity of F as a function of the first block–component. This contradiction establishes that $x_1(t_{k+1}) - x_1(t_k)$ converges to zero. In particular, $z^1(t_k)$ converges to x^*.

    From the definition (3.13) of the algorithm, we have

$$F\big(z^1(t_k)\big) \leq F\big(x_1, x_2(t_k), \ldots, x_m(t_k)\big), \qquad \forall x_1 \in X_1.$$

Taking the limit as k tends to infinity, we obtain

$$F(x^*) \leq F(x_1, x_2^*, \ldots, x_m^*), \qquad \forall x_1 \in X_1.$$

Using the optimality conditions for constrained optimization (Prop. 3.1), we conclude that

$$\nabla_1 F(x^*)'(x_1 - x_1^*) \geq 0, \qquad \forall x_1 \in X_1.$$

Let us now consider the sequence $\{z^1(t_k)\}$. We have already shown that $z^1(t_k)$ converges to x^*. A verbatim repetition of the preceding argument shows that $x_2(t_{k+1}) - x_2(t_k)$ converges to zero and $\nabla_2 F(x^*)'(x_2 - x_2^*) \geq 0$ for every $x_2 \in X_2$. Continuing inductively, we obtain $\nabla_i F(x^*)'(x_i - x_i^*) \geq 0$ for every $x_i \in X_i$ and for every i. Adding these inequalities, and using the Cartesian product structure of the set X, we conclude that $\nabla F(x^*)'(x - x^*) \geq 0$ for every $x \in X$. In view of the convexity of F, this shows that x^* minimizes F over the set X (Prop. 3.1).   **Q.E.D.**

Notice that by letting $X_i = \Re^{n_i}$ in this proposition, we have also established the convergence of the nonlinear Gauss–Seidel algorithm for unconstrained optimization (Prop. 2.5).

The convergence of the nonlinear Jacobi algorithm can be established under suitable contraction assumptions on the mapping $x := x - \gamma \nabla F(x)$. (Sufficient conditions for this to be a contraction mapping have been furnished in Subsection 3.1.3.) In particular, the following result extends and provides a proof for the corresponding unconstrained optimization result (Prop. 2.6 in Section 3.2).

Proposition 3.10.   (*Convergence of Nonlinear Algorithms under Contraction Assumptions*) Let $F : \Re^n \mapsto \Re$ be continuously differentiable, let γ be a positive scalar, and suppose that the mapping $R : X \mapsto \Re^n$, defined by $R(x) = x - \gamma \nabla F(x)$, is a contraction with respect to the block–maximum norm $\|x\| = \|(x_1, \dots, x_m)\| = \max_i \|x_i\|_i / w_i$, where each $\| \cdot \|_i$ is the Euclidean norm on $\Re^{n_i}$ and each w_i is a positive scalar. Then, there exists a unique vector x^* which minimizes F over X. Furthermore, the nonlinear Jacobi and Gauss–Seidel algorithms are well defined, that is, a minimizing x_i in Eqs. (3.12) and (3.13) always exists. Finally, the sequence $\{x(t)\}$ generated by either of these algorithms converges to x^* geometrically.

Proof. The contraction assumption on R and the nonexpansive property of the projection [Prop. 3.2(c)] imply that the mapping $T : X \mapsto X$ defined by $T(x) = [x - \gamma \nabla F(x)]^+$, is also a contraction. In particular, T has a unique fixed point $x^* \in X$, and the iteration $x := T(x)$ converges to x^* geometrically. Our first task is to show that x^* minimizes F over the set X.

Since R is a contraction, we have

$$\gamma \|\nabla F(x) - \nabla F(y)\| = \|(x - y) - (R(x) - R(y))\| \leq \|x - y\| + \|R(x) - R(y)\| \leq 2\|x - y\|.$$

This proves that ∇F satisfies the Lipschitz Continuity Assumption 3.1(b).

We now introduce the notation R^δ and T^δ to denote the mappings obtained from R and T, respectively, when the stepsize parameter γ is replaced by δ. For every $\delta \in (0, \gamma]$, we have $R^\delta(x) = (1 - \delta/\gamma)x + (\delta/\gamma)R(x)$. Thus,

$$\|R^{\delta}(x) - R^{\delta}(y)\| \le \left(1 - \frac{\delta}{\gamma}\right)\|x - y\| + \frac{\delta}{\gamma}\|R(x) - R(y)\| \le \left(1 - \frac{\delta}{\gamma} + \frac{\alpha\delta}{\gamma}\right)\|x - y\|,$$

where α is the contraction modulus of R. Since $\alpha < 1$, it is seen that R^{δ} is a contraction. It follows that T^{δ} is also a contraction for every $\delta \in (0, \gamma]$. By Prop. 3.3(b), we see that $x \in X$ is a fixed point of T^{δ} if and only if $(y - x)'\nabla F(x) \ge 0$ for all $y \in X$. Since this condition is independent of the value of δ, we conclude that the fixed point x^* of T is also the unique fixed point of T^{δ} for every $\delta \in (0, \gamma]$.

Let us now consider some $\delta \in (0, \gamma]$ which is sufficiently small so that the iteration $x := T^{\delta}(x)$ has the property $F\big(T^{\delta}(x)\big) \le F(x) - A\|T^{\delta}(x) - x\|^2$ for every $x \in X$, where A is some positive constant. [Such a δ exists because of the descent properties of gradient projection iterations; see Prop. 3.3(a).] Consider some $x(0) \in X$ different from x^* and let $x(t + 1) = T^{\delta}\big(x(t)\big)$, for $t = 0, 1, \ldots$. Since $x(0) \ne x^*$, we have $T^{\delta}\big(x(0)\big) \ne x(0)$, and the preceding remarks imply that $F\big(x(1)\big) < F\big(x(0)\big)$. Furthermore, $x(t)$ converges to x^*, and the sequence $\big\{F\big(x(t)\big)\big\}$ is monotonically nonincreasing and converges to $F(x^*)$. Therefore, $F(x^*) \le F\big(x(1)\big) < F\big(x(0)\big)$. Since this inequality is true whenever $x(0) \in X$ and $x(0) \ne x^*$, it follows that x^* is the unique minimizing point of the function F.

Let us now fix some index i and represent the vector x in the form $x = (x_i, \bar{x})$ where $x_i \in X_i$ and $\bar{x}$ is the vector with the remaining block–components of x. We fix $\bar{x}$ and view $F(x) = F(x_i, \bar{x})$ as a function of x_i alone. The mapping $R_i : X_i \mapsto \Re^{n_i}$, defined by $R_i(x_i) = x_i - \gamma\nabla_i F(x_i, \bar{x})$ inherits the contraction property of R. (This is because a block–maximum norm is employed.) Our previous arguments can be repeated to establish that for any fixed $\bar{x}$, there exists a unique $x_i \in X_i$ which satisfies $x_i = \big[x_i - \gamma\nabla_i F(x_i, \bar{x})\big]_i^+$, and such an x_i is the unique minimizer of $F(x_i, \bar{x})$ over the set X_i. This is exactly the type of minimization carried out in Eqs. (3.12) and (3.13). Thus, the nonlinear Jacobi and Gauss–Seidel algorithms are well defined.

We now consider the component solution method for solving the fixed point problem $T(x) = x$. We recall from Subsection 3.1.2 that given some current vector $x(t)$, the component solution method determines $x_i(t + 1)$ by solving the equation $x_i = T_i(x) = \big[x_i - \gamma\nabla_i F(x)\big]_i^+$ for x_i while fixing the remaining block–components of x at the values determined by $x(t)$. Given the discussion of the preceding paragraph, this is equivalent to determining x_i by minimizing F over all $x_i \in X_i$ while keeping the values of the remaining block–components fixed. But this is precisely the nonlinear Jacobi algorithm. Similarly, the nonlinear Gauss–Seidel algorithm coincides with the Gauss–Seidel version of the component solution method. We now apply our earlier convergence results for component solution methods for solving fixed point problems involving block–contractions (Prop. 1.7 in Subsection 3.1.2) to conclude that the sequences generated by the algorithms under consideration converge geometrically to the unique fixed point of T which as we have already established, is the unique minimizer of F over the set X.   **Q.E.D.**

The nonlinear Jacobi algorithm can be parallelized by assigning a separate processor to each block–component x_i. The nonlinear Gauss–Seidel algorithm can be also parallelized, provided that a coloring scheme can be applied (see Subsection 1.2.4).

We may also consider hybrid methods which combine certain features of the Jacobi and Gauss–Seidel methods. For example, we could split the m block–components of x into two groups: $(x_1, \dots, x_k)$ and $(x_{k+1}, \dots, x_m)$ and use the update equations

$$x_i(t+1) = \arg\min_{x_i \in X_i} F\Big(x_1(t), \dots, x_{i-1}(t), x_i, x_{i+1}(t), \dots, x_m(t)\Big),$$

if $1 \leq i \leq k$, and

$$x_i(t+1) = \arg\min_{x_i \in X_i} F\Big(x_1(t+1), \dots, x_k(t+1), x_{k+1}(t), \dots, x_{i-1}(t), x_i, x_{i+1}(t), \dots, x_m(t)\Big),$$

if $k+1 \leq i \leq m$. Thus each group of components is updated in Jacobi fashion but the updates of the second group incorporate the results of the update for the first group, as in Gauss–Seidel iterations. (Generalizations to more than two groups are clearly possible.) As long as the number of processors is smaller than the number of components in each group, we obtain the same parallelism as for the nonlinear Jacobi method, while convergence could be faster due to the Gauss–Seidel element. The convergence result of Prop. 3.10 remains true for such hybrid methods as well.

Notice that a nonlinear method can be viewed as a procedure whereby at each stage, an infinite number of iterations of a linearized algorithm is performed on the same component, until the cost function is minimized with respect to that component. We could have also considered intermediate methods whereby a limited number of linearized iterations on the same component is performed at each stage. Such methods are also convergent under the block–contraction assumption of Prop. 3.10; their convergence is most easily established by viewing them as special cases of asynchronous iterations of the type studied in Chapter 6.

EXERCISES

3.1. (Projection on a Subspace.) Let X be a subspace of $\Re^n$ and consider the mapping $f : \Re^n \mapsto \Re^n$, defined by $f(x) = [x]^+$.

    (a) Show that $y = f(x)$ if and only if $y \in X$ and $(y - x)'z = 0$ for every $z \in X$.

    (b) Show that $f(ax + by) = af(x) + bf(y)$ for every x, $y \in \Re^n$ and every a, $b \in \Re$. This establishes that the mapping f is of the form $f(x) = Px$, where P is an $n \times n$ matrix.

    (c) Show that the matrix P defined in (b) has the following properties:

        (i) $Px = x$ for every $x \in X$.

        (ii) $P^2 = P$.

        (iii) $\|x\|_2^2 = \|Px\|_2^2 + \|(I - P)x\|_2^2$ for every $x \in \Re^n$.

        (iv) P is symmetric.

    (d) Suppose that the subspace X is of the form $X = \{x \mid Ax = 0\}$, where A is an $m \times n$ matrix with the property that AA' is nonsingular. Find a formula for the matrix P of part (b) in terms of A.

Hint: To establish symmetry of P, show that $x'Py = x'P'y$ for all $x, y \in \Re^n$. In part (d), formulate the problem defining the projection of a vector on X and apply the optimality conditions.

3.2. Prove Prop. 3.7.

Hints: For part (a), show that $(x-y)'M(t)(x-y)$ is a strictly convex function of y when y is restricted to X. For part (b), use the optimality conditions of Prop. 3.1. For part (c), mimic the proof of Prop. 3.2 to show that

$$\left([y]_t^+ - [x]_t^+\right)' M(t)\left([y]_t^+ - [x]_t^+\right) \le \left([y]_t^+ - [x]_t^+\right)' M(t)(x-y). \qquad (3.15)$$

Then use inequality (3.9) for the left hand side of inequality (3.15), and the Schwartz inequality for the right hand side. For part (d), continue as in Prop. 3.2, using the norm $\|x\| = \left\|\left(M(t)\right)^{1/2} x\right\|_2$. For part (e), apply Prop. 3.1 to the minimization problem of Eq. (3.8). For part (f), use the optimality conditions for the problem in Eq. (3.8) and then proceed as in part (c). For part (g), proceed as in the proof of Prop. 3.3 and use inequality (3.9). Finally, for part (h), show that

$$\left(y - x(t+1)\right)' \left(M(t)\left(x(t+1) - x(t)\right) + \gamma \nabla F\left(x(t)\right)\right) \le 0, \qquad \forall y \in X,$$

and take the limit along a sequence $\{t_k\}$ such that $x(t_k)$ and $x(t_k + 1)$ converge to x^*.

3.3. **[Ber82b]** As illustrated in Fig. 3.3.3, the iteration (3.6) given by

$$x(t+1) = \left[x(t) - \gamma\left(M(t)\right)^{-1} \nabla F\left(x(t)\right)\right]^+ \qquad (3.16)$$

may increase the value of F, no matter how $\gamma > 0$ is chosen. For this reason, the iteration was modified as in Eq. (3.7), so that the projection on X is carried out with respect to the norm corresponding to $M(t)$. An alternative for the case where X is the positive orthant is to suitably restrict the form of the matrix $M(t)$ in Eq. (3.16) so that for γ sufficiently small, a cost improvement is obtained.

Let $X = \{x \mid x_i \ge 0, \ i = 1, \dots, n\}$. Suppose that $M(t)$ is symmetric positive definite and its elements satisfy

$$[M(t)]_{ij} = 0, \qquad \text{if } i \in I(t) \text{ and } i \ne j,$$

where

$$I(t) = \left\{i \ \middle| \ x_i(t) = 0 \text{ and } \frac{\partial F}{\partial x_i}\left(x(t)\right) < 0\right\}.$$

Show that if $x(t)$ is not optimal, there exists some $\bar{\gamma} > 0$ such that $F\left(x(t+1)\right) < F\left(x(t)\right)$ for every choice of γ in $(0, \bar{\gamma}]$. Modify this result for the case where $X = \{x \mid a_i \le x_i \le b_i, \ i = 1, \dots, n\}$, for given scalars a_i and b_i.

3.4 PARALLELIZATION AND DECOMPOSITION OF OPTIMIZATION PROBLEMS

In the last two sections, we analyzed several optimization methods that are well suited for parallelization, such as the Jacobi, Gauss–Seidel, gradient–like, and approximate Newton algorithms. These methods are not always applicable, e.g., when there is a constraint set that is not the Cartesian product of simpler sets. In this section, we show how to exploit structural problem features and enhance parallelization by means of suitable problem transformations. We thus switch our focus from parallelization based on method structure to parallelization based on problem structure.

Our approach is based on the duality theory of Appendix C. The idea here is to consider a dual optimization problem that may be more suitable for parallel solution than the original. Related approaches, known as *decomposition methods*, have been applied for many years to large problems with special structure (see e.g., [Las70]). These methods involve the solution of many simple optimization subproblems of small dimension in place of the original problem. When a parallel computing system is available, decomposition methods typically become even more attractive because the simple subproblems can be solved in parallel.

We begin in Subsection 3.4.1 with a strictly convex quadratic programming problem. This problem arises often in applications, or as a subroutine in more complex calculations (e.g. the gradient projection method). The dual cost here is also quadratic and has a gradient that can be conveniently calculated.

In Subsection 3.4.2, we consider another class of problems with special structure. Here the (primal) cost function is separable and strictly convex. The strict convexity property is important because it implies differentiability of the dual cost function (see the Differentiability Theorem in Appendix C). The separability property is important because it facilitates parallelization.

The remainder of the section is devoted to methods for dealing with lack of strict convexity of the primal cost, and the attendant lack of differentiability of the dual cost. This difficulty arises, for example, in the important special case of a linear programming problem. In Subsections 3.4.3 and 3.4.4, we show how the dual problem can be converted into a differentiable optimization problem, and can be solved by methods similar to those used for the separable strictly convex problem of Subsection 3.4.2. An alternative possibility, which we will not consider in this text, is to solve the dual problem by a nondifferentiable optimization method (see [Sha79] and [Pol87]). An example of such a method for linear network flow problems will be developed in Chapter 5.

Throughout this section, we use the duality framework of Appendix C, which is restricted for simplicity to optimization problems with convex cost functions and linear constraints. The reader who is familiar with duality theory will have no difficulty applying the parallelization approaches of this section to more general duality frameworks.

3.4.1 Quadratic Programming

Consider the quadratic programming problem

$$\text{minimize} \quad \tfrac{1}{2}x'Qx - b'x$$
$$\text{subject to} \quad Ax \le c, \tag{4.1}$$

where Q is a given $n \times n$ positive definite symmetric matrix, A is a given $m \times n$ matrix, and $b \in \Re^n$ and $c \in \Re^m$ are given vectors. This is an important problem that arises naturally in many contexts, and also provides a convenient vehicle for reformulation of other problems. For example, the feasibility problem of finding a point in the set $\{x \mid Ax \leq c\}$ can be formulated as the quadratic programming problem of projecting any given point on that set. As another example, a solution of a linear programming problem can be obtained by solving a finite number of quadratic programming problems (see Subsection 3.4.3).

We use the duality theory developed in Appendix C. The dual of the quadratic programming problem (4.1) is given by

$$\text{minimize} \quad \tfrac{1}{2}u'Pu + r'u, \tag{4.2}$$

$$\text{subject to} \quad u \geq 0,$$

where

$$P = AQ^{-1}A', \qquad r = c - AQ^{-1}b. \tag{4.3}$$

It is shown in Appendix C that if u^* solves the dual problem, then $x^* = Q^{-1}\left(b - A'u^*\right)$ solves the primal problem (4.1). The dual problem has a simple constraint set, so it is amenable to the use of parallel algorithms.

Let a_j denote the jth column of A'. We assume that a_j is nonzero for all j (if $a_j = 0$, then the corresponding constraint $a_j'x \leq c_j$ is meaningless and can be eliminated). Since Q is symmetric and positive definite, the jth diagonal element of P, given by $p_{jj} = a_j'Q^{-1}a_j$, is positive. This means that for every j, the dual cost function is strictly convex along the jth coordinate. Therefore, the strict convexity assumption of Prop. 3.9 in Section 3.3 is satisfied and it is possible to use the nonlinear Gauss–Seidel algorithm. Because the dual cost is quadratic, the minimization with respect to u can be done analytically, and the iteration can be written explicitly as we proceed to show.

The first partial derivative of the dual cost function with respect to u_j is given by

$$r_j + \sum_{k=1}^{m} p_{jk}u_k, \tag{4.4}$$

where p_{jk} and r_j are the corresponding elements of the matrix P and the vector r, respectively. Setting the derivative to zero, we see that the unconstrained minimum of the dual cost along the jth coordinate starting from u is attained at $\tilde{u}_j$ given by

$$\tilde{u}_j = -\frac{1}{p_{jj}}\left(r_j + \sum_{k \neq j} p_{jk}u_k\right) = u_j - \frac{1}{p_{jj}}\left(r_j + \sum_{k=1}^{m} p_{jk}u_k\right).$$

Taking into account the nonnegativity constraint $u_j \geq 0$, we see that the Gauss–Seidel iteration, when the jth coordinate is updated, has the form

$$u_j := \max\{0, \tilde{u}_j\} = \max\Big\{0, u_j - \frac{1}{p_{jj}}\Big(r_j + \sum_{k=1}^{m} p_{jk} u_k\Big)\Big\},$$

(4.5)

$$u_i := u_i, \qquad \forall\, i \neq j.$$

We can also consider a linearized projected Jacobi method [cf. the discussion following Eq. (3.6) in Section 3.3]. This is a special case of the scaled gradient projection method. In particular, the scaling matrix $M(t)$ is diagonal and its jth diagonal entry is equal to p_{jj}. Taking into account the form of the first partial derivative of the dual cost with respect to u_j given by Eq. (4.4), we see that the method is given by

$$u_j(t+1) = \max\Big\{0, u_j(t) - \frac{\gamma}{p_{jj}}\Big(r_j + \sum_{k=1}^{m} p_{jk} u_k(t)\Big)\Big\}, \qquad j = 1, \ldots, m,$$

(4.6)

where $\gamma > 0$ is the stepsize parameter. This iteration is more suitable for parallelization than the Gauss–Seidel iteration (4.5). On the other hand, for convergence, the stepsize γ should be chosen sufficiently small, and some experimentation may be needed to obtain the appropriate range for γ. Convergence can be shown when $\gamma = 1/m$ (Exercise 4.1) but this value may be too small for some problems, and can lead to an unnecessarily slow rate of convergence. A frequently more practical scheme is a hybrid Gauss–Seidel and Jacobi method, whereby the index set $\{1, \ldots, n\}$ is partitioned in subsets and at each iteration, the coordinates of only one of the subsets are updated according to Eq. (4.6). In this way, one may enlarge the range of stepsizes γ for which convergence is obtained.

The matrix A often has a sparse structure in practice, and one would like to take advantage of this structure. Unfortunately, the matrix $P = AQ^{-1}A'$ typically has a less advantageous sparsity structure than A. Furthermore, it may be undesirable to calculate and store the elements of P, particularly when m is large. It turns out that the Gauss–Seidel iteration (4.5) can be performed without explicit knowledge of the elements p_{jk} of the matrix P; only the elements of the matrix AQ^{-1} are needed instead. To see how this can be done, consider the vector

$$y = -A'u.$$

(4.7)

We have

$$Pu = AQ^{-1}A'u = -AQ^{-1}y,$$

and the jth component of this vector equation yields

$$\sum_{k=1}^{m} p_{jk} u_k = -w_j' y,$$

(4.8)

where w_j' is the jth row of AQ^{-1}. We also have

$$p_{jj} = w'_j a_j, \tag{4.9}$$

where a_j is the jth column of A'. The Gauss–Seidel iteration (4.5) can now be written, using Eqs. (4.8) and (4.9), as

$$u_j := \max\left\{0, u_j - \frac{1}{w'_j a_j}(r_j - w'_j y)\right\},$$

$$u_i := u_i, \qquad \forall\, i \neq j,$$

or, equivalently,

$$u := u - \min\left\{u_j, \frac{1}{w'_j a_j}(r_j - w'_j y)\right\} e_j, \tag{4.10}$$

where e_j is the jth unit vector (all its elements are zero except for the jth, which is unity). The corresponding iteration for the vector y of Eq. (4.7) is obtained by multiplication of Eq. (4.10) with $-A'$ yielding

$$y := y + \min\left\{u_j, \frac{1}{w'_j a_j}(r_j - w'_j y)\right\} a_j. \tag{4.11}$$

The (nonlinear) Gauss–Seidel method can now be summarized as follows. Initially, u is any vector in the nonnegative orthant and $y = -A'u$. At each iteration, a coordinate index j is chosen and u and y are iterated simultaneously using Eqs. (4.10) and (4.11). For problems with special structure, it is possible to parallelize the Gauss–Seidel method by observing that the iterations corresponding to any indices j_1 and j_2 are decoupled and can be carried out in parallel if there is no coordinate which is nonzero for both a_{j_1} and w_{j_2}. To see this, suppose that starting with the vectors u and y, the iteration corresponding to index j_1 yields u_1 and y_1. Let also u_2 and y_2 be the vectors obtained by an iteration corresponding to index j_2 starting with the vectors u_1 and y_1. It is seen from Eq. (4.11) that y and y_1 differ in a given coordinate only if the corresponding coordinate of a_{j_1} is nonzero. Thus, if there is no coordinate which is nonzero for both a_{j_1} and w_{j_2}, we have $w'_{j_2} y = w'_{j_2} y_1$. It follows from Eqs. (4.10) and (4.11) that the values of u_2 and y_2 will be the same, regardless of whether the iteration corresponding to j_1 precedes or is carried out simultaneously with the iteration corresponding to j_2.

When Q is the identity matrix and $b = 0$, the problem is equivalent to projecting the origin on the constraint set. In this case, iteration (4.11) has a nice interpretation as a "modified projection" of y on the halfspace $H_j = \{x \mid a'_j x \leq c_j\}$, as illustrated in Fig. 3.4.1. The Gauss–Seidel algorithm therefore involves, at each iteration, a sequence of modified projections on a halfspace, to update y, while simultaneously updating the corresponding coordinates of u. The Jacobi algorithm involves simultaneous projections on all halfspaces of this type. These and related algorithms have proved successful on very large problems arising, for example, in image reconstruction (see e.g., [CeH87] for a survey).

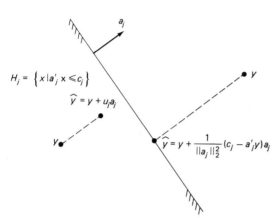

Figure 3.4.1 Interpretation of iteration (4.11) as a projection when $Q = I$ and $b = 0$. Then $w_j = a_j$, $r_j = c_j$, and the iteration takes the form

$$y := y + \min \left\{ u_j, \frac{1}{\|a_j\|_2^2}(c_j - a_j'y) \right\} a_j.$$

When $y \notin H_j$, we have $c_j - a_j'y < 0$ and, because $u_j \geq 0$, y is set to the vector

$$\hat{y} = y + \frac{1}{\|a_j\|_2^2}(c_j - a_j'y)a_j,$$

which is the orthogonal projection of y on H_j. When $y \in H_j$, then y is set to the projection of y on the boundary of H_j if $u_j \geq \left(1/\|a_j\|_2^2\right)(c_j - a_j'y)$, and, otherwise, is set to $\hat{y} = y + u_j a_j$, which lies between y and the boundary of H_j.

3.4.2 Separable Strictly Convex Programming

Suppose that the space $\Re^n$ is represented as the Cartesian product of spaces $\Re^{n_i}$, where $n_1 + \cdots + n_m = n$, and consider the problem

$$\text{minimize} \quad \sum_{i=1}^m F_i(x_i)$$

$$\text{subject to } e_j'x = s_j, \qquad j = 1, \ldots, r, \tag{4.12}$$

$$x_i \in P_i, \qquad i = 1, \ldots, m,$$

where $F_i : \Re^{n_i} \mapsto \Re$ are strictly convex functions, x_i are the components of x, e_j are given vectors in $\Re^n$, s_j are given scalars, and P_i are given bounded polyhedral subsets of $\Re^{n_i}$. We note that if the constraints $e_j'x = s_j$ were not present, it would be possible to decompose this problem into independent subproblems. This motivates us to consider a dual problem that involves Lagrange multipliers for these constraints. In accordance with the theory of Appendix C, this dual problem has the form

$$\text{maximize} \quad q(p)$$

$$\text{subject to} \quad p \in \Re^r. \tag{4.13}$$

The dual function is given by

$$
q(p) = \min_{x_i \in P_i} \left\{ \sum_{i=1}^{m} F_i(x_i) + \sum_{j=1}^{r} p_j(e_j'x - s_j) \right\} = \sum_{i=1}^{m} q_i(p) - p's, \qquad (4.14)
$$

where $p's = \sum_{j=1}^{r} p_j s_j$, and

$$
q_i(p) = \min_{x_i \in P_i} \left\{ F_i(x_i) + \sum_{j=1}^{r} p_j e_{ji}' x_i \right\}, \qquad i = 1, \ldots, m, \qquad (4.15)
$$

with e_{ji} denoting the appropriate subvector of e_j that corresponds to x_i. An important observation is that due to the separable structure of the problem, the evaluation of the dual function is amenable to parallel computation with a separate processor calculating each component $q_i(p)$ of $q(p)$.

By applying the Differentiability Theorem of Appendix C, we see that strict convexity of F_i implies that the dual function is continuously differentiable, and that if the minimum in Eq. (4.15) is attained at the point $x_i(p)$, the partial derivative of q with respect to p_j is given by

$$
\frac{\partial q(p)}{\partial p_j} = e_j' x(p) - s_j, \qquad (4.16)
$$

where $x(p) = \big(x_1(p), \ldots, x_m(p)\big)$. Since the dual function is differentiable, we can apply methods considered earlier in this chapter, such as Gauss–Seidel, Jacobi, and gradient methods, that are amenable to parallel implementation. This is possible because, in contrast with the primal problem (4.12), the dual problem (4.13) is unconstrained. [If the primal problem (4.12) had inequality constraints in place of the equality constraints, the dual problem would have nonnegativity constraints but the parallelizable Gauss–Seidel, Jacobi, and gradient projection methods would still be applicable.] Note also that the calculation of the ith component $q_i(p)$ of the dual cost [Eq. (4.15)] yields $x_i(p)$ and therefore also the ith components $e_{ji}'x_i(p)$ of the dual cost derivatives $\partial q(p)/\partial p_j$ of Eq. (4.16). In a message–passing parallel computing system, where there is a separate processor assigned to the ith component, the calculation of the dual cost gradient via Eq. (4.16) requires a single or multinode accumulation (cf. Subsection 1.3.4). The gradient $\nabla q(p)$ can then be distributed to all processors, if necessary, by means of a single or multinode broadcast [depending on whether all coordinates of $\nabla q(p)$ are accumulated at a single node or not].

In some problems where the separability structure of problem (4.12) is not present, it may be desirable to create this structure through some transformation in order to make the application of parallel methods possible. We provide an example:

Example 4.1.   *Minimizing the Sum of Strictly Convex Functions*

Consider the problem

$$\text{minimize} \quad \sum_{i=0}^{m} F_i(x)$$

$$\text{subject to } x \in P_i, \qquad i = 0, 1, \ldots, m,$$

(4.17)

where $F_i : \Re^n \mapsto \Re$, $i = 0, 1, \ldots, m$ are strictly convex functions, and P_i are bounded polyhedral subsets of $\Re^n$. An interesting special case of this problem arises when minimizing an expected cost $E\big[F(x, w)\big]$, subject to $x \in P(w)$, where w is a random variable taking a finite number of values, each with a given probability, $F(x, w)$ is strictly convex for each w, and $P(w)$ is a bounded polyhedral set for each w.

We consider the equivalent separable problem

$$\text{minimize} \quad F_0(x) + \sum_{i=1}^{m} F_i(x_i)$$

$$\text{subject to } x_i = x, \qquad i = 1, \ldots, m,$$

$$x \in P_0, \qquad x_i \in P_i, \qquad i = 1, \ldots, m,$$

(4.18)

where $x_i \in \Re^n$, $i = 1, \ldots m$, are additional (artificial) variables. Based on the theory of Appendix C, the corresponding dual problem is given by

$$\text{maximize} \quad q(p) = q_0(p_1 + p_2 + \cdots + p_m) + \sum_{i=1}^{m} q_i(p_i)$$

$$\text{subject to } p_i \in \Re^n, \qquad i = 1, 2, \ldots, m,$$

(4.19)

where

$$q_0(p_1 + p_2 + \cdots + p_m) = \min_{x \in P_0} \{F_0(x) - (p_1 + p_2 + \cdots + p_m)'x\}, \qquad (4.20)$$

$$q_i(p_i) = \min_{x_i \in P_i} \{F_i(x_i) + p_i'x_i\}. \qquad (4.21)$$

By the Differentiability Theorem of Appendix C, the dual cost is continuously differentiable, and its gradient is given by

$$\frac{\partial q(p)}{\partial p_i} = x_i(p) - x(p), \qquad i = 1, 2, \ldots, m,$$

where $x(p)$ and $x_i(p)$ are the unique minimizing vectors in Eqs. (4.20) and (4.21), respectively. Note that $x(p)$ and $x_i(p)$ can be computed in parallel, and that the dual problem is well suited for solution using parallel gradient methods. An alternative gradient–like dual method for this problem that does not require strict convexity of the functions F_i will be given in Subsection 3.4.4.

3.4.3 The Proximal Minimization Algorithm

We mentioned earlier that strict convexity of the primal cost function is an important property, since it implies differentiability of the dual cost function. When the dual cost function is not differentiable, one might try to solve the dual problem using a method that can handle nondifferentiabilities (see [BaW75], [Sha79], and [Pol87]). A different approach, considered in this subsection, is to make the primal cost function strictly convex by adding a quadratic term to it. We use this approach to develop an algorithm, called the *proximal minimization algorithm*. We show how this algorithm allows us to transform a linear programming problem into a strictly convex quadratic programming problem that can be solved, for example, using the dual methods of Subsection 3.4.1. In the next subsection we look at the proximal minimization algorithm in a dual setting, thereby obtaining decomposition methods for separable problems that are not strictly convex.

Consider the problem

$$\text{minimize} \quad F(x)$$
$$\text{subject to} \quad x \in X, \tag{4.22}$$

where $F : \Re^n \mapsto \Re$ is a given convex function, and X is a nonempty closed convex set. We introduce an additional vector $y \in \Re^n$, and consider the following equivalent optimization problem

$$\text{minimize} \quad F(x) + \frac{1}{2c}\|x - y\|_2^2$$
$$\text{subject to} \quad x \in X, \ y \in \Re^n,$$

where c is a positive scalar parameter, and $\|\cdot\|_2$ is the standard Euclidean norm. This problem can be solved by the nonlinear Gauss–Seidel method of Subsection 3.3.5, which alternately minimizes the cost over $x \in X$ while keeping y fixed, then minimizes the cost over $y \in \Re^n$ while keeping x fixed, and repeats. The method is given by

$$x(t + 1) = \arg\min_{x \in X} \left\{ F(x) + \frac{1}{2c}\|x - y(t)\|_2^2 \right\},$$
$$y(t + 1) = x(t + 1),$$

or, equivalently,

$$x(t + 1) = \arg\min_{x \in X} \left\{ F(x) + \frac{1}{2c}\|x - x(t)\|_2^2 \right\}. \tag{4.23}$$

It will be shown as part of the following Prop. 4.1 that the minimum in Eq. (4.23) is uniquely attained for any given $x(t) \in \Re^n$. As a result the method is well defined.

Figures 3.4.2 through 3.4.4 illustrate how the method converges, and how the parameter c affects the rate of convergence. Note that when the cost function F is linear, then a straightforward calculation shows that the iteration (4.23) can be written as

$$x(t+1) = \left[x(t) - c\nabla F\big(x(t)\big) \right]^{+},$$

where $[\cdot]^{+}$ denotes projection on the set X, so for this case, iteration (4.23) can be viewed as a gradient projection iteration.

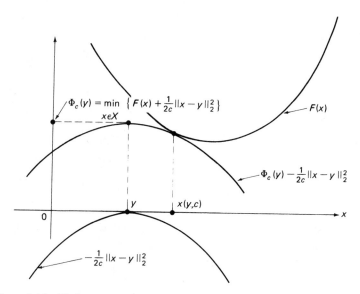

Figure 3.4.2   Finding the minimum of $F(x) + (1/2c)\|x - y\|_2^2$ over X for a given y and c. The minimum is attained at the unique point $x(y, c)$ at which the graph of the quadratic function $-(1/2c)\|x - y\|_2^2$ raised up or down just touches the graph of $F(x)$.

Since the cost function $F(x) + (1/2c)\|x - y\|_2^2$ is strictly convex with respect to x for fixed y, and strictly convex with respect to y for fixed x, our nonlinear Gauss–Seidel convergence result (Prop. 3.9 in Section 3.3) can be applied assuming that F is continuously differentiable. Figure 3.4.3 suggests that convergence occurs even if F is not differentiable, and even if c increases from one iteration to the next. Figure 3.4.5 suggests that convergence is finite under certain circumstances. We show these facts in the following proposition:

Proposition 4.1.   Let $F : \Re^n \mapsto \Re$ be a convex function, and X be a nonempty closed convex set. Denote also by X^* the set of points that minimize $F(x)$ over $x \in X$

$$X^* = \{ x^* \in X \mid F(x^*) \leq F(x),\ \forall\, x \in X \}. \tag{4.24}$$

(a) For every $y \in \Re^n$ and $c > 0$, the minimum of $F(x) + (1/2c)\|x - y\|_2^2$ over $x \in X$ is attained at a unique point denoted by $x(y, c)$.

(b) The function $\Phi_c : \Re^n \mapsto \Re$ defined by

$$\Phi_c(y) = \min_{x \in X} \left\{ F(x) + \frac{1}{2c}\|x - y\|_2^2 \right\} \tag{4.25}$$

is convex and continuously differentiable, and its gradient is given by

$$\nabla\Phi_c(y) = \frac{y - x(y, c)}{c}. \tag{4.26}$$

Furthermore, x^* minimizes $\Phi_c(y)$ over $y \in \Re^n$ if and only if x^* minimizes $F(x)$ over $x \in X$, that is,

$$X^* = \left\{ x^* \,\middle|\, \Phi_c(x^*) = \min_{y \in \Re^n} \Phi_c(y) \right\}, \qquad \forall\, c > 0. \tag{4.27}$$

(c) Assume that X^* is nonempty. A sequence generated by the iteration

$$x(t + 1) = \arg\min_{x \in X} \left\{ F(x) + \frac{1}{2c(t)}\|x - x(t)\|_2^2 \right\}, \tag{4.28}$$

where $\{c(t)\}$ is a sequence of positive numbers with $\liminf_{t \to \infty} c(t) > 0$, converges to an element of X^*.

(d) Assume that X^* is nonempty, and that there exists a scalar $\beta > 0$ such that

$$F(x) \geq F^* + \beta\rho(x; X^*), \qquad \forall\, x \in X, \tag{4.29}$$

where

$$F^* = \min_{x \in X} F(x), \qquad \text{and} \qquad \rho(x; X^*) = \min_{x^* \in X^*} \|x - x^*\|_2. \tag{4.30}$$

Then

$$x(y, c) = \arg\min_{x \in X^*} \|x - y\|_2, \qquad \text{if } \rho(y; X^*) \leq c\beta. \tag{4.31}$$

In particular, the algorithm (4.28) converges finitely [i.e., there exists $\bar{t} > 0$, depending on $x(0)$, such that $x(t) \in X^*$ for all $t \geq \bar{t}$], and, for a given $x(0)$, it converges in a single iteration if $c(0)$ is sufficiently large.

Note: The condition (4.29) is illustrated in Fig. 3.4.6. It can be shown to hold in the case of a linear programming problem, that is, when F is a linear function and X is a polyhedral set (see Exercise 4.3).

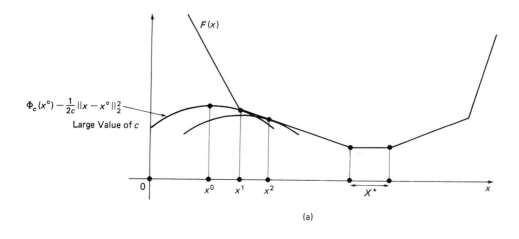

$\Phi_c(x^\circ) - \dfrac{1}{2c}\|x - x^\circ\|_2^2$

Large Value of c

(a)

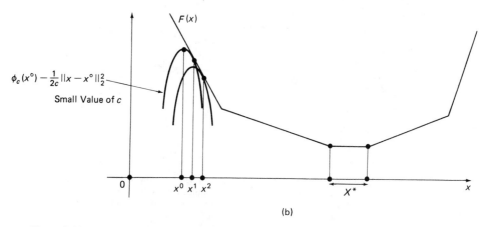

$\phi_c(x^\circ) - \dfrac{1}{2c}\|x - x^\circ\|_2^2$

Small Value of c

(b)

Figure 3.4.3 Illustration of the role of the parameter c in the convergence process of the proximal minimization algorithm. (a) Case of large value of c. The graph of the quadratic term is "blunt" and the method makes fast progress toward the optimal solution set X^*. (b) Case of a small value of c. The graph of the quadratic term is "pointed" and the method makes slow progress.

Proof.

(a) It will suffice to show that for all $c > 0$ and $y \in \Re^n$, the level sets

$$\left\{ x \in X \,\Big|\, F(x) + \frac{1}{2c}\|x - y\|_2^2 \le \alpha \right\}, \qquad \alpha \in \Re, \tag{4.32}$$

are bounded. It will follow then that we can equivalently search for the minimum of $F(x) + (1/2c)\|x - y\|_2^2$ over a compact subset of X instead of X. Weierstrass' theorem (Prop. A.8 in Appendix A) can then be used to show that the minimum of $F(x) + (1/2c)\|x - y\|_2^2$ over X is attained, necessarily at a unique point in view of

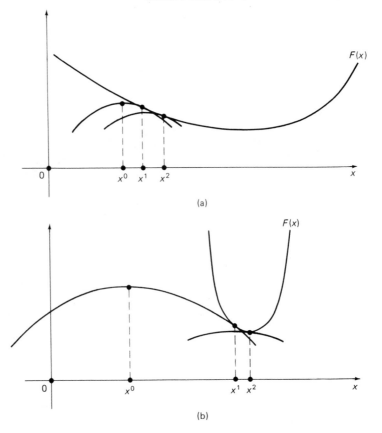

Figure 3.4.4 Illustration of the role of the growth properties of the function F in the convergence process of the proximal minimization algorithm (see Exercise 4.2). (a) Case where $F(x)$ grows slowly, and the convergence is slow. (b) Case where $F(x)$ grows fast, and the convergence is fast.

the strict convexity of the quadratic term $(1/2c)\|x - y\|_2^2$. [Proving boundedness of the set of Eq. (4.32) is very simple if X^* is nonempty or more generally if $F(x)$ is bounded below over X; the following argument primarily addresses the case where $\inf_{x \in X} F(x) = -\infty$, and is based on the idea that a convex function cannot decrease along any one direction at faster than linear rate while the term $(1/2c)\|x - y\|_2^2$ increases at a quadratic rate.]

We argue by contradiction. Suppose that for some $c > 0$ and $y \in \Re^n$, there exists a sequence $\{x^k\}$ such that

$$\|x^k - y\|_2 \to \infty, \qquad F(x^k) + \frac{1}{2c}\|x^k - y\|_2^2 \le \alpha, \qquad \forall\, k. \qquad (4.33)$$

Denote $\beta_k = \|x^k - y\|_2$, and assume without loss of generality that $\beta_k \ge 1$ for all k. Define also $z^k = (x^k - y)/\beta_k$, and consider the convex function $\hat{F}(x) = F(x + y)$.

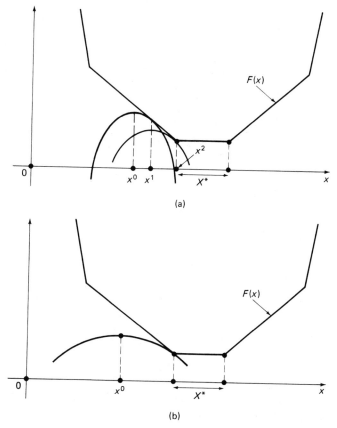

Figure 3.4.5 Finite convergence of the proximal minimization algorithm when $F(x)$ grows at a linear rate near the optimal solution set X^*. (a) Finite convergence for a small value of c. (b) Convergence in a single iteration for a large enough value of c.

From Eq. (4.33) we obtain

$$\hat{F}(\beta_k z^k) + \frac{(\beta_k)^2}{2c} = \hat{F}(x^k - y) + \frac{1}{2c}\|x^k - y\|_2^2 \leq \alpha, \qquad \forall\, k. \qquad (4.34)$$

By convexity of $\hat{F}$ we have

$$\min_{\|z\|_2=1} \hat{F}(z) \leq \hat{F}(z^k) \leq \frac{1}{\beta_k}\hat{F}\left(\beta_k z^k\right) + \left(1 - \frac{1}{\beta_k}\right)\hat{F}(0),$$

from which we obtain

$$(1 - \beta_k)\hat{F}(0) + \beta_k \min_{\|z\|_2=1} \hat{F}(z) \leq \hat{F}\left(\beta_k z^k\right).$$

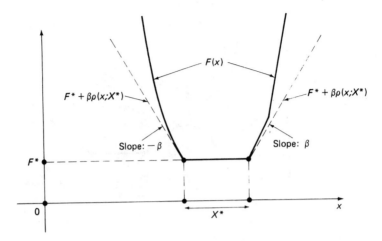

Figure 3.4.6 Illustration of the condition (4.29). Here $F(x)$ majorizes the function $F^* + \beta\rho(x; X^*)$ which grows at a rate $\beta > 0$ with the distance of x from the optimal solution set X^*.

Combining this relation with Eq. (4.34), we obtain

$$\hat{F}(0) + \beta_k \left(\min_{\|z\|_2 = 1} \hat{F}(z) - \hat{F}(0) \right) + \frac{(\beta_k)^2}{2c} \le \alpha, \qquad \forall \, k.$$

Since $\beta_k \to \infty$, we reach a contradiction.

(b) To show convexity of Φ_c, let y_1 and y_2 be any vectors in $\Re^n$ and let α be a scalar in $[0, 1]$. Denote $x_1 = x(y_1, c)$ and $x_2 = x(y_2, c)$. We have, using the convexity of F and of the norm function $\|\cdot\|_2$,

$$
\begin{aligned}
\alpha \Phi_c(y_1) + (1 - \alpha)\Phi_c(y_2) = {}& \alpha \left[F(x_1) + \frac{1}{2c}\|x_1 - y_1\|_2^2 \right] \\
& + (1 - \alpha)\left[F(x_2) + \frac{1}{2c}\|x_2 - y_2\|_2^2 \right] \\
\ge {}& F\big(\alpha x_1 + (1 - \alpha)x_2\big) \\
& + \frac{1}{2c}\|\alpha x_1 + (1 - \alpha)x_2 - \alpha y_1 - (1 - \alpha)y_2\|_2^2 \\
\ge {}& \min_{x \in X} \left\{ F(x) + \frac{1}{2c}\|x - \alpha y_1 - (1 - \alpha)y_2\|_2^2 \right\} \\
= {}& \Phi_c\big(\alpha y_1 + (1 - \alpha)y_2\big).
\end{aligned}
$$

This proves the convexity of Φ_c.

To show differentiability of Φ_c, let us consider any $y \in \Re^n$, $d \in \Re^n$, and $\alpha > 0$. We have

$$F\big(x(y,c)\big) + \frac{1}{2c}\|x(y,c) - (y+\alpha d)\|_2^2 \geq \Phi_c(y+\alpha d) \geq \Phi_c(y) + \alpha\Phi_c'(y;d)$$

$$= F\big(x(y,c)\big) + \frac{1}{2c}\|x(y,c) - y\|_2^2 + \alpha\Phi_c'(y;d), \qquad (4.35)$$

where the second inequality follows from the convexity of Φ_c and the definition of the directional derivative $\Phi_c'(y;d)$. By expanding the quadratic form in the left–hand side of Eq. (4.35), by collecting terms, and then by dividing by α, we obtain

$$\left[\frac{y - x(y,c)}{c}\right]' d + \frac{\alpha}{2c}\|d\|_2^2 \geq \Phi_c'(y;d), \qquad \forall\, \alpha > 0,\ d \in \Re^n.$$

Taking the limit as $\alpha \to 0$, it follows that

$$\left[\frac{y - x(y,c)}{c}\right]' d \geq \Phi_c'(y;d), \qquad \forall\, d \in \Re^n.$$

By replacing d with $-d$ in the preceding relation, we obtain

$$-\left[\frac{y - x(y,c)}{c}\right]' d \geq \Phi_c'(y;-d) \geq -\Phi_c'(y;d),$$

where the second inequality follows from Eq. (A.16) in Appendix A. The last two relations imply that

$$\left[\frac{y - x(y,c)}{c}\right]' d = \Phi_c'(y;d), \qquad \forall\, d \in \Re^n,$$

or equivalently, that Φ_c is differentiable with gradient equal to $\big[y - x(y,c)\big]/c$. We note also that since Φ_c is a convex function, its gradient is continuous (Prop. A.42 in Appendix A).

We finally show that the minimizing points of $\Phi_c(y)$ over $\Re^n$ and of $F(x)$ over X coincide. We first note that the function $F(x) + (1/2c)\|x - y\|_2^2$ takes the value $F(y)$ for $x = y$, from which it follows that

$$\Phi_c(y) \leq F(y), \qquad \forall\, y \in X. \qquad (4.36)$$

If y^* minimizes $F(x)$ over $x \in X$ then using Eq. (4.36) we have

$$\Phi_c(y^*) \leq F(y^*) \leq F\big(x(y,c)\big) \leq F\big(x(y,c)\big) + \frac{1}{2c}\|x(y,c) - y^*\|_2^2 = \Phi_c(y), \quad \forall y \in \Re^n,$$

which implies that y^* minimizes $\Phi_c(y)$ over $\Re^n$. Conversely, if y^* minimizes $\Phi_c(y)$ over $\Re^n$, then $c\nabla\Phi_c(y^*) = y^* - x(y^*, c) = 0$. This implies that $y^* \in X$ and, using also Eq. (4.36), it is seen that

$$F(y^*) = \Phi_c(y^*) \leq \Phi_c(y) \leq F(y), \qquad \forall\, y \in X.$$

Therefore y^* minimizes $F(y)$ over $y \in X$.

(c) The proof proceeds in two stages. We first show that all limit points of $\{x(t)\}$ belong to X^*, and then we show that $\{x(t)\}$ is bounded and has a unique limit point.

We have, using Eq. (4.28),

$$F\big(x(t+1)\big) + \frac{1}{2c(t)}\|x(t+1) - x(t)\|_2^2 \leq F(x) + \frac{1}{2c(t)}\|x - x(t)\|_2^2, \qquad \forall\, x \in X,$$
(4.37)

from which, by setting $x = x(t)$ we obtain

$$F\big(x(t+1)\big) + \frac{1}{2c(t)}\|x(t+1) - x(t)\|_2^2 \leq F\big(x(t)\big), \qquad \forall\, t.$$
(4.38)

Let $\{x(t)\}_{t\in T}$ be a subsequence converging to a vector $x_\infty \in X$. From Eq. (4.38), it follows that $F\big(x(t)\big)$ decreases monotonically to $F(x_\infty)$ and that

$$\lim_{t\to\infty}\|x(t+1) - x(t)\|_2 = 0.$$
(4.39)

Furthermore, Eq. (4.39) implies that the subsequence $\{x(t+1)\}_{t\in T}$ also converges to x_∞. Let $x^* \in X^*$, and $\alpha \in (0,1)$. By setting $x = \alpha x^* + (1-\alpha)x(t+1)$ in Eq. (4.37) and using the convexity of F, we obtain

$$F\big(x(t+1)\big) + \frac{1}{2c(t)}\|x(t+1) - x(t)\|_2^2$$

$$\leq F\big(\alpha x^* + (1-\alpha)x(t+1)\big) + \frac{1}{2c(t)}\|\alpha x^* + (1-\alpha)x(t+1) - x(t)\|_2^2$$

$$\leq \alpha F(x^*) + (1-\alpha)F\big(x(t+1)\big) + \frac{1}{2c(t)}\|\alpha\big(x^* - x(t+1)\big) + x(t+1) - x(t)\|_2^2.$$

Taking the limit as $t \to \infty$, $t \in T$, and using Eq. (4.39), we obtain

$$F(x_\infty) - F(x^*) \leq \frac{\alpha\|x^* - x_\infty\|_2^2}{2\liminf_{t\to\infty} c(t)}, \qquad \forall\, \alpha \in (0,1).$$
(4.40)

Since this relation holds for all $\alpha \in (0, 1)$, it follows that $F(x_\infty) = F(x^*)$, implying that $x_\infty \in X^*$. We have thus proved that every limit point of $\{x(t)\}$ is an optimal solution.

There remains to show that $\{x(t)\}$ converges. From Eq. (4.37) we obtain

$$\|x(t+1) - x(t)\|_2 \leq \|x - x(t)\|_2, \qquad \forall \, x \in X \text{ with } F(x) \leq F\big(x(t+1)\big), \qquad (4.41)$$

from which it follows that $x(t+1)$ is the unique projection of $x(t)$ on the convex set $\{x \in X \mid F(x) \leq F\big(x(t+1)\big)\}$. From the Projection Theorem (Prop. 3.2 in Section 3.3) we obtain

$$\big(x(t+1) - x(t)\big)'\big(x - x(t+1)\big) \geq 0, \qquad \forall \, x \in X \text{ with } F(x) \leq F\big(x(t+1)\big). \,\, (4.42)$$

For every optimal solution $x^* \in X^*$, we have

$$\|x^* - x(t)\|_2^2 = \|x^* - x(t+1)\|_2^2 + 2\big(x(t+1) - x(t)\big)'\big(x^* - x(t+1)\big) + \|x(t+1) - x(t)\|_2^2,$$

and by using Eq. (4.42) in this relation we obtain

$$\|x^* - x(t+1)\|_2 \leq \|x^* - x(t)\|_2, \qquad \forall \, x^* \in X^*. \qquad (4.43)$$

From Eq. (4.43) we see that $\{x(t)\}$ is bounded, so it must have one or more limit points. We have already proved that all limit points of $\{x(t)\}$ belong to X^*. If x^* is a limit point, then Eq. (4.43) implies that the distance of $x(t)$ from x^* cannot increase at any iteration. Therefore, $\{x(t)\}$ cannot have a second limit point, and must converge to x^*.

(d) See Fig. 3.4.7.   **Q.E.D.**

The operator that assigns to y the unique minimizing point $x(y, c)$ in the definition (4.25) of Φ_c is known as the *prox operator* [Mor65]; this explains the name proximal minimization algorithm for the iteration (4.28).

Note that when $c(t)$ is constant [say $c(t) = c$ for all t], the proximal minimization algorithm (4.28) can also be written, based on the gradient expression (4.26), as

$$x(t+1) = x(t) - c\nabla\Phi_c\big(x(t)\big),$$

so it can be viewed as a gradient method for minimizing Φ_c. The rate of convergence of the iteration depends on c and improves as c becomes larger, as indicated in Fig. 3.4.3 and in Exercise 4.2. Computational experience has shown that using an increasing sequence $\{c(t)\}$ often works considerably better than using a constant value of c. Note that one may not wish to use a very high value of c because this can lead to numerical difficulties in minimizing $F(x) + (1/2c)\|x - y\|_2^2$.

The gradient interpretation also suggests the variation

$$x(t+1) = x(t) - \gamma(t)\nabla\Phi_c\big(x(t)\big),$$

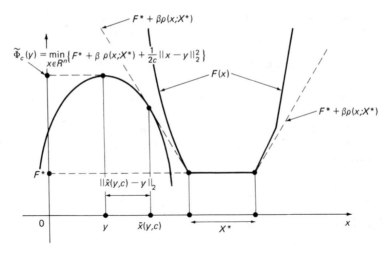

Figure 3.4.7   Proof of part (d) of Prop. 4.1. We first note that the function $\rho(x; X^*) = \min_{x^* \in X^*} \|x - x^*\|_2$ is convex, and that

$$\nabla \rho(x; X^*) = \frac{x - \hat{x}}{\rho(x; X^*)}, \qquad \forall \; x \notin X^*,$$

where $\hat{x}$ denotes the unique projection of x on X^*. The verification of convexity is left for the reader. The formula for $\nabla \rho(x; X^*)$ is obtained by differentiating in the equation $\rho(x; X^*) = \sqrt{2c\hat{\Phi}_c(x)}$ where $\hat{\Phi}_c(x) = \min_{x^* \in X^*} (1/2c)\|x - x^*\|_2^2$, and by using the fact $\nabla \hat{\Phi}_c(x) = (x - \hat{x})/c$ [cf. Eq. (4.26)].

Consider the function $\tilde{\Phi}_c : \Re^n \mapsto \Re$ defined by

$$\tilde{\Phi}_c(y) = \min_{x \in \Re^n} \left\{ F^* + \beta \rho(x; X^*) + \frac{1}{2c}\|x - y\|_2^2 \right\},$$

(compare with the figure). From part (a) of Prop. 4.1, the minimum in the definition of $\tilde{\Phi}_c(y)$ is attained at a unique point denoted $\tilde{x}(y, c)$. Suppose that $\tilde{x}(y, c) \notin X^*$. By setting to zero the gradient of $F^* + \beta\rho(x; X^*) + (1/2c)\|x - y\|_2^2$ at $\tilde{x}(y, c)$ we obtain

$$\frac{\beta\big(\tilde{x}(y, c) - \hat{x}(y, c)\big)}{\rho\big(\tilde{x}(y, c); X^*\big)} + \frac{\tilde{x}(y, c) - y}{c} = 0,$$

where $\hat{x}(y, c)$ is the projection of $\tilde{x}(y, c)$ on X^*. It follows that $\|\tilde{x}(y, c) - y\|_2 = c\beta$. Using the analog of Eq. (4.41) with $F(x)$ replaced by $F^* + \beta\rho(x; X^*)$, we have that $\tilde{x}(y, c)$ is the projection of y on the set $\big\{\tilde{x} \in X \mid \rho(x; X^*) \leq \rho\big(\tilde{x}(y, c); X^*\big)\big\}$, which contains X^*. Therefore, $\rho(y; X^*) > \|\tilde{x}(y, c) - y\|_2 = c\beta$. We have thus shown that $\tilde{x}(y, c) \notin X^*$ implies that $\rho(y; X^*) > c\beta$. It follows that if $\rho(y; X^*) \leq c\beta$, then $\tilde{x}(y, c) \in X^*$.

Suppose now that the condition (4.29) holds. We will show that if $\tilde{x}(y, c) \in X^*$, then $x(y, c) = \tilde{x}(y, c)$ (as can be seen from the figure). Indeed condition (4.29) implies that $\tilde{\Phi}_c(y) \leq \Phi_c(y) \leq F(x) + (1/2c)\|x - y\|_2^2$ for all $x \in X$. On the other hand if $\tilde{x}(y, c) \in X^*$, then

$$\tilde{\Phi}_c(y) = F^* + \beta\rho\big(\tilde{x}(y, c); X^*\big) + \frac{1}{2c}\|\tilde{x}(y, c) - y\|_2^2 = F\big(\tilde{x}(y, c)\big) + \frac{1}{2c}\|\tilde{x}(y, c) - y\|_2^2,$$

showing that the minimum of $F(x) + (1/2c)\|x - y\|_2^2$ is attained at $\tilde{x}(y, c)$. Therefore $\tilde{x}(y, c) = x(y, c)$. It follows that $x(y, c) \in X^*$ if $\rho(y; X^*) \leq c\beta$. Also since $x(y, c)$ minimizes $F(x) + (1/2c)\|x - y\|_2^2$ over X, we obtain that $\|x(y, c) - y\|_2 \leq \|x^* - y\|_2$ for all $x^* \in X^*$, so $x(y, c)$ is the projection of y on X^*.

where $\gamma(t)$ is a stepsize parameter, possibly different than c. Exercise 4.4 develops a related convergence result for the choice $\gamma(t) \in (0, 2c)$.

We finally note that the cost function $F(x) + (1/2c)\|x - y\|_2^2$ is strictly convex with respect to x, so when F has the separable form $F(x) = \sum_{i=1}^{m} F_i(x_i)$, the dual methods discussed in Subsection 3.4.2 are applicable. The price for this is that we must solve a sequence of separable (strictly convex) problems instead of a single problem (which, however, may not be strictly convex, and may involve a nondifferentiable dual problem). An interesting alternative will be explored in the next subsection.

3.4.4 Augmented Lagrangian Methods

We now consider a dual approach for overcoming the lack of strict convexity of the primal cost, which is based again on adding a quadratic term to the cost function. The resulting algorithm, with proper interpretation, turns out to be equivalent to the proximal minimization algorithm of the previous subsection.

Consider the constrained optimization problem

$$\begin{aligned} \text{minimize} \quad & F(x) \\ \text{subject to} \quad & e_j'x = s_j, \qquad j = 1, \ldots, r \\ & x \in P, \end{aligned} \qquad (4.44)$$

where $F : \Re^n \mapsto \Re$ is a convex function, e_j are given vectors in $\Re^n$, s_j are given scalars, and P is a nonempty polyhedral subset of $\Re^n$. This is the optimization problem that we used to develop the duality theory of Appendix C, except that here we have disregarded linear inequality constraints of the form $a_j'x \leq t_j$. It turns out that this does not involve a loss of generality (see Exercise 4.5). We will also assume for simplicity that P is bounded; the subsequent analysis, however, can be generalized considerably (see [Ber82a], [Roc76b], and [Roc76c]).

We can consider in place of the original problem (4.44), the equivalent problem

$$\begin{aligned} \text{minimize} \quad & F(x) + \frac{c}{2}\|Ex - s\|_2^2 \\ \text{subject to} \quad & Ex = s, \\ & x \in P, \end{aligned}$$

where c is a positive scalar parameter, and $Ex = s$ is a compact notation for the constraints $e_j'x = s_j$, that is, E is the matrix with rows e_j', and s is the vector with coordinates s_j. The dual problem is

$$\begin{aligned} \text{maximize} \quad & q_c(p) = \inf_{x \in P} L_c(x, p) \\ \text{subject to} \quad & p \in \Re^m, \end{aligned}$$

where $L_c(x, p)$ is the *Augmented Lagrangian* function

$$L_c(x, p) = F(x) + p'(Ex - s) + \frac{c}{2}\|Ex - s\|_2^2.$$

An important method using the Augmented Lagrangian function, called the *method of multipliers* ([HaB70], [Hes69], and [Pow69]), consists of successive minimizations of the form

$$x(t + 1) = \arg\min_{x \in P} L_{c(t)}(x, p(t)), \tag{4.45}$$

followed by updates of the vector $p(t)$ according to

$$p(t + 1) = p(t) + c(t)(Ex(t + 1) - s). \tag{4.46}$$

The initial vector $p(0)$ is arbitrary, and $\{c(t)\}$ is a nondecreasing sequence of positive numbers. Note that the minimum of the Augmented Lagrangian in Eq. (4.45) is attained based on our earlier assumption that P is bounded and the Weierstrass theorem (Prop. A.8 in Appendix A). In the case where this minimum is not uniquely attained, the vector $x(t + 1)$ in Eq. (4.45) is chosen arbitrarily from the set of minimizing points of $L_{c(t)}(\cdot, p(t))$.

It turns out that the iteration (4.45)–(4.46) is in reality the proximal minimization algorithm (4.28) in disguise. To see this, we introduce an auxiliary vector $z \in \Re^m$, and write

$$\min_{x \in P} L_{c(t)}(x, p(t)) = \min_{x \in P}\left\{ F(x) + p(t)'(Ex - s) + \frac{c(t)}{2}\|Ex - s\|_2^2 \right\}$$

$$= \min_{Ex - s = z,\ x \in P,\ z \in \Re^m}\left\{ F(x) + p(t)'z + \frac{c(t)}{2}\|z\|_2^2 \right\}. \tag{4.47}$$

We view the problem on the right–hand side in Eq. (4.47) as a constrained optimization problem in the variables x and z. The vector pair $(x(t + 1), z(t + 1))$, where

$$z(t + 1) = Ex(t + 1) - s, \tag{4.48}$$

is an optimal solution to this problem. Let $\bar{y}$ be a corresponding optimal dual solution, that is,

$$\bar{y} = \arg\max_{y \in \Re^m}\left\{ \min_{x \in P,\ z \in \Re^m}\left\{ F(x) + y'(Ex - s - z) + p(t)'z + \frac{c(t)}{2}\|z\|_2^2 \right\} \right\}$$

$$= \arg\max_{y \in \Re^m}\left\{ \min_{x \in P}\{F(x) + y'(Ex - s)\} + \min_{z \in \Re^m}\left\{ (p(t) - y)'z + \frac{c(t)}{2}\|z\|_2^2 \right\} \right\}. \tag{4.49}$$

(An optimal dual solution is guaranteed to exist by the Duality Theorem of Appendix C.) Then $z(t+1)$ attains the minimum in the right–hand side of the above equation when $y = \bar{y}$, which implies that

$$z(t+1) = \frac{\bar{y} - p(t)}{c(t)}$$

or equivalently using Eqs. (4.46) and (4.48),

$$\bar{y} = p(t+1). \tag{4.50}$$

A straightforward calculation shows that

$$\min_{z \in \Re^m} \left\{ \left(p(t) - y\right)' z + \frac{c(t)}{2} \|z\|_2^2 \right\} = -\frac{1}{2c(t)} \|y - p(t)\|_2^2,$$

so from Eqs. (4.49) and (4.50) we obtain

$$p(t+1) = \arg\max_{y \in \Re^m} \left\{ q(y) - \frac{1}{2c(t)} \|y - p(t)\|_2^2 \right\}, \tag{4.51}$$

where $q(y)$ is the dual functional of the original problem (4.44)

$$q(y) = \min_{x \in P} \left\{ F(x) + y'(Ex - s) \right\}.$$

Thus, from Eq. (4.51) we see that the multiplier iteration (4.45)–(4.46) is equivalent to the proximal minimization algorithm applied to the problem of minimizing the real–valued convex function $-q$ or equivalently to the dual problem of maximizing q.

By applying now the convergence result of Prop. 4.1(c), we see that the sequence $\{p(t)\}$ generated by the method of multipliers converges to some dual optimal solution. Furthermore, convergence in a finite number of iterations is obtained in the case of a linear programming problem [cf. Prop. 4.1(d) and Exercise 4.3 applied to the dual problem, which is also a linear programming problem]. We also claim that every limit point of the generated sequence $\{x(t)\}$ is an optimal solution of the primal problem (4.44). To see this, note that from the multiplier update formula (4.46) we obtain

$$Ex(t+1) - s \to 0, \qquad c(t)\big(Ex(t+1) - s\big) \to 0.$$

We also have

$$L_{c(t)}\big(x(t+1), p(t)\big) = \min_{x \in P} \left\{ F(x) + p(t)'(Ex - s) + \frac{c(t)}{2} \|Ex - s\|_2^2 \right\}.$$

The last two relations yield

$$\limsup_{t \to \infty} F\big(x(t+1)\big) = \limsup_{t \to \infty} L_{c(t)}\big(x(t+1), p(t)\big) \le F(x), \qquad \forall\, x \in P, \text{ with } Ex = s,$$

so if $x^* \in P$ is a limit point of $\{x(t)\}$, we obtain

$$F(x^*) \leq F(x), \qquad \forall\ x \in P, \text{ with } Ex = s,$$

as well as $Ex^* = s$ [in view of $Ex(t+1) - s \to 0$]. Therefore any limit point x^* of the generated sequence $\{x(t)\}$ is an optimal solution of the primal problem (4.44).

The method of multipliers of Eqs. (4.45) and (4.46) is an excellent general purpose method for constrained optimization, and applies to considerably more general problems than the one treated here. For example, it can be used for problems involving nonconvex cost functions and constraint equations. It involves a sequence of minimizations of $L_{c(t)}\big(x, p(t)\big)$, but each of these minimizations is subject to fewer constraints and is presumably easier than solving the original problem (4.44). For this, it is necessary that the parameter $c(t)$ is not too large in order to avoid "ill–conditioning" the minimization of the Augmented Lagrangian. Practical experience has shown that it is best to start with a moderate value of c (perhaps obtained through some preliminary experimentation), and either to keep c constant, or to increase c by some factor (say, 2 to 10) with each minimization of the Augmented Lagrangian. There are a number of practical ways to use the results of one minimization in the next minimization (see [Ber82a]).

One difficulty with the method of multipliers is that even if the cost function $F(x)$ is separable, the Augmented Lagrangian $L_c\big(\cdot, p(t)\big)$ is typically nonseparable because it involves the quadratic term $\|Ex - s\|_2^2$. With some reformulation, however, it is possible to preserve a good deal of the separable structure, as shown in the following examples.

Example 4.2.   *Minimizing the Sum of Convex Functions*

Consider the problem

$$\text{minimize}\ \sum_{i=1}^{m} F_i(x)$$

$$\text{subject to}\ \ x \in P_i, \qquad i = 1, \dots, m, \tag{4.52}$$

where $F_i : \Re^n \mapsto \Re$, $i = 0, 1, \dots, m$, are convex functions, and P_i are bounded polyhedral subsets of $\Re^n$. Note the difference with the related Example 4.1; here the functions F_i are not necessarily strictly convex.

We consider the equivalent separable problem

$$\text{minimize}\ \sum_{i=1}^{m} F_i(x_i)$$

$$\text{subject to}\ \ x_i = x, \qquad i = 1, \dots, m,$$

$$x_i \in P_i, \qquad i = 1, \dots, m,$$

where $x_i \in \Re^n$, $i = 1, \dots m$, are additional (artificial) variables. We apply the method of multipliers to this problem. It takes the form

$$p_i(t+1) = p_i(t) + c(t)\big(x(t+1) - x_i(t+1)\big), \qquad i = 1, \dots, m, \tag{4.53}$$

where $x_i(t+1)$ and $x(t+1)$ solve the problem

$$\text{minimize} \ \sum_{i=1}^{m}\left\{ F_i(x_i) + p_i(t)'(x - x_i) + \frac{c(t)}{2}\|x - x_i\|_2^2 \right\} \tag{4.54}$$

$$\text{subject to} \ \ x \in \Re^n, \quad x_i \in P_i, \quad i = 1, \ldots, m.$$

Note that there is coupling in this problem between x and the vectors x_i, so this problem cannot be decomposed into separate minimizations with respect to some of the variables. On the other hand, the problem (4.54) has a Cartesian product constraint set, and a structure that is suitable for the application of the nonlinear Gauss–Seidel method. In particular, we can consider a method that minimizes the Augmented Lagrangian with respect to x with the iteration

$$x := \frac{\sum_{i=1}^{m} x_i}{m} - \frac{\sum_{i=1}^{m} p_i(t)}{mc(t)}, \tag{4.55}$$

then minimizes the Augmented Lagrangian with respect to x_i with the iteration

$$x_i := \arg\min_{x_i \in P_i}\left\{ F_i(x_i) - p_i(t)x_i + \frac{c(t)}{2}\|x - x_i\|_2^2 \right\}, \quad \forall \ i = 1, \ldots, m, \tag{4.56}$$

and repeats until convergence to a minimum of the Augmented Lagrangian. Note that the method can be parallelized to a great extent because the minimizations in Eq. (4.56) can be done in parallel. In a message–passing system, the "averaging" step of Eq. (4.55) used to update x can be performed by means of a single node accumulation algorithm at some processor (cf. Subsection 1.3.4). The resulting vector x can then be distributed to all processors by using a single node broadcast.

The next example is essentially a special case of the preceding one. It has the property that a single minimization of the Augmented Lagrangian is needed because the primal cost function is identically zero and the corresponding dual function has the property of Eq. (4.29) with β arbitrarily large [cf. part (d) of Prop. 4.1].

Example 4.3. *Finding a Point in a Set Intersection by Parallel Projections*

We are given m closed convex sets $C_1, C_2, \ldots, C_m$ in $\Re^n$, and we want to find a point in their intersection. An equivalent problem is

$$\text{minimize} \ \frac{1}{2}\sum_{i=1}^{m} \|x_i - x\|_2^2 \tag{4.57}$$

$$\text{subject to} \ x \in \Re^n, \ x_i \in C_i, \ i = 1, \ldots, m.$$

Here the variables of the optimization are $x, x_1, \ldots, x_m$ and if the intersection $C_1 \cap \cdots \cap C_m$ is nonempty, an optimal solution $(x^*, x_1^*, \ldots, x_m^*)$ of the above problem is such that $x^* = x_i^*$ for all i, and x^* belongs to the intersection. The problem (4.57) may also be viewed as a minimization of the Augmented Lagrangian function (4.54) of the preceding example, where $c(t) = 1$, $F_i(x_i) = 0$, and $p_i(t) = 0$.

Let us now apply the nonlinear Gauss–Seidel method to problem (4.57). The order of variable updating is $x, x_1, \ldots, x_m$, repeated cyclically. Minimization of the cost with respect to each one of $x, x_1, \ldots, x_m$, while all the other variables are fixed, yields the algorithm

$$x(t+1) = \frac{1}{m} \sum_{i=1}^{m} x_i(t), \tag{4.58}$$

$$x_i(t+1) = P_i\big(x(t+1)\big), \qquad i = 1, \ldots, m, \tag{4.59}$$

where $P_i(\cdot)$ denotes projection on C_i. Note that the strict convexity assumption of Prop. 3.9 in Section 3.3 is satisfied in problem (4.57), so the convergence result of that proposition applies. Exercise 4.6 refines this result, showing convergence to an element of the intersection.

Figure 3.4.8 illustrates the parallelizable character of the method and shows that its convergence rate can be slow under some circumstances.

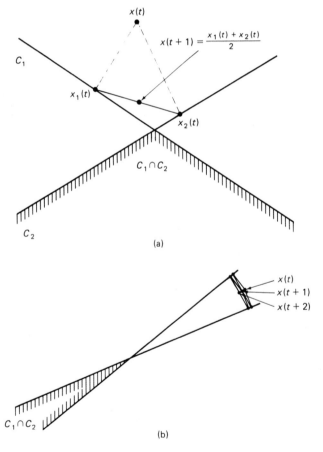

(a)

(b)

Figure 3.4.8 (a) Illustration of the parallel character of the method of Eqs. (4.58)–(4.59) for the feasibility problem of finding a point in the intersection $C_1 \cap \cdots \cap C_m$. (b) Example illustrating how the rate of convergence of the method can be poor.

Example 4.4. *Separable Problems*

Consider the separable problem of Subsection 3.4.2

$$
\begin{aligned}
\text{minimize} \quad & \sum_{i=1}^{m} F_i(x_i) \\
\text{subject to} \quad & e_j' x = s_j, \qquad j = 1, \ldots, r, \\
& x_i \in P_i, \qquad i = 1, \ldots, m,
\end{aligned}
\tag{4.60}
$$

with the difference that we assume that the functions $F_i : \Re^{n_i} \mapsto \Re$ are convex but not necessarily strictly convex. Recall here that $x = (x_1 \ldots, x_m)$, where x_i is a subvector of dimension n_i, and P_i is a bounded polyhedral set.

Let e_{ji} denote the subvector of e_j that corresponds to x_i, and for a given j, let $I(j)$ be the set of indices i of subvectors x_i that appear in the jth constraint $e_j' x = s_j$, that is

$$
I(j) = \{i \mid e_{ji} \neq 0\}, \qquad j = 1, \ldots, r.
$$

We transform the problem by introducing additional variables z_{ji}, $i \in I(j)$, as follows

$$
\begin{aligned}
\text{minimize} \quad & \sum_{i=1}^{m} F_i(x_i) \\
\text{subject to} \quad & e_{ji}' x_i = z_{ji}, \qquad j = 1, \ldots, r, \ i \in I(j), \\
& \sum_{i \in I(j)} z_{ji} = s_j, \qquad j = 1, \ldots, r, \\
& x_i \in P_i, \qquad i = 1, \ldots, m.
\end{aligned}
\tag{4.61}
$$

For each $j = 1, \ldots, r$, we consider Lagrange multipliers p_{ji} for the equality constraints $e_{ji}' x_i = z_{ji}$, $i \in I(j)$. The method of multipliers consists of

$$
p_{ji}(t+1) = p_{ji}(t) + c(t) \left(e_{ji}' x_i(t+1) - z_{ji}(t+1) \right), \qquad j = 1, \ldots, r, \ i \in I(j),
\tag{4.62}
$$

where $x_i(t+1)$ and $z_{ji}(t+1)$ minimize the Augmented Lagrangian

$$
\sum_{i=1}^{m} F_i(x_i) + \sum_{j=1}^{r} \sum_{i \in I(j)} p_{ji}(t) \left(e_{ji}' x_i - z_{ji} \right) + \frac{c(t)}{2} \sum_{j=1}^{r} \sum_{i \in I(j)} \left(e_{ji}' x_i - z_{ji} \right)^2,
$$

subject to $\sum_{i \in I(j)} z_{ji} = s_j, j = 1, \ldots, r$, and $x_i \in P_i, i = 1, \ldots, m$. Similarly as in Example 4.2 [cf. Eqs. (4.55) and (4.56)], this minimization can be done iteratively by alternate minimizations with respect to the vectors x_i, and the vectors z_{ji}.

The iteration has the form

$$
x_i := \arg\min_{\xi_i \in P_i} \left\{ F_i(\xi_i) + \sum_{\{j \mid i \in I(j)\}} \left\{ p_{ji}(t) e'_{ji}\xi_i + \frac{c(t)}{2} \left(e'_{ji}\xi_i - z_{ji} \right)^2 \right\} \right\},
$$

$$
\forall \, i = 1, \ldots, m, \tag{4.63}
$$

$$
\{z_{ji} \mid i \in I(j)\}
$$

$$
:= \underset{\left\{ \zeta_{ji} \mid i \in I(j), \; \sum_{i \in I(j)} \zeta_{ji} = s_j \right\}}{\arg\min} \left\{ -\sum_{i \in I(j)} p_{ji}(t)\zeta_{ji} + \frac{c(t)}{2} \sum_{i \in I(j)} \left(e'_{ji}x_i - \zeta_{ji} \right)^2 \right\}
$$

$$
\forall \, j = 1, \ldots, r. \tag{4.64}
$$

Note that the minimization with respect to $\{\zeta_{ji} \mid i \in I(j)\}$ in the above equation involves a separable quadratic cost and a single equality constraint, and can be carried out analytically. In particular, the minimum is attained for

$$
\zeta_{ji} = e'_{ji}x_i + \frac{p_{ji}(t) - \lambda_j}{c(t)}, \qquad j = 1, \ldots, r, \; i \in I(j), \tag{4.65}
$$

where λ_j is a scalar Lagrange multiplier, chosen so that the constraint $\sum_{i \in I(j)} \zeta_{ji} = s_j$ is satisfied or equivalently

$$
\lambda_j = \frac{1}{m_j} \sum_{i \in I(j)} p_{ji}(t) + \frac{c(t)}{m_j} \left[\sum_{i \in I(j)} e'_{ji}x_i - s_j \right], \qquad j = 1, \ldots, r, \tag{4.66}
$$

where m_j is the number of elements of $I(j)$, that is

$$
m_j = |I(j)|.
$$

Using the preceding equations we can simplify the update formula (4.62) for p_{ji}. Suppose we have found the optimal values $x_i(t+1)$. Then from Eq. (4.65), the optimal values $z_{ij}(t+1)$ are given by

$$
z_{ji}(t+1) = e'_{ji}x_i(t+1) + \frac{p_{ji}(t) - \lambda_j(t+1)}{c(t)}, \qquad j = 1, \ldots, r, \; i \in I(j),
$$

where $\lambda_j(t+1)$ is given by Eq. (4.66) after x_i is replaced by $x_i(t+1)$. By comparing this equation with Eq. (4.62) we see that

$$
p_{ji}(t+1) = \lambda_j(t+1), \qquad \forall \, j = 1, \ldots, r, \; i \in I(j).
$$

Thus the single multiplier variable λ_j can be used in place of the m_j variables $p_{ji}, \; i \in I(j)$. By writing the multiplier update formula (4.62) for $i \in I(j)$ and by adding we obtain

$$\lambda_j(t+1) = \lambda_j(t) + \frac{c(t)}{m_j} \left[\sum_{i \in I(j)} \left(e'_{ji} x_i(t+1) - z_{ji}(t+1) \right) \right], \qquad j = 1, \ldots, r,$$

or equivalently,

$$\lambda_j(t+1) = \lambda_j(t) + \frac{c(t)}{m_j} \left(e'_j x(t+1) - s_j \right), \qquad j = 1, \ldots, r. \tag{4.67}$$

By replacing $p_{ji}(t)$ by $\lambda_j(t)$ in Eqs. (4.65) and (4.66), we obtain the following updating formula for z_{ji}

$$z_{ji} := e'_{ji} x_i + \frac{\lambda_j(t) - \lambda_j}{c(t)}, \qquad j = 1, \ldots, r, \ i \in I(j),$$

where λ_j is given by

$$\lambda_j = \lambda_j(t) + \frac{c(t)}{m_j} \left[\sum_{i \in I(j)} e'_{ji} x_i - s_j \right], \qquad j = 1, \ldots, r.$$

By combining these two equations, the iteration for z_{ji} becomes

$$z_{ji} := e'_{ji} x_i - \frac{1}{m_j} (e'_j x - s_j), \qquad j = 1, \ldots, r, \ i \in I(j).$$

This relation can be used to eliminate z_{ji} from Eq. (4.63), thereby obtaining the following highly parallelizable iteration for minimizing the Augmented Lagrangian:

$$x_i := \arg \min_{\xi_i \in P_i} \left\{ F_i(\xi_i) + \sum_{\{j | i \in I(j)\}} \left\{ \lambda_j(t) e'_{ji} \xi_i + \frac{c(t)}{2} \left(e'_{ji}(\xi_i - x_i) + w_j \right)^2 \right\} \right\},$$

$$\forall \ i = 1, \ldots, m, \tag{4.68}$$

where w_j is given in terms of x by

$$w_j = \frac{1}{m_j} (e'_j x - s_j), \qquad j = 1, \ldots, r. \tag{4.69}$$

Example 4.5.   *Multiplier Methods for Linear Programming*

Consider the linear program

$$\text{minimize} \ a'x$$

$$\text{subject to} \ Ex = s, \qquad 0 \le x \le b,$$

where $a \in \Re^m$, $b \in \Re^m$, $s \in \Re^r$, and E is a given $r \times m$ matrix. The method of multipliers is given by

$$x(t+1) = \arg \min_{0 \leq x \leq b} \left\{ a'x + p(t)'(Ex - s) + \frac{c(t)}{2} \|Ex - s\|_2^2 \right\},$$

$$p(t+1) = p(t) + c(t)\left(Ex(t+1) - s \right).$$

By expanding the quadratic form $\|Ex - s\|_2^2$, collecting terms, and neglecting those terms that do not depend on x, we can write the minimization of the Augmented Lagrangian as

$$\text{minimize} \ \frac{c(t)}{2} x' E' E x + \left[a + E'\left(p(t) - c(t)s \right) \right]' x$$

$$\text{subject to } 0 \leq x \leq b.$$

This quadratic program can be solved using the Gauss–Seidel method of Eqs. (4.10) and (4.11), suitably modified to take into account the additional upper bound constraint $x \leq b$. In this modification, the unconstrained minimum of the cost function along each coordinate i is projected on the interval $[0, b_i]$ instead of being projected on the interval $[0, \infty)$ as in Eq. (4.5).

Let $e_i \in \Re^m$ be the ith column of E. Initially we choose $x \geq 0$ and we let $y = -Ex$. At each iteration, we select an index $i \in \{1, \ldots, n\}$ and we update x and y according to

$$x := \left[x_i - \frac{1}{c(t)\|e_i\|_2^2} \left[a_i + e_i'\left(p(t) - c(t)(s + y) \right) \right] \right]^+ v_i, \qquad (4.70a)$$

where $[\cdot]^+$ denotes projection on the interval $[0, b_i]$, v_i is the ith unit vector, and

$$y := y + \left\{ x_i - \left[x_i - \frac{1}{c(t)\|e_i\|_2^2} \left[a_i + e_i'\left(p(t) - c(t)(s + y) \right) \right] \right]^+ \right\} e_i. \qquad (4.70b)$$

Note that similarly as for the Gauss–Seidel algorithm of Eqs. (4.10)–(4.11), the iterations of any two indices i_1 and i_2 are decoupled if there is no coordinate that is nonzero for both e_{i_1} and e_{i_2}. Thus the method is highly parallelizable for favorable sparsity structures of the matrix E. There are a number of variations of this method including hybrid Gauss–Seidel and Jacobi schemes as discussed in Subsection 3.4.1.

An alternative to the preceding method is obtained by viewing the linear program as a separable problem and by applying the corresponding multiplier method given by Eqs. (4.67)–(4.69). By using the identifications $n_i = 1$, $F_i(x_i) = a_i x_i$, $P_i = \{x_i \mid 0 \leq x_i \leq b_i\}$, for all i, it is straightforward to verify that this method is given by the multiplier iteration [cf. Eq. (4.67)]

$$\lambda_j(t+1) = \lambda_j(t) + \frac{c(t)}{m_j}\left(e_j' x_i(t+1) - s_j \right), \qquad j = 1, \ldots, r,$$

where $x(t+1)$ minimizes the corresponding Augmented Lagrangian and is obtained via the iteration [cf. Eqs. (4.68) and (4.69)]

$$x_i := \arg \min_{0 \le \xi_i \le b_i} \left\{ \left(a_i + \sum_{\{j|i \in I(j)\}} \lambda_j(t) e_{ji} \right) \xi_i + \frac{c(t)}{2} \sum_{\{j|i \in I(j)\}} \left(e_{ji}(\xi_i - x_i) + w_j \right)^2 \right\},$$
$$i = 1, \ldots, m,$$

where

$$w_j = \frac{1}{m_j}(e_j' x - s_j), \qquad j = 1, \ldots, r.$$

The above one–dimensional quadratic minimization can be carried out analytically yielding, after some calculation, the iteration

$$x_i := \left[x_i - \frac{1}{c(t)\|e_i\|_2^2} \left[a_i + e_i'\big(\lambda(t) + c(t)w\big) \right] \right]^+, \tag{4.71}$$

where $[\cdot]^+$ denotes projection on the interval $[0, b_i]$, e_i is the ith column of E, and $\lambda(t)$ and w are the vectors with coordinates $\lambda_j(t)$ and w_j, respectively. This iteration bears considerable resemblance with the alternative iteration (4.70), but it is of the Jacobi type, that is, it can be executed simultaneously for all i.

The main potential difficulty with the preceding methods of multipliers is that the Gauss–Seidel iterations used to minimize the Augmented Lagrangian may converge very slowly. In such cases, it may be useful to try to accelerate convergence by using Newton-like methods specially designed for minimizing quadratic functions subject to upper and lower bounds on the variables (see [Ber82a], [Ber82b], and [Tho87]).

A number of modifications to the method of multipliers have been suggested in order to make it more suitable for decomposition techniques. One such modification is discussed in the following.

The Alternating Direction Method of Multipliers

We draw motivation for this method from Example 4.2 which involves the problem

$$\text{minimize} \quad \sum_{i=1}^{m} F_i(x)$$

$$\text{subject to} \quad x \in P_i, \qquad i = 1, \ldots, m.$$

We saw that one implementation of the method of multipliers for this problem alternately updates x and x_i, and changes the multipliers $p_i(t)$ only after (typically) many updates of x and x_i (enough to minimize the Augmented Lagrangian within adequate precision). An interesting variation is to perform only a small number, k, of minimizations with respect to x and x_i before changing the multipliers. In the extreme case where $k = 1$, the method takes the form

$$x(t+1) = \frac{\sum_{i=1}^{m} x_i(t)}{m} - \frac{\sum_{i=1}^{m} p_i(t)}{mc}, \tag{4.72}$$

$$x_i(t+1) = \arg \min_{x_i \in P_i} \left\{ F_i(x_i) - p_i(t)x_i + \frac{c}{2} \| x(t+1) - x_i \|_2^2 \right\}, \qquad \forall\, i = 1, \ldots, m, \tag{4.73}$$

$$p_i(t+1) = p_i(t) + c \big(x(t+1) - x_i(t+1) \big), \qquad \forall\, i = 1, \ldots, m. \tag{4.74}$$

Thus, this method operates in cycles, where in each cycle we minimize the Augmented Lagrangian with respect to one set of variables, then minimize it with respect to the remaining variables, and then carry out a multiplier update. We use the name *alternating direction multiplier method* to refer to this type of algorithm. The name comes from its similarity with some methods for solving differential equations, known as alternating direction methods (see [FoG83] and [GIL87] for detailed explanations).

Consider next the separable problem of Example 4.4:

$$\text{minimize } \sum_{i=1}^{m} F_i(x_i)$$

$$\text{subject to } e_j' x = s_j, \qquad j = 1, \ldots, r,$$

$$x_i \in P_i, \qquad i = 1, \ldots, m.$$

The natural alternating direction multiplier method is given by [cf. Eqs. (4.67)–(4.69)]

$$x_i(t+1) = \arg \min_{x_i \in P_i} \left\{ F_i(x_i) + \sum_{\{j \mid i \in I(j)\}} \left\{ \lambda_j(t) e_{ji}' x_i + \frac{c}{2} \big(e_{ji}'(x_i - x_i(t)) + w_j(t) \big)^2 \right\} \right\},$$

$$i = 1, \ldots, m, \tag{4.75a}$$

$$\lambda_j(t+1) = \lambda_j(t) + c w_j(t+1), \qquad j = 1, \ldots, r, \tag{4.75b}$$

where

$$w_j(t) = \frac{1}{m_j} \big(e_j' x(t) - s_j \big), \qquad j = 1, \ldots, r, \tag{4.75c}$$

and the initial vectors $x(0)$ and $\lambda(0)$ are arbitrary. It is seen that this is a highly parallelizable method, which applies to convex separable problems that are not necessarily strictly convex, including general linear programs.

We now formulate more precisely the alternating direction method of multipliers and prove its convergence. The starting point is the optimization problem

$$\text{minimize} \quad G_1(x) + G_2(Ax)$$
$$\text{subject to} \quad x \in C_1, \ Ax \in C_2. \tag{4.76}$$

Here, $G_1 : \Re^n \mapsto \Re$ and $G_2 : \Re^m \mapsto \Re$ are convex functions, A is an $m \times n$ matrix, and $C_1 \subset \Re^n$ and $C_2 \subset \Re^m$ are nonempty polyhedral sets. As in our earlier development, we are assuming polyhedral constraint sets to be able to use the duality theory developed in Appendix C. The subsequent algorithm and convergence result can be formulated for more general convex constraint sets.

We will make the following assumption:

Assumption 4.1. The optimal solution set X^* of problem (4.76) is nonempty. Furthermore, either C_1 is bounded or else the matrix $A'A$ is invertible.

A slightly more general version of Assumption 4.1 requires that the level sets $\{x \in C_1 \mid G_1(x) \le \alpha\}$ be compact for all $\alpha \in \Re$ in place of the condition that C_1 be compact. The subsequent convergence result can also be proved under this version of Assumption 4.1 using a somewhat more complicated analysis.

We introduce an additional vector $z \in \Re^m$ and reformulate the problem as

$$\text{minimize} \quad G_1(x) + G_2(z)$$
$$\text{subject to} \quad x \in C_1, \ z \in C_2, \ Ax = z. \tag{4.77}$$

We assign a Lagrange multiplier vector $p \in \Re^m$ to the equality constraint $Ax = z$, and we consider the Augmented Lagrangian function

$$L_c(x, z, p) = G_1(x) + G_2(z) + p'(Ax - z) + \frac{c}{2}\|Ax - z\|_2^2. \tag{4.78}$$

The alternating direction method of multipliers is given by

$$x(t+1) = \arg\min_{x \in C_1} \left\{ G_1(x) + p(t)'Ax + \frac{c}{2}\|Ax - z(t)\|_2^2 \right\}, \tag{4.79}$$

$$z(t+1) = \arg\min_{z \in C_2} \left\{ G_2(z) - p(t)'z + \frac{c}{2}\|Ax(t+1) - z\|_2^2 \right\}, \tag{4.80}$$

$$p(t+1) = p(t) + c\big(Ax(t+1) - z(t+1)\big). \tag{4.81}$$

The parameter c is any positive number, and the initial vectors $p(0)$ and $z(0)$ are arbitrary. Note that the functions G_1 and G_2, and the constraint sets C_1 and C_2 have been decoupled in the minimization problems of Eqs. (4.79) and (4.80); this turns out to be very useful in some problems.

Prop. 4.1(a) shows that the minimum with respect to z in Eq. (4.80) is attained. The minimum with respect to x in Eq. (4.79) is attained if C_1 is compact by the Weierstrass theorem (Prop. A.8 in Appendix A) or if the matrix $A'A$ is invertible, in which case the quadratic term in Eq. (4.79) is positive definite, and a slight modification of the proof of Prop. 4.1(a) applies. Therefore, under Assumption 4.1, the minima in Eqs. (4.79) and (4.80) are attained, and the algorithm is well defined.

Note that we can consider changing c from one iteration of the algorithm to the next, but there is no clear reason why we would want to do so in the alternating direction method. (This is in contrast with the method of multipliers, where increasing c is often useful in practice.) Furthermore, practical experience shows that the proper choice of c may require considerably more experimentation in this method than in the method of multipliers.

It can be seen that both algorithms of Eqs. (4.72)–(4.74) and Eq. (4.75) are special cases of the general alternating direction multiplier method of Eqs. (4.79)–(4.81). Indeed, the algorithm of Eqs. (4.72)–(4.74) for minimizing the sum of convex functions $\sum_{i=1}^{m} F_i(x)$ over $x \in \cap_{i=1}^{m} P_i$ is obtained with the identifications

$$G_1(x) = 0, \qquad C_1 = \Re^n,$$

$$A = \begin{bmatrix} I \\ I \\ \vdots \\ I \end{bmatrix}, \qquad (I \text{ is the } n \times n \text{ identity matrix}),$$

$$G_2(z_1, \ldots, z_m) = \sum_{i=1}^{m} F_i(z_i), \qquad C_2 = P_1 \times P_2 \times \ldots \times P_m.$$

The algorithm of Eq. (4.75) for minimizing the separable function $\sum_{i=1}^{m} F_i(x_i)$ subject to the constraints $Ex = s$ and $x_i \in P_i$ is obtained with the identifications

$$G_1(x) = \sum_{i=1}^{m} F_i(x_i), \qquad C_1 = P_1 \times P_2 \times \ldots \times P_m,$$

$$G_2(z) = 0, \qquad C_2 = \left\{ z \ \bigg| \ \sum_{i \in I(j)} z_{ji} = s_j, \ j = 1, \ldots, r \right\},$$

and with A being the matrix that maps x into the vector having coordinates $e'_{ji} x_i$, $j = 1, \ldots, r, \ i \in I(j)$.

The following proposition gives the main convergence properties of the alternating direction method.

Proposition 4.2. Let Assumption 4.1 hold. A sequence $\{x(t), z(t), p(t)\}$ generated by the algorithm of Eqs. (4.79)–(4.81) is bounded, and every limit point of $\{x(t)\}$ is an optimal solution of the original problem (4.76). Furthermore $\{p(t)\}$ converges to an optimal solution p^* of the dual problem [cf. Eq. (4.77)]

$$\text{maximize}\ \ H_1(p) + H_2(p)$$
$$\text{subject to}\ \ p \in \Re^m,$$
(4.82)

where for all $p \in \Re^n$,

$$H_1(p) = \inf_{x \in C_1} \{G_1(x) + p'Ax\}, \qquad H_2(p) = \inf_{z \in C_2} \{G_2(z) - p'z\}. \tag{4.83}$$

The following lemma will be useful for proving Prop. 4.2.

Lemma 4.1.   If $y^* = \arg\min_{y \in Y} \{J_1(y) + J_2(y)\}$, where $J_1 : \Re^n \mapsto \Re$ and $J_2 : \Re^n \mapsto \Re$ are convex functions, Y is a polyhedral subset of $\Re^n$, and J_2 is continuously differentiable, then

$$y^* = \arg\min_{y \in Y} \{J_1(y) + \nabla J_2(y^*)'y\}. \tag{4.84}$$

Proof. We have that

$$(y^*, y^*) = \arg\min_{y \in Y,\ z \in \Re^n,\ z=y} \{J_1(y) + J_2(z)\}.$$

By the Lagrange Multiplier Theorem of Appendix C, there exists $\lambda \in \Re^n$ such that

$$y^* = \arg\min_{y \in Y} \{J_1(y) + \lambda'y\}, \tag{4.85}$$

$$y^* = \arg\min_{z \in \Re^n} \{J_2(z) - \lambda'z\}. \tag{4.86}$$

From Eq. (4.86) we obtain $\lambda = \nabla J_2(y^*)$, which together with Eq. (4.85) proves the result.   **Q.E.D.**

Proof of Prop. 4.2.   By applying Lemma 4.1 with the identifications $Y = C_1$, $J_1(x) = G_1(x)$, $J_2(x) = p(t)'Ax + (c/2)\|Ax - z(t)\|_2^2$ [cf. Eq. (4.79)] we obtain

$$G_1\big(x(t+1)\big) + \big[p(t) + c\big(Ax(t+1) - z(t)\big)\big]' Ax(t+1)$$
$$\leq G_1(x) + \big[p(t) + c\big(Ax(t+1) - z(t)\big)\big]' Ax, \qquad \forall\, x \in C_1. \tag{4.87}$$

Similarly we obtain [cf. Eq. (4.80)]

$$G_2\big(z(t+1)\big) - \big[p(t) + c\big(Ax(t+1) - z(t+1)\big)\big]' z(t+1)$$
$$\leq G_2(z) - \big[p(t) + c\big(Ax(t+1) - z(t+1)\big)\big]' z, \qquad \forall\, z \in C_2. \tag{4.88}$$

Let (x^*, z^*) be an optimal solution of problem (4.77) and let p^* be an optimal solution of its dual problem (4.82). By applying Eq. (4.87) with $x = x^*$, and Eq. (4.88) with $z = z^*$, and by using also the multiplier update formula (4.81) we have

$$G_1\big(x(t+1)\big) + p(t+1)'Ax(t+1) + c\big(z(t+1) - z(t)\big)'Ax(t+1)$$
$$\leq G_1(x^*) + p(t+1)'Ax^* + c\big(z(t+1) - z(t)\big)'Ax^*,$$
$$G_2\big(z(t+1)\big) - p(t+1)'z(t+1) \leq G_2(z^*) - p(t+1)'z^*.$$

By adding these two relations and using also the fact $Ax^* = z^*$, we obtain

$$G_1\big(x(t+1)\big) + G_2\big(z(t+1)\big) + p(t+1)'\big(Ax(t+1) - z(t+1)\big) + c\big(z(t+1) - z(t)\big)'A\big(x(t+1) - x^*\big)$$
$$\leq G_1(x^*) + G_2(z^*). \tag{4.89}$$

By the Saddle Point Theorem of Appendix C, we must have

$$G_1(x^*) + G_2(z^*) \leq G_1\big(x(t+1)\big) + G_2\big(z(t+1)\big) + p^{*\prime}\big(Ax(t+1) - z(t+1)\big), \qquad \forall\, t. \tag{4.90}$$

By adding Eqs. (4.89) and (4.90) we obtain

$$\big(p(t+1) - p^*\big)'\big(Ax(t+1) - z(t+1)\big) + c\big(z(t+1) - z(t)\big)'A\big(x(t+1) - x^*\big) \leq 0. \tag{4.91}$$

We now denote for all t

$$\bar{x}(t) = x(t) - x^*, \qquad \bar{z}(t) = z(t) - z^*, \qquad \bar{p}(t) = p(t) - p^*,$$

and we observe that, since $Ax^* = z^*$, we can write the multiplier update formula (4.81) as

$$\bar{p}(t+1) = \bar{p}(t) + c\big(A\bar{x}(t+1) - \bar{z}(t+1)\big),$$

and

$$\bar{p}(t+1) = \bar{p}(t) + c\big(Ax(t+1) - z(t+1)\big).$$

By using the preceding relations in Eq. (4.91), we obtain after collecting terms

$$\frac{1}{c}\bar{p}(t+1)'\big(\bar{p}(t+1) - \bar{p}(t)\big) + c\big(\bar{z}(t+1) - \bar{z}(t)\big)'\bar{z}(t+1) + \big(\bar{z}(t+1) - \bar{z}(t)\big)'\big(\bar{p}(t+1) - \bar{p}(t)\big) \leq 0. \tag{4.92}$$

We estimate each of the three terms in the preceding relation. We have

$$\bar{p}(t+1)'\big(\bar{p}(t+1) - \bar{p}(t)\big) = \tfrac{1}{2}\|\bar{p}(t+1) - \bar{p}(t)\|_2^2 + \tfrac{1}{2}\|\bar{p}(t+1)\|_2^2 - \tfrac{1}{2}\|\bar{p}(t)\|_2^2, \tag{4.93}$$

$$\big(\bar{z}(t+1) - \bar{z}(t)\big)'\bar{z}(t+1) = \tfrac{1}{2}\|\bar{z}(t+1) - \bar{z}(t)\|_2^2 + \tfrac{1}{2}\|\bar{z}(t+1)\|_2^2 - \tfrac{1}{2}\|\bar{z}(t)\|_2^2. \tag{4.94}$$

To estimate the third term in Eq. (4.92), we consider the optimality relation (4.88) with $z = z(t)$, that is,

$$G_2\big(z(t+1)\big) - p(t+1)'z(t+1) \leq G_2\big(z(t)\big) - p(t+1)'z(t), \qquad (4.95)$$

and we consider also Eq. (4.88) at iteration t with $z = z(t+1)$, that is,

$$G_2\big(z(t)\big) - p(t)'z(t) \leq G_2\big(z(t+1)\big) - p(t)'z(t+1). \qquad (4.96)$$

Adding Eqs. (4.95) and (4.96) we obtain $0 \leq \big(z(t+1) - z(t)\big)'\big(p(t+1) - p(t)\big)$ or equivalently

$$0 \leq \big(\bar{z}(t+1) - \bar{z}(t)\big)'\big(\bar{p}(t+1) - \bar{p}(t)\big). \qquad (4.97)$$

We now use Eqs. (4.93), (4.94), and (4.97) in inequality (4.92). We obtain

$$\|\bar{p}(t+1) - \bar{p}(t)\|_2^2 + c^2\|\bar{z}(t+1) - \bar{z}(t)\|_2^2 \leq \big(\|\bar{p}(t)\|_2^2 + c^2\|\bar{z}(t)\|_2^2\big) - \big(\|\bar{p}(t+1)\|_2^2 + c^2\|\bar{z}(t+1)\|_2^2\big). \qquad (4.98)$$

It follows that

$$\bar{p}(t+1) - \bar{p}(t) \to 0, \qquad \bar{z}(t+1) - \bar{z}(t) \to 0. \qquad (4.99)$$

Since $\bar{p}(t+1) - \bar{p}(t) = c\big(Ax(t+1) - z(t+1)\big)$, we obtain from Eqs. (4.89) and (4.90)

$$\lim_{t\to\infty} \big[G_1\big(x(t+1)\big) + G_2\big(z(t+1)\big)\big] = G_1(x^*) + G_2(z^*) = \min_{x\in C_1,\ z\in C_2,\ Ax=z} \{G_1(x) + G_2(z)\}. \qquad (4.100)$$

Furthermore, for every limit point $(\tilde{x}, \tilde{z})$ of $\big\{\big(x(t), z(t)\big)\big\}$ we have that $A\tilde{x} = \tilde{z}$, and that $\tilde{x}$ is an optimal solution of the original problem (4.76).

From Eq. (4.98) we obtain that $\{p(t)\}$ and $\{z(t)\}$ are bounded, and from Eqs. (4.81) and (4.99) we see that $\|Ax(t) - z(t)\|_2^2 \to 0$. In view of Assumption 4.1 it follows that $\{x(t)\}$ is also bounded. Consider a convergent subsequence $\big\{\big(x(t), z(t), p(t)\big) \mid t \in T\big\}$, and let $(\tilde{x}, \tilde{z}, \tilde{p})$ be its limit. Then, as shown earlier, $\tilde{x}$ is an optimal solution of the original problem (4.76). To show that $\tilde{p}$ is a solution of the dual problem (4.82), define $\hat{p}(t+1) = p(t) + c\big(Ax(t+1) - z(t)\big)$. From the definitions (4.83), and Eqs. (4.87) and (4.88) we see that

$$H_1\big(\hat{p}(t+1)\big) = G_1\big(x(t+1)\big) + \hat{p}(t+1)'Ax(t+1) \leq G_1(x) + \hat{p}(t+1)'Ax, \qquad \forall\, x \in C_1, \qquad (4.101)$$

$$H_2\big(p(t+1)\big) = G_2\big(z(t+1)\big) - p(t+1)'z(t+1) \leq G_2(z) - p(t+1)'z, \qquad \forall\, z \in C_2. \qquad (4.102)$$

By taking limits in these relations and using the fact that $\tilde{p}$ is also the limit of the subsequence $\{p(t+1) \mid t \in T\}$ [cf. Eq. (4.99)], we obtain

$$\limsup_{t \to \infty, \ t \in T} \ H_1\big(\hat{p}(t+1)\big) \le G_1(x) + \tilde{p}' A x, \qquad \forall \ x \in C_1,$$

$$\limsup_{t \to \infty, \ t \in T} \ H_2\big(p(t+1)\big) \le G_2(z) - \tilde{p}' z, \qquad \forall \ z \in C_2,$$

so

$$\limsup_{t \to \infty, \ t \in T} \ H_1\big(\hat{p}(t+1)\big) \le H_1(\tilde{p}), \qquad \limsup_{t \to \infty, \ t \in T} \ H_2\big(p(t+1)\big) \le H_2(\tilde{p}). \qquad (4.103)$$

On the other hand by adding Eqs. (4.101) and (4.102), and using the fact $A\tilde{x} = \tilde{z}$, we obtain

$$\lim_{t \to \infty, \ t \in T} \big[H_1\big(\hat{p}(t+1)\big) + H_2\big(p(t+1)\big) \big] = G_1(\tilde{x}) + G_2(\tilde{z})$$

$$= \min_{x \in C_1, \ z \in C_2, \ Ax=z} \{ G_1(x) + G_2(z) \}. \qquad (4.104)$$

Since by the Duality Theorem of Appendix C, we have

$$\max_{p \in \Re^n} \{ H_1(p) + H_2(p) \} = \min_{x \in C_1, \ z \in C_2, \ Ax=z} \{ G_1(x) + G_2(z) \},$$

we obtain from Eqs. (4.103) and (4.104) that $\tilde{p}$ is an optimal solution of the dual problem (4.82).

We now show that $\big\{ \big(z(t), p(t) \big) \big\}$ has a unique limit point. Indeed Eq. (4.98) shows that

$$\| p(t) - p^* \|_2^2 + c^2 \| z(t) - z^* \|_2^2$$

is a nondecreasing sequence for *every* choice of optimal solutions (x^*, z^*) and p^* of the primal problem (4.77) and the dual problem (4.82), respectively. In particular, any limit point $(\tilde{z}, \tilde{p})$ of $\big\{ \big(z(t), p(t) \big) \big\}$ can be used in place of (z^*, p^*) in Eq. (4.98). It follows that $\big\{ \big(z(t), p(t) \big) \big\}$ cannot have more than one limit point.   **Q.E.D.**

Note that in the course of the preceding proof, we showed that the sequence $\{z(t)\}$ converges, and that $Ax(t) - z(t) \to 0$. It follows that if the matrix $A'A$ is invertible, then $\{x(t)\}$ must also converge, necessarily to an optimal solution of the original problem.

To see what can happen when $A'A$ is not invertible, consider the case where $n = 1$, $C_1 = [0, 1]$, $C_2 = \Re$, $A = 0$, and $G_1(x) = 0$, $G_2(x) = 0$ for all x. Here, the optimal solution set X^* is $[0, 1]$ and Assumption 4.1 is satisfied because C_1 is compact. It can be verified that the sequence $\big\{ \big(z(t), p(t) \big) \big\}$ generated by the algorithm converges to $(0, 0)$ in one iteration, but the sequence $\{x(t)\}$ need not converge; it can be any sequence in $[0, 1]$. By changing C_1 to be equal to $\Re$, we obtain an example where X^* is nonempty, but Assumption 4.1 is violated and the generated sequence $\{x(t)\}$ can be unbounded.

We finally mention that there are several variations of the alternating direction method of multipliers. An example is the iteration

$$x(t + 1) = \arg\min_{x \in C_1} \left\{ G_1(x) + p(t)'Ax + \frac{c}{2} \|Ax - z(t)\|_2^2 \right\}, \tag{4.105}$$

$$\hat{p}(t) = p(t) + c\big(Ax(t + 1) - z(t)\big). \tag{4.106}$$

$$z(t + 1) = \arg\min_{z \in C_2} \left\{ G_2(z) - \hat{p}(t)'z + \frac{c}{2} \|Ax(t + 1) - z\|_2^2 \right\}, \tag{4.107}$$

$$p(t + 1) = \hat{p}(t) + c\big(Ax(t + 1) - z(t + 1)\big), \tag{4.108}$$

which is the same as the method of Eqs. (4.79)–(4.81) given earlier except for the additional multiplier update (4.106) executed between the updates of x and z. A convergence analysis and a discussion of this and other related methods is given in [GIL87].

EXERCISES

4.1. Consider the problem

$$\text{minimize} \quad F(x) = \frac{1}{2}x'Px + r'x$$

$$\text{subject to} \quad x \geq 0,$$

where P is a nonnegative definite symmetric $n \times n$ matrix with positive diagonal elements and $r \in \Re^n$ is given. Let K be the largest eigenvalue of P and assume that $K > 0$.
  (a) Show that all the limit points of the sequence generated by the gradient projection method

$$x(t + 1) = \Big[x(t) - \gamma \nabla F\big(x(t)\big) \Big]^+,$$

  are optimal solutions provided that $\gamma \in (0, 2/K)$. *Hint:* Do Exercise 2.3 in Section 3.2.
  (b) Show that the sum of the diagonal elements of P is an upper bound for K.
  (c) Consider the linearized Jacobi method

$$x(t + 1) = \Big[x(t) - \gamma M^{-1} \nabla F\big(x(t)\big) \Big]^+,$$

  where M is the diagonal matrix with diagonal elements equal to the corresponding diagonal elements of P. Show that if $\gamma \in (0, 2/n)$, all limit points of the sequence $\{x(t)\}$ are optimal solutions. *Hint:* Consider the transformation of variables $y(t) = M^{1/2}x(t)$ and use part (b).

4.2. (Convergence Rate of the Proximal Minimization Algorithm [KoB76].) Assume that there exist $\beta > 0$, $\delta > 0$, and $\alpha > 1$ such that

$$F^* + \beta\big(\rho(x; X^*)\big)^\alpha \leq F(x), \qquad \forall\, x \in X \text{ with } \rho(x; X^*) \leq \delta.$$

Let $\{x(t)\}$ be a sequence generated by the proximal minimization algorithm and assume that $\liminf_{t\to\infty} c(t) > 0$. Show that:

(a) If $\alpha < 2$, then

$$\limsup_{t\to\infty} \frac{\rho\big(x(t+1); X^*\big)}{\big(\rho\big(x(t); X^*\big)\big)^{1/(\alpha-1)}} < \infty.$$

This is known as superlinear convergence of order $1/(\alpha-1)$.

Hint: Part (a) and the following parts (b) and (c) are based on the relation

$$\rho\big(x(t+1); X^*\big) + \beta c(t)\big(\rho\big(x(t+1); X^*\big)\big)^{\alpha-1} \le \rho\big(x(t); X^*\big).$$

To show this relation, let $\hat{x}$ denote the projection of any x on X^* and let $d = \hat{x}(t+1) - x(t+1)$. Consider the scalar convex function

$$H(\gamma) = F\big(x(t+1) + \gamma d\big) + \frac{1}{2c(t)}\|x(t+1) + \gamma d - x(t)\|_2^2.$$

Since H is minimized at $\gamma = 0$, its right derivative $H^+(0)$ is nonnegative, from which we obtain

$$0 \le H^+(0) = F'\big(x(t+1); d\big) + \frac{1}{c(t)}\big(x(t+1) - x(t)\big)'\big(\hat{x}(t+1) - x(t+1)\big)$$

$$\le F^* - F\big(x(t+1)\big) + \frac{1}{c(t)}\big(x(t+1) - x(t)\big)'\big(\hat{x}(t+1) - x(t+1)\big).$$

Using the hypothesis, it follows that

$$\beta c(t)\big(\rho\big(x(t+1); X^*\big)\big)^\alpha \le \big(x(t+1) - x(t)\big)'\big(\hat{x}(t+1) - x(t+1)\big),$$

for t sufficiently large. We now add to both sides $\big(x(t+1)-\hat{x}(t)\big)'\big(x(t+1)-\hat{x}(t+1)\big)$ and we use the fact

$$\|x(t+1) - \hat{x}(t+1)\|_2^2 \le \big(x(t+1) - \hat{x}(t+1)\big)'\big(x(t+1) - \hat{x}(t+1)\big),$$

(which follows from the Projection Theorem) to obtain

$$\|x(t+1)-\hat{x}(t+1)\|_2^2+\beta c(t)\big(\rho\big(x(t+1); X^*\big)\big)^\alpha \le \|x(t)-\hat{x}(t)\|_2\|x(t+1)-\hat{x}(t+1)\|_2,$$

from which the desired relation follows.

(b) If $\alpha = 2$ and $\lim_{t\to\infty} c(t) = \bar{c} < \infty$ then

$$\limsup_{t\to\infty} \frac{\rho\big(x(t+1); X^*\big)}{\rho\big(x(t); X^*\big)} \le \frac{1}{1 + \beta\bar{c}}.$$

(c) If $\alpha = 2$ and $\lim_{t\to\infty} c(t) = \infty$, then

$$\limsup_{t\to\infty} \frac{\rho\big(x(t+1); X^*\big)}{\rho\big(x(t); X^*\big)} = 0.$$

This is known as superlinear convergence.

(d) If F is a positive definite quadratic function, $X = \Re^n$, $\alpha = 2$ and $\lim_{t\to\infty} c(t) = \bar{c} < \infty$, then

$$\limsup_{t\to\infty} \frac{\rho\big(x(t+1); X^*\big)}{\rho\big(x(t); X^*\big)} \leq \frac{1}{1 + 2\beta\bar{c}}.$$

Show by example that this estimate is tight. *Hint:* Let x^* be the minimizing point of F over $x \in \Re^n$, and let $\tilde{y}$ denote the unique vector that minimizes $\beta\|x - x^*\|_2^2 + (1/2c)\|x - y\|_2^2$ over $x \in \Re^n$. Show that $y - x^* = (1 + 2\beta c)(\tilde{y} - x^*)$, and that $\|x(y, c) - x^*\|_2 \leq \|\tilde{y} - x^*\|_2$.

(e) Prove that

$$F\big(x(t+1)\big) - F^* \leq \frac{\rho\big(x(t); X^*\big)^2}{2c(t)},$$

and use this relation to show that

$$\limsup_{t\to\infty} \frac{\rho\big(x(t+1); X^*\big)}{\rho\big(x(t); X^*\big)^{2/\alpha}} < \infty.$$

For $\alpha > 2$, this is known as sublinear convergence.

4.3. Show that the condition (4.29) holds when F is a linear function, X is a polyhedral set, and X^* is nonempty. *Hint:* Suppose that X has the form $\{x \mid a_j'x \leq t_j, \ j = 1, \ldots, m\}$ for some vectors a_j and scalars t_j, and that $F(x) = c'x$ for some vector c. For $x \in X$, let $p(x)$ be the projection of x on X^*, and consider the cone of $\Re^{n+1}$

$$C_x = \{(z, \mu) \mid c'z \leq \mu, \ a_j'z \leq 0 \text{ for all } j \text{ such that } a_j'p(x) = t_j\},$$

and the cones

$$M_x = \{(z, \mu) \in C_x \mid \mu = 0\},$$

$$Z_x = \{(z, \mu) \in C_x \mid \text{the projection of } (z, \mu) \text{ on } M_x \text{ is the origin } (0, 0)\}.$$

Show that the collection of distinct sets C_x is finite, and that for each such set there exists $\theta_x > 0$ such that

$$|\mu| \geq \theta_x \|z\|_2, \qquad \forall \ (z, \mu) \in Z_x.$$

Take $\beta = \min_{x \in X} \theta_x$ in condition (4.29).

4.4. Consider the variation of the proximal minimization algorithm given by

$$x(t+1) = x(t) - \gamma(t)\nabla\Phi_c\big(x(t)\big),$$

where $\gamma(t)$ is a stepsize parameter satisfying $\gamma(t) \in [\delta, 2c - \delta]$ for all t and some $\delta \in (0, c]$. Show that all limit points of the sequences that the algorithm generates are optimal solutions. *Hint:* Modify the proof of part (c) of Prop. 4.1.

4.5. (The Method of Multipliers for Inequality Constraints [Roc71].) Consider the problem of Subsection 3.4.4 for the case where we have the inequality constraints $a'_j x - t_j \leq 0$ instead of the equality constraints $e'_j x - s_j = 0$. Replace these inequality constraints by the equality constraints $a'_j x - t_j + w_j = 0$, where w_j is constrained to be nonnegative, and show that the method of multipliers takes the form

$$x(t+1) = \arg\min_{x \in P} \left\{ F(x) + \frac{1}{2c(t)} \sum_{j=1}^{r} \Big[\max\{0, p_j(t) + c(t)(a'_j x - t_j)\} \Big]^2 \right\},$$

$$p_j(t+1) = \max\left\{0, p_j(t) + c(t)\big(a'_j x(t+1) - t_j\big)\right\}, \qquad \forall\, j = 1, \ldots, r.$$

4.6. Consider the set intersection problem of Example 4.3 and assume that the intersection is nonempty. Show that the parallel projection method of Eqs. (4.58)–(4.59) converges to an element of the intersection. *Hint:* Show that for all $x^* \in C_1 \cap \cdots \cap C_m$ we have $\|x(t+1) - x^*\|_2 \leq \|x(t) - x^*\|_2$.

4.7. Show convergence of the method of Eqs. (4.58)–(4.59), if Eq. (4.58) is replaced by

$$x(t+1) = \sum_{i=1}^{m} \lambda_j x_i(t),$$

where $\lambda_1, \ldots, \lambda_m$ are positive scalars summing to unity.

3.5 VARIATIONAL INEQUALITIES

The variational inequality problem is as follows. We are given a set $X \subset \Re^n$ and a function $f : \Re^n \mapsto \Re^n$, and our objective is to find a vector $x^* \in X$ such that

$$(x - x^*)' f(x^*) \geq 0, \qquad \forall x \in X. \tag{5.1}$$

As a shorthand notation, we will refer to this problem as VI(X, f). It will be assumed throughout that X is nonempty, closed, and convex.

3.5.1 Examples of Variational Inequality Problems

Several interesting problems can be formulated as variational inequality problems and some examples follow.

(a) *Solution of Systems of Equations.* Let $X = \Re^n$ and let $f : \Re^n \mapsto \Re^n$ be a given function. It is easy to see that a vector $x^* \in \Re^n$ solves the problem VI($\Re^n, f$) if and only if $f(x^*) = 0$. Indeed, if $f(x^*) = 0$ then inequality (5.1) holds with equality. Conversely, if x^* satisfies Eq. (5.1), let $x = x^* - f(x^*)$. By Eq. (5.1), we have $-\|f(x^*)\|_2^2 \geq 0$, which implies that $f(x^*) = 0$.

(b) *Constrained and Unconstrained Optimization.* Let X be nonempty, closed, and convex and let $F : \Re^n \mapsto \Re$ be a continuously differentiable function that is convex on the set X. Using the optimality conditions for convex optimization (Prop. 3.1), a vector $x^* \in X$ minimizes F over the set X if and only if $(x - x^*)'\nabla F(x^*) \geq 0$ for all $x \in X$, that is, if and only if x^* solves the variational inequality problem VI$(X, \nabla F)$. In particular, if we let $X = \Re^n$, we see that unconstrained convex optimization is also a variational inequality problem. In the optimization context, the function f of Eq. (5.1) has a special structure because it is the gradient of a scalar function F. In particular, the line integral of f depends only on the end points of the path of integration and not on the path itself. In more general variational inequality problems, this path independence property is absent and such problems cannot be formulated as optimization problems; this restricts the tools available for establishing convergence of an algorithm. In particular, the descent approach cannot be applied.

(c) *Traffic Assignment.* We are given a directed graph $G = (N, A)$, which is viewed as a model of a transportation network. The arcs of the graph represent transportation links such as highways, rail lines, etc. The nodes of the graph represent junction points where traffic can exit from one transportation link and enter another. We are also given a set W of node pairs, referred to as origin–destination (OD) pairs. For OD pair $w = (i, j)$, there is a known input $r_w > 0$ representing traffic entering the network at the origin node i of w and exiting the network at the destination node j of w. For each $w \in W$, the input r_w is to be divided among a given collection P_w of simple positive paths starting at the origin node of w and ending at the destination node of w (i.e., these paths have no cycles and their arcs are oriented as in the graph G). We denote by x_p the portion of r_w carried by path p (also called the flow of path p). Let x be the vector having as coordinates all the path flows x_p, $p \in P_w$, $w \in W$. Thus, x must belong to the set

$$X = \left\{ x \; \middle| \; \sum_{p \in P_w} x_p = r_w, \; \forall w \in W, \text{ and } x_p \geq 0, \; \forall p \in P_w, \; \forall w \in W \right\}.$$

For each path p, we are given a function $t_p(x)$, called the travel time of path p. This function models the time required for traffic to travel from the start node to the end node of path p as a function of the path flow vector x. The problem is to find a path flow vector $x^* \in X$ that consists of path flows that are positive only on paths of minimum travel time. That is, for all $w \in W$ and paths $p \in P_w$, we require that

$$x_p^* > 0 \quad \Longrightarrow \quad t_p(x^*) \leq t_{p'}(x^*), \qquad \forall p' \in P_w. \tag{5.2}$$

This problem is based on a transportation hypothesis called the *user–optimization principle*, which asserts that traffic network equilibrium is established when each user of the network chooses, among all available paths, a path requiring minimum travel time.

We claim that a vector $x^* \in X$ satisfies the user–optimization condition (5.2) if and only if x^* is a solution of the variational inequality

$$\sum_{w \in W} \sum_{p \in P_w} (x_p - x_p^*) t_p(x^*) \geq 0, \qquad \forall x \in X, \tag{5.3}$$

which is the variational inequality problem $\text{VI}(X, f)$, with $f(x)$ being the function with components $t_p(x)$. To see this, assume that $x^* \in X$ satisfies the condition (5.2), and let

$$T_w^* = \min_{p \in P_w} t_p(x^*).$$

We have for every $x \in X$, $\sum_{p \in P_w} (x_p - x_p^*) = 0$, so that

$$0 = \sum_{p \in P_w} (x_p - x_p^*) T_w^* \leq \sum_{\{p \in P_w | x_p > x_p^*\}} (x_p - x_p^*) t_p(x^*) + \sum_{\{p \in P_w | x_p < x_p^*\}} (x_p - x_p^*) T_w^*.$$

Condition (5.2) implies that $t_p(x^*) = T_w^*$ if $x_p^* > 0$, so T_w^* can be replaced by $t_p(x^*)$ in the right–hand side of the previous inequality, thereby yielding

$$0 \leq \sum_{p \in P_w} (x_p - x_p^*) t_p(x^*), \qquad \forall x \in X, \ \forall w \in W.$$

By adding this inequality over all OD pairs $w \in W$, we see that x^* satisfies the variational inequality (5.3).

Conversely, assume that x^* satisfies the variational inequality (5.3). Let $p \in P_w$ be a path of some OD pair w with $x_p^* > 0$, and let $\bar{p} \in P_w$ be a path of the same OD pair with $t_{\bar{p}}(x^*) = T_w^*$. Then, either $p = \bar{p}$, in which case the condition (5.2) holds, or $p \neq \bar{p}$, in which case by taking $x_p = 0$, $x_{\bar{p}} = x_{\bar{p}}^* + x_p^*$, and $x_{p'} = x_{p'}^*$ for all other paths $p' \neq p$, $\bar{p}$, we obtain from Eq. (5.3) $x_p^* \big(T_w^* - t_p(x^*)\big) \geq 0$. Since $x_p^* > 0$, we obtain $t_p(x^*) \leq T_w^*$, thereby showing that the condition (5.2) holds.

(d) *Game Theory and Saddle Point Problems.* A *Nash game* is defined as follows. There are m players. Each player i chooses a strategy x_i belonging to a closed convex set $X_i \subset \Re^{n_i}$. Then, the ith player is penalized by an amount equal to $F_i(x_1, \ldots, x_m)$, where each $F_i : \Re^{n_i} \mapsto \Re$ is a continuously differentiable function. A set $x^* = (x_1^*, \ldots, x_m^*) \in \prod_{i=1}^m X_i$ of strategies is said to be *in equilibrium* if no player is able to reduce the incurred penalty by unilaterally modifying the chosen strategy. That is,

$$F_i\big(x_1^*, \ldots, x_{i-1}^*, x_i^*, x_{i+1}^*, \ldots, x_m^*\big) \leq F_i\big(x_1^*, \ldots, x_{i-1}^*, x_i, x_{i+1}^*, \ldots, x_m^*\big), \quad \forall x_i \in X_i, \forall i.$$

Let us assume that each one of the functions F_i is convex on the set X_i when viewed as a function of x_i alone and the other components are fixed. Using the optimality conditions for convex optimization (Prop. 3.1), we see that a set of strategies x^* is in equilibrium if and only if $(x_i - x_i^*)' \nabla_i F_i(x^*) \geq 0$ for every $x_i \in X_i$ and every i. Adding these conditions, we conclude that x^* must be a solution of the variational inequality $(x - x^*)' f(x^*) \geq 0$, where $f : \prod_{i=1}^m \Re^{n_i} \mapsto \prod_{i=1}^m \Re^{n_i}$ is given by $f(x) = \big(\nabla_1 F_1(x), \dots, \nabla_m F_m(x) \big)$. In fact, under our convexity assumptions, the reverse is also true: any solution of the above defined variational inequality provides a set of strategies in equilibrium (this can be seen using Prop. 5.7 to be proved later in this section).

A related problem is the *saddle point problem*, in which we are given a function $F : X \times Y \mapsto \Re$ and our objective is to find a pair $(x^*, y^*) \in X \times Y$ such that

$$F(x^*, y) \leq F(x^*, y^*) \leq F(x, y^*), \qquad \forall x \in X, \ \forall y \in Y.$$

The saddle point problem is seen to be a special case of a Nash game, provided that we let $F_1 = F$ and $F_2 = -F$. Our convexity assumptions for the Nash game translate to a requirement that the function F is convex in x for each fixed y, and concave in y for each fixed x.

An important application of saddle point problems arises in duality theory for constrained convex optimization. The Saddle Point Theorem of Appendix C shows that an optimal primal solution x^* of a primal optimization problem, and an optimal dual solution $y^* = (p^*, u^*)$ of the corresponding dual optimization problem can be found as a saddle point of the Lagrangian function. The latter function has the form $F(x, y)$, is convex in x for each fixed y, and concave in y for each fixed x. It is thus possible to approach the solution of a constrained optimization problem by considering the associated saddle point problem, and by subsequently applying variational inequality algorithms presented in this section. In some situations, where the optimization problem has separable structure (e.g., the problem considered in Subsection 3.4.2), the saddle point problem can be amenable to decomposition and parallelization (see Exercise 5.2).

3.5.2 Preliminaries

A useful necessary and sufficient condition for x^* to be a solution of VI(X, f) is given by the following result, illustrated in Fig. 3.5.1.

Proposition 5.1.   (*Fixed Point Characterization of Solutions*) Let γ be a positive scalar and let G be a symmetric positive definite matrix. A vector x^* is a solution of VI(X, f) if and only if $[x^* - \gamma G^{-1} f(x^*)]_G^+ = x^*$, where $[\cdot]_G^+$ is the projection on X with respect to norm $\|x\|_G = (x'Gx)^{1/2}$.

Proof. Suppose that $x^* = [x^* - \gamma G^{-1} f(x^*)]_G^+$. Then, the Scaled Projection Theorem [Prop. 3.7(b)] yields $(x - x^*)' \big(-\gamma f(x^*) \big) \leq 0$ for all $x \in X$, and since γ is positive, it follows that x^* solves VI(X, f). Conversely, suppose that x^* solves VI(X, f). Then, Eq. (5.1) yields

$$(x - x^*)' G \Big(x^* - \big(x^* - G^{-1} \gamma f(x^*) \big) \Big) \geq 0$$

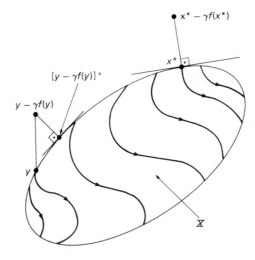

Figure 3.5.1 Illustration of the necessary and sufficient condition for x^* to be a solution of VI(X, f). The function f can be thought of as a vector field on the set X. At the point x^* that solves the variational inequality $(x - x^*)' f(x^*) \geq 0$, the vector field is normal to the boundary and points inwards. For this reason, the projection of $x^* - \gamma f(x^*)$ is equal to x^*, whereas this property is false for other points, such as y.

for all $x \in X$, and the Scaled Projection Theorem implies that $x^* = [x^* - G^{-1}\gamma f(x^*)]_G^+$. **Q.E.D.**

For a fixed positive scalar γ and a symmetric positive definite matrix G, let $R_G : X \mapsto \Re^n$ and $T_G : X \mapsto X$ be the mappings defined by

$$R_G(x) = x - \gamma G^{-1} f(x)$$

and

$$T_G(x) = \left[x - \gamma G^{-1} f(x) \right]_G^+ = \left[R_G(x) \right]_G^+.$$

According to Prop. 5.1, solving the variational inequality VI(X, f) is equivalent to finding a fixed point of the mapping T_G. This allows us to use all of the results on fixed point problems developed in Section 3.1. For instance, we obtain the following existence and uniqueness results.

Proposition 5.2. (*Existence*) Suppose that X is compact and that $f : \Re^n \mapsto \Re^n$ is continuous. Then, there exists a solution to the variational inequality VI(X, f).

Proof. Fix a positive scalar γ and a symmetric positive definite matrix G. If f is continuous then R_G is continuous. Since the projection is a continuous operation (Prop. 3.2), it follows that T_G is continuous as well, and the Leray–Schauder–Tychonoff Fixed Point Theorem (Prop. 1.3) shows that T_G has a fixed point which, by Prop. 5.1, is a solution of VI(X, f). **Q.E.D.**

Figure 3.5.2 shows that if X is not convex, VI(X, f) could have no solutions.

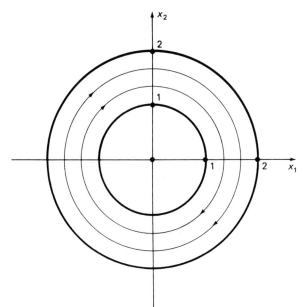

Figure 3.5.2 Illustration of a variational inequality that has no solution. Let $X = \{x \mid 1 \le \|x\|_2 \le 2\}$, which is closed but nonconvex. Let $f(x) = (x_2, -x_1)$. The figure shows the corresponding vector field and it is seen that the variational inequality $(x - x^*)'f(x^*) \ge 0$ has no solution.

Proposition 5.3.   (*Existence and Uniqueness*) Suppose that there exists some $\gamma > 0$, some symmetric positive definite matrix G, and some $\alpha \in [0, 1)$ such that the mapping R_G satisfies

$$\|R_G(x) - R_G(y)\|_G \le \alpha \|x - y\|_G, \qquad \forall x, y \in X. \tag{5.4}$$

Then, the problem $\mathrm{VI}(X, f)$ has a unique solution.

Proof. Proposition 3.7(d) states that the projection $[\cdot]_G^+$ is nonexpansive with respect to the norm $\|x\|_G = (x'Gx)^{1/2}$. Therefore,

$$\|T_G(x) - T_G(y)\|_G \le \|R_G(x) - R_G(y)\|_G \le \alpha \|x - y\|_G.$$

Thus, T_G is a contraction with respect to the norm $\| \cdot \|_G$ and has a unique fixed point x^*. By Prop. 5.1, x^* is the unique solution of $\mathrm{VI}(X, f)$.   **Q.E.D.**

Recall that some sufficient conditions for the mapping R_G to be a contraction mapping have been furnished in Subsection 3.1.3.

3.5.3 The Projection Algorithm

Since our objective is to find a fixed point of the mapping T_G, it is natural to employ the iteration

$$x(t + 1) = T_G\big(x(t)\big) = \Big[x(t) - \gamma G^{-1} f\big(x(t)\big)\Big]_G^+, \qquad t = 0, 1, \ldots, \tag{5.5}$$

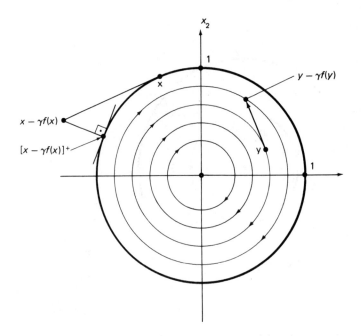

Figure 3.5.3 Illustration of failure of the projection method. Let $X = \{x \mid \|x\|_2 \leq 1\}$ and let $f(x) = (x_2, -x_1)$. The set X is convex and the variational inequality $(x - x^*)' f(x^*) \geq 0$ has the unique solution $x^* = 0$. (Compare with Fig. 3.5.2.) On the other hand, if the projection method is initialized on the boundary, it always stays on the boundary and does not converge. Also, if it is initialized at any nonzero interior point, it moves toward the boundary.

which is called the *projection algorithm*. Here, G is a symmetric positive definite matrix and γ is a positive scalar. Notice that in the special case where f is the gradient of a scalar function F, the projection algorithm of Eq. (5.5) is identical with the scaled gradient projection algorithm of Section 3.3. Unlike the constrained optimization case, the projection algorithm is not guaranteed to converge, as illustrated in Fig. 3.5.3. On the other hand it is guaranteed to converge if the mapping T_G is a contraction. This is always the case if the mapping R_G is a contraction with respect to the norm $\| \cdot \|_G$, because of the nonexpansive property of the projection [Prop. 3.7(d)]. Sufficient conditions for R_G to be such a contraction are provided by Props. 1.12–1.13, specialized to the case of a single block–component ($m = 1$). In particular, we obtain the following result.

Proposition 5.4. (*Convergence of the Projection Algorithm*) Suppose that:

(a) (*Lipschitz Continuity*) There exists some constant K such that

$$\|f(x) - f(y)\|_2 \leq K \|x - y\|_2, \qquad \forall x, y \in X.$$

(b) (*Strong Monotonicity*) There exists some $\alpha > 0$ such that

$$(x - y)'\big(f(x) - f(y)\big) \geq \alpha\|x - y\|_2^2, \qquad \forall x, y \in X. \tag{5.6}$$

Let G be a symmetric positive definite matrix. Then, there exists some $\gamma_0 > 0$ such that for any $\gamma \in (0, \gamma_0]$, T_G is a contraction mapping with respect to the norm $\| \cdot \|_G$. In particular, the problem VI(X, f) has a unique solution and for $\gamma \in (0, \gamma_0]$, the sequence $\{x(t)\}$ generated by the projection algorithm (5.5) converges to it geometrically.

Proof. We use Prop. 1.12 of Subsection 3.13, for the case of a single block–component, to see that R_G is a contraction mapping with respect to the norm $\| \cdot \|_G$, when $\gamma > 0$ is sufficiently small. We then use the nonexpansive property of the projection [Prop. 3.7(d)] to conclude that T_G is also a contraction with respect to the same norm. The result follows from the convergence theorem for contracting iterations.   **Q.E.D.**

If f is a function of the form $f(x) = Ax + b$, then the strong monotonicity condition (5.6) is equivalent to the nonnegative definiteness of $A - \alpha I$. In particular, the matrix A must be positive definite.

For another special case, suppose that f is the gradient of a cost function $F : \Re^n \mapsto \Re^n$. Then, the strong monotonicity assumption is equivalent to the requirement that F is strongly convex on the set X. Furthermore, for this particular case, the projection algorithm (with G being the identity matrix) is identical to the gradient algorithm of Section 3.2 (if $X = \Re^n$) or the gradient projection algorithm of Section 3.3 (if X is a convex subset of $\Re^n$). Proposition 5.4 therefore establishes the geometric convergence of the gradient and the gradient projection algorithms in the strongly convex case (Props. 2.4 and 3.5 in Sections 3.2 and 3.3, respectively).

Strong monotonicity is essential for the result of Prop. 5.4 and its geometric significance is illustrated in Fig. 3.5.4. In case f satisfies only the *monotonicity* condition

$$(x - y)'\big(f(x) - f(y)\big) \geq 0, \qquad \forall x, y \in X,$$

then convergence is not guaranteed. For instance, in the example of Fig. 3.5.3, we have $(x - y)'\big(f(x) - f(y)\big) = 0$ for all x, y, the monotonicity condition is satisfied, but strong monotonicity fails to hold and the projection algorithm does not converge. Exercise 5.1 provides a modification of the projection algorithm that converges appropriately under the monotonicity assumption.

The next result is a restatement of Prop. 5.4 for the case where f is affine.

Proposition 5.5.   (*Convergence of the Projection Algorithm for Linear Problems*) Suppose that $f(x) = Ax + b$, where b is a vector in $\Re^n$ and A is a positive definite (not necessarily symmetric) $n \times n$ matrix. Then, the variational inequality VI(X, f) has a unique solution x^* and for any positive definite symmetric matrix G, the projection algorithm $x(t + 1) = T_G\big(x(t)\big)$ converges to x^* geometrically, provided that γ is small enough.

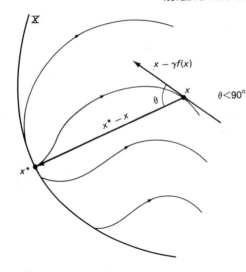

Figure 3.5.4 Interpretation of the strong monotonicity condition (5.6). Let x^* satisfy $(x - x^*)'f(x^*) \geq 0$ for all $x \in X$. Suppose that Eq. (5.6) is true and consider the trajectories determined by the vector field f. Using Eq. (5.6), with $y = x^*$, we obtain

$$(x - x^*)'f(x) \geq (x - x^*)'f(x^*)$$
$$+ \alpha \|x - x^*\|_2^2$$
$$\geq \alpha \|x - x^*\|_2^2.$$

In particular, if $x \neq x^*$, then the angle between $-f(x)$ and $x^* - x$ is smaller than 90 degrees. This means that if the trajectories of the vector field are followed in the reverse direction, the distance from x^* decreases. The projection method for the case where G is the identity matrix can be visualized as an attempt to follow these trajectories. This is done most accurately when γ is very small. Of course, a very small value of γ is undesirable because it slows convergence. In any case, with γ sufficiently small, the projection method inherits the properties of the vector field, that is, the distance from x^* is decreased at each step.

> **Proof.** We have $(x - y)'\big(f(x) - f(y)\big) = (x - y)'A(x - y) = \frac{1}{2}(x - y)'(A + A')(x - y) \geq \alpha\|x - y\|_2^2$ for some $\alpha > 0$, because $A + A'$ is symmetric and positive definite. The result follows from Proposition 5.4.   **Q.E.D.**

We now discuss an application of the projection algorithm to constrained optimization problems with equality constraints. For simplicity, we only consider the case of a quadratic cost function and linear equality constraints, although the following discussion generalizes to broader classes of problems. Let B and C be matrices of dimensions $n \times n$ and $m \times n$, respectively. Consider the problem of minimizing the cost function $\frac{1}{2}x'Bx$ over all $x \in \Re^n$ satisfying the equality constraint $Cx = b$, where b is a vector in $\Re^m$. We assume that B is symmetric positive definite, which implies that the cost function under consideration is strictly convex. We form the Lagrangian

$$L(x, p) = \tfrac{1}{2}x'Bx + p'Cx - p'b,$$

where p is an m–dimensional vector. Let $\nabla_x L$ and $\nabla_p L$ be the vectors of partial derivatives of the Lagrangian with respect to the components of the vectors x and p, respectively. In the present context, $\nabla_x L(x, p) = Bx + C'p$ and $\nabla_p L(x, p) = Cx - b$. As shown in Appendix C and as discussed in the saddle point example in the beginning of this section, a possible approach for solving the constrained optimization problem is to look for a saddle point of the function L. This is equivalent to solving the variational inequality $VI(X, f)$, where $X = \Re^{n+m}$ and the function $f : \Re^{n+m} \mapsto \Re^{n+m}$ is given by

$$f(x,p) = \begin{bmatrix} \nabla_x L(x,p) \\ -\nabla_p L(x,p) \end{bmatrix} = \begin{bmatrix} Bx + C'p \\ -Cx + b \end{bmatrix} = \begin{bmatrix} B & C' \\ -C & 0 \end{bmatrix} \begin{bmatrix} x \\ p \end{bmatrix} + \begin{bmatrix} 0 \\ b \end{bmatrix}.$$

The projection algorithm for this problem is given by

$$x(t+1) = x(t) - \gamma Bx(t) - \gamma C'p(t),$$

$$p(t+1) = p(t) + \gamma Cx(t) - \gamma b.$$

Even though the matrix B is assumed positive definite, the matrix

$$A = \begin{bmatrix} B & C' \\ -C & 0 \end{bmatrix}$$

is not positive definite because of the zero block in the lower right–hand corner. For this reason, the strong monotonicity condition (5.6) fails to hold. A direct calculation yields

$$\begin{bmatrix} x' & p' \end{bmatrix} \begin{bmatrix} B & C' \\ -C & 0 \end{bmatrix} \begin{bmatrix} x \\ p \end{bmatrix} = x'Bx \geq 0, \qquad \forall x, p,$$

and this shows that inequality (5.6) is satisfied with $\alpha = 0$. Thus, the monotonicity (as opposed to strong monotonicity) condition holds. In particular, the extragradient method of Exercise 5.1 is applicable and is guaranteed to converge. It turns out that the projection method is also guaranteed to converge for this example, provided that the matrix C has full rank; a proof can be found in [Ber82a, p. 232].

3.5.4 Linearized Algorithms

Let x^0 be an element of X and let G be symmetric positive definite. Using the Scaled Projection Theorem [Prop. 3.7(b)], we see that $T_G(x^0)$ could be defined as the unique vector $x^1 \in X$ satisfying

$$(x - x^1)'G\left(x^1 - x^0 + \gamma G^{-1}f(x^0)\right) \geq 0, \qquad \forall x \in X.$$

Equivalently, since $\gamma > 0$, we see that x^1 satisfies

$$(x - x^1)'\left(f(x^0) + \mu G(x^1 - x^0)\right) \geq 0, \qquad \forall x \in X, \tag{5.7}$$

where $\mu = 1/\gamma$, which is again a variational inequality. In particular, it is the variational inequality problem VI(X, g), where $g(x) = f(x^0) + \mu G(x - x^0)$. However, it is in general easier to solve than the original variational inequality VI(X, f) because the function g is linear in the variable x. We can thus think of the projection algorithm as a method that solves a variational inequality by successively solving a sequence of simpler variational inequalities. Based on this observation, a variety of different algorithms are obtained by choosing differently the variational inequality to be solved at each stage. These algorithms are classified as *linearized* or *nonlinear*, depending on whether the variational inequality solved at each stage involves a linear or a nonlinear function, respectively.

In a general linearized algorithm [Daf83], having computed $x(t)$, we compute $x(t + 1)$ by solving the variational inequality $VI(X, g_t)$, where the function g_t has the form

$$g_t(x) = f(x(t)) + A(x(t))(x - x(t)).$$

Equivalently, we are looking for a vector $x(t + 1)$ satisfying

$$(x - x(t + 1))'\left(f(x(t)) + A(x(t))(x(t + 1) - x(t))\right) \geq 0, \qquad \forall x \in X.$$

Here, $A(x(t))$ is a positive definite (not necessarily symmetric) scaling matrix, depending on $x(t)$. It follows (Prop. 5.5) that the previous variational inequality has a unique solution and the linearized algorithm is well–defined.

Different linearized algorithms correspond to different choices of the scaling matrices $A(x)$. [Accordingly, we will be referring to "the linearized algorithm determined by $\{A(x) \mid x \in X\}$".] Once these scaling matrices have been fixed, a linearized algorithm can be cast into the standard form

$$x(t + 1) = T(x(t)),$$

where $T(x)$ is defined as the unique element of X satisfying

$$(y - T(x))'\left(f(x) + A(x)(T(x) - x)\right) \geq 0, \qquad \forall y \in X. \tag{5.8}$$

As a concrete example, if $A(x) = \mu G$, for all x, where G is symmetric positive definite and $\mu > 0$, we recover the projection algorithm [see the variational inequality (5.7)]. To motivate some reasonable choices of $A(x)$, we consider the unconstrained optimization context, where $f(x) = \nabla F(x)$ for some cost function F and $X = \Re^n$. In this case, the solution of the variational inequality (5.8) is

$$T(x) = x - \left(A(x)\right)^{-1}\nabla F(x). \tag{5.9}$$

In this context, it is desirable to let $A(x)$ be an approximation of $\nabla^2 F(x) = \nabla f(x)$. Generalizing this prescription, a common choice is to let $A(x)$ be a diagonal matrix whose diagonal entries are equal to the diagonal entries of the matrix $\nabla f(x)$.

The following is a general result on the convergence of linearized algorithms, although its conditions are not always easy to verify. The proof is omitted because it is a special case of Prop. 5.8, which is proved later.

Proposition 5.6. (*Convergence of Linearized Algorithms*) Suppose that the variational inequality $VI(X, f)$ has a solution x^*. Consider the linearized algorithm determined by $\{A(x) \mid x \in X\}$. Suppose that there exists a symmetric positive definite matrix G and some $\delta > 0$ such that the matrix $A(x) - \delta G$ is nonnegative definite for every $x \in X$. Furthermore, suppose that for some $\alpha \in [0, 1)$,

$$\left\| G^{-1}\Big(f(x) - f(y) - A(y)(x - y)\Big) \right\|_G \leq \delta\alpha\|x - y\|_G, \qquad \forall x, y \in X, \qquad (5.10)$$

where $\|z\|_G = (z'Gz)^{1/2}$. Then the sequence $\{x(t)\}$ generated by the linearized algorithm converges to x^* geometrically, and x^* is the unique solution of $\mathrm{VI}(X, f)$.

As discussed earlier, in the projection method, we have $A(x) = G/\gamma$. Thus, if we let $\delta = 1/\gamma$, then $A(x) - \delta G = 0$, which is nonnegative definite, and the hypothesis (5.10) in this proposition is equivalent to the statement that the mapping R_G, given by $R_G(x) = x - \gamma G^{-1} f(x)$, is a contraction. Thus, Prop. 5.6 generalizes our earlier results on the convergence of the projection method (Prop. 5.4).

3.5.5 The Cartesian Product Case: Parallel Implementations

From now on we assume that X is a Cartesian product $X = \prod_{i=1}^m X_i$, where each set X_i is of dimension n_i and $\sum_{i=1}^m n_i = n$. Any vector $x \in X$ is accordingly decomposed as $x = (x_1, \ldots, x_m)$, with $x_i \in X_i$. We still assume that X is nonempty, closed, and convex, and these properties are then implied for each one of the sets X_i. The Cartesian product assumption holds for several important problems such as the solution of systems of nonlinear equations in n variables, the traffic assignment problem, Nash games (see Subsection 3.5.1), as well for many important economic equilibrium problems ([Pan85], [Ahn79], [Nag87]). As in constrained optimization (Subsection 3.3.4), this assumption provides the possibility for parallel algorithms, as will be shown next.

A key observation for the product set case is that a variational inequality decomposes into m coupled variational inequalities of smaller dimensions.

Proposition 5.7.   (*Decomposition Lemma*) A vector $x^* \in X$ solves the variational inequality $\mathrm{VI}(X, f)$ if and only if

$$(x_i - x_i^*)' f_i(x^*) \geq 0, \qquad \forall x_i \in X_i, \ \forall i. \qquad (5.11)$$

Proof. If Eq. (5.11) is satisfied for each i, we add these inequalities to conclude that $(x - x^*)' f(x^*) \geq 0$. Conversely, suppose that $x^* \in X$ solves the problem $\mathrm{VI}(X, f)$. Choose some vector x such that $x_j = x_j^*$ for all $j \neq i$ and $x_i \in X_i$. Because of the Cartesian product assumption, we have $x \in X$ and using the inequality $(x - x^*)' f(x^*) \geq 0$, we see that Eq. (5.11) holds.   **Q.E.D.**

Consider now a linearized algorithm determined by a collection $\{A(x) \mid x \in X\}$ of scaling matrices. Such an algorithm is not easily parallelizable in general. For example, in the case of unconstrained optimization [see Eq. (5.9)], a system of linear equations has to be solved at each step and this task cannot be easily decomposed into a set of independent subtasks. Rather, a parallel algorithm for systems of linear equations is needed at each step and this requires a greater degree of coordination between processors. On the other hand, if the matrix $A(x)$ is block–diagonal for each x, the ith block $A_i(x)$ being of dimension $n_i \times n_i$, the problem decouples naturally, as we proceed to show. Let $T : X \mapsto X$ be the mapping describing one iteration of the linearized algorithm, that is, $T(x)$ satisfies Eq. (5.8). Under the assumption that $A(x)$ is block–diagonal, the ith block–component of the function $f(x) + A(x)\big(T(x) - x\big)$ is equal to $f_i(x) + A_i(x)\big(T_i(x) - x_i\big)$, and using the Decomposition Lemma, we conclude that $T_i(x)$ satisfies

$$\big(y_i - T_i(x)\big)' \Big(f_i(x) + A_i(x)\big(T_i(x) - x_i\big) \Big) \geq 0, \qquad \forall y_i \in X_i. \qquad (5.12)$$

This shows that each component of $T_i(x)$ can be found by solving a variational inequality of smaller dimension, and this can be done independently for each i. In particular, each one of these smaller variational inequalities can be solved by a different processor.

We return to the convergence analysis of linearized algorithms. Let us fix a choice of the scaling matrices $A(x)$, assumed to be block–diagonal, as discussed earlier. We assume that each diagonal block $A_i(x)$ of $A(x)$ is positive definite for each x, which guarantees that each subproblem (5.12) has a unique solution (Prop. 5.5) and the linearized algorithm is well–defined. The following result establishes the convergence of the iteration $x := T(x)$ as well as of the associated Gauss–Seidel algorithm, under the standing assumption that X is a Cartesian product and the scaling matrices $A(x)$ are block–diagonal.

Proposition 5.8. (*Linearized Algorithm Convergence in the Product Case*) Suppose that the problem VI(X, f) has a solution x^*. Suppose that there exist symmetric positive definite matrices G_i and some $\delta > 0$ such that $A_i(x) - \delta G_i$ is nonnegative definite for every i and $x \in X$, and that there exists some $\alpha \in [0, 1)$ such that

$$\left\| G_i^{-1} \Big(f_i(x) - f_i(y) - A_i(y)(x_i - y_i) \Big) \right\|_i \leq \delta \alpha \max_j \|x_j - y_j\|_j, \qquad \forall x, y \in X, \quad (5.13)$$

where $\|x_i\|_i = (x_i' G_i x_i)^{1/2}$. Then, the iteration mapping T of the linearized algorithm determined by $\{A(x) \mid x \in X\}$ has the property

$$\|T_i(x) - x_i^*\|_i \leq \alpha \max_j \|x_j - x_j^*\|_j, \qquad \forall x \in X, \ i = 1, \ldots, m. \qquad (5.14)$$

In particular, x^* is the unique solution of VI(X, f) and the linearized algorithm $x(t+1) = T\big(x(t)\big)$, as well as the Gauss–Seidel algorithm based on T, converge to x^* geometrically.

Proof. Fix some $x \in X$. Since $x_i^* \in X_i$, inequality (5.12) yields

$$\big(x_i^* - T_i(x)\big)' \Big(f_i(x) + A_i(x)\big(T_i(x) - x_i\big) \Big) \geq 0. \qquad (5.15)$$

We also have

$$\left(T_i(x) - x_i^*\right)' f_i(x^*) \geq 0, \tag{5.16}$$

because x^* solves VI(X, f) and because of the Decomposition Lemma. We add inequalities (5.15) and (5.16) and rearrange terms to obtain

$$\left(T_i(x) - x_i^*\right)' A_i(x)\left(T_i(x) - x_i^*\right) \leq \left(T_i(x) - x_i^*\right)' \left(f_i(x^*) - f_i(x) - A_i(x)(x_i^* - x_i)\right). \tag{5.17}$$

The left–hand side of inequality (5.17) is bounded below by $\delta\|T_i(x) - x_i^*\|_i^2$ because of the nonnegative definiteness of $A_i(x) - \delta G_i$. Also, the right–hand side of inequality (5.17) is equal to

$$\left(T_i(x) - x_i^*\right)' G_i\left[G_i^{-1}\left(f_i(x^*) - f_i(x) - A_i(x)(x_i^* - x_i)\right)\right]. \tag{5.18}$$

From the Schwartz inequality [Prop. A.28(e) in Appendix A] and inequality (5.13), the expression (5.18) is bounded above by $\|T_i(x) - x_i^*\|_i \cdot \delta\alpha \max_j \|x_j - x_j^*\|_j$. We have thus shown that

$$\delta\|T_i(x) - x_i^*\|_i^2 \leq \|T_i(x) - x_i^*\|_i \cdot \delta\alpha \max_j \|x_j - x_j^*\|_j,$$

from which inequality (5.14) follows. In particular, T is a pseudocontraction and x^* is the unique fixed point of T. The rest of the result follows from the convergence theorem for pseudocontracting iterations and their Gauss–Seidel versions (Props. 1.2 and 1.5 of Section 3.1).   **Q.E.D.**

Notice that this proof remains valid under the assumption that VI(X, f) has a solution x^* and that inequality (5.13) holds when $y = x^*$. On the other hand, given that x^* is unknown, this weaker version is usually not any easier to verify.

In the special case where $A(x)$ is symmetric positive definite and independent of x we obtain the projection algorithm and the previous proposition can be strengthened a little. In particular, we do not need to assume the existence of a solution x^*.

Proposition 5.9.   Let $\gamma > 0$, let G_i, $i = 1, \ldots, m$, be symmetric positive definite matrices, and let $\|\cdot\|_i$ be the norm $\|x\|_i = (x'G_ix)^{1/2}$. Suppose that

$$\left\|\gamma G_i^{-1}\left(f_i(x) - f_i(y)\right) - (x_i - y_i)\right\|_i \leq \alpha \max_j \|x_j - y_j\|_j, \qquad \forall x, y \in X, \tag{5.19}$$

where $\alpha \in [0, 1)$. Then, the problem VI(X, f) has a unique solution x^*. Let G be a block–diagonal matrix whose ith diagonal block is equal to G_i. Then, the sequence $\{x(t)\}$ generated by the projection algorithm $x(t+1) = \left[x(t) - \gamma G^{-1}f\left(x(t)\right)\right]^+$ converges to x^* geometrically. The same is true concerning the corresponding Gauss–Seidel algorithm.

Proof. The condition (5.19) states that the mapping $R_G(x) = x - \gamma G^{-1} f(x)$ is a contraction with respect to the block–maximum norm $\|x\| = \max_i \|x\|_i$. It follows that the mapping $T_G(x) = [x - \gamma G^{-1} f(x)]_G^+$ is also a contraction and has a unique fixed point. Existence and uniqueness of a solution follow from our general existence and uniqueness results (Prop. 5.3). Convergence of the projection algorithm follows from the convergence theorem for contracting iterations (Prop. 1.1) and their Gauss–Seidel variants (Prop. 1.4).   **Q.E.D.**

Sufficient conditions for condition (5.19) to hold are provided by Props. 1.10 and 1.11 of Subsection 3.1.3.

3.5.6 Nonlinear Algorithms

We still assume that X is a Cartesian product $X = \prod_{i=1}^m X_i$. According to the Decomposition Lemma, the variational inequality $\text{VI}(X, f)$ is equivalent to a system of m variational inequalities that must be solved simultaneously. A nonlinear algorithm proceeds by solving for each i the ith variational inequality

$$(x_i - x_i^*)' f_i(x^*) \geq 0, \qquad \forall x_i \in X_i,$$

with respect to the ith block–component of x^*, while keeping the other block–components fixed. To be more precise, fix some $x^0 \in X$. Starting from x^0, the new value of the ith block–component, produced by an iteration of a nonlinear algorithm, is equal to some $Q_i(x^0)$ satisfying

$$\left(x_i - Q_i(x^0)\right)' f_i\left(x_1^0, \ldots, x_{i-1}^0, Q_i(x^0), x_{i+1}^0, \ldots, x_m^0\right) \geq 0, \qquad \forall x_i \in X_i. \quad (5.20)$$

Notice that (5.20) is itself a variational inequality. It is the problem $\text{VI}(X_i, g)$, where $g(x_i) = f\left(x_1^0, \ldots, x_{i-1}^0, x_i, x_{i+1}^0, \ldots, x_m^0\right)$. Therefore, $Q_i(x^0)$ can be found using any one of the algorithms presented earlier. Furthermore, (5.20) should be easier to solve than the original problem (5.1) because the sets X_i are of smaller dimension.

It is assumed in the sequel that for every $x^0 \in X$, there exists some $Q_i(x^0)$ satisfying (5.20). Since (5.20) is itself a variational inequality in the unknown $Q_i(x^0)$, sufficient conditions for the existence of a solution are provided by our general existence results (Props. 5.2–5.3). In case that there are several solutions, we assume that $Q_i(x^0)$ has been arbitrarily defined to be equal to one of them. Then, the nonlinear algorithm is well defined.

We let $Q(x^0) = \left(Q_1(x^0), \ldots, Q_m(x^0)\right)$ and this determines a mapping $Q : X \mapsto X$. Accordingly, the nonlinear Jacobi algorithm is defined by the iteration

$$x(t + 1) = Q\big(x(t)\big).$$

With the nonlinear Jacobi algorithm, all block–components $x_i(t + 1)$ are simultaneously computed on the basis of $x(t)$. Alternatively, with a nonlinear Gauss–Seidel algorithm, the block–components of $x(t + 1)$ are computed in succession. In the terminology of Section 3.1, the latter is the Gauss–Seidel algorithm based on the mapping Q.

We briefly interpret the above defined nonlinear algorithm in the context of the specific examples discussed in Subsection 3.5.1.

(a) *(Systems of equations)* Here $X = \Re^n$ and the objective is to find a solution of $f(x) = 0$. For this example, $Q_i(x)$ is the value of x_i obtained by solving the ith equation $f_i(x) = 0$, while keeping the other components of x constant.

(b) *(Optimization)* Here X is a closed convex set and $f(x) = \nabla F(x)$, where F is a continuously differentiable convex cost function. Given a current vector x^0, the new value $\tilde{x}_i = Q_i(x^0)$ of the ith block–component is obtained by solving the variational inequality

$$(y_i - \tilde{x}_i)' \nabla_i F\left(x_1^0, \ldots, x_{i-1}^0, \tilde{x}_i, x_{i+1}^0, \ldots, x_m^0\right) \geq 0, \qquad \forall y_i \in X_i.$$

This is equivalent to minimizing F with respect to the ith block–component. In particular, the nonlinear methods of this section contain as special cases the nonlinear methods of Sections 3.2 and 3.3.

(c) *(Game theory)* Consider a Nash game and let F_i be the cost function of the ith player. Assuming that each F_i is convex in the variable x_i (the strategy of the ith player), it is easily seen that at each iteration of the nonlinear algorithm, the strategy of each player is optimized while holding the strategies of the other players constant.

In Sections 3.2 and 3.3, we presented certain results on the convergence of the nonlinear Gauss–Seidel algorithm for optimization problems (Props. 2.5 and 3.9). The proof of these results was based on the descent property: the value of the cost function was nonincreasing in the course of the algorithm. For more general variational inequalities, the descent approach is inapplicable. We therefore rely instead on the theory of contraction mappings of Section 3.1 together with the observation that the nonlinear Jacobi algorithm is identical to the component solution method of Section 3.1.2, which is proved next.

Proposition 5.10. *(Nonlinear Algorithms are Component Solution Methods)* Let $T : X \mapsto X$ be the mapping corresponding to one iteration of a linearized algorithm determined by a collection of scaling matrices $\{A(x) \mid x \in X\}$ assumed to be block–diagonal and positive definite. Then, an iteration $x := Q(x)$ of the nonlinear Jacobi algorithm coincides with an iteration of the component solution method for solving the fixed point problem $x = T(x)$.

Proof. We only need to show that $Q_i(x)$ solves the ith equation of the system $x = T(x)$, that is, we need to show that the equality

$$Q_i(x) = T_i\big(x_1,\ldots,x_{i-1},Q_i(x),x_{i+1},\ldots,x_m\big) \tag{5.21}$$

holds for every i and every $x \in X$. Let us fix some $x \in X$. From Eq. (5.20) we have

$$\big(z_i - Q_i(x)\big)' f_i\big(x_1,\ldots,x_{i-1},Q_i(x),x_{i+1},\ldots,x_m\big) \geq 0, \qquad \forall z_i \in X_i.$$

This can be rewritten as

$$\big(z_i - Q_i(x)\big)'\Big(f_i\big(x_1,\ldots,x_{i-1},Q_i(x),x_{i+1},\ldots,x_m\big)$$
$$+ A_i\big(x_1,\ldots,x_{i-1},Q_i(x),x_{i+1},\ldots,x_m\big)\big(Q_i(x)-Q_i(x)\big)\Big) \geq 0, \qquad \forall z_i \in X_i,$$

which shows that $Q_i(x)$ solves (for the unknown y_i) the variational inequality

$$(z_i - y_i)'\Big(f_i\big(x_1,\ldots,x_{i-1},Q_i(x),x_{i+1},\ldots,x_m\big)$$
$$+ A_i\big(x_1,\ldots,x_{i-1},Q_i(x),x_{i+1},\ldots,x_m\big)\big(y_i-Q_i(x)\big)\Big) \geq 0, \qquad \forall z \in X_i. \tag{5.22}$$

On the other hand this is exactly the variational inequality solved by the linearized algorithm [see Eq. (5.12)], if the current vector is $(x_1,\ldots,x_{i-1},Q_i(x),x_{i+1},\ldots,x_m)$. Furthermore, a solution is unique, because $A(x)$ has been assumed positive definite (Prop. 5.5). Therefore, by the definition of T, we obtain $Q_i(x) = T_i(x_1,\ldots,x_{i-1},Q_i(x),x_{i+1},\ldots,x_m)$, as desired.   **Q.E.D.**

Convergence of nonlinear algorithms can be now demonstrated using our general results on the convergence of component solution methods (Subsection 3.1.2). In particular, if the mapping T corresponding to a linearized algorithm is a contraction or a pseudocontraction, with respect to a block–maximum norm, the same property holds for the mapping Q describing the nonlinear Jacobi algorithm (Props. 1.7 and 1.9 in Subsection 3.1.2). Furthermore, in the case where T is a contraction, it has been shown in Section 3.1 (Prop. 1.6) that the component solutions $Q_i(x)$ are uniquely defined for every $x \in X$. We now state two results that follow directly from Prop. 5.10 and the preceding discussion.

Proposition 5.11. Let $T : X \mapsto X$ be the mapping corresponding to one iteration of a linearized algorithm determined by a collection of scaling matrices $\{A(x) \mid x \in X\}$ assumed to be block–diagonal and positive definite. Suppose also that T is a pseudo-contraction, with respect to a block–maximum norm. Let x^* be the fixed point of T. If the nonlinear Jacobi algorithm $x(t+1) = Q\big(x(t)\big)$ is well defined [meaning that the variational inequality (5.20) always has a solution] then the sequence $\{x(t)\}$ converges to x^* geometrically, and the same is true for the nonlinear Gauss–Seidel algorithm.

It should be recalled here that Prop. 5.8 provides sufficient conditions for a linearized algorithm to be a pseudocontraction with respect to a block–maximum norm.

Proposition 5.12. Let $T : X \mapsto X$ be the mapping corresponding to one iteration of a linearized algorithm determined by a collection of scaling matrices $\{A(x) \mid x \in X\}$ assumed to be block–diagonal and positive definite. Suppose also that T is a contraction with respect to a block–maximum norm. Then the problem $\mathrm{VI}(X, f)$ has a unique solution x^*, the nonlinear Jacobi and Gauss–Seidel algorithms are well defined, and they converge to x^* geometrically.

An example of a linearized algorithm that is a block–maximum norm contraction is the projection algorithm under the assumption (5.19) of Prop. 5.9. Conditions for the latter assumption to hold have been presented in Subsection 3.1.3.

3.5.7 Decomposition Methods for Variational Inequalities

Some of the decomposition techniques developed in Section 3.4 for convex constrained optimization problems can be extended to more general variational inequality problems. As an example, consider the following natural extension of the separable problem of Subsection 3.4.4 (Example 3.4), where we want to find a vector $x^* = (x_1^*, \ldots, x_m^*)$ in a product set $P_1 \times \cdots \times P_m$ which satisfies the linear coupling constraints

$$e_j' x^* = s_j, \qquad j = 1, \ldots, r,$$

and solves the separable variational inequality

$$\sum_{i=1}^m f_i(x_i^*)'(x_i - x_i^*) \geq 0, \qquad \forall\, x \in P_1 \times \cdots \times P_m, \text{ with } e_j' x = s_j, \, j = 1, \ldots, r. \quad (5.23)$$

Here P_i is a polyhedral subset of $\Re^{n_i}$, $e_j \in \Re^n$ are given vectors, and $s_j \in \Re$ are given scalars, where $n = n_1 + \cdots + n_m$. If $f_i(x_i) = \nabla F_i(x_i)$, where $F_i : \Re^{n_i} \mapsto \Re$ is a convex function for each i, we obtain a separable optimization problem.

Let e_{ji} be the subvector of e_j that corresponds to x_i, let

$$I(j) = \{i \mid e_{ji} \neq 0\}, \qquad j = 1, \ldots, r,$$

and let m_j be the number of elements of $I(j)$. In the typical iteration of the natural alternating direction method of multipliers (cf. Subsection 3.4.4), we obtain for $i = 1, \ldots, m$, a solution $x_i(t+1) \in P_i$ of the variational inequality

$$\left[f_i\big(x_i(t+1)\big) + \sum_{\{j \mid i \in I(j)\}} e_{ji}\big[\lambda_j(t) + c\big(e_{ji}'(x_i(t+1) - x_i(t)) + w_j(t)\big)\big] \right]'(x_i - x_i(t+1)) \geq 0,$$

$$\forall\, x_i \in P_i, \qquad (5.24)$$

where

$$w_j(t) = \frac{1}{m_j}\big(e_j' x(t) - s_j\big), \qquad j = 1, \ldots, r, \qquad (5.25)$$

and we update $\lambda_j(t)$ according to

$$\lambda_j(t+1) = \lambda_j(t) + cw_j(t+1), \qquad j = 1, \ldots, r. \tag{5.26}$$

Here c is a positive scalar and the initial vectors $x_i(0)$ and $\lambda_j(0)$ are arbitrary. Note that this is a highly parallelizable method.

To establish the validity of the preceding method we consider (cf. Subsection 3.4.4) the variational inequality problem of finding $x^* \in \Re^n$ such that $x^* \in C_1$, $Ax^* \in C_2$ and

$$f(x^*)'(x - x^*) \geq 0, \qquad \forall x \in C_1 \cap \{\xi \mid A\xi \in C_2\}. \tag{5.27}$$

Here A is an $m \times n$ matrix, and $C_1 \subset \Re^n$ and $C_2 \subset \Re^m$ are nonempty polyhedral sets.

There is a natural extension of the alternating direction method of multipliers of Subsection 3.4.4 for the above problem. In the typical iteration of this method, we obtain $x(t+1)$ that solves the variational inequality

$$\left[f\big(x(t+1)\big) + A'\big[p(t) + c\big(Ax(t+1) - z(t)\big)\big] \right]' (x - x(t+1)) \geq 0, \qquad \forall x \in C_1, \tag{5.28}$$

and we update $z(t)$ and $p(t)$ by

$$z(t+1) = \arg\min_{z \in C_2} \left\{ -p(t)'z + \frac{c}{2} \|Ax(t+1) - z\|_2^2 \right\}, \tag{5.29}$$

$$p(t+1) = p(t) + c\big(Ax(t+1) - z(t+1)\big). \tag{5.30}$$

The parameter c is assumed positive, and the initial vectors $p(0)$ and $z(0)$ are arbitrary.

As in Subsection 3.4.4, the method (5.24)–(5.26) is obtained as a special case of the method (5.28)–(5.30) with the identifications

$$f(x) = \sum_{i=1}^m f_i(x_i), \qquad C_1 = P_1 \times P_2 \times \cdots \times P_m,$$

$$C_2 = \left\{ z \mid \sum_{i \in I(j)} z_{ji} = s_j, \; j = 1, \ldots, r \right\},$$

and with A being the matrix that maps x into the vector having coordinates $e'_{ji}x_i$, $j = 1, \ldots, r$, $i \in I(j)$.

We will make the following assumption (cf. Assumption 4.1 in Subsection 3.4.4):

Assumption 5.1. The optimal solution set X^* of problem (5.27) is nonempty, and the function f is Lipschitz continuous and monotone, that is, for some K

$$\|f(x) - f(y)\|_2 \leq K\|x - y\|_2, \qquad (x - y)'\big(f(x) - f(y)\big) \geq 0, \qquad \forall x, y \in C_1. \tag{5.31}$$

Furthermore, either C_1 is bounded, or else the matrix $A'A$ is invertible.

It is possible to show that under Assumption 5.1, a solution $x(t+1)$ of the variational inequality of Eq. (5.28) exists. Indeed if C_1 is compact, existence follows from Prop. 5.2. If $A'A$ is invertible the variational inequality of Eq. (5.28) involves a strongly monotone map because f is monotone and $A'A$ is positive definite, so existence (as well as uniqueness) follows from Prop. 5.4. The following convergence result parallels Prop. 4.2 in Subsection 3.4.4.

Proposition 5.13.   Let Assumption 5.1 hold. A sequence $\{x(t), z(t), p(t)\}$ generated by the algorithm (5.28)–(5.30) is bounded, and every limit point of $\{x(t)\}$ is a solution of the original variational inequality (5.27).

Proof. The proof closely resembles the proof of Prop. 4.2 in Subsection 3.4.4. Let x^* be a solution of the variational inequality (5.27), let $z^* = Ax^*$, and let p^* be a Lagrange multiplier associated with the equality constraint $z = Ax$ in the problem

$$\text{minimize } f(x^*)'x$$
$$\text{subject to } x \in C_1, \ z \in C_2, \ z = Ax. \tag{5.32}$$

Then (x^*, z^*) is an optimal solution of the above optimization problem. By using the multiplier update formula (5.30) we can write the condition (5.28) as

$$f\big(x(t{+}1)\big)'\big(x(t{+}1){-}x\big)+\big[p(t{+}1)+c\big(z(t{+}1){-}z(t)\big)\big]'A\big(x(t{+}1){-}x\big) \le 0, \qquad \forall\, x \in C_1, \tag{5.33}$$

while by using the necessary optimality condition of Prop. 3.1 of Section 3.3 we obtain from Eq. (5.29)

$$p(t + 1)'\big(z - z(t + 1)\big) \le 0, \qquad \forall\, z \in C_2. \tag{5.34}$$

By applying Eq. (5.33) with $x = x^*$ we have

$$f\big(x(t + 1)\big)'\big(x(t + 1) - x^*\big) + \big[p(t + 1) + c\big(z(t + 1) - z(t)\big)\big]'A\big(x(t + 1) - x^*\big) \le 0,$$

and by applying Eq. (5.34) with $z = z^*$ we have

$$p(t + 1)'\big(z^* - z(t + 1)\big) \le 0.$$

By adding these two relations, and using also the fact $Ax^* = z^*$, we obtain

$$f\big(x(t + 1)\big)'\big(x(t + 1) - x^*\big) + p(t + 1)'\big(Ax(t + 1) - z(t + 1)\big)$$
$$+ c\big(z(t + 1) - z(t)\big)'A\big(x(t + 1) - x^*\big) \le 0. \tag{5.35}$$

Since (x^*, z^*) is an optimal solution and p^* is a Lagrange multiplier for problem (5.32), we have

$$0 \leq f(x^*)'(x(t+1) - x^*) + p^{*'}(Ax(t+1) - z(t+1)), \qquad \forall\, t. \tag{5.36}$$

By adding Eqs. (5.35) and (5.36) we obtain

$$[f(x(t+1)) - f(x^*)]'(x(t+1) - x^*) + (p(t+1) - p^*)'(Ax(t+1) - z(t+1))$$
$$+ c(z(t+1) - z(t))'A(x(t+1) - x^*) \leq 0. \tag{5.37}$$

Using the monotonicity of f, we see that the first term on the left–hand side of Eq. (5.37) is nonnegative, so we obtain

$$(p(t+1) - p^*)'(Ax(t+1) - z(t+1)) + c(z(t+1) - z(t))'A(x(t+1) - x^*) \leq 0. \tag{5.38}$$

We now denote for all t

$$\tilde{x}(t) = x(t) - x^*, \qquad \tilde{z}(t) = z(t) - z^*, \qquad \tilde{p}(t) = p(t) - p^*,$$

and we use the calculation given in the proof of Prop. 4.2 to obtain

$$\|\tilde{p}(t+1) - \tilde{p}(t)\|_2^2 + c^2\|\tilde{z}(t+1) - \tilde{z}(t)\|_2^2 \leq \left(\|\tilde{p}(t)\|_2^2 + c^2\|\tilde{z}(t)\|_2^2\right) - \left(\|\tilde{p}(t+1)\|_2^2 + c^2\|\tilde{z}(t+1)\|_2^2\right). \tag{5.39}$$

It follows that $\{z(t)\}$ and $\{p(t)\}$ are bounded and

$$\tilde{p}(t+1) - \tilde{p}(t) \to 0, \qquad \tilde{z}(t+1) - \tilde{z}(t) \to 0. \tag{5.38}$$

Since $Ax(t) - z(t) = (\tilde{p}(t) - \tilde{p}(t-1))/c \to 0$ and $\{z(t)\}$ is bounded, we obtain by using Assumption 5.1 that $\{x(t)\}$ is bounded. Furthermore, for every limit point $(\tilde{x}, \tilde{z})$ of $\{(x(t), z(t))\}$ we have $A\tilde{x} = \tilde{z}$. Let $(\tilde{x}, \tilde{z}, \tilde{p})$ be a limit point of the sequence $\{(x(t), z(t), p(t))\}$. Then by taking the limit in Eq. (5.33) we obtain

$$f(\tilde{x})'(\tilde{x} - x) + \tilde{p}'A(\tilde{x} - x) \leq 0, \qquad \forall\, x \in C_1, \tag{5.39}$$

while by taking the limit in Eq. (5.34) we obtain

$$\tilde{p}'(z - \tilde{z}) \leq 0, \qquad \forall\, z \in C_2. \tag{5.40}$$

By adding Eqs. (5.39) and (5.40), and by using the fact $A\tilde{x} = \tilde{z}$ we obtain

$$f(\tilde{x})'(x - \tilde{x}) + \tilde{p}'(Ax - z) \geq 0, \qquad \forall\, x \in C_1, \; z \in C_2. \tag{5.41}$$

By using the Lagrange Multiplier Theorem of Appendix C we see that Eq. (5.41) implies that $\tilde{x}$ and $\tilde{z}$ are an optimal solution of the problem

$$\text{minimize}\ \ f(\tilde{x})'x$$

$$\text{subject to}\ \ x \in C_1,\ z \in C_2,\ z = Ax,$$

or equivalently that $\tilde{x}$ is a solution of the original variational inequality (5.27).   **Q.E.D.**

We note that it is possible to show convergence of the sequences $\{z(t)\}$ and $\{p(t)\}$ as in the proof of Prop. 4.2. Exercise 5.3 provides an alternating direction method of multipliers for a generalized version of the variational inequality (5.27).

EXERCISES

5.1. (**The Extragradient Method [Kor76].**) This exercise provides a modification of the projection algorithm that converges appropriately to a solution of $VI(X, f)$, assuming that the monotonicity condition

$$(x - y)'\big(f(x) - f(y)\big) \geq 0, \qquad \forall x, y \in X,$$

holds, and that there exists a constant A such that

$$\|f(x) - f(y)\|_2 \leq A\|x - y\|_2, \qquad \forall x, y \in X.$$

(As shown in Fig. 3.5.3, the projection algorithm need not converge, for any value of the stepsize, under the preceding conditions; a strong monotonicity condition is needed.)
　　Consider the modified projection method

$$x(t + 1) = \Big[x(t) - \gamma f\big(\bar{x}(t)\big)\Big]^+,$$

where $\bar{x}(t)$ is given by

$$\bar{x}(t) = \Big[x(t) - \gamma f\big(x(t)\big)\Big]^+,$$

and γ is a positive scalar. [Thus, the method, at each iteration, uses the value of f at $\bar{x}(t)$ rather than the one at $x(t)$.]
　　(**a**) Show that for any solution x^* of $VI(X, f)$ we have

$$\|x(t + 1) - x^*\|_2^2 \leq \|x(t) - x^*\|_2^2 - (1 - \gamma^2 A^2)\|x(t) - \bar{x}(t)\|_2^2,$$

and conclude that for $\gamma \in (0, 1/A)$, the method converges to some solution of $\mathrm{VI}(X, f)$, if at least one such solution exists. *Hint:* The monotonicity condition and the fact that x^* is a solution imply that

$$
\begin{aligned}
0 \le \Big(f\big(\bar{x}(t)\big) - f(x^*)\Big)' \big(\bar{x}(t) - x^*\big) &= f\big(\bar{x}(t)\big)' \big(\bar{x}(t) - x^*\big) - f(x^*)' \big(\bar{x}(t) - x^*\big) \\
&\le f\big(\bar{x}(t)\big)' \big(\bar{x}(t) - x^*\big) \\
&= f\big(\bar{x}(t)\big)' \big(\bar{x}(t) - x(t+1)\big) \\
&\quad + f\big(\bar{x}(t)\big)' \big(x(t+1) - x^*\big),
\end{aligned}
$$

and, finally,

$$
f\big(\bar{x}(t)\big)' \big(x^* - x(t+1)\big) \le f\big(\bar{x}(t)\big)' \big(\bar{x}(t) - x(t+1)\big). \tag{5.42}
$$

Since $x(t+1)$ is the projection of $x(t) - \gamma f\big(\bar{x}(t)\big)$ on X and $x^* \in X$ we have, also using Eq. (5.42),

$$
\begin{aligned}
\|x(t+1) - x^*\|_2^2 &\le \|x(t) - \gamma f\big(\bar{x}(t)\big) - x^*\|_2^2 - \|x(t) - \gamma f\big(\bar{x}(t)\big) - x(t+1)\|_2^2 \\
&= \|x(t) - x^*\|_2^2 - \|x(t) - x(t+1)\|_2^2 + 2\gamma f\big(\bar{x}(t)\big)' \big(x^* - x(t+1)\big) \\
&\le \|x(t) - x^*\|_2^2 - \|x(t) - \bar{x}(t)\|_2^2 - \|\bar{x}(t) - x(t+1)\|_2^2 \\
&\quad - 2\big(x(t) - \bar{x}(t)\big)' \big(\bar{x}(t) - x(t+1)\big) + 2\gamma f\big(\bar{x}(t)\big)' \big(\bar{x}(t) - x(t+1)\big)
\end{aligned}
$$

and, finally,

$$
\begin{aligned}
\|x(t+1) - x^*\|_2^2 &\le \|x(t) - x^*\|_2^2 - \|x(t) - \bar{x}(t)\|_2^2 - \|\bar{x}(t) - x(t+1)\|_2^2 \\
&\quad + 2\big(x(t+1) - \bar{x}(t)\big)' \big(x(t) - \gamma f\big(\bar{x}(t)\big) - \bar{x}(t)\big).
\end{aligned} \tag{5.43}
$$

Since $\bar{x}(t)$ is the projection of $x(t) - \gamma f\big(x(t)\big)$ on X and $x(t+1) \in X$ we have, also using the Lipschitz continuity of f,

$$
\begin{aligned}
\big(x(t+1) - \bar{x}(t)\big)' &\big(x(t) - \gamma f\big(\bar{x}(t)\big) - \bar{x}(t)\big) \\
&= \big(x(t+1) - \bar{x}(t)\big)' \big(x(t) - \gamma f\big(x(t)\big) - \bar{x}(t)\big) \\
&\quad + \gamma \big(x(t+1) - \bar{x}(t)\big)' \big(f\big(x(t)\big) - f\big(\bar{x}(t)\big)\big) \\
&\le \gamma \big(x(t+1) - \bar{x}(t)\big)' \big(f\big(x(t)\big) - f\big(\bar{x}(t)\big)\big) \\
&\le \gamma A \|x(t+1) - \bar{x}(t)\|_2 \cdot \|x(t) - \bar{x}(t)\|_2.
\end{aligned} \tag{5.44}
$$

Using inequality (5.44) to strengthen inequality (5.43), we obtain

$$\|x(t+1) - x^*\|_2^2 \le \|x(t) - x^*\|_2^2 - \|x(t) - \bar{x}(t)\|_2^2 - \|\bar{x}(t) - x(t+1)\|_2^2$$

$$+ 2\gamma A\|x(t) - \bar{x}(t)\|_2 \cdot \|\bar{x}(t) - x(t+1)\|_2$$

$$= \|x(t) - x^*\|_2^2 - (1 - \gamma^2 A^2)\|x(t) - \bar{x}(t)\|_2^2$$

$$- \left(\gamma A\|x(t) - \bar{x}(t)\|_2 - \|\bar{x}(t) - x(t+1)\|_2\right)^2$$

$$\le \|x(t) - x^*\|^2 - (1 - \gamma^2 A^2)\|x(t) - \bar{x}(t)\|_2^2.$$

(b) Demonstrate the convergence of the method when applied to the example of Fig. 3.5.3.

5.2. (Separable Constrained Optimization Problems.) Consider the separable, convex constrained optimization problem

$$\text{minimize} \quad \sum_{i=1}^{m} F_i(x_i)$$

$$\text{subject to} \quad a_j' x \le t_j, \quad j = 1, \dots, r,$$

$$x_i \in P_i, \quad i = 1, \dots, m,$$

similar to the one considered in Subsection 3.4.4, where $F_i : \Re^{n_i} \mapsto \Re$ is a convex differentiable function.

(a) Verify that this problem is equivalent to the variational inequality problem of finding $x_i^* \in P_i$ and $u_j^* \ge 0$ such that

$$\sum_{i=1}^{m} \left(\nabla F_i(x_i^*) + \sum_{j=1}^{r} u_j^* a_{ji}\right)' (x_i - x_i^*) + \sum_{j=1}^{r} (t_j - a_j' x^*)(u_j - u_j^*) \ge 0,$$

$$\forall x_i \in P_i, \ u_j \ge 0.$$

(b) Discuss the use of the extragradient method of Exercise 5.1 for solving the problem.

5.3. Consider the problem of finding $x^* \in \Re^n$ such that $x^* \in C_1$, $Ax^* \in C_2$ and

$$f(x^*)'(x - x^*) + G(Ax) - G(Ax^*) \ge 0, \qquad \forall\, x \in C_1 \cap \{\xi \mid A\xi \in C_2\}.$$

Here $G : \Re^m \mapsto \Re$ is a convex function, A is an $m \times n$ matrix, and $C_1 \subset \Re^n$, $C_2 \subset \Re^m$ are nonempty polyhedral sets. Let Assumption 5.1 hold, and consider the algorithm (5.28)–(5.30) except that Eq. (5.29) is replaced by

$$z(t+1) = \arg\min_{z \in C_2} \left\{ G(z) - p(t)'z + \frac{c}{2}\|Ax(t+1) - z\|_2^2 \right\}.$$

Show that a sequence $\{x(t), z(t), p(t)\}$ generated by the algorithm is bounded, and every limit point of $\{x(t)\}$ is a solution of the above inequality.

5.4. Develop an alternating direction method of multipliers for the variational inequality

$$\sum_{i=1}^{m} f_i(x^*)'(x - x^*) \geq 0, \qquad \forall\, x \in \cap_{i=1}^{m} P_i,$$

based on the algorithm (5.24)–(5.26).

NOTES AND SOURCES

3.1. Most of the material in this section is classical; see, e.g., [OrR70] and [Lue69]. Some of the sufficient conditions for contraction mappings (Props. 1.10–1.13) are inspired from related results of [PaC82a].

3.2. Unconstrained optimization algorithms are discussed in many textbooks, e.g., [Avr76], [Ber82a], [DeS83], [GMW81], [KoO68], [Lue84], [OrR70], [Pol71], [Pol87], [Zan69], and [Zou76]. A special type of approximate Newton method, called the *truncated Newton method* and based on the conjugate gradient method is analyzed in [DES82]. An example showing that some form of strict convexity assumption is needed to guarantee convergence of the nonlinear Gauss–Seidel method is given in [Pow73]. Parallel conjugate direction methods for unconstrained optimization are given in [ChM70], [Sut83], [Han86], and [BSS88]. For an overview of parallel optimization methods, see [LoR88] and [MeZ88].

3.3. Many of the above mentioned books on unconstrained optimization also contain discussions of constrained optimization. The gradient projection method was proposed independently in [Gol64] and [LeP65]. For some further developments and analysis see [Ber76a] and [Dun81]. Variants of the gradient projection method that aim at acceleration of its convergence rate while maintaining its simplicity are given in [Ber82b], [BeG83], [Bon83], [GaB84], and [CaM87]. The results on the well–posedness of the nonlinear Jacobi and Gauss–Seidel methods and their global convergence to a minimizing point (Prop. 3.10) appear to be new.

We have not discussed in this section or elsewhere in this book the simplex method for linear programming because this method contains some operations that are difficult to parallelize. In particular each iteration of the simplex method consists of two steps (see e.g. [Dan63], [Chv83], [Lue84]): a) choosing a new basic variable and b) performing a pivot operation. The first of these steps lends itself to parallelization but the second generally does not. While much depends on the parallelization approach used and the structure of the problem solved, parallel versions of the simplex method have produced thus far only limited speedup in computational experiments. For a representative computational study that discusses various approaches see [Pet88].

3.4. The uses of duality in large–scale optimization are discussed in numerous sources, including the books [Las70], [MMT70], [Sin77], and [FBB80], the edited volumes [Wis71] and [HoM76], and the journal special issue [IEE78].

The dual quadratic programming algorithm of Subsection 3.4.1 is given in [Hil57]; for related work see [Lue69], [Cry71], [Man77], [MaD86], and [MaD87]. The given implementation for sparse problems has been used extensively (with some variations) in image processing applications [HLL78], [HeL78], [Cen81], and [CeH87].

Dual methods have been used extensively for the solution of various types of separable problems. An early reference is [Eve63]; see also [Las70], [Wis71], [Geo72], [Las73], [BLT76], and [Lue84]. Nondifferentiable optimization methods (see, e.g., [Pol69], [BaW75], [Sha79], and [Pol87]) have also been popular in this context.

The proximal minimization algorithm was introduced in [Mar70], and was also understood through the studies of its dual equivalent, the method of multipliers. Reference [Ber82a] provides an extensive treatment of the latter method, and contains a large number of references on the subject; see also the survey papers [Ber76b] and [Roc76c]. The finiteness of the method when applied to linear programs was shown independently in [PoT74] and [Ber75]. The method of multipliers has been advocated for linear programs with structure that is unfavorable for the use of the simplex method [Ber76c], [BLS83], [Man84]. An extension of the proximal minimization algorithm for nonconvex problems is given in [Ber79a]; see also [TaM85].

The problem of solving systems of linear inequalities or, more generally, finding a point in the intersection of several convex sets has a long history; see [Cim38], [Agm54], [MoS54], [Bre67], [Tan71], [Aus76], [Jer79], [Elf80], and [Gof80]. References [Spi85a], [Spi87], and [Han88] are similar in spirit to the material in this section.

The alternating direction method of multipliers was proposed in [GlM75] and [GaM76], and was further developed in [Gab79]. It was generalized in [LiM79], where the connection with alternating direction methods for solving differential equations was pointed out. Discussions of the method and its applications in large boundary–value problems are given in [FoG83] and [GlL87]. Related work includes [Gol85b], [Spi85b], [Gol86a], [HaL88], and [RoW87]. An extension which addresses the problem of finding a zero of the sum of monotone operators is given in [Gol87b]. The decomposition algorithms for separable and linear programs of Subsection 3.4.4 (derived with assistance from J. Eckstein) are simpler and involve updating fewer variables than other related algorithms in the literature.

A generalization of the proximal minimization algorithm, called the *proximal point algorithm* was introduced in [Mar70] and [Mar72]. This algorithm applies also to variational inequalities under monotonicity assumptions. An extensive analysis and further development of the algorithm is given in [Roc76a], [Roc76b]. A rate of convergence analysis is given in [Luq84]. Extensions are given in [Luq86a] and [Luq86b]; in the case of the proximal minimization algorithm, these extensions involve the use of a nonquadratic additive term. The proximal point algorithm solves the problem of finding a zero of a maximal monotone operator and contains as special cases all of the algorithms discussed in Subsections 3.4.3 and 3.4.4 together with several other related methods. In particular the proximal minimization algorithm and the method of multipliers are special cases as shown in [Roc76a], [Roc76b]. The method of partial inverses of [Spi85b] was also developed as a special case of the proximal point algorithm. One of the splitting algorithms of [LiM79] contains as special cases both the method of partial inverses and the alternating direction method of Section 3.4.4. It is shown in [Eck88] that the proximal point algorithm contains as a special case the algorithm of [LiM79] and *a fortiori* the alternating direction method. Therefore a substantial amount of analysis can be shared by all of the methods mentioned above. As an example, we could use known results on the proximal point algorithm to obtain a more elegant and insightful convergence analysis for the alternating direction method of multipliers than the one we gave here. We have not pursued this analysis because of its advanced mathematical character.

As mentioned in Subsection 3.4.4, the quadratic term used in the method of multipliers tends to affect adversely the separability structure of the problem. The alternating direction method can be viewed as one way of coping with this difficulty for some separable problems. A different approach, which also lends itself well to parallelization, was introduced in [StW75], and was further developed in [Sto77], [WNM78], and [CoZ83]; see also [Coh78].

3.5. For more background on variational inequalities, see [Aus76], [KiS80], and [GLT81]. Methods for solving the traffic assignment problem are given in [AaM81], [BeG82], [BeG83], [CaG74], [Daf71], [Daf80], [FlN74], [HLN84], [HLV87], and [LaH84]. The projection method for variational inequalities satisfying the strong monotonicity assumption of Prop. 5.4 was proposed in [Sib70]. This assumption was relaxed somewhat in [BeG82]. The extragradient method of [Kor76] (see Exercise 5.1) bypasses altogether the need for strong monotonicity, and is therefore applicable to linear programs (see Exercise 5.2). A general class of algorithms, generalizing the projection method has been introduced and analyzed in [Daf83]. The results concerning the product set case and nonlinear algorithms are adapted from [PaC82a], [PaC82b], and [Pan85], although the derivations here, using the general theory of contraction mappings, are different. The alternating direction method for variational inequalities was proposed in [Gab79]; see also [Gab83].

4

Shortest Paths and Dynamic Programming

The shortest path problem is a classical and important combinatorial problem that arises in many contexts. We are given a directed graph and a cost or "length" a_{ij} for each arc (i, j). The length of a path $(i, i_1, i_2, \ldots, i_k, 1)$ from node i to node 1 with arcs $(i, i_1), (i_1, i_2), \ldots, (i_{k-1}, i_k), (i_k, 1)$ is defined to be the sum of the arc lengths $\left(a_{ii_1} + a_{i_1 i_2} + \cdots + a_{i_{k-1} i_k} + a_{i_k 1}\right)$. The problem is to find a path of minimum length (or shortest path) from each node i to node 1.

There are many applications of the shortest path problem. One example, of particular relevance to distributed computation, arises in the context of routing data within a computer communication network. Here the length a_{ij} represents a measure of cost (such as average delay) for crossing link (i, j). Thus, a shortest path is a minimum cost path and can be viewed as a desirable path for routing data. An interesting feature here is that the communication network defines the graph of the shortest path problem, and each node is a processor that can participate in the numerical solution.

Shortest path applications arise also in other types of routing problems, involving, for example, the flow of vehicles, materials, etc. Other examples include problems of heuristic search, and deterministic optimal control problems, where the trajectory of a dynamic system is to be optimized over a given time interval [Ber87]. Here the number of nodes is often very large, and parallel computation may be required to reduce the computation time to an acceptable level.

Finally, the shortest path problem frequently arises as a subroutine in algorithms for solving other, more complicated problems. In this context, the shortest path subroutine may have to be called many times, so its fast parallel execution can be critical for the success of the overall algorithm.

The shortest path problem formulation is a special case of a more general modeling technique known as dynamic programming, which deals with the issue of making optimal decisions sequentially. Each decision results in a cost, but also affects the options of subsequent decisions, so the objective is to strike a balance between incurring a low cost for the present decision and avoiding future situations where high costs are inevitable. We can also view the shortest path problem as a problem of sequential decision making. Starting at node i, the first decision is to select an incident arc (i, i_1) of node i, then to select an arc (i_1, i_2), and so on until the destination node is reached through a final arc $(i_k, 1)$. In the first decision one must balance the desire to select an arc (i, j) with small length a_{ij} with the desire to avoid going to a node j that is "far" from the destination. This tradeoff is captured in the equation

$$x_i^* = \min_j(a_{ij} + x_j^*), \qquad i = 2, \ldots, n,$$

$$x_1^* = 0,$$

which, as we shall see, is satisfied by the shortest path lengths x_i^*, $i = 1, \ldots, n$. The dynamic programming algorithm for the shortest path problem has the form

$$x_i := \min_j(a_{ij} + x_j), \qquad i = 2, \ldots, n,$$

$$x_1 := 0,$$

which is reminiscent of the relaxation methods of Chapters 2 and 3. This algorithm is particularly well suited for parallel or distributed implementation since the minimization over j in the previous equation can be carried out in parallel for all nodes $i \neq 1$. Its convergence to the shortest path lengths will be shown in Subsection 4.1.1 for a broad range of initial conditions. In Subsection 4.1.2, we will analyze the complexity of other shortest path methods that are well suited for distributed implementation, and we will compare them with the preceding algorithm.

In this chapter, we will also discuss dynamic programming problems that are more general than the shortest path problem in that, once a decision is selected at a given node, the next node is not predictable, but rather is chosen according to a known probability distribution that depends on the selected decision. This leads to a model involving a finite–state Markov chain, the transition probabilities of which are influenced by the choice of decision. We first consider this model in Section 4.2 for the simpler case where there are no decisions to be made or, equivalently, the transition probabilities are independent of the decision. We then consider the effect of decisions in Section 4.3. Much of our dynamic programming analysis is based on a monotonicity property of the mapping underlying the dynamic programming algorithm [Prop. 3.1(a) in Section

4.3]. Under additional conditions, this mapping is also a contraction with respect to a maximum norm [Prop. 3.1(c) and Exercise 3.3]. We use these two properties to show convergence of the algorithm to the correct solution. In Chapter 6, we show that these properties also guarantee convergence in a totally asynchronous distributed environment.

4.1 THE SHORTEST PATH PROBLEM

The shortest path problem is defined in terms of a directed graph consisting of n nodes, which are numbered $1, \ldots, n$. We denote by $A(i)$ the set of all nodes j for which there is an outgoing arc (i, j) from node i. Node 1 is a special node called the *destination*. We assume that $A(1)$ is empty, that is, the destination has no outgoing arcs. We are given a scalar a_{ij} for each arc (i, j), which we call the length of (i, j). We define the *length* of a path $\{(i, i_1), (i_1, i_2), \ldots, (i_k, j)\}$ starting from node i and ending at node j to be the sum of the lengths of its arcs $(a_{ii_1} + a_{i_1 i_2} + \cdots + a_{i_k j})$. The problem is to find a path of minimum length (or shortest path) from each node i to the destination. Note here that we are optimizing over paths consisting exclusively of forward arcs (such paths are called positive; see Appendix B). When we refer to a path or a cycle in connection with the shortest path problem, we implicitly assume that it is positive. We assume the following:

> **Assumption 1.1.** (*Connectivity*) There exists a path from every node $i = 2, \ldots, n$ to the destination node 1.

> **Assumption 1.2.** (*Positive Cycle*) Every cycle has positive length.

We will show that the shortest path lengths x_i^*, $i = 1, \ldots, n$, also called *shortest distances*, are the unique solution of the system

$$x_i^* = \min_{j \in A(i)} (a_{ij} + x_j^*), \qquad i = 2, \ldots, n, \tag{1.1a}$$

$$x_1^* = 0 \tag{1.1b}$$

(known as *Bellman's equation*). Furthermore, we will show that the iteration

$$x_i := \min_{j \in A(i)} (a_{ij} + x_j), \qquad i = 2, \ldots, n, \tag{1.2a}$$

$$x_1 := 0 \tag{1.2b}$$

(also known as the *Bellman–Ford algorithm*) converges to this solution for an arbitrary initial vector x with $x_1 = 0$.

Note that the Bellman–Ford algorithm is particularly well suited for parallel and distributed implementations since the iteration for each node i can be carried out simultaneously with the iteration for every other node. The version of the Bellman–Ford algorithm that we will focus on in this section can be viewed as a Jacobi relaxation method for solving the system of n nonlinear equations with n unknowns specified by Bellman's equation (1.1). There is also a Gauss–Seidel version, which is considered in Exercise 1.2, and can be viewed as a coordinate ascent method in the context of a dual network optimization problem (see Subsection 5.2.1). A totally asynchronous implementation of the Bellman–Ford algorithm will be discussed in Section 6.4.

One possible set of initial conditions in the Bellman–Ford algorithm is $x_i = \infty$ for $i \neq 1$ and $x_1 = 0$; this is the choice most often discussed in the literature. Indeed, in the absence of additional information, this is a good choice, and results in polynomially bounded running time for the algorithm, as will be shown shortly. Our interest in arbitrary initial conditions stems from certain applications where the shortest path problem must be solved repeatedly and in real time, as the arc lengths change by small increments. A small change in the arc lengths implies a small change in the shortest path lengths, so it may be advantageous in terms of speed of convergence to restart the Bellman–Ford algorithm using as initial conditions the previous shortest path lengths (or approximations thereof). Another advantage of this approach in a distributed implementation is that it does not require a potentially complex and time–consuming restart/resynchronization procedure to inform all the processors of the change in problem data and to restart the algorithm with a predetermined set of initial conditions. In this context, the processors of the distributed system can simply incorporate the changes of the arc lengths in their iterations at the time that they become aware of them. In other words, the processors keep on executing their portion of the iteration (1.2) using the latest information available regarding the values of the arc lengths. Naturally, in order for this scheme to be workable, the arc lengths should not change too frequently relative to the speed of convergence of the Bellman–Ford algorithm. For further discussion of this type of algorithm in the context of routing data in a communication network, we refer the reader to Subsection 5.2.4 of [BeG87].

4.1.1 The Bellman–Ford Algorithm

The kth iteration of the Bellman–Ford algorithm has the form

$$x_i^k = \min_{j \in A(i)} (a_{ij} + x_j^{k-1}), \qquad i = 2, \ldots, n, \tag{1.3a}$$

$$x_1^k = 0. \tag{1.3b}$$

Regarding initial conditions, we assume that $x_1^0 = 0$, and that for $i = 2, \ldots, n$, x_i^0 is either a real number or $+\infty$. We say that the algorithm *terminates after k iterations* if $x_i^k = x_i^{k-1}$ for all i.

Given nodes $i \neq 1$ and $j \neq 1$, we define

$$w_{ij}^k = \text{minimum path length over all paths from } i \text{ to } j,$$
$$\text{and having } k \text{ arcs } (w_{ij}^k = \infty \text{ if there is no such path}). \tag{1.4}$$

To complete the definition of w_{ij}^k, we define for all $i \neq 1$

$$w_{i1}^k = \text{minimum path length over all paths from } i \text{ to } 1 \text{ having } k \text{ arcs or less}$$
$$(w_{i1}^k = \infty \text{ if there is no such path}). \tag{1.5}$$

Note that the path of minimum length in the definition of w_{ij}^k can contain cycles; this will certainly happen if $j \neq 1$ and $k \geq n - 1$.

The following lemma is very useful:

Lemma 1.1.   There holds

$$x_i^k = \min_{j=1,\dots,n} (w_{ij}^k + x_j^0), \qquad \forall\, i = 2,\dots,n, \text{ and } k \geq 1. \tag{1.6}$$

Proof. We use induction. By the definitions of x_i^1 and w_{ij}^1 [Eqs. (1.3)–(1.5)], the result holds for $k = 1$. Assume that it holds for some $k \geq 1$. For any nodes $i \neq 1$ and j, let us denote by P_{ij}^k the set of paths appearing in the definition of w_{ij}^k [Eqs. (1.4)–(1.5)]. We have, using the convention $a_{i1} = \infty$ if $1 \notin A(i)$,

$$\min_{j=1,\dots,n} \left(w_{ij}^{k+1} + x_j^0 \right) = \min_{\substack{(i,i_1,\dots,i_m,j)\in P_{ij}^{k+1} \\ j=1,\dots,n}} \left(a_{ii_1} + a_{i_1 i_2} + \cdots + a_{i_m j} + x_j^0 \right)$$

$$= \min \left(a_{i1}, \min_{i_1 \in A(i), i_1 \neq 1} \left(a_{ii_1} + \min_{\substack{(i_1,i_2,\dots,i_m,j)\in P_{i_1 j}^k \\ j=1,\dots,n}} \left(a_{i_1 i_2} + \cdots + a_{i_m j} + x_j^0 \right) \right) \right)$$

$$= \min \left(a_{i1}, \min_{i_1 \in A(i), i_1 \neq 1} \left(a_{ii_1} + \min_{j=1,\dots,n} \left(w_{i_1 j}^k + x_j^0 \right) \right) \right)$$

$$= \min_{i_1 \in A(i)} \left(a_{ii_1} + x_{i_1}^k \right)$$

$$= x_i^{k+1}, \tag{1.7}$$

where we used the induction hypothesis to establish the next to last equality. The induction is complete.   **Q.E.D.**

The preceding lemma yields the following result:

Proposition 1.1.   Let the Connectivity and Positive Cycle Assumptions 1.1 and 1.2 hold:

(a) There exists a shortest path from every node $i \neq 1$ to node 1. Furthermore, every one of these shortest paths has at most $n - 1$ arcs.

(b) For any set of initial conditions, the Bellman–Ford algorithm terminates after some finite number k of iterations, with x_i^k equal to the shortest distances x_i^*, $i = 1, \ldots, n$.

(c) If $x_i^0 \geq x_i^*$ for all $i \neq 1$, then the Bellman–Ford algorithm yields the shortest distances in at most m^* iterations, and terminates after at most $m^* + 1$ iterations, where

$$m^* = \max_{i=2,\ldots,n} m_i \leq n - 1, \tag{1.8}$$

and m_i is the smallest number of arcs contained in a shortest path from i to 1.

(d) The shortest distances x_i^*, $i = 1, \ldots, n$, are the unique solution of Bellman's equation (1.1).

Proof.

(a) A path from a node $i \neq 1$ to node 1 containing more than $n - 1$ arcs must contain one or more cycles, which, by the Positive Cycle Assumption 1.2, have positive length. By deleting the cycles from the path, we can obtain a shorter path with no more than $n - 1$ arcs. Therefore, only paths with $n - 1$ or less arcs are candidates for optimality. By the Connectivity Assumption 1.1, there exists at least one path having $n - 1$ or less arcs, and there is a finite number of such paths. Therefore, there must exist a shortest path.

(b) Since all cycles have positive length, we have for all $i \neq 1$ and $j \neq 1$, $w_{ij}^k \to \infty$ as $k \to \infty$, and $w_{i1}^k = x_i^* < \infty$ for all $k \geq n - 1$. From Lemma 1.1 [cf. Eq. (1.6)], it follows that $x_i^k = x_i^*$ for all sufficiently large k.

(c) Consider first the initial conditions $x_i^0 = \infty$, for all $i \neq 1$. Then from Lemma 1.1 we see that, for each $i \neq 1$ and k, x_i^k is the shortest distance from i to 1 using paths with k arcs or less. Hence $x_i^k = x_i^*$ for all i and $k \geq m^*$. Consider next any set of initial conditions with $x_i^* \leq x_i^0$ for all $i \neq 1$. From part (b) we have that the shortest distances x_i^* solve Bellman's equations. Therefore

$$x_i^* = \min_{j \in A(i)} (a_{ij} + x_j^*) \leq \min_{j \in A(i)} (a_{ij} + x_j^0) = x_i^1, \qquad \forall\, i = 2, \ldots, n,$$

and by repeating this argument, we obtain

$$x_i^* \leq x_i^k, \qquad \forall\, i \text{ and } k.$$

Let $\tilde{x}_i^k$ be the iterates of the Bellman–Ford algorithm, starting from the initial conditions $\tilde{x}_i^0 = \infty$, $i = 2, \ldots, n$. We have, using a similar argument as before,

$$x_i^* \leq x_i^k \leq \tilde{x}_i^k, \qquad \forall\, i \text{ and } k.$$

Since, as shown earlier, we have $\tilde{x}_i^k = x_i^*$ for all i and $k \geq m^*$, the desired conclusion follows.

(d) If we start the Bellman–Ford algorithm with a solution of Bellman's equation, we terminate after a single iteration, so by part (b), this solution must equal the shortest distances. **Q.E.D.**

Figure 4.1.1 gives an example showing how Prop. 1.1 fails if the cycle lengths are assumed nonnegative instead of positive.

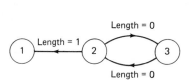

Length = 1
Length = 0
Length = 0

Figure 4.1.1 Shortest path problem involving a cycle of zero length. Here the shortest distances are $x_1^* = 0$, $x_2^* = x_3^* = 1$ and satisfy Bellman's equation. The zero vector also satisfies Bellman's equation, and if the Bellman–Ford algorithm is started with that vector, it will make no progress toward the shortest distance vector.

When the Bellman–Ford algorithm does not terminate, and the Connectivity Assumption 1.1 is known to hold, it follows from Prop. 1.1 that the Positive Cycle Assumption 1.2 is violated, and there exists a cycle with nonpositive length. If all cycle lengths are assumed nonnegative (rather than positive), then it is clear that there exist shortest paths with $n - 1$ arcs or less from every $i \neq 1$ to the destination. Lemma 1.1 then implies that the algorithm finds the shortest distances in $n - 1$ steps or less when the initial conditions

$$x_i^0 = \infty, \qquad \forall \, i \neq 1 \tag{1.9}$$

are used. If there is a cycle of negative length, then for the same initial conditions, we will have $x_i^n < x_i^{n-1}$ for some $i \neq 1$ (Exercise 1.1), and this can be used to detect the presence of a negative length cycle.

Generally, the number of iterations for termination depends strongly on the initial conditions. This number is $m^* + 1$ when the initial conditions $x_i^0 = \infty$, $i \neq 1$, are used, as shown in Prop. 1.1. For other initial conditions, this number can be much larger, and may depend on the size of the arc lengths (see Fig. 4.1.2). It appears plausible that the number of iterations will often be smaller than m^* if the initial conditions x_i^0 are chosen to be close to their eventual final values x_i^*. A typical situation occurs when the initial conditions are the shortest distances corresponding to arc lengths that either differ slightly from the arc lengths of the problem at hand or else are the same except for a few relatively inconsequential arcs. The following analysis is geared toward estimating the number of iterations for initial conditions of this type. Simple examples show that even if a single arc length changes by a small amount, it is possible that the number of iterations required is as large as $n - 1$. In special cases, however, the number is much smaller (see e.g. Exercise 1.4). The following proposition estimates the number of iterations in terms of the scalars

$$\beta = \max_{i=2,\dots,n} (x_i^* - x_i^0), \tag{1.10}$$

$$L = \min_{\text{All cycles}} \frac{\text{Length of the cycle}}{\text{Number of arcs on the cycle}}. \tag{1.11}$$

The scalar L of Eq. (1.11) is defined only for graphs that contain at least one cycle, and is known as the *minimum cycle mean*. Algorithms for computing L are considered in [Law67] and [Kar78].

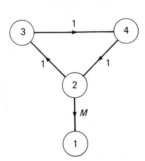

Figure 4.1.2 Example shortest path problem where the number of iterations of the Bellman–Ford algorithm depends on the size of the arc lengths. Here arcs (2,3), (3,4), and (4,2) have length 1, and arc (2,1) has a large length M. If initially $x_i^0 = 0$ for all i then, for all $k \le M$, after k iterations we have

$$x_i^k = k, \quad i = 2, 3, 4,$$

$$x_1^k = 0,$$

so the algorithm terminates after $M + 3$ iterations. By contrast, $m^* = 3$, and only 4 iterations are needed for the initial condition $x_i^0 = \infty$, $i = 2, 3, 4$. Similarly, the number of iterations is $\Theta(M)$ when the initial conditions are the shortest distances corresponding to unity length for all arcs. Therefore a large, length–dependent number of iterations may be necessary to recompute the shortest distances following a length increase of a single arc lying on a shortest path.

Proposition 1.2. Let the Connectivity and Positive Cycle Assumptions 1.1 and 1.2 hold. The Bellman–Ford algorithm terminates after at most $\bar{k} + 1$ iterations ($x_i^k = x_i^*$ for all i and $k \ge \bar{k}$), where

$$\bar{k} = \begin{cases} m^*, & \text{if } \beta \le 0, \\ n - 1, & \text{if } \beta > 0 \text{ and the graph is acyclic,} \\ n - 2 + \lceil \beta/L \rceil, & \text{if } \beta > 0 \text{ and the graph has cycles,} \end{cases} \tag{1.12}$$

m^* is given by

$$m^* = \max_{i=2,\dots,n} m_i \le n - 1, \tag{1.13}$$

and m_i is the smallest number of arcs contained in a shortest path from i to 1.

Proof. If $\beta \le 0$, then $\bar{k} = m^*$ and the result has already been proved in Prop. 1.1(c). Assume $\beta > 0$ and suppose that, for some $k \ge m^*$, the algorithm has not found the shortest distances after k iterations, i.e., $x_i^* \ne x_i^k$ for some i. Since $w_{i1}^k = x_i^*$ for $k \ge m^*$, by Lemma 1.1 we must have $x_i^* \ge x_i^k$ for all i, and furthermore, for some i, and $j \ne 1$, we must have

$$x_i^* > x_i^k = w_{ij}^k + x_j^0.$$

Consider a minimum length path from i to j involved in the definition of w_{ij}^k. This path has k arcs, it does not pass through node 1, and either it contains no cycles, or else it can be decomposed into a simple path from i to j with length L_{ij}, and a nonempty collection of cycles with total length $w_{ij}^k - L_{ij}$ (see the Path Decomposition Theorem of Appendix B). In the former case we obtain $k < n - 1$. In the latter case we argue as follows: since the number of arcs in the simple path is no more than $n - 2$, the number of arcs in the cycles is no less than $k - (n - 2)$, and therefore

$$w_{ij}^k - L_{ij} \geq \left[k - (n - 2)\right]L,$$

where L is given by Eq. (1.11). It follows that

$$x_i^* > x_i^k = w_{ij}^k + x_j^0 \geq L_{ij} + x_j^0 + \left[k - (n - 2)\right]L.$$

Using the relations $x_j^0 \geq x_j^* - \beta$ and $L_{ij} + x_j^* \geq x_i^*$, we obtain

$$x_i^* > L_{ij} + x_j^* - \beta + \left[k - (n - 2)\right]L \geq x_i^* - \beta + \left[k - (n - 2)\right]L.$$

Therefore, $k < \max\{n - 1, n - 2 + \lceil \beta/L \rceil\} = n - 2 + \lceil \beta/L \rceil$. Thus we have shown that if $\beta > 0$ and the algorithm has not found the shortest distances at iteration k, then either $k < n - 1$ (if the graph is acyclic) or $k < n - 2 + \lceil \beta/L \rceil$ (if the graph has cycles). This completes the proof.   **Q.E.D.**

Figure 4.1.3 shows that the estimate of Prop. 1.2 on the number of iterations is tight in the case of a graph with cycles. To show that the estimate is tight for acyclic graphs, consider the graph with arcs $(i + 1, i)$, $i = 1, \ldots, n - 1$, and $(n, 1)$. Let $a_{(i+1)i} = 1$, let $a_{n1} = n - (3/2)$, and consider the algorithm with zero initial conditions. A straightforward calculation shows that the algorithm finds the shortest distances after $n - 1$ iterations while $m^* = n - 2$.

From Prop. 1.2, it is seen that the number of iterations is guaranteed to be relatively small if the initial conditions x_i^0 are not much smaller than the true shortest distances x_i^*. If x_i^0 is much smaller than x_i^* for some i, we may ignore the given initial conditions, and start the algorithm from the infinite initial conditions of Eq. (1.9), thereby guaranteeing termination in $m^* + 1$ iterations. A related procedure which changes selectively some of the initial conditions is given in Exercise 1.4.

Timing Analysis of the Bellman–Ford Algorithm

It can be seen that each iteration of the Bellman–Ford algorithm involves $O(|A|)$ additions and comparisons, where $|A|$ is the number of arcs. Hence, for the initial conditions $x_i^0 = \infty$, $i \neq 1$, the serial solution time for the problem is $O(m^*|A|)$. For other initial conditions, the solution time is $O(\bar{k}|A|)$ where $\bar{k}$ is the estimate on the number of iterations given by Eq. (1.12).

We consider now two types of synchronous parallel implementations of the Bellman–Ford algorithm. In the first type, we have a distributed system involving an interconnection network of n processors that is identical with the graph of the shortest path

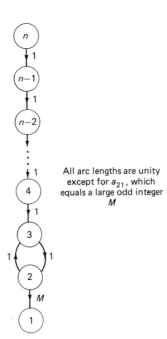

All arc lengths are unity except for a_{21}, which equals a large odd integer M

Figure 4.1.3 Example shortest path problem showing that the estimate of Prop. 1.2 on the number of iterations of the Bellman–Ford algorithm is tight. Here all arcs have unity length except for (2,1) which has length equal to the positive *odd* integer M. The initial conditions are

$$x_i^0 = \max\{0, i - 2\}, \qquad i = 1, \ldots, n.$$

The generated sequence of iterates for nodes 2 and 3 are

$$\{x_2^k\} = \{0, 2, 2, 4, 4, \ldots,$$

$$2\lfloor M/2 \rfloor, 2\lfloor M/2 \rfloor, M, M, \ldots\},$$

$$\{x_3^k\} = \{0, 1, 3, 3, 5, \ldots, 2\lfloor M/2 \rfloor - 1,$$

$$2\lfloor M/2 \rfloor + 1, 2\lfloor M/2 \rfloor + 1,$$

$$M + 1, \ldots\}.$$

For $i \geq 2$ the shortest distance $x_i^* = i - 2 + M$ is found in $i - 2 + M$ iterations. At iteration $n - 2 + M$ all shortest distances have been obtained. In this problem $\beta = M$, $L = 1$, so the estimate of Prop. 1.2 is tight.

problem in the sense that for every arc (i, j) of the latter problem, there is a bidirectional communication link connecting processors i and j. An iteration consists of the update

$$x_i := \min_{j \in A(i)} (a_{ij} + x_j), \tag{1.14}$$

at each processor $i \neq 1$, followed by a transmission of the result to the neighbor processors j with $i \in A(j)$. It is clear then that the time per iteration is $O(r)$, where r is the maximum number of outgoing arcs from a node in the graph, that is,

$$r = \max_{i \neq 1} |A(i)|. \tag{1.15}$$

Note that if each processor itself consists of a parallel computing system with r processors, then the time per iteration becomes $O(\log r)$, assuming negligible communication delays. It is natural to synchronize this implementation using the local synchronization method, whereby a processor can proceed to the next iteration once it receives the results of the previous iteration from its neighboring processors. It is still necessary for each processor to send its shortest distance estimate to all its neighbors at the end of every iteration, even if this estimate has not changed over the previous iteration. This can be wasteful both in terms of time and in terms of communication resources. In Section

6.4, we will see that it is advantageous in this respect to use an asynchronous version of the Bellman–Ford algorithm, where shortest distance estimates are transmitted only when they change values, and processors do not have to wait for messages from all their neighbors before updating their estimate of shortest distance.

The second type of synchronous parallel implementation involves the use of a regular interconnection network of processors such as a hypercube. The situation here is quite similar as for the matrix–vector type of calculations discussed in Subsection 1.3.6. This becomes evident when we compare the term

$$\min_{j \in A(i)} (a_{ij} + x_j) \tag{1.16}$$

in the Bellman–Ford iteration, with the ith coordinate of the product Ax

$$[Ax]_i = \sum_{j \in A(i)} a_{ij} x_j, \tag{1.17}$$

where A is the matrix with entries a_{ij} for $j \in A(i)$ and 0 for $j \notin A(i)$. The difference is that addition and minimization in the Bellman–Ford iteration term (1.16) are replaced by multiplication and summation, respectively, in the matrix–vector product term (1.17). Thus the computational requirements for a single Bellman–Ford iteration are essentially identical with those for the matrix–vector product Ax. The algorithms and results of Subsection 1.3.6 apply except for the fact that in that subsection, we assumed that A is a fully dense matrix, whereas here A has a sparsity structure determined by the neighbor node sets $A(i)$.

Assume first that we have a system of p processors, with p less than or equal to the number of nodes n, and for simplicity assume that n is divisible by p. It is then natural to let the jth processor update the distance estimates of nodes $(j - 1)k + 1$ through jk, where $k = n/p$. Let us assume that the jth processor holds the vector x and the lengths a_{ij} for all $j \in A(i)$, and $i = (j - 1)k + 1$ through $i = jk$. Then the updating of the corresponding coordinates of x according to the Bellman–Ford iteration takes time $O(kr) = O(nr/p)$ for each processor, where $r = \max_{i \neq 1} |A(i)|$ [cf. Eq. (1.15)]. To communicate the results of the updating to the other processors, a multinode broadcast of packets, each containing k numbers, is necessary. If a linear array is used for communication, the results of Subsection 1.3.4 show that the multinode broadcast takes $O(kp) = O(n)$ time. The total time per iteration is then $O\big(\max(n, nr/p)\big)$. If instead a hypercube with p processors is used, the multinode broadcast time becomes $O(n/\log p)$, and the total time per iteration becomes $O\big(\max(n/\log p, nr/p)\big)$. Note that as the maximum number of outgoing arcs r becomes larger, the ratio of computation to communication time increases, and the communication penalty becomes less significant. This means that as r becomes larger, more processors can be fruitfully employed to solve the problem without incurring prohibitive delays due to communications, thereby resulting in higher speedup.

Assume now that a hypercube with n^2 processors arranged in an $n \times n$ array is available, where n is a power of 2. Assume also that at the beginning of each iteration, each processor (i, j), with $j \in A(i)$, holds x_j and a_{ij}. Then, based on the relationship of the Bellman–Ford iteration with the matrix–vector multiplication described previously, the $O(\log n)$ algorithm for matrix–vector multiplication of Fig. 1.3.26 in Subsection 1.3.6 applies.

We have considered so far a single destination. In the all–pairs version of the problem, we want to find a shortest path from every node to every other node. For this purpose we can apply the Bellman–Ford algorithm separately for each destination. Suppose that p processors ($p \leq n$) are available and assume for simplicity that n is divisible by p. Then we can assign n/p destinations to each processor and apply the (serial) Bellman–Ford algorithm for each of these destinations. This requires $O(|A|n/p)$ time per iteration. (We ignore here the possibility that the shortest distances corresponding to one destination may provide useful information about the shortest distances corresponding to other destinations [FNP81].)

Suppose next that a mesh of n^2 processors is available. The mesh can emulate n independent linear arrays, each having n processors. We can use each of these arrays to solve in parallel a different single destination shortest path problem, in time $O(n)$ per iteration (based on the linear array result given earlier for $p = n$). It is similarly seen that based on the single destination results for a hypercube with $p = n$ and $p = n^2$ given earlier, we can solve the all–pairs problem in $O\big(\max(n/\log n, r)\big)$ time per iteration using a hypercube with $p = n^2$ processors, and in $O(\log n)$ time per iteration using a hypercube with $p = n^3$ processors.

To obtain upper bounds on the running time of the Bellman–Ford algorithm, we should multiply the times per iteration given above with the number of required iterations for termination. This number is $m^* + 1$ for the case of the initial conditions $x_i = \infty$, $i \neq 1$, where m^* is the maximum number of arcs in a shortest path [cf. Prop. 1.1(c)]. In practice, m^* is often much smaller than its upper bound $n - 1$, so one cannot accurately predict the running time for the algorithm without additional knowledge about the problem at hand. In the next subsection, we describe several other algorithms for the all–pairs problem, and we compare them with the Bellman–Ford method.

4.1.2 Other Parallel Shortest Path Methods

Consider the all–pairs shortest path problem where we want to find a shortest path from each node to each other node. We first consider the possibility of assigning a processor to each destination and applying a good serial algorithm to the corresponding single destination problem. Thus, if T_S is the serial time complexity of the single destination algorithm, we obtain a T_S time complexity with n processors, assuming the required problem data are available at each processor. When all arc lengths are nonnegative, we can use Dijkstra's method; this is a popular method for solving the single destination shortest path problem with nonnegative arc lengths (see, e.g., [PaS82]). There are implementations of this method that take time $O(|A| + n \log n)$ (see [FrT84]). For problems where some of the arc lengths are negative, a preprocessing phase is required to transform the problem into a shortest path problem with nonnegative arc lengths. This can be done by replacing a_{ij} with

$$a'_{ij} = a_{ij} + p_j - p_i$$

where p_i is a set of numbers such that $a'_{ij} \geq 0$ (see Exercise 1.3). Finding such a set of numbers is equivalent to solving an assignment problem (see Exercise 1.3 in Section 5.1), and can be done in $O\left(n^{1/2}|A|\log(nC)\right)$ time, where $C = \max_{(i,j)}|a_{ij}|$ and the lengths a_{ij} are assumed integer (see [GaT87] and Exercise 4.5 in Section 5.4). Note that to execute the algorithm, a processor must know the lengths of all arcs, whereas in the Bellman–Ford algorithm, it requires only the lengths of its incident arcs. To broadcast all arc lengths from some node to all other nodes over an optimally chosen spanning tree takes $O(d + |A|) = O(|A|)$ time (by sending each arc length in a separate packet and pipelining the packets, cf. Exercise 3.19 in Section 1.3), where d is the diameter of the interconnection network. Hence, the communication time is of order that is comparable to the order of the computation time. Thus, the time to solve the all–pairs shortest path problem using Dijkstra's method and a network of n processors, each handling a different destination, is $O(|A|+n\log n)$ if all arc lengths are nonnegative, and $O\left(n^{1/2}|A|\log(nC)\right)$ otherwise. The timing estimate obtained earlier for the Bellman–Ford algorithm using n processors is $O(m^*|A|)$, so it is seen that the preceding estimate for Dijkstra's method is superior when all arc lengths are nonnegative; the situation is less clear when some arc lengths are negative.

We now discuss two algorithms that are specially designed for the all–pairs problem, and have a worst case serial running time which is better than the one of the Bellman–Ford method. These algorithms are not any faster when applied to the single destination problem, and are better suited for dense rather than sparse graphs, as they cannot take advantage of sparsity. By contrast, the serial version of the Bellman–Ford algorithm is speeded up by a factor of n when applied to the single destination problem, and it is also speeded up when the graph is sparse. Furthermore, the Bellman–Ford algorithm has an additional advantage in that it is naturally suited to distributed systems where the processor interconnection network coincides with the graph of the problem, and it also admits an asynchronous implementation (see Section 6.4).

In the following complexity analysis, we consider a message–passing system and we assume that the transmission times of all packets along any link of the processor interconnection network are the same, and are also nonnegligible. Furthermore, we assume that each processor can compute, and simultaneously transmit and receive on all its incident links. The Connectivity and Positive Cycle Assumptions 1.1 and 1.2 are in effect for each destination, but we relax the assumption that a destination node has no outgoing arcs.

The *Floyd–Warshall* algorithm starts with the initial condition

$$x_{ij}^0 = \begin{cases} a_{ij}, & \text{if } j \in A(i), \\ \infty, & \text{otherwise,} \end{cases}$$

and generates sequentially for all $k = 0, 1, \ldots, n-1$, and all nodes i and j

$$x_{ij}^{k+1} = \begin{cases} \min\left\{ x_{ij}^k, \ x_{i(k+1)}^k + x_{(k+1)j}^k \right\}, & \text{if } j \neq i, \\ \infty, & \text{otherwise.} \end{cases}$$

An induction argument shows that x_{ij}^k gives the shortest distance from node i to node j using only nodes from 1 to k as intermediate nodes. The serial solution time is $O(n^3)$, which is superior to the corresponding estimate $O(nm^*|A|)$ for the Bellman–Ford algorithm when the graph is dense.

A parallel implementation of a single iteration of the Floyd–Warshall algorithm on a hypercube with n^2 processors can be shown to take $O(\log n)$ time (see Exercise 1.6). Therefore, if the iterations are synchronized using the global synchronization method (i.e., no processor starts a new iteration before all processors complete the previous iteration and the results of the iteration are communicated to the relevant processors, cf. Subsection 1.4.1), the total time for the n iterations is $O(n \log n)$. This is slower by a factor of $\log n$ over the bound $O(n)$ for the time taken by the algorithm when all communication is instantaneous. On the other hand, it is possible to implement the Floyd–Warshall algorithm on a square mesh of n^2 processors (and *a fortiori* on a hypercube of n^2 processors) using the local synchronization method, whereby each processor executes an iteration once it receives all the necessary information (cf. Subsection 1.4.1). This implementation is described in Exercise 1.7 and takes $O(n)$ time to solve the all–pairs problem, which is the same order of time as when communication is instantaneous.

The *doubling algorithm* is given by

$$x_{ij}^1 = \begin{cases} a_{ij}, & \text{if } j \in A(i), \\ 0, & \text{if } i = j, \\ \infty, & \text{otherwise,} \end{cases}$$

$$x_{ij}^{k+1} = \begin{cases} \min_m \{ x_{im}^k + x_{mj}^k \}, & \text{if } i \neq j, \ k = 1, 2, \ldots, \lceil \log(n-1) \rceil, \\ 0, & \text{if } i = j, \ k = 1, 2, \ldots, \lceil \log(n-1) \rceil. \end{cases}$$

An induction argument shows that for $i \neq j$, x_{ij}^k gives the shortest distance from i to j using paths with 2^{k-1} arcs or less. A serial implementation takes $O(n^3 \log m^*)$ time, where m^* is the maximum number of arcs in a shortest path over all shortest paths [cf. Eq. (1.8)]. This is inferior to the serial running time of the Floyd–Warshall algorithm, and roughly comparable to that of the Bellman–Ford algorithm when the graph is dense and m^* is small.

Regarding a synchronous parallel implementation of the doubling algorithm, we observe that each iteration has the same structure as the multiplication of two $n \times n$ matrices (the multiplications and additions of matrix multiplication are replaced by additions and minimizations, respectively, in the doubling algorithm iteration). Therefore, the types of algorithms for matrix–matrix multiplication given in Subsection 1.3.6 apply. In particular, we see that the doubling algorithm iteration takes time $O(n)$ using an $n \times n$ mesh of processors and an algorithm that is very similar to the one of Fig. 1.3.27 in Subsection 1.3.6. The total time for the algorithm is $O(n \log m^*)$. It is also possible to implement the doubling algorithm in $O\big((\log n)(\log m^*)\big)$ time using a hypercube of n^3

processors, and the ideas of the matrix–matrix multiplication algorithm of Fig. 1.3.28 in Subsection 1.3.6. This is the minimum known order of solution time for the all–pairs problem, even assuming that communication is instantaneous (a smaller order of solution time can be obtained with a different model of computation than the one we have been using [Kuc82]).

Table 1.1 provides a comparison of the Bellman–Ford, Floyd–Warshall, and doubling algorithms. The estimates given are based on specific implementations of each method, and have either been derived earlier or can be inferred from those derived earlier. For example, the $O(n^3/p)$ estimate for the Floyd–Warshall using a linear array of p processors follows from the $O(n)$ estimate for an $n \times n$ mesh, since each processor of the linear array can emulate n^2/p mesh processors with a slowdown factor of at most n^2/p. The entries of the table suggest that the Bellman–Ford algorithm is superior for the single destination problem, particularly when m^* is relatively small; the Floyd–Warshall and the doubling algorithms are designed for the all–pairs problem, and they are not any faster when applied to the single destination problem. For the all–pairs problem, the Floyd–Warshall is superior to the doubling algorithm when a linear array or an $n \times n$ mesh is used, but the doubling algorithm achieves the smallest known order of solution time when a hypercube with n^3 processors is used. Under some circumstances, where m^* is small and the problem is sparse, the Bellman–Ford algorithm is superior to the Floyd–Warshall using a linear array with $p \leq n$ processors.

Table 1.1: Solution times of shortest path algorithms using various interconnection networks. The times for the single destination problem are the same as for the all–pairs problem for both the Floyd–Warshall and the doubling algorithms. Here n is the number of nodes, r is the maximum number of outgoing arcs from a node [cf. Eq. (1.15)], p is the number of processors, and m^* is the maximum number of arcs in a shortest path [cf. Eq. (1.8)].

Problem	Network	Bellman–Ford	Floyd–Warshall	Doubling
Single Destination	Linear Array $p \leq n$	$O\left(m^* \max\left(n, \frac{nr}{p}\right)\right)$		
	Hypercube $p \leq n$	$O\left(m^* \max\left(\frac{n}{\log p}, \frac{nr}{p}\right)\right)$		
	Hypercube $p = n^2$	$O(m^* \log n)$		
All–Pairs	Linear Array $p \leq n$	$O\left(\frac{m^*|A|n}{p}\right)$	$O\left(\frac{n^3}{p}\right)$	$O\left(\frac{n^3 \log m^*}{p}\right)$
	Mesh $p = n^2$	$O(m^* n)$	$O(n)$	$O(n \log m^*)$
	Hypercube $p = n^2$	$O\left(m^* \max\left(\frac{n}{\log n}, r\right)\right)$		
	Hypercube $p = n^3$	$O\left(m^* \log n\right)$		$O\left((\log n)(\log m^*)\right)$

EXERCISES

1.1. Consider the Bellman–Ford algorithm for the initial conditions $x_i^0 = \infty$, $i \neq 1$. Use Lemma 1.1 to show that we have $x_i^n < x_i^{n-1}$ for some i if and only if there exists a cycle of negative length.

1.2. (Gauss–Seidel Version of the Bellman–Ford Algorithm.) Consider the shortest path problem under the Connectivity and Positive Cycle Assumptions.

(a) Viewing the Bellman–Ford algorithm as a Jacobi relaxation method, construct its Gauss–Seidel version, and show that it terminates finitely for any initial condition vector x^0 with $x_1^0 = 0$. *Hint:* Let $J : \Re^n \mapsto \Re^n$ and $G : \Re^n \mapsto \Re^n$ be the Jacobi and Gauss–Seidel relaxation mappings, respectively. Let u be the vector with all coordinates equal to 1 except for $u_1 = 0$. Show that for any scalar $\gamma > 0$ we have

$$x^* - \gamma u \le J(x^* - \gamma u) \le G(x^* - \gamma u) \le x^* \le G(x^* + \gamma u) \le J(x^* + \gamma u) \le x^* + \gamma u.$$

For any initial condition vector x^0 with $x_1^0 = 0$, consider $\gamma > 0$ such that $x^* - \gamma u \le x^0 \le x^* + \gamma u$.

(b) For the case of the initial conditions $x_i^0 = \infty$ for all $i \ne 1$, $x_1 = 0$, show that the Gauss–Seidel version converges at least as fast as the Jacobi version.

(c) Assume that the graph is acyclic. Show that there exists a node relaxation order for which the Gauss–Seidel version converges in a single iteration.

1.3. Let the Connectivity and Positive Cycle Assumptions hold, and consider the shortest path problem with arc lengths a_{ij} and shortest distances x_i^*. Let p_i, $i = 1, \ldots, n$, be any scalars. Consider also the shortest path problem with arc lengths $a'_{ij} = a_{ij} + p_j - p_i$.

(a) Show that the length of every cycle with respect to a_{ij} is equal to its length with respect to a'_{ij}, and, therefore, the Positive Cycle Assumption holds for the arc lengths a'_{ij}.

(b) Show that a path is shortest with respect to a_{ij} if and only if it is shortest with respect to a'_{ij}, and that the shortest distances x'_i with respect to a'_{ij} satisfy

$$x_i^* = x'_i + p_i - p_1, \qquad \forall \, i = 1, \ldots, n.$$

1.4. Let $\tilde{x}_i$ be the shortest distances corresponding to a set of arc lengths $\tilde{a}_{ij}$. Consider the shortest path problem for another set of arc lengths a_{ij} and assume that the Connectivity and Positive Cycle Assumptions 1.1 and 1.2 hold.

(a) Assume that $a_{ij} - \tilde{a}_{ij} \ge 0$ for all arcs (i, j), and that $a_{ij} - \tilde{a}_{ij} > 0$ only for arcs (i, j) such that $\tilde{x}_i < \tilde{a}_{ij} + \tilde{x}_j$. Show that the Bellman–Ford algorithm starting from the initial conditions $x_i^0 = \tilde{x}_i$ for all i terminates in one iteration.

(b) Define for $k = 1, 2, \ldots$

$$N_1 = \{i \mid \text{for some arc } (i, j) \text{ with } a_{ij} > \tilde{a}_{ij} \text{ we have } \tilde{x}_i = \tilde{a}_{ij} + \tilde{x}_j\},$$

$$N_{k+1} = \{i \mid \text{for some arc } (i, j) \text{ with } j \in N_k \text{ we have } \tilde{x}_i = \tilde{a}_{ij} + \tilde{x}_j\}.$$

Show that the Bellman–Ford algorithm starting from the initial conditions $x_i^0 = \tilde{x}_i$ for $i \notin \cup_k N_k$ and $x_i^0 = \infty$ for $i \in \cup_k N_k$ terminates in no more than $m^* + 1$ iterations. *Hint:* Show that for $i \notin \cup_k N_k$, $\tilde{x}_i$ is not smaller than the shortest distance of i with respect to lengths a_{ij}.

1.5. Consider the shortest path problem for the case where the graph is a 2–dimensional grid with mk nodes in each dimension (all links are bidirectional). Consider the Bellman–Ford algorithm on a $m \times m$ mesh array of processors with each processor handling the computations for a $k \times k$ "square" block of nodes. Verify that the parallel computation time per iteration is $O(k^2)$, and that the corresponding communication time is equal to the time needed to transmit a message carrying k numbers plus overhead over a mesh link. Discuss the implication of this result for the upper bound on speedup imposed by the communication penalty, and quantify the role of packet overhead (cf. the analysis of Subsections 1.3.4 and 1.3.5).

1.6. Consider the following implementation of the Floyd–Warshall algorithm on a hypercube of n^2 processors. We asssume that n is a power of 2 and that the processors are arranged in an $n \times n$ array. At the beginning of the algorithm, each processor (i, j) holds a_{ij}. At the kth iteration, processor (i, j) (with $i \neq j$) computes x_{ij}^k. Show that the computation and the communication times per iteration are $O(1)$ and $O(\log n)$, respectively. Assuming that the computations of an iteration can only start after the previous iteration has been completed, establish that the overall time taken by the algorithm is $O(n \log n)$.

1.7. (Parallel $O(n)$ Implementation of the Floyd–Warshall Algorithm.) Consider the following parallel implementation of the Floyd–Warshall algorithm on a square mesh of n^2 processors using the local synchronization method (cf. Subsection 1.4.1). At the beginning of the algorithm each processor (i, j) with $i \neq j$ holds a_{ij}, where $a_{ij} = \infty$ if $(i, j) \notin A$. Processor (i, j) calculates for $k = 0, 1, \dots, n-1$,

$$
x_{ij}^{k+1} = \begin{cases} \min\left\{x_{ij}^k, \ x_{i(k+1)}^k + x_{(k+1)j}^k\right\}, & \text{if } j \neq i, \\ \infty, & \text{otherwise,} \end{cases}
$$

once it has calculated x_{ij}^k and has received $x_{i(k+1)}^k$ and $x_{(k+1)j}^k$ from its neighboring nodes. Processor (i, j) transmits x_{ij}^{j-1} to its neighboring nodes $(i, j-1)$ and $(i, j+1)$ (if they exist) immediately upon calculating x_{ij}^{j-1}; transmits x_{ij}^{i-1} to its neighboring nodes $(i-1, j)$ and $(i+1, j)$ (if they exist) immediately upon calculating x_{ij}^{i-1}; transmits to processor $(i, j-1)$ (if it exists) whatever it receives from processor $(i, j+1)$; transmits to processor $(i, j+1)$ (if it exists) whatever it receives from processor $(i, j-1)$; transmits to processor $(i-1, j)$ (if it exists) whatever it receives from processor $(i+1, j)$; and transmits to processor $(i+1, j)$ (if it exists) whatever it receives from processor $(i-1, j)$. Assuming that an addition followed by a comparison requires unit time and that transmission of a single number on any one link also requires unit time, show that the algorithm terminates after $O(n)$ time.

1.8. (Parallel Computation of Minimum Weight Spanning Trees [MaP88].) We are given an undirected graph $G = (N, A)$ with a set of nodes $N = \{1, 2, \dots, n\}$, and a scalar a_{ij} for each arc (i, j) ($a_{ij} = a_{ji}$) called the *weight* of (i, j). The *weight of a spanning tree* of G is defined to be the sum of its arc weights. We refer to the maximum over all the weights of the arcs contained in a given walk as the *critical weight* of the walk. Consider the problem of finding a minimum weight spanning tree (MST).

(a) Show that an arc (i, j) belongs to an MST if and only if the critical weight of every walk starting at i and ending at j is greater than or equal to a_{ij}.

(b) Consider the following iterative algorithm:

$$
x_{ij}^0 = \begin{cases} a_{ij}, & \text{if } (i, j) \in A, \\ \infty, & \text{otherwise,} \end{cases}
$$

$$
x_{ij}^{k+1} = \begin{cases} \min\left\{x_{ij}^k, \ \min\left\{x_{i(k+1)}^k, x_{(k+1)j}^k\right\}\right\}, & \text{if } j \neq i, \\ \infty, & \text{otherwise.} \end{cases}
$$

Show that x_{ij}^k is the minimum over all critical weights of walks that start at i, end at j, and use only nodes 1 to k as intermediate nodes.

    (c) Show how to compute x_{ij}^n in $O(n)$ time using a square mesh with n^2 processors, assuming that processor (i, j) holds initially a_{ij}. *Hint:* Observe the similarity with the Floyd–Warshall algorithm and use Exercise 1.7.

1.9. **(Transitive Closure of a Boolean Matrix.)** Consider a Boolean $n \times n$ matrix B, that is, a matrix with elements b_{ij} being either zero or one. The transitive closure of B is the matrix B^* obtained by repeated multiplication of $I + B$ with itself, that is, $B^* = \lim_{k \to \infty} (I + B)^k$, where I is the identity matrix, and binary addition and multiplication are replaced by logical OR and logical AND, respectively. Consider the directed graph G with nodes $1, 2, \ldots, n$, and the arc set $\{(i, j) \mid i \neq j \text{ and } b_{ij} = 1\}$.

    (a) Show that the ijth element of $(I + B)^k$ is 1 if and only if either $i = j$ or else $i \neq j$ and there exists a directed path from i to j in G having k arcs or less.

    (b) Use the result of (a) to show that $B^* = (I + B)^k$ for all k greater or equal to some $\bar{k}$, and characterize $\bar{k}$ in terms of properties of the graph G.

    (c) Show how B^* can be computed with a variation of the Floyd–Warshall algorithm.

1.10. **(Shortest Path Calculation by Forward Search.)** Consider the problem of finding a shortest path from a single origin s to the destination 1. We assume that the Connectivity Assumption 1.1 holds and furthermore $a_{ij} \geq 0$ for all $(i, j) \in A$. The following algorithm makes use of a set of nodes L and of a scalar d_i for each node i. Initially $L = \{s\}$, $d_i = \infty$ for all $i \neq s$, and $d_s = 0$. Let $h_i \geq 0$ be a known underestimate of the shortest distance from node $i \neq 1$ to the destination 1 and let $h_1 = 0$. (One can always take $h_i = 0$ for all i, but the knowledge of sharper underestimates is beneficial.) The algorithm consists of the following steps:

Step 1: Let M be the set of nodes j with $j \in A(i)$ for at least one $i \in L$, and let $\tilde{M}$ be the set

$$\tilde{M} = \left\{ j \in M \mid \min_{\{i \in L \mid j \in A(i)\}} (d_i + a_{ij}) < \min\{d_j, d_1 - h_j\} \right\}.$$

Set $d_j = \min_{\{i \in L \mid j \in A(i)\}} (d_i + a_{ij})$ for all $j \in \tilde{M}$, and set $L = \{j \in \tilde{M} \mid j \neq 1\}$.

Step 2: If L is empty stop; else go to Step 1.

    (a) Show that the algorithm terminates, and that upon termination d_1 is equal to the shortest distance from s to 1.

    (b) Show that the conclusion of (a) holds for the (Gauss–Seidel) version of the algorithm where Step 1 is replaced by the following:

Step 1: Remove a node i from L. For each $j \in A(i)$, if $d_i + a_{ij} < \min\{d_j, d_1 - h_j\}$ set $d_j = d_i + a_{ij}$, and if $j \neq 1$ and j is not in L, place j in L.

    (c) Supplement the algorithms of (a) and (b) with a procedure that allows the construction of a shortest path following termination.

Hint: Show that for both algorithms of parts (a) and (b), the scalar d_i is at all times either ∞ or the length of some path from s to i. Use this fact to show that the algorithms terminate finitely.

4.2 MARKOV CHAINS WITH TRANSITION COSTS

In this section, we lay the groundwork for the formulation of stochastic dynamic programming models, which will be introduced in the next section.

Consider a stationary discrete–time Markov chain with state space

$$S = \{1, 2, \ldots, n\},$$

and transition probability matrix P with elements p_{ij} (see Appendix D for a review of Markov chains). Suppose that if the state is $s(t) = j$ at time t, there is a cost $\alpha^t c_j$ incurred, where c_j and α are given scalars. We assume that $0 < \alpha \le 1$, and we refer to α as the *discount factor*. The implication here is that the cost for being at state j at some time is reduced by a factor α over the cost for being at j one period earlier. Thus, when $\alpha < 1$, costs accumulate primarily during the early periods. Since we have

$$\Pr\big(s(t) = j \mid s(0) = i\big) = [P^t]_{ij},$$

the total expected cost associated with the system starting at state i is

$$x_i^* = \sum_{t=0}^{\infty} \alpha^t E\left[c_{s(t)} \mid s(0) = i\right] = \sum_{t=0}^{\infty} \alpha^t \left[P^t c\right]_i.$$

Equivalently, we have

$$x^* = \sum_{t=0}^{\infty} \alpha^t P^t c, \tag{2.1}$$

where x^* and c are the vectors with coordinates x_i^* and c_i, respectively. In this section, we show, under reasonable assumptions, that the series defining x^* in Eq. (2.1) is convergent and that $x^* = c + \alpha P x^*$. We then consider the iteration

$$x := c + \alpha P x,$$

which can be implemented in both Gauss–Seidel and Jacobi modes (cf. Chapter 2), and we show that it converges to x^*. We differentiate between the two cases where $0 < \alpha < 1$ and $\alpha = 1$.

Assumption 2.1. $0 < \alpha < 1$.

Under Assumption 2.1 the cost is said to be *discounted*. In this case, the series defining the cost vector x^* in Eq. (2.1) can be shown to be convergent. Indeed, we have

$$\|P\|_\infty = \max_i \sum_{j=1}^{n} p_{ij} = 1,$$

where $\| \cdot \|_\infty$ denotes the maximum norm. Consider the equation $x = c + \alpha P x$. It has a unique solution since $\rho(\alpha P) \leq \alpha \|P\|_\infty = \alpha < 1$. This solution, call it $\tilde{x}$, satisfies

$$\tilde{x} = c + \alpha P(c + \alpha P \tilde{x}) = \cdots = \sum_{t=0}^{m-1} \alpha^t P^t c + \alpha^m P^m \tilde{x}, \qquad \forall m. \qquad (2.2)$$

By taking the limit in this equation as $m \to \infty$, we obtain that the series in Eq. (2.1) is convergent and that $\tilde{x} = x^*$. Therefore, the optimal cost vector x^* is well defined and satisfies

$$x^* = c + \alpha P x^*. \qquad (2.3)$$

Consider now the iteration

$$x := c + \alpha P x \qquad (2.4)$$

for an arbitrary initial condition. Since $\|\alpha P\|_\infty = \alpha$, the function $c + \alpha P x$ is a contraction of modulus α with respect to the maximum norm when $0 < \alpha < 1$. It follows that the iteration $x := c + \alpha P x$ converges to the unique fixed point x^* [cf. Eq. (2.3)] when implemented in a synchronous parallel setting, as discussed in Chapter 2. This is true for both a Jacobi and a Gauss–Seidel mode of implementation (Props. 6.7 and 6.8 in Section 2.6).

We now turn to the case $\alpha = 1$, and consider the question whether the series in Eq. (2.1) defining the cost vector x^* is convergent and whether $x^* = c + P x^*$ [cf. Eq. (2.3)]. The equation $x = c + P x$ may or may not have a solution. If it has a solution x, it will have an infinite number of solutions (for every scalar r, the vector with coordinates $x_i + r$ is also a solution). To delineate situations where a solution exists, we draw motivation from the special case where $c \geq 0$ and we reason as follows. If $c \geq 0$ and for some state i, the cost x_i^* is finite, then starting from i, the system must enter eventually (with probability one) a set of zero–cost states, and stay within that set permanently; otherwise the number of times a positive cost state is visited would be infinite with positive probability, contradicting the finiteness of x_i^*. Therefore, if x_i^* is finite for some i, there is a nonempty subset of the set of zero–cost states,

$$\bar{S} \subset \{j \in S \mid c_j = 0\},$$

which is *absorbing* in the sense

$$p_{jm} = 0, \qquad \forall \, j \in \bar{S}, \; m \notin \bar{S}, \qquad (2.5)$$

and is such that there is a sequence of positive probability transitions leading from i to at least one state in $\bar{S}$. To guarantee that x_i^* is finite for all i, we consequently lump all states in $\bar{S}$ into a single state, say state 1, and consider the following assumption.

Assumption 2.2. $\alpha = 1$, state 1 is absorbing and cost–free ($p_{11} = 1, c_1 = 0$), and there exists some $\bar{t} > 0$ such that state 1 is reached with positive probability after at most $\bar{t}$ transitions regardless of the initial state ($[P^{\bar{t}}]_{i1} > 0$ for all i).

To establish the equation $x^* = c + Px^*$ under the preceding assumption, we write P in the form

$$P = \begin{bmatrix} 1 & 0 \ldots 0 \\ p_{21} & \\ \vdots & \tilde{P} \\ p_{n1} & \end{bmatrix}. \tag{2.6}$$

It was shown in Prop. 8.4 of Section 2.8 that for some $\delta > 0$, we have

$$\rho(\tilde{P}^{\bar{t}}) \leq \|\tilde{P}^{\bar{t}}\|_\infty \leq 1 - \delta. \tag{2.7}$$

Since $c_1 = 0$, it is seen from Eq. (2.6) that for all $t \geq 0$, we have

$$P^t c = \begin{bmatrix} 0 \\ \tilde{P}^t \tilde{c} \end{bmatrix}, \tag{2.8}$$

where

$$\tilde{c} = \begin{bmatrix} c_2 \\ \vdots \\ c_n \end{bmatrix}.$$

From Eq. (2.7) we see that the spectral radius $\rho(\tilde{P})$ of $\tilde{P}$ satisfies $\rho(\tilde{P}) < 1$. Therefore the equation $\tilde{x} = \tilde{c} + \tilde{P}\tilde{x}$ has a unique solution. This solution, call it $\tilde{x}^*$, satisfies

$$\tilde{x}^* = \tilde{c} + \tilde{P}(\tilde{c} + \tilde{P}\tilde{x}^*) = \cdots = \sum_{t=0}^{m-1} \tilde{P}^t \tilde{c} + \tilde{P}^m \tilde{x}^*, \qquad \forall m. \tag{2.9}$$

Since $\rho(\tilde{P}) < 1$, we have $\lim_{m \to \infty} \tilde{P}^m \tilde{x}^* = 0$. Therefore, by taking the limit in Eq. (2.9) as $m \to \infty$, we obtain that the series $\sum_{t=0}^\infty P^t c$ defining the optimal cost vector x^* is convergent and that

$$\tilde{x}^* = \begin{bmatrix} x_2^* \\ \vdots \\ x_n^* \end{bmatrix}.$$

Since $\tilde{x}^* = \tilde{c} + \tilde{P}\tilde{x}^*$, $c_1 = 0$, and $x_1^* = 0$, it follows using Eq. (2.6) that x^* satisfies the equation $x^* = c + Px^*$. Furthermore, since $\rho(\tilde{P}) < 1$, the iteration

$$\tilde{x} := \tilde{c} + \tilde{P}\tilde{x},$$

converges to $\tilde{x}^*$ starting from an arbitrary initial condition. In Section 6.3, we will see that this iteration converges even if executed in a totally asynchronous environment.

EXERCISES

2.1. (Upper and Lower Bounds on the Cost Vector.) Let $0 < \alpha < 1$, let x be an arbitrary vector in $\Re^n$, and let

$$\bar{x} = c + \alpha P x,$$

$$\bar{\gamma} = \max_i(\bar{x}_i - x_i), \qquad \gamma = \min_i(\bar{x}_i - x_i).$$

Show that

$$x + \frac{\gamma}{1-\alpha}e \le \bar{x} + \frac{\alpha\gamma}{1-\alpha}e \le x^* \le \bar{x} + \frac{\alpha\bar{\gamma}}{1-\alpha}e \le x + \frac{\bar{\gamma}}{1-\alpha}e,$$

where x^* is the unique solution of the system $x = c + \alpha P x$, and e is the vector $(1, 1, \dots, 1)$.

2.2. Let Assumption 2.2 hold, and let t_i denote the mean first passage time from state i to state 1, that is, the average number of steps required to reach state 1 starting from state i. Show that these times are the unique solution of the system of equations

$$t_i = 1 + \sum_{j=2}^{n} p_{ij} t_j, \qquad i = 2, \dots, n,$$

$$t_1 = 0.$$

4.3 MARKOVIAN DECISION PROBLEMS

We now generalize the problem of the previous section by allowing the transition probability matrix at each stage to be subject to optimal choice. At each state i, we are given a finite set of decisions or controls $U(i)$. If the state is i and control u is chosen at time t, the cost incurred is $\alpha^t c_i(u)$, where $\alpha > 0$, $c_i(u)$ are given scalars; the system then moves to state j with given probability $p_{ij}(u)$. Consider the finite set of functions μ that map states i into controls $\mu(i) \in U(i)$, that is, the set

$$M = \big\{\mu \mid \mu(i) \in U(i), \ i = 1, \dots, n\big\}.$$

We can identify each μ with a rule for choosing a control as a function of the state. Similarly we identify a sequence $\{\mu_0, \mu_1, \ldots\}$ ($\mu_t \in M$ for all t), with a rule for choosing at time t and at state i the control $\mu_t(i)$. Such a sequence is called a *policy* and if μ_t is the same for all t, it is called a *stationary policy*.

Let $P(\mu)$ be the transition probability matrix corresponding to μ, that is, the matrix with elements

$$\left[P(\mu)\right]_{ij} = p_{ij}\big(\mu(i)\big), \qquad i, j = 1, \ldots, n.$$

Define also the cost vector $c(\mu)$ corresponding to $\mu \in M$,

$$c(\mu) = \begin{bmatrix} c_1\big(\mu(1)\big) \\ \vdots \\ c_n\big(\mu(n)\big) \end{bmatrix}.$$

For any policy $\pi = \{\mu_0, \mu_1, \ldots\}$, we have

$$\Pr\big(\text{State is } j \text{ at time } t \mid \text{Initial state is } i, \text{ and } \pi \text{ is used}\big) = \big[P(\mu_0)P(\mu_1)\ldots P(\mu_{t-1})\big]_{ij}.$$

Therefore, if $x_i(\pi)$ is the expected cost corresponding to initial state i and policy $\pi = \{\mu_0, \mu_1, \ldots\}$, and $x(\pi)$ is the vector with coordinates $x_1(\pi), \ldots, x_n(\pi)$, we have

$$x(\pi) = \sum_{t=0}^{\infty} \alpha^t \big[P(\mu_0)P(\mu_1)\cdots P(\mu_{t-1})\big] c(\mu_t), \tag{3.1}$$

assuming the above series converges. Conditions for convergence will be introduced shortly. When the above series is not known to converge, we use the definition

$$x(\pi) = \limsup_{k \to \infty} \sum_{t=0}^{k} \alpha^t \big[P(\mu_0)P(\mu_1)\cdots P(\mu_{t-1})\big] c(\mu_t). \tag{3.2}$$

For a stationary policy $\{\mu, \mu, \ldots\}$, the corresponding cost vector is denoted

$$x(\mu) = \limsup_{k \to \infty} \sum_{t=0}^{k} \alpha^t P(\mu)^t c(\mu). \tag{3.3}$$

We define the optimal expected cost starting at state i as

$$x_i^* = \inf_{\pi} x_i(\pi), \qquad \forall\, i. \tag{3.4}$$

We say that the policy π^* is optimal if

$$x_i(\pi^*) = \inf_{\pi} x_i(\pi), \qquad \forall\, i.$$

It is convenient to introduce the mappings $T_\mu : \Re^n \mapsto \Re^n$ and $T : \Re^n \mapsto \Re^n$ defined by

$$T_\mu(x) = c(\mu) + \alpha P(\mu)x, \qquad \mu \in M, \tag{3.5}$$

$$T(x) = \min_{\mu \in M} \left[c(\mu) + \alpha P(\mu)x \right] = \min_{\mu \in M} T_\mu(x). \tag{3.6}$$

The minimization in the preceding equation is meant to be separate for each coordinate, that is, the ith coordinate of $T(x)$ is

$$\left[T(x) \right]_i = \min_{u \in U(i)} \left[c_i(u) + \alpha \sum_{j=1}^n p_{ij}(u)x_j \right]. \tag{3.7}$$

Note that T_μ is the mapping involved in the iteration $x := c + \alpha Px$ of the previous section, with c and P replaced by $c(\mu)$ and $P(\mu)$, respectively. A straightforward calculation verifies that for all $k \geq 1$ and x

$$(T_{\mu_0} T_{\mu_1} \cdots T_{\mu_k})(x) = \alpha^{k+1} P(\mu_0)P(\mu_1) \cdots P(\mu_k)x + \sum_{t=0}^k \alpha^t \left[P(\mu_0)P(\mu_1) \cdots P(\mu_{t-1}) \right] c(\mu_t)$$

where $(T_{\mu_0} T_{\mu_1} \cdots T_{\mu_k})$ is the composition of the mappings $T_{\mu_0}, \ldots, T_{\mu_k}$. Therefore, we can write [cf. Eqs. (3.1)–(3.3)]

$$x(\pi) = \limsup_{k \to \infty} (T_{\mu_0} T_{\mu_1} \cdots T_{\mu_k})(x^0), \tag{3.8}$$

$$x(\mu) = \limsup_{k \to \infty} T_\mu^k(x^0), \tag{3.9}$$

where x^0 is the zero vector

$$x^0 = (0, 0, \ldots, 0),$$

and T_μ^k is the composition of T_μ with itself k times.

Our main result will be to show, under reasonable conditions, that the optimal cost vector x^* is a fixed point of the mapping T, that is,

$$x^* = T(x^*),$$

and that x^* can be obtained in the limit through the iteration

$$x := T(x),$$

known as the *dynamic programming* iteration.

The following proposition gives some basic properties of T and T_μ.

Proposition 3.1.   The following hold for the mappings T and T_μ of Eqs. (3.5) and (3.6):

(a) T and T_μ are monotone in the sense

$$x \le x' \quad \Rightarrow \quad T(x) \le T(x'),$$

$$x \le x' \quad \Rightarrow \quad T_\mu(x) \le T_\mu(x'), \qquad \forall\, \mu \in M.$$

(b) For all $x \in \Re^n$, scalars r, integers $t > 0$, and functions $\mu_1, \ldots, \mu_t \in M$, we have

$$T^t(x + re) = T^t(x) + \alpha^t re,$$

$$(T_{\mu_1} T_{\mu_2} \cdots T_{\mu_t})(x + re) = (T_{\mu_1} T_{\mu_2} \cdots T_{\mu_t})(x) + \alpha^t re,$$

where e is the vector $(1, 1, \ldots, 1)$.

(c) For all x and $x' \in \Re^n$, we have

$$\|T(x) - T(x')\|_\infty \le \alpha \|x - x'\|_\infty,$$

$$\left\|T_\mu(x) - T_\mu(x')\right\|_\infty \le \alpha \|x - x'\|_\infty, \qquad \forall\, \mu \in M.$$

In particular, if $\alpha < 1$, then T and T_μ are contraction mappings with respect to the maximum norm $\|\cdot\|_\infty$.

Proof. Assertion (a) is obtained using the nonnegativity of the elements of $\alpha P(\mu)$. Assertion (b) is obtained for $t = 1$ using the fact $P(\mu)e = e$, and is generalized to arbitrary t using induction. To prove (c), we note that

$$T(x) = \min_\mu \left[c(\mu) + \alpha P(\mu)x' + \alpha P(\mu)(x - x') \right]$$

$$= \min_\mu \left[T_\mu(x') + \alpha P(\mu)(x - x') \right] \le T(x') + \alpha \|x - x'\|_\infty e.$$

Similarly,

$$T(x') \le T(x) + \alpha \|x - x'\|_\infty e.$$

Combining these two inequalities, we obtain

$$-\alpha \|x - x'\|_\infty e \le T(x) - T(x') \le \alpha \|x - x'\|_\infty e,$$

which shows that

$$\|T(x) - T(x')\|_\infty \le \alpha \|x - x'\|_\infty.$$

A similar argument shows that $\left\|T_\mu(x) - T_\mu(x')\right\|_\infty \leq \alpha\|x - x'\|_\infty$ for all $\mu \in M$.
Q.E.D.

4.3.1 Discounted Problems

Consider now the case where there is a discount factor.

Assumption 3.1. *(Discounted Cost)* $0 < \alpha < 1$.

The main results follow from the contraction property of Prop. 3.1(c).

Proposition 3.2. Under the Discounted Cost Assumption 3.1 the following hold:

(a) The optimal cost vector x^* is the unique fixed point of T within $\Re^n$.

(b) For every $x \in \Re^n$ and $\mu \in M$, there holds

$$\lim_{t\to\infty} T^t(x) = x^*, \qquad \lim_{t\to\infty} T_\mu^t(x) = x(\mu),$$

and the convergence is geometric.

(c) A stationary policy $\{\mu^*, \mu^*, \ldots\}$ is optimal if and only if

$$T_{\mu^*}(x^*) = T(x^*).$$

Proof.

(a) By Prop. 3.1(c), T is a contraction mapping and hence has a unique fixed point $\tilde{x}$. We will show that $\tilde{x} = x^*$. Let x^0 be the zero vector. For any policy $\pi = \{\mu_0, \mu_1, \ldots\}$, we see from the definition (3.6) of T that $T(x^0) \leq T_{\mu_t}(x^0)$, and by using the monotonicity of T, we obtain

$$T^2(x^0) \leq (TT_{\mu_t})(x^0) \leq (T_{\mu_{t-1}}T_{\mu_t})(x^0).$$

Proceeding similarly, we obtain for all t,

$$T^{t+1}(x^0) \leq (T_{\mu_0}T_{\mu_1}\cdots T_{\mu_t})(x^0).$$

By taking the limit superior as $t \to \infty$, and using the definition (3.8) of $x(\pi)$, and the fact $\lim_{t\to\infty} T^{t+1}(x^0) = \tilde{x}$, we obtain for all π

$$\tilde{x} \leq x(\pi).$$

Therefore,

$$\tilde{x} \leq x^*. \tag{3.10}$$

To prove the reverse inequality, we select a function $\mu \in M$ such that

$$T_\mu(\tilde{x}) = T(\tilde{x}).$$

Applying T_μ repeatedly and using the fact $T(\tilde{x}) = \tilde{x}$ we obtain

$$T_\mu^t(\tilde{x}) = \tilde{x}.$$

We showed in the previous section that $\lim_{t\to\infty} T_\mu^t(\tilde{x}) = x(\mu)$, so we must have

$$x(\mu) = \tilde{x}.$$

Since $x^* \leq x(\mu)$, we obtain $x^* \leq \tilde{x}$, which, combined with the inequality $x^* \geq \tilde{x}$ proved earlier, shows that $x^* = \tilde{x}$.

(b) This follows from the contraction property of T and T_μ, and part (a).

(c) Suppose that $T_{\mu^*}(x^*) = T(x^*)$. Using part (a), we have $T(x^*) = x^*$. It follows that $T_{\mu^*}(x^*) = x^*$, and by the analysis of the previous section, we obtain $x(\mu^*) = x^*$, so $\{\mu^*, \mu^*, \ldots\}$ is optimal. Conversely, suppose $\{\mu^*, \mu^*, \ldots\}$ is optimal. Then x^* is the cost corresponding to μ^*, so x^* is the unique fixed point of T_{μ^*} as well as the unique fixed point of T [by part (a)]. Hence, $T_{\mu^*}(x^*) = x^* = T(x^*)$. **Q.E.D.**

Note that Prop. 3.2(b) guarantees the validity of the dynamic programming algorithm that starts from an arbitrary vector x and successively generates $T(x)$, $T^2(x), \ldots$. This algorithm yields in the limit x^*, and from x^* one can obtain an optimal stationary policy using Prop. 3.2(c) (see also Exercise 3.1). The contraction property of T guarantees also that the Gauss–Seidel algorithm based on T converges to x^* (Prop. 1.4 in Section 3.1).

4.3.2 Undiscounted Problems—Stochastic Shortest Paths

When $\alpha = 1$, the problem is of interest primarily when there is a cost–free state, say state 1, which is absorbing (this is similar to the case of a single policy in the previous section). The objective then is to reach this state at minimum expected cost. We say that a stationary policy $\{\mu, \mu, \ldots\}$ is *proper* if $\lim_{t\to\infty} \left[P^t(\mu)\right]_{i1} = 1$ for all $i \in S$; otherwise, we say that π is *improper*. We will operate under the following assumption:

Assumption 3.2. (*Undiscounted Cost*) $\alpha = 1$, $p_{11}(u) = 1$, and $c_1(u) = 0$ for all $u \in U(1)$, and there exists at least one proper stationary policy. Furthermore, each improper stationary policy yields infinite cost for at least one initial state, that is, for each improper $\{\mu, \mu, \ldots\}$, there is a state i such that $\limsup_{k\to\infty} \left[\sum_{t=0}^{k} P^t(\mu)c(\mu)\right]_i = \infty$.

The shortest path problem of Section 4.1 is an important example of a dynamic programming problem where the above assumption holds. To establish this fact, we view the nodes of the given graph as the states of a Markov chain. A stationary policy

$\{\mu, \mu, \ldots\}$ is identified with a rule that assigns to each node $i \neq 1$ a neighbor node $\mu(i) = j$ with $(i, j) \in A(i)$. Given such a μ, the transitions are deterministic and the cost of the transition at i is $a_{i\mu(i)}$ (see Fig. 4.3.1). The destination node 1 has no outgoing arcs by assumption, and is viewed as an absorbing and cost–free state for all μ. For each initial state $i \neq 1$ and each stationary policy, there are two possibilities. The first is that the sequence of generated states does not contain state 1, in which case the policy is improper; in this case, the Positive Cycle Assumption 1.2, implies that this state is associated with infinite cost. The second possibility is that the policy is proper, so the system eventually reaches state 1 and subsequently stays there, in which case, the total cost equals the sum of the transition costs up to the time state 1 is reached first. In this case, the sequence of transitions defines a simple path starting at i and ending at 1, and the corresponding total cost equals the length of the path. It is seen, therefore, that optimal stationary policies are those that correspond to shortest paths. The Connectivity Assumption 1.1 is seen to be equivalent to the existence of at least one proper policy, while the Positive Cycle Assumption 1.2 is seen to be equivalent to the existence of an infinite cost state for every improper policy. Therefore, the assumptions made in Section 4.1 are, in effect, equivalent with the Undiscounted Cost Assumption 3.2 as applied to the shortest path problem. We may view the general problem under Assumption 3.2 as a stochastic version of the shortest path problem whereby at any given node, instead of choosing a successor node, we choose a probability distribution over the successor nodes with the objective of minimizing the expected length of the path that will be traveled from the given node to the destination node 1.

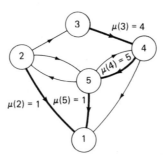

Figure 4.3.1 Viewing a shortest path problem as a (deterministic) dynamic programming problem. The figure shows the paths corresponding to a stationary policy $\{\mu, \mu, \ldots\}$. The control $\mu(i)$ associated with a node $i \neq 1$ is a node adjacent to i. The policy shown is proper because the path from every state leads to the destination.

Exercise 3.2 explores conditions under which the Undiscounted Cost Assumption 3.2 is guaranteed to hold. If *all* stationary policies are proper, it can be shown (Exercise 3.3) that the mapping T is a contraction over the subspace $X = \{x \in \Re^n \mid x_1 = 0\}$ with respect to some weighted maximum norm. This is not true in general, however, as the example of Fig. 4.3.2 shows. Despite this fact, essentially the same results as for the Discounted Cost case hold (cf. Prop. 3.2).

Proposition 3.3. Let the Undiscounted Cost Assumption 3.2 hold. Then:

(a) The optimal cost vector x^* is the unique fixed point of T within the subspace

$$X = \{x \in \Re^n \mid x_1 = 0\}.$$

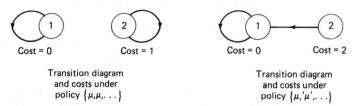

Transition diagram
and costs under
policy $\{\mu, \mu, \ldots\}$

Transition diagram
and costs under
policy $\{\mu', \mu', \ldots\}$

Figure 4.3.2 Example problem where the Undiscounted Cost Assumption 3.2 is satisfied, but the mapping T is not a contraction mapping over the subspace $X = \{x \in \Re^n \mid x_1 = 0\}$. Here $M = \{\mu, \mu'\}$ with transition probabilities and costs as shown. The mapping T over the set $X = \{(x_1, x_2) \mid x_1 = 0\}$ is given by

$$\left[T(x)\right]_1 = 0,$$

$$\left[T(x)\right]_2 = \min\{1 + x_2, 2\}.$$

Thus for $x = (0, x_2)$ and $x' = (0, x_2')$, with $x_2 < 1$ and $x_2' < 1$ we have

$$\left| \left[T(x)\right]_2 - \left[T(x')\right]_2 \right| = |(1 + x_2) - (1 + x_2')| = |x_2 - x_2'|.$$

Therefore, T is not a contraction mapping with respect to any weighted maximum norm.

(b) For every $x \in X$, there holds

$$\lim_{t \to \infty} T^t(x) = x^*.$$

(c) A stationary policy $\pi = \{\mu^*, \mu^*, \ldots\}$ is optimal if and only if

$$T_{\mu^*}(x^*) = T(x^*).$$

Proof. We first show the following:

Lemma 3.1.   Let Assumption 3.2 hold:

(a) If the stationary policy $\{\mu, \mu, \ldots\}$ is proper, then $x(\mu)$ is the unique fixed point of T_μ within X. Furthermore, $\lim_{t \to \infty} T_\mu^t(x) = x(\mu)$ for all $x \in X$.
(b) If $x \geq T_\mu(x)$ for some $x \in X$, then $\{\mu, \mu, \ldots\}$ is proper.

Proof.

(a) If $\{\mu, \mu, \ldots\}$ is proper, then Assumption 2.2 of Section 4.2 is satisfied and the conclusion follows from the results of that section.

(b) If $x \in X$ and $x \geq T_\mu(x)$, then by the monotonicity of T_μ,

$$x \geq T_\mu^t(x) = P^t(\mu)x + \sum_{k=0}^{t-1} P^k(\mu)c(\mu), \qquad \forall \, t \geq 1. \tag{3.11}$$

If $\{\mu, \mu, \ldots\}$ were improper, then some subsequence of $\sum_{k=0}^{t-1} P^k(\mu)c(\mu)$ would have a coordinate that tends to infinity, thereby contradicting the above inequality. **Q.E.D.**

We now return to the proof of Prop. 3.3. We first show that T has at most one fixed point within X. Indeed, if x and x' are two fixed points in X, then we select μ and μ' such that $x = T(x) = T_\mu(x)$ and $x' = T(x') = T_{\mu'}(x')$. By Lemma 3.1(b), we have that $\{\mu, \mu, \ldots\}$ and $\{\mu', \mu', \ldots\}$ are proper, and furthermore $x = x(\mu)$ and $x' = x(\mu')$. We have $x = T^t(x) \leq T_{\mu'}^t(x)$ for all $t \geq 1$, and by Lemma 3.1(a), we obtain $x \leq \lim_{t \to \infty} T_{\mu'}^t(x) = x(\mu') = x'$. Similarly, $x' \leq x$, showing that $x = x'$ and that T has at most one fixed point within X.

We next show that T has a fixed point within X. Let $\{\mu, \mu, \ldots\}$ be a proper policy. Choose $\mu' \in M$ such that $T_{\mu'}\big(x(\mu)\big) = T\big(x(\mu)\big)$. Then we have $x(\mu) = T_\mu\big(x(\mu)\big) \geq T_{\mu'}\big(x(\mu)\big)$. By Lemma 3.1(b), $\{\mu', \mu', \ldots\}$ is proper, and by the monotonicity of $T_{\mu'}$, we obtain

$$x(\mu) \geq \lim_{t \to \infty} T_{\mu'}^t\big(x(\mu)\big) = x(\mu'). \tag{3.12}$$

If $x(\mu) = x(\mu')$, then we obtain $x(\mu) = x(\mu') = T_{\mu'}\big(x(\mu')\big) = T_{\mu'}\big(x(\mu)\big) = T\big(x(\mu)\big)$ and $x(\mu)$ is a fixed point of T. If $x(\mu) \neq x(\mu')$, then, from Eq. (3.12), $x(\mu) \geq x(\mu')$ and $x_i(\mu) > x_i(\mu')$ for at least one state i. We then replace μ by μ' and continue the process. Since the set of proper policies is finite, we must obtain eventually two successive proper policies with equal cost vectors, thereby showing that T has a fixed point within X.

Next we show that the unique fixed point of T within X is equal to the optimal cost vector x^*, and that $T^t(x) \to x^*$ for all $x \in X$. Indeed, the construction of the preceding paragraph provides a proper policy $\{\mu, \mu, \ldots\}$ such that $T_\mu\big(x(\mu)\big) = T\big(x(\mu)\big) = x(\mu)$. We will show that $T^t(x) \to x(\mu)$ for all $x \in X$, and that $x(\mu) = x^*$. Let Δ be the vector with coordinates

$$\Delta_i = \begin{cases} 0, & \text{if } i = 1, \\ \delta, & \text{if } i \neq 1, \end{cases} \tag{3.13}$$

where $\delta > 0$ is some scalar, and let x^Δ be the vector in X satisfying

$$T_\mu(x^\Delta) = x^\Delta - \Delta. \tag{3.14}$$

[There is a unique such vector because the equation $x^\Delta = c(\mu) + \Delta + P(\mu)x^\Delta$ ($= T_\mu(x^\Delta) + \Delta$) has a unique solution within X by the analysis of Section 4.2.] Since x^Δ

is the cost vector corresponding to μ for $c(\mu)$ replaced by $c(\mu) + \Delta$, we have $x^{\Delta} \geq x(\mu)$. Furthermore, for any $x \in X$, there exists $\Delta > 0$ such that $x \leq x^{\Delta}$. We have

$$x(\mu) = T\big(x(\mu)\big) \leq T(x^{\Delta}) \leq T_{\mu}(x^{\Delta}) = x^{\Delta} - \Delta \leq x^{\Delta}.$$

Using the monotonicity of T and the previous relation, we obtain

$$x(\mu) = T^{t}\big(x(\mu)\big) \leq T^{t}(x^{\Delta}) \leq T^{t-1}(x^{\Delta}) \leq x^{\Delta}, \qquad \forall\, t \geq 1. \tag{3.15}$$

Hence, $T^{t}(x^{\Delta})$ converges to some $\tilde{x} \in X$, and by continuity of T, we must have $\tilde{x} = T(\tilde{x})$. By the uniqueness of the fixed point of T shown earlier, we must have $\tilde{x} = x(\mu)$. It is also seen using the fact $x_{1}(\mu) = 0$, that

$$x(\mu) - \Delta = T\big(x(\mu)\big) - \Delta \leq T\big(x(\mu) - \Delta\big) \leq T\big(x(\mu)\big) = x(\mu), \tag{3.16}$$

so $x(\mu) - \Delta \leq \lim_{t \to \infty} T^{t}\big(x(\mu) - \Delta\big) \leq x(\mu)$. Similarly, as earlier, it follows that $\lim_{t \to \infty} T^{t}\big(x(\mu) - \Delta\big) = x(\mu)$. For any $x \in X$, we can find $\delta > 0$ such that

$$x(\mu) - \Delta \leq x \leq x^{\Delta}.$$

By monotonicity of T, we then have

$$T^{t}\big(x(\mu) - \Delta\big) \leq T^{t}(x) \leq T^{t}(x^{\Delta}), \qquad \forall\, t \geq 1, \tag{3.17}$$

and since $\lim_{t \to \infty} T^{t}\big(x(\mu) - \Delta\big) = \lim_{t \to \infty} T^{t}(x^{\Delta}) = x(\mu)$, it follows that $\lim_{t \to \infty} T^{t}(x) = x(\mu)$. To show that $x(\mu) = x^{*}$, take any policy $\pi = \{\mu_{0}, \mu_{1}, \dots\}$. We have

$$(T_{\mu_{0}} \cdots T_{\mu_{t-1}})(x^{0}) \geq T^{t}(x^{0}),$$

where x^{0} is the zero vector. Taking the limit superior in the preceding inequality, we obtain

$$x(\pi) \geq x(\mu),$$

so $\{\mu, \mu, \dots\}$ is an optimal policy and $x(\mu) = x^{*}$.

To prove part (c), we note that if $\{\mu^{*}, \mu^{*}, \dots\}$ is optimal, then $x(\mu^{*}) = x^{*}$, so $T_{\mu^{*}}(x^{*}) = T_{\mu^{*}}\big(x(\mu^{*})\big) = x(\mu^{*}) = x^{*} = T(x^{*})$. Conversely, if $x^{*} = T(x^{*}) = T_{\mu^{*}}(x^{*})$ it follows from Lemma 3.1 that $\{\mu^{*}, \mu^{*}, \dots\}$ is proper, and by using the results of Section 4.2, we obtain $x^{*} = x(\mu^{*})$. Therefore, $\{\mu^{*}, \mu^{*}, \dots\}$ is optimal.   **Q.E.D.**

We note that the convergence property of Prop. 3.3(b) can also be shown for the Gauss–Seidel algorithm based on T (Exercise 3.7). An alternative method of proof for Prop. 3.3 is outlined in Exercise 3.4 under somewhat different assumptions.

The results of Prop. 3.3 may not hold if the Assumption 3.2 or the undiscounted cost model are modified in seemingly minor ways. Figure 4.3.3 gives an example where there is a (nonoptimal) improper policy that yields finite cost for all initial states and Prop. 3.3 fails to hold. Exercise 3.8 gives an example where Prop. 3.3 fails to hold when the set of decisions $U(i)$ is not finite, even though all stationary policies are proper.

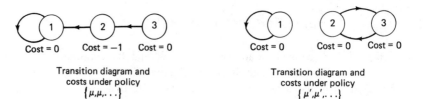

Transition diagram and
costs under policy
$\{\mu,\mu,\ldots\}$

Transition diagram and
costs under policy
$\{\mu',\mu',\ldots\}$

Figure 4.3.3 Example where Prop. 3.3 fails to hold. Here there are two stationary policies, $\{\mu,\mu,\ldots\}$ and $\{\mu',\mu',\ldots\}$ with transition probabilities and costs as shown. The equation $x = T(x)$ over the subspace $X = \{(x_1, x_2, x_3) \mid x_1 = 0\}$ is given by

$$x_1 = 0,$$

$$x_2 = \min\{-1, x_3\},$$

$$x_3 = x_2,$$

and is satisfied by any vector of the form $x = (0, \delta, \delta)$ with $\delta \le -1$. Here the proper policy $\{\mu,\mu,\ldots\}$ is optimal and the corresponding optimal cost vector is $x^* = (0, -1, -1)$. The difficulty is that there is the nonoptimal improper policy $\{\mu',\mu',\ldots\}$ that has finite (zero) cost for all initial states. This example depends on the existence of a negative state cost (see Exercise 3.4).

The construction used in the proof of Prop. 3.3 to show that T has a fixed point constitutes an algorithm, known as *policy iteration*, for obtaining an optimal proper policy starting with an arbitrary proper policy. In the typical iteration of this algorithm, given a proper policy $\{\mu,\mu,\ldots\}$ and the corresponding cost vector $x(\mu)$, one obtains a new proper policy $\{\mu',\mu',\ldots\}$ satisfying the equation $T_{\mu'}\big(x(\mu)\big) = T\big(x(\mu)\big)$, or, equivalently,

$$\mu'(i) = \arg\min_{u \in U(i)} \left[c_i(u) + \sum_{j=2}^{n} p_{ij}(u) x_j(\mu) \right], \qquad i = 2, 3, \ldots, n.$$

The new policy is strictly better if the current policy is nonoptimal; indeed, it was shown by Eq. (3.12) and the discussion following that equation that $x(\mu') \le x(\mu)$, with strict inequality $x_i(\mu') < x_i(\mu)$ for at least one state x_i, if the policy $\{\mu,\mu,\ldots\}$ is nonoptimal. Because the number of stationary policies is finite, it follows that this policy iteration algorithm terminates after a finite number of iterations with an optimal proper policy. Note that each iteration involves a "policy evaluation" step, whereby, given $\mu \in M$, we obtain the corresponding cost vector $x(\mu)$ by solving the system of equations $x(\mu) = c(\mu) + P(\mu)x(\mu)$ subject to the constraint $x_1(\mu) = 0$. This step can be very time–consuming when the number of states is large. If a powerful parallel machine is available, however, the policy evaluation step can be speeded up a great deal [to as little as $O(n)$ as shown in Section 2.2, or $O(\log^2 n)$ as shown in Section 2.9]. Under these circumstances, the policy iteration algorithm can be attractive, since it typically requires very few iterations for termination. We note also that a similar finitely terminating policy iteration algorithm can be shown to yield an optimal stationary policy under the Discounted Cost Assumption 3.1 starting from an arbitrary stationary policy [Ber87].

4.3.3 Parallel Implementation of the Dynamic Programming Iteration

We now consider the implementation of the dynamic programming (D.P.) iteration

$$x_i := \min_{u \in U(i)} \left[c_i(u) + \alpha \sum_{j=1}^{n} p_{ij}(u)x_j \right]$$

in a message–passing system [cf. Eq. (3.7)]. The situation here is similar as for the matrix–vector type of calculations discussed in Subsection 1.3.6. The main difference is the presence of the minimization over $u \in U(i)$. Indeed when $U(i)$ consists of a single element, the D.P. iteration consists of a matrix–vector multiplication followed by a vector addition [cf. Eq. (3.5) in Subsection 1.3.6].

We first assume that there are p processors, with p less than or equal to the number of states n, and for simplicity, we assume that n is divisible by p. It is then natural to let the jth processor update the cost of states $(j-1)k+1$ through jk, where $k = n/p$. Let us assume that each set $U(i)$ contains r elements, $p_{ij}(u)$ is nonzero for all u [so the matrix $P(u)$ is dense], and the jth processor holds the vector x and the values $c_i(u)$, and $p_{im}(u)$ for all $u \in U(i)$, m, and $i = (j-1)k+1$ through $i = jk$. Then the updating of the corresponding coordinates of x according to the D.P. iteration takes $O(knr)$ time for each processor. To communicate the results of the updating to the other processors, a multinode broadcast of packets, each containing k numbers, is necessary. If a linear array is used for communication, then we see, using the results of Subsection 1.3.4, that the multinode broadcast takes $O(kp) = O(n)$ time. Thus, the total time per iteration is $O(knr) = O(n^2r/p)$.

Assume now that a hypercube with n^2 processors is available. We assume that n is a power of 2, and that the processors are arranged in an $n \times n$ array, with each "row" of n processors being itself a hypercube (cf. the algorithm for matrix–vector multiplication of Fig. 1.3.26 in Subsection 1.3.6). We also assume that at the beginning of each iteration, each processor (i, j) holds x_j and $p_{ij}(u)$ for all $u \in U(i)$. Furthermore, every processor (i, i) holds $c_i(u)$ for all $u \in U(i)$. Each D.P. iteration consists of four phases. In the first phase, each processor (i, j) forms the product $p_{ij}(u)x_j$ for all $u \in U(i)$; this takes $O(r)$ time. In the second phase, the sums $c_i(u) + \sum_{j=1}^{n} p_{ij}(u)x_j$, for all $u \in U(i)$, are formed at node (i, i) by using r single node accumulations along the ith row hypercube; these can be pipelined (cf. Exercise 3.19 in Section 1.3) so that they take $O(r + \log n)$ time. In the third phase, each processor (i, i) computes the new value of x_i, which is the minimum over $u \in U(i)$ of the sums $c_i(u) + \sum_{j=1}^{n} p_{ij}(u)x_j$ over all $u \in U(i)$; this takes $O(r)$ time. Finally, in the fourth phase, each processor (i, i) broadcasts the new value of x_i to all processors (j, i), $j = 1, 2, \ldots, n$ along the ith column hypercube, requiring $O(\log n)$ time. The total time taken by the D.P. iteration is $O(r + \log n)$.

Suppose, finally, that a hypercube with $n^2 r$ processors is available. We assume that both r and n are powers of 2, and that the processors are arranged in an $n \times n \times r$ array, with each "row" of n or r processors being itself a hypercube. We number the r elements of $U(i)$ as $1, 2, \ldots, r$, and we assume that at the beginning of each iteration, each processor (i, j, u) holds x_j and $p_{ij}(u)$, and each processor (i, i, u) holds $c_i(u)$. Then the D.P. iteration can be implemented similarly as in the preceding paragraph, but with modifications to take advantage of the additional processors. One difference is that the first and second phases are parallelized over u, so that they take time $O(1)$ and $O(\log n)$, respectively; furthermore, the minimization over $u \in U(i)$ of the third phase yielding x_i is done in time $O(\log r)$ using a single node accumulation at node $(i, i, 1)$. Finally, at the fourth phase, x_i is transmitted from processor $(i, i, 1)$ to all processors (j, i, u) in time $O\big(\log(rn)\big)$ using a single node broadcast. If $r \leq n$, the total time per D.P. iteration is $O(\log n)$.

Note that the bound on the order of time per D.P. iteration given above for each case of number of processors and interconnection network cannot be improved in the absence of additional problem structure, even if all communication is assumed instantaneous.

EXERCISES

3.1. Let Assumption 3.1 hold, $e = (1, 1, \ldots, 1)$, and $\epsilon > 0$ be a given scalar:

(a) Show that if $\mu \in M$ is such that

$$T_\mu(x^*) \leq T(x^*) + \epsilon e,$$

then

$$x(\mu) \leq x^* + \frac{\epsilon}{1 - \alpha} e.$$

(b) Suppose that x satisfies $|x_i - x_i^*| \leq \epsilon$ for all i. Show that if $\mu \in M$ is such that $T_\mu(x) = T(x)$, then

$$x^* \leq x(\mu) \leq x^* + \frac{2\alpha\epsilon}{1 - \alpha} e.$$

3.2. Assume that $\alpha = 1$, $p_{ii}(u) = 0$ for all $i \neq 1$ and $u \in U(i)$, and $p_{11}(u) = 1$ for all $u \in U(1)$. For an improper policy $\{\mu, \mu, \ldots\}$, consider the directed graph having nodes $1, 2, \ldots, n$, and an arc (i, j) for each pair of nodes i and j such that $p_{ij}\big(\mu(i)\big) > 0$. Define the length of a cycle $(i_1, i_2, \ldots, i_k, i_1)$ as the sum $c_{i_1}\big(\mu(i_1)\big) + \cdots + c_{i_k}\big(\mu(i_k)\big)$. Show that if all cycles have positive length, the policy yields infinite cost for at least one initial state (cf. Assumption 3.2).

3.3. Assume that $\alpha = 1$, $p_{11}(u) = 1$ and $c_1(u) = 0$ for all $u \in U(1)$, and, furthermore, all stationary policies are proper. Show that the mappings T and T_μ of Eqs. (3.5) and (3.6), respectively, are contraction mappings with respect to some weighted maximum norm $\|\cdot\|_\infty^w$ over the subspace

$$X = \{x \in \Re^n \mid x_1 = 0\}.$$

Abbreviated proof.   Partition the state space as follows. Let $S_1 = \{1\}$ and for $k = 2, 3, \ldots$, define sequentially

$$S_k = \left\{i \;\Big|\; i \notin S_1 \cup \cdots \cup S_{k-1} \text{ and } \min_{u \in U(i)} \max_{j \in S_1 \cup \cdots \cup S_{k-1}} p_{ij}(u) > 0\right\}.$$

Let S_m be the last of these sets that is nonempty. We claim that the sets S_k cover the entire state space, that is, $\cup_{k=1}^m S_k = S$. To see this, suppose that the set $S_\infty = \left\{i \mid i \notin \cup_{k=1}^m S_k\right\}$ is nonempty. Then for each $i \in S_\infty$, there exists some $u_i \in U(i)$ such that $p_{ij}(u_i) = 0$ for all $j \notin S_\infty$. Take any μ such that $\mu(i) = u_i$ for all $i \in S_\infty$. The stationary policy $\{\mu, \mu, \ldots\}$ satisfies $\left[P^t(\mu)\right]_{ij} = 0$ for all $i \in S_\infty$, $j \notin S_\infty$, and t, and, therefore, cannot be proper, which contradicts the hypothesis.

We will choose a vector $w > 0$ so that T is a contraction with respect to $\|\cdot\|_\infty^w$ on the set X. We will take the ith coordinate w_i to be the same for states i in the same set S_k. In particular, we will choose the coordinates w_i of the vector w by

$$w_i = y_k \qquad \text{if} \qquad i \in S_k,$$

where $y_1, \ldots, y_m$ are appropriately chosen scalars satisfying

$$1 = y_1 < y_2 < \cdots < y_m. \tag{3.18}$$

Let

$$\epsilon = \min_{k=2,\ldots,m} \min_{\mu \in M} \min_{i \in S_k} \sum_{j \in S_1 \cup \cdots \cup S_{k-1}} \left[P(\mu)\right]_{ij}, \tag{3.19}$$

and note that $0 < \epsilon \leq 1$. We will show that it is sufficient to choose $y_2, \ldots, y_m$ so that for some $\gamma < 1$, we have

$$\frac{y_m}{y_k}(1 - \epsilon) + \frac{y_{k-1}}{y_k}\epsilon \leq \gamma < 1, \qquad k = 2, \ldots, m. \tag{3.20}$$

and then show that such a choice of $y_2, \ldots, y_m$ exists.

Indeed, for $x, x' \in X$, let $\mu \in M$ be such that $T_\mu(x) = T(x)$. Then we have for all i,

$$[T(x') - T(x)]_i = [T(x') - T_\mu(x)]_i \leq [T_\mu(x') - T_\mu(x)]_i = \sum_{j=1}^n p_{ij}\big(\mu(i)\big)(x'_j - x_j). \quad (3.21)$$

Let $k(j)$ be such that j belongs to the set $S_{k(j)}$. Then we have, for any constant c,

$$\|x' - x\|_\infty^w \leq c \quad \Rightarrow \quad x'_j - x_j \leq c y_{k(j)}, \qquad j = 2, \ldots, n,$$

and Eq. (3.21) implies that for all i,

$$\frac{\big[T(x')\big]_i - \big[T(x)\big]_i}{c y_{k(i)}} \leq \frac{1}{y_{k(i)}} \sum_{j=1}^n p_{ij}\big(\mu(i)\big) y_{k(j)}$$

$$\leq \frac{y_{k(i)-1}}{y_{k(i)}} \sum_{j \in S_1 \cup \cdots \cup S_{k(i)-1}} p_{ij}\big(\mu(i)\big) + \frac{y_m}{y_{k(i)}} \sum_{j \in S_{k(i)} \cup \cdots \cup S_m} p_{ij}\big(\mu(i)\big)$$

$$= \left(\frac{y_{k(i)-1}}{y_{k(i)}} - \frac{y_m}{y_{k(i)}}\right) \sum_{j \in S_1 \cup \cdots \cup S_{k(i)-1}} p_{ij}\big(\mu(i)\big) + \frac{y_m}{y_{k(i)}}$$

$$\leq \left(\frac{y_{k(i)-1}}{y_{k(i)}} - \frac{y_m}{y_{k(i)}}\right) \epsilon + \frac{y_m}{y_{k(i)}} \leq \gamma,$$

where the second inequality follows from Eq. (3.18), the third inequality uses Eq. (3.19) and the fact $y_{k(i)-1} - y_m \leq 0$, and the last inequality follows from (3.20). Thus, we have

$$\frac{\big[T(x')\big]_i - [T(x)]_i}{w_i} \leq c\gamma, \qquad i = 1, \ldots, n,$$

so we obtain

$$\max_i \frac{\big[T(x')\big]_i - [T(x)]_i}{w_i} \leq c\gamma,$$

or

$$\big\|T(x) - T(x')\big\|_\infty^w \leq c\gamma, \qquad \text{for all } x, x' \in X \text{ with } \|x - x'\|_\infty^w \leq c.$$

It follows that T is a contraction mapping with respect to $\|\cdot\|_\infty^w$ over X.

We now show how to choose the scalars $y_1, y_2, \ldots, y_m$ so that Eqs. (3.18) and (3.20) hold. Let $y_0 = 0$, $y_1 = 1$, and suppose that $y_1, y_2, \ldots, y_k$ have been chosen. If $\epsilon = 1$, we choose $y_{k+1} = y_k + 1$. If $\epsilon < 1$, we choose y_{k+1} to be

$$y_{k+1} = \frac{1}{2}(y_k + M_k),$$

where

$$M_k = \min_{1 \le i \le k} \left[y_i + \frac{\epsilon}{1-\epsilon}(y_i - y_{i-1}) \right].$$

Using the fact

$$M_{k+1} = \min \left\{ M_k, y_{k+1} + \frac{\epsilon}{1-\epsilon}(y_{k+1} - y_k) \right\},$$

it is seen by induction that for all k,

$$y_k < y_{k+1} < M_{k+1}.$$

In particular, we have

$$y_m < M_m = \min_{1 \le i \le m} \left[y_i + \frac{\epsilon}{1-\epsilon}(y_i - y_{i-1}) \right],$$

which implies Eq. (3.20).

3.4. Prove Prop. 3.3 under a variation of Assumption 3.2, whereby, instead of assuming that every improper policy yields infinite cost for some initial state, we assume that $c_i(u) \ge 0$ for all i and $u \in U(i)$, and that there exists an optimal proper policy. The set X is now defined as $X = [x | x \ge 0, x_1 = 0]$. *Hint:* Lemma 3.1 is not valid, so a somewhat different argument is needed. The assumptions guarantee that x^* is finite and $x^* \in X$. [We have $x^* \ge 0$ because $c_i(u) \ge 0$, and $x_i^* < \infty$ because a proper policy exists.] The idea now is to show that $x^* \ge T(x^*)$, and then to choose μ such that $T_\mu(x^*) = T(x^*)$ and show that $\{\mu, \mu, \ldots\}$ is optimal and proper. Let $\pi = \{\mu_0, \mu_1, \ldots\}$ be a policy. We have for all i,

$$\left[x(\pi)\right]_i = c_i\big(\mu_0(i)\big) + \sum_{j=1}^{n} p_{ij}\big(\mu_0(i)\big) \left[x(\pi_1)\right]_j$$

where π_1 is the policy $\{\mu_1, \mu_2, \ldots\}$. Since $x(\pi_1) \ge x^*$, we obtain

$$\left[x(\pi)\right]_i \ge c_i\big(\mu_0(i)\big) + \sum_{j=1}^{n} p_{ij}\big(\mu_0(i)\big) x_j^* = \left[T_{\mu_0}(x^*)\right]_i \ge \left[T(x^*)\right]_i.$$

Taking the infimum over π in the preceding equation, we obtain

$$x^* \ge T(x^*). \tag{3.22}$$

Let $\mu \in M$ be such that $T_\mu(x^*) = T(x^*)$. From Eq. (3.22), we have $x^* \ge T_\mu(x^*)$, and using the monotonicity of T_μ, we obtain

$$x^* \ge T_\mu^t(x^*) = P^t(\mu)x^* + \sum_{k=0}^{t-1} P^k(\mu)c(\mu) \ge \sum_{k=0}^{t-1} P^k(\mu)c(\mu), \qquad \forall\, t \ge 1. \tag{3.23}$$

By taking limit superior as $t \to \infty$, we obtain $x^* \geq x(\mu)$. Hence, $\{\mu, \mu, \ldots\}$ is an optimal proper policy, and $x^* = x(\mu)$. Since μ was selected so that $T_\mu(x^*) = T(x^*)$, we obtain, using $x^* = x(\mu)$ and $x(\mu) = T_\mu\big(x(\mu)\big)$, $x^* = T(x^*)$. For the rest of the proof, use the vector Δ similarly as in the proof of Prop. 3.3.

3.5. Under the Discounted Cost Assumption 3.1, show that if $x \in \Re^n$ is such that $T(x) \geq x$, then $x^* \geq x$. Use this fact to show that x^* solves the linear program

$$\text{maximize} \quad \beta' x$$

$$\text{subject to} \quad c_i(u) + \alpha \sum_{j=1}^{n} p_{ij}(u)x_j \geq x_i, \qquad i = 1, \ldots, n, \ u \in U(i),$$

where β is a nonzero vector with nonnegative coordinates. Derive a similar result under the Undiscounted Cost Assumption 3.2.

3.6. [Tse85] Consider the linear program in $\Re^n$:

$$\text{maximize} \quad \beta' x$$

$$\text{subject to} \quad C_k x \leq d_k, \qquad k = 1, \ldots, m$$

where β is a nonzero vector with nonnegative coordinates, d_k are given vectors, and C_k are square $n \times n$ matrices with positive elements on the diagonal and nonpositive elements off the diagonal. Assume that all matrices C_k are diagonally dominant. Use the result of Exercise 3.5 to transform the problem into a dynamic programming problem.

3.7. Under the Undiscounted Cost Assumption 3.2 show that the Gauss–Seidel algorithm based on T (as defined in Subsection 3.1.2 of Chapter 3), converges to x^* for any initial vector $x \in X$. *Hint:* Compare with Exercise 1.4 in Section 3.1.

3.8. (**The Blackmailer's Dilemma** [Whi83].) The analysis given for undiscounted problems in this section relies on the finiteness of the set $U(i)$ of available decisions at state i. This exercise shows that if $U(i)$ is not finite, then Prop. 3.3 need not hold even if all stationary policies are proper. In particular, the optimal cost may be $-\infty$ for some initial states, there may exist an optimal nonstationary policy but no optimal stationary policy, and the dynamic programming algorithm may converge to a wrong point for some initial conditions.

Consider a controlled Markov chain with two states, 1 and 2. State 1 is absorbing and cost–free. In state 2 we must choose a control u from the interval $(0, 1]$ and incur a cost $-u$; we then move to state 1 at no cost with probability u^β, where β is a fixed positive scalar, and we stay in state 2 with probability $1 - u^\beta$. (We may view here u as a demand made by a blackmailer, and state 2 as the situation where the victim complies. State 1 is the situation where the victim refuses to pay and denounces the blackmailer to the police. The problem of this exercise models the blackmailer's effort to maximize the total expected gain through balancing at each time the desire for a high demand u with a low probability u^β that the victim will not comply.)

The mapping T takes the form

$$\big[T(x)\big]_1 = 0, \qquad \big[T(x)\big]_2 = \inf_{u \in (0,1]} \big[-u + \big(1 - u^\beta\big) x_2\big].$$

Show that:
  (a) All stationary policies are proper and yield finite cost.
  (b) If $\beta > 1$, then the optimal cost x_2^* starting from state 2 is $-\infty$. Show also that if $\beta = 2$ then the nonstationary policy that chooses in state 2 the control $u_k = \gamma/(k+1)$ at time k is optimal provided $\gamma \in (0, 1/2]$. *Hint:* Use the fact that $\sum_{k=1}^{\infty} 1/k = \infty$, and also that the product $\prod_{k=1}^{\infty} \left(1 - \gamma^2/k^2\right)$ is greater than $1 - \gamma^2 \sum_{k=1}^{\infty}(1/k^2)$ and is therefore positive for $\gamma \in (0, 1/2]$.
  (c) If $\beta \leq 1$ then $x_2^* = -1$, and for all x with $x_1 = 0$, $x_2 \geq -1$ we have $T(x) = x^*$. On the other hand we have $x = T(x)$ for all x with $x_1 = 0$, $x_2 < -1$.

NOTES AND SOURCES

4.1 The shortest path problem is discussed in nearly every book on combinatorial and network optimization, see, e.g., [Law76], [PaS82], and [Roc84]. For a literature survey, see [DeP84] and for an extensive computational study, see [DGK79]. The Bellman–Ford algorithm is derived in [Bel57] and [For56]. Our treatment of arbitrary initial conditions (Prop. 1.2 in particular), appears to be new. The distributed Bellman–Ford algorithm as well as a parallel form of Dijkstra's method with a separate processor assigned to each origin node have been used in routing algorithms for data networks, including the ARPANET (see [BeG87], [Eph86], [MRR80], and [ScS80]). For distributed shortest path algorithms, appropriate for message–passing systems and data networks, see [Gal82] and [AwG87]. The parallel implementation of the Floyd–Warshall algorithm of Exercise 1.7 is similar to implementations on array processors and systolic arrays (see [AtK84], [DNS81], and [Kun88]). The parallel solution of a number of graph problems using various processor interconnection networks is discussed in [DNS81]. Shortest path algorithms based on forward search (cf. Exercise 1.10) are commonly used in artificial intelligence applications and are related to some branch–and–bound methods for integer programming; see [Ber87] and [Pea84].

4.2 Treatments of dynamic programming can be found in many textbooks, including [Bel57], [Ber87], [BeS78], [HeS82], [KuV86], [Nem66], [Ros83b], [Whi82], and [Whi83].

4.3 Discounted Markovian decision problems have been exhaustively analyzed and a detailed account with references and additional computational methods can be found in [Ber87].

Special cases of undiscounted Markovian decision problems, called *stopping problems* or *first passage problems*, have been considered extensively in the literature (see [Ber87] for an account and references). The theory existing up to now assumes that state costs are either all nonnegative or all nonpositive. Our treatment extends the theory to the case where both positive and negative state costs are allowed. Because our assumptions generalize naturally the standard Connectivity and Positive Cycle assumptions of the shortest path problem, we refer to the undiscounted problem as the stochastic shortest path problem.

Contraction mappings in dynamic programming are treated in [Den67] and [BeS78]. The weighted maximum norm contraction result of Exercise 3.3 has been attributed to A. J. Hoffman. The monotonicity of the dynamic programming mapping is emphasized in [Ber77], [BeS78], and [VeP87]; it will play an important role in the asynchronous version of the Bellman–Ford algorithm discussed in Section 6.4.

The complexity analysis of [PaT87b] strongly suggests that in contrast with the shortest path problem, there do not exist any parallel algorithms for solving the dynamic programming problems of this section in time $O\left(\log^k n\right)$ for any integer k.

5

Network Flow Problems

Network flow problems are the most frequently solved class of optimization problems. They include as special cases combinatorial problems such as the assignment, transportation, max–flow, and shortest path problems, and they arise naturally in the analysis of large systems such as manufacturing, communication, and transportation networks. Among network problems, those involving linear cost are by far the most common. Traditionally, these problems are solved using primal–simplex (see [Dan63]), primal–dual (see [FoF62]), or relaxation methods (see [Ber82c], [BeT85], and Section 5.2). Highly sophisticated codes based on these methods are presently available [AaM76], [BBG77], [BeT85], [GKK74], [GrH80], [KeH80], and [Mul78]. Unfortunately, none of these methods seems inherently well–suited for parallel computation. In this chapter, we consider several methods that are similar in spirit to the Gauss–Seidel and Jacobi methods examined in Chapters 2 and 3. They are based on a dual network flow optimization problem involving a single dual variable per network node. At each iteration, a single node is chosen, and its dual variable or its incident arc flows are changed in an attempt to improve the dual cost. This approach is well suited for massive parallelization, whereby each node is a processor adjusting its own dual variable on the basis of local information communicated by adjacent processors/nodes.

In Section 5.1, we introduce the linear network flow problem (otherwise known as the *transshipment* or *minimum cost flow* problem), along with several important special cases. We formulate a dual problem based on linear programming duality theory. This is an unconstrained optimization problem with a structure that is suitable for application of the Gauss–Seidel relaxation method discussed in Section 3.2, but with a cost function that violates the differentiability requirement of the analysis of that section. We explain the associated difficulties in Section 5.2, and we discuss potential approaches for overcoming these difficulties. A highly parallelizable method, called ϵ–*relaxation*, is introduced in Section 5.3. A closely related method for the assignment problem, called the *auction* algorithm, is also discussed. The complexity analysis of these methods is given in Section 5.4.

The last two sections of the chapter deal with nonlinear problems. In Section 5.5, we consider nonlinear network flow problems with strictly convex arc costs, and the associated duality theory. Here the dual cost is differentiable, so the application of the Gauss–Seidel relaxation method is much easier than for the linear cost case. Nonetheless, the analysis is nontrivial because the dual cost is not strictly convex, and the results of Section 3.2 for the nonlinear Gauss–Seidel method do not apply. The algorithm can be extended to the class of convex problems with separable cost and linear constraints, also known as *monotropic programming problems* [Roc84], but we will not go into this here; see [TsB87a]. It turns out that the Jacobi version of the relaxation algorithm is not guaranteed to converge to an optimal solution. We will show in Sections 6.6 and 7.2 that modified relaxation algorithms are convergent when either a Jacobi–like or an asynchronous implementation is used. Finally, in Section 5.6, we consider nonlinear multicommodity network flow problems of the type often arising in communication and transportation networks. The method considered here is based on the gradient projection method discussed in Section 3.3.

Throughout this chapter, we consider synchronous algorithms. Totally and partially asynchronous versions are discussed in the next two chapters.

5.1 THE LINEAR NETWORK FLOW PROBLEM AND ITS DUAL

The optimal network flow problem with linear arc costs of this section is a special case of a linear programming problem, and the duality formulation to be given is a special case of linear programming duality (see Appendix C).

Consider a directed graph with a set of nodes N and a set of arcs A. Each arc (i, j) has associated with it an integer a_{ij} referred to as the cost coefficient of (i, j). Let f_{ij} be the flow of the arc (i, j), and consider the problem

$$\text{minimize} \quad \sum_{(i,j) \in A} a_{ij} f_{ij} \qquad \text{(LNF)}$$

$$\text{subject to} \quad \sum_{\{j | (i,j) \in A\}} f_{ij} - \sum_{\{j | (j,i) \in A\}} f_{ji} = s_i, \qquad \forall \, i \in N, \qquad (1.1)$$

$$b_{ij} \leq f_{ij} \leq c_{ij}, \qquad \forall \, (i, j) \in A, \qquad (1.2)$$

where a_{ij}, b_{ij}, c_{ij}, and s_i are given integers. We refer to b_{ij} and c_{ij}, and the interval $[b_{ij}, c_{ij}]$ as the *flow bounds* and the *feasible flow range* of arc (i, j), respectively. We refer to s_i as the *supply* of node i and to $-s_i$ as the *demand* of node i. We refer to the constraints (1.1) and (1.2) as the *conservation of flow constraints* and the *capacity constraints* respectively. We assume that $\sum_{i \in N} s_i = 0$; by adding the constraints (1.1), we see that this condition is necessary for problem feasibility. As discussed in Appendix B, we also assume that there is at most one arc in each direction between any pair of nodes; this assumption is made in order to simplify notation and can be easily dispensed with (Exercise 1.5). The numbers of nodes and arcs are denoted $|N|$ and $|A|$, respectively.

The linear network flow problem (LNF) is a classical problem that has been studied extensively. The assignment, max–flow, and shortest path problems are special cases, as shown in Figs. 5.1.1 through 5.1.3. These problems are particularly interesting within our context, each for different reasons.

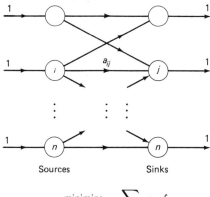

Sources   Sinks

Figure 5.1.1 In the assignment problem, there are $2n$ nodes, n of which (the sources) have supply of 1 unit of flow, and the other n (the sinks) have a demand of 1 unit. Each arc (i, j) connects a source i to a sink j and has an arc cost coefficient a_{ij}. All arcs flows must satisfy $0 \le f_{ij} \le B$, where B is a given positive integer. [An alternative and equivalent formulation uses only the constraint $0 \le f_{ij}$; the resulting problem, however, is not a special case of the linear network flow problem (LNF).] The problem is

$$\text{minimize} \quad \sum_{(i,j) \in A} a_{ij} f_{ij}$$

$$\text{subject to} \quad \sum_{\{j \mid (i,j) \in A\}} f_{ij} = 1, \qquad \forall\, i = 1, \ldots, n,$$

$$\sum_{\{i \mid (i,j) \in A\}} f_{ij} = 1, \qquad \forall\, j = 1, \ldots, n,$$

$$0 \le f_{ij} \le B, \qquad \forall\, (i, j) \in A.$$

It will be shown as a by–product of our analysis in the next section that if there exists a feasible solution for problem (LNF), there exists an *integer* optimal solution for both (LNF) and its dual. For the assignment problem, such an optimal solution consists of arc flows that are zero or one, and assigns exactly one source to each sink.

The assignment problem can be viewed as the canonical special case because it can be shown that problem (LNF) can be transformed into an assignment problem (see Fig. 5.1.4). This means that algorithms that can be developed or understood using the rich intuition afforded by the assignment problem can be made to work for the general problem (LNF).

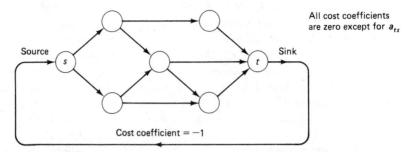

Figure 5.1.2 In the max–flow problem, there are two special nodes, the *source* (s) and the *sink* (t), which are connected by an arc (t, s). All arcs have zero cost coefficient except for (t, s) which has a cost coefficient of -1. The lower bound for all arc flows is zero, and the upper bound c_{ts} is greater than or equal to $\sum_i c_{it}$. We have $s_i = 0$ for all nodes i. At the optimum, the flow f_{ts} equals the maximum flow that can be sent from s to t through the subgraph obtained by deleting arc (t, s).

Figure 5.1.3 In the shortest path problem, each arc (i, j) has a length a_{ij}, and the objective is to find a minimum length simple path from every node to node 1. We can write the problem into the form of the linear network flow problem (LNF) as follows

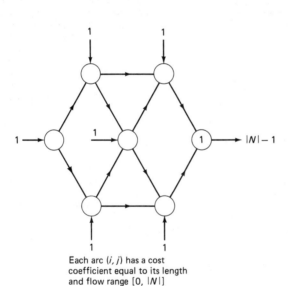

Each arc (i, j) has a cost coefficient equal to its length and flow range $[0, |N|]$

minimize $\displaystyle\sum_{(i,j)\in A} a_{ij} f_{ij}$

subject to $\displaystyle\sum_{\{j \,|\,(i,j)\in A\}} f_{ij} - \sum_{\{j \,|\,(j,i)\in A\}} f_{ji} = 1,$

$$\forall\, i = 2, \ldots, |N|,$$

$$\sum_{\{j \,|\,(j,1)\in A\}} f_{j1} = |N| - 1,$$

$$0 \le f_{ij} \le |N|, \quad \forall\, (i,j) \in A.$$

This equivalence holds provided every cycle has a positive length.

The max–flow problem is characterized by the fact that the range of values of arc cost coefficients is small ($[-1, 0]$; see Fig. 5.1.2), and this will turn out to be significant within the context of the ϵ–relaxation algorithm of Secion 5.3.

Finally, the shortest path problem is fundamental in the analysis of the linear network flow problem (LNF) and often appears as a subroutine in various algorithms for solving (LNF). We will see in the next section that the relaxation method for solving the shortest path problem is closely related to the Bellman–Ford algorithm discussed in Section 4.3.

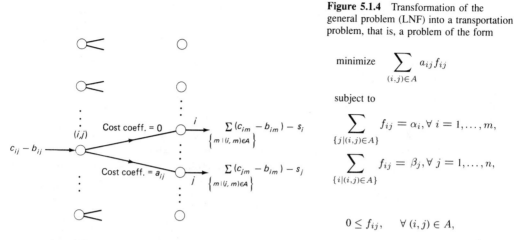

Figure 5.1.4 Transformation of the general problem (LNF) into a transportation problem, that is, a problem of the form

$$\text{minimize} \quad \sum_{(i,j)\in A} a_{ij} f_{ij}$$

subject to

$$\sum_{\{j|(i,j)\in A\}} f_{ij} = \alpha_i, \forall\, i = 1,\ldots,m,$$

$$\sum_{\{i|(i,j)\in A\}} f_{ij} = \beta_j, \forall\, j = 1,\ldots,n,$$

$$0 \le f_{ij}, \quad \forall\, (i,j) \in A,$$

where α_i, and β_j are positive integers. In the transportation problem we take as sources the arcs of the original network, and as sinks the nodes of the original network. Each transportation problem source has two outgoing arcs with cost coefficients as shown. The supply of each transportation problem source is the feasible flow range length of the corresponding original network arc. The demand of each transportation problem sink is the sum of the feasible flow range lengths of the outgoing arcs from the corresponding original network node minus the supply of that node as shown. An arc flow f_{ij} in (LNF) corresponds to flows equal to f_{ij} and $c_{ij} - b_{ij} - f_{ij}$ on the transportation problem arcs $\big((i,j),j\big)$ and $\big((i,j),i\big)$ respectively. The transportation problem can be converted to an assignment problem by creating α_i unit supply sources (β_j unit capacity sinks) for each transportation problem source i (sink j respectively).

The Dual Problem

We formulate a dual problem associated with (LNF) by associating a Lagrange multiplier p_i with the ith conservation of flow constraint (1.1) as discussed in Appendix C. By denoting by f and p the vectors with elements f_{ij}, $(i,j) \in A$, and p_i, $i \in N$, respectively, we can write the corresponding Lagrangian function as

$$
\begin{aligned}
L(f,p) &= \sum_{(i,j)\in A} a_{ij} f_{ij} + \sum_{i\in N} p_i \left(\sum_{\{j|(j,i)\in A\}} f_{ji} - \sum_{\{j|(i,j)\in A\}} f_{ij} + s_i \right) \\
&= \sum_{(i,j)\in A} (a_{ij} + p_j - p_i) f_{ij} + \sum_{i\in N} s_i p_i.
\end{aligned}
\tag{1.3}
$$

The dual function value $q(p)$ at a vector p is obtained by minimizing $L(f,p)$ over all f satisfying the capacity constraints (1.2). This leads to the dual problem

$$\text{maximize} \quad q(p) \tag{1.4}$$

$$\text{subject to no constraint on } p,$$

with the dual functional q given by

$$q(p) = \min_{\substack{b_{ij} \le f_{ij} \le c_{ij} \\ (i,j) \in A}} L(f,p) = \sum_{(i,j) \in A} q_{ij}(p_i - p_j) + \sum_{i \in N} s_i p_i, \qquad (1.5)$$

where each q_{ij} is the scalar function defined by

$$q_{ij}(p_i - p_j) = \min_{b_{ij} \le f_{ij} \le c_{ij}} (a_{ij} + p_j - p_i) f_{ij}. \qquad (1.6)$$

The function q_{ij} is shown in Fig. 5.1.5. We henceforth refer to (LNF) as the *primal problem*, and note that based on the duality results of Appendix C, the optimal primal cost equals the optimal dual cost. The dual variable p_i will be referred to as the *price* of node i.

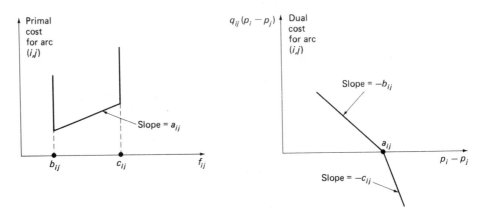

Figure 5.1.5 Primal and dual costs for arc (i,j). Note that the break points for each function correspond to slopes of linear segments in the other function.

For any flow vector f and node i, the scalar

$$g_i = \sum_{\{j|(j,i) \in A\}} f_{ji} - \sum_{\{j|(i,j) \in A\}} f_{ij} + s_i \qquad (1.7)$$

is called the *surplus* of node i. It represents the difference of total flow imported and total flow exported by the node. The conservation of flow constraint (1.1) is also written as

$$g_i = 0, \qquad \forall \ i \in N. \qquad (1.8)$$

The necessary and sufficient conditions for a pair (f, p) to be an optimal primal and dual solution pair are primal feasibility and complementary slackness [relations (C.16) and (C.17) in Appendix C]. To state these conditions, we first introduce some terminology. For any price vector p, we say that an arc (i, j) is

$$\text{Inactive if} \qquad p_i < a_{ij} + p_j,$$

$$\text{Balanced if} \qquad p_i = a_{ij} + p_j,$$

$$\text{Active if} \qquad p_i > a_{ij} + p_j.$$

We say that a pair (f, p) satisfies *complementary slackness* (abbreviated CS) if

$$f_{ij} = b_{ij}, \qquad\qquad \text{for all inactive arcs } (i, j), \qquad\qquad (1.9)$$

$$b_{ij} \le f_{ij} \le c_{ij}, \qquad\qquad \text{for all balanced arcs } (i, j), \qquad\qquad (1.10)$$

$$f_{ij} = c_{ij}, \qquad\qquad \text{for all active arcs } (i, j), \qquad\qquad (1.11)$$

(see Fig. 5.1.6). Notice that a pair (f, p) satisfies CS if and only if each f_{ij} attains the minimum in the definition of the dual arc cost of Eq. (1.6). The optimality conditions of Appendix C translated to our problem yield the following result:

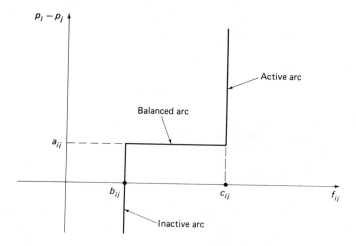

Figure 5.1.6 Illustration of the complementary slackness conditions (1.9)–(1.11). For each arc (i, j), the pair of flow f_{ij} and price differential $p_i - p_j$ should lie on the diagram shown.

Proposition 1.1. (*Optimality Conditions*)

(a) A flow vector f is primal optimal if and only if it is primal feasible, and there exists a price vector p that together with f satisfies the CS conditions (1.9)–(1.11).

(b) A flow vector f and a price vector p are primal and dual optimal, respectively, if and only if they satisfy the conservation of flow constraint (1.8) and the CS conditions (1.9)–(1.11).

An alternative optimality condition is given in Exercise 1.2. Another important property is that if there exists a feasible solution for problem (LNF), then there exist *integer* optimal solutions to both (LNF) and its dual. We will show this constructively in the next section by means of a method that computes such solutions.

EXERCISES

1.1. Let p be any price vector, and consider a problem that is the same as the linear network flow problem (LNF) except that the cost coefficient of each arc (i, j) is $a_{ij} + p_j - p_i$ instead of a_{ij}. Show that this problem has the same optimal solutions as (LNF), and that its optimal cost is less than the optimal cost of (LNF) by $\sum_{i \in N} p_i s_i$.

1.2. Show that a flow vector f is optimal for (LNF) if and only if f is feasible, and for every directed cycle Y for which

$$f_{ij} < c_{ij}, \qquad \forall \, (i, j) \in Y^+,$$

$$b_{ij} < f_{ij}, \qquad \forall \, (i, j) \in Y^-,$$

we have

$$\sum_{(i,j) \in Y^+} a_{ij} - \sum_{(i,j) \in Y^-} a_{ij} \geq 0,$$

where Y^+ and Y^- are the sets of forward and backward arcs of Y, respectively. *Hint:* Use the optimality condition of Prop. 3.1 in Section 3.3, and the Conformal Realization Theorem of Appendix B; see also the proof of Prop. 3.1 in Section 5.3.

1.3. In some situations, it is useful to have a price vector for which all arcs are inactive or balanced; for example, to convert the problem to one where all the arc cost coefficients are nonnegative (see Exercise 1.1). This exercise characterizes situations where this is possible, and shows that a corresponding price vector can be obtained by solving an assignment problem.

    (a) Consider the assignment problem of Fig. 5.1.1 for the case where $B > 1$. Show that the dual problem can be written as

$$\text{maximize} \quad \sum_{i=1}^{n} r_i - \sum_{j=1}^{n} p_j$$

$$\text{subject to} \quad a_{ij} + p_j \geq r_i, \qquad \forall \, (i, j) \in A.$$

    (b) Consider the linear network problem (LNF). Assume that each cycle that consists of forward arcs (a positive cycle) has a nonnegative arc cost sum. Show that a price vector such that all arcs are inactive or balanced [$a_{ij} + p_j \geq p_i$, for all $(i, j) \in A$] can be found by solving the dual of an assignment problem. Conversely, show that if one can find a price vector such that all arcs are inactive or balanced, then each cycle consisting of forward arcs has a nonnegative arc cost sum. *Hint:* For each node i, create a source i and a sink i'. For each arc (i, j) with cost a_{ij}, create an arc from source i to sink j' with cost a_{ij}. Create also an arc (i, i') with zero cost for each i. Use the result of Exercise 1.2 to show that assigning i to i' for each i is an optimal solution if and only if each positive cycle has a nonnegative arc cost sum.

1.4. There are several ways to convert problem (LNF) to a problem where the flow is constrained to be a circulation. One way is to introduce a new node v and for every node i with $s_i \neq 0$, introduce an arc (v, i) with zero arc cost coefficient and a feasible arc flow range $[s_i, s_i]$. This exercise provides a different conversion, which has the property that if the zero flow vector satisfies the arc capacity constraints of (LNF), then the zero flow vector is a feasible circulation after the conversion; this is sometimes useful in algorithms and theoretical studies. Introduce two new nodes v and w. For each node i with $s_i > 0$, introduce an arc (v, i) with zero arc cost coefficient and feasible arc flow range $[0, s_i]$. For each node i with $s_i < 0$ introduce an arc (i, w) with zero arc cost coefficient and feasible arc flow range $[0, -s_i]$. Introduce an arc (w, v) with feasible arc flow range $[0, c_{wv}]$, where $c_{wv} \geq \frac{1}{2} \sum_{i \in N} |s_i|$. Show that an optimal flow vector of the problem involving the enlarged network yields an optimal flow vector of (LNF) if the arc cost coefficient a_{wv} is less than $-L$, where L is defined as follows: for every simple path p from v to w, let L_p be the sum of the forward arc costs of the path minus the backward arc costs of the path, and let $L = \max_p L_p$. *Hint:* Consider an optimal flow vector f of the enlarged network problem, and assume that $f_{wv} < \frac{1}{2} \sum_{i \in N} |s_i|$. Use the result of Exercise 1.2 and the Conformal Realization Theorem to arrive at a contradiction.

1.5. Show that the version of problem (LNF) where multiple arcs are allowed between a pair of nodes can be converted to the single arc version by introducing an extra node for each multiple arc.

1.6. Show how to convert a network problem with convex piecewise linear arc costs to one with linear arc costs. *Hint:* Convert each arc with a piecewise linear cost into several arcs with linear costs. Use also Exercise 1.5.

1.7. (**A Method of Multipliers for Transportation Problems.**) Consider the (capacitated) transportation problem

$$\text{minimize} \quad \sum_{(i,j) \in A} a_{ij} f_{ij}$$

$$\text{subject to} \quad \sum_{\{j | (i,j) \in A\}} f_{ij} = \alpha_i, \quad \forall \, i = 1, \ldots, m,$$

$$\sum_{\{i | (i,j) \in A\}} f_{ij} = \beta_j, \quad \forall \, j = 1, \ldots, n,$$

$$0 \leq f_{ij} \leq c_{ij}, \quad \forall \, (i, j) \in A,$$

and the first of the two methods of multipliers introduced in Example 4.5 of Subsection 3.4.4. Show that the iteration that minimizes the Augmented Lagrangian has the form

$$f_{ij} := \left[f_{ij} + \frac{1}{2c(t)} \big(r_i(t) + p_i(t) - a_{ij} + c(t)(y_i + w_j) \big) \right]^+, \quad \forall \, (i, j) \in A,$$

where $[\cdot]^+$ denotes projection on the interval $[0, c_{ij}]$, and y_i and w_j are given in terms of f by

$$y_i = \alpha_i - \sum_{\{j|(i,j)\in A\}} f_{ij}, \qquad \forall\, i = 1, \ldots, m,$$

$$w_j = \beta_j - \sum_{\{i|(i,j)\in A\}} f_{ij}, \qquad \forall\, j = 1, \ldots, n.$$

At the end of the minimization yielding $f_{ij}(t+1)$, $y_i(t+1)$, and $w_j(t+1)$, the prices r_i and p_j are updated according to

$$r_i(t+1) = r_i(t) + c(t)y_i(t+1), \qquad \forall\, i = 1, \ldots, m,$$

$$p_j(t+1) = p_j(t) + c(t)w_j(t+1), \qquad \forall\, j = 1, \ldots, n.$$

1.8. (An Alternating Direction Method for Transportation Problems.) Consider the transportation problem of Exercise 1.7. Show that the following iteration is a special case of the alternating direction method of multipliers given in Subsection 3.4.4:

$$f_{ij}(t+1) := \left[f_{ij}(t) + \frac{1}{2c}\left[r_i(t) + p_i(t) - a_{ij} + c(y_i(t) + w_j(t)) \right] \right]^+, \qquad \forall\, (i,j) \in A,$$

$$r_i(t+1) = r_i(t) + cy_i(t+1), \qquad \forall\, i = 1, \ldots, m,$$

$$p_j(t+1) = p_j(t) + cw_j(t+1), \qquad \forall\, j = 1, \ldots, n,$$

where $y_i(t)$ and $w_j(t)$ are given in terms of $f(t)$ by

$$y_i(t) = \frac{1}{d_i}\left(\alpha_i - \sum_{\{j|(i,j)\in A\}} f_{ij}(t) \right), \qquad \forall\, i = 1, \ldots, m,$$

$$w_j(t) = \frac{1}{d_j}\left(\beta_j - \sum_{\{i|(i,j)\in A\}} f_{ij}(t) \right), \qquad \forall\, j = 1, \ldots, n,$$

and d_i (or d_j) is the number of incident arcs to i (or j, respectively).

5.2 THE RELAXATION METHOD

Consider the dual cost functional given by

$$q(p) = \sum_{(i,j)\in A} q_{ij}(p_i - p_j) + \sum_{i\in N} s_i p_i, \qquad (2.1a)$$

where

$$q_{ij}(p_i - p_j) = \begin{cases} (a_{ij} + p_j - p_i)b_{ij}, & \text{if } a_{ij} + p_j - p_i \geq 0, \\ (a_{ij} + p_j - p_i)c_{ij}, & \text{if } a_{ij} + p_j - p_i < 0, \end{cases} \qquad (2.1b)$$

[cf. Eqs. (1.5), (1.6) and Fig. 5.1.5]. An important characteristic of this function is that it has a separable form that motivates solution by a Gauss–Seidel relaxation (or coordinate ascent) method. In this section, we explore various possibilities in this direction. The idea is to choose a single node i, and to change its price p_i in a direction of improvement of the dual cost while keeping the other prices unchanged. Since p_i appears only in the terms $q_{ij}, (i, j) \in A$, and $q_{ji}, (j, i) \in A$, in the dual cost expression (2.1), the change in p_i requires a relatively small amount of computation.

To understand how to implement this type of iteration, we first focus on the dual cost $q(p)$ along a single price coordinate p_i, that is, for a given price vector p, we consider the function of the scalar ξ

$$Q_p^i(\xi) = q\big(p_1, \ldots, p_{i-1}, \xi, p_{i+1}, \ldots, p_{|N|}\big).$$

This function is the sum of linear and piecewise linear functions [cf. Eq. (2.1)], and is, therefore, piecewise linear as shown in Fig. 5.2.1. It is seen that the break points of the function correspond to the values of ξ at which one or more arcs incident to node i are balanced, that is, the values

$$p_j + a_{ij} \qquad \text{for outgoing arcs } (i, j) \in A,$$

$$p_j - a_{ji} \qquad \text{for incoming arcs } (j, i) \in A.$$

At a break point of $Q_p^i(\xi)$, we must distinguish between the left derivative g_i^- and the right derivative g_i^+ of $Q_p^i(\xi)$. In view of the dual cost equations (2.1) and Fig. 5.1.5, for given values of p and ξ, we have

$$g_i^+ = \sum_{\substack{(j,i):\ \text{active}}} c_{ji} + \sum_{\substack{(j,i):\ \text{inactive or balanced}}} b_{ji}$$

$$- \sum_{\substack{(i,j):\ \text{active or balanced}}} c_{ij} - \sum_{\substack{(i,j):\ \text{inactive}}} b_{ij} + s_i, \tag{2.2a}$$

$$g_i^- = \sum_{\substack{(j,i):\ \text{active or balanced}}} c_{ji} + \sum_{\substack{(j,i):\ \text{inactive}}} b_{ji}$$

$$- \sum_{\substack{(i,j):\ \text{active}}} c_{ij} - \sum_{\substack{(i,j):\ \text{inactive or balanced}}} b_{ij} + s_i. \tag{2.2b}$$

Note that within an open interval where $Q_p^i(\xi)$ is linear, the right and left derivatives are equal ($g_i^+ = g_i^-$), and there are no balanced arcs. Note also that g_i^+ (g_i^-) are the minimum (maximum, respectively) surplus of node i over all flow vectors that satisfy complementary slackness (CS) together with p [cf. conditions (1.9)–(1.11) in the preceding section].

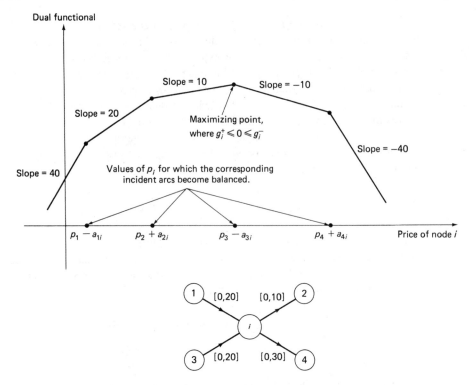

Figure 5.2.1 Illustration of $Q_p^i(\xi)$, the dual cost along price p_i, together with the left and right derivatives g_i^- and g_i^+, respectively (all other prices are kept fixed). Here node i has four incident arcs $(1, i)$, $(3, i)$, $(i, 2)$, $(i, 4)$ with flow ranges $[0,20]$, $[0,20]$, $[0,10]$, and $[0,30]$, respectively, and $s_i = 0$. The break points of the dual cost correspond to the values of p_i at which one or more incident arcs to node i become balanced. For values of p_i strictly between two successive break points, there are no balanced arcs.

A direct analog of the Gauss–Seidel relaxation method of Chapters 2 and 3 is obtained by choosing at each iteration a node i and by changing the price p_i so as to optimize the dual cost, that is,

$$p_i := \arg\ \max_{\xi} Q_p^i(\xi) = \arg\ \max_{\xi} q\big(p_1, \ldots, p_{i-1}, \xi, p_{i+1}, \ldots, p_{|N|}\big).$$

In particular, p_i is changed to a break point for which

$$g_i^+ \le 0 \le g_i^- \tag{2.3}$$

(see Fig. 5.2.1).

The algorithm terminates when the condition $g_i^+ \le 0 \le g_i^-$ holds for all $i \in N$. If the starting prices are integer and the optimal dual value is finite (as it will be when the primal problem is feasible; see Appendix C), the algorithm will terminate after a finite number of iterations. To see this, first note that throughout the algorithm the node prices and the break points of all functions $Q_p^i(\xi)$ are integer. Next observe that each time a node price changes, there will be an improvement of the dual cost by an integer amount, since both the price increment and the corresponding rate of improvement of the dual cost are integer. Therefore, there can only be a finite number of dual cost improvements and the algorithm must terminate finitely.

The difficulty with this algorithm is that it can terminate at a nonoptimal price vector, depending on the starting price vector and the problem data. This is illustrated graphically in Fig. 5.2.2 and analytically in the context of the shortest path problem in the following subsection.

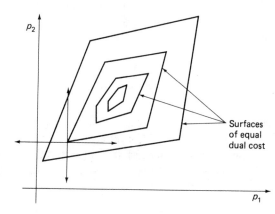

Figure 5.2.2 The difficulty with the relaxation method. At the indicated corner point, it is impossible to improve the dual cost by changing any *single* price coordinate.

5.2.1 Application to the Shortest Path Problem

Consider the shortest path problem formulation shown in Fig. 5.1.3, where node 1 is the destination. It can be shown that if p^* is a dual optimal price vector, then $p_i^* - p_1^*$ is the shortest distance from i to 1. Indeed, by the optimality conditions of Prop. 1.1(b), p^* satisfies CS together with every primal optimal flow vector. We can construct such a flow vector by sending the supply of each node i to the destination node 1 along a shortest path from i to 1, and by accumulating the total flow on each arc. Each arc of this shortest path must be balanced [it cannot be inactive because its flow is positive and it cannot be active because no optimal arc flow can exceed $|N| - 1$ (the sum of all node supplies) while the arc flow upper bound is $|N|$]. By adding the condition $p_i^* - p_j^* = a_{ij}$ for a balanced arc (i, j) along a shortest path, we obtain that $p_i^* - p_1^*$ equals the length of the shortest path.

The left and right derivatives of the dual cost $Q_p^i(\xi)$ along the ith price coordinate are given by [cf. Eq. (2.2)]

$$g_i^- = 1 + |N| \cdot [\text{number of active or balanced arcs (j,i)} - \text{number of active arcs (i,j)}],$$
$$\text{if } i \neq 1,$$

$$g_1^- = 1 - |N| + |N| \cdot [\text{number of active or balanced arcs (j,1)}],$$

$$g_i^+ = 1 + |N| \cdot [\text{number of active arcs (j,i)} - \text{number of active or balanced arcs (i,j)}],$$
$$\text{if } i \neq 1,$$

$$g_1^+ = 1 - |N| + |N| \cdot [\text{number of active arcs (j,1)}].$$

Consider the relaxation algorithm whereby at each iteration, a single node price p_i is changed so as to maximize the dual cost along p_i, that is, p_i is set to a point where the condition $g_i^+ \leq 0 \leq g_i^-$ is satisfied [cf. Eq. (2.3)]. It is seen from the above equations that this can be accomplished by setting the price p_i of a node $i \neq 1$ to the smallest breakpoint at which there are fewer active incoming arcs (j, i) than active and balanced outgoing arcs (i, j); the price p_1 should be set to the value at which there is no active arc $(j, 1)$, and there are one or more than one balanced arc $(j, 1)$.

Suppose now that a price vector p is such that all arcs are inactive or balanced, that is,

$$\max_{\{j|(j,i)\in A\}} (p_j - a_{ji}) \leq p_i \leq \min_{\{j|(i,j)\in A\}} (p_j + a_{ij}), \qquad \forall\, i \in N. \tag{2.4}$$

[Such a price vector exists assuming that all cycles have positive length; see Exercise 1.3 in the previous section. In particular, if $a_{ij} \geq 0$ for all arcs (i, j), it is seen that for the zero price vector, all arcs are inactive or balanced.] It can be seen then (Fig. 5.2.3) that, for $i \neq 1$, the relaxation iteration sets p_i to the smallest value such that at least one outgoing arc becomes balanced, and takes the form

$$p_i := \min_{\{j|(i,j)\in A\}} (p_j + a_{ij}), \qquad \forall\, i \neq 1, \tag{2.5}$$

and that, for $i = 1$, the iteration takes the form

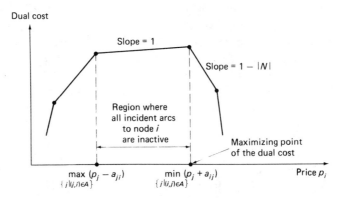

Figure 5.2.3 Illustration of the relaxation iteration at a node $i \neq 0$ when the condition

$$\max_{\{j|(j,i)\in A\}} (p_j - a_{ji}) \leq p_i \leq \min_{\{j|(i,j)\in A\}} (p_j + a_{ij}), \qquad \forall\, i \in N,$$

[cf. Eq. (2.4)] holds in the shortest path problem.

$$p_1 := \max_{\{j|(j,1)\in A\}}(p_j - a_{j1}).$$ (2.6)

It can be seen also that this iteration creates no active arcs. Thus, if initially there are no active arcs, then the same will be true for all iterations, and the relaxation algorithm will be given by the preceding Eqs. (2.5) and (2.6). Under these circumstances, it is seen that the prices p_i, $i \neq 1$, cannot decrease as a result of iteration (2.5) since for this to happen, it is necessary that some arc (i, j) is active. Similarly, the price p_1 cannot increase as a result of iteration (2.6) since for this to happen, it is necessary that some arc $(j, 1)$ is active. Furthermore, since the prices p_j, $j \neq 1$, cannot decrease, it follows that the price p_1 can decrease at most once as a result of iteration (2.6). Therefore, following the first execution of iteration (2.6), the price p_1 will be constant and the algorithm will become essentially equivalent to the Bellman–Ford algorithm discussed in Section 4.1. Upon termination (which, as discussed earlier, will occur if the shortest path problem has at least one feasible solution), it will yield a vector p^* satisfying

$$p_i^* = \min_{\{j|(i,j)\in A\}} (p_j^* + a_{ij}), \qquad \forall\, i \neq 1.$$

By subtracting p_1^* from both sides of this equation, we see that the scalars

$$x_i^* = p_i^* - p_1^*, \qquad i \in N$$

satisfy Bellman's equation

$$x_i^* = \min_{\{j|(i,j)\in A\}} (a_{ij} + x_j^*), \qquad \forall\, i \neq 1,$$

$$x_1^* = 0.$$

This guarantees that for all nodes i, x_i^* is the shortest distance from i to 1 under the condition that all cycles have a positive length (Section 4.1).

In conclusion, the relaxation algorithm of this section, when applied to the shortest path problem, is essentially equivalent to the Bellman–Ford method provided that there are no active arcs for the initial price vector [cf. Eq. (2.4)].

Unfortunately, the relaxation method may not work well for other initial price vectors. Figure 5.2.4 gives an example where it terminates with the wrong answer. It is thus necessary to modify the basic relaxation algorithm in order to improve its convergence properties. Two ways for doing so will be given. The first method, presented in the next subsection, leads to good practical sequential algorithms but does not naturally lend itself to parallelization. The second method is the subject of the next two sections, and is highly parallelizable.

5.2.2 Multiple Node Relaxation Method

The idea here is to change the prices of several nodes simultaneously when a search along a single price coordinate does not produce a dual cost improvement (see Fig.

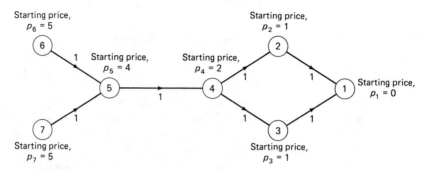

Figure 5.2.4   Example of a shortest path problem where the relaxation iteration terminates with the wrong answer when the initial price vector violates condition (2.4), that is, there is at least one active arc. The starting prices are as shown. All arcs have unity length, and they are all balanced except for arc (5,4), which is active. It can be verified that for each node i, we have $g_i^+ \leq 0 \leq g_i^-$, so the relaxation method terminates without obtaining an optimal price vector.

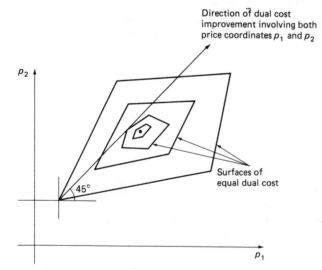

Figure 5.2.5   Illustration of the idea of the multiple node relaxation method. At the indicated corner point, it is impossible to improve the dual cost by changing a single price coordinate. A dual cost improvement is effected by changing simultaneously both price coordinates by equal amounts; this corresponds to dual ascent along the direction of the form (2.7) involving nodes 1 and 2.

5.2.5). Equivalently, at a nonoptimal price vector p, we would like to use some direction of dual cost improvement, similarly as we did in gradient methods for optimization in Chapter 3. A remarkable fact about our problem, which will be shown shortly, is that such a direction of improvement can be found within the finite set of directions having the form

$$d_L = \left(d_1, d_2, \ldots, d_{|N|}\right), \tag{2.7a}$$

where

$$d_i = \begin{cases} 1 & \text{if } i \in L, \\ 0 & \text{if } i \notin L, \end{cases} \tag{2.7b}$$

and $L \subset N$ is the node set of a connected subgraph of the graph (N, A) with $L \neq N$.

From the dual cost expression (2.1) and Fig. 5.1.5, it is seen that the directional derivative of the dual cost along a vector d_L of the form (2.7) is given by

$$
\begin{aligned}
q'(p; d_L) = &\lim_{\alpha \downarrow 0} \frac{q(p + \alpha d_L) - q(p)}{\alpha} \\
= &\sum_{\substack{(j,i):\ \text{active, } j \notin L, i \in L}} c_{ji} \\
&+ \sum_{\substack{(j,i):\ \text{inactive or balanced, } j \notin L, i \in L}} b_{ji} \\
&- \sum_{\substack{(i,j):\ \text{active or balanced, } i \in L, j \notin L}} c_{ij} \\
&- \sum_{\substack{(i,j):\ \text{inactive, } i \in L, j \notin L}} b_{ij} \\
&+ \sum_{i \in L} s_i.
\end{aligned}
\tag{2.8}
$$

Thus, the directional derivative $q'(p; d_L)$ is the difference between inflow and outflow across the node set L when the flows of the inactive and active arcs are set at their lower and upper bounds, respectively, and the flow of each balanced arc incident to L is set to its lower or upper bound depending on whether the arc is coming into L or coming out of L. Equivalently, $q'(p; d_L)$ is the minimum of the total surplus of the nodes in L over all flow vectors that satisfy CS together with p.

In principle, we could search over the set of vectors d_L of the form (2.7) and find a direction of improvement, that is, one for which the directional derivative (2.8) is positive, but this brute force approach requires computation that is exponential in $|N|$ because there are exponentially many vectors of the form (2.7). A more effective alternative, which we now describe, is based on maintaining a flow vector f satisfying CS together with p. This helps to organize the search for a direction of improvement. From the definition of the surplus, Eq. (1.7), we obtain

$$\sum_{i \in L} g_i = \sum_{\{(j,i) \in A \mid j \notin L, i \in L\}} f_{ji} - \sum_{\{(i,j) \in A \mid i \in L, j \notin L\}} f_{ij} + \sum_{i \in L} s_i. \tag{2.9}$$

Therefore, if f satisfies CS together with p, we have using Eqs. (2.8) and (2.9)

$$\sum_{i \in L} g_i = q'(p; d_L) + \sum_{(j,i): \text{ balanced, } j \notin L, i \in L} (f_{ji} - b_{ji})$$

$$+ \sum_{(i,j): \text{ balanced, } i \in L, j \notin L} (c_{ij} - f_{ij}) \tag{2.10}$$

$$\geq q'(p; d_L).$$

We see, therefore, that only a node set L that has positive total surplus is a candidate for generating a direction d_L of dual cost improvement. The next lemma makes this idea precise and provides the basis for the subsequent algorithm.

Lemma 2.1.   Suppose that f and p satisfy the CS conditions. Let d_L be a direction vector of the form (2.7), and assume that

$$\sum_{i \in L} g_i > 0.$$

Then either d_L is a dual ascent direction, that is,

$$q'(p; d_L) > 0,$$

or else there exist nodes $i \in L$ and $j \notin L$ such that either (i, j) is a balanced arc and $f_{ij} < c_{ij}$, or (j, i) is a balanced arc and $b_{ji} < f_{ji}$.

Proof. Follows from Eq. (2.10).   **Q.E.D.**

The typical iteration of the following algorithm starts with an integer price–flow vector pair satisfying the CS conditions, and operates in steps. At the beginning of each step, we have a connected subset of nodes L such that

$$\sum_{i \in L} g_i > 0;$$

initially L consists of an arbitrary node i_1 with positive surplus. According to the preceding lemma, there are two possibilities: Either (a) d_L given by Eq. (2.7) is a direction of dual cost improvement, or (b) L can be enlarged by adding a node $j \notin L$ with the property described in the lemma. In case (b), there are two possibilities: either (b1) $g_j \geq 0$, in which case,

$$\sum_{i \in L \cup \{j\}} g_i > 0,$$

and the process can be continued with

$$L \cup \{j\}$$

replacing L, or (b2) $g_j < 0$, in which case, it can be seen that there is a path originating at the starting node i_1 and ending at node j with the property that all arcs on the path have room for a flow increase in the direction from i_1 to j. Such a path is called an *augmenting path* (see Fig. 5.2.6). By increasing the flow of the forward arcs (direction from i_1 to j) of the path and by decreasing the flow of the backward arcs (direction from j to i_1) of the path, we can bring both surpluses g_{i_1} and g_j closer to zero by an integer amount while leaving the surplus of all other nodes unaffected and maintaining CS. Once $\sum_{i \in N} |g_i|$ is reduced to zero, the corresponding flow and price vectors are optimal by Prop. 5.1, so it follows that in a finite number of iterations, a direction of dual cost improvement will be found at any nonoptimal price vector.

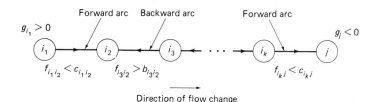

Figure 5.2.6   Illustration of an augmenting path. The initial node i_1 and the final node j have positive and negative surplus, respectively. Each arc on the path has room for flow change in the direction from i_1 to j. A flow change of magnitude $\delta > 0$ in this direction reduces the total absolute surplus $\sum_{i \in N} |g_i|$ by 2δ provided $\delta \leq \min\{g_{i_1}, -g_j\}$.

We now formalize the preceding procedure. The algorithm starts with any integer pair (f, p) satisfying CS. One possibility is to choose arbitrarily the integer vector p and to set $f_{ij} = b_{ij}$ if (i, j) is inactive or balanced, and $f_{ij} = c_{ij}$ otherwise. (Prior knowledge could be built into the initial choice of p and f based, for example, on the results of an earlier optimization.) It will be seen that the algorithm preserves the integrality and CS property of the pair (f, p) throughout.

At the start of the typical iteration, we have an integer pair (f, p) satisfying CS, and we select a node i_1 with positive surplus. The iteration indicates that the primal problem is infeasible, or else indicates that (f, p) is optimal, or else transforms this pair into another pair (f, p) satisfying CS. In the latter case the iteration terminates under two possible circumstances:

(a) When we find an augmenting path, in which case the flows of the arcs of the path are changed as illustrated in Fig. 5.2.6 (see Step 4 below). In this case the price vector (and hence also the dual cost) does not change, but the total absolute surplus $\sum_{i \in N} |g_i|$ is reduced by an integer amount.

(b) When we find a node set L such that d_L [cf. Eq. (2.7)] is a dual ascent direction. In this case the prices of the nodes in L are increased by an integer amount and the dual cost is improved by an integer amount (see Step 5 below). The amount of price increase is the minimum required to either make some arc (i, j) with $i \in L$, $j \notin L$ balanced from inactive or to make some arc (j, i) with $j \notin L$, $i \in L$ balanced from active. With a little thought, it is seen that the price increase corresponds to moving from the current price vector to the next breakpoint of the (piecewise linear) dual function along the direction d_L.

To implement the iteration efficiently, we introduce a simple data structure of *labels* (more sophisticated data structures are possible, but for simplicity we will not go into this). The label of a node i is simply the ID number of another node (or "0" if i is the starting node i_1 of the iteration), or else an indication that node i has no label. In the former case, node i is said to be *labeled*, whereas in the latter case, it is said to be *unlabeled*. At the start of the iteration all nodes are unlabeled except for the starting node i_1. Labels are helpful in constructing an augmenting path once a node j with negative surplus is identified. The corresponding augmenting path $(j, i_k, i_{k-1}, \ldots, i_2, i_1)$ (cf. Fig. 5.2.6) is constructed backwards by taking i_k to be the label of j, and for $m = k, \ldots, 2$, by taking i_{m-1} to be the label of i_m, until the starting node i_1 is encountered (and recognized because of its distinctive label "0"). This construction is used in Step 4 below.

During an iteration, the current node set L that is a candidate for yielding a dual ascent direction d_L is maintained in a list. In the following algorithm, the nodes of L are said to have been *scanned*, loosely indicating the fact that these nodes have been "selected" and "examined" during the iteration. The nodes which are not yet scanned, that is, do not belong to the current set L, are said to be *unscanned*. A node must be labeled before it can be scanned and the algorithm also maintains a list of the nodes that are labeled but unscanned. This list is used to keep track of the set of nodes that are candidates for entering the set L.

Multiple Node Relaxation Iteration

Step 1: (*Initialization*) Choose a node i_1 with $g_{i_1} > 0$. (The iteration can be started also from a node i_1 with $g_{i_1} < 0$; the steps are similar.) If no such node can be found terminate the algorithm; the current pair (f, p) is primal and dual optimal. Else give the label "0" to i_1, set $L :=$ empty, and go to Step 2.

Step 2: (*Choose a node to scan*) Select a labeled but unscanned node i, set $L := L \cup \{i\}$, and go to Step 3.

Step 3: (*Scan a node*) Scan the labeled node i as follows: give the label "i" to all unlabeled nodes j such that either (j, i) is balanced and $f_{ji} > b_{ji}$ or (i, j) is balanced and $f_{ij} < c_{ij}$. If

$$q'(p; d_L) > 0$$

[cf. Eq. (2.8)] go to Step 5. Else if for any of the nodes j given the label "i" earlier in this step, we have $g_j < 0$, go to Step 4. Else go to Step 2.

Step 4: (*Flow Augmentation*) An augmenting path H has been found that begins at the starting node i_1 and ends at the node j identified in Step 3. The path is constructed by tracing labels backwards starting from j, and is such that we have

$$f_{mn} < c_{mn}, \qquad \forall \, (m,n) \in H^+,$$

$$f_{mn} > b_{mn}, \qquad \forall \, (m,n) \in H^-,$$

where H^+ and H^- are the sets of forward and backward arcs of H, respectively, given by

$$H^+ = \{(m,n) \in H \mid (m,n) \text{ is oriented in the direction from } i_1 \text{ to } j\},$$

$$H^- = \{(m,n) \in H \mid (m,n) \text{ is oriented in the direction from } j \text{ to } i_1\}.$$

Let

$$\delta = \min\Big\{g_{i_1}, -g_j, \{c_{mn} - f_{mn} \mid (m,n) \in H^+\}, \{f_{mn} - b_{mn} \mid (m,n) \in H^-\}\Big\}.$$

Increase by δ the flows of all arcs $(m,n) \in H^+$, decrease by δ the flows of all arcs $(m,n) \in H^-$, and go to the next iteration.

Step 5: (*Price Change*) Set

$$f_{ij} := c_{ij}, \qquad \forall \text{ balanced arcs } (i,j) \text{ with } i \in L, j \notin L, j \in M, \text{ (2.11a)}$$

$$f_{ji} := b_{ji}, \qquad \forall \text{ balanced arcs } (j,i) \text{ with } i \in L, j \notin L, j \in M, \text{ (2.11b)}$$

where L is the set of scanned nodes constructed in Step 2, and M is the set of currently labeled nodes. Let

$$\gamma = \min_{\xi \in S^+ \cup S^-} \xi, \tag{2.12}$$

where

$$S^+ = \{p_j + a_{ij} - p_i \mid (i,j)\text{: inactive}, i \in L, j \notin L\},$$

$$S^- = \{p_j - a_{ji} - p_i \mid (j,i)\text{: active}, i \in L, j \notin L\}.$$

Set

$$p_i := \begin{cases} p_i + \gamma, & \text{if } i \in L, \\ 0, & \text{otherwise.} \end{cases} \tag{2.13}$$

Go to the next iteration. (*Note:* If there is no active arc (i,j) with $i \in L$, $j \notin L$, or inactive arc (j,i) with $i \in L$, $j \notin L$, then the price increment γ can be taken infinite, which indicates that the dual optimal value is infinite or, equivalently, that the primal problem is infeasible; see Exercise 2.1).

It is clear that all operations of the algorithm preserve the integrality of the price–flow vector pair. To see that CS is also maintained, note that a flow augmentation step changes only flows of balanced arcs and, therefore, cannot destroy CS; the flow change of Eq. (2.11) and the price change of Eq. (2.13) maintain CS because they set the flows of the balanced arcs that the price change renders active (or inactive) to the corresponding upper (or lower) bounds. Assuming the optimal dual value is finite (otherwise the primal problem is infeasible), termination of the algorithm is guaranteed by the fact that each price change improves the dual cost by an integer amount. Furthermore, it is impossible to have an infinite number of flow augmentation steps, since each of these reduces the total absolute surplus by an integer amount. Finally, termination can occur only when all nodes have zero surplus, which together with CS guarantees optimality of the final price–flow vector pair. Since the algorithm maintains integrality of flows and prices, the optimal flow and price vector obtained upon termination will be integer. We have thus shown constructively that if problem (LNF) is feasible, there exist optimal *integer* flow and price vectors. If the problem is infeasible, this can be detected either in Step 5 (see the note given there) or through the fact that some prices increase to infinity (see also Exercise 2.1).

Figure 5.2.7 traces the steps of the algorithm for a simple shortest path example. The figure illustrates that in an efficient implementation of the algorithm, more than one iterations can be "combined" in a single iteration in order to save computation time.

The stepsize γ of Eq. (2.12) corresponds to the first break point of the dual function along the ascent direction d_L. It is also possible to calculate through a line search an optimal stepsize that maximizes the dual function along d_L. We leave it for the reader to verify that this computation can be done quite economically, using Eq. (2.8) or Eq. (2.10) to test the sign of the directional derivative of the dual function at successive break points along d_L. Computational experience shows that a line search is beneficial in practice. Consider now the case where there is a price change via Step 5 and the set L consists of just the starting node i_1. This happens when the multiple node iteration scans i_1 and finds (at the first time Step 3 is entered) that the corresponding coordinate direction leads to a dual cost improvement $[q'(p; d_{\{i_1\}}) > 0]$. If line search of the type just described is performed, the price p_{i_1} is changed to a break point where $g_{i_1}^+ \leq 0 \leq g_{i_1}^-$. In this case the multinode iteration becomes identical with the (single node) relaxation iteration examined earlier in this section (cf. Fig. 5.2.1). Computational experience shows that such single node iterations are very frequent in the early stages of the algorithm and account for most of the total dual cost improvement, but become much less frequent near the algorithm's termination.

In practice, the method should be implemented using iterations that start from both positive and negative surplus nodes. This seems to improve substantially the performance of the method. It can be shown that the algorithm terminates properly under these circumstances (Exercise 2.2). Another important practical issue has to do with the initial choice of flows and prices. One possibility is to try to choose an initial price vector that is as close to optimal as possible (for example, using the results of some earlier optimization); one can then choose the arc flows to satisfy the CS conditions.

Computational experiments show that the method based on multiple node relaxation iterations has excellent practical performance. Its computational complexity, however,

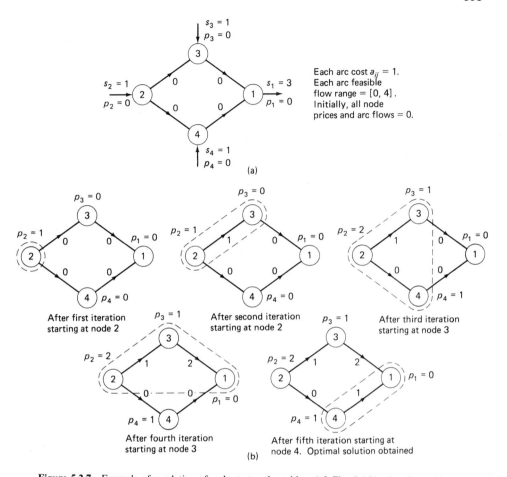

Figure 5.2.7 Example of a solution of a shortest path problem (cf. Fig. 5.1.3) using the multiple node relaxation method. The numbers next to the arcs are the arc flows. All problem data and initial conditions are as shown in part (a). The problem is solved in five iterations as shown in part (b). [The iteration sequence generated by the algorithm depends on the rule for choosing the starting node of an iteration; the sequence shown in part (b) is one possible iteration sequence.] The broken curves indicate the set of labeled nodes in each iteration. A description of the iterations follows:

(1) Iteration 1 starts at node 2 and raises the price of node 2 by one unit through Step 5.

(2) Iteration 2 starts at node 2, identifies the augmenting path $2 \rightarrow 3$, and increases the flow of arc $(2, 3)$ by one unit through Step 4.

(3) Iteration 3 starts at node 3, labels node 2, and then node 4. It then raises the prices of nodes 2, 3, and 4 by one unit through Step 5.

(4) Iteration 4 starts at node 3, identifies the augmenting path $3 \rightarrow 1$, and increases the flow of arc $(3, 1)$ by two units through Step 4.

(5) Iteration 5 starts at node 4, identifies the augmenting path $4 \rightarrow 1$, and increases the flow of arc $(4, 1)$ by one unit through Step 4.

A more efficient implementation of the algorithm tries to identify an augmenting path following a price change. Then iterations 1 and 2 can be combined in a single iteration. Iterations 3 and 4 can be similarly combined.

depends on the size of the arc cost coefficients. To see this, consider the shortest path problem with positive arc lengths. The Bellman–Ford algorithm starting from the zero initial conditions is a special case of the relaxation method, as discussed earlier, and in Section 4.1 we saw that its complexity depends on the maximum arc length (cf. Fig. 4.1.2 in Chapter 4). It is possible to improve the theoretical complexity of the method by using the technique of scaling the arc cost coefficients, which is discussed in Section 5.4 (see Exercise 4.2).

We finally note that multiple node relaxation iterations are less suited for parallelization than the earlier single node iterations. The difficulty is that while multiple node iterations can start simultaneously from two different nodes with positive surplus, it is possible that the corresponding sets of labeled nodes may intersect at some point, in which case, only one of the two iterations can proceed. This has an adverse effect on the degree of parallelism afforded by the algorithm. It is still possible, however, to construct a parallel implementation of the method by using an arbitration mechanism that allows only one out of two or more simultaneous and interfering multiple node iterations to proceed while the others are temporarily suspended. The details of this are somewhat complicated and will not be discussed.

EXERCISES

2.1. **[Ber86a]** This exercise illustrates a type of argument that is central in the complexity analysis of relaxation algorithms for linear network flow problems. Consider the multiple node relaxation algorithm, let p_i^0 be the initial price of node i, and let S be the set of nodes that have negative surplus initially. For every simple path p that ends at a node $j \in S$, let L_p be the sum of the costs of the forward arcs of the path minus the sum of the costs of the backward arcs of the path, and let $L = \max_p L_p$. Assume that only nodes with positive surplus are chosen as starting nodes in the relaxation iteration. Show that, if the problem is feasible, then during the course of the algorithm, the price of any positive surplus node cannot exceed its initial price by more than $L + \max_{j \in S} p_j^0 - \min_{i \in N} p_i^0$. *Hint:* Use the fact that at any point in the algorithm the prices of all nodes with negative surplus have not changed since the start of the algorithm. Show also that if i is a node with positive surplus, there must exist some node with negative surplus j and a path starting at i and ending at j such that all forward arcs of the path are inactive or balanced, and all backward arcs of the path are active or balanced.

2.2. Write the form of the multiple node relaxation iteration starting from *both* positive and negative surplus nodes. Show that the method terminates at an optimal flow–price vector pair if a feasible solution exists.

2.3. **(The Primal–Dual Method [FoF62].)** The purpose of this exercise is to clarify the relation of the multiple node relaxation method and two versions of a classical ascent method for solving the dual problem, which is commonly referred to as the *primal–dual* method.

    (a) One version of the primal–dual method for (LNF) can be obtained through a small (but significant) change in the description of the multiple node iteration. Simply replace the statement "If $q'(p; d_L) > 0$ [cf. Eq. (2.8)] go to Step 5" of Step 3 by the statement "If the set of scanned nodes is equal to the set of labeled nodes go to Step 5". Show that the resulting method terminates in a finite number of iterations.

(b) Another version of the primal–dual method is obtained by making the change described in part (a), and also by giving in Step 1 the label "0" to all nodes i with positive surplus instead of just to a single node with positive surplus. Show that the resulting method also terminates in a finite number of iterations, and that the direction of ascent used in Step 5 maximizes the directional derivative $q'(p; d_L)$ over all vectors d_L of the form (2.7).

5.3 THE ϵ – RELAXATION METHOD

In the preceding section, we discussed one possible method for resolving the difficulty due to the nondifferentiability of the dual cost illustrated in Fig. 5.2.2. In this section, we consider an alternative method. The main idea is illustrated in Fig. 5.3.1. We allow single node price changes even if these worsen the dual cost. The rationale is that if the cost deterioration is small, then the algorithm can approach eventually the optimal solution. Indeed, we will show that this is so, and in fact an *exact* solution of the problem can be obtained in a finite number of iterations owing to the integer nature of the problem data. A key idea is that each price change improves the dual cost of a perturbed problem, where some of the arc cost coefficients are modified by a small amount ϵ. Implementation of this idea is based on a notion of approximate complementary slackness, which we now introduce.

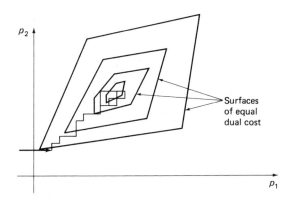

Surfaces of equal dual cost

Figure 5.3.1 Illustration of the idea of the ϵ–relaxation method. By making small changes in the coordinate directions, it is possible to approach the optimal solution even if each step does not result in a dual cost improvement. The method eventually reaches a small neighborhood of the optimal solution.

For any price vector p and $\epsilon > 0$, we say that an arc (i, j) is

$$\epsilon - \text{Inactive} \qquad \text{if } p_i < a_{ij} + p_j - \epsilon, \tag{3.1a}$$

$$\epsilon^- - \text{Balanced} \qquad \text{if } p_i = a_{ij} + p_j - \epsilon, \tag{3.1b}$$

$$\epsilon - \text{Balanced} \qquad \text{if } a_{ij} + p_j - \epsilon \le p_i \le a_{ij} + p_j + \epsilon, \tag{3.1c}$$

$$\epsilon^+ - \text{Balanced} \qquad \text{if } p_i = a_{ij} + p_j + \epsilon, \tag{3.1d}$$

$$\epsilon - \text{Active} \qquad \text{if } p_i > a_{ij} + p_j + \epsilon. \tag{3.1e}$$

Given $\epsilon \geq 0$, we say that a vector pair (f, p) satisfies ϵ–*complementary slackness* (ϵ–CS) if for each arc (i, j),

$$f_{ij} = b_{ij} \qquad \text{if } (i, j) \text{ is } \epsilon\text{–inactive,} \tag{3.2a}$$

$$b_{ij} \leq f_{ij} \leq c_{ij} \qquad \text{if } (i, j) \text{ is } \epsilon\text{–balanced,} \tag{3.2b}$$

$$f_{ij} = c_{ij} \qquad \text{if } (i, j) \text{ is } \epsilon\text{–active.} \tag{3.2c}$$

An equivalent statement of the ϵ–CS conditions is that the flows f_{ij} satisfy the capacity constraints (1.2), and that

$$f_{ij} < c_{ij} \qquad \Rightarrow \qquad p_i - p_j \leq a_{ij} + \epsilon, \tag{3.3a}$$

$$b_{ij} < f_{ij} \qquad \Rightarrow \qquad p_i - p_j \geq a_{ij} - \epsilon \tag{3.3b}$$

(see Fig. 5.3.2). A useful way to think about ϵ–CS is that if the pair (f, p) satisfies it, then the primal cost to be obtained by moving flow around a cycle Y without violating the capacity constraints decreases at a rate that is at most $|Y|\epsilon$, where $|Y|$ is the number of arcs of Y. This fact is the essence of the proof of Prop. 3.1 that follows.

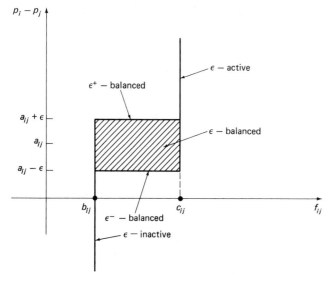

Figure 5.3.2 Illustration of ϵ–CS. All pairs of arc flows f_{ij} and price differentials $p_i - p_j$ should either lie on the thick–line diagram or in the shaded area between the thick lines.

The algorithm to be described shortly maintains at all times a price vector p and a flow vector f satisfying ϵ–CS. It terminates when the flow vector f satisfies the primal feasibility condition $g_i = 0$ for all $i \in N$. A key fact is that if ϵ is sufficiently small, then the final flow vector f is optimal. The proof given uses our earlier assumption that the arc cost coefficients a_{ij} are integer, but does not use the assumption that the flow bounds b_{ij} and c_{ij} are also integer.

Proposition 3.1.   If $\epsilon < 1/|N|$ and the flow vector f together with the price vector p satisfy ϵ–CS and primal feasibility ($g_i = 0$ for all $i \in N$), then f is optimal for (LNF).

Proof.   If f is not optimal, there must exist a nonzero flow vector $y = \{y_{ij} \mid (i,j) \in A\}$ such that $f + y$ is primal feasible, and has lower cost than f, that is, y is a circulation and

$$b_{ij} \leq f_{ij} + y_{ij} \leq c_{ij}, \qquad \forall\,(i,j) \in A,$$

$$\sum_{(i,j)\in A} a_{ij} y_{ij} < 0.$$

By the Conformal Realization Theorem (Appendix B) the circulation y can be decomposed into the sum of a finite number of simple circulations $y^1, \ldots, y^m$ that conform to y ($y_{ij}^k > 0$ or $y_{ij}^k < 0$ implies $y_{ij} > 0$ or $y_{ij} < 0$ respectively). Therefore $f + y^k$ is primal feasible for all $k = 1, \ldots, m$, and at least one circulation y^k defines a direction of descent, that is,

$$\sum_{(i,j)\in A} a_{ij} y_{ij}^k < 0.$$

Let Y^+ and Y^- be the sets of arcs (i,j) of the cycle corresponding to y^k for which $y_{ij}^k > 0$ and $y_{ij}^k < 0$, respectively. Since y^k is a simple circulation, we have that $|y_{ij}^k|$ is equal to some $\delta > 0$ on all arcs (i,j) for which $y_{ij}^k \neq 0$. Therefore, by dividing the preceding condition by δ we obtain

$$\sum_{(i,j)\in Y^+} a_{ij} - \sum_{(i,j)\in Y^-} a_{ij} < 0, \qquad\qquad (3.4)$$

$$f_{ij} < c_{ij}, \qquad \forall\,(i,j) \in Y^+,$$

$$b_{ij} < f_{ij}, \qquad \forall\,(i,j) \in Y^-.$$

By ϵ–CS [cf. Eq. (3.3)], we have

$$p_i \leq p_j + a_{ij} + \epsilon, \qquad \forall\,(i,j) \in Y^+,$$

$$p_j \leq p_i - a_{ij} + \epsilon, \qquad \forall\,(i,j) \in Y^-,$$

which, by adding and using the hypothesis $\epsilon < 1/|N|$, yields

$$\sum_{(i,j)\in Y^+} a_{ij} - \sum_{(i,j)\in Y^-} a_{ij} \geq -|N|\epsilon > -1.$$

Since the a_{ij} are integer, we obtain a contradiction of Eq. (3.4).   **Q.E.D.**

A strengthened form of Prop. 3.1 which remains valid even if the arc cost coefficients and flow bounds are not integer, is obtained by replacing the condition $\epsilon < 1/|N|$ with the condition

$$\epsilon < \min_{\text{All cycles } Y} \left\{ -\frac{\text{Length of cycle } Y}{\text{Number of arcs of } Y} \mid \text{Length of } Y < 0 \right\},$$

where

$$\text{Length of cycle } Y = \sum_{(i,j) \in Y^+} a_{ij} - \sum_{(i,j) \in Y^-} a_{ij}.$$

The proof is obtained by suitably modifying the last relation in the proof of Prop. 3.1.

The *ϵ-relaxation method* uses a fixed value of $\epsilon > 0$, and starts with a pair (f, p) such that ϵ–CS is satisfied and f_{ij} are all integer. The algorithm preserves the ϵ–CS and flow integrality properties throughout. A possible starting procedure is to arbitrarily choose the vector p, and to set $f_{ij} = b_{ij}$ if (i, j) is inactive or balanced, and $f_{ij} = c_{ij}$ otherwise. At the start of each iteration, a node i with positive surplus g_i is chosen. (If all nodes have zero surplus the algorithm terminates; then f is primal feasible and, together with p, satisfies ϵ–CS, so Prop. 3.1 applies.) At the end of the iteration, the surplus g_i is driven to zero, while another pair (f, p) satisfying ϵ–CS is obtained. During an iteration, all node prices stay unchanged except possibly for the price of the chosen node i. Similarly, all arc flows stay unchanged except for the flows of some of the arcs incident to node i. As a result of these flow changes, the surplus of some of the nodes adjacent to i is increased. In order for the flow of an arc (i, j) to change, the arc must be ϵ^+–balanced and $f_{ij} < c_{ij}$ (such an arc is called *ϵ^+–unblocked*). Similarly, in order for the flow of an arc (j, i) to change, the arc must be ϵ^-–balanced and $b_{ji} < f_{ji}$ (such an arc is called *ϵ^-–unblocked*). The price of node i at the end of the iteration is usually $\bar{p}_i + \epsilon$, where $\bar{p}_i$ is one of the maximizing points of $Q_i^p(\xi)$, the dual function along the ith price coordinate. This price level is reached through possibly several price increases at Step 4 below (see the subsequent discussion and Exercise 3.1). Each price increase may be preceded and followed by flow changes of incident arcs of node i to maintain ϵ–CS and to reduce the surplus g_i to zero (Steps 2 and 3 below).

Positive Surplus Node Iteration (or Up Iteration):

Let (f, p) satisfy ϵ–CS, and let i be a node with $g_i > 0$.

Step 1: (*Scan incident arc*) Select a node j such that (i, j) is an ϵ^+–unblocked arc and go to Step 2, or select a node j such that (j, i) is an ϵ^-–unblocked arc and go to Step 3. If no such node can be found go to Step 4.

Step 2: (*Decrease surplus by increasing f_{ij}*) Let $\delta = \min\{g_i, c_{ij} - f_{ij}\}$. Update f_{ij}, g_i, and g_j according to

$$f_{ij} := f_{ij} + \delta,$$

$$g_i := g_i - \delta, \qquad g_j := g_j + \delta.$$

If the updated values g_i and f_{ij} satisfy $g_i = 0$ and $f_{ij} < c_{ij}$, stop; else go to Step 1.

Step 3: (*Decrease surplus by reducing f_{ji}*) Let $\delta = \min\{g_i, f_{ji} - b_{ji}\}$. Update f_{ji}, g_i, and g_j according to

$$f_{ji} := f_{ji} - \delta,$$

$$g_i := g_i - \delta, \qquad g_j := g_j + \delta.$$

If the updated values g_i and f_{ji} satisfy $g_i = 0$ and $b_{ji} < f_{ji}$, stop; else go to Step 1.

Step 4: (*Increase price of node i*) Set

$$p_i := \min_{\xi \in R^+ \cup R^-} \xi, \tag{3.5}$$

where

$$R_i^+ = \left\{ p_j + a_{ij} + \epsilon \mid (i,j) \in A \text{ and } f_{ij} < c_{ij} \right\},$$

$$R_i^- = \left\{ p_j - a_{ji} + \epsilon \mid (j,i) \in A \text{ and } b_{ji} < f_{ji} \right\}.$$

Go to Step 1. (Note: If $g_i > 0$ and the set $R_i^+ \cup R_i^-$ over which the minimum in Eq. (3.5) is taken is empty, the problem is infeasible and the algorithm terminates; see the comments that follow. If this set is empty and $g_i = 0$, we leave p_i unchanged and stop.)

To see that Eq. (3.5) leads to a price increase, note that when Step 4 is entered, we have $f_{ij} = c_{ij}$ for all (i,j) such that $p_i \geq p_j + a_{ij} + \epsilon$, and we have $b_{ji} = f_{ji}$ for all (j,i) such that $p_i \geq p_j - a_{ji} + \epsilon$. Therefore, when Step 4 is entered, we have

$$p_i < \min R_i^+ = \min \left\{ p_j + a_{ij} + \epsilon \mid (i,j) \in A \text{ and } f_{ij} < c_{ij} \right\},$$

$$p_i < \min R_i^- = \min \left\{ p_j - a_{ji} + \epsilon \mid (j,i) \in A \text{ and } b_{ji} < f_{ji} \right\}.$$

It follows that p_i must be increased via Eq. (3.5) when the set $R_i^+ \cup R_i^-$ over which the minimum is taken is nonempty. In the case where this set is empty, we have $f_{ij} = c_{ij}$ for all (i,j) outgoing from i and $b_{ji} = f_{ji}$ for all (j,i) incoming to i, so maximum flow is going out of i while minimal flow is coming in. Therefore, if $g_i > 0$ and $R_i^+ \cup R_i^-$ is empty, we can terminate the algorithm with the assurance that the problem is infeasible.

Figure 5.3.3 illustrates an up iteration. It is seen that each time Step 2 or 3 is executed, flow is pushed away from i along an ϵ^+−unblocked or an ϵ^-−unblocked arc, respectively. If no more flow can be pushed and $g_i > 0$, the price of i is increased in Step 4.

Figures 5.3.3 and 5.3.4 illustrate the sequence of price changes of an up iteration in the cases where the dual cost has one and multiple maximizing points, respectively, with respect to p_i. It is seen in these figures that at the end of the iteration, the price of the node i equals ϵ plus some value that maximizes the dual cost with respect to p_i with all other prices kept fixed (this property can be shown for the case where $p_i + \epsilon$ is less than the minimal maximizing point of the dual cost; see Exercise 3.1). We thus obtain an interpretation of the algorithm as a relaxation (or coordinate ascent) method, although "approximate relaxation" may be a more appropriate term.

Consider now the case where there is a bounded interval $[\underline{p}_i, \bar{p}_i]$ of maximizing points with $\underline{p}_i < \bar{p}_i$ [see Fig. 5.3.4(a)]. A careful examination of the steps of the algorithm shows that it has a tendency to set the price p_i close to the largest maximizing point $\bar{p}_i$. This is due to the fact that the iteration does not stop when $g_i = 0$ and $f_{ij} = c_{ij}$ (in Step 2) or $f_{ji} = b_{ji}$ (in Step 3). As a result Step 4 may be entered with $g_i = 0$ with an additional price increase resulting over the version of the iteration that always stops when $g_i = 0$ in Step 2 or 3. The latter version tends to set the price p_i near the smallest maximizing point $\underline{p}_i$ and seems to work worse in practice. The reasons for this are not entirely clear, but the complexity analysis of the next section provides some justification since it suggests that the algorithm terminates faster when the price changes are as large as possible.

Note that a symmetric iteration can be used for nodes with negative surplus (called *down iteration*). One can construct an example (see Exercise 3.2) showing that the algorithm may not terminate if up and down iterations are mixed arbitrarily. It is therefore necessary to impose some assumptions either on the problem structure or on the method by which up and down iterations are interleaved. We henceforth assume that the algorithm consists of up iterations only.

Proposition 3.2. If problem (LNF) is feasible, the algorithm terminates with (f, p) satisfying ϵ–CS, and with f being integer and primal feasible.

Proof. The following facts can be verified based on the construction of the up iteration:

(1) The integrality of f and the ϵ–CS property of (f, p) are preserved throughout the algorithm.

(2) The prices of all nodes are monotonically nondecreasing during the algorithm.

(3) Once a node has nonnegative surplus, its surplus stays nonnegative thereafter. (This follows from the fact that an up iteration at some node i cannot drive the surplus of i below zero, and can only increase the surplus of its adjacent nodes.)

(4) If at some time a node has negative surplus, it must have never been iterated on up to that time, and therefore its price must be equal to its initial price. [This is a consequence of (3) above and the fact that only nodes with positive surplus are iterated on by up iterations.]

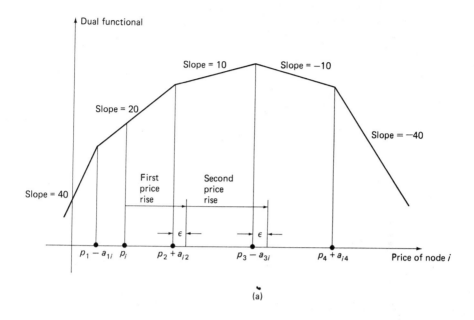

(a)

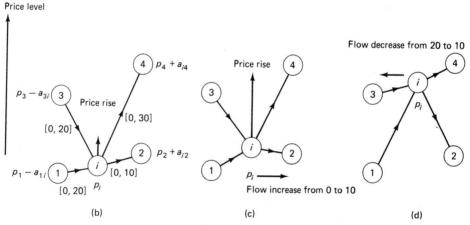

(b)   (c)   (d)

Figure 5.3.3   Illustration of an up iteration involving a single node i and the arcs $(1, i)$, $(3, i)$, $(i, 2)$, and $(i, 4)$ with feasible arc flow ranges [0,20], [0,20], [0,10], and [0,30], respectively, and $s_i = 0$. (a) Form of the dual functional along p_i for given values of p_1, p_2, p_3, and p_4. The breakpoints correspond to the levels of p_i for which the corresponding arcs become balanced. For values of p_i between two successive breakpoints, there are no balanced arcs incident to node i. The corresponding slope of the dual cost is equal to the surplus g_i resulting when all active arc flows are set to their upper bounds and all inactive arc flows are set to their lower bounds; compare with Eq. (2.1). (b) Illustration of a price rise of p_i from a value between the first two breakpoints to a value ϵ above the breakpoint at which $(i, 2)$ becomes balanced (Step 4). (c) Price rise of p_i to a value ϵ above the breakpoint at which arc $(3, i)$ becomes balanced. When this is done, arc $(i, 2)$ has changed from ϵ^+–balanced to ϵ–active, and its flow has increased from 0 to 10, maintaining ϵ–CS. (d) Step 3 of the algorithm reduces the flow of arc $(3, i)$ from 20 to 10, driving the surplus of node i to zero.

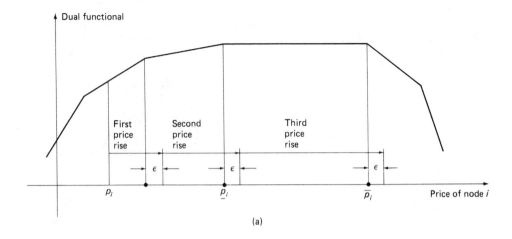

(a)

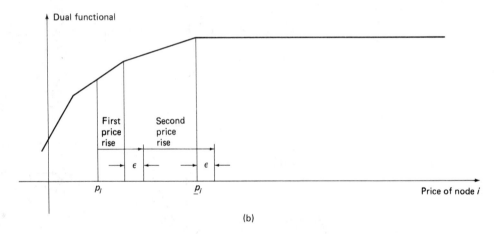

(b)

Figure 5.3.4 Illustration of an up iteration in the case where there are multiple maximizing points of the dual cost with respect to p_i. In case (a), the set of maximizing points is bounded, and at the end of the iteration, p_i is set at ϵ plus the largest maximizing point $\bar{p}_i$. In case (b), the set of maximizing points is unbounded, and at the end of the iteration, p_i is set at ϵ plus the smallest maximizing point $\underline{p}_i$.

Based on (2) there are two possibilities: either (a) the prices of a nonempty subset N^∞ of N diverge to $+\infty$ or else (b) the prices of all nodes in N stay bounded from above.

Suppose that case (a) holds. Then, since N^∞ is nonempty, it follows that the algorithm never terminates, implying that at all times there must exist a node with negative surplus which, by (4), must have a constant price. It follows that N^∞ is a proper subset of N. To preserve ϵ–CS, we must have, after a sufficient number of iterations,

$$f_{ij} = c_{ij} \qquad \text{for all } (i,j) \in A \text{ with } i \in N^\infty, j \notin N^\infty,$$

$$f_{ji} = b_{ij} \qquad \text{for all } (j,i) \in A \text{ with } i \in N^\infty, j \notin N^\infty,$$

while the sum of surpluses of the nodes in N^∞ must be positive. This means that even with as much flow as arc capacities allow coming out of N^∞ to nodes $j \notin N^\infty$ and as little flow as arc capacities allow coming into N^∞ from nodes $j \notin N^\infty$, the total surplus of nodes in N^∞ is positive. It follows that there is no feasible flow vector contradicting the hypothesis. Therefore, case (b) holds (all prices of nodes in N stay bounded).

We now show by contradiction that the algorithm terminates. If that is not so, then there must exist a node $i \in N$ at which an infinite number of iterations are executed. There must also exist an adjacent ϵ^-–balanced arc (j,i) or ϵ^+–balanced arc (i,j) whose flow is decreased or increased, respectively, by an integer amount during an infinite number of iterations. For this to happen, the flow of (j,i) or (i,j) must be increased or decreased, respectively, an infinite number of times due to iterations at the adjacent node j. This implies that the arc (j,i) or (i,j) must become ϵ^+–balanced or ϵ^-–balanced from ϵ^-–balanced or ϵ^+–balanced, respectively, an infinite number of times. For this to happen, the price of the adjacent node j must be increased an infinite number of times by at least 2ϵ. It follows that $p_j \to \infty$, which contradicts the boundedness of all node prices shown earlier. Therefore the algorithm must terminate.   **Q.E.D.**

Note that Prop. 3.2 holds for all $\epsilon > 0$. If $\epsilon < 1/|N|$, however, we see, by combining Props. 3.1 and 3.2, that the algorithm terminates with an *optimal* flow vector. Note also that the integrality of a_{ij} was not needed for the proof of Prop. 3.2, while the integrality of b_{ij}, c_{ij}, s_i, and the starting flow vector were only needed to establish that the flow change increments are bounded from below during the course of the algorithm. The integrality assumptions are essential, however, for the complexity analysis of the next section.

Proposition 3.2 applies without modification to the variation of the algorithm, where up iterations are not necessarily carried to completion. In this variation, it is permissible to execute only *partial* up iterations, in which the algorithm can select a new node for iteration immediately following the completion of any Step 2, 3, or 4, even if the current node surplus is not yet zero.

While it is possible for a price change in Step 4 of the up iteration to degrade the dual cost, there is still an interesting interpretation of Step 4 as a dual cost improvement. It can be seen from Eq. (2.1) that the sign of the directional derivatives g_i^+ and g_i^- can change if the cost coefficients of some of the ϵ–balanced arcs incident to node i are perturbed by a small ϵ amount. It follows that price changes in Step 4 yield a dual cost improvement of a *perturbed* problem where some of the arc cost coefficients are slightly changed.

A final issue has to do with detection of infeasibility (assuming it is not detected at Step 4 of some iteration). By using the argument of the proof of Prop. 3.2, it follows that for an infeasible problem, the prices of some nodes diverge to $+\infty$. In Section 5.4, we derive a precomputable upper bound for the prices when the problem is feasible [Eq. (4.7)]. Once this bound is exceeded, we know that the problem is infeasible.

5.3.1 The Auction Algorithm for the Assignment Problem

The main idea of the ϵ–relaxation iteration is to increase a single price coordinate so as to approximately optimize a dual cost with respect to that coordinate. This process can be applied to several other network duality formulations. As an illustration, we consider an alternative duality formulation of the assignment problem that leads to an effective computational method.

The method, called the *auction algorithm*, can be intuitively understood in terms of an economic process, and will be consequently described in those terms. Sources and sinks are viewed as persons and objects, respectively. The algorithm operates like an auction, whereby unassigned persons bid simultaneously for objects, thereby raising their prices. Once all bids are in, objects are awarded to the highest bidder. The serial or Gauss–Seidel version of the algorithm can be interpreted as a variation of the ϵ–relaxation method (see Exercise 3.5 for the precise relation).

Consider n persons wishing to divide among themselves n objects. For each person i, there is a nonempty subset $A(i)$ of objects that can be assigned to i, and there is a given integer value a_{ij} that person i associates with each object j. An *assignment* S is a (possibly empty) set of person–object pairs (i, j) such that $j \in A(i)$ for all $(i, j) \in S$; for each person i, there is at most one pair $(i, j) \in S$; and for each object j, there is at most one pair $(i, j) \in S$. In the context of a given assignment S, we say that person i is *assigned* if there exists an object j such that $(i, j) \in S$; otherwise, we say that i is *unassigned*. We use similar terminology for objects. A *complete assignment* is an assignment containing n pairs (i.e., every person is assigned to a distinct object). We want to find a complete assignment that maximizes

$$\sum_{(i,j)\in S} a_{ij}$$

over all complete assignments S. This problem is equivalent to the linear programming problem

$$\text{maximize} \quad \sum_{i=1}^{n} \sum_{j \in A(i)} a_{ij} f_{ij}$$

$$\text{subject to} \quad \sum_{j \in A(i)} f_{ij} = 1, \qquad \forall\, i = 1, \ldots, n,$$

$$\sum_{\{i \mid j \in A(i)\}}^{n} f_{ij} = 1, \qquad \forall\, j = 1, \ldots, n, \tag{3.6}$$

$$0 \leq f_{ij}, \qquad \forall\, i = 1, \ldots, n, \quad j \in A(i).$$

A dual problem is given by (cf. Appendix C)

$$\text{minimize} \quad \sum_{i=1}^{n} r_i + \sum_{j=1}^{n} p_j \tag{3.7}$$

$$\text{subject to} \quad r_i + p_j \geq a_{ij}, \qquad \forall \, i, \, j \in A(i).$$

We are considering a maximization as in Eq. (3.6) rather than a minimization problem in order to make the economic interpretation of the algorithm more transparent. It is also convenient for our purposes to use the constraint $0 \leq f_{ij}$ rather than $0 \leq f_{ij} \leq B$, with $B \geq 1$. None of these changes are of consequence, and problem (3.6) is essentially identical with the assignment problem considered earlier (cf. Fig. 5.1.1). Therefore, there is an integer optimal solution that assigns each person i to a distinct object $j_i \in A(i)$ so that

$$\sum_{i=1}^{n} a_{ij_i}$$

is maximized over all such assignments.

We see from Eq. (3.7) that the cost of the dual problem is minimized when r_i equals the maximum value of $a_{ij} - p_j$ over $j \in A(i)$. Thus, an equivalent form of the dual problem is

$$\text{minimize} \quad q(p) \tag{3.8}$$

$$\text{subject to no constraints on } p,$$

where p is the vector of object prices p_j, and

$$q(p) = \sum_{i=1}^{n} \max_{j \in A(i)} \{a_{ij} - p_j\} + \sum_{j=1}^{n} p_j. \tag{3.9}$$

For a given price vector p, the scalar

$$\pi_i = \max_{j \in A(i)} \{a_{ij} - p_j\} \tag{3.10}$$

is called the *profit margin* of person i corresponding to p. It is helpful to think of p_j as the amount of money that a person must pay when assigned to j. Therefore, for a given price vector p, $a_{ij} - p_j$ can be thought of as the benefit person i associates with being assigned to object j. In this context, the name "profit margin" for π_i as given by Eq. (3.10) becomes meaningful.

It is straightforward to verify that the complementary slackness conditions for an assignment S (not necessarily complete) and a price vector p can be written as

$$a_{ij_i} - p_{j_i} = \max_{j \in A(i)} \{a_{ij} - p_j\}, \qquad \forall \ (i, j_i) \in S.$$

A necessary and sufficient condition for S and p to be primal and dual optimal is that S is complete and that S and p satisfy complementary slackness. Thus, at an optimal assignment, each person is assigned to an object attaining the maximum in the profit margin definition (3.10).

A relaxation of the complementary slackness condition is to allow persons to be assigned to objects that come within ϵ of attaining the maximum in Eq. (3.10). This can be seen to be equivalent to the ϵ–CS condition (3.2) specialized to the assignment problem. Formally, we say that an assignment S and a price vector p satisfy ϵ–CS if

$$\pi_i - \epsilon = \max_{k \in A(i)} \{a_{ik} - p_k\} - \epsilon \leq a_{ij} - p_j, \qquad \forall \ (i, j) \in S, \tag{3.11}$$

where π_i is given by Eq. (3.10), and ϵ is a nonnegative constant.

We now describe formally the auction algorithm. We fix $\epsilon > 0$, and we start with some assignment (possibly empty) and price vector satisfying ϵ–CS. The algorithm proceeds iteratively and terminates when a complete assignment is obtained. At the start of the generic iteration we have an assignment S and a price vector p satisfying ϵ–CS. The iteration preserves the ϵ–CS condition and consists of two phases: the *bidding phase* and the *assignment phase* described in the following.

Bidding Phase:

For each person i that is unassigned under the assignment S:

1. Compute the "current value" of each object $j \in A(i)$ given by

$$v_{ij} = a_{ij} - p_j. \tag{3.12}$$

2. Find a "best" object j^* having maximum value

$$v_{ij^*} = \max_{j \in A(i)} v_{ij},$$

and find the best value offered by objects other than j^*

$$w_{ij^*} = \max_{j \in A(i), j \neq j^*} v_{ij}. \tag{3.13}$$

[If j^* is the only object in $A(i)$, we define w_{ij^*} to be $-\infty$ or, for computational purposes, a number that is much smaller than v_{ij^*}.]

3. Compute the "bid" of person i given by

$$b_{ij^*} = p_{j^*} + v_{ij^*} - w_{ij^*} + \epsilon = a_{ij^*} - w_{ij^*} + \epsilon. \tag{3.14}$$

[We characterize this situation by saying that person i bid for object j^*, and that object j^* received a bid from person i. The algorithm works if the bid has any value between $p_{j^*} + \epsilon$ and $p_{j^*} + v_{ij^*} - w_{ij^*} + \epsilon$, but it tends to work fastest for the maximal choice of Eq. (3.14).]

Assignment Phase:

For each object j:

Let $P(j)$ be the set of persons from which j received a bid in the bidding phase of the iteration. If $P(j)$ is nonempty, increase p_j to the highest bid:

$$p_j := \max_{i \in P(j)} b_{ij}, \tag{3.15}$$

remove from the assignment S any pair (i, j) (if j was assigned to some i under S), and add to S the pair (i^*, j), where i^* is a person in $P(j)$ attaining the maximum above.

It is seen that during an iteration, the objects whose prices are changed are the ones that received a bid during the iteration. Each price change involves an increace of at least ϵ. To see this, note that from Eqs. (3.12) to (3.14) we have $b_{ij^*} = a_{ij^*} - w_{ij^*} + \epsilon \geq a_{ij^*} - v_{ij^*} + \epsilon = p_{j^*} + \epsilon$, and the conclusion follows from Eq. (3.15). At the end of the iteration, we have a new assignment that differs from the preceding one in that each object that received a bid is now assigned to some person that was unassigned at the start of the iteration. However, the assignment at the end of the iteration need not have more pairs than the one at the start of the iteration, because it is possible that all objects that received a bid were assigned at the start of the iteration.

A first important fact is that the algorithm preserves ϵ–CS throughout its execution, that is, if the assignment and price vector available at the start of an iteration satisfy ϵ–CS, the same is true for the assignment and price vector obtained at the end of the iteration. To see this, suppose that object j^* received a bid from person i and was assigned to i during the iteration. Let p_j and p'_j be the object prices before and after the assignment phases, respectively. Then we have [cf. Eqs. (3.14) and (3.15)]

$$p'_{j^*} = b_{ij^*} = a_{ij^*} - w_{ij^*} + \epsilon. \tag{3.16}$$

Using this equation and the fact $p'_j \geq p_j$ for all j, it follows that

$$a_{ij^*} - p'_{j^*} = a_{ij^*} - b_{ij^*} = w_{ij^*} - \epsilon = \max_{j \in A(i), j \neq j^*} \{a_{ij} - p'_j\} - \epsilon. \tag{3.17}$$

This equation implies that

$$a_{ij^*} - p'_{j^*} \geq \max_{j \in A(i)} \{a_{ij} - p'_j\} - \epsilon, \tag{3.18}$$

which shows that the ϵ–CS condition (3.11) continues to hold after the assignment phase of an iteration for a pair (i, j^*) that entered the assignment during the iteration. Consider also any pair (i, j^*) that belonged to the assigment just before an iteration, and also belongs to the assignment after the iteration. Then j^* must not have received a bid during the iteration, so $p'_{j^*} = p_{j^*}$. Therefore, Eq. (3.18) holds in view of the ϵ–CS condition that holds prior to the iteration and the fact $p'_j \geq p_j$ for all j.

Figure 5.3.5 indicates how each bidding and subsequent assignment phase can be interpreted as a Jacobi–like relaxation step for minimizing the dual function $q(p)$ of Eq. (3.9). In particular, *the price p_j of each object j that received a bid during the assignment phase is increased to either a value that minimizes $q(p)$ when all other prices are kept constant or else exceeds the largest such value by no more than ϵ.* To see this, suppose that at some iteration, there is a bid for object j, raising its price from p_j to p'_j. Then

$$p'_j = \max\{a_{ij} - w_{ij} \mid i \text{ was unassigned}, j \in A(i), \text{ and } j \text{ received a bid from } i \} + \epsilon, \tag{3.19}$$

$$p_j \geq \max\{a_{ij} - w_{ij} \mid i \text{ was unassigned}, j \in A(i), \text{ and } j \text{ did not receive a bid from } i\}. \tag{3.20}$$

Since whenever an object receives a bid, its price increases by at least ϵ, we have

$$p'_j \geq p_j + \epsilon,$$

so from Eqs. (3.19) and (3.20), we obtain

$$p'_j \geq \max\{a_{ij} - w_{ij} \mid i \text{ was unassigned and } j \in A(i)\} + \epsilon. \tag{3.21}$$

Since the algorithm maintains the ϵ–CS condition (3.11) throughout, we have that if at the start of the iteration person i was assigned to some $k \neq j$ and $j \in A(i)$, then

$$a_{ij} - p_j \leq \pi_i \leq a_{ik} - p_k + \epsilon \leq w_{ij} + \epsilon.$$

Using this relation and the fact $p'_j \geq p_j + \epsilon$, we obtain

$$p'_j \geq p_j + \epsilon \geq a_{ij} - w_{ij}$$

and

$$p'_j \geq \max\{a_{ij} - w_{ij} \mid i \text{ was assigned to some } k \neq j, \text{ and } j \in A(i)\}. \tag{3.22}$$

Combining Eqs. (3.21) and (3.22), we obtain

$$p'_j \geq \max\{a_{ij} - w_{ij} \mid i \text{ was not assigned to } j, \text{ and } j \in A(i)\}.$$

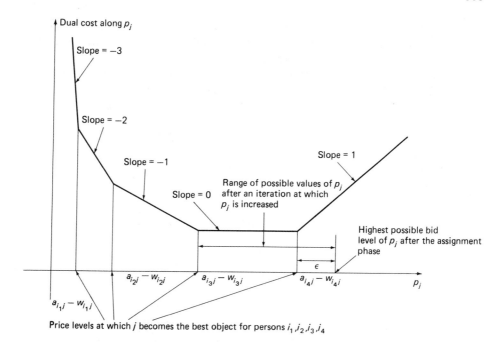

Figure 5.3.5 Form of the dual cost along the price coordinate p_j. From Eq. (3.9), the right directional derivative of q along p_j is

$$d_j^+ = 1 - (\text{number of persons } i \text{ with } j \in A(i) \text{ and } p_j < a_{ij} - w_{ij})$$

where w_{ij} is given by Eq. (3.13). The break points are $a_{ij} - w_{ij}$ for all i such that $j \in A(i)$. If $p_j < a_{ij} - w_{ij}$, then an unassigned person i bids for object j the amount $a_{ij} - w_{ij} + \epsilon$. The price p_j after the assignment phase is increased to ϵ plus the highest level $a_{ij} - w_{ij}$ over all unassigned persons i with $j \in A(i)$.

Since there can be at most one person assigned to j, it follows from the form of the dual cost shown in Fig. 5.3.5, that p_j' is no less than the smallest value of p_j that minimizes $q(p)$. Combining this fact with Eq. (3.19), we see that p_j' has the property stated in the beginning of this paragraph.

Note that the dual cost (3.9) can deteriorate after a price increase. However, the cost deterioration is at most ϵ. Similarly with the ϵ–relaxation method, for ϵ small enough, an optimal solution can still be obtained thanks to the rounding introduced by the integer nature of the problem data and the fact that ϵ–CS holds at termination [cf. Eq. (3.11)].

Figure 5.3.5 suggests a variation of the algorithm, whereby, in addition to all unassigned persons, each *assigned* person i bids for its *own* assigned object j the amount $a_{ij} - w_{ij} + \epsilon$. This variation can be useful under some circumstances.

The above algorithm can be viewed as a *Jacobi* version of the relaxation idea since the bids of all unassigned persons bid are calculated simultaneously and the prices of objects that receive a bid are raised simultaneously. An alternative is a *Gauss–Seidel* version, whereby a single unassigned person bids for an object and the price rise of the object is taken into account when the next bid by an unassigned person takes place. This version is just as valid as the Jacobi version and in fact tends to converge somewhat faster in practice, but is generally less parallelizable because the corresponding dependency graph can be quite dense (cf. the discussion of Subsection 1.2.4).

Suppose now that the algorithm terminates with the final (complete) assignment $\{(i, j_i) \mid i = 1, \ldots, n\}$, the object prices p_j, and the profit margins π_i given by Eq. (3.10). Then, by adding the ϵ–CS condition (3.11) over i, it is seen that

$$\sum_{i=1}^{n} a_{ij_i} \geq \sum_{i=1}^{n} (\pi_i + p_{j_i}) - n\epsilon.$$

If A* is the optimal primal value and the (equal) optimal dual value, we have, using the relation above,

$$A^* \geq \sum_{i=1}^{n} a_{ij_i} \geq \sum_{i=1}^{n} (\pi_i + p_{j_i}) - n\epsilon \geq A^* - n\epsilon,$$

where the last step follows from the feasibility of the scalars π_i and p_{j_i} for the dual problem (3.7). Therefore, the assignment $\{(i, j_i) \mid i = 1, \ldots, n\}$ is within $n\epsilon$ of being optimal. Since a_{ij} are integer, an optimal assignment is obtained when $\epsilon < 1/n$. Thus, we have shown the following:

Proposition 3.3. An assignment $\{(i, j_i) \mid i = 1, \ldots, n\}$ obtained upon termination of the auction algorithm is within $n\epsilon$ of being optimal, and is optimal if $\epsilon < 1/n$.

The next result asserts that the algorithm terminates assuming existence of at least one feasible assignment. The proof relies on the following facts:

(a) Once an object is assigned, it remains assigned throughout the remainder of the algorithm's duration. Furthermore, except at termination, there will always exist at least one object that has never been assigned, and has a price equal to its initial price. This is because a bidding and assignment phase can result in a reassignment of an already assigned object to a different person, but cannot result in the object becoming unassigned.

(b) Each time an object receives a bid, its price increases by at least ϵ [cf. Eqs. (3.14) and (3.15)]. Therefore if the object receives a bid an infinite number of times, its price increases to ∞.

(c) For every $|A(i)|$ bids by person i, where $|A(i)|$ is the number of objects in the set $A(i)$, the profit margin π_i as defined by Eq. (3.10) decreases by at least ϵ. This is because a bid by person i either decreases π_i by at least ϵ, or else leaves π_i unchanged because there is more than one object j attaining the maximum in Eq. (3.10). However, in the latter case, the price of the object j^* receiving the bid will increase by at least ϵ, and object j^* will not receive another bid by person i until π_i decreases by at least ϵ. The conclusion is that if a person i bids an infinite number of times, π_i must decrease to $-\infty$.

Proposition 3.4.   If at least one complete assignment exists, the algorithm terminates in a finite number of steps.

Proof. If the algorithm continues indefinitely, the prices of a proper [cf. (a) above] subset J^∞ of objects increases to ∞, while the profit margins π_i of a subset I^∞ of persons decrease to $-\infty$, [cf. (c) above]. Furthermore, eventually, in view of Eq. (3.11), at any given time, each object in J^∞ can only be assigned to a person from I^∞ , and a person from I^∞ will either be assigned to an object in J^∞ or be unassigned. Also, in view of (c) above, eventually only persons from I^∞ will be unassigned. Therefore, the cardinality of I^∞ is greater than the cardinality of J^∞, while, in view of Eq. (3.11), we have $J^\infty \supset A(i)$ for all i in I^∞. This contradicts the existence of a complete assignment. **Q.E.D.**

Practical experience with the serial version of the auction algorithm has shown that it is at least competitive with the best alternative serial algorithms for the assignment problem, particularly for sparse problems [Ber88], [BeE88]. It is sometimes important, however, to combine the algorithm with the scaling technique described in the next subsection.

5.3.2 Parallel Versions of the ϵ–Relaxation and the Auction Algorithms

In this subsection, we discuss the parallel implementation aspects of the auction and ϵ–relaxation algorithms. It is clear that both the bidding and the assignment phases of the auction algorithm are highly parallelizable. In the extreme case of a fine grain parallel computing environment, where there is a processor associated with each person and a processor associated with each object, all unassigned persons/processors can compute their bids simultaneously and communicate them to the relevant objects/processors. Those object/processors that receive at least one bid can determine the highest bidder simultaneously and communicate to the relevant persons/processors the changes in the current assignment and price vector. A similar implementation is possible in systems where there are relatively few processors communicating via an interconnection network such as a hypercube. Each processor is given the responsibility of computing the bids of several persons, and of updating the assignments and prices of several objects. At the end of the bidding phase, the bids are transmitted to the appropriate processors using some form of total exchange algorithm that depends on the interconnection network and on the sparsity structure of the assignment problem graph (cf. Subsection 1.3.4). At the end of the assignment phase, the updated object assignments and prices are transmitted to all processors via a multinode broadcast.

The auction algorithm is also well suited for implementation in a shared memory machine. Here the processors of the system perform tasks such as bid calculations, object assignments, and price updates. A synchronization mechanism is required for strict separation of the bidding and the assignment phases. In particular, it is necessary that the bids of all unassigned persons are calculated before the price or assignment of any object is updated. This separation is not necessary in an asynchronous implementation of the type to be discussed in the next chapter.

We now discuss how the ϵ-relaxation algorithm can be implemented in a message-passing system that assigns a separate processor to each node. This processor is charged with the responsibility of carrying out up iterations at the node and communicating the results to the adjacent processor/nodes. Our discussion applies with minor modifications to systems with few processors, where several nodes are assigned to each processor.

There are three basic parallel implementation modes for the ϵ-relaxation method. The first two, discussed here, are synchronous and will be referred to as the Gauss–Seidel and Jacobi versions in view with their similarity with the Gauss–Seidel and Jacobi relaxation methods discussed in Chapter 3. The third is a totally asynchronous version, and will be discussed in the next chapter (Section 6.5).

The synchronous algorithms are operated in phases, as discussed in Section 1.4. Some nodes/processors i with $g_i > 0$ at the start of the phase execute a complete or partial up iteration during the phase, and the results of the iteration are communicated to all adjacent nodes. A node cannot proceed to the next phase before it knows the results of the computation (if any) at all adjacent nodes during the preceding phase.

In the synchronous Gauss–Seidel version, the set of nodes is partitioned into subsets. Each subset should not contain a pair of nodes joined by an arc. In each phase, a single subset is selected and the positive surplus nodes of this subset only execute an up iteration. Because no two adjacent nodes execute an up iteration concurrently, it is seen that the Gauss–Seidel version is mathematically equivalent to a sequential version with a specific order for choosing nodes to execute an up iteration [see the discussion in Subsection 1.2.4; the dependency graph here contains the bidirectional arc (i, j) if either (i, j) or (j, i) is an arc of the graph of the problem]. Note that for transportation problems, we can use just two subsets; the subset of all sources and the subset of all sinks.

The Gauss–Seidel version has the drawback that some positive surplus nodes may be idle during some phases. This motivates the synchronous Jacobi version, whereby all positive surplus nodes execute an up iteration at every phase based on the prices and flows of adjacent nodes and arcs at the start of the phase. At the end of the phase, the price of each node and the flows of all its incident arcs are communicated to its corresponding adjacent nodes. There is an issue here on how two adjacent nodes i and j agree on a common value of the flow of the arc (i, j) joining them. The problem is that f_{ij} may be simultaneously modified by both i and j during a phase. When only one of the nodes i and j increases its price during a phase, we require that the value of f_{ij} as set by the node that increased its price is accepted by the other node. We resolve situations where both nodes i and j increase their prices during a phase as follows: if at the end of phase k, the prices p_i and p_j have become such that (i, j) is ϵ-active (or ϵ-inactive), then f_{ij} is set to c_{ij} (or b_{ij}) by both nodes i and j; otherwise, both nodes i and j set f_{ij} at the value of f_{ij} that prevailed at the start of phase k.

It can be seen that with this rule, ϵ–CS is preserved, and that at the end of each phase k, we have $g_i \geq 0$ for all nodes i having $g_i \geq 0$ at the start of phase k. With these observations, the proof of Prop. 3.2 goes through almost verbatim, thereby showing that the Jacobi version of the algorithm terminates in a finite number of phases.

An interesting question relates to the speedup that can be attained with a parallel implementation of the ϵ–relaxation method. We first note here that the maximum number of processors that can be executing up iterations in parallel at any one time cannot exceed the number of nodes with positive surplus. Computational experimentation shows that this number is typically quite large in the early stages of the computation. Near termination of the algorithm, however, most nodes have zero surplus, so the number of processors actively engaged in iterations is quite small. In fact, we give an example at the end of the next subsection where a parallel implementation of the algorithm leads to no appreciable speedup over a serial implementation. This example represents worst case behavior. Limited experience with parallel implementations of the ϵ–relaxation method and with the auction algorithm indicates that a speedup of the order of 10 should be attainable in many computing systems. This is only a rough estimate. Further experimentation and research is needed to establish the potential of parallel implementations of the ϵ–relaxation method and to provide a comparison with parallel implementations of the multiple node relaxation method of the previous section.

EXERCISES

3.1. Assume that for some price vector p, the dual cost along the ith price coordinate, $q(p_1, \ldots, p_{i-1}, \xi, p_{i+1}, \ldots, p_{|N|})$, attains a maximum over ξ in the interval $[\underline{p}_i, \bar{p}_i]$. Show that an up iteration at node i starting at a price value $p_i < \underline{p}_i - \epsilon$ sets p_i to $\bar{p}_i + \epsilon$, [cf. Fig. 5.3.4(a)]. Assume instead that the maximum is attained in the interval $[\underline{p}_i, \infty)$. Show that an up iteration at node i starting at a price value $p_i < \underline{p}_i - \epsilon$ sets p_i to $\underline{p}_i + \epsilon$, [cf. Fig. 5.3.4(b)]. Show that under either one of the preceding assumptions, p_i is set to a value that is within ϵ of some maximizing point of the dual cost along the ith price coordinate.

3.2. (Mixing of Up and Down Iterations, [Tse86] and [Eck87].) Define a *down iteration*, which is similar to an up iteration, but only applies to nodes i with $g_i < 0$, increases g_i, and decreases p_i.

    (a) Discuss briefly how to modify the proof of Prop. 3.2 to show the finiteness of the following algorithm: while there exists a node $i \in N$ with $g_i < 0$, select such an i and perform a down iteration upon it.

    (b) Consider the following algorithm: while there exists an $i \in N$ with $g_i \neq 0$, select such an i and perform an up iteration if $g_i > 0$ or a down iteration if $g_i < 0$. Consider also the following network problem: $N = \{1, 2, 3, 4\}$, $A = \{(1,2), (1,3), (2,4), (3,4)\}$, $s_1 = 1$, $s_2 = s_3 = 0$, $s_4 = -1$, $a_{ij} = 0$, $b_{ij} = 0$, and $c_{ij} = 2$ for all $(i,j) \in A$. Show that for this problem the algorithm is not guaranteed to be finite for $\epsilon = 1$ and the initial price vector $p = 0$. *Hint:* Give a sequence of price and flow modifications meeting the specifications of the algorithm, in which the state $p_1 = 1$, $p_2 = p_3 = 0$, $p_4 = -1$, $f_{12} = 1$, $f_{13} = f_{24} = 0$, $f_{34} = 1$ recurs infinitely many times.

3.3. Consider the multiple node relaxation iteration of Section 5.2, and also the primal–dual methods of Exercise 2.3. Show that if the terms "balanced", "active", and "inactive" are replaced by "ϵ–balanced", "ϵ–active", and "ϵ–inactive", respectively, then the resulting methods terminate in a finite number of iterations and that the final pairs (f, p) obtained satisfy ϵ–CS.

3.4. In this exercise, we consider a variation of an up iteration that involves *degenerate price increases*. A degenerate price increase raises the price of a node that currently has zero surplus to the maximum possible value that does not violate ϵ–CS with respect to the current flow vector (assuming there exists such a maximum value). One example of such a price increase occurs when Step 4 of the up iteration is executed with $g_i = 0$. Show that Prop. 3.2 holds even if degenerate price rises are allowed in the up iteration.

3.5. (Relation of the ϵ–Relaxation Method and the Auction Algorithm.) Consider the assignment problem of Fig. 5.1.1 having n sources, n sinks, and an arbitrary set A of source-to-sink arcs. We say that source i is assigned to sink j if (i, j) has positive flow. We consider a version of the ϵ–relaxation algorithm in which up iterations are organized as follows: between iterations (and also at initialization), only source nodes i can have positive surplus. Each iteration does the following: (1) finds any unassigned source i (i.e., one with positive surplus), and performs an up iteration at i; and (2) takes the sink j to which i was consequently assigned, and performs an up iteration at j, even if j has zero surplus. (If j has zero surplus, such an up iteration will consist of just a degenerate price rise; see Exercise 3.4.)

     More specifically, an iteration by an unassigned source i works as follows: (a) Source node i sets its price to $p_j + a_{ij} + \epsilon$, where j minimizes $p_k + a_{ik} + \epsilon$ over all k for which $(i, k) \in A$. It then sets $f_{ij} = 1$, assigning itself to j. (b) Node i then raises its price to $p_{j'} + a_{ij'} + \epsilon$, where j' minimizes $p_k + a_{ik} + \epsilon$ for $k \neq j$, $(i, k) \in A$. (c) If sink j had a previous assignment $f_{i'j} = 1$, it breaks the assignment by setting $f_{i'j} := 0$ (one can show inductively that if this occurs, $p_j = p_{i'} - a_{i'j} + \epsilon$). (d) Sink j then raises its price p_j to

$$p_i - a_{ij} + \epsilon = p_{j'} + a_{ij'} - a_{ij} + 2\epsilon.$$

Show that the corresponding algorithm is equivalent to the sequential (Gauss–Seidel) version of the auction algorithm.

3.6. (The Auction Algorithm with Similar Objects [BeC87].) Given the assignment problem of Subsection 5.3.1, we say that two objects j and j' are *similar*, and write $j \sim j'$, if for all persons $i = 1, \dots, n$, we have

$$j \in A(i) \quad \Rightarrow \quad j' \in A(i) \quad \text{and} \quad a_{ij} = a_{ij'}.$$

For each object j, the set of all objects similar to j is called the similarity class of j and is denoted $M(j)$. Consider a variation of the auction algorithm that is the same as the one of Subsection 5.3.1 except for one difference: in the bidding phase, w_{ij*} is defined now as

$$w_{ij*} = \max_{j \in A(i), j \notin M(j*)} v_{ij}$$

(instead of $w_{ij*} = \max_{j \in A(i), j \neq j*} v_{ij}$). Show that, assuming the initial assignment S satisfies ϵ–CS together with the initial vector $\hat{p}$ defined by

$$\hat{p}_j = \min_{k \in M(j)} p_k, \qquad j = 1, \ldots, n,$$

that is,

$$\max_{k \in A(i)} \{a_{ik} - \hat{p}_k\} - \epsilon \leq a_{ij} - \hat{p}_j, \qquad \forall \, (i,j) \in S,$$

the same is true of the assignment and the vector $\hat{p}$ obtained at the end of each assignment phase. Show also that the algorithm terminates finitely with an optimal assignment if $\epsilon < 1/n$.

3.7. **(The Auction Algorithm for Network Problems with Unit Capacity Bounds.)** Consider the linear network flow problem (LNF) for the case where the feasible flow range of each arc (i,j) is $0 \leq f_{ij} \leq 1$. Convert this problem into a transportation problem, as in Fig. 5.1.4 of Section 5.1, and describe the application of the auction algorithm of Exercise 3.6.

3.8. **(The Auction Algorithm for Transportation Problems [BeC87].)** Consider the assignment problem. We say that two persons i and i' are *similar*, and write $i \sim i'$, if for all objects $j = 1, \ldots, N$, we have

$$j \in A(i) \qquad \Rightarrow \qquad j \in A(i') \qquad \text{and} \qquad a_{ij} = a_{i'j}.$$

The set of all persons similar to i is called the similarity class of i.
   (a) Generalize the auction algorithm with similar objects given in Exercise 3.6 so that it takes into account both similar persons and similar objects. *Hint:* Consider simultaneous bids by all persons in the same similarity class.
   (b) Show how the algorithm of part (a) can be applied to transportation problems.

3.9. **(The Auction Algorithm for Incomplete Assignment Problems.)**
   (a) Derive a variation of the auction algorithm for an assignment problem where the number of persons m is greater than the number of objects n. All objects must be assigned to distinct persons. *Hint:* Introduce $m - n$ additional objects connected to all persons with zero cost arcs. Use the auction algorithm with similar objects of Exercise 3.7.
   (b) Repeat part (a) for the case where $m < n$ and all persons must be assigned to distinct objects. *Hint:* Introduce $n - m$ additional persons which are similar (cf. Exercise 3.8).
   (c) Repeat part (b) for the case where a person need not be assigned to an object, that is, the constraints of the problem are

$$\sum_{j \in A(i)} f_{ij} \leq 1, \qquad \sum_{\{i \mid j \in A(i)\}} f_{ij} \leq 1, \qquad f_{ij} \geq 0.$$

3.10. **(An Auction–Like Algorithm Based on the Alternating Direction Method.)** Consider a transportation problem of the form

$$\text{minimize} \quad \sum_{(i,j)\in A} a_{ij} f_{ij}$$

subject to

$$\sum_{j\in O(i)} f_{ij} = \alpha_i, \qquad \forall \, i = 1,\ldots,m$$

$$\sum_{i\in I(j)} f_{ij} = \beta_j, \qquad \forall \, j = 1,\ldots,n$$

$$0 \le f_{ij}, \qquad \forall \, (i,j) \in A,$$

where for all i and j,

$$O(i) = \{j \mid (i,j) \in A\}, \qquad I(j) = \{i \mid (i,j) \in A\}.$$

Consider an iteration where we first calculate, for all sources i in parallel,

$$\left\{ f_{ij}(t+1) \,|\, j \in O(i) \right\}$$

$$= \arg \min_{\substack{\sum_{j\in O(i)} f_{ij} = \alpha_i \\ f_{ij} \ge 0}} \left\{ \sum_{j\in O(i)} \left[\big(a_{ij} + p_j(t)\big) f_{ij} + \frac{c}{2}\big(f_{ij} - f_{ij}(t) + \bar{g}_j(t)\big)^2 \right] \right\},$$

and then we calculate, for all sinks j in parallel,

$$p_j(t+1) = p_j(t) + c\bar{g}_j(t+1),$$

where for all j and t,

$$\bar{g}_j(t) = \frac{1}{d_j} \left(\sum_{i\in I(j)} f_{ij}(t) - \beta_j \right)$$

and d_j is the number of sources in $I(j)$. The initial flows $f_{ij}(0)$ and prices $p_j(0)$ are arbitrary, and c is a positive constant. Show that this method is a special case of the alternating direction method of multipliers of Subsection 3.4.4.

5.4 COMPLEXITY ANALYSIS OF THE ϵ–RELAXATION METHOD AND ITS SCALED VERSION

In this section, we derive a bound on the order of time taken by the ϵ–relaxation algorithm. We then introduce a scaled version of the method with a particularly favorable time bound. Our analysis assumes the following:

Assumption 4.1. There exists at least one feasible solution of problem (LNF).

Assumption 4.2.   All arc cost coefficients are integer multiples of ϵ.

Assumption 4.3.   All starting prices are integer multiples of ϵ, all starting flows are integer, and together they satisfy ϵ–CS. Furthermore, initially there are no ϵ^+–unblocked or ϵ^-–unblocked arcs.

To achieve the last property required in Assumption 4.3 we can simply take initially $f_{ij} = c_{ij}$ for all ϵ^+–balanced arcs (i, j) and $f_{ij} = b_{ij}$ for all ϵ^-–balanced arcs (i, j), but better choices may be possible in particular situations.

A notion that is central in the subsequent complexity analysis is the so called *admissible graph*, which consists of the ϵ^+–unblocked arcs and of the ϵ^-–unblocked arcs with their directions reversed (i.e., the arcs along which flow is allowed to change according to the rules of the algorithm, with each arc oriented in the direction of the flow change). Formally, the admissible graph is defined as $G^* = (N, A^*)$, where an arc (i, j) belongs to A^* if and only if it is possible to "push" flow from i to j without an intervening price change according to the rules of the algorithm in Step 2 or 3. In other words, A^* contains an arc (i, j) if either (i, j) is an ϵ^+–unblocked arc of A or (j, i) is an ϵ^-–unblocked arc of A. Note that the admissible graph depends on the current pair (f, p) that satisfies ϵ–CS and changes as the pair (f, p) changes during the course of the algorithm. In particular, when flow is increased (or decreased) to the upper bound of an ϵ^+–unblocked arc in Step 2 (or the lower bound of an ϵ^-–unblocked arc in Step 3, respectively) of the up iteration, the arc is removed from A^*. Furthermore, when there is a price increase of a node i during Step 4 of the up iteration, all the incident arcs of node i that belonged to A^* prior to the price increase are removed from A^*, and the incident arcs (i, j) or (j, i) that become ϵ^+–unblocked or ϵ^-–unblocked, respectively, following the price increase [i.e., those for which the minimum in Eq. (3.5) is attained] are added to A^*.

To organize the computation efficiently, it is necessary to maintain the admissible graph in a data structure. In particular, the incident arcs of each node i that belong to the admissible graph are maintained in a list L_i, which is updated as necessary after each execution of a Step 2, 3, or 4 of an up iteration. We assume that the list L_i is organized in a way that the addition and deletion of a single arc takes $O(1)$ computation; this is true, for example, if L_i is a doubly linked list [Kru87]. Then it is seen that updating L_i at the end of Steps 2, 3, and 4 of the up iteration takes $O(1)$, $O(1)$, and $O(d_i)$ time, respectively, where d_i is the number of incident arcs of node i. As a result, updating the list L_i does not affect the order of time needed for these steps.

The role of the admissible graph can be understood in terms of the example of Fig. 5.4.1. Here the admissible graph contains the cycle 2–3–2. As a result, arc flows change along the cycle by small increments for a number of times that can be as large as the arc flow bounds. We call this phenomenon *flow looping*. It can occur only when the admissible graph has cycles. It does not arise when $\epsilon < 1/|N|$, because then the admissible graph is always acyclic. To see this, note that if there existed a cycle, then by adding the condition for an ϵ^+–balanced or ϵ^-–balanced arc along the cycle, we obtain that the sum of the arc costs of the ϵ^-–balanced arcs minus the sum of the arc costs of the ϵ^+–balanced arcs on the cycle equals ϵ times the number of arcs on the cycle. This is impossible when the coefficients a_{ij} are integer and $\epsilon < 1/|N|$. When $\epsilon \geq 1/|N|$, it is necessary to choose the initial flows and prices so that the admissible graph is initially acyclic. Then all up iterations maintain the acyclicity of this graph, as will be shown in the proof of Prop. 4.1. Assumption 4.3 guarantees that the admissible graph initially has no arcs and is therefore trivially acyclic.

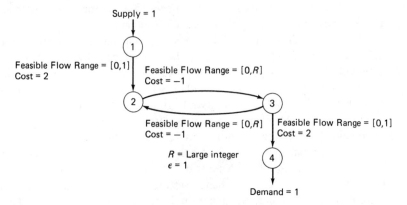

Figure 5.4.1 An example demonstrating the role of Assumption 4.3 on the initial conditions. Initially, we choose $f = 0$ and $p = 0$, which do satisfy 1–CS, but not Assumption 4.3. The algorithm will push one unit of flow R times around the cycle 2–3–2, implying $\Omega(R)$ solution time.

In order to maintain the acyclicity of the admissible graph, we need a special data structure and a restriction in the way the algorithm is operated. We introduce an order for choosing nodes in iterations. A *cycle* is a set of iterations whereby all nodes are chosen once in a given order, and an up iteration is executed at each node having positive surplus at the time its turn comes. The order in which nodes are taken up in a cycle can change from one cycle to the next. This node order is maintained in a linked list that is traversed from the first to the last element in each cycle. Each time a node i changes price as a result of its up iteration within a cycle, node i is removed from its present list position and is placed in the first list position. (This does not change the order in which the remaining nodes are taken up in the current cycle; only the order for the subsequent cycle is affected.) The initial list is arbitrary. It will be shown as part of the proof of the subsequent Prop. 4.1 that with the above method for operating the algorithm, the admissible graph is always acyclic.

Assumption 4.4.   The algorithm is operated in cycles as described above.

The motivation for the linked list data structure is illustrated in Fig. 5.4.2, and is based on the admissible graph, which is acyclic at all times and defines a partial order on the nodes. Within any one cycle, and up to the point where a price change occurs, flow can only be pushed from a higher ranking (first in the list) to a lower ranking node according to the order at the beginning of the cycle. Therefore, it is most efficient to iterate on higher ranking nodes first. Choosing the lower ranking node first may be wasteful since its surplus will be set to zero through an up iteration and can become positive again within the same cycle through an up iteration at a higher ranking node; this cannot happen if nodes are chosen according to the partial order induced by the admissible graph. This order will be shown to be consistent with the order of nodes in the linked list previously described. As a result, during a cycle, high ranking nodes are taken up for iteration before low ranking nodes. This effect can be described as sweeping the positive surplus along the admissible graph from top to bottom, so we call the corresponding implementation of the ϵ–relaxation method *sweep implementation*.

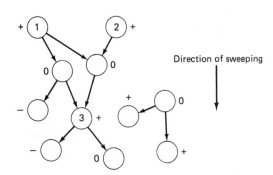

Figure 5.4.2 Illustration of the admissible graph consisting of the ϵ^+–unblocked arcs and the ϵ^-–unblocked arcs with their directions reversed. These arcs specify the direction along which flow can be changed according to the rules of the algorithm. A "+" (or "−" or "0") indicates a node with positive (or negative or zero) surplus. The algorithm is operated so that the admissible graph is acyclic at all times. The sweep implementation, based on the linked list data structure, requires that the high ranking nodes (e.g., nodes 1 and 2 in the graph) are chosen for iteration before the low ranking nodes (e.g., node 3 in the graph).

Direction of sweeping

We begin the complexity analysis by introducing some notation and terminology. For any path H, we denote by $s(H)$ and $t(H)$ the start and end nodes of H, respectively, and by H^+ and H^- the sets of forward and backward arcs of H, respectively, as the path is traversed in the direction from $s(H)$ to $t(H)$. For any price vector p and simple path H, we define

$$
\begin{aligned}
d_H(p) &= \max\left\{0, \sum_{(i,j)\in H^+}(p_i - p_j - a_{ij}) - \sum_{(i,j)\in H^-}(p_i - p_j - a_{ij})\right\} \\
&= \max\left\{0, \ p_{s(H)} - p_{t(H)} - \sum_{(i,j)\in H^+}a_{ij} + \sum_{(i,j)\in H^-}a_{ij}\right\}.
\end{aligned}
\tag{4.1}
$$

Note that the second term in the maximum can be viewed as a "reduced cost length of H", being the sum of the reduced costs $p_i - p_j - a_{ij}$ over all arcs $(i, j) \in H^+$ less the sum of $p_i - p_j - a_{ij}$ over all arcs $(i, j) \in H^-$. For any flow vector f satisfying the capacity constraints (1.2) we say that a simple path H is *unblocked with respect to f* if we have $f_{ij} < c_{ij}$ for all arcs $(i, j) \in H^+$ and we have $f_{ij} > b_{ij}$ for all arcs $(i, j) \in H^-$. In words, H is unblocked with respect to f if there is margin for sending positive flow along H (in addition to f) from $s(H)$ to $t(H)$ without violating the capacity constraints.

For any price vector p and flow vector f satisfying both the conservation of flow and the capacity constraints (1.1) and (1.2), denote

$$D(p, f) = \max\{d_H(p) \mid H \text{ is a simple unblocked path with respect to } f\}. \quad (4.2)$$

In the exceptional case where there is no simple unblocked path with respect to f, we define $D(p, f) = 0$. In this case, we must have $b_{ij} = c_{ij}$ for all (i, j) since any arc (i, j) with $b_{ij} < c_{ij}$ gives rise to a one–arc unblocked path with respect to f.

Let

$$\beta(p) = \min\{D(p, f) \mid f \text{ satisfies constraints (1.1) and (1.2)}\}. \quad (4.3)$$

Since for a given p, there is only a finite number of values that $D(p, f)$ can take, it follows that the minimum in Eq. (4.3) is attained by some f. The following lemma shows that $\beta(p)$ provides a measure of suboptimality of the price vector p. The solution time estimate for the algorithm to be obtained shortly is proportional to $\beta(p^0)$, where p^0 is the initial price vector:

Lemma 4.1.

(a) If there exists a flow vector f satisfying the conservation of flow and the capacity constraints (1.1) and (1.2), and satisfying γ–CS together with p for some $\gamma \geq 0$, then

$$0 \leq \beta(p) \leq (|N| - 1)\gamma. \quad (4.4)$$

(b) p is dual optimal if and only if $\beta(p) = 0$.

Proof.

(a) For each simple path H that is unblocked with respect to f and has $|H|$ arcs, we have, by adding the γ–CS condition along H and using Eq. (4.1), $d_H(p) \leq |H|\gamma \leq (|N| - 1)\gamma$ and the result follows from Eqs. (4.2) and (4.3).

(b) If p is optimal, then it satisfies complementary slackness together with some primal optimal vector f, so from Eq. (4.4) (with $\gamma = 0$), we obtain $\beta(p) = 0$. Conversely, if $\beta(p) = 0$, then from Eq. (4.3), we see that there must exist a primal feasible f such that $D(p, f) = 0$. Hence, $d_H(p) = 0$ for all unblocked simple paths H with respect to f. Applying this fact to single–arc paths H and using the definition (4.1), we obtain that f together with p satisfy complementary slackness. It follows that p and f satisfy all the optimality conditions (1.8)–(1.11), and p is optimal. **Q.E.D.**

Proposition 4.1.   Under Assumptions 4.1 – 4.4, the ϵ–relaxation algorithm terminates in $O(|N|^3 + |N|^2\beta(p^0)/\epsilon)$ time, where p^0 is the initial price vector.

Proof. To economize on notation, we write β in place of $\beta(p^0)$. We first show the following:

Lemma 4.2. The number of price increases at each node is $O(|N| + \beta/\epsilon)$.

Proof. Let f^0 be a flow vector attaining the minimum in the definition (4.3) of $\beta(p^0)$. To explain the main argument better, we assume that f^0 is the zero vector. This can be done without loss of generality because we can transform the problem by replacing c_{ij}, b_{ij}, f_{ij} and s_i by $c_{ij} - f_{ij}^0$, $b_{ij} - f_{ij}^0$, $f_{ij} - f_{ij}^0$ and 0, respectively. The transformation does not change the surplus of any node, and does not change the prices generated by the algorithm. Let (f, p) be a vector pair generated by the algorithm. If $g_t > 0$ for some node t, there must exist a node s with $g_s < 0$ and a simple path H with $s(H) = s$, $t(H) = t$, and such that $f_{ij} > 0$ for all $(i, j) \in H^+$ and $f_{ij} < 0$ for all $(i, j) \in H^-$. [This follows from the Conformal Realization Theorem (Appendix B). It can also be shown quickly from first principles: take $T_0 = \{t\}$, and given T_k, define

$$T_{k+1} = T_k \cup \left\{ j \notin T_k \mid \text{there is a node } i \in T_k, \right.$$

$$\text{and either an arc } (i, j) \text{ such that } f_{ij} < 0, \text{ or an arc } (j, i) \text{ such that } f_{ji} > 0 \Big\}.$$

If none of the negative surplus nodes belongs to any of the T_k, then the total surplus of the nodes in $\cup T_k$ is positive, while the forward arcs of the arc set separating $\cup T_k$ and its complement have nonnegative flow and the backward arcs have nonpositive flow. This is a contradiction, showing that a node s with $g_s < 0$ and the aforementioned properties can be found.]

We thus conclude that the path H is unblocked with respect to f^0. Hence, from Eq. (4.2), we must have $d_H(p^0) \leq D(p^0, f^0) = \beta$, and by using Eq. (4.1),

$$p_s^0 - p_t^0 - \sum_{(i,j)\in H^+} a_{ij} + \sum_{(i,j)\in H^-} a_{ij} \leq \beta. \tag{4.5}$$

Also, using ϵ–CS, we have $p_j + a_{ij} \leq p_i + \epsilon$ for all $(i, j) \in H^+$ and $p_i \leq p_j + a_{ij} + \epsilon$ for all $(i, j) \in H^-$. By adding these conditions along H, we obtain

$$-p_s + p_t + \sum_{(i,j)\in H^+} a_{ij} - \sum_{(i,j)\in H^-} a_{ij} \leq |H|\epsilon \leq (|N| - 1)\epsilon \tag{4.6}$$

where $|H|$ is the number of arcs of H. We have $p_s^0 = p_s$, since the condition $g_s < 0$ implies that the price of s has not yet changed. Therefore, by adding Eqs. (4.5) and (4.6), we obtain

$$p_t - p_t^0 < (|N| - 1)\epsilon + \beta \tag{4.7}$$

throughout the algorithm for all nodes t with $g_t > 0$. Since all the starting prices and arc cost coefficients are integer multiples of ϵ, it follows that the size of a price increase is a positive integer multiple of ϵ, and we see from Eq. (4.7) that the number of price increases of each node is $O(|N| + \beta/\epsilon)$.   **Q.E.D.**

Note that the price bound (4.7) ensures that an infeasible problem instance can be detected by checking whether the total price rise of any node exceeds a known upper bound to $(|N| - 1)\epsilon + \beta$.

We now proceed with the proof of Prop. 4.1. The dominant computational requirements are:

(1) The computation required for price increases in Step 4.

(2) The computation required for Steps 2 or 3 for which the flow of the corresponding arc is set to its upper or its lower bound.

(3) The computation required for Steps 2 or 3 for which the flow of the corresponding arc is set to a value strictly between its upper and its lower bound.

We first make the general observation that by using the lists L_i that hold the arcs of the admissible graph, the computation time to examine any one arc in the algorithm is $O(1)$. In particular, the time to execute Steps 1, 2, 3, and 4 (including the updating of the lists L_i) is $O(1)$, $O(1)$, $O(1)$, and $O(d_i)$, respectively, where d_i is the number of incident arcs of the node i iterated on. Since there are $O(|N| + \beta/\epsilon)$ price increases for each node, the requirements in (1) above are $O(|A|(|N| + \beta/\epsilon))$ operations. Whenever an arc flow is set to either the upper or the lower bound due to an iteration at one of the end nodes, it takes a price increase of at least 2ϵ by the opposite end node before the arc flow can change again. Therefore, there are $O(|N| + \beta/\epsilon)$ Steps 2 or 3 per arc for which the flow of the arc is set to its upper or lower bound. The computation time for each of these steps is $O(1)$, so the total requirements for (2) above are $O(|A|(|N| + \beta/\epsilon))$ operations.

There remains to estimate the computational requirements for (3) above. At this point, we will use the fact that the algorithm is operated in cycles with the node order in each cycle determined by a linked list that is restructured in the course of the algorithm, as described earlier. We will demonstrate that the number of cycles up to termination is $O(|N|(|N| + \beta/\epsilon))$. Given this, the proof of Prop. 4.2 can be completed as follows: for each cycle, there can only be one arc flow per node set to a value strictly between the upper and lower arc flow bound in Step 2 or 3. Therefore the total number of operations required for these steps [cf. (3) above] is $O(|N|^2(|N| + \beta/\epsilon))$. Adding the computational requirements for (1) and (2) calculated earlier, we obtain an $O(|N|^2(|N| + \beta/\epsilon)) + O(|A|(|N| + \beta/\epsilon))$ or $O(|N|^2(|N| + \beta/\epsilon))$ time bound.

To show that the number of cycles up to termination is $O(|N|(|N| + \beta/\epsilon))$, we use the admissible graph $G^* = (N, A^*)$ and we argue as follows: a node i is called a *predecessor* of a node j if a directed path exists from i to j in G^*. First, we claim that immediately following a price rise at node j, there are no arcs (i, j) in A^* that are incoming to j, and hence j has no predecessors. To see this, note that if $(i, j) \in A$ is ϵ^+–balanced after the price change, it must have been ϵ–active beforehand, and, hence, $f_{ij} = c_{ij}$, implying that (i, j) is not in A^*. The ϵ^-–balanced case is similar, establishing the claim. We next claim that G^* is always acyclic. This is true initially because Assumption 4.3 implies that A^* is empty. Flow change operations (Steps 2 and 3) can only remove arcs from A^*, so G^* can acquire a cycle only immediately after a price rise at some node j, and the cycle must include that node. But since j must then have no incoming incident arcs in the admissible graph, no such cycle is possible. This establishes the second claim. Finally, we claim that the node list maintained by the algorithm will always be compatible with the partial order induced by G^*, in the sense that every node will always appear in the list after all its predecessors. Again this is initially true because A^* starts out empty. Furthermore a flow change operation does not create new predecessor relationships, while after the price of some node i rises, i can have no predecessors and is moved to the head of the list before any possible descendants. This establishes the claim.

Let N^+ be the set of nodes with positive surplus that have no predecessor with positive surplus, and let N^0 be the set of nodes with nonpositive surplus that have no predecessor with positive surplus. Then, as long as no price increase takes place, all nodes in N^0 remain in N^0, and execution of a complete up iteration at a node $i \in N^+$ moves i from N^+ to N^0. If no node changed price during a cycle, then all nodes of N^+ will be added to N^0 by the end of the cycle, which implies that the algorithm terminates. Therefore, there will be a node price change during every cycle except possibly for the last one. Since the number of price increases per node is $O(|N| + \beta/\epsilon)$, there can be only $O(|N|(|N| + \beta/\epsilon))$ cycles, leading to an $O(|N|^2(|N| + \beta/\epsilon))$ overall time bound based on the argument given earlier.   **Q.E.D.**

An upper bound for $\beta(p^0)$ is given by $(|N| - 1)C + p^+ - p^-$, where

$$p^+ = \max_{i \in N} p_i^0,$$

$$p^- = \min_{i \in N} p_i^0,$$

and C is the arc cost range:

$$C = \max_{(i,j) \in A} |a_{ij}|. \tag{4.8}$$

Assuming that $p^+ - p^- = O(1)$, we obtain the time bound $O\left(|N|^3 C/\epsilon\right)$. The algorithm is indeed sensitive to C, as shown in the example of Fig. 5.4.3.

Application to the Max–Flow Problem

For classes of problems with special structure, a better estimate of $\beta(p^0)$ may be possible. As an example, consider the max–flow problem formulation shown in Fig. 5.1.2. The artificial arc (t, s) connecting the sink t with the source s has cost coefficient -1, and flow bounds $\beta_{ts} = 0$ and $c_{ts} = \sum_i c_{si}$. We assume that $a_{ij} = 0$ and $b_{ij} = 0 < c_{ij}$ for all other arcs (i, j), and that $s_i = 0$ for all i. We apply the ϵ-relaxation algorithm with initial prices

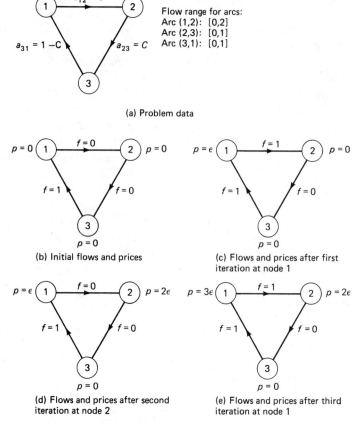

(a) Problem data

Flow range for arcs:
Arc (1,2): [0,2]
Arc (2,3): [0,1]
Arc (3,1): [0,1]

(b) Initial flows and prices

(c) Flows and prices after first
iteration at node 1

(d) Flows and prices after second
iteration at node 2

(e) Flows and prices after third
iteration at node 1

Figure 5.4.3 Example showing that the pure form of the algorithm can take time that is proportional to the cost–dependent factor C. Here up iterations at node 1 alternate with up iterations at node 2 until the time when p_1 rises to the level $C - 1 + \epsilon$ and arc (3,1) becomes ϵ^-–balanced, so that a unit of flow can be pushed back along that arc. At this time, the optimal solution is obtained. Since prices rise by increments of no more than 2ϵ, the number of up iterations is $\Omega(C/\epsilon)$.

and arc flows satisfying ϵ–CS, where $\epsilon = 1/(|N| + 1)$ and $p^+ - p^- = O(1)$. Because there is only one arc that has nonzero (-1) cost coefficient, we obtain $d_H(p^0) = O(1)$ for all paths H. Therefore, $\beta(p^0) = O(1)$ and Prop. 4.1 yields an $O(|N|^3)$ time bound. This bound is competitive with that of other max–flow algorithms [PaS82], and can only be improved through the use of sophisticated data structures [GoT86], [AhO86].

5.4.1 The Scaled Version of the Algorithm

Since the algorithm is sensitive to the arc cost range C, it is natural to consider cost scaling procedures involving solution of a sequence of approximations to the original problem, gradually increasing the accuracy of the cost coefficient data.

Consider the problem obtained from (LNF) by multiplying all arc cost coefficients by $|N| + 1$, that is, the problem with arc cost coefficients

$$a'_{ij} = (|N| + 1)a_{ij}, \qquad \forall \ (i, j) \in A.$$

We refer to this problem as (SNLF). If a pair (f', p') satisfies 1–CS (namely, ϵ–CS with $\epsilon = 1$) with respect to (SLNF), then clearly the pair

$$(f, p) = \left(f', \frac{p'}{|N| + 1} \right)$$

satifies $(|N| + 1)^{-1}$–CS with respect to (LNF), and hence f' is optimal for (LNF) by Prop. 4.1. In the scaled algorithm, we seek a 1–CS solution to (SLNF).

Let

$$M = \lfloor \log_2(|N| + 1)C \rfloor + 1 = O\big(\log(|N|C)\big), \tag{4.9}$$

where $C = \max_{(i,j) \in A} |a_{ij}|$. In the scaled algorithm, we solve M subproblems. The mth subproblem is a minimum cost flow problem, where the cost coefficient of each arc (i, j) is

$$a_{ij}(m) = \text{Trunc} \left(\frac{a'_{ij}}{2^{M-m}} \right), \tag{4.10}$$

where Trunc($\cdot$) denotes integer rounding in the direction of 0, that is, down for positive and up for negative numbers. Note that $|a_{ij}(m)|$ is the integer consisting of the m most significant bits in the M–bit binary representation of $|a'_{ij}|$. In particular each $a_{ij}(1)$ is 0, $+1$, or -1, while $a_{ij}(m+1)$ is obtained by doubling $a_{ij}(m)$ and adding (subtracting) 1 if the $(m + 1)$st bit of the M–bit representation of $|a_{ij}|$ is a 1 and a_{ij} is positive (negative). Note also that

$$a_{ij}(M) = a'_{ij},$$

so the last problem of the sequence is (SLNF).

All problems in the sequence are solved by applying the ϵ–relaxation algorithm using $\epsilon = 1$, yielding upon termination a pair $\big(f^t(m), p^t(m) \big)$ satisfying 1–CS with respect to the cost coefficients $a_{ij}(m)$. The algorithm is operated in cycles as per Assumption 4.4.

The starting pair $\big(f^0(1), p^0(1) \big)$ for the first problem must be integer and must satisfy 1–CS. The starting price vector for the $(m + 1)$st problem $(m = 1, 2, ..., M - 1)$ is

$$p^0(m + 1) = 2p^t(m), \tag{4.11}$$

where $p^t(m)$ is the final price vector obtained from solution of the mth problem. Doubling $p^t(m)$ as above roughly maintains complementary slackness since $a_{ij}(m)$ is roughly doubled when passing to the $(m + 1)$st problem. Indeed, it can be seen that every arc that was 1–balanced (1–active, 1–inactive) upon termination of the algorithm for the mth problem will be 3–balanced (1–active, 1–inactive, respectively) at the start of the $(m + 1)$st problem.

The starting flow vector $f^0(m + 1)$ for the $(m + 1)$st problem is obtained from the final flow vector $f^t(m)$ of the preceding problem by setting

$$f_{ij}^0(m + 1) = f_{ij}^t(m) \qquad \text{for all balanced arcs } (i, j),$$

$$f_{ij}^0(m + 1) = c_{ij} \qquad \text{for all active arcs } (i, j),$$

$$f_{ij}^0(m + 1) = b_{ij} \qquad \text{for all inactive arcs } (i, j).$$

(The definitions of balanced, active, and inactive arcs used above are those given in Section 5.2, that is, they correspond to $\epsilon = 0$.) Note that this initialization method implies that the starting price and flow vector will be integer, and that there will be no 1^+–unblocked and 1^-–unblocked arcs initially for the $(m + 1)$st problem. These facts guarantee that Assumptions 4.2 and 4.3 are satisfied for the subproblems. A more refined initial flow vector choice for the subproblems is given in Exercise 4.1.

Based on Prop. 4.1, the scaled form of the algorithm solves the problem in $O(|N|^3 + |N|^2 B)$ time, where

$$B = \sum_{m=1}^{M} \beta_m \left[p^0(m) \right], \tag{4.12}$$

and $\beta_m(\cdot)$ is defined by Eqs. (4.1)–(4.3) but with the modified cost coefficients $a_{ij}(m)$ replacing a_{ij} in the definition (4.1). We will show that $\beta_m[p^0(m)] = O(|N|)$ for every m, thereby obtaining the following proposition:

Proposition 4.2. Assume that for the initial subproblem, Assumptions 4.1-4.3 are satisfied and that $p_i^0 - p_j^0 = O(1)$ for all arcs (i, j). The scaled form of the algorithm solves the problem in $O\left(|N|^3 \log(|N|C)\right)$ time, where $C = \max_{(i,j) \in A} |a_{ij}|$.

   Proof. Since initially we have $p_i - p_j = O(1)$ and $a_{ij}(1) = O(1)$ for all arcs (i, j), we obtain $d_H\left(p^0(1)\right) = O(|N|)$ for all H, and $\beta_1\left[p^0(1)\right] = O(|N|)$. We also have that the final flow vector $f^t(m)$ obtained from the mth problem satisfies constraints (1.1) and (1.2), and together with $p^0(m + 1)$ it can be seen to satisfy 3–CS. It follows from Lemma 4.1(a) that $\beta_{m+1}[p^0(m + 1)] \leq 3(|N| - 1) = O(|N|)$ and the result follows from Eq. (4.12) as discussed above.   **Q.E.D.**

5.4.2 Application to the Assignment Problem

Consider the special case of the assignment problem shown in Fig. 5.1.1, with the feasible flow range for all arcs taken to be [0,1]. Since all flows generated by the algorithm are integer, it follows that at no Step 2 or 3 of the ϵ–relaxation method, an arc flow is set strictly between the corresponding upper and the lower bound. Therefore, the computation required for such steps can be eliminated from the accounting of the proof of Prop. 4.1 leading to a time bound $O\big(|A|(|N| + \beta(p^0)/\epsilon)\big)$ for the ϵ–relaxation method and $O\big(|A||N|\log(|N|C)\big)$ for the scaled version.

The auction algorithm described in the previous section can also be shown to have an $O\big(|A|(|N| + \beta(p^0)/\epsilon)\big)$ time bound in its pure form and an $O\big(|A||N|\log(|N|C)\big)$ bound in its scaled version. This can be done by first modifying the proof of Lemma 4.2 to show that the number of times the profit margin of each person decreases or the price of each object increases is $O\big(|N| + \beta(p^0)/\epsilon\big)$. Then, one uses the argument of the proof of Prop. 4.2 while excluding from the time accounting the computation for steps for which an arc flow is set strictly between the upper and lower bounds. Note here that to achieve the stated time bound, it is still necessary to maintain the arcs of the admissible graph in appropriate lists, one per person and one per object. For an unassigned person i, this list consists of the arcs (i,j) for which $\pi_i = \max_{k \in A(i)}\{a_{ik} - p_k\} = a_{ij} - p_j$, and person i can detect at the start of an iteration if its list contains more than one arc. The iterations in which this happens are the ones for which the profit margin π_i does not change. In such an iteration, it can be seen that the bid b_{ij^*} of Eq. (3.14) is simply $p_{j^*} + \epsilon$ and can be calculated in $O(1)$ time. With this observation, the complexity analysis of the auction algorithm closely parallels the one of the ϵ–relaxation method (see also [BeE88]). Note, however, that maintaining the lists of arcs of the admissible graph, while useful for theoretical analysis purposes, can actually slow down the algorithm in practice.

Computational experience has shown that the serial scaled version of the auction algorithm performs very well, outperforming some highly efficient implementations of alternative methods. There is also some experience with parallel implementations of the auction algorithm in shared memory machines showing a modest speedup of up to about ten over the serial version of the algorithm. This is probably the maximum speedup that can be expected from a parallel version of the auction algorithm, because near termination there are typically very few persons that are unassigned thereby diminishing the method's potential for concurrency.

We finally mention that it is possible to combine the auction algorithm with the primal–dual method (Exercises 2.4 and 3.8) with the purpose of improving its serial time bound. This method is described in Exercise 4.5 and takes time $O\big(|A||N|^{\frac{1}{2}}\log(|N|C)\big)$. Its practical performance, however, does not appear to be better than the performance of the pure auction algorithm with scaling.

An Example of Poor Performance of the ϵ–Relaxation Method

In spite of the good theoretical time bound obtained for the scaled ϵ–relaxation method, there are problems where it can perform poorly compared with alternative methods. In particular, there is sometimes a tendency for each node to make a large number of small price rises, and the actual amount of work involved in price rises is then of the same order as its theoretical bound. Figure 5.4.4 presents an example of such behavior. It is an assignment problem with $2n$ nodes, nodes $s_1, ..., s_n$ being persons and $t_1, ..., t_n$ being objects. The arcs are (s_k, t_k) for $k = 1, ..., n$, and (s_k, t_{k+1}) for $k = 1, ..., n-1$. All arcs have unit capacity and zero cost. The problem may also be viewed as a max–flow problem by adjoining a "super source" node s and arcs (s, s_k), along with a "super sink" node t and arcs (t_k, t). Suppose that the (scaled or pure) ϵ–relaxation algorithm is applied to the assignment version of this example, with $\epsilon = 1$, initial node order $1, 2, ..., n$, and the rule that whenever it is possible to push flow away from a node on more than one arc, the one that is uppermost in Fig. 5.4.4 is selected. After the first n price rises, the prices and flows will be as shown in Fig. 5.4.5(a).

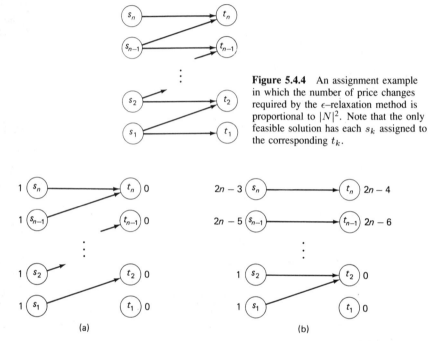

Figure 5.4.4 An assignment example in which the number of price changes required by the ϵ–relaxation method is proportional to $|N|^2$. Note that the only feasible solution has each s_k assigned to the corresponding t_k.

(a)   (b)

Figure 5.4.5 (a) The assignment example after n price rises. Prices are shown next to the corresponding node. Only arcs with positive flow are depicted. (b) The intermediate result after $(n - 1)^2 + 1$ price rises.

Claim. The ϵ–relaxation algorithm as applied to the example of Fig. 5.4.4 requires n^2 price rises. The final price of node s_k is $2k - 1$, and that of t_k is $2k - 2$.

Proof. By induction. When $n = 1$, a single price rise at s_1 and the ensuing flow adjustment yield a solution in which s_1 has price 1, t_1 has price 0, and s_1 is assigned to t_1. This establishes the base case of the induction. Now assume the claim is true for the problem of size $n - 1$; we establish it for the problem of size n. After n price rises, the configuration of Fig. 5.4.5(a) will be attained. This leaves nodes $s_2, ..., s_n$ and $t_2, ..., t_n$ in precisely the same state as after $n - 1$ price changes in a problem of size $n - 1$. By induction, after another

$$(n - 1)^2 - (n - 1) = n^2 - 3n + 2$$

price changes, the algorithm reaches the configuration of Fig. 5.4.5(b). Following the rules of ϵ–relaxation, the reader can confirm that the sequence of nodes now iterated on is $t_2, s_2, t_3, s_3, \ldots, t_n, s_n$, and the promised prices are obtained after $2(n-1)$ further price rises. Following this, the nodes are processed in the opposite order, and a primal feasible solution is obtained in $2n$ additional iterations (but no further price rises). The total number of price changes is

$$n + (n^2 - 3n + 2) + 2(n-1) = n^2.$$

This establishes the induction.   **Q.E.D.**

The total number of nodes in the example is $|N| = 2n$; hence the number of price changes is $(|N|/2)^2 = |N|^2/4 = \Omega(|N|^2)$, and increases with $|N|$ at the same rate as its theoretical bound. Since all arc costs are zero, scaling cannot be of any help in this situation. Note also that there is little opportunity for parallelism here, because there is never more than one node with a positive surplus at any time after the first n iterations.

It can be verified that the auction algorithm performs much better than the ϵ–relaxation method for the preceding example, requiring only $O(n)$ iterations in its Gauss–Seidel version (Exercise 4.3).

EXERCISES

4.1. Consider a variation of the initial flow vector choice for the subproblems of the scaled method of Subsection 5.4.1, whereby the flow of each arc (i, j) that belonged to the admissible graph at the end of the previous subproblem, and which is 1–balanced at the start of the current subproblem, is left unchanged, that is, $f_{ij}^0(m + 1) = f_{ij}^t(m)$. Show that the estimate of Prop. 4.2 remains unchanged.

4.2. **(Time Bound for the Multiple Node Relaxation Method.)** Consider the multiple node relaxation method of Section 5.2, where iterations start only from nodes with positive surplus.
   (a) Use an argument similar to the one of Lemma 4.2 to show that the number of iterations that result in a price increase is $O(|N|\beta(p^0))$, and, therefore, the total amount of time to solve the problem is $O(|N|\beta(p^0)F)$, where F is the amount of time for flow augmentations between two successive price increases. [If nodes are scanned in the order they are labeled, it is possible to show that $F = O(|N|^5)$; see [PaS82] and [Law76]. With a more sophisticated implementation, F can be reduced further considerably.]
   (b) Show that if cost scaling is used as described in this section, the time estimate becomes $O(|N|^2 F \log C)$.

4.3. Apply the Gauss–Seidel version of the auction algorithm to the example of Fig. 5.4.4 and show that it requires $O(n)$ price increases.

4.4. **(ϵ–Scaling.)** Consider the assignment problem. An alternative to the cost scaling procedure given in this section is to apply the auction algorithm for a decreasing sequence $\{\epsilon_k\}$ of values of ϵ, while transferring price and assignment information from one application to the next. The general form of this procedure is as follows: initially, we replace all arc cost coefficients a_{ij} with $a'_{ij} = (n+1)a_{ij}$, we select a scalar $\theta \in (0,1)$, we set $\epsilon_0 = \max_{(i,j)\in A} |a'_{ij}|$, and for $k = 1, 2, \ldots$ we set $\epsilon_k = \lceil \theta \epsilon_{k-1} \rceil$. We apply the auction algorithm for $k = 0, 1, \ldots, \bar{k}$ with $\epsilon = \epsilon_k$, where $\bar{k}$ is the first integer k for which $\epsilon_k = 1$. (Note here that the admissible graph should be maintained in appropriate lists, as discussed in Subsection 5.4.2.) Let p^k and S^k be the price vector and complete assignment, respectively, obtained at the end of the kth application of the algorithm. The starting price vector and assignment for the $(k+1)$st application of the algorithm are p^k and $\{(i,j) \in S^k \mid \pi_i^k - \epsilon_{k+1} \le a_{ij} - p_j^k\}$, respectively, where π_i^k is the profit margin of i corresponding to p^k. The starting price vector and assignment for the initial application of the algorithm must satisfy ϵ^0–CS. Show that the algorithm finds an optimal assignment in $O\big(n|A|\log(nC)\big)$ time.

4.5. **(Hybrid Auction Algorithm with Running Time** $O\big(n^{1/2}|A|\log(nC)\big)$**) [AhO87].)** This exercise shows how the auction algorithm can be combined with a more traditional primal–dual method to obtain an algorithm with an improved running time bound. The auction algorithm is used to assign the first $n - O\big(n^{1/2}\big)$ persons and the primal–dual method is used to assign the rest. Consider the solution of the assignment problem by the Gauss–Seidel variant of the scaled auction algorithm ($\epsilon = 1$ throughout).

    (a) Extend Lemma 4.2 to show that in any subproblem of the scaled auction algorithm we have $\sum_{i\in I}(\pi_i^0 - \pi_i) \le 8\epsilon n$, where I is the set of unassigned persons, $\pi_i^0 = \max_{j\in A(i)}\{a_{ij} - p_j^0\}$, and p^0 is the vector of prices prevailing at the outset of the subproblem.

    (b) Suppose that at the outset of each subproblem we use a modified Gauss–Seidel auction procedure in which only persons i with profit margins π_i greater than or equal to $\pi_i^0 - (8n)^{1/2}\epsilon$ are allowed to place bids. Show that this procedure can be implemented so that at most $(8n)^{1/2} + 1$ iterations are performed at each person node i, and that it terminates in $O(n^{1/2}|A|)$ time. Furthermore the number of unassigned persons after termination is at most $(8n)^{1/2}$.

    (c) Assume that there exists some algorithm X which, given an incomplete assignment S and a price vector p obeying ϵ–CS, produces a new pair (S', p') obeying ϵ–CS in $O(|A|)$ time, with S' containing one more assignment than S (Exercise 3.3 indicates how such an algorithm may be constructed). Outline how one would construct an $O\big(n^{1/2}|A|\log(nC)\big)$ assignment algorithm.

5.5 NETWORK FLOW PROBLEMS WITH STRICTLY CONVEX COST

We now consider the nonlinear cost version of the problem of the past four sections:

$$\text{minimize} \quad \sum_{(i,j)\in A} a_{ij}(f_{ij}) \qquad\qquad (CNF)$$

subject to

$$\sum_{\{j\mid(i,j)\in A\}} f_{ij} - \sum_{\{j\mid(j,i)\in A\}} f_{ji} = s_i, \qquad \forall\, i \in N, \qquad (5.1)$$

$$b_{ij} \le f_{ij} \le c_{ij}, \qquad \forall\, (i,j) \in A. \qquad (5.2)$$

The difference from the linear cost problem (LNF) is that in place of the linear arc cost functions $a_{ij}f_{ij}$, we now have the nonlinear cost functions $a_{ij}(f_{ij})$. We make the following assumption:

Assumption 5.1. (*Strict Convexity*)   The functions $a_{ij}(\cdot)$, $(i,j) \in A$, are strictly convex real–valued functions, and problem (CNF) has at least one feasible solution.

Assumption 5.1 implies that (CNF) has a unique optimal solution. To see this note that existence of a solution follows from the Weierstrass theorem (Prop. A.8 in Appendix A), since the cost function is continuous (being real–valued and convex; Prop. A.36 in Appendix A), and the constraint set of Eqs. (5.1) and (5.2) is compact. Uniqueness follows from the strict convexity of the cost function [Prop. A.35(g) in Appendix A].

As in the linear cost case, we will develop an unconstrained dual problem involving a dual variable or price for each node. There is a fundamental difference, however, because the strict convexity of the arc cost functions implies differentiability of the dual cost as demonstrated at the end of Appendix C, and as will also be shown shortly. As a result, the relaxation method for the dual problem encounters none of the difficulties with corner points that were addressed in the previous sections.

Problem (CNF) and the analysis outlined above admit considerable extension. One possibility is to eliminate the upper bounds c_{ij} and/or the lower bounds b_{ij}, and replace them by growth conditions on the arc cost functions (see the analysis later in this section). A more substantial extension is to allow the cost function to be nonseparable and/or to replace the network conservation of flow constraints (5.1) with more general linear constraints (see Exercise 5.1). Still, as long as the corresponding dual cost is differentiable, the application of relaxation methods is straightforward. The degree of parallelism afforded by these methods, however, depends on the dependency graph associated with the relaxation method for the dual problem (Subsection 1.2.4), and is greatly affected by the structure of the linear constraints.

The Dual Problem

The formulation of the dual problem for (CNF) is similar to the formulation of Section 5.1 (see also Appendix C). The Lagrangian function is given by

$$
\begin{aligned}
L(f,p) &= \sum_{(i,j)\in A} a_{ij}(f_{ij}) + \sum_{i\in N} p_i \left(\sum_{\{j|(j,i)\in A\}} f_{ji} - \sum_{\{j|(i,j)\in A\}} f_{ij} + s_i \right) \\
&= \sum_{(i,j)\in A} \left(a_{ij}(f_{ij}) + (p_j - p_i)f_{ij} \right) + \sum_{i\in N} s_i p_i.
\end{aligned}
\tag{5.3}
$$

The dual function value $q(p)$ at a price vector p is obtained by minimizing $L(f,p)$ over all f satisfying the capacity constraints (5.2). This leads to the dual problem

$$
\text{maximize} \quad q(p)
\tag{5.4}
$$

$$
\text{subject to no constraint on } p,
$$

with the dual functional q given by

$$q(p) = \min_{\substack{b_{ij} \le f_{ij} \le c_{ij} \\ (i,j) \in A}} L(f, p) = \sum_{(i,j) \in A} q_{ij}(p_i - p_j) + \sum_{i \in N} s_i p_i, \qquad (5.5a)$$

where

$$q_{ij}(p_i - p_j) = \min_{b_{ij} \le f_{ij} \le c_{ij}} \left\{ a_{ij}(f_{ij}) - (p_i - p_j)f_{ij} \right\}. \qquad (5.5b)$$

The minimization in the definition (5.5b) of q_{ij} involves a continuous function and a compact constraint set. Therefore, the minimum is attained (Weierstrass' theorem given as Prop. A.8 in Appendix A), and it follows that q_{ij} is real–valued. Note also that q_{ij} is concave as it is the pointwise minimum of linear functions [Prop. A.35(d) in Appendix A]. The form of q_{ij} is illustrated in Fig. 5.5.1.

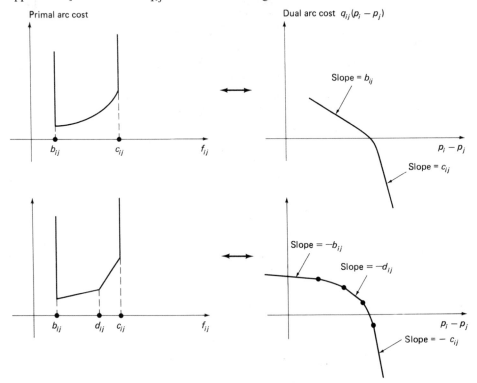

Figure 5.5.1 Illustration of primal and dual arc cost function pairs. Points where the primal function is nondifferentiable correspond to linear segments of the dual function.

The necessary and sufficient conditions for a pair (f, p) to be primal and dual optimal are given by the Duality Theorem in Appendix C. When specialized to our problem, these conditions are similar to (and indeed generalize) the conditions of Prop.

1.1 for the linear cost problem (LNF). There is the primal feasibility condition that the surplus of each node i should be zero:

$$g_i = \sum_{\{j|(j,i)\in A\}} f_{ji} - \sum_{\{j|(i,j)\in A\}} f_{ij} + s_i = 0, \qquad \forall\, i \in N. \qquad (5.6)$$

The role of the cost coefficients a_{ij} of the linear cost problem is played by the right and left derivatives of the arc cost functions defined by

$$a_{ij}^+(f_{ij}) = \lim_{\delta \downarrow 0} \frac{a_{ij}(f_{ij} + \delta) - a_{ij}(f_{ij})}{\delta},$$

$$a_{ij}^-(f_{ij}) = \lim_{\delta \downarrow 0} \frac{a_{ij}(f_{ij}) - a_{ij}(f_{ij} - \delta)}{\delta}.$$

The generalization of the complementary slackness (CS) conditions for a flow–price vector pair (f, p) is that f_{ij} attains the minimum in the definition (5.5b) of q_{ij} for all arcs (i, j) (see the Duality Theorem in Appendix C). Thus, denoting

$$t_{ij} = p_i - p_j,$$

these conditions take the following form, which generalizes the corresponding CS conditions (1.9)–(1.11) for the linear cost problem:

$$t_{ij} \le a_{ij}^+(b_{ij}) \quad \Rightarrow \quad f_{ij} = b_{ij}, \qquad (5.7)$$

$$t_{ij} \ge a_{ij}^-(c_{ij}) \quad \Rightarrow \quad f_{ij} = c_{ij}, \qquad (5.8)$$

$$a_{ij}^+(b_{ij}) < t_{ij} < a_{ij}^-(c_{ij}) \quad \Rightarrow \quad b_{ij} < f_{ij} < c_{ij}, \quad \text{and} \quad a_{ij}^-(f_{ij}) \le t_{ij} \le a_{ij}^+(f_{ij}), \quad (5.9)$$

as illustrated in Fig. 5.5.2. A key observation is that because of the strict convexity of a_{ij}, for each price differential $t_{ij} = p_i - p_j$ there is a *unique* flow f_{ij} attaining the minimum in the definition (5.5b) of q_{ij}, and satisfying the CS conditions. It will be shown shortly [Lemma 5.1(d) to follow] that this unique arc flow is equal to minus the derivative of the dual arc cost at t_{ij}, that is,

$$f_{ij} \text{ and } t_{ij} \text{ satisfy the CS conditions (5.7)–(5.9)} \quad \Longleftrightarrow \quad f_{ij} = -\nabla q_{ij}(t_{ij}). \qquad (5.10)$$

This fact will be of central importance in the relaxation algorithm to be described shortly.

By using the Lagrange Multiplier and Duality Theorems of Appendix C, we obtain:

Proposition 5.1.   Let Assumption 5.1 hold:

(a) A flow vector f is primal optimal if and only if f is primal feasible and there exists a price vector p satisfying together with f the CS conditions (5.7)–(5.9).

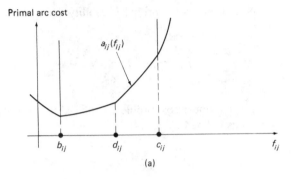

(a)

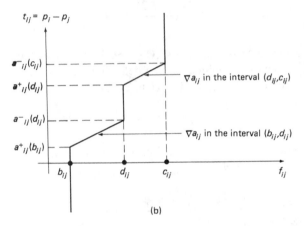

(b)

Figure 5.5.2 Illustration of the CS conditions for the case where $b_{ij} < c_{ij}$. (a) A primal cost function with a single point of nondifferentiability in the interval (b_{ij}, c_{ij}). (b) For CS to be satisfied, the pair of f_{ij} and t_{ij} should lie on the diagram. Note that, because a_{ij} is strictly convex, the gradient ∇a_{ij} is monotonically increasing and there is a unique f_{ij} corresponding to each t_{ij}.

(b) For every dual optimal solution p^*, we have

$$q(p^*) = \sum_{(i,j)\in A} a_{ij}(f_{ij}^*),$$

where $f^* = \left\{ f_{ij}^* \mid (i,j) \in A \right\}$ is the unique optimal flow vector. Furthermore, there exists at least one dual optimal solution.

(c) A flow vector f and a price vector p are primal and dual optimal, respectively, for (CNF) if and only if they satisfy primal feasibility and the CS conditions (5.7)–(5.9).

The proofs of the theorems of Appendix C require differentiability of the primal cost function. For the problem of this section, however, a fairly simple proof that does not require differentiability is possible (see Exercise 5.6).

From the definition of the dual function (5.5), it is seen (using the fact $\sum_{i\in N} s_i = 0$, which is a requirement for feasibility) that if $\{p_i^* \mid i \in N\}$ is an optimal set of prices, the same is true for $\{p_i^* + c \mid i \in N\}$, where c is any constant. Therefore, Prop. 5.1(b) shows that the dual problem has an infinite number of solutions. This implies in particular that the dual function q is not strictly concave. In fact, it can be seen through simple examples (compare with Fig. 5.5.1) that q need not be strictly concave along any single coordinate direction, so the convergence analysis of the Jacobi and Gauss–Seidel methods for maximizing q (cf. Section 3.2) does not apply.

The Gradient of the Dual Function

According to the Dual Function Differentiability Theorem of Appendix C, the strict convexity of the primal cost implies differentiability of the dual function q. We provide a simple independent proof of this property and we derive the form of the gradient ∇q.

The relation between the primal and dual arc cost functions a_{ij} and q_{ij} is a special case of a conjugacy relation that is central in the theory of convex functions ([Roc70], [Roc84], and [StW70]). More precisely, $-q_{ij}(t_{ij})$ is the *conjugate convex function* of the extended real–valued function $\tilde{a}_{ij}(f_{ij})$ given by

$$\tilde{a}_{ij}(f_{ij}) = \begin{cases} a_{ij}(f_{ij}), & \text{if } b_{ij} \leq f_{ij} \leq c_{ij} \\ +\infty, & \text{otherwise.} \end{cases} \tag{5.11}$$

Several interesting facts regarding the relation of $\tilde{a}_{ij}$ and q_{ij}, including the differentiability of q_{ij}, can be obtained by appealing to the theory of conjugate convex functions. To keep the presentation simple, however, we prove only the facts needed for our analysis in the following lemma:

Lemma 5.1.   Let $a_{ij}(\cdot)$ be a strictly convex real–valued function. Then $a_{ij}(\cdot)$ and the function

$$q_{ij}(t_{ij}) = \min_{b_{ij} \leq f_{ij} \leq c_{ij}} \{a_{ij}(f_{ij}) - t_{ij}f_{ij}\} \tag{5.12}$$

[cf. Eq. (5.5b)] are related by

$$\sup_{t_{ij}}\{q_{ij}(t_{ij}) + t_{ij}f_{ij}\} = \begin{cases} a_{ij}(f_{ij}), & \text{if } b_{ij} \leq f_{ij} \leq c_{ij} \\ +\infty, & \text{otherwise.} \end{cases} \tag{5.13}$$

Furthermore, q_{ij} is differentiable, and the following statements are equivalent for two scalars t_{ij} and $f_{ij} \in [b_{ij}, c_{ij}]$:

(a) $t_{ij}f_{ij} = a_{ij}(f_{ij}) - q_{ij}(t_{ij})$.
(b) f_{ij} attains the minimum in Eq. (5.12).
(c) t_{ij} attains the supremum in Eq. (5.13).
(d) $\nabla q_{ij}(t_{ij}) = -f_{ij}$.
(e) f_{ij} and t_{ij} satisfy the CS conditions (5.7)–(5.9).

Proof. Figure 5.5.3 sketches a proof of Eq. (5.13); it is left for the reader to complete the details. From Eq. (5.12) we see that (b) is equivalent with (a). Similarly, from

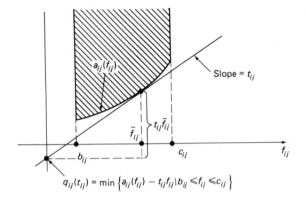

$$q_{ij}(t_{ij}) = \min \left\{ a_{ij}(f_{ij}) - t_{ij}f_{ij} \mid b_{ij} \leq f_{ij} \leq c_{ij} \right\}$$

(a)

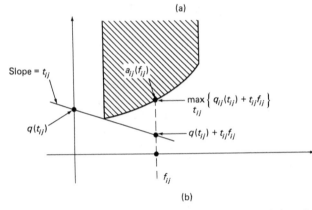

(b)

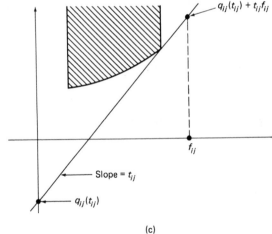

(c)

Figure 5.5.3 Sketch of the proof that $\sup_{t_{ij}}\{q_{ij}(t_{ij}) + t_{ij}f_{ij}\}$ is equal to $a_{ij}(\bar{f}_{ij})$ if $b_{ij} \leq f_{ij} \leq c_{ij}$ and is equal to ∞ otherwise [cf. Eq. (5.13)]:
(a) For any t_{ij}, the value of $q_{ij}(t_{ij})$ is obtained by constructing a supporting line with slope t_{ij} to the shaded convex set

$$\left\{(f_{ij}, \mu) \mid b_{ij} \leq f_{ij} \leq c_{ij}, \, \mu \geq a_{ij}(f_{ij})\right\},$$

and by obtaining the point where this line intercepts the vertical axis.
(b) For a given $f_{ij} \in [b_{ij}, c_{ij}]$, the value of $q_{ij}(t_{ij}) + t_{ij}f_{ij}$ is obtained by intercepting the vertical line passing through $\left(f_{ij}, a_{ij}(f_{ij})\right)$ with the line of slope t_{ij} that supports the shaded set. This point of intercept cannot lie higher than $a_{ij}(f_{ij})$, and with proper choice of t_{ij} lies exactly at $a_{ij}(f_{ij})$. This proves that $\sup_{t_{ij}}\{q_{ij}(t_{ij}) + t_{ij}f_{ij}\} = a_{ij}(f_{ij})$ for $f_{ij} \in [b_{ij}, c_{ij}]$.
(c) For $f_{ij} \notin [b_{ij}, c_{ij}]$, the construction given shows that $\sup_{t_{ij}}\left\{q_{ij}(t_{ij}) + t_{ij}f_{ij}\right\} = \infty$.

Eq. (5.13) we see that (c) is equivalent with (a). Therefore, (b) and (c) are equivalent. To prove differentiability of q_{ij}, let us fix t_{ij}, and let $q_{ij}^+(t_{ij})$ and $q_{ij}^-(t_{ij})$ be the right and left directional derivatives of q_{ij}, respectively, at t_{ij}. A scalar y satisfies

$$q_{ij}^+(t_{ij}) \leq y \leq q_{ij}^-(t_{ij}), \tag{5.14}$$

where q_{ij}^+ and q_{ij}^- are the right and left derivatives, respectively, of q_{ij}, if and only if t_{ij} maximizes $q_{ij}(\xi) - \xi y$ over all ξ, which is true [by the equivalence of (b) and (c)] if and only if $-y$ attains the minimum in Eq. (5.12). Since a_{ij} is strictly convex there is only one minimizing scalar in Eq. (5.12), call it f_{ij}, and $-f_{ij}$ is the only scalar y satisfying Eq. (5.14). Therefore, q_{ij} is differentiable, and (b) implies (d). Conversely, if $\nabla q_{ij}(t_{ij}) = -f_{ij}$, then t_{ij} attains the supremum in Eq. (5.13), and [since (c) implies (b)] f_{ij} attains the minimum in Eq. (5.12). The equivalence of (b) and (d) follows. Finally, the CS conditions (5.7)–(5.9) are equivalent to (b), so the proof is complete.   **Q.E.D.**

We can now derive the gradient of the dual cost given a price vector p. We have for all $i \in N$

$$
\begin{aligned}
\frac{\partial q(p)}{\partial p_i} &= \sum_{(m,n) \in A} \frac{\partial q_{mn}(p_m - p_n)}{\partial p_i} + s_i \\
&= -\sum_{\{j|(j,i) \in A\}} \nabla q_{ji}(p_j - p_i) + \sum_{\{j|(i,j) \in A\}} \nabla q_{ij}(p_i - p_j) + s_i.
\end{aligned}
\tag{5.15}
$$

By Lemma 5.1, the derivatives above are equal to minus the unique arc flows satisfying the CS conditions (5.7)–(5.9) together with p. Therefore, comparing the preceding relation with the definition of surplus (5.6), we obtain

$$\frac{\partial q(p)}{\partial p_i} = g_i(p) \tag{5.16a}$$

where

$$
\begin{aligned}
g_i(p) = \; &\text{Surplus of node } i \text{ corresponding to the unique } f \\
&\text{satisfying the CS conditions (5.7)–(5.9) together with } p.
\end{aligned}
\tag{5.16b}
$$

5.5.1 The Relaxation Method

The relaxation method is simply the coordinate ascent (or nonlinear Gauss–Seidel) method of Subsection 3.2.4 applied to the maximization of the dual function. We generalize the method somewhat by allowing the maximization along each coordinate to be inexact to some extent, and to be controlled by a given scalar $\delta \in [0,1)$.

At the start of the typical iteration we have a price vector p. If the corresponding surplus $g_i(p)$ of Eq. (5.16) is zero for all nodes i, then p and the unique vector f satisfying CS together with p are dual and primal optimal, respectively, and the algorithm terminates. Otherwise:

Relaxation Iteration.   Choose any node i. If the surplus $g_i(p)$ is zero do nothing. Otherwise change the ith coordinate of p, obtaining a vector $\bar{p}$ which is such that

$$0 \le g_i(\bar{p}) \le \delta g_i(p) \quad \text{if} \quad g_i(p) > 0,$$

$$\delta g_i(p) \le g_i(\bar{p}) \le 0 \quad \text{if} \quad g_i(p) < 0.$$

Figure 5.5.4 illustrates the relaxation iteration when $\delta = 0$, in which case we have $g_i(\bar{p}) = \partial q(\bar{p})/\partial p_i = 0$, and the coordinate maximization is exact [cf. Eq. (5.16)]. There is a great deal of flexibility regarding the order in which nodes are taken up for relaxation. The only assumption we make is the following:

Assumption 5.2.   Every node is chosen as the node i in the relaxation iteration an infinite number of times.

The relaxation iteration is well defined, in the sense that it is always possible to adjust the price p_i as required. To see this, suppose that $g_i(p) > 0$ and that there does not exist a $\gamma > 0$ such that $g_i(p + \gamma e_i) \le \delta g_i(p)$, where e_i denotes the ith coordinate vector. Consider the price differentials $t_{ij}(\gamma)$, $(i, j) \in A$ and $t_{ji}(\gamma)$, $(j, i) \in A$ corresponding to the price vector $p + \gamma e_i$. We have $t_{ij}(\gamma) = p_i - p_j + \gamma \to \infty$ and $t_{ji}(\gamma) = p_j - p_i - \gamma \to -\infty$ as $\gamma \to \infty$. Therefore, the corresponding unique arc flows satisfying the CS conditions (5.7)–(5.9) become $f_{ij} = c_{ij}$ and $f_{ji} = b_{ji}$ as $\gamma \to \infty$, and using the definition (5.16) of $g_i(\cdot)$, it is seen that

$$\lim_{\gamma \to \infty} g_i(p + \gamma e_i) = \sum_{\{j|(j,i) \in A\}} b_{ji} - \sum_{\{j|(i,j) \in A\}} c_{ij} + s_i \ge \delta g_i(p) > 0.$$

This implies that the surplus of node i is positive for any flow vector f satisfying the capacity constraints (5.2), and contradicts the existence of a feasible flow (Assumption 5.1). An analogous argument can be made for the case where $g_i(p) < 0$.

It is evident that the relaxation algorithm admits synchronous parallel Gauss–Seidel or Jacobi implementations similar to the ϵ–relaxation method of Section 5.3. We now show that the Gauss–Seidel version of the algorithm is convergent. Simple examples show that the Jacobi version is not convergent (see Fig. 5.5.5), but in the next two chapters, it will be seen that when suitably modified, the algorithm is convergent under reasonable conditions when implemented in either the Jacobi or an asynchronous mode.

5.5.2 Convergence Analysis

In order to obtain our convergence result, we must show that the sequence of flow vectors generated by the relaxation algorithm approaches the linear manifold defined by the conservation of flow constraint (5.1). The line of argument that we will use is as follows: we will bound from below the improvement in the dual functional q per iteration by a positive quantity. We will then show that if the sequence of flow vectors does not approach the constraint manifold, the quantity itself can be lower bounded by

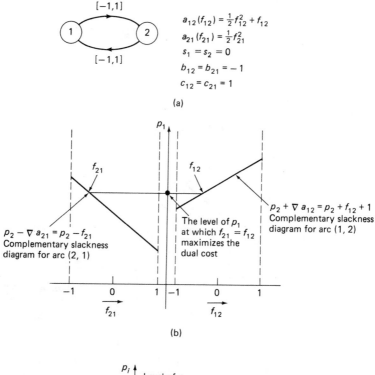

$$a_{12}(f_{12}) = \tfrac{1}{2}f_{12}^2 + f_{12}$$
$$a_{21}(f_{21}) = \tfrac{1}{2}f_{21}^2$$
$$s_1 = s_2 = 0$$
$$b_{12} = b_{21} = -1$$
$$c_{12} = c_{21} = 1$$

(a)

(b)

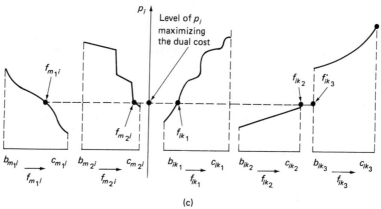

(c)

Figure 5.5.4 Illustration of the relaxation iteration. (a) An example problem involving two nodes with zero supplies, and two arcs with the arc costs and flow bounds shown. (b) Adjustment of the price p_1 so as to maximize the dual function along the first coordinate. The CS diagrams for arcs (1,2) and (2,1) are superimposed, and p_1 is set at the level at which the flows f_{12} and f_{21} obtained from these diagrams are equalized. (c) Illustration of the same process for the case where the node i chosen for relaxation has more than two incident arcs. The price p_i is set at the level at which the sum of outgoing arc flows (obtained from the CS diagrams) equals the sum of the corresponding incoming arc flows plus s_i.

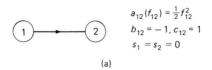

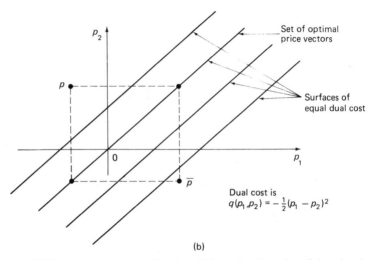

Figure 5.5.5 (a) An example problem for which the Jacobi version of the relaxation algorithm does not converge to an optimal price vector. (b) The Jacobi version of the relaxation method (with exact minimization along each price coordinate), starting from p yields $\bar{p}$, and starting from $\bar{p}$ yields p. By contrast, the Gauss–Seidel version finds an optimal price vector in a single iteration (assuming again exact maximization along each price coordinate).

a positive constant, which implies that the optimal dual cost is ∞. This will contradict the finiteness of the optimal primal cost (Prop. 5.1 and Assumption 5.1). We will denote the price vector generated at the kth iteration by p^k, $k = 0, 1, \ldots$, and the node operated on at the kth iteration by i^k, $k = 0, 1, \ldots$. We will also use the notation

$$t_{ij}^k = p_i^k - p_j^k, \qquad f_{ij}^k = -\nabla q_{ij}(p^k).$$

Note that by Lemma 5.1, f_{ij}^k is the unique flow satisfying, together with $t_{ij}^k = p_i^k - p_j^k$ the CS conditions (5.7)–(5.9). For any directed cycle Y of the network, we denote

$$Y^+ = \{(i,j) \mid (i,j) \text{ is a forward arc of } Y\},$$
$$Y^- = \{(i,j) \mid (i,j) \text{ is a backward arc of } Y\}.$$

We also denote [cf. Eq. (5.11)]

$$\tilde{a}_{ij}^+(f_{ij}) = \begin{cases} a_{ij}^+(f_{ij}), & \text{if } b_{ij} \le f_{ij} < c_{ij} \\ +\infty, & \text{if } f_{ij} = c_{ij}, \end{cases} \qquad (5.17a)$$

$$\tilde{a}_{ij}^-(f_{ij}) = \begin{cases} a_{ij}^-(f_{ij}), & \text{if } b_{ij} < f_{ij} \le c_{ij} \\ -\infty, & \text{if } b_{ij} = f_{ij}, \end{cases} \qquad (5.17b)$$

that is, $\tilde{a}_{ij}^-$ and $\tilde{a}_{ij}^+$ denote the left and right derivatives of the function $\tilde{a}_{ij}$ of Eq. (5.11). Note that the conditions for f_{ij} and t_{ij} to satisfy CS can be written as

$$b_{ij} \le f_{ij} \le c_{ij}, \qquad \tilde{a}_{ij}^-(f_{ij}) \le t_{ij} \le \tilde{a}_{ij}^+(f_{ij}). \qquad (5.18)$$

We first show a few preliminary results:

Lemma 5.2.   We have for all k such that $p^{k+1} \ne p^k$ [i.e., $g_{i^k}(p^k) \ne 0$]

$$q(p^{k+1}) - q(p^k) \ge \sum_{(i,j) \in A} \left[a_{ij}(f_{ij}^{k+1}) - a_{ij}(f_{ij}^k) - (f_{ij}^{k+1} - f_{ij}^k)t_{ij}^k \right] > 0, \qquad (5.19)$$

with equality holding in the left inequality if $g_{i^k}(p^{k+1}) = 0$ (i.e., the exact maximum of the dual cost along the i^kth coordinate is found at the kth iteration).

Proof.   Fix an index $k \ge 0$. Denote $\gamma = p_{i^k}^{k+1} - p_{i^k}^k$. From the definition of the dual function (5.5), Lemma 5.1, and the definitions of t_{ij}^k and f_{ij}^k, we have

$$q(p^k) = \sum_{(i,j) \in A} \left[a_{ij}(f_{ij}^k) - t_{ij}^k f_{ij}^k \right] + \sum_{i \in N} s_i p_i^k, \qquad \forall\, k \ge 0.$$

Therefore, denoting $e_{ij} = 1$ if $i = i^k$, $e_{ij} = -1$ if $j = i^k$, and $e_{ij} = 0$ otherwise, we have

$$q(p^{k+1}) - q(p^k) = \sum_{(i,j) \in A} \left[a_{ij}(f_{ij}^{k+1}) - t_{ij}^{k+1} f_{ij}^{k+1} \right] - \sum_{(i,j) \in A} \left[a_{ij}(f_{ij}^k) - t_{ij}^k f_{ij}^k \right]$$
$$+ \sum_{i \in N} \left(p_i^{k+1} - p_i^k \right) s_i$$

$$= \sum_{(i,j) \in A} \left[a_{ij}(f_{ij}^{k+1}) - (t_{ij}^k + e_{ij}\gamma) f_{ij}^{k+1} \right] - \sum_{(i,j) \in A} \left[a_{ij}(f_{ij}^k) - t_{ij}^k f_{ij}^k \right] + \gamma s_{i^k}$$

$$= \sum_{(i,j) \in A} \left[a_{ij}(f_{ij}^{k+1}) - a_{ij}(f_{ij}^k) - (f_{ij}^{k+1} - f_{ij}^k)t_{ij}^k \right] + \gamma \left(s_{i^k} - \sum_{(i,j) \in A} e_{ij} f_{ij}^{k+1} \right)$$

$$= \sum_{(i,j) \in A} \left[a_{ij}(f_{ij}^{k+1}) - a_{ij}(f_{ij}^k) - (f_{ij}^{k+1} - f_{ij}^k)t_{ij}^k \right] + \gamma g_{i^k}(p^{k+1}).$$

When $\gamma > 0$ (that is, $p_{i^k}^k$ is increased), the new price $p_{i^k}^{k+1}$ of i^k either maximizes the cost with respect to p_{i^k}, in which case $g_{i^k}(p^{k+1}) = 0$ or $p_{i^k}^{k+1}$ is smaller than all prices that maximize the dual cost, in which case $g_{i^k}(p^{k+1}) > 0$. Thus, we have $\gamma g_{i^k}(p^{k+1}) \geq 0$ when $\gamma > 0$. A similar argument shows that $\gamma g_{i^k}(p^{k+1}) \geq 0$ when $\gamma < 0$, and from the above equation, we obtain the left side of Eq. (5.19). The right side of Eq. (5.19) follows from the strict convexity of a_{ij}, the fact $f^{k+1} \neq f^k$ (since the surplus of i^k has changed), and the fact that f_{ij}^k, by Lemma 5.1, minimizes $a_{ij}(f_{ij}) - t_{ij}^k f_{ij}$ over $f_{ij} \in [b_{ij}, c_{ij}]$. **Q.E.D.**

The next result is remarkable in that it shows that under a mild restriction on the way the relaxation iteration is carried out (which is typically very easy to satisfy in practice), the sequence of price vectors approaches the dual optimal set in an unusual manner. In particular, the distance of the current iterate from *any* optimal price vector with respect to the maximum norm never increases.

Lemma 5.3.   Let p be a price vector, i be a node, and $\bar{p}$ be a dual price vector obtained by applying the relaxation iteration to p using node i. Assume in addition that $\bar{p}$ is chosen so that

$$g_i(p) > 0 \quad \Rightarrow \quad g_i\big(\bar{p} + \gamma(p - \bar{p})\big) > 0, \qquad \forall \ \gamma > 0, \qquad (5.20a)$$

$$g_i(p) < 0 \quad \Rightarrow \quad g_i\big(\bar{p} + \gamma(p - \bar{p})\big) < 0, \qquad \forall \ \gamma > 0. \qquad (5.20b)$$

Then for all optimal dual price vectors p^*, we have

$$\min_{m \in N}\{p_m - p_m^*\} \leq \min_{m \in N}\{\bar{p}_m - p_m^*\} \leq \max_{m \in N}\{\bar{p}_m - p_m^*\} \leq \max_{m \in N}\{p_m - p_m^*\}. \quad (5.21)$$

Note: When $g_i(p) > 0$ [or $g_i(p) < 0$], the assumption (5.20) is equivalent to assuming that $\bar{p}_i$ is chosen less (greater) than or equal to the smallest (largest) maximizing point of the dual cost along the ith coordinate starting from p. It is automatically satisfied if there is a unique maximizing point along the ith coordinate.

Proof.   The desired assertion (5.21) holds if $g_i(p) = 0$ since then we have $\bar{p} = p$. Assume that $g_i(p) > 0$, and fix an optimal dual price vector p^*. Consider the vector $\hat{p}$ defined by

$$\hat{p}_j = \begin{cases} p_j, & \text{if } j \neq i \\ p_i^* + \max_{m \in N}\{p_m - p_m^*\}, & \text{if } j = i. \end{cases}$$

We have

$$\hat{p}_i - \hat{p}_m \geq p_i^* - p_m^*, \qquad \forall \ (i, m) \in A,$$

$$\hat{p}_m - \hat{p}_i \leq p_m^* - p_i^*, \qquad \forall \ (m, i) \in A.$$

Since each ∇q_{ij} is a nonincreasing function (being the gradient of a concave function), we have

$$\nabla q_{im}(\hat{p}_i - \hat{p}_m) \leq \nabla q_{im}(p_i^* - p_m^*), \qquad \forall\ (i, m) \in A,$$

$$\nabla q_{mi}(\hat{p}_m - \hat{p}_i) \geq \nabla q_{mi}(p_m^* - p_i^*), \qquad \forall\ (m, i) \in A.$$

By adding over all m and by using Eqs. (5.15) and (5.16), we obtain $g_i(\hat{p}) \leq g_i(p^*) = 0$. Therefore, using assumption (5.20), we have $\bar{p}_i \leq \hat{p}_i$, while at the same time $p_i < \bar{p}_i$, and $p_m = \bar{p}_m$ for all $m \neq i$. The assertion (5.21) follows. The proof is similar when $g_i(p) < 0$.   **Q.E.D.**

Lemma 5.3 implies, among other things, that if care is taken so that the condition (5.20) is satisfied at all iterations, the sequence $\{p^k\}$ generated by the relaxation method is bounded. Furthermore, the lemma shows that if $\{p^k\}$ has a limit point that is an optimal price vector, then $\{p^k\}$ must converge to that vector. We are now ready to show our main result.

Proposition 5.2.   Let $\{p^k, f^k\}$ be a sequence generated by the relaxation method for strictly convex arc costs. Then:

(a)
$$\lim_{k \to \infty} g_i(p^k) = 0, \qquad \forall\ i \in N. \tag{5.22}$$

(b)
$$\lim_{k \to \infty} f^k = f^*, \tag{5.23}$$

where f^* is the unique optimal flow vector.

(c)
$$\lim_{k \to \infty} q(p^k) = \max_p q(p).$$

(d) If each iteration is carried out so that the condition (5.20) is satisfied, then

$$\lim_{k \to \infty} p^k \to p^*, \tag{5.24}$$

where p^* is some optimal price vector.

Proof.

(a) We first show that

$$\lim_{k \to \infty} g_{i^k}(p^k) = 0. \tag{5.25}$$

Indeed, if this were not so, there must exist an $\epsilon > 0$ and a subsequence K such that $|g_{i^k}(p^k)| \geq \epsilon$ for all $k \in K$. Without loss of generality, we assume that $g_{i^k}(p^k) \geq \epsilon$ for all $k \in K$. Since $\delta |g_{i^k}(p^k)| \geq |g_{i^k}(p^{k+1})|$, we have that at the kth iteration, some arc incident to node i^k must change its flow by at least Δ, where $\Delta = (1 - \delta)\epsilon / |A|$. By passing to a subsequence, if necessary, we assume that this happens for the same arc, say (i, j), for all $k \in K$, and that $f_{ij}^{k+1} - f_{ij}^k \geq \Delta$, and $i^k = i$ for all $k \in K$ (the case $f_{ij}^{k+1} - f_{ij}^k < \Delta$ and $i^k = j$ for all $k \in K$ can be treated analogously). Using the boundedness of $\{f^k\}$ we can also assume that the subsequence $\{f_{ij}^k\}_{k \in K}$ converges to some f_{ij}. We note that all terms $a_{ij}(f_{ij}^{k+1}) - a_{ij}(f_{ij}^k) - (f_{ij}^{k+1} - f_{ij}^k)t_{ij}^k$ in the sum of Eq. (5.19) in Lemma 5.2 are nonnegative. Therefore, we have from Eq. (5.19)

$$q(p^{k+1}) - q(p^k) \geq a_{ij}(f_{ij}^{k+1}) - a_{ij}(f_{ij}^k) - (f_{ij}^{k+1} - f_{ij}^k)t_{ij}^k$$

$$\geq a_{ij}(f_{ij}^k + \Delta) - a_{ij}(f_{ij}^k) - \Delta t_{ij}^k$$

$$\geq a_{ij}(f_{ij}^k + \Delta) - a_{ij}(f_{ij}^k) - \Delta a_{ij}^+(f_{ij}^k),$$

where the second inequality follows from the fact that $a_{ij}(f_{ij}^k + \delta) - a_{ij}(f_{ij}^k) - \delta t_{ij}^k$ is a monotonically increasing function of δ (since t_{ij}^k is a subgradient of a_{ij} at f_{ij}^k), and the last inequality follows from the fact $\Delta > 0$ (implying $f_{ij}^k < c_{ij}$) and the CS condition (5.18). Taking the limit as $k \to \infty$, $k \in K$, and using the facts $f_{ij}^k \to f_{ij}$ and $\liminf_{k \to \infty} a_{ij}^+(f_{ij}^k) \leq a_{ij}^+(f_{ij})$ (in view of the fact that a_{ij}^+ is monotonically nondecreasing and right–continuous), we obtain

$$\liminf_{k \in K, k \to \infty} \left[q(p^{k+1}) - q(p^k) \right] \geq a_{ij}(f_{ij} + \Delta) - a_{ij}(f_{ij}) - \Delta a_{ij}^+(f_{ij}) > 0.$$

This implies that $\lim_{k \to \infty} q(p^k) = \infty$, contradicting the equality of the optimal dual value and the optimal primal value (which is finite), and proving Eq. (5.25).

We now show that $\lim_{k \to \infty} g_i(p^k) = 0$ [cf. Eq. (5.22)]. Choose any $i \in N$. Take any $\epsilon > 0$ and let K be the set of indices k such that $g_i(p^k) > 2\epsilon$. Assume without loss of generality that $g_i(p^k) < \epsilon$ for all k with $i = i^k$ [cf. Eq. (5.25)]. For every $k \in K$, let k' be the first index with $k' > k$ such that $i = i^{k'}$. Then during iterations $k, k+1, \ldots, k'-1$ node i is not chosen for relaxation while its surplus decreases from greater than 2ϵ to lower than ϵ. We claim that during these iterations the total absolute surplus $\sum_{j \in N} |g_j(p)|$ is decreased by a total of more than 2ϵ. To see this, we first note that the total absolute surplus cannot increase due to an iteration because a flow change on an arc reflects itself in a change of the surplus of its start node and an opposite change in the surplus of its end node; furthermore, the surplus of the node chosen for relaxation at an iteration cannot increase in absolute value or change sign during that iteration. Next observe that for any of the iterations $k, k+1, \ldots, k'-1$, say $\bar{k}$, for which the surplus of i is decreased by an amount $\xi > 0$ from a positive value $g_i(p^{\bar{k}}) > 0$, the node $s = i^{\bar{k}}$ chosen for relaxation must be adjacent to i and must have a negative surplus $g_s(p^{\bar{k}}) < 0$. Since all of the increase in $g_s(p^{\bar{k}})$ during the iteration must be matched by decreases of the surpluses of the neighbor nodes of s, and, furthermore, the surplus of s will remain nonpositive after the iteration, it follows that the total absolute surplus will be decreased by at least $2\min\{\xi, g_i(p^{\bar{k}})\}$ during the iteration. This shows that during iterations $k, k+1, \ldots, k'-1$, the total absolute surplus must decrease by more than 2ϵ. Therefore, the set K of indices k for which $g_i(p^k) > 2\epsilon$ cannot be infinite.

Since $\epsilon > 0$ is arbitrary, we obtain $\limsup_{k \to \infty} g_i(p^k) \le 0$. Similarly, we can show that $\liminf_{k \to \infty} g_i(p^k) \ge 0$ and therefore $g_i(p^k) \to 0$.

(b)–(c) Since $\{f_{ij}^k\}$ is bounded, it has a subsequence converging to some f^* which is primal feasible in view of part (a). We will show that f^* is the unique optimal flow vector, and, therefore, the entire sequence $\{f_{ij}^k\}$ actually converges to f^*. For every arc (i, j) for which $b_{ij} < c_{ij}$, there are three possibilities for the corresponding subsequence of $\{t_{ij}^k\}$:

(1) $\{t_{ij}^k\}$ is bounded.

(2) $f_{ij}^* = c_{ij}$, and $-\infty < \liminf_{k \to \infty} t_{ij}^k \le \limsup_{k \to \infty} t_{ij}^k = \infty$.

(3) $f_{ij}^* = b_{ij}$, and $-\infty = \liminf_{k \to \infty} t_{ij}^k \le \limsup_{k \to \infty} t_{ij}^k < \infty$.

For an arc (i, j) with $b_{ij} = c_{ij}$ we must have $f_{ij}^* = f_{ij}^k$ for all k. From these facts, it is seen that we can construct a subsequence K such that

$$\sum_{(i,j) \in A} t_{ij}^k(f_{ij}^k - f_{ij}^*) \le \sum_{(i,j) \in B} t_{ij}^k(f_{ij}^k - f_{ij}^*), \qquad \forall \, k \in K,$$

where B is a set of arcs (i, j) such that $\{t_{ij}^k\}_K$ is bounded. We have, using the definition of the dual functional (5.5), Lemma 5.1 and the fact $\sum_{(i,j) \in A} t_{ij}^k f_{ij}^* = \sum_{i \in N} p_i s_i$,

$$\sum_{(i,j) \in A} a_{ij}(f_{ij}^k) - q(p^k) = \sum_{(i,j) \in A} t_{ij}^k f_{ij}^k - \sum_{i \in N} p_i s_i$$

$$= \sum_{(i,j) \in A} t_{ij}^k(f_{ij}^k - f_{ij}^*) \le \sum_{(i,j) \in B} t_{ij}^k(f_{ij}^k - f_{ij}^*).$$

Since $f_{ij}^k \to f_{ij}^*$ and $\{t_{ij}^k\}_K$ is bounded for $(i, j) \in B$, we obtain by taking the limit above

$$\sum_{(i,j) \in A} a_{ij}(f_{ij}^*) \le \lim_{k \to \infty, \, k \in K} q(p^k).$$

Since f^* is primal feasible and $q(p)$ is less than or equal to the optimal primal cost, the optimality of f^* follows. Since $q(p^k)$ is monotonically nondecreasing, and therefore converges, it also follows from the relation above that it converges to the dual optimal value.

(d) Under the condition (5.20), Lemma 5.3 implies that $\{p^k\}$ is bounded. Let $\{p^k\}_{k \in K}$ be a subsequence converging to a vector p^*, and let t^* be the vector with elements $t_{ij}^* = p_i^* - p_j^*$. We have for all $(i, j) \in A$,

$$\tilde{a}_{ij}^-(f_{ij}^k) \le t_{ij}^k \le \tilde{a}_{ij}^+(f_{ij}^k), \qquad \forall \, k \in K.$$

It follows, using part (b) and the fact that $\tilde{a}_{ij}^-$ (or $\tilde{a}_{ij}^+$) is nondecreasing and left continuous (or nondecreasing and right–continuous, respectively) (Prop. A.38 in Appendix A), that for all $(i, j) \in A$,

$$\tilde{a}_{ij}^-(f_{ij}^*) \le t_{ij}^* \le \tilde{a}_{ij}^+(f_{ij}^*),$$

where f^* is the optimal flow vector. Therefore, t^* satisfies together with f^* the CS condition (5.18) for all $(i, j) \in A$, and must be dual optimal. Lemma 5.3 shows that $\{p^k\}$ cannot have two different dual optimal price vectors as limit points and the conclusion follows. **Q.E.D.**

5.5.3 The Problem without Arc Flow Bounds

Consider the variation of the convex cost network flow problem (CNF), where there are no arc flow bounds, that is, the problem

$$\text{minimize} \quad \sum_{(i,j)\in A} a_{ij}(f_{ij}) \qquad\qquad\qquad (UCNF)$$

$$\text{subject to} \quad \sum_{\{j|(j,i)\in A\}} f_{ji} - \sum_{\{j|(i,j)\in A\}} f_{ij} = s_i, \qquad \forall \ i \in N. \qquad (5.26)$$

In place of Assumption 5.1, we assume that the arc cost functions a_{ij} grow at an infinite rate as f_{ij} approaches the boundaries of the domain of a_{ij} (see Fig. 5.5.6):

Assumption 5.2. For each arc (i, j), there is a nonempty open interval (b_{ij}, c_{ij}), where $b_{ij} \in [-\infty, \infty)$ and $c_{ij} \in (-\infty, \infty]$, and such that the real–valued function a_{ij} is defined and is strictly convex over (b_{ij}, c_{ij}). Furthermore, a_{ij} satisfies

$$\lim_{f_{ij}\downarrow b_{ij}} a_{ij}(f_{ij}) = \infty, \qquad \lim_{f_{ij}\uparrow c_{ij}} a_{ij}(f_{ij}) = \infty, \qquad (5.27a)$$

and its directional derivatives satisfy

$$\lim_{f_{ij}\downarrow b_{ij}} a_{ij}^-(f_{ij}) = -\infty, \qquad \lim_{f_{ij}\uparrow c_{ij}} a_{ij}^+(f_{ij}) = \infty. \qquad (5.27b)$$

In addition the problem (UCNF) has at least one feasible solution.

One consequence of the above assumption is that the primal problem (UCNF) has a unique optimal solution (a_{ij} is seen to be continuous and the level sets of the cost function are compact, so Weierstrass' theorem, given as Prop. A.8 in Appendix A, applies). Similarly as earlier, the dual function is defined by [cf. Eq. (5.5)]

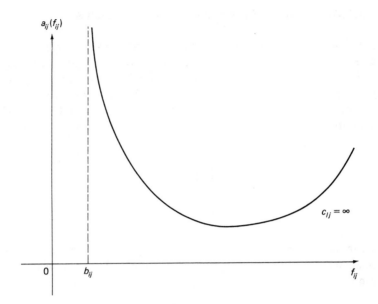

Figure 5.5.6 Illustration of the conditions (5.27). The function a_{ij} grows to ∞ as f_{ij} approaches the endpoints of the (open) domain (b_{ij}, c_{ij}). The rate of increase also approaches infinity.

$$q(p) = \sum_{(i,j)\in A} q_{ij}(p_i - p_j) + \sum_{i\in N} s_i p_i, \qquad (5.28a)$$

where

$$q_{ij}(p_i - p_j) = \min_{f_{ij}\in(b_{ij},c_{ij})} \{a_{ij}(f_{ij}) - (p_i - p_j)f_{ij}\}. \qquad (5.28b)$$

A second consequence of Assumption 5.2 is that the minimum in the preceding equation is attained for all p, so the dual function value is finite. Using these facts, one can derive variations of Prop. 5.1 and Lemma 5.1 (Exercise 5.3), as well as a modified version of the relaxation algorithm. The CS conditions (5.7)–(5.9) are replaced by the condition

$$a_{ij}^-(f_{ij}) \le t_{ij} \le a_{ij}^+(f_{ij}).$$

It is seen that the strict convexity of a_{ij} implies that, given p, there exists a unique flow vector satisfying the condition above together with p. Using this, one can verify the dual gradient expressions (5.15) and (5.16), and carry out a convergence analysis of the corresponding relaxation algorithm that is similar to the one given earlier.

Similar results hold for the case of hybrid problems where some of the arc flows are subject to upper and lower bounds, as in problem (CNF), while other arc flows are subject to no such constraints.

5.5.4 An Example: Constrained Matrix Problems

A problem that arises in a variety of contexts is to find an $n \times m$ matrix F that has given row sums and column sums, and approximates a given $n \times m$ matrix M in some optimal sense. It is often appropriate to formulate such a problem in terms of a bipartite graph consisting of n sources and m sinks. In this graph, the set of arcs A consists of the pairs (i, j) for which the corresponding entry f_{ij} of the matrix F is allowed to be nonzero. The given row sums r_i and the given column sums c_j imply the constraints

$$\sum_{\{j | (i,j) \in A\}} f_{ij} = r_i, \qquad i = 1, \ldots, n,$$

$$\sum_{\{i | (i,j) \in A\}} f_{ij} = c_j, \qquad j = 1, \ldots, m.$$

There may be also bounds for the entries f_{ij} of F. Thus, the structure of this problem is similar to the structure of a transportation problem. The cost function to be optimized can take the form

$$\sum_{(i,j) \in A} a_{ij}(f_{ij}).$$

Commonly used examples expressing the objective of making the entries of F close to the corresponding entries of M are the quadratic function

$$a_{ij}(f_{ij}) = \tfrac{1}{2} \sum_{(i,j) \in A} w_{ij}(f_{ij} - m_{ij})^2, \tag{5.29}$$

where w_{ij} are given positive weights, and the logarithmic function

$$a_{ij}(f_{ij}) = f_{ij} \left[\ln \left(\frac{f_{ij}}{m_{ij}} \right) - 1 \right], \tag{5.30}$$

where we assume that $m_{ij} > 0$ for all $(i, j) \in A$. Note that the logarithmic arc cost function (5.30) is not defined for $f_{ij} \leq 0$, but it can be seen that this does not cause difficulties either in the dual problem definition or in the corresponding relaxation algorithm, since the growth conditions (5.27) are satisfied for $b_{ij} = 0$ and $c_{ij} = \infty$.

Let us denote by π_i, $i = 1, \ldots, n$ the prices corresponding to the rows of F, and by p_j, $j = 1, \ldots, m$, the prices corresponding to the columns of F. For the quadratic cost function (5.29), the dual problem (assuming no bound constraints on the entries of F) is

$$\text{maximize} \qquad q(p) = \sum_{(i,j) \in A} \left(-\frac{(\pi_i - p_j)^2}{2w_{ij}} + m_{ij}(\pi_i - p_j) \right) - \sum_{i=1}^{n} r_i \pi_i + \sum_{j=1}^{m} c_j p_j$$

subject to no constraints on π and p.

For every set of prices (π, p), the unique flow vector that satisfies the CS conditions is

$$f_{ij} = m_{ij} - \frac{\pi_i - p_j}{w_{ij}}, \qquad (i,j) \in A.$$

The relaxation iteration with exact maximization along each price coordinate is given by

$$\pi_i := \frac{1}{\sum_{j \in O(i)} 1/w_{ij}} \left(\sum_{j \in O(i)} \left(\frac{p_j}{w_{ij}} + m_{ij} \right) - r_i \right), \qquad i = 1, \ldots, n,$$

$$p_j := \frac{1}{\sum_{i \in I(j)} 1/w_{ij}} \left(\sum_{i \in I(j)} \left(\frac{\pi_i}{w_{ij}} - m_{ij} \right) + c_j \right), \qquad j = 1, \ldots, m,$$

where

$$O(i) = \left\{ j \mid (i,j) \in A \right\}, \qquad I(j) = \left\{ i \mid (i,j) \in A \right\}.$$

Note that a synchronous parallel implementation of the method is possible, whereby in each iteration, the prices of all rows are updated simultaneously followed by simultaneous updating of the prices of all columns. Since no two rows (columns) are connected by an arc, this method is equivalent to the Gauss–Seidel method of this section with a particular order of choosing nodes for relaxation.

For the logarithmic cost function (5.30) the dual problem has the form

$$\text{maximize} \qquad q(p) = - \sum_{(i,j) \in A} m_{ij} e^{p_j - \pi_i} - \sum_{i=1}^{n} r_i \pi_i + \sum_{j=1}^{m} c_j p_j$$

subject to no constraints on π and p.

The corresponding relaxation iteration sets π_i to the value $\tilde{\pi}_i$, for which

$$\left(\sum_{j \in O(i)} m_{ij} e^{p_j} \right) e^{-\tilde{\pi}_i} = r_i, \qquad i = 1, \ldots, n,$$

and sets p_j to the value $\tilde{p}_j$, for which

$$\left(\sum_{i \in I(j)} m_{ij} e^{-\pi_i} \right) e^{\tilde{p}_j} = c_j, \qquad j = 1, \ldots, m.$$

If we make the change of variables

$$y_i = e^{-\pi_i}, \qquad z_j = e^{p_j},$$

we obtain the iterations

$$y_i := \frac{r_i}{\sum_{j \in O(i)} m_{ij} z_j}, \qquad i = 1, \ldots, n, \tag{5.31}$$

$$z_j := \frac{c_j}{\sum_{i \in I(j)} m_{ij} y_i}, \qquad j = 1, \ldots, m. \tag{5.32}$$

The iterative method consisting of alternative updating of y_i using Eq. (5.31) and updating of z_j using Eq. (5.32) is known as *Kruithof's method* and dates to 1937 [Kru37]. It is used in telephony to predict traffic between n origins and m destinations based on predictions of the total traffic of origins and destinations. In this context, the known values m_{ij} represent traffic intensity from origins i to destinations j as measured during some earlier period.

5.5.5 Parallel Implementations of the Relaxation Method

The parallel implementation aspects of the relaxation method of this subsection are similar to those of the ϵ–relaxation method (Subsection 5.3.2). We assume that there is a processor assigned to each node, which has the responsibility of carrying out relaxation iterations at the node and communicating the results to adjacent processors/nodes. Minor modifications in the following are required in the case where several nodes are assigned to each processor. A possibility for further parallelization in executing approximately the coordinate minimization in the relaxation iteration is described in Exercise 5.7, and requires that a separate processor be used for each arc in each direction.

There are three main possibilities. The first is the synchronous Gauss–Seidel implementation, where the set of nodes is partitioned in subsets by means of a coloring scheme (cf. Subsection 1.2.4); there is no pair of nodes connected by an arc that is contained in the same subset. The algorithm is operated in phases. In each phase, a subset is selected, and a relaxation iteration is executed using each node of the subset. The iterations of the nodes in the same subset can be done in parallel. The method is then mathematically equivalent to a serial algorithm for which the convergence analysis of this section applies. Note that when the graph is bipartite as in the case of the constrained matrix problems of Subsection 5.5.4, it is possible to use just two subsets of nodes and execute a relaxation iteration at every node in just two phases.

The other possibilities are a synchronous Jacobi implementation and an asynchronous implementation. It was seen earlier (Fig. 5.5.5) that the synchronous Jacobi method need not converge to an optimal solution because adding the same constant to all prices leaves the dual cost unchanged. To overcome this difficulty, we consider in Section 6.5 a variation of the relaxation method, whereby the price of a single node, say node 1, is kept fixed, and we assume that there is a unique dual optimal vector p with p_1 equal to the given fixed value. Under these circumstances, we show that the synchronous Jacobi method and a totally asynchronous relaxation method converge to that vector. A variation to be described in Chapter 7, that involves the use of a relaxation parameter and a partially asynchronous implementation, will be shown to converge as desired without fixing the price of any node and without making any assumptions on the nature of the set of dual optimal price vectors.

The limited computational experience available with parallel implementations of the relaxation method of this section ([ZeM86] and [ZeL87]) indicates that the speedup obtained is substantial. This is due to the experimentally observed fact that there are many nodes with nonzero surplus throughout the algorithm. This observation is not supported by any analysis at present.

EXERCISES

5.1. Consider the problem

$$\text{minimize} \quad \sum_{j=1}^{n} f_j(x_j)$$

$$\text{subject to} \quad Ax = s, \qquad b_j \leq x_j \leq c_j, \qquad j = 1, \ldots, n,$$

where $f_j : \Re \mapsto \Re$ are strictly convex functions, A is a given $m \times n$ matrix, s is a given vector in $\Re^m$, and b_j, c_j are given scalars.
  (a) Dualize the constraints $Ax = s$ and write the dual problem.
  (b) Calculate the gradient of the dual function and describe the corresponding relaxation method. Under what circumstances is the method highly parallelizable?
  (c) Repeat parts (a) and (b) for the case where the cost is a general strictly convex function $f : \Re^n \mapsto \Re$.
5.2. (Necessary and Sufficient Optimality Condition.) This exercise generalizes the necessary and sufficient optimality conditions for linear network flow problems (cf. Exercise 1.2). Show that a flow vector $f = \{f_{ij} \mid (i,j) \in A\}$ is optimal for the convex network flow problem (CNF) if and only if f is feasible, and for every directed cycle Y for which

$$f_{ij} < c_{ij}, \qquad \forall \, (i,j) \in Y^+,$$

$$b_{ij} < f_{ij}, \qquad \forall \, (i,j) \in Y^-,$$

we have

$$\sum_{(i,j) \in Y^+} a_{ij}^+(f_{ij}) - \sum_{(i,j) \in Y^-} a_{ij}^-(f_{ij}) \geq 0.$$

Hint: The rate of change of the primal cost at a feasible flow vector f in the direction of a circulation y is given by

$$d(f; y) = \sum_{\{(i,j) \mid y_{ij} > 0\}} a_{ij}^+(f_{ij}) y_{ij} + \sum_{\{(i,j) \mid y_{ij} < 0\}} a_{ij}^-(f_{ij}) y_{ij}.$$

If f is feasible but not optimal, there must exist a circulation y such that $d(f; y) < 0$. Use the Conformal Realization Theorem of Appendix B to show that the given optimality condition is then violated.

5.3. State and prove analogs of Lemma 5.1 and Prop. 5.1 for problem (UCNF) under Assumption 5.2.

5.4. (**A Problem of Agreement.**) The following problem will be reencountered in more general form in Chapter 7, where it will play a significant role in the analysis. Consider a connected undirected graph (N, A). Each node i has a scalar value $p_i(t)$ at time t. At each time t, a node i is selected and its value is set to a convex combination of its value and a weighted average of the values of its neighbors, that is,

$$p_i(t + 1) = \delta_i p_i(t) + (1 - \delta_i) \sum_{j \in A(i)} a_{ij} p_j(t),$$

where $\delta_i \in [0, 1)$ is a given scalar, $A(i)$ is the set of nodes connected to i with an arc, and a_{ij} are positive scalars such that $a_{ij} = a_{ji}$ and $\sum_{j \in A(i)} a_{ij} = 1$ for all i. Assuming each node is selected infinitely often, show that the nodes will asymptotically agree on a common value, that is, there exists some scalar p^* such that

$$\lim_{t \to \infty} p_i(t) = p^*, \qquad \forall\, i \in N.$$

Hint: Replace each undirected arc $(i, j) \in A$ with two directed arcs (i, j) and (j, i). To each directed arc (i, j) of the resulting network, assign the arc cost function $a_{ij}(f_{ij}) = (1/2a_{ij})f_{ij}^2$ and consider the problem of minimizing $\sum_{(i,j)} a_{ij}(f_{ij})$ subject to the constraint that f is a circulation. Show that a price vector is optimal if and only if all its coordinates are equal. Apply the relaxation method.

5.5. (**Feasible Differential Theorem.**) Consider a directed graph (N, A). For each arc $(i, j) \in A$, we are given two scalars $a_{ij}^- \in [-\infty, \infty)$ and $a_{ij}^+ \in (-\infty, \infty]$, with $a_{ij}^- \leq a_{ij}^+$. Show that there exists a price vector p satisfying

$$a_{ij}^- \leq p_i - p_j \leq a_{ij}^+, \qquad \forall\, (i, j) \in A,$$

if and only if for every directed cycle Y, we have

$$0 \leq \sum_{(i,j) \in Y^+} a_{ij}^+ - \sum_{(i,j) \in Y^-} a_{ij}^-. \qquad (5.33)$$

Hint: Consider the instance of (CNF) involving the piecewise linear arc cost functions

$$a_{ij}(f_{ij}) = \max\left\{a_{ij}^- f_{ij}, a_{ij}^+ f_{ij}\right\},$$

and the constraint that f is a circulation (that is, $s_i = 0$ for all i, and there are no arc flow bounds). Show that if Eq. (5.33) holds for all Y, then $f = 0$ is an optimal solution of this piecewise linear cost problem, and otherwise there is no optimal solution. Convert this problem to a linear programming problem, and use the linear programming duality theory of Appendix C.

5.6. (Proof of the Duality Theorem.) Use Lemma 5.1, and the results of Exercises 5.2 and 5.5 to prove Prop. 5.1. *Hint:* We have

$$q(p') \leq \sum_{(i,j) \in A} a_{ij}(f'_{ij})$$

for all p' and feasible f' [cf. Eq. (C.12) in Appendix C]. If f and p satisfy primal feasibility and the CS conditions (5.7)–(5.9), argue that f_{ij} attains the minimum in the definition (5.5b) of the dual arc function q_{ij}, and use Lemma 5.1 to show that equality is obtained above. Conversely, suppose that f is optimal. Combine the results of Exercises 5.2 and 5.5 to show that there exists a price vector p such that

$$a_{ij}^-(f_{ij}) \leq p_i - p_j \leq a_{ij}^+(f_{ij}), \qquad \forall \, (i, j) \in A.$$

Show that this price vector is dual optimal.

5.7. (Parallelization of Stepsize Selection [Tse87].) Consider a relaxation iteration where a node i with $g_i(p) > 0$ is chosen, and we wish to find a stepsize $\bar{\gamma}$ such that for some $\delta \in [0, 1)$, we have $0 \leq g_i(\bar{p}) \leq \delta g_i(p)$, where $\bar{p}_i = p_i + \bar{\gamma}$ and $\bar{p}_j = p_j$ for $j \neq i$. The following is a parallelizable procedure for computing a suitable stepsize $\bar{\gamma}$. Let μ be any scalar with $\mu \in (0, 1)$, and define for all $\gamma \in \Re$ and all incident arcs to node i

$$f_{ij}(\gamma) = \arg \min_{b_{ij} \leq \xi \leq c_{ij}} \{a_{ij}(\xi) - (p_i - p_j + \gamma)\xi\},$$

$$f_{ji}(\gamma) = \arg \min_{b_{ji} \leq \xi \leq c_{ji}} \{a_{ji}(\xi) - (p_j - p_i - \gamma)\xi\}.$$

Let n_i be the number of arcs (i, j) that are outgoing from i and satisfy $f_{ij} < c_{ij}$, plus the number of arcs (j, i) that are incoming to i and satisfy $f_{ji} > b_{ji}$. For each arc (i, j) that is outgoing from i and $f_{ij} < c_{ij}$, set

$$\gamma_{ij} = \infty, \quad \text{if} \quad f_{ij}(\gamma) - f_{ij} < \frac{\mu}{n_i} g_i(p), \qquad \forall \, \gamma \geq 0,$$

and otherwise let γ_{ij} be a scalar such that

$$\frac{\mu}{n_i} g_i(p) \leq f_{ij}(\gamma_{ij}) - f_{ij} \leq \frac{1}{n_i} g_i(p).$$

Similarly, for each arc (j, i) that is incoming to i and $f_{ji} > b_{ji}$ set

$$\gamma_{ji} = \infty, \quad \text{if} \quad f_{ji} - f_{ji}(\gamma) < \frac{\mu}{n_i} g_i(p), \qquad \forall \, \gamma \geq 0,$$

and otherwise let γ_{ji} be a scalar such that

$$\frac{\mu}{n_i} g_i(p) \leq f_{ji} - f_{ji}(\gamma_{ji}) \leq \frac{1}{n_i} g_i(p).$$

(Note that all the scalars γ_{ij} and γ_{ji} can be computed in parallel in a system that assigns a separate processor to each incident arc to node i.) Let

$$\bar{\gamma} = \min \left\{ \min_{\{j|(i,j)\in A\}} \gamma_{ij}, \ \min_{\{j|(j,i)\in A\}} \gamma_{ji} \right\}.$$

(a) Show that $\bar{\gamma} > 0$, and that

$$0 \le g_i(\bar{p}) \le \left(1 - \frac{\mu}{n_i}\right) g_i(p).$$

(b) Provide a similarly parallelizable stepsize procedure for the case where $g_i(p) < 0$.

5.8. (ϵ–**Complementary Slackness [BHT87].**) Consider the convex network problem (CNF). Given $\epsilon \ge 0$, we say that a flow–price vector pair (f, p) satisfies ϵ–complementary slackness (ϵ–CS) if for all $(i, j) \in A$, we have $f_{ij} \in [b_{ij}, c_{ij}]$ and

$$\tilde{a}_{ij}^-(f_{ij}) - \epsilon \le p_i - p_j \le \tilde{a}_{ij}^+(f_{ij}) + \epsilon,$$

where $\tilde{a}_{ij}^+(f_{ij})$ and $\tilde{a}_{ij}^-(f_{ij})$ are defined by Eqs. (5.17a) and (5.17b), respectively. Verify that this definition contains as a special case the corresponding definition of Section 5.3, and show that if (f, p) satisfies ϵ–CS, then

$$0 \le \sum_{(i,j)\in A} a_{ij}(f_{ij}) - q(p) \le \epsilon \sum_{(i,j)\in A} (c_{ij} - b_{ij}).$$

5.6 NONLINEAR MULTICOMMODITY FLOW PROBLEMS–ROUTING APPLICATIONS

In this section, we consider a network flow routing model that is more complex than the models of the previous sections in that we distinguish between several independently constrained types of flow (commodities) that share the arcs of the given network. Typical applications of this model arise in routing of data in computer communication networks, and in equilibrium studies of transportation networks. The size of the problems encountered in the context of these applications is often very large, so it may be essential to speedup the solution method through parallelization in order to meet practical solution time constraints. In the case of routing in a data network, a distributed on–line implementation is often desirable; we refer to [BeG87] for a description of some of the practical issues arising in this context.

We are given a network and a set W of ordered pairs w of distinct nodes referred to as the origin and the destination of w. We refer to w as an OD pair. For each w, we are given a scalar r_w referred to as the input traffic of w. In the context of routing in a data network, r_w (measured in data units/second) is the arrival rate of traffic entering and exiting the network at the origin and the destination of w, respectively. The routing objective is to divide each r_w among the many paths from origin to destination in a way that the resulting total arc flow pattern minimizes a suitable cost function. We denote:

P_w: A given set of simple positive paths that start at the origin and end at the destination of w.

x_p: The flow of path p.

The collection of all path flows $\{x_p \mid w \in W, p \in P_w\}$ must satisfy the constraints

$$\sum_{p \in P_w} x_p = r_w, \qquad \forall \; w \in W, \tag{6.1}$$

$$x_p \geq 0, \qquad \forall \; p \in P_w, \; w \in W, \tag{6.2}$$

as shown in Fig. 5.6.1. The total flow F_{ij} of arc (i,j) is the sum of all path flows traversing the arc:

$$F_{ij} = \sum_{\substack{\text{all paths } p \\ \text{containing } (i,j)}} x_p. \tag{6.3}$$

Consider a cost function of the form

$$\sum_{(i,j)} D_{ij}(F_{ij}). \tag{6.4}$$

The problem is to find a set of path flows $\{x_p\}$ that minimize this cost function subject to the constraints of Eqs. (6.1) to (6.3).

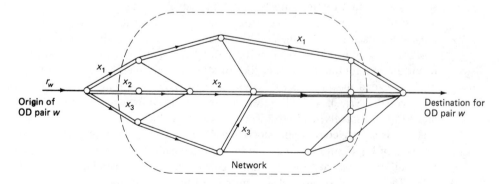

Figure 5.6.1 Constraints for the path flows of an OD pair w. The path flows should be nonnegative and add up to the given traffic input r_w of the OD pair.

A frequently used function D_{ij} in packet routing applications is

$$D_{ij}(F_{ij}) = \frac{F_{ij}}{C_{ij} - F_{ij}} + d_{ij}F_{ij}, \tag{6.5}$$

where C_{ij} is the transmission capacity of arc (i, j) measured in the same units as F_{ij}, and d_{ij} is the processing and propagation delay. (This function is defined for $F_{ij} \in [0, C_{ij})$ and is usually modified during algorithmic solution so that it is defined as a convex function for all $F_{ij} \geq 0$.) With this formula, the cost function (6.4) expresses the average number of packets in the system based on the hypothesis that each queue behaves as an M/M/1 queue of packets [BeG87].

By expressing the total flows F_{ij} in terms of the path flows in the cost function (6.4) [using Eq. (6.3)], the problem can be formulated in terms of the path flow variables $\{x_p \mid p \in P_w, \ w \in W\}$ as

$$\text{minimize} \quad D(x)$$

$$\text{subject to} \quad \sum_{p \in P_w} x_p = r_w, \qquad \forall \ w \in W, \tag{6.6}$$

$$x_p \geq 0, \qquad \forall \ p \in P_w, \ w \in W,$$

where

$$D(x) = \sum_{(i,j)} D_{ij} \left(\sum_{\substack{\text{all paths } p \\ \text{containing } (i,j)}} x_p \right)$$

and x is the vector of path flows x_p.

We now turn to the characterization of an optimal solution. In particular, we will show that optimal routing directs traffic exclusively along paths that are shortest with respect to some arc lengths that depend on the flows carried by the arcs. For this, we assume that each D_{ij} is defined on $[0, \infty)$ and is twice differentiable on $(0, \infty)$. The case where D_{ij} is defined in an interval $[0, C_{ij})$, where C_{ij} is a positive number [the capacity of the arc in a routing context, cf. Eq. (6.5)] can be handled by extending the definition of D_{ij} beyond the interval $[0, C_{ij})$, and by suitably modifying $D_{ij}(F_{ij})$ for F_{ij} near C_{ij}; see [BeG87], p. 416. The first and second derivatives of D_{ij} are denoted by D'_{ij} and D''_{ij}, respectively, and are assumed positive for all F_{ij}. This implies in particular that D_{ij} is strictly convex and monotonically increasing. It is seen that the optimization problem of Eq. (6.6), viewed as a problem in the path flow variables $\{x_p\}$, has a convex twice differentiable cost function and a convex, compact constraint set.

The partial derivative of D with respect to x_p is given by

$$\frac{\partial D(x)}{\partial x_p} = \sum_{\substack{\text{all arcs } (i,j) \\ \text{on path } p}} D'_{ij}, \tag{6.7}$$

where the first derivatives D'_{ij} are evaluated at the arc flows F_{ij} corresponding to x. From this equation, it is seen that $\partial D/\partial x_p$ *is the length of path p when the length of each arc (i, j) is taken to be the first derivative D'_{ij} evaluated at x.* Consequently, in what follows, $\partial D/\partial x_p$ is called the *first derivative length of path p.*

According to Prop. 3.1 in Section 3.3, $x^* = \{x_p^*\}$ is an optimal path flow vector if and only if it is feasible, that is, it satisfies the constraints

$$\sum_{p\in P_w} x_p = r_w, \qquad x_p \geq 0, \qquad \forall\ p \in P_w,\ w \in W, \tag{6.8}$$

and the rate of change of the cost function is nonnegative along every "feasible direction", that is,

$$\sum_{w\in W}\sum_{p\in P_w} \frac{\partial D(x^*)}{\partial x_p}(x_p - x_p^*) \geq 0, \tag{6.9}$$

for all $\{x_p\}$ that are feasible. Note that the optimality conditions (6.8) and (6.9) represent a variational inequality which is identical to the one encountered in the traffic assignment problem (Section 3.5) if the path travel time $t_p(x)$ in the latter problem is identified with the first derivative length of path p, that is,

$$t_p(x) = \frac{\partial D(x)}{\partial x_p}. \tag{6.10}$$

From the equivalence of Eqs. (5.2) and (5.3) in Section 3.5, it is seen that the optimality conditions (6.8) and (6.9) are equivalent to having, for all $w \in W$ and $p \in P_w$

$$x_p^* > 0 \quad \text{only if} \quad \left[\frac{\partial D(x^*)}{\partial x_{p'}} \geq \frac{\partial D(x^*)}{\partial x_p}, \qquad \forall\ p' \in P_w\right]. \tag{6.11}$$

In words, the above condition says that *a set of path flows is optimal if and only if path flow is positive only on paths with a minimum first derivative length.* This parallels the minimum travel time condition implied by the user optimization principle in the traffic assignment problem. The condition of Eq. (6.11) also implies that at an optimum, the paths along which the input flow r_w of OD pair w is split must have *equal* length (and less than or equal length to that of all other paths of w).

We now consider iterative algorithms for solving the optimal routing problem. One possible method is based on the scaled gradient projection method discussed in Section 3.3. To apply this method, we write the optimization problem of Eq. (6.6) as

$$\begin{aligned}
\text{minimize} \quad & D(x) \\
\text{subject to} \quad & x_w \in X_w, \qquad \forall\ w \in W,
\end{aligned} \tag{6.12}$$

where x_w is the vector of path flows of OD pair w:

$$x_w = \{x_p \mid p \in P_w\}, \tag{6.13}$$

and X_w is the feasible set for x_w:

$$X_w = \left\{ x_w \,\bigg|\, \sum_{p \in P_w} x_p = r_w, \ x_p \geq 0, \ p \in P_w \right\}. \tag{6.14}$$

The gradient projection method replaces the current iterates x_w, $w \in W$, with the corresponding solutions $\bar{x}_w$ of the quadratic programming problems

$$\begin{aligned} \text{minimize} \quad & (\bar{x}_w - x_w)' \nabla_w D(x) + \tfrac{1}{2}(\bar{x}_w - x_w)' M_w (\bar{x}_w - x_w) \\ \text{subject to} \quad & \bar{x}_w \in X_w, \end{aligned} \tag{6.15}$$

where $\nabla_w D$ denotes the gradient of D with respect to x_w, and M_w is a matrix that satisfies $x_w' M_w x_w > 0$, for every nonzero x_w in the subspace

$$\left\{ x_w \,\bigg|\, \sum_{p \in P_w} x_p = 0 \right\}. \tag{6.16}$$

A suitable practical choice is to select M_w diagonal with the scalars

$$\frac{1}{\gamma} \frac{\partial^2 D(x)}{\partial x_p^2}, \qquad p \in P_w$$

along the diagonal, where γ is a positive stepsize parameter. This choice corresponds to an approximation of a constrained form of Newton's method, where the off–diagonal terms of the Hessian matrix have been set to zero. Note that M_w can change from one iteration to the next. The convergence properties of the algorithm can be inferred from the convergence result for the gradient projection method given in Section 3.3 (Prop. 3.6). Note that the algorithm admits massive parallelism, since the OD pairs w can be assigned to separate processors that can solve the quadratic subproblems (6.15) in parallel.

Another gradient projection algorithm (which in fact can be shown to be a special case of the preceding one for a particular choice of the matrices M_w) is based on converting the simplex constraints of the optimization problem (6.6) (for the purpose of the next iteration) into nonnegativity constraints. This is done as follows: at each iteration, we calculate for each OD pair $w \in W$ a path $\bar{p}_w$ of minimum first derivative length (MFDL). We then express the flows of the MFDL paths $\bar{p}_w$ in terms of the other path flows while eliminating the equality constraints

$$\sum_{p \in P_w} x_p = r_w$$

in the process. For each w, we eliminate $x_{\bar{p}_w}$ from the cost function $D(x)$ using the equation

$$x_{\overline{p}_w} = r_w - \sum_{\substack{p \in P_w \\ p \neq \overline{p}_w}} x_p, \tag{6.17}$$

thereby obtaining a problem of the form

$$\begin{aligned} \text{minimize} \quad & \tilde{D}(\tilde{x}) \\ \text{subject to} \quad & x_p \geq 0, \quad \forall\; w \in W,\; p \in P_w,\; p \neq \overline{p}_w, \end{aligned} \tag{6.18}$$

where $\tilde{x}$ is the vector of all path flows x_p with $p \neq \overline{p}_w$ for all $w \in W$. Note that the constraint $x_{\overline{p}_w} \geq 0$ has been ignored because the flow $x_{\overline{p}_w}$ can only be increased during the iteration as will be seen shortly. Note also that the path $\overline{p}_w$ may change from one iteration to the next, so the vector $\tilde{x}$ and the function $\tilde{D}$ depend on the iteration count, but for simplicity we have not shown this dependence.

Using Eq. (6.17) and the definition of $\tilde{D}(\tilde{x})$, we obtain

$$\frac{\partial \tilde{D}(\tilde{x}^k)}{\partial x_p} = \frac{\partial D(x^k)}{\partial x_p} - \frac{\partial D(x^k)}{\partial x_{\overline{p}_w}}, \quad \forall\; p \in P_w,\; p \neq \overline{p}_w,\; w \in W. \tag{6.19}$$

Regarding second derivatives, a straightforward differentiation of the first derivative expressions (6.19) and (6.7) shows that

$$\frac{\partial^2 \tilde{D}(\tilde{x}^k)}{\partial x_p^2} = \sum_{(i,j) \in L_p} D_{ij}''(F_{ij}^k), \quad \forall\; w \in W,\; p \in P_w,\; p \neq \overline{p}_w, \tag{6.20}$$

where, for each p,

L_p: Set of arcs belonging to either p or the corresponding MFDL path $\overline{p}_w$, but not both.

We now use the gradient projection iteration for positivity constraints and diagonal second derivative scaling applied to the "reduced" cost function $\tilde{D}(\tilde{x})$. The iteration takes the form

$$x_p^{k+1} = \max\{0, x_p^k - \gamma^k H_p^{-1}(d_p - d_{\overline{p}_w})\}, \quad \forall\; w \in W,\; p \in P_w,\; p \neq \overline{p}_w, \tag{6.21}$$

where d_p and $d_{\overline{p}_w}$ are the first derivative lengths of the paths p and $\overline{p}_w$, respectively, given by [cf. Eq. (6.7)]

$$d_p = \sum_{\substack{\text{all arcs } (i,j) \\ \text{on path } p}} D_{ij}'(F_{ij}^k), \qquad d_{\overline{p}_w} = \sum_{\substack{\text{all arcs } (i,j) \\ \text{on path } \overline{p}_w}} D_{ij}'(F_{ij}^k), \tag{6.22}$$

and H_p is the "second derivative length"

$$H_p = \sum_{(i,j) \in L_p} D_{ij}''(F_{ij}^k) \tag{6.23}$$

given by Eq. (6.20). The stepsize γ^k is some positive scalar which may be chosen by a variety of methods to be discussed shortly.

The following observations can be made regarding the gradient projection iteration (6.21):

1. Since for each OD pair $w \in W$, we have $d_p \geq d_{\overline{p}_w}$ for all $p \neq \overline{p}_w$, it follows that all the nonshortest path flows x_p ($p \neq \overline{p}_w$) that are positive will be reduced with the corresponding increment of flow being shifted to the MFDL path $\overline{p}_w$.

2. Those nonshortest path flows x_p, $p \neq \overline{p}_w$, that are zero will stay at zero. Therefore, the calculation indicated in the gradient projection iteration (6.21) should only be carried out for paths that carry positive flow.

3. Only paths that carried positive flow at the start or were MFDL paths at some previous iteration can carry positive flow at the beginning of an iteration. This is important in that it tends to keep the number of flow carrying paths small with a corresponding reduction in the amount of calculation and overhead needed at each iteration.

Regarding the choice of the stepsize γ^k, there are several possibilities. It is possible to select γ^k to be constant ($\gamma^k \equiv \gamma$ for all k). With this choice, it can be shown that given any starting set of path flows, there exists $\overline{\gamma} > 0$ such that if $\gamma \in (0, \overline{\gamma}]$, then a sequence generated by the gradient projection iteration (6.21) converges to the optimal cost of the problem [this can be proved by viewing the iteration as a special case of the gradient projection method based on Eq. (6.15) for a particular choice of M_w, and will also be proved in more general form in Chapter 7]. A crucial question has to do with the magnitude of the constant stepsize. It is known from nonlinear programming experience and analysis that a stepsize equal to unity usually works well with Newton's method as well as diagonal approximations to Newton's method that employ scaling based on second derivatives ([Ber82a] and [Lue84]). Experience has verified that a choice of the stepsize γ^k in iteration (6.21) near unity typically works quite well regardless of the values of the input flows r_w [BGV79]. On a serial machine, better performance is usually obtained if iteration (6.21) is carried out *one OD pair (or one origin) at a time*, that is, first carry out the iteration with $\gamma^k = 1$ for a single OD pair (or origin), adjust the corresponding total arc flows to account for the effected change in the path flows of this OD pair (or origin), and continue with the next OD pair until all OD pairs are taken up cyclically. This is a form of linearized block Gauss–Seidel method of the type discussed in Section 3.3. The rationale here is based on the fact that dropping the off–diagonal terms of the Hessian matrix, in effect, neglects the interaction between the flows of different OD pairs. In other words, iteration (6.21) is based to some extent on the premise that each OD pair will adjust its own path flows while the other OD pairs will keep theirs unchanged. Carrying out iteration (6.21) one OD pair at a time reduces the potentially detrimental effect of the neglected off–diagonal terms of the Hessian, and increases the likelihood that the unity stepsize is appropriate and effective. Under these circumstances, experience shows that iteration (6.21) typically works well with a unity stepsize.

For serial computation, it is possible to choose γ^k by a simple form of line search. For example, start with a unity stepsize, evaluate the corresponding cost, and if no reduction is obtained over $D(x^k)$, successively reduce the stepsize until a cost reduction $D(x^{k+1}) < D(x^k)$ is obtained. (It is noted that this scheme cannot be shown to converge to the optimal solution. However, it typically works well in practice. Similar schemes with better theoretical convergence properties are described in [Ber76a] and [Ber82b].)

The projection algorithm typically yields rapid convergence to a neighborhood of an optimal solution. Once it comes near a solution (how "near" depends on the problem), it tends to slow down. For a projection algorithm to converge fast after it approaches an optimal solution, it is necessary that the off–diagonal terms of the Hessian matrix are taken into account. Surprisingly, it is possible to implement sophisticated methods of this type (see [BeG83]), but we will not go into this topic further. These methods are based on a more accurate approximation of a constrained version of Newton's method (using the conjugate gradient method) near an optimal solution. However, when far from a solution, their speed of convergence is usually only slightly superior to that of the simple diagonally scaled gradient projection iteration (6.21). Furthermore, these methods are typically less suitable for parallelization than iteration (6.21).

Consider now synchronous parallel and distributed implementations of the gradient projection iteration (6.21). There are two main situations of interest. The first arises in a distributed data network routing context, where each node (arc) of the network flow problem is also a node (communication link) of the data network. The most straightforward possibility for distributed implementation is for all nodes i to broadcast to all other nodes the current total flows F_{ij}^k of their outgoing arcs (i,j) [BeG87]. Each node can then compute the MFDL paths of OD pairs for which it is the origin, and can execute iteration (6.21) for some fixed stepsize. The method can also be implemented in an asynchronous, distributed format, whereby the computation and information reception are not synchronized at each node. An analysis under these conditions is given in Chapter 7.

The second type of synchronous parallel implementation involves the use of a regular interconnection network of processors such as a hypercube. The ith processor is then assigned to updating the path flows of all OD pairs in a subset W_i by using iteration (6.21); for example, W_i can consist of all OD pairs that have a given node as origin. Let us assume for concreteness that each P_w is the set of all simple positive paths connecting the origin node and the destination node of w. To execute the kth iteration, processor i must know the shortest paths of its own OD pairs $w \in W_i$; this requires a shortest path computation of the type discussed in Section 4.1, using the link flows F_{ij}^k (from which the corresponding first derivative lengths $D'_{ij}(F_{ij}^k)$ can be obtained). (If additional processors are available, the shortest path computation can be parallelized along the lines discussed in Section 4.1.) Processor i can then proceed to update the path flows of the OD pairs in W_i using iteration (6.21) and the corresponding first and second derivative lengths. The processors must then cooperatively calculate the arc flows F_{ij}^{k+1} needed for the next iteration. One way to do this is for each processor i to calculate the change of the flow of every arc that results from its own updating of the path flows of the OD pairs in W_i. These arc flow changes can be communicated to all other nodes using a multinode broadcast (cf. Subsection 1.3.4). Upon reception from all processors of the corresponding changes of all arc flows, each processor, knowing the arc flows of the previous iteration F_{ij}^k, can calculate the arc flows F_{ij}^{k+1} needed for the next iteration.

NOTES AND SOURCES

5.1 There are a number of standard references on network flow optimization ([BaJ77], [Dan63], [FoF62], [JeB80], [KeH80], [Law76], [Min78], [PaS82], [Roc84], and [Zou76]). Of these, [Roc84] emphasizes duality and is closest in spirit to the material of the chapter. For parallel implementations of network simplex methods see [Pet88]. Methods of multipliers (Exercises 1.7 and 1.8) are interesting but untested possibilities for massively parallel solution of network flow problems.

5.2.2 The relaxation method with multiple node price changes was first proposed in the context of the assignment problem in [Ber81]. Its extension to the general linear network flow problem is due to [Ber82c] and [BeT85]. The method is implemented in a public domain code called RELAX, which is described in [BeT85] and [BeT88]. The main difference between this method and the more traditional primal–dual method (cf. Exercise 2.3) is that the direction of ascent used in the primal–dual method is the vector of the form (2.7) along which the directional derivative of the dual cost is maximized, whereas the direction used in the relaxation method is the first found vector of the form (2.7) along which the directional derivative is positive. Thus the direction of ascent is usually obtained with a lot less computation in the relaxation method than in the primal–dual method, while the "quality" of the ascent directions used in the relaxation method is typically not much worse than for the primal–dual method. For this reason the relaxation method, for most practical problems, terminates much faster than the primal–dual method. The method of this subsection has been extended to network flow problems with gains ([BeT85] and [Tse86]), to general linear programs ([Tse86] and [TsB87b]), to network flow problems with nonlinear arc cost functions [BHT87], to separable convex problems with linear constraints ([Tse86] and [TsB87c]), and to linear programs with decomposable structure of the type discussed in Section 3.4 [Tse86].

5.3 The ϵ–relaxation method is due to [Ber86a] and [Ber86b]. The auction algorithm was first given together with a complexity analysis in [Ber79b] (see also [Ber85] and [Ber88]). As shown in Exercise 3.5, it is possible to obtain the auction algorithm by means of a variation of the ϵ–relaxation method. The reverse is also true. The general linear network flow problem (LNF) can be converted first into a transportation problem and then into an assignment problem (see Fig. 5.1.4). By applying the auction algorithm to this assignment problem, one can derive a generic form of the ϵ–relaxation method.

The notion of ϵ–complementary slackness was first introduced in connection with the auction algorithm [Ber79b], and later in the context of linear and nonlinear network flow problems ([BeT85] and [BHT87]), and convex separable problems with linear constraints [TsB87c]. It was also developed independently in the analysis of [Tar85] for the special case where the flow vector f is feasible. There is a conceptual relationship between the use of the ϵ–complementary slackness idea in the relaxation methods of this section, and the use of the notion of an ϵ–subgradient in nondifferentiable optimization methods [BeM73], [Lem74], [Lem75], and [Roc84].

5.4 The sweep implementation was first given, except for some details, in [Ber86a] together with its complexity analysis without the use of scaling. The max–flow version of the ϵ–relaxation method bears a close resemblance with the max–flow algorithm of [Gol85a] and [GoT86], which was developed independently of the relaxation and auction ideas. This max–flow algorithm uses node labels that estimate distances over usable paths. In the context of the ϵ–relaxation approach, these labels can be viewed as dual prices. Because all arc costs are zero in the max–flow formulation of Fig. 5.1.2, the value of ϵ is immaterial as long as it is positive ($\epsilon = 1$ is used in [Gol85a] and [GoT86]). The max–flow version of the ϵ–relaxation method, first given in [Ber86b], is simpler than the algorithm of [Gol85a], [GoT86] in that it obtains an optimal primal solution in a single phase rather than two (a single phase algorithm was also given later in [Gol87a]). It can also be initialized with arbitrary prices whereas in the max–flow algorithm of [GoT86] the initial prices must satisfy $p_i \leq p_j + 1$ for all arcs (i, j). Our complexity analysis uses the general line of argument given for the max–flow algorithm of [GoT86]. In contrast with the latter algorithm, however, the ϵ–relaxation method requires the use of the admissible graph and either the sweep implementation or some other implementation that maintains the acyclicity of the admissible graph. It is also necessary to use the admissible graph and something like the sweep implementation in the max–flow version of the ϵ–relaxation method when the initial prices are arbitrary. We note that sharper complexity results are possible for the max–flow problem than for the general linear problem [AhO86]. A different type of parallel max–flow algorithm is given in [ScV82]. Parallel algorithms for the problem of maximal matching are given in [IsS86] and [KiC87].

5.4.1 Scaling is the standard technique for improving the complexity of network flow algorithms ([BlJ85], [EdK72], and [Roc80]). There are two main scaling approaches in connection with the ϵ–relaxation method. The first is based on scaling the arc costs similarly as the method given in Section 5.4. The second is based on scaling the value of ϵ and consists of applying the ϵ–relaxation method repeatedly with successively smaller values of ϵ, starting with a large value and ending with a value less than $1/|N|$ (see Exercise 4.4). This method, called ϵ–*scaling*, was mentioned in [Ber79] as a method for improving the performance of the auction algorithm based on the result of computational experimentation. ϵ–scaling was first analyzed for the general linear network flow problem in [Gol86b], where an algorithm with an $O\big(|N||A| \log(|N|) \log(|N|C)\big)$ running time was suggested. The timing estimate for this algorithm, which uses a dynamic tree data structure, was more fully established in [Gol87a] and [GoT87], where algorithms with $O\big(|N|^{5/3}|A|^{2/3} \log(|N|C)\big)$, and $O\big(|N|^3 \log(|N|C)\big)$ running times were also given. The $O\big(|N|^3 \log(|N|C)\big)$ algorithm uses the sweep implementation. The scaling analysis given here is due to [BeE87a] (see also [BeE88]), and uses some of the earlier ideas of [Gol86b]. Related work includes [BlJ85], which provides a scaling analysis of an $O\left(|N|^4 \log C\right)$ algorithm based on the traditional primal–dual method (cf. Exercise 2.3).

5.5.1 The relaxation algorithm has been applied to the dual problem of a convex programming problem by a number of authors ([CDZ86], [CoP82], [Cry71], [Hil57], and [OhK84]). [Roc84] introduces the class of monotropic programming problems, and gives an extensive analysis of the corresponding duality framework. The convergence analysis given here is due to [BHT87], which also provides an algorithm for network problems with arc cost functions that are not strictly convex. This algorithm generalizes both the relaxation algorithm of Section 5.5 and the multiple node relaxation algorithm of Subsection 5.2.2. Extensions of the convergence analysis of this section to problems that do not have a network structure are given in [TsB87a] and [TsB87c].

5.5.3 Constrained matrix problems and special cases thereof have a long history in telephone communications and other contexts ([BaK78], [BaK80], [ChC58], [Cot84], [Gra71], [Kru37], [LaS81], and [Mac79]).

5.6 Multicommodity network flow problems have been considered by many authors in the context of the traffic assignment problem (see the references for Section 3.5). Distributed routing algorithms for data networks were introduced in [Gal77] (whose algorithm bears a relation with the gradient projection method; see [Ber79c], [Gaf79], and [BGG84]), and [Ste77] (which is a dual relaxation method, similar to the ones discussed in Section 5.5). The method of [Gal77] is suitable for distributed real–time implementation. The algorithm of this section was introduced in [Ber80] (see also [BeG82], [BeG83], and [TsB86]).

PART 2
Asynchronous Algorithms

6

Totally Asynchronous Iterative Algorithms

In this chapter and the next, we discuss asynchronous counterparts of many of the algorithms analyzed earlier. We have in mind a situation where an algorithm is parallelized by separating it into several local algorithms operating concurrently at different processors. The main characteristic of an asynchronous algorithm is that the local algorithms do not have to wait at predetermined points for predetermined messages to become available. We thus allow some processors to compute faster and execute more iterations than others, we allow some processors to communicate more frequently than others, and we allow the communication delays to be substantial and unpredictable. We also allow the communication channels to deliver mesages out of order, that is, in a different order than the one in which they were transmitted.

The advantages one hopes to gain from asynchronism are twofold. First, a reduction of the synchronization penalty and a potential speed advantage over synchronous algorithms in some problems, perhaps at the expense of higher communication complexity (see Subsection 1.4.2, and Sections 6.3 and 6.4). Second, a greater implementation flexibility and tolerance to problem data changes during the algorithm's execution, as discussed in Section 1.4.

On the negative side, we will find that the conditions for validity of an asynchronous algorithm may be more stringent than the corresponding conditions for its synchronous counterpart. Furthermore the detection of termination tends to be somewhat more difficult for asynchronous than for synchronous algorithms (see the discussion of Section 8.1).

An interesting fact is that some asynchronous algorithms, called *totally asynchronous*, or *chaotic*, can tolerate arbitrarily large communication and computation delays, while other asynchronous algorithms, called *partially asynchronous*, are not guaranteed to work unless there is an upper bound on these delays. The convergence mechanisms at work in each of these two cases are genuinely different and so are their analyses. In the present chapter, we concentrate on totally asynchronous algorithms, and in the next chapter we take up the partially asynchronous case.

In the next section, we describe the totally asynchronous algorithmic model in the context of fixed point problems. In Section 6.2, we formulate a general convergence theorem for the natural distributed version of the general fixed point iteration discussed in Subsection 1.2.4. In Section 6.3, we present a number of examples involving mappings that are contractions with respect to a weighted maximum norm. Sufficient conditions for convergence are given for general nonlinear problems, and necessary conditions for convergence are given for linear problems. We also provide a rate of convergence analysis and a comparison between synchronous and asynchronous algorithms. In Section 6.4, we consider iterations involving monotone mappings, including the shortest path problem. We provide examples showing that the asynchronous version of the Bellman–Ford algorithm can require many more message transmissions than its synchronous counterpart, even though it finds the shortest distances at least as fast (and often faster). On the other hand, the number of message transmissions that the asynchronous algorithm requires on the average is probably acceptable in most practical situations. In Section 6.5, we consider linear network flow problems and a distributed asynchronous version of the ϵ–relaxation method of the previous chapter. In Section 6.6 we consider nonlinear network flow problems, and the corresponding asynchronous distributed relaxation method. Finally, in Section 6.7, we consider relaxation methods for solving ordinary differential equations and two–point boundary value problems.

6.1 THE TOTALLY ASYNCHRONOUS ALGORITHMIC MODEL

In this section, we consider a general fixed point problem and provide an algorithm which is a natural distributed version of the fixed point iteration discussed in Subsection 1.2.4. In the next section, we formulate a convergence theorem of broad applicability. Subsequent sections make extensive use of this theorem.

Let $X_1, X_2, \ldots, X_n$ be given sets, and let X be their Cartesian product:

$$X = X_1 \times X_2 \times \cdots \times X_n.$$

Elements of X are written as n–tuples of their "components", that is, for $x \in X$, we write

$$x = (x_1, x_2, \ldots, x_n),$$

where x_i are the corresponding elements of X_i, $i = 1, \ldots, n$. We assume that there is a notion of sequence convergence defined on X. Let $f_i : X \mapsto X_i$ be given functions, and let $f : X \mapsto X$ be the function defined by

$$f(x) = \big(f_1(x), f_2(x), \ldots, f_n(x)\big), \qquad \forall\, x \in X.$$

The problem is to find a fixed point of f, that is, an element $x^* \in X$ with $x^* = f(x^*)$ or, equivalently,

$$x_i^* = f_i(x^*), \qquad \forall\, i = 1, \ldots, n.$$

We now describe a distributed asynchronous version of the iterative method

$$x_i := f_i(x), \qquad i = 1, \ldots, n.$$

Let

$$x_i(t) \;=\; \text{Value of ith component at time } t.$$

We assume that there is a set of times $T = \{0, 1, 2, \ldots\}$ at which one or more components x_i of x are updated by some processor of a distributed computing system. Let

$$T^i \;=\; \text{Set of times at which } x_i \text{ is updated.}$$

We assume that the processor updating x_i may not have access to the most recent value of the components of x; thus, we assume that

$$x_i(t + 1) = f_i\Big(x_1\big(\tau_1^i(t)\big), \ldots, x_n\big(\tau_n^i(t)\big)\Big), \qquad \forall\, t \in T^i, \tag{1.1a}$$

where $\tau_j^i(t)$ are times satisfying

$$0 \le \tau_j^i(t) \le t, \qquad \forall\, t \in T.$$

At all times $t \notin T^i$, x_i is left unchanged:

$$x_i(t + 1) = x_i(t), \qquad \forall\, t \notin T^i. \tag{1.1b}$$

The elements of T should be viewed as the indices of the sequence of physical times at which updates take place. The sets T^i, as well as the sequences of physical times that they represent need not be known to any one processor, since their knowledge is not required to execute iteration (1.1). Thus, there is no requirement for a shared global clock or synchronized local clocks at the processors. The difference $\big(t - \tau_j^i(t)\big)$ between the current time t and the time $\tau_j^i(t)$ corresponding to the jth component available at the processor updating $x_i(t)$ can be viewed as a form of communication delay; see the following examples. A useful conceptual model is that some processor awakes spontaneously at the times $t \in T^i$, receives by some mechanism the values $x_1\big(\tau_1^i(t)\big), \ldots, x_n\big(\tau_n^i(t)\big)$, and then updates x_i using Eq. (1.1a) without knowing any other quantity such as t, $\tau_1^i(t), \ldots, \tau_n^i(t)$ or any element of T^j, $j = 1, \ldots, n$. In a real computational environment, some of these quantities may be known to some of the processors, but as long as they are not used in iteration (1.1a), it is still appropriate to regard them as unknown.

Note that the Jacobi, Gauss–Seidel, and block iterative methods discussed in previous chapters are special cases of the asynchronous iteration (1.1). It will be seen in this chapter that the conditions for satisfactory convergence of this iteration are, generally speaking, not much more stringent than the corresponding conditions for the above methods.

We describe two examples of situations covered by the model:

Example 1.1. *Message–Passing System*

Consider a network of n processors, each having its own local memory. Processor i stores the vector

$$x^i(t) = \big(x_1^i(t), \ldots, x_n^i(t)\big),$$

updates its ith component $x_i^i(t)$ at times $t \in T^i$ according to

$$x_i^i(t + 1) = f_i\big(x^i(t)\big),$$

and occasionally, at some unspecified times, communicates its stored value of the ith component x_i^i to the other processors. When processor j receives (after some unspecified communication delay) the value of x_i^i, it stores this value in place of its currently stored ith component of x^j. Immediately after this happens, we have

$$x_i^j(t) = x_i^i\big(\tau_i^j(t)\big),$$

so we can view $\big(t - \tau_i^j(t)\big)$ as a communication delay. It is natural to assume also that $\tau_i^i(t) = t$. The asynchronous iteration model (1.1) applies with the identification

$$x_i(t) \sim x_i^i(t).$$

Thus, the components of the vector

$$x(t) = \big(x_1^1(t), x_2^2(t), \ldots, x_n^n(t)\big)$$

generated by the algorithm are distributed among the processors, with processor i holding $x_i^i(t)$. The distributed vector $x(t)$ and the "local" vectors $x^1(t), \ldots, x^n(t)$ stored at the processors need not be equal at any time; see the example of Fig. 6.1.1. Note that we do not assume that the communication channels between processors preserve the order of the messages transmitted; neither do we assume that a processor can determine whether an update received from another processor is older than the corresponding value stored in its memory.

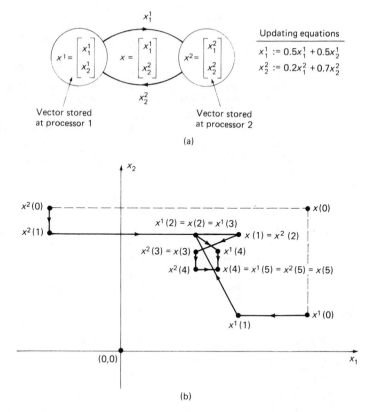

Figure 6.1.1   (a) An example of an asynchronous algorithm involving two processors and a problem with two variables. Processor i, $(i = 1, 2)$, stores $x^i = (x_1^i, x_2^i)$, updates the variable x_i^i at times $t \in T^i$, and transmits it to the other processor. (b) Evolution of the vector $x(t) = \left(x_1^1(t), x_2^2(t)\right)$, and the vectors $x^i(t) = \left(x_1^i(t), x_2^i(t)\right)$, $(i = 1, 2)$, stored at the processors using the iteration

$$x_1 := 0.5x_1 + 0.5x_2, \qquad x_2 := 0.2x_1 + 0.7x_2$$

for the initial conditions $x^i(0)$ shown and the following sequence of events:

t=0: Processor 1 updates x_1^1 and transmits it to processor 2, where it is received at a time between $t = 1$ and $t = 2$. Processor 2 updates x_2^2 and transmits it to processor 1, where it is received at a time between $t = 1$ and $t = 2$.

t=1: Processor 1 updates x_1^1 and transmits it to processor 2, where it is received at a time between $t = 2$ and $t = 3$. [Processor 2 does not update X_2^2 but X_1^2 will change at some time $t \in (1, 2)$ because of the reception of $X_1^1(1)$; for this reason, $x^2(1) \neq x^2(2)$ as shown in the figure.]

t=2: Processor 2, having received $x_1^1(1)$, updates x_2^2 and transmits it to processor 1, where it is received at a time between $t = 3$ and $t = 4$. [Processor 1 does not update X_1^1 and does not receive a value of X_2^2 from Processor 2 at any time $t \in (2, 3)$; for this reason, $X^1(2) = X^1(3)$ as shown in the figure.]

t=3: Processor 1, having received $x_2^2(1)$ [at some time $t \in (1, 2)$], updates x_1^1 and transmits it to processor 2, where it is received at a time between $t = 4$ and $t = 5$. Processor 2, having received $x_1^1(2)$, updates x_2^2 and transmits it to processor 1, where it is received at a time between $t = 4$ and $t = 5$.

t=4: Processor 1 has already received $x_2^2(3)$; no updating takes place.

t=5: Processor 1 has already received $x_2^2(4)$ and processor 2 has already received $x_1^1(4)$.

Example 1.2. *Shared Memory System*

Consider a shared memory multiprocessor, where the memory has registers for $x_1, x_2, \ldots, x_n$, with the ith register storing at time t the value $x_i(t)$. A processor starts reading the values of components from the memory at some time, performs the iteration (1.1a), and eventually, at another time, writes the new value of the corresponding component; see Fig. 6.1.2. It is not necessary to have a one–to–one correspondence between processors and components in this model. Furthermore, it is possible that $\tau_i^i(t) < t$ for $t \in T^i$. Note, however, that by requiring that there can be no more than one processor simultaneously executing an iteration of the ith component, we can be sure that x_i will not change between a time $t \in T^i$ and the corresponding time $\tau_i^i(t)$. Under these circumstances, we can assume without loss of generality that

$$\tau_i^i(t) = t, \qquad \forall\, t \in T^i.$$

This condition will play a significant role in one of the partially asynchronous models of Chapter 7 [see Assumption 7.1(c) in Section 7.1, as well as the discussion following Proposition 3.1 and Example 3.1 in Section 6.3].

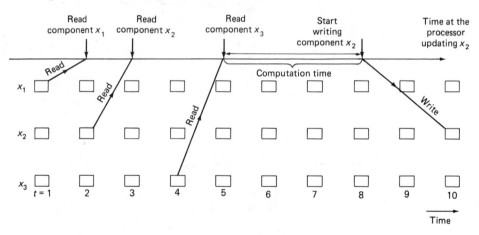

Figure 6.1.2 Illustration of a component update in a shared memory multiprocessor. Here x_2 is viewed as being updated at time $t = 9$ ($9 \in T^2$), with $\tau_1^2(9) = 1$, $\tau_2^2(9) = 2$, and $\tau_4^2(9) = 4$. The updated value of x_2 is entered at the corresponding register at $t = 10$. Several components can be simultaneously in the process of being updated, and the values of $\tau_j^i(t)$ can be unpredictable.

Throughout this chapter, we make the following standing assumption:

Assumption 1.1. *(Total Asynchronism)* The sets T^i are infinite, and if $\{t_k\}$ is a sequence of elements of T^i that tends to infinity, then $\lim_{k \to \infty} \tau_j^i(t_k) = \infty$ for every j.

This assumption guarantees that each component is updated infinitely often, and that old information is eventually purged from the system. More precisely, given any time t_1, there exists a time $t_2 > t_1$ such that

$$\tau_j^i(t) \geq t_1, \qquad \forall\, i, j, \text{ and } t \geq t_2. \tag{1.2}$$

In words, given any time t_1, values of components generated prior to t_1 will not be used in updates after a sufficiently long time t_2. On the other hand, the amounts $t - \tau_j^i(t)$ by which the variables used in iterations are outdated can become unbounded as t increases. This is the main difference with the partial asynchronism assumptions that will be introduced in connection with the asynchronous algorithms of Chapter 7.

6.2 A GENERAL CONVERGENCE THEOREM

In this section, we establish a pattern for proving convergence of the asynchronous algorithm of the previous section. The idea is to provide a set of sufficient conditions, which, when satisfied in a given fixed point problem, guarantee convergence of the algorithm.

> **Assumption 2.1.**   There is a sequence of nonempty sets $\{X(k)\}$ with
>
> $$\cdots \subset X(k+1) \subset X(k) \subset \cdots \subset X \qquad (2.1)$$
>
> satisfying the following two conditions:
>
> **(a)** (*Synchronous Convergence Condition*) We have
>
> $$f(x) \in X(k+1), \qquad \forall \, k \text{ and } x \in X(k). \qquad (2.2)$$
>
> Furthermore, if $\{y^k\}$ is a sequence such that $y^k \in X(k)$ for every k, then every limit point of $\{y^k\}$ is a fixed point of f.
>
> **(b)** (*Box Condition*) For every k, there exist sets $X_i(k) \subset X_i$ such that
>
> $$X(k) = X_1(k) \times X_2(k) \times \cdots \times X_n(k).$$

Note that the Synchronous Convergence Condition implies that the limit points of sequences generated by the (synchronous) iteration $x := f(x)$ are fixed points of f, assuming that the initial x belongs to $X(0)$. Note also that the Box Condition implies that by combining components of vectors in $X(k)$, we obtain vectors in $X(k)$, that is, if $x \in X(k)$ and $\bar{x} \in X(k)$, and we replace the ith component of x with the ith component of $\bar{x}$, we obtain an element of $X(k)$. A typical example where the box condition holds is when $X(k)$ is a sphere in $\Re^n$ with respect to some weighted maximum norm.

Our main result is the following:

> **Proposition 2.1.**   (*Asynchronous Convergence Theorem*) If the Synchronous Convergence and Box Conditions of Assumption 2.1 hold, and the initial solution estimate
>
> $$x(0) = \big(x_1(0), \ldots, x_n(0)\big)$$
>
> belongs to the set $X(0)$, then every limit point of $\{x(t)\}$ is a fixed point of f.

Proof. We show by induction that for each $k \geq 0$, there is a time t_k such that:

(a) $x(t) \in X(k)$ for all $t \geq t_k$.

(b) For all i and $t \in T^i$ with $t \geq t_k$, we have $x^i(t) \in X(k)$, where

$$x^i(t) = \Big(x_1\big(\tau_1^i(t)\big), x_2\big(\tau_2^i(t)\big), \ldots, x_n\big(\tau_n^i(t)\big)\Big), \qquad \forall\, t \in T^i.$$

[In words, after some time, all solution estimates will be in $X(k)$ and all estimates used in iteration (1.1a) will come from $X(k)$.]

The induction hypothesis is true for $k = 0$, since the initial estimate is assumed to be in $X(0)$. Assuming it is true for a given k, we will show that there exists a time t_{k+1} with the required properties. For each $i = 1, \ldots, n$, let t^i be the first element of T^i such that $t^i \geq t_k$. Then by the Synchronous Convergence Condition, we have $f\big(x^i(t^i)\big) \in X(k+1)$, implying (in view of the Box Condition) that

$$x_i(t^i + 1) = f_i\big(x^i(t^i)\big) \in X_i(k+1).$$

Similarly, for every $t \in T^i$, $t \geq t^i$, we have $x_i(t+1) \in X_i(k+1)$. Between elements of T^i, $x_i(t)$ does not change. Thus,

$$x_i(t) \in X_i(k+1), \qquad \forall\, t \geq t^i + 1.$$

Let $t_k' = \max_i\{t^i\} + 1$. Then, using the Box Condition we have

$$x(t) \in X(k+1), \qquad \forall\, t \geq t_k'.$$

Finally, since by the Continuing Update Assumption 1.1, we have $\tau_j^i(t) \to \infty$ as $t \to \infty$, $t \in T^i$, we can choose a time $t_{k+1} \geq t_k'$ that is sufficiently large so that $\tau_j^i(t) \geq t_k'$ for all i, j, and $t \in T^i$ with $t \geq t_{k+1}$. We then have, $x_j\big(\tau_j^i(t)\big) \in X_j(k+1)$, for all $t \in T^i$ with $t \geq t_{k+1}$ and all $j = 1, \ldots, n$, which (by the Box Condition) implies that

$$x^i(t) = \Big(x_1\big(\tau_1^i(t)\big), x_2\big(\tau_2^i(t)\big), \ldots, x_n\big(\tau_n^i(t)\big)\Big) \in X(k+1).$$

The induction is complete.   **Q.E.D.**

A number of useful extensions of the Asynchronous Convergence Theorem are provided in Exercises 2.1–2.3.

The Asynchronous Convergence Theorem is a powerful aid in showing convergence of totally asynchronous algorithms in a variety of contexts. The challenge in applying the theorem is to identify a suitable sequence of sets $\{X(k)\}$. In many cases, this is straightforward, but in other cases, it requires creative analysis. This is reminiscent of the process of identifying a Lyapunov function in the stability analysis of nonlinear dynamic systems ([Bro70] and [Vid78]). In fact, our theorem is conceptually related to Lyapunov stability theorems, with the sets $X(k)$ playing the role of the level sets of a Lyapunov function. When application of the Asynchronous Convergence Theorem to a given algorithm seems unlikely, this is a strong indication that the algorithm does not converge under totally asynchronous conditions. We will make this statement rigorous in the next section for the case of a linear mapping f (see, however, Exercise 2.4 for the case where f is nonlinear).

EXERCISES

2.1. Formulate and prove an appropriate extension of the Asynchronous Convergence Theorem for the case where the update equation is time dependent, that is,

$$x_i(t+1) = f_i\Big(x_1\big(\tau_1^i(t)\big),\ldots,x_n\big(\tau_n^i(t)\big),t\Big), \qquad \forall \, t \in T^i.$$

2.2. In some cases, a component of x may occur several times in the formula for $f(x)$, [e.g., $f_1(x_1,x_2) = x_1x_2 + x_1$, or $f_i(x) = g_i\big(h_1^i(x), h_2^i(x),\ldots, h_m^i(x)\big)$, where g_i and h_j^i are given functions]. It is then possible that the values used for different occurrences of the same component have incurred different delays; for example when the value of f is determined by the values of several *functions* of x and these values become available at a processor with differing delays. This leads to a generalization of the asynchronous iteration (1.1a) described by

$$x_i(t+1) = f_i\Big(x_1\big(\tau_1^i(t,1)\big),\ldots,x_1\big(\tau_1^i(t,m)\big), x_2\big(\tau_2^i(t,1)\big),\ldots,x_2\big(\tau_2^i(t,m)\big),$$

$$\ldots, x_n\big(\tau_n^i(t,1)\big),\ldots,x_n\big(\tau_n^i(t,m)\big)\Big), \qquad i=1,\ldots,n,$$

where m is the number of occurences of each component. Formulate and prove an appropriate extension of the Asynchronous Convergence Theorem.

2.3. Formulate and prove an appropriate extension of the Asynchronous Convergence Theorem for the case where $f_i(x)$ is a subset of X_i for each $x \in X$ and we want to find an $x \in X$ such that $x_i \in f_i(x)$ for all i.

2.4. This exercise provides an example where the Asynchronous Convergence Theorem does not apply even though the asynchronous iteration (1.1) converges appropriately for all starting points. Consider the function $f : \Re^2 \mapsto \Re^2$ defined by $f_1(x_1,x_2) = 0$ for all (x_1,x_2) and defined by $f_2(x_1,x_2) = 2x_2$ when $x_1 \neq 0$ and $f_2(0,x_2) = x_2/2$ when $x_1 = 0$. Show that a sequence $\{x(t)\}$ generated by the iteration (1.1) converges to the unique fixed point of f. Show also that there is no sequence of sets $\{X(k)\}$ satisfying the Synchronous Convergence and Box Conditions for which $X(0)$ contains a vector $x = (x_1,x_2)$ with $x_1 \neq 0$.

6.3 APPLICATIONS TO PROBLEMS INVOLVING MAXIMUM NORM CONTRACTION MAPPINGS

In this section, we provide several examples of application of the Asynchronous Convergence Theorem of the previous section. All these examples involve mappings that are contractions or pseudocontractions with respect to a weighted maximum norm

$$\|x\|_\infty^w = \max_i \frac{|x_i|}{w_i}$$

on $\Re^n$, where $w \in \Re^n$ is a vector with positive coordinates. The key property of a weighted maximum norm in this regard is that its unit sphere has the box property that is central in Assumption 2.1.

Suppose that $f : \Re^n \mapsto \Re^n$ is a contraction mapping with respect to the norm above, and suppose that $X_i = \Re$ for $i = 1, \ldots, n$ and $X = \Re^n$ in the definition of the algorithmic model of Section 6.1. Define the sets

$$X(k) = \left\{ x \in \Re^n \mid \|x - x^*\|_\infty^w \le \alpha^k \|x(0) - x^*\|_\infty^w \right\},$$

where x^* is the unique fixed point of f, and $\alpha < 1$ is the contraction modulus (cf. Prop. 1.1 in Section 3.1). It is evident that the Synchronous Convergence and the Box Conditions of Assumption 2.1 are satisfied. Therefore, asynchronous convergence in the sense of the theorem of the previous section is guaranteed. A similar conclusion holds if f is a pseudocontraction mapping with respect to the norm above (cf. Prop. 1.2 in Section 3.1).

We now consider several problems, discussed in previous chapters, that involve weighted maximum norm contractions.

6.3.1 Solution of Linear Systems of Equations

Consider the case where

$$f(x) = Ax + b$$

for a given $n \times n$ matrix A and vector $b \in \Re^n$. Thus, we wish to find x^* such that

$$x^* = Ax^* + b$$

by means of the asynchronous version of the relaxation iteration $x := Ax + b$ given by

$$x_i(t+1) = \sum_{j=1}^n a_{ij} x_j\big(\tau_j^i(t)\big) + b_i, \qquad t \in T^i, \tag{3.1}$$

$$x_i(t+1) = x_i(t), \qquad t \notin T^i, \tag{3.2}$$

where a_{ij} is the ijth entry of A. The Asynchronous Convergence Theorem applies provided A corresponds to a weighted maximum norm contraction. In Section 2.6, we saw that this is equivalent to the condition

$$\rho(|A|) < 1,$$

where $\rho(|A|)$ is the spectral radius of the matrix $|A|$ having as elements the absolute values $|a_{ij}|$.

As an example, consider the iteration

$$\tilde{\pi}(t+1) = \tilde{\pi}(t)\tilde{P} + \pi_1(0)a$$

for finding the invariant distribution of a Markov chain [cf. Eq. (8.6) in Section 2.8]. Here $\tilde{P}$ is the matrix obtained from the transition probability matrix P of the chain after deleting the first row and the first column, and a is the row vector consisting of the elements p_{12} through p_{1n} of P. Assuming that the transition probability graph contains a positive path from every state to state 1, we have $\rho(\tilde{P}') = \rho(\tilde{P}) < 1$, as shown in Prop. 8.4 of Section 2.8. It follows that $\tilde{P}'$ corresponds to a weighted maximum norm contraction, and the above iteration fulfills the conditions for asynchronous convergence.

The following proposition shows that the condition $\rho(|A|) < 1$ is also, in effect, necessary for asynchronous convergence.

Proposition 3.1.   Let A be an $n \times n$ matrix such that $I - A$ is invertible. Then the following are equivalent:

(i) $\rho(|A|) < 1$;

(ii) For any initialization $x(0)$, for any $b \in \Re^n$, for any choice of the sets T^i of computation times such that each T^i is infinite, and for any choice of the variables $\tau_j^i(t)$ satisfying $t - 2 \le \tau_j^i(t) \le t$ for all t, the sequence $\{x(t)\}$ produced by the asynchronous relaxation iteration (3.1)–(3.2) converges to $(I - A)^{-1}b$.

Proof. The fact that (i) implies (ii) follows from the Asynchronous Convergence Theorem of the previous section. We thus concentrate on the reverse implication. We assume that condition (i) fails to hold, and we will show that condition (ii) also fails to hold, i.e. that there is a choice of b, namely $b = 0$, a choice of $x(0)$, a choice of times $\tau_j^i(t)$, and a choice of sets T^i under which the sequence $x(t)$ produced by the algorithm does not converge to zero.

Since we are assuming that (i) fails to hold, we have $\rho(|A|) \ge 1$. The Perron–Frobenius theorem [Prop. 6.6(b) in Section 2.6] implies that there exists a vector $w \ge 0$ such that $w \ne 0$ and $|A|w \ge w$.

To explain the proof better, let us temporarily assume that $x(0)$ and $x(1)$ satisfy $x(0) \ge w$ and $x(1) \le -w$. Suppose that T^i is the set of all nonnegative integers for each i. We define the variables $\tau_j^i(t)$ as follows:

If t is even and nonzero,

$$\tau_j^i(t) = t - 1, \quad \text{if } a_{ij} \geq 0, \tag{3.3}$$

$$\tau_j^i(t) = t - 2, \quad \text{otherwise.} \tag{3.4}$$

If t is odd,

$$\tau_j^i(t) = t - 1, \quad \text{if } a_{ij} \geq 0, \tag{3.5}$$

$$\tau_j^i(t) = t, \quad\quad\; \text{otherwise.} \tag{3.6}$$

We then have

$$x_i(2) = \sum_{\{j \mid a_{ij} \geq 0\}} a_{ij} x_j(0) + \sum_{\{j \mid a_{ij} < 0\}} a_{ij} x_j(1)$$

$$\geq \sum_{\{j \mid a_{ij} \geq 0\}} a_{ij} w_j + \sum_{\{j \mid a_{ij} < 0\}} a_{ij}(-w_j)$$

$$= \sum_{j=1}^{n} |a_{ij}| w_j \geq w_i,$$

where the last inequality uses the definition of w. A similar argument yields $x_i(3) \leq -w_i$. Then the argument can be repeated inductively to show that $x_i(t) \geq w_i$ for every even t, and $x_i(t) \leq -w_i$, for every odd t. Clearly then, $x(t)$ does not converge. Nevertheless, this argument is not a proof of the desired result for the following reason. While we are free to choose $x(0)$ to be larger than w, $x(1)$ has to be generated from $x(0)$ according to Eqs. (3.1)–(3.2) and it will usually be impossible to satisfy the inequality $x(1) \leq -w$. The argument that we present in the following is essentially the same as the one just presented, except that we exercise some care in order to get around the inability to choose $x(1)$ arbitrarily.

Since $I - A$ is assumed nonsingular, there exists some $x \in \Re^n$ satisfying $Ax = x - w$. This particular x we take as the initialization $x(0)$. Again, we let each T^i be the set of all nonnegative integers. We let $\tau_j^i(t)$ be defined by (3.3)–(3.6), for $t \geq 1$. We also let $\tau_j^i(0) = 0$. Notice that with this choice of $\tau_j^i(0)$, we have $x(1) = Ax(0)$, which is equal to $x(0) - w$, because of the way we chose $x(0)$. We will now demonstrate that $x(t)$ does not converge by showing that $x(t) - x(t+1) \geq w$ for every even t. We prove this statement by induction on the set of nonnegative even integers. This statement is obviously true for $t = 0$, because $x(0) - x(1) = w$. Let us assume that t is even and $x(t) - x(t+1) \geq w$; we will then show that $x(t+2) - x(t+3) \geq w$.

We have

$$x_i(t+2) = \sum_{\{j \mid a_{ij} \geq 0\}} a_{ij} x_j(t) + \sum_{\{j \mid a_{ij} < 0\}} a_{ij} x_j(t+1).$$

Similarly,

$$x_i(t+3) = \sum_{\{j|a_{ij} \geq 0\}} a_{ij} x_j(t+1) + \sum_{\{j|a_{ij} < 0\}} a_{ij} x_j(t).$$

Subtracting these two equations, we get

$$x_i(t+2) - x_i(t+3) = \sum_{\{j|a_{ij} \geq 0\}} a_{ij} \left[x_j(t) - x_j(t+1) \right] - \sum_{\{j|a_{ij} < 0\}} a_{ij} \left[x_j(t) - x_j(t+1) \right]$$

$$= \sum_{j=1}^{n} |a_{ij}| \left[x_j(t) - x_j(t+1) \right] \geq \sum_{j=1}^{n} |a_{ij}| w_j \geq w_i$$

as desired. This completes the induction and the proof is complete.   **Q.E.D.**

The proposition shows that "delays" $t - \tau_j^i(t)$ as small as two are sufficient to induce divergence when $\rho(|A|) \geq 1$, even if $\rho(A) < 1$. Notice that the choice of $\tau_j^i(t)$ used in the proof to construct a nonconvergent sequence $x(t)$ does not have the property $\tau_i^i(t) = t$. This may be unnatural in certain contexts, particularly in message–passing systems. It would be therefore preferable if we were able to construct for every matrix A with $\rho(|A|) \geq 1$, an asynchronously generated divergent sequence under the constraint $\tau_i^i(t) = t$. This turns out to be impossible, however, when there is a fixed bound on the delays $t - \tau_j^i(t)$, as will be seen in Chapter 7. In other words, when $\tau_i^i(t) = t$, the required size of $t - \tau_j^i(t)$, for $i \neq j$, to demonstrate nonconvergence may depend on the entire matrix A and not just on $\rho(|A|)$; see Example 3.1 in the next subsection and Example 1.3 in Section 7.1.

6.3.2 Unconstrained Optimization

We now consider asynchronous algorithms for unconstrained optimization. We concentrate on the case of a quadratic cost function F and the gradient method. Our conclusions can be extended to the case of a continuously differentiable convex function F for which the mapping $f(x) = x - \gamma \nabla F(x)$ is a weighted maximum norm contraction for some $\gamma > 0$ (see Prop. 1.11 and Exercise 1.3 in Section 3.1). Similarly, they can be extended to the case of a nonlinear Jacobi method (Prop. 2.6 in Subsection 3.2.4). These extensions are left as exercises for the reader.

The problem is

$$\text{minimize} \quad F(x) = \tfrac{1}{2} x' A x - b' x$$

$$\text{subject to} \quad x \in \Re^n,$$

where A is an $n \times n$ positive definite symmetric matrix and $b \in \Re^n$ is a given vector. Consider the gradient iteration

$$x := x - \gamma \nabla F(x) = x - \gamma(Ax - b),$$

or

$$x := (I - \gamma A)x + \gamma b,$$

where γ is a positive scalar stepsize. Note that for γ sufficiently small, the synchronous version of this iteration is convergent (see Section 3.2), so we have $\rho(I - \gamma A) < 1$.

To guarantee asynchronous convergence, it is sufficient that γ and A are such that $I - \gamma A$ is a weighted maximum norm contraction. This will be true in particular if the maximum row sum of $|I - \gamma A|$ is less than 1:

$$|1 - \gamma a_{ii}| + \sum_{\{j|j \neq i\}} \gamma |a_{ij}| < 1, \qquad i = 1, \ldots, n.$$

This will be so if

$$\gamma \leq \frac{1}{a_{ii}}, \qquad \forall \, i, \tag{3.7}$$

and

$$a_{ii} > \sum_{\{j|j \neq i\}} |a_{ij}|, \qquad \forall \, i. \tag{3.8}$$

The requirement of Eq. (3.7) places an upper bound on the stepsize as in the synchronous case (Section 3.2). The requirement of Eq. (3.8) is a *diagonal dominance* condition on A. Generally, some kind of diagonal dominance condition is needed in nonlinear unconstrained optimization to be able to assert that the gradient iteration mapping is a weighted maximum norm contraction, thereby establishing asynchronous convergence (see Subsection 3.1.3).

The following example shows what can happen if the diagonal dominance condition is violated.

Example 3.1.

Consider the problem

$$\min_{x \in \Re^3} \; \frac{1}{4} \left[(x_1 + x_2 + x_3)^2 + (3 - x_1 - x_2 - x_3)^2 + 2\epsilon(x_1^2 + x_2^2 + x_3^2) \right], \tag{3.9}$$

where

$$0 < \epsilon < 1.$$

For this problem, we have

$$A = \begin{bmatrix} 1+\epsilon & 1 & 1 \\ 1 & 1+\epsilon & 1 \\ 1 & 1 & 1+\epsilon \end{bmatrix},$$

so the diagonal dominance condition (3.8) is violated. Consider now the asynchronous gradient method in a message–passing system where there is a processor assigned to each coordinate. Each processor executes the gradient iteration with a fixed stepsize γ satisfying $0 < \gamma < 1/(1 + \epsilon)$ [cf. Eq. (3.7)]. Suppose that we have initially

$$x_1(0) = x_2(0) = x_3(0) = c,$$

for some constant c. Let all processors execute their gradient iteration an equal and very large number of times without receiving any message from the other processors. In doing so, processor i, in effect, is solving the problem

$$\min_{x_i} \tfrac{1}{4}\left[(x_i + 2c)^2 + (3 - x_i - 2c)^2 + 2\epsilon(x_i^2 + 2c^2)\right],$$

that is, the single coordinate problem resulting when the other coordinates are set to the constant c. The solution of this problem is calculated to be

$$x_i = \frac{3}{2(1 + \epsilon)} - \frac{2}{(1 + \epsilon)}c.$$

After sufficiently many iterations, the coordinates x_i will be arbitrarily close to this value, so if after many iterations, the processors exchange the values of their coordinates, they will all have $x_i = \bar{c}$, with

$$\bar{c} \approx \frac{3}{2(1 + \epsilon)} - \frac{2}{(1 + \epsilon)}c.$$

For ϵ in the interval $(0, 1)$, this iteration is unstable, so if we repeat the process of a large number of gradient iterations followed by a single interprocessor communication, we will obtain a growing oscillation of the coordinates stored in the processors' memories. This example illustrates that an asynchronous gradient iteration, under a particular sequence of events, can be very similar to the nonlinear Jacobi method of Subsection 3.2.4. In particular, if the nonlinear Jacobi method diverges, then convergence of the asynchronous gradient iteration is very likely to fail.

Note that in the preceding example, we do not have $\tau_i^i(t) < t$, which was the characteristic feature of the example of the proof of Prop. 3.1. The difficulty comes from the fact that the "delays" $t - \tau_j^i(t)$, for $i \neq j$, can be arbitrarily large, in conjunction with the fact $\rho(|I - \gamma A|) > 1$ for all $\gamma > 0$. It turns out that if we imposed a bound $t - \tau_j^i(t) \leq B$ on the delays, we would be able to find sufficiently small $\bar{\gamma}(B) > 0$ such that for $0 < \gamma \leq \bar{\gamma}(B)$, the gradient iteration converges to the correct solution. The upper bound $\bar{\gamma}(B)$ and the speed of convergence depends on B. An analysis of asynchronous gradient methods when $\tau_i^i(t) = t$ and the communication delays $t - \tau_j^i(t)$ are bounded will be given in Chapter 7. The preceding example in particular will be reconsidered under a boundedness assumption on the communication delays (see Example 1.3 in Section 7.1).

6.3.3 Constrained Optimization and Variational Inequalities

Consider the problem of finding a solution $x^* \in X$ of the variational inequality

$$(x - x^*)' f(x^*) \geq 0, \qquad \forall\, x \in X, \tag{3.10}$$

where X is the Cartesian product

$$X = X_1 \times X_2 \times \cdots \times X_m \tag{3.11}$$

of nonempty closed convex sets $X_i \subset \Re^{n_i}$, $i = 1, \ldots, m$, and $f : \Re^n \mapsto \Re^n$, $n = n_1 + \cdots + n_m$, is a given function. When f is the gradient of some convex function F, that is, $f(x) = \nabla F(x)$, the variational inequality is equivalent to the optimization problem $\min_{x \in X} F(x)$ (cf. Section 3.5).

We discussed in Subsection 3.5.5 the variational inequality (3.10) and, under certain conditions on f (in effect, generalized diagonal dominance conditions), we proved convergence of several parallelizable algorithms. These are the linearized algorithm (Prop. 5.8, Subsection 3.5.5), the projection algorithm (Prop. 5.9, Subsection 3.5.5), and their nonlinear counterparts (Props. 5.11 and 5.12, Subsection 3.5.6).

In all of these algorithms, the convergence proof consists of establishing that under certain assumptions the corresponding algorithmic mapping, call it T, is a special type of pseudocontraction. In particular, T satisfies

$$\|T(x) - x^*\| \leq \alpha \|x - x^*\|, \qquad \forall\, x \in X,$$

where x^* is the unique solution of the variational inequality (3.10), $\alpha \in (0, 1)$ is some scalar, $\|\cdot\|$ is the block maximum norm $\|x\| = \max_{i=1,\ldots,m} \|x_i\|_i$ with $\|\cdot\|_i$ being some norm on $\Re^{n_i}$, and $x_i \in \Re^{n_i}$ is the ith component of x. By choosing the sets $X(k)$ as

$$X(k) = \left\{ x \in \Re^n \mid \|x - x^*\| \leq \alpha^k \|x(0) - x^*\| \right\},$$

it follows that the Synchronous Convergence and Box Conditions of Assumption 2.1 are satisfied. Therefore, the corresponding iterations converge as desired when executed asynchronously.

6.3.4 Dynamic Programming

Consider the case of a Markovian decision problem of the type discussed in Section 4.3. Here we have [cf. Eq. (3.6) in Section 4.3]

$$f(x) = T(x) = \min_{\mu \in M} \left[c(\mu) + \alpha P(\mu) x \right],$$

where $c(\mu)$ and $P(\mu)$ are the cost vector and transition probability matrix, respectively, corresponding to the stationary policy $\{\mu, \mu, \ldots\}$, and α is the discount factor. We saw in Section 4.3 that T is a contraction mapping with respect to the maximum norm when $0 < \alpha < 1$ (Prop. 3.1 of Section 4.3); see also Exercise 3.3 in Section 4.3 for the case where $\alpha = 1$. In these cases, the iteration

$$x := T(x)$$

converges to the unique fixed point of T when executed asynchronously according to the model of Section 6.1.

6.3.5 Convergence Rate Comparison of Synchronous and Asynchronous Algorithms

We now consider the convergence rate of the asynchronous fixed point algorithm

$$x_i(t + 1) = f_i\Big(x_1\big(\tau_1^i(t)\big), \ldots, x_n\big(\tau_n^i(t)\big)\Big), \qquad \forall\, t \geq 0. \tag{3.12}$$

We assume that f is a contraction with respect to the maximum norm, with a unique fixed point denoted by x^*. The reader should have no difficulty in extending the results to the case of a more general (weighted) maximum norm. Our analysis can be understood in terms of the discussion of Subsection 1.4.2, and the example given in that subsection. We show that with bounded communication delays, the convergence rate is geometric and, under certain conditions, it is superior to the convergence rate of the corresponding synchronous iteration.

For simplicity, we will assume that the time required for a variable update is constant and, without loss of generality, equal to one time unit. We are primarily interested in a comparison with the corresponding synchronous algorithm in which the next iteration is executed only after all messages from the previous iteration are received. To make a fair comparison, we will assume that in the asynchronous algorithm, the processors keep computing at the maximum possible speed, while simultaneously transmitting messages to other processors. Thus, all variables are updated according to Eq. (3.12) at every time t. We also assume that the communication delays are bounded; otherwise the algorithm could be arbitrarily slow. We thus assume that there exists an integer B such that

$$t - B \leq \tau_j^i(t) \leq t, \qquad \forall\, i, j, t. \tag{3.13}$$

A characteristic feature of the asynchronous algorithm is that different variables are incorporated in the computations with different communication delays. To simplify the following analysis, we assume only two sizes of communication delays; extensions to more general cases are possible (Exercise 3.2). In particular, we assume that for each index i, there is a nonempty subset of coordinates $F(i)$ and a nonnegative integer b such that

$$0 \le b < B,$$

$$t - \tau_j^i(t) \le b, \qquad \forall\, t,\ i = 1,\ldots,n,\ \text{and}\ j \in F(i). \tag{3.14}$$

The interpretation here is that the variables x_j, $j \in F(i)$, are "special" in that they are communicated "fast" to the processor updating x_i (within $b < B$ time units). An example is when each processor i updates only variable x_i, and keeps the latest value of x_i in local memory, in which case, we can take $F(i) = \{i\}$ and $b = 0$. Another example arises in a hierarchical processor interconnection network when $F(i)$ represents a cluster of processors within which communication is fast.

We will consider the following two conditions:

Assumption 3.1.   There exist scalars $\alpha \in [0,1)$ and $A \in [0,1)$ such that

$$|f_i(x) - x_i^*| \le \max\left\{ \alpha \max_{j \in F(i)} |x_j - x_j^*|,\ A \max_{j \notin F(i)} |x_j - x_j^*| \right\}, \qquad \forall\, x \in \Re^n,\ i = 1,\ldots,n. \tag{3.15}$$

Assumption 3.2.   There exist scalars $\alpha \ge 0$ and $A \ge 0$ with $\alpha + A < 1$, and such that

$$|f_i(x) - x_i^*| \le \alpha \max_{j \in F(i)} |x_j - x_j^*| + A \max_{j \notin F(i)} |x_j - x_j^*|, \qquad \forall\, x \in \Re^n,\ i = 1,\ldots,n. \tag{3.16}$$

When f is linear of the form $f(x) = Qx + b$, where Q is an $n \times n$ matrix with elements denoted q_{ij}, then Eq. (3.16) holds with

$$\alpha = \max_{i=1,\ldots,n} \sum_{j \in F(i)} |q_{ij}|, \qquad A = \max_{i=1,\ldots,n} \sum_{j \notin F(i)} |q_{ij}|.$$

The primary interest is in the case $A < \alpha$, in which case there is "strong coupling" between x_i and the "special" variables x_j, $j \in F(i)$, which are communicated "fast" to the processor updating x_i [cf. Eq. (3.14)].

The following proposition gives a bound on the convergence rate of the asynchronous iteration (3.12):

Proposition 3.2.   The sequence of vectors generated by the asynchronous iteration (3.12) satisfies

$$\|x(t) - x^*\|_\infty \le \rho_A^t \|x(0) - x^*\|_\infty \tag{3.17}$$

where:

(a) If Assumption 3.1 holds, ρ_A is the unique nonnegative solution of the equation

$$\rho = \max\left\{ \alpha \rho^{-b},\ A \rho^{-B} \right\}. \tag{3.18}$$

(b) If Assumption 3.2 holds, ρ_A is the unique nonnegative solution of the equation

$$\rho = \alpha\rho^{-b} + A\rho^{-B}. \tag{3.19}$$

Proof. Let Assumption 3.1 hold. We use induction. For $t = 0$, the desired relation (3.17) holds. Assume that it holds for all t up to some $\bar{t}$. Since there is an update at $\bar{t}$ by assumption, we have

$$x_i(\bar{t} + 1) = f_i\Big(x_1\big(\tau_1^i(\bar{t})\big), \ldots, x_n\big(\tau_n^i(\bar{t})\big)\Big).$$

Therefore, using the assumptions (3.14), (3.15), (3.18) and the induction hypothesis

$$|x_i(\bar{t}+1) - x_i^*| \leq \max\left\{\alpha \max_{j \in F(i)} |x_j\big(\tau_j^i(\bar{t})\big) - x_j^*|, \; A \max_{j \notin F(i)} |x_j\big(\tau_j^i(\bar{t})\big) - x_j^*|\right\}$$

$$\leq \max\left\{\alpha\rho_A^{\bar{t}-b}, \; A\rho_A^{\bar{t}-B}\right\}\|x(0) - x^*\|_\infty = \rho_A^{\bar{t}+1}\|x(0) - x^*\|_\infty,$$

and the induction proof is complete. The proof under Assumption 3.2 is entirely similar and is omitted.   **Q.E.D.**

Figure 6.3.1 illustrates the method for determining the asynchronous convergence rate coefficient ρ_A and compares it with ρ_S, which is the corresponding coefficient for the synchronous version of the fixed point iteration (3.12). It can be seen that $\rho_A < \rho_S$ if $A < \alpha$ and Assumption 3.1 holds or if $0 < \alpha$ and Assumption 3.2 holds. In these cases the convergence rate estimate of the asynchronous algorithm is superior to that of its synchronous counterpart. Its communication complexity, however, can be worse, as discussed in Subsection 1.4.2.

EXERCISES

3.1. Use the function $f : \Re^2 \mapsto \Re^2$ defined by $f_1(x_1, x_2) = 0$ and $f_2(x_1, x_2) = x_1 x_2$ to construct a counterexample to the following statement (which is true when f is linear):

If $X = \Re^n$, f is continuous and has a unique fixed point x^* within $\Re^n$, and all the sequences $\{x(t)\}$ generated by the asynchronous iteration (1.1) converge to x^*, then there must exist $w > 0$ such that

$$\|f(x) - x^*\|_\infty^w < \|x - x^*\|_\infty^w, \qquad \forall \, x \neq x^*.$$

3.2. For each i consider a partition $F_1(i) \cup \cdots \cup F_m(i)$ of the index set $\{1, \ldots, n\}$, where $m \geq 2$ is some integer, and suppose that for some nonnegative integers $b_1, \ldots, b_m$, we have

$$t - \tau_j^i(t) \leq b_k, \qquad \forall \, t, \; i = 1, \ldots, n, \; \text{and} \; j \in F_k(i).$$

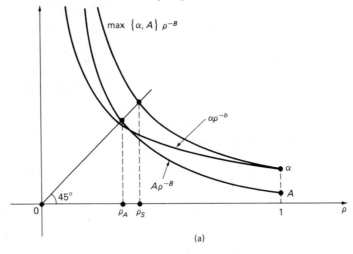

(a)

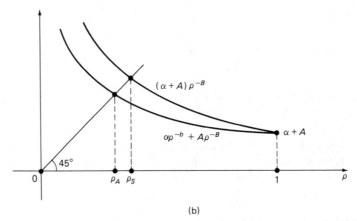

(b)

Figure 6.3.1 Comparison of the convergence rates of the asynchronous iteration (3.12) and its synchronous counterpart under (a) Assumption 3.1 and (b) Assumption 3.2. The synchronous algorithm executes an iteration every $(B + 1)$ time units, after the results of all updates from the previous iteration are known to all processors. Its convergence rate coefficient is $\rho_S = \left(\max\{\alpha, A\}\right)^{1/(B+1)}$ under Assumption 3.1, and $\rho_S = (\alpha + A)^{1/(B+1)}$ under Assumption 3.2. The convergence rate of the asynchronous algorithm is superior when $A < \alpha$ and Assumption 3.1 holds or $0 < \alpha$ and Assumption 3.2 holds.

Provide an analog of Prop. 3.2 under the assumption

$$|f_i(x) - x_i^*| \leq \max_{k=1,\ldots,m}\left\{\alpha_k \max_{j \in F_k(i)} |x_j - x_j^*|\right\}, \qquad i = 1,\ldots,n,$$

where $\alpha_k \in [0, 1)$, and under the assumption

$$|f_i(x) - x_i^*| \leq \sum_{k=1}^{m} \alpha_k \max_{j \in F_k(i)} |x_j - x_j^*|,$$

where $\sum_{k=1}^{m} \alpha_k < 1$, $\alpha_k \geq 0$.

6.4 APPLICATIONS TO MONOTONE MAPPINGS AND THE SHORTEST PATH PROBLEM

In this section, we show how the Asynchronous Convergence Theorem can be applied to fixed point iterations involving monotone mappings. A special case is the Bellman–Ford algorithm for the shortest path problem discussed in Section 4.3.

Consider the asynchronous algorithmic model of Section 6.1. Suppose that each set X_i is a subset of $[-\infty, +\infty]$, and that f is monotone in the sense that for all x and y in the set $X = \prod_{i=1}^{n} X_i$ we have

$$x \leq y \quad \Longrightarrow \quad f(x) \leq f(y), \tag{4.1}$$

where the inequalities are interpreted coordinatewise.

Suppose also that there exists a unique fixed point x^* of f in X and two vectors $\underline{x}$ and $\bar{x}$ in X such that

$$\underline{x} \leq f(\underline{x}) \leq f(\bar{x}) \leq \bar{x}, \tag{4.2}$$

and

$$\lim_{k \to \infty} f^k(\underline{x}) = \lim_{k \to \infty} f^k(\bar{x}) = x^*. \tag{4.3}$$

In the preceding equation $f^k(\cdot)$ is the composition of f with itself k times, and $f^0(\cdot)$ is the identity mapping. The monotonicity condition (4.2) implies that

$$f^k(\underline{x}) \leq f^{k+1}(\underline{x}) \leq x^* \leq f^{k+1}(\bar{x}) \leq f^k(\bar{x}), \qquad \forall \ k,$$

and, therefore, also implies the convergence condition (4.3) if $X \subset R^n$ and f is a continuous function on X.

Define the sets

$$X(k) = \big\{ x \mid f^k(\underline{x}) \leq x \leq f^k(\bar{x}) \big\}. \tag{4.4}$$

It is seen that the Synchronous Convergence and Box Conditions of Assumption 2.1 are satisfied, and, therefore, the Asynchronous Convergence Theorem applies.

The main difficulty in using the theorem is to establish the existence of vectors $\underline{x}$ and $\bar{x}$ for which the monotonicity and convergence conditions (4.2) and (4.3) hold. To prove this, one must use special features of the problem at hand.

One situation where the underlying mapping is monotone arises in network flow problems. As an example, consider the constrained matrix problem of Subsection 5.5.4. The relaxation mappings corresponding to the quadratic and logarithmic cost functions given there can be seen to be monotone. As a result, asynchronous convergence can be shown for a modified version of the relaxation method of Section 5.5. This will be shown in more general form in Section 6.6.

The underlying mapping is also monotone in the Markovian decision problems of Section 4.3. Based on the Undiscounted Cost Assumption 3.2 and Props. 3.1 and 3.3 of that section, it is seen that the monotonicity and convergence conditions (4.2) and (4.3) are satisfied for the undiscounted problem with

$$\underline{x}_i = x_i^* - \Delta, \qquad \bar{x}_i = x_i^* + \Delta, \qquad i = 2, \ldots, n, \tag{4.5a}$$

$$\underline{x}_1 = x_1 = \bar{x}_1 = 0, \tag{4.5b}$$

where x_i^* is the optimal cost starting at state i, and Δ is any positive scalar. In the case of a shortest path problem we can also choose $\bar{x}_i = \infty$ for $i \neq 1$ (see Prop. 1.1 in Section 4.1). Therefore, the Asynchronous Convergence Theorem applies, showing that the dynamic programming algorithm converges from arbitrary initial conditions when executed asynchronously. We now discuss the special case of the Bellman–Ford algorithm for the shortest path problem in more detail.

The Shortest Path Problem

Consider the shortest path problem under the Connectivity and Positive Cycle Assumptions 1.1 and 1.2 of Section 4.1 (node 1 is the only destination). It was seen in that section that if the initial condition in the Bellman–Ford algorithm

$$x_i := \min_{j \in A(i)} (a_{ij} + x_j), \qquad i = 2, \ldots, n, \tag{4.6a}$$

$$x_1 = 0, \tag{4.6b}$$

is chosen to be equal to either the vector $\underline{x}$ or the vector $\bar{x}$ of Eq. (4.5), then convergence is obtained in a finite number of iterations. Therefore, for all k sufficiently large, the sets $X(k)$ of Eq. (4.4) consist of just the shortest distance vector x^*. It follows from the Asynchronous Convergence Theorem that the asynchronous version of the Bellman–Ford iteration

$$x_i(t+1) = \min_{j \in A(i)} \left(a_{ij} + x_j\big(\tau_j^i(t)\big) \right), \qquad i = 2, \ldots, n, \ t \in T^i,$$

$$x_1(t+1) = 0,$$

terminates with the correct shortest distances in finite time.

We will now consider an implementation of the asynchronous Bellman–Ford algorithm, which is of particular relevance to communication networks; see Chapter 5 of [BeG87]. We will compare this algorithm with its synchronous counterpart for the initial conditions $\bar{x}_i = \infty$, $i \neq 1$, in terms of the amount of time, and communication needed to solve the problem. We assume that at each node $i \neq 1$, there is a processor updating x_i according to the Bellman–Ford iteration (4.6a). The value of x_i available at node i at time t is denoted by $x_i(t)$. For each arc (i, j), $j \in A(i)$, there is a communication link along which j can send messages to i. When x_j is updated and, as a result, its value actually changes, the new value of x_j is immediately sent to every processor i for which (i, j) is an arc. If the updating leaves the value of x_j unchanged, no communication takes place. Let t_{ij} be the time required for a message to traverse arc (i, j) in the direction from j to i. We assume that this time is the same for all messages that traverse (i, j), and, in particular, that the messages are received on each arc in the order they are sent. When a processor i receives a message containing a value of x_j, for some $j \in A(i)$, it stores it in place of the preexisting value of x_j and updates x_i according to the Bellman–Ford iteration (4.6a) using the values of $x_{j'}$ latest received from all $j' \in A(i)$ (if no value of $x_{j'}$ has been received as yet, node i uses $x_{j'} = \infty$ for $j' \neq 1$ and $x_1 = 0$ for $j' = 1$). It is assumed that an update requires negligible time, modeling a situation where an update requires much less time than a message transmission. We adopt the convention that if there is an update at node j at time t, $x_j(t)$ is the value of x_j just *after* the update. Regarding initialization, we assume that each node j sends at time 0 its initial estimate

$$x_j(0) = \begin{cases} 0, & \text{if } j = 1, \\ \infty, & \text{otherwise,} \end{cases} \tag{4.7}$$

to all nodes i with $j \in A(i)$. We say that the algorithm terminates at time t if, for each i, $x_i(t)$ is equal to the shortest distance x_i^* from i to 1. Because of the preceding choice of initial conditions and the monotonicity of the Bellman–Ford iteration (4.6), it is seen that the estimates $x_i(t)$ are monotonically nonincreasing to their final values x_i^*.

To visualize the asynchronous algorithm, it is helpful to consider (somewhat informally) an equivalent algorithmic process. Imagine, for each path p that ends at node 1, a "token" that travels along the path in the reverse direction, starting from node 1 at time 0, and requiring the same time to traverse each link as any other message. If the token reaches a node i on the path at time t, and the sum of the lengths of the arcs that it has traversed is lower than the estimate of the shortest distance of i at the time of arrival, then $x_i(t)$ is set equal to this sum and the token is allowed to proceed to the next node on the path (if any); otherwise the token is discarded and its travel is stopped. (If more than one token arrives at a node simultaneously, only the ones with smallest sum of arc lengths are allowed to proceed to the next node on their respective paths, assuming that they cause a reduction of the estimate of shortest distance of the node.) It can be seen then that link traversals by the tokens can be associated, on a one–to–one basis, with transmissions of messages carrying shortest distance estimates in the asynchronous Bellman–Ford algorithm. Furthermore, for each node i, $x_i(t)$ is equal to the minimum length over all lengths of paths that terminate at i and whose tokens have arrived at i at some time $t' \leq t$.

We denote the length of a path p consisting of arcs $(i_1, i_2), \ldots, (i_k, i_{k+1})$ by

$$L_p = \sum_{m=1}^{k} a_{i_m i_{m+1}}, \tag{4.8}$$

and we define the communication time of p as

$$t_p = \sum_{m=1}^{k} t_{i_m i_{m+1}}. \tag{4.9}$$

Denote for any $i \neq 1$

$$P_i(t) = \text{Set of paths } p \text{ with } t_p \leq t \text{ that start at } i \text{ and end at } 1. \tag{4.10}$$

From the preceding observations, it is seen with a little thought that the shortest distance estimate of node i at time t is

$$x_i(t) = \begin{cases} \infty, & \text{if } P_i(t) \text{ is empty,} \\ \min_{p \in P_i(t)} L_p, & \text{otherwise.} \end{cases} \tag{4.11}$$

Consider now a synchronous version of the algorithm. Here each processor i performs the $(k+1)$st update·immediately upon receiving the results of the kth update from all processors $j \in A(i)$, that is, the local synchronization method of Subsection 1.4.1 is used. Note that we require that each processor j send the result of each update to all processors i for which $j \in A(i)$, whether or not this result is different from the result of the previous update. For $i \neq 1$, let P_i^k be the set of paths that start at i, end at 1, and have k arcs or less. Denote

$$k_i(t) = \max\{k \mid t_p \leq t, \ \forall \ p \in P_i^k\}. \tag{4.12}$$

Thus, $k_i(t)$ is the number of synchronous Bellman–Ford iterations reflected by the shortest distance estimate of i at time t. Then it is seen (Exercise 4.3) that the shortest distance estimate at node i at time t for the synchronous algorithm is

$$x_i^S(t) = \begin{cases} \infty, & \text{if } P_i^{k_i(t)}(t) \text{ is empty,} \\ \min_{p \in P_i^{k_i(t)}(t)} L_p, & \text{otherwise.} \end{cases} \tag{4.13}$$

We now observe that for all i and t, we have $P_i^{k_i(t)} \subset P_i(t)$. The reason is that for each path $p \in P_i^{k_i(t)}$, we have from Eq. (4.12) $t_p \leq t$, which, using Eq. (4.10), implies that $p \in P_i(t)$. It follows from Eqs. (4.11) and (4.13) that

$$x_i(t) \leq x_i^S(t), \qquad \forall \ t,$$

and hence the synchronous algorithm cannot terminate faster than the asynchronous algorithm.

Unfortunately, the asynchronous Bellman–Ford algorithm can require many more message transmissions than synchronous versions of the algorithm. Figures 6.4.1 and

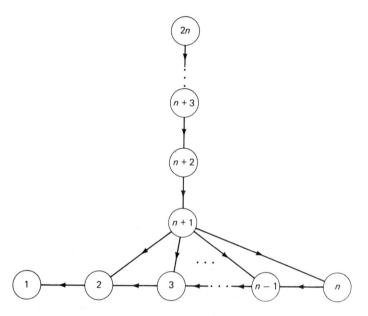

Figure 6.4.1   An example where the asynchronous version of the Bellman–Ford algorithm requires many more message transmissions than a synchronous version (from [BeG87]). All arc lengths are unity. The initial estimates of shortest distance of all nodes are ∞. Consider the following sequence of events:

1. Node 2 updates its shortest distance and communicates the result to node 3. Node 3 updates and communicates the result to 4.... Node $n - 1$ updates and communicates the result to node n. Node n updates and communicates the result to $n + 1$. (These are $n - 1$ messages.)

2. Node $n + 1$ updates and communicates the result to node $n + 2$.... Node $2n - 1$ updates and communicates the result to node $2n$. Node $2n$ updates. (These are $n - 1$ messages.)

3. For $i = n - 1, n - 2, \ldots, 2$, in that order, node i communicates its update to node $n + 1$ and the sequence of step 2 is repeated. [These are $n(n - 2)$ messages.]

The total number of messages is $n^2 - 2$. Only $\Theta(n)$ messages would be needed in a synchronous version of the algorithm where the global synchronization method with timeouts is used (cf. Subsection 1.4.1), and where a message is sent by a node j to all nodes i with $j \in A(i)$ only when an update changes the value x_j. The difficulty in the asynchronous version is that a great deal of unimportant information arrives at node $n + 1$ early and triggers many unnecessary messages starting from $n + 1$ and proceeding all the way to $2n$. The total number of distance changes in this example is $\Theta(n^2)$. Generally, for a shortest path problem with n nodes and unity arc lengths it can be shown that in the asynchronous Bellman–Ford algorithm with $x_i(0) = \infty$, $i \neq 1$, there can be at most $n - 1$ distance changes for each node (Exercise 4.2). By contrast, only one distance change per node is needed in the synchronous version of the algorithm.

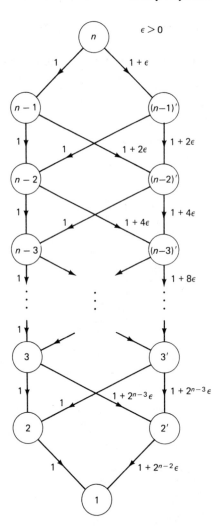

Figure 6.4.2 An example of a shortest path problem where the asynchronous Bellman–Ford algorithm requires an exponentially large number of messages for termination starting from the initial condition $x_i(0) = \infty$, $i \neq 1$ (due to E. M. Gafni and R. G. Gallager, a private communication). The arc lengths are shown next to the arcs. Suppose that the communication delays of the arcs are such that the communication time of a path from each node i to node 1 is larger as the length of the path is smaller, that is, for all paths p and p', we have

$$L_p < L_{p'} \quad \Rightarrow \quad t_p > t_{p'},$$

(such a choice of arc delays is possible for this example). Then the distance $x_n(t)$ of node n will change a number of times equal to the number of paths from n to 1, which is 2^{n-2}.

6.4.2 provide two examples. Both examples represent worst case (and rather unlikely) scenarios.

EXERCISES

4.1. This exercise comes from packet radio communications ([BeG87], p. 277). We have a set of n transmitters that transmit data in intervals of unit time (also called *slots*). Each transmitter i transmits in a slot with probability p_i independently of the history of past transmissions. For each transmitter i, there is a set S_i of other transmitters such that if i transmits simultaneously with one or more transmitters in S_i, the transmission is unsuccessful. Then the success rate (or throughput) of transmitter i is

$$t_i = p_i \prod_{j \in S_i} (1 - p_j).$$

We want to find the probabilities p_i, $i = 1, \ldots, n$, that realize a given set of throughputs t_i, $i = 1, \ldots, n$, that is, solve the system of the above n nonlinear equations for the n unknowns p_j. For this, we use the iteration

$$p_i := \frac{t_i}{\prod_{j \in S_i} (1 - p_j)}$$

implemented in totally asynchronous format. Show that, if there exists a set of feasible probabilities, the iteration will converge to a unique such set of probabilities when initiated at $p_i = 0$ for all i.

4.2. Consider the asynchronous Bellman–Ford algorithm for an n–node shortest path problem with all arc lengths being unity. Assume that initially $x_i(0) = \infty$ for all $i \neq 1$. Show that there are less than n changes of x_i at each node i. *Hint:* Each node's estimate of shortest distance is nonincreasing and can only take the values $1, 2, \ldots, n - 1$ and ∞.

4.3. Consider the synchronous Bellman–Ford algorithm with the local synchronization method, and show Eq. (4.13). *Hint:* Define

$$t_i(0) = 0, \qquad \forall \, i = 1, \ldots, n,$$

$$t_i(k + 1) = \begin{cases} \max_{\{j \mid (i,j) \in A\}} \{t_{ij} + t_j(k)\}, & \text{if } i \neq 1 \\ 0, & \text{otherwise.} \end{cases}$$

Show that each node $i \neq 1$ will execute its kth iteration at time $t_i(k)$.

4.4. (Asynchronous Forward Search.) Consider an asynchronous version of the forward search shortest path algorithm of Exercise 1.10(a) of Section 4.1 (we use the same notation as in that exercise). In this version, d_j is updated at times $t \in T^j$ according to

$$d_j(t + 1) = \begin{cases} \min_{i \in L^j(t)} \left(d_i \left(\tau_i^j(t) \right) + a_{ij} \right), & \text{if } \min_{i \in L^j(t)} \left(d_i \left(\tau_i^j(t) \right) + a_{ij} \right) \\ & \qquad < \min \left\{ d_j(t), d_1 \left(\tau_1^j(t) \right) - h_j \right\}, \\ d_j(t), & \text{otherwise,} \end{cases}$$

$$(4.14)$$

where $L^j(t)$ is a subset of the set $\{i \mid j \in A(i)\}$. Assume that $d_s(0) = 0$ and $d_j(0) = \infty$ for all $j \neq s$. Assume also that for every j, each node $i \in \{k \mid j \in A(k)\}$ belongs to infinitely many sets $L^j(t)$, $t \in T^j$ and that the Total Asynchronism Assumption 1.1 holds. [Note, however, that we have $\tau_j^j(t) = t$ in Eq. (4.14).] Show that $d_1(t)$ will be equal to the shortest distance from s to 1 for all sufficiently large t. *Hint:* Show that for each i, $d_i(t)$ is monotonically nonincreasing and can take only a finite number of values.

6.5 LINEAR NETWORK FLOW PROBLEMS

In this section, we discuss some of the asynchronous distributed implementation aspects of the linear network flow problems of Chapter 5. There is a natural asynchronous version of the auction algorithm of Subsection 5.3.1 in an environment where there is a processor assigned to each person and a processor assigned to each object, and the processors communicate with each other via an interconnection network. Here there is no strict separation between the bidding and the assignment phases, and each unassigned person/processor can bid at arbitrary times on the basis of object price information that can be outdated because of additional bidding of which the person is not informed. Furthermore, the assignment of objects can be decided even if some potential bidders have not been heard from. We can show the same termination properties as for the synchronous version of the algorithm subject to two conditions stated somewhat informally:

(a) An unassigned person/processor will bid for some object within finite time and cannot simultaneously bid for more than one object (i.e., it cannot bid for a second object while waiting for a response regarding the disposition of an earlier bid for another object).

(b) Whenever one or more bids are received that raise the price of an object, then within finite time, the updated price of the object must be communicated (not necessarily simultaneously) to all persons that can be assigned to the object. Furthermore, the new person that is assigned to the object must be informed of this fact simultaneously with receiving the new price.

A similar implementation is possible when there are relatively few processors and each processor is assigned to several persons and objects. There is also a straightforward asynchronous implementation of the auction algorithm in a shared memory machine, which is similar to a synchronous implementation except that there is no strict separation between the bidding and the assignment phases; some processors may be calculating person bids while some other processors may be simultaneously updating object prices. We do not give a precise formulation and a proof of validity of these implementations. We will concentrate instead on the more challenging case of the general linear network flow problem

$$\text{minimize} \quad \sum_{(i,j)\in A} a_{ij} f_{ij} \tag{LNF}$$

$$\text{subject to} \quad \sum_{\{j|(i,j)\in A\}} f_{ij} - \sum_{\{j|(j,i)\in A\}} f_{ji} = s_i, \quad \forall\, i \in N,$$

$$b_{ij} \leq f_{ij} \leq c_{ij}, \quad \forall\, (i,j) \in A,$$

where a_{ij}, b_{ij}, c_{ij}, and s_i are given integers. We introduce a distributed totally asynchronous version of the ϵ–relaxation method of Section 5.3, and show that it converges finitely.

We assume that each node i is a processor that updates its own price and incident arc flows, and exchanges information with its forward adjacent nodes

$$F_i = \{j \mid (i,j) \in A\},$$

and its backward adjacent nodes

$$B_i = \{j \mid (j, i) \in A\}.$$

The following distributed asynchronous implementation applies to both the ϵ-relaxation method of Section 5.3 and to the subproblems of the scaled version discussed in Section 5.4. The information available at node i for any time t is as follows:

$p_i(t)$: The price of node i

$p_j(i, t)$: The price of node $j \in F_i \cup B_i$ communicated by j at some earlier time

$f_{ij}(i, t)$: The estimate of the flow of arc (i, j), $j \in F_i$, available at node i at time t

$f_{ji}(i, t)$: The estimate of the flow of arc (j, i), $j \in B_i$, available at node i at time t

$g_i(t)$: The estimate of the surplus of node i at time t given by

$$g_i(t) = \sum_{(j,i) \in A} f_{ji}(i, t) - \sum_{(i,j) \in A} f_{ij}(i, t) + s_i. \tag{5.1}$$

A more precise description of the algorithmic model is possible, but for brevity, we will keep our description somewhat informal. We assume that for every node i, the quantities just listed do not change except possibly at an increasing sequence of times $t_0, t_1, \ldots$, with $t_m \to \infty$. At each of these times, generically denoted by t, and at each node i, one of three events happens:

Event 1. Node i does nothing.

Event 2. Node i checks $g_i(t)$. If $g_i(t) < 0$, node i does nothing further. Otherwise node i executes either an up iteration or a partial up iteration (cf. Section 5.3) based on the available price and flow information

$$p_i(t), \qquad p_j(i, t), \; j \in F_i \cup B_i, \qquad f_{ij}(i, t), \; j \in F_i, \qquad f_{ji}(i, t), \; j \in B_i,$$

and accordingly changes

$$p_i(t), \qquad f_{ij}(i, t), \; j \in F_i, \qquad f_{ji}(i, t), \; j \in B_i.$$

Event 3. Node i receives, from one or more adjacent nodes $j \in F_i \cup B_i$, a message containing the corresponding price and arc flow $\big(p_j(t'), f_{ij}(j, t')\big)$ (in the case $j \in F_i$) or $\big(p_j(t'), f_{ji}(j, t')\big)$ (in the case $j \in B_i$) stored at j at some earlier time $t' < t$. If

$$p_j(t') < p_j(i, t),$$

node i discards the message and does nothing further. Otherwise node i stores the received value $p_j(t')$ in place of $p_j(i, t)$. In addition, if $j \in F_i$, node i stores $f_{ij}(j, t')$ in place of $f_{ij}(i, t)$ if

$$p_i(t) < p_j(t') + a_{ij}, \qquad \text{and} \qquad f_{ij}(j, t') < f_{ij}(i, t),$$

and otherwise leaves $f_{ij}(i, t)$ unchanged; in the case $j \in B_i$, node i stores $f_{ji}(j, t')$ in place of $f_{ji}(i, t)$ if

$$p_j(t') \geq p_i(t) + a_{ji}, \qquad \text{and} \qquad f_{ji}(j, t') > f_{ji}(i, t),$$

and otherwise leaves $f_{ji}(i, t)$ unchanged. (Thus, in case of a balanced arc, the "tie" is broken in favor of the flow of the start node of the arc.)

Let T^i be the set of times for which an update by node i is attempted as in Event 2, and let $T^i(j)$ be the set of times when a message is received at i from j, as in Event 3. We assume the following:

Assumption 5.1. Nodes never stop attempting to execute an up iteration, and receiving messages from all their adjacent nodes, that is, T^i and $T^i(j)$ have an infinite number of elements for all i and $j \in F_i \cup B_i$.

Assumption 5.2. Old information is eventually purged from the system, that is, given any time t_k, there exists a time $t_m \geq t_k$ such that the time of generation of the price and flow information received at any node after t_m (i.e., the time t' in Event 3), exceeds t_k.

Assumption 5.3. For each i, the initial arc flows $f_{ij}(i, t_0)$, $j \in F_i$, and $f_{ji}(i, t_0)$, $j \in B_i$, are integer and satisfy ϵ–CS together with $p_i(t_0)$ and $p_j(i, t_0)$, $j \in F_i \cup B_i$. Furthermore, there holds

$$p_i(t_0) \geq p_i(j, t_0), \qquad \forall\, j \in F_i \cup B_i,$$

$$f_{ij}(i, t_0) \geq f_{ij}(j, t_0), \qquad \forall\, j \in F_i.$$

Assumptions 5.1 and 5.2 are similar to the Total Asynchronism Assumption 1.1 of Section 6.1. One set of initial conditions satisfying Assumption 5.3 but requiring very little cooperation between processors is $p_j(i, t_0) \approx -\infty$ for all i and $j \in F_i \cup B_i$, $f_{ij}(i, t_0) = c_{ij}$ and $f_{ij}(j, t_0) = b_{ij}$ for all i and $j \in F_i$. Assumption 5.3 guarantees that for all $t \geq t_0$,

$$p_i(t) \geq p_i(j, t''), \qquad \forall\, j \in F_i \cup B_i,\ t'' \leq t. \tag{5.2}$$

To see this, note that $p_i(t)$ is monotonically nondecreasing in t and $p_i(j, t'')$ equals $p_i(t')$ for some $t' < t''$.

An important fact is that for all nodes i and times t, $f_{ij}(i, t)$ and $f_{ji}(i, t)$ are integer and satisfy ϵ–CS together with $p_i(t)$ and $p_j(i, t)$, $j \in F_i \cup B_i$. This is seen from Eq. (5.2), the logic of the up iteration, and the rules for accepting information from adjacent nodes.

Another important fact is that for all i and $t > t_0$

$$f_{ij}(i, t) \geq f_{ij}(j, t), \qquad \forall\, j \in F_i, \tag{5.3}$$

that is, the start node of an arc has at least as high an estimate of arc flow as the end node. For a given $(i, j) \in A$, condition (5.3) holds initially by Assumption 5.3 and it is preserved by up iterations since an up iteration at i cannot decrease $f_{ij}(i, t)$ and an up iteration at j cannot increase $f_{ij}(j, t)$. Therefore, Eq. (5.3) can first be violated only at the time of a message reception. To show that this cannot happen throughout the algorithm, we argue by contradiction: suppose Eq. (5.3) first fails to hold at some time t, implying

$$f_{ij}(i, t) < f_{ij}(j, t). \tag{5.4}$$

Let r be the last time up to or including t that i accepted a message from j that reduced i's flow estimate for (i, j), and let r' be the time that this message originated at j. Similarly, let s be the last time up to or including t that j increased its flow estimate for (i, j), and s' be the time the message responsible was sent from i. Using Assumption 5.3, it can be seen that both of these times must exist, for otherwise the violation of Eq. (5.4) cannot have occurred (note also that $t = \max\{r, s\}$). The acceptance of these messages at times r and s implies

$$p_i(r) < p_j(r') + a_{ij}, \tag{5.5}$$

$$p_i(s') \geq p_j(s) + a_{ij}. \tag{5.6}$$

It also follows that $r' \leq s$ and $s' \leq r$ or, again, the violation at time t could not have occurred. By the monotonicity of prices, it then follows that

$$p_i(r') \leq p_i(s), \qquad p_i(s') \leq p_i(r).$$

Substituting these into Eqs. (5.5) and (5.6), respectively, one obtains

$$p_i(r) < p_j(s) + a_{ij}, \tag{5.7a}$$

$$p_i(r) \geq p_j(s) + a_{ij}, \tag{5.7b}$$

a contradiction. Thus, Eq. (5.3) must always hold for all $(i, j) \in A$.

Note that once a node i has nonnegative surplus $g_i(t) \geq 0$, it maintains a nonnegative surplus for all subsequent times. The reason is that an up iteration at i can at most decrease $g_i(t)$ to zero, whereas, in view of the rules for accepting a communicated arc flow, a message exchange with an adjacent node j can only increase $g_i(t)$. Note also that from Eq. (5.3) we obtain

$$\sum_i g_i(t) \leq 0, \qquad \forall\, t \geq t_0. \tag{5.8}$$

This implies that at any time t, there is at least one node i with negative surplus $g_i(t)$ if there is a node with positive surplus. This node i must not have executed any up iteration up to t, and, therefore, its price $p_i(t)$ must still be equal to the initial price $p_i(t_0)$.

We say that the algorithm *terminates* if there is a time t_k such that for all $t \geq t_k$, we have

$$g_i(t) = 0, \qquad\qquad \forall\, i \in N, \tag{5.9}$$

$$f_{ij}(i,t) = f_{ij}(j,t), \qquad \forall\, (i,j) \in A, \tag{5.10}$$

$$p_j(t) = p_j(i,t), \qquad\quad \forall\, j \in F_i \cup B_i, \tag{5.11}$$

a flow–price vector pair satisfying ϵ–CS is then obtained. Termination can be detected by using a method to be discussed in Section 8.1.

Proposition 5.1.   If problem (LNF) is feasible and Assumptions 5.1–5.3 hold, the algorithm terminates.

Proof.   Suppose no up iterations are executed at any node after some time t^*. Then Eq. (5.9) must hold for large enough t. Because no up iterations occur after t^*, all the $p_i(t)$ must remain constant after t^*, and Assumption 5.1, Eq. (5.2), and the message acceptance rules imply Eq. (5.11). After t^*, furthermore, no flow estimates can change except by message reception. By Eq. (5.11), the nodes will eventually agree on whether each arc is active, inactive, or balanced. The message reception rules, Eq. (5.3), Assumptions 5.1 and 5.2 then imply the eventual agreement on arc flows as in Eq. (5.10). (Eventually, the start node of each inactive arc will accept the flow of the end node, and the end node of a balanced or active arc will accept the flow of the start node.)

We assume, therefore, the contrary, that is, that up iterations are executed indefinitely, and, hence, for every t, there is a time $t' > t$ and a node i such that $g_i(t') > 0$. There are two possibilities: the first is that $p_i(t)$ converges to a finite value p_i for every i. In this case, we assume without loss of generality that there is at least one node i at which an infinite number of up iterations are executed and an adjacent arc (i,j) whose flow $f_{ij}(i,t)$ is changed by an integer amount an infinite number of times with (i,j) being ϵ^+–balanced. For this to happen, there must be a reduction of $f_{ij}(i,t)$ through communication from j an infinite number of times. This means that $f_{ij}(j,t)$ is reduced an infinite number of times, which can happen only if an infinite number of up iterations are executed at j with (i,j) being ϵ^-–balanced. But this is impossible since, when p_i and p_j converge, arc (i,j) cannot become both ϵ^+–balanced and ϵ^-–balanced an infinite number of times.

The second possibility is that there is a nonempty subset of nodes N^∞ whose prices increase to ∞. From Eq. (5.8), it is seen that there is at least one node that has negative surplus for all t and, therefore, also a constant price. It follows that N^∞ is a strict subset of N. Since the algorithm maintains ϵ–CS, we have for all sufficiently large t that

$$f_{ij}(i,t) = f_{ij}(j,t) = c_{ij} \qquad \forall \ (i,j) \in A \ \text{ with } \ i \in N^\infty, \ j \in N^\infty,$$

$$f_{ji}(i,t) = f_{ji}(j,t) = b_{ji} \qquad \forall \ (j,i) \in A \ \text{ with } \ i \in N^\infty, \ j \in N^\infty.$$

Note now that all nodes in N^∞ have nonnegative surplus, and each must have positive surplus infinitely often. Adding Eq. (5.1) for all i in N^∞, and using both Eq. (5.3) and the preceding relations, we find that the sum of c_{ij} over all $(i,j) \in A$ with $i \in N^\infty$ and $j \in N^\infty$ is less than the sum of b_{ji} over all $(j,i) \in A$ with $i \in N^\infty$ and $j \in N^\infty$, plus the sum of s_i over $i \in N^\infty$. Therefore, there can be no feasible solution, violating the hypothesis. It follows that the algorithm must terminate.   **Q.E.D.**

6.6 NONLINEAR NETWORK FLOW PROBLEMS

In this section, we consider the nonlinear network flow problem of Section 5.5

$$\text{minimize} \quad \sum_{(i,j)\in A} a_{ij}(f_{ij}) \tag{CNF}$$

$$\text{subject to} \quad \sum_{\{j|(i,j)\in A\}} f_{ij} - \sum_{\{j|(j,i)\in A\}} f_{ji} = s_i, \qquad \forall \ i \in N, \tag{6.1}$$

$$b_{ij} \leq f_{ij} \leq c_{ij}, \qquad \forall \ (i,j) \in A, \tag{6.2}$$

under the following assumption (made also in Section 5.5).

Assumption 6.1.   (*Strict Convexity*) The functions a_{ij}, $(i,j) \in A$, are strictly convex real–valued functions, and problem (CNF) has at least one feasible solution.

Our purpose is to develop a distributed asynchronous version of the relaxation method described in Section 5.5 and to analyze its convergence properties.

We showed that the method of Section 5.5 converges appropriately when implemented in a Gauss–Seidel version. Figure 5.5.5 of Section 5.5 shows that this is not true when the method is implemented in a Jacobi version, and, therefore, it cannot be true for an asynchronous version. The difficulty is due to the structure of the optimal dual solution set; in particular, by adding the same constant to all coordinates of an optimal price vector, we still obtain an optimal price vector. We are thus motivated to consider the variation of the method where a single price, say p_1, is fixed, thereby effectively restricting the dual optimal solution set.

Consider the dual functional q given by

$$q(p) = \sum_{(i,j)\in A} q_{ij}(p_i - p_j) + \sum_{i\in N} s_i p_i, \tag{6.3}$$

where

$$q_{ij}(p_i - p_j) = \min_{b_{ij}\le f_{ij}\le c_{ij}} \left\{ a_{ij}(f_{ij}) - (p_i - p_j)f_{ij} \right\}. \tag{6.4}$$

Consider also the following version of the dual problem:

$$\text{maximize} \quad q(p) \tag{6.5}$$

$$\text{subject to} \quad p \in P,$$

where P is the *reduced set of price vectors*

$$P = \left\{ p \in \Re^{|N|} \mid p_1 = c \right\},$$

and c is a fixed scalar. If we add the same constant to all prices, the dual function value (6.3) does not change (since, for feasibility, $\sum_{i\in N} s_i = 0$). Therefore, the constrained version (6.5) of the dual problem is equivalent to the unconstrained version considered in Section 5.5 in the sense that the optimal values of the two problems are equal, and the optimal price vectors of the latter problem are obtained from the optimal price vectors of the former by adding a multiple of the vector $(1, 1, \ldots, 1)$.

Recall the definition of the surplus of a node i:

$$g_i = \sum_{\{j|(j,i)\in A\}} f_{ji} - \sum_{\{j|(i,j)\in A\}} f_{ij} + s_i. \tag{6.6}$$

In Section 5.5, we calculated the gradient of the dual functional as

$$\frac{\partial q(p)}{\partial p_i} = g_i(p), \tag{6.7}$$

where

$$g_i(p) = \text{Surplus of node } i \text{ corresponding to the unique } f$$

$$\text{satisfying complementary slackness together with } p. \tag{6.8}$$

For $i = 1, \ldots, |N|$, consider the point–to–set mapping R_i, which assigns to a price vector $p \in P$ the interval of all prices ξ that maximize the dual cost along the ith price starting from p, that is,

$$R_i(p) = \left\{ \xi \mid g_i(p_1, \ldots, p_{i-1}, \xi, p_{i+1}, \ldots, p_{|N|}) = 0 \right\}$$

$$= \left\{ \xi \middle| \sum_{\{j \mid (j,i) \in A\}} \nabla q_{ji}(p_j - \xi) = \sum_{\{j \mid (i,j) \in A\}} \nabla q_{ij}(\xi - p_j) + s_i \right\}. \tag{6.9}$$

We call $R_i(p)$ the *ith relaxation mapping*, and note that $R_i(p)$ is nonempty for all p, as shown in Section 5.5 following Assumption 5.2. We will need a more precise characterization of $R_i(p)$. To this end we note that by assumption there exists a flow vector that satisfies both the conservation of flow constraints (6.1) and the capacity constraints (6.2), thereby implying that

$$\sum_{\{j \mid (i,j) \in A\}} b_{ij} - \sum_{\{j \mid (j,i) \in A\}} c_{ji} \le s_i \le \sum_{\{j \mid (i,j) \in A\}} c_{ij} - \sum_{\{j \mid (j,i) \in A\}} b_{ji}.$$

The following lemma shows that the form of $R_i(p)$ depends on whether equality holds in the above inequalities.

Lemma 6.1.   For all $p \in \Re^{|N|}$ the set of real numbers $R_i(p)$ of Eq. (6.9) is nonempty closed and convex. Furthermore, it is bounded below if and only if

$$\sum_{\{j \mid (i,j) \in A\}} b_{ij} - \sum_{\{j \mid (j,i) \in A\}} c_{ji} < s_i,$$

and it is bounded above if and only if

$$s_i < \sum_{\{j \mid (i,j) \in A\}} c_{ij} - \sum_{\{j \mid (j,i) \in A\}} b_{ji}.$$

Proof.   We have for all i and p,

$$\lim_{\xi \to -\infty} g_i(p_1, \ldots, p_{i-1}, \xi, p_{i+1}, \ldots, p_{|N|}) = \sum_{\{j \mid (j,i) \in A\}} c_{ji} - \sum_{\{j \mid (i,j) \in A\}} b_{ij} + s_i,$$

$$\lim_{\xi \to \infty} g_i(p_1, \ldots, p_{i-1}, \xi, p_{i+1}, \ldots, p_{|N|}) = \sum_{\{j \mid (j,i) \in A\}} b_{ji} - \sum_{\{j \mid (i,j) \in A\}} c_{ij} + s_i.$$

Furthermore $R_i(p)$ is nonempty and $g_i(p)$ is the ith partial derivative $\partial q(p)/\partial p_i$ of the concave dual function q. These facts imply the desired form of $R_i(p)$.   **Q.E.D.**

We now define the (point–to–point) mappings

$$\overline{R}_i(p) = \max_{\xi \in R_i(p)} \xi, \qquad \forall\, i \text{ such that } s_i < \sum_{\{j \mid (i,j) \in A\}} c_{ij} - \sum_{\{j \mid (j,i) \in A\}} b_{ji}, \tag{6.10}$$

$$\underline{R}_i(p) = \min_{\xi \in R_i(p)} \xi, \qquad \forall \, i \text{ such that } \sum_{\{j|(i,j)\in A\}} b_{ij} - \sum_{\{j|(j,i)\in A\}} c_{ji} < s_i. \quad (6.11)$$

We call $\overline{R}_i$ the *ith maximal relaxation mapping*, and $\underline{R}_i$ the *ith minimal relaxation mapping*. They give the maximal and minimal maximizing points, respectively, of the dual cost along the ith coordinate with all other coordinates held fixed; these points exist for all i satisfying the conditions of Eqs. (6.10) and (6.11) in view of Lemma 6.1. When $\overline{R}_i$ is defined for all $i = 2, \ldots, |N|$, we denote by $\overline{R}$ the (point–to–point) mapping from $\Re^{|N|}$ to $\Re^{|N|}$ defined by

$$\overline{R}(p) = \left[c, \overline{R}_2(p), \ldots, \overline{R}_{|N|}(p) \right]. \quad (6.12)$$

Similarly, when $\underline{R}_i$ is defined for all $i = 2, \ldots, |N|$, we denote by $\underline{R}$ the (point–to–point) mapping from $\Re^{|N|}$ to $\Re^{|N|}$ defined by

$$\underline{R}(p) = \left[c, \underline{R}_2(p), \ldots, \underline{R}_{|N|}(p) \right]. \quad (6.13)$$

We also denote by $\overline{R}^k$ and $\underline{R}^k$ the composition of $\overline{R}$ and $\underline{R}$, respectively, with themselves k times.

A key fact about the mappings $\overline{R}_i$ and $\underline{R}_i$ is that they are continuous and monotone. This can be visualized as in Figs. 6.6.1 and 6.6.2, and is shown in the following proposition:

Proposition 6.1. The ith maximal and minimal relaxation mappings $\overline{R}_i$ and $\underline{R}_i$, given by Eqs. (6.10) and (6.11), are continuous on $\Re^{|N|}$. Furthermore $\overline{R}_i$ and $\underline{R}_i$ are monotone on $\Re^{|N|}$ in the sense that for all p and $p' \in \Re^{|N|}$ we have

$$\overline{R}_i(p') \leq \overline{R}_i(p) \qquad \text{if } p' \leq p, \quad (6.14)$$

$$\underline{R}_i(p') \leq \underline{R}_i(p) \qquad \text{if } p' \leq p. \quad (6.15)$$

Proof. To show continuity of $\overline{R}_i$, we argue by contradiction. Suppose there exists a sequence $\{p^k\}$ that converges to a vector p such that the corresponding sequence $\{\overline{R}_i(p^k)\}$ does not converge to $\overline{R}_i(p)$. By passing to a subsequence, if necessary, suppose that for some $\epsilon > 0$, we have

$$\overline{R}_i(p) \geq \overline{R}_i(p^k) + \epsilon, \qquad \forall \, k, \quad (6.16)$$

(the proof is similar if $\epsilon < 0$ and the inequality is reversed). By the definition of $\overline{R}_i$, we have

$$\sum_{\{j|(j,i)\in A\}} \nabla q_{ji}\big(p_j - \overline{R}_i(p)\big) = \sum_{\{j|(i,j)\in A\}} \nabla q_{ij}\big(\overline{R}_i(p) - p_j\big) + s_i, \quad (6.17)$$

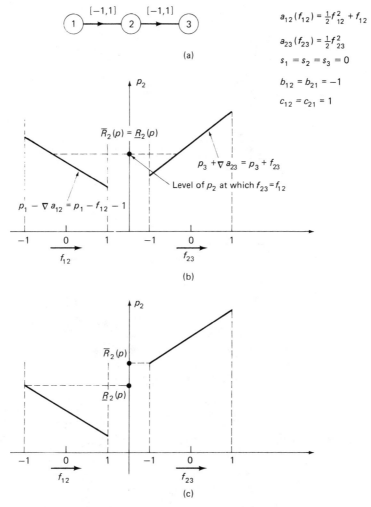

Figure 6.6.1   Illustration of mappings $\underline{R}_i$, $\overline{R}_i$, and R_i. (a) An example problem involving three nodes with zero supplies and two arcs with the arc costs and flow bounds shown. (b) Here $R_2(p)$ consists of a single element. (c) Here $\underline{R}_2(p) < \overline{R}_2(p)$ and $R_2(p)$ consists of the interval $\left[\underline{R}_2(p), \overline{R}_2(p)\right]$. In both (b) and (c), it is evident that $\overline{R}_2(p)$ and $\underline{R}_2(p)$ change continuously and monotonically with p_1 and p_3.

$$\sum_{\{j|(j,i)\in A\}} \nabla q_{ji}\left(p_j^k - \overline{R}_i(p^k)\right) = \sum_{\{j|(i,j)\in A\}} \nabla q_{ij}\left(\overline{R}_i(p^k) - p_j^k\right) + s_i, \quad \forall\, k. \tag{6.18}$$

Since $p^k \to p$, it follows using Eq. (6.16) that for sufficiently large k, we have

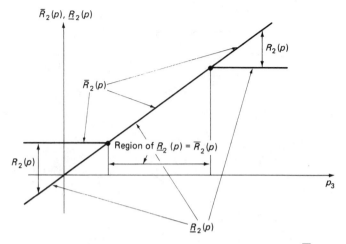

Figure 6.6.2 Illustration of continuity and monotonicity of $\underline{R}_2(p)$ and $\overline{R}_2(p)$ in the example of Fig. 6.1. The figure shows $\underline{R}_2(p)$, $\overline{R}_2(p)$, and $R_2(p)$ as p_1 is fixed and p_3 varies.

$$p_j^k - \overline{R}_i(p^k) > p_j - \overline{R}_i(p), \qquad \forall\, (j, i) \in A,$$

$$\overline{R}_i(p^k) - p_j^k < \overline{R}_i(p) - p_j, \qquad \forall\, (i, j) \in A.$$

Therefore, for sufficiently large k, we have, using the concavity of q_{ji} and q_{ij},

$$\nabla q_{ji}\left(p_j^k - \overline{R}_i(p^k)\right) \leq \nabla q_{ji}\left(p_j - \overline{R}_i(p)\right), \qquad \forall\, (j, i) \in A,$$

$$\nabla q_{ij}\left(\overline{R}_i(p^k) - p_j^k\right) \geq \nabla q_{ij}\left(\overline{R}_i(p) - p_j\right), \qquad \forall\, (i, j) \in A.$$

Using these relations together with Eqs. (6.17) and (6.18), we obtain for all sufficiently large k

$$\nabla q_{ji}\left(p_j - \overline{R}_i(p)\right) = \nabla q_{ji}\left(p_j^k - \overline{R}_i(p^k)\right), \qquad \forall\, (j, i) \in A, \qquad (6.19)$$

$$\nabla q_{ij}\left(\overline{R}_i(p) - p_j\right) = \nabla q_{ij}\left(\overline{R}_i(p^k) - p_j^k\right), \qquad \forall\, (i, j) \in A. \qquad (6.20)$$

Consider the intervals I_{ji} and I_{ij} given by

$$I_{ji} = \left\{ t \mid \nabla q_{ji}(t) = \nabla q_{ji}\left(p_j - \overline{R}_i(p)\right) \right\}, \qquad \forall\, (j, i) \in A, \qquad (6.21)$$

$$I_{ij} = \left\{ t \mid \nabla q_{ij}(t) = \nabla q_{ij}\left(\overline{R}_i(p) - p_j\right) \right\}, \qquad \forall\, (i, j) \in A. \qquad (6.22)$$

For k sufficiently large so that Eqs. (6.19) and (6.20) hold, we have

$$\overline{R}_i(p) = \max\{\xi \mid \xi \in (p_j - I_{ji}),\ (j, i) \in A,\ \xi \in (I_{ij} - p_j),\ (i, j) \in A\},$$

$$\overline{R}_i(p^k) = \max\{\xi \mid \xi \in (p_j^k - I_{ji}),\ (j, i) \in A,\ \xi \in (I_{ij} - p_j^k),\ (i, j) \in A\}.$$

Since $p^k \to p$, it is evident from these relations that $\overline{R}_i(p^k) \to \overline{R}_i(p)$, thereby contradicting the hypothesis $\overline{R}_i(p) \geq \overline{R}_i(p^k) + \epsilon$ for all k [cf. Eq. (6.16)].

To show monotonicity of $\overline{R}_i$, let $p \in P$ and $p' \in P$ be such that $p \geq p'$. The concavity of q_{ij} and q_{ji} implies that

$$\nabla q_{ji}\big(p_j - \overline{R}_i(p')\big) \leq \nabla q_{ji}\big(p'_j - \overline{R}_i(p')\big), \qquad \forall\, (j,i) \in A, \tag{6.23}$$

$$\nabla q_{ij}\big(\overline{R}_i(p') - p_j\big) \geq \nabla q_{ij}\big(\overline{R}_i(p') - p'_j\big), \qquad \forall\, (i,j) \in A. \tag{6.24}$$

Thus,

$$0 = s_i + \sum_{\{j|(i,j)\in A\}} \nabla q_{ij}\big(\overline{R}_i(p') - p'_j\big) - \sum_{\{j|(j,i)\in A\}} \nabla q_{ji}\big(p'_j - \overline{R}_i(p')\big)$$

$$\leq s_i + \sum_{\{j|(i,j)\in A\}} \nabla q_{ij}\big(\overline{R}_i(p') - p_j\big) - \sum_{\{j|(j,i)\in A\}} \nabla q_{ji}\big(p_j - \overline{R}_i(p')\big).$$

Since $s_i + \sum_{\{j|(i,j)\in A\}} \nabla q_{ij}(\xi - p_j) - \sum_{\{j|(j,i)\in A\}} \nabla q_{ji}(p_j - \xi)$ is negative for any $\xi > \overline{R}_i(p)$, we must have $\overline{R}_i(p') \leq \overline{R}_i(p)$.

The proof of continuity and monotonicity of $\underline{R}_i$ is analogous to the one just given for $\overline{R}_i$ and is omitted.   **Q.E.D.**

We now consider the *restricted dual optimal solution set* defined as

$$P^* = \big\{ p^* \in P \mid q(p^*) = \max_{p\in P} q(p) \big\}.$$

In order to characterize this set, we introduce some terminology. We say that P^* is *bounded above* if there exists $\hat{p} \in P$ such that $p^* \leq \hat{p}$ for all $p^* \in P^*$, and we say that P^* is *bounded below* if there exists $\hat{p} \in P$ such that $\hat{p} \leq p^*$ for all $p^* \in P^*$. Note that if P^* is bounded above, then the set $R_i(p^*)$ is bounded above for all i and $p^* \in P^*$, so by Lemma 6.1, we have

$$s_i < \sum_{\{j|(i,j)\in A\}} c_{ij} - \sum_{\{j|(j,i)\in A\}} b_{ji}, \qquad \forall\, i = 2,\ldots,|N|, \tag{6.25}$$

and the maximal relaxation mapping $\overline{R}_i$ is defined for all $i = 2,\ldots,|N|$ [cf. Eq. (6.10)]. Similarly, if P^* is bounded below, then the minimal relaxation mapping $\underline{R}_i$ is defined for all $i = 2,\ldots,|N|$.

The following proposition shows an interesting property of P^*.

Proposition 6.2.   If the restricted dual optimal solution set P^* is bounded above, then there exists a maximal element of P^*, that is, an element $\overline{p} \in P^*$ such that

$$p^* \leq \overline{p}, \qquad \forall\, p^* \in P^*.$$

Similarly, if P^* is bounded below, then there exists a minimal element of P^*, that is, an element $\underline{p} \in P^*$ such that

$$\underline{p} \leq p^*, \qquad \forall \, p^* \in P^*.$$

Proof. Assume that P^* is bounded above. Then, since P^* is also closed, it must contain elements $p^1, p^2, \ldots, p^{|N|}$ such that for all $p \in P^*$ and $i = 1, 2, \ldots, |N|$ we have $p_i^i \geq p_i$. We claim that the vector $\bar{p}$ given by

$$\bar{p}_i = p_i^i, \qquad \forall \, i = 1, 2, \ldots, |N|,$$

is the maximal element of P^*. By construction, $\bar{p} \geq p$ for all $p \in P^*$, so it only remains to show that $\bar{p} \in P^*$. Since $\bar{p}_i = \max\left\{p_i^1, \ldots, p_i^{|N|}\right\}$, it suffices to show that for any $p' \in P^*$ and $p'' \in P^*$, the vector $\hat{p}$ with coordinates given by

$$\hat{p}_i = \max\{p_i', p_i''\}, \qquad \forall \, i = 1, 2, \ldots, |N|, \tag{6.26}$$

belongs to P^*. Denote $I = \{i \mid p_i' > p_i''\}$ and let f^* be the unique optimal flow vector. The concavity of q_{ij} and the optimality of p' and p'' imply that

$$-f_{ji}^* = \nabla q_{ji}(p_j' - p_i') \geq \nabla q_{ji}(p_j'' - p_i') \geq \nabla q_{ji}(p_j'' - p_i'') = -f_{ji}^*,$$
$$\forall \, (j, i) \in A \text{ with } i \in I, \, j \notin I, \tag{6.27}$$

$$-f_{ij}^* = \nabla q_{ij}(p_i' - p_j') \leq \nabla q_{ij}(p_i' - p_j'') \leq \nabla q_{ij}(p_i'' - p_j'') = -f_{ij}^*,$$
$$\forall \, (i, j) \in A \text{ with } i \in I, \, j \notin I. \tag{6.28}$$

We also have

$$\nabla q_{ij}(p_i' - p_j') = -f_{ij}^*, \qquad \forall \, (i, j) \in A \text{ with } i \in I, \, j \in I, \tag{6.29}$$

$$\nabla q_{ij}(p_i'' - p_j'') = -f_{ij}^*, \qquad \forall \, (i, j) \in A \text{ with } i \notin I, \, j \notin I. \tag{6.30}$$

By combining Eqs. (6.26) through (6.30) we obtain $\nabla q_{ij}(\hat{p}_i - \hat{p}_j) = -f_{ij}^*$ for all $(i, j) \in A$. Therefore $\hat{p} \in P^*$.

The proof of existence of a minimal element $\underline{p}$ is similar.   **Q.E.D.**

Figures 6.6.3 and 6.6.4 provide examples of problems where P^* is bounded above and/or below and illustrates the maximal and/or minimal elements of P^*. Exercise 6.1 provides conditions under which boundedness above and/or below of P^* can be verified. A typical case where P^* is unbounded above as well as below occurs when the graph contains two disconnected components; in this case, the dual function value is unchanged if a constant is added to the prices of the nodes of the first component and a different constant is added to the prices of the nodes of the second component.

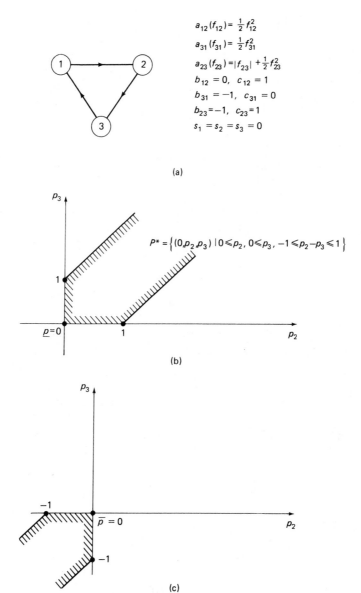

(a)

(b)

(c)

Figure 6.6.3 Illustration of situations where P^* is unbounded above or below; cf. Exercise 6.1. (a) An example problem with data as shown. The optimal flow vector is $(0, 0, 0)$. (b) The form of P^* for the problem of part (a). (c) The form of P^* when the flow bounds of arcs (1,2) and (3,1) are changed to $b_{12} = -1$, $c_{12} = 0$, and $b_{31} = 0$, $c_{31} = 1$, respectively.

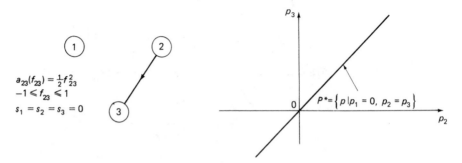

Figure 6.6.4 An example where the reduced dual optimal solution set P^* is not bounded below or above.

We now consider a distributed asynchronous algorithm based on the relaxation mapping R_i. This algorithm is cast into the algorithmic model of Section 6.1 by taking $X_1 = \{c\}$, X_i equal to the real line for $i = 2, \ldots, |N|$, $x = p$, and

$$f_1(p) = c \qquad \text{for } i = 1,$$

$$f_i(p) \in R_i(p) \qquad \text{for } i = 2, \ldots, |N|.$$

We call this algorithm the *asynchronous relaxation method* (ARM). The price vector generated by ARM at time t is denoted $p(t)$, and its ith coordinate is denoted $p_i(t)$. We have the following proposition:

Proposition 6.3. Let the initial vector $p(0)$ be arbitrary subject to $p_1(0) = c$.

(a) If the restricted dual optimal solution set P^* is bounded above, every limit point of a sequence $\{p(t)\}$ generated by the ARM belongs to the set

$$\overline{P} = \{p \in P \mid p \le \overline{p}\}, \tag{6.31}$$

where $\overline{p}$ is the maximal element of P^* (cf. Prop. 6.2).

(b) If P^* is bounded below, every limit point of a sequence $\{p(t)\}$ generated by the ARM belongs to the set

$$\underline{P} = \{p \in P \mid \underline{p} \le p\}, \tag{6.32}$$

where $\underline{p}$ is the minimal element of P^* (cf. Prop. 6.2).

(c) If P^* consists of a unique element p^*, we have

$$\lim_{t \to \infty} p(t) = p^*. \tag{6.33}$$

Proof.

(a) Let $\hat{p}$ be the vector defined by $\hat{p}_i = \overline{p}_i + \delta$ for all $i = 1, 2, \ldots, |N|$, where $\delta > 0$ is a positive constant chosen large enough so that $p(0) \leq \hat{p}$. Consider the mapping $\overline{R}$ of Eq. (6.12). We have using the definition (6.9) of $R_i(p)$,

$$\overline{R}_i(\hat{p}) = \overline{R}_i(\overline{p}) + \delta = \overline{p}_i + \delta, \qquad \forall\, i = 2, \ldots, |N|,$$

while the first coordinates of $\overline{R}(\hat{p})$ and $\overline{R}(\overline{p})$ are both equal to c. Therefore we have $\overline{p} \leq \overline{R}(\hat{p}) \leq \hat{p}$ and by using the monotonicity of the components of the mapping $\overline{R}$, we obtain

$$\overline{p} \leq \overline{R}^{k+1}(\hat{p}) \leq \overline{R}^{k}(\hat{p}), \qquad \forall\, k.$$

From this relation, we see that the sequence $\{\overline{R}^{k}(\hat{p})\}$ converges to some p, and by the continuity of $\overline{R}$, we must have $p = \overline{R}(p)$ as well as $p \geq \overline{p}$. Since $p = \overline{R}(p)$ implies that $p \in P^*$ and since $\overline{p}$ is the maximal element of P^*, we see that $\overline{p} = p = \lim_{k \to \infty} \overline{R}^{k}(\hat{p})$. We now consider the sets

$$\overline{P}(k) = \left\{ p \in P \mid p \leq \overline{R}^{k}(\hat{p}) \right\}, \qquad k = 0, 1, \ldots, \tag{6.34}$$

and note that the sequence $\{\overline{P}(k)\}$ is nested, and its intersection is the set $\overline{P} = \{p \in P \mid p \leq \overline{p}\}$ of Eq. (6.31). We apply the Asynchronous Convergence Theorem of Section 6.2 with the sets $\overline{P}(k)$ in place of $X(k)$. It is evident that these sets satisfy the Synchronous Convergence and Box Conditions of Assumption 2.1, so the result follows.

(b) Similar with the proof of part (a).

(c) Follows from parts (a) and (b), since $\overline{p}$ and $\underline{p}$ coincide with p^*.   **Q.E.D.**

Proposition 6.3 shows that the ARM has satisfactory convergence properties when P^* has a unique element. One way to check this condition is to consider the optimal solution f^* of the primal problem (CNF), and the subset of arcs

$$\tilde{A} = \left\{ (i, j) \in A \mid b_{ij} < f_{ij}^* < c_{ij} \text{ and } a_{ij} \text{ is differentiable at } f_{ij}^* \right\}.$$

For every optimal price vector p^*, we must have $p_i^* - p_j^* = \nabla a_{ij}(f_{ij}^*)$ for all $(i, j) \in \tilde{A}$, so if the graph $(N, \tilde{A})$ is connected, it is seen that P^* must consist of a unique element. In order to improve the convergence properties when P^* has more then one element, it is necessary to modify the ARM so that a price relaxation at node i replaces p_i with $\overline{R}_i(p)$ [not just any element of $R_i(p)$]. We call this method the *maximal ARM*. If in place of $\overline{R}_i(p)$ we use $\underline{R}_i(p)$ the resulting method is called the *minimal ARM*.

Proposition 6.4.

(a) Assume that the restricted dual optimal solution set P^* is bounded above and $\overline{p}$ is its maximal element. If the initial vector $p(0)$ satisfies $p_1(0) = c$ and $\overline{p} \le p(0)$, then a sequence generated by the maximal ARM converges to $\overline{p}$.

(b) Assume that P^* is bounded below and $\underline{p}$ is its minimal element. If the initial vector $p(0)$ satisfies $p_1(0) = c$ and $p(0) \le \underline{p}$, then a sequence generated by the minimal ARM converges to $\underline{p}$.

Proof. The proof of part (a) is identical to the one of Prop. 6.3(a) except that the sets $P(k)$ of Eq. (6.34) are replaced by $\left\{ p \in P \mid \overline{p} \le p \le \overline{R}^k(\hat{p}) \right\}$. The proof of part (b) is similar.   **Q.E.D.**

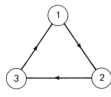

Figure 6.6.5 A three node network example. The arc cost functions and the lower and upper arc flow bounds are

$$a_{12}(f_{12}) = |f_{12}| + (f_{12})^2, \quad -1 \le f_{12} \le 1,$$

$$a_{23}(f_{23}) = (f_{23})^2, \qquad -1 \le f_{23} \le 1,$$

$$a_{31}(f_{31}) = |f_{23}| + (f_{31})^2, \quad -1 \le f_{31} \le 1.$$

The node supplies are zero. The optimal primal solution is $f_{12}^* = f_{23}^* = f_{31}^* = 0$. The reduced dual optimal solution set for $c = 0$ is

$$P^* = \{ p \mid p_1 = 0, \ p_2 = p_3,$$

$$-1 \le p_2 \le 1, \ -1 \le p_3 \le 1 \}.$$

To illustrate the results of Props. 6.3 and 6.4, consider the example of Fig. 6.6.5. The regions of initial price vectors for which the ARM, the maximal ARM, and the minimal ARM converge to the optimal solutions are shown in Fig. 6.6.6. This example shows that the results of Props. 6.3 and 6.4 cannot be improved even for the special case of the synchronous Jacobi relaxation version. A method to overcome the difficulty in this example is discussed in Subsection 7.2.3.

EXERCISES

6.1. Show that the restricted dual optimal solution set P^* is unbounded above if and only if there exists a nonempty subset $S \subset N$ such that $1 \notin S$ and for all $(i, j) \in A$ with $i \in S$ and $j \notin S$, we have $f_{ij}^* = c_{ij}$, and for all $(i, j) \in A$ with $i \in S$ and $j \notin S$, we have $f_{ij}^* = b_{ij}$. Formulate a similar condition for P^* to be unbounded below. *Hint:* If P^* is unbounded

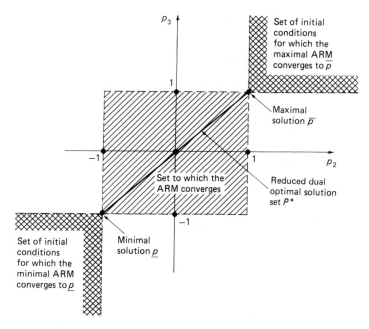

Figure 6.6.6 The structure of the reduced dual optimal solution set, the convergence regions of the ARM, the maximal ARM, and the minimal ARM for the example of Fig. 6.6.5.

above, there must exist vectors p^* and u in $\Re^{|N|}$ such that $p^* + \alpha u \in P^*$ for all $\alpha \geq 0$, and, furthermore, the set $S = \{i \in N \mid u_i > 0\}$ is nonempty. Use the fact that the unique optimal flow vector f^* must satisfy complementary slackness with $p^* + \alpha u$ for all $\alpha \geq 0$ in order to show that the set S has the required property. Conversely, if S has the stated property, and $p^* \in P^*$, then $p^* + \alpha u \in P^*$ for all $\alpha \geq 0$, where the ith coordinate of u is 1 if $i \in S$ and is 0 otherwise.

6.7 ASYNCHRONOUS RELAXATION FOR ORDINARY DIFFERENTIAL EQUATIONS AND TWO–POINT BOUNDARY VALUE PROBLEMS

Consider a dynamical system consisting of m interconnected subsystems. Let $x_i(t) \in R^{n_i}$ be the state vector of the ith subsystem at time t.   Suppose that the initial state $x_i(0)$ of each subsystem has been fixed, and suppose that the dynamics of the system are described by the following set of linear differential equations:

$$\frac{dx_i}{dt}(t) + D_i(t)x_i(t) = \sum_{j=1}^{m} B_{ij}(t)x_j(t) + u_i(t), \qquad i = 1, \ldots, m. \qquad (7.1)$$

Here $D_i(t)$ and $B_{ij}(t)$ are matrices of dimensions $n_i \times n_i$ and $n_i \times n_j$, respectively, and $u_i(t)$ is a known vector of dimension n_i. The matrix $D_i(t)$ is supposed to describe the internal dynamics of the ith subsystem, and the matrices $B_{ij}(t)$ are meant to describe the interaction of the ith subsystem with other subsystems. Let $n = \sum_{i=1}^{m} n_i$ be the dimension of the overall system. Let $D(t)$ be the block–diagonal matrix of size $n \times n$, which has $D_i(t)$ as its ith block; let $B(t)$ be the $n \times n$ matrix consisting of the blocks $B_{ij}(t)$. With this notation, the system (7.1) can be written compactly as

$$\frac{dx}{dt}(t) + D(t)x(t) = B(t)x(t) + u(t). \tag{7.2}$$

We will assume throughout this section that each element of $D_i(\cdot)$, $B_{ij}(\cdot)$ and $u_i(\cdot)$ is a continuous and bounded function of time, over the time interval $[0, \infty)$. This guarantees that the system (7.1) has a unique solution over $[0, \infty)$ for any initial conditions, as discussed in Appendix A (Prop. A.44).

In this section, we describe an asynchronous relaxation algorithm for solving numerically the system (7.1) over a time interval of the form $[0, T]$, where T is a positive real number, or over the time interval $[0, \infty)$. Relaxation algorithms for solving ordinary differential equations are based on the following idea. Suppose that we have available some approximation of the trajectories of the different subsystems. We use these approximate trajectories in the right–hand side of the differential equation (7.1), and then solve this equation for the trajectory of the ith subsystem. (This step is called *relaxing* the ith equation.) This is done for each subsystem, and then the procedure is repeated until eventually convergence to a set of sufficiently good approximate solutions is obtained. The situation is the same as when solving systems of equations. The only difference is that the objects that we are solving for are not vectors in a finite dimensional vector space but belong to an infinite dimensional space of time functions. Similarly, as with systems of equations with a finite number of unknowns, there are several variations of the above described algorithm. The equations (7.1) can be relaxed one after the other, which corresponds to a Gauss–Seidel algorithm, or they can be relaxed simultaneously, which corresponds to a Jacobi algorithm. More generally, these equations can be relaxed in an arbitrary order by a set of parallel processors operating asynchronously, according to the model introduced in Section 6.1.

6.7.1 The Asynchronous Relaxation Algorithm

Let X_i be the set of functions $x_i(\cdot)$ that are continuous over the time interval of interest $([0, T]$ or $[0, \infty))$, and whose initial value $x_i(0)$ agrees with the given initial conditions. Let $X = X_1 \times \cdots \times X_m$. We define a mapping $f_i : X \mapsto X_i$ as follows. Given functions $x_j(\cdot) \in X_j$, $j = 1, ..., m$, let

$$y_i(\cdot) = f_i\big(x_1(\cdot), \ldots, x_m(\cdot)\big)$$

be the solution of the differential equation

$$\frac{dy_i}{dt}(t) + D_i(t)y_i(t) = \sum_{j=1}^{m} B_{ij}(t)x_j(t) + u_i(t), \tag{7.3}$$

subject to the initial condition $y_i(0) = x_i(0)$. In view of the continuity assumption on D_i, B_{ij}, and u_i, the solution $y_i(\cdot)$ of this differential equation exists, is unique, and belongs to X_i. Furthermore, $y(\cdot)$ has the following explicit representation (see Prop. A.44 in Appendix A)

$$y_i(t) = \int_0^t \Phi_i(t, \tau) \left[\sum_{j=1}^{m} B_{ij}(\tau)x_j(\tau) + u_i(\tau) \right] d\tau + \Phi_i(t, 0)x_i(0), \tag{7.4}$$

where $\Phi_i(t, \tau)$ is the matrix–valued function that satisfies the differential equation

$$\frac{\partial \Phi_i(t, \tau)}{\partial t} = -D_i(t)\Phi_i(t, \tau), \tag{7.5}$$

and the initial condition $\Phi_i(\tau, \tau) = I$, where I is the $n_i \times n_i$ identity matrix. Let $f : X \mapsto X$ be the mapping whose ith component is the mapping f_i, and let $x^*(\cdot)$ be the solution of the system (7.1) subject to the given initial conditions. Then $x^*(\cdot)$ satisfies the integral equation

$$x_i^*(t) = \int_0^t \Phi_i(t, \tau) \left[\sum_{j=1}^{m} B_{ij}(\tau)x_j^*(\tau) + u_i(\tau) \right] d\tau + \Phi_i(t, 0)x_i(0), \tag{7.6}$$

and from Eq. (7.4) it is seen that $x^*(\cdot)$ is a fixed point of f.

Having defined the mapping f, we consider the corresponding asynchronous algorithm in accordance with the model of Section 6.1. We assume that the algorithm is initialized with functions $x_i(\cdot)$ belonging to X_i for each i. Application of the mapping f_i corresponds to updating the ith component x_i by a processor. In the present context, each component x_i is a vector time function, an infinite dimensional object. This does not pose any mathematical difficulty because the Asynchronous Convergence Theorem of Section 6.2 has been proved without assuming that the underlying space X is finite dimensional.

In practice, one should have available a numerical method for solving the differential equation (7.3). This issue is not directly related to the issues of parallelism and asynchronism and has to be dealt with even in a uniprocessor environment. We do not discuss this issue further and refer the reader to textbooks on numerical analysis [CoL55], [Hen64], and [Hil74].

Pointwise Convergence Over the Interval $[0, \infty)$

We now prove that the sequence of trajectories produced by the asynchronous relaxation algorithm converges pointwise to $x^*(\cdot)$. We will need the following lemma, which is proved in Prop. A.44 of Appendix A.

Lemma 7.1.   For every i, there exist constants $C_i \geq 0$ and $c_i \geq 0$ such that

$$||\Phi_i(t, \tau)||_\infty \leq C_i e^{c_i(t-\tau)}, \qquad \forall \, t \geq \tau, \tag{7.7}$$

where $|| \cdot ||_\infty$ is the matrix norm induced by the maximum norm.

Let A be an upper bound on $||B_{ij}(t)||_\infty$, let $K > 0$ be an arbitrary constant, and let g and G be constants larger than all the constants c_i and C_i of Lemma 7.1, respectively. For any nonnegative integer k, let

$$X(k) = \left\{ x(\cdot) \in X \middle| \, ||x(t) - x^*(t)||_\infty \leq K \frac{(mGAt)^k}{k!} e^{gt}, \, \forall \, t \geq 0 \right\}.$$

The sets $X(k)$ satisfy the Box Condition of Section 6.2 and will be used in a subsequent application of the Asynchronous Convergence Theorem. The following lemma shows that the Synchronous Convergence Condition of Section 6.2 is also satisfied.

Lemma 7.2.   The mapping f maps $X(k)$ into $X(k+1)$ for every $k \geq 0$.

Proof.   Let us assume that $x(\cdot) \in X(k)$ and let $y(\cdot) = f\big(x(\cdot)\big)$. Using the representations (7.4) and (7.6), Lemma 7.1, and the definition of A, we have

$$
\begin{aligned}
||y_i(t) - x_i^*(t)||_\infty &= \left\| \int_0^t \Phi_i(t, \tau) \left[\sum_{j=1}^m B_{ij}(\tau)\big(x_j(\tau) - x_j^*(\tau)\big) \right] d\tau \right\|_\infty \\
&\leq \int_0^t G e^{g(t-\tau)} mAK \frac{(mGA\tau)^k}{k!} e^{g\tau} \, d\tau \\
&= K(mGA)^{k+1} e^{gt} \int_0^t \frac{\tau^k}{k!} \, d\tau \\
&= K(mGA)^{k+1} e^{gt} \frac{t^{k+1}}{(k+1)!}.
\end{aligned}
$$

Q.E.D.

It can be shown by using an argument similar to the one of Prop. A.44 in Appendix A, that there exist positive constants f and F such that $||x^*(t)||_\infty \leq Fe^{ft}$. Suppose that the algorithm is initialized with a time function $z(\cdot) \in X$ that is bounded by some constant H. It follows that $||z(t) - x^*(t)||_\infty \le K e^{ft}$, where $K = H + F$. Therefore, if the algorithm is initialized with a bounded and continuous time function satisfying the given initial conditions, this time function belongs to the set $X(0)$ for a suitable choice of the constants K, g, G. We can then apply the Asynchronous Convergence Theorem, showing that the algorithm will eventually enter and stay in the set $X(k)$ for any k. In particular, for any fixed t, the maximum norm of $(x(t) - x^*(t))$ eventually becomes smaller than $K(mGAt)^k e^{gt}/k!$, which converges to zero as $k \to \infty$. This proves the following:

Proposition 7.1.   The sequence of time functions produced by the asynchronous algorithm based on the mapping f, initialized with a bounded and continuous function satisfying the given initial conditions, converges pointwise to the solution of the system (7.1).

Uniform Convergence on $[0, T]$

If we are interested only in a finite interval $[0, T]$, with $T < \infty$, we can define the sets $X(k)$ by

$$X(k) = \left\{ x(\cdot) \in X \middle| \; ||x(t) - x^*(t)||_\infty \le K \frac{(mGAt)^k}{k!} e^{gt}, \; \forall \, t \in [0, T] \right\}.$$

We then repeat the argument in Lemma 7.2 and conclude again that f maps $X(k)$ into $X(k+1)$, and, therefore, the time functions produced by the algorithm eventually enter every set $X(k)$. This implies that, for every k, the quantity $\max_{t \in [0,T]} ||x(t) - x^*(t)||_\infty$ eventually becomes smaller than $K(mGAT)^k e^{gT}/k!$, which converges to zero as $k \to \infty$. We have thus proved the following:

Proposition 7.2.   If $T < \infty$, then the sequence of time functions generated by the asynchronous algorithm, initialized by an arbitrary continuous function satisfying the given initial conditions, converges uniformly to the solution of the system (7.1).

Uniform Convergence on $[0, \infty)$

The uniform convergence result of Prop. 7.2 seems encouraging because in practice we would only want to solve the system (7.1) over a finite time interval. However, the speed of convergence implicit in this result is unsatisfactory. Suppose that we are interested in obtaining a true solution within some $\epsilon > 0$. The argument preceding Prop. 7.2 suggests that we should wait until $x(\cdot)$ enters the set $X(k)$, where k is large enough so that $K(mGAT)^k e^{gT}/k! < \epsilon$. If we choose k according to this requirement, it is clear that k should be chosen larger when T is larger. This suggests that a larger number of iterations is needed in order to solve the system (7.1) over a larger time interval. Suppose now that the asynchronous algorithm were to converge uniformly over the interval $[0, \infty)$. Then, convergence over a smaller time interval could only be faster, implying that for any finite time interval $[0, T]$, the algorithm would converge uniformly at least as fast as for the interval $[0, \infty)$. In other words, the number of iterations required to attain a certain accuracy would have a bound independent of T. This is the main reason for our interest in uniform convergence over the interval $[0, \infty)$.

To be able to show uniform convergence over $[0, \infty)$, it is essential to impose several additional assumptions on the system (7.1). There is a need for some type of stability assumption to guarantee that the solution $x^*(t)$ stays bounded as $t \to \infty$; otherwise, uniform convergence may not occur. There is also a need for further assumptions of the type needed for relaxation methods for (algebraic) systems of linear equations, such as diagonal dominance conditions (cf. Sections 2.6 and 6.3). The reason for this will become apparent shortly, in the proof of Prop. 7.4, where we will show an intimate connection between the limit (as $t \to \infty$) of the solution $x^*(t)$ of the differential system (7.1), and the solution of an associated linear (algebraic) system of equations. Diagonal dominance conditions needed for asynchronous convergence of relaxation methods for the linear algebraic system will be translated into corresponding conditions for convergence of relaxation methods for the differential system (7.1). The reader may find it easier to understand why stability and diagonal dominance conditions are not needed for pointwise convergence by considering the corresponding case of a system of difference equations discussed at the end of the present section.

For the remainder of this subsection we restrict the set of functions X_i to include only bounded functions; that is, for $i = 1, \ldots, m$, X_i is the set of all bounded and continuous functions $x_i(\cdot)$ satisfying the given initial conditions. We introduce some convenient norms. Let $w \in R^n$ be a vector of the form $w = (w_1, \ldots, w_m)$, where $w_i \in R^{n_i}$ are some positive vectors. For any $x_i \in R^{n_i}$, let $||x_i||_\infty^{w_i}$ be its weighted maximum norm, as defined in Appendix A. We define a norm $|| \cdot ||_i$ on X_i by letting, for any $x_i(\cdot) \in X_i$,

$$||x_i(\cdot)||_i = \sup_{t \in [0,\infty)} ||x_i(t)||_\infty^{w_i}. \tag{7.8}$$

We finally define a norm $|| \cdot ||$ on X by letting, for any $x(\cdot) \in X$,

$$||x(\cdot)|| = \max_i ||x_i(\cdot)||_i.$$

We are interested in conditions on $D_i(\cdot)$ and $B_{ij}(\cdot)$ for which the iteration mapping f is a contraction with respect to the $|| \cdot ||$ norm; in that case, convergence will follow from the theory of Sections 6.2 and 6.3. We first assume that the functions $D_i(\cdot)$, $B_{ij}(\cdot)$ are constant (independent of time), and $n_i = 1$ for all i, that is, each subsystem is one-dimensional. In addition, we assume that $D_i > 0$ for all i. [†] The solution of Eq. (7.5) is then $\Phi_i(t, \tau) = e^{-(t-\tau)D_i}$, and by using Eqs. (7.4) and (7.6), we obtain

$$y_i(t) - x_i^*(t) = \int_0^t e^{-(t-\tau)D_i} \sum_{j=1}^m B_{ij}\big(x_j(\tau) - x_j^*(\tau)\big) d\tau. \tag{7.9}$$

[†] This asssumption is motivated by the following consideration. If $D_i \le 0$, then even if $x(\cdot)$ and $u(\cdot)$ are bounded functions, $f_i\big(x(\cdot)\big)$ will be in general unbounded and uniform convergence becomes impossible, except for a few trivial cases.

We divide both sides of this equation by w_i, and then take absolute values to obtain

$$
\left| \frac{y_i(t) - x_i^*(t)}{w_i} \right| \leq \int_0^t e^{-(t-\tau)D_i} \sum_{j=1}^m \left| B_{ij} \frac{w_j}{w_i} \right| \cdot \left| \frac{x_j(\tau) - x_j^*(\tau)}{w_j} \right| d\tau
$$

$$
\leq \int_0^t e^{-(t-\tau)D_i} \sum_{j=1}^m \left| B_{ij} \frac{w_j}{w_i} \right| \cdot ||x(\cdot) - x^*(\cdot)|| \, d\tau
$$

$$
= \frac{1}{D_i} \left(1 - e^{-tD_i} \right) \sum_{j=1}^m \left| B_{ij} \frac{w_j}{w_i} \right| \cdot ||x(\cdot) - x^*(\cdot)||
$$

$$
\leq \frac{1}{D_i} \sum_{j=1}^m \left| B_{ij} \frac{w_j}{w_i} \right| \cdot ||x(\cdot) - x^*(\cdot)||.
$$

(7.10)

Taking the maximum over all i and t, it follows that the function f that maps $x(\cdot)$ to $y(\cdot)$ is a pseudocontraction (with respect to the norm $|| \cdot ||$) if

$$
\frac{1}{D_i} \sum_{j=1}^m |B_{ij}| \frac{w_j}{w_i} < 1, \qquad \forall \, i. \tag{7.11}
$$

[In fact f is seen to be a contraction due to its linearity properties; cf. Eq. (7.4).] In accordance with the notation introduced in the beginning of this section, let D be a diagonal matrix, with D_i being the ith diagonal element, and let $|B|$ be a matrix whose ijth element is equal to $|B_{ij}|$. The inequality (7.11) is equivalent to

$$
D^{-1}|B|w < w. \tag{7.12}
$$

Asynchronous convergence is obtained if the above condition holds for *some* choice of $w > 0$. We recall Corollary 6.1 of Section 2.6 which states that this condition holds for some choice of $w > 0$ if and only if $\rho(D^{-1}|B|) < 1$. We have, therefore, proved the following:

Proposition 7.3.   Assume that $n_i = 1$ for all i, that the functions $D_i(\cdot)$ and $B_{ij}(t)$ do not depend on time, that $D_i > 0$ for all i, and that $\rho(D^{-1}|B|) < 1$. Then the sequence of time functions generated by the asynchronous algorithm, initialized with any bounded and continuous function satisfying the given initial conditions, converges uniformly over the interval $[0, \infty)$ to the solution of the system (7.1).

Interestingly enough, the above proposition has a converse that provides necessary conditions for uniform convergence on $[0, \infty)$.

Proposition 7.4.   Suppose that $n_i = 1$ for all i, that the functions $D(\cdot)$ and $B_{ij}(\cdot)$ do not depend on time, and that $D_i > 0$ for all i. If the sequence of time functions generated by the asynchronous algorithm converges uniformly over the time interval $[0, \infty)$ to the solution of the system (7.1) for every choice of bounded and continuous functions $U_i(\cdot)$ and every initial choice of functions $x_i(\cdot) \in X_i$, then $\rho(D^{-1}|B|) < 1$.

Proof. By assumption, the algorithm converges in the special case where $u_i(t) = 0$ for all i and t. We take this to be the case. Let Y_i be the set of time functions $x_i(\cdot) \in X_i$ for which the limit of $x_i(t)$, as $t \to \infty$, exists. Let $Y = Y_1 \times \cdots \times Y_m$. For any $x(\cdot) \in Y$, we denote by $x(\infty)$ the value of this limit. It is an easy consequence of our assumption $D_i > 0$ that the mapping f maps Y into itself. [This can be proved by using Eq. (7.4).] In particular,

$$(f(x))(\infty) = D^{-1}Bx(\infty).$$

Thus, considering only the limiting values of the time functions generated in the course of the asynchronous algorithm, we see that they are identical to those generated by an asynchronous execution of the finite–dimensional iteration

$$x(\infty) := D^{-1}Bx(\infty). \tag{7.13}$$

Since we have assumed that the algorithm converges for every initial choice of time functions [and therefore, for every initial choice of $x(\infty)$], the asynchronous iteration (7.13) also converges. This is an iteration for the solution of a system of linear equations of the type considered in Section 6.3. Proposition 3.1 of that section is, therefore, applicable and shows that $\rho(D^{-1}|B|) < 1$.   **Q.E.D.**

We will now generalize Prop. 7.3 to the multidimensional and time–varying case. We shall need some more elaborate notation: we use $x_{i,p}$ to denote the pth component of any vector $x_i \in R^{n_i}$. Accordingly, let $D_{i,pq}(t)$, $B_{ij,pq}(t)$ be the pqth entry of $D_i(t)$ and $B_{ij}(t)$, respectively.

Proposition 7.5.   Assume that there exists a positive vector $w \in R^n$ and some $\epsilon > 0$ such that

$$D_{i,pp}(t)(1-\epsilon)w_{i,p} > \sum_{\{q|q\neq p\}} |D_{i,pq}(t)|w_{i,q} + \sum_{j=1}^{m}\sum_{q=1}^{n_j} |B_{ij,pq}(t)|w_{j,q}, \quad \forall\, i,j,p,t. \tag{7.14}$$

Then the mapping f is a contraction with respect to the norm $||\cdot||$, and uniform convergence on $[0, \infty)$ of the asynchronous algorithm follows.

Proof. In order to keep the proof simple, we assume that the input $u(t)$ and the initial conditions $x(0)$ are all zero. [It then follows that $x^*(t) = 0$ for all t.] The proof for the general case is identical provided that $x(t)$ and $y(t)$ are replaced throughout by $x(t) - x^*(t)$ and $y(t) - x^*(t)$, respectively. Let us assume that $||x(\cdot)|| \le 1$ and let $y(\cdot) = f(x(\cdot))$. Suppose that at some time t we have $||y(t)|| \le 1$. Let us consider the ith subsystem and suppose that some component $y_{i,p}(t)$ of $y(t)$ satisfies $y_{i,p}(t) \in \left[(1 - \epsilon)w_{i,p}, w_{i,p}\right]$. We then claim that $(dy_{i,p}/dt)(t) < 0$. Indeed,

$$\frac{dy_{i,p}}{dt}(t) = -D_{i,pp}(t)y_{i,p}(t) - \sum_{\{q\,|\,q \neq p\}} D_{i,pq}(t)y_{i,q}(t) + \sum_{j=1}^{m}\sum_{q=1}^{n_j} B_{ij,pq}(t)x_{j,q}(t)$$

$$\leq -D_{i,pp}(t)(1 - \epsilon)w_{i,p} + \sum_{\{q\,|\,q \neq p\}} |D_{i,pq}(t)|w_{i,q} + \sum_{j=1}^{m}\sum_{q=1}^{n_j} |B_{ij,pq}(t)|w_{j,q} < 0,$$

because of assumption (7.14). A similar argument shows that if $||y(t)|| \leq 1$ and $y_{i,p}(t) \in \left[-w_{i,p}, -(1 - \epsilon)w_{i,p}\right]$, then $(dy_{i,p}/dt)(t) > 0$.

At the time origin, we have $||y(0)|| = 0$, since $y(\cdot)$ is initialized at zero and the above proved inequalities on the derivative of $y(\cdot)$ suggest that $||y(t)||$ can never exceed $(1 - \epsilon)$. We prove this formally. Suppose that this statement is false. Then there exists some $\delta > 0$, some indices i and p and some time t such that $|y_{i,p}(t)| \geq (1 - \epsilon + \delta)w_{i,p}$. Let t_2 be the first time at which this event occurs and let i and p be the corresponding indices. Let t_1 be the last time t before t_2 at which $|y_{i,p}(t)| = (1 - \epsilon)w_{i,p}$. During the time interval $[t_1, t_2]$, we have $||y(t)|| \leq 1$ and $|y_{i,p}(t)| \in \left[(1 - \epsilon)w_{i,p}, w_{i,p}\right]$. Hence, by our previous observations, we have $d|y_{i,p}(s)|/dt < 0$, for all $s \in [t_1, t_2]$. Thus, $|y_{i,p}(t_2)| \leq (1 - \epsilon)w_{i,p}$, which is a contradiction and proves the desired result.

We conclude that $||y(t)||$ never exceeds $(1 - \epsilon)$. Thus, $||f(x(\cdot))|| \leq (1 - \epsilon)||x(\cdot)||$ for every $x \in X$ satisfying $||x|| \leq 1$ and, since f is linear, it follows that f is a contraction with respect to the norm $|| \cdot ||$.   **Q.E.D.**

6.7.2 Two–Point Boundary Value Problems

Two–point boundary value problems are similar to the problem of solving the system of differential equations (7.1) over a finite time interval $[0, T]$, except that we are not given initial conditions for each subsystem. Rather, we are given initial conditions for some of the subsystems and final conditions for the remaining ones. Let I be the set of all i for which an initial condition for $x_i(0)$ is given and let J be the set of all i for which a final condition $x_i(T)$ is given.

A relaxation algorithm is also applicable in this case. The equation for $x_i(\cdot)$, $i \in I$, is integrated forward, while the equation for $x_j(\cdot)$, $j \in J$, is integrated backward in time, starting with the final condition at time T. Unlike the case of initial value problems treated earlier, pointwise convergence becomes a nontrivial issue; not even the synchronous (Jacobi–like) relaxation algorithm is guaranteed to converge. Convergence at a rate independent of T is obtained in the following proposition, under diagonal dominance conditions similar to those assumed in Prop. 7.5.

Proposition 7.6.   Assume that the diagonal entries of D are positive for those subsystems for which initial conditions are prescribed and negative for those subsystems for which final conditions are prescribed. Assume that there exists a vector $w > 0$ and some $\epsilon > 0$ such that

$$|D_{i,pp}(t)|(1 - \epsilon)w_{i,p} > \sum_{\{q|q \neq p\}} |D_{i,pq}(t)|w_{i,q} + \sum_{j=1}^{m} \sum_{q=1}^{n_j} |B_{ij,pq}(t)|w_{j,q}, \quad \forall\, i, j, p, t.$$

(7.15)

Then the two–point boundary value problem has a unique solution, and the sequence of time functions generated by the asynchronous algorithm converges uniformly to it.

Proof. We argue that the mapping f is a contraction with respect to the norm $||\cdot||$. This will show that the equation $f(x^*(\cdot)) = x^*(\cdot)$ has a unique solution, and will also imply asynchronous convergence based on the theory of Sections 6.2 and 6.3.

We assume that $||x(t) - x^*(t)|| \leq 1$ for all t, and we want to prove that $||y_i(t) - x_i^*(t)||_i \leq (1 - \epsilon)$ for all t, where y_i is the time function obtained by solving the equation for the ith subsystem. If we have initial conditions for the ith subsystem, then the argument is identical to the argument in the proof of Prop. 7.5. If, instead, final conditions are given, then the same argument is again applicable, except that time is reversed. **Q.E.D.**

6.7.3 The Discrete Time Case

All of the preceding continuous time results have discrete time counterparts in which the differential equation (7.1) is replaced by the difference equation

$$x_i(t + 1) + D_i(t)x_i(t) = \sum_{j=1}^{m} B_{ij}(t)x_j(t) + u_i(t),$$

(7.16)

together with initial conditions prescribing $x(0)$. We collect below the relevant results, and we leave the proof as an exercise because it is a simple repetition of the proof of the continuous time results. Let us simply say that the pointwise convergence result is somewhat trivial. The reason is that once every equation is relaxed, then $x(1)$ assumes the correct value and never changes thereafter. Proceeding by induction, for any t, the value of $x(t)$ generated by the algorithm will in finite time become exactly equal to the corresponding value of the solution of the difference equation (7.16). In general, however, it will take at least t iterations for $x(t)$ to be obtained. As in the case of continuous time systems, we are interested in uniform convergence over $[0, \infty)$, because in that case, the value of $x(t)$ is obtained within a desired accuracy after a number of iterations that does not depend on t.

Proposition 7.7. Consider the asynchronous relaxation algorithm for solving the system of difference equations (7.16).

(a) For any t, the value of $x(t)$ generated by the asynchronous algorithm becomes eventually equal to the corresponding value for the true solution.

(b) Assume that there exists a vector $w > 0$ and a scalar $\epsilon > 0$ such that $\big(|D(t)| + |B(t)|\big)w \leq (1-\epsilon)w$ for all t. Then the sequence of time functions generated by the asynchronous relaxation algorithm, initialized with an arbitrary bounded function, converges uniformly to the solution of Eq. (7.16).

(c) Assume that each subsystem is time–invariant and one–dimensional, that is, $n_i = 1$, and that $|D_i| < 1$ for each i. Then the condition in part (b) is equivalent to the condition $\rho\big((I-|D|)^{-1}|B|\big) < 1$. Furthermore, the condition $\rho\big(|(I+D)^{-1}B|\big) < 1$ is necessary for uniform convergence on the interval $[0,\infty)$. *Note:* When the entries of D are all negative (which occurs when the difference equation arises from a simple discretization of a differential equation) the preceding necessary condition and the preceding sufficient condition coincide.

NOTES AND SOURCES

6.1 Totally asynchronous algorithmic models were introduced in [ChM69] in the context of iterative solution of linear systems of equations. Sometimes these models are also referred to as *chaotic relaxation models*. They have been subsequently studied by several authors [Bau78], [Ber82d], [Ber83], [Boj84b], [Don71], [MiS85], [Mie75], [Mit87], [RCM75], [Rob76], [Tsi87], [UrD86], [UrD88a], and [UrD88b].

6.2 The Asynchronous Convergence Theorem is due to [Ber83]. Necessary conditions for asynchronous convergence are discussed in [Tsi87].

6.3 Totally asynchronous relaxation was studied in [Rob76] and [Bau78] in connection with nonlinear problems involving maximum norm contractions. A study of some time–varying nonlinear asynchronous iterations that asymptotically approximate a maximum norm contraction is given in [LiB87].

6.3.1 The observation that the invariant distribution of a Markov chain can be found by a totally asynchronous algorithm after fixing the value of a single coordinate of the distribution vector is new. Earlier work [LuM86], which is discussed in Section 7.3, gave a partially asynchronous algorithm in which all elements of the distribution vector are updated. In practice it may be better to perform a few iterations on all coordinates before fixing the value of a single coordinate. Proposition 3.1 is due to [ChM69]; we give a somewhat different proof.

6.3.3 The material in this subsection is new. For related results see [Spi84].

6.3.5 The rate of convergence material in this subsection is new.

6.4 Totally asynchronous relaxation methods involving monotone mappings such as those arising in Dynamic Programming and the shortest path problem were studied in [Ber82d]. The asynchronous Bellman–Ford algorithm has been used in the context of the original routing algorithm in the ARPANET (1969) and subsequently in several other data communication networks (see [BeG87], [McW77], and [MRR80] for details). An analysis of some related asynchronous shortest path routing algorithms is given in [Taj77] for the case where all arcs have unit length.

6.5 The material in this section is due to [Ber86a] and [BeE87a].

6.6 The material in this section is due to [BeE87b].

6.7 Relaxation methods for differential equations are used extensively in electric circuit simulation problems (see [NeS83] and [LRS82]). Parallel synchronous methods for solving ordinary differential equations are discussed in [Gea86] and [Gea87].

6.7.1 Asynchronous relaxation methods for differential equations were proposed in [Mit87], where Props. 7.3 and 7.5 and their generalizations to nonlinear equations were shown. The pointwise convergence result of Prop. 7.1, and the necessary condition of Prop. 7.4 are new.

6.7.2 The results in this subsection are new. Asynchronous algorithms for two–point boundary value problems arising in optimal control have been studied in [LMS86] and [Spi86].

7

Partially Asynchronous Iterative Methods

In Chapter 6, we studied asynchronous algorithms under minimal interprocessor synchronization assumptions. We merely required that no processor quits forever. In particular, we allowed the possibility of arbitrarily large communication delays and arbitrary differences in the frequency of computation of different processors. We saw that excessive asynchronism can be detrimental to the convergence of some natural algorithms, such as the gradient algorithm (Example 3.1 in Subsection 6.3.2). It turns out that the desired convergence properties of several interesting algorithms are recovered, provided that certain bounds are imposed on the amount of asynchronism present in the execution of the algorithm, and this is the subject of this chapter. In particular, we shall assume that there exists a constant B (which we call the *asynchronism measure*) such that:

(a) Each processor performs an update at least once during any time interval of length B.

(b) The information used by any processor is outdated by at most B time units.

An asynchronous algorithm satisfying these two conditions will be called a *partially asynchronous* algorithm, as opposed to the totally asynchronous algorithms of Chapter 6. The convergence analysis of partially asynchronous algorithms cannot be reduced to a single general convergence result such as the Asynchronous Convergence Theorem of

Section 6.2. In fact, it will be seen in this chapter that there are two different types of partially asynchronous algorithms:

(a) Algorithms that do not converge totally asynchronously, but their partially asynchronous execution converges for any choice of the asynchronism measure B, as long as B is finite.

(b) Algorithms that converge partially asynchronously if the asynchronism measure B is small enough, and diverge if B is large.

This chapter can be roughly divided along the above lines. Sections 7.2–7.4 and 7.8 deal with algorithms of the first type, and Sections 7.5 and 7.6 deal with algorithms of the second type. We start in Section 7.1, with a definition of the partially asynchronous algorithmic model, and prove a general result that is sometimes useful in establishing convergence. This result is exploited in Section 7.2, where we prove partially asynchronous convergence of certain iterative algorithms involving nonexpansive mappings (with respect to the maximum norm). Two applications are provided: partially asynchronous convergence is established for a certain class of linear iterative algorithms, as well as for the dual relaxation algorithm for the solution of strictly convex network flow problems. In Section 7.3, we consider an iterative process whereby a set of processors try to reach agreement by receiving tentative values from other processors and forming convex combinations. We then proceed to show that the convergence of the agreement algorithm also implies partially asynchronous convergence of the algorithm $\pi := \pi P$ for computing the invariant distribution of an irreducible Markov chain. In Section 7.4, we consider an algorithm for load balancing in a computer network in which processors keep transferring parts of their own load to their lightly loaded neighbors. In Section 7.5, we study descent (gradient–like) algorithms for unconstrained and constrained optimization. Partially asynchronous convergence is established provided that the stepsize employed is small enough. We will also see that if the value of the asynchronism measure B is increased, a smaller stepsize is required. Thus, for a fixed stepsize, the algorithm converges if B is small enough, but can diverge when B is large. In Section 7.6, we consider the problem of optimal routing in a data communication network, which we formulate as a multicommodity network flow problem (cf. Section 5.6). We prove partially asynchronous convergence of an algorithm of the gradient projection type, under fairly realistic assumptions. In Section 7.7, we refine the model of computation of Section 7.1, by allowing the possibility that several processors update the same component of the vector being iterated. This can result in disagreement between different processors and we employ the scheme of Section 7.3 to eliminate this disagreement. Then, in Section 7.8, we consider asynchronous stochastic gradient–like algorithms. In such algorithms, processors have access to noisy measurements of the gradient of a cost function being optimized; it is then reasonable to have several processors update the same component, in the hope that the effects of the noise are averaged out. Thus, the extended model of computation introduced in Section 7.7 becomes applicable.

Several sections in this chapter can be omitted without any loss of continuity. In particular, the results in each one of Sections 7.2, 7.4, 7.5, and 7.6 are not used elsewhere. Furthermore, the results of Section 7.3 are only used in Sections 7.7 and 7.8.

7.1 THE PARTIALLY ASYNCHRONOUS ALGORITHMIC MODEL

In this section, we present a model of partially asynchronous iterative algorithms, provide some illustrative examples, and prove a result that is sometimes useful in establishing convergence. The model we use is the same as the totally asynchronous model of Section 6.1 except that certain bounds are placed on the time between consecutive updates by each processor and on the magnitude of the communication delays. We keep the same notation as in Chapter 6, which we now review.

Let $X_1, X_2, \ldots, X_n$ be given subsets of Euclidean spaces and let $X = X_1 \times X_2 \times \cdots \times X_n$ be their Cartesian product. Accordingly, elements of X are decomposed into block–components, that is, $x = (x_1, x_2, \ldots, x_n)$, with $x_i \in X_i$. We are given functions $f_i : X \mapsto X_i$, $i = 1, \ldots, n$, and we consider the asynchronous iteration

$$x_i := f_i(x), \qquad i = 1, \ldots, n.$$

An execution of this iteration is completely determined by the following:

(a) Initial conditions $x(t) \in X$ for each $t \leq 0$.

(b) A set T^i of times at which the ith component x_i is updated.

(c) A variable $\tau_j^i(t)$ for each i and j, and each $t \in T^i$. These variables determine the amount by which the information used in an update of x_i is outdated and satisfy $0 \leq \tau_j^i(t) \leq t$. For the purposes of mathematical analysis, it is sometimes convenient to allow $\tau_j^i(t)$ to be negative; this is the reason why we require initial conditions $x(t)$ for negative times.

The equations describing the algorithm are, for $t \geq 0$:

$$x_i(t + 1) = x_i(t), \qquad \text{if } t \notin T^i, \tag{1.1}$$

$$x_i(t + 1) = f_i\Big(x_1\big(\tau_1^i(t)\big), x_2\big(\tau_2^i(t)\big), \ldots, x_n\big(\tau_n^i(t)\big) \Big), \qquad \text{if } t \in T^i. \tag{1.2}$$

Any particular choice of the sets T^i and the values of the variables $\tau_j^i(t)$ will be called a *scenario*. It is seen that for any fixed scenario, the value of $x(t)$, for $t > 0$, is uniquely determined by the initial conditions. However, the values obtained under different scenarios could be very different. The assumption that follows is a restriction on the set of scenarios under consideration and should be contrasted with the Total Asynchronism Assumption of Section 6.1.

Assumption 1.1.   (*Partial Asynchronism*) There exists a positive integer B such that:

(a) For every i and for every $t \geq 0$, at least one of the elements of the set $\{t, t + 1, \ldots, t + B - 1\}$ belongs to T^i.

(b) There holds

$$t - B < \tau_j^i(t) \leq t, \tag{1.3}$$

for all i and j, and all $t \geq 0$ belonging to T^i.

(c) There holds $\tau_i^i(t) = t$ for all i and $t \in T^i$.

The partial asynchronism assumption is often easy to enforce in a practical implementation. It is by no means assumed that the time variable t is accessible to the processors; rather, t should be viewed as a time variable measured by an external observer. In fact, t need not correspond to real time; it could simply be an artificial variable used to index the events of interest (e.g., the times at which some variables are updated). The following example demonstrates that Assumption 1.1 is typically easy to satisfy in message–passing systems.

Example 1.1.

Let τ denote the true (global) time. Suppose that the value of τ is unknown to the processors and that each processor maintains its own clock. Let $t_i(\tau)$ be the reading of the clock of processor i when τ is the true time. Let us now assume that the local clocks can be neither arbitrarily fast nor arbitrarily slow compared to the true time. In particular, we assume that

$$A_1|\tau - \tau'| \leq |t_i(\tau) - t_i(\tau')| \leq A_2|\tau - \tau'|, \qquad \forall \tau, \tau', \ \forall i,$$

where A_1 and A_2 are some positive constants. Suppose that an update by any processor takes anywhere between A_3 and A_4 time units, and that a processor can remain idle up to A_5 time units before initiating the next update. Here A_3, A_4, and A_5 are positive constants and time is measured by the local clock of the processor under consideration. Finally, suppose that the local time difference between the initiation of two consecutive broadcasts of any variable x_i is bounded by some A_6 and that such a broadcast takes up to A_7 global time units to be completed.

We introduce an index variable t that is incremented by 1 whenever some processor has completed a variable update, and we identify it with the time variable in the model of Eqs. (1.1) and (1.2). Under these assumptions, it is not hard to verify that the mathematical description (1.1)–(1.2) of the algorithm satisfies parts (a) and (b) of Assumption 1.1 (Exercise 1.1).

Part (c) of Assumption 1.1 is very natural and holds automatically in message–passing systems where the ith processor maintains the latest version of x_i and is the only processor that is allowed to update x_i. In shared memory systems, however, this assumption is not necessarily valid although it can be enforced quite easily (recall also the discussion of Example 1.2 in Section 6.1). It will be seen (Exercise 2.1 in the next section) that if Assumption 1.1(c) is violated, an otherwise convergent algorithm can diverge.

We continue with two examples that illustrate the different types of convergence behavior exhibited by partially asynchronous algorithms.

Example 1.2.   *Convergence for All Values of the Asynchronism Measure*

We consider the linear iteration $x := Ax$, where A is a 2×2 matrix given by

$$A = \begin{bmatrix} \frac{1}{2} & \frac{1}{2} \\ \frac{1}{2} & \frac{1}{2} \end{bmatrix}.$$

It is seen that the set X^* of fixed points of the mapping $f(x) = Ax$ is the set of all vectors $(x_1, x_2) \in \Re^2$ such that $x_1 = x_2$. Notice that the synchronous iteration $x(t+1) = Ax(t)$ converges in a single step to the vector $x = (y, y)$, where $y = (x_1 + x_2)/2$.

We consider the following scenario. There are two processors $i = 1, 2$, and each processor i updates the variable x_i at each time step. At certain times $t_1, t_2, \ldots$, each processor transmits its value, which is received with zero delay and is immediately incorporated into the computations of the other processor. We then have

$$x_1(t+1) = \frac{x_1(t)}{2} + \frac{x_2(t_k)}{2}, \qquad t_k \leq t < t_{k+1},$$

$$x_2(t+1) = \frac{x_1(t_k)}{2} + \frac{x_2(t)}{2}, \qquad t_k \leq t < t_{k+1}.$$

Thus,

$$x_1(t_{k+1}) = (\tfrac{1}{2})^{t_{k+1}-t_k} x_1(t_k) + \left(1 - (\tfrac{1}{2})^{t_{k+1}-t_k}\right) x_2(t_k),$$

$$x_2(t_{k+1}) = (\tfrac{1}{2})^{t_{k+1}-t_k} x_2(t_k) + \left(1 - (\tfrac{1}{2})^{t_{k+1}-t_k}\right) x_1(t_k).$$

Subtracting these two equations, we obtain

$$|x_2(t_{k+1}) - x_1(t_{k+1})| = \left(1 - 2(\tfrac{1}{2})^{t_{k+1}-t_k}\right)|x_2(t_k) - x_1(t_k)| = (1 - \epsilon_k)|x_2(t_k) - x_1(t_k)|,$$

where $\epsilon_k = 2(\tfrac{1}{2})^{t_{k+1}-t_k}$. In particular, the quantity $|x_2(t_k) - x_1(t_k)|$ keeps decreasing. Nevertheless, convergence to a vector in X^* is not guaranteed unless $\prod_{k=1}^{\infty}(1 - \epsilon_k) = 0$, which is not necessarily the case. For example, it can be shown that $\prod_{k=1}^{\infty}(1 - k^{-2}) > 0$, and if we choose the differences $t_{k+1} - t_k$ to be large enough so that $\epsilon_k < k^{-2}$, then convergence to a vector in X^* does not take place. (See Fig. 7.1.1 for an illustration.) This shows that the iteration $x := Ax$ does not converge totally asynchronously. On the other hand, if the partial asynchronism assumption is imposed, we must have $t_{k+1} - t_k \leq B$ in the scenario just described. We then obtain $\epsilon_k > 1/2^B$ and $\prod_{k=1}^{\infty}(1 - \epsilon_k) = 0$, which proves that $x_1(t_k) - x_2(t_k)$ converges to zero, and the sequence $\{x(t_k)\}$ converges to the set X^*. This conclusion will be generalized in Section 7.3, where convergence is proved for every partially asynchronous scenario.

This example is typical of algorithms that converge partially asynchronously for every choice of B, but do not converge totally asynchronously. In such algorithms, there is usually a function that measures distance from the set X^* of fixed points and that is guaranteed to decrease once in a while. However, the factor by which this distance function decreases is reduced when the communication delays increase. We then need to assume that communication delays are bounded in order to guarantee that the distance function decreases at a fixed rate.

Example 1.3.   *Convergence Only When the Asynchronism Measure is Small*

Consider the linear iteration $x := x - \gamma Ax$, where γ is a small positive stepsize, the matrix A is given by

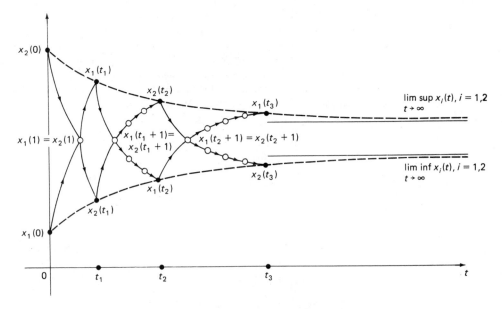

Figure 7.1.1 Nonconvergence under a totally asynchronous scenario in Example 1.2. Here, for each integer t in the range $[t_k, t_{k+1})$, each processor i averages its value $x_i(t)$ with the value $x_j(t_k)$ of the other processor j computed $t - t_k$ time units earlier. The difference $|x_1(t_k) - x_2(t_k)|$ is monotonically decreasing, but does not converge to zero if the intervals $[t_k, t_{k+1}]$ are increasingly large.

$$A = \begin{bmatrix} 1+\epsilon & 1 & 1 \\ 1 & 1+\epsilon & 1 \\ 1 & 1 & 1+\epsilon \end{bmatrix} = \begin{bmatrix} \epsilon & 0 & 0 \\ 0 & \epsilon & 0 \\ 0 & 0 & \epsilon \end{bmatrix} + \begin{bmatrix} 1 \\ 1 \\ 1 \end{bmatrix} [1 \quad 1 \quad 1],$$

and ϵ is a scalar satisfying $0 < \epsilon < 1$. (Notice that A is positive definite.) This iteration is the gradient algorithm for minimizing the quadratic cost function $\frac{1}{2}x'Ax$ and, if γ is small enough, it converges synchronously (Chapters 2 and 3). The present example is the same as Example 3.1 of Section 6.3.2, where it was shown that the corresponding totally asynchronous iteration does not converge. We now consider a partially asynchronous scenario whereby each processor performs an iteration at each time step and information is exchanged once every B time units. We let $t_k = kB$, and the update equation for x_1 is given by

$$x_1(t + 1) = x_1(t) - \gamma\big((1 + \epsilon)x_1(t) + x_2(t_k) + x_3(t_k)\big), \qquad t_k \leq t < t_{k+1}. \tag{1.4}$$

Similar equations are valid for x_2 and x_3. We solve the difference equation (1.4) to obtain

$$x_1(t_{k+1}) = \big(1 - \gamma(1 + \epsilon)\big)^B x_1(t_k) - \frac{1 - \big(1 - \gamma(1 + \epsilon)\big)^B}{1 + \epsilon}\big(x_2(t_k) + x_3(t_k)\big),$$

and similar equations hold for $x_2(t_k)$ and $x_3(t_k)$. We conclude that for this particular scenario, we have

$$x(t_{k+1}) = Cx(t_k),$$

where

$$C = \begin{bmatrix} \alpha & \beta & \beta \\ \beta & \alpha & \beta \\ \beta & \beta & \alpha \end{bmatrix},$$

$$\alpha = \left(1 - \gamma(1+\epsilon)\right)^B, \qquad \beta = -\frac{1 - \left(1 - \gamma(1+\epsilon)\right)^B}{1+\epsilon}.$$

The eigenvalues of C are equal to $\alpha + 2\beta$ and $\alpha - \beta$, the latter with multiplicity two. [This is because $C = (\alpha - \beta)I + \beta ee'$, where $e \in \Re^3$ is the vector with all entries equal to 1. It is then seen that the eigenvalues of ee' are equal to 3 and 0, the latter with multiplicity two.] As B increases to infinity, α approaches 0 and β approaches $-1/(1+\epsilon)$, assuming that γ is small enough to satisfy $\gamma(1+\epsilon) < 1$. In particular, $\alpha + 2\beta$ approaches $-2/(1+\epsilon)$, which is larger than 1 in magnitude. It follows that for B sufficiently large, we have $\rho(C) > 1$ and the iteration does not converge under the previously considered partially asynchronous scenario. On the other hand, if B is a moderate number and γ is very small, we have $\alpha \approx 1 - B\gamma(1+\epsilon)$ and $\beta \approx -B\gamma$, where we have neglected terms of the order of γ^2 or smaller. Thus, the eigenvalues of C are approximately equal to $1 - B\gamma(3+\epsilon)$ and $1 - B\gamma\epsilon$. Assuming that γ is sufficiently small so that $B\gamma(3+\epsilon) < 1$, we see that the eigenvalues of C are smaller than 1 in magnitude and convergence follows for the previously considered scenario.

A different approach for establishing convergence, which is also easier to generalize, is to notice that the differences $x_2(t) - x_2(t_k)$ and $x_3(t) - x_3(t_k)$ for $t_k \leq t < t_{k+1}$ are of the order of γB. It then follows that the update $x_1(t+1) - x_1(t)$ in Eq. (1.4) differs from the synchronous update $-\gamma\big((1+\epsilon)x_1(t) + x_2(t) + x_3(t)\big)$ by a factor of the order of $B\gamma^2$. Thus, even though the values in Eq. (1.4) are outdated, this can only have effects of the order of $B\gamma^2$. As long as $B\gamma$ is much smaller than 1, the effects of asynchronism are small compared with the magnitude of the updates and the algorithm can be approximated (up to first order terms in γ) with the synchronous algorithm that is known to be convergent. On the other hand, if $B\gamma$ is larger than 1, then the effect of asynchronism on an update becomes comparable to the magnitude of that update and is therefore big enough to cause divergence. Although this argument is somewhat sketchy, it will be made rigorous in Section 7.5.

This example is representative of algorithms that converge partially asynchronously when B is small and can diverge when B is large. A typical property of such algorithms is that the effects of asynchronism are negligible when delays are small, but can become significant when delays are large. Such a property is naturally present in algorithms that employ a small stepsize.

We continue by developing some background on the structure of partially asynchronous iterations. An important consequence of Eqs. (1.1) and (1.2) and Assumption 1.1 is that the value of $x(t+1)$ depends only on $x(t), x(t-1), \ldots, x(t-B+1)$, and not on any earlier information $x(\tau)$, $\tau \leq t - B$. Thus, old information is purged from the system after at most B time units, and this suggests that we introduce the vector

$$z(t) = \big(x(t), x(t-1), \ldots, x(t-B+1)\big),$$

which summarizes all unpurged information. From the preceding discussion, for any given scenario, the value of $x(t+1)$ can be determined from knowledge of $z(t)$. It follows that $z(t+1)$ can be determined from $z(t)$. Proceeding inductively, we can see that for any fixed scenario and any positive integer s, the value of $z(t+s)$ is uniquely determined by $z(t)$. Another important observation is that if the function f is continuous, then for any fixed scenario and any $s > 0$, $z(t+s)$ is a continuous function of $z(t)$.

We denote by X^* the set $\{x \in X \mid x = f(x)\}$ of fixed points of f, and by Z the Cartesian product of B copies of X. We also use Z^* to denote the set of all elements of Z of the form $(x^*, x^*, \ldots, x^*)$, where x^* is an arbitrary element of X^*. It is not hard to see that if $z(t) = z^* \in Z^*$, then $z(t+s) = z^*$ for every $s > 0$ and for every scenario.

The result that follows is sometimes useful in establishing convergence of a partially asynchronous algorithm to X^* and will be invoked in Section 7.2. It involves a distance function $d : Z \mapsto [0, \infty)$, which measures the progress of $z(t)$ toward the set Z^* and an assumption that this function has to decrease once in a while. In this respect, Prop. 1.1 has the flavor of a Lyapunov stability theorem and can be successfully applied only if a suitable function d is available.

Proposition 1.1. (*Lyapunov Theorem*) Consider the asynchronous iteration (1.1)–(1.2). Suppose that f is continuous and that Assumption 1.1 (partial asynchronism) holds. Suppose also that there exists some positive integer t^* and a continuous function $d : Z \mapsto [0, \infty)$ with the following properties:

(a) For every $z(0) \notin Z^*$ and for every scenario, we have $d\big(z(t^*)\big) < d\big(z(0)\big)$.

(b) For every $z(0) \in Z$, for every $t \geq 0$, and for every scenario, we have $d\big(z(t+1)\big) \leq d\big(z(t)\big)$.

Then, we have $z^* \in Z^*$ for every limit point $z^* \in Z$ of the sequence $\{z(t)\}$.

Proof. By the continuity of f and our earlier discussion, $z(t^*)$ is a continuous function of $z(0)$ for every scenario. Using the continuity of d, $d\big(z(t^*)\big)$ is also a continuous function of $z(0)$ for every scenario. We define a function $h : Z \mapsto \Re$ by letting

$$h\big(z(0)\big) = \max\big\{d\big(z(t^*)\big) - d\big(z(0)\big)\big\}, \tag{1.5}$$

where the maximum is taken over all possible scenarios. Although there are infinitely many possible scenarios, if we consider the iteration over a time interval of t^* units, there are only a finite number of choices. This is because we have to deal with only a finite number of variables $\tau_j^i(t)$, $0 \leq t \leq t^*$, and because each one of these variables can take a finite number B of different values. Therefore, the maximum in the definition of h is over a finite number of choices. For each such choice, $d\big(z(t^*)\big) - d\big(z(0)\big)$ is a continuous function of $z(0)$. It is not hard to see that the maximum of a finite number of continuous functions is continuous. It follows that h is continuous. Furthermore, for every scenario and every $z(0) \notin Z^*$, we have $d\big(z(t^*)\big) - d\big(z(0)\big) < 0$, from which it follows that $h(z) < 0$ for every $z \notin Z^*$.

Notice that if there exists a scenario that starts with some $z(0) = z$ at time 0 and generates some $z(t^*) = \tilde{z}$ at time t^*, then there also exists a scenario that starts with $z(t) = z$ at time t and produces $z(t + t^*) = \tilde{z}$ at time $t + t^*$. The converse is also true. For this reason, the function h defined by Eq. (1.5) is also given by

$$h\big(z(t)\big) = \max\big\{d\big(z(t + t^*)\big) - d\big(z(t)\big)\big\}, \qquad (1.6)$$

where the maximum is again taken over all scenarios.

Let us now fix a scenario and a choice of $z(0)$. From condition (b) in the statement of the proposition, the sequence $\big\{d\big(z(t)\big)\big\}$ is nonincreasing. Furthermore, it is bounded below by zero and, therefore, converges to a limit that will be denoted by d^*. Let $z^* \in Z$ be a limit point of the sequence $\{z(t)\}$ and choose a sequence $\{t_k\}$ of times such that $z(t_k)$ converges to z^*. From Eq. (1.6) and the continuity of h,

$$d^* = \lim_{k \to \infty} d\big(z(t_k + t^*)\big) \le \lim_{k \to \infty} d\big(z(t_k)\big) + \lim_{k \to \infty} h\big(z(t_k)\big) = d^* + h(z^*).$$

Since, as observed earlier, we have $h(z) < 0$ for all $z \notin Z^*$, it follows that $z^* \in Z^*$. **Q.E.D.**

Proposition 1.1 does not deal with convergence rates and is in fact too general to have useful convergence rate implications. However, it can be shown (Exercise 1.2) that for the case of linear iterative algorithms, convergence is guaranteed to be geometric.

EXERCISES

1.1. Show that for a sufficiently large B, parts (a) and (b) of Assumption 1.1 are satisfied in the context of Example 1.1.

1.2. (**Geometric Convergence of Linear Partially Asynchronous Iterations.**) Consider a partially asynchronous iteration in which $X = \Re^n$ and the iteration function f is of the form $f(x) = Ax$, where A is an $n \times n$ matrix. Notice that the set X^* of fixed points of f is a subspace of $\Re^n$. Let Z and Z^* be as defined in this section, and let $\| \cdot \|$ be some vector norm on Z. For any $z \in Z$, we define $d(z) = \inf_{z^* \in Z^*} \|z - z^*\|$.

  (**a**) Show that the infimum in the definition of d is attained and that the function d is continuous.

  (**b**) Show that $d(cz) = cd(z)$ and $d(z - z^*) = d(z)$ for every $z \in Z$, $z^* \in Z^*$, and every positive scalar c.

  (**c**) Suppose that conditions (a) and (b) of Prop. 1.1 are satisfied. Show that $d\big(z(t)\big)$ converges to zero geometrically.

  (**d**) Extend the result of part (b) to the case where f is of the form $f(x) = Ax + b$, where b is a given vector in $\Re^n$, assuming that the function f has a fixed point.

  Hints: For part (a), see the proof of Prop. 2.1 in the next section. For part (c), we let $S(z^*) = \big\{z \in Z \mid d(z) = \|z - z^*\|\big\}$ for any $z^* \in Z^*$. We also let $R(c) = \{z \in Z \mid d(z) = c\}$ and

$$\rho = \sup \frac{d\big(z(t^*)\big)}{d\big(z(0)\big)}, \tag{1.7}$$

where the supremum is over all $z(0) \in S(0) \cap R(1)$ and all scenarios. Use the continuity of d and the compactness of $S(0) \cap R(1)$ to show that $\rho < 1$. Then notice that for any scenario, the mapping that determines $z(t)$ as a function of $z(0)$ is linear. Show that the value of ρ remains the same if the supremum in Eq. (1.7) is taken over all $z(0) \in S(0)$ such that $z(0) \notin Z^*$. Next, notice that if $z^* \in Z^*$ and $z(0)$ is changed to $z(0) - z^*$, then for any fixed scenario, $z(t^*)$ is changed to $z(t^*) - z^*$. Use the property $d(z) = d(z - z^*)$ to conclude that ρ remains the same if the supremum in Eq. (1.7) is taken over all $z(0) \notin Z^*$. For part (d), use a change of variables to replace b by the zero vector.

1.3. Formulate and prove an extension of Prop. 1.1 for the case where Eq. (1.2) is generalized to

$$x_i(t + 1) = f_i\Big(x_1\big(\tau_1^i(t)\big), x_2\big(\tau_2^i(t)\big), \dots, x_n\big(\tau_n^i(t)\big), \theta_i(t)\Big), \qquad \text{if } t \in T^i.$$

Here each $\theta_i(t)$ is a parameter belonging to a compact set Θ. *Hint:* The maximum in Eq. (1.5) has to be taken over all choices of the parameters $\theta_i(t)$.

7.2 ALGORITHMS FOR FIXED POINTS OF NONEXPANSIVE MAPPINGS

We consider a partially asynchronous iteration of the form $x := f(x)$, where $f : \Re^n \mapsto \Re^n$. We let $X^* = \{x \in \Re^n \mid f(x) = x\}$ be the set of fixed points of f, and we study the case where f has the following properties:

Assumption 2.1.

(a) The set X^* is nonempty.

(b) The function f is continuous.

(c) The function f is *nonexpansive*, that is, it satisfies

$$\|f(x) - x^*\|_\infty \le \|x - x^*\|_\infty, \qquad \forall x \in \Re^n, \ \forall x^* \in X^*. \tag{2.1}$$

We develop a general convergence result (Prop. 2.3) which we then apply to two specific problems: solution of systems of equations involving a weakly diagonally dominant matrix (Subsection 7.2.2) and nonlinear convex network flow problems (Subsection 7.2.3).

7.2.1 A Convergence Result

For any $x \in \Re^n$, we denote by $g(x)$ the distance of x from X^*, defined by

$$g(x) = \inf_{x^* \in X^*} \|x - x^*\|_\infty. \tag{2.2}$$

The following preliminary result will be needed in the sequel.

Proposition 2.1.   Suppose that $f : \Re^n \mapsto \Re^n$ satisfies Assumption 2.1. Then:

(a) The set X^* is closed.

(b) For every $x \in \Re^n$, there exists some $x^* \in X^*$ such that $g(x) = \|x - x^*\|_\infty$.

(c) The function $g : X \mapsto \Re^n$, is continuous.

(d) For every $x \in \Re^n$ we have $g(f(x)) \leq g(x)$.

Proof.

(a) Let $\{x^k\}$ be a sequence of elements of X^* converging to some x^*. Using the continuity of f, we have

$$f(x^*) = \lim_{k \to \infty} f(x^k) = \lim_{k \to \infty} x^k = x^*,$$

and x^* belongs to X^*. This shows that the set X^* contains all of its limit points and is therefore closed.

(b) Let us fix some $x \in \Re^n$, and let y^* be an arbitrary element of X^*. A definition equivalent to Eq. (2.2) is

$$g(x) = \inf_{\{x^* \in X^* \mid \|x - x^*\|_\infty \leq \|x - y^*\|_\infty\}} \|x - x^*\|_\infty.$$

The set over which this minimization is carried out is the intersection of the closed set X^* with a closed and bounded set. It is therefore itself closed and bounded. Furthermore, the function being minimized is continuous and it follows (Prop. A.8 in Appendix A) that the infimum is attained at some element of X^*.

(c) Let $x, y \in \Re^n$ and let $x^* \in X^*$ be such that $\|x - x^*\|_\infty = g(x)$. Then

$$g(y) \leq \|y - x^*\|_\infty \leq \|y - x\|_\infty + \|x - x^*\|_\infty = \|y - x\|_\infty + g(x).$$

A similar argument shows that $g(x) \leq \|x - y\|_\infty + g(y)$. Thus, $|g(y) - g(x)| \leq \|y - x\|_\infty$, which shows that g is continuous.

(d) Let $x \in \Re^n$ and let x^* be such that $\|x - x^*\|_\infty = g(x)$. Then

$$g(f(x)) \leq \|f(x) - x^*\|_\infty \leq \|x - x^*\|_\infty = g(x).$$

Q.E.D.

We introduce some more notation. Given any $x \in \Re^n$ and $x^* \in X^*$ we let $I(x; x^*)$ be the set of indices of coordinates of x that are farthest away from x^*. That is,

$$I(x; x^*) = \{ i \mid |x_i - x_i^*| = \|x - x^*\|_\infty \}. \tag{2.3}$$

Notice that $I(x; x^*)$ is always nonempty. We also let

$$U(x; x^*) = \left\{ y \in \Re^n \;\middle|\; y_i = x_i \text{ for all } i \in I(x; x^*), \right.$$

$$\left. \text{and } |y_i - x_i^*| < \|x - x^*\|_\infty \text{ for all } i \notin I(x; x^*) \right\}. \tag{2.4}$$

Notice that $I(x; x^*) = I(y; x^*)$ and $\|x - x^*\|_\infty = \|y - x^*\|_\infty$ for every $y \in U(x; x^*)$. Furthermore, $x \in U(x; x^*)$. Loosely speaking, $U(x; x^*)$ is the set of all vectors y with $\|y - x^*\|_\infty = \|x - x^*\|_\infty$ that agree with x in the components that are farthest away from x^* (see Fig. 7.2.1).

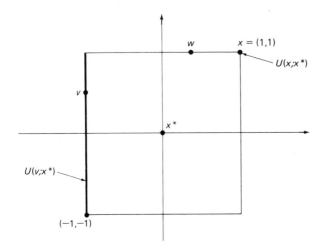

Figure 7.2.1 Illustration of the sets $I(\cdot; x^*)$ and $U(\cdot; x^*)$. Let $n = 2$ and suppose that $x^* = (0, 0) \in X^*$. For the indicated points x, v, and w, we have $I(x; x^*) = \{1, 2\}$, $I(v; x^*) = \{1\}$, $I(w; x^*) = \{2\}$. The set $U(v; x^*)$ is the set of all vectors of the form $(-1, c)$, where c satisfies $-1 < c < 1$, which is the segment joining the points $(-1, -1)$ and $(-1, 1)$, the endpoints excluded. Similarly, $U(w; x^*) = \{(c, 1) \mid -1 < c < 1\}$. Finally, we have $U(x; x^*) = \{x\}$.

Our convergence result uses the following assumption on f.

Assumption 2.2.

(a) The set X^* is convex.

(b) For every $x \in \Re^n$ and $x^* \in X^*$ such that $\|x - x^*\|_\infty = g(x) > 0$, there exists some $i \in I(x; x^*)$ such that $f_i(y) \neq y_i$ for all $y \in U(x; x^*)$.

(c) If $x \in \Re^n$, $f_i(x) \neq x_i$, and $x^* \in X^*$, then $|f_i(x) - x_i^*| < \|x - x^*\|_\infty$.

We interpret Assumption 2.2(b). Consider some $x \notin X^*$. Then $f(x) \neq x$, and there exists some i such that $f_i(x) \neq x_i$. Assumption 2.2(b) imposes the additional requirement that such an i can be found among the set of worst indices, that is, i belongs to the set $I(x; x^*)$ of indices corresponding to components farthest away from a closest element of X^*. Furthermore, if we change some of the components of x to obtain another vector $y \in U(x; x^*)$, we still retain the property $f_i(y) \neq y_i$, for this particular i. Assumption 2.2(b) can be difficult to verify, in general, but it will be shown to be true for two interesting problems in the next two subsections.

The following result shows that Assumption 2.2(c) is automatically true for certain algorithms involving a relaxation parameter.

Proposition 2.2.   Suppose that a function $h : \Re^n \mapsto \Re^n$ satisfies Assumptions 2.1, 2.2(a), and 2.2(b). Let $\gamma \in (0, 1)$. Then the mapping $f : \Re^n \mapsto \Re^n$ defined by

$$f(x) = (1 - \gamma)x + \gamma h(x)$$

satisfies Assumptions 2.1 and 2.2.

Proof.   We first notice that f and h have the same set X^* of fixed points. Thus, f satisfies Assumptions 2.1(a) and 2.2(a). Since h is assumed continuous, f is also continuous and satisfies Assumption 2.1(b). Furthermore, for any $x \in \Re^n$ and $x^* \in X^*$, we have

$$|f_i(x) - x_i^*| = \left| (1-\gamma)(x_i - x_i^*) + \gamma \big(h_i(x) - x_i^* \big) \right| \le (1-\gamma)|x_i - x_i^*| + \gamma\|x - x^*\|_\infty \le \|x - x^*\|_\infty.$$

Therefore, Eq. (2.1) holds for f and Assumption 2.1(c) is satisfied. Finally, we have $f_i(x) \ne x_i$ if and only if $h_i(x) \ne x_i$; since h satisfies Assumption 2.2(b), so does f.

We now fix some $x \in \Re^n$ such that $f_i(x) \ne x_i$ and some $x^* \in X^*$. Since $f_i(x) \ne x_i$, we have $x \notin X^*$, $x \ne x^*$ and $\|x - x^*\|_\infty > 0$. Consider the interval

$$A = \big\{ y_i \mid |y_i - x_i^*| \le \|x - x^*\|_\infty \big\}.$$

Clearly, $x_i \in A$. Also, by the nonexpansive property of h, we have $|h_i(x) - x_i^*| \le \|x - x^*\|_\infty$ and $h_i(x)$ also belongs to A. Since $f_i(x) \ne x_i$, we also have $h_i(x) \ne x_i$ and $f_i(x)$ is a convex combination of two distinct points in the interval A. Since $\gamma \ne 0$ and $\gamma \ne 1$, such a convex combination must lie in the interior of the interval. This shows that $|f_i(x) - x_i^*| < \|x - x^*\|_\infty$ and f satisfies Assumption 2.2(c).   **Q.E.D.**

We now explore the consequences of Assumption 2.2. Part (b) states that one of the components of x farthest away from the closest element x^* of X^* will move when the mapping f is applied; part (c) states that when this happens, the new value of that component will be closer to the corresponding component of x^*; this guarantees that the algorithm makes positive progress toward the set X^*. In fact, a convergence proof for the synchronous iteration $x(t + 1) = f\big(x(t)\big)$ under Assumptions 2.1 and 2.2 is fairly straightforward and the key ideas are illustrated in Fig. 7.2.2. The proof of asynchronous convergence (Prop. 2.3) will follow the same reasoning as in Fig. 7.2.2. A key difference, however, is that once the cardinality of the set $I\big(x(t); x^*\big)$ is reduced, it takes up to B time units for this information to be incorporated into the information available to other processors, and it can take an additional B time units for the other processors to perform an update using this new information. For this reason, the distance function employed in the proof of Prop. 2.3 is guaranteed to decrease once every (approximately) $2nB$ time units, as opposed to n time units in the argument outlined in Fig. 7.2.2. Another difference is that neither the convexity of X^* nor the full power of Assumption 2.2(b) are used in Fig. 7.2.2, but they play an essential role in the proof of asynchronous convergence.

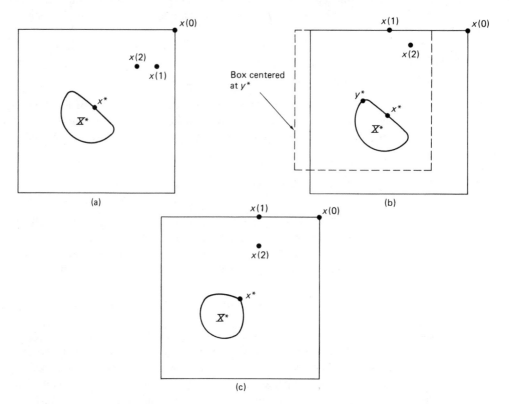

Figure 7.2.2 Illustration of a convergence proof for the synchronous iteration $x(t+1) = f\big(x(t)\big)$ under Assumptions 2.1 and 2.2. Suppose that $n = 2$ and let $x(0)$, $x^* \in X^*$ be as indicated. Suppose that $g\big(x(0)\big) = \|x(0) - x^*\|_\infty$. Since $x(0) \notin X^*$, there exists some $i \in \{1, 2\}$ such that $x_i(1) \neq x_i(0)$. Let us assume that $i = 1$. There are three cases to consider.

(a) If $x_2(1) \neq x_2(0)$, then Assumption 2.2(c) implies that $g\big(x(2)\big) \le g\big(x(1)\big) \le \|x(1) - x^*\|_\infty < \|x(0) - x^*\|_\infty = g\big(x(0)\big)$.

(b) If $x_2(1) = x_2(0)$ and if there exists some $y^* \in X^*$ such that $\|x(1) - y^*\|_\infty < \|x(1) - x^*\|_\infty$, then $g\big(x(2)\big) \le g\big(x(1)\big) \le \|x(1) - y^*\|_\infty < \|x(1) - x^*\|_\infty \le g\big(x(0)\big)$.

(c) If $x_2(1) = x_2(0)$ and $\|x(1) - y^*\|_\infty \ge \|x(1) - x^*\|_\infty$ for all $y^* \in X^*$, then $g\big(x(1)\big) = \|x(1) - x^*\|_\infty$. Furthermore, $I\big(x(1); x^*\big) = \{2\}$. It follows from Assumption 2.2(b) that $x_2(2) \neq x_2(1)$ and from Assumption 2.2(c), $|x_2(2) - x_2^*| < \|x(1) - x^*\|_\infty = g\big(x(0)\big)$.

In all three cases, we have $g\big(x(2)\big) < g\big(x(0)\big)$ and convergence follows from Prop. 1.1 of Section 7.1 applied to the function g. In the more general case of n–dimensional problems, a similar argument would yield $g\big(x(n)\big) < g\big(x(0)\big)$.

Proposition 2.3.   Suppose that $f : \Re^n \mapsto \Re^n$ satisfies Assumptions 2.1 and 2.2. Suppose that Assumption 1.1 (partial asynchronism) holds. Then the sequence $\{x(t)\}$ generated by the asynchronous iteration $x := f(x)$ converges to some element of X^*.

Proof. As in Section 7.1, we consider vectors of the form $z = (x^1, \dots, x^B)$, where each x^i belongs to $\Re^n$, and we let Z be the set of all such vectors. We also let $Z^* = \{(x^*, \dots, x^*) \in Z \mid x^* \in X^*\}$. Given any $z = (x^1, \dots, x^B)$ and $x^* \in X^*$, we let

$$D(z; x^*) = \max_{1 \le i \le B} \|x^i - x^*\|_\infty$$

and

$$d(z) = \inf_{x^* \in X^*} D(z; x^*).$$

Our intention is to apply Prop. 1.1 of Section 7.1 to the function d. We start by noticing that the function d is continuous and that the infimum in its definition is attained at some $x^* \in X^*$. (The proof of these assertions is identical to the proof of Prop. 2.1.)

We continue with a useful property of the function d, illustrated in Fig. 7.2.3.

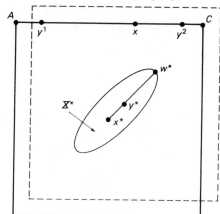

Figure 7.2.3 Illustration of the proof of Lemma 2.1. Let X^*, x, and x^* be as indicated. Let $B = 2$. Notice that $I(x; x^*) = \{2\}$ and that $U(x, x^*)$ is the segment AC, excluding the end points. Here $w^* \ne x^*$ is the fixed point closest to the vector x. We fix some $y^1, y^2 \in U(x; x^*)$ and we let y^* be a point on the segment joining x^* and w^*. The dashed–line rectangle is the set of all points y satisfying $\|y - y^*\|_\infty \le \|x - x^*\|_\infty$. We notice that if y^* is chosen close enough to x^*, then y^1 and y^2 both lie strictly inside the dashed–line rectangle. Thus, $\|y^1 - y^*\|_\infty < \|x - x^*\|_\infty$ and $\|y^2 - y^*\|_\infty < \|x - x^*\|_\infty$, which shows that $d(y^1, y^2) < g(x)$.

Lemma 2.1.   Suppose that $x \notin X^*$, $x^* \in X^*$, and that $g(x) = \inf_{w^* \in X^*} \|x - w^*\|_\infty < \|x - x^*\|_\infty$. Consider a vector $z \in Z$ of the form $z = (y^1, \dots, y^B)$, with each y^k belonging to $U(x; x^*)$. Then $d(z) < \|x - x^*\|_\infty$.

Proof. Let $w^* \in X^*$ be such that $\|x - w^*\|_\infty = g(x)$. Let ϵ be a small positive scalar to be determined later and let $y^* = (1 - \epsilon)x^* + \epsilon w^*$. In particular, if $0 < \epsilon < 1$, then $y^* \in X^*$, because of the convexity of X^*. We will now show that $D(z; y^*) < g(x)$ when ϵ is chosen sufficiently small.

Fix some k and consider the vector y^k. For any $i \in I(x; x^*)$, we have $y_i^k = x_i$, because $y^k \in U(x; x^*)$. Therefore,

$$|y_i^k - y_i^*| = |x_i - y_i^*| \le (1-\epsilon)|x_i - x_i^*| + \epsilon|x_i - w_i^*| \le (1-\epsilon)\|x - x^*\|_\infty + \epsilon g(x) < \|x - x^*\|_\infty.$$

Also, if $i \notin I(x; x^*)$, we have $|y_i^k - x_i^*| < \|x - x^*\|_\infty$, because $y^k \in U(x; x^*)$. Let $\alpha > 0$ be such that $\|x - x^*\|_\infty - |y_i^k - x_i^*| > \alpha$ for every k and every $i \notin I(x; x^*)$. Then

$$|y_i^k - y_i^*| \le |y_i^k - x_i^*| + |y_i^* - x_i^*| < \|x - x^*\|_\infty - \alpha + \epsilon \|w^* - x^*\|_\infty < \|x - x^*\|_\infty,$$

where the last inequality is valid provided that ϵ is chosen so that it satisfies $\epsilon \|w^* - x^*\|_\infty < \alpha$. With such a choice of ϵ, we have $\|y^k - y^*\|_\infty < \|x - x^*\|_\infty$ for all k. This shows that $d(z) \le D(z; y^*) < \|x - x^*\|_\infty$.   **Q.E.D.**

As in Section 7.1, we let $z(t) = \big(x(t), x(t-1), \ldots, x(t - B + 1)\big)$. We also use the notation, for $t \in T^i$,

$$x^i(t) = \Big(x_1\big(\tau_1^i(t)\big), \ldots, x_n\big(\tau_n^i(t)\big)\Big).$$

Lemma 2.2.

(a) If $x^* \in X^*$, then $\|x^i(t) - x^*\|_\infty \le D\big(z(t); x^*\big)$ for every $t \in T^i$.

(b) If $x^* \in X^*$, then $D\big(z(t+1); x^*\big) \le D\big(z(t); x^*\big)$ for all $t \ge 0$.

(c) There holds $d\big(z(t+1)\big) \le d\big(z(t)\big)$ for all $t \ge 0$.

Proof.

(a) By definition, $|x_j(\tau) - x_j^*| \le D\big(z(t); x^*\big)$ for all τ satisfying $t - B + 1 \le \tau \le t$, and the result follows because $t - B + 1 \le \tau_j^i(t) \le t$.

(b) If $t \in T^i$, we have $|x_i(t+1) - x_i^*| = |f\big(x^i(t)\big) - x_i^*| \le \|x^i(t) - x^*\|_\infty \le D\big(z(t); x^*\big)$, where the last step made use of part (a). Also, if $t \notin T^i$, then $|x_i(t+1) - x_i^*| = |x_i(t) - x_i^*| \le D\big(z(t); x^*\big)$. We thus conclude that $\|x(t+1) - x^*\|_\infty \le D\big(z(t); x^*\big)$, from which the desired conclusion follows.

(c) Let x^* be such that $d\big(z(t)\big) = D\big(z(t); x^*\big)$. Then $d\big(z(t+1)\big) \le D\big(z(t+1); x^*\big) \le D\big(z(t); x^*\big) = d\big(z(t)\big)$.   **Q.E.D.**

Notice that part (c) of Lemma 2.2 establishes that condition (b) in Prop. 1.1 is valid. In the remainder of the proof, we will show that if $z(0) \notin Z^*$, then $d\big(z(2nB + B)\big) < d\big(z(0)\big)$. This will establish that condition (a) of Prop. 1.1 is also valid, with $t^* = 2nB + B$.

Let us fix some $z(0) \notin Z^*$ and a particular scenario satisfying Assumption 1.1. We use the notation $d^* = d\big(z(0)\big)$ and from now on, we use x^* to indicate a particular element of X^* for which $d^* = d\big(z(0)\big) = D\big(z(0); x^*\big)$. We let

$$J(t) = \big\{i \mid |x_i(t) - x_i^*| = d^*\big\}.$$

Lemma 2.3.

(a) If $x_i(t+1) \neq x_i(t)$ for some $t \geq 0$, then $i \notin J(t+1)$.

(b) For every $t \geq 0$, we have $J(t+1) \subset J(t)$.

Proof.

(a) If $x_i(t+1) \neq x_i(t)$, we have $t \in T^i$. Furthermore, $f_i(x^i(t)) = x_i(t+1) \neq x_i(t) = x_i^i(t)$, where the last equality follows from Assumption 1.1(c). Using Assumption 2.2(c), we obtain

$$|x_i(t+1) - x_i^*| = |f_i(x^i(t)) - x_i^*| < \|x^i(t) - x^*\|_\infty \leq D(z(t); x^*) \leq D(z(0); x^*) = d^*.$$

(We have made use of parts (a) and (b) of Lemma 2.2.)

(b) If $i \in J(t+1)$, then part (a) shows that $x_i(t) = x_i(t+1)$, which implies that $i \in J(t)$.   **Q.E.D.**

For any finite set J, we use $|J|$ to denote its cardinality.

Lemma 2.4.   Suppose that $d^* = d(z(0)) > 0$. Then at least one of the following is true:

(i) Either $d(z(2nB + B)) < d^*$,

(ii) Or for every t_0 in the range $0 \leq t_0 \leq 2(n-1)B$, if $|J(t_0)| > 0$, then $|J(t_0 + 2B)| < |J(t_0)|$.

Proof. Suppose that $d(z(2nB + B)) = d^*$. We shall prove that if $|J(0)| > 0$, then $|J(2B)| < |J(0)|$, which will establish alternative (ii), at least for $t_0 = 0$. The argument for the case of an arbitrary t_0 in the given range is identical. Assume, in order to obtain a contradiction, that $J(0)$ is nonempty and that $|J(0)| = |J(2B)|$. Then Lemma 2.3 shows that $J(t) = J(0)$ for every t satisfying $0 \leq t \leq 2B$; furthermore, for any such t and every $i \in J(0)$, we have $x_i(t) = x_i(0)$.

Consider some t satisfying $0 \leq t \leq 2B$. Then $\|x(t) - x^*\|_\infty \leq D(z(t); x^*) \leq D(z(0); x^*) = d^*$; also, since $J(t)$ is nonempty, we have $\|x(t) - x^*\|_\infty \geq d^*$. Thus, $\|x(t) - x^*\|_\infty = d^*$ and $J(0) = J(t) = I(x(t); x^*)$. This implies that $x_i(t) = x_i(0)$ for every $i \in I(x(t); x^*) = I(x(0); x^*)$ and, from the definition of $U(x; x^*)$, it is seen that $x(t) \in U(x(0); x^*)$.

Consider now some $t \in T^i$ satisfying $B - 1 < t \leq 2B - 1$. Then $0 \leq \tau_j^i(t) \leq 2B - 1$ and this implies that $x_j^i(t) = x_j(\tau_j^i(t)) = x_j(0)$ for every $j \in J(0)$. Also, $|x_j(\tau_j^i(t)) - x_j^*| < d^*$ for every $j \notin J(\tau_j^i(t)) = J(0)$. We conclude that $x^i(t) \in U(x(0); x^*)$.

We will now apply Assumption 2.2(b). We distinguish two cases:

Case A. Suppose that $g(x(0)) < \|x(0) - x^*\|_\infty = d^*$. Since $x(t) \in U(x(0); x^*)$ for $t = 0, 1, \ldots, B$, Lemma 2.1 implies that $d(z(B)) < d^*$. Since $d(z(t))$ is monotonically nonincreasing, this contradicts our assumption that $d\big(z(2nB + B)\big) = d^*$.

Case B. Suppose that $g\big(x(0)\big) = \|x(0) - x^*\|_\infty = d^*$. Assumption 2.2(b) states that there exists some $i \in I\big(x(0); x^*\big) = J(0)$ such that $f_i(y) \neq y_i$ for all $y \in U\big(x(0); x^*\big)$. Let t_i be an element of T^i such that $B - 1 < t_i \leq 2B - 1$. As shown earlier, $x^i(t_i) \in U\big(x(0); x^*\big)$ and it follows that $x_i(t_i + 1) \neq x_i(t_i)$. This implies that $i \notin J(t_i + 1)$. Therefore, $|J(2B)| \leq |J(t_i + 1)| < |J(0)|$, which contradicts the assumption made in the beginning of the proof of the lemma and concludes the proof.   **Q.E.D.**

Proof of Proposition 2.3. (cont.)   According to Lemma 2.4, if $d\big(z(0)\big) > 0$, then there are two cases to consider. Either $d\big(z(2nB + B)\big) < d\big(z(0)\big)$ or the cardinality of $J(t)$ decreases every $2B$ time units until it is empty. In the latter case, we conclude that $J(2nB)$ is empty. Using Lemma 2.3, it follows that $J(t)$ is empty and $\|x(t) - x^*\|_\infty < d^*$ for all t satisfying $2nB \leq t \leq 2(n + 1)B$. This implies that $d\big(z(2nB + B)\big) < d^*$. We have, therefore, reached the conclusion that the inequality $d\big(z(2nB + B)\big) < d\big(z(0)\big)$ holds in both cases. This establishes condition (a) of Prop. 1.1. Notice that the sequence $\{z(t)\}$ is bounded, because of Lemma 2.2(b), and therefore has a limit point z^*. By Prop. 1.1, $z^* \in Z^*$. Let x^* be such that $z^* = (x^*, \ldots, x^*)$. Then $x^* \in X^*$ and $\liminf_{t \to \infty} D\big(z(t); x^*\big) = 0$. Since $D\big(z(t); x^*\big)$ is nonincreasing, we conclude that it converges to zero. This establishes that $z(t)$ converges to z^* and $x(t)$ converges to x^*. **Q.E.D.**

It should be pointed out that the limit of $x(t)$ in Prop. 2.3 depends in general on the particular scenario as well as on the initial conditions.

7.2.2 Weakly Diagonally Dominant Systems of Linear Equations

Consider a system $Ax = b$ of linear equations, where A is an $n \times n$ matrix with entries a_{ij}, and b is a vector in $\Re^n$. We study the case where A and b have the following properties.

Assumption 2.3.

(a) For every i, we have

$$|1 - a_{ii}| + \sum_{j \neq i} |a_{ij}| \leq 1. \tag{2.5}$$

(b) The set X^* of solutions of the equation $Ax = b$ is nonempty.

(c) The matrix A is irreducible.

Notice that Assumption 2.3(a) implies that $a_{ii} \in [0, 2]$. For the special case where $0 \leq a_{ii} \leq 1$, inequality (2.5) is equivalent to the condition $\sum_{j \neq i} |a_{ij}| \leq a_{ii}$, which is a weak row diagonal dominance condition. Notice also that an alternative statement of condition (2.5) is that $\|I - A\|_\infty \le 1$. It should be pointed out that no conclusions can be drawn from this condition on the existence and uniqueness of solutions of $Ax = b$. Existence is explicitly assumed in Assumption 2.3(b), but X^* could have several elements.

We consider the partially asynchronous iteration

$$x := f(x) = x - \gamma(Ax - b), \tag{2.6}$$

where γ is a relaxation parameter belonging to $(0, 1)$. Notice that the iteration matrix in Eq. (2.6) is equal to $I - \gamma A$. Under Assumption 2.3(a), we have

$$\|I - \gamma A\|_\infty \le (1 - \gamma) + \gamma \|I - A\|_\infty \le (1 - \gamma) + \gamma = 1.$$

If we had $\|I - A\|_\infty < 1$, then the last inequality would be strict and totally asynchronous convergence would be guaranteed, according to the results of Section 6.3. Thus, the following result is interesting primarily in the case where $\|I - A\|_\infty = 1$.

Proposition 2.4.   If Assumption 2.3 holds and if $0 < \gamma < 1$, then the mapping f of Eq. (2.6) satisfies Assumptions 2.1 and 2.2. In particular, under Assumption 1.1 (partial asynchronism), the asynchronous iteration (2.6) converges to some x^* satisfying $Ax^* = b$.

Proof.   Consider the mapping h defined by $h(x) = x - (Ax - b)$ and notice that $f(x) = (1 - \gamma)x + \gamma h(x)$. In view of Prop. 2.2, it is sufficient to show that h satisfies Assumptions 2.1, 2.2(a), and 2.2(b).

The set of fixed points of h is nonempty by Assumption 2.3(b). The function h is clearly continuous. Let x^* satisfy $Ax^* = b$. Then $\|h(x) - x^*\|_\infty = \|x - Ax + b - x^* + Ax^* - b\|_\infty = \|(I - A)(x - x^*)\|_\infty \le \|I - A\|_\infty \cdot \|x - x^*\|_\infty \le \|x - x^*\|_\infty$, where the last inequality follows from Eq. (2.5). We conclude that h satisfies Assumption 2.1.

Suppose that $x^* \in X^*$ and $y^* \in X^*$. Then $Ax^* = Ay^* = b$, which implies that $cAx^* + (1 - c)Ay^* = b$ for every scalar c. Thus, $cx^* + (1 - c)y^* \in X^*$. This shows that X^* is convex and Assumption 2.2(a) holds.

It remains to establish the validity of Assumption 2.2(b) for the function h. Fix some $x \in \Re^n$ and some $x^* \in X^*$ such that $\|x - x^*\|_\infty = g(x) > 0$, and let $S = I(x; x^*) = \{i \mid |x_i - x_i^*| = \|x - x^*\|_\infty\}$. If Assumption 2.2(b) fails to hold, then for every $i \in S$, there exists a vector $y^i \in U(x; x^*)$ such that $h_i(y^i) = y_i^*$; equivalently, $[Ay^i]_i - b_i = 0$. We now fix some $i \in S$ and a vector y^i with these properties. Since $y^i \in U(x; x^*)$, we have $|y_j^i - x_j^*| = \|x - x^*\|_\infty$ for $j \in S$ and $|y_j^i - x_j^*| < \|x - x^*\|_\infty$ for $j \notin S$. Since $Ax^* = b$, we obtain $[A(y^i - x^*)]_i = 0$, which can be written as

$$y_i^i - x_i^* = (1 - a_{ii})(y_i^i - x_i^*) - \sum_{\{j \in S \mid j \ne i\}} a_{ij}(y_j^i - x_j^*) - \sum_{j \notin S} a_{ij}(y_j^i - x_j^*).$$

Taking absolute values, we obtain

$$\|x - x^*\|_\infty = |y_i^i - x_i^*|$$

$$\leq |1 - a_{ii}| \cdot |y_i^i - x_i^*| + \sum_{\{j \in S | j \neq i\}} |a_{ij}| \cdot |y_j^i - x_j^*| + \sum_{j \notin S} |a_{ij}| \cdot |y_j^i - x_j^*|$$

$$\leq \left(|1 - a_{ii}| + \sum_{j \neq i} |a_{ij}| \right) \|x - x^*\|_\infty \leq \|x - x^*\|_\infty. \tag{2.7}$$

Therefore, equality holds throughout. However, for the second inequality in Eq. (2.7) to be an equality, we need

$$\sum_{j \notin S} |a_{ij}| \cdot |y_j^i - x_j^*| = \sum_{j \notin S} |a_{ij}| \cdot \|x - x^*\|_\infty.$$

Since $|y_j^i - x_j^*| < \|x - x^*\|_\infty$ for $j \notin S$, we conclude that $\sum_{j \notin S} |a_{ij}| = 0$, which shows that $a_{ij} = 0$ for every $j \notin S$. Since this is true for every $i \in S$ and since A is irreducible, we conclude that $S = \{1, \ldots, n\}$. We therefore have $U(x; x^*) = \{x\}$. Thus, $y^i = x$ for all i, and since $[Ay^i]_i = b_i$, we conclude that $Ax = b$ and $x \in X^*$. Thus, $g(x) = 0 < \|x - x^*\|_\infty$. This contradicts our initial assumptions for $g(x)$ and shows that Assumption 2.2(b) is satisfied. Convergence of the iteration (2.6) follows from Prop. 2.3.   **Q.E.D.**

According to Exercise 1.2, the convergence of the partially asynchronous iteration (2.6) is guaranteed to be geometric. (This is because, convergence was proved by appealing to Prop. 2.3 which, in turn was proved by showing that the conditions of Prop. 1.1 are satisfied. But these are precisely the conditions assumed in Exercise 1.2.) On the other hand, convergence is not guaranteed, in general, if the relaxation parameter γ is equal to 1 (see Example 2.1 to follow or Example 3.1 in the next section). Furthermore, convergence fails to hold, in general, if the iteration is executed totally asynchronously (see Example 1.2). The following example shows that a relaxation parameter $\gamma \in (0, 1)$ may be needed even if the matrix A is invertible, in which case, the set X^* of vectors x^* satisfying $Ax^* = b$ consists of a single element.

Example 2.1.

   Let

$$A = \begin{bmatrix} 1 & -1 \\ 1 & 1 \end{bmatrix}$$

and $b = 0$. Then the iteration $x := x - Ax$ takes the form $x_1 := x_2$ and $x_2 := -x_1$. This iteration does not converge when executed in Gauss–Seidel fashion [see Fig. 7.2.4(a)]. Since Gauss–Seidel execution is a special case of partially asynchronous execution, it follows that the partially asynchronous iteration $x := x - Ax$ does not converge. On the other hand, if a relaxation parameter $\gamma \in (0, 1)$ is introduced, the iteration $x := x - \gamma Ax$ converges when executed in Gauss–Seidel fashion [see Fig. 7.2.4(b)]. Furthermore, it is seen that

Assumption 2.3 is satisfied and, according to Prop. 2.4, the partially asynchronous iteration $x := x - \gamma Ax$ converges to zero.

7.2.3 Strictly Convex Network Flow Problems

Consider the nonlinear network flow problem of Sections 5.5 and 6.6:

$$\text{minimize} \quad \sum_{(i,j)\in A} a_{ij}(f_{ij}) \qquad\qquad (CNF)$$

$$\text{subject to} \quad \sum_{\{j|(i,j)\in A\}} f_{ij} - \sum_{\{j|(j,i)\in A\}} f_{ji} = s_i, \qquad \forall\, i \in N, \qquad (2.8)$$

$$b_{ij} \le f_{ij} \le c_{ij}, \qquad \forall\, (i,j) \in A, \qquad (2.9)$$

under the assumption of Sections 5.5 and 6.6:

Assumption 2.4.   (*Strict Convexity*) The functions $a_{ij}(\cdot)$, $(i,j) \in A$, are strictly convex real–valued functions, and problem (CNF) has at least one feasible solution.

We recall from Section 5.5 that for a given flow vector f, the surplus of a node i is

$$g_i = \sum_{\{j|(j,i)\in A\}} f_{ji} - \sum_{\{j|(i,j)\in A\}} f_{ij} + s_i.$$

The gradient of the dual functional is given by

$$\frac{\partial q(p)}{\partial p_i} = \sum_{\{j|(i,j)\in A\}} \nabla q_{ij}(p_i - p_j) - \sum_{\{j|(j,i)\in A\}} \nabla q_{ji}(p_j - p_i) + s_i = g_i(p), \qquad (2.10)$$

where

$$\nabla q_{ij}(p_i - p_j) = -\,[\text{the unique flow } f_{ij} \text{ of arc } (i,j) \text{ satisfying}$$

$$\text{complementary slackness together with } p],$$

$$g_i(p) = \text{surplus of node } i \text{ corresponding to the unique } f$$

$$\text{satisfying complementary slackness together with } p.$$

For $i = 1, \ldots, |N|$, we consider, as in Section 6.6, the point–to–set mapping R_i that assigns to a price vector p the interval of all prices ξ that maximize the dual cost along the ith price starting from p, that is,

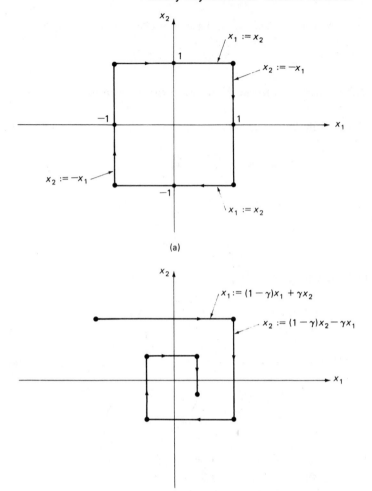

Figure 7.2.4 The need for a relaxation parameter in the iteration $x_1 := x_2$ and $x_2 := -x_1$. In part (a), the trajectory corresponding to a nonconvergent Gauss–Seidel execution is shown. When a relaxation parameter $\gamma \in (0,1)$ is introduced, the iteration becomes $x_1 := (1 - \gamma)x_1 + \gamma x_2$ and $x_2 := (1 - \gamma)x_2 - \gamma x_1$, and Gauss–Seidel convergence is obtained [part (b)].

$$R_i(p) = \left\{\xi \mid g_i(p_1, \ldots, p_{i-1}, \xi, p_{i+1}, \ldots, p_{|N|}) = 0\right\}$$

$$= \left\{\xi \; \middle| \; \sum_{\{j|(j,i)\in A\}} \nabla q_{ji}(p_j - \xi) = \sum_{\{j|(i,j)\in A\}} \nabla q_{ij}(\xi - p_j) + s_i\right\}.$$

It was shown in Section 5.5 that $R_i(p)$ is nonempty for all i and p. We also recall from Lemma 6.1 in Section 6.6 that the set $R_i(p)$ is bounded above for every p if and only if we have

$$s_i < \sum_{\{j|(i,j)\in A\}} c_{ij} - \sum_{\{j|(j,i)\in A\}} b_{ji}. \tag{2.11}$$

Similarly, the set $R_i(p)$ is bounded below for every p if and only if we have

$$\sum_{\{j|(i,j)\in A\}} b_{ij} - \sum_{\{j|(j,i)\in A\}} c_{ji} < s_i. \tag{2.12}$$

We consider the mappings

$$\overline{R}_i(p) = \sup_{\xi\in R_i(p)} \xi, \tag{2.13}$$

$$\underline{R}_i(p) = \inf_{\xi\in R_i(p)} \xi, \tag{2.14}$$

and the mapping $\tilde{R} : R^{|N|} \to R^{|N|}$ given by

$$\tilde{R}_i(p) = \begin{cases} p_i, & \text{if } g_i(p) = 0, \\ \overline{R}_i(p), & \text{if } g_i(p) < 0, \\ \underline{R}_i(p), & \text{if } g_i(p) > 0. \end{cases} \tag{2.15}$$

Note that $g_i(p) \geq \sum_{\{j|(j,i)\in A\}} b_{ji} - \sum_{\{j|(i,j)\in A\}} c_{ij} + s_i$, so if $g_i(p) < 0$, then inequality (2.11) holds and we have that $\overline{R}_i(p)$ is finite for all p. Similarly, if $g_i(p) > 0$, then $\underline{R}_i(p)$ is finite for all p. As a result, the mapping $\tilde{R}(p)$ is well defined by Eq. (2.15). Another fact that will be useful to us is that $\overline{R}_i(p)$ is continuous whenever it is finite, that is, when inequality (2.11) holds. This was proved in Prop. 6.1 in Section 6.6. Similarly, $\underline{R}_i(p)$ is continuous whenever it is finite, that is, when inequality (2.12) holds.

We now focus on the relaxation iteration

$$p := R^\gamma(p),$$

where $R^\gamma(p)$ is defined for all $\gamma \in (0, 1]$ by

$$R^\gamma(p) = p + \gamma\big(\tilde{R}(p) - p\big). \tag{2.16}$$

We note that the set of all dual optimal price vectors $\hat{P}$ coincides with the set of all fixed points of R^γ, that is, we have

$$\hat{P} = \{p \mid p = R^\gamma(p)\}, \qquad \forall \, \gamma \in (0, 1].$$

We will show that the function $\tilde{R}$ satisfies Assumptions 2.1, 2.2(a), and 2.2(b) (with f, x, and X^* in these assumptions replaced by $\tilde{R}$, p, and $\hat{P}$, respectively). In view of Props. 2.2 and 2.3, this implies partially asynchronous convergence of the iteration $p := R^\gamma(p)$ for all $\gamma \in (0, 1)$.

Proposition 2.5.   If Assumption 2.4 holds, the function $\tilde{R}$ satisfies Assumptions 2.1, 2.2(a), and 2.2(b). In particular, under Assumption 1.1 (partial asynchronism), the asynchronous iteration $p := R^{\gamma}(p)$, where $\gamma \in (0, 1)$, converges to some element of $\hat{P}$.

Proof.   The set $\hat{P}$ is convex because it is the optimal solution set of the unconstrained dual maximization problem which has a concave cost function, and it was shown to be nonempty in Section 5.5, so Assumptions 2.1(a) and 2.2(a) are satisfied. Lemma 5.3 shows that for all $p \in R^{|N|}$ and $p^* \in P^*$, we have

$$\min_{i \in N}\{p_i - p_i^*\} \leq \min_{i \in N}\{\tilde{R}_i(p) - p_i^*\} \leq \max_{i \in N}\{\tilde{R}_i(p) - p_i^*\} \leq \max_{i \in N}\{p_i - p_i^*\}.$$

It follows that

$$\|\tilde{R}(p) - p^*\|_\infty \leq \|p - p^*\|_\infty, \qquad \forall\, p \in R^{|N|},\ p^* \in \hat{P},$$

so $\tilde{R}$ is nonexpansive and Assumption 2.1(c) is satisfied.

We now show that Assumption 2.1(b) is satisfied, that is, $\tilde{R}$ is continuous. This is a straightforward consequence of the continuity of the mappings $\underline{R}_i$ and $\overline{R}_i$, which was shown in Section 6.6. More specifically, let $\{p(t)\}$ be a sequence converging to some p. If $g_i(p) > 0$, then $\tilde{R}_i\big(p(t)\big) = \underline{R}_i\big(p(t)\big)$ for t sufficiently large, so by continuity of $\underline{R}_i$ (Prop. 6.1 in Section 6.6), we have $\tilde{R}_i\big(p(t)\big) \to \tilde{R}_i(p)$. Similarly, we show that if $g_i(p) < 0$, then $\tilde{R}_i\big(p(t)\big) \to \tilde{R}_i(p)$. Finally, if $g_i(p) = 0$, there are four possibilities: (a) $p_i = \underline{R}_i(p) < \overline{R}_i(p)$, (b) $p_i = \overline{R}_i(p) > \underline{R}_i(p)$, (c) $p_i = \underline{R}_i(p) = \overline{R}_i(p)$, and (d) $\underline{R}_i(p) < p_i < \overline{R}_i(p)$. In case (a) [or (b)], we have for sufficiently large t, either $\tilde{R}\big(p(t)\big) = p(t)$ or $\tilde{R}\big(p(t)\big) = \underline{R}_i\big(p(t)\big)$ $[\tilde{R}\big(p(t)\big) = \overline{R}_i\big(p(t)\big)$, respectively], and the continuity of $\underline{R}_i$ and $\overline{R}_i$ implies that $\tilde{R}_i\big(p(t)\big) \to \tilde{R}_i(p)$. In case (c), the continuity of $\underline{R}_i$ and $\overline{R}_i$ implies that

$$\lim_{t \to \infty} \underline{R}_i\big(p(t)\big) = \lim_{t \to \infty} \overline{R}_i\big(p(t)\big) = p_i = \tilde{R}_i(p),$$

and since we have for all t, $\underline{R}_i\big(p(t)\big) \leq \tilde{R}_i\big(p(t)\big) \leq \overline{R}_i\big(p(t)\big)$, we obtain $\tilde{R}_i\big(p(t)\big) \to \tilde{R}_i(p)$. Finally, in case (d), we have $\tilde{R}\big(p(t)\big) = p(t)$ for sufficiently large t, and since $p(t) \to p$, we have $\tilde{R}_i\big(p(t)\big) \to \tilde{R}_i(p)$. Thus, $\tilde{R}$ is continuous.

There remains to show that Assumption 2.2(b) holds. Fix some $p \in R^{|N|}$ and some $p^* \in \hat{P}$ such that $\|p - p^*\|_\infty = \min_{\hat{p} \in \hat{P}} \|p - \hat{p}\|_\infty > 0$, and let

$$I^+ = \big\{i \mid p_i - p_i^* = \|p - p^*\|_\infty\big\},$$

$$I^- = \big\{i \mid p_i - p_i^* = -\|p - p^*\|_\infty\big\},$$

$$U(p; p^*) = \Big\{\tilde{p} \ \Big|\ \tilde{p}_i = p_i,\ \forall\, i \in I^+ \cup I^-,$$

$$\text{and } |\tilde{p}_i - p_i^*| < \|p - p^*\|_\infty,\ \forall\, i \notin I^+ \cup I^-\Big\}.$$

We want to show that there exists some $i \in I^+ \cup I^-$ such that $\tilde{R}_i(\tilde{p}) \neq \tilde{p}_i$ for all $\tilde{p} \in U(p; p^*)$. We argue by contradiction. Assume that for every $i \in I^+ \cup I^-$, there exists a price vector $p^i \in U(p; p^*)$ such that $\tilde{R}_i(p^i) = p_i^i$ or, equivalently, the surplus of the ith node corresponding to p^i is zero:

$$g_i(p^i) = 0.$$

Define the positive scalar δ by

$$\delta = \begin{cases} \|p - p^*\|_\infty, & \text{if } I^+ \cup I^- = \{1, \dots, |N|\}, \\ \|p - p^*\|_\infty - \beta & \text{otherwise,} \end{cases}$$

where

$$\beta = \max_{i \notin I^+ \cup I^-, \ k \in I^+ \cup I^-} |p_i^k - p_i^*|.$$

We assume in what follows that both I^+ and I^- are nonempty; if either I^+ or I^- is empty, a similar (and in fact simpler) proof can be used.

We have for each $i \in I^+$,

$$p_i^i - p_j^i \geq p_i^* - p_j^* + \delta, \qquad \forall \, j \notin I^+, \tag{2.17}$$

$$p_i^i - p_j^i = p_i^* - p_j^*, \qquad \forall \, j \in I^+. \tag{2.18}$$

Let f_{mn}^i (or f_{mn}^*) be the unique flow of each arc (m, n) that satisfies complementary slackness together with p^i (or p^*, respectively). Using inequality (2.17) and Eq. (2.18), we obtain for all $i \in I^+$,

$$f_{ij}^i = -\nabla q_{ij}(p_i^i - p_j^i) \geq -\nabla q_{ij}(p_i^* - p_j^* + \delta) \geq -\nabla q_{ij}(p_i^* - p_j^*) = f_{ij}^*,$$
$$\text{if } j \notin I^+ \text{ and } (i, j) \in A,$$

$$f_{ji}^i = -\nabla q_{ji}(p_j^i - p_i^i) \leq -\nabla q_{ji}(p_j^* - p_i^* - \delta) \leq -\nabla q_{ji}(p_j^* - p_i^*) = f_{ji}^*,$$
$$\text{if } j \notin I^+ \text{ and } (j, i) \in A,$$

$$f_{ij}^i = -\nabla q_{ij}(p_i^* - p_j^*) = f_{ij}^*, \qquad \text{if } j \in I^+ \text{ and } (i, j) \in A,$$

$$f_{ji}^i = -\nabla q_{ji}(p_j^* - p_i^*) = f_{ji}^*, \qquad \text{if } j \in I^+ \text{ and } (j, i) \in A.$$

By adding the preceding inequalities, we obtain

$$g_i(p^i) = \sum_{\{j|(j,i)\in A\}} f_{ji}^i - \sum_{\{j|(i,j)\in A\}} f_{ij}^i + s_i$$

$$\leq - \sum_{\{j|(j,i)\in A, j\notin I^+\}} \nabla q_{ji}(p_j^* - p_i^* - \delta) - \sum_{\{j|(j,i)\in A, j\in I^+\}} \nabla q_{ji}(p_j^* - p_i^*)$$

$$+ \sum_{\{j|(i,j)\in A, j\notin I^+\}} \nabla q_{ij}(p_i^* - p_j^* + \delta) + \sum_{\{j|(i,j)\in A, j\in I^+\}} \nabla q_{ij}(p_i^* - p_j^*) + s_i$$

$$\leq \sum_{\{j|(j,i)\in A\}} f_{ji}^* - \sum_{\{j|(i,j)\in A\}} f_{ij}^* + s_i$$

$$= g_i(p^*).$$

Since $g_i(p^i) = g_i(p^*) = 0$, we obtain

$$- \sum_{\{j|(j,i)\in A, j\notin I^+\}} \nabla q_{ji}(p_j^* - p_i^* - \delta) - \sum_{\{j|(j,i)\in A, j\in I^+\}} \nabla q_{ji}(p_j^* - p_i^*) $$

$$+ \sum_{\{j|(i,j)\in A, j\notin I^+\}} \nabla q_{ij}(p_i^* - p_j^* + \delta) + \sum_{\{j|(i,j)\in A, j\in I^+\}} \nabla q_{ij}(p_i^* - p_j^*) + s_i = 0$$

or equivalently, $g_i(\tilde{p}) = 0$ for all $i = 1, \ldots, |N|$, where the vector $\tilde{p}$ is given by

$$\tilde{p}_i = \begin{cases} p_i^* + \delta, & \text{if } i \in I^+, \\ p_i^*, & \text{if } i \notin I^+. \end{cases}$$

Therefore $\tilde{p} \in \hat{P}$. By construction we have

$$\|p - \tilde{p}\|_\infty = \|p - p^*\|_\infty = \min_{\hat{p} \in \hat{P}} \|p - \hat{p}\|_\infty \tag{2.19}$$

$$p_i - \tilde{p}_i = -\|p - \tilde{p}\|_\infty, \qquad \forall \, i \in I^-, \tag{2.20}$$

$$|p_i - \tilde{p}_i| < \|p - \tilde{p}\|_\infty, \qquad \forall \, i \notin I^-. \tag{2.21}$$

It follows that we can choose $\epsilon > 0$ which is sufficiently small so that the vector $\hat{p}$ with coordinates $\hat{p}_i = \tilde{p}_i - \epsilon$ for all i satisfies

$$\|p - \hat{p}\|_\infty = \|p - \tilde{p}\|_\infty - \epsilon. \tag{2.22}$$

Since the coordinates of $\hat{p}$ differ from those of $\tilde{p}$ by the same constant, we have $\hat{p} \in \hat{P}$. Therefore Eq. (2.22) contradicts Eq. (2.19).   **Q.E.D.**

Figure 7.2.5 illustrates the convergence process of the synchronous Jacobi version of the algorithm in a simple two node example and shows why taking $\gamma < 1$ is essential for convergence.

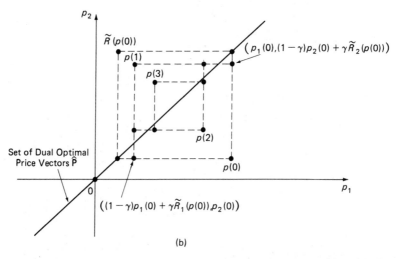

$$a_{12}(f_{12}) = \tfrac{1}{2}f_{12}^2$$
$$b_{12} = -1, c_{12} = 1$$
$$s_1 = s_2 = 0$$

(a)

(b)

Figure 7.2.5 (a) Two node example, with data as shown, where the Jacobi version of the relaxation method does not converge to an optimal price vector (cf. Fig. 5.5.5 in Section 5.5). (b) Sequence $\{p(0), p(1), \ldots\}$ generated by the synchronous Jacobi method $p(t+1) = (1-\gamma)p(t) + \gamma \tilde{R}\big(p(t)\big)$ when a relaxation parameter $\gamma \in (0,1)$ is used.

EXERCISES

2.1. Suppose that a function $h : \Re^n \mapsto \Re^n$ satisfies Assumptions 2.1, 2.2(a), and 2.2(b). Let Assumption 1.1 hold (partial asynchronism), and let γ be a scalar satisfying $0 < \gamma < 1$. Propositions 2.2 and 2.3 show that the asynchronous iteration

$$x_i(t+1) = (1-\gamma)x_i(t) + \gamma h_i\big(x^i(t)\big), \qquad t \in T^i, \tag{2.23}$$

converges to a fixed point of h. In this exercise, we allow $\tau_i^i(t)$ to be different than t, as long as it satisfies $t - B < \tau_i^i(t) \le t$, that is, we relax Assumption 1.1(c).

   (a) Show that the sequence $\{x(t)\}$ generated by the asynchronous iteration (2.23) is still guaranteed to converge to a fixed point of h.

   (b) Show that the sequence $\{x(t)\}$ generated by the asynchronous iteration

$$x_i(t+1) = x_i(t) + \gamma\Big(h_i\big(x^i(t)\big) - x_i\big(\tau_i^i(t)\big)\Big), \qquad t \in T^i,$$

can be unbounded and divergent.

(c) Show that the sequence $\{x(t)\}$ generated by the asynchronous iteration

$$x_i(t+1) = (1-\gamma)x_i\big(\tau_i^i(t)\big) + \gamma h_i\big(x^i(t)\big), \qquad t \in T^i,$$

is guaranteed to be bounded, but does not necessarily converge to a fixed point of h. *Hints:* For part (a), only a minor modification of the proof of Prop. 2.3 is needed. For part (b), use the function $h(x) = -x$ as an example. For part (c), use the example $h(x) = Ax$, where

$$A = \begin{bmatrix} 0 & 1 \\ -1 & 0 \end{bmatrix},$$

and apply Prop. 3.1 of Section 6.3.

2.2. Let A be a nonnegative and irreducible matrix of dimensions $n \times n$, with the property $\sum_{j=1}^{n} a_{ij} \leq 1$. Suppose that all of the diagonal entries of A are positive. Show that under Assumption 1.1, the asynchronous iteration $x := Ax$ converges to a vector x^* satisfying $Ax^* = x^*$. *Hint:* Let δ be the smallest diagonal entry of A. The iteration $x := Ax$ can be written as [cf. Eq. (2.6)]

$$x := x - (1-\delta)\frac{I-A}{1-\delta}x.$$

Show that the matrix $(I-A)/(1-\delta)$ satisfies Assumption 2.3.

7.3 ALGORITHMS FOR AGREEMENT AND FOR MARKOV CHAIN PROBLEMS

We now consider a set of processors that try to reach agreement on a common scalar value by exchanging tentative values and combining them by forming convex combinations. Although this algorithm is of limited use on its own, it has interesting applications in certain contexts, such as the computation of invariant distributions of Markov chains (Subsection 7.3.2) and an extended model of asynchronous computation (Section 7.7).

7.3.1 The Agreement Algorithm

Consider a set $N = \{1, \ldots, n\}$ of processors, and suppose that the ith processor has a scalar $x_i(0)$ stored in its memory. We would like these processors to exchange messages and eventually agree on an intermediate value y, that is, the agreed upon value should satisfy

$$\min_{i \in N} x_i(0) \leq y \leq \max_{i \in N} x_i(0).$$

A trivial solution to this problem is to have a particular processor (say processor 1) communicate (directly or indirectly) its own value to all other processors and then all processors can agree on the value $x_1(0)$. We shall impose an additional requirement that excludes such a solution. In particular, we postulate the existence of a set $D \subset N$ of *distinguished* processors and we are interested in guaranteeing that the values initially possessed by distinguished processors influence the agreed upon value y. For example, if $k \in D$, $x_k(0) > 0$, and $x_i(0) = 0$ for all $i \neq k$, then we would like y to be influenced by $x_k(0)$ and be positive. Such a requirement can be met if the processors simply cooperate to compute the average of their initial values. This, however, may require a certain amount of coordination between the processors. We shall instead postulate an asynchronous iterative process whereby each processor receives tentative values from other processors and combines them with its own value by forming a convex combination. We let $x_i(t)$ be the value in the memory of the ith processor at time t, and we consider the asynchronous execution of the iteration

$$x_i := \sum_{j=1}^{n} a_{ij} x_j, \qquad i = 1, \ldots, n,$$

where the coefficients a_{ij} are nonnegative scalars such that

$$\sum_{j=1}^{n} a_{ij} = 1, \qquad \forall i. \tag{3.1}$$

A precise description of the algorithm, referred to as the *agreement algorithm*, is

$$x_i(t+1) = x_i(t), \qquad \text{if } t \notin T^i, \tag{3.2}$$

$$x_i(t+1) = \sum_{j=1}^{n} a_{ij} x_j\left(\tau_j^i(t)\right), \qquad \text{if } t \in T^i. \tag{3.3}$$

Here T^i and $\tau_j^i(t)$ are as in Section 7.1 and will be assumed to satisfy the partial asynchronism Assumption 1.1. In the present context, it would be natural to assume that $0 \leq \tau_j^i(t)$. It is convenient, however, to consider a more general case, allowing $\tau_j^i(t)$ to be negative (as long as Assumption 1.1 is satisfied), and allowing $x_i(t)$, for $t < 0$, to be different from $x_i(0)$.

Let A be the matrix whose ijth entry is equal to a_{ij}. We are then dealing with the special case of the model of Section 7.1, where the mapping f is of the form

$$f(x) = Ax.$$

Notice that any vector $x \in \Re^n$ whose components are all equal is a fixed point of f, because of the condition $\sum_{j=1}^{n} a_{ij} = 1$ for all i. In the sequel, we derive conditions under which the sequence $\{x(t)\}$ of the vectors generated by the partially asynchronous agreement algorithm of Eqs. (3.2) and (3.3) converges to such a fixed point. A result of this type is readily obtained if the matrix A is irreducible, a relaxation parameter $\gamma \in (0, 1)$ is employed, and the iteration $x := Ax$ is modified to $x := (1 - \gamma)x + \gamma Ax = x - \gamma(I - A)x$. This is because the matrix $I - A$ satisfies Assumption 2.3 of Section

7.2 and Prop. 2.4 in that section applies. Even if no relaxation parameter is used, Prop. 2.4 can be again invoked as long as all of the diagonal entries of A are positive (see Exercise 2.2 in the preceding section). The result derived in this section is more general in that it allows most of the diagonal entries of A to be zero. Let us also mention that the agreement problem can be related to a network flow problem with quadratic costs (see Exercise 5.4 in Section 5.5.) We now consider some examples to motivate our assumptions.

Example 3.1.

Suppose that

$$A = \begin{bmatrix} 0 & 1 \\ 1 & 0 \end{bmatrix}.$$

Here the set of fixed points of f is $X^* = \{(x_1, x_2) \mid x_1 = x_2\}$, but the iteration $x := f(x)$ is not guaranteed to converge to X^*, even if it is executed synchronously. To see this, notice that if the synchronous execution is initialized with $x(0) = (1, 0)$, then $x(t)$ alternates between $(0, 1)$ and $(1, 0)$ (Fig. 7.3.1). The possibility of such nonconvergent oscillations will be eliminated by assuming that some diagonal entry of the matrix A is nonzero. Such an entry has the effect of a relaxation parameter and serves as a damping factor.

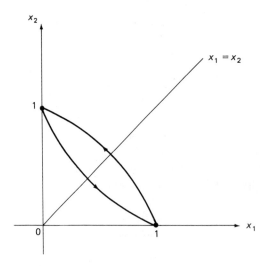

Figure 7.3.1 Nonconvergence in Example 3.1. Here when $x(t)$ is updated synchronously, it alternates between $(1, 0)$ and $(0, 1)$. The oscillation can be eliminated by introducing a relaxation parameter $\gamma \in (0, 1)$ thereby replacing the iteration $x_1(t + 1) = x_2(t)$ and $x_2(t + 1) = x_1(t)$ with $x_1(t + 1) = (1 - \gamma)x_1(t) + \gamma x_2(t)$ and $x_2(t + 1) = (1 - \gamma)x_2(t) + \gamma x_1(t)$. This amounts to introducing positive diagonal elements in the iteration matrix A.

To justify the partial asynchronism assumption, consider the matrix

$$A = \begin{bmatrix} \frac{1}{2} & \frac{1}{2} \\ \frac{1}{2} & \frac{1}{2} \end{bmatrix}.$$

The agreement algorithm for this choice of A is the same as the iteration considered in Example 1.2 of Section 7.1, where it was established that failure to converge is possible if part (b) of the partial asynchronism Assumption 1.1 is violated. There also exist examples that demonstrate that parts (a) and (c) of Assumption 1.1 are also necessary for convergence (Exercise 3.1).

We define a directed graph $G = (N, A)$, where $N = \{1, \ldots, n\}$, and $A = \{(i, j) \mid i \neq j$ and $a_{ji} \neq 0\}$. Notice that $(i, j) \in A$ if and only if the value possessed by processor i directly influences the value of processor j. Convergence will be proved under the following assumption on the matrix A.

Assumption 3.1.   There exists a nonempty set $D \subset N$ of "distinguished" processors such that:

(a) For every $i \in D$, we have $a_{ii} > 0$.
(b) For every $i \in D$ and every $j \in N$, there exists a positive path from i to j in the previously defined graph G.

This assumption is quite natural. Since we wish the initial values of any distinguished processor to affect the value that is eventually agreed upon, we have imposed the condition that every distinguished processor can indirectly affect the value of every other processor [part (b)]. Part (a) of the assumption ensures that a distinguished processor does not forget its initial value when it executes its first iteration; it also serves to eliminate nonconvergent oscillations (cf. Example 3.1).

Proposition 3.1.   Consider the agreement algorithm of Eqs. (3.2) and (3.3) and let Assumptions 1.1 (partial asynchronism) and 3.1 hold. Let $\alpha > 0$ be the smallest of the nonzero entries of A. Then there exist constants $\eta > 0$, $C > 0$, $\rho \in (0, 1)$, depending only on the number n of processors, on α, and on the asynchronism measure B of Assumption 1.1, such that for any initial values $x_i(t)$, $t \leq 0$, and for any scenario allowed by Assumption 1.1, the following are true:

(a) The sequence $\{x_i(t)\}$ converges and its limit is the same for each processor i.
(b) There holds

$$\max_i x_i(t) - \min_i x_i(t) \leq C\rho^t \left(\max_i \max_{-B+1 \leq \tau \leq 0} x_i(\tau) - \min_i \min_{-B+1 \leq \tau \leq 0} x_i(\tau) \right).$$

(c) If $0 \leq x_i(\tau)$ for every i and every $\tau \leq 0$, and if $k \in D$, then $y \geq \eta x_k(0)$, where y is the common limit whose existence is asserted in part (a).

Proof. We define

$$M(t) = \max_i \max_{t-B+1 \leq \tau \leq t} x_i(\tau), \tag{3.4}$$

$$m(t) = \min_i \min_{t-B+1 \leq \tau \leq t} x_i(\tau). \tag{3.5}$$

Notice that because of Assumption 1.1, we have $m(t) \le x_j(\tau_j^i(t)) \le M(t)$ for every i, j, $t \in T^i$, a fact that will be often used. The proof consists of showing that the difference $M(t) - m(t)$ is reduced to zero in the course of the algorithm (see Fig. 7.3.2 for an illustration of the main idea of the proof).

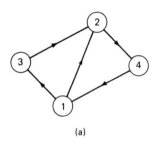

(a)

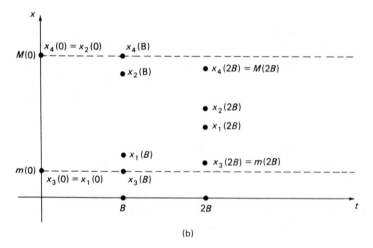

(b)

Figure 7.3.2   (a) A possible graph G associated to a matrix A in the agreement algorithm. (b) Illustration of the convergence of the agreement algorithm for the graph of part (a). For simplicity, we assume that $a_{11} > 0$, $a_{44} > 0$, and that information is never outdated. Let the initial conditions be as indicated and let I be the interval $[m(0), M(0)]$. Since $a_{11} > 0$ and $a_{44} > 0$, we have $x_1(t) < M(0)$ and $x_4(t) > m(0)$ for all times t. Within the first B time units, processor 2 performs an iteration and x_2 is pulled by x_1 to a value smaller than $M(0)$. Similarly, x_1 is pulled by x_4 to a value larger than $m(0)$. After an additional B time units, the variables x_3 and x_4 are pulled by x_1 and x_2, respectively, into the interior of I. At that point, all the components of $x(2B)$ lie in the interior of I and the maximum disagreement $M(2B) - m(2B)$ is smaller than the initial maximum disagreement $M(0) - m(0)$.

Lemma 3.1.

(a) For every $t \ge 0$, we have $m(t+1) \ge m(t)$ and $M(t+1) \le M(t)$.

(b) For every t and $t' \ge t - B + 1$, we have $m(t) \le x_i(t') \le M(t)$.

Proof. Fix some i and t. If $t \notin T^i$, then $x_i(t+1) = x_i(t) \geq m(t)$. If $t \in T^i$, then

$$x_i(t+1) = \sum_{j=1}^{n} a_{ij} x_j\big(\tau_j^i(t)\big) \geq \sum_{j=1}^{n} a_{ij} m(t) = m(t).$$

Thus, in either case, $x_i(t+1) \geq m(t)$ for all i, and, using the definition of $m(t+1)$, it is seen that $m(t+1) \geq m(t)$. The proof of the inequality $M(t+1) \leq M(t)$ is similar. Finally, for $t' \geq t - B + 1$, we use the definition of $m(t' + B - 1)$ and part (a) of the lemma to obtain $x_i(t') \geq m(t' + B - 1) \geq m(t)$. The inequality $x_i(t') \leq M(t)$ is proved similarly.   **Q.E.D.**

For the remainder of the proof of the proposition, we fix some $k \in D$. We let $D_0 = \{k\}$ and we let D_ℓ be the set of all $i \in N$ such that ℓ is the minimum number of arcs in a positive path, in the graph G, from node k to node i. By Assumption 3.1(b), there exists a path from k to every other processor. It follows that every $i \in N$ belongs to one of the sets $D_0, D_1, \ldots, D_{n-1}$. Furthermore, for every $i \in D_\ell$, there exists some $j \in D_{\ell-1}$, such that $(j, i) \in A$. Let $L \leq n - 1$ be such that $D_0 \cup \cdots \cup D_L = N$.

Lemma 3.2.   For every $\ell \in \{0, 1, \ldots, L\}$, there exists some $\eta_\ell > 0$ (depending only on n, α, B) such that for every positive integer s, for every $t \in [s + 2\ell B + 1, s + 2LB + B]$, and for every $i \in D_\ell$, we have

$$x_i(t) \geq m(s) + \eta_\ell\big(x_k(s) - m(s)\big) \tag{3.6}$$

and

$$x_i(t) \leq M(s) - \eta_\ell\big(M(s) - x_k(s)\big). \tag{3.7}$$

Proof. Throughout the proof of this lemma, $k \in D$ is fixed. Without loss of generality, we only consider the case where $s = 0$. Suppose that $t \in T^k$. Then

$$x_k(t+1) - m(0) = \sum_{j=1}^{n} a_{kj}\Big(x_j\big(\tau_j^k(t)\big) - m(0)\Big) \geq a_{kk}\big(x_k(t) - m(0)\big) \geq \alpha\big(x_k(t) - m(0)\big),$$

where we made use of the property $\tau_k^k(t) = t$ [cf. Assumption 1.1(c)]. If $t \notin T^k$, then $x_k(t+1) - m(0) = x_k(t) - m(0) \geq \alpha\big(x_k(t) - m(0)\big)$. It follows that for $t \in [0, 2LB+B]$, we have

$$x_k(t) - m(0) \geq \alpha^t\big(x_k(0) - m(0)\big) \geq \eta_0\big(x_k(0) - m(0)\big),$$

where $\eta_0 = \alpha^{2LB+B}$. This proves inequality (3.6) for $i = k$. Since $D_0 = \{k\}$, inequality (3.6) has been proved for all $i \in D_0$.

We now proceed by induction on ℓ. Suppose that inequality (3.6) is true for some $\ell < L$. Let i be an element of $D_{\ell+1}$. We shall prove inequality (3.6) for i.

Let $j \in D_\ell$ be such that $(j,i) \in A$. Suppose now that t belongs to T^i and satisfies $(2\ell+1)B \leq t \leq 2LB + B$. We then have $2\ell B + 1 \leq \tau_j^i(t) \leq t \leq 2LB + B$ and, by the induction hypothesis,

$$x_j\big(\tau_j^i(t)\big) - m(0) \geq \eta_\ell\big(x_k(0) - m(0)\big).$$

Consequently,

$$x_i(t+1) - m(0) = \sum_{q=1}^{n} a_{iq}\Big(x_q\big(\tau_q^i(t)\big) - m(0)\Big) \geq a_{ij}\Big(x_j\big(\tau_j^i(t)\big) - m(0)\Big)$$

$$\geq \alpha\eta_\ell\big(x_k(0) - m(0)\big) = \eta_{\ell+1}\big(x_k(0) - m(0)\big), \tag{3.8}$$

where $\eta_{\ell+1} = \alpha\eta_\ell$. Let t_i be an element of T^i such that $(2\ell+1)B \leq t_i \leq 2(\ell+1)B$. Such a t_i exists because of Assumption 1.1(a). Inequality (3.8) has been proved for $t = t_i$, as well for any subsequent $t \in T^i$ such that $t \leq 2LB + B$. Furthermore, since $x_i(t) = x_i(t+1)$, if $t \notin T^i$, we conclude that inequality (3.8) holds for all t such that $t_i \leq t \leq (2L+1)B$. Since $t_i \leq 2(\ell+1)B$, we conclude that (3.8) holds for every t such that $2(\ell+1)B \leq t \leq 2LB + B$. This establishes inequality (3.6) for $i \in D_{\ell+1}$ and for $s = 0$. This completes the induction and the proof of (3.6) for the case $s = 0$. The proof for the case of a general s is identical. Finally, inequality (3.7) is proved by a symmetrical argument.   **Q.E.D.**

Proof of Proposition 3.1. (cont.)   We now complete the proof of the proposition. We have $m(t) \leq M(t) \leq M(0)$. Furthermore, the sequence $\{m(t)\}$ is nondecreasing. Since it is bounded above, it converges to a limit denoted by $\bar{m}$. Let $\bar{M}$ be the limit of $M(t)$, which exists by a similar argument. Let $\eta = \min\{\eta_0, \ldots, \eta_L\}$. Using Lemma 3.2 we obtain, for every $t \geq 0$,

$$m(t + 2LB + B) = \min_\ell \min_{i \in D_\ell} \min_{t+2LB+1 \leq \tau \leq t+2LB+B} x_i(\tau) \geq m(t) + \min_\ell \eta_\ell\big(x_k(t) - m(t)\big)$$

$$= m(t) + \eta\big(x_k(t) - m(t)\big).$$

Similarly,

$$M(t + 2LB + B) \leq M(t) + \eta\big(x_k(t) - M(t)\big).$$

Subtracting these two inequalities, we obtain

$$M(t + 2LB + B) - m(t + 2LB + B) \leq (1 - \eta)\big(M(t) - m(t)\big). \tag{3.9}$$

Thus, $M(t) - m(t)$ decreases at the rate of a geometric progression and $\bar{M} = \bar{m}$. Let y be the common value of $\bar{M}$ and $\bar{m}$. Since $m(t) \leq x_i(t) \leq M(t)$ for every i and

t, it follows that the sequence $\{x_i(t)\}$ also converges to y at the rate of a geometric progression. This establishes parts (a) and (b) of the proposition.

We now prove part (c). We have $m(0) \geq 0$, and using Lemma 3.2, we obtain $y \geq m(2LB + B) \geq \eta x_k(0)$.   **Q.E.D.**

It should be emphasized that the value y on which agreement is reached usually depends on the particular scenario.

7.3.2 An Asynchronous Algorithm for the Invariant Distribution of a Markov Chain

Notice that the iteration matrix A in the agreement algorithm was a stochastic matrix. This suggests some similarities between the agreement algorithm and the iterative algorithms of Section 2.8 for computing the invariant distribution of a Markov chain. In this subsection, we let P be an irreducible stochastic matrix and we establish partially asynchronous convergence of the iteration $\pi := \pi P$ by suitably exploiting the convergence result for the agreement algorithm. It should be recalled that the totally asynchronous version of this iteration converges if one of the components of π is not iterated (Subsection 6.3.1). If all of the components of π are iterated, then totally asynchronous convergence is not guaranteed (this can be seen from either Example 3.1 of this section or Example 1.2 of Section 7.1) and, therefore, the partial asynchronism assumption is essential.

Let P be an irreducible and aperiodic stochastic matrix of dimensions $n \times n$ and let p_{ij} denote its ijth entry. Let π^* be the row vector of invariant probabilities of the corresponding Markov chain. Proposition 8.3 of Section 2.8 states that each component π_i^* of π^* is positive and $\lim_{t \to \infty} \pi(0)P^t = \pi^*$ for any row vector $\pi(0)$ whose entries add to 1. This leads to the iterative algorithm $\pi := \pi P$ of Section 2.8 and the corresponding synchronous parallel implementation. We now consider its asynchronous version.

We employ again the model of Section 7.1, except that the vector being iterated is denoted by π and is a row vector. The iteration function f is defined by $f(\pi) = \pi P$. The iteration is described by the equations

$$\pi_i(t+1) = \pi_i(t), \qquad\qquad t \notin T^i, \qquad (3.10)$$

$$\pi_i(t+1) = \sum_{j=1}^{n} \pi_j\big(\tau_j^i(t)\big)p_{ji}, \qquad t \in T^i. \qquad (3.11)$$

Proposition 3.2.   Suppose that the matrix P is stochastic, irreducible, and that there exists some i^* such that $p_{i^* i^*} > 0$. Furthermore, suppose that the iteration (3.10)–(3.11) is initialized with positive values [$\pi_i(\tau) > 0$ for $\tau \leq 0$]. Then for every scenario allowed by Assumption 1.1, there exists a positive number c such that $\lim_{t \to \infty} \pi(t) = c\pi^*$. Also, convergence takes place at the rate of a geometric progression.

Proof.   We prove this result by showing that it is a special case of the convergence result for the agreement algorithm (Prop. 3.1). We introduce a new set of variables $x_i(t)$ defined by

$$x_i(t) = \frac{\pi_i(t)}{\pi_i^*}.$$

These new variables are well defined because $\pi_i^* > 0$ for all i as a consequence of irreducibility. In terms of the new variables, Eqs. (3.10) and (3.11) become

$$x_i(t+1) = x_i(t), \qquad\qquad t \notin T^i, \qquad\qquad (3.12)$$

$$x_i(t+1) = \sum_{j=1}^{n} \frac{p_{ji}\pi_j^*}{\pi_i^*} x_j\big(\tau_j^i(t)\big), \quad t \in T^i. \qquad\qquad (3.13)$$

By letting

$$a_{ij} = \frac{p_{ji}\pi_j^*}{\pi_i^*}, \qquad\qquad (3.14)$$

Eq. (3.13) becomes

$$x_i(t+1) = \sum_{j=1}^{n} a_{ij} x_j\big(\tau_j^i(t)\big), \qquad t \in T^i,$$

which is identical to Eq. (3.3) in the agreement algorithm. Furthermore, notice that $a_{ij} \geq 0$ and that

$$\sum_{j=1}^{n} a_{ij} = \sum_{j=1}^{n} \frac{p_{ji}\pi_j^*}{\pi_i^*} = \frac{1}{\pi_i^*}\sum_{j=1}^{n} p_{ji}\pi_j^* = \frac{\pi_i^*}{\pi_i^*} = 1,$$

where we have used the property $\pi^* = \pi^* P$. Thus, Eq. (3.1) holds as well.

We now verify that the remaining assumptions in Prop. 3.1 are satisfied. Let i^* be such that $p_{i^*i^*} > 0$, and let $D = \{i^*\}$. Then $a_{i^*i^*} > 0$ and Assumption 3.1(a) holds. Also, since P is irreducible, the coefficients a_{ij} satisfy Assumption 3.1(b).

Therefore, Prop. 3.1 applies and shows that there exists a constant c such that

$$\lim_{t\to\infty} x_i(t) = c, \qquad \forall i.$$

Equivalently,

$$\lim_{t\to\infty} \pi_i(t) = c\pi_i^*, \qquad \forall i.$$

Geometric convergence follows from part (b) of Prop. 3.1.

Let $m(0) = \min_i \min_{-B+1 \leq \tau \leq 0} x_i(\tau)$. Since the algorithm is initialized with positive values, $m(0)$ is positive. As shown in the convergence proof for the agreement algorithm, the limit c of $x_i(t)$ is no smaller than $m(0)$. Thus, c is positive. **Q.E.D.**

As in the agreement algorithm, the constant c whose existence is asserted by Prop. 3.2 depends on the particular scenario. This does not cause any difficulties because π^* can be recovered from the limiting value of $\pi(t)$ by normalizing it so that its entries add to 1.

If P is stochastic and irreducible, but all of its diagonal entries are zero, the iteration of Eqs. (3.10) and (3.11) does not converge, in general (see Example 3.1). However, we can let

$$Q = \gamma P + (1 - \gamma)I,$$

and apply the algorithm with P replaced by Q. Here γ is a constant belonging to $(0, 1)$, and I is the identity matrix. Then Q satisfies the assumptions of Prop. 3.2, and we obtain convergence to a multiple of the invariant distribution vector of Q. This is all we need because it is easily seen that P and Q have the same invariant distribution.

As a final extension, suppose that P is nonnegative, irreducible, with $\rho(P) = 1$, but not necessarily stochastic. Then the Perron–Frobenius theorem (Prop. 6.6 in Section 2.6), applied to the transpose of P, guarantees the existence of a positive row vector π^* such that $\pi^* = \pi^* P$, and the proof of Prop. 3.2 remains valid without any modifications whatsoever.

EXERCISES

3.1.   **(a)** Suppose that Assumption 1.1(a) is replaced by the requirement that T^i is infinite, for all i. Show that Props. 3.1 and 3.2 are no longer true.
   (b) Suppose that Assumption 1.1(c) is replaced by the requirement $t - B + 1 \leq \tau_i^i(t) \leq t$ for all i and $t \in T^i$. Show that Props. 3.1 and 3.2 are no longer true.
   Hints: For part (a), let

$$A = \begin{bmatrix} \frac{1}{2} & 0 & \frac{1}{2} \\ \frac{1}{2} & \frac{1}{2} & 0 \\ 0 & \frac{1}{2} & \frac{1}{2} \end{bmatrix}$$

and show that if each processor in turn executes a large number of iterations, the algorithm behaves similarly with the iteration $x_1 := x_3$, $x_3 := x_2$, and $x_2 := x_1$ executed in Gauss–Seidel fashion. For part (b), let

$$A = \begin{bmatrix} \frac{1}{2} & \frac{1}{2} \\ \frac{1}{2} & \frac{1}{2} \end{bmatrix}.$$

Arrange the initial conditions and a scenario so that for every t, we have $x(t) = x(t + 2)$, but $x(t + 1) \neq x(t)$.

3.2. We consider a variant of the agreement algorithm whereby processors receive messages from other processors, and upon reception, these messages are immediately taken into account by forming convex combinations. Let $G = (N, A)$ be a directed graph, with $N = \{1, \ldots, n\}$ and with $(j, i) \in A$ if and only if processor j communicates to processor i. For any $(j, i) \in A$, let T_j^i be the set of times that processor i receives a message $x_j\big(\tau_j^i(t)\big)$ from processor j. We assume that for any fixed i, the sets T_j^i, $j \neq i$, are disjoint. Let the algorithm be described by the equations

$$x_i(t + 1) = a_{ij}x_j\big(\tau_j^i(t)\big) + (1 - a_{ij})x_i(t), \qquad t \in T_j^i,$$

and $x_i(t + 1) = x_i(t)$ if t does not belong to any T_j^i. Assume that $0 < a_{ij} < 1$ for every i and j such that $(j, i) \in A$.

(a) Reformulate appropriately Assumptions 1.1 and 3.1, redefine the constant α of Prop. 3.1, and then show that the conclusions of Prop. 3.1 hold for the present algorithm as well.

(b) What happens in this algorithm if one of the processors breaks down and stops transmitting any messages?

(c) Answer the question of part (b) for the original algorithm of Eqs. (3.2) and (3.3).

3.3. For each i we let $\{\epsilon_i(t)\}$ be a sequence of real numbers that converges geometrically to zero. We consider a perturbed version of the agreement algorithm, whereby Eq. (3.3) is replaced by

$$x_i(t + 1) = \sum_{j=1}^{n} a_{ij}x_j\big(\tau_j^i(t)\big) + \epsilon_i(t), \qquad \text{if } t \in T^i.$$

Let Assumptions 1.1 and 3.1 hold, and show that for every scenario and each i, the sequence $\{x_i(t)\}$ converges geometrically to a limit independent of i. *Hint:* Fix some positive integer s. For any scenario, define $v(t)$ by letting $v(t) = x(t)$ if $t \leq s$,

$$v_i(t + 1) = \sum_{j=1}^{n} a_{ij}v_j\big(\tau_j^i(t)\big), \qquad \text{if } t \geq s, \ t \in T^i,$$

and $v_i(t + 1) = v(t)$ if $t \geq s$ and $t \notin T^i$. Let $q(t) = \min_i \min_{t-B+1 \leq \tau \leq t} v_i(\tau)$ and $Q(t) = \max_i \max_{t-B+1 \leq \tau \leq t} v_i(\tau)$. From Prop. 3.1 we have $Q(s+2LB+B) - q(s+2LB+B) \leq \eta\big(Q(s) - q(s)\big)$. Furthermore, $x_i(s + 2LB + B) - v_i(s + 2LB + B)$ can be bounded by a constant which tends to zero geometrically as s goes to infinity. Combine these two observations to show that $M(s+2B+B) - m(s+2B+B) \leq (1-\eta)\big(M(s)-m(s)\big) + \delta(s)$, where $\{\delta(s)\}$ is a sequence that converges to zero geometrically.

3.4. Let all of the assumptions in Prop. 3.2 hold except for the irreducibility of P. Assume instead that the Markov chain corresponding to P has a single ergodic class and that the nonzero diagonal entry $p_{i^*i^*}$ corresponds to a recurrent state i^*. Show that the sequence $\{\pi(t)\}$ generated by the partially asynchronous iteration (3.10)–(3.11), initialized with positive values, converges geometrically to a positive multiple of the vector of invariant probabilities of the Markov chain. *Hint:* We are dealing with the asynchronous iterations $\pi^{(1)} := \pi^{(1)}P_{11}$ and $\pi^{(2)} := \pi^{(1)}P_{12} + \pi^{(2)}P_{22}$, where $\pi^{(1)}$ and $\pi^{(2)}$ are appropriate subvectors of π, and P_{11}, P_{12} and P_{22} are appropriate submatrices of P. Show that $\rho(P_{11}) < 1$ and that $\pi^{(1)}(t)$ converges to zero geometrically. For the second iteration, use a suitable change of variables and the result of Exercise 3.3.

7.4 LOAD BALANCING IN A COMPUTER NETWORK

Consider a network of n processors, described by a connected undirected graph $G = (N, A)$, where $N = \{1, \ldots, n\}$, and A is the set of arcs connecting different processors. These processors are cooperating in the execution of some computational task. We assume that the computation consists of the execution of independent subtasks and that each subtask can be executed by any processor. For maximum speed, it is desired to spread the subtasks among processors as evenly as possible. We consider a situation in which the load is initially distributed unevenly and we assume that the highly loaded processors try to remedy this by transferring some load to the less loaded processors. We shall assume that this process of load exchange takes place asynchronously, which is reasonable for a loosely coupled network of processors. Finally, we shall make the simplifying assumption that there is a very large number of very small subtasks, so that the load of each processor can be described by a continuous variable.

Let $x_i(t) \geq 0$ be the load handled by processor i at time t, where t is a nonnegative integer time variable. Let L be the total load. Let $A(i)$ be the set of neighbors of the ith processor. Each processor i keeps in its memory an estimate $x_j^i(t)$ of the load carried by each neighboring processor $j \in A(i)$. Due to communication delays and asynchronism, this estimate can be outdated and we assume that

$$x_j^i(t) = x_j\left(\tau_j^i(t)\right), \tag{4.1}$$

where $\tau_j^i(t)$ is an integer variable satisfying $0 \leq \tau_j^i(t) \leq t$.

There is a set of times T^i at which processor i compares its load with the load of its neighbors, and if it finds that it is overloaded, transfers some of its load, according to the following rule. For each neighboring processor $j \in A(i)$, if $x_i(t) > x_j^i(t)$, then a nonnegative amount of load, denoted by $s_{ij}(t)$, is transferred from i to j; no load is transferred if $x_i(t) \leq x_j^i(t)$, in which case, we let $s_{ij}(t) = 0$. For notational convenience, we also let $s_{ij}(t) = 0$ if $t \notin T^i$. We assume that a load transfer can take some time to be completed. We use $v_{ij}(t)$ to denote the amount of load that has been sent from processor i to processor j before time t, but has not been received by processor j before time t. Let $r_{ij}(t)$ be the load received by processor j from processor i at time t. We then have

$$x_i(t + 1) = x_i(t) - \sum_{j \in A(i)} s_{ij}(t) + \sum_{j \in A(i)} r_{ji}(t) \tag{4.2}$$

and

$$v_{ij}(t) = \sum_{\tau=0}^{t-1} \left(s_{ij}(\tau) - r_{ij}(\tau)\right), \tag{4.3}$$

where we are making the implicit assumption that $v_{ij}(0) = 0$. Since no load is assumed to be in transit at time zero, we have $\sum_{i=1}^{n} x_i(0) = L$, and using Eqs. (4.2) and (4.3), we easily obtain the load conservation equation

$$\sum_{i=1}^{n}\left(x_i(t) + \sum_{j \in A(i)} v_{ij}(t)\right) = L, \qquad \forall t \geq 0. \tag{4.4}$$

We now introduce two assumptions without which load equalization can fail to take place asymptotically (Exercise 4.1).

Assumption 4.1. *(Partial Asynchronism)* There exists a positive integer B such that:

(a) For every i and for every $t \geq 0$, at least one of the elements of the set $\{t, t + 1, \ldots, t + B - 1\}$ belongs to T^i.

(b) There holds

$$t - B < \tau_j^i(t) \leq t,$$

for all i and t, and all $j \in A(i)$.

(c) The load $s_{ij}(t)$ sent from processor i to processor j at some time $t \in T^i$ is received by processor j before time $t + B$.

Assumption 4.1(c) implies that $v_{ij}(t)$, the load in transit just before time t, consists exclusively of pieces of the load that were sent during the time interval $(t - B, t - 1]$. Accordingly, we have

$$v_{ij}(t) \leq \sum_{\tau=t-B+1}^{t-1} s_{ij}(\tau), \qquad \forall i, \ \forall j \in A(i). \tag{4.5}$$

The next assumption has two parts. Part (a) postulates that when processor i detects a load imbalance, it will transfer a nonnegligible portion of its excess load to some lightest loaded neighbor. Of course, that does not preclude that it also sends some load to other neighbors as well. However, no load is transferred to neighbors carrying a larger load. Part (b) prohibits processor i from transferring a very large amount of load and creating a load imbalance in the opposite direction. The latter assumption is introduced in order to preclude the possibility that two nodes keep sending load to each other back and forth, without ever reaching equilibrium.

Assumption 4.2.

(a) There exists some constant $\alpha \in (0, 1)$ such that for every i and every $t \in T^i$, there exists some $j \in A(i)$ satisfying $x_j^i(t) = \min_{k \in A(i)} x_k^i(t)$ and $s_{ij}(t) \geq \alpha\big(x_i(t) - x_j^i(t)\big)$. Furthermore, if $x_i(t) \leq x_j^i(t)$, then $s_{ij}(t) = 0$.

(b) For any i, any $t \in T^i$, and any $j \in A(i)$ such that $x_i(t) > x_j^i(t)$, we have

$$x_i(t) - \sum_{k \in A(i)} s_{ik}(t) \geq x_j^i(t) + s_{ij}(t). \tag{4.6}$$

The algorithm of this section resembles the agreement algorithm in certain respects, but its convergence cannot be derived from the corresponding result for the agreement algorithm. Still, the general ideas in the proof of convergence are similar. In particular, we will show that if there is a load imbalance, then the load of the lightest loaded processors will eventually increase, thus reducing the load imbalance. The main result is the following.

Proposition 4.1.   Under Assumptions 4.1 and 4.2, we have $\lim_{t \to \infty} x_i(t) = L/n$ for all i.

Proof. For notational convenience, we define $x_i(t) = x_i(0)$ for $t < 0$. Let

$$m(t) = \min_i \ \min_{t-B < \tau \leq t} x_i(\tau), \tag{4.7}$$

and notice that $x_j^i(t) = x_j(\tau_j^i(t)) \geq m(t)$, for every i, j, and t. The proof is based on the following lemmas:

Lemma 4.1.   There exists some $\beta \in (0, 1)$ such that

$$x_i(t + 1) \geq m(t) + \beta(x_i(t) - m(t)), \qquad \forall i, t. \tag{4.8}$$

In particular, β can be chosen equal to $1/n$.

Proof. Let us fix some i and t. If $t \notin T^i$, then $x_i(t + 1) = x_i(t) = m(t) + (x_i(t) - m(t))$. Since $x_i(t)$ is larger than or equal to $m(t)$, inequality (4.8) follows for any $\beta \in (0, 1)$. Now suppose that $t \in T^i$, consider the set $A' = \{j \mid j \in A(i), \ x_i(t) > x_j^i(t)\}$, and let K be its cardinality. Equations (4.2) and (4.6) imply that $x_i(t+1) \geq x_j^i(t) + s_{ij}(t)$ for all $j \in A'$, and adding over all $j \in A'$, we obtain

$$Kx_i(t + 1) \geq \sum_{j \in A'} x_j^i(t) + \sum_{j \in A'} s_{ij}(t). \tag{4.9}$$

Furthermore, from Eq. (4.2) and the fact $s_{ij}(t) = 0$ for $j \notin A'$, we obtain

$$\sum_{j \in A'} s_{ij}(t) = \sum_{j \in A(i)} s_{ij}(t) \geq x_i(t) - x_i(t + 1). \tag{4.10}$$

Combining Eqs. (4.9) and (4.10) and using the definition of $m(t)$, we obtain $Kx_i(t+1) \geq Km(t) + (x_i(t) - x_i(t + 1))$, which can be rewritten as

$$x_i(t+1) \geq \frac{K}{K+1}m(t) + \frac{1}{K+1}x_i(t) = m(t) + \frac{1}{K+1}(x_i(t) - m(t)) \geq m(t) + \frac{1}{n}(x_i(t) - m(t)).$$

This proves inequality (4.8) with $\beta = 1/n$.   **Q.E.D.**

Lemma 4.2.

(a) The sequence $m(t)$ is nondecreasing and converges.

(b) For every i and every $t, s \geq 0$, we have

$$x_i(t+s) \geq m(t) + \beta^s \big(x_i(t) - m(t)\big), \qquad (4.11)$$

where β is the constant of Lemma 4.1.

Proof.

(a) Lemma 4.1 implies that $x_i(t+1) \geq m(t)$ and the inequality $m(t+1) \geq m(t)$ follows. Furthermore, $x_i(t)$ is bounded by the total load L. Therefore, $m(t)$ is also bounded by L, and since it is monotonic, it converges.

(b) The proof is by induction on s. Lemma 4.1 shows that inequality (4.11) is true for $s = 1$. Assuming that it is true for some general s, we use again Lemma 4.1 and the monotonicity of $m(t)$ to obtain

$$x_i(t+s+1) \geq m(t+s) + \beta\big(x_i(t+s) - m(t+s)\big) \geq m(t) + \beta\big(x_i(t+s) - m(t)\big)$$
$$\geq m(t) + \beta^{s+1}\big(x_i(t) - m(t)\big),$$

where the last step follows from the induction hypothesis.   **Q.E.D.**

We could have also considered using the variable $M(t) = \max_i \max_{t-B < \tau \leq t} x_i(\tau)$ in the analysis. However, unlike the agreement algorithm of Section 7.3, this variable is not monotonically nonincreasing (Exercise 4.2). This is a major difference with the agreement algorithm (compare with Lemma 3.1 of Section 7.3).

Let us fix a processor i and some time t_0. For any $j \in A(i)$ and any time $t \geq t_0$, we say that the event $E_j(t)$ occurs if the following two conditions are true:

(i)
$$x_j^i(t) < m(t_0) + \tfrac{\alpha}{2}\beta^{t-t_0}\big(x_i(t_0) - m(t_0)\big). \qquad (4.12)$$

(ii) Processor j is a lightest loaded neighbor of i to which some load is transferred, as in Assumption 4.2(a), and in particular,

$$s_{ij}(t) \geq \alpha\big(x_i(t) - x_j^i(t)\big). \qquad (4.13)$$

Lemma 4.3.   If $j \in A(i)$, $t_1 \geq t_0$, $t_1 \in T^i$, and the event $E_j(t_1)$ occurs, then the event $E_j(\tau)$ does not occur, for any $\tau \geq t_1 + 2B$ such that $\tau \in T^i$.

Proof. Suppose that $t_1 \geq t_0$, $t_1 \in T^i$, $j \in A(i)$, and the event $E_j(t_1)$ occurs. In particular, inequalities (4.12) and (4.13) are valid for $t = t_1$. Lemma 4.2(b) yields

$$x_i(t_1) \geq m(t_0) + \beta^{t_1-t_0}\big(x_i(t_0) - m(t_0)\big). \qquad (4.14)$$

We subtract inequality (4.12) (with $t = t_1$) from (4.14) and use the fact $\alpha < 1$ to obtain

$$x_i(t_1) - x_j^i(t_1) \geq \tfrac{1}{2} \beta^{t_1 - t_0} \big(x_i(t_0) - m(t_0) \big).$$

Then, inequality (4.13) (with $t = t_1$) yields

$$s_{ij}(t_1) \geq \frac{\alpha}{2} \beta^{t_1 - t_0} \big(x_i(t_0) - m(t_0) \big). \tag{4.15}$$

Processor j will receive the load $s_{ij}(t_1)$ at some time t_2 satisfying $t_1 \leq t_2 < t_1 + B$ [Assumption 4.1(c)]. If $t_2 \notin T^j$ or, more generally, if $s_{jk}(t_2) = 0$ for all $k \in A(j)$, then Eq. (4.2) yields

$$x_j(t_2 + 1) = x_j(t_2) + \sum_{k \in A(j)} r_{kj}(t_2) \geq x_j(t_2) + r_{ij}(t_2)$$

$$\geq x_j(t_2) + s_{ij}(t_1) \geq m(t_2) + s_{ij}(t_1).$$

If, on the other hand, $t_2 \in T^j$ and there exists some $k^* \in A(j)$ such that $s_{jk^*}(t_2) > 0$, then Eqs. (4.2) and (4.6) yield

$$x_j(t_2+1) = x_j(t_2) - \sum_{k \in A(j)} s_{jk}(t_2) + \sum_{k \in A(j)} r_{kj}(t_2) \geq x_{k^*}^j(t_2) + r_{ij}(t_2) \geq m(t_2) + s_{ij}(t_1).$$

In both cases, we have using inequality (4.15),

$$x_j(t_2 + 1) \geq m(t_2) + s_{ij}(t_1) \geq m(t_0) + \frac{\alpha}{2} \beta^{t_1 - t_0} \big(x_i(t_0) - m(t_0) \big)$$

$$\geq m(t_0) + \frac{\alpha}{2} \beta^{t_2 + 1 - t_0} \big(x_i(t_0) - m(t_0) \big).$$

We use Lemma 4.2 to conclude that

$$
\begin{aligned}
x_j(t) &\geq m(t_2 + 1) + \beta^{t - t_2 - 1} \big(x_j(t_2 + 1) - m(t_2 + 1) \big) \\
&\geq m(t_0) + \beta^{t - t_2 - 1} \big(x_j(t_2 + 1) - m(t_0) \big) \\
&\geq m(t_0) + \beta^{t - t_2 - 1} \frac{\alpha}{2} \beta^{t_2 + 1 - t_0} \big(x_i(t_0) - m(t_0) \big) \\
&\geq m(t_0) + \frac{\alpha}{2} \beta^{t - t_0} \big(x_i(t_0) - m(t_0) \big), \qquad \forall t \geq t_2 + 1.
\end{aligned}
\tag{4.16}
$$

Since $t_2 < t_1 + B$, we see that inequality (4.16) holds for all $t \geq t_1 + B$.

Let t_3 satisfy $t_3 \in T^i$ and $t_3 \geq t_1 + 2B$. Then $\tau_j^i(t_3) > t_3 - B \geq t_1 + B$. Inequality (4.16) applies and yields

$$x_j^i(t_3) - m(t_0) = x_j\big(\tau_j^i(t_3)\big) - m(t_0) \geq \frac{\alpha}{2} \beta^{\tau_j^i(t_3) - t_0} \big(x_i(t_0) - m(t_0) \big)$$

$$\geq \frac{\alpha}{2} \beta^{t_3 - t_0} \big(x_i(t_0) - m(t_0) \big).$$

Thus, inequality (4.12) does not hold for $t = t_3$, and the event $E_j(t_3)$ does not occur.
Q.E.D.

Lemma 4.4. There exists some $\eta > 0$ such that for any i, t_0, $j \in A(i)$, and any $t \geq t_0 + 3nB$, we have

$$x_j(t) \geq m(t_0) + \eta \beta^{t-t_0} \big(x_i(t_0) - m(t_0)\big).$$

Proof. Let us fix i and t_0. Let $t_1, \ldots, t_n$ be elements of T^i such that $t_{k-1} + 2B < t_k \leq t_{k-1} + 3B$, $k = 1, \ldots, n$. According to Lemma 4.3, if $j \in A(i)$ and $k \neq \ell$, then the events $E_j(t_k)$ and $E_j(t_\ell)$ cannot both occur. It follows that for some t_k ($1 \leq k \leq n$), the event $E_j(t_k)$ does not occur for any $j \in A(i)$. According to Assumption 4.2(a) inequality (4.13) must be true for some j^* satisfying

$$x_{j^*}^i(t_k) \leq x_j^i(t_k), \qquad \forall j \in A(i).$$

Since $E_{j^*}(t_k)$ does not occur, inequality (4.12) must be violated for $j = j^*$, and we obtain

$$x_j\big(\tau_j^i(t_k)\big) = x_j^i(t_k) \geq x_{j^*}^i(t_k) \geq m(t_0) + \frac{\alpha}{2}\beta^{t_k - t_0}\big(x_i(t_0) - m(t_0)\big), \qquad \forall j \in A(i).$$

For any t satisfying $t \geq t_0 + 3nB$, we have $t \geq t_k \geq \tau_j^i(t_k)$ and Lemma 4.2 yields

$$x_j(t) \geq m\big(\tau_j^i(t_k)\big) + \beta^{t - \tau_j^i(t_k)}\Big(x_j\big(\tau_j^i(t_k)\big) - m\big(\tau_j^i(t_k)\big)\Big)$$

$$\geq m(t_0) + \beta^{t - \tau_j^i(t_k)}\Big(x_j\big(\tau_j^i(t_k)\big) - m(t_0)\Big)$$

$$\geq m(t_0) + \beta^{t - \tau_j^i(t_k)}\frac{\alpha}{2}\beta^{t_k - t_0}\big(x_i(t_0) - m(t_0)\big)$$

$$\geq m(t_0) + \frac{\alpha}{2}\beta^B \beta^{t - t_0}\big(x_i(t_0) - m(t_0)\big),$$

where the last inequality follows because $t_k - \tau_j^i(t_k) \leq B$. This proves the lemma with $\eta = \alpha\beta^B/2$. **Q.E.D.**

By repeatedly applying Lemma 4.4, we obtain:

Lemma 4.5. For any i, t_0, any j that can be reached from i by traversing ℓ arcs, and for any $t \geq t_0 + 3\ell nB$, we have

$$x_j(t) \geq m(t_0) + \big(\eta \beta^{t-t_0}\big)^\ell \big(x_i(t_0) - m(t_0)\big).$$

Proof. Lemma 4.4 establishes Lemma 4.5 for the case $\ell = 1$. We proceed by induction on ℓ. Assume that the result is true for every j at distance ℓ from i. Suppose that k is at distance $\ell + 1$ from i. Then $k \in A(j)$ for some j at distance ℓ from i. We apply the induction hypothesis to processor j to obtain

$$x_j(t_0 + 3\ell n B) \geq m(t_0) + \left(\eta \beta^{3\ell n B}\right)^\ell \left(x_i(t_0) - m(t_0)\right).$$

We then apply Lemma 4.4 to processor k, with t_0 replaced by $t_0 + 3\ell n B$ to obtain for any $t \geq t_0 + 3\ell n B + 3nB$,

$$
\begin{aligned}
x_k(t) &\geq m(t_0 + 3\ell n B) + \eta \beta^{t - t_0 - 3\ell n B}\left(x_j(t_0 + 3\ell n B) - m(t_0 + 3\ell n B)\right) \\
&\geq m(t_0) + \eta \beta^{t - t_0 - 3\ell n B}(\eta \beta^{3\ell n B})^\ell \left(x_i(t_0) - m(t_0)\right) \\
&\geq m(t_0) + \eta \beta^{t - t_0}(\eta \beta^{t - t_0})^\ell \left(x_i(t_0) - m(t_0)\right) \\
&= m(t_0) + (\eta \beta^{t - t_0})^{\ell + 1} \left(x_i(t_0) - m(t_0)\right),
\end{aligned}
$$

which concludes the induction and proves the lemma.   **Q.E.D.**

We now conclude the proof of the proposition. Let us again fix some processor i and a time t_0. Since every processor is at a distance smaller than n from i, Lemma 4.5 yields

$$x_j(t) \geq m(t_0) + \left(\eta \beta^{3n^2 B + B}\right)^n \left(x_i(t_0) - m(t_0)\right), \qquad \forall j, \ \forall t \in \left[t_0 + 3n^2 B, t_0 + 3n^2 B + B\right].$$

Consequently, there exists some $\delta > 0$ such that

$$m(t_0 + 3n^2 B + B) \geq m(t_0) + \delta\left(x_i(t_0) - m(t_0)\right).$$

This inequality is true for every i and therefore,

$$m(t_0 + 3n^2 B + B) \geq m(t_0) + \delta\left(\max_i x_i(t_0) - m(t_0)\right). \tag{4.17}$$

If $\max_i x_i(t) - m(t)$ does not converge to zero, then inequality (4.17) shows that $m(t)$ will increase to infinity, which contradicts the boundedness of $m(t)$. Therefore, $\max_i x_i(t) - m(t)$ converges to zero. Furthermore, $m(t)$ converges to some constant c [Lemma 4.2(a)]. It follows that $\lim_{t \to \infty} \max_i x_i(t) = c$. Since $m(t) \leq x_j(t) \leq \max_i x_i(t)$ for every j and t, we see that $x_j(t)$ also converges to c, for every j. In view of inequality (4.6) we obtain $\lim_{t \to \infty} s_{ij}(t) = 0$ for all $(i, j) \in A$. We then use inequality (4.5) to conclude that $\lim_{t \to \infty} v_{ij}(t) = 0$ for all $(i, j) \in A$. Using Eq. (4.4) we obtain $nc = \lim_{t \to \infty} \sum_{i=1}^n x_i(t) = L$, from which we conclude that $c = L/n$.   **Q.E.D.**

It can be shown that convergence of the algorithm takes place geometrically (Exercise 4.3).

It should be noted that this algorithm operates without the processors knowing the value of L. If the value of L changes to L' while the algorithm is executed, then each $x_i(t)$ will converge to L'/n, and this happens without the processors being informed of the change from L to L'. Thus, the algorithm is able to adapt to changes in the problem data without a need for being restarted, which is a characteristic feature of asynchronous algorithms.

EXERCISES

4.1. Show by means of examples that Prop. 4.1 fails to hold in the following cases:

(a) If part (b) of Assumption 4.1 is replaced by the assumption that $\lim_{t\to\infty} \tau_j^i(t) = \infty$.

(b) If part (c) of Assumption 4.1 is replaced by the assumption that the load sent by any processor eventually reaches its destination.

(c) If part (a) of Assumption 4.2 is replaced by the following requirement: for any $t \in T^i$, let $A' = \{j \mid j \in A(i), x_j^i(t) < x_i(t)\}$, and assume that if A' is nonempty, there exists some $j \in A'$ such that $s_{ij}(t) \geq \alpha\big(x_i(t) - x_j^i(t)\big)$, where α is a constant belonging to $(0, 1)$.

(d) If part (b) of Assumption 4.2 is replaced by the requirement that $x_i(t) - \sum_{k\in A(i)} s_{ik}(t) \geq x_j^i(t)$, for all $j \in A(i)$ and all $t \in T^i$.

4.2. Let $M(t) = \max_i \max_{t-B\leq t\leq t} x_i(\tau)$. Show by means of an example that $M(t)$ is not necessarily monotonically nonincreasing.

4.3. (**Geometric Convergence.**) Let, for each i and t,

$$y_i(t) = x_i(t) + \sum_{j\in A(i)} v_{ji}(t).$$

(a) Fix some t. Show that there exists some $t' \in [t+1, t+B]$ for which

$$\sum_{j\in A(i)} r_{ji}(t') \geq \frac{y_i(t) - x_i(t)}{B}.$$

(b) Show that for some $\beta \in (0, 1)$,

$$x_i(t' + 1) \geq m(t) + \beta^{t'-t}\big(x_i(t) - m(t)\big) + \frac{y_i(t) - x_i(t)}{B}.$$

(c) Show that there exists some $\gamma > 0$ such that

$$x_i(t + B + 1) \geq m(t) + \gamma\big(y_i(t) - m(t)\big).$$

(d) Show that

$$\max_i x_i(t + B + 1) - m(t) \geq \gamma\left(\frac{L}{n} - m(t)\right).$$

(e) Use inequality (4.17) to prove that $m(t)$, as well as each $x_i(t)$, converges geometrically to L/n.

4.4. [Cyb87] Suppose that the network of processors is a d–cube and consider the following synchronous algorithm. At the ith phase of the algorithm ($i = 1, \ldots, d$) each processor exchanges load with its neighbor whose identity differs in the ith bit. Furthermore, the load exchanged is such that after the exchange, the load of these two processors is the same. Show that all processors have the same load at the end of the dth phase.

7.5 GRADIENT–LIKE OPTIMIZATION ALGORITHMS

In this section, we take a new look at gradient–like algorithms for unconstrained and constrained optimization. We recall that the totally asynchronous gradient algorithm is guaranteed to converge if the Hessian matrix $\nabla^2 F$ of the cost function satisfies a diagonal dominance condition, guaranteeing that the iteration $x := x - \gamma \nabla F(x)$ is a maximum norm contraction mapping for sufficiently small γ (see Section 6.3). On the other hand, if such a condition is not satisfied, then the totally asynchronous algorithm can be nonconvergent, no matter how small the stepsize γ is chosen, as demonstrated in Example 3.1 of Subsection 6.3.2. We will show that the desired convergence properties of asynchronous gradient–like algorithms are recovered once we impose the assumption of partial asynchronism.

The results to be derived in this section differ from those of Sections 7.2–7.4 in an important respect. In those sections, we established convergence of certain algorithms under the assumption that the asynchronism measure B was finite but otherwise arbitrary. In contrast, in this section, we can establish convergence of the iteration $x := x - \gamma \nabla F(x)$ only if the stepsize γ is small compared to $1/B$; equivalently, only if B is small compared to $1/\gamma$. This is not a deficiency of the method of proof. As demonstrated in Example 1.3 of Section 7.1, the partially asynchronous gradient algorithm, with a fixed value of γ, does not converge, in general, if B is sufficiently large. In other words, asynchronous gradient–like algorithms can only tolerate a limited amount of asynchronism.

Throughout this section, $\| \cdot \|$ stands for the Euclidean norm $\| \cdot \|_2$.

7.5.1 The Algorithm and its Convergence

Let $F : \Re^n \mapsto \Re$ be a cost function to be minimized subject to no constraints. We impose the same assumptions on F as in Section 3.2, which dealt with synchronous algorithms for unconstrained optimization.

Assumption 5.1.

(a) There holds $F(x) \geq 0$ for every $x \in \Re^n$.

(b) (*Lipschitz Continuity of ∇F*) The function F is continuously differentiable and there exists a constant K_1 such that

$$\|\nabla F(x) - \nabla F(y)\| \leq K_1 \|x - y\|, \qquad \forall x, y \in \Re^n. \tag{5.1}$$

The asynchronous gradient algorithm is the asynchronous iteration

$$x := x - \gamma \nabla F(x). \tag{5.2}$$

A more general version will be considered here. Our model is similar to the one introduced in Section 7.1 and is the following. The algorithm iterates on a vector $x(t)$ whose ith coordinate, denoted by $x_i(t)$, is updated by processor i according to

$$x_i(t + 1) = x_i(t) + \gamma s_i(t), \qquad i = 1, \ldots, n, \tag{5.3}$$

where γ is a positive stepsize, and $s_i(t)$ is the update direction. We let T^i be the set of times when the ith processor performs an update. Thus, we assume that

$$s_i(t) = 0, \qquad \forall t \notin T^i. \tag{5.4}$$

Processor i has knowledge at any time t of a vector $x^i(t)$ that is a possibly outdated version of $x(t)$. That is,

$$x^i(t) = \Big(x_1\big(\tau_1^i(t)\big), \ldots, x_n\big(\tau_n^i(t)\big)\Big). \tag{5.5}$$

Here the variables $\tau_j^i(t)$ have the same meaning as in the model of Section 7.1. They are assumed to be defined for all t and to satisfy $0 \le \tau_j^i(t) \le t$ for all $t \ge 0$.

For those times t that belong to T^i, we assume that the update direction is such that the cost function does not increase; equivalently, $s_i(t)$ should have the opposite sign from $\nabla_i F(x)$, where x is the vector in the memory of the processor in charge of this update. We thus assume the following:

Assumption 5.2.

(a) *(Descent Property Along Each Coordinate)* For every i and t, we have

$$s_i(t)\nabla_i F\big(x^i(t)\big) \le 0. \tag{5.6}$$

(b) There exist positive constants K_2 and K_3 such that

$$K_2\big|\nabla_i F\big(x^i(t)\big)\big| \le |s_i(t)| \le K_3\big|\nabla_i F\big(x^i(t)\big)\big|, \qquad \forall t \in T^i, \ \forall i. \tag{5.7}$$

The lower bound on $|s_i(t)|$ provided by Eq. (5.7) is introduced because otherwise $s_i(t)$ could be always equal to zero, in which case, convergence cannot be demonstrated. The upper bound in Eq. (5.7) is also essential, because otherwise $s_i(t)$ could be chosen so large that the algorithm would exhibit unstable oscillations.

Assumption 5.2 roughly requires that $s(t)$ is in the same quadrant as $-\nabla F(x)$ and is quite general. For example, if we let $s_i(t) = -\nabla_i F\big(x^i(t)\big)$, for $t \in T^i$, we recover the asynchronous gradient algorithm of Eq. (5.2). For this example, part (a) of Assumption 5.2 is satisfied and part (b) holds with $K_2 = K_3 = 1$.

As another example, consider an asynchronous Jacobi algorithm (cf. Section 3.2). In this case we assume that F is twice differentiable and we let

$$s_i(t) = -\frac{\nabla_i F\big(x^i(t)\big)}{\nabla_{ii}^2 F\big(x^i(t)\big)}, \qquad t \in T^i.$$

Assumption 5.2 is satisfied provided that the cost function F has the property $0 < K_2 \le 1/\nabla_{ii}^2 F(x) \le K_3$ for some constants K_2 and K_3 and for all $x \in \Re^n$.

The partial asynchronism assumption that follows is almost identical to Assumption 1.1 of Section 7.1, except that we do not need the condition $\tau_i^i(t) = t$.

Assumption 5.3.   (*Partial Asynchronism*) There exists a positive integer B such that:

(a) For every i and for every $t \geq 0$, at least one of the elements of the set $\{t, t + 1, \ldots, t + B - 1\}$ belongs to T^i.

(b) There holds

$$\max\{0, t - B + 1\} \leq \tau_j^i(t) \leq t,$$

for all i and j and all $t \geq 0$.

Proposition 5.1 to follow states that under the above assumptions, convergence is obtained provided that the stepsize is small enough. The proof follows the same steps as the proof of convergence of synchronous gradient–like algorithms (Props. 2.1 and 2.2 in Section 3.2) and the reader is advised to consult these proofs at this point. The main difference is that asynchronism introduces a few additional error terms, because the processors are using outdated information. Given the bound B of Assumption 5.3 and given the fact that the processors can only make small steps (γ is small), we show that these error terms are small enough to be inconsequential.

Proposition 5.1.   Under Assumptions 5.1–5.3, there exists some $\gamma_0 > 0$ (depending on n, B, K_1, and K_3) such that if $0 < \gamma < \gamma_0$, then $\lim_{t \to \infty} \nabla F(x(t)) = 0$.

Proof. For notational convenience, we define $s(t)$ to be zero for $t < 0$. We use the descent lemma (Prop. A.32 in Appendix A) and Assumptions 5.1 and 5.2, to obtain

$$
\begin{aligned}
F(x(t+1)) &= F(x(t) + \gamma s(t)) \\
&\leq F(x(t)) + \gamma \sum_{i=1}^{n} s_i(t) \nabla_i F(x(t)) + K_1 \gamma^2 \|s(t)\|^2 \\
&= F(x(t)) + \gamma \sum_{i=1}^{n} s_i(t) \nabla_i F(x^i(t)) + \gamma \sum_{i=1}^{n} s_i(t) \Big(\nabla_i F(x(t)) - \nabla_i F(x^i(t)) \Big) \\
&\qquad + K_1 \gamma^2 \|s(t)\|^2 \qquad\qquad (5.8) \\
&\leq F(x(t)) - \gamma \sum_{i=1}^{n} \frac{1}{K_3} |s_i(t)|^2 + \gamma K_1 \sum_{i=1}^{n} |s_i(t)| \cdot \|x(t) - x^i(t)\| + K_1 \gamma^2 \|s(t)\|^2.
\end{aligned}
$$

We now proceed to bound $\|x^i(t) - x(t)\|$. We have

$$|x_j^i(t) - x_j(t)| = |x_j(\tau_j^i(t)) - x_j(t)| = \gamma \left| \sum_{\tau=\tau_j^i(t)}^{t-1} s_j(\tau) \right| \leq \gamma \sum_{\tau=t-B}^{t-1} |s_j(\tau)|.$$

Therefore, the inequality

$$|x^i(t) - x(t)| \leq \gamma \sum_{\tau=t-B}^{t-1} |s(\tau)|$$

holds (componentwise). Using this and the triangle inequality, we obtain

$$\|x^i(t) - x(t)\| \leq \gamma \left\| \sum_{\tau=t-B}^{t-1} |s(\tau)| \right\| \leq \gamma \sum_{\tau=t-B}^{t-1} \|s(\tau)\|. \tag{5.9}$$

We now substitute inequality (5.9) in inequality (5.8) to obtain

$$F\bigl(x(t+1)\bigr) \leq F\bigl(x(t)\bigr) - \gamma \left(\frac{1}{K_3} - K_1\gamma \right) \|s(t)\|^2 + \gamma^2 K_1 \sum_{i=1}^{n} |s_i(t)| \sum_{\tau=t-B}^{t-1} \|s(\tau)\|.$$

We then use the inequality

$$|s_i(t)| \cdot \|s(\tau)\| \leq |s_i(t)|^2 + \|s(\tau)\|^2,$$

to obtain

$$F\bigl(x(t+1)\bigr) \leq F\bigl(x(t)\bigr) - \gamma \left(\frac{1}{K_3} - K_1\gamma \right) \|s(t)\|^2 + \gamma^2 K_1 \sum_{i=1}^{n} \sum_{\tau=t-B}^{t-1} \left(|s_i(t)|^2 + \|s(\tau)\|^2 \right)$$

$$= F\bigl(x(t)\bigr) - \gamma \left(\frac{1}{K_3} - K_1\gamma \right) \|s(t)\|^2 + \gamma^2 K_1 \left(B\|s(t)\|^2 + n \sum_{\tau=t-B}^{t-1} \|s(\tau)\|^2 \right)$$

$$= F\bigl(x(t)\bigr) - \gamma \left(\frac{1}{K_3} - K_1\gamma - K_1\gamma B \right) \|s(t)\|^2 + \gamma^2 n K_1 \sum_{\tau=t-B}^{t-1} \|s(\tau)\|^2. \tag{5.10}$$

We have an inequality of the form (5.10) for each different t. By adding those inequalities, we obtain

$$F\bigl(x(t+1)\bigr) \leq F\bigl(x(0)\bigr) - \gamma \left(\frac{1}{K_3} - K_1\gamma - K_1\gamma B \right) \sum_{\tau=0}^{t} \|s(\tau)\|^2 + nB\gamma^2 K_1 \sum_{\tau=0}^{t} \|s(\tau)\|^2$$

$$= F\bigl(x(0)\bigr) - \gamma \left(\frac{1}{K_3} - K_1\gamma - K_1\gamma B - nB\gamma K_1 \right) \sum_{\tau=0}^{t} \|s(\tau)\|^2. \tag{5.11}$$

Let $\gamma_0 = 1/\bigl[(1 + B + nB)K_1 K_3\bigr]$, and assume that $\gamma \in (0, \gamma_0)$. Then $C = (1/K_3) - K_1\gamma - K_1\gamma B - nBK_1\gamma$ is positive, and we can divide both sides of inequality (5.11) by C, without reversing the inequality. Since F is assumed nonnegative, we have $F\big(x(t+1)\big) \geq 0$ and inequality (5.11) becomes

$$\sum_{\tau=0}^{t} \|s(\tau)\|^2 \leq \frac{1}{C\gamma} F\big(x(0)\big). \tag{5.12}$$

Inequality (5.12) holds for every $t \geq 0$. Therefore,

$$\sum_{\tau=0}^{\infty} \|s(\tau)\|^2 \leq \frac{1}{C\gamma} F\big(x(0)\big) < \infty,$$

which implies that

$$\lim_{t\to\infty} s(t) = 0. \tag{5.13}$$

Using Eq. (5.3), we conclude that

$$\lim_{t\to\infty} \|x(t+1) - x(t)\| = 0, \tag{5.14}$$

and using inequality (5.9) we also obtain

$$\lim_{t\to\infty} \|x^i(t) - x(t)\| = 0. \tag{5.15}$$

We now combine Eq. (5.13) and the left hand side of Eq. (5.7) to conclude that $\nabla_i F\big(x^i(t)\big)$ converges to zero, as $t \to \infty$, along any sequence of times that belong to T^i. Given any time t, let $r_i(t)$ be an element of T^i such that $|t - r_i(t)| \leq B$. Such an $r_i(t)$ exists because of Assumption 5.3(a). As t tends to infinity, $r_i(t)$ also tends to infinity, and we have $\lim_{t\to\infty} \nabla_i F\big(x^i(r_i(t))\big) = 0$. Using Eq. (5.15) and the Lipschitz continuity of ∇F, we obtain $\lim_{t\to\infty} \nabla_i F\big(x(r_i(t))\big) = 0$; finally, Eq. (5.14) implies that $\lim_{t\to\infty} \|x(t) - x\big(r_i(t)\big)\| = 0$, which, together with the Lipschitz continuity of ∇F, implies that $\lim_{t\to\infty} \nabla_i F\big(x(t)\big) = 0$ and completes the proof of the proposition. **Q.E.D.**

Suppose now that $F(x) = \frac{1}{2}x'Ax$, where A is a positive definite symmetric matrix such that the totally asynchronous version of the gradient algorithm $x := x - \gamma Ax$ diverges for every choice of $\gamma > 0$. (The existence of such a matrix was demonstrated in Example 3.1 of Subsection 6.3.2.) Proposition 3.1 of Section 6.3 shows that $\rho(|I - \gamma A|) \geq 1$ for every $\gamma > 0$, and, furthermore, for any $\gamma > 0$, there exists a scenario, with $B = 2$, under which the asynchronous algorithm diverges. On the other hand, Prop. 5.1 shows that if $B = 2$ and γ is sufficiently small, then the asynchronous algorithm converges. The reason for the apparent contradiction lies in a minor difference between the model of this section and the model of Section 6.3. In particular, according to the model of Section 6.3, the asynchronous iteration $x := x - \gamma Ax$ is described by the equation

$$x_i(t+1) = x_i\big(\tau_i^i(t)\big) - \gamma \sum_{j=1}^{n} a_{ij}x_j\big(\tau_j^i(t)\big), \quad t \in T^i,$$

whereas the asynchronous gradient algorithm of this section, applied to the minimization of $\frac{1}{2}x'Ax$, is described by

$$x_i(t+1) = x_i(t) - \gamma \sum_{j=1}^{n} a_{ij}x_j\big(\tau_j^i(t)\big), \quad t \in T^i.$$

The two iterations are different if we allow $\tau_i^i(t)$ to be different from t. As we have just seen, this seemingly small difference is important enough to affect convergence.

7.5.2 The Role of the Various Parameters

There are some interesting qualitative observations that can be made regarding the relationship between the maximum stepsize γ_0, the allowed amount of asynchronism B, and the structure of the cost function, the latter being captured by the various constants K_i introduced in the assumptions. Let us recall that in the course of the proof of Prop. 5.1, we found the choice

$$\gamma_0 = \frac{1}{K_3 K_1 (1 + B + nB)} \qquad (5.16)$$

to be sufficient for convergence. This formula suggests that the stepsize should be made smaller as the asynchronism measure B increases. This is very intuitive: if processors make larger steps, then they should inform the others more often. In particular, suppose that we had the objective of keeping the quantity $|x_i(t) - x_i^j(t)|$ bounded. Assuming that $\|s(t)\|$ is bounded, Eq. (5.9) suggests that the product γB should be bounded, consistently with Eq. (5.16).

It should be stressed here that Eq. (5.16) is associated with a sufficient, not necessary, condition for convergence. Nevertheless, this equation has the right qualitative properties. It can be shown that if nothing is known about the optimization problem at hand, other than the constants K_1 and K_3, then in order to guarantee convergence, it is necessary to take γ_0 smaller than c/B, where c is some constant, depending on K_1 and K_3 (Exercise 5.1).

A further issue of interest concerns the relation between γ_0 and the constants K_1 and K_3. We first consider the constant K_3 of Eq. (5.7). The quantity that matters in the algorithm is not γ itself, but the product $\gamma s_i(t)$; it follows from Eq. (5.7), that only the product γK_3 matters. This explains why γ_0 and K_3 are inversely proportional in Eq. (5.16).

The dependence on K_1 is more involved. Even for synchronous algorithms, if K_3 is kept constant, it is a necessary condition for convergence to pick γ_0 inversely proportional to K_1, consistently with Eq. (5.16). Equation (5.16), however, suggests another tradeoff: if γ_0 is held constant, then B should be made smaller as K_1 increases. This is again natural: if K_1 is larger, a change in x_i produces a larger change in $\nabla_j F$.

Therefore, if we want $\nabla_j F(x^j(t)) - \nabla_j F(x(t))$ to stay bounded, a smaller change in $x_i(t)$ is tolerated before processor j receives new information from processor i, and B should be smaller.

Suppose now that there are only two processors and that $F(x) = F^1(x_1) + F^2(x_2)$; we thus have two decoupled optimization problems. Clearly, convergence is obtained even if the processors never communicate; in particular, B can be arbitrarily large. Suppose that we add a coupling term $F^3(x_1, x_2)$ to the cost function. The presence of this term now requires that the two processors communicate to each other. Intuition suggests that the frequency of communication should depend primarily on the properties of the coupling term F^3. To formalize this effect, we refine Assumption 5.1(b) in a way that allows us to quantify the strength of coupling between different components. Assumption 5.4 that follows is a diagonal dominance assumption, similar to Assumptions 3.1 and 3.2, introduced in Section 6.3.

Assumption 5.4.   There exists a constant K_4 such that $|\nabla_i F(x) - \nabla_i F(y)| \leq K_4 \|x - y\|$ for every i and for all $x, y \in \Re^n$ satisfying $x_i = y_i$.

In the case of decoupled problems, we have $K_4 = 0$; the case where K_4 is small can be taken as the definition of a weakly coupled problem. Using Assumption 5.4, the inequalities in the proof of Prop. 5.1 can be somewhat improved. In particular, consider the term $\gamma K_1 \sum_{i=1}^n |s_i(t)| \cdot \|x(t) - x^i(t)\|$ arising in the right–hand side of inequality (5.8); if we impose the additional assumption that $\tau_i^i(t) = t$, we obtain $x_i(t) = x_i^i(t)$, and K_1 can be replaced by K_4. Tracing the steps in the proof, we are finally led to the following sufficient condition for convergence:

$$0 < \gamma < \gamma_0 = \frac{1}{K_3(K_1 + K_4 B + n K_4 B)}.$$

Thus, the asynchronism measure B must be inversely proportional to the strength of coupling between different components, as quantified by the constant K_4. However, even this prescription on the allowed delay is too restrictive when K_4 becomes very small. To see this, assume that F is twice continuously differentiable and that there exists some $\alpha > 0$ such that $\nabla_{ii}^2 F(x) \geq \alpha$ for every $x \in \Re^n$ and for every i. It is easily shown that if K_4 is sufficiently small, then the matrix $\nabla^2 F$ is diagonally dominant, the iteration $x := x - \gamma \nabla F(x)$ is a maximum norm contraction mapping for sufficiently small γ (Prop. 1.11 in Section 3.1), the totally asynchronous gradient algorithm converges (Section 6.3), and no bound on B is needed. Such a diagonal dominance condition cannot be exploited sufficiently well in the proof of Prop. 5.1 because this proof relies on cost reduction rather than reduction of the error $\|x(t) - x^*\|$, where x^* is a minimizer of F.

Finally, let us remark that the dependence of γ on n in Eq. (5.16) is fairly conservative and should not be taken at face value.

7.5.3 Block–Iterative Algorithms

Proposition 5.1 can be extended to the case where each component x_i is not one–dimensional, but rather a vector of dimension n_i. Thus, x is a vector of dimension

$\sum_{i=1}^{m} n_i$, which has been decomposed into block–components $x_1, \ldots, x_m$, and m is the number of processors. Accordingly, we let s_i be a vector of dimension n_i. In this context, we can relax the requirement that each one–dimensional component of x is updated in a descent direction. Rather, it is sufficient to require that each block–component be updated in a descent direction. In particular, we replace Assumption 5.2 with the following.

Assumption 5.5.   There exist positive constants K_2 and K_3 such that:

(a) (*Block–Descent*) There holds $s_i(t)'\nabla_i F(x^i(t)) \leq -\|s_i(t)\|^2/K_3$ for all i and all $t \in T^i$.

(b) There holds $\|s_i(t)\| \geq K_2\|\nabla_i F(x^i(t))\|$ for all i and all $t \in T^i$.

In the above assumption, the notation $\nabla_i F$ stands for the vector of dimension n_i with the partial derivatives of F with respect to the (scalar) components of x corresponding to the subvector x_i. We have the following extension of Prop. 5.1.

Proposition 5.2.   Under Assumptions 5.1, 5.3, and 5.5, there exists some $\gamma_0 > 0$ (depending on n, B, K_1, and K_3) such that, if $0 < \gamma < \gamma_0$, then $\lim_{t \to \infty} \nabla F(x(t)) = 0$.

The proof of Prop. 5.2 is almost the same as the proof of Prop. 5.1 and is left as an exercise.

7.5.4 Gradient Projection Algorithms

We consider a partially asynchronous implementation of the gradient projection algorithm for constrained optimization. For simplicity, we only consider the case of identity scaling, but the discussion applies to more general scaling rules as well. Let $X \subset \Re^n$ be nonempty, closed, and convex, and let $F : \Re^n \mapsto \Re$ be a convex continuously differentiable cost function. We assume that X is a Cartesian product $X = \prod_{i=1}^{m} X_i$ of lower dimensional sets, where $X_i \subset \Re^{n_i}$ and $\sum_{i=1}^{m} n_i = n$. The ith processor updates the ith block–component x_i according to

$$x_i(t+1) = \left[x_i(t) - \gamma \nabla_i F(x^i(t))\right]^+, \qquad t \in T^i, \qquad (5.17)$$

where $[\cdot]^+$ denotes projection on the set X_i and where the vector $x^i(t)$ is defined as in Eq. (5.5). Naturally, we let $x_i(t+1) = x_i(t)$ if $t \notin T^i$. We represent this algorithm in the form of Eq. (5.3) by defining $s_i(t) = 0$, if $t \notin T^i$, and

$$s_i(t) = \frac{1}{\gamma}\big(x_i(t+1) - x_i(t)\big) = \frac{1}{\gamma}\left(\left[x_i(t) - \gamma \nabla_i F(x^i(t))\right]^+ - x_i(t)\right), \qquad t \in T^i.$$

Lemma 5.1.   For any i and t, we have

$$s_i(t)'\nabla_i F(x^i(t)) \leq -\|s_i(t)\|^2. \qquad (5.18)$$

Proof. If $t \notin T^i$, then inequality (5.18) is trivially true since both sides are zero. If $t \in T^i$, the Projection Theorem (Prop. 3.2 in Section 3.3) yields

$$\left(\left[x_i(t)-\gamma\nabla_i F\big(x^i(t)\big)\right]^+ -x_i(t)\right)'\left(\left[x_i(t)-\gamma\nabla_i F\big(x^i(t)\big)\right]^+ -x_i(t)+\gamma\nabla_i F\big(x^i(t)\big)\right) \le 0.$$

Equivalently,

$$\gamma s_i(t)'\left(\gamma s_i(t) + \gamma\nabla_i F\big(x_i(t)\big)\right) \le 0, \qquad t \in T^i,$$

from which inequality (5.18) follows.   **Q.E.D.**

Lemma 5.1 establishes a block–descent property for the gradient projection algorithm [cf. Assumption 5.5(a)]. This property can be exploited to obtain the following result.

Proposition 5.3.   Let $X \subset \Re^n$ be as before. Suppose that $F : \Re^n \mapsto \Re$ is convex, nonnegative, and its gradient satisfies the Lipschitz continuity condition (5.1). Let Assumption 5.3 (partial asynchronism) hold. Then there exists some $\gamma_0 > 0$ such that if $0 < \gamma < \gamma_0$, then any limit point x^* of the sequence $\{x(t)\}$ generated by the partially asynchronous gradient projection algorithm minimizes F over X.

Proof. We follow the proof of Prop. 5.1. The only differences are the following. The term $s_i(t)\nabla_i F\big(x^i(t)\big)$ is replaced by the inner product $s_i(t)'\nabla_i F\big(x^i(t)\big)$ and the term $|s_i(t)|$ is replaced by $\|s_i(t)\|$. Also, K_3 is replaced by 1. All the steps up to Eq. (5.15) remain valid, and we obtain $\lim_{t\to\infty} s_i(t) = 0$ for each i. Let x^* be a limit point of $x(t)$, let $\{t_k\}$ be a sequence such that $\lim_{k\to\infty} x(t_k) = x^*$, and let τ_k be such that $|t_k - \tau_k| \le B$ and $\tau_k \in T^i$. Then, Eqs. (5.14) and (5.15) imply that $x(\tau_k)$ and $x^i(\tau_k)$ converge to x^*. We then have

$$\left[x_i^*-\gamma\nabla_i F(x^*)\right]^+ -x_i^* = \lim_{k\to\infty}\left(\left[x_i(\tau_k)-\gamma\nabla_i F\big(x^i(\tau_k)\big)\right]^+ -x_i(\tau_k)\right) = \lim_{k\to\infty} \gamma s_i(\tau_k) = 0.$$

Since this is true for each i, it follows that x^* minimizes F (Prop. 3.3 in Section 3.3). **Q.E.D.**

EXERCISES

5.1. Consider Example 1.3 of Section 7.1 for which the totally asynchronous gradient algorithm diverges. Show that a necessary condition for convergence of the partially asynchronous gradient algorithm is $0 < \gamma \le c/B$, where c is a suitable constant independent of B or γ.

5.2. Identify the modifications needed in the proof of Prop. 5.1 in order to prove Prop. 5.2.

7.6 DISTRIBUTED ASYNCHRONOUS ROUTING IN DATA NETWORKS

We consider here and prove convergence of a distributed asynchronous implementation of the gradient projection method for solving an optimal routing problem in a data communication network, assuming that the routing problem has been formulated as a nonlinear multicommodity network flow problem, as in Section 5.6. Our model incorporates a number of aspects of actual data networks, such as asynchronism and the transients that occur when a routing strategy is changed. Our model can also serve as a prototype for the analysis of other asynchronous iterative models involving imperfectly known dependencies on several past iterates.

Throughout this section, $\| \cdot \|$ stands for the Euclidean vector norm $\| \cdot \|_2$.

7.6.1 Problem Definition

The reader may wish to review Section 5.6, where the routing problem has been defined. We repeat here the key features and notation. We are given a network (directed graph), a set W of origin–destination (OD) pairs, and for each OD pair $w \in W$, a set of simple positive paths P_w from the origin to the destination. Let $r_w > 0$ be the flow that has to be routed from the origin to the destination of OD pair w, and let x_p denote the flow through a particular path $p \in P_w$. These path flows satisfy the constraints

$$\sum_{p \in P_w} x_p = r_w, \qquad \forall w \in W, \tag{6.1}$$

$$x_p \geq 0, \qquad \forall p \in P_w, \quad \forall w \in W. \tag{6.2}$$

Let x_w be the vector consisting of the path flows x_p, $p \in P_w$, and let x be the vector of all path flows; the latter vector is formed by arranging all the vectors x_w in a single vector.

For any directed arc (i, j) in the network, F_{ij}, the flow through that arc, is given by

$$F_{ij} = \sum_{p \in P_{ij}} x_p, \tag{6.3}$$

where P_{ij} is the set of all paths traversing arc (i, j). We wish to minimize a cost function of the form

$$\sum_{(i,j)} D_{ij}(F_{ij}),$$

where the summation runs over all arcs (i, j) in the network. From Eq. (6.3), this cost function can be expressed in terms of the vector x of path flows to yield a cost function $D(x)$ defined by

$$D(x) = \sum_{(i,j)} D_{ij} \left(\sum_{p \in P_{ij}} x_p \right). \tag{6.4}$$

We make the following assumption.

Assumption 6.1.   For every arc (i, j), the function $D_{ij} : \Re \mapsto \Re$ is convex, twice continuously differentiable, and its second derivative is bounded.

Assumption 6.1 implies that D is also convex, twice continuously differentiable, and its Hessian matrix is bounded. In particular, the boundedness of the Hessian matrix implies that there exists a constant K such that

$$\|\nabla D(x) - \nabla D(y)\| \le K \|x - y\|, \qquad \forall x, y. \tag{6.5}$$

We are faced here with the problem of minimizing a twice differentiable convex function over the closed convex constraint set defined by Eqs. (6.1) and (6.2), and any variant of the gradient projection algorithm can be used. However, when such an algorithm is implemented in real time in an operating data network, the network is likely to behave quite differently from the mathematical description of the algorithm. This is due to several reasons:

(a) Information is inexact: the gradient projection method requires the evaluation of the derivatives of the cost function with respect to the path flows. This requires knowledge of the arc flows through the arcs of interest. Such information is obtained in practice by having the end nodes of each arc measure the average flow through the arc, over a sufficiently long period of time, and then transmit this value to all other nodes that need this value. Due to communication delays, when this information reaches its destination, it can be outdated.

(b) Updates occur asynchronously: the reason is that it is fairly difficult to synchronize a large and geographically distributed data network.

(c) The above problems notwithstanding, even if a node in the network performs a computation and decides to update the path flows under its control, it may be unable to do so instantaneously. For example, if the traffic through the network consists of sessions between users (e.g., telephone conversations), it may be difficult to reroute ongoing sessions; it may be preferable to reroute the traffic by waiting for the current sessions to terminate and assigning different routes to newly generated sessions.

The mathematical model that follows takes into account all of the above considerations. The only missing element from a fully realistic model are the stochastic fluctuations in the amount of traffic that has to be routed. Still, the analysis to follow is asymptotically exact, if one assumes that there is a very large number of users with very small communication rate, in which case, the laws of large numbers take over and eliminate the stochastic fluctuations.

7.6.2 The Algorithm and its Convergence

Let t be a discrete (integer) time variable used to index the events of interest (routing updates). If $p \in P_w$, let $x_p(t)$ be the amount of traffic for OD pair w routed through path p at time t. We define vectors $x_w(t)$ and $x(t)$ analogously. That is, the components of $x_w(t)$ are the variables $x_p(t)$, $p \in P_w$, and $x(t)$ consists of all the vectors $x_w(t)$ arranged in a single vector. Let $F_{ij}(t)$ be the flow through arc (i, j) at time t. In particular, Eq. (6.3) holds for all times t. We assume that a separate processor w is assigned the responsibility of updating x_w. Let T^w be the set of times that such an update is performed. The algorithm is assumed to start at some negative time and we assume that by time 0, each processor w has performed at least one update. That is, for each w, there exists some $t \in T^w$ such that $t \leq 0$. We assume that processor w knows $x_w(t)$ and r_w exactly. This is reasonable, for example, if this processor is located at the origin node of the OD pair w. However, this processor does not know exactly the values of the partial derivatives $(\partial D / \partial x_p)(x(t))$, for $p \in P_w$, but has access to estimates denoted by $\lambda_p(t)$.

We now describe how each $\lambda_p(t)$ is formed. We assume that for every arc (i, j), node i estimates the amount of traffic through that arc by averaging a few recent values of measured traffic. Accordingly, at each time t, node i has available an estimate

$$\tilde{F}_{ij}(t) = \sum_{\tau=t-Q}^{t} c_{ij}(t, \tau) F_{ij}(\tau). \tag{6.6}$$

Here $c_{ij}(t, \tau)$ are (generally unknown) nonnegative scalars satisfying

$$\sum_{\tau=t-Q}^{t} c_{ij}(t, \tau) = 1, \qquad \forall t.$$

The constant Q is a bound on the time over which measurements are being averaged. These estimates are broadcast from time to time (asynchronously and possibly with some variable communication delay). We assume that the times between consecutive broadcasts and the communication delays are bounded, and, consequently, the information available to any other processor can be outdated by at most R time units, where R is some constant. That is, at any time t, each processor w knows the value of an estimate $\tilde{F}_{ij}(\sigma)$ for some σ satisfying $t - R \leq \sigma \leq t$. This, together with Eq. (6.6) implies that at each time t, each processor w has access to an estimate $\hat{F}_{ij,w}(t)$ satisfying

$$\hat{F}_{ij,w}(t) = \sum_{\tau=t-C}^{t} d_{ij,w}(t, \tau) F_{ij}(\tau), \tag{6.7}$$

where $C = R + Q$, and $d_{ij,w}(t, \tau)$ are (generally unknown) nonnegative coefficients satisfying

$$\sum_{\tau=t-C}^{t} d_{ij,w}(t,\tau) = 1, \qquad \forall t. \tag{6.8}$$

We now notice that for every path p, we have [cf. Eq. (6.4)]

$$\frac{\partial D}{\partial x_p}(x(t)) = \sum_{\text{all arcs } (i,j) \text{ on path } p} D'_{ij}(F_{ij}(t)), \qquad \forall t \in T^w,$$

where D'_{ij} denotes the derivative of the function D_{ij}. As the exact value of $F_{ij}(t)$ is unavailable, we assume that processor w forms an estimate $\lambda_p(t)$ by letting

$$\lambda_p(t) = \sum_{\text{all arcs } (i,j) \text{ on path } p} D'_{ij}(\hat{F}_{ij,w}(t)), \qquad \forall t \in T^w. \tag{6.9}$$

We then let $\lambda_w(t)$ be a vector of the same dimension as x_w, whose coordinates are the estimates $\lambda_p(t)$ corresponding to the paths p belonging to P_w.

Using the estimate $\lambda_w(t)$, processor w can compute a vector of desired path flows for OD pair w denoted by $\bar{x}_w(t)$, whose components are $\bar{x}_p(t)$, $p \in P_w$. The actual flows, however, do not settle instantly to their desired values. Rather, we assume that they approach the desired values geometrically. In particular, we assume that there exist scalars $\alpha > 0$, $a_p(t)$, such that

$$a_p(t) \geq \alpha, \qquad \forall p, t, \tag{6.10}$$

and such that

$$x_p(t+1) = a_p(t)\bar{x}_p(t) + \big(1 - a_p(t)\big)x_p(t), \qquad \forall p, t. \tag{6.11}$$

Thus, the flow $x_p(t)$ moves toward the desired value by a nonnegligible factor, during each time unit. The validity of this assumption depends on the particular method that the processors use for rerouting the traffic toward a preferred set of routes; it is satisfied by several rerouting methods (Exercise 6.1). In addition to Eq. (6.11), it is, of course, assumed that the equation $\sum_{p \in P_w} x_p(t) = r_w$ is valid for all t and all w.

It remains to describe the heart of the algorithm, which is the method for computing the desired flows. If $t \notin T^w$, we simply let $\bar{x}_w(t) = \bar{x}_w(t-1)$. If $t \in T^w$, then processor w determines $\bar{x}_w(t)$ by performing an iteration of a version of the gradient projection method [see Eqs. (6.21)–(6.23) of Section 5.6]. In more detail, processor w finds a MFDL (minimum first derivative length) path $p_w(t)$, that is, a path with the smallest associated value of $\lambda_p(t)$. Let

$$\tilde{\lambda}_w(t) = \min_{p \in P_w} \lambda_p(t) = \lambda_{p_w(t)}(t).$$

For any $p \in P_w$, $p \neq p_w(t)$, let $H_p(t)$ be a scaling factor. Usually, $H_p(t)$ is an estimate of the second derivative length of path p [see Eq. (6.23), Section 5.6], but for our purposes, we only need to assume that there exist constants h and H such that

$$0 < h \leq H_p(t) \leq H, \qquad \forall t, p. \tag{6.12}$$

(If $H_p(t)$ is the second derivative length [as in Eq. (6.23) of Section 5.6], and if the second derivative D_{ij}'' is bounded above and below by positive numbers for each arc (i, j), then condition (6.12) will be satisfied.) For any $p \in P_w$, $p \neq p_w(t)$, $\bar{x}_p(t)$ is determined by [cf. Eq. (6.21), Section 5.6]

$$\bar{x}_p(t) = \max\left\{0, x_p(t) - \frac{\gamma}{H_p(t)}\left(\lambda_p(t) - \tilde{\lambda}_w(t)\right)\right\}, \qquad t \in T^w. \tag{6.13}$$

For $p = p_w(t)$, we let

$$\bar{x}_{p_w(t)}(t) = r_w - \sum_{p \in P_w, \ p \neq p_w(t)} \bar{x}_p(t), \qquad t \in T^w. \tag{6.14}$$

The description of the algorithm is now complete. The main equations are Eq. (6.3), describing the dependence of the arc flows on the path flows, Eq. (6.9), describing the dependence of the estimates $\lambda_p(t)$ on the arc flows, Eqs. (6.13) and (6.14), describing the dependence of the desired flows on $\lambda_p(t)$, and Eq. (6.11), which closes the loop by describing the dependence of the actual path flows on the desired ones.

The main ideas in the proof of the following result are similar with the convergence proof for partially asynchronous gradient–like algorithms presented in the preceding section (Prop. 5.1). We show again that the updates are in a descent direction. Furthermore, the errors caused by asynchronism are of second order in γ and are inconsequential when γ is small. Some additional complications are caused by the transients when actual flows move towards their desired values. In particular, we have to ensure that these transients do not destroy the descent properties of the algorithm.

Proposition 6.1. Assume that the difference between consecutive elements of T^w is bounded by some constant B for each OD pair w. Then there exists some $\gamma_0 > 0$ such that if $0 < \gamma < \gamma_0$, then $D\big(x(t)\big)$ converges to the minimum of $D(x)$ over the set of feasible path flow vectors x, and every limit point of the sequence $\{x(t)\}$ minimizes D.

Proof. Throughout the proof, $K_1, K_2, \ldots$, will be constants that do not depend on t or γ. Notice that for any $p \in P_w$, $\lambda_p(t)$ is defined and used only for $t \in T^w$ [Eqs. (6.9) and (6.13)]. To simplify notation, we also define $\lambda_p(t)$ for $t \notin T^w$, $t \geq 0$, by $\lambda_p(t) = \lambda_p(t_0)$, where t_0 is the largest element of T^w satisfying $t_0 \leq t$. (Such a t_0 is well defined, because we have assumed that each set T^w contains a nonpositive element.) Similarly, we use the convention $\tilde{\lambda}_w(t) = \tilde{\lambda}_w(t_0)$.

For any t and $p \in P_w$, we define variables $s_p(t)$ and $\bar{s}_p(t)$ by

$$s_p(t) = x_p(t+1) - x_p(t), \tag{6.15}$$

$$\bar{s}_p(t) = \begin{cases} \bar{x}_p(t) - x_p(t), & t \in T^w, \\ 0, & t \notin T^w. \end{cases} \tag{6.16}$$

We define vectors $s_w(t)$, $\bar{s}_w(t)$, $s(t)$, and $\bar{s}(t)$ analogously. Our first lemma relates $s(t)$ to $\bar{s}(t)$.

Lemma 6.1.

(a) There holds

$$s_p(t) = a_p(t)\bar{s}_p(t), \qquad \forall p \in P_w, \ \forall t \in T^w, \ \forall w. \tag{6.17}$$

(b) Given some w and $t \geq 0$, let t_0 be the largest element of T^w satisfying $t_0 \leq t$. Then for $p \in P_w$,

$$\text{sign}\big(s_p(t)\big) = \text{sign}\big(\bar{s}_p(t_0)\big), \tag{6.18}$$

$$|s_p(t)| \leq |\bar{s}_p(t_0)|, \tag{6.19}$$

where we are using the convention $\text{sign}(0) = 0$.

(c) There exist constants K_1 and K_1' such that

$$\sum_{\tau=0}^{t} |s_p(\tau)|^2 \leq K_1 \sum_{\tau=0}^{t} |\bar{s}_p(\tau)|^2 + K_1', \qquad \forall t \geq 0, \ \forall p \in P_w, \ \forall w. \tag{6.20}$$

Proof.

(a) Immediate from Eq. (6.11) and the definitions (6.15) and (6.16).

(b) Let t_1 be the first element of T^w larger than t_0. Suppose that $\bar{s}_p(t_0) \geq 0$. An easy induction shows that

$$x_p(t_0) \leq x_p(t) \leq x_p(t+1) \leq \bar{x}_p(t_0), \qquad \forall t \in [t_0, t_1),$$

and the result follows for this case. The argument for the case $\bar{s}_p(t_0) \leq 0$ is identical.

(c) Let $p \in P_w$. Part (b) yields, for any successive nonnegative elements t_0 and t_1 of T^w,

$$\sum_{\tau=t_0}^{t_1-1} |s_p(\tau)|^2 \leq (t_1 - t_0)|\bar{s}_p(t_0)|^2 \leq B|\bar{s}_p(t_0)|^2. \tag{6.21}$$

Let t_w (t'_w, respectively) be the smallest element of T^w such that $t_w \geq 0$ ($t'_w > t$, respectively). We sum inequality (6.21) over all $t_0 \in T^w$ such that $t_w \leq t_0 < t'_w$, and use the property $\bar{s}_p(\tau) = 0$ for $\tau \notin T^w$ to obtain

$$\sum_{\tau=t_w}^{t'_w-1} |s_p(\tau)|^2 \leq B \sum_{\{\tau \in T^w \mid t_w \leq \tau < t'_w\}} |\bar{s}_p(\tau)|^2 = B \sum_{\tau=0}^{t} |\bar{s}_p(\tau)|^2.$$

Since $t'_w > t$, we obtain

$$\sum_{\tau=0}^{t} |s_p(\tau)|^2 \leq \sum_{\tau=0}^{t_w-1} |s_p(\tau)|^2 + \sum_{\tau=t_w}^{t'_w-1} |s_p(\tau)|^2 \leq K'_1 + B \sum_{\tau=0}^{t} |\bar{s}_p(\tau)|^2.$$

Notice that $t_w \leq B$ and, therefore, K'_1 can be chosen equal to B times the maximum possible value of $|s_p(t)|$, which is finite because $s_p(t)$ belongs to a bounded set. **Q.E.D.**

We next show that the steps taken by the algorithm possess a certain descent property (cf. Lemma 5.1 in Section 7.5).

Lemma 6.2.   There exists a constant $K_2 > 0$ such that

$$\lambda_w(t)'s_w(t) \leq -\frac{K_2}{\gamma}\|\bar{s}_w(t)\|^2, \qquad \forall t \geq 0, w. \tag{6.22}$$

Proof. Notice that

$$\sum_{p \in P_w} s_p(t) = \sum_{p \in P_w} x_p(t+1) - \sum_{p \in P_w} x_p(t) = r_w - r_w = 0, \qquad \forall t, w. \tag{6.23}$$

Consequently,

$$\lambda_w(t)'s_w(t) = \sum_{p \in P_w} \lambda_p(t)s_p(t) = \sum_{p \in P_w} s_p(t)\big(\lambda_p(t) - \tilde{\lambda}_w(t)\big). \tag{6.24}$$

We first consider the case $t \notin T^w$, in which the right–hand side of inequality (6.22) is zero. Let t_0 be again the largest element of T^w satisfying $t_0 \leq t$, as in Lemma 6.1(b). We have, by definition, $\lambda_p(t) - \tilde{\lambda}_w(t) = \lambda_p(t_0) - \tilde{\lambda}_w(t_0) \geq 0$ for every $p \in P_w$. Furthermore, Eq. (6.13) shows that $\bar{s}_p(t_0) \leq 0$ for every $p \neq p_w(t)$. Using Eq. (6.18) we obtain $s_p(t) \leq 0$ for every $p \neq p_w(t)$, $p \in P_w$. Therefore, each summand in Eq. (6.24), with $p \neq p_w(t)$, is less than or equal to zero. The summand corresponding to $p_w(t)$ is equal to zero, because $\tilde{\lambda}_w(t) = \lambda_{p_w(t)}(t)$, by definition. This proves inequality (6.22) for the case $t \notin T^w$.

We now assume that $t \in T^w$. Equation (6.24) becomes

$$\lambda_w(t)'s_w(t) = \sum_{p \in P_w} a_p(t)\bar{s}_p(t)\big(\lambda_p(t) - \tilde{\lambda}_w(t)\big)$$

$$= - \sum_{p \in P_w} a_p(t)|\bar{s}_p(t)| \cdot |\lambda_p(t) - \tilde{\lambda}_w(t)|$$

$$\leq -\alpha \sum_{p \in P_w} |\bar{s}_p(t)| \cdot |\lambda_p(t) - \tilde{\lambda}_w(t)|$$

$$\leq -\frac{\alpha h}{\gamma} \sum_{p \in P_w, \ p \neq p_w(t)} |\bar{s}_p(t)|^2.$$

(6.25)

[Here the first equality follows from Eq. (6.17); the second follows from the same reasoning as in the preceding paragraph; the next inequality follows from inequality (6.10); and the last inequality follows because Eqs. (6.12) and (6.13) yield $|\bar{s}_p(t)| \leq (\gamma/h)|\lambda_p(t) - \tilde{\lambda}_w(t)|$ for $p \neq p_w(t)$.] Equation (6.14) leads to

$$\bar{s}_{p_w(t)}(t) = - \sum_{p \in P_w, \ p \neq p_w(t)} \bar{s}_p(t) \qquad (6.26)$$

and by squaring both sides of Eq. (6.26), we obtain

$$|\bar{s}_{p_w(t)}(t)|^2 \leq K_3 \sum_{p \in P_w, \ p \neq p_w(t)} |\bar{s}_p(t)|^2,$$

where K_3 is an upper bound on the cardinality of each P_w. Therefore,

$$\sum_{p \in P_w, \ p \neq p_w(t)} |\bar{s}_p(t)|^2 \geq \frac{1}{2} \sum_{p \in P_w, \ p \neq p_w(t)} |\bar{s}_p(t)|^2 + \frac{1}{2K_3}|\bar{s}_{p_w(t)}(t)|^2 \geq \frac{1}{2K_3}\|\bar{s}_w(t)\|^2.$$

(6.27)

Using Eqs. (6.25) and (6.27), we obtain

$$\lambda_w(t)'s_w(t) \leq -\frac{\alpha h}{2\gamma K_3}\|\bar{s}_w(t)\|^2,$$

which proves inequality (6.22) for the case $t \in T^w$ with $K_2 = \alpha h/2\gamma K_3$.   **Q.E.D.**

The next lemma bounds the error in the estimated gradient, caused by asynchronism.

Lemma 6.3.   There exists some constant K_4 such that

$$\big\|\lambda(t) - \nabla D\big(x(t)\big)\big\| \leq K_4 \sum_{\tau=t-B-C}^{t} \|s(\tau)\|, \qquad \forall t \geq 0, \qquad (6.28)$$

where C is the constant in Eq. (6.7).

Proof. Let us fix some $p \in P_w$ and some $t \geq 0$. Let t_0 be the largest element of T^w satisfying $t_0 \leq t$. Then, using Eq. (6.9),

$$\left| \lambda_p(t) - \frac{\partial D}{\partial x_p}(x(t)) \right| = \left| \lambda_p(t_0) - \frac{\partial D}{\partial x_p}(x(t)) \right| \leq \sum_{(i,j)} \left| D'_{ij}(\hat{F}_{ij,w}(t_0)) - D'_{ij}(F_{ij}(t)) \right|,$$
(6.29)

where the last summation is over all arcs traversed by path p. Let K_5 be the maximum of the number of arcs in any given path. Let K_6 be a bound on the second derivatives D''_{ij}. Then inequality (6.29) becomes

$$\begin{aligned}
\left| \lambda_p(t) - \frac{\partial D}{\partial x_p}(x(t)) \right| &\leq K_5 K_6 \max_{(i,j)} \left| \hat{F}_{ij,w}(t_0) - F_{ij}(t) \right| \\
&\leq K_5 K_6 \max_{(i,j)} \sum_{\tau=t_0-C}^{t_0} d_{ij,w}(t_0, \tau) \left| F_{ij}(\tau) - F_{ij}(t) \right| \\
&\leq K_5 K_6 \max_{(i,j)} \max_{t_0-C \leq \tau \leq t_0} \left| F_{ij}(\tau) - F_{ij}(t) \right| \\
&\leq K_5 K_6 \max_{(i,j)} \max_{t-B-C \leq \tau \leq t} \left| F_{ij}(\tau) - F_{ij}(t) \right| \\
&\leq K_5 K_6 K_7 \max_{t-B-C \leq \tau \leq t} \left\| x(\tau) - x(t) \right\| \\
&\leq K_8 \sum_{\tau=t-B-C}^{t} \left\| s(\tau) \right\|.
\end{aligned}$$
(6.30)

Here $K_8 = K_5 K_6 K_7$. For the constant K_7, we can use the induced norm of the linear mapping in Eq. (6.3), which determines the arc flows F_{ij} in terms of the path flows x_p. In the previous inequalities, we have also made use of Eqs. (6.7) and (6.8).

The desired result follows from inequality (6.30) and the triangle inequality. **Q.E.D.**

We can now carry out the main part of the proof, which follows the same steps as the proof of Prop. 5.1 in the preceding section. Using the descent lemma (Prop. A.32 in Appendix A) and Lemmas 6.2 and 6.3, we obtain

$$\begin{aligned}
D(x(t+1)) &\leq D(x(t)) + s(t)' \nabla D(x(t)) + \frac{K}{2} \|s(t)\|^2 \\
&\leq D(x(t)) + s(t)' \lambda(t) + \|\lambda(t) - \nabla D(x(t))\| \cdot \|s(t)\| + \frac{K}{2} \|s(t)\|^2 \\
&\leq D(x(t)) - \frac{K_2}{\gamma} \|\bar{s}(t)\|^2 + K_4 \sum_{\tau=t-B-C}^{t} \|s(\tau)\| \cdot \|s(t)\| + \frac{K}{2} \|s(t)\|^2
\end{aligned}$$

$$\leq D\big(x(t)\big) - \frac{K_2}{\gamma}\big\|\bar{s}(t)\big\|^2 + K_4 \sum_{\tau=t-B-C}^{t} \big(\|s(\tau)\|^2 + \|s(t)\|^2\big) + \frac{K}{2}\|s(t)\|^2$$

$$\leq D\big(x(t)\big) - \frac{K_2}{\gamma}\big\|\bar{s}(t)\big\|^2 + K_9 \sum_{\tau=t-B-C}^{t} \|s(\tau)\|^2, \tag{6.31}$$

where $K_9 = K_4(B + C + 1) + K/2$. By adding inequality (6.31) for different values of t, and rearranging terms, we obtain

$$D\big(x(t+1)\big) \leq D\big(x(0)\big) - \frac{K_2}{\gamma} \sum_{\tau=0}^{t}\big\|\bar{s}(t)\big\|^2 + K_9(B+C+1) \sum_{\tau=-B-C}^{t} \|s(\tau)\|^2$$

$$\leq D\big(x(0)\big) - \left(\frac{K_2}{\gamma} - K_1 K_9(B+C+1)\right) \sum_{\tau=0}^{t}\big\|\bar{s}(\tau)\big\|^2$$

$$+ K_1' K_9(B+C+1) + \sum_{\tau=-B-C}^{-1} \|s(\tau)\|^2,$$

where in the last step we made use of inequality (6.20). Let γ be small enough so that $K_2 > \gamma K_1 K_9(B + C + 1)$. Notice that $D\big(x(t+1)\big)$ is bounded from below [because D is continuous and $x(t+1)$ belongs to a compact set]. Since the sum $\sum_{\tau=-B-C}^{-1}\|s(\tau)\|^2$ is finite, we conclude that the series $\sum_{\tau=0}^{t}\|\bar{s}(\tau)\|^2$ is bounded. Therefore,

$$\lim_{t\to\infty} \|\bar{s}(t)\| = 0. \tag{6.32}$$

Using inequality (6.19), we obtain

$$\lim_{t\to\infty} \|s(t)\| = 0. \tag{6.33}$$

Then Lemma 6.3 yields

$$\lim_{t\to\infty} \Big(\lambda(t) - \nabla D\big(x(t)\big)\Big) = 0. \tag{6.34}$$

Let x^* be a limit point of the sequence $\{x(t)\}$. Such a limit point exists because $x(t)$ is constrained to lie in a compact set. Let us fix some $w \in W$. Since $x(t+1) - x(t) = s(t)$ converges to zero and since the difference between consecutive elements of T^w is bounded, it follows that there exists a sequence of elements of T^w along which $x(t)$ converges to x^*. Let $\{t_k\}$ be a subsequence of that sequence such that $p_w(t_k)$ is the same and equal to some $p^* \in P_w$ for all t_k. Let us also fix some $p \in P_w$ for which $x_p^* > 0$. Since $\bar{s}_p(t)$ converges to zero, the update equation (6.13), implies that

$$\lim_{k\to\infty} \big(\lambda_p(t_k) - \lambda_{p^*}(t_k)\big) = 0.$$

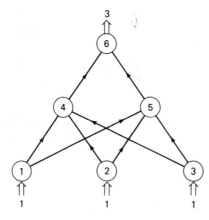

Figure 7.6.1 The routing problem of Example 6.1. If the communication delays are excessively large, the flows can oscillate between the two available paths for each OD pair.

By the definition of p^*, $\lambda_{p^*}(t_k) \leq \lambda_{p'}(t_k)$ for every k and for every $p' \in P_w$. Thus,

$$\limsup_{k\to\infty} \big(\lambda_p(t_k) - \lambda_{p'}(t_k)\big) \leq 0, \qquad \forall p' \in P_w.$$

Using Eq. (6.34), we obtain

$$\limsup_{k\to\infty} \left[\frac{\partial D}{\partial x_p}\big(x(t_k)\big) - \frac{\partial D}{\partial x_{p'}}\big(x(t_k)\big)\right] \leq 0, \qquad \forall p' \in P_w.$$

Since $x(t_k)$ converges to x^*, we use the continuity of $\partial D/\partial x_p$ to conclude that

$$\frac{\partial D}{\partial x_p}(x^*) \leq \frac{\partial D}{\partial x_{p'}}(x^*), \qquad \forall p' \in P_w.$$

This inequality has been shown to be true for every w and for every $p \in P_w$ such that $x_p^* > 0$. But these are precisely the sufficient conditions for optimality of Section 5.6 [Eq. (6.11) in Section 5.6]. Therefore, x^* is an optimal vector of path flows.

Consider now any sequence $\{t_k\}$ such that $D\big(x(t_k)\big)$ converges. By restricting to a subsequence, we can assume that $x(t_k)$ also converges to some x^*. As shown already, x^* is an optimal vector and, therefore, $D\big(x(t_k)\big)$ converges to the optimal value of D, denoted by D^*. The sequence $\big\{D\big(x(t)\big)\big\}$ is bounded and we have just shown that all of its limit points are equal to D^*. Thus, $D\big(x(t)\big)$ converges to D^*, which completes the proof of the proposition.   **Q.E.D.**

7.6.3 Discussion

The proof of Prop. 6.1 made essential use of the assumption that the information available to the processors cannot be arbitrarily out of date (see Lemma 6.3, for example). In the absence of such an assumption, the flows through the network can oscillate back and forth to what the nodes incorrectly perceive as underutilized paths and the algorithm does not converge. A simple example follows.

Example 6.1.

Consider the network of Fig. 7.6.1. There are three origin nodes (nodes 1, 2, and 3), whose input arrival rates are all 1, and a single destination node (node 6). For each OD pair, there are two paths. For each origin node i, let x_i denote the flow routed through the path containing node 4. Let $D_{ij}(F_{ij}) = F_{ij}^2$ for $(i,j) = (4,6)$ or $(5,6)$, and $D_{ij}(F_{ij}) = 0$, for all other arcs. In terms of the variables x_1, x_2, and x_3, the cost becomes

$$D(x_1, x_2, x_3) = (x_1 + x_2 + x_3)^2 + (3 - x_1 - x_2 - x_3)^2.$$

We assume that the settling time is zero, so that we need not distinguish between actual and desired flows, and that each node i, $i = 1, 2, 3$, knows x_i exactly and is able to transmit it instantaneously to the remaining nodes. Suppose that initially $x_1 = x_2 = x_3 = 1$ and that each node executes a large number of gradient projection iterations with a small stepsize before communicating the current value of x_i to the other nodes. Then, effectively, each node i solves the problem

$$\min_{0 \le x_i \le 1} \{(x_i + 2)^2 + (1 - x_i)^2\},$$

thereby obtaining the value $x_i = 0$. At that point, the processors broadcast their current values of x_i. If that sequence of events is repeated, a symmetrical argument shows that each x_i will become again equal to 1. So, (x_1, x_2, x_3) oscillates between $(1,1,1)$ and $(0,0,0)$, and does not converge to an optimal routing. The same behavior is observed if the cost function is modified by adding a term $\epsilon(x_1^2 + x_2^2 + x_3^2)$, which makes it strictly convex, as long as ϵ is positive and very small.

An important virtue of the algorithm of this section is that it is able to adapt to changes in the input traffic r_w without having to be restarted. Simply, whenever r_w changes, the processor in charge of OD pair w continues performing gradient projection iterations, using the new value of r_w. As long as the time variations in r_w are slow compared to the speed of convergence of the algorithm, the algorithm will keep generating flows that at any time are close to the optimal ones, given the current value of r_w.

There is an alternative distributed implementation of the algorithm, in which the estimates $\lambda_p(t)$ are formed somewhat differently. In particular, let node i evaluate the derivative $D'_{ij}(\tilde{F}_{ij})$, where $\tilde{F}_{ij}$ is defined by Eq. (6.6), and then transmit this value to all other nodes. Then the node in control of the variable x_p evaluates λ_p by adding these derivatives along the path p. Essentially, this amounts to substituting $\tilde{F}_{ij}$ for $\hat{F}_{ij}$ in Eq. (6.9). With this modification, the proof of Prop. 6.1 remains valid, with a minor change in the proof of Lemma 6.4.

We finally mention another form of the algorithm in which the basic iteration (6.13)–(6.14) is replaced by the scaled gradient projection iteration

$$\bar{x}_w(t+1) = \left[\bar{x}_w(t) - \gamma M_w^{-1}(t)\lambda_w(t)\right]_{M_w(t)}^+, \qquad t \in T^w. \qquad (6.35)$$

Here $M_w(t)$ is a positive definite symmetric matrix, and $[\cdot]_{M_w(t)}^+$ denotes projection on the set

$$\left\{ x_w \mid \sum_{p \in P_w} x_p = r_w \text{ and } x_p \geq 0, \ \forall p \in P_w \right\}$$

[cf. Eqs. (6.1) and (6.2)], with respect to the norm $\|x_w\|_{M_w(t)} = \left(x'_w M_w(t) x_w \right)^{1/2}$ (see Subsection 3.3.3). This algorithm also converges (Exercise 6.2); however, it has the undesirable feature that the next value $\bar{x}_w(t+1)$ is determined in terms of the current value $\bar{x}_w(t)$ of the desired flows, as opposed to the current value $x_w(t)$ of the actual path flows, and this can slow down the adaptation to sudden changes in the problem data r_w. A more reasonable alternative, in which $x_w(t)$ replaces $\bar{x}_w(t)$ in Eq. (6.35), might be

$$\bar{x}_w(t) = \left[x_w(t) - \gamma M_w^{-1}(t) \lambda_w(t) \right]^+_{M_w(t)}, \qquad t \in T^w. \tag{6.36}$$

Surprisingly, however, this algorithm need not have the descent property and is not guaranteed to converge (see Exercise 6.3).

EXERCISES

6.1. This exercise provides an example of a rerouting method for which the model of Eqs. (6.10) and (6.11) is valid. Consider a particular OD pair w and the associated paths P_w. We assume that at any given time t, the traffic of such an OD pair consists of a number $n(t)$ of sessions that are simultaneously active. Each active session generates a constant flow of δ bits per second, which has to be routed from the origin to the destination. We assume that there is a very large number of sessions, each generating a very small flow, which allows us to view the total traffic $r(t) = \delta n(t)$ as a continuous variable. We assume that new sessions are "born" at a rate of λ per second, and that existing sessions terminate at a rate of $\mu n(t)$ per second, where λ and μ are positive constants. Thus, the total traffic $r(t)$ satisfies the differential equation

$$\frac{dr}{dt}(t) = \delta\lambda - \mu r(t).$$

In the long run, equilibrium is reached, we have $(dr/dt)(t) = 0$, and the traffic $r(t)$ is constant and equal to $r^* = \delta\lambda/\mu$.

Let $x_p(t)$ be the traffic routed through a particular path $p \in P_w$, and let $\bar{x}_p(t)$ be the corresponding desired flow. Suppose that once a session is born, it is assigned to some path and it cannot be reassigned before it terminates. Thus, routing can be only controlled by assigning paths to new sessions. Let $\rho_p(t)$ be the proportion of new sessions generated at time t that are assigned to path p. Then the path flow $x_p(t)$ satisfies the equation

$$\frac{dx_p}{dt}(t) = \delta\lambda\rho_p(t) - \mu x_p(t).$$

Suppose that $\rho_p(t) = \bar{x}_p(t)/r^*$. Furthermore, suppose that the desired path flows $\bar{x}_p(t)$ can only change at integer times. Show that Eqs. (6.10) and (6.11) hold for every integer time t.

6.2. Suppose that the update equations (6.13) and (6.14) are replaced by Eq. (6.35). We assume that the matrices $M_w(t)$ are symmetric, bounded, and that there exists some $h > 0$ such that $M_w(t) - hI$ is nonnegative definite for each w and t. Show that Prop. 6.1 remains valid. Assume for simplicity, that $x(0) = \bar{x}(0)$.

Hints: Let $s(t) = \bar{x}(t+1) - \bar{x}(t)$. Use the Scaled Projection Theorem of Section 3.3 to show that

$$\lambda_w(t)' s_w(t) \leq -\frac{A}{\gamma} \|s_w(t)\|^2, \qquad \forall t,$$

where A is a positive constant (this replaces Lemma 6.2). Then show that there exist constants $A > 0$ and $\rho \in (0,1)$ such that

$$\left\| \lambda(t) - \nabla D\big(x(t)\big) \right\| \leq A \sum_{\tau=0}^{t} \rho^{t-\tau} \left\| s(\tau) \right\|, \qquad \forall t.$$

(This replaces Lemma 6.3.) Next, use the inequality

$$D\big(\bar{x}(t+1)\big) \leq D\big(\bar{x}(t)\big) + s(t)' \nabla D\big(\bar{x}(t)\big) + \frac{K}{2} \|s(t)\|^2$$

and proceed as in inequality (6.31) to show that $s(t)$ converges to zero.

6.3. Suppose that the update equations (6.13) and (6.14) are replaced by Eq. (6.36). Consider the simple case where there is a single OD pair (we accordingly suppress the superscript or subscript w from our notation). Furthermore, consider the synchronous scenario where the set T of update times is the set of all nonnegative integers, $\lambda(t) = \nabla D\big(x(t)\big)$ for all t, and the scaling matrix $M(t)$ is equal to a fixed symmetric positive definite matrix M. Let $A(t)$ be a diagonal matrix with $a_p(t)$ being the pth diagonal entry. Then the iteration (6.36) and the flow adjustment equation (6.11) become

$$\bar{x}(t) = \left[x(t) - \gamma M^{-1} \nabla D\big(x(t)\big) \right]_M^+, \tag{6.37}$$

$$x(t+1) = x(t) + A(t)\big(\bar{x}(t) - x(t)\big). \tag{6.38}$$

It is assumed, of course, that the coefficients $a_p(t)$ satisfy the conditions $0 < \alpha \leq a_p(t) \leq 1$ and

$$\sum_p a_p(t)\big(\bar{x}_p(t) - x_p(t)\big) = 0$$

so that Eq. (6.38) keeps $x(t+1)$ in the feasible set. Show (possibly by means of a figure) that the iteration (6.37)–(6.38) is not guaranteed to have the descent property $D\big(x(t+1)\big) \leq D\big(x(t)\big)$ no matter how small γ is chosen. *Hint:* The matrix $A(t)M^{-1}$ is not necessarily positive definite.

7.7 A MODEL IN WHICH SEVERAL PROCESSORS UPDATE THE SAME VARIABLES

We now present a model of distributed iterative computation in which several processors are allowed to update the same component of the vector being iterated. As the updates of different processors will be generally different, the agreement algorithm of Section 7.3 will be used to reconcile the individual updates. This model will be used in the next section in the context of a stochastic gradient–like algorithm.

We motivate the model of this section by means of a simple example. Let y be a random variable with unknown finite mean m and variance σ^2. Suppose that there are p processors and that the ith processor observes, at times $t = 1, 2, \ldots$, an independent realization (sample value) of y, to be denoted by $y_i(t)$. [For instance, the processors might be generating $y_i(t)$ by Monte Carlo simulation; alternatively, the observations $y_i(t)$ could be sensor data obtained at geographically distributed sensor sites.] The objective of the processors is to estimate the mean of y. At any time $t \geq 1$, each processor can compute the estimate $m_i(t) = \left(\sum_{\tau=1}^{t} y_i(\tau)\right)/t$ based on its own data. Furthermore, the computation of $m_i(t)$ can be carried out recursively by means of the formula

$$m_i(t+1) = m_i(t) + \frac{1}{t+1}\big(y_i(t+1) - m_i(t)\big),$$

initialized with $m_i(0) = 0$. This equation resembles the equation $x(t+1) = x(t) + \gamma s(t)$ of Section 7.5 [cf. Eq. (5.3)]; here $1/(t+1)$ plays the role of a (time–varying and decreasing) stepsize γ and $y_i(t+1) - m_i(t)$ plays the role of $s(t)$.

The variance $E\big[(m_i(t) - m)^2\big]$ of $m_i(t)$ is equal to σ^2/t. A better estimate, with variance $\sigma^2/(tp)$, is obtained if the processors were to exchange their individual estimates at time t and compute their average. This averaging could be performed once and for all at the end of the algorithm. However, it may be desirable that the processors obtain good estimates of m while the generation of new observations $y_i(t)$ is in progress. This necessitates that the averaging of their individual estimates be performed more frequently. One possibility is that at each time t, once the processors obtain the new realizations $y_i(t)$ and compute their new individual estimates, they exchange and average their estimates. In this case, the computation consists of interleaved phases involving computation of $y_i(t)$ and averaging. This is a synchronous algorithm, which may be undesirable if, say, some processors are faster than others or if communication delays are too long.

An alternative approach is to overlap the individual computations and the averaging process. This can be done by letting the processors execute the agreement algorithm of Section 7.3, trying to agree on a common estimate, while they keep obtaining new samples $y_i(t)$, which they immediately incorporate into their estimates. We are faced here with two opposing effects: the agreement algorithm tends to bring the estimates of the processors closer together, whereas the generation of new samples has the potential of increasing the difference of their estimates. The interaction of these two effects substantially complicates the question of asynchronous convergence.

We now proceed to the formal description of the model to be employed. The reader is advised at this point that the notation to be introduced is somewhat different from earlier sections. This is because components will no more be associated with a unique processor; an additional superscript will be used to specify the processor transmitting a message with the value of some component. The general notational convention to be followed here and in the next section is that superscripts denote processors and subscripts denote components.

We consider an algorithm that iterates on a vector x belonging to the vector space $\Re^n$. Furthermore, we assume that $\Re^n$ is expressed as a Cartesian product of m subspaces of lower dimensions, that is, $\Re^n = \Re^{n_1} \times \cdots \times \Re^{n_m}$, where $n_1 + \cdots + n_m = n$. Accordingly, any vector $x \in \Re^n$ is decomposed as $x = (x_1, \ldots, x_m)$, with x_ℓ belonging to $\Re^{n_\ell}$. We refer to x_ℓ as the ℓth component of x.

Let there be p processors. Each processor i has available at each time t a vector $x^i(t) \in \Re^n$, with components $x_\ell^i(t) \in \Re^{n_\ell}$, $\ell = 1, \ldots, m$. For every component index ℓ, we let $C_\ell \subset \{1, \ldots, p\}$ be the set of processors who are in charge of updating the ℓth component x_ℓ, based on their own measurements or computations. We call C_ℓ the set of *computing processors* for component ℓ and we assume that it is nonempty for each ℓ. If $i \in C_\ell$, we let T_ℓ^i be the set of times at which processor i updates x_ℓ.

For every processor i, any component x_ℓ, and any time t, let $\gamma_\ell^i(t)s_\ell^i(t)$ be the update in x_ℓ due to a computation by processor i. Here $\gamma_\ell^i(t)$ is a positive stepsize and $s_\ell^i(t) \in \Re^{n_\ell}$ is an update direction. We could, without loss of generality, absorb $\gamma_\ell^i(t)$ into $s_\ell^i(t)$; our choice of notation is dictated by the application to be considered in the next section. Naturally, we assume that if $i \notin C_\ell$ or if $t \notin T_\ell^i$, then no computation is performed and $s_\ell^i(t) = 0$.

For every component index ℓ, there is a directed graph $G_\ell = (N, A_\ell)$ used to model the exchange of messages carrying a value of x_ℓ. The node set N is the set $\{1, \ldots, p\}$ of processors and the arc set A_ℓ is the set of all pairs (j, i) such that processor j keeps sending messages x_ℓ to processor i. For $(j, i) \in A_\ell$, we let T_ℓ^{ij} be the set of times that such a message is received by processor i and we assume that this set is infinite. For any $t \in T_\ell^{ij}$, we use $\tau_\ell^{ij}(t)$ to denote the time at which the message x_ℓ^j (received by i at time t) was transmitted by processor j. Thus, the message received by processor i at time t is equal to $x_\ell^j\big(\tau_\ell^{ij}(t)\big)$. We assume that $1 \leq \tau_\ell^{ij}(t) \leq t$. We also use the convention that T_ℓ^{ii} is the set of all nonnegative integers and that $\tau_\ell^{ii}(t) = t$, for all t.

The algorithm is initialized at time 1 with each processor i having a vector $x^i(1) \in \Re^n$ in its memory. Processor i can, at any time t, receive messages $x_\ell^j\big(\tau_\ell^{ij}(t)\big)$ from other processors, incorporate these messages into its memory by forming a convex combination with its own value $x_\ell^i(t)$, and finally incorporate the result $\gamma_\ell^i(t)s_\ell^i(t)$ of its own computations. We thus postulate that for every i and ℓ, the variable $x_\ell^i(t)$ is updated according to the formula

$$x_\ell^i(t+1) = \sum_{\{j \mid t \in T_\ell^{ij}\}} a_\ell^{ij}(t)x_\ell^j\big(\tau_\ell^{ij}(t)\big) + \gamma_\ell^i(t)s_\ell^i(t), \tag{7.1}$$

where the coefficients $a_\ell^{ij}(t)$ are nonnegative scalars satisfying

$$\sum_{\{j \mid t \in T_\ell^{ij}\}} a_\ell^{ij}(t) = 1, \qquad \forall \ell, t, i.$$

Equation (7.1) is the general description of the algorithm but it takes somewhat simpler forms in special cases. For example, if processor i receives no messages x_ℓ^j at time t, then $\{j \mid t \in T_\ell^{ij}\} = \{i\}$ and Eq. (7.1) simplifies to

$$x_\ell^i(t + 1) = x_\ell^i(t) + \gamma_\ell^i(t) s_\ell^i(t).$$

Similarly, if $i \notin C_\ell$ or if $t \notin T_\ell^i$, then $s_\ell^i(t) = 0$ and Eq. (7.1) becomes

$$x_\ell^i(t + 1) = \sum_{\{j \mid t \in T_\ell^{ij}\}} a_\ell^{ij}(t) x_\ell^j\big(\tau_\ell^{ij}(t)\big). \tag{7.2}$$

Equation (7.2) resembles the equations defining the agreement algorithm of Section 7.3, although it is somewhat more general, due to the dependence of the coefficients $a_\ell^{ij}(t)$ on time. In any case, the iteration (7.2) will be referred to as the *underlying agreement algorithm*. Notice that we essentially have a decoupled set of agreement algorithms, one for each component x_ℓ. Coupling between components can arise, however, in Eq. (7.1) because $s_\ell^i(t)$ can depend on the entire vector $x^i(t)$.

Given our motivation of the model (7.1), we want to ensure that the underlying agreement algorithm (7.2) works properly. That is, we would like the values of the variables x_ℓ^i, possessed by different processors, to converge to a common value in the absence of further computations. This turns out to be the case under some reasonable assumptions.

Example 7.1.

We show that the agreement algorithm of Section 7.3 is a special case of Eq. (7.2). Suppose that for each processor i and for every j who communicates x_ℓ to i [i.e., if $(j, i) \in A_\ell$], the set T_ℓ^{ij} does not depend on j. We are thus assuming that $T_\ell^{ij} = R_\ell^i$ for all j such that $(j, i) \in A_\ell$, where R_ℓ^i is some set. Accordingly, at any time t, either $t \notin R_\ell^i$ and processor i receives no message x_ℓ^j or $t \in R_\ell^i$ and processor i receives simultaneously messages x_ℓ^j from all processors j that are supposed to send such messages. This is not as unrealistic as it sounds. For example, processor i might physically receive these messages at different times, store them in a buffer, and then read them all at the same time t. As far as the mathematical description of the algorithm is concerned, this situation is identical to the case of simultaneous receptions.

We now assume for each $(j, i) \in A_\ell$ and $t \in R_\ell^i$, that the value of the coefficient $a_\ell^{ij}(t)$ is positive and independent of t, and will be denoted by a_ℓ^{ij}. Let us define for convenience $a_\ell^{ij} = 0$ if $j \neq i$ and $(j, i) \notin A_\ell$. Then Eq. (7.2) can be rewritten as

$$x_\ell^i(t + 1) = \sum_{j=1}^{p} a_\ell^{ij} x_\ell^j\big(\tau_\ell^{ij}(t)\big), \qquad \text{if } t \in R_\ell^i,$$

$$x_\ell^i(t + 1) = x_\ell^i(t), \qquad \text{if } t \notin R_\ell^i.$$

These two equations are identical to those describing the agreement algorithm of Section 7.3 [cf. Eqs. (3.2) and (3.3)], except for somewhat different notation. If we now introduce the partial asynchronism assumption and assume that there exists some i such that $a_\ell^{ii} > 0$ and such that there exists a positive path (in the graph G_ℓ) from i to all other processors, then the sequence generated by Eq. (7.2) is guaranteed to converge to agreement, geometrically.

Example 7.2.

We now consider an alternative to Example 7.1, in which received messages are immediately incorporated in the memory of the receiving processor. For any i and ℓ and any $j \neq i$ such that $(j, i) \in A_\ell$, we are given a constant $a_\ell^{ij} \in (0, 1)$. Furthermore, we assume that each processor i receives at most one message x_ℓ^j at each time unit; equivalently, the sets T_ℓ^{ij}, with $j \neq i$, are disjoint for any fixed i. In practice, physical message receptions could be simultaneous, but a processor can always place incoming messages in a buffer and read them one at a time. Thus, our assumption is not entirely unrealistic. Suppose that for every $t \in T_\ell^{ij}$, the incoming message $x_\ell^j\big(\tau_\ell^{ij}(t)\big)$ is taken into account by processor i by letting

$$x_\ell^i(t+1) = a_\ell^{ij} x_\ell^j\big(\tau_\ell^{ij}(t)\big) + (1 - a_\ell^{ij})x_\ell^i(t) + \gamma_\ell^i(t)s_\ell^i(t), \qquad t \in T_\ell^{ij}.$$

We also let $x_\ell^i(t+1) = x_\ell^i(t) + \gamma_\ell^i(t)s_\ell^i(t)$ if t does not belong to any T_ℓ^{ij}. It is easily seen that we are dealing with a special case of Eq. (7.1). The underlying agreement algorithm is identical to the one considered in Exercise 3.2 of Section 7.3. According to the result of that exercise, such an agreement algorithm is guaranteed to converge geometrically if the partial asynchronism assumption holds and provided that for some i, there exists a positive path (in the graph G_ℓ) from i to every other processor j.

Examples 7.1 and 7.2 demonstrate that we can realistically assume that the underlying agreement algorithm (7.2) converges geometrically and such an assumption will be introduced shortly. Before doing so, we shall develop an alternative representation that is equivalent to Eq. (7.1) but easier to work with.

Suppose that we have fixed the sets T_ℓ^{ij} and the values of the coefficients $a_\ell^{ij}(t)$ and $\tau_\ell^{ij}(t)$ for all ℓ, i, j, $t \in T_\ell^{ij}$. (We refer to any fixed choice of these sets and variables as a *realization* of the underlying agreement algorithm.) Let us now fix some component index ℓ. It is seen from Eq. (7.1) that for any fixed t and i, the value of $x_\ell^i(t)$ is a linear function of the variables $\{x^j(1) \mid j = 1, \ldots, p\}$ and $\{\gamma_\ell^j(\tau)s_\ell^j(\tau) \mid j = 1, \ldots, p, \ \tau = 1, \ldots, t-1\}$. (This is easily proved by induction, using the fact that the composition of two linear functions is linear.) It follows that there exist scalar coefficients $\Phi_\ell^{ij}(t, \tau)$, $t > \tau \geq 0$, such that

$$x_\ell^i(t) = \sum_{j=1}^p \Phi_\ell^{ij}(t, 0)x_\ell^j(1) + \sum_{\tau=1}^{t-1} \sum_{j=1}^p \Phi_\ell^{ij}(t, \tau)\gamma_\ell^j(\tau)s_\ell^j(\tau). \tag{7.3}$$

Equation (7.3) is more explicit than the original Eq. (7.1). On the other hand, the coefficients $\Phi_\ell^{ij}(t, \tau)$ depend on the particular realization of the underlying agreement algorithm and are therefore usually unknown.

Example 7.3.

The best way of visualizing the coefficient $\Phi_\ell^{ij}(t, \tau)$ is by considering the following sequence of events. Let us fix j, ℓ, and τ. For simplicity, suppose that each component is one–dimensional ($n_\ell = 1$) and that $x_\ell^k(1) = 0$ for all k. Suppose that processor j performs a computation at time τ and obtains $\gamma_\ell^j(\tau)s_\ell^j(\tau) = 1$. Furthermore, suppose that this is the only computation ever to be performed by any processor, that is $s_\ell^k(\sigma) = 0$, unless $k = j$ and $\sigma = \tau$. For such a sequence of events, Eq. (7.3) shows that for $t > \tau$, $\Phi_\ell^{ij}(t, \tau) = x_\ell^i(t)$. In other words, $\Phi_\ell^{ij}(t, \tau)$ is the value (at time t and at processor i) generated by the underlying agreement algorithm, initialized at time $\tau + 1$ with $x^j(\tau+1) = 1$, $x^k(\tau+1) = 0$ for $k \neq j$, and with all messages in transit at time $\tau + 1$ equal to zero.

There are several conclusions that can be drawn from Example 7.3. First, we must have

$$0 \leq \Phi_\ell^{ij}(t, \tau) \leq 1, \qquad \forall i, j, \ell, t > \tau.$$

Furthermore, if the underlying agreement algorithm is geometrically convergent (as is the case in Examples 7.1 and 7.2), then the coefficients $\Phi_\ell^{ij}(t, \tau)$ converge geometrically, as t tends to infinity, to a limit independent of i. We introduce the notation $\Phi_\ell^j(\tau)$ to denote this common limit. The variable $\Phi_\ell^j(\tau)$ is interpreted as the value of the component x_ℓ on which all processors would agree under the sequence of events specified in Example 7.3.

Finally, let us notice that if i is a computing processor for component ℓ (that is, if $i \in C_\ell$), then it is desirable that each update $\gamma_\ell^i(t)s_\ell^i(t)$ of processor i can influence the value of x_ℓ^j for all other processors j by a nonnegligible amount in the long run. This can be expressed mathematically by requiring that there exists a positive constant η such that $\Phi_\ell^i(\tau) \geq \eta$ for all $i \in C_\ell$ and all $\tau \geq 0$.

Example 7.1. (*cont.*)

Suppose that for every computing processor i for component ℓ (i.e., $i \in C_\ell$), we have $a_\ell^{ii} > 0$ and that there exists a positive path in the graph G_ℓ from processor i to every other processor j. Then processor i is a "distinguished" processor in the terminology of Section 7.3 and part (c) of Prop. 3.1 applies. In particular, if $x_\ell^k(1) = 0$ for every k and ℓ, and if $\gamma_\ell^i(\tau)s_\ell^i(\tau) = 1$ is the only nonzero update in the course of the algorithm (as in Example 7.3), then the value on which the processors will eventually agree is no smaller than the positive constant η of Prop. 3.1(c). We have already shown that the agreed upon value is equal to $\Phi_\ell^i(\tau)$ (Example 7.3). We conclude that the inequality $\Phi_\ell^i(\tau) \geq \eta > 0$ holds for all $\tau \geq 0$. A similar argument can be made for the agreement algorithm of Example 7.2.

We summarize the above discussion in Assumption 7.1 to follow. In particular, we have shown that Assumption 7.1 is satisfied when the underlying agreement algorithm is as in Example 7.1 or Example 7.2, provided that for each component ℓ, there is a communication path from every computing processor to every other processor. This assumption can be also shown to hold for more general choices of the underlying agreement algorithm [Tsi84].

Assumption 7.1. The sets T_ℓ^{ij} and the variables $a_\ell^{ij}(t)$, $\tau_\ell^{ij}(t)$, defining a realization of the underlying agreement algorithm [cf. Eqs. (7.1) and (7.2)], are such that the following hold:

(a) For all i, j, and $t > \tau \geq 0$, we have $0 \leq \Phi_\ell^{ij}(t, \tau) \leq 1$.

(b) For any i, j, and $\tau \geq 0$, the limit of $\Phi_\ell^{ij}(t, \tau)$, as t tends to infinity, exists, is the same for all i, and is denoted by $\Phi_\ell^j(\tau)$.

(c) There exists some $\eta > 0$ (independent of the particular realization) such that $\Phi_\ell^j(\tau) \geq \eta$ for all $j \in C_\ell$ and $\tau \geq 0$.

(d) There exist constants $A > 0$ and $\rho \in (0, 1)$ (independent of the particular realization) such that

$$|\Phi_\ell^{ij}(t, \tau) - \Phi_\ell^j(\tau)| \leq A\rho^{t-\tau}, \qquad \forall t > \tau \geq 0.$$

Equation (7.3) has a simple structure, but is still difficult to manipulate when it comes to the analysis of specific algorithms. The reason is that we have one such equation for each ℓ and i, and all of these equations are, in general, coupled. Thus, we need to keep track of all the vectors $x^1(t), \ldots, x^p(t)$, simultaneously. Analysis would be easier if we could associate with the algorithm a single vector $y(t)$ that summarizes the information contained in the vectors $x^i(t)$. It turns out that this is possible and the following choice of $y(t)$ is particularly useful. We define the ℓth component of $y(t)$ by

$$y_\ell(t) = \sum_{i=1}^{p} \Phi_\ell^i(0)x_\ell^i(1) + \sum_{\tau=1}^{t-1}\sum_{i=1}^{p} \Phi_\ell^i(\tau)\gamma_\ell^i(\tau)s_\ell^i(\tau), \qquad \ell = 1, \ldots, m. \qquad (7.4)$$

The interpretation of $y(t)$ is quite interesting. Let us fix some time $\bar{t}$ and suppose that $\gamma_\ell^i(\tau)s_\ell^i(\tau) = 0$ for all $\tau \geq \bar{t}$. Consider Eq. (7.3) and take the limit as $t \to \infty$. We only need to keep the summands for $\tau < \bar{t}$ and we are left with the defining expression for $y_\ell(\bar{t})$. In other words, if the processors stop performing any updates at time $\bar{t}$, but keep communicating and forming convex combinations of their states, as in the underlying agreement algorithm, they will asymptotically agree and $y(\bar{t})$ is precisely the vector on which they will agree.

The vector $y(t)$ is a very convenient tool for analysis, primarily because it is generated by the recursion

$$y_\ell(t + 1) = y_\ell(t) + \sum_{i=1}^{p} \Phi_\ell^i(t)\gamma_\ell^i(t)s_\ell^i(t), \qquad \ell = 1, \ldots, m, \qquad (7.5)$$

which is an immediate consequence of Eq. (7.4)

Example 7.4. *Specialized Computation*

We now show that our earlier model of asynchronous computation in which each processor is associated with a different component (e.g., as in Section 7.5) is a special case of the present model, and we evaluate the coefficients $\Phi_\ell^i(t)$ for this particular context. Let the number m of components be the same as the number p of processors, and let processor j be the only computing processor for component j, that is, $C_j = \{j\}$. Each processor j broadcasts its value of x_j from time to time to all other processors and these values are received after some bounded delay. Processor i, upon receiving at time t a value of x_j that has been sent at some time $\tau_j^{ij}(t) \le t$ by some processor $j \ne i$ [thus, processor i receives the message $x_j^j\left(\tau_j^{ij}(t)\right)$], lets

$$x_j^i(t+1) = x_j^j\left(\tau_j^{ij}(t)\right). \tag{7.6}$$

Also, processor i lets

$$x_j^i(t+1) = x_j^i(t), \tag{7.7}$$

if no message is received from processor $j \ne i$ at time t. Equations (7.6) and (7.7) are a trivial special case of an agreement algorithm. Comparing with Eq. (7.1), we have $a_j^{ij}(t) = 1$, if processor i receives a message x_j^j from j at time t. In this example, if processor j stops performing any computations, the values $x_j^i(t)$ possessed by different processors all agree, within finite time. (Finite time convergence can be viewed as a special case of geometric convergence.) Furthermore, the value on which they agree is the value possessed by the computing processor j. Using the interpretation of the coefficients $\Phi_i^j(t)$ provided by Example 7.3, we see that $\Phi_j^j(t) = 1$ for all j and t, and $\Phi_i^j(t) = 0$ if $i \ne j$.

The model we have developed will be used in the next section, in the context of a stochastic gradient algorithm.

7.8 STOCHASTIC GRADIENT ALGORITHMS

Let $F : \Re^n \mapsto \Re$ be a differentiable cost function to be minimized, subject to no constraints. Suppose, however, that we only have access to noisy measurements of the gradient. That is, for any $x \in \Re^n$, we cannot compute $\nabla F(x)$, but we have access to $\nabla F(x) + w$, where w is a random variable representing measurement or observation noise. Such a situation often arises in statistics or in system identification ([RoM51], [Lju77], [LjS83], and [PoT73]).

One could still try to use the gradient algorithm, as if no noise was present, which gives rise to the equation

$$x(t+1) = x(t) - \gamma\left(\nabla F\big(x(t)\big) + w(t)\right), \tag{8.1}$$

where $w(t)$ is the noise in the measurement of $\nabla F\big(x(t)\big)$. This algorithm does not converge, in general, to the minimum of F. For example, suppose that for each t, the random variable $w(t)$ is independent of $x(t)$ and has variance $\sigma^2 > 0$. It follows from Eq. (8.1) that the variance of $x(t)$ is at least $\gamma^2 \sigma^2$ and, therefore, $x(t)$ fails to converge (in the mean square sense). What may happen, at best, is that $x(t)$ reaches a neighborhood of a (local) minimum x^* of F and moves randomly around x^*. The mean square distance of $x(t)$ from x^* increases with the variance of $x(t)$ and can be made small only if γ is chosen small. On the other hand, if γ is excessively small, it can take a very large number of steps to reach a neighborhood of a local minimum. We can strike a balance between these two effects by employing a time–varying stepsize $\gamma(t)$ and replacing Eq. (8.1) by

$$x(t+1) = x(t) - \gamma(t)\Big(\nabla F\big(x(t)\big) + w(t)\Big). \tag{8.2}$$

The stepsize $\gamma(t)$ is initially large, which allows a rapid approach to the vicinity of a minimizing point, and then is decreased to zero so that, hopefully, the variance of $x(t)$ also decreases to zero.

Some typical conditions on the choice of the stepsize are

$$\sum_{t=1}^{\infty} \gamma(t) = \infty, \tag{8.3}$$

$$\sum_{t=1}^{\infty} \gamma^2(t) < \infty. \tag{8.4}$$

Condition (8.3) is needed because, otherwise, $x(t)$ might not be able to travel far enough to get to a minimum of F; this condition would be required even if no noise was present. Condition (8.4) is used to ensure that the variance of $x(t)$ converges to zero. A choice for $\gamma(t)$, satisfying conditions (8.3) and (8.4) and commonly used in analytical studies, is $\gamma(t) = 1/t$.

Example 8.1.

Let x be one–dimensional and $F(x) = \frac{1}{2}x^2$. Then Eq. (8.2) becomes $x(t+1) = \big(1 - \gamma(t)\big)x(t) + \gamma(t)w(t)$. Let $V(t)$ be the variance of $x(t)$. If $w(t)$ is independent of $x(t)$ and has variance σ^2, then the variance of $x(t+1)$ is the sum of the variances of $\big(1 - \gamma(t)\big)x(t)$ and $\gamma(t)w(t)$. Thus,

$$V(t+1) = \big(1 - \gamma(t)\big)^2 V(t) + \gamma^2(t)\sigma^2.$$

Assuming that conditions (8.3) and (8.4) hold, it can be shown that $V(t)$ converges to zero (Exercise 8.1).

The algorithm (8.2) admits a straightforward distributed implementation, similar to the distributed deterministic gradient algorithm of Section 7.5, whereby each processor is assigned the task of updating a particular component of x. However, in the presence of noise, it makes sense to have several processors work on the same component of x. In particular, if the noise in the measured value of the gradient is independent for different processors, then the different processors can average their individual updates and come up with a common update. This is expected to improve the speed of convergence because the averaging of independent identically distributed random variables always reduces the variance. Nevertheless, we might wish to avoid a synchronous implementation of this updating and averaging procedure, and this leads us to the model introduced in Section 7.7.

7.8.1 Description of the Algorithm and Assumptions

Throughout this section, $\|\cdot\|$ will stand for the Euclidean norm $\|\cdot\|_2$. We make the same assumptions on F as in Section 7.5.

Assumption 8.1.

(a) There holds $F(x) \geq 0$ for every $x \in \Re^n$.

(b) *(Lipschitz Continuity of ∇F)* The function F is continuously differentiable and there exists a constant K_1 such that

$$\|\nabla F(x) - \nabla F(y)\| \leq K_1 \|x - y\|, \qquad \forall x, y \in \Re^n. \tag{8.5}$$

We assume that vectors in $\Re^n$ are decomposed into m components. As in Section 7.7, we assume that the algorithm is described by the equation [cf. Eq. (7.1)]

$$x_\ell^i(t+1) = \sum_{\{j \mid t \in T_\ell^{ij}\}} a_\ell^{ij}(t) x_\ell^j \left(\tau_\ell^{ij}(t)\right) + \gamma_\ell^i(t) s_\ell^i(t).$$

Furthermore, the underlying agreement algorithm is described by [cf. Eq. (7.2)]

$$x_\ell^i(t+1) = \sum_{\{j \mid t \in T_\ell^{ij}\}} a_\ell^{ij}(t) x_\ell^j \left(\tau_\ell^{ij}(t)\right),$$

and will be assumed to satisfy Assumption 7.1. We assume that the sets T_ℓ^{ij} and the variables $a_\ell^{ij}(t)$, $\tau_\ell^{ij}(t)$, defining the underlying agreement algorithm, are *deterministic*. (This does not imply that they are known ahead of time by the processors; it only means that they are not modeled as random variables.) We also assume that the initializations $x_\ell^i(1)$ are deterministic.

Concerning the stepsizes, we assume that there exist positive constants K_2 and K_3 such that

$$\frac{K_2}{t} \leq \gamma_\ell^i(t) \leq \frac{K_3}{t}, \qquad \forall i, \ell, t. \tag{8.6}$$

As a practical matter, a stepsize satisfying condition (8.6) can be enforced without assuming that the processors know the current value of t. For example, suppose that each processor i uses the following rule: let the current value of γ_ℓ^i be the reciprocal of the number of times that i has performed an update. Assuming that the time between consecutive updates by each processor is bounded above and below by positive constants, it is easily verified that the resulting stepsizes satisfy inequality (8.6).

It remains to specify the update directions $s_\ell^i(t)$. An interesting special case suggested by Eq. (8.2) is to let $s_\ell^i(t) = -\left(\nabla_\ell F(x^i(t)) + w_\ell^i(t)\right)$ for $t \in T_\ell^i$, where the random variables $w_\ell^i(t)$ are independent identically distributed with finite variance. We shall actually introduce a somewhat more general set of assumptions.

We consider the set $\mathcal{F}(t)$ of random variables defined by

$$\mathcal{F}(t) = \left\{ s_\ell^i(\tau) \mid i \in \{1, ..., p\}, \ \ell \in \{1, ..., m\}, \ \tau < t \right\}.$$

Given our earlier assumptions on the deterministic nature of the underlying agreement algorithm and the initial conditions, the variables in the set $\mathcal{F}(t)$ are the only sources of randomness up to time t. We may therefore view $\mathcal{F}(t)$ as a representation of the entire history of the algorithm up to the moment that the update directions $s_\ell^i(t)$ are to be generated. Furthermore, for any choice of initial conditions and any fixed realization of the underlying agreement algorithm, it is seen that $x_\ell^i(t)$ is a uniquely determined function of the random variables in the set $\mathcal{F}(t)$.

Assumption 8.2.   (*Stochastic Descent*) There exist positive constants K_4, K_5 and K_6 such that

$$\nabla_\ell F\big(x^i(t)\big)' E\big[s_\ell^i(t) \mid \mathcal{F}(t)\big] \leq -K_4 \big\|\nabla_\ell F\big(x^i(t)\big)\big\|^2, \quad \forall t \in T_\ell^i, \tag{8.7}$$

$$E\Big[\big\|s_\ell^i(t)\big\|^2 \mid \mathcal{F}(t)\Big] \leq K_5 \big\|\nabla_\ell F\big(x^i(t)\big)\big\|^2 + K_6, \quad \forall t \in T_\ell^i. \tag{8.8}$$

Furthermore $s_\ell^i(t) = 0$, for all $t \notin T_\ell^i$.

Assumption 8.2 is similar to Assumptions 5.2 and 5.5 of Section 7.5. Inequality (8.7) requires that the expected direction of the update $s_\ell^i(t)$, given the past history $\mathcal{F}(t)$ of the algorithm, is a descent direction. Notice the presence of the constant K_6 in inequality (8.8). This constant allows the algorithm to make nonzero updates even if a minimum has been reached. This is natural because a noisy measurement of the gradient at the minimum may be nonzero.

7.8.2 A Convergence Result

The synchronous version of the algorithm considered in this section is known to be convergent [PoT73]. The proof we provide here follows the same steps as the corresponding proof in [PoT73] and establishes that convergence is preserved in the presence of partial asynchronism. The main idea is that we use the vector $y(t)$ [cf. Eq. (7.4)] as a summary of the state of the algorithm at time t, we monitor the progress of the cost $F\big(y(t)\big)$, and we obtain an inequality of the form [cf. Eq. (8.16)]

$$F\big(y(t+1)\big) \leq F\big(y(t)\big) - \gamma(t)G(t) + O\big(\gamma(t)^2\big).$$

Here the term $G(t)$ is nonnegative in a probabilistic sense, meaning that $E[G(t) \mid \mathcal{F}(t)] \geq 0$. The errors due to asynchronism are all incorporated into the $O\big(\gamma(t)^2\big)$ term. The proof is then completed using reasoning analogous to the deterministic case (Section 7.5) although some of the technical issues are more difficult.

Proposition 8.1.   We assume the model of Section 7.7. We assume that T_ℓ^i is infinite for every computing processor i for component ℓ, and that the difference between consecutive elements of T_ℓ^i is bounded by some $B > 0$. We also assume that the underlying agreement algorithm satisfies Assumption 7.1 of Section 7.7. Finally, we suppose that Assumptions 8.1 and 8.2 hold and that the stepsizes satisfy condition (8.6). Then the following are true:

(a) The limit of $F\big(x^i(t)\big)$, as $t \to \infty$, exists and is the same for all i, with probability 1.
(b) The limit of $x^i(t) - x^j(t)$, as $t \to \infty$, is equal to zero with probability 1 and in the mean square sense.
(c) For every i, $\liminf_{t\to\infty} \nabla F\big(x^i(t)\big) = 0$.
(d) Suppose that the set $\{x \mid F(x) \le c\}$ is bounded for every $c \in \Re$, that there exists a unique vector x^* at which F is minimized, and that this is the unique vector at which ∇F vanishes. Then $x^i(t)$ converges to x^* for each i with probability 1.

Proof.   We only prove the result under the assumption $x_\ell^i(1) = 0$ for all i and ℓ. There are only a few minor modifications needed to cover the general case.

Let us define $\bar{s}_\ell^i(t) = \big(t\gamma_\ell^i(t)\big)s_\ell^i(t)$ and view $\bar{s}_\ell^i(t)$ as the update direction, with stepsize $1/t$. Using inequality (8.6), we see that conditions (8.7) and (8.8) also hold for $\bar{s}_\ell^i(t)$, possibly with a different choice of constants K_4, K_5, K_6. Thus, without loss of generality, we can and will assume that $\gamma_\ell^i(t) = 1/t$ for all i, ℓ, and t.

We use the notations $\Phi_\ell^{ij}(t,\tau)$, $\Phi_\ell^i(t)$, and $y(t)$ as in Section 7.7. We also define

$$b(t) = \sum_{i=1}^{p}\sum_{\ell=1}^{m} \|s_\ell^i(t)\|, \quad t \ge 1, \tag{8.9}$$

$$G(t) = -\sum_{i=1}^{p}\sum_{\ell=1}^{m} \Big(\nabla_\ell F\big(x^i(t)\big)\Big)' \Phi_\ell^i(t)s_\ell^i(t), \quad t \ge 1. \tag{8.10}$$

Lemma 8.1.

(a) If $t \in T_\ell^i$, then

$$E\big[G(t)\,|\,\mathcal{F}(t)\big] \ge K_4\eta \sum_{\{(i,\ell)\,|\,t\in T_\ell^i\}} \big\|\nabla_\ell F\big(x^i(t)\big)\big\|^2 \ge 0,$$

where $\eta > 0$ is the constant in Assumption 7.1(c).
(b) If $t \ge 1$, then

$$E\big[b^2(t)\,|\,\mathcal{F}(t)\big] \le A_1 E\big[G(t)\,|\,\mathcal{F}(t)\big] + A_2,$$

where $A_1 = (mpK_5)/(\eta K_4)$ and $A_2 = m^2p^2K_6$.

Proof. Using inequality (8.7) and the fact that $s_\ell^i(t) = 0$ for $t \notin T_\ell^i$, we obtain

$$E\big[G(t) \mid \mathcal{F}(t)\big] = - \sum_{\{(i,\ell)\mid t \in T_\ell^i\}} \nabla_\ell F\big(x^i(t)\big)' \Phi_\ell^i(t) E\big[s_\ell^i(t) \mid \mathcal{F}(t)\big]$$

$$\geq \sum_{\{(i,\ell)\mid t \in T_\ell^i\}} K_4 \big\|\nabla_\ell F\big(x^i(t)\big)\big\|^2 \Phi_\ell^i(t) \tag{8.11}$$

$$\geq \eta K_4 \sum_{\{(i,\ell)\mid t \in T_\ell^i\}} \big\|\nabla_\ell F\big(x^i(t)\big)\big\|^2.$$

This proves part (a) of the lemma. For part (b), we use inequality (8.8) to obtain

$$E\big[b^2(t) \mid \mathcal{F}(t)\big] = E\left[\left(\sum_{i=1}^p \sum_{\ell=1}^m \big\|s_\ell^i(t)\big\| \right)^2 \;\middle|\; \mathcal{F}(t) \right] \leq pm \sum_{i=1}^p \sum_{\ell=1}^m E\left[\big\|s_\ell^i(t)\big\|^2 \;\middle|\; \mathcal{F}(t) \right]$$

$$\leq pm \sum_{\{(i,\ell)\mid t \in T_\ell^i\}} \left(K_5 \big\|\nabla_\ell F\big(x^i(t)\big)\big\|^2 + K_6 \right) \tag{8.12}$$

$$\leq \frac{pmK_5}{\eta K_4} E\big[G(t) \mid \mathcal{F}(t)\big] + p^2 m^2 K_6,$$

where the last inequality follows from part (a).   **Q.E.D.**

Lemma 8.2.   For every $t \geq 1$, we have

$$\big\|y(t) - x^i(t)\big\| \leq A \sum_{\tau=1}^{t-1} \frac{1}{\tau} \rho^{t-\tau} b(\tau), \tag{8.13}$$

where $A > 0$ and $\rho \in (0, 1)$ are the constants of Assumption 7.1(d).

Proof. We subtract Eq. (7.3) from Eq. (7.4) to obtain

$$y_\ell(t) - x_\ell^i(t) = \sum_{\tau=1}^{t-1} \sum_{j=1}^p \frac{1}{\tau} \left[\Phi_\ell^j(\tau) - \Phi_\ell^{ij}(t,\tau) \right] s_\ell^j(\tau). \tag{8.14}$$

We then use Assumption 7.1(d) to obtain

$$\big\|y_\ell(t) - x_\ell^i(t)\big\| \leq \sum_{\tau=1}^{t-1} \frac{1}{\tau} \sum_{j=1}^p A\rho^{t-\tau} \big\|s_\ell^j(\tau)\big\|. \tag{8.15}$$

We then sum inequality (8.15) over all components ℓ and use the definition of $b(\tau)$ to obtain inequality (8.13).   **Q.E.D.**

We use Eq. (7.5) and the descent lemma (Prop. A.32 in Appendix A) to obtain

$$F\big(y(t+1)\big) \le F\big(y(t)\big) + \frac{1}{t}\sum_{i=1}^{p}\sum_{\ell=1}^{m}\nabla_\ell F\big(y(t)\big)' \Phi_\ell^i(t)s_\ell^i(t) + \frac{K_1}{2t^2}\sum_{\ell=1}^{m}\Big\|\sum_{i=1}^{p}\Phi_\ell^i(t)s_\ell^i(t)\Big\|^2$$

$$\le F\big(y(t)\big) + \frac{1}{t}\sum_{i=1}^{p}\sum_{\ell=1}^{m}\nabla_\ell F\big(x^i(t)\big)' \Phi_\ell^i(t)s_\ell^i(t)$$

$$+ \frac{1}{t}\sum_{i=1}^{p}\sum_{\ell=1}^{m}\Big\|\nabla_\ell F\big(x^i(t)\big) - \nabla_\ell F\big(y(t)\big)\Big\| \cdot \big\|\Phi_\ell^i(t)s_\ell^i(t)\big\| + \frac{K_1}{2t^2}b^2(t)$$

$$\le F\big(y(t)\big) - \frac{1}{t}G(t) + \frac{1}{t}\sum_{i=1}^{p}\sum_{\ell=1}^{m}K_1\big\|x^i(t) - y(t)\big\| \cdot \big\|s_\ell^i(t)\big\| + \frac{K_1}{2t^2}b^2(t)$$

$$\le F\big(y(t)\big) - \frac{1}{t}G(t) + \frac{K_1}{t}\sum_{i=1}^{p}\sum_{\ell=1}^{m}A\sum_{\tau=1}^{t-1}\frac{1}{\tau}\rho^{t-\tau}b(\tau)\big\|s_\ell^i(\tau)\big\| + \frac{K_1}{2t^2}b^2(t)$$

$$= F\big(y(t)\big) - \frac{1}{t}G(t) + K_1 A\sum_{\tau=1}^{t-1}\frac{1}{t\tau}\rho^{t-\tau}b(\tau)b(t) + \frac{K_1}{2t^2}b^2(t)$$

$$\le F\big(y(t)\big) - \frac{1}{t}G(t) + K_1 A\sum_{\tau=1}^{t-1}\rho^{t-\tau}\Big(\frac{b^2(\tau)}{\tau^2} + \frac{b^2(t)}{t^2}\Big) + \frac{K_1}{2t^2}b^2(t)$$

$$\le F\big(y(t)\big) - \frac{1}{t}G(t) + A_3\sum_{\tau=1}^{t}\rho^{t-\tau}\frac{b^2(\tau)}{\tau^2}, \tag{8.16}$$

where $A_3 = K_1 A/(1 - \rho) + K_1/2$.

Lemma 8.3.   There holds

$$\sum_{t=1}^{\infty}\frac{1}{t}E\big[G(t)\big] < \infty. \tag{8.17}$$

Proof. We take expectations of both sides of inequality (8.16) and use Lemma 8.1(b) to bound $E\big[b^2(t)\big]$. This yields

$$E\big[F\big(y(t+1)\big)\big] \le E\big[F\big(y(t)\big)\big] - \frac{1}{t}E\big[G(t)\big] + A_3\sum_{\tau=1}^{t}\rho^{t-\tau}\frac{1}{\tau^2}\big(A_1 E\big[G(\tau)\big] + A_2\big). \tag{8.18}$$

We add inequality (8.18) for t running from 1 to $\bar{t}$; after cancellations, we obtain

$$E\left[F\left(y(\bar{t}+1)\right)\right] \le F\left(y(1)\right) - \sum_{t=1}^{\bar{t}} \frac{1}{t} E\left[G(t)\right] + A_2 A_3 \sum_{t=1}^{\bar{t}} \sum_{\tau=1}^{t} \rho^{t-\tau} \frac{1}{\tau^2}$$

$$+ A_1 A_3 \sum_{t=1}^{\bar{t}} \sum_{\tau=1}^{t} \rho^{t-\tau} \frac{1}{\tau^2} E\left[G(\tau)\right]$$

$$= F\left(y(1)\right) - \sum_{t=1}^{\bar{t}} \frac{1}{t} E\left[G(t)\right] \left(1 - A_1 A_3 \frac{1}{t} \sum_{\tau=t}^{\bar{t}} \rho^{\tau-t}\right) \tag{8.19}$$

$$+ A_2 A_3 \sum_{t=1}^{\bar{t}} \sum_{\tau=1}^{t} \rho^{t-\tau} \frac{1}{\tau^2}$$

$$\le F\left(y(1)\right) - \sum_{t=1}^{\bar{t}} \frac{1}{t} E\left[G(t)\right] \left(1 - \frac{A_1 A_3}{t(1-\rho)}\right) + A_2 A_3 \sum_{\tau=1}^{\bar{t}} \frac{1}{\tau^2(1-\rho)}.$$

Notice that $A_2 A_3 \sum_{\tau=1}^{\bar{t}} 1/\left(\tau^2(1-\rho)\right)$ is bounded above by some finite constant A_4, because the infinite sum $\sum_{\tau=1}^{\infty} 1/\tau^2$ is finite. Furthermore, $1 - A_1 A_3/\left(t(1-\rho)\right)$ is larger than $1/2$ when t is sufficiently large. If $\sum_{t=1}^{\infty} E[G(t)]/t$ was equal to infinity, then the right–hand side of inequality (8.19) would be equal to minus infinity. However, the left–hand side of inequality (8.19) is nonnegative [Assumption 8.1(a)]. This proves the lemma.   **Q.E.D.**

Lemma 8.4.   The sequence $\left\{F\left(y(t)\right)\right\}$ converges, with probability 1.

Proof. We take the conditional expectation of both sides of inequality (8.16), conditioned on $\mathcal{F}(t)$, and use Lemma 8.1(a) to obtain

$$E\left[F\left(y(t+1)\right) \mid \mathcal{F}(t)\right] \le F\left(y(t)\right) + A_3 \sum_{\tau=1}^{t} \rho^{t-\tau} \frac{1}{\tau^2} E\left[b^2(\tau) \mid \mathcal{F}(t)\right]. \tag{8.20}$$

Let

$$Z(t) = \sum_{\tau=1}^{t} \rho^{t-\tau} \frac{1}{\tau^2} E[b^2(\tau) \mid \mathcal{F}(t)].$$

Using Lemma 8.1(b) and Lemma 8.3, we have

$$\sum_{t=1}^{\infty} E[Z(t)] = \frac{1}{1-\rho} \sum_{t=1}^{\infty} \frac{1}{t^2} E\left[b^2(t)\right] \le \frac{1}{1-\rho} \sum_{t=1}^{\infty} \frac{1}{t^2} \left(A_1 E[G(t)] + A_2\right) < \infty. \tag{8.21}$$

With inequalities (8.20) and (8.21) available, a variant of the Supermartingale Convergence Theorem (Prop. D.7 in Appendix D) applies and shows that $F\left(y(t)\right)$ converges, with probability 1.   **Q.E.D.**

Lemma 8.5.   For each i, we have $\lim_{t\to\infty} \|y(t) - x^i(t)\| = 0$, with probability 1.

Proof. Inequality (8.21) has shown that

$$\sum_{t=1}^{\infty} \frac{1}{t^2} E[b^2(t)] < \infty. \tag{8.22}$$

Using the Monotone Convergence Theorem (Prop. D.4 in Appendix D), the infinite sum $\sum_{t=1}^{\infty} b^2(t)/t^2$ is finite and, in particular, $b(t)/t$ converges to zero, with probability 1. Given some $\epsilon > 0$, let T be such that $b(t)/t \leq \epsilon$ for all $t \geq T$. Using inequality (8.13) for $t \geq T$, we obtain

$$\|y(t) - x^i(t)\| \leq A \left(\sum_{\tau=1}^{T-1} \frac{1}{\tau} \rho^{t-\tau} b(\tau) + \sum_{\tau=T}^{t-1} \frac{1}{\tau} \rho^{t-\tau} b(\tau) \right) \leq A\rho^{t-T} \sum_{\tau=1}^{T-1} \frac{b(\tau)}{\tau} + \frac{A\epsilon}{1-\rho},$$

which converges to $A\epsilon/(1-\rho)$, as t tends to ∞. Since ϵ was arbitrary, the result follows. **Q.E.D.**

Lemma 8.6.   For every i, we have $\lim_{t\to\infty} E[\|x^i(t) - y(t)\|^2] = 0$.

Proof. From Lemma 8.1(b) and Lemma 8.3,

$$\lim_{t\to\infty} E\left[\frac{b^2(t)}{t} \right] \leq \lim_{t\to\infty} \left(\frac{A_1}{t} E[G(t)] + \frac{A_2}{t} \right) = 0.$$

We now square both sides of inequality (8.13), use the elementary inequality $\left(\sum_{\tau=1}^{t-1} a_i \right)^2 \leq (t-1) \sum_{\tau=1}^{t-1} a_i^2$, and take expectations to obtain

$$E\left[\|y(t) - x^i(t)\|^2 \right] \leq tA^2 \sum_{\tau=1}^{t-1} \frac{1}{\tau^2} \rho^{2(t-\tau)} E[b^2(\tau)].$$

Given some $\epsilon > 0$, let T be such that $E[b^2(\tau)/\tau] \leq \epsilon$ for all $\tau \geq T$. Let $Q = \max_{\tau \leq T} E[b^2(\tau)/\tau]$. Then for $t > T$,

$$E\left[\|y(t) - x^i(t)\|^2 \right] \leq tA^2 \sum_{\tau=1}^{T-1} \frac{1}{\tau} \rho^{t-\tau} Q + \epsilon tA^2 \sum_{\tau=T}^{t-1} \frac{1}{\tau} \rho^{t-\tau}$$

$$\leq t\rho^{t-T} A^2 TQ + \epsilon A^2 \sum_{\tau=T}^{t-1} (t - \tau + 1)\rho^{t-\tau}.$$

[We have used the trivial inequality $t/\tau = (t - \tau + \tau)/\tau \leq t - \tau + 1$.] As t tends to infinity, $t\rho^t$ converges to zero, which shows that the first term in the right–hand side of the previous inequality vanishes. The limit of the second term is bounded by $\epsilon A^2 \sum_{\tau=0}^{\infty}(\tau + 1)\rho^{\tau}$, which is finite. By taking ϵ arbitrarily small, the result follows. **Q.E.D.**

Part (b) of the proposition follows from Lemmas 8.5 and 8.6 and the triangle inequality $\|x^i(t) - x^j(t)\| \leq \|x^i(t) - y(t)\| + \|y(t) - x^j(t)\|$.

Lemma 8.7.   For every $x \in \Re^n$, we have $\|\nabla F(x)\|^2 \leq 2K_1 F(x)$.

Proof. Using the nonnegativity of F and Prop. A.32 in Appendix A, we have

$$0 \leq F\left(x - \frac{1}{K_1}\nabla F(x)\right) \leq F(x) - \frac{1}{K_1}\|\nabla F(x)\|^2 + \frac{K_1}{2}\frac{1}{K_1^2}\|\nabla F(x)\|^2$$

$$= F(x) - \frac{1}{2K_1}\|\nabla F(x)\|^2.$$

Q.E.D.

Since $F(y(t))$ converges (Lemma 8.4), it is bounded. By Lemma 8.7, $\|\nabla F(y(t))\|$ is also bounded by some constant A_5. Therefore, using Prop. A.32 in Appendix A,

$$\left|F(x^i(t)) - F(y(t))\right| \leq A_5\|x^i(t) - y(t)\| + \frac{K_1}{2}\|x^i(t) - y(t)\|^2, \qquad (8.23)$$

which converges to 0, with probability 1, by Lemma 8.5. Therefore, for each i, $F(x^i(t))$ converges, with probability 1, to the same limit as $F(y(t))$, which proves part (a) of the proposition.

Lemma 8.8.   There holds $\lim_{t\to\infty}\|y(t+1) - y(t)\| = 0$, with probability 1.

Proof. Equation (7.5) yields $\|y(t+1) - y(t)\| \leq b(t)/t$. But we have already shown, in the course of the proof of Lemma 8.5, that $b(t)/t$ converges to 0, with probability 1. **Q.E.D.**

We now recall Lemma 8.3 and the fact $E[G(t)\,|\,\mathcal{F}(t)] \geq 0$ (Lemma 8.1). We apply the Monotone Convergence Theorem to conclude that

$$E\left[\sum_{t=1}^{\infty}\frac{1}{t}E[G(t)\,|\,\mathcal{F}(t)]\right] = \sum_{t=1}^{\infty}E\left[\frac{1}{t}E[G(t)\,|\,\mathcal{F}(t)]\right] = \sum_{t=1}^{\infty}\frac{1}{t}E[G(t)] < \infty.$$

This implies that

$$\sum_{t=1}^{\infty} \frac{1}{t} E\big[G(t)\,|\,\mathcal{F}(t)\big] < \infty, \tag{8.24}$$

with probability 1. Let B be a bound on the difference between successive elements of T_ℓ^i for every ℓ and every computing processor i for component ℓ. Since $\sum_{t=1}^{\infty} 1/t = \infty$, inequality (8.24) implies that

$$\liminf_{t\to\infty} \sum_{\tau=t}^{t+B} E\big[G(\tau)\,|\,\mathcal{F}(\tau)\big] = 0.$$

Using Lemma 8.1(a), we obtain

$$\liminf_{t\to\infty} \sum_{\tau=t}^{t+B} \sum_{\{(i,\ell)\,|\,\tau\in T_\ell^i\}} \big\|\nabla_\ell F\big(x^i(\tau)\big)\big\|^2 = 0.$$

By taking t sufficiently large, the quantity $\max\big\{\big\|y(t) - x^i(\tau)\big\| \mid t \le \tau \le t + B\big\}$ can be made arbitrarily small, because of Lemmas 8.5 and 8.8. We then use the Lipschitz continuity of ∇F to obtain

$$\liminf_{t\to\infty} \sum_{\tau=t}^{t+B} \sum_{\{(i,\ell)\,|\,\tau\in T_\ell^i\}} \big\|\nabla_\ell F\big(y(t)\big)\big\|^2 = 0. \tag{8.25}$$

By the definition of B and the assumption that there is at least one computing processor for each component, we see that for every component ℓ and time t, there exists some processor i and some time $\tau \in [t, t + B]$ such that $\tau \in T_\ell^i$. Therefore, in the sum (8.25), the summand $\big\|\nabla_\ell F\big(y(t)\big)\big\|^2$ appears at least once for each ℓ. Therefore,

$$\liminf_{t\to\infty} \nabla F\big(y(t)\big) = 0.$$

Since $\big\|x^i(t) - y(t)\big\|$ converges to zero and ∇F is Lipschitz continuous, part (c) of the proposition follows.

We now turn to the proof of part (d). Let x^* be the unique minimizer of F and fix some i. Consider a sequence of times along which $\nabla F\big(x^i(t)\big)$ converges to zero, which exists because of part (c) of the proposition. We restrict to a subsequence $\{t_k\}$ such that the sequence $\{x^i(t_k)\}$ converges to some y^*. [Such a sequence exists because $F\big(x^i(t)\big)$ is bounded (since it converges) and because F is assumed to have bounded level sets; this implies that $x^i(t)$ is bounded and, therefore, has a convergent subsequence.] From the triangle inequality,

$$\big\|\nabla F(y^*)\big\| \le \lim_{k\to\infty} \big\|\nabla F(y^*) - \nabla F\big(x^i(t_k)\big)\big\| + \lim_{k\to\infty} \big\|\nabla F\big(x^i(t_k)\big)\big\| = 0.$$

Therefore, $\nabla F(y^*) = 0$ and, by our assumptions, $y^* = x^*$. Since x^* is a limit point of the sequence $\{x^i(t)\}$, we conclude that $F(x^*)$ is equal to the limit of $F(x^i(t))$. Let z be an arbitrary limit point of $x^i(t)$. Then $F(z)$ is a limit point of $F(x^i(t))$ and, since the latter converges to $F(x^*)$, we conclude that $z = x^*$. Therefore, x^* is the unique limit point of $x^i(t)$. Since the sequence $x^i(t)$ is bounded, it converges to x^*.   **Q.E.D.**

7.8.3 Discussion and Extensions

In the assumptions preceding Prop. 8.1 and in the proof, we have treated the coefficients $\Phi^i_\ell(t)$ as unknown but deterministic. This allowed us to go through the crucial step, in inequality (8.11),

$$E\left[\nabla_\ell F\big(x^i(t)\big)' \Phi^i_\ell(t) s^i_\ell(t) \mid \mathcal{F}(t)\right] = \Phi^i_\ell(t) \nabla_\ell F\big(x^i(t)\big)' E\left[s^i_\ell(t) \mid \mathcal{F}(t)\right]. \qquad (8.26)$$

However, if $\Phi^i_\ell(t)$ is a random variable, then Eq. (8.26) is not valid, in general.

To illustrate how Eq. (8.26) can fail to hold, suppose that the processors decide when to send messages to other processors, based on the results of their recent computations. For example, a processor could decide to inform the others whenever a substantial change in its state of computation occurs. This implies that the decision whether to transmit becomes a function of the random variables $s^i_\ell(t)$. In such a context, the underlying agreement algorithm has some probabilistic aspects and the coefficient $\Phi^i_\ell(t)$ will be, in general, a random variable. Under such circumstances, neither Eq. (8.26) nor the proof of Prop. 8.1 is valid. This is not a deficiency of the proof: one can construct examples in which the dependence of the transmission times on the state of computation of a processor can cause divergence of an otherwise convergent algorithm. The essence of such examples is that the processors can choose to communicate only when their most recent update is a direction of ascent. Then the coefficient $\Phi^i_\ell(t)$ will tend to be larger if $s^i_\ell(t)$ is a direction of ascent and the inner product $\nabla_\ell F\big(x^i(t)\big)' E\left[\Phi^i_\ell(t) s^i_\ell(t) \mid \mathcal{F}(t)\right]$ could become positive even though $\nabla_\ell F\big(x^i(t)\big)' E\left[s^i_\ell(t) \mid \mathcal{F}(t)\right]$ is assumed to be negative.

Notice that in the case of a "specialized computation" (exactly one processor per component; see Example 7.4 of the preceding section), the coefficients $\Phi^i_\ell(t)$ are exactly known and are deterministic, even if the underlying process of message receptions is random. For this particular case, Eq. (8.26) and the proof of Prop. 8.1 remain valid.

We indicate a few extensions. Notice that as time goes to infinity, the changes in the state of computation of each processor are smaller due to the stepsize decrease. Intuition then suggests that processors should be allowed to communicate to each other less and less frequently. This is in fact correct: convergence can be proved under the assumption that $t - \tau^{ij}_\ell(t)$ is bounded by t^β, where β is a positive number smaller than 1, even though the geometric convergence of $\Phi^{ij}_\ell(t, \tau)$ [Assumption 7.1(d)] is lost ([Tsi84] and [TBA86]).

A last, but important, extension concerns the case where the stochastic descent assumption (8.7) fails to hold. An alternative and substantially weaker assumption requires that if $x^i(t)$ is kept fixed and a sequence of steps s_ℓ^i is generated, then the long–run average of these steps is a descent direction. When the stepsize is very small, which is the case as t tends to infinity, $x^i(t)$ remains approximately constant sufficiently long. Therefore, under a suitable continuity assumption on the dependence of $s_\ell^i(t)$ on $x^i(t)$, the average value of $s_\ell^i(\tau)$ (averaged over a time interval of the form $[t, t + T]$, where T is large) is approximately the same as the average value of the steps s_ℓ^i generated at the constant (frozen) value of $x^i(t)$. But, the latter average was assumed to be a descent direction. This argument can be made rigorous and, under a suitable set of assumptions, convergence to a stationary point of F can be proved ([Tsi84], [KuY87a], and [KuY87b]).

EXERCISES

8.1. Verify that $V(t)$ converges to zero in Example 8.1. *Hints:* Use condition (8.4) to establish that $V(t)$ is bounded above. Conclude that there exist $\epsilon(t)$ such that $\sum_{t=1}^{\infty} \epsilon(t) < \infty$ and $V(t + 1) \leq V(t) - 2\gamma(t)V(t) + \epsilon(t)$. Finally, use Eq. (8.3) to establish that $V(t)$ converges to zero.

NOTES AND SOURCES

7.1. Proposition 1.1 and the geometric convergence result for partially asynchronous linear iterations (Exercise 1.2) are new.

7.2. The results of this section are from [TBT88] which also contains simulation results and additional examples. Some convergence results for synchronous nonexpansive iterations can be found in [BrP67] and references therein.

7.3. The asynchronous agreement algorithm and its convergence proof are from [Tsi84], where a more general version is considered. A different class of distributed agreement algorithms is studied in [BoV82] and [TsA84]. The partially asynchronous algorithm for Markov chain problems (Subsection 7.3.2) is from [LuM86], where partially asynchronous convergence was established. The relation of this algorithm to the agreement algorithm and the corresponding convergence proof are new.

7.4. The synchronous version of the load equalization algorithm has been suggested in [Cyb87], where a convergence proof is provided. The asynchronous algorithm and the convergence proof are new.

7.5. This section is based on the results of [Tsi84] and [TBA86], except for Prop. 5.3 which is new. Similar convergence results can be proved for more general classes of algorithms which can be made arbitrarily slow (through a stepsize parameter), provided that their synchronous version remains convergent under diagonal scaling of the update directions.

7.6. The algorithm and the results of this section are based on [TsB86]. The behavior of the algorithm in the presence of stochastic fluctuations was investigated in [Tsa86], where it was shown that the conclusions of the deterministic analysis are valid in the limit of a large number of small users in the network. This reference, as well as [TTB86], contains a discussion of alternative implementations of the adjustment of the path flows, for a given OD pair, to their desired values. A related asynchronous flow control algorithm is analyzed in [San88].

7.7. The model of this section and its properties are from [Tsi84] and [TBA86].

7.8. Synchronous stochastic gradient–like algorithms have been extensively studied (see, e.g., [RoM51], [PoT73], and [Lju77]) and have found applications in several areas [LjS83]. The asynchronous convergence result of this section is from [Tsi84] and [TBA86] and the proof is patterned after the proof in [PoT73] for the synchronous case. Some extensions and some applications to system identification problems can be found in [Tsi84]. Stochastic algorithms have also been studied using the so called ODE approach ([Lju77] and [Kus84]). In this approach, convergence is established by approximating the sequence generated by the algorithm by the solution of a deterministic differential equation. The ODE approach has been used to analyze asynchronous stochastic algorithms in [Tsi84] and in [KuY87a] and [KuY87b], the latter two references using the machinery of weak convergence theory.

8

Organizing an Asynchronous Network of Processors for Distributed Computation

We have considered so far synchronous and asynchronous algorithms for the solution of a variety of problems on a network of processors. The focus has been on questions of convergence and rate of convergence, and on the computation and communication complexity of these algorithms. These questions can, to a large extent, be viewed separately from the issue of organizing the processor network itself to execute distributed algorithms in either a synchronous or an asynchronous mode. There are a number of questions related to this issue. For example, how does one start a distributed algorithm in an asynchronous processor network? How does one abort a distributed algorithm that is in progress? How does one detect the termination of a distributed algorithm? How can a processor broadcast messages to all other processors? If an algorithm is synchronous, how does one synchronize its computations across the processors of the network? How does one schedule the use of scarce resources among different processors? How can the above be accomplished when the processors and/or the communication links that connect them are subject to failure and repair? We have touched upon some of these topics in previous chapters, and in this chapter, we will provide a more systematic discussion.

The subject of this chapter is very broad and we cannot address it comprehensively within the framework of this book. Our treatment is, therefore, selective and focuses on problems that are most relevant to the numerical computation methods of the earlier chapters. Our treatment is also somewhat nonrigorous because we often do not adhere to formal models of distributed computation. This serves the dual purpose of curtailing the length of the exposition and of emphasizing the more intuitive aspects of the algorithms discussed. We justify, however, our algorithms in sufficient detail to convince the reader of their essential correctness and to provide a starting point for rigorous proofs of their validity.

Throughout this chapter we restrict ourselves to message–passing systems. In Section 8.1, we discuss the problem of detecting the (global) termination of an algorithm based on local termination conditions at the processors of a distributed system. In Section 8.2, we present a snapshot algorithm that can be used to detect certain properties of the global state of a distributed system such as deadlock, for example. In Section 8.3, we consider algorithms for scheduling the resources of an asynchronous processor network when there are restrictions on the simultaneous use of some resources by several processors. In Section 8.4, we discuss a synchronization method, based on rollback, that provides an alternative to the global and local synchronization methods of Section 1.4, and is particularly relevant to simulation of discrete event dynamical systems. In Sections 8.1 through 8.4, we assume that the topology of the processor network does not change with time. In Section 8.5, we consider networks whose topology can change unpredictably due to processor or link failures and repairs. We discuss two fundamental problems within this framework: communication of all processors with a single special processor and communication of a single special processor with all other processors.

8.1 DETECTING TERMINATION OF A DISTRIBUTED ALGORITHM

In many of the algorithms considered in the preceding chapters, there are situations where the computation can naturally be viewed as terminated. For example, the Bellman–Ford algorithm comes to an end when Bellman's equation is satisfied for each node. Similarly one may terminate the iterative solution of a linear system of equations when relaxation of any one of the equations changes the corresponding variable by no more than a given $\epsilon >$ 0. These are examples of situations where a global termination condition is decomposed into a collection of local termination conditions, one for each processor. In some cases, for example, when using the global synchronization method of Subsection 1.4.1 based on phase termination messages, there is a processor that can observe simultaneously all the local termination conditions, and can, therefore, detect the global termination condition. In an alternative scheme, a special processor checks (with some delay) whether the system satisfied the global termination condition at the end of some phase, in which case, it issues a command to stop all computation. In a related scheme, a processor issues a special "local termination" message when it reaches the local termination condition, and issues a special "restart" message when it exits that condition. A special processor collects the local termination and restart messages. When the difference between the number of local termination messages and the number of restart messages equals the number of processors, the special processor issues a command to stop the computation, perhaps after some delay to guard against the possibility that additional restart messages are forthcoming. There is no guarantee, however, that this algorithm will always detect termination correctly, particularly when the delays of messages along communication links are unpredictable. The preceding types of schemes are, nonetheless, often adequate in practice, despite the fact that their theoretical properties may not be fully satisfactory.

In this section, we describe, somewhat informally, an alternative method for detecting termination that is theoretically more sound than the methods just described. We have a network of processors connected with bidirectional communication links. We assume that each packet transmitted on a link is correctly received after a finite but unspecified time delay. We do not assume, however, that the links preserve the order of packet transmissions.

It is useful for our purposes to ignore the precise nature of the algorithm whose termination is to be detected and to focus instead on its communication aspects. We use the term "message" to refer to a special type of packet that is related in some way to the algorithm. The examples that follow illustrate the nature of messages in specific contexts. We assume that the algorithm is started when a special processor, referred to as the *initiator*, sends a message to one or more other processors. Subsequently, a number of messages are exchanged by the processors. The implication here is that each processor follows some rules according to which it generates and sends messages to other processors; however, the nature of these rules and the contents of the messages are immaterial for our purposes.

We consider a situation where during execution of the algorithm, each processor is able to monitor its own computations and decide whether a certain "local termination condition" holds. We do not need to specify the precise nature of this condition, but we assume the following:

Assumption 1.1.   If the local termination condition holds at some processor, then no messages can be transmitted by that processor. Furthermore, once true, the local termination condition remains true until a message from some other processor is received.

We say that *termination has occurred* at some time t if:

(a) The local termination condition holds at all processors at time t.
(b) No message is in transit along any communication link at time t.

We say that *termination occurs* at time $\bar{t}$, if $\bar{t}$ is the smallest time t for which the above conditions (a) and (b) hold. Our objective is to detect the termination within finite time after it occurs. Notice that if termination has occurred at some time t, then the same is true for every subsequent time $t' > t$, since no messages will be transmitted after time t and the local termination condition will remain true at all processors.

We illustrate the nature of messages and of the termination condition by means of some examples:

Example 1.1. *Asynchronous Fixed Point Iterations*

Consider a network of n processors and the totally asynchronous execution of the iteration $x := f(x)$, where $f : \Re^n \mapsto \Re^n$, as discussed in Section 6.1 (cf. Example 1.1). Each processor i stores the vector

$$x^i(t) = \left(x_1^i(t), \ldots, x_n^i(t) \right), \tag{1.1}$$

it updates its ith coordinate at some times according to

$$x_i^i := f_i(x^i), \tag{1.2}$$

and it subsequently communicates this updated value to the other processors. Here the messages of the algorithm are the updated values of the coordinates. The preceding algorithm, as stated, will execute an infinite number of iterations. To convert it into a finitely terminating algorithm, we assume that the update (1.2) is not executed (and the attendant communication of the updated coordinate does not take place) if

$$|x_i^i - f_i(x^i)| \leq \epsilon, \tag{1.3}$$

where ϵ is a given positive scalar. This is the local termination condition at i. Thus, termination occurs when Eq. (1.3) holds simultaneously for all processors i and there is no message in transit along any communication link. Note the nature of the difficulty here; each processor i can verify its own local termination condition (1.3), but cannot easily detect whether this condition holds simultaneously for all processors and whether there is any message in transit.

Example 1.2. *Asynchronous Bellman–Ford Algorithm*

In the context of the preceding example, consider the asynchronous Bellman–Ford algorithm discussed in Section 6.4 for finding the shortest distances of all nodes to node 1. The algorithm updates the shortest distance estimate of a node $i \neq 1$ according to

$$x_i := \min_{j \in A(i)} (a_{ij} + x_j), \tag{1.4}$$

where $A(i)$ is the set of all nodes such that (i, j) is an arc, and the updated value is communicated to the processors j such that $i \in A(j)$. Thus, the messages of this algorithm are the updated values of the shortest distance estimates. We assume that when the iteration (1.4) does not change the value of x_i, this value is not communicated to any other processor. The local termination condition here holds at i if execution of iteration (1.4) does not change the value of x_i. Based on the results of Section 6.4, the number of messages generated by the algorithm is finite, and termination occurs within finite time after all processors have found their shortest distance to the destination.

Our termination detection procedure is based on message acknowledgments. In particular, messages received by processor i from processor j, are acknowledged by i by sending to j special acknowledgment packets (abbreviated ACKs). Note that ACKs are distinct from messages and are not acknowledged by further ACKs. We assume that each message and each ACK arrives at its destination after some positive (but finite) time from the time it was transmitted. Furthermore, each processor can transmit only a finite number of messages and ACKs within any bounded time interval, can transmit at most one message or ACK to another prossesor at any one instant of time, can receive at most one message or ACK at any one instant of time, and is not allowed to transmit (a message or ACK) and simultaneously receive (a message or ACK) at any instant of time. These assumptions do not diminish the practical relevance of our analysis. For example, they would be appropriate for a practical situation where there can be multiple simultaneous transmissions and receptions at a processor, but the processor has a way of establishing unambiguously the relative temporal order of these transmissions and receptions. Our assumptions are used to resolve in a simple manner ambiguities about the algorithmic rules that will be described shortly. They also allow us to simplify the presentation by assuming without loss of generality that communication events, that is, transmissions and receptions of messages and ACKs, occur at integer times $t \geq 0$ and that the initial transmission of the initiator occurs at time $t = 0$. Accordingly, in all subsequent references to communication events, we imply that *these events occur instantaneously at integer times*. The expression "just after time t", where t is an integer, will refer to all times that are larger than t and smaller than $t + 1$.

There are two possible states for a processor at any one time: the *inactive state* (in which the processor is called *inactive*) and the *active state* (in which the processor is called *active*). We describe these states, the restrictions that a processor must obey at each state, and the circumstances under which a processor changes states. All changes of state occur at integer times, and we will adopt the convention that when a processor changes its state from A to B at time t, then the state is A at time t and it is B just after time t.

In the inactive state, a processor i can send no messages or ACKs. It will move from the inactive state to the active state at a time t if it receives a message at time t from some other processor j. This message and the corresponding processor j play a special role for the period between t and the next time t' at which processor i returns to the inactive state. During this period, the message is called the *critical message*, j is called the *parent* of i, whereas i is called a *child* of j.

In the active state a processor may transmit any number of messages to any one of its neighbors (subject to the limitation of one per neighbor and time instant assumed earlier). It must also acknowledge within a finite number of time units each message that it receives except for the critical message. An active processor becomes inactive simultaneously with transmitting an ACK for its critical message. This ACK is transmitted at the first time t for which the following conditions hold:

(a) No message is received by the processor at time t.

(b) The local termination condition holds at the processor at time t.

(c) The processor has transmitted prior to t an ACK for each message it has received except for the critical message.

(d) The processor has received prior to t an ACK for each message it has transmitted.

The preceding rule for changing to the inactive state is also imposed on an active processor without a parent, except that the references to the critical message are unnecessary. It will be seen shortly that under our assumptions, the initiator is the only processor that is ever active without having a parent. Note that the parent i of a processor j must be active, since i must still be awaiting the ACK for the critical message it sent to j. A diagram summarizing the algorithm is given in Fig. 8.1.1.

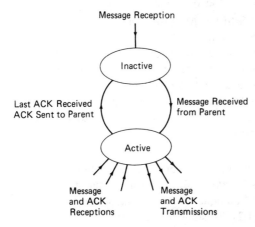

Figure 8.1.1 States of a processor during the termination detection algorithm. In the inactive state a processor transmits no messages or acknowledgments (ACKs), and changes to the active state upon receiving a message from some other processor, which then becomes the processor's parent. In the active state, a processor trasmits messages and sends an ACK for each message it receives. The processor changes its state to inactive upon sending an ACK to its parent, and is allowed to send this ACK only after it receives an ACK for each of the messages it has transmitted, and in addition, its local termination condition holds.

Initially, at time $t = 0$, the initiator is active and all other processors are inactive. Furthermore, at $t = 0$, the local termination condition holds at all processors except for the initiator. It can be seen that based on the rules of the algorithm, if a processor is inactive at time t, the following are true:

(a) Its local termination condition holds at t.

(b) It has transmitted ACKs for all the messages it has received prior to t.

(c) It has received ACKs for all the messages it has transmitted prior to t.

If the processor is active at time t, at least one of the above conditions is violated.

We say that *termination is detected*, at the first time when the initiator becomes inactive. It follows that up to the time that termination is detected, the initiator will never receive a critical message and acquire a parent, whereas every other processor will always have a parent while it is active.

We will show that the procedure we have described has the following two properties:

(a) If termination is detected at time t', then termination occurred at some time $t \le t'$.

(b) If termination occurs at time t, then termination is detected at some time $t' \ge t$.

The key concept for showing these properties is the *activity graph* (abbreviated AG), which at each time t, consists of all the processors that are active together with the directed arcs that connect the parents of these processors with the processors themselves. We make the following observations regarding the AG:

(1) At all times prior to termination detection, the initiator is active and therefore belongs to the AG.

(2) At all times, the parent of any processor that belongs to the AG (other than the initiator) is unique and must also belong to the AG.

(3) If a processor j belongs to the AG just after time t, then its parent i belongs to the AG at all times in the interval $(t - 2, t + 2)$. (The reason is that the critical message sent from i to j must have been transmitted at a time $t' \le t - 1$ and the corresponding ACK will not be transmitted by j prior to time $t + 1$ and will not be received by i prior to time $t + 2$; we are using here the assumption that all messages and ACKs take at least one time unit to reach their recipients. Based on this observation, we see that only childless processors are added to or removed from the AG at any one time.)

An important fact is that at all times prior to termination detection, *the AG is a tree of directed arcs that is rooted at the initiator* (meaning that it has no cycles, it contains the initiator and also contains a unique positive path from the initiator to every one of its other processors; see Fig. 8.1.2). To show this, it will be sufficient, in view of the above observations (1) and (2), to show that at all times prior to termination detection the AG does not contain a positive cycle. Indeed, initially the AG consists of just the initiator and if the AG first acquired a positive cycle C just after time t, then each processor of C is the parent of another processor of C which is active just after time t. By the above observation (3), it follows that each processor of C is active just after time $t - 1$. Since the AG is acyclic just after time $t - 1$, it follows that some arc of the cycle C was added to the AG at time t, joining two already active processors. This, however, is impossible since an arc (i, j) is added to the AG only when the processor j changes from inactive to active.

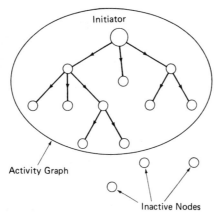

Figure 8.1.2 The activity graph at a given time consists of all the processors that are active at that time together with directed arcs connecting the parents of the active processors with the processors themselves. At all times, the graph is a tree of directed arcs that is rooted at the initiator in the sense that it has no cycles, it contains the initiator and also contains a unique positive path from the initiator to every one of its other nodes.

Assume now that termination is detected at time t'. We claim that the activity graph becomes empty at t' and that termination must have occurred at time t'. To show this, we first observe that just after time $t' - 1$, the initiator must be the only processor in the AG since otherwise, the initiator would be the parent of some processor just after time $t' - 1$ and by the above observation (3), the initiator would not become inactive at time t'. We next observe that a processor cannot become active at time t' since by the above observation (3), its parent must be active in the interval $(t' - 2, t' + 2)$; the parent cannot be different than the initiator because it must be inactive just after time $t' - 1$ as shown earlier, and it cannot be the initiator which turns inactive at time t' by assumption. Therefore, at time t', the activity graph becomes empty and all processors are inactive. From the rules by which processors become inactive, it follows that the local termination condition holds at all processors and that there are no messages in transit at time t'. This means that termination has occurred at time t'.

Suppose finally that termination occurs at time t. We will show that termination is detected (necessarily at some time $t' \geq t$, based on what has been proved so far). Indeed after t, no processor can change its state from inactive to active because no further messages will be received by any processor, so if termination is never detected, the activity graph must not change after some time while being nonempty. This, however, cannot happen because each processor i that is active and has no child in the final activity graph will eventually receive an ACK for each message it sent to the other processors (once termination occurs and the activity graph stops changing, processor i will never again have a child, so each processor must either have sent an ACK to i or will send eventually an ACK to i for every message it has received from i). Since the local termination condition holds at processor i after termination has occurred, i must eventually become inactive, thereby contradicting the hypothesis that it stays active indefinitely. We see, therefore, that the activity graph will eventually become empty at which time termination is detected.

We now consider the communication overhead that can be attributed to the termination detection procedure. Since there is one ACK per message, we see that when the procedure is used, the total number of packet transmissions is doubled. On the other hand, the ACKs can be incorporated in some way into an existing data link control scheme such as those discussed in Subsection 1.3.2, in which case, the communication overhead for termination detection is almost negligible.

Consider next the delay associated with the termination detection procedure, that is, the difference between the time when termination is detected and the time when termination occurs. Let us consider the activity graph at the time when termination occurs. It can be seen that the delay for termination detection is the time needed for the ACKs to propagate to the initiator along the links of the AG, starting from the childless nodes and proceeding toward the initiator. Thus the delay for termination detection is $O(r)$, where r is the maximum number of links on a path of the AG that connects the initiator with a node of the AG. Since r is less than the number p of processors of the distributed system, the delay for termination detection can be estimated as $O(p)$.

There are a number of variations of the termination detection procedure just described. For example, it is possible that a single ACK can acknowledge several messages

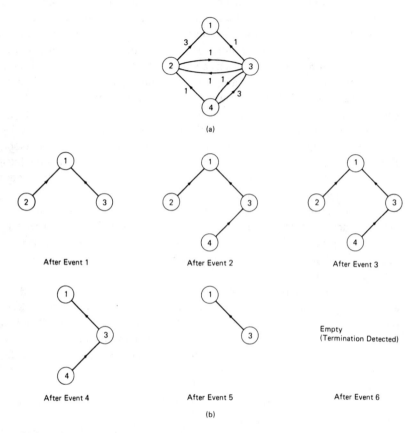

Figure 8.1.3 Illustration of the termination detection procedure for the asynchronous Bellman–Ford algorithm. (a) Shortest path problem data. The number next to each arc is the length of the arc. (b) The activity graphs corresponding to the following sequence of events involving updates according to the Bellman–Ford iteration, and message and ACK transmissions. Each event may require several time units.

Event 1: Nodes 2 and 3 receive message "$x_1 = 0$" from node 1. Node 2 becomes active due to the message from node 1, declares node 1 as its parent, and sends message "$x_2 = 3$" to nodes 3 and 4. Node 3 becomes active due to the message from node 1, declares node 1 as its parent, and sends message "$x_3 = 1$" to nodes 2 and 4. All these messages are received before event 2 begins. The 3–to–4 message is received before the 2–to–4 message (so node 4 will declare node 3 as its parent).

Event 2: Node 3 sends ACK to node 2. Node 2 sends message "$x_2 = 2$" to nodes 3 and 4, and then sends ACK to node 3. Node 3 sends (a second) ACK to node 2. Node 4 becomes active, declares node 3 as its parent, sends message "$x_4 = 4$" to node 3, and sends ACK to node 2. All messages and ACKs are received before event 3 begins.

Event 3: Node 3 sends ACK to node 4. Node 4 sends message "$x_4 = 3$" to node 3, and sends ACK to node 2. All messages and ACKs are received before event 4 begins.

Event 4: Node 2 sends ACK to node 1 and becomes inactive. Node 3 sends ACK to node 4. These ACKs are received before event 5 begins.

Event 5: Node 4 sends ACK to node 3 and becomes inactive. The ACK is received before event 6 begins.

Event 6: Node 3 sends ACK to node 1 and becomes inactive. Node 1 receives the ACK of node 3, becomes inactive, and termination is detected.

simultaneously. Furthermore, it is not crucial that each ACK is tied to a specific message. What is important for the execution of the algorithm is that each node keeps track of the difference between the number of messages transmitted and ACKs received along each link. When this difference becomes zero, the node knows that no more ACKs are pending from the opposite end processor of that link.

Figure 8.1.3 illustrates the termination detection procedure in the context of the asynchronous Bellman–Ford algorithm (Example 1.2) for a particular sequence of message and ACK receptions. The following is another example of a termination detection algorithm.

Example 1.3.   *Verifying the Reception of Broadcast Information*

Consider a network of processors connected with bidirectional communication links. Suppose that some processor, referred to as the *initiator*, wishes to send some information, call it I, to all other processors and to verify the reception of I by all other processors. The following algorithm uses two types of packets, denoted M and A, which are assumed to be received within finite time from the start of their transmission. The packets M carry the value of I and the packets A play the role of acknowledgments of reception of packets M. The algorithm operates as follows:

The initiator starts the algorithm by sending M to all its neighbor processors.

When processor i receives M for the first time, say from processor $f(i)$, it stores the identity number of $f(i)$ and sends M to all its neighbors except for $f(i)$, if it has at least one such neighbor; otherwise it sends A to $f(i)$.

When processor i receives M for the second and subsequent times, say from processor j, it sends A to j.

When processor i receives A from all neighboring processors other than $f(i)$, it sends A to $f(i)$.

By associating M with messages and A with ACKs, and by viewing $f(i)$ as the parent of processor i, we see that the preceding algorithm is a special case of the termination detection procedure. It follows that the initiator will eventually receive A from all its neighbors and that at that time, all processors will have received M. Figure 8.1.4 illustrates the operation of the algorithm.

Algorithms such as the one of the preceding example are often useful in data networks. For instance, the reader may wish to construct a similar algorithm that allows the initiator to determine the number and/or identities of all the processors in the network.

8.2 SNAPSHOTS

Each processor in a distributed computing system typically has access only to local information, that is, its own state of computation as well as the messages it sends and receives. Now suppose that we wish to detect whether the global state of the distributed system has certain properties. For instance, we might wish to detect whether the system

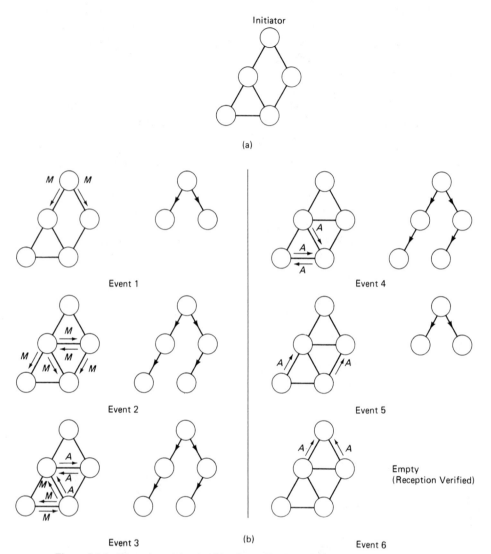

Figure 8.1.4 Illustration of the algorithm for verification of the reception of broadcast information of Example 1.3. (a) Graph over which the information is broadcast by the initiator. (b) A sequence of message and ACK transmissions (shown on the left) together with the corresponding activity graphs following these transmissions (shown on the right). M indicates a message transmission and A indicates an ACK transmission.

is deadlocked, whether the vector generated by an asynchronous iterative algorithm has come sufficiently close to a solution, or to monitor the progress of some distributed algorithm. Ideally, such a task might be accomplished by having the processors simultaneously record and then transmit their local states to a central processor. However, simultaneous recording of local states is generally impossible if the processors do not have access to a global clock and if messages (that could be used for synchronization) are subject to unknown delays. For this reason, we will settle for the lesser goal of having the processors record their local states at a set of times that are *possibly simultaneous*, meaning that the information available to the processors does not contradict the simultaneity of these times. We provide an algorithm (known as the snapshot algorithm) that achieves this goal and we then show how the recorded information can be used to detect certain properties of the true global state of the system.

We start by stating the assumptions on the operation of the distributed system. Let $G = (N, A)$ be a directed graph. The set N of nodes corresponds to the processors and each arc (i, j) represents a unidirectional, never failing, and error–free communication link. We assume that G is strongly connected, meaning that there exists a positive path from every processor to every other processor. Concerning the communication links, we assume that for each $(i, j) \in A$, a message sent by processor i to processor j reaches its destination after a positive but finite amount of time, and, furthermore, messages are received by processor j in the order in which they were transmitted. The latter assumption (often called FIFO, for first in, first out) is crucial for the correct operation of the snapshot algorithm to be presented later. It can be enforced by using an appropriate protocol for data link control (Subsection 1.3.2).

We associate a local clock with each processor. The current value t_i of the local clock of processor i will be called i's *local time*, as opposed to *global time*, denoted by τ, which is the time in the clock of an external observer. We make the assumption that distinct global times correspond to distinct local times, and conversely. In particular, the global time can be written as $h_i(t_i)$, where t_i is the local time of processor i and h_i is a strictly increasing function. The material in this section could have been presented without introducing the notion of global time. This is because global time (equivalently, the function h_i) is not known by any processor and its value cannot have any effect on the algorithms being implemented. Nevertheless, the concept of global time simplifies the presentation.

We assume that the processors are engaged in some collective computation and that at any time, the state of computation of processor i is specified by a *local state* x_i belonging to some state space X_i. [For example, the local state variable x_i could consist of the values of all variables in the memory of the ith processor that are related to the collective computation. In the special case of an asynchronous iteration of the form $y := f(y)$, the local state variable x_i is naturally identified with the value of the vector y kept in the memory of processor i.] The computation involves the exchange of messages. For any $(i, j) \in A$, let M_{ij} be the set of all possible messages from i to j. The *state of a communication link* $(i, j) \in A$, at some global time, is defined to consist of all messages that have been transmitted through that link and have not yet been received. A collection of local states (a variable x_i for each processor i) and of link states [a sequence of messages m_{ij} for every $(i, j) \in A$] is called a *global state*. If the processor and link states in a global state s are the actual states at some global time τ, we say that s is *the global state at (global) time* τ. We use S to denote the set of all global states.

The computations performed by each processor are modeled as a sequence of *events*. When an event occurs at processor i, the state x_i of that processor may change and certain messages m_{ij} to other processors may be generated. Events can be of two types: they can be *self–induced*, in which case, the state x_i changes spontaneously to a new value, or they can be *message–induced*; in the latter case, an event occurs upon reception of a message $m_{ji} \in M_{ji}$ from some processor j with $(j, i) \in A$. In the sequel, the following assumption will be in effect. It is somewhat stronger than necessary, but helps in simplifying the discussion.

Assumption 2.1.

(a) Events are instantaneous: each event at any processor i takes a zero amount of time. (Accordingly, it is meaningful to talk about "the time that an event occurs" or *event time*, for brevity.)

(b) Distinct events at the same processor occur at different local times.

(c) Only a finite number of events can occur during a time interval of finite length.

(d) Different messages received by the same processor are received at distinct local times. In particular, a message–induced event is caused by exactly one message.

Let us consider local times t_i, t_j, and t_k at three respective processors i, j, and k. Suppose that a message m_{ij} is transmitted by processor i at a local time larger than t_i, and that this message is received by j at a local time smaller than t_j. In such a case, there is sufficient information to determine that $h_i(t_i) < h_j(t_j)$. If, in addition, some other message m_{jk} from j to k testifies to the fact that $h_j(t_j) < h_k(t_k)$, then it can be inferred that $h_i(t_i) < h_k(t_k)$. If, on the other hand, two local times t_i and t_j are such that no inference of the form $h_i(t_i) < h_j(t_j)$ can be made, we will say that the local times are *possibly simultaneous*. We shall make this notion precise and then present an algorithm that records the state of each processor, and of each link, at possibly simultaneous times.

We define a collection $\{t_i \mid i \in N\}$ of local times to be *possibly simultaneous* if every message m_{ij} sent by i at or after t_i is received by j after t_j, and this property holds for every $(i, j) \in A$. We define the *snapshot* corresponding to a collection $\{t_i \mid i \in N\}$ of possibly simultaneous times to be the global state consisting of the local states x_i of each processor i at local time t_i and, for each $(i, j) \in A$, of the sequence of all messages sent by i before t_i and received by j after t_j (Fig. 8.2.1). This definition could be ambiguous if some t_i is an event time at processor i (do we record the state x_i immediately before or immediately after the event?) and for this reason, we shall subsequently ensure that none of the times t_i is an event time.

We now present an algorithm by means of which a snapshot of the system is taken. The algorithm uses special *marker* messages. We assume that these marker messages do not interfere with the underlying collective computation carried out by the processors. In particular, any sequence of events and message transmissions related to the underlying computation that was possible in the absence of the marker messages is also assumed to be possible when the marker messages are present, and conversely.

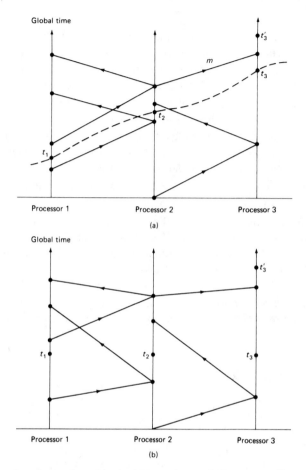

Figure 8.2.1   Illustration of a set of possibly simultaneous times and of a corresponding snapshot. Each axis represents the progress of each processor as global time increases. Each node in the diagram represents an event and each arc represents a message. Although the vertical axes stand for global time, the labels t_1, t_2, t_3, and t_3' are the local times of the respective processors at the indicated points. Times t_2 and t_3' are not possibly simultaneous because of the presence of the message m. However, the times t_1, t_2, and t_3 are possibly simultaneous. In part (b), we show an alternative timing of the different events that is indistinguishable from the one in part (a) as far as the sequence of events in each processor is concerned and in which the local times t_1, t_2, and t_3 correspond to the same global time.

It can be shown that a timing diagram as in (a) can be always redrawn to an equivalent diagram (meaning that for each processor, the same events occur in the same order) so that a given set of possibly simultaneous times is transformed into truly simultaneous times.

The dashed line in (a) illustrates a snapshot. The state of each processor i is recorded at local time t_i and the link states consist of all message that cross the dashed line. In this example, the recorded states of links $(1, 2)$ and $(2, 3)$ consist of the empty sequence and the recorded states of links $(2, 1)$ and $(3, 2)$ consist of one message.

Notice that messages crossing the dashed line can only start below the dashed line and end above it; otherwise the possible simultaneity of the times t_1, t_2, and t_3 would be contradicted.

The Snapshot Algorithm [ChL85]

(A1) *(Initialization)* One or more processors initiate the algorithm by recording their respective local states and immediately sending a marker message to each of their neighbors. For every initiating processor i, let t_i^* be its local time upon initiation. It is assumed that t_i^* is not an event time at processor i.

(A2) *(Recording of processor states)* Each processor i that is not an initiator records its local state at the first local time t_i^* that it receives a marker message. (If the first reception of a marker message by processor i occurs at an event time, we assume that the marker reception is artificially delayed by a negligible amount, thus ensuring that t_i^* is not an event time.)

(A3) *(Marker generation)* If processor i is not an initiator, it sends a marker message along each of its outgoing arcs at local time t_i^*.

(A4) *(Recording of link states)* For any $(i, j) \in A$, let t_{ij}^* be the first local time that processor j receives a marker message from processor i. Processor j records the state of link (i, j) by recording the sequence of all messages received by j on that link between local times t_j^* and t_{ij}^*.

Figure 8.2.2 illustrates the algorithm and shows that the global state recorded by a snapshot can be different from any one of the true global states at the different global times.

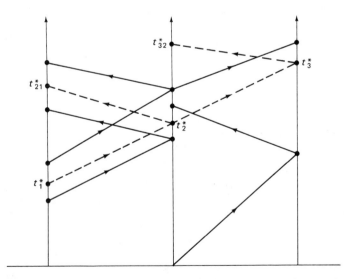

Figure 8.2.2 Illustration of the snapshot algorithm for the sequence of events shown in Fig. 8.2.1. The algorithm is initiated at local time t_1^* by processor 1. The dashed lines indicate the travel of marker messages. Processor 1 records the state of link $(2, 1)$ to consist of all messages received between local times t_1^* and t_{21}^*. This is the set of all messages that were generated by processor 2 in the "past" (that is, before time t_2^*) and received by processor 1 in the "future" (that is, after time t_1^*).

We now show that the snapshot algorithm performs as desired. We first show that the algorithm eventually terminates with every processor having recorded its local state as well as the states of its incoming links. Because of the marker generation rule (A3), and because the graph G has been assumed strongly connected, it follows that every processor that is not an initiator eventually receives a marker message. In particular, t_i^* is well defined for each i, and every processor eventually records its local state. We then see [cf. (A1) and (A3)] that exactly one marker message is transmitted along each arc $(i, j) \in A$. In particular, t_{ij}^* is well defined and finite for every $(i, j) \in A$. Thus, each link's state is recorded. We conclude that the snapshot algorithm eventually terminates.

Next we show that the local times t_i^* at which the processors record their states are possibly simultaneous. Suppose that $(i, j) \in A$ and that a message m_{ij} is transmitted from processor i to processor j after time t_i^*. We see that this message is transmitted after the transmission of a marker message from i to j. Using the FIFO assumption, the message m_{ij} is received by processor j subsequent to the reception time t_{ij}^* of the marker message. Since $t_{ij}^* \geq t_j^*$, it follows that m_{ij} is received after time t_j^*. This proves that the times $\{t_i^* \mid i \in N\}$ are possibly simultaneous.

In order to complete the proof that the states recorded by the algorithm form a snapshot, it remains to show that the recorded state of a link (i, j) is the sequence of messages sent along that link before t_i^* and received after t_j^*. According to (A4), the recorded messages are those received by processor j between local times t_j^* and t_{ij}^*. From the FIFO assumption, this is the same as the set of messages sent by i before time t_i^* and received by j after t_j^*, which completes the proof.

As just shown, the snapshot algorithm is guaranteed to terminate. Termination can be detected by the processors as follows. As soon as a processor records its own state and the states of its incoming links, it broadcasts to all processors a termination message. As soon as a processor receives a termination message from all other processors, it knows that the snapshot algorithm has terminated. Furthermore, the processors can send the recorded states to a particular processor, designated as a center, which could analyze the data provided by the snapshot and draw inferences on the global state of the distributed system. It was indicated earlier that the states recorded in a snapshot need not correspond to a true global state of the distributed system. Despite that, it will be shown that the information contained in a snapshot is sufficient for detecting certain interesting properties of the true global state.

Let S_0 be a subset of the set S of all global states. We say that S_0 is *invariant* if it has the following property: if the global state at some global time τ belongs to S_0, then the same is true for every possible global state at any subsequent global time $\tau' > \tau$.

It has been shown [ChL85] that a snapshot can be employed to detect membership in an invariant set, under certain assumptions. We are interested, in particular, in the following two properties:

Property P1.   If the global state of the system at global time τ belongs to S_0 and if the snapshot algorithm is initiated after global time τ, then the global state recorded by the snapshot algorithm also belongs to S_0.

Property P2. If the global state recorded by the snapshot algorithm belongs to S_0, then the global state of the system also belongs to S_0 at any global time τ subsequent to the termination of the snapshot algorithm.

We will prove the above two properties for the special case where the invariant set S_0 has a simple Cartesian product structure. A more general result can be found in [ChL85].

Let there be given a subset X_i^* of X_i and a subset M_{ij}^* of M_{ij} for each $i \in N$ and each $(i, j) \in A$, respectively.

Assumption 2.2.

(a) If the local state x_i of processor i belongs to X_i^* prior to a self–induced event, then it belongs to X_i^* after the event as well. Furthermore, any messages m_{ij} generated by that event belong to the set M_{ij}^*.

(b) Part (a) of this assumption holds for message–induced events as well, provided that the message m_{ji} causing the event belongs to M_{ji}^*.

Let S_0 be the set of all global states for which the local state x_i of each processor i belongs to X_i^* and every message in the state of a link $(i, j) \in A$ belongs to M_{ij}^*. We see that under Assumption 2.2, the set S_0 is invariant.

We now verify Properties P1 and P2 when S_0 is defined as above and Assumption 2.2 holds. Property P1 is obvious because if the global state at some global time τ belongs to S_0, then every subsequent local state of processor i belongs to X_i^* and every subsequently generated message belongs to a set M_{ij}^*, which establishes that the global state recorded by a subsequent snapshot belongs to S_0.

We now assume that a snapshot corresponding to a set of possibly simultaneous times $\{t_i^* \mid i \in N\}$ has recorded a state in S_0, and we verify Property P2. We will say that an event at processor i has Property P if the state of processor i after the event belongs to X_i^* and any message m_{ij} generated by that event belongs to M_{ij}^*. We assume that Property P2 does not hold, in order to derive a contradiction. Then there exists an event that occurs at some processor i at some local time $t_i > t_i^*$ that does not have Property P. Let us choose a processor i and such an event for which the corresponding global time $h_i(t_i)$ is as small as possible. If this event is self–induced, then Assumption 2.2(a) implies that the state of processor i did not belong to X_i^* before the event. However, x_i belonged to X_i^* at time t_i^* and we conclude that some event must have occurred between local times t_i^* and t_i that does not have Property P. This contradicts our definition of t_i. We now consider the case where the event at time t_i is message–induced. Using Assumption 2.2(b) and the same reasoning as before, we conclude that the message m_{ji} inducing this event does not belong to M_{ji}^*. We distinguish two subcases. If the message m_{ji} was transmitted by processor j before local time t_j^*, then this message is one of the messages recorded in the state of link (j, i) and, therefore, belongs to M_{ji}^*, a contradiction. In the second subcase, the message m_{ji} was transmitted after time t_j^*. It follows that this message was generated by some event at processor j at some (local) time t_j satisfying $t_j > t_j^*$ and, furthermore, since $m_{ji} \notin M_{ji}^*$, the event at processor j did not have property P. On the other hand, we have $h_j(t_j) < h_i(t_i)$, which again contradicts our choice of i and t_i, and completes the proof.

Example 2.1.   *Termination Detection*

For each processor i, let X_i^* be the set of states x_i from which any self–induced event leaves x_i unchanged and generates no messages. (The condition $x_i \in X_i^*$ is to be interpreted as a local termination condition for processor i.) For every link $(i,j) \in A$, let M_{ij}^* be the empty set. It is clear that the sets X_i^* and M_{ij}^* satisfy Assumption 2.2, and the corresponding set S_0 is invariant. It is seen that the global state of the system belongs to S_0 if and only if the underlying computation has terminated. We conclude that a snapshot can be usefully employed for termination detection.

Another interesting application of snapshots will be seen in Section 8.4 on asynchronous simulation.

EXERCISES

2.1. [Gaf86] Suppose that each one of the sets $\{t_i \mid i \in N\}$ and $\{t_i' \mid i \in N\}$ is a collection of possibly simultaneous local times. Show that the same is true for each one of the sets $\{\max\{t_i, t_i'\} \mid i \in N\}$ and $\{\min\{t_i, t_i'\} \mid i \in N\}$.

8.3 RESOURCE SCHEDULING

We consider an asynchronous network of processors, described by an undirected graph $G = (N, A)$, where $N = \{1, \ldots, n\}$ is the set of processors, and A is the set of undirected arcs. Each arc represents a perfectly reliable bidirectional communication link joining processors i and j. We assume that the processors participate in some computational task and that they perform certain operations once in a while. We assume, however, that each arc (i, j) is associated with some shared resource R_{ij}, which is necessary for either processor i or j to perform an operation, and that this resource can only be possessed by one processor at a time. Therefore, for the computation to proceed, we need a processor i to gain control of all resources associated with its incident arcs. As shown in Fig. 8.3.1, it is possible that the processors become deadlocked if each one is idle waiting for some needed resource. We will present a simple algorithm under which deadlock is avoided and all processors have a chance to operate an infinite number of times.

This problem, also known as the *dining philosophers problem*, is of fundamental importance in synchronization and deadlock avoidance in distributed systems, and applies to a variety of situations. The example closest to the applications discussed in this book relates to the distributed execution of an iteration of the form

$$x_i := f_i(x_1, \ldots, x_n), \qquad i = 1, \ldots, n. \tag{3.1}$$

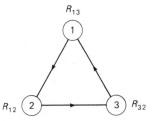

R_{13}

R_{12} R_{32}

Figure 8.3.1 Illustration of deadlock. Each processor has taken hold of one of the two resources it needs and waits to take hold of the second. A direction is assigned to each arc (i,j) to indicate the processor holding the corresponding resource R_{ij}. As the situation of each processor is completely symmetrical, they are faced with a deadlock.

Here we let G be the corresponding undirected dependency graph, that is, an arc (i,j) is present if and only if f_i depends on x_j or f_j depends on x_i. Consider a serial execution of iteration (3.1), whereby at each time t, some processor $i(t)$ executes Eq. (3.1) and informs the other processors about the new value of $x_{i(t)}$. Suppose that such a serial algorithm is convergent for all possible choices of $i(1)$, $i(2),\ldots$, provided that each processor executes an infinite number of times. This is the case, for example, for the dual relaxation algorithms for network flow problems, which were studied in Chapter 5. The same is true in several situations in which there is an underlying cost function that decreases whenever a single processor performs an update. Coordinate descent methods, such as the Gauss–Seidel algorithm for linear equations or the nonlinear Gauss–Seidel algorithm for nonlinear problems, are some examples. In some such algorithms, convergence can be lost if two neighboring processors i and j [with $(i,j) \in A$] are allowed to perform an update simultaneously. For example, the nonlinear Gauss–Seidel algorithm for strictly convex optimization problems is guaranteed to converge, but this is not always the case for the nonlinear Jacobi algorithm in which all processors update simultaneously. We conclude that there are several circumstances in which we wish iteration (3.1) to be executed in a way that is mathematically equivalent to a serial execution (one processor at a time). To guarantee this, it is sufficient to require that no two adjacent processors operate simultaneously. This, in turn, will be accomplished by means of a resource R_{ij} that cannot be simultaneously held by processors i and j.

A synchronous solution to our problem is obtained by using a coloring scheme, as discussed in Subsection 1.2.4. Here we associate a particular "color" with each processor in the graph, subject to the constraint that no two adjacent processors have the same color. Let the different colors be numbered from 1 to K. The computation proceeds in stages. At the first stage, all processors with the first color operate, then processors with the second color, all the way to the last color, and then we restart with the first color. Such a scheme is *fair* in the sense that the number of operations performed by different processors can differ by at most one. The example in Fig. 8.3.2 shows that the coloring approach is not necessarily the most efficient possible synchronous scheduling method. In an inherently asynchronous system, the previously outlined synchronous solution can be implemented using a synchronization mechanism (Section 1.4). In particular, a global synchronization method could be used, but the overhead involved is unwarranted. We do not discuss the use of a local synchronization method for this problem because it leads to an algorithm similar to the one to be presented.

We motivate our algorithm in terms of the resource allocation problem mentioned in the beginning of this section. With each arc $(i,j) \in A$, we associate a resource R_{ij}.

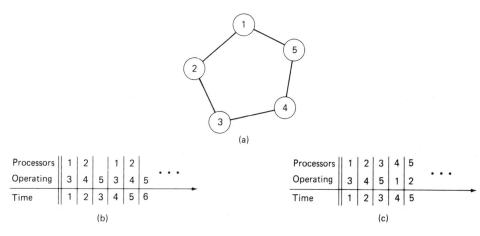

Figure 8.3.2 An example where optimal coloring cannot achieve the concurrency attainable by an optimal schedule. We consider the dependency graph in (a) and we require that no two neighbors operate simultaneously. Let processors 1 and 3 have color 1, processors 2 and 4 have color 2, and processor 5 have color 3. The synchronous schedule based on this coloring is shown in (b) and the average number of processors operating per time unit is 5/3. With the schedule in (c), however, there are two processors operating at each time unit.

At any point in time, either one of the two processors i and j is in control of R_{ij} or the resource is traveling from one processor to the other. When a processor i takes control of the resources R_{ij} associated with all of its incident arcs, it is allowed to perform an operation, and we assume that it will do so in finite time. Subsequently, and for each j such that $(i, j) \in A$, the resource R_{ij} is transferred to processor j. This is done by sending an appropriate message to each adjacent processor j. The resource is said to be traveling while this message is in transit and as soon as that message reaches processor j, the resource R_{ij} is under the control of processor j. The state of this scheduling procedure, at any given time, can be described compactly by assigning a particular direction to each arc $(i, j) \in A$, thus converting G to a directed graph. In particular, we orient arc (i, j) to point toward processor j if and only if the resource R_{ij} is under the control of j or is traveling toward j. Given a current orientation of the arcs in the graph G, we say that processor i is a *sink* if and only if all of its incident arcs $(i, j) \in A$ are oriented to point toward i. It is seen that a processor that is a sink eventually has control of all relevant resources and performs an operation. The subsequent transfer of these resources to the neighbors of i is then equivalent to reversing the directions of all arcs incident to i. We notice that if the previously described directed graph has no sink, then the graph remains forever unchanged. In that case, no processor ever becomes a sink, no processor ever operates, and the system is deadlocked. (This is the case, for example, in Fig. 8.3.1.) It will be shown that we can guarantee the existence of a sink at any given time, provided that the directions with which the scheduling algorithm is initialized make G a *directed acyclic graph*, that is, a directed graph with no cycles consisting exclusively of forward arcs.

In terms of the directed graphs just defined, the algorithm can be simply described as follows (see Fig. 8.3.3 for an illustration).

Arc Reversal Algorithm.   The algorithm is initialized by assigning a direction to each arc $(i, j) \in A$ so that the resulting directed graph is acyclic. Any processor who is a sink performs an operation, within a finite amount of time, and reverses the directions of its incident arcs.

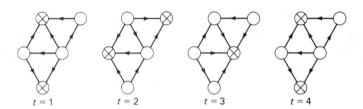

Figure 8.3.3   Illustration of the arc reversal algorithm. Processors marked with an X are those that are ready to operate and reverse the directions of their incident arcs.

We now verify that if a directed graph is acyclic and if the orientation of each arc incident to a sink is reversed, then the resulting directed graph is also acyclic. Let i be a sink that has performed an arc reversal. After the arc reversal, there can be no positive cycle going through i because there are no arcs oriented toward i. Furthermore, the directions of all arcs not incident to i are unchanged by the arc reversal. Assuming that the directed graph was acyclic before the arc reversal, we see that no positive cycles not involving i are created by the reversal. We conclude that the directed graph maintained by the arc reversal algorithm is at all times acyclic.

We next verify that any directed acyclic graph has a sink. To see this, suppose that there was no sink. Then we could construct an arbitrarily long path by starting at an arbitrary node and choosing each time an outgoing path from the current node. In particular, if the path has at least n arcs, then some node has to be visited at least twice, thereby contradicting acyclicity and proving the existence of a sink.

This discussion shows that at any given time, the directed graph maintained by the algorithm has a sink. It follows that for any given time t, there exists a subsequent time t' at which some processor operates. In particular, deadlock is never reached. We continue by verifying a fairness property of the algorithm. Let $X_i(t)$ be the number of operations performed by processor i until time t. Between consecutive operations by processor i, all of its neighbors must operate at least once, in order to reset the corresponding arcs so that they point toward i. It follows that $|X_i(t) - X_j(t)| \leq 1$ for all arcs (i, j). Thus, if the graph G is connected, we have

$$|X_i(t) - X_j(t)| \leq d, \qquad \forall i, j, \tag{3.2}$$

where d is the diameter of the graph. Hence, no processor can be arbitrarily far ahead of the others, as far as the number of operations is concerned.

In the context of the distributed execution of iteration (3.1), the scheduling algorithm is implemented as follows. Each arc is initially assigned a direction, so that the resulting directed graph is acyclic. Each processor i that is initially a sink learns the initial value of x_j for each neighbor j and updates x_i according to Eq. (3.1). It then transmits the new value of x_i to all its neighbors. When a neighbor j of i receives a value of x_i, it interprets this as a signal that the direction of the arc (j, i) has now been reversed to point toward j. Eventually, processor j becomes a sink, performs an update of x_j, etc. To summarize, it is seen that a processor performs an update as soon as it has received new values from all of its neighbors and transmits to them its new value as soon as it has performed its own update. The similarity with the local synchronization method of Section 1.4 should be evident. The only difference is that here we are dealing with a Gauss–Seidel rather than a Jacobi iteration, and that the algorithm uses the *undirected* dependency graph as a starting point.

We now investigate the choice of the directed acyclic graph with which the scheduling algorithm is initialized. For the sake of analysis, let us assume that the algorithm starts at time 1, that an operation by a processor takes exactly one time unit, and that communication between processors is instantaneous. (In particular, processors adjacent to a sink are instantaneously informed about the arc reversal when it occurs.) We finally assume that a processor starts its operation as soon as it becomes a sink. Let $G(t)$ denote the directed acyclic graph at time t. We notice that the set of all possible graphs $G(t)$ is finite, since there is only a finite number of possible orientations of the arcs in the graph G. Since $G(t)$ changes deterministically, it must eventually become a periodic function of time. We let $M(t)$ be the number of sinks in $G(t)$. We see that $M(t)$ eventually becomes periodic and, therefore, the limit

$$M = \lim_{t \to \infty} \frac{\sum_{\tau=1}^{t} M(\tau)}{t}$$

exists. The number M is the average number of operations per time unit and should be thought of as a measure of concurrency. We notice that

$$\sum_{\tau=1}^{t} M(\tau) = \sum_{i=1}^{n} X_i(t+1).$$

We divide both sides by nt, take the limit as t tends to infinity, and use inequality (3.2) to obtain

$$\frac{M}{n} = \lim_{t \to \infty} \frac{X_i(t)}{t}, \qquad \forall i.$$

The number M depends strongly on the directed acyclic graph $G(1)$ with which the algorithm is initialized. In particular, for the same underlying undirected graph G, M could be as large as $n/2$ and as small as 1 (see Fig. 8.3.4 for an example). It turns out that with an optimal choice of $G(1)$, the scheduling method under consideration achieves the maximum concurrency over all schemes where a processor must operate once between two consecutive operations by any neighbor [BaG87]. Unfortunately, the problem of choosing $G(1)$ so as to maximize M is an intractable combinatorial problem (NP–hard) [BaG87], although it is often easy to solve when G has a special structure (Exercise 3.2).

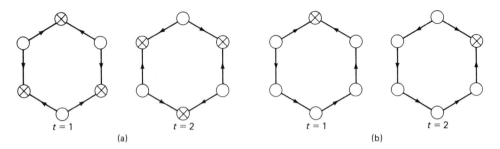

Figure 8.3.4 The effects of the initial assignment of directions to the arcs on the resulting measure of concurrency M. (a) A good choice of $G(1)$. Here $M = 3$. (b) A bad choice of $G(1)$. Here there is only one sink at a time and $M = 1$. More generally, if we have a ring of n nodes, with n even, a best choice of $G(1)$ leads to $M = n/2$, whereas a bad choice leads to $M = 1$.

EXERCISES

3.1. Let $G(1) = (N, A(1))$ be the directed acyclic graph with which the arc reversal algorithm is initialized. Suppose that there exist nodes $i_1, \ldots, i_K \in N$ such that $(i_1, i_K) \in A(1)$ and $(i_k, i_{k+1}) \in A(1)$ for $k = 1, \ldots, K - 1$. Show that the concurrency measure M is bounded above by n/K. *Hint:* See Figure 8.3.4.

3.2. Suppose that the graph G is a d–dimensional mesh. Assign initial orientations to the arcs of G so that the value of the concurrency measure M in the resulting scheduling algorithm, is as large as possible. *Hint:* Generalize the red–black ordering of Subsection 1.2.4 to the d–dimensional case.

8.4 SYNCHRONIZATION USING ROLLBACK: ASYNCHRONOUS SIMULATION

We have seen in Subsection 1.4.1 that a synchronous algorithm can be implemented in an inherently asynchronous parallel or distributed computing system, using either global or local synchronization methods. However, these methods have drawbacks that in certain contexts can be significant. For example, in global synchronization, several processors can be idle, waiting for other processors to complete the computations of the current phase. Also, the local synchronization method works well if each processor knows from which processors it is going to receive a message at the current phase, but involves substantial communication overhead (dummy messages) in case such knowledge is missing (see the discussion in Subsection 1.4.1). The synchronization method presented here is based on an entirely different principle: each processor keeps computing at its own pace under the assumption that no message is going to be received from other processors; in the case that such a message is actually received, the processor invalidates its computations and starts over again, taking the received message properly into account. This mechanism, called *rollback*, is a general purpose synchronization procedure and can be used in the implementation of any synchronous algorithm in an asynchronous computing system. It has been applied mainly in concurrency control of distributed databases and in the simulation of dynamical systems. We use simulation as our working example in this section, but it should be kept in mind that the method is of more general validity.

A Model of Discrete Time Dynamical Systems

We wish to simulate a discrete time dynamical system (referred to as the *physical system*) consisting of n interacting subsystems. It is natural to carry out the simulation using a parallel computing system with a different processor assigned to the task of simulating a different subsystem. The processors have to exchange messages, in the course of the simulation, in order to handle the interactions between subsystems.

To be more specific, let S_i be the ith subsystem and let its state at time t be described by a state variable $x_i(t)$ belonging to some state space X_i. Here t is an integer time variable, running from 0 to some final time T, which represents *physical* time in the system being simulated. It should be distinguished from *real* time, which is the time in the clock of an observer looking at the computing system used for the simulation. The initial states $x_i(0)$ in the physical system are assumed to be known. Let $G = (N, A)$ be a directed graph. The set N of nodes is equal to $\{1, \ldots, n\}$, with node i representing subsystem S_i. The presence of an arc (i, j) indicates the possibility that the state of subsystem S_i influences the state of subsystem S_j. For any $(i, j) \in A$ and any (physical) time t, let $m_{ij}(t)$ be a variable, taking values in a space M_{ij}, which models the interaction of subsystems S_i and S_j in a way to be made precise shortly. We postulate a functional dependence of the form

$$m_{ij}(t) = g_{ij}\big(x_i(t)\big), \qquad (i, j) \in A, \tag{4.1}$$

where g_{ij} is a function from X_i into M_{ij}. We wish to allow for the possibility that even if $(i, j) \in A$, subsystems S_i and S_j do not interact at every time instance. We thus assume that m_{ij} can take a special (null) value, denoted by π. The equality $m_{ij}(t) = \pi$ is interpreted as the absence of any interaction from S_i to S_j at physical time t. Let $z_i(t)$ be the vector consisting of all interaction variables $m_{ji}(t)$, where $(j, i) \in A$. We assume that we have a model of the form

$$x_i(t + 1) = f_i\big(x_i(t), z_i(t)\big), \tag{4.2}$$

for each subsystem S_i. Equations (4.1) and (4.2) define completely the computations that we would like to carry out. In fact, such equations can be used to describe a broad variety of synchronous algorithms and for this reason, the discussion that follows is of much more general applicability.

A Synchronous Simulation Algorithm

We assign a separate processor P_i to each subsystem S_i. The computation proceeds as follows. If processor P_i knows the value of $x_i(t)$ and has received a message from processor P_j containing the value of $m_{ji}(t)$ for every j such that $(j, i) \in A$, then processor P_i computes $x_i(t + 1)$ and $m_{ik}(t + 1)$ for each k such that $(i, k) \in A$, using Eqs. (4.2) and (4.1), respectively. Subsequently, for every k such that $(i, k) \in A$, the message $m_{ik}(t + 1)$ is transmitted to the corresponding processor P_k. [Such a message is transmitted even if $m_{ik}(t + 1)$ has the null value π.] We allow for the possibility that messages are not received in the order in which they were transmitted. In order for the receiver to be able to interpret correctly the received messages, we assume that the messages also contain a timestamp (see Fig. 8.4.1). For concreteness, let us assume that messages have the format (t, m, i, j). Reception of such a message informs the recipient that $m_{ij}(t) = m$. We refer to t as the *timestamp* of the message.

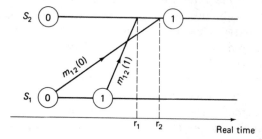

Figure 8.4.1 Illustration of the need for timestamps. Here there are two subsystems and subsystem S_1 affects S_2, but not conversely $[A = \{(1, 2)\}]$. The nodes in this figure indicate the real times at which the values of the variables $x_i(t)$ are computed. Processor P_2 receives two messages at real times r_1 and r_2, respectively, but if these messages carry no timestamps, it has no way of telling which one is $m_{12}(0)$ and which one is $m_{12}(1)$.

Assuming that all messages eventually reach their destinations, it is evident that the previously described algorithm correctly simulates the system described by Eqs. (4.1) and (4.2). Consider the special case where each stage requires C time units of computation by each processor and assume that each message reaches its destination with a delay of D time units. Then the total time until the completion of the simulation is equal to $(C + D)T$. This is the best possible if the subsystems interact all of the time.

The method just described is precisely the local synchronization method of Subsection 1.4.1. It is an appropriate method if subsystems S_i and S_j interact at every physical time step for each i and j such that $(i, j) \in A$. On the other hand, if such interactions are rarely present, then $m_{ij}(t)$ is equal to the null value π, most of the time. Then processor P_j will often have to wait to receive a message m_{ij}, only to discover that it carries the uninformative value π. The objective of the synchronization method to be presented is precisely to avoid waiting for these null messages.

The Rollback Mechanism

Let us consider the following scheme. Each processor continues updating according to Eq. (4.2) and keeps sending messages containing values of the interaction variables, generated according to Eq. (4.1). We assume again that messages have the generic format (t, m, i, j) and that they are guaranteed to reach their destination after some finite but unknown real time and not necessarily in the order that they were sent. Whenever processor P_i needs [in order to execute Eq. (4.2)] the value of some interaction variable $m_{ji}(t)$ and a message (t, m, j, i) has not been received, then processor P_i uses the default value π. In effect, processor P_i takes a gamble that interactions will be absent. If interactions are indeed absent for all times and for all pairs of subsystems, then it is evident that the simulation is completed in the least possible time, since each processor continues computing at full speed. Now suppose that during the simulation, a nonnull interaction variable $m_{ij}(t) \neq \pi$ is generated. When processor P_j receives the corresponding message (t, m, i, j), there are two distinct possibilities that we now discuss.

Suppose that at the real time instance when $m_{ij}(t)$ is received, $x_j(t + 1)$ has not been computed. Then when processor P_j eventually reaches the point where $x_j(t+1)$ is to be generated, it will have available and will be able to use the correct value of $m_{ij}(t)$.

Now suppose that processor P_j has already computed $x_j(t + 1)$, before receiving $m_{ij}(t)$, while assuming, incorrectly, that $m_{ij}(t) = \pi$. Then the value of $x_j(t+1)$ and all subsequent values $x_j(t')$, $t' > t$, that have already been computed are incorrect and must be recomputed. (We then say that processor P_j is *rolling back*; see Fig. 8.4.2.) In order to recompute these values, processor P_j must remember the value of $x_j(t)$ and all messages $m_{kj}(t')$, $t' \geq t$, it has received. Furthermore, all messages $m_{jk}(t')$, $t' > t$, sent by processor P_j are incorrect because they were evaluated from Eq. (4.1) on the basis of an incorrect value of $x_j(t')$. Therefore, processor P_j has to transmit special messages to the other processors, informing them that certain messages transmitted in the past are invalid. We refer to these special messages as *antimessages*. For concreteness, we assume that the antimessage invalidating the message (t, m, j, k) has the format $(t, m, j, k, *)$. Notice that the transmission of appropriate antimessages requires each processor to keep a record of the messages it has transmitted in the past. Whenever a processor P_k receives an antimessage $(t, m, j, k, *)$, some of the results of earlier computations by that processor can be invalidated, which can invalidate some messages that have been already sent by P_k. Thus, P_k may have to send antimessages as well. In particular, each antimessage can trigger the transmission of an arbitrary number of further antimessages (see Fig. 8.4.3). Finally, notice that a processor can receive an antimessage $(t, m, i, j, *)$ without first receiving the corresponding message (t, m, i, j), because we allow messages to be received out of order, and we must specify how such a situation is to be handled.

We continue with a full description of the simulation algorithm, but we first make the key observation that null messages of the form (t, π, i, j) are inconsequential: processor P_j performs the same computations whether or not such a message has been received. The reason is that π is the default value to be used in the absence of a message. It follows that processor P_i does not have to transmit a message if the value of the interaction variable $m_{ij}(t)$ is equal to π. This modification can save a substantial amount of communication and is one of the reasons for introducing the rollback mechanism.

We assume that for each $(i, j) \in A$, there is a buffer B_{ij} in which messages from P_i to P_j are placed upon reception until they are processed by P_j. We also assume that each processor P_i keeps the following in its memory:

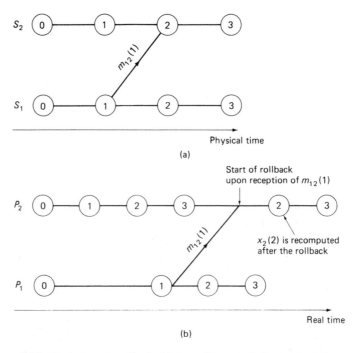

Figure 8.4.2 Illustration of a rollback. (a) A possible scenario for the physical system being simulated. Here the state of subsystem S_1 at time 1 affects the state of S_2 at time 2. (b) A possible scenario for the simulation. A node labeled t stands for the point in time that $x_i(t)$ was computed by processor P_i. In this scenario, processor P_1 is slow and the communication delay of the message $m_{12}(1)$ is large enough so that this message reaches processor P_2 after $x_2(3)$ is computed. Receipt of such a message invalidates the computation of $x_2(2)$ and $x_2(3)$, which have to be recomputed.

(a) An integer variable τ_i initialized with $\tau_i = -1$. [This variable is interpreted as the largest value of t such that $x_i(t)$ has been computed and the computed value has not been invalidated.]

(b) A record containing a value $x_i(\tau)$ for every τ such that $0 \le \tau \le \tau_i$.

(c) A record of all messages (t, m, j, i) it has received and processed and for which a corresponding antimessage $(t, m, j, i, *)$ has not been received and processed.

(d) A record of all antimessages $(t, m, j, i, *)$ it has received and processed and for which a corresponding message (t, m, j, i) has not been received and processed.

(e) A record of all messages (t, m, i, j) it has sent and for which it has not sent a corresponding antimessage.

Initially, the records (b) to (e) are empty. During the algorithm, processor P_i executes the following three instructions. (Several improvements are possible; see e.g. Exercise 4.2.)

1. If a message (t, m, j, i) exists in one of the buffers B_{ji}, remove it from the buffer and do the following:

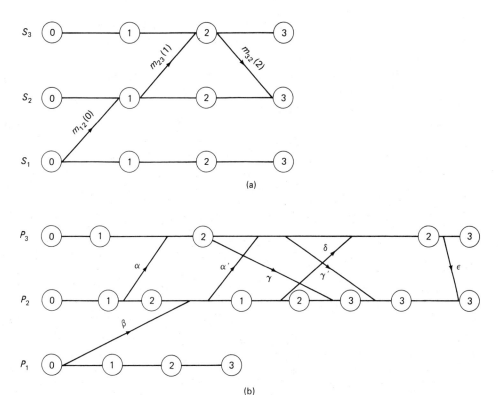

Figure 8.4.3 Illustration of a rollback that causes a further rollback at another processor. (a) A possible scenario for a physical system consisting of three subsystems. Here the arrows stand for nonnull interactions. For example, $x_1(0)$ affects $x_2(1)$ by means of an interaction $m_{12}(0)$. (b) A corresponding possible scenario for the simulation. Processor P_2 computes $x_2(1)$ and sends a message $\alpha = m_{23}(1)$ to processor P_3. However, the message $\beta = m_{12}(0)$ reaches processor P_2 after $x_2(2)$ has been computed, causes a rollback, and invalidates the values of $x_2(1)$ and $x_2(2)$. This rollback triggers an antimessage α' from processor P_2 to processor P_3 to invalidate the message α. In the meantime, processor P_3 has sent a message γ to processor P_2 based on its computation of $x_3(2)$. However, when the antimessage α' is received, the value of $x_3(2)$ is invalidated and an antimessage γ' is sent to processor P_2 to cancel the message γ. Eventually, $x_2(1)$ is recomputed and a new message δ is sent to processor P_3, carrying the correct value of $m_{23}(1)$. Then processor P_3 eventually computes the correct value of $x_3(2)$ and sends a message ϵ with the correct value of $m_{32}(2)$. This message causes one more rollback at processor P_2 which recomputes $x_2(3)$.

1.1. If the antimessage $(t, m, j, i, *)$ is found in the record (d) of antimessages, then delete it and discard the message (t, m, j, i).

1.2. If the antimessage $(t, m, j, i, *)$ is not found in the record (d), then place the message (t, m, j, i) in the record (c) of messages received and processed. If $t \geq \tau_i$, no further action is required. If $t < \tau_i$, then do the following:

1.2.1. (Rolling back) Assign to the variable τ_i the new value t and delete $x_i(t')$ from record (b) for all $t' > t$.

      1.2.2. (Canceling incorrect messages) Remove all messages of the form (t', m, i, k), $t' > t$, from the record (e) of messages sent and send corresponding antimessages $(t', m, i, k, *)$.

2. If an antimessage $(t, m, j, i, *)$ exists in one of the buffers B_{ji}, remove it from the buffer and do the following:

    2.1. If the message (t, m, j, i) is not found in the record (c) of messages, then place the antimessage in the record (d) of antimessages received and processed.

    2.2. If the message (t, m, j, i) is found in the record (c), then delete it from that record and discard the antimessage. If $t \geq \tau_i$, no further action is required. If $t < \tau_i$, then do the following:

        2.2.1. Assign to the variable τ_i the new value t and delete $x_i(t')$ from record (b) for all $t' > t$.

        2.2.2. Remove all messages of the form (t', m, i, k), $t' > t$, from the record (e) of messages sent and send corresponding antimessages $(t', m, i, k, *)$.

3. If $\tau_i < T$, then do the following:

    3.1. Compute $x_i(\tau_i + 1)$ and $m_{ik}(\tau_i + 1)$ for each k such that $(i, k) \in A$, using Eqs. (4.1) and (4.2). [In the special case where $\tau_i = -1$, instead of using Eq. (4.2), simply fetch the value of $x_i(0)$, which is viewed as an external input.] If the computation of $x_i(\tau_i + 1)$ requires the value of $m_{ji}(\tau_i)$ [i.e., if $(j, i) \in A$], look for it in the record of messages received and processed. If it is not found, use the default value π. If several messages from P_j with the same timestamp τ_i are found in that record, choose one of them arbitrarily.

    3.2. Increment τ_i to $\tau_i + 1$.

    3.3. If $\tau_i < T$, then for each k such that $(i, k) \in A$ and $m_{ik}(\tau_i) \neq \pi$, send a message (τ_i, m, i, k) to processor P_k, with $m = m_{ik}(\tau_i)$, and place this message in the record (e) of messages sent.

    The algorithm terminates when $\tau_i = T$ for each i, and there are no messages or antimessages that have been transmitted but have not yet been received and processed.

    We assume that each processor keeps executing instructions 1, 2, and 3 at its own pace and in an arbitrary order. For example, if several messages and antimessages have been placed in the buffers B_{ji} of processor P_i, then this processor has the option of executing either instruction 1 or 2, and handle any one of the received and yet unprocessed messages and antimessages. Still, we assume that every transmitted message or antimessage is received correctly and is processed after a finite amount of time, in the course of some execution of instruction 1 or 2. We also assume that if $\tau_i < T$, then processor P_i will eventually execute instruction 3. It is assumed that each one of the three instructions is indivisible: for example, processor P_i will never interrupt the execution of instruction 2 to start executing instruction 1.

    We now argue that the algorithm eventually terminates with the correct values of $x_i(t)$ for each i and $t \in \{0, 1, \ldots, T\}$, where a value is called *correct* if it is the one generated by a synchronous execution of Eqs. (4.1) and (4.2). To reach this conclusion, we will show that for each physical time t, there exists some real time r_t such that the following are true:

(a) We have $\tau_i \geq t$ for each i.

(b) There are no messages or antimessages in transit (i.e., sent but not yet received and processed) with a timestamp smaller than t.

We start by noticing that if (a) and (b) are true at some real time r_t, then they remain true for all real times $r > r_t$. To see this, we examine the nature of instructions 1 to 3 and verify that there is no possibility for (a) or (b) to become false. For example, if instruction 3 is executed, τ_i becomes $\tau_i + 1 \geq t + 1 \geq t$, messages generated have the timestamp $\tau_i + 1 \geq t + 1$, and no antimessages are generated. If instruction 1 is executed, it involves a message with a timestamp no smaller than t. Thus, even if a rollback occurs, the new value of τ will be no smaller than t, and any antimessages caused by this rollback have a timestamp no smaller than $t + 1$. If instruction 2 is executed, the argument is similar.

We now proceed by induction. We observe that for $t = 0$, condition (b) always holds and condition (a) becomes and remains true as soon as instruction 3 is executed at least once by each processor. Consider now some $t < T$ and suppose that (a) and (b) are true at some real time r_t. The argument of the preceding paragraph shows that (a) and (b) remain forever true and, furthermore, no new messages or antimessages with a timestamp smaller than $t + 1$ will be generated in the future. In particular, any messages and antimessages with a timestamp t will eventually reach their destinations and be processed. (This argument is correct if we assume that there is only a finite number of messages or antimessages in transit. Otherwise, it might take an infinite amount of time until all of them are received and processed, even though each one is received and processed in finite time. This issue is, however, of no concern because it can be proved that only a finite number of messages and antimessages is generated in the course of the algorithm; see Exercise 4.1.) We conclude that there exists some real time r'_t after which condition (b) will be satisfied for $t + 1$. Similarly, after real time r_t, the value of each τ_i never becomes smaller than t. Moreover, at the first time after r'_t that instruction 3 is executed, τ_i is incremented to a value no smaller than $t + 1$ and is never going to decrease below $t + 1$ because no message or antimessage with a timestamp smaller than $t + 1$ will be received in the future. Therefore, there exists a real time $r_{t+1} > r'_t$ such that condition (a) is true for every real time $r \geq r_{t+1}$.

We conclude that there exists some time r_T at which $\tau_i = T$, for each i, no messages or antimessages are in transit, and, therefore, the algorithm has terminated. It remains to show that at termination, all the values $x_i(t)$ and $m_{ij}(t)$ in the records of the processors are correct for each t. This is obviously true for $t = 0$ and we proceed again by induction. Assuming that it is true for some physical time t, the messages $m_{ij}(t)$ in the buffers of processor P_j have the correct values and this implies that the value of $x_j(t + 1)$ is also correct. Therefore, the only messages $m_{jk}(t + 1)$ that have been sent and have not been invalidated by subsequent antimessages have the correct values. Since, at termination, there are no messages or antimessages in transit, it follows that the messages $m_{jk}(t + 1)$ in the buffers of all processors P_k have the correct values, which completes the induction.

Let us now make the additional assumption that messages and antimessages are received in the same order as they are transmitted. In this case, the antimessages invalidating past erroneous values of $m_{ji}(t)$ reach processor P_i before the final correct message. Therefore, as soon as the correct messages are received, processor P_i can compute the correct value of $x_i(t)$ without any further delay. We conclude that in this case, the algorithm proceeds as fast as possible: correct values are computed at the first instance of time when the required data have been received. To be more specific, suppose that computations take zero time and the transmission delay of a message or antimessage from P_i to P_j takes T_{ij} time units. Let $r_{i,t}$ be the real time of the last (and, therefore, correct) computation of $x_i(t)$. Assume that $r_{i,0} = 0$ and it can be seen that

$$ r_{i,t+1} = \max\left\{ r_{i,t}, \max\left\{ r_{j,t} + T_{ji} \mid (j,i) \in A, \ m_{ji}(t) \neq \pi \right\} \right\}, $$

where we use the convention that $\max\{c \mid c \in C\} = -\infty$ when C is the empty set. On the other hand, given our assumptions on communication delays, no other algorithm could evaluate $x_i(t)$ before real time $r_{i,t}$, even if we knew ahead of time which of the interaction variables $m_{ij}(t)$ are absent (null). We therefore have an optimal algorithm as far as time is concerned.

The argument in the preceding paragraph refers to an idealized situation. It is based on the assumption that communication delays are independent of the particular algorithm being used and ignores the overhead associated with the rollback mechanism. In fact, rollback involves several types of overhead:

(a) Computational overhead due to invalid computations: computational resources are wasted in computing often incorrect values of $x_i(t)$ to be invalidated later. Suppose that a processor can stop a computation immediately upon reception of an invalidating message and start a new computation using the message value received. Then the computational overhead does not slow down the computation because any processor engaged in a computation to be invalidated later only has the alternative option of staying idle. On the other hand, if computations cannot be interrupted and take a long time to be completed, this overhead should be taken into account.

(b) Communication overhead: this can be quite severe in the worst case. One can envisage multiple rollbacks triggering further rollbacks, each one generating large numbers of antimessages that result in queueing delays. Even if communication resources are abundant, excessive communication can drain the computational resources of the processors, since each message requires some amount of processing. On the other hand, it is hoped that for a class of interesting systems, rollbacks will exhibit some temporal and spatial locality: if a processor rolls back, it may only roll back a few time units, and if any further rollbacks are triggered, these will involve only a few neighboring processors. However, this hypothesis has not been established theoretically or experimentally as yet.

(c) Finally, the algorithm has significant memory requirements. Processors have to keep records of all messages sent and received, and of the values of $x_i(t)$ that have been computed. There are two partial remedies to this problem that we now discuss.

Assuming that messages are relatively infrequent, the main memory requirement comes from having to remember old values of $x_i(t)$. This requirement is reduced if a processor saves $x_i(t)$ only once in a while, say once every A time units, where A is some integer. This introduces a new problem: if a processor has to roll back to some time t for which the value of $x_i(t)$ has not been saved, then it must go even further back, use an earlier value of x_i, and reconstruct $x_i(t)$. So, the savings in memory are offset by increased computational requirements each time that a rollback occurs. A reasonable compromise is to save all values $x_i(t)$ for t close to τ_i, and save a few old values just in case that a rollback to the distant past occurs. Again, whether this scheme would work well depends on the validity of the hypothesis of temporal locality of rollbacks.

Another reduction of the memory requirements is suggested by the following observation. If $\tau_i \geq t$ for all i, and if there are no messages or antimessages in transit (transmitted but not received and processed) with timestamps smaller than t, then there is nothing that could cause a rollback resetting τ_i to a value smaller than t. This means that the values of $x_i(\tau)$ and $m_{ij}(\tau)$ for $\tau < t$ can be discarded. Unfortunately, such a memory management mechanism cannot be easily implemented in a distributed manner, because it involves global properties of the algorithm, as opposed to the local information available to each processor. It can be implemented, however, by employing the snapshot algorithm of Section 8.2 (under the FIFO assumption). To see this, we say that the state of computation of processor P_i belongs to the set X_i^* if $\tau_i \geq t$ and any messages or antimessages in the buffers B_{ji} (that is, received but not processed) have timestamps greater than or equal to t. Also, we let M_{ij}^* be the set of all possible messages or antimessages from i to j with timestamps greater than or equal to t. These sets have the invariance properties considered in Section 8.2, and, therefore, the snapshot algorithm can be used to detect whether the local state of computation of each processor P_i belongs to X_i^* and each message or antimessage in transit from i to j belongs to M_{ij}^*.

A related problem with the algorithm is that the processors cannot detect termination based on their own local information. Rather, termination has to be detected either by a host computer supervising the simulation or by a distributed termination detection algorithm of the type discussed in Section 8.1. Alternatively, if the snapshot algorithm is used to monitor the progress of the algorithm, the snapshots can also be used for the purpose of termination detection.

Simulation of Continuous Time Discrete Event Systems

Asynchronous distributed simulation with rollback has been actually proposed not for discrete time systems described by equations of the form (4.1)–(4.2), but for so called *discrete event* systems. These latter systems evolve in continuous time, but their state changes only at a discrete set of times. (An example of a discrete event system is a queueing network with random arrivals and service times.) Some new difficulties arise because the times at which these discrete events can occur are not a priori known.

We describe a model of a discrete event system and suggest some algorithms. The issues are similar to those discussed in the context of the simulation of discrete time systems, and for this reason, the presentation here will be less detailed.

We again have n subsystems $\mathcal{S}_1, \ldots, \mathcal{S}_n$ and a directed graph $G = (N, A)$ indicating the possible interactions between subsystems. Let $x_i(t)$ be the state of the ith subsystem at time t. Here t is a continuous time variable, taking values in $[0, T]$. We constrain $x_i(t)$ to be a piecewise constant function of time, and for concreteness, we assume that it is right–continuous. The times of discontinuity of $x_i(t)$ are called *event times*. Whenever an event occurs at subsystem $\mathcal{S}_i$, it can trigger an interaction with another subsystem $\mathcal{S}_j$, assuming that $(i, j) \in A$. Whether this is the case or not depends on the state $x_i(t)$ just after the event. To keep the discussion simple, we assume that interactions are not instantaneous, that is, if an event occurs at subsystem $\mathcal{S}_i$ at time t, the resulting interaction can affect another subsystem $\mathcal{S}_j$ only after some positive amount of time, although we allow this time to be arbitrarily small. At the time that such an interaction affects subsystem $\mathcal{S}_j$, an event is triggered at the latter subsystem. Events can also be self–induced. In particular, if an event occurs at subsystem $\mathcal{S}_i$ at time t, then a new event time t' is generated, as a function of the state $x_i(t)$ right after the event. The value of t' is the time of the next event at subsystem $\mathcal{S}_i$, unless an event is triggered earlier due to an interaction from another subsystem.

The above description of a discrete event system is not very rigorous. The following sequential algorithm simulates a discrete event system, and can also be taken as a definition of the dynamics of such a system. Assume that the system has been simulated up to a certain time t, including t itself. Each event that has already occurred determines the times at which certain events will occur in the future. Choose that event that is scheduled to occur first among all those future events. (For simplicity, we prohibit simultaneous events at different subsystems. This is no loss of generality: since we do not allow simultaneous interactions, if two events were to occur simultaneously, they could not be causally dependent and their times could be perturbed by an infinitesimal amount to make them appear non–simultaneous.) Suppose that the first future event is scheduled to occur at subsystem $\mathcal{S}_i$ at time $t' > t$. We can then simulate all subsystems up to time t' as follows. No events occur at any of the remaining subsystems during the interval $[t, t']$, and, therefore, the state of these subsystems remains unchanged. Concerning subsystem $\mathcal{S}_i$, we have to simulate the particular event under consideration. That is, we have to generate the new state of $\mathcal{S}_i$ after the event, determine the times of interaction with other subsystems caused by this event (if any), and determine the time of the next self–generated event at subsystem $\mathcal{S}_i$. We can then proceed to the simulation of the next event.

The above algorithm can be used to simulate an arbitrary number of events. In particular, if only a finite number of events can occur during a finite time interval, the algorithm can simulate the system for any arbitrary length of time. On the other hand, this algorithm is inherently sequential, because after the occurrence of each event, we need to determine the minimum event time over all events due to occur in the future and all subsystems. Several modifications of this algorithm which are more parallelizable have been studied. However, they are susceptible to deadlock and require, in general, special deadlock resolution procedures or special assumptions on the nature of interactions between subsystems [Mis86].

An alternative distributed simulation algorithm is based on the rollback scheme and is almost identical to the algorithm provided earlier for discrete time systems. Each processor P_i keeps simulating its subsystem S_i arbitrarily far into the future. At each stage, it determines the time of the next event due to occur at S_i, using the information available. Whenever an event is simulated by P_i, messages are transmitted to other processors P_j to inform them about events to be triggered at S_j caused by the event simulated at S_i. If processor P_j receives a message stating that an event is to occur at some time t at S_j and processor P_j has already simulated S_j up to some time $t' > t$, then it has to undo and repeat its simulation for the interval $[t, t']$. As before, appropriate antimessages should be sent to invalidate any incorrect messages. The details are the same as for the simulation of discrete time systems. In particular, if we assume that all messages and antimessages reach their destinations and are processed in finite (real) time, and if only a finite number of events can occur during a finite (physical) time interval, then the rollback algorithm eventually simulates the system correctly, arbitrarily far into the future.

An Example: Shortest Path Computation

In the example to be discussed here, the physical system to be simulated involves a directed graph $G = (N, A)$. With each arc (i, j), there is an associated positive arc length a_{ij}. The physical system operates as follows: initially, all nodes have a state $x_i(0) = \infty$, except for node 1 for which $x_i(0) = 0$. Node 1 emits a signal along its outgoing arcs. When a node receives for the first time a signal along one of its incoming arcs, it immediately retransmits it along all of its outgoing arcs. Signals to be received later are not retransmitted. Let t_i be the time at which subsystem S_i receives a signal for the first time. We define the dynamics of the state variables x_i: we have $x_i(t) = \infty$ for $t < t_i$, and when a signal is first received by node i at time t_i, the value of x_i becomes t_i and stays at that value thereafter. Assume that the travel time of the signal along an arc (i, j) is equal to the arc length a_{ij}. It is then obvious that t_i is equal to the length of a shortest path from node 1 to node i.

This physical system can be viewed as a discrete event system. The event times are the times at which the nodes receive signals. Notice that the state of a node changes only at the first event at that node. We now describe a simulation of the system using the rollback algorithm.

We use a network of n processors interconnected according to the topology determined by the graph G. The algorithm to be executed by processor P_i is the following: initially, $x_i(0) = \infty$ for $i \neq 1$, and $x_1(0) = 0$. Messages along an arc of the computing system simulate signals along the same arc in the physical system. The only useful information in these signals is the physical time at which the signal is received. Accordingly, messages only carry a timestamp indicating the time that the corresponding signal should reach its destination in the physical system.

Recall that the essence of the rollback scheme is that each processor simulates its own subsystem, [the time function $x_i(\cdot)$] as far into the future as it can under the assumption that all messages it has received are correct, and that no further messages are to be received. Notice that in the present example, the time function $x_i(\cdot)$ corresponding to a set of messages is straightforward to determine: $x_i(t)$ is infinite for t less than the smallest timestamp s_i of the received, processed, and not invalidated messages, and $x_i(t)$ is equal to s_i thereafter. Thus, the time function $x_i(\cdot)$ is uniquely determined by the single number s_i, and we can assume that processor P_i only keeps s_i in its memory, rather than the time function $x_i(\cdot)$. It follows that the rollback scheme amounts to the following. Each processor P_i, $i \neq 1$, keeps a number s_i initialized at infinity. Whenever a processor P_i receives a message, it reads the timestamp t. If $t \geq s_i$, it leaves s_i unchanged. If $t < s_i$, then s_i is reset to t. The messages sent by P_i, triggered by the reception of a message with timestamp t, are determined as follows. If $t \geq s_i$, no message is sent, corresponding to the fact that a signal is emitted from the subsystem $\mathcal{S}_i$ only at the first time that the subsystem receives a signal. If on the other hand, $t < s_i$, then the old value of s_i is invalidated, which invalidates the signals already sent by P_i. Thus, processor P_i must sent antimessages as well as new messages based on the new value of s_i. The message sent to processor P_j should be equal to the sum of the new value of s_i and a_{ij}; this is the time at which a signal is received by $\mathcal{S}_j$ if this signal was emitted from $\mathcal{S}_i$ at a time equal to the new value of s_i. In fact, it is not hard to see that antimessages are redundant in this context. If processor P_j receives a new message with a smaller timestamp it automatically knows that the old messages are invalid.

An equivalent and more compact description of the above scheme is the following. Each processor P_i, $i \neq 1$, maintains a number s_i initialized at infinity. Whenever processor P_j receives a message from processor P_i with a timestamp $s_j' = s_i + a_{jj}$ which is less than s_j, it resets s_j to be equal to s_j' and sends a message $s_j' + a_{jk}$ to every processor k such that $(j, k) \in A$. It is assumed that all messages are received after some unspecified delay. We recognize this as being equivalent to the asynchronous Bellman–Ford algorithm analyzed in Section 6.4. We now recall that the asynchronous Bellman–Ford algorithm has, under a worst case scenario, exponential communication complexity (see Fig. 6.4.2 in Section 6.4). This proves, in particular, that it is possible for the rollback scheme to generate a number of messages and antimessages that is an exponential function of the number of nonnull interactions in the physical system being simulated.

EXERCISES

4.1. Show that the total number of messages and antimessages generated during the asynchronous simulation of a discrete time system over a finite time interval $[0, T]$, using the rollback mechanism, is bounded by some function of T and the number of subsystems. *Hint:* Show that the number of rollbacks that reset τ_i to a value less than or equal to t is bounded by a function of the number of messages and antimessages with a timestamp smaller than or equal to t. Then bound the number of messages and antimessages with a timestamp equal to $t + 1$ and proceed by induction.

4.2. Consider a processor P_i that computes $x_i(t + 1)$ by executing instruction 3. Suppose, furthermore, that processor P_i finds two messages (t, m, j, i) and (t, m', j, i) in the record of messages received and processed, and that the message (t, m, j, i) is used to compute $x_i(t+1)$. Suppose that the antimessage $(t, m', j, i, *)$ is received later. Such an antimessage causes a rollback at processor P_i and the recomputation of $x_i(t + 1)$ (cf. instruction 2). On the other hand, it is intuitively clear that if a message has not been used in computations, its cancellation by a corresponding antimessage does not invalidate any computations and should not cause a rollback.

(a) Modify the algorithm so that no rollback occurs in a situation such as the one described above and explain why the algorithm still produces the correct results.

(b) Show that the situation under consideration cannot arise if messages and antimessages are received in the order in which they are transmitted.

8.5 MAINTAINING COMMUNICATION WITH A CENTER

We consider an asynchronous network of processors described by an undirected graph $G = (N, A)$, where $N = \{0, 1, \ldots, n\}$ is the set of processors, and A is the set of undirected arcs. Each arc (i, j) indicates the existence of a bidirectional communication link between processors i and j. Processor 0 represents a center and we are interested in an algorithm that guarantees that each processor maintains a set of simple (loop–free) paths through which it can communicate with the center. Furthermore, we would like such an algorithm to be able to adapt itself to unpredictable topological changes such as the removal or the addition of communication links. Finally, the algorithm should be distributed, with the actions of each processor depending only on locally available information.

The above problem has applications in a few different contexts. For example, in certain data networks, such as mobile packet radio networks, topological changes can be very frequent and the task of maintaining communication with a center can be quite challenging. Another context is provided by geographically distributed sensor networks in which data obtained by the sensors must be relayed to a central processing station. Finally, one might envisage loosely coupled distributed computing systems operating in an uncertain environment with failure–prone communications.

A simple solution to our problem could be a *centralized* one. Here the processors transmit topological information to the center. Then the center, based on its knowledge of the topology of the network, computes a set of simple paths, from each processor to the center, and communicates these paths to the individual processors. This is not as straightforward as it seems because for the processors to transmit topological information to the center, they need to have already established communication paths, which is the problem that we were trying to solve in the first place. For this reason, the task of transmitting the topological information to the center becomes rather complex. It can be solved by flooding or by running a topology broadcast algorithm (see the end of this section). Both of these solutions can be undesirable, however, because they can involve an excessive amount of message transmissions and considerable overhead.

A distributed alternative is based on the solution of a shortest path problem. Let us assign a length of 1 to every arc in the network and let the processors execute the asynchronous Bellman–Ford algorithm, with processor 0 playing the role of the destination. If the topology of the network does not change and if the network is connected, this algorithm will eventually terminate and a set of shortest paths from every processor to the center will be obtained. Since the arc lengths are positive, such shortest paths will be simple, as desired (Fig. 8.5.1). Furthermore, if topological changes occur,

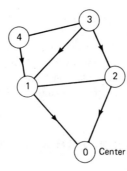

Figure 8.5.1 Simple paths from every processor to the center obtained by solving a shortest path problem. An arrow on the arc (i, j) indicates that this arc belongs to a shortest path from i to the center.

the processors will keep executing the Bellman–Ford algorithm, which is then guaranteed to converge to a set of shortest paths for the new topology of the network.

While the shortest path approach provides a distributed algorithm for our problem, it has two undesirable properties:

(a) The paths obtained when the algorithm reaches quiescence are guaranteed to be simple, but this is not necessarily true while the algorithm is executing. If a processor attempts to communicate with the center before the algorithm has terminated, the messages it sends might travel in a cycle before they reach their destination (Fig. 8.5.2).

(b) If a topological change (say the addition of an arc) does not disrupt previously established paths from the processors to the center, it might be reasonable to continue using these paths. Nevertheless, the shortest path algorithm may lead to major changes in the paths (Fig. 8.5.3).

We now proceed to develop a class of algorithms for the problem under consideration. In these algorithms, starting with the original undirected graph G, we convert it into a directed graph G' by assigning a direction to each one of its arcs. If the assigned directions are such that G' is acyclic (i.e., there are no cycles consisting exclusively of forward arcs), we say that G' is a directed acyclic graph (*DAG*). If G' is a DAG and node 0 is the only sink, we say that G' is *oriented* toward the center; otherwise, we call it *disoriented*. Notice that if we manage to assign directions to the arcs so that G' is acyclic and oriented, we have obtained a solution to our problem. In particular, starting from any node i, consider any path obtained by traversing consecutive arcs in accordance to their assigned directions. Such a path must eventually come to an end because G' is acyclic. When it comes to an end, a sink must have been reached and, since G' is oriented, that sink must be node 0 (Fig. 8.5.4).

The algorithms to be presented maintain at all times a direction for each arc and rely on the following properties:

Property A. The algorithm is initialized by assigning directions to the arcs so that the resulting directed graph is acyclic.

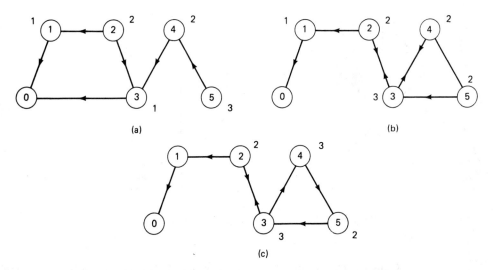

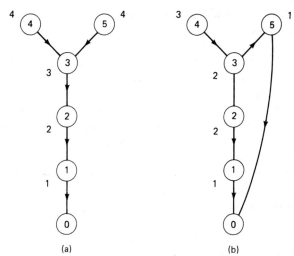

Figure 8.5.2 Formation of a cycle when the paths are chosen by a shortest path algorithm. (a) Original shortest paths. The labels next to each node indicate estimates of the distance from the center. Also, an arrow on arc (i, j) pointing toward j indicates that node i perceives this arc as belonging to a shortest path to the center. (b) Arc $(3,0)$ is removed from the network and arc $(5,3)$ is added. Processors 3 and 5 perform simultaneously an iteration of the Bellman–Ford algorithm to obtain new distance estimates of 3 and 2, respectively. (c) Processor 4 performs an iteration to obtain a distance estimate of 3. The shortest paths perceived by each processor are such that a cycle is formed. In particular, if processor 4 attempts to send a message to the center, that message could circulate in the cycle until eventually the processors perform more iterations and obtain the correct shortest distances.

Figure 8.5.3   (a) A network and corresponding shortest distances. (b) Arc $(5,0)$ is added to the network. Although the old shortest paths can still be used for communication with the center, the new shortest paths are different.

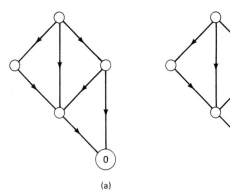

Figure 8.5.4 (a) An oriented DAG. (b) A disoriented DAG.

(a)   (b)

Property B.   The direction of any arc can only be changed in a way that preserves acyclicity.

Property C.   In the absence of topological changes and assuming that the undirected graph G is connected, the algorithm eventually terminates and, at termination, processor 0 is the only sink.

Property D.   When an arc is added, it is assigned a direction so that the new directed graph is still acyclic.

Clearly, any algorithm with these four properties provides a solution to our problem. Acyclicity is preserved throughout, resulting in loop–free paths, and at termination, we have an oriented DAG.

A simple way for initializing any algorithm is by letting arc (i, j) point toward processor j if and only if $i > j$. This results in a DAG because any path in the directed graph can only go toward processors with smaller identity numbers and cannot, therefore, contain a cycle.

It is assumed in the sequel that the direction of an arc is under the control of the processor to which it points from the time that this processor learns this direction until the time that the direction is changed. In particular, if a processor is in control, it knows the correct direction. Also, our subsequent algorithms are such that a processor that is not in control remains passive. It follows that no actions will ever by taken by processors with incorrect knowledge of the direction of an arc. In order to keep the discussion simple, we will assume that every processor always knows the current directions of its incident arcs (i.e., arc reversal information is instantaneously transmitted and received along an arc whenever its direction is reversed), but the above discussion implies that this assumption is not really necessary.

Our first algorithm is very simple:

Full Reversal Algorithm.   The algorithm is initialized by assigning arc directions so that the resulting directed graph is acyclic. Each processor knows the directions of its incident arcs. If all arcs incident to processor i point toward i (i.e., if i is a sink) and if $i \neq 0$, then processor i will, after some finite amount of time, reverse the directions of all these arcs.

Arc reversals by a processor i in this algorithm are assumed to be instantaneous operations and, in particular, all arcs involved are simultaneously reversed and the neighbors of i are informed about this reversal after a finite amount of time. We now verify that the full reversal algorithm has Properties B and C. Concerning Property B, it has already been shown in Section 8.3 that an arc reversal by a sink in a directed acyclic graph preserves acyclicity. For Property C, let $X_i(t)$ be the number of times that processor i has performed a full arc reversal until time t. Let j be a neighbor of i. After an arc reversal by processor i, the arc (i, j) points toward processor j. In order for processor i to perform another arc reversal, it must become a sink and this is possible only if processor j performs an arc reversal in between. This shows that a full arc reversal is performed by processor j between any two consecutive full arc reversals by processor i. Hence $|X_i(t) - X_j(t)| \leq 1$ for all times t and for all pairs i and j, of neighboring processors. Furthermore, processor 0 never performs an arc reversal and we have $X_0(t) = 0$ for all t. Assuming that the underlying graph is connected, we obtain $X_i(t) \leq d$ for all times t, where d is the largest distance from processor 0 to any other processor i. We thus see that in the absence of topological changes, each processor performs at most d full arc reversals and the algorithm terminates after a total of less than nd arc reversals. After termination, no processor $i \neq 0$ can be a sink because if it were a sink, it would eventually perform an arc reversal, thereby contradicting termination. Figure 8.5.5 illustrates the algorithm for a particular example and Exercise 5.1 shows that the worst case estimate $O(nd)$ on the total number of full arc reversals is tight.

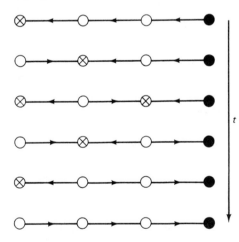

Figure 8.5.5 Illustration of the full reversal algorithm. The black node corresponds to the center and an X denotes a sink ready to perform an arc reversal.

We have not yet mentioned how the full reversal algorithm copes with topological changes, additions of new arcs in particular. It can be seen (Exercise 5.2) that there always exists a direction that can be assigned to a new arc, so that acyclicity is preserved, but this cannot be done, in general, using only the local information available to the processors (Fig. 8.5.6). For this reason, we modify the algorithm so that more information is available to the processors.

Numbered Full Reversal Algorithm.   This is the same as our earlier full reversal algorithm except that each processor i maintains an integer number a_i. Initially, these integers satisfy $a_i > a_j$ for every arc (i, j) that points toward j. Whenever processor $i \neq 0$ becomes a sink, it performs an arc reversal and updates a_i by letting

$$a_i := 1 + \max_{j \in A(i)} a_j,$$

where $A(i)$ is the set of neighbors of i. Furthermore, when a neighbor of i becomes aware of an arc reversal by i, it also learns the new value of a_i. Finally, whenever a new arc (i, j) is added to the network, it is oriented to point to processor j if and only if $a_i > a_j$ or $a_i = a_j$ and $i > j$.

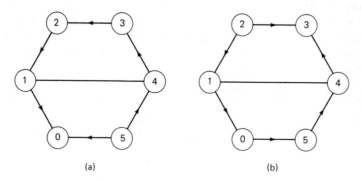

Figure 8.5.6 Difficulties in assigning a direction to a newly created arc using only local information. In (a) and (b), we show two directed acyclic graphs. Arc $(1, 4)$ has just been added to the graph and is to be assigned a direction while preserving acyclicity. In (a), this arc must point toward node 1, whereas in (b), it must point toward node 4. However, in both examples, the local information available to processors 1 and 4 is the same and is therefore insufficient for assigning a direction to arc $(1, 4)$.

The initialization of the numbers a_i is easy. For example, we can let $a_i = i$ for all i, and orient every arc (i, j) to point to the processor with the smaller identity. We call the pair $v_i = (a_i, i)$ the *value* of processor i. We order values lexicographically, that is, we let $(a_i, i) > (a_j, j)$ if $a_i > a_j$ or if $a_i = a_j$ and $i > j$. With this ordering, the set of all possible values is totally ordered and, furthermore, no two processors can ever have the same value. We notice that the algorithm maintains throughout the property that an arc $(i, j) \in A$ is oriented toward processor j if and only if $v_i > v_j$. In particular, this property is preserved when arcs are added to or removed from the network, which guarantees that we have an acyclic graph at all times and Property D holds. Properties B and C remain valid by our earlier discussion. We conclude that this algorithm satisfies all of our requirements.

As the numbered full reversal algorithm continues to be executed and as more topological changes occur (resulting in more and more arc reversals) the numbers a_i will grow unbounded. It may thus be necessary to have the center obtain a global view of the network and reassign new and relatively small numbers to the processors once in a while. Alternatively, a processor can reduce its number a_i on its own, provided that this does not change the direction of any arc.

We continue with a modification of the full reversal algorithm that, in the absence of topological changes, tends to terminate with a substantially smaller number of arc reversals.

Partial Reversal Algorithm.   The algorithm is initialized by assigning arc directions so that the resulting directed graph is acyclic. Each processor $i \neq 0$ maintains a list of its incident arcs (i, j) that have been recently reversed by processor j. (Initially this list is empty.) If processor i becomes a sink, then it reverses the directions of all incident arcs that *do not* appear in the list and empties the list. An exception arises if the list contains all arcs incident to i, in which case, all of them are reversed and the list is emptied.

In the absence of topological changes, the partial reversal algorithm tends to involve fewer arc reversals than the full reversal algorithm (see Fig. 8.5.7 for an illustration), even though the best bound we have available is exponential in d. Exercise 5.3 provides such a bound and also proves that the algorithm eventually terminates. The difficult part in the proof of correctness of this algorithm is in verifying that acyclicity is preserved throughout. Furthermore, as discussed earlier, in the context of the full reversal algorithm, locally available information is not sufficient to handle topological changes. For this reason, a set of auxiliary integer variables will be introduced. Each processor i is assumed to maintain a value v_i that is a triple $v_i = (a_i, b_i, i)$. Values are again ordered lexicographically. That is, $v_i > v_j$ if and only if one of the following three occurs: (i) $a_i > a_j$, or (ii) $a_i = a_j$ and $b_i > b_j$, or (iii) $a_i = a_j$, $b_i = b_j$, and $i > j$. The processors' values are to be updated as in the following algorithm.

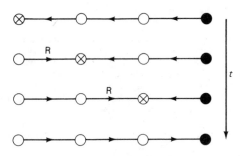

Figure 8.5.7 Illustration of the partial reversal algorithm for the same graph and initialization as in Fig. 8.5.5. An arc labeled R and pointing toward processor i belongs to the list (maintained by processor i) of recently reversed arcs.

Numbered Partial Reversal Algorithm.   The algorithm is initialized by assigning arc directions so that the resulting directed graph is acyclic. Each processor i maintains a triple $v_i = (a_i, b_i, i)$; an arc (i, j) is oriented toward j if and only if $v_i > v_j$. If processor $i \neq 0$ becomes a sink [i.e., if $v_i < v_j$ for all $j \in A(i)$], then processor i lets

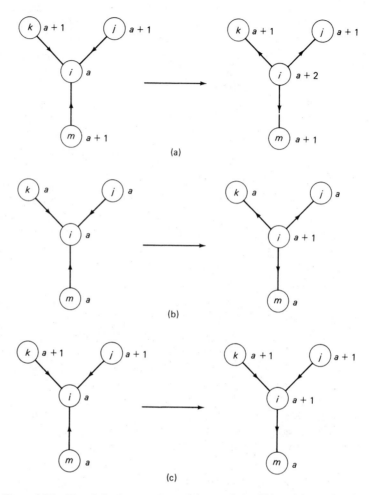

Figure 8.5.8   The relation between the partial reversal algorithm and the numbered partial reversal algorithm, in the absence of topological changes. Suppose that the numbered partial reversal algorithm is initialized with $a_i = b_i = c$ for all $i \neq 0$, where c is some constant. We show that throughout the algorithm we have (i) $|a_i - a_j| \leq 1$ for any two neighboring processors i and j, and (ii) $a_i = a_j + 1$ if and only if processor i has recently reversed the direction of arc (i, j) and processor j has not yet performed a partial arc reversal. Indeed these properties are true at initialization. Suppose that these properties are true before a partial arc reversal by processor i. Parts (a), (b), and (c) consider the three possible cases. All arcs are reversed in cases (a) and (b). In (c), we have right after the partial arc reversal, $a_i = a_j = a_k$, $b_i < b_j$, and $b_i < b_k$. Thus, arcs (j, i) and (k, i) are not reversed. This shows that properties (i) and (ii) remain valid throughout the algorithm. Given that property (ii) holds, we conclude that the set $\{i \mid a_i = a_j + 1\}$ in the numbered partial reversal algorithm is equal to the list of recently reversed arcs maintained by processor j in the partial reversal algorithm, and the two algorithms are identical.

$$a_i := 1 + \min_{j \in A(i)} a_j, \tag{5.1}$$

$$b_i := \min_{j \in A(i)} b_j - 1, \tag{5.2}$$

reverses the directions of its adjacent arcs (i, j) for which the new value of v_i is larger than v_j, and communicates the new value of v_i to its neighbors. If a new arc (i, j) is added to the network, it is oriented toward j if and only if $v_i > v_j$.

This algorithm coincides with our original partial reversal algorithm, provided that it is initialized appropriately and no topological changes occur (Fig. 8.5.8). The algorithm can also be interpreted as a version of the Bellman–Ford shortest path algorithm [cf. Eq. (5.1)]. The role of the coefficients b_i is to provide a tie breaking mechanism under which acyclicity is preserved. The number of partial arc reversals until the algorithm terminates behaves similarly with the Bellman–Ford algorithm: it tends to be small when the coefficients a_i are initialized appropriately (e.g., very large; see Section 4.1), but can also be arbitrarily large under certain circumstances (Fig. 8.5.9).

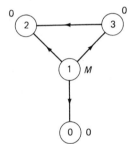

Figure 8.5.9 An example of slow performance of the numbered partial reversal algorithm. Suppose that the algorithm is initialized with $a_0 = 0$, $a_1 = M$, and $a_2 = a_3 = 0$, where M is a large integer. Processor 1 never becomes a sink and the value of a_1 stays constant. The values of a_2 and a_3 increase by steps of size $\Theta(1)$, and it is seen that the algorithm undergoes a total of $\Theta(M)$ partial arc reversals before it terminates.

We now verify that this algorithm has the desired properties. In our arguments, we will assume that processors adjacent to i receive all relevant information instantaneously after an arc reversal by processor i. Similarly, if a topological change involving arc (i, j) occurs, both processors i and j are instantaneously informed. The proof for the case where these instantaneity assumptions fail to hold follows the same lines, but the details are more tedious. Property A holds by definition. The values v_i of successive processors along any positive path in the directed graph are strictly decreasing, which shows that acyclicity is maintained throughout, and, therefore, Properties B and D hold.

To verify Property C, we assume that there are no topological changes and that the graph is connected, and we first prove that the algorithm eventually terminates. Let us denote by $a_i(t)$ the value of a_i at time t. Suppose that the function $a_i(t)$ is unbounded above for some i. From Eq. (5.1), it follows that $a_j(t)$ is also unbounded above for every j that is a neighbor of i. Since the graph is connected, $a_j(t)$ must be unbounded above for all processors. But this is impossible because processor 0 never performs an arc reversal and a_0 stays constant at its initial value. We conclude that each $a_i(t)$ is bounded above. We also notice from Eq. (5.1) that the quantity $\min_i a_i$ cannot decrease when a processor performs an arc reversal. We conclude that the functions $a_i(t)$ are also bounded below. In particular, each function $a_i(t)$ has a smallest limit point to be denoted by c_i.

We denote by NT the set of processors that perform an infinite number of partial arc reversals, and let T be its complement. We assume, in order to derive a contradiction, that NT is nonempty. Let t_0 be some time such that $a_i(\tau) \geq c_i$ for all $\tau \geq t_0$ and all i. Such a time exists because otherwise some function $a_i(t)$ would have a limit point smaller than or equal to $c_i - 1$. Notice that for every $i \in T$, the function $a_i(t)$ eventually becomes and stays equal to c_i. Thus, by choosing t_0 sufficiently large, we have $a_i(t) = c_i$ for all $i \in T$ and $t \geq t_0$. Let $i^* \in NT$ be a processor such that $c_{i^*} \leq c_i$ for all $i \in NT$. We consider two cases:

(i) If processor i^* has a neighbor $j \in T$ with $c_j < c_{i^*}$, then $a_{i^*}(t) \geq c_{i^*} > c_j = a_j(t)$ for all $t \geq t_0$. Thus, processor i^* cannot be a sink at any time after t_0, contradicting our assumption that $i^* \in NT$.

(ii) Now suppose that $c_j \geq c_{i^*}$ for all neighbors $j \in T$ of i^*. Since $c_j \geq c_{i^*}$ for all $j \in NT$ (this follows from the definition of i^*), we obtain $a_j(t) \geq c_j \geq c_{i^*}$ for all neighbors j of i^* and for all times greater than t_0. In particular, at each time after t_0 that processor i^* performs an arc reversal, the new value of a_{i^*} is at least as large as $c_{i^*} + 1$. In between consecutive arc reversals by processor i^*, the value of a_{i^*} remains constant. We conclude that $a_{i^*}(t) \geq c_{i^*} + 1$ subsequent to the first arc reversal by processor i^* that occurs after time t_0. In particular, every limit point of $a_{i^*}(t)$ is larger than c_{i^*}. This contradicts the definition of c_{i^*}.

We have thus contradicted the existence of an element of NT. It follows that the algorithm eventually terminates. At termination, processor 0 is by necessity the only sink, and we conclude that the algorithm has Property C and performs as desired.

We now show that the reversal algorithms do not have the undesirable properties of the shortest path methods that were mentioned in the beginning of this section. Suppose that a reversal algorithm has not yet terminated and that a processor i sends a message to a neighboring processor j, attempting to communicate with the center. If the direction of the arc (i, j) is reversed by processor j before the message is forwarded by j, it is conceivable that the message is returned to processor i. Such a scenario can be repeated, thus demonstrating that a message can circulate in a cycle as long as the reversal algorithm has not terminated. It can be shown, however, that the number of arcs traversed by such a message is bounded by a function of the number of arc reversals performed by the processors. In the absence of further topological changes, the number of arc reversals is bounded, and, therefore, the total number of arcs traversed by a message is also bounded (Exercise 5.4). This is in contrast to the shortest path method, in which a cycle can be formed and a message can circulate an unbounded number of times in that cycle (cf. Fig. 8.5.2).

For the second property, we claim that if a numbered reversal algorithm has terminated, resulting in a particular DAG and a set P of simple positive paths, and if a topological change occurs, then any path in P that is unaffected by the topological change is also unaffected by future iterations of the algorithm. To see this, first suppose that a new arc is added. Since at termination, processor 0 was the only sink and no new sinks can be created by the addition of an arc, we conclude that the new DAG is also oriented and therefore does not change in the future. Now suppose that an arc is removed, but that a path $p = (i_1, i_2, \ldots, i_K, 0) \in P$ from a processor i_1 to 0 is unaffected. Since the arc $(i_K, 0)$ has not been removed and processor 0 never reverses its arcs, processor i_K never becomes a sink. Thus, processor i_K does not reverse its incident arcs and, therefore, processor i_{K-1} never becomes a sink. Proceeding backwards, we see that none of the processors on the path p ever becomes a sink and the path p remains unaffected. This is a major difference with our earlier algorithm that was based on the shortest path problem (compare with Fig. 8.5.3).

Information Broadcast in a Failure–Prone Network

We have considered so far the problem of establishing loop–free paths along which the nodes of the network can communicate with the center. These paths can also be used to solve the reverse problem, whereby the center wishes to communicate with the processors. In particular these paths can be used to broadcast some information from the center to every node. We discuss briefly some approaches to this problem.

Suppose that the center has some information that we model as a variable V taking values from some set. The value of this variable changes with time, and the center wishes, roughly speaking, that every other processor is to know, after a while, the current value of this variable. For example, V could represent the status of one of the outgoing communication links from the center; in this case, when the information broadcast algorithm is executed with every node independently playing the role of the center, it is usually called a *topology broadcast algorithm*. Alternatively, V could be a command from the center to start a certain distributed algorithm together with the information needed by each processor to execute this algorithm.

More precisely, we assume that after some initial time, several changes of V and several changes of the network topology occur, but there is some time after which there are no changes of either V or the network topology. We wish to design an algorithm by which all processors, after a finite time from the last change, are to know the correct value of V.

The simplest solution to the broadcast problem, widely used in data communication networks, is the so called *flooding* scheme, whereby the center (which holds the value of V) sends an update message with the most recent value of V to all its neighbors following each change of V. The neighbors send the message to their neighbors except for the one that they heard the message from, etc. To avoid infinite circulation of messages, a sequence number is appended to the value of V. This number is incremented with each new message issued by the center. A processor then accepts a new value of V and propagates it further only if it carries a sequence number that is larger than the one stored in its memory; otherwise it simply discards the corresponding message. To cope with situations where the network becomes disconnected, we require that when a link becomes operational after being down, the end processors exchange their stored values of V together with the corresponding sequence numbers. This flooding scheme works fairly well in practice, and requires less than $2|A|$ messages per new value of V, where

$|A|$ is the number of bidirectional network links. In fact, the scheme does not require the assumption that links preserve the order of transmission of messages; the sequence numbers can be used to recognize the correct order of messages.

One drawback of this flooding scheme is the extra overhead required for the sequence number. Usually, this number is encoded in a binary field of fixed length, which must be large enough to ensure that wraparound will never occur between startup and shutdown of the system. A second drawback is that when a processor crashes, it must remember the last sequence number it used at the time of the crash if there is a possibility that the processor will be repaired before the entire system is shut down.

We now discuss briefly an alternative to the use of sequence numbers. Here each processor i stores in its memory the value V_j^i latest received from each of its neighbors j and also maintains in its memory the value of V_i it thinks is the correct one. Each time V_i changes, its value is transmitted to all neighbors of i along each of the currently operating links incident to i; also, when a link (i, j) becomes operational after being down, the end nodes i and j exchange their current values V_i and V_j, that is, i sends V_i to j, which is stored as V_i^j, and j sends V_j to i, which is stored as V_j^i.

The algorithm description will be completed once we give the rule for changing the value V_i of each processor i. There are a number of possibilities along these lines, but the main idea is as follows.

Suppose we have an algorithm running in our system that maintains a tree of directed paths from all processors to the center (i.e., a tree rooted at the center; see Fig. 8.5.10). What we mean here is that this algorithm constructs such a tree within finite time following the last change in the network topology. Every node i except for the center has a unique successor $s(i)$ in such a tree, and we assume that this successor eventually becomes known to i. The rule for changing V_i then is for node i to make it equal to the value $V_{s(i)}^i$ latest transmitted by the successor $s(i)$ within finite time after either the current successor transmits a new value or the successor itself changes. It is evident, under these assumptions, that each node i will have the correct value V_i within finite time following the last change in V or in the network topology.

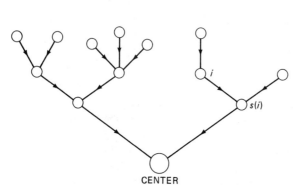

CENTER

Figure 8.5.10 Information broadcast over a tree rooted at the center that initially holds the value V. Here there is a unique directed path from every processor to the center and a unique successor $s(i)$ of every node i on the tree. The idea of the algorithm to broadcast V is to maintain such a tree (in the presence of topological changes) and to require each node i to (eventually) adopt the latest received message from its successor $s(i)$ (i.e., $V_i = V_{s(i)}^i$). This guarantees that the correct information will eventually be propagated and adopted along the tree even after a finite number of topological changes that may require the restructuring of the tree several times.

It should be clear that there are many candidate algorithms that maintain a tree rooted at the center in the face of topological changes. Two possibilities are the full and partial reversal algorithms of this section, where the successor $s(i)$ of a node i is selected arbitrarily among the neighbors j for which the arc (i, j) is oriented from i to j. Another scheme is given in [Spi85c] and [SpG87], where the idea of information broadcast without sequence numbers was first introduced. A detailed presentation, together with additional discussion of topological change broadcasting is given in Section 5.3 of [BeG87].

EXERCISES

5.1. Consider the graph $G = (N, A)$, where $N = \{0, 1, \ldots, n\}$, and $A = \{(i, i + 1) \mid 0 \leq i \leq n - 1\}$. Suppose that each arc $(i, i + 1)$ is initially oriented to point toward node $i + 1$. Calculate the total number of full arc reversals to be performed by the processors before the full reversal algorithm terminates. Check your answer with Fig. 8.5.5 for the case $n = 3$.

5.2. Let $G = (N, A)$ be a directed acyclic graph and suppose that $(i, j) \notin A$ and $(j, i) \notin A$ for some $i, j \in N$. Let $A' = A \cup \{(i, j)\}$ and $A'' = A \cup \{(j, i)\}$. Show that at least one of the graphs (N, A') and (N, A'') is acyclic.

5.3. Consider the partial reversal algorithm on a connected graph with a fixed topology. Let $X_i(t)$ be the number of times, up to time t, that processor i has performed a partial arc reversal.

    (a) Show that if $(i, j) \in A$, then between any three consecutive partial arc reversals by processor i, processor j must have performed at least one partial arc reversal.

    (b) Show that $X_i(t) \leq 2X_j(t) + 2$ for all $(i, j) \in A$.

    (c) Show that the algorithm eventually terminates and bound the total number of partial arc reversals until termination.

5.4. Suppose that the processors are using either the full or the partial reversal algorithm and that some processor sends a message, attempting to communicate with the center, before the algorithm terminates. This message is forwarded by other processors along arcs that are oriented away from the forwarding processor. Assuming that no topological changes occur, show that the total number of arcs traversed by the message, until it reaches the center, is bounded by some function of the number of processors. *Hint:* For the partial reversal algorithm, use the result of Exercise 5.3.

NOTES AND SOURCES

8.1 The idea of detecting termination through the use of acknowledgments is implicit in some distributed shortest path routing and network resynchronization algorithms developed for use in data communication networks (cf. Example 8.3; see [Gal76], [SMG78], [Fin79], and [Seg83]). The termination detection procedure of this section is due to [DiS80]. For related work see [Apt86], [ChM82], [DFV83], [Eri88], [Fra80], [HaZ87], [MiC82], [SSP85], and [Ver87].

8.2 The snapshot algorithm is from [ChL85]. A discussion of local and global clocks, and of the issues related to the comparison of the times at which different events take place at different processors can be found in [Lam78]. See [GaB87] for the use of snapshots in the context of a distributed implementation of simulated annealing.

8.3 A version of the resource allocation problem has been first formulated in [Dij71]. A probabilistic algorithm for this problem was given in [LeR81]. The algorithm presented in this section is from [ChM84] and is closely related to the arc reversal algorithm of Section 8.5. See [Bar86] and [BaG87] for the analysis and the optimization of the concurrency measure M.

8.4 Methods for the simulation of discrete event systems that do not use rollback are surveyed in [Mis86]. See also [ChM81] for a particular such method. Synchronization by rollback has been introduced in [Jef85]. The rate of progress of a simulation when the rollback mechanism is used has been studied in a probabilistic framework in [LMS83] and [MiM84], for the case of two processors. The use of the snapshot algorithm for monitoring the progress of the simulation is discussed in [Sam85b] and [Gaf86]. The relation between rollback and the asynchronous Bellman–Ford algorithm, and its communication complexity implications, are new.

8.5 The arc reversal algorithms of this section are from [GaB81]. The topology broadcast problem is discussed in [Spi85c], [Gaf86], [HuS87a], [HuS87b], and [SpG87]. The idea of maintaining a tree in the face of topological changes along which to broadcast information, is implicit in [Spi85c] and [SpG87], and was articulated by E. M. Gafni (private communication). Flooding is used in many data networks for information broadcast, including the ARPANET. Some difficulties with the ARPANET algorithm are discussed in [Per83] and [BeG87]. For a complexity analysis of flooding, see [Top87].

A

Linear Algebra and Analysis

In this appendix, we collect definitions, notational conventions, and several results on linear algebra and analysis that are used extensively in the book. We omit some proofs that are either elementary or too involved. In any case, it is assumed that the reader has some basic background on the subject. Related and additional material can be found in [Gan59], [HoK71], [LaT85], and [Str76] (linear algebra), and in [Rud76] and [Ash72] (analysis).

We will be considering both real and complex vectors and matrices. Many results are stated for the complex case, but the reader should have no difficulty in converting them to the real case.

Notation

If S is a set and x is an element of S, we write $x \in S$. A set can be specified in the form $S = \{x \mid x \text{ satisfies } P\}$, as the set of all elements satisfying property P. The union of two sets S and T is denoted by $S \cup T$ and their intersection by $S \cap T$. The symbols $\exists$ and $\forall$ have the meanings "there exists" and "for all," respectively.

Let $\Re$ be the set of real numbers and let $\bar{\Re}$ be the set of real numbers together with ∞ and $-\infty$. If $a, b \in \bar{\Re}$ and $a \leq b$, the notation $[a, b]$ stands for the set of all $x \in \bar{\Re}$ such that $a \leq x \leq b$. Similarly, if $a < b$, the notation (a, b) stands for the set of all $x \in \Re$ such that $a < x < b$. Notations such as $[a, b)$ and $(a, b]$ are to be interpreted accordingly.

If f is a function, we use the notation $f : A \mapsto B$ to indicate the fact that f is defined on a set A (its *domain*) and takes values in a set B (its *range*).

Let A be some subset of $\Re$ and let $f : A \mapsto \Re$ and $g : A \mapsto \Re$ be some functions. The notation $f(x) = O\big(g(x)\big)$ [respectively, $f(x) = \Omega\big(g(x)\big)$] means that there exists a positive constant c and some x_0 such that for every $x \in A$ satisfying $x \geq x_0$, we have $|f(x)| \leq cg(x)$ [respectively, $f(x) \geq cg(x)$]. The notation $f(x) = \Theta\big(g(x)\big)$ means that both $f(x) = O\big(g(x)\big)$ and $f(x) = \Omega\big(g(x)\big)$ are true.

Throughout the text, we use $\log x$ to denote the base 2 logarithm of x and $\ln n$ to denote the natural logarithm of x, that is, $x = 2^{\log x} = e^{\ln x}$.

Vectors and Matrices

Let $\mathcal{C}$ be the set of complex numbers. For any $c \in \mathcal{C}$, let $\bar{c}$ be its complex conjugate, and let $|c|$ be its magnitude. Let $\Re^n$ (respectively, $\mathcal{C}^n$) be the set of n–dimensional real (respectively, complex) vectors. For any $x \in \mathcal{C}^n$, we use x_i to indicate its ith *coordinate*, also called its ith *component*. Vectors in $\mathcal{C}^n$ will be viewed as column vectors, unless the contrary is explicitly stated. For any $x \in \mathcal{C}^n$, we let x' be its transpose, which is an n–dimensional row vector; we also let x^* be the conjugate transpose of x. For any two vectors $x, y \in \mathcal{C}^n$, their *inner product* $\langle x, y \rangle$ is defined to be equal to $x^* y = \sum_{i=1}^n \bar{x}_i y_i$. For real vectors $x, y \in \Re^n$, their inner product is equal to $x'y$. Any two vectors $x, y \in \mathcal{C}^n$ satisfying $x^* y = 0$ are called *orthogonal*.

For any matrix A, we use A_{ij}, $[A]_{ij}$, or a_{ij} to denote its ijth entry. The *transpose* of A, denoted by A', is defined by $[A']_{ij} = a_{ji}$ and its complex conjugate transpose, denoted by A^*, is defined by $[A^*]_{ij} = \bar{a}_{ji}$. For any two matrices A and B of compatible dimensions, we have $(AB)' = B'A'$ and $(AB)^* = B^* A^*$.

Let A be a square matrix. We say that A is *symmetric* if $A' = A$. We say that A is *diagonal* if $[A]_{ij} = 0$ whenever $i \neq j$. It is *tridiagonal* if $[A]_{ij} = 0$ for all i and j such that $|i - j| > 1$. It is *lower triangular* if $[A]_{ij} = 0$ whenever $i < j$ and *strictly lower triangular* if $[A]_{ij} = 0$ whenever $i \leq j$. It is *upper* (respectively, *strictly upper*) *triangular* if its transpose is lower (respectively, strictly lower) triangular. It is *triangular* if it is upper or lower triangular. We use I to denote the identity matrix. The *determinant* of A is denoted by $\det(A)$.

Positive Vectors and Matrices

If w is a vector in $\Re^n$, the notations $w > 0$ and $w \geq 0$ indicate that all coordinates of w are positive or nonnegative, respectively. Similarly, if A is a real matrix, the notations $A > 0$ and $A \geq 0$ indicate that all entries of A are positive or nonnegative, respectively. For any two vectors w, v, the notation $w > v$ means $w - v > 0$. The notations $w \geq v$, $w < v$, $A < B$, etc. are to be interpreted accordingly.

Given a vector $w \in \mathcal{C}^n$, we denote by $|w|$ the vector whose ith coordinate is equal to the magnitude of the ith coordinate of w. Similarly, for any matrix A, we denote by $|A|$ the matrix whose entries are equal to the magnitudes of the corresponding entries of A.

Subspaces and Linear Independence

A subset S of C^n is called a *subspace* of C^n if $ax + by \in S$ for every $x, y \in S$ and every $a, b \in C$. If S is a subspace of C^n and x is some vector in C^n, then the set $x + S = \{z \in C^n \mid z - x \in S\}$ is called a *linear manifold*. Given a finite collection $F = \{x^1, \ldots, x^K\}$ of elements of C^n, the *span* of F is the subspace of C^n defined as the set of all vectors y of the form $y = \sum_{k=1}^{K} a_k x^k$, where each a_k is a complex scalar. The vectors $x^1, \ldots, x^K \in C^n$ are called *linearly independent* if there exists no set of complex coefficients $a_1, \ldots, a_K$ such that $\sum_{k=1}^{K} a_k x^k = 0$, unless $a_k = 0$ for each k. An equivalent definition is that $x^1 \neq 0$ and for every $k > 1$, the vector x^k does not belong to the span of $x^1, \ldots, x^{k-1}$. It can be seen that if the vectors $x^1, \ldots, x^K$ are nonzero and mutually orthogonal, then they are automatically linearly independent. Given a subspace S of C^n, a *basis* for S is a collection of vectors that are linearly independent and whose span is equal to S. Every basis of a given subspace has the same number of vectors and this number is called the *dimension* of S. In particular, the dimension of C^n is equal to n. Another important fact is that every subspace has an *orthogonal basis*, that is, a basis consisting of mutually orthogonal vectors.

Vector Norms

Definition A.1.   A *norm* $\| \cdot \|$ on C^n is a mapping that assigns a real number $\|x\|$ to every $x \in C^n$ and that has the following properties:

(a) $\|x\| \geq 0$ for all $x \in C^n$.
(b) $\|cx\| = |c| \cdot \|x\|$ for every $c \in C$ and every $x \in C^n$.
(c) $\|x\| = 0$ if and only if $x = 0$.
(d) $\|x + y\| \leq \|x\| + \|y\|$ for all $x, y \in C^n$.

A norm on $\Re^n$ is defined by replacing C and C^n by $\Re$ and $\Re^n$, respectively, in the above.

The *Euclidean norm* $\| \cdot \|_2$ is defined by

$$\|x\|_2 = (x^* x)^{1/2} = \left(\sum_{i=1}^{n} |x_i|^2 \right)^{1/2}, \tag{A.1}$$

and $\Re^n$, equipped with this norm, is called a *Euclidean space*. The Euclidean norm satisfies the *Schwartz inequality*

$$|x^* y| \leq \|x\|_2 \cdot \|y\|_2, \tag{A.2}$$

and the following theorem:

Proposition A.1.   (*Pythagorean Theorem*) If x and y are orthogonal then $\|x + y\|_2^2 = \|x\|_2^2 + \|y\|_2^2$.

The *maximum norm* $\| \cdot \|_\infty$ (also called *sup–norm* or ℓ_∞–*norm*) is defined by

$$\|x\|_\infty = \max_i |x_i|. \tag{A.3}$$

For any positive vector w ($w > 0$), we define the *weighted maximum norm* $\| \cdot \|_\infty^w$ by

$$\|x\|_\infty^w = \max_i \left| \frac{x_i}{w_i} \right|. \tag{A.4}$$

The ℓ_1–*norm* $\| \cdot \|_1$ is defined by

$$\|x\|_1 = \sum_{i=1}^{n} |x_i|. \tag{A.5}$$

Proposition A.2. For any $x \in \mathcal{C}^n$, we have:

(a) $\|x\|_\infty \le \|x\|_2 \le n^{1/2}\|x\|_\infty$.
(b) $\|x\|_1 \le n^{1/2}\|x\|_2 \le n^{1/2}\|x\|_1$.

Proof.

(a) This is a straightforward consequence of Eqs. (A.1) and (A.3).
(b) Let e be the vector with all coordinates equal to 1. Using Eqs. (A.5) and (A.2), we have

$$\|x\|_1 = e'|x| \le \|e\|_2 \cdot \|x\|_2 = n^{1/2}\|x\|_2.$$

The inequality $\|x\|_2 \le \|x\|_1$ is an easy consequence of Eqs. (A.1) and (A.5).
Q.E.D.

Sequences, Limits, and Continuity

A sequence $\{x^k \mid k = 1, 2, \ldots\}$ (or $\{x^k\}$ for short) of complex numbers is said to *converge* to a complex number x if for every $\epsilon > 0$ there exists some K such that $|x^k - x| < \epsilon$ for every $k \ge K$. A real sequence $\{x^k\}$ is said to converge to ∞ (respectively, $-\infty$) if for every A there exists some K such that $x^k \ge A$ (respectively, $x^k \le A$) for all $k \ge K$. If a sequence converges to some x (possibly infinite), we say that x is the *limit* of x^k; symbolically, $\lim_{k \to \infty} x^k = x$.

A sequence $\{x^k\}$ is said to converge *geometrically* (or *at the rate of a geometric progression*) to x^* if there exist constants $A \ge 0$ and $\alpha \in [0, 1)$ such that $|x^k - x^*| \le A\alpha^k$ for all k.

A sequence $\{x^k\}$ is called a *Cauchy sequence* if for every $\epsilon > 0$, there exists some K such that $|x^k - x^m| < \epsilon$ for all $k \ge K$ and $m \ge K$.

A real sequence $\{x^k\}$ is said to be *bounded above* (respectively, *below*) if there exists some real number A such that $x^k \le A$ (respectively, $x^k \ge A$) for all k. A real sequence is said to be *nonincreasing* (respectively, *nondecreasing*) if $x^{k+1} \leq x^k$ (respectively, $x^{k+1} \geq x^k$) for all k. A complex sequence $\{x^k\}$ is called *bounded* if the sequence $\{|x^k|\}$ is bounded above.

Proposition A.3.   Every nonincreasing or nondecreasing real sequence converges to a possibly infinite number. If it is also bounded, then it converges to a finite real number.

The *supremum* of a nonempty set $A \subset \Re$, denoted by $\sup A$, is defined as the smallest real number x such that $x \geq y$ for all $y \in A$. If no such real number exists, we say that the supremum of A is infinite. Similarly, the *infimum* of A, denoted by $\inf A$, is defined as the largest real number x such that $x \leq y$ for all $y \in A$, and is equal to $-\infty$ if no such real number exists. Given a sequence $\{x^k\}$ of real numbers, the supremum of the sequence, denoted by $\sup_k x^k$, is defined as $\sup\{x^k \mid k = 1, 2, \ldots\}$. The infimum of a sequence is similarly defined. Given a sequence $\{x^k\}$, let $y^m = \sup\{x^k \mid k \geq m\}$, $z^m = \inf\{x^k \mid k \geq m\}$. The sequences $\{y^m\}$ and $\{z^m\}$ are nonincreasing and nondecreasing, respectively, and therefore have a (possibly infinite) limit (Prop. A.3). The limit of y^m is denoted by $\limsup_{m \to \infty} x^m$ and the limit of z^m is denoted by $\liminf_{m \to \infty} x^m$.

Proposition A.4.   Let $\{x^k\}$ be a real sequence.

(a) There holds

$$\inf_k x^k \leq \liminf_{k \to \infty} x^k \leq \limsup_{k \to \infty} x^k \leq \sup_k x^k.$$

(b) The sequence $\{x^k\}$ converges if and only if $\liminf_{k \to \infty} x^k = \limsup_{k \to \infty} x^k$ and, in that case, both of these quantities are equal to the limit of x^k.

A sequence $\{x^k\}$ of vectors in $\mathcal{C}^n$ is said to converge to some $x \in \mathcal{C}^n$ if the ith coordinate of x^k converges to the ith coordinate of x for every i. The notation $\lim_{k \to \infty} x^k = x$ is used again. Convergence is said to occur geometrically if each coordinate of x^k converges geometrically. Finally, a sequence of vectors is called a Cauchy sequence (respectively, bounded) if each coordinate is a Cauchy sequence (respectively, bounded).

Definition A.2.   We say that some $x \in \mathcal{C}^n$ is a *limit point* of a sequence $\{x^k\}$ in $\mathcal{C}^n$ if there exists a subsequence of $\{x^k\}$ that converges to x. Let A be a subset of $\mathcal{C}^n$. We say that $x \in \mathcal{C}^n$ is a limit point of A if there exists a sequence $\{x^k\}$, consisting of elements of A, that converges to x.

Proposition A.5.

(a) A bounded sequence of vectors in $\mathcal{C}^n$ converges if and only if it has a unique limit point.

(b) A sequence in $\mathcal{C}^n$ converges if and only if it is a Cauchy sequence.

(c) Every bounded sequence in C^n has at least one limit point.

(d) If $\{x^k\}$ is a real sequence and $\limsup_{k\to\infty} x^k$ (respectively, $\liminf_{k\to\infty} x^k$) is finite, then it is the largest (respectively, smallest) limit point of the sequence $\{x^k\}$.

Definition A.3.   A set $A \subset C^n$ is called *closed* if it contains all of its limit points. It is called *open* if its complement is closed. It is called *bounded* if there exists some $c \in \Re$ such that the magnitude of any coordinate of any element of A is less than c. A closed and bounded subset of C^n is called *compact*. Let $\|\cdot\|$ be a vector norm on C^n. If $A \subset C^n$ and $x \in A$, we say that x is an *interior* point of A if there exists some $\epsilon > 0$ such that $\{y \in C^n \mid \|x - y\| < \epsilon\} \subset A$.

Proposition A.6.

(a) The union of finitely many closed sets is closed.

(b) The intersection of closed sets is closed.

(c) The union of open sets is open.

(d) The intersection of finitely many open sets is open.

(e) A subset of C^n is open if and only if all of its elements are interior points.

Let A be a subset of C^m and let $f : A \mapsto C^n$ be some function. Let x be a limit point of A. If the sequence $\{f(x^k)\}$ has a common limit z for every sequence $\{x^k\}$ of elements of A such that $\lim_{k\to\infty} x^k = x$, we write $\lim_{y\to x} f(y) = z$. If A is a subset of $\Re$ and x is a limit point of A, the notation $\lim_{y\uparrow x} f(y)$ [respectively, $\lim_{y\downarrow x} f(y)$] will stand for the limit of $f(x^k)$, where $\{x^k\}$ is any sequence of elements of A converging to x and satisfying $x^k \leq x$ (respectively, $x^k \geq x$), assuming that the limit exists and is independent of the choice of the sequence $\{x^k\}$.

Definition A.4.   Let A be a subset of C^m.

(a) A function $f : A \mapsto C^n$ is said to be *continuous* at a point $x \in A$ if $\lim_{y\to x} f(y) = f(x)$. It is said to be continuous on A if it is continuous at every point $x \in A$.

(b) A real valued function $f : A \mapsto \Re$ is called *upper semicontinuous* (respectively, *lower semicontinuous*) at a vector $x \in A$ if $f(x) \geq \limsup_{k\to\infty} f(x^k)$ [respectively, $f(x) \leq \liminf_{k\to\infty} f(x^k)$] for every sequence $\{x^k\}$ of elements of A converging to x.

(c) Let A be a subset of $\Re$. A function $f : A \mapsto C^n$ is called *right–continuous* (respectively, *left–continuous*) at a point $x \in A$ if $\lim_{y\downarrow x} f(y) = f(x)$ [respectively, $\lim_{y\uparrow x} f(y) = f(x)$].

It is easily seen that when A is a subset of $\Re$, a nondecreasing and right–continuous (respectively, left–continuous) function $f : A \mapsto \Re$ is upper (respectively, lower) semicontinuous.

Proposition A.7.

(a) The composition of two continuous functions is continuous.

(b) Any vector norm on C^n is a continuous function.

(c) Let $f : C^m \mapsto C^n$ be continuous, and let $A \subset C^n$ be open (respectively, closed). Then the set $\{x \in C^m \mid f(x) \in A\}$ is open (respectively, closed).

Proposition A.8.   (*Weierstrass' Theorem*) Let A be a nonempty compact subset of C^n. If $f : A \mapsto \Re$ is continuous, then there exist $x, y \in A$ such that $f(x) = \inf_{z \in A} f(z)$ and $f(y) = \sup_{z \in A} f(z)$.

Proof. Let $\{z^k\}$ be a sequence of elements of A such that $\lim_{k \to \infty} f(z^k) = \inf_{z \in A} f(z)$. Since A is bounded, this sequence has at least one limit point x [Prop. A.5(c)]. Since A is closed, x belongs to A. Finally, the continuity of f implies that $f(x) = \lim_{k \to \infty} f(z^k) = \inf_{z \in A} f(z)$. The proof concerning the supremum of f is similar.   **Q.E.D.**

Proposition A.9.   For any two norms $\| \cdot \|$ and $\| \cdot \|'$ on C^n, there exists some positive constant $c \in \Re$ such that $\|x\| \le c\|x\|'$ for all $x \in C^n$.

Proof. Let a be the minimum of $\|x\|'$ over the set of all $x \in C^n$ such that $\|x\| = 1$. The latter set is closed and bounded and, therefore, the minimum is attained at some $\tilde{x}$ (Prop. A.8) that must be nonzero since $\|\tilde{x}\| = 1$. For any $x \in C^n$, $x \ne 0$, the $\| \cdot \|$ norm of $x/\|x\|$ is equal to 1. Therefore,

$$0 < a = \|\tilde{x}\|' \le \left\| \frac{x}{\|x\|} \right\|' = \frac{\|x\|'}{\|x\|}, \qquad \forall x \ne 0,$$

which proves the desired result with $c = 1/a$.   **Q.E.D.**

Proposition A.10.   The set of interior points of a set $A \subset C^n$ does not depend on the choice of norm.

Proposition A.11.   Let $\| \cdot \|$ be an arbitrary vector norm. A sequence $\{x^k\}$ converges to x if and only if $\lim_{k \to \infty} \|x^k - x\| = 0$. In particular, x^k converges to x geometrically if and only if $\|x^k - x\|$ converges to zero geometrically.

Proof. By definition, x^k converges to x if and only if $\lim_{k \to \infty} \|x^k - x\|_\infty = 0$ and the first result follows from Prop. A.9. The result concerning geometric convergence follows similarly.   **Q.E.D.**

Definition A.5.   Let A be a subset of C^m. Let $\{f^k\}$ be a sequence of functions from A into C^n. We say that f^k converges *pointwise* to a function $f : A \mapsto C^n$ if $\lim_{k \to \infty} f^k(x) = f(x)$ for every $x \in A$. We say that f^k converges to f *uniformly* if for every $\epsilon > 0$, there exists some K such that $\|f^k(x) - f(x)\| < \epsilon$ for all $k \ge K$ and $x \in A$.

(Using Prop. A.9, it is seen that uniform convergence is independent of the choice of the norm $\| \cdot \|$.)

Matrix Norms

A norm $\| \cdot \|$ on the set of $n \times n$ complex matrices is a mapping that assigns to any $n \times n$ matrix A a real number $\|A\|$ and that has the same properties as vector norms do when the matrix is viewed as an element of C^{n^2}.

We are mainly interested in *induced norms*, which are constructed as follows. Given any vector norm $\| \cdot \|$, the corresponding induced matrix norm, also denoted by $\| \cdot \|$, is defined by

$$\|A\| = \max_{\{x \in C^n | \; \|x\|=1\}} \|Ax\|. \tag{A.6}$$

The set over which the maximization takes place in Eq. (A.6) is closed [Prop. A.7(c)] and bounded; the function being maximized is continuous [Prop. A.7(b)] and therefore the maximum is attained (Prop. A.8). It is easily verified that for any vector norm, Eq. (A.6) defines a bona fide matrix norm having all the required properties. Induced norms have the following additional properties:

Proposition A.12. Let $\| \cdot \|$ be an induced norm on the set of $n \times n$ matrices. Then:

   (a) $\|A\| = \max_{x \neq 0} \|Ax\|/\|x\|$.
   (b) $\|Ax\| \leq \|A\| \cdot \|x\|$ for all $x \in C^n$.
   (c) $\|AB\| \leq \|A\| \cdot \|B\|$, where A and B are $n \times n$ matrices.

     Proof. Part (a) follows because any nonzero vector x can be scaled so that its norm is equal to 1, without changing the value of the ratio $\|Ax\|/\|x\|$. Part (b) then follows immediately. For part (c), we use part (b) twice to obtain $\|ABx\| \leq \|A\| \cdot \|Bx\| \leq \|A\| \cdot \|B\| \cdot \|x\|$. Since this is true for all x, the result follows from Eq. (A.6).   **Q.E.D.**

     The examples of vector norms given earlier induce certain matrix norms and, by abuse of notation, we use the same symbols to denote them. They have the following properties:

Proposition A.13. Let A be an $n \times n$ matrix. Then:

   (a) $\|A\|_\infty^w = \max_i \frac{1}{w_i} \sum_{j=1}^n |a_{ij}| w_j$.   (A.7)
   (b) $\|A\|_1 = \max_j \sum_{i=1}^n |a_{ij}|$.   (A.8)
   (c) $\|A\|_1 = \|A'\|_\infty$.
   (d) $\|A\|_\infty \leq n^{1/2} \|A\|_2$.
   (e) $\|A\|_1 \leq n^{1/2} \|A\|_2$.
   (f) $\|A\|_\infty \cdot \|A\|_1 \leq n \|A\|_2^2$.

Proof.

(a) Let x be such that $\|x\|_\infty^w = 1$. We then have $|x_i| \le w_i$ for all i and it follows that

$$\|Ax\|_\infty^w = \max_i \frac{1}{w_i} \left| \sum_{j=1}^n a_{ij} x_j \right| \le \max_i \frac{1}{w_i} \sum_{j=1}^n |a_{ij}| w_j.$$

Since this is true for all such x, we conclude that $\|A\|_\infty^w$ is no larger than the right–hand side of Eq. (A.7). Let i be an index for which the maximum in the right–hand side of Eq. (A.7) is attained. Let x be a vector whose jth coordinate x_j satisfies $a_{ij} x_j = |a_{ij}| w_j$ for each j. In particular, $|x_j| = w_j$ for each j and $\|x\|_\infty^w = 1$. Furthermore, the ith coordinate of Ax is equal to $\sum_{j=1}^n |a_{ij}| w_j$. Therefore, $\|Ax\|_\infty^w$ is at least as large as the right–hand side of Eq. (A.7). This implies the same inequality for $\|A\|_\infty^w$ and completes the proof.

(b) The proof is similar. A little algebra shows that $\|A\|_1$ is no larger than the right–hand side of Eq. (A.8). Then consider a vector x with all entries equal to zero, except for the entry corresponding to the maximizing index in Eq. (A.8), which is equal to 1. For this vector, $\|x\|_1 = 1$ and $\|Ax\|_1$ is equal to the right–hand side of Eq. (A.8), which shows that $\|A\|_1$ is no smaller than the right–hand side of Eq. (A.8).

(c) This is immediate from Eqs. (A.7) and (A.8).

(d) Using Prop. A.2, we have

$$\|Ax\|_\infty \le \|Ax\|_2 \le \|A\|_2 \cdot \|x\|_2 \le \|A\|_2 n^{1/2} \|x\|_\infty.$$

By dividing with $\|x\|_\infty$ and taking the maximum over all $x \ne 0$, the result is obtained.

(e) The result follows, similarly with part (d), from the inequalities

$$\|Ax\|_1 \le n^{1/2} \|Ax\|_2 \le n^{1/2} \|A\|_2 \cdot \|x\|_2 \le n^{1/2} \|A\|_2 \cdot \|x\|_1.$$

(f) This is obtained by combining parts (d) and (e).   **Q.E.D.**

A more general class of induced matrix norms is defined as follows. Let $\| \cdot \|$ and $\| \cdot \|'$ be vector norms on $\mathcal{C}^m$ and $\mathcal{C}^n$, respectively. (The two norms could be different even if $m = n$.) This pair of vector norms induces a matrix norm defined by

$$\|A\| = \max_{\|x\|' = 1} \|Ax\|,$$

where A is an $m \times n$ matrix. Parts (a) and (b) of Prop. A.12 remain valid, provided that $\|x\|$ is replaced by $\|x\|'$.

Eigenvalues

Definition A.6.   A square matrix A is called *singular* if its determinant is zero. Otherwise it is called *nonsingular* or *invertible*.

Proposition A.14.

(a) Let A be an $n \times n$ matrix. The following are equivalent:
   (i) The matrix A is nonsingular.
   (ii) The matrix A' is nonsingular.
   (iii) For every nonzero $x \in C^n$, we have $Ax \neq 0$.
   (iv) For every $y \in C^n$, there exists a unique $x \in C^n$ such that $Ax = y$.
   (v) There exists a matrix B such that $AB = I = BA$.
   (vi) The columns of A are linearly independent.

(b) Assuming that A is nonsingular, the matrix B of statement (v) (called the *inverse* of A and denoted by A^{-1}) is unique. Furthermore, if A is real, then A^{-1} is also real.

(c) For any two square invertible matrices A and B of the same dimensions, we have $(AB)^{-1} = B^{-1}A^{-1}$.

Definition A.7.   The *characteristic polynomial* ϕ of an $n \times n$ matrix A is defined by $\phi(\lambda) = \det(\lambda I - A)$, where I is the identity matrix of the same size as A. The n (possibly repeated) roots of ϕ are called the *eigenvalues* of A. A vector $x \in C^n$ such that $Ax = \lambda x$ is called an *eigenvector* of A associated with λ.

We note that the eigenvalues and eigenvectors of A could be complex even if A is real.

Proposition A.15.

(a) A complex number λ is an eigenvalue of a square matrix A if and only if there exists a nonzero eigenvector associated with λ.

(b) A square matrix A is singular if and only if it has an eigenvalue that is equal to zero.

Definition A.8.

(a) A matrix J of size $m \times m$ is said to be a *Jordan block* if it is of the form

$$
J = \begin{bmatrix} \lambda & 1 & 0 & 0 \\ 0 & \ddots & \ddots & 0 \\ \vdots & \ddots & \ddots & 1 \\ 0 & \cdots & 0 & \lambda \end{bmatrix}.
$$

That is, $J_{i,i+1} = 1$ $(1 \le i \le m-1)$, $J_{ii} = \lambda$ $(1 \le i \le m)$, and $J_{ij} = 0$ if $j \ne i$ and $j \ne i+1$.

(b) A square matrix J is said to be a *Jordan matrix* if it has the structure

$$
J = \begin{bmatrix}
J_1 & 0 & \cdots & 0 \\
0 & \ddots & \ddots & \vdots \\
\vdots & \ddots & \ddots & 0 \\
0 & \cdots & 0 & J_L
\end{bmatrix},
$$

where each J_ℓ, $\ell = 1, \ldots, L$, is a Jordan block. That is, J is block–diagonal and each diagonal block is a Jordan block.

Proposition A.16.   (*Jordan Normal Form*)

(a) Every square matrix A can be represented in the form $A = SJS^{-1}$, where S is a nonsingular matrix and J is a Jordan matrix.

(b) The Jordan matrix J associated with A is unique up to the rearrangement of its blocks.

(c) The diagonal entries of J are the eigenvalues of A repeated according to their multiplicities.

Proposition A.17.

(a) The eigenvalues of a triangular matrix are equal to its diagonal entries.

(b) If S is a nonsingular matrix and $B = SAS^{-1}$, then the eigenvalues of A and B coincide.

(c) The eigenvalues of $cI + A$ are equal to $c + \lambda_1, \ldots, c + \lambda_n$, where $\lambda_1, \ldots, \lambda_n$ are the eigenvalues of A.

(d) The eigenvalues of A^k are equal to $\lambda_1^k, \ldots, \lambda_n^k$, where $\lambda_1, \ldots, \lambda_n$ are the eigenvalues of A.

(e) If A is nonsingular, then the eigenvalues of A^{-1} are the reciprocals of the eigenvalues of A.

(f) The eigenvalues of A and A' coincide.

Proof.

(a) If a_{ii} is the ith diagonal entry of a triangular $n \times n$ matrix A, then $\det(\lambda I - A) = \prod_{i=1}^{n} (\lambda - a_{ii})$, which has roots $a_{11}, \ldots, a_{nn}$.

(b) Let $A = S_1 J S_1^{-1}$, where J is a Jordan matrix associated with A (Prop. A.16). Then $B = (SS_1)J(SS_1)^{-1}$. Thus, J is a Jordan matrix associated with B. From Prop. A.16(c), A and B have the same eigenvalues.

(c) If $A = SJS^{-1}$, where J is a Jordan matrix, then $cI + A = S(cI + J)S^{-1}$. It is easy to see that $cI + J$ is a Jordan matrix and its ith diagonal entry is equal to $\lambda_i + c$, where λ_i is the ith diagonal entry of J. The result follows from Prop. A.16(c).

(d) If $A = SJS^{-1}$, where J is a Jordan matrix, then $A^k = SJ^kS^{-1}$. From part (b) of the present proposition, the eigenvalues of A^k coincide with the eigenvalues of J^k. Since J is triangular, J^k is also triangular and its eigenvalues are equal to its diagonal entries; the latter are equal to the kth powers of the diagonal entries of J, that is, the kth powers of the eigenvalues of A.

(e) If $A = SJS^{-1}$, then $A^{-1} = SJ^{-1}S^{-1}$ and, by part (b), the eigenvalues of A^{-1} are equal to the eigenvalues of J^{-1}. It is easy to show that the inverse of a triangular matrix is also triangular and the diagonal entries of the inverse are the reciprocals of the diagonal entries of the original matrix. From part (a), the eigenvalues of J^{-1} are equal to the reciprocals of the diagonal entries of J; they are, therefore, equal to the reciprocals of the eigenvalues of A.

(f) Notice that $A' = (S^{-1})'J'S'$. From part (b), the eigenvalues of A' coincide with the eigenvalues of J'. From part (a), the eigenvalues of J' are its diagonal entries; these coincide with the diagonal entries of J, which are the eigenvalues of A. **Q.E.D.**

Given a polynomial ϕ and a square matrix A, we define $\phi(A)$ by substituting A for the free variable λ of the polynomial.

Proposition A.18.   (*Cayley–Hamilton Theorem*) If ϕ is the characteristic polynomial of a square matrix A, then $\phi(A) = 0$.

Definition A.9.   The *spectral radius* $\rho(A)$ of a square matrix A is defined as the maximum of the magnitudes of the eigenvalues of A.

It is known that the roots of a polynomial depend continuously on the coefficients of the polynomial. For this reason, the eigenvalues of a square matrix A depend continuously on A, and we obtain the following.

Proposition A.19. $\rho(A)$ is a continuous function of A.

Proposition A.20.   For any induced matrix norm $\| \cdot \|$ and any $n \times n$ matrix A we have

$$\lim_{k \to \infty} \|A^k\|^{1/k} = \rho(A) \leq \|A\|.$$

Proof. Let λ be an eigenvalue of A such that $|\lambda| = \rho(A)$. Let $x \neq 0$ be an eigenvector of A corresponding to the eigenvalue λ normalized so that $\|x\| = 1$. Then $\|A\| \geq \|Ax\| = \|\lambda x\| = |\lambda| = \rho(A)$, which proves the right–hand side inequality. Furthermore, $\|A^k\| \geq \|A^k x\| = \|\lambda^k x\| = |\lambda|^k = \rho(A)^k$, which shows that $\liminf_{k \to \infty} \|A^k\|^{1/k} \geq \rho(A)$. We will now prove a reverse inequality. Let $A = SJS^{-1}$, where J is a Jordan matrix. Then $A^k = SJ^kS^{-1}$ and

$$\|A^k\| \leq \|S\| \cdot \|J^k\| \cdot \|S^{-1}\|.$$

Thus,

$$\limsup_{k \to \infty} \|A^k\|^{1/k} \leq \limsup_{k \to \infty} \left(\|S\| \cdot \|S^{-1}\|\right)^{1/k} \limsup_{k \to \infty} \|J^k\|^{1/k} = \limsup_{k \to \infty} \|J^k\|^{1/k},$$

where we used the fact that $\lim_{k \to \infty} a^{1/k} = 1$ for any positive number a.

Let $\bar{J}$ be one of the Jordan blocks in J, of size $m \times m$. Let λ be the value of its diagonal entries [thus, $|\lambda| \leq \rho(A)$]. A direct computation shows that for $k \geq m$, the entries of $\bar{J}^k$ are given by

$$[\bar{J}^k]_{ij} = \begin{cases} 0, & 0 < j < i, \\ \binom{k}{j-i} \lambda^{k-(j-i)}, & i \leq j \leq m, \end{cases}$$

where

$$\binom{k}{\ell} = \frac{k!}{\ell!(k-\ell)!}$$

is the binomial coefficient. Using the inequality

$$\binom{k}{j-i} \leq k(k-1)\cdots(k-j+i+1) \leq k(k-1)\cdots(k-m+1) \leq k^m,$$

we see that each one of the entries of $\bar{J}^k$ is bounded in magnitude by $k^m |\lambda|^{k-(j-i)} \leq ck^n \rho(A)^k$, where c is a constant such that $|\lambda|^{-(j-i)} \leq c$ for every nonzero eigenvalue λ and any i and j between 1 and n. The same bound is obtained for all entries of J^k. Let c_{ij} be the norm of a matrix with all entries equal to 0, except for the ijth entry, which is equal to 1. Let $C = \sum_{i=1}^n \sum_{j=1}^n c_{ij}$. From the triangle inequality,

$$\|J^k\| \leq Cck^n \rho(A)^k \qquad (A.9)$$

and

$$\limsup_{k \to \infty} \|J^k\|^{1/k} \leq \rho(A) \lim_{k \to \infty} (Cck^n)^{1/k} = \rho(A),$$

which completes the proof. We have used here the fact $\lim_{k \to \infty} k^{1/k} = 1$, which is easily proved by taking logarithms.   **Q.E.D.**

As a corollary of Prop. A.20, we obtain:

Proposition A.21.   Let A be a square matrix. We have $\lim_{k \to \infty} A^k = 0$ if and only if $\rho(A) < 1$.

Proof. If $\rho(A) \geq 1$, then $\|A^k\| \geq \rho(A^k) = \rho(A)^k \geq 1$ and A^k does not converge to zero. If $\rho(A) < 1$, let $\epsilon > 0$ be such that $\rho(A) + \epsilon < 1$. Using Prop. A.20, we have $\|A^k\|^{1/k} \leq \rho(A) + \epsilon < 1$ for all sufficiently large k. It follows that A^k converges to zero. **Q.E.D.**

Definition A.10. The *trace* of a square matrix A, denoted by $\mathrm{tr}(A)$, is defined as the sum of the diagonal entries of A.

Proposition A.22.

(a) The trace of A is equal to the sum of the eigenvalues of A counted according to their multiplicities.

(b) The trace of A^k is equal to the sum of the kth powers of the eigenvalues of A counted according to their multiplicities.

Proof. Consider the characteristic polynomial $\det(\lambda I - A) = c_0 + c_1 \lambda + \cdots + c_{n-1}\lambda^{n-1} + \lambda^n$. From the formula for the determinant, it can be seen that the coefficient c_{n-1} is equal to the negative of the sum of the diagonal entries of A. On the other hand, $\det(\lambda I - A) = \prod_{i=1}^{n}(\lambda - \lambda_i)$, where $\lambda_1, \ldots, \lambda_n$ are the eigenvalues of A. The coefficient of λ^{n-1} is seen to be equal to $-\sum_{i=1}^{n}\lambda_i$ and the result of part (a) follows. Part (b) follows from part (a) and Prop. A.17(d). **Q.E.D.**

Properties of Symmetric and Positive Definite Matrices

Proposition A.23. Let A be a real and symmetric $n \times n$ matrix. Then:

(a) The eigenvalues of A are real.

(b) The Jordan matrix associated to A is diagonal.

(c) The matrix A has a set of n mutually orthogonal, real, and nonzero eigenvectors $x^1, \ldots, x^n$, associated to its eigenvalues $\lambda_1, \ldots, \lambda_n$.

(d) Suppose that the eigenvectors in part (c) have been normalized so that $\|x^k\|_2 = 1$ for each k. Then

$$A = \sum_{k=1}^{n} \lambda_k x^k (x^k)'.$$

Proof.

(a) Let λ be an eigenvalue of A and let x be an associated nonzero eigenvector. Since A is real and symmetric, we have $(x^* A x)^* = x^* A^* x = x^* A x$. Therefore, the expression $x^* A x = x^* \lambda x = \lambda \|x\|_2^2$ is real, which shows that λ is real.

(b) We represent A in the form $A = SJS^{-1}$, where S and J are as in Prop. A.16. Suppose, to derive a contradiction, that J is not diagonal. Consider the smallest i such that $[J]_{i,i+1} = 1$. Let $\lambda = [J]_{ii}$ and let x and y be the ith and $(i+1)$st column, respectively, of the matrix S. By reading the ith and $(i+1)$st column of the equation $AS = SJ$, we obtain $Ax = \lambda x$ and $Ay = x + \lambda y$. The first equation yields $y^*Ax = \lambda y^*x$. The second yields $x^*Ay = x^*x + \lambda x^*y$. We combine these two equalities and the assumption that A is real and symmetric to obtain

$$\lambda y^*x = y^*Ax = (x^*A^*y)^* = (x^*Ay)^* = (x^*x + \lambda x^*y)^* = x^*x + \lambda y^*x,$$

from which we conclude that $x^*x = 0$. Therefore, $x = 0$, which means that a column of S is zero. Using the equivalence of conditions (i) and (vi) in Prop. A.14(a), we see that S is singular, which is a contradiction.

(c) Suppose that λ is an eigenvalue of A and that it has multiplicity m as a root of the characteristic polynomial of A. Then m of the diagonal entries of the Jordan matrix J are equal to λ. Let $x^1, \ldots, x^m$ be the columns of the matrix S corresponding to these diagonal entries. Since J is diagonal and $AS = SJ$, we see that each x^k, $k = 1, \ldots, m$, is an eigenvector of A associated to λ. Furthermore, these eigenvectors are linearly independent because otherwise the matrix S would not be invertible.

Let Q be the span of the vectors $x^1, \ldots, x^m$; its dimension is m because these vectors are linearly independent. For $k = 1, \ldots, m$, let v^k, w^k, be the real and imaginary parts, respectively, of the vector x^k. Since A is a real matrix and since its eigenvalues are real, the equation $Ax^k = \lambda x^k$ implies that $Av^k = \lambda v^k$ and $Aw^k = \lambda w^k$. The span in $\mathcal{C}^n$ of the set of vectors $U = \{v^1, w^1, \ldots, v^m, w^m\}$ contains Q and therefore has dimension at least equal to m. Thus, the set U contains m linearly independent vectors. Furthermore, these vectors are real and they therefore span an m–dimensional subspace H of $\Re^n$. Let $z^1, \ldots, z^m$ be an orthogonal basis for the subspace H. We have already shown that each element of U is an eigenvector of A, with eigenvalue λ. The vectors $z^1, \ldots, z^m$ are, by construction, linear combinations of the elements of U and are themselves eigenvectors.

We have shown so far that to every eigenvalue of multiplicity m, we can associate m real, nonzero, and mutually orthogonal eigenvectors. The proof is completed by observing that eigenvectors associated to different eigenvalues are also orthogonal. Indeed, suppose that $Ax = \lambda_1 x$, $Ay = \lambda_2 y$, and $\lambda_1 \neq \lambda_2$. Then

$$\lambda_1 y^*x = y^*Ax = \left(x^*Ay\right)^* = \lambda_2(x^*y)^* = \lambda_2 y^*x,$$

which shows that $y^*x = 0$.

(d) Let $\lambda_1, \ldots, \lambda_n$ be the eigenvalues of A and let $x^1, \ldots, x^n$ be associated real mutually orthogonal eigenvectors, normalized so that $\|x^k\|_2 = 1$ for each k. These eigenvectors are linearly independent and they therefore span $\Re^n$. Thus, any vector $y \in \Re^n$ can be expressed in the form $y = \sum_{k=1}^{n} c_k x^k$, where $c_1, \ldots, c_n$ are suitable real coefficients. Using the orthogonality of the eigenvectors, we obtain $c_k = y'x^k$. We now notice that

$$\sum_{k=1}^{n} \lambda_k x^k (x^k)' y = \sum_{k=1}^{n} \lambda_k c_k x^k = \sum_{k=1}^{n} c_k A x^k = Ay.$$

Since this equality is true for every $y \in \Re^n$, the proof of part (d) is complete.   **Q.E.D.**

Proposition A.24.   If A is a real and symmetric $n \times n$ matrix, then:

(a) $\|A\|_2 = \rho(A)$.
(b) $\|A\|_2 = \max_{\{x \in \Re^n \mid \|x\|_2 = 1\}} |x' A x|$.

Proof.

(a) We already know that $\|A\|_2 \geq \rho(A)$ (Prop. A.20) and we need to show the reverse inequality. Let $x^1, \ldots, x^n$ and $\lambda_1, \ldots, \lambda_n$ be mutually orthogonal nonzero eigenvectors of A and the corresponding eigenvalues, respectively. We express an arbitrary vector $x \in \mathcal{C}^n$ in the form $x = \sum_{i=1}^{n} c_i x^i$, where each c_i is a suitable complex scalar. Using the orthogonality of the vectors x^i and Prop. A.1, we obtain $\|x\|_2^2 = \sum_{i=1}^{n} |c_i|^2 \cdot \|x^i\|_2^2$. Using Prop. A.1 again, we obtain

$$\|Ax\|_2^2 = \left\| \sum_{i=1}^{n} \lambda_i c_i x^i \right\|_2^2 = \sum_{i=1}^{n} |\lambda_i|^2 \cdot |c_i|^2 \cdot \|x^i\|_2^2 \leq \rho^2(A) \|x\|_2^2.$$

Since this is true for every x, we obtain $\|A\|_2 \leq \rho(A)$ and the desired result follows.
(b) Let λ be an eigenvalue of A such that $|\lambda| = \rho(A) = \|A\|_2$ and let $y \neq 0$ be a corresponding real eigenvector normalized so that $\|y\|_2 = 1$. Then

$$\max_{\{x \in \Re^n \mid \|x\|_2 = 1\}} |x' A x| \geq |y' A y| = |\lambda| \cdot \|y\|_2^2 = \|A\|_2.$$

For the reverse inequality, let $x \in \Re^n$, with $\|x\|_2 = 1$, be arbitrary and decompose it as $x = \sum_{i=1}^{n} c_i x^i$, as in the proof of part (a). Using the orthogonality of the eigenvectors, we obtain

$$|x' A x| = \sum_{i=1}^{n} |c_i|^2 \cdot |\lambda_i| \cdot \|x^i\|_2^2 \leq \rho(A) \|x\|_2^2 = \rho(A) = \|A\|_2.$$

Q.E.D.

Proposition A.25.   Let A be a real square matrix. Then:
(a) $\|A\|_2 = \max_{\|y\|_2 = \|x\|_2 = 1} |y' A x|$, where the maximization is carried out in $\Re^n$.
(b) $\|A\|_2 = \|A'\|_2$.
(c) If A is symmetric then $\|A^k\|_2 = \|A\|_2^k$ for any positive integer k.
(d) $\|A\|_2^2 = \|A' A\|_2 = \|A A'\|_2$.

(e) $\|A\|_2^2 \leq \|A\|_\infty \cdot \|A\|_1$.

(f) If A is symmetric and nonsingular, then $\|A^{-1}\|_2$ is equal to the reciprocal of the smallest of the absolute values of the eigenvalues of A.

Proof.

(a) It is easily seen that the Euclidean vector norm satisfies $\|x\|_2 = \max_{\|y\|_2=1} |y'x|$. It follows that $\|A\|_2 = \max_{\|x\|_2=1} \|Ax\|_2 = \max_{\|y\|_2=\|x\|_2=1} |y'Ax|$.

(b) This is an immediate consequence of part (a) and the fact $y'Ax = x'A'y$.

(c) If A is symmetric then A^k is symmetric. Using Prop. A.24(a), we have $\|A^k\|_2 = \rho(A^k)$. Using Prop. A.17(d), we obtain $\rho(A^k) = \rho(A)^k$, which is equal to $\|A\|_2^k$ by Prop. A.24(a).

(d) For any vector x such that $\|x\|_2 = 1$, we have, using the Schwartz inequality (A.2),

$$\|Ax\|_2^2 = x^*A'Ax \leq \|x\|_2 \cdot \|A'Ax\|_2 \leq \|x\|_2 \cdot \|A'A\|_2 \cdot \|x\|_2 = \|A'A\|_2.$$

Thus, $\|A\|_2^2 \leq \|A'A\|_2$. On the other hand, $\|A'A\|_2 \leq \|A'\|_2 \cdot \|A\|_2 = \|A\|_2^2$. Therefore, $\|A\|_2^2 = \|A'A\|_2$. The second equality is obtained by replacing A by A' and using the result of part (b).

(e) Using part (d) and Prop. A.24(a), we have $\|A\|_2^2 = \|AA'\|_2 = \rho(AA')$. We now recall Prop. A.20, which shows that $\rho(AA') \leq \|AA'\|_\infty$. Finally, we use Prop. A.13(c) to obtain $\|AA'\|_\infty \leq \|A\|_\infty \cdot \|A'\|_\infty = \|A\|_\infty \cdot \|A\|_1$, which completes the proof.

(f) This follows by combining Prop. A.17(e) with Prop. A.24(a).   **Q.E.D.**

Definition A.11.   A square matrix A of dimensions $n \times n$ is called *positive definite* if A is real and $x'Ax > 0$ for all $x \in \Re^n$, $x \neq 0$. It is called *nonnegative definite* if it is real and $x'Ax \geq 0$ for all $x \in \Re^n$.

Proposition A.26.

(a) For any real matrix A, the matrix $A'A$ is symmetric and nonnegative definite. It is positive definite if and only if A is nonsingular.

(b) A square symmetric real matrix is nonnegative definite (respectively, positive definite) if and only if all of its eigenvalues are nonnegative (respectively, positive).

(c) The inverse of a symmetric positive definite matrix is symmetric and positive definite.

Proof.

(a) Symmetry is obvious. For any vector $x \in \Re^n$, we have $x'A'Ax = \|Ax\|_2^2 \geq 0$, which establishes nonnegative definiteness. Positive definiteness is obtained if and only if the inequality is strict for every $x \neq 0$, which is the case if and only if $Ax \neq 0$ for every $x \neq 0$. This is equivalent to A being nonsingular.

(b) Let λ, $x \neq 0$, be an eigenvalue and a corresponding real eigenvector of a symmetric nonnegative definite matrix A. Then $0 \leq x'Ax = \lambda x'x = \lambda \|x\|_2^2$, which proves that $\lambda \geq 0$. For the converse result, let x be an arbitrary real vector. Let $\lambda_1, \ldots, \lambda_n$ be the eigenvalues of A, assumed to be nonnegative, and let $x^1, \ldots, x^n$ be a corresponding set of nonzero, real, and orthogonal eigenvectors. Let us express x in the form $x = \sum_{i=1}^{n} c_i x^i$. Then $x'Ax = (\sum_{i=1}^{n} c_i x^i)'(\sum_{i=1}^{n} c_i \lambda_i x^i)$. From the orthogonality of the eigenvectors, the latter expression is equal to $\sum_{i=1}^{n} c_i^2 \lambda_i \|x^i\|_2^2 \geq 0$, which proves that A is nonnegative definite. The proof for the case of positive definite matrices is similar.

(c) Let A be symmetric positive definite. We have $AA^{-1} = I$, which implies $I = (A^{-1})'A' = (A^{-1})'A$, which shows that $(A^{-1})' = A^{-1}$ and A^{-1} is symmetric. Since A is positive definite, we have for every real nonzero vector x, $x'A^{-1}x = x'A^{-1}AA^{-1}x = (A^{-1}x)'A(A^{-1}x) > 0$, which shows that A^{-1} is positive definite. **Q.E.D.**

Proposition A.27.   Let A be a square symmetric nonnegative definite matrix.

(a) There exists a symmetric matrix $A^{1/2}$ with the property $A^{1/2}A^{1/2} = A$, called a *symmetric square root* of A.

(b) The matrix $A^{1/2}$ is invertible if and only if A is invertible; its inverse is denoted by $A^{-1/2}$.

(c) There holds $A^{-1/2}A^{-1/2} = A^{-1}$.

(d) There holds $AA^{1/2} = A^{1/2}A$.

Proof.

(a) Let $\lambda_1, \ldots, \lambda_n$ be the eigenvalues of A and let $x^1, \ldots, x^n$ be corresponding nonzero, real, and orthogonal eigenvectors normalized so that $\|x^k\|_2 = 1$ for each k. We let

$$A^{1/2} = \sum_{k=1}^{n} \lambda_k^{1/2} x^k (x^k)',$$

where $\lambda_k^{1/2}$ is the nonnegative square root of λ_k. We then have

$$A^{1/2}A^{1/2} = \sum_{i=1}^{n}\sum_{k=1}^{n} \lambda_i^{1/2} \lambda_k^{1/2} x^i (x^i)' x^k (x^k)' = \sum_{\{(i,k) \mid i=k\}} \lambda_i^{1/2} \lambda_k^{1/2} x^i (x^k)'$$

$$= \sum_{k=1}^{n} \lambda_k x^k (x^k)' = A.$$

Here the second equality follows from the orthogonality of distinct eigenvectors; the last equality follows from Prop. A.23(d). We now notice that each one of the matrices $x^k (x^k)'$ is symmetric and it follows that $A^{1/2}$ is also symmetric.

(b) This follows from the fact that the eigenvalues of A are the squares of the eigenvalues of $A^{1/2}$ [Prop. A.17(d)].

(c) We have $(A^{-1/2}A^{-1/2})A = A^{-1/2}(A^{-1/2}A^{1/2})A^{1/2} = A^{-1/2}IA^{1/2} = I$.

(d) We have $AA^{1/2} = A^{1/2}A^{1/2}A^{1/2} = AA^{1/2}$.   **Q.E.D.**

A symmetric square root of A is not unique. For example, let $A^{1/2}$ be as in the proof of Prop. A.27(a) and notice that the matrix $-A^{1/2}$ also has the property $(-A^{1/2})(-A^{1/2}) = A$. However, if A is positive definite, it can be shown that the matrix $A^{1/2}$ we have constructed is the only symmetric and positive definite square root of A.

Proposition A.28.   Let G be a symmetric positive definite $n \times n$ matrix. For $x \in \Re^n$, let $\|x\|_G = (x'Gx)^{1/2}$. Let $G^{1/2}$ be a symmetric square root of G.

(a) There holds $\|x\|_G = \|G^{1/2}x\|_2$ for all $x \in \Re^n$.

(b) $\|\cdot\|_G$ is a vector norm.

(c) There exist positive constants K_1 and K_2, such that $K_1 x'G^{-1}x \leq x'Gx \leq K_2 x'G^{-1}x$ for all $x \in \Re^n$.

(d) There exists some $\alpha > 0$ such that $x'Gx \geq \alpha\|x\|_2^2$ for all $x \in \Re^n$.

(e) (*Schwartz inequality*) There holds $x'Gy \leq \|x\|_G \cdot \|y\|_G$ for all $x, y \in \Re^n$.

Proof. Part (a) is trivial and part (b) follows easily from part (a) and the fact that $\|\cdot\|_2$ is a norm. For part (c), notice that $(x'G^{-1}x)^{1/2}$ is also a vector norm, because G^{-1} is symmetric and positive definite [Prop. A.26(c)], and the result follows from Prop. A.9. Part (d) follows similarly from Prop. A.9. Part (e) follows from the Schwartz inequality applied to the vectors $G^{1/2}x$ and $G^{1/2}y$.   **Q.E.D.**

Proposition A.29.   Let G and H be symmetric positive definite matrices of dimensions $m \times m$ and $n \times n$, respectively. Consider the norm on $m \times n$ matrices defined by $\|A\| = \max_{\|x\|_H=1} \|Ax\|_G$, where $\|\cdot\|_G$ and $\|\cdot\|_H$ are defined as in Prop. A.28. Then $\|A\| = \|G^{1/2}AH^{-1/2}\|_2$.

Proof. Since $\|x\|_H = \|H^{1/2}x\|_2$, we obtain

$$\|A\| = \max_{\{x|\ \|H^{1/2}x\|_2=1\}} \|G^{1/2}Ax\|_2 = \max_{\{y|\ \|y\|_2=1\}} \|G^{1/2}AH^{-1/2}y\|_2 = \|G^{1/2}AH^{-1/2}\|_2.$$

Q.E.D.

Derivatives

Let $f : \Re^n \mapsto \Re$ be some function, fix some $x \in \Re^n$, and consider the expression

$$\lim_{\alpha \to 0} \frac{f(x + \alpha e^i) - f(x)}{\alpha},$$

where e^i is the ith unit vector. If the above limit exists, it is called a *partial derivative* of f at the point x and is denoted by $(\partial f/\partial x_i)(x)$. If all of these partial derivatives exist, we let $\nabla f(x)$, called the *gradient* of f, be the column vector whose ith coordinate, denoted by $\nabla_i f(x)$, is equal to the partial derivative $(\partial f/\partial x_i)(x)$. For any $y \in \Re^n$, we define $f'(x; y)$, the one-sided *directional derivative* of f in the direction y, to be equal to

$$\lim_{\alpha \downarrow 0} \frac{f(x + \alpha y) - f(x)}{\alpha},$$

provided that the limit exists. [Notice that if $f'(x; e^i) = -f'(x; -e^i)$, then $f'(x; e^i) = (\partial f/\partial x_i)(x)$.] If all directional derivatives of f at a point x exist and $f'(x; y)$ is a linear function of y, we say that f is *differentiable* at x. It is seen that f is differentiable at x if and only if the gradient $\nabla f(x)$ exists and satisfies $y'\nabla f(x) = f'(x; y)$ for every $y \in \Re^n$. The function f is called differentiable if it is differentiable at every $x \in \Re^n$. In particular, f is differentiable if $\nabla f(x)$ exists for every x and is a continuous function of x, in which case f is said to be *continuously differentiable*. It is seen that a continuously differentiable function is always continuous. Finally, continuously differentiable functions have the property

$$\lim_{y \to 0} \frac{f(x + y) - f(x) - y'\nabla f(x)}{\|y\|} = 0, \qquad \forall x,$$

where $\| \cdot \|$ is an arbitrary vector norm.

Notice that the definitions concerning differentiability of f at a point x only involve the values of f in a neighborhood of x, that is, in an open set containing x. Thus, f does not have to be defined on all of $\Re^n$, as long as it is defined in a neighborhood of the point at which the derivative is computed.

If $f : \Re^n \mapsto \Re^m$ is a vector valued function, it is called differentiable (respectively, continuously differentiable) if each component f_i of f is differentiable (respectively, continuously differentiable), and we let $\nabla f(x)$ be the matrix of dimensions $n \times m$ whose ith column is the gradient $\nabla f_i(x)$ of f_i. Thus,

$$\nabla f(x) = \Big[\nabla f_1(x) \cdots \nabla f_m(x) \Big].$$

The transpose of ∇f is called the *Jacobian* of f and is a matrix whose ijth entry is equal to the partial derivative $\partial f_i/\partial x_j$.

Now suppose that each one of the partial derivatives of a function $f : \Re^n \mapsto \Re$ is a continuously differentiable function of x. We use the notation $(\partial^2 f/\partial x_i \partial x_j)(x)$ to indicate the ith partial derivative of $\partial f/\partial x_j$ at a point $x \in \Re^n$. We define $\nabla^2 f(x)$, called the *Hessian* of f, as the matrix whose ijth entry, denoted by $\nabla^2_{ij} f(x)$, is equal to $(\partial^2 f/\partial x_i \partial x_j)(x)$. We have $(\partial^2 f/\partial x_i \partial x_j)(x) = (\partial^2 f/\partial x_j \partial x_i)(x)$ for every x, which implies that $\nabla^2 f(x)$ is symmetric.

Let $f : \Re^k \mapsto \Re^m$ and $g : \Re^m \mapsto \Re^n$ be continuously differentiable functions and let $h = g \circ f$ be their composition, that is, $h(x) = g(f(x))$. Then, the *chain rule* for differentiation states that

$$\nabla h(x) = \nabla f(x) \nabla g(f(x)), \qquad \forall x \in \Re^k.$$

Proposition A.30.   (*Mean Value Theorem*) If $f : \Re \mapsto \Re$ is continuously differentiable, then for every $x, y \in \Re$, there exists some $z \in [x, y]$ such that

$$f(y) - f(x) = f'(z)(y - x),$$

where f' is the derivative of f.

Proposition A.31.   (*Second Order Taylor Series*) Let $f : \Re^n \mapsto \Re$ be twice continuously differentiable.

(a) For any $x \in \Re^n$, there exists a function $h : \Re^n \mapsto \Re$ satisfying

$$\lim_{\|y\| \to 0} \frac{h(y)}{\|y\|^2} = 0$$

and such that

$$f(x + y) = f(x) + y' \nabla f(x) + \tfrac{1}{2} y' \nabla^2 f(x) y + h(y), \qquad \forall y \in \Re^n. \qquad \text{(A.10)}$$

(b) For any $x, y \in \Re^n$, there exists some $\alpha \in [0, 1]$ such that

$$f(x + y) = f(x) + y' \nabla f(x) + \tfrac{1}{2} y' \nabla^2 f(x + \alpha y) y.$$

Proposition A.32.   (*Descent Lemma*) If $f : \Re^n \mapsto \Re$ is continuously differentiable and has the property $\|\nabla f(x) - \nabla f(y)\|_2 \le K \|x - y\|_2$ for every $x, y \in \Re^n$, then

$$f(x + y) \le f(x) + y' \nabla f(x) + \frac{K}{2} \|y\|_2^2.$$

Proof. Let t be a scalar parameter and let $g(t) = f(x + ty)$. The chain rule yields $(dg/dt)(t) = y' \nabla f(x + ty)$. Now

$$f(x+y) - f(x) = g(1) - g(0) = \int_0^1 \frac{dg}{dt}(t)\, dt = \int_0^1 y'\nabla f(x+ty)\, dt$$

$$\leq \int_0^1 y'\nabla f(x)\, dt + \left| \int_0^1 y'\big(\nabla f(x+ty) - \nabla f(x)\big)\, dt \right|$$

$$\leq \int_0^1 y'\nabla f(x)\, dt + \int_0^1 \|y\|_2 \cdot \|\nabla f(x+ty) - \nabla f(x)\|_2\, dt$$

$$\leq y'\nabla f(x) + \|y\|_2 \int_0^1 Kt\|y\|_2\, dt$$

$$= y'\nabla f(x) + \tfrac{1}{2}K\|y\|_2^2.$$

Q.E.D.

Proposition A.33. Let $f : \Re \mapsto \Re$ be twice continuously differentiable and fix some $x \in \Re$. Then

$$\frac{d^2 f}{dx^2}(x) = \frac{f(x+\Delta) + f(x-\Delta) - 2f(x)}{\Delta^2} + h(\Delta),$$

where h is some function satisfying $\lim_{\Delta \to 0} h(\Delta) = 0$.

Proof. We apply Prop. A.31(a) twice: once with $y = \Delta$ and once with $y = -\Delta$. By adding the two equalities obtained, the desired result follows.   **Q.E.D.**

Definition A.12. Let $X \subset \Re^n$ and let $f : X \mapsto \Re$ be a given function. A vector $x \in X$ is called a *local minimum* of f (over the set X) if there exists some $\epsilon > 0$ such that $f(y) \geq f(x)$ for every $y \in X$ satisfying $\|x - y\| \leq \epsilon$, where $\|\cdot\|$ is some vector norm. A vector $x \in X$ is called a *global minimum* of f (over the set X) if $f(y) \geq f(x)$ for every $y \in X$. A local or global maximum is defined similarly.

Proposition A.34. Let $f : \Re^n \mapsto \Re$ be a continuously differentiable function. If some $x \in \Re^n$ is a local minimum of f over $\Re^n$, then $\nabla f(x) = 0$.

Proof. Fix some $y \in \Re^n$. Then

$$y'\nabla f(x) = \lim_{t\downarrow 0} \frac{f(x+ty) - f(x)}{t} \geq 0,$$

where the last inequality follows from the assumption that x is a local minimum. Since y is arbitrary, the same inequality holds with y replaced by $-y$. Therefore, $y'\nabla f(x) = 0$ for all $y \in \Re^n$, which shows that $\nabla f(x) = 0$.   **Q.E.D.**

Convexity

Definition A.13.   Let C be a subset of $\Re^n$. We say that C is *convex* if

$$\alpha x + (1 - \alpha)y \in C, \qquad \forall x, y \in C, \ \forall \alpha \in [0, 1].$$

Let C be a convex subset of $\Re^n$. A function $f : C \mapsto \Re$ is called *convex* if

$$f\big(\alpha x + (1 - \alpha)y\big) \leq \alpha f(x) + (1 - \alpha)f(y), \qquad \forall x, y \in C, \ \forall \alpha \in [0, 1]. \qquad \text{(A.12)}$$

The function f is called *concave* if $-f$ is convex. The function f is *strictly convex* if for every $x, y \in C$, $x \neq y$, we have

$$f\big(\alpha x + (1 - \alpha)y\big) < \alpha f(x) + (1 - \alpha)f(y), \qquad \forall \alpha \in (0, 1).$$

We occasionally deal with convex functions that can take the value of infinity. An extended real valued function $f : C \mapsto \Re \cup \{\infty\}$ is also called convex if condition (A.12) holds.

Proposition A.35.   Let $C \subset \Re^n$ be a convex set.

(a) If $f : C \mapsto \Re$ is convex, $x^1, \ldots, x^m \in C$, $a_1, \ldots, a_m \geq 0$, and $\sum_{i=1}^{m} a_i = 1$, then

$$f\left(\sum_{i=1}^{m} a_i x^i\right) \leq \sum_{i=1}^{m} a_i f(x^i).$$

(b) A linear function is convex.

(c) The weighted sum of convex functions, with positive weights, is convex.

(d) If I is an index set and $f_i : C \mapsto \Re$ is convex for each $i \in I$, then the extended real valued function $h : C \mapsto \Re \cup \{\infty\}$ defined by $h(x) = \sup_{i \in I} f_i(x)$ is also convex.

(e) Any vector norm is convex.

(f) If x is a local minimum of a convex function $f : C \mapsto \Re$, then it is also a global minimum.

(g) If $f : C \mapsto \Re$ is strictly convex, then there exists at most one global minimum of f.

Proof. Part (a) is obtained by repeated application of inequality (A.12). Parts (b) and (c) are immediate consequences of the definition of convexity.

For part (d), let us fix some $x, y \in C$, $\alpha \in [0, 1]$, and let $z = \alpha x + (1 - \alpha)y$. For every $i \in I$, we have

$$f_i(z) \leq \alpha f_i(x) + (1 - \alpha)f_i(y) \leq \alpha h(x) + (1 - \alpha)h(y).$$

Taking the supremum over all $i \in I$, we conclude that $h(z) \leq \alpha h(x) + (1 - \alpha)h(y)$, and h is convex.

Let $\| \cdot \|$ be a vector norm. For any $x, y \in \Re^n$ and any $\alpha \in [0, 1]$, we have

$$\|\alpha x + (1 - \alpha)y\| \leq \|\alpha x\| + \|(1 - \alpha)y\| = \alpha \|x\| + (1 - \alpha)\|y\|,$$

which proves part (e).

Suppose that x is a local minimum of f but not a global minimum. Then there exists some $y \neq x$ such that $f(y) < f(x)$. Using inequality (A.12), we conclude that $f(\alpha x + (1 - \alpha)y) < f(x)$ for every $\alpha \in [0, 1)$. This contradicts the assumption that x is a local minimum and proves part (f). To prove part (g), suppose that two global minima x and y existed. Then their average $(x + y)/2$ would belong to C, since C is convex, and the value of f would be smaller at that point by the strict convexity of f.   **Q.E.D.**

Proposition A.36.   If $f : \Re^n \mapsto \Re$ is convex, then it is continuous.   More generally, if $C \subset \Re^n$ is convex and $f : C \mapsto \Re$ is convex, then f is continuous in the interior of C.

Proof. Without any loss of generality, it is sufficient to prove continuity at the origin, assuming that $0 \in C$ and that the unit cube $S = \{z \mid \|x\|_\infty \leq 1\}$ is contained in C. Let e^i, $i = 1, \ldots, 2^n$, be the corners of S, that is, each e^i is a vector whose entries belong to $\{-1, 1\}$. It is not difficult to see that any $x \in S$ can be expressed in the form $x = \sum_{i=1}^{2^n} a_i e^i$, where each a_i is a nonnegative scalar and $\sum_{i=1}^{2^n} a_i = 1$. Let $A = \max_i f(e^i)$. From Prop. A.35(a), it follows that $f(x) \leq A$ for every $x \in S$.

Let $\{x^k\}$ be a sequence in $\Re^n$ that converges to zero. For the purpose of proving continuity at zero, we can assume that $x^k \in S$ for all k. Using (A.12), we have

$$f(x^k) \leq (1 - \|x^k\|_\infty)f(0) + \|x^k\|_\infty f\left(\frac{x^k}{\|x^k\|_\infty}\right).$$

Letting k tend to infinity, $\|x^k\|_\infty$ goes to zero and we obtain

$$\limsup_{k \to \infty} f(x^k) \leq f(0) + A \limsup_{k \to \infty} \|x^k\|_\infty = f(0).$$

Inequality (A.12) also implies that

$$f(0) \leq \frac{\|x^k\|_\infty}{\|x^k\|_\infty + 1} f\left(\frac{-x^k}{\|x^k\|_\infty}\right) + \frac{1}{\|x^k\|_\infty + 1} f(x^k)$$

and letting k tend to infinity, we obtain $f(0) \leq \liminf_{k \to \infty} f(x^k)$. Thus, $\lim_{k \to \infty} f(x^k) = f(0)$ and f is continuous at zero.   **Q.E.D.**

Proposition A.37.   Let $I \subset \Re$ be convex. (Thus, I is an interval.) Let $f : I \mapsto \Re$ be convex. If $x, y, z \in I$ and $x < y < z$, then

$$\frac{f(y) - f(x)}{y - x} \leq \frac{f(z) - f(x)}{z - x} \leq \frac{f(z) - f(y)}{z - y}.$$

Proof. Using inequality (A.12), we obtain

$$f(y) \leq \left(\frac{y - x}{z - x}\right) f(z) + \left(\frac{z - y}{z - x}\right) f(x)$$

and either of the desired inequalities follows by appropriately rearranging terms.   **Q.E.D.**

Let $I \subset \Re$ be an interval and let $f : I \mapsto \Re$ be convex. Let a and b be the infimum and the supremum, respectively, of I. For any $x \in I$, $x \neq b$, and for any $\alpha > 0$ such that $x + \alpha \in I$, we define

$$s^{+}(x, \alpha) = \frac{f(x + \alpha) - f(x)}{\alpha}.$$

Let $0 < \alpha \leq \alpha'$. We use the first inequality in Prop. A.37 with $y = x + \alpha$ and $z = x + \alpha'$ to obtain $s^{+}(x, \alpha) \leq s^{+}(x, \alpha')$. Therefore, $s^{+}(x, \alpha)$ is a nondecreasing function of α and, as α decreases to zero, it converges either to a finite number or to $-\infty$. Let $f^{+}(x)$ be the value of the limit, which we call the *right derivative* of f at the point x. Similarly, if $x \in I$, $x \neq a$, $\alpha > 0$, and $x - \alpha \in I$, we define

$$s^{-}(x, \alpha) = \frac{f(x) - f(x - \alpha)}{\alpha},$$

which is, by a symmetrical argument, a nonincreasing function of α. Its limit as α decreases to zero, denoted by $f^{-}(x)$, is called the *left derivative* of f at the point x, and is either finite or equal to ∞.

In case the end points a and b belong to the domain I of f, we define for completeness $f^{-}(a) = -\infty$ and $f^{+}(b) = \infty$.

Proposition A.38.   Let $I \subset \Re$ be convex and let $f : I \mapsto \Re$ be a convex function. Let a and b be the end points of I as above.

  (a) We have $f^{-}(y) \leq f^{+}(y)$ for every $y \in I$.
  (b) If x belongs to the interior of I, then $f^{+}(x)$ and $f^{-}(x)$ are finite.
  (c) If $x, z \in I$ and $x < z$, then $f^{+}(x) \leq f^{-}(z)$.
  (d) The functions $f^{-}, f^{+} : I \mapsto [-\infty, +\infty]$ are nondecreasing.
  (e) The function f^{+} (respectively, f^{-}) is right– (respectively, left–) continuous at every interior point of I. Also, if $a \in I$ (respectively, $b \in I$) and f is continuous at a (respectively, b), then f^{+} (respectively, f^{-}) is right– (respectively, left–) continuous at a (respectively, b).

(f) If f is differentiable at a point x belonging to the interior of I, then $f^+(x) = f^-(x) = (df/dx)(x)$.

(g) For any $x, z \in I$ and any d satisfying $f^-(x) \le d \le f^+(x)$, we have

$$f(z) \ge f(x) + d(z - x).$$

(h) The function $f^+ : I \mapsto (-\infty, \infty]$ [respectively, $f^- : I \mapsto [-\infty, \infty)$] is upper (respectively, lower) semicontinuous at every $x \in I$.

Proof.

(a) If y is an end point of I, the result is trivial because $f^-(a) = -\infty$ and $f^+(b) = \infty$. We assume that y is an interior point, we let $\alpha > 0$, and use Prop. A.37, with $x = y - \alpha$ and $z = y + \alpha$, to obtain $s^-(y, \alpha) \le s^+(y, \alpha)$. Taking the limit as α decreases to zero, we obtain $f^-(y) \le f^+(y)$.

(b) Let x belong to the interior of I and let $\alpha > 0$ be such that $x - \alpha \in I$. Then $f^-(x) \ge s^-(x, \alpha) > -\infty$. For similar reasons, we obtain $f^+(x) < \infty$. Part (a) then implies that $f^-(x) < \infty$ and $f^+(x) > -\infty$.

(c) We use Prop. A.37, with $y = (z + x)/2$, to obtain $s^+\big(x, (z - x)/2\big) \le s^-\big(z, (z - x)/2\big)$. The result then follows because $f^+(x) \le s^+\big(x, (z - x)/2\big)$ and $s^-\big(z, (z - x)/2\big) \le f^-(z)$.

(d) This follows by combining parts (a) and (c).

(e) Fix some $x \in I$, $x \ne b$, and some positive δ and α such that $x + \delta + \alpha < b$. We allow x to be equal to a, in which case f is assumed to be continuous at a. We have $f^+(x + \delta) \le s^+(x + \delta, \alpha)$. We take the limit, as δ decreases to zero, to obtain $\lim_{\delta \downarrow 0} f^+(x + \delta) \le s^+(x, \alpha)$. We have used here the fact that $s^+(x, \alpha)$ is a continuous function of x, which is a consequence of the continuity of f (Prop. A.36). We now let α decrease to zero to obtain $\lim_{\delta \downarrow 0} f^+(x + \delta) \le f^+(x)$. The reverse inequality is also true because f^+ is nondecreasing and this proves the right–continuity of f^+. The proof for f^- is similar.

(f) This is immediate from the definition of f^+ and f^-.

(g) Fix some $x, z \in I$. The result is trivially true for $x = z$. We only consider the case $x < z$; the proof for the case $x > z$ is similar. Since $s^+(x, \alpha)$ is nondecreasing in α, we have $\big(f(z) - f(x)\big)/(z - x) \ge s^+(x, \alpha)$ for α belonging to $(0, z - x)$. Letting α decrease to zero, we obtain $\big(f(z) - f(x)\big)/(z - x) \ge f^+(x) \ge d$ and the result follows.

(h) This follows from parts (d), (e), and the definition of semicontinuity (Definition A.4).   **Q.E.D.**

Any $d \in \Re$ satisfying $f^-(x) \le d \le f^+(x)$ is called a *subgradient* of f at x. The following result generalizes Prop. A.38(g) to the case of a multivariable and differentiable convex function.

Proposition A.39.   Let $C \subset \Re^n$ be a convex set and let $f : \Re^n \mapsto \Re$ be differentiable.

(a) The function f is convex on the set C if and only if

$$f(z) \geq f(x) + (z - x)'\nabla f(x), \qquad \forall x, z \in C. \tag{A.13}$$

(b) If the inequality (A.13) is strict whenever $x \neq z$, then f is strictly convex on C.

(c) Suppose that $C = \Re^n$ and that f is convex. We have $\nabla f(x) = 0$ if and only if x is a global minimum of f.

Proof.

(a) Suppose that f is convex on C. Let $x \in C$ and $z \in C$. By the convexity of C, we obtain $x + \alpha(z - x) \in C$ for every $\alpha \in [0, 1]$. Furthermore,

$$\lim_{\alpha \downarrow 0} \frac{f\big(x + \alpha(z - x)\big) - f(x)}{\alpha} = (z - x)'\nabla f(x).$$

Using the convexity of f, we have

$$f\big(x + \alpha(z - x)\big) \leq \alpha f(z) + (1 - \alpha)f(x), \qquad \forall \alpha \in [0, 1].$$

Using this inequality to replace the $f\big(x + \alpha(z - x)\big)$ term in the previous inequality, we obtain (A.13).

For the proof of the converse, suppose that inequality (A.13) is true. We fix some $x, y \in C$ and some $\alpha \in [0, 1]$. Let $z = \alpha x + (1 - \alpha)y$. Using inequality (A.13) twice, we obtain

$$f(x) \geq f(z) + (x - z)'\nabla f(z),$$

$$f(y) \geq f(z) + (y - z)'\nabla f(z).$$

We multiply the first inequality by α, the second by $(1 - \alpha)$, and add them to obtain

$$\alpha f(x) + (1 - \alpha)f(y) \geq f(z) + \big(\alpha x + (1 - \alpha)y - z\big)'\nabla f(z) = f(z),$$

which proves that f is convex.

(b) The proof for the strictly convex case is almost identical to the proof for part (a) and is omitted.

(c) If $\nabla f(x) = 0$, then inequality (A.13) shows that $f(z) \geq f(x)$ for all $z \in \Re^n$, and x is a global minimum. Conversely, if x is a global minimum, then it is also a local minimum, and Prop. A.34 shows that $\nabla f(x) = 0$.   **Q.E.D.**

Proposition A.40. Let $f : \Re^n \mapsto \Re$ be twice continuously differentiable, and let A be a real symmetric $n \times n$ matrix.

(a) The function f is convex if and only if $\nabla^2 f(x)$ is nonnegative definite for all x.

(b) If $\nabla^2 f(x)$ is positive definite for every x, then f is strictly convex.

(c) The function $f(x) = x'Ax$ is convex if and only if A is nonnegative definite.

(d) The function $f(x) = x'Ax$ is strictly convex if and only if A is positive definite. In particular, $\|x\|_2^2 = x'Ix$ is strictly convex.

Proof.

(a) If $\nabla^2 f(x)$ is nonnegative definite for all x, then Prop. A.31(b) shows that $f(x + y) \geq f(x) + y'\nabla f(x)$ for all $x, y \in \Re^n$. Using Prop. A.39(a), we conclude that f is convex. Conversely, suppose that f is convex and suppose, to derive a contradiction, that there exist some x, y such that $y'\nabla^2 f(x)y < 0$. Using the continuity of $\nabla^2 f$, we see that we can choose the magnitude of y to be small enough so that $y'\nabla^2 f(x + \alpha y)y < 0$ for every $\alpha \in [0, 1]$. Then Prop. A.31(b) yields $f(x + y) < f(x) + y'\nabla f(x)$, which, in view of Prop. A.39(a), contradicts the convexity of f.

(b) The proof is similar to the proof of the corresponding statement in part (a).

(c) An easy calculation shows that $\nabla^2 f(x) = 2A$ for all $x \in \Re^n$, and the result follows from part (a).

(d) If A is positive definite, then strict convexity of f follows from part (b). For the converse, suppose that f is strictly convex. Then part (c) implies that A is nonnegative definite and it remains to show that A is actually positive definite. In view of Prop. A.26(b), it suffices to show that zero is not an eigenvalue of A. Suppose the contrary. Then there exists some $x \neq 0$ such that $Ax = -Ax = 0$. It follows that $\frac{1}{2}\bigl(f(x) + f(-x)\bigr) = 0 = f(0)$, which contradicts the strict convexity of f. **Q.E.D.**

Proposition A.41. *(Strong Convexity)* Let $f : \Re^n \mapsto \Re^n$ be continuously differentiable and let α be a positive constant. If f satisfies the condition

$$\bigl(\nabla f(x) - \nabla f(y)\bigr)'(x - y) \geq \alpha\|x - y\|_2^2, \qquad \forall x, y \in \Re^n, \qquad (A.14)$$

then f is strictly convex. Furthermore, if f is twice continuously differentiable, then the condition (A.14) is equivalent to the nonnegative definiteness of $\nabla^2 f(x) - \alpha I$ for every $x \in \Re^n$, where I is the identity matrix.

Proof. Fix some $x, y \in \Re^n$ such that $x \neq y$, and define the function $h : \Re \mapsto \Re$ by $h(t) = f\bigl(x + t(y - x)\bigr)$. Consider some $t, t' \in \Re$ such that $t < t'$. Using the chain rule and Eq. (A.14), we have

$$(t' - t)\left(\frac{dh}{dt}(t') - \frac{dh}{dt}(t)\right) = \left(\nabla f\big(x + t'(y - x)\big) - \nabla f\big(x + t(y - x)\big)\right)'(y - x)(t' - t)$$

$$\geq \alpha(t' - t)^2 \|x - y\|_2^2 > 0.$$

Thus, dh/dt is strictly increasing and for any $t \in (0, 1)$, we have

$$\frac{h(t) - h(0)}{t} = \frac{1}{t}\int_0^t \frac{dh}{d\tau}(\tau)\,d\tau < \frac{1}{1 - t}\int_t^1 \frac{dh}{d\tau}(\tau)\,d\tau = \frac{h(1) - h(t)}{1 - t}.$$

Equivalently, $th(1) + (1 - t)h(0) > h(t)$. The definition of h yields $tf(y) + (1 - t)f(x) > f\big(ty + (1 - t)x\big)$. Since this inequality has been proved for arbitrary $t \in (0, 1)$ and $x \neq y$, we conclude that f is strictly convex.

Suppose now that f is twice continuously differentiable and Eq. (A.14) holds. Let c be a scalar variable. We use Proposition A.31(b) twice to obtain

$$f(x + cy) = f(x) + cy'\nabla f(x) + \frac{c^2}{2}y'\nabla^2 f(x + tcy)y,$$

and

$$f(x) = f(x + cy) - cy'\nabla f(x + cy) + \frac{c^2}{2}y'\nabla^2 f(x + scy)y,$$

for some t and s belonging to $[0, 1]$. Adding these two inequalities and using (i) we obtain

$$\frac{c^2}{2}y'\left(\nabla^2 f(x + scy) + \nabla^2 f(x + tcy)\right)y = \left(\nabla f(x + cy) - \nabla f(x)\right)'(cy) \geq \alpha c^2\|y\|_2^2.$$

We divide both sides by c^2 and then take the limit as c tends to zero to conclude that $y'\nabla^2 f(x)y \geq \alpha\|y\|_2^2$. Since this inequality is valid for every $y \in \Re^n$, it follows that $\nabla^2 f(x) - \alpha I$ is nonnegative definite.

For the converse, assume that $\nabla^2 f(x) - \alpha I$ is nonnegative definite for all $x \in \Re^n$. Consider the function $g : \Re \mapsto \Re$ defined by

$$g(t) = \nabla f\big(tx + (1 - t)y\big)'(x - y).$$

Using the Mean Value Theorem (Prop. A.30), we have $\left(\nabla f(x) - \nabla f(y)\right)'(x - y) = g(1) - g(0) = (dg/dt)(t)$ for some $t \in [0, 1]$. The result follows because

$$\frac{dg}{dt}(t) = (x - y)'\nabla^2 f\big(tx + (1 - t)y\big)(x - y) \geq \alpha\|x - y\|_2^2,$$

where the last inequality is a consequence of the nonnegative definiteness of $\nabla^2 f(tx + (1-t)y) - \alpha I$.   **Q.E.D.**

Notice that the directional derivative $f'(x; y)$ of a convex function $f : \Re^n \mapsto \Re$ at a vector $x \in \Re^n$ in the direction $y \in \Re^n$ is equal to the right derivative $F_y^+(0)$ of the convex scalar function $F_y(\alpha) = f(x + \alpha y)$ at $\alpha = 0$, that is,

$$f'(x; y) = \lim_{\alpha \downarrow 0} \frac{f(x + \alpha y) - f(x)}{\alpha}, \qquad (A.15)$$

and, in particular, the limit in Eq. (A.15) is guaranteed to exist. Similarly, the left derivative $F_y^-(0)$ of F_y is equal to $-f'(x; -y)$ and, by using Prop. A.38(a), we obtain

$$-f'(x; -y) \leq f'(x; y), \qquad \forall y \in \Re^n. \qquad (A.16)$$

The following proposition generalizes the upper semicontinuity property of right derivatives of scalar convex functions [Prop. A.38(h)], and shows that if f is differentiable, then its gradient is continuous.

Proposition A.42.   Let $f : \Re^n \mapsto \Re$ be convex, and let $\{f_k\}$ be a sequence of convex functions $f_k : \Re^n \mapsto \Re$ with the property that $\lim_{k \to \infty} f_k(x_k) = f(x)$ for every $x \in \Re^n$ and every sequence $\{x_k\}$ that converges to x. Then for any $x \in \Re^n$ and $y \in \Re^n$, and any sequence $\{x_k\}$ converging to x, we have

$$\limsup_{k \to \infty} f_k'(x_k; y) \leq f'(x; y). \qquad (A.17)$$

Furthermore, if f is differentiable at all $x \in \Re^n$, then its gradient $\nabla f(x)$ is a continuous function of x.

Proof. For any $\mu > f'(x; y)$, there exists an $\alpha > 0$ such that

$$\frac{f(x + \alpha y) - f(x)}{\alpha} < \mu.$$

Hence, for all sufficiently large k, we have

$$\frac{f_k(x_k + \alpha y) - f_k(x_k)}{\alpha} < \mu,$$

and since $f_k'(x_k; y)$ does not exceed the left–hand side of the last inequality, we obtain that

$$\limsup_{k \to \infty} f_k'(x_k; y) < \mu.$$

Since this is true for all $\mu > f'(x; y)$, inequality (A.17) follows.

If f is differentiable at all $x \in \Re^n$, then using the continuity of f and the part of the proposition just proved, we have for every $\{x_k\}$ converging to x and every $y \in \Re^n$,

$$\limsup_{k \to \infty} \nabla f(x_k)'y = \limsup_{k \to \infty} f'(x_k; y) \le f'(x; y) = \nabla f(x)'y.$$

By replacing y by $-y$ in the preceding argument, we obtain

$$-\liminf_{k \to \infty} \nabla f(x_k)'y = \limsup_{k \to \infty}\left(-\nabla f(x_k)'y\right) \le -\nabla f(x)'y.$$

Therefore, we have $\nabla f(x_k)'y \to \nabla f(x)'y$ for every y, which implies that $\nabla f(x_k) \to \nabla f(x)$. Hence, the gradient is continuous.   **Q.E.D.**

We will encounter functions of the form $f(x) = \max_{z \in Z} \phi(x, z)$ when dealing with dual optimization problems (see Appendix C). The following result characterizes the directional derivatives of f.

Proposition A.43.   (*Danskin's Theorem* [Dan67]) Let $Z \subset \Re^m$ be a compact set, and let $\phi : \Re^n \times Z \mapsto \Re$ be a continuous function such that $\phi(\cdot, z) : \Re^n \mapsto \Re$, viewed as a function of its first argument, is convex for each $z \in Z$.

(a) The function $f : \Re^n \mapsto \Re$ given by

$$f(x) = \max_{z \in Z} \phi(x, z)$$

is convex and has directional derivative given by

$$f'(x; y) = \max_{z \in Z(x)} \phi'(x, z; y), \tag{A.18}$$

where $\phi'(x, z; y)$ is the directional derivative of the function $\phi(\cdot, z)$ at x in the direction y, and

$$Z(x) = \{\bar{z} \mid \phi(x, \bar{z}) = \max_{z \in Z} \phi(x, z)\}. \tag{A.19}$$

In particular, if $Z(x)$ consists of a unique point $\bar{z}$ and $\phi(\cdot, \bar{z})$ is differentiable at x, then f is differentiable at x, and $\nabla f(x) = \nabla_x \phi(x, \bar{z})$, where $\nabla_x \phi(x, \bar{z})$ is the vector with coordinates $(\partial \phi / \partial x_i)(x, \bar{z})$, $i = 1, \ldots, n$.

(b) The conclusion of (a) also holds if, instead of assuming that Z is compact, we assume that $Z(x)$ is nonempty for all $x \in \Re^n$, and that ϕ and Z are such that for every sequence $\{x_k\}$ converging to some x, there exists a bounded sequence $\{z_k\}$ with $z_k \in Z(x_k)$ for all k.

Proof. We only prove part (a). The proof of part (b) is almost identical. The convexity of f has been established in Prop. A.35(d). We note that since ϕ is continuous and Z is compact, the set $Z(x)$ is nonempty by Weierstrass' theorem (Prop. A.8) and f is finite. For any $z \in Z(x)$, $y \in \Re^n$, and $\alpha > 0$, we use the definition of f to obtain

$$\frac{f(x + \alpha y) - f(x)}{\alpha} \geq \frac{\phi(x + \alpha y, z) - \phi(x, z)}{\alpha}.$$

Taking the limit as α decreases to zero, we obtain $f'(x; y) \geq \phi'(x, z; y)$. Since this is true for every $z \in Z(x)$, we conclude that

$$f'(x; y) \geq \sup_{z \in Z(x)} \phi'(x, z; y), \qquad \forall \, y \in \Re^n. \tag{A.20}$$

To prove the reverse inequality and that the supremum in the right–hand side of inequality (A.20) is attained, consider a sequence $\{\alpha_k\}$ of positive scalars that converges to zero and let $x_k = x + \alpha_k y$. For each k, let z_k be a vector in $Z(x_k)$. Since $\{z_k\}$ belongs to the compact set Z, it has a subsequence converging to some $\bar{z} \in Z$. Without loss of generality, we assume that the entire sequence $\{z_k\}$ converges to $\bar{z}$. We have

$$\phi(x_k, z_k) \geq \phi(x_k, z), \qquad \forall \, z \in Z,$$

so by taking the limit as $k \to \infty$ and by using the continuity of ϕ, we obtain

$$\phi(x, \bar{z}) \geq \phi(x, z), \qquad \forall \, z \in Z.$$

Therefore, $\bar{z} \in Z(x)$. We now have

$$f'(x; y) \leq \frac{f(x + \alpha_k y) - f(x)}{\alpha_k} = \frac{\phi(x + \alpha_k y, z_k) - \phi(x, \bar{z})}{\alpha_k} \leq \frac{\phi(x + \alpha_k y, z_k) - \phi(x, z_k)}{\alpha_k}$$

$$\leq -\phi'(x + \alpha_k y, z_k; -y) \leq \phi'(x + \alpha_k y, z_k; y), \tag{A.21}$$

where the last inequality follows from inequality (A.16). We apply Prop. A.42 to the functions f_k defined by $f_k(\cdot) = \phi(\cdot, z_k)$, and with $x_k = x + \alpha_k y$, to obtain

$$\limsup_{k \to \infty} \phi'(x + \alpha_k y, z_k; y) \leq \phi'(x, \bar{z}; y). \tag{A.22}$$

We take the limit in inequality (A.21) as $k \to \infty$, and use inequality (A.22) to conclude that

$$f'(x; y) \leq \phi'(x, \bar{z}; y).$$

This relation together with inequality (A.20) proves Eq. (A.18).

For the last statement of part (a), if $Z(x)$ consists of the unique point $\bar{z}$, Eq. (A.18) and the differentiability assumption on ϕ yield

$$f'(x; y) = \phi'(x, \bar{z}; y) = y'\nabla_x\phi(x, \bar{z}), \qquad \forall y \in \Re^n,$$

which implies that $\nabla f(x) = \nabla_x\phi(x, \bar{z})$.   **Q.E.D.**

Linear Differential Equations

Consider the differential equation

$$\frac{dx}{dt}(t) = A(t)x(t) + B(t)u(t). \tag{A.23}$$

Here $x(t) \in \Re^n$, $u(t) \in \Re^m$, and $A(t)$, $B(t)$ are matrices of dimensions $n \times n$ and $n \times m$, respectively. We assume that $u(t)$, $A(t)$, and $B(t)$ are continuous functions of t. Then it can be shown that for any given initial condition $x(0) = x_0 \in \Re^n$, the differential equation (A.23) has a unique solution over the interval $[0, \infty)$ [CoL55].

Proposition A.44.

(a) Under the above continuity assumptions, the solution of Eq. (A.23) admits the representation

$$x(t) = \int_0^t \Phi(t, \tau)B(\tau)u(\tau)\, d\tau + \Phi(t, 0)x_0, \tag{A.24}$$

where $\Phi(t, \tau)$ is an $n \times n$ matrix satisfying $\Phi(\tau, \tau) = I$ for every $\tau \geq 0$, and

$$\frac{d\Phi}{dt}(t, \tau) = A(t)\Phi(t, \tau), \qquad \forall \tau, \; \forall t \geq \tau. \tag{A.25}$$

(b) Suppose that $A(t)$ is a continuous and bounded function of time. Let $\|\cdot\|$ be some induced matrix norm. Then there exist constants C and c such that

$$\|\Phi(t, \tau)\| \leq Ce^{c(t-\tau)}, \qquad \forall \tau \geq 0, \; \forall t \geq \tau. \tag{A.26}$$

Proof.

(a) We first notice that Eq. (A.25) defines $\Phi(t, \tau)$ uniquely, because of the existence and uniqueness result quoted earlier. Let us define $x(t)$, $t \geq 0$, by Eq. (A.24). We notice that $x(t)$ satisfies the initial condition $x(0) = x_0$ and, by differentiating the right–hand side of Eq. (A.24), we see that $x(t)$ also satisfies Eq. (A.23). The result follows because Eq. (A.23) has a unique solution.

(b) Let D_1 be a bound on $\|A(t)\|$. Let $D_2 = \|I\|$. Let $c = D_1$ and $C = 2D_2$. Notice that inequality (A.26) is true if $t = \tau$. Fix some $\tau \geq 0$. Suppose, to derive a contradiction, that there exists some $t > \tau$ such that inequality (A.26) fails to hold. Let t^* be the infimum of the set of all such t. Since $\Phi(t, \tau)$ is a continuous function of t, it follows that inequality (A.26) holds with equality at time t^*. We integrate Eq. (A.25) and take the norm of both sides to obtain

$$2D_2 e^{D_1(t^*-\tau)} = \|\Phi(t^*, \tau)\| \leq \left\| \int_\tau^{t^*} A(t)\Phi(t, \tau)\, dt \right\| + \|\Phi(\tau, \tau)\|$$

$$\leq \int_\tau^{t^*} \|A(t)\| \cdot \|\Phi(t, \tau)\|\, dt + D_2$$

$$\leq \int_\tau^{t^*} D_1 2 D_2 e^{D_1(t-\tau)}\, dt + D_2$$

$$= 2D_2 e^{D_1(t^*-\tau)} - 2D_2 + D_2 < 2D_2 e^{D_1(t^*-\tau)},$$

which is a contradiction.   **Q.E.D.**

B

Graph Theory

In this appendix, we collect the definitions and notational conventions relating to graph theory that we will use throughout the book. For further material, consult [Chr75], [Har69], [Law76], [PaS82], and [Roc84].

Undirected Graphs

We define a *graph*, $G = (N, A)$, to be a finite nonempty set N of *nodes* and a collection A of pairs of distinct nodes from N. Each pair of nodes in A is called an *arc* (or *link* in some contexts). An arc (i, j) is viewed as an unordered pair, and is indistinguishable from the pair (j, i); thus $(i, j) = (j, i)$. If (i, j) is an arc, we say that (i, j) is *incident* to i and to j, and we say that i and j are *adjacent* nodes (or *neighboring* nodes or *neighbors*). The *degree* of a node i is the number of arcs that are incident to i. The numbers of nodes and arcs of G are denoted by $|N|$ and $|A|$, respectively.

Note that we have disallowed self–arcs, that is, arcs connecting a node with itself. We have also disallowed multiple arcs between the same pair of nodes, and thus we can refer unambiguously to the arc between nodes i and j as arc (i, j). This was done for notational convenience; all of our analysis can be simply extended to the case of graphs that can have multiple arcs between any pair of distinct nodes. The standard method for doing this is to replace each arc between nodes i and j by an additional node, call it n, together with the two arcs (i, n) and (n, j).

A *walk* in a graph G is a finite sequence of nodes $(n_1, n_2, \ldots, n_k)$ such that $(n_1, n_2), (n_2, n_3), \ldots, (n_{k-1}, n_k)$ are arcs of G. A walk $(n_1, \ldots, n_k)$ with $n_1 = n_k$, $k \geq 3$, is called a *cycle*. A walk is said to be *simple* if it contains no repeated nodes, except possibly for the start and end nodes, in which case it is a (simple) cycle. We say that a graph is *connected* if for each node i, there is a walk $(i = n_1, n_2, \ldots, n_k = j)$ to each other node j.

We say that $G' = (N', A')$ is a *subgraph* of $G = (N, A)$ if G' is a graph, $N' \subset N$, and $A' \subset A$. A *tree* is a connected graph that contains no cycles. A *spanning tree* of a graph G is a subgraph of G that is a tree and that includes all the nodes of G. The following proposition gives a basic result on trees and spanning trees:

Proposition B.1.   Let $G = (N, A)$ be a connected graph with $|N|$ nodes and $|A|$ arcs. Then:

(a) G contains a spanning tree.

(b) $|A| \geq |N| - 1$.

(c) G is a tree if and only if $|A| = |N| - 1$.

Proof.

(a) We show that the following algorithm constructs a spanning tree:
1. Let n be an arbitrary node in N. Let $N' = \{n\}$, $A' = $ empty.
2. If $N' = N$, then stop [$G' = (N', A')$ is a spanning tree]; else go to Step 3.
3. Let $(i, j) \in A$ be an arc with $i \in N'$ and $j \notin N'$. Update N' and A' by

$$N' := N' \cup \{j\},$$
$$A' := A' \cup \{(i, j)\}.$$

Go to Step 2.

To see why the algorithm works, note that Step 3 is only entered when N' is a proper subset of N, so that the existence of the arc (i, j) in Step 3 follows from the connectedness of G. We use induction on successive executions of Step 3 to show that $G' = (N', A')$ is always a tree. Initially, $G' = (\{n\}, \text{empty})$ is trivially a tree, so assume that $G' = (N', A')$ is a tree before the update of Step 3. This ensures that there is a walk between each pair of nodes in N' using arcs of A'. After node j and arc (i, j) are added, each node has a walk to j simply by adding j to the walk to i, and, similarly, j has a walk to each other node. Finally, node j cannot be in any cycles since (i, j) is the only arc of G' incident to j. Furthermore, there are no cycles not including j by the induction hypothesis.

(b) Observe that the algorithm starts with a subgraph having one node and zero arcs, and adds one node and one arc on each execution of Step 3. This means that the spanning tree G' resulting from the algorithm always has $|N|$ nodes and $|N| - 1$ arcs. Since G' is a subgraph of G, the number of arcs $|A|$ in G must satisfy $|A| \geq |N| - 1$.

(c) Assume that $|A| = |N| - 1$. This means that the algorithm uses all arcs of G in the spanning tree G', so that $G = G'$ and G must be a tree itself. Conversely, if $|A| \geq |N|$, then G contains at least one arc (i, j) not in the spanning tree G' generated by the algorithm. Letting $(j, \ldots, i)$ be the walk from j to i in G', it is seen that $(i, j, \ldots, i)$ is a cycle in G and G cannot be a tree.   **Q.E.D.**

Directed Graphs

A *directed graph* or *digraph* $G = (N, A)$ is a finite nonempty set N of nodes and a collection A of *ordered* pairs of distinct nodes from N; each ordered pair of nodes in A is called a *directed arc* (or simply arc). Thus, a directed graph can be viewed as a graph where each arc has a direction associated with it. We do not allow more than one arc between a pair of nodes in the same direction, but we do not exclude the possibility that there is a separate arc connecting a pair of nodes in each of the two directions. If (i, j) is a directed arc, we say that (i, j) is an *outgoing* arc from node i, and an *incoming* arc to node j; we also say that (i, j) is *incident* to i and to j, and that i and j are *adjacent* nodes (or *neighboring* nodes or *neighbors*).

A *path* P in a directed graph is a sequence of nodes $(n_1, n_2, \ldots, n_k)$ with $k \geq 2$ and a corresponding sequence of $k - 1$ arcs such that the ith arc in the sequence is either (n_i, n_{i+1}) (in which case it is called a *forward* arc of the path) or (n_{i+1}, n_i) (in which case, it is called a *backward* arc of the path). We denote by P^+ and P^- the sets of forward and backward arcs of P, respectively. The arcs in P^+ and P^- are said to *belong* to P. Nodes n_1 and n_k are called the *start node* (or *origin*) and *end node* (or *destination*) of P, respectively.

A *directed cycle* (or simply *cycle* when confusion cannot arise) is a path for which the start and end nodes are the same. A path is said to be *simple* if it contains no repeated nodes except possibly for the start and end nodes, in which case, it is a (simple) cycle. A path is said to be *positive* (or *negative*) if all of its arcs are forward (respectively, backward) arcs. We refer similarly to a positive and a negative cycle. A digraph that does not contain any positive cycles is said to be *acyclic*.

A digraph is said to be *connected* if for each pair of nodes i and j, there is a path starting at i and ending at j; it is said to be *strongly connected* if for each pair of nodes i and j, there is a positive path starting at i and ending at j.

Flows

A *flow vector* f in a directed graph (N, A) is a set of real numbers $\{f_{ij} \mid (i, j) \in A\}$. We refer to f_{ij} as the flow of the arc (i, j). The *divergence vector* y associated with a flow vector is the $|N|$–dimensional vector with coordinates

$$y_i = \sum_{\{j \mid (i, j) \in A\}} f_{ij} - \sum_{\{j \mid (i, j) \in A\}} f_{ji}, \qquad \forall \, i \in N. \tag{B.1}$$

Thus, y_i is the total flow departing from node i less the total flow arriving at i. We say that node i is a *source* (respectively, *sink*) for the flow vector f if $y_i > 0$ (respectively, $y_i < 0$). If $y_i = 0$ for all $i \in N$, then f is called a *circulation*.

We say that a path P *conforms* to a flow vector f if $f_{ij} > 0$ for all $(i, j) \in P^+$ and $f_{ij} < 0$ for all $(i, j) \in P^-$, and either P is a cycle or else the start and end nodes of P are a source and a sink of f, respectively. A *simple path flow* is a flow vector f of the form

$$f_{ij} = \begin{cases} a & \text{if } (i, j) \in P^+, \\ -a & \text{if } (i, j) \in P^-, \\ 0 & \text{otherwise,} \end{cases} \tag{B.2}$$

where a is a positive scalar, and P^+ and P^- are the sets of forward and backward arcs, respectively, of a simple path P. We say that a simple path flow f^s *conforms* to a flow vector f if the path P corresponding to f^s via Eq. (B.2) conforms to f. The following is an important result proved in several sources, (e.g., [Roc84], p. 103).

Conformal Realization Theorem. A nonzero flow vector f can be decomposed into the sum of finitely many simple path flow vectors $f^1, f^2, \ldots, f^k$ that conform to f. If f is integer, then $f^1, f^2, \ldots, f^k$ can also be chosen to be integer. If f is a circulation, then $f^1, f^2, \ldots, f^k$ can be chosen to be circulations.

Proof. We first assume that f is a circulation. Our proof consists of showing how to obtain from f a simple circulation f' such that

$$0 \leq f_{ij} \quad \Rightarrow \quad 0 \leq f'_{ij} \leq f_{ij}, \tag{B.3a}$$

$$f_{ij} \leq 0 \quad \Rightarrow \quad f_{ij} \leq f'_{ij} \leq 0, \tag{B.3b}$$

$$f_{ij} = f'_{ij} \neq 0 \qquad \text{for at least one arc } (i, j). \tag{B.3c}$$

Once this is done, we have $f_{ij} - f'_{ij} > 0 \, (< 0)$ only if $f_{ij} > 0 \, (f_{ij} < 0)$, and $f_{ij} - f'_{ij} = 0$ for at least one arc (i, j) with $f_{ij} \neq 0$. If f is integer, then f' and $f - f'$ will also be integer. We then repeat the process with the circulation f replaced by the circulation $f - f'$ and so on until the zero flow is obtained. This is guaranteed to happen eventually because $f - f'$ has at least one more arc with zero flow than f.

We now describe the procedure by which f' with the properties (B.3) is obtained. Choose an arc (i, j) with $f_{ij} \neq 0$. Assume that $f_{ij} > 0$. (A similar procedure can be used when $f_{ij} < 0$.) Take $T_0 = \{j\}$. Given T_k, let

$$T_{k+1} = \big\{ n \notin \cup_{p=0}^k T_p \, \big| \text{ there is a node } m \in T_k, \text{ and either an arc } (m, n)$$

$$\text{such that } f_{mn} > 0, \text{ or an arc } (n, m) \text{ such that } f_{nm} < 0 \big\},$$

and mark each node $n \in T_{k+1}$ with the label "m", where m is a node of T_k such that $f_{mn} > 0$ or $f_{nm} < 0$. We claim that one of the sets T_k contains node i. To see this note that there is no outgoing arc from $\cup_k T_k$ with positive flow and no incoming arc into $\cup_k T_k$ with negative flow. If i did not belong to $\cup_k T_k$, there would exist at least one incoming arc into $\cup_k T_k$ with positive flow, namely, the arc (i, j). Thus, the total incoming flow into $\cup_k T_k$ would not be equal to the total outgoing flow from $\cup_k T_k$, and this contradicts the fact that f is a circulation. Therefore, one of the sets T_k contains node i.

We now trace labels backwards from i until node j is reached. (This will happen eventually because if "m" is the label of node n and $n \in T_{k+1}$, then $m \in T_k$, so a "cycle" of labels cannot be formed before reaching j.) In particular, let "i_1" be the label of i, let "i_2" be the label of i_1, etc., until a node i_k with label "j" is found. The cycle $C = (j, i_k, i_{k-1}, \ldots, i_1, i, j)$ is simple, it contains (i, j) as a forward arc, and is such that all its forward arcs have positive flow and all its backward arcs have negative flow (see Fig. B.1). Let $a = \min_{(m,n) \in C} |f_{mn}| > 0$. Then the circulation f', where

$$f'_{ij} = \begin{cases} a & \text{if } (i,j) \in C^+, \\ -a & \text{if } (i,j) \in C^-, \\ 0 & \text{otherwise,} \end{cases} \tag{B.4}$$

has the required properties (B.3).

If f is not a circulation, we introduce a new node s and for each node $i \in N$, an arc (s, i) with flow f_{si} equal to the divergence y_i of Eq. (B.1). Then the resulting flow vector is a circulation, and application of the decomposition result just shown for circulations proves the proposition.   **Q.E.D.**

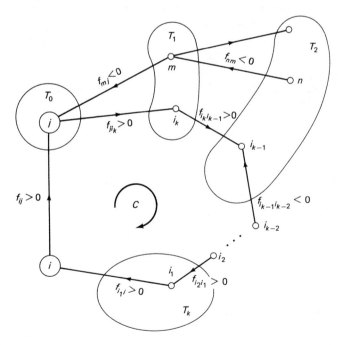

Figure B.1 Construction of a cycle of nonzero flow arcs used in the proof of the Conformal Realization Theorem.

We close this appendix by using the Conformal Realization Theorem to prove a useful fact. We first introduce some definitions. For any positive path $P = (n_1, n_2, \ldots, n_k)$, the *multiplicity* of an arc belonging to P is the number of times that it appears in the sequence $(n_1, n_2), (n_2, n_3), \ldots, (n_{k-1}, n_k)$. We say that the positive path P is *decomposed* into a set of positive paths $P_1, P_2, \ldots, P_d$ if:

(a) an arc belongs to P if and only if it belongs to at least one of the paths $P_1, P_2, \ldots, P_d$;

(b) the multiplicity of an arc belonging to P is equal to the sum of the multiplicities of the arc in those paths $P_1, P_2, \ldots, P_d$ to which it belongs.

We have the following result:

Path Decomposition Theorem. A positive path P can be decomposed into a (possibly empty) collection of simple positive cycles, together with a simple positive path $\bar{P}$ that has the same start node and end node as P.

Proof. For every arc (i, j) that belongs to P, let f_{ij} be equal to its multiplicity, and for every other arc (i, j) let $f_{ij} = 0$. Assume first that P is a cycle. Then, for each node i, the number of arcs that are outgoing from i and belong to P is equal to the number of arcs that are incoming to i and belong to P. Hence, the flow vector f is a circulation, and the result follows by applying the Conformal Realization Theorem. If P is not a cycle, introduce a new node s and the arcs (s, i_1) and (i_k, s) where i_1 and i_k are the start node and end node of P, respectively. Let $f_{si_1} = f_{i_k s} = 1$. Then the flow vector f is a circulation in the expanded graph. By applying the Conformal Realization Theorem, we see that f is decomposed into a collection of simple positive cycles, of which only one contains the arcs (s, i_1) and (i_k, s). This latter cycle is used to determine the simple positive path $\bar{P}$ that has the same start and end node as P.   **Q.E.D.**

C

Duality Theory

In this appendix, we develop a Lagrange multiplier theorem and an associated duality theorem for convex optimization problems with linear constraints. For additional material on duality, consult [Roc70], [Roc84], and [StW70]. Our line of development is based on a simple result known as Farkas' Lemma. To understand this lemma, we introduce some notions related to cones in $\Re^n$.

Definition C.1. A set $C \subset \Re^n$ is said to be a *cone* if $ax \in C$ for all $a \geq 0$ and $x \in C$.

Definition C.2. The *polar cone* of a cone C is the cone given by

$$C^{\perp} = \{y \mid y'z \leq 0, \ \forall \ x \in C\}. \tag{C.1}$$

Figure C.1 illustrates these definitions.

To develop an example of a cone that is particularly interesting to us, let $e_1, e_2, \ldots, e_m$ and $a_1, a_2, \ldots, a_r$ be given vectors in $\Re^n$. Then it can be seen that the set

$$C = \left\{ x \ \middle| \ x = \sum_{i=1}^{m} p_i e_i + \sum_{j=1}^{r} u_j a_j, \ p_i \in \Re, \ u_j \geq 0 \right\} \tag{C.2}$$

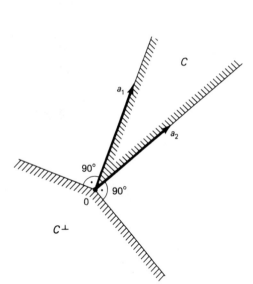

C

a_1

a_2

90°

90°

0

$C^\perp$

Figure C.1 Illustration of a cone and its polar in $\Re^2$. Here $C = \{x \mid x = u_1 a_1 + u_2 a_2,\ u_1 \geq 0,\ u_2 \geq 0\}$ and $C^\perp = \{y \mid y'a_1 \leq 0,\ y'a_2 \leq 0\}$, where a_1 and a_2 are the vectors shown; compare with Eqs. (C.2) and (C.3).

is a closed cone with a polar cone given by

$$C^\perp = \{y \mid y'e_i = 0,\ y'a_j \leq 0,\ \forall\ i = 1, \ldots, m,\ j = 1, \ldots, r\}. \tag{C.3}$$

The following result, when specialized to the cones C and $C^\perp$ of Eqs. (C.2) and (C.3), respectively, yields what is usually referred to as Farkas' lemma [PaS82].

Polar Cone Theorem.   For any closed convex cone C, we have $(C^\perp)^\perp = C$.

Proof. See Fig. C.2.

Consider now the optimization problem

$$
\begin{aligned}
\text{minimize} \quad & F(x) \\
\text{subject to} \quad & e_i'x = s_i, \qquad i = 1, \ldots, m, \\
& a_j'x \leq t_j, \qquad j = 1, \ldots, r, \\
& x \in P,
\end{aligned}
\tag{P}
$$

where $F : \Re^n \mapsto \Re$ is a convex function, e_i and a_j are given vectors in $\Re^n$, s_i and t_j are given scalars, and P is a nonempty polyhedral subset of $\Re^n$. (A polyhedral set P is one that is specified by a finite collection of linear inequalities; we admit the possibility that $P = \Re^n$.) A vector x satisfying the constraints of problem (P) will be referred to as *primal feasible* (or simply *feasible*). Define the *Lagrangian* function

$$L(x, p, u) = F(x) + \sum_{i=1}^{m} p_i(e_i'x - s_i) + \sum_{j=1}^{r} u_j(a_j'x - t_j), \tag{C.4}$$

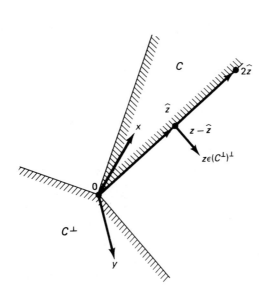

Figure C.2 Proof of the Polar Cone Theorem. If $x \in C$, then for all $y \in C^{\perp}$, we have $x'y \leq 0$, which implies that $x \in (C^{\perp})^{\perp}$. Hence, $C \subset (C^{\perp})^{\perp}$. To prove the reverse inclusion, take $z \in (C^{\perp})^{\perp}$, and let $\hat{z}$ be the unique projection of z on C, as shown in the figure. The projection exists because C is closed; see Prop. 3.2 in Section 3.3, which also implies that

$$(z - \hat{z})'(x - \hat{z}) \leq 0, \qquad \forall \, x \in C.$$

By taking $x = 0$ and $x = 2\hat{z}$ in the preceding relation, it is seen that

$$(z - \hat{z})'\hat{z} = 0.$$

Combining the last two relations, we obtain $(z - \hat{z})'x \leq 0$ for all $x \in C$. Therefore, $(z - \hat{z}) \in C^{\perp}$, and since $z \in (C^{\perp})^{\perp}$, we obtain $(z - \hat{z})'z \leq 0$, which when added to $(z - \hat{z})'\hat{z} = 0$ yields $\|z - \hat{z}\|_2^2 \leq 0$. Therefore, $z = \hat{z}$ and $z \in C$. It follows that $(C^{\perp})^{\perp} \subset C$.

where p and u are the vectors $(p_1, \ldots, p_m)$ and $(u_1, \ldots, u_r)$, respectively. Consider also the *dual functional* $q : \Re^{m+r} \mapsto [-\infty, \infty)$ defined by

$$q(p, u) = \inf_{x \in P} L(x, p, u). \tag{C.5}$$

The *dual problem* is

$$\begin{aligned} \text{maximize} \quad & q(p, u) \\ \text{subject to} \quad & p \in \Re^m, \quad u \in \Re^r, \quad u \geq 0. \end{aligned} \tag{D}$$

Note that if the polyhedron P is bounded, then the dual functional takes real values, but in general, $q(p, u)$ can take the value $-\infty$. Thus we generally view q as an extended real valued function. A pair (p, u) satisfying the constraints of problem (D) will be referred to as *dual feasible* (or simply *feasible*). From Eqs. (C.4) and (C.5) we see that q is obtained as the infimum of a collection of linear functions of p and u (one for each $x \in P$). It follows that q is *concave* [Prop. A.35(d) in Appendix A]. Figure C.3 provides a geometric interpretation of the dual functional, and illustrates why the optimal value of the original problem (P) is "normally" equal to the optimal dual value.

The following theorems hold for general convex functions $F : \Re^n \mapsto \Re$, but will be shown under the additional assumption that F is differentiable. The proof without this assumption requires a more refined version of Farkas' lemma (see [Roc70], pp. 187 and 277). These theorems will be proved in Section 5.5 without assuming differentiability

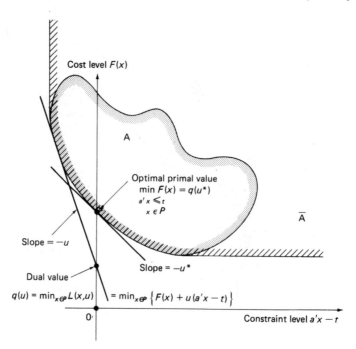

Figure C.3 Geometrical interpretation of the dual functional for the case of the single inequality constraint problem

$$\text{minimize} \quad F(x)$$

$$\text{subject to} \quad a'x \le t, \qquad x \in P.$$

We construct the set of constraint–cost pairs $A = \left\{ \left(a'x - t, F(x) \right) \mid x \in P \right\}$. Given $u \ge 0$, the dual value $q(u)$ is obtained by "supporting" A from below with a line of slope $-u$. The point where this line intercepts the vertical axis is $q(u)$. As u varies, $q(u)$ is always below the optimal primal value and for a particular value u^*, $q(u^*)$ equals the optimal primal value. This happens because the convexity of F can be used to show that the set $\bar{A} = \left\{ (z, y) \mid a'x - t \le z, \ F(x) \le y \text{ for some } x \in P \right\}$ shown in the figure is convex.

of F in the special case of a network flow problem with a separable cost function. They also have extensions to more general convex optimization problems, where the inequality constraints are specified by convex nonlinear functions and the constraint set P is a convex set which is not necessarily polyhedral (see [Roc70] and [StW70]).

Lagrange Multiplier Theorem. A vector x^* is an optimal solution of problem (P) if and only if x^* is feasible and there exist vectors $p^* = (p_1^*, \dots, p_m^*)$ and $u^* = (u_1^*, \dots, u_r^*)$ with $u^* \ge 0$ such that

$$F(x^*) = L(x^*, p^*, u^*) = \min_{x \in P} L(x, p^*, u^*), \tag{C.6}$$

$$u_j^* = 0, \qquad \forall\, j \text{ such that } a_j'x^* < t_j. \tag{C.7}$$

Proof. (Assuming that F is differentiable.) Let x^* be feasible. If there exist p^* and u^* with the given property, we have for all x that are feasible for (P),

$$F(x^*) \leq L(x, p^*, u^*) = F(x) + \sum_{i=1}^{m} p_i^*(e_i'x - s_i) + \sum_{j=1}^{r} u_j^*(a_j'x - t_j) \leq F(x), \tag{C.8}$$

where the last inequality follows from the condition $u^* \geq 0$ and the feasibility of x. Hence, x^* is optimal for (P).

Conversely, assume that x^* is optimal for (P). We will first prove the version of the result where $P = \Re^n$ or, equivalently, where the linear inequalities defining P are lumped together with the inequality constraints $a_j'x \leq t_j$, $j = 1, \ldots, r$. We will then use the result for this special case together with the just shown forward part of the theorem to prove the result for the general case.

The optimality of x^* implies that for every feasible z, the rate of change of F starting from x^* and going toward z is nonnegative, that is,

$$\nabla F(x^*)'(z - x^*) \geq 0, \qquad \forall \text{ feasible } z, \tag{C.9}$$

(cf. Prop. 3.1 in Section 3.3). Consider a representation of the polyhedral set P as

$$P = \{x \mid a_j'x \leq t_j, \ j = r+1, \ldots, \bar{r}\},$$

where a_j and t_j, $j = r+1, \ldots, \bar{r}$, are some vectors and scalars, respectively. Let J be the set of indices for which the corresponding inequalities $a_j'x \leq t_j$ hold as equalities at x^*, that is,

$$J = \{j \mid a_j'x^* = t_j, \ j = 1, \ldots, \bar{r}\}.$$

Consider the cone

$$C = \left\{ y \ \middle|\ y = \sum_{i=1}^{m} p_i e_i + \sum_{j \in J} u_j a_j, \ p_i \in \Re, \ u_j \geq 0 \right\}, \tag{C.10}$$

and its polar given by [cf. Eqs. (C.2) and (C.3)]

$$C^\perp = \{y \mid y'e_i = 0, \ y'a_j \leq 0, \ \forall\, i = 1, \ldots, m, \ j \in J\}.$$

It is seen that we have $y \in C^\perp$ if and only if $y = \gamma(z - x^*)$ for some $\gamma > 0$ and some feasible z. Thus, from the condition $\nabla F(x^*)'(z - x^*) \geq 0$ [cf. Eq. (C.9)] we obtain

$$\nabla F(x^*)'y \geq 0, \qquad \forall\, y \in C^\perp.$$

Hence, $-\nabla F(x^*)$ belongs to $(C^\perp)^\perp$, which, by the Polar Cone Theorem, is equal to C. It follows from the representation of C [cf. Eq. (C.10)] that there exist p^* and $w^* \geq 0$ such that $w_j^* = 0$ for all $j \notin J$ and

$$\nabla F(x^*) + \sum_{i=1}^{m} p_i^* e_i + \sum_{j=1}^{r} w_j^* a_j + \sum_{j=r+1}^{\bar{r}} w_j^* a_j = 0. \tag{C.11}$$

Define $u^* = (w_1^*, \ldots, w_r^*)$ and consider the problem

$$\text{minimize} \quad L(x, p^*, u^*)$$

$$\text{subject to} \quad a_j' x \leq t_j, \qquad j = r+1, \ldots, \bar{r}.$$

The function $L(x, p^*, u^*) + \sum_{j=r+1}^{\bar{r}} w_j^*(a_j' x - t_j)$ is the Lagrangian function for this problem and is convex with respect to x. From Eq. (C.11), it follows that x^* minimizes this function over $\Re^n$. By using the earlier shown forward part of the theorem, we obtain that x^* solves the above problem, that is, minimizes $L(x, p^*, u^*)$ over all $x \in P$. Using the properties of u^* and the feasibility of x^* we see that (C.7) holds and that $F(x^*) = L(x^*, p^*, u^*)$.   **Q.E.D.**

Duality Theorem.

(a) If the primal problem (P) has an optimal solution, the dual problem (D) also has an optimal solution and the two optimal values are equal.

(b) In order for x^* to be an optimal primal solution and (p^*, u^*) to be an optimal dual solution it is necessary and sufficient that x^* be primal feasible, (p^*, u^*) be dual feasible, and

$$F(x^*) = L(x^*, p^*, u^*) = \min_{x \in P} L(x, p^*, u^*).$$

Proof.

(a) We have, using the definitions of the Lagrangian and the dual functions [cf. Eqs. (C.4) and (C.5)]

$$q(p, u) \leq L(x, p, u) \leq F(x), \qquad \forall \text{ primal feasible } x, \text{ and dual feasible } (p, u). \tag{C.12}$$

Furthermore, the Lagrange Multiplier Theorem implies that if x^* is a primal optimal solution, then there exist dual feasible p^* and u^* such that $q(p^*, u^*) = F(x^*)$. From Eq. (C.12), it follows that (p^*, u^*) is dual optimal and that the primal and dual optimal values are equal.

(b) If x^* is primal optimal and (p^*, u^*) is dual optimal, then using the equality of the optimal primal and dual values [part (a)], Eq. (C.12), and the definition of the dual functional, we obtain

$$F(x^*) = L(x^*, p^*, u^*) = q(p^*, u^*) = \min_{x \in P} L(x, p^*, u^*).$$

Conversely, the relation $F(x^*) = \min_{x \in P} L(x, p^*, u^*)$ can be written as $F(x^*) = q(p^*, u^*)$, and, since x^* is primal feasible and (p^*, u^*) is dual feasible, Eq. (C.12) implies that x^* is primal optimal and (p^*, u^*) is dual optimal.   **Q.E.D.**

Saddle Point Theorem.   In order for x^* to be an optimal primal solution and (p^*, u^*) to be an optimal dual solution, it is necessary and sufficient that $x^* \in P$, $u^* \geq 0$, and

$$L(x^*, p, u) \leq L(x^*, p^*, u^*) \leq L(x, p^*, u^*), \qquad \forall \ x \in P, \ p \in \Re^m, \ u \geq 0. \qquad \text{(C.13)}$$

Proof. If x^* is primal optimal and (p^*, u^*) is dual optimal, then $x^* \in P$ and $u^* \geq 0$. Furthermore, from part (b) of the Duality Theorem, we obtain

$$L(x^*, p^*, u^*) = \min_{x \in P} L(x, p^*, u^*),$$

thereby proving the right–hand side of Eq. (C.13). We also have for all p and $u \geq 0$, using Eq. (C.12) and part (b) of the Duality Theorem,

$$L(x^*, p, u) \leq F(x^*) = L(x^*, p^*, u^*),$$

which shows the left–hand side of Eq. (C.13).

Conversely, assume that $x^* \in P$, $u^* \geq 0$, and Eq. (C.13) holds. It is seen from the definition of the Lagrangian function (C.4) that

$$\sup_{u \geq 0, p} L(x^*, p, u) = \begin{cases} F(x^*), & \text{if } e_i' x^* = s_i, \ \forall \ i, \ a_j' x^* \leq t_j, \ \forall \ j, \\ +\infty, & \text{otherwise.} \end{cases}$$

Therefore, from Eq. (C.13), we obtain that x^* is primal feasible and

$$F(x^*) = L(x^*, p^*, u^*) = \min_{x \in P} L(x, p^*, u^*).$$

The primal optimality of x^* and the dual optimality of (p^*, u^*) follow from part (b) of the Duality Theorem.   **Q.E.D.**

Examples of Dual Problems

As an example of application of the preceding theorems, consider the linear program

$$\begin{aligned} \text{minimize} \quad & a'x \\ \text{subject to} \quad & e_i' x = s_i, \qquad i = 1, \dots, m, \\ & b_j \leq x_j \leq c_j, \qquad j = 1, \dots, n, \end{aligned} \qquad \text{(LP)}$$

where a and e_i are given vectors in $\Re^n$, and s_i are given scalars. The jth component of the vector e_i is denoted by e_{ij}. Using the definition of the dual functional q [cf. Eqs. (C.4) and (C.5)], we obtain

$$q(p) = \min_{b_j \leq x_j \leq c_j, \; j=1,\ldots,n} \left\{ \sum_{j=1}^{n} \left(a_j + \sum_{i=1}^{m} p_i e_{ij} \right) x_j - \sum_{i=1}^{m} p_i s_i \right\}.$$

This minimization can be carried out separately for each x_j, leading to the form

$$q(p) = \sum_{j=1}^{n} q_j(p) - \sum_{i=1}^{m} p_i s_i, \tag{C.14}$$

where

$$q_j(p) = \begin{cases} \left(a_j + \sum_{i=1}^{m} p_i e_{ij} \right) b_j, & \text{if } a_j + \sum_{i=1}^{m} p_i e_{ij} \geq 0, \\ \left(a_j + \sum_{i=1}^{m} p_i e_{ij} \right) c_j, & \text{if } a_j + \sum_{i=1}^{m} p_i e_{ij} < 0. \end{cases} \tag{C.15}$$

The dual problem is

$$\begin{aligned} &\text{maximize} \quad q(p) \\ &\text{subject to} \quad p \in \Re^m. \end{aligned} \tag{DLP}$$

From part (b) of the Duality Theorem, we also obtain that x^* and p^* are primal and dual optimal, respectively, if and only if

$$e_i' x^* = s_i, \qquad \forall \, i = 1, \ldots, m, \tag{C.16}$$

and x_j^* minimizes $\left(a_j + \sum_{i=1}^{m} p_i^* e_{ij} \right) x_j$ subject to $b_j \leq x_j \leq c_j$ for each j. The latter minimizing property of x_j^* is equivalent to

$$x_j^* = b_j, \qquad \text{if } a_j + \sum_{i=1}^{m} p_i^* e_{ij} > 0, \tag{C.17a}$$

$$x_j^* = c_j, \qquad \text{if } a_j + \sum_{i=1}^{m} p_i^* e_{ij} < 0, \tag{C.17b}$$

$$b_j \leq x_j^* \leq c_j, \qquad \text{if } a_j + \sum_{i=1}^{m} p_i^* e_{ij} = 0. \tag{C.17c}$$

The relations (C.17) are known as the *complementary slackness conditions*.

Consider also the linear program

$$\text{minimize} \quad a'x$$

$$\text{subject to} \quad e_i'x = s_i, \qquad i = 1, \ldots, m, \tag{LP$'$}$$

$$0 \le x_j, \qquad j = 1, \ldots, n,$$

where a, e_i, and s_i are as in the previous linear program (LP). Using the definition of the dual functional q of Eqs. (C.4) and (C.5), we obtain

$$q(p) = \inf_{0 \le x_j, \; j=1,\ldots,n} \left\{ \sum_{j=1}^{n} \left(a_j + \sum_{i=1}^{m} p_i e_{ij} \right) x_j - \sum_{i=1}^{m} p_i s_i \right\},$$

so $q(p) = -\infty$ if $a_j + \sum_{i=1}^{m} p_i e_{ij} < 0$ for some j, and $q(p) = -\sum_{i=1}^{m} p_i s_i$ otherwise. Thus, the dual problem is

$$\text{maximize} \quad -\sum_{i=1}^{m} p_i s_i$$

$$\text{subject to} \quad a_j + \sum_{i=1}^{m} p_i e_{ij} \ge 0, \qquad \forall\, j = 1, \ldots, n.$$

By making the change of variables $\pi_i = -p_i$, this problem is written in the following form, which is the one usually encountered in linear programming textbooks,

$$\text{maximize} \quad \sum_{i=1}^{m} \pi_i s_i$$

$$\text{subject to} \quad \sum_{i=1}^{m} \pi_i e_{ij} \le a_j, \qquad \forall\, j = 1, \ldots, n. \tag{DLP$'$}$$

As an example of a special case of the linear program (LP$'$), consider the following version of the assignment problem [see Section 5.3, Eq. (3.6)]

$$\text{maximize} \quad \sum_{i=1}^{n} \sum_{j \in A(i)} a_{ij} f_{ij}$$

$$\text{subject to} \quad \sum_{j \in A(i)} f_{ij} = 1, \qquad \forall\, i = 1, \ldots, n,$$

$$\sum_{\{i \mid j \in A(i)\}} f_{ij} = 1, \qquad \forall\, j = 1, \ldots, n, \tag{AP}$$

$$0 \le f_{ij}, \qquad \forall\, i = 1, \ldots, n, \quad j \in A(i),$$

where each $A(i)$ is a subset of $\{1, \ldots, n\}$. This problem becomes a special case of (LP') once the sign of a_{ij} is reversed and maximization is replaced by minimization. By carrying out this transformation, writing the corresponding dual problem (DLP'), and changing sign of the dual variables while replacing minimization by maximization, we obtain the dual problem

$$\text{minimize} \quad \sum_{i=1}^{n} r_i + \sum_{j=1}^{n} p_j \tag{DAP}$$

$$\text{subject to} \quad r_i + p_j \geq a_{ij}, \qquad \forall \ i, \ j \in A(i).$$

Here the dual variables r_i (respectively, p_j) correspond to the first (respectively, second) set of equality constraints of the assignment problem (AP).

As another example of a duality relation, consider the quadratic programming problem

$$\text{minimize} \quad \tfrac{1}{2}x'Qx - b'x$$

$$\text{subject to} \quad Ax \leq c, \tag{QP}$$

where Q is a given $n \times n$ positive definite symmetric matrix, A is a given $m \times n$ matrix, and $b \in \Re^n$ and $c \in \Re^m$ are given vectors. The dual functional is

$$q(u) = \inf_x \left\{ \tfrac{1}{2}x'Qx - b'x + u'(Ax - c) \right\}.$$

The infimum is attained for $x = Q^{-1}(b - A'u)$, and, after substitution of this expression in the preceding relation for q, a straightforward calculation yields

$$q(u) = -\tfrac{1}{2}u'AQ^{-1}A'u - u'(c - AQ^{-1}b) - \tfrac{1}{2}b'Q^{-1}b.$$

The dual problem, after a sign change that converts it to a minimization problem, is equivalent to

$$\text{minimize} \quad \tfrac{1}{2}u'Pu + r'u$$

$$\text{subject to} \quad u \geq 0, \tag{DQP}$$

where

$$P = AQ^{-1}A', \qquad r = c - AQ^{-1}b.$$

If u^* is any optimal solution of the dual problem (DQP), then the optimal solution of the primal quadratic programming problem (QP) is given by $x^* = Q^{-1}(b - A'u^*)$.

Differentiability Properties of the Dual Functional

We finally consider the question of differentiability of the dual function q of Eq. (C.5) when P is a bounded polyhedron. Since $L(\cdot, p, u)$ is convex, it is continuous (Prop. A.36 in Appendix A) and it follows that the infimum of $L(x, p, u)$ over $x \in P$ is attained for all (p, u) by the Weierstrass theorem (Prop. A.8 in Appendix A). Thus, the concave function q is everywhere finite and is therefore continuous (Prop. A.36 in Appendix A). Situations where q is differentiable can be characterized by using Danskin's theorem (Prop. A.43 in Appendix A). This theorem applies to functions of the form $\max_{z \in Z} \phi(y, z)$ where ϕ is convex with respect to y for every fixed z. Equivalently, by changing the sign of ϕ, the theorem applies to functions of the form $\min_{z \in Z} \psi(y, z)$, where ψ is concave with respect to y for every fixed z. The dual functional is of the latter form, provided that we identify ψ, y, z, and Z with L, (p, u), x, and P respectively, and we notice that L is linear (and hence concave) with respect to (p, u) for each fixed x. Since P is compact and L is continuous, it follows from Danskin's theorem that if the infimum of $L(x, p, u)$ over $x \in P$ is attained at a unique point, then q is differentiable at (p, u). Thus, by using also the fact that a convex differentiable function has a continuous gradient (Prop. A.42 in Appendix A), we obtain the following result:

Dual Function Differentiability Theorem.   Assume that F is a strictly convex function and that the polyhedron P is bounded. Then the dual functional q is continuously differentiable and for all (p, u), we have

$$\frac{\partial q(p, u)}{\partial p_i} = e_i' \bar{x} - s_i, \qquad i = 1, \ldots, m,$$

$$\frac{\partial q(p, u)}{\partial u_j} = a_j' \bar{x} - t_j, \qquad j = 1, \ldots, r,$$

where $\bar{x}$ is the unique vector that minimizes $L(x, p, u)$ over $x \in P$ for the given pair (p, u).

D

Probability Theory and Markov Chains

We now present some background material on probability theory. We start with two results on exponentially distributed random variables needed for Exercise 4.1 in Section 1.4. We continue with the basic definitions and properties of finite state Markov chains. Finally, we present some more advanced results that are needed for Section 7.8. It is assumed that the reader is already familiar with the basic concepts of probability theory, such as random variables, independence, expectations, and conditional expectations. A rigorous proof of some of the results to be presented requires measure theory ([Ash72] and [Rud74]). Still, knowledge of measure theory is not needed for understanding the contents of this appendix. For more information, the reader could consult [Ash70], [Fel68], and [WoH85] for probability theory, and [Ash70] and [Ros83a] for Markov chains.

We use the notation $\Pr(A)$ to denote the probability of an event A. A piecewise continuous function $p : \Re \mapsto [0, \infty)$ is called the *density* of a real valued random variable X if

$$\Pr\bigl(X \in [a, b]\bigr) = \int_a^b p(x)\, dx,$$

for every $a, b \in \Re$ such that $a < b$. The *expectation* of a real valued random variable X with density p is given by

$$E[X] = \int_{-\infty}^{\infty} xp(x)\,dx,$$

and its *variance* by

$$\text{Var}(X) = E\left[(X - E[X])^2\right] = \int_{-\infty}^{\infty} (x - E[X])^2 p(x)\,dx,$$

provided that the integrals exist. If X is a random variable that takes only nonnegative values, then its expectation satisfies the *Markov inequality*

$$E[X] \geq a\text{Pr}(X \geq a), \tag{D.1}$$

for every scalar a. Suppose now that X is nonnegative and that $\lim_{x \to \infty} x\text{Pr}(X \geq x) = 0$. We notice that the function $x\text{Pr}(X \geq x)$ also vanishes at zero and infinity and its derivative is equal to $\text{Pr}(X \geq x) - xp(x)$. It follows that

$$E[X] = \int_{0}^{\infty} xp(x)\,dx = \int_{0}^{\infty} \text{Pr}(X \geq x)\,dx. \tag{D.2}$$

Properties of Exponential Random Variables

A random variable X is said to have an *exponential* distribution, with mean λ, if it has the density

$$p(x) = \begin{cases} 0, & x < 0, \\ \lambda e^{-\lambda x}, & x \geq 0. \end{cases}$$

Notice that if X has an exponential distribution, then

$$\text{Pr}(X \geq x) = \int_{x}^{\infty} \lambda e^{-\lambda y}\,dy = e^{-\lambda x}.$$

Proposition D.1.   Let $\{X_i\}$ be a sequence of independent exponentially distributed random variables, with mean one. Then

$$\ln n \leq E\left[\max_{1 \leq i \leq n} X_i\right] \leq 1 + \ln n, \qquad \forall n \geq 1.$$

(Here ln is the natural logarithm.)

Proof. Let $a_n = E\left[\max_{1 \leq i \leq n} X_i\right]$. Then $a_1 = 1$. For $n \geq 2$, we use Eq. (D.2) to obtain

$$
\begin{aligned}
a_n &= \int_0^\infty \Pr\left(\max_{1 \leq i \leq n} X_i \geq x\right) dx \\
&= \int_0^\infty \left(1 - (1 - e^{-x})^n\right) dx \\
&= \int_0^\infty \left(1 - (1 - e^{-x})^{n-1}\right) dx + \int_0^\infty e^{-x}(1 - e^{-x})^{n-1}\, dx \\
&= a_{n-1} + \frac{1}{n}(1 - e^{-x})^n \Big|_0^\infty = a_{n-1} + \frac{1}{n}.
\end{aligned}
$$

Thus, $a_n = 1 + (1/2) + \cdots + (1/n)$. We then notice that

$$
\ln n = \int_1^n \frac{1}{x}\, dx \leq \sum_{i=1}^n \frac{1}{i} \leq 1 + \int_1^n \frac{1}{x}\, dx = 1 + \ln n,
$$

which proves the desired result.   **Q.E.D.**

Proposition D.2. Let $\{X_i\}$ be a sequence of independent exponentially distributed random variables, with mean one. Then there exist positive constants α and K, such that

$$
\Pr\left(\sum_{i=1}^n X_i \geq nk\right) \leq e^{-\alpha k n}, \tag{D.3}
$$

for every positive integer n and any k larger than K.

Proof. Fix some $\beta \in (0, 1)$, and let γ be a positive scalar. A direct calculation yields

$$
E\left[e^{\beta(X_i - \gamma)}\right] = \int_0^\infty e^{\beta(x - \gamma)} e^{-x}\, dx = e^{-\beta\gamma}\frac{1}{1 - \beta}.
$$

In particular, we can choose γ sufficiently large so that

$$
E\left[e^{\beta(X_i - \gamma)}\right] < 1.
$$

Using the independence of the random variables X_i, we obtain

$$
E\left[e^{\beta \sum_{i=1}^n (X_i - \gamma)}\right] = \prod_{i=1}^n E\left[e^{\beta(X_i - \gamma)}\right] < 1.
$$

Using the Markov inequality (D.1), we obtain

$$e^{\beta mn} \Pr\left(e^{\beta \sum_{i=1}^{n}(X_i - \gamma)} > e^{\beta mn}\right) < 1.$$

This in turn implies that

$$\Pr\left(\sum_{i=1}^{n} X_i \geq n(m + \gamma)\right) = \Pr\left(e^{\beta \sum_{i=1}^{n}(X_i - \gamma)} > e^{\beta mn}\right) < e^{-\beta mn}.$$

Let $k = 2m$ and $K = 2\gamma$. Then if $k \geq K$, we have $m \geq \gamma$ and

$$\Pr\left(\sum_{i=1}^{n} X_i \geq nk\right) = \Pr\left(\sum_{i=1}^{n} X_i \geq n2m\right) \leq \Pr\left(\sum_{i=1}^{n} X_i \geq n(m + \gamma)\right)$$

$$< e^{-\beta mn} = e^{-\alpha kn},$$

where $\alpha = \beta/2$.   **Q.E.D.**

Markov Chains

A discrete time, finite state, homogeneous *Markov chain* is a sequence $\{X_k \mid k = 0, 1, 2, \ldots\}$ of random variables that take values in a finite set (state space) $\{1, \ldots, n\}$ and such that

$$\Pr\left(X_{k+1} = j \mid X_1, \ldots, X_{k-1}, X_k = i\right) = p_{ij}, \qquad \forall k \geq 0, \qquad \text{(D.4)}$$

where each p_{ij} is a given nonnegative scalar. In particular, the probability distribution of the next state X_{k+1} depends on the past only through the current state X_k. Furthermore, since the coefficients p_{ij} do not depend on the time index k, the *transition probabilities* $\Pr(X_{k+1} = j \mid X_k = i)$ are independent of k.

The sum over all j of the transition probabilities $\Pr(X_{k+1} = j \mid X_k = i)$ has to be equal to 1. Thus,

$$\sum_{j=1}^{n} p_{ij} = 1, \qquad \forall i.$$

We form an $n \times n$ matrix P with entries p_{ij}. The sum of the entries in any row of P is equal to 1; furthermore, all entries of P are nonnegative. Any square matrix possessing these two properties is called *stochastic*.

Proposition D.3.   The product of two stochastic matrices of the same dimensions is a stochastic matrix.

Proof. Let P and Q be $n \times n$ stochastic matrices. Since $P \geq 0$ and $Q \geq 0$, it follows that $PQ \geq 0$. Also, for any i, we have

$$\sum_{j=1}^{n}[PQ]_{ij} = \sum_{j=1}^{n}\sum_{k=1}^{n}[P]_{ik}[Q]_{kj} = \sum_{k=1}^{n}\sum_{j=1}^{n}[P]_{ik}[Q]_{kj}$$

$$= \sum_{k=1}^{n}[P]_{ik}\sum_{j=1}^{n}[Q]_{kj} = \sum_{k=1}^{n}[P]_{ik} = 1,$$

where the last two equalities followed from the assumption that Q and P are stochastic. **Q.E.D.**

As a special case of Prop. D.3, if P is stochastic and t is a positive integer, then P^t is also stochastic and its entries have the following probabilistic interpretation:

$$[P^t]_{ij} = \Pr(X_t = j \mid X_0 = i). \tag{D.5}$$

To see this, assume that Eq. (D.5) holds for $t - 1$ and use Eq. (D.4) to obtain

$$\Pr(X_t = j \mid X_0 = i) = \sum_{k=1}^{n}\Pr(X_t = j \mid X_{t-1} = k, X_0 = i) \cdot \Pr(X_{t-1} = k \mid X_0 = i)$$

$$= \sum_{k=1}^{n}\Pr(X_t = j \mid X_{t-1} = k)[P^{t-1}]_{ik} = \sum_{k=1}^{n}p_{kj}[P^{t-1}]_{ik} = [P^t]_{ij}.$$

Let π be an n–dimensional nonnegative row vector whose entries sum to 1. Such a vector defines a probability distribution for the initial state X_0 by means of the formula $\Pr(X_0 = i) = \pi_i$. Using Eq. (D.5), we obtain

$$[\pi P^t]_i = \sum_{j=1}^{n}\pi_j[P^t]_{ji} = \sum_{j=1}^{n}\Pr(X_t = i \mid X_0 = j) \cdot \Pr(X_0 = j) = \Pr(X_t = i).$$

In particular, if π has the property $\pi P = \pi$, then $\Pr(X_t = i) = \pi_i = \Pr(X_0 = i)$ for all t and all i, and the distribution of X_t does not change with time. Such a π is called an *invariant* or *steady–state distribution* of the Markov chain associated with P.

A useful classification of the states of a Markov chain is obtained by forming a directed graph $G = (N, A)$, with $N = \{1, \ldots, n\}$ and $A = \{(i, j) \mid i \neq j \text{ and } p_{ij} \neq 0\}$. For any state $i \in N$, let R_i be the set consisting of state i and all states $j \neq i$ such that there exists a positive path from i to j (that is, all arcs in the path are forward arcs). A state i is called *transient* if there exists some $j \in N$ such that $j \in R_i$ but $i \notin R_j$. Nontransient states are called *recurrent*.

If $j \in R_i$, we say that i communicates to j. It can be seen that the set of recurrent states can be partitioned into a collection of disjoint sets $C_1, \ldots, C_\ell$ such that any two states in the same set C_i communicate to each other and no two states in distinct sets C_i and C_j, $i \neq j$, communicate. Each one of the sets C_i is called an *ergodic* class (see Fig. D.1 for an illustration). We say that the matrix P is *irreducible* if $j \in R_i$ for every

$i, j \in N$. An equivalent condition is that there are no transient states and there exists a single ergodic class.

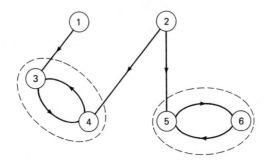

Figure D.1 The transition diagram of a Markov chain. States 1 and 2 are transient. There are two ergodic classes, namely, $\{3, 4\}$ and $\{5, 6\}$.

Suppose that the Markov chain associated with a stochastic matrix P has m_0 transient states and ℓ ergodic classes, with m_i states in the ith ergodic class C_i. Let us assume that the states have been renumbered so that the transient states have the smallest indices and so that the states in C_i have smaller indices than the states in C_j if $i < j$. Since states in an ergodic class C_i communicate only to other states in C_i, the matrix P has the structure

$$P = \begin{bmatrix} A_{00} & \cdots & \cdots & A_{0\ell} \\ 0 & A_{11} & 0 & 0 \\ \vdots & \ddots & \ddots & 0 \\ 0 & \cdots & 0 & A_{\ell\ell} \end{bmatrix},$$

where each A_{0i} and A_{ii} is a matrix of size $m_0 \times m_i$ and $m_i \times m_i$, respectively.

A stochastic matrix P is called *periodic* if there exists some $k > 1$ and disjoint nonempty subsets $N_0, \ldots, N_{k-1}$ of the state space N such that if $i \in N_\ell$ and $p_{ij} > 0$ then $j \in N_{\ell+1(\text{mod } k)}$. We say that P is *aperiodic* if it is not periodic.

Convergence of Random Variables and their Expectations

A sequence $\{X_i\}$ of random variables is said to converge to a random variable X, *with probability one*, if

$$\Pr\left(\lim_{i \to \infty} X_i = X \right) = 1.$$

More generally, we say that an event A occurs with probability one ("w.p.1," for short) if $\Pr(A) = 1$. The sequence $\{X_i\}$ converges to X in the *mean square* sense if

$$\lim_{i \to \infty} E\left[(X_i - X)^2 \right] = 0.$$

Finally, it converges to X *in probability* if

$$\lim_{i \to \infty} \Pr\left(|X_i - X| \geq \delta \right) = 0,$$

for every $\delta > 0$. Convergence with probability one (respectively, in the mean square sense, in probability) of vector valued random variables is defined by requiring convergence with probability one (respectively, in the mean square sense, in probability) of each component. It is a basic fact that convergence with probability one implies convergence in probability (see, e.g., [Ash72], p.94).

The following result allows us to interchange summation and expectation, under certain assumptions ([Ash72], p.44).

Proposition D.4.   (*Lebesgue's Monotone Convergence Theorem*) Let $\{X_i\}$ be a sequence of nonnegative random variables and suppose that $\sum_{i=1}^{\infty} E[X_i] < \infty$. Let $Y_k = \sum_{i=1}^{k} X_i$. Then:

(a) The sequence $\{Y_k\}$ converges, w.p.1, to a finite valued random variable Y.

(b) There holds $E[Y] = \sum_{i=1}^{\infty} E[X_i]$.

Given a finite set $\mathcal{F} = \{X_1, \ldots, X_m\}$ of random variables, we use the notation $E[X \mid \mathcal{F}]$ to denote the conditional expectation of a random variable X, given the random variables $X_1, \ldots, X_m$.[†] The conditional expectation $E[X \mid \mathcal{F}] = E[X \mid X_1, \ldots, X_m]$ is a function of $X_1, \ldots, X_m$ and is therefore itself a random variable. We define $M(\mathcal{F})$ as the set of all random variables X of the form $X = f(X_1, \ldots, X_m)$, where f is an arbitrary function from $\Re^m$ into $\Re$. In particular, $E[X \mid \mathcal{F}] \in M(\mathcal{F})$.[††]

The following result provides some properties of conditional expectations (see, e.g., [Ash72], Section 6.5).

Proposition D.5.   Let $X, Y, X_1, \ldots, X_m, Y_i, i \geq 0$, be random variables with finite expectations, and let $\mathcal{F} = \{X_1, \ldots, X_m\}$, $\mathcal{G} = \{X_1, \ldots, X_n\}$. Then:

(a) There holds

$$E\big[E[X \mid \mathcal{F}]\big] = E[X].   \tag{D.6}$$

(b) If $n \leq m$ (equivalently, $\mathcal{G} \subset \mathcal{F}$), then

$$E\big[E[X \mid \mathcal{F}] \mid \mathcal{G}\big] = E[X \mid \mathcal{G}], \quad \text{w.p.1}.   \tag{D.7}$$

(c) If $Y \in M(\mathcal{F})$, then

$$E[X \cdot Y \mid \mathcal{F}] = Y \cdot E[X \mid \mathcal{F}], \quad \text{w.p.1}.   \tag{D.8}$$

[†] The reader familiar with measure theory should interpret $\mathcal{F}$ as the σ–field generated by $X_1, \ldots, X_m$, and $E[X \mid \mathcal{F}]$ becomes the usual notion of conditional expectation given a σ–field [Ash72]. We also point out that conditional expectations can be uniquely defined only on a set of probability 1. (That is, there can exist different versions of $E[X \mid \mathcal{F}]$ which are different with probability zero but which are not always equal.) For this reason, any statements involving conditional expectations are only valid w.p.1.

[††] Actually, only "measurable" functions [Ash72] should be allowed in the definition of $M(\mathcal{F})$, which excludes certain pathological functions. This is not a concern for our purposes.

(d) If $E[|X|] < \infty$, then $E[X \mid \mathcal{F}]$ is well defined and finite, w.p.1.

(e) If each Y_i is nonnegative and $\sum_{i=1}^{\infty} E[Y_i] < \infty$, then

$$E\left[\sum_{i=1}^{\infty} Y_i \;\middle|\; \mathcal{F}\right] = \sum_{i=1}^{\infty} E[Y_i \mid \mathcal{F}], \tag{D.9}$$

where the infinite sums are interpreted as limits with probability 1. Furthermore, both sides of Eq. (D.9) are finite, with probability 1.

The following result can be viewed as a generalization, to a probabilistic context, of the fact that a bounded monotonic sequence converges ([Ash72], Section 7.4).

Proposition D.6.   (*Supermartingale Convergence Theorem*) Let $\{Y_i\}$ be a sequence of random variables and let $\{\mathcal{F}_i\}$ be a sequence of finite sets of random variables such that $\mathcal{F}_i \subset \mathcal{F}_{i+1}$ for each i. Suppose that:

(a) Each Y_i is nonnegative and belongs to $M(\mathcal{F}_i)$.

(b) For each i, we have $E[Y_i] < \infty$.

(c) For each i, we have $E[Y_{i+1} \mid \mathcal{F}_i] \leq Y_i$, w.p.1.

Then there exists a nonnegative random variable Y such that the sequence $\{Y_i\}$ converges to Y, w.p.1.

In Section 7.8, we use the following extension of the Supermartingale Convergence Theorem.

Proposition D.7.   Let $\{Y_i\}$ and $\{Z_i\}$ be two sequences of random variables. Let $\{\mathcal{F}_i\}$ be a sequence of finite sets of random variables such that $\mathcal{F}_i \subset \mathcal{F}_{i+1}$ for each i. Suppose that:

(a) The random variables Y_i and Z_i are nonnegative, have finite expectations, and belong to $M(\mathcal{F}_i)$ for each i.

(b) There holds

$$E[Y_{i+1} \mid \mathcal{F}_i] \leq Y_i + Z_i, \qquad \forall i, \text{ w.p.1.} \tag{D.10}$$

(c) There holds

$$\sum_{i=1}^{\infty} E[Z_i] < \infty. \tag{D.11}$$

Then there exists a nonnegative random variable Y such that the sequence $\{Y_i\}$ converges to Y, w.p.1.

Proof. Proposition D.5(e) states that $V_k = E\left[\sum_{i=k}^{\infty} Z_i \mid \mathcal{F}_k\right]$ is finite, w.p.1, for every k. We define random variables W_k by

$$W_k = Y_k + V_k = Y_k + E\left[\sum_{i=k}^{\infty} Z_i \mid \mathcal{F}_k\right].$$

Then, from Prop. D.5(b) and inequality (D.10),

$$E[W_{k+1} \mid \mathcal{F}_k] = E[Y_{k+1} \mid \mathcal{F}_k] + E\left[E\left[\sum_{i=k+1}^{\infty} Z_i \mid \mathcal{F}_{k+1}\right] \mid \mathcal{F}_k\right]$$

$$\leq Y_k + Z_k + E\left[\sum_{i=k+1}^{\infty} Z_i \mid \mathcal{F}_k\right] = W_k, \qquad \text{w.p.1.}$$

Notice that each W_k is nonnegative, belongs to $M(\mathcal{F}_k)$, and has finite expectation. Thus, Prop. D.6 applies to the sequence $\{W_k\}$ and shows that it converges, with probability one, to a nonnegative random variable W.

We will now prove that V_k converges to zero, with probability one. This will imply that $Y_k = W_k - V_k$ converges to W, with probability one, and will complete the proof. Using Prop. D.5(b), we have

$$E[V_{k+1} \mid \mathcal{F}_k] = E\left[E\left[\sum_{i=k+1}^{\infty} Z_i \mid \mathcal{F}_{k+1}\right] \mid \mathcal{F}_k\right] = E\left[\sum_{i=k+1}^{\infty} Z_i \mid \mathcal{F}_k\right]$$

$$= V_k - E[Z_k \mid \mathcal{F}_k] \leq V_k, \qquad \text{w.p.1,}$$

where the last inequality follows from the nonnegativity of Z_k. We apply Prop. D.6 to the sequence $\{V_k\}$ to see that it converges to a nonnegative random variable V, with probability one. We now use the Monotone Convergence Theorem to obtain

$$E[V_k] = E\left[\sum_{i=k}^{\infty} Z_i\right] = \sum_{i=k}^{\infty} E[Z_i],$$

which converges to zero as k tends to infinity, because of Eq. (D.11). Suppose that V is nonzero with positive probability. Then there exist some $\delta > 0$ and $\epsilon > 0$ such that $\Pr(V \geq \delta) \geq \epsilon$. On the other hand, V_k converges to V in probability and this implies that we can find some k_0 such that $\Pr\big(|V_k - V| \geq \delta/2\big) \leq \epsilon/2$ for every $k \geq k_0$. Therefore, for $k \geq k_0$,

$$\Pr\left(V_k \geq \delta/2\right) \geq \Pr\left(V \geq \delta \text{ and } |V_k - V| \leq \delta/2\right)$$
$$\geq \Pr\left(V \geq \delta\right) - \Pr\left(|V_k - V| \geq \delta/2\right) \geq \epsilon/2.$$

This implies that $E[V_k] \geq (\delta\epsilon)/4$ for every $k \geq k_0$, contradicts the convergence of $E[V_k]$ to zero, and shows that $V = 0$.   **Q.E.D.**

References

[AaM76] Aashtiani, H. A., and T. L. Magnanti. 1976. Implementing primal-dual network flow algorithms. Operations Research Center, Working Paper OR-055-76, Massachusetts Institute of Technology, Cambridge.

[AaM81] Aashtiani, H. A., and T. L. Magnanti. 1981. Equilibria on a congested transportation network. *SiAM J. Algeb. & Disc. Math.* 2:213–26.

[ADM82] Ahmed, H. M., J.-M. Delosme, and M. Morf. 1982. Highly concurrent computing structures for matrix arithmetic and signal processing. *Computer* 15:65–82.

[Agm54] Agmon, S. 1954. The relaxation method for linear inequalities. *Can. J. Math.* 6:382–92.

[Ahn79] Ahn, B. H. 1979. *Computation of Market Equilibria for Policy Analysis: The Project Independence Evaluation Study (PIES) Approach.* New York:Garland.

[AhO86] Ahuja, R. K., and J. B. Orlin. 1986. A fast and simple algorithm for the maximum flow problem. Working paper. Sloan School of Management, Massachusetts Institute of Technology, Cambridge.

[AhO87] Ahuja, R. K., and J. B. Orlin. 1987. Private communication.

[AHU74] Aho, A. V., J. E. Hopcroft, and J. D. Ullman. 1974. *The Design and Analysis of Computer Algorithms.* Reading, MA: Addison-Wesley.

680

[AHV85] Andre, F., D. Herman, and J.-P. Verjus. 1985. *Synchronization of Parallel Programs.* Cambridge, MA: The MIT Press.

[Akl85] Akl, S. G. 1985. *Parallel Sorting Algorithms.* Orlando, FL: Academic Press.

[Ame77] Ames, W. F. 1977. *Numerical Methods for Partial Differential Equations.* New York: Academic Press.

[Apt86] Apt, K. R. 1986. Correctness proofs of distributed termination algorithms. *ACM Trans. Prog. Lang. & Syst.* 8:388–405.

[Ash70] Ash, R. B. 1970. *Basic Probability Theory.* New York: Wiley.

[Ash72] Ash, R. B. 1972. *Real Analysis and Probability.* New York: Academic Press.

[AtK84] Atallah, M. J., and S. R. Kosaraju. 1984. Graph problems on a mesh-connected processor array. *J. ACM.* 31:649–67.

[Aus76] Auslender, A. 1976. *Optimization: Methodes Numeriques.* Paris: Mason.

[Avr76] Avriel, M. 1976. *Nonlinear Programming: Analysis and Methods.* Englewood Cliffs, NJ: Prentice-Hall.

[Awe85] Awerbuch, B. 1985. Complexity of network synchronization. *J. ACM.* 32:804–23.

[AwG87] Awerbuch, B., and R. G. Gallager. 1987. A new distributed algorithm to find breadth first search trees. *IEEE Trans. Inf. Theory.* IT-33:315–22.

[BaG87] Barbosa, V. C., and E. M. Gafni. 1987. Concurrency in heavily loaded neighborhood-constrained systems. *Proc. 7th Int. Conf. Distr. Comput. Sys.*

[BaJ77] Bazaraa, M. S., and J. J. Jarvis. 1977. *Linear Programming and Network Flows.* New York: Wiley.

[BaK78] Bachem, A., and B. Korte. 1978. An algorithm for quadratic optimization over transportation polytopes. *Z. Angew. Math. & Mech.* 58:T459–61.

[BaK80] Bachem, A., and B. Korte. 1980. Minimum norm problems over transportation polytopes. *Lin. Algeb. & Appl.* 31:102–18.

[Bar86] Barbosa, V. C. 1986. Concurrency in systems with neighborhood constraints. Doctoral dissertation. Computer Science Dept., UCLA.

[Bau78] Baudet, G. M. 1978. Asynchronous iterative methods for multiprocessors. *J. ACM.* 15:226–44.

[BaW75] Balinski, M., and P. Wolfe (eds.) 1975. *Nondifferentiable Optimization, Math. Prog. Study 3.* Amsterdam: North-Holland.

[BBG77] Bradley, G. H., G. G. Brown, and G. W. Graves. 1977. Design and implementation of large-scale primal transshipment problems. *Manag. Sci.* 24:1–34.

[BBK84] Bojanczyk, A., R. P. Brent, and H. T. Kung. 1984. Numerically stable solution of linear equations using mesh-connected processors. *SiAM J. Sci. & Stat. Comput.* 5:95–104.

[BeC87] Bertsekas, D. P., and D. A. Castanon. 1987. The auction algorithm for transportation problems. Unpublished report.

[BeE87a] Bertsekas, D. P., and J. Eckstein. 1987. Distributed asynchronous relaxation methods for linear network flow problems. *Proc. IFAC '87.*

[BeE87b] Bertsekas, D. P., and D. El Baz. 1987. Distributed asynchronous relaxation methods for convex network flow problems. *SiAM J. Contr. & Optim.* 25:74–85.

[BeE88] Bertsekas, D. P., and J. Eckstein. 1988. Dual coordinate step methods for linear network flow problems. Laboratory for Information and Decision Systems Report LIDS-P-1768, Massachusetts Institute of Technology, Cambridge. *Math. Prog.* Series B. (in press).

[BeG82] Bertsekas, D. P., and E. M. Gafni. 1982. Projection methods for variational inequalities with application to the traffic assignment problem. In D. C. Sorensen and R. J.-B Wets (eds.), *Mathematical Programming Studies*, Volume 17, 139–59. Amsterdam: North-Holland.

[BeG83] Bertsekas, D. P., and E. M. Gafni. 1983. Projected Newton methods and optimization of multicommodity flows. *IEEE Trans. Auto. Contr.* AC-28:1090–6.

[BeG87] Bertsekas, D. P., and R. G. Gallager. 1987. *Data Communication Networks*. Englewood Cliffs, NJ: Prentice-Hall.

[Bel57] Bellman, R. 1957. *Dynamic Programming*. Princeton, NJ: Princeton University Press.

[BeM73] Bertsekas, D. P., and S. K. Mitter. 1973. Descent numerical methods for optimization problems with nondifferentiable cost functions. *SiAM J. Contr.* 11:637–52.

[Ber74] Bertsekas, D. P. 1974. Partial conjugate gradient methods for a class of optimal control problems. *IEEE Trans. Auto. Contr.* 19:209–17.

[Ber75] Bertsekas, D. P. 1975. Necessary and sufficient conditions for a penalty method to be exact. *Math. Prog.* 9:87–99.

[Ber76a] Bertsekas, D. P. 1976. On the Goldstein-Levitin-Polyak gradient projection method. *IEEE Trans. Auto. Contr.* AC-21:174–84.

[Ber76b] Bertsekas, D. P. 1976. Multiplier methods: A survey. *Automatica.* 12:133–45.

[Ber76c] Bertsekas, D. P. 1976. Newton's method for linear optimal control problems. *Proc. IFAC Symp. Large Scale Sys.*, 353–9.

[Ber77] Bertsekas, D. P. 1977. Monotone mappings with application in dynamic programming. *SiAM J. Contr. & Optim.* 15:438–64.

[Ber79a] Bertsekas, D. P. 1979. Convexification procedures and decomposition methods for nonconvex optimization problems. *JOTA.* 29:169–97.

[Ber79b] Bertsekas, D. P. 1979. A distributed algorithm for the assignment problem. Laboratory for Information and Decision Systems, Working Paper, Massachusetts Institute of Technology, Cambridge.

[Ber79c] Bertsekas, D. P. 1979. Algorithms for nonlinear multicommodity network flow problems. In A. Bensoussan and J. L. Lions (eds.), *International Symposium on Systems Optimization and Analysis*, 210–24. New York: Springer-Verlag.

[Ber80] Bertsekas, D. P. 1980. A class of optimal routing algorithms for communication networks. *Proc. 5th Intl. Conf. Comput. Commun.*, 71–6.

[Ber81] Bertsekas, D. P. 1981. A new algorithm for the assignment problem. *Math. Prog.* 21:152–71.

[Ber82a] Bertsekas, D. P. 1982. *Constrained Optimization and Lagrange Multiplier Methods.* New York: Academic Press.

[Ber82b] Bertsekas, D. P. 1982. Projected Newton methods for optimization problems with simple constraints. *SiAM J. Contr. & Optim.* 20:221–46.

[Ber82c] Bertsekas, D. P. 1982. A unified framework for minimum cost network flow problems. Laboratory for Information and Decisions Systems Report LIDS-P-1245-A, Massachusetts Institute of Technology, Cambridge. Also in *Math. Prog.* (1985), 125–45.

[Ber82d] Bertsekas, D. P. 1982. Distributed dynamic programming, *IEEE Trans. Auto. Contr.* AC-27:610–16.

[Ber83] Bertsekas, D. P. 1983. Distributed asynchronous computation of fixed points. *Math. Prog.* 27:107–20.

[Ber85] Bertsekas, D. P. 1985. A distributed asynchronous relaxation algorithm for the assignment problem. *Proc. 24th IEEE Conf. Dec. & Contr.*, 1703–4.

[Ber86a] Bertsekas, D. P. 1986. Distributed asynchronous relaxation methods for linear network flow problems. Laboratory for Information and Decisions Systems Report LIDS-P-1606, revision of Nov. 1986, Massachusetts Institute of Technology, Cambridge.

[Ber86b] Bertsekas, D. P. 1986. Distributed relaxation methods for linear network flow problems. *Proc. 25th IEEE Conf. Dec. & Contr.*, 2101–6.

[Ber87] Bertsekas, D. P. 1987. *Dynamic Programming: Deterministic and Stochastic Models.* Englewood Cliffs, NJ: Prentice-Hall.

[Ber88] Bertsekas, D. P. 1988. The auction algorithm: A distributed relaxation method for the assignment problem. *Ann. Oper. Res.* (in press).

[BeS78] Bertsekas, D. P., and S. E. Shreve. 1978. *Stochastic Optimal Control: The Discrete Time Case.* New York: Academic Press.

[BeT85] Bertsekas, D. P., and P. Tseng. 1985. Relaxation methods for minimum cost ordinary and generalized network flow problems. Laboratory for Information and Decision Systems Report LIDS-P-1462, Massachusetts Institute of Technology, Cambridge. Also in *Oper. Res. J.* (1988) 36:93–114.

[BeT88] Bertsekas, D. P., and P. Tseng. 1988. RELAX: A computer code for minimum cost network flow problems. *Ann. Oper. Res.* 13:125–90.

[BGG84] Bertsekas, D. P., E. M. Gafni, and R. G. Gallager. 1984. Second derivative algorithms for minimum delay distributed routing in networks. *IEEE Trans. Commun.* COM-32:911–19.

[BGV79] Bertsekas, D. P., E. M. Gafni, and K. S. Vastola. 1979. Validation of algorithms for optimal routing of flow in networks. *Proc. 18th IEEE Conf. Dec. & Contr*, 220–227.

[BhI85] Bhatt, S. N., and I. C. F. Ipsen. 1985. How to embed trees in hypercubes. Dept. of Computer Science, Research Report YALEU/DCS/RR-443, Yale University, New Haven, CT.

[BHT87] Bertsekas, D. P., P. Hossein, and P. Tseng. 1987. Relaxation methods for network flow problems with convex arc costs. *SiAM J. Contr. & Optim.* 25:1219–43.

[Bin84] Bini, D. 1984. Parallel solution of certain Toeplitz linear systems. *SiAM J. Comput.* 13:268–76.

[BlJ85] Bland, R. G., and D. L. Jensen. 1985. On the computational behavior of a polynomial-time network flow algorithm. School of Operations Research and Industrial Engineering, Technical Report 661, Cornell University, Ithaca, NY.

[BLS83] Bertsekas, D. P., G. S. Lauer, N. R. Sandell, Jr., and T. A. Posbergh. 1983. Optimal short term scheduling of large-scale power systems. *IEEE Trans. Auto. Contr.* AC-28:1–11.

[BLT76] Bensoussan, A., J. L. Lions, and R. Temam. 1976. Sur les methodes de decomposition, de decentralisation et de coordination et applications. In J. L. Lions and G. I. Marchouk (eds.), *Methodes Numeriques pour les Sciences Physiques at Economiques.* Paris:Dunod.

[Boj84a] Bojanczyk, A. 1984. Complexity of solving linear systems in different models of computation. *SiAM J. Numer. Analy.* 21:591–603.

[Boj84b] Bojanczyk, A. 1984. Optimal asynchronous Newton method for the solution of nonlinear equations. *J. ACM.* 32:792–803.

[Bok81] Bokhari, S. H. 1981. On the mapping problem. *IEEE Trans. Comput.* C-30:207–14.

[BoM75] Borodin, A., and I. Munro. 1975. *The Computational Complexity of Algebraic and Numeric Problems.* New York: American Elsevier.

[Bon83] Bonnans, J. F. 1983. A variant of a projected variable metric method for bound constrained optimization problems. Research Report 242. INRIA, France.

[BoV82] Borkar, V., and P. Varaiya. 1982. Asymptotic agreement in distributed estimation. *IEEE Trans. Auto. Contr.* AC-27:650–5.

[BrH83] Broomell, G., and J. R. Heath. 1983. Classification categories and historical development of circuit switching topologies. *Computing Surveys.* 15:95–134.

[BrL85] Brent, R. P., and F. T. Luk. 1985. The solution of singular-value and symmetric eigenvalue problems on multiprocessor arrays. *SiAM J. Sci. Stat. Comput.* 6:69–84.

[BrP67] Browder, F. E., and W. V. Petryshyn. 1967. Construction of fixed points of nonlinear mappings in Hilbert space. *J. Math. Anal. & Appl.* 20:197–228.

[Bra81] Brandt, A. 1981. Muligrid solvers on parallel computers. In M. H. Schultz (ed.), *Elliptic Problem Solvers.* New York: Academic Press.

[Bre67] Bregman, L. M. 1967. The relaxation method for finding the common point of convex sets and its application to the solution of problems in convex programming. *USSR Comput. Math. & Math. Phys.* 7:200–17.

[Bre74] Brent, R. P. 1974. The parallel evaluation of general arithmetic expressions. *J. ACM.* 21:201–6.

[Bro70] Brockett, R. W. 1970. *Finite Dimensional Linear Systems.* New York: Wiley.

[BSS88] Byrd, R. H., R. B. Schnabel, and G. A. Shultz. 1988. Parallel quasi-Newton methods for unconstrained optimization. Dept. of Computer Science, Technical Report CU-CS-396-88, University of Colorado-Boulder.

[CaG74] Cantor, D. G., and M. Gerla. 1974. Optimal routing in a packet switched computer network. *IEEE Trans. Comput.* C-23:1062–9.

[CaM87] Calamai, P. H., and J. J. More. 1987. Projected gradient methods for linearly constrained problems. *Math. Prog.* 38:93–116.

[Cap87] Cappello, P. C. 1987. Gaussian elimination on a hypercube automaton. *J. Parallel & Dist. Comput.* 4:288–308.

[CDZ86] Cottle, R. W., S. G. Duvall, and K. Zikan. 1986. A Lagrangean relaxation algorithm for the constrained matrix problem. *Naval Res. Logist. Quart.* 33:55–76.

[CeH87] Censor, Y., and G. T. Herman. 1987. On some optimization techniques in image reconstruction from projections. *Appl. Numer. Math.* 3:365–91.

[Cen81] Censor, Y. 1981. Row-action methods for huge and sparse systems and their applications. *SiAM Rev.* 23:444–91.

[ChC58] Charnes, A., and W. W. Cooper. 1958. Nonlinear network flows and convex programming over incidence matrices. *Naval Res. Logist. Quart.* 5:321–40.

[ChL85] Chandy, K. M., and L. Lamport. 1985. Distributed snapshots: Determining global states of distributed systems. *ACM Trans. Comput. Syst.* 3:63–75.

[ChM69] Chazan, D., and W. L. Miranker. 1969. Chaotic relaxation. *Lin. Algeb. & Appl.* 2:199–222.

[ChM70] Chazan, D., and W. L. Miranker. 1970. A nongradient and parallel algorithm for unconstrained minimization. *SiAM J. Contr.* 8:207–17.

[ChM81] Chandy, K. M., and J. Misra. 1981. Asynchronous distributed simulation via a sequence of parallel computations. *Commun. ACM.* 24:198–206.

[ChM82] Chandy, K. M., and J. Misra. 1982. Distributed computation on graphs: Shortest path algorithms. *Commun. ACM.* 25:833–7.

[ChM84] Chandy, K. M., and J. Misra. 1984. The drinking philosophers problem. *ACM Trans. Prog. Lang. & Sys.* 6:632–46.

[Chr75] Christofides, N. 1975. *Graph Theory: An Algorithmic Approach.* New York: Academic Press.

[ChS85] Chan, T. F., and R. Schreiber. 1985. Parallel networks for multi-grid algorithms: Architecture and complexity. *SiAM J. Sci. & Stat. Comput.* 6:698–711.

[ChS86] Chan, T. F., and Y. Saad. 1986. Multigrid algorithms on the hypercube multiprocessor. *IEEE Trans. Comput.* C-35:969–77.

[Chv83] Chvatal, V. 1983. *Linear Programming.* New York: W. H. Freeman.

[Cim38] Cimmino, G. 1938. Calcolo approssimato per le soluzioni dei sistemi di equazioni lineari. *Ricerca Sci.* XVI Ser. II, Anno IX, 1:326–33.

[Cof76] Coffman, E. G., Jr. (ed.). 1976. *Computer and Job Shop Scheduling Theory.* Englewood Cliffs, NJ: Prentice-Hall.

[Coh78] Cohen, G. 1978. Optimization by decomposition and coordination: A unified approach. *IEEE Trans. Auto. Contr.* AC-23:222–32.

[CoL55] Coddington, E. A., and N. Levinson. 1955. *Theory of Ordinary Differential Equations.* New York: McGraw-Hill.

[Coo81] Cook, S. A. 1981. Towards a complexity theory of synchronous parallel computation. *Enseigne. Math.* 27:99–124.

[CoP82] Cottle, R. W., and J. S. Pang. 1982. On the convergence of a block successive overrelaxation method for a class of linear complementarity problems. In D.C. Sorensen and R. J.-B. Wets (eds.), *Mathematical Programming Studies*, Volume 17, 126–38. Amsterdam: North-Holland.

[CoR86] Cosnard, M., and Y. Robert. 1986. Complexity of parallel QR factorization. *J. ACM.* 33:712–23.

[Cot84] Cottle, R. W. 1984. Application of a block successive overrelaxation method to a class of constrained matrix problems. In R. W. Cottle, M. L. Kelmanson, and B. Korte (eds.), *Mathematical Programming*, 89–103. Amsterdam: North-Holland.

[CoZ83] Cohen, G., and D. L. Zhu. 1983. Decomposition and coordination methods in large scale optimization problems. The nondifferentiable case and the use of augmented Lagrangians. In J. B. Cruz, Jr. (ed.), *Advances in Large Scale Systems, Theory and Applications*, Vol. 1. Greenwich, CT: JAI Press.

[Cry71] Cryer, C. W. 1971. The solution of a quadratic programming problem using systematic overrelaxation. *SiAM J. Contr.* 9:385–92.

[Csa76] Csanky, L. 1976. Fast parallel matrix inversion algorithms. *SiAM J. Comput.* 5:618–23.

[Cyb87] Cybenko, G. 1987. Dynamic load balancing for distributed memory multiprocessors. Dept. of Computer Science, Technical Report 87-1, Tufts University, Medford, MA.

[Daf71] Dafermos, S. C. 1971. An extended traffic assignment model with applications to two-way traffic. *Trans. Sci.* 5:366–89.

[Daf80] Dafermos, S.C 1980. Traffic equilibrium and variational inequalities. *Trans. Sci.* 14:42–54.

[Daf83] Dafermos, S. C. 1983. An iterative scheme for variational inequalities. *Math. Prog.* 26:40–7.

[Dan63] Dantzig, G. B. 1963. *Linear Programming and Extensions.* Princeton, NJ: Princeton University Press.

[Dan67] Danskin, J. M. 1967. *Theory of Max-Min and Its Application in Weapons Allocation Problems.* New York: Springer-Verlag.

[Dat85] Datta, K. 1985. Parallel complexities and computations of Cholesky's decomposition and QR factorization. *Intl. J. Comput. Math.* 18:67–82.

[Den67] Denardo, E. V. 1967. Contraction mappings in the theory underlying dynamic programming. *SiAM Rev.* 9:165–77.

[DeP84] Deo, N., and C. Pang. 1984. Shortest path algorithms: Taxonomy and annotation. *Networks.* 14:275–323.

[DES82] Dembo, R. S., S. C. Eisenstadt, and T. Steihaug. 1982. Inexact Newton methods. *SiAM J. Numer. Anal.* 19:400–8.

[DeS83] Dennis, J. E., Jr., and R. B. Schnabel. 1983. *Numerical Methods for Unconstrained Optimization and Nonlinear Equations.* Englewood Cliffs, NJ: Prentice-Hall.

[DFV83] Dijkstra, E. W., W. H. J. Feijen, and A. J. M. Van Gasteren. 1983. Derivation of a termination algorithm for distributed computations. *Inf. Proc. Lett.* 15:217–19.

[DGK79] Dial, R., F. Glover, D. Karney, and D. Klingman. 1979. A computational analysis of alternative algorithms and labeling techniques for finding shortest path trees. *Networks.* 9:215–48.

[Dij71] Dijkstra, E. W. 1971. Hierarchical ordering of sequential processes. *Acta Informatica.* 1:115–38.

[DiS80] Dijkstra, E. W., and C. S. Sholten. 1980. Termination detection for diffusing computations. *Inf. Proc. Lett.* 11:1–4.

[DNS81] Dekel, E., D. Nassimi, and S. Sahni. 1981. Parallel matrix and graph algorithms. *SiAM J. Comput.* 10:657–73.

[Don71] Donnelly, J. D. P. 1971. Periodic chaotic relaxation. *Lin. Algeb. & Appl.* 4:117–28.

[DoS87] Dongarra, J. J., and D. C. Sorensen. 1987. A fully parallel algorithm for the symmetric eigenvalue problem. *SiAM J. Sci. Stat. Comput.* 8:s139–54.

[DuB82] Dubois, M., and F. A. Briggs. 1982. Performance of synchronized iterative processes in multiprocessor systems. *IEEE Trans. Software Eng.* SE-8:419–31.

[Dun81] Dunn, J. C. 1981. Global and asymptotic convergence rate estimates for a class of projected gradient processes. *SiAM J. Contr. & Optim.* 19:368–400.

[DuS63] Dunford, N., and J. T. Schwartz. 1963. *Linear Operators.* New York: Wiley.

[Eck87] Eckstein, J. 1987. Private communication.

[Eck88] Eckstein, J. 1988. The Lions-Mercier splitting algorithm and the alternating direction method are instances of the proximal point algorithm. Laboratory for Information and Decision Systems Report LIDS-P-1769, Massachusetts Institute of Technology, Cambridge.

[EdK72] Edmonds, J., and R. M. Karp. 1972. Theoretical improvements in algorithmic efficiency for network flow problems. *J. ACM.* 19:248–64.

[Elf80] Elfving, T. 1980. Block-iterative methods for consistent and inconsistent linear equations. *Numer. Math.* 35:1–12.

[ElT82] El Tarazi, M. N. 1982. Some convergence results for asynchronous algorithms. *Numer. Math.* 39:325–40.

[Eph86] Ephremides, A. 1986. The routing problem in computer networks. In I. F. Blake and H. V. Poor (eds.), *Communication and Networks*, 299–325. New York: Springer-Verlag.

[Eri88] Eriksen, O. 1988. A termination detection protocol and its formal verification. *J. Parallel & Distr. Comput.* 5:82–91.

[Eve63] Everett, H. 1963. Generalized Lagrange multiplier method for solving problems of optimum allocation of resources. *Oper. Res.* 11:399–417.

[FaF63] Fadeev, D. K., and V. N. Fadeeva. 1963. *Computational Methods of Linear Algebra*. San Francisco: W. H. Freeman.

[FBB80] Findeisen, W., F. N. Bailey, M. Brdys, K. Malinowski, P. Tatjewski, and A. Wozniak. 1980. *Control and Coordination in Hierarchical Systems*. New York: Wiley.

[Fel68] Feller, W. 1968. *An Introduction to Probability Theory and Its Applications*. New York: Wiley.

[Fin79] Finn, S. G. 1979. Resynch procedures and a failsafe network protocol. *IEEE Trans. Commun.* COM-27:840–6.

[FJL88] Fox, G., M. Johnson, G. Lyzenga, S. Otto, J. Salmon, and D. Walker. 1988. *Solving Problems on Concurrent Processors*, Vol. 1. Englewood Cliffs, NJ: Prentice-Hall.

[FlN74] Florian, M., and S. Nguyen. 1974. A method for computing network equilibrium with elastic demand. *Trans. Sci.* 8:321–32.

[Fly66] Flynn, M. J. 1966. Very high-speed computing systems. *Proc. IEEE.* 54:1901–9.

[FNP81] Florian, M. S., S. Nguyen, and S. Pallottino. 1981. A dual simplex algorithm for finding all shortest paths. *Networks.* 11:367–78.

[FoF62] Ford, L. R., Jr., and D. R. Fulkerson. 1962. *Flow in Networks*. Princeton, NJ: Princeton University Press.

[FoG83] Fortin, M., and R. Glowinski. 1983. On decomposition-coordination methods using an augmented Lagrangian. In M. Fortin and R. Glowinski (eds.), *Augmented Lagrangian Methods: Applications to the Numerical Solution of Boundary-Value Problems*. 97–146. Amsterdam: North-Holland.

[FoM67] Forsythe, G. E., and C. B. Moler. 1967. *Computer Solution of Linear Algebraic Systems*. Englewood Cliffs, NJ: Prentice-Hall.

[For56] Ford, L. R., Jr. 1956. Network flow theory. Report P-923, The Rand Corp., Santa Monica, CA.

[FoW78] Fortune, S., and J. Wyllie. 1978. Parallelism in random access machines. *Proc. 10th ACM STOC.*, 114–18.

[Fra80] Francez, N. 1980. Distributed termination. *ACM Trans. Prog. Lang. & Sys.* 2:42–5.

[FrT84] Fredman, M. L., and R. E. Tarjan. 1984. Fibonacci heaps and their uses in improved network optimization algorithms. *Proc. 25th Annual Symp. Found. Comput. Sci.*, 338–46.

[Gab79] Gabay, D. 1979. Methodes numeriques pour l'optimisation non-lineaire. These de Doctorat d'Etat et Sciences Mathematiques, Universite Pierre et Marie Curie (Paris VI).

[GaB81] Gafni, E. M., and D. P. Bertsekas. 1981. Distributed algorithms for generating loopfree routes in networks with frequently changing topology. *IEEE Trans. Commun.* COM-29:11–18.

[Gab83] Gabay, D. 1983. Applications of the method of multipliers to variational inequalities. In M. Fortin and R. Glowinski (eds.), *Augmented Lagrangian Methods: Applications to the Numerical Solution of Boundary-Value Problems*. 299–331. Amsterdam: North-Holland.

[GaB84] Gafni, E. M., and D. P. Bertsekas. 1984. Two-metric projection methods for constrained optimization. *SiAM J. Contr. & Optim.* 22:936–64.

[GaB86] Gafni, E. M., and V. C. Barbosa. 1986. Optimal snapshots and the maximum flow in precedence graphs. *Proc. 24th Allerton Conf.* 1089–97.

[Gaf79] Gafni, E. M. 1979. Convergence of a routing algorithm. MS thesis. Dept. of Electrical Engineering, University of Illinois-Urbana.

[Gaf86] Gafni, E. M. 1986. Perspectives on distributed network protocols: A case for building blocks. Computer Science Dept., UCLA; MILCOM '86, Monterey, CA.

[GaJ79] Garey, M. R., and D. S. Johnson. 1979. *Computers and Intractability: A Guide to the Theory of NP-Completeness*. San Francisco: W. H. Freeman.

[Gal68] Gallager, R. G. 1968. *Information Theory and Reliable Communications*. New York: Wiley.

[Gal76] Gallager, R. G. 1976. A shortest path routing algorithm with automatic resynch. Unpublished note.

[Gal77] Gallager, R. G. 1977. A minimum delay routing algorithm using distributed computation. *IEEE Trans. Commun.* COM-23:73–85.

[Gal82] Gallager, R. G. 1982. Distributed minimum hop algorithm. Laboratory for Information and Decision Systems Report LIDS-P-1175, Massachusetts Institute of Technology, Cambridge.

[Gal85] Gallopoulos, E. 1985. Processor arrays for problems in computational physics. PhD thesis. Dept. of Computer Science, University of Illinois-Urbana.

[GaM76] Gabay, D., and B. Mercier. 1976. A dual algorithm for the solution of nonlinear variational problems via finite-element approximations. *Comput. and Math. Appl.* 2:17–40.

[Gan59] Gantmacher, F. R. 1959. *The Theory of Matrices*. New York: Chelsea.

[GaT87] Gabow, H. N., and R. E. Tarjan. 1987. Faster scaling algorithms for graph matching. Unpublished manuscript.

[GaV84] Gannon, D. B., and J. Van Rosendale. 1984. On the impact of communication complexity on the design of parallel numerical algorithms. *IEEE Trans. Comput.* C-32:1180–94.

[Gea86] Gear, C. W. 1986. The potential for parallelism in ordinary differential equations. Dept. of Computer Science, Report No. UIUCDCS-R-86-1246, University of Illinois at Urbana-Champaign; also presented at the Second International Conference of Computational Mathematics, University of Benin, Benin City, Nigeria.

[Gea87] Gear, C. W. 1987. Parallel methods for ordinary differential equations. Dept. of Computer Science, Report No. UIUCDCS-R-87-1369, University of Illinois at Urbana-Champaign.

[GeK81] Gentleman, W. M., and H. T. Kung. 1981. Matrix triangularization by systolic arrays. *Proc. SPIE 298, Real Time Signal Processing IV*, 19–26.

[Gen78] Gentleman, W. M. 1978. Some complexity results for matrix computations on parallel processors. *J. ACM*. 25:112–15.

[Geo72] Geoffrion, A. M. 1972. Generalized Benders decomposition. *JOTA*. 10:237–60.

[GHN87] Geist, G. A., M. T. Heath, and E. Ng. 1987. Parallel algorithms for matrix computations. In L. H. Jamieson, D. B. Gannon, and R. J. Douglass (eds.), *The Characteristics of Parallel Algorithms*. 233–51. Cambridge, MA: The MIT Press.

[GKK74] Glover, F., D. Karney, D. Klingman, and A. Napier. 1974. A computation study on start procedures, basis change criteria, and solution algorithms for transportation problems. *Manage. Sci.* 20:793–819.

[GKK87] Gohberg. I., T. Kailath, I. Koltracht, and P. Lancaster. 1987. Linear complexity algorithms for linear systems of equations with recursive structure. *Lin. Algeb. & Appl.* 88/89:271–315.

[GlL87] Glowinski, R., and P. Le Tallec. 1987. Augmented Lagrangian methods for the solution of variational problems. Mathematics Research Center, Technical Summary Report 2965, University of Wisconsin-Madison.

[GlM75] Glowinski, R., and A. Marrocco. 1975. Sur l'approximation par elements finis d'ordre un et la resolution par penalisation-dualite d'une classe de problemes de Dirichlet non lineaires. *Revue Francaise d'Automatique Informatique Recherche Operationnelle, Analyse numerique*. R-2:41–76.

[GLT81] Glowinski, R., J. L. Lions, and R. Tremolieres. 1981. *Numerical Analysis of Variational Inequalities*. Amsterdam: North-Holland.

[GMW81] Gill, P. E., W. Murray, and M. H. Wright. 1981. *Practical Optimization*. New York: Academic Press.

[Gof80] Goffin, J. L. 1980. The relaxation method for solving problems of linear inequalities. *Math. Oper. Res.* 5:388–414.

[Gol64] Goldstein, A. A. 1964. Convex programming in Hilbert Space. *Bull. Am. Math. Soc.* 70:709–10.

[Gol78] Goldschlager, L. M. 1978. A unified approach to models of synchronous parallel machines. *Proc. 10th ACM STOC.*, 89–94.

[Gol85a] Goldberg, A. V. 1985. A new max-flow algorithm. Laboratory for Computer Science, Tech. Mem. MIT/LCS/TM-291, Massachusetts Institute of Technology, Cambridge.

[Gol85b] Golshtein, E. G. 1985. A decomposition method for linear and convex programming problems. *Ekon. i Mat. Metody* [translated as *Matecon*]. 21:1077–91.

[Gol86a] Golshtein, E. G. 1986. The block method of convex programming. *Sov. Math. Doklady*. 33:584–7.

[Gol86b] Goldberg, A. V. 1986. Solving minimum-cost flow problems by successive approximations. Extended abstract. Submitted to *19th ACM STOC*.

[Gol87a] Goldberg, A. V. 1987. Efficient graph algorithms for sequential and parallel computers. Laboratory for Computer Science, Technical Report TR-374, Massachusetts Institute of Technology, Cambridge.

[Gol87b] Golshtein, E. G. 1987. A general approach to decomposition of optimization systems. *Sov. J. Comput. & Sys. Sci.* 25:105–14 [translated from *Tekhnicheskaya Kibernetika* (1987). 1:59–69].

[GoT86] Goldberg, A. V., and R. E. Tarjan. 1986. A new approach to the maximum flow problem. *Proc. 18th ACM STOC*. 136–46.

[GoT87] Goldberg, A. V., and R. R. Tarjan. 1987. Solving minimum cost flow problems by successive approximation. *Proc. 19th ACM STOC*. 7–18.

[GoV83] Golub, G. H., and C. F. Van Loan. 1983. *Matrix Computations*. Baltimore: The Johns Hopkins University Press.

[Gra71] Grad, J. 1971. Matrix balancing. *Comput. J.* 14:280–4.

[GrH80] Grigoriadis, M. D., and T. Hsu. 1980. The Rutgers minimum cost network flow subroutines. RNET Documentation. Dept. of Computer Science Report, Rutgers University, New Brunswick, NJ.

[GrS81] Grcar, J., and A. Sameh. 1981. On certain parallel Toeplitz linear system solvers. *SiAM J. Sci. & Stat. Comput.* 2:238–56.

[GuP74] Guillemin, V., and A. Pollack. 1974. *Differential Topology*. Englewood Cliffs, NJ: Prentice-Hall.

[HaB70] Haarhoff, P. C., and J. D. Buys. 1970. A new method for the optimization of a nonlinear function subject to nonlinear constraints. *The Comput. J.* 13:178–84.

[Hac85] Hackbush, W. 1985. *Multi-Grid Methods and Applications*. New York: Springer-Verlag.

[HaC87] Hajek, B., and R. L. Cruz. 1987. Delay and routing in interconnection networks. In A. R. Odoni, L. Bianco, and G. Szego (eds.), *Flow Control of Congested Networks*. 235–42. New York: Springer-Verlag.

[HaL88] Han, S. P., and G. Lou. 1988. A parallel algorithm for a class of convex programs. *SiAM J. Contr. & Optim.* 26:345–55.

[Ham86] Hamming, R. W. 1986. *Coding and Information Theory*. Englewood Cliffs, NJ: Prentice-Hall.

[Han86] Han, S. P. 1986. Optimization by updated conjugate subspaces. In D. F. Griffiths and G. A. Watson (eds.), *Numerical Analysis: Pitman Research Notes in Mathematics Series 140*, 82–97. Burnt Mill, England: Longman Scientific and Technical.

[Han88] Han, S. P. 1988. A successive projection method. *Math. Prog.* 40:1–14.

[Har69] Harary, F. 1969. *Graph Theory*. Reading, MA: Addison-Wesley.

[HaY81] Hageman, L. A., and D. M. Young. 1981. *Applied Iterative Methods*. New York: Academic Press.

[Hay84] Hayes, J. F. 1984. *Modeling and Analysis of Computer Communications Networks*. New York: Plenum.

[HaZ87] Haxari, C., and H. Zedan. 1987. A distributed algorithm for distributed termination. *Inf. Proc. Lett.* 24:293–7.

[HeL78] Herman, G. T., and A. Lent. 1978. A family of iterative quadratic optimization algorithms for pairs of inequalities, with application in diagnostic radiology. *Math. Prog. Studies.* 9:15–29.

[Hel74] Heller, D. 1974. On the efficient computation of recurrence relations. Dept. of Computer Science, Technical Report, Carnegie-Mellon University, Pittsburgh, PA.

[Hel76] Heller, D. 1976. Some aspects of the cyclic reduction algorithm for block tridiagonal linear systems. *SiAM J. Numer. Anal.* 13:484–96.

[Hel78] Heller, D. 1978. A survey of parallel algorithms in numerical linear algebra. *SiAM Rev.* 20:740–77.

[Hen64] Henrici, P. 1964. *Elements of Numerical Analysis*. New York: Wiley.

[HeS52] Hestenes, M. R., and E. L. Stiefel. 1952. Methods of conjugate gradients for solving linear systems. *J. Res. Nat. Bur. Standards Sect. 5.* 49:409–36.

[Hes69] Hestenes, M. R. 1969. Multiplier and gradient methods. *JOTA.* 4:303–20.

[HeS82] Heyman, D. P., and M. J. Sobel. 1982. *Stochastic Models in Operations Research*. New York: McGraw-Hill.

[Hil57] Hildreth, C. 1957. A quadratic programming procedure. *Naval Res. Logist. Quart.* 4:79–85. See also "Erratum," *Naval Res. Logist. Quart.* 4:361.

[Hil74] Hildebrand, F. B. 1974. *Introduction to Numerical Analysis*. New York: McGraw-Hill.

[Hil85] Hillis, W. D. 1985. *The Connection Machine*. Cambridge, MA: The MIT Press.

[HLL78] Herman, G. T., A. Lent, and P. H. Lutz. 1978. Relaxation methods for image reconstruction. *Commun. ACM.* 21:152–8.

[HLN84] Hearn, D. W., S. Lawphongpanich, and S. Nguyen. 1984. Convex programming formulation of the asymmetric traffic assignment problem. *Trans. Res.* 18B:357–65.

[HLV87] Hearn, D. W., S. Lawphongpanich, and J. A. Ventura. 1987. Restricted simplicial decomposition: Computation and extensions. *Math. Programming Studies.* 31:99–118.

[Hoc65] Hockney, R. W. 1965. A fast direct solution of Poisson's equation using Fourier analysis. *J. ACM.* 12:95–113.

[Hoc85] Hockney, R. W. 1985. MIMD computing in the USA—1984. *Parallel Comput.* 2:119–36.

[HoJ81] Hockney, R. W., and C. R. Jesshope. 1981. *Parallel Computers*. Bristol, England: Adam Hilger.

[HoK71] Hoffman, K., and R. Kunze. 1971. *Linear Algebra*. Englewood Cliffs, NJ: Prentice-Hall.

[HoM76] Ho, Y. C., and S. K. Mitter (eds.). 1976. *Directions in Large Scale Systems*. New York: Plenum.

[Hou64] Householder, A. S. 1964. *The Theory of Matrices in Numerical Analysis*. New York: Dover.

[HuS87a] Humblet, P. A., and S. R. Soloway. 1987. A fail-safe layer for distributed network algorithms and changing topologies. Laboratory for Information and Decision Systems Report LIDS-P-1702, Massachusetts Institute of Technology, Cambridge.

[HuS87b] Humblet, P. A., and S. R. Soloway. 1987. Topology broadcast algorithms. Laboratory for Information and Decisions Systems Report LIDS-P-1692, Massachusetts Institute of Technology, Cambridge.

[Hwa84] Hwang, K., (ed.). 1984. *Supercomputers: Design and Applications*. Silver Springs, MD: IEEE Computer Society Press.

[Hwa87] Hwang, K. 1987. Advanced parallel processing with supercomputer architectures. *Proc. IEEE*. 75:1348–79.

[HwB84] Hwang, K., and F. A. Briggs. 1984. *Computer Architecture and Parallel Processing*. New York: McGraw-Hill.

[HyK77] Hyafil, L., and H. T. Kung. 1977. The complexity of parallel evaluation of linear recurrences. *J. ACM*. 24:513–21.

[IEE78] *IEEE Trans. Auto. Contr.* 1978. Special Issue on Large-Scale Systems and Decentralized Control, Vol. AC-23.

[IEE87] *IEEE Computer*. 1987. Special Issue on Interconnection Networks, Vol. 20.

[IpS85] Ipsen, I. C. F., and Y. Saad. 1985. The impact of parallel architectures on the solution of eigenvalue problems. Dept. of Computer Science, Research Report YALEU/DCS/RR-444, Yale University, New Haven, CT.

[IsK66] Isacson, E., and H. B. Keller. 1966. *Analysis of Numerical Methods*. New York: Wiley.

[ISS86] Ipsen, I. C. F., Y. Saad, and M. H. Schultz. 1986. Complexity of dense-linear-system solution on a multiprocessor ring. *Lin. Algeb. & Appl.* 77:205–39.

[IsS86] Israeli, A., and Y. Schiloach. 1986. An improved parallel algorithm for maximal matching. *Inf. Proc. Lett.* 22:57–60.

[JeB80] Jensen, P. A., and J. W. Barnes. 1980. *Network Flow Programming*. New York: Wiley.

[Jef85] Jefferson, D. R. 1985. Virtual time. *ACM Trans. Prog. Lang. & Sys.* 7:404–25.

[Jer79] Jeroslow, R. G. 1979. Some relaxation methods for linear inequalities. *Cahiers du C.E.R.O.* 21:43–53.

[Joh85a] Johnsson, S. L. 1985. Cyclic reduction on a binary tree. *Comput. Phys. Commun.* 37:195–203.

[Joh85b] Johnsson, S. L. 1985. Solving narrow banded systems on ensemble architectures. *ACM Trans. Math. Software.* 11:271–88.

[Joh87a] Johnsson, S. L. 1987. Communication efficient basic linear algebra computations on hypercube architectures. *J. Parallel & Distr. Comput.* 4:133–72.

[Joh87b] Johnsson, S. L. 1987. Solving tridiagonal systems on ensemble architectures. *SiAM J. Sci. & Stat. Comput.* 8:354–92.

[Kar78] Karp, R. M. 1978. A characterization of the minimum cycle mean in a digraph. *Disc. Math.* 23:309–11.

[KeH80] Kennington, J., and R. Helgason. 1980. *Algorithms for Network Programming.* New York: Wiley.

[KiC87] Kim, T., and K.-T. Chwa. 1987. An O(n log n log log n) parallel maximum matching algorithm for bipartite graphs. *Inf. Proc. Lett.* 24:15–17.

[KiL86] Kindervater, G. A. P., and J. K. Lenstra. 1986. An introduction to parallelism in combinatorial optimization. *Disc. Appl. Math.* 14:135–56.

[KiS80] Kinderlehrer, D., and G. Stampacchia. 1980. *An Introduction to Variational Inequalities and their Applications.* New York: Academic Press.

[KMW67] Karp, R. M., R. E. Miller, and S. Winograd. 1967. The organization of computations for uniform recurrence equations. *J. ACM.* 14:563–90.

[KoB76] Kort, B. W., and D. P. Bertsekas. 1976. Combined primal-dual and penalty methods for convex programming. *SiAM J. Contr.* 14:268–94.

[KoO68] Kowalik, J., and M. R. Osborne. 1968. *Methods for Unconstrained Optimization Problems.* New York: Elsevier.

[Kor76] Korpelevich, G. M. 1976. The extragradient method for finding saddle points and other problems. *Ekon. i Mat. Metody* [translated as *Matecon*]. 12:747–56.

[Kru37] Kruithof, J. 1937. Calculation of telephone traffic. *De Ingenieur (E. Electrotechnik 3).* 52:E15–25.

[Kru87] Kruse, R. L. 1987. *Data Structures and Program Design.* Englewood Cliffs, NJ: Prentice-Hall.

[KSS81] Kung, H. T., B. Sproul, and G. Steele (eds.). 1981. *VLSI Systems and Computations.* Rockville, MD: Computer Science Press.

[Kuc82] Kucera, L. 1982. Parallel computation and conflicts in memory access. *Inf. Proc. Lett.* 14:93–96.

[Kun76a] Kung, H. T. 1976. New algorithms and lower bounds for the parallel evaluation of certain rational expressions and recurrences. *J. ACM.* 23:252–61.

[Kun76b] Kung, H. T. 1976. Synchronized and asynchronous parallel algorithms for multiprocessors. In J. F. Traub (ed.), *Algorithms and Complexity*, 153–200. New York: Academic Press.

[Kun82] Kung, H. T. 1982. Why systolic architectures? *Computer.* 15:37–45.

[Kun88] Kung, S. Y. 1988. *VLSI Array Processors.* Englewood Cliffs, NJ: Prentice-Hall.

[KuP81] Kuhn, R. M., and D. A. Padua (eds.). 1981. *Tutorial on Parallel Processing.* Silver Springs, MD: IEEE Computer Society Press.

[Kus84] Kushner, H. J. 1984. *Approximation and Weak Convergence Methods for Random Processes.* Cambridge, MA: The MIT Press.

[KuV86] Kumar, P. R., and P. P. Varaiya. 1986. *Stochastic Systems: Estimation, Identification, and Adaptive Control.* Englewood Cliffs, NJ: Prentice-Hall.

[KuY87a] Kushner, H. J., and G. Yin. 1987. Stochastic approximation algorithms for parallel and distributed processing. *Stochastics.* 22:219–50.

[KuY87b] Kushner, H. J., and G. Yin. 1987. Asymptotic properties of distributed and communicating stochastic approximation algorithms. *SiAM J. Contr. & Optim.* 25:1266–90.

[KVC88] Krumme, D. W., K. N. Venkataraman, and G. Cybenko. 1988. The token exchange problem. Dept. of Applied Math. Technical Report 88-2. Tufts University, Medford, MA.

[LaF80] R. E. Ladner, and M. J. Fischer. 1980. Parallel prefix computation. *J. ACM.* 27:831–8.

[LaH84] Lawphongpanich, S., and D. W. Hearn. 1984. Simplicial decomposition of the asymmetric traffic assignment problems. *Trans. Res.* 18B:123–33.

[Lam78] Lamport, L. 1978. Time, clocks, and the ordering of events in a distributed system. *Commun. ACM.* 21:558–65.

[LaS81] Lamond, B., and N. F. Stewart. 1981. Bregman's balancing method. *Trans. Res.* 15B:239–48.

[Las70] Lasdon, L. S. 1970. *Optimization Theory for Large Systems.* New York: Macmillan.

[Las73] Lasdon, L. S. 1973. Decomposition in resource allocation. In D. M. Himmelblau (ed.), *Decomposition of Large-Scale Problems*, 207–31. Amsterdam: North-Holland.

[LaT85] Lancaster, P., and M. Tismenetsky. 1985. *The Theory of Matrices.* New York: Academic Press.

[Law67] Lawler, E. L. 1967. Optimal cycles in doubly weighted linear graphs. In P. Rosenstiehl (ed.), *Theory of Graphs*, 209–14. Paris: Dunod; New York: Gordon & Breach.

[Law76] Lawler, E. 1976. *Combinatorial Optimization: Networks and Matroids.* New York: Holt, Rinehart & Winston.

[Lem74] Lemarechal, C. 1974. An algorithm for minimizing convex functions. In J. L. Rosenfeld (ed.), *Information Processing '74*, 552–6. Amsterdam: North-Holland.

[Lem75] Lemarechal, C. 1975. An extension of Davidon methods to nondifferentiable problems. *Math. Prog. Studies.* 3:95–109.

[LeP65] Levitin, E. S., and B. T. Poljak. 1965. Constrained minimization methods. *Z. Vycisl. Mat. i Mat. Fiz.* 6:787–823. English translation in *USSR Comput. Math. Phys.* 6:1–50.

[LeR81] Lehmann, D., and M. Rabin. 1981. On the advantages of free choice: A symmetric solution of the dining philosophers problem. *Proc. 8th ACM Symp. Princ. Prog. Lang.*, 133–8.

[LeV40] Le Verrier, U. J. J. 1840. Sur les variations seculaires des elements elliptiques des sept planets principales. *J. Math. Pures Appl.* 5:220–54.

[LiB87] Li, S. and T. Basar. 1987. Asymptotic agreement and convergence of asynchronous stochastic algorithms. *IEEE Trans. Auto. Contr.* AC-32:612–18.

[LiM79] Lions, P. L., and B. Mercier. 1979. Splitting algorithms for the sum of two nonlinear operators. *SiAM J. Numer. Analy.* 16:964–79.

[LjS83] Ljung, L., and T. Soderstrom. 1983. *Theory and Practice of Recursive Identification.* Cambridge, MA: The MIT Press.

[Lju77] Ljung, L. 1977. Analysis of recursive stochastic algorithms. *IEEE Trans. Auto. Contr.* AC-22:551–75.

[LKK83] Lord, R. E., J. S. Kowalik, and S. P. Kumar. 1983. Solving linear algebraic expressions on an MIMD computer. *J. ACM.* 30:103–17.

[LMS83] Lavenberg, S., R. Muntz, and B. Samadi. 1983. Performance analysis of a rollback method for distributed simulation. In A. K. Agrawala and S. K. Tripathi (eds.), *Performance '83,* 117–32. Amsterdam: North-Holland.

[LMS86] Lang, B., J. C. Miellou, and P. Spiteri. 1986. Asynchronous relaxation algorithms for optimal control problems. *Math. & Comput. Simul.* 28:227–42.

[LoR88] Lootsma, F. A., and K. M. Ragsdell. 1988. State of the art in parallel nonlinear optimization. *Parallel Comput.* 6:131–55.

[LPS87] Lo, S.-S., B. Philippe, and A. Sameh. 1987. A multiprocessor algorithm for the symmetric tridiagonal eigenvalue problem. *SiAM J. Sci. & Stat. Comput.* 8:s155–65.

[LRS82] Lelarasmee, E., A. E. Ruehli, and A. L. Sangiovanni-Vincentelli. 1982. The waveform relaxation method for the time-domain analysis of large scale integrated circuits. *IEEE Trans. Comput.-Aided Des. Integ. Circ.* CAD-1:131–45.

[Lue69] Luenberger, D. G. 1969. *Optimization by Vector Space Methods.* New York: Wiley.

[Lue84] Luenberger, D. G. 1984. *Linear and Nonlinear Programming.* Reading, MA: Addison-Wesley.

[LuM86] Lubachevsky, B., and D. Mitra. 1986. A chaotic asynchronous algorithm for computing the fixed point of a nonnegative matrix of unit spectral radius. *J. ACM.* 33:130–50.

[Luo87] Luo, Z.-Q. 1987. Private communication.

[Luq84] Luque, F. J. 1984. Asymptotic convergence analysis of the proximal point algorithm. *SiAM J. Contr. & Optim.* 22:277–93.

[Luq86a] Luque, F. J. 1986. The nonlinear proximal point algorithm and multiplier methods. Laboratory for Information and Decision Systems Report LIDS-P-1596, Massachusetts Institute of Technology, Cambridge.

[Luq86b] Luque, F. J. 1986. The nonlinear proximal point algorithm. Laboratory for Information and Decision Systems Report LIDS-P-1598, Massachusetts Institute of Technology, Cambridge.

[Mac79] Macgill, S. H. 1979. Convergence and related properties for a modified biproportional problem. *Envir. Plan A.* 11:499–506.

[MaD86] Mangasarian, O. L., and R. De Leone. 1986. Parallel gradient projection successive overrelaxation for symmetric linear complementarity problems and linear programs. Computer Sciences Dept. Technical Report 659, University of Wisconsin-Madison.

[MaD87] Mangasarian, O. L., and R. De Leone. 1987. Parallel successive overrelaxation methods for symmetric linear complementarity problems and linear programs. *JOTA*. 54:437–46.

[Man77] Mangasarian, O. L. 1977. Solution of symmetric linear complementarity problems by iterative methods. *JOTA*. 22:465–85.

[Man84] Mangasarian, O. L. 1984. Sparsity-preserving SOR algorithms for separable quadratic and linear programming. *Comput. & Oper. Res.* 11:105–12.

[MaP88] Maggs, B. M., and S. A. Plotkin. 1988. Minimum-cost spanning tree as a path-finding problem. *Inf. Proc. Lett.* 26:291–3.

[Mar70] Martinet, B. 1970. Regularisation d'inequations variationnelles par approximations successives. *Rev. Francaise Inf. Rech. Oper.* 4:154–59.

[Mar72] Martinet, B. 1972. Determination approchee d'un point fixe d'une application pseudocontractante. *C. R. Acad. Sci. Paris.* 274A:163–5.

[Mar73] Maruyama, K. 1973. On the parallel evaluation of polynomials. *IEEE Trans. Comput.* C-22:2–5.

[McV87] McBryan, O. A., and E. F. Van de Velde. 1987. Hypercube algorithms and implementations. *SiAM J. Sci. Stat. Comput.* 8:s227–87.

[McW77] McQuillan, J. M., and D. C. Walden. 1977. The ARPANET design decisions. *Computer Networks.* 1:243–89.

[MeC80] Mead, C., and L. Conway. 1980. *Introduction to VLSI Systems.* Reading, MA: Addison-Wesley.

[MeZ88] Meyer, R. R., and S. A. Zenios (eds.). 1988. *Parallel Optimization on Novel Computer Architectures, Annals of Operations Research.* Bazel, Switzerland: A. C. Baltzer.

[MiC82] Misra, J., and K. M. Chandy. 1982. Termination detection of diffusing computations in communicating sequential processes. *ACM Trans. Prog. Lang. & Sys.* 4:37.

[MiC87] Mitra, D., and R. A. Cieslak. 1987. Randomized parallel communications on an extension of the Omega network. *J. ACM.* 34:802–24.

[Mie75] Miellou, J. C. 1975. Algorithmes de relaxation chaotique a retards. *R.A.I.R.O.* 9:55–82.

[MiM84] Mitra, D., and I. Mitrani. 1984. Analysis and optimum performance of two message-passing parallel processors synchronized by rollback. In E. Gelenbe (ed.), *Performance '84*, 35–50. New York: Elsevier.

[Min78] Minieka, E. 1978. *Optimization Algorithms for Networks and Graphs.* New York: Marcel Dekker.

[MiR85] Miller, G. L., and J. Reif. 1985. Parallel tree contraction and its applications. *Proc. 26th Annual Symp. Found. Comput. Sci.*, 478–89.

[MiS85] Miellou, J. C., and P. Spiteri. 1985. Un critere de convergence pour des methodes generales de point fixe. *Math. Modelling & Numer. Analy.* 19:645–69.

[Mis86] Misra, J. 1986. Distributed discrete-event simulation. *Comput. Surv.* 18:39–65.

[Mit87] Mitra, D. 1987. Asynchronous relaxations for the numerical solution of differential equations by parallel processors. *SiAM J. Sci. Stat. Comput.* 8:s43–58.

[MMT70] Mesarovic, M. D., D. Macko, and Y. Takahara. 1970. *Theory of Hierarchical Multilevel Systems.* New York: Academic Press.

[Mor65] Moreau, J. J. 1965. Proximite et dualite dans un espace Hilbertien. *Bull. Soc. Math. France.* 93:273–99.

[MoS54] Motzkin, T. S., and I. J. Schoenberg. 1954. The relaxation method for linear inequalities. *Can. J. Math.* 6:393–404.

[MRR80] McQuillan, J. M., I. Richer, and E. C. Rosen. 1980. The new routing algorithm for the ARPANET. *IEEE Trans. Commun.* COM-28:711–19.

[Mul78] Mulvey, J. M. 1978. Testing of a large-scale network optimization program. *Math. Prog.* 15:291–314.

[MuP73] Munro, I., and M. Paterson. 1973. Optimal algorithms for parallel polynomial evaluation. *J. Comput. & Sys. Sci.* 7:189–98.

[MuP76] Muller, D. E., and F. P. Preparata. 1976. Restructuring of arithmetic expressions for parallel evaluation. *J. ACM.* 23:534–43.

[Nag87] Nagurney, A. 1987. Competitive equilibrium problems, variational inequalities and regional science. *J. Reg. Sci.* 27:503–17.

[NaS80] Nassimi, D., and S. Sahni. 1980. An optimal routing algorithm for mesh-connected parallel computers. *J. ACM.* 27:6–29.

[Nem66] Nemhauser, G. L. 1966. *Introduction to Dynamic Programming.* New York: Wiley.

[NeS83] Newton, A. R., and A. L. Sangiovanni-Vincentelli. 1983. Relaxation-based electrical simulation. *IEEE Trans. Electron. Devices.* ED-30:1184–1207.

[OhK84] Ohuchi, A., and I. Kaji. 1984. Lagrangian dual coordinatewise maximization algorithm for network transportation problems with quadratic costs. *Networks.* 14:515–30.

[OLR85] O'hEigeartaigh, M., S. K. Lenstra, and A. H. G. Rinnoy Kan (eds.). 1985. *Combinatorial Optimization: Annotated Bibliographies.* New York: Wiley.

[Orc74] Orcutt, S. E., Jr. 1974. Computer organization and algorithms for very high-speed computations. PhD Thesis, Dept. of Electrical Engineering, Stanford University, Stanford, CA.

[OrR70] Ortega, J. M., and W. C. Rheinboldt. 1970. *Iterative Solution of Nonlinear Equations in Several Variables.* New York: Academic Press.

[OrV85] Ortega, J. M., and R. G. Voigt. 1985. Solution of partial differential equations on vector and parallel computers. *SiAM Rev.* 27:149–240.

[Ozv87] Ozveren, C. 1987. Communication aspects of parallel processing. Laboratory for Information and Decision systems Report LIDS-P-1721, Massachusetts Institute of Technology, Cambridge.

[PaC82a] Pang, J. S., and D. Chan. 1982. Gauss-Seidel methods for variational inequality problems over product sets. Unpublished manuscript. School of Management, University of Texas-Dallas.

[PaC82b] Pang, J. S., and D. Chan. 1982. Iterative methods for variational and complementarity problems. *Math. Prog.* 24:284–313.

[Pan85] Pang, J. S. 1985. Asymmetric variational inequality problems over product sets: Applications and iterative methods. *Math. Prog.* 31:206–19.

[PaR85] Pan, V., and J. Reif. 1985. Efficient parallel solution of linear systems. *Proc. 17th ACM STOC.*, 143–52.

[PaS82] Papadimitriou, C. H., and K. Steiglitz. 1982. *Combinatorial Optimization: Algorithms and Complexity.* Englewood Cliffs, NJ: Prentice-Hall.

[PaT87a] Papadimitriou, C. H., and J. N. Tsitsiklis. 1987. Unpublished research.

[PaT87b] Papadimitriou, C. H., and J. N. Tsitsiklis. 1987. The complexity of Markov decision processes. *Math. Oper. Res.* 12:441–50.

[PaY88] Papadimitriou, C. H., and M. Yannakakis. 1988. Towards an architecture-independent analysis of parallel algorithms. *Proc. 20th ACM STOC.* 510–3.

[Pea84] Pearl, J. 1984. *Heuristics.* Reading, MA: Addison-Wesley.

[Per83] Perlman, R. 1983. Fault-tolerant broadcast of routing information. *Comput. Netw.* 7:395–405.

[Pet88] Peters, J. 1988. A parallel algorithm for minimal cost network flow problems. Computer Sciences Dept., Technical Report 762, University of Wisconsin-Madison.

[Pol69] Poljak, B. T. 1969. Minimization of unsmooth functionals. *USSR Comput. Math. Phys.* 9:14–29.

[Pol71] Polak, E. 1971. *Computational Methods in Optimization: A Unified Approach.* New York: Academic Press.

[Pol87] Poljak, B. T. 1987. *Introduction to Optimization.* New York: Optimization Software.

[PoT73] Poljak, B. T., and Y. Z. Tsypkin. 1973. Pseudogradient adaptation and training algorithms. *Auto. & Rem. Contr.* 12:83–94.

[PoT74] Poljak, B. T., and N. V. Tretjakov. 1974. An iterative method for linear programming and its economic interpretation. *Matecon.* 10:81–100.

[Pow69] Powell, M. J. D. 1969. A method for nonlinear constraints in minimization problems. In R. Fletcher (ed.), *Optimization*, 283–98. New York: Academic Press.

[Pow73] Powell, M. J. D. 1973. On search directions for minimization algorithms. *Math. Prog.* 4:193–201.

[PrS78] Preparata, F. P., and D. V. Sarwate. 1978. An improved parallel processor bound in fast matrix inversion. *Inf. Proc. Lett.* 7:148–9.

[QuD84] Quinn, M. J., and N. Deo. 1984. Parallel graph algorithms. *Comput. Surv.* 16:338–48.

[Qui87] Quinn, M. J. 1987. *Designing Efficient Algorithms for Parallel Computers.* New York: McGraw-Hill.

[RaK88] Rao, S. K., and T. Kailath. 1988. Regular iterative algorithms and their implementation on processor arrays. *Proc. IEEE.* 76:259–69.

[RAP87] Reed, D. A., L. M. Adams, and M. L. Patrick. 1987. Stencils and problem partitionings: Their influence on the performance of multiple processor systems. *IEEE Trans. Comput.* C-36:845–58.

[RCM75] Robert, F., M. Charnay, and F. Musy. 1975. Iterations chaotiques serie-parallele pour des equations non-lineaires de point fixe. *Aplikace Mat.* 20:1–38.

[Rib87] Ribeiro, C. C. 1987. Parallel computer models and combinatorial algorithms. *Ann. Disc. Math.* 31:325–64.

[Rob76] Robert, F. 1976. Contraction en norme vectorielle: Convergence d'iterations chaotiques pour des equations non lineaires de point fixe a plusieurs variables. *Lin. Algeb. & Appl.* 13:19–35.

[Roc70] Rockafellar, R. T. 1970. *Convex Analysis.* Princeton, NJ: Princeton University Press.

[Roc71] Rockafellar, R. T. 1971. New applications of duality in convex programming. *Proc. 4th Conf. Prob.*, 73–81.

[Roc76a] Rockafellar, R. T. 1976. Monotone operators and the proximal point algorithm. *SiAM J. Contr. & Optim.* 14:877–98.

[Roc76b] Rockafellar, R. T. 1976. Augmented Lagrangians and applications of the proximal point algorithm in convex programming. *Math. Oper. Res.* 1:97–116.

[Roc76c] Rockafellar, R. T. 1976. Solving a nonlinear programming problem by way of a dual problem. *Symp. Mat.* 27:135–60.

[Roc80] Rock, H. 1980. Scaling techniques for minimal cost network flows. In V. Page (ed.), *Discrete Structures and Algorithms.* Munich: Carl Hansen. 181–91

[Roc84] Rockafellar, R. T. 1984. *Network Flows and Monotropic Programming.* New York: Wiley.

[RoM51] Robbins, H., and S. Monro. 1951. A stochastic approximation method. *Ann. Math. Stat.* 22:400–7.

[Ros83a] Ross, S. 1983. *Stochastic Processes.* New York: Wiley.

[Ros83b] Ross, S. 1983. *Introduction to Dynamic Programming.* New York: Academic Press.

[RoW87] Rockafellar, R. T., and R. J.-B. Wets. 1987. Scenarios and policy aggregation in optimization under uncertainty. International Institute of Systems Analysis, Working Paper WP-87-119, Laxenburg, Austria.

[Rud76] Rudin, W. 1976. *Real Analysis.* New York: McGraw-Hill.

[Saa86] Saad, Y. 1986. Communication complexity of the Gaussian elimination algorithm on multiprocessors. *Lin. Algeb. & Appl.* 77:315–40.

[SaK77] Sameh, A. H., and D. J. Kuck. 1977. A parallel QR algorithm for symmetric tridiagonal matrices. *IEEE Trans. Comput.* C-26:147–53.

[SaK78] Sameh, A. H., and D. J. Kuck. 1978. On stable parallel linear solvers. *J. ACM.* 25:81–91.

[Sam77] Sameh, A. H. 1977. Numerical parallel algorithms: A survey. In D. J. Kuck, D. H. Lawrie, and A. H. Sameh (eds.), *High Speed Computer and Algorithm Organization,* 207–28. New York: Academic Press.

[Sam81] Sameh, A. H. 1981. Parallel algorithms in numerical linear algebra. Paper presented at the CREST Conference on the Design of Numerical Algorithms for Parallel Processing, Bergamo, Italy.

[Sam85a] Sameh, A. H. 1985. On some parallel algorithms on a ring of processors. *Comput. Phys. Commun.* 37:159–66.

[Sam85b] Samadi, B. 1985. Distributed simulation: Algorithms and performance analysis. PhD dissertation. Computer Science Dept., UCLA.

[San88] Sanders, B. A. 1988. An asynchronous distributed flow control algorithm for rate allocation in computer networks. *IEEE Trans. Comput.* 37:779–87.

[SaS85] Saad, Y., and M. H. Schultz. 1985. Data communication in hypercubes. Dept. of Computer Sciences, Research Report YALEU/DCS/RR-428, Yale University, New Haven, CT.

[SaS86] Saad, Y., and M. H. Schultz. 1986. Data communication in parallel architectures. Dept. of Computer Sciences, Research Report, Yale University, New Haven, CT.

[SaS87] Saad, Y., and M. H. Schultz. 1987. Parallel direct methods for solving banded linear systems. *Lin. Algeb. & Appl.* 88/89:623–50.

[SaS88] Saad, Y., and M. H. Schultz. 1988. Topological properties of hypercubes. *IEEE Trans. Comput.* 37:867–72.

[Sch80] Schwartz, J. T. 1980. Ultracomputers. *ACM Trans. Prog. Lang. & Sys.* 2:484–521.

[Sch84] Schendel, U. 1984. *Introduction to Numerical Methods for Parallel Computers.* Chichester, England: Ellis Horwood.

[Sch87] Schwartz, M. 1987. *Telecommunication Networks.* Reading, MA: Addison-Wesley.

[ScS80] Schwartz, M., and T. E. Stern. 1980. Routing techniques used in computer communication networks. *IEEE Trans. Commun.* COM-28:539–52.

[ScV82] Schiloach, Y., and V. Vishkin. 1982. An $O(n^2 \log n)$ parallel max-flow algorithm. *J. Algor.* 3:128–46.

[Seg83] Segall, A. 1983. Distributed network protocols. *IEEE Trans. Inf. Theory.* IT-29:23–35.

[Sen81] Seneta, E. 1981. *Non-Negative Matrices and Markov Chains.* New York: Springer-Verlag.

[Sha79] Shapiro, J. F. 1979. *Mathematical Programming.* New York: Wiley.

[Sib70] Sibony, M. 1970. Methodes iteratives pour les equations et inequations aux derivees partielles nonlineaires de type monotone. *Calcolo.* 7:65–183.

[Sin77] Singh, M. G. 1977. *Dynamical Hierarchical Control.* Amsterdam: North-Holland.

[SMG78] Segall, A., P. M. Merlin, and R. G. Gallager. 1978. A recoverable protocol for loop-free distributed routing. *Proc. ICC.*

[SpG87] Spinelli, J. M., and R. G. Gallager. 1987. Broadcasting topology information in computer networks. Laboratory for Information and Decision Systems Report LIDS-P-1543, Massachusetts Institute of Technology, Cambridge.

[Spi84] Spiteri, P. 1984. Contribution a l'etude de grands systemes non lineaires. Doctoral thesis. L'Universite de Franche-Comte, Besancon, France.

[Spi85a] Spingarn, J. E. 1985. A primal-dual projection method for solving systems of linear inequalities. *Lin. Algeb. & Appl.* 65:45–62.

[Spi85b] Spingarn, J. E. 1985. Applications of the method of partial inverses to convex programming: Decomposition. *Math. Prog.* 32:199–223.

[Spi85c] Spinelli, J. M. 1985. Broadcasting topology and routing information in computer networks. Laboratory for Information and Decision Systems Report LIDS-TH-1470, Massachusetts Institute of Technology, Cambridge.

[Spi86] Spiteri, P. 1986. Parallel asynchronous algorithms for solving boundary value problems. In M. Cosnard et al. (eds.) *Parallel Algorithms and Architectures.* 73–84. New York: Elsevier.

[Spi87] Spingarn, J. E. 1987. A projection method for least-squares solutions to overdetermined systems of linear inequalities. *Lin. Algeb. & Appl.* 86:211–36.

[SSP85] Szymanski, B., Y. Shi, and N. Prywes. 1985. Terminating iterative solution of simultaneous equations in distributed message passing systems. *J. ACM.* 32:287–92.

[Sta85] Stallings, W., 1985. *Data and Computer Communications.* New York: Macmillan.

[Sta87] Stallings, W. 1987. *Local Networks.* New York: Macmillan.

[Ste73] Stewart, G. W. 1973. *Introduction to Matrix Computations.* New York: Academic Press.

[Ste77] Stern, T. E. 1977. A class of decentralized routing algorithms using relaxation. *IEEE Trans. Commun.* COM-25:1092–1102.

[Sto75] Stone, H. S. 1975. Parallel tridiagonal equation solvers. *ACM Trans. Math. Software.* 1:289–307.

[Sto77] Stoilow, E. 1977. The augmented Lagrangian method in two-level static optimization. *Arch. Auto. Telemech.* 22:219–37.

[Str76] Strang, G. 1976. *Linear Algebra and Its Applications.* New York: Academic Press.

[StW70] Stoer, J., and C. Witzgall. 1970. *Convexity and Optimization in Finite Dimensions I.* New York: Springer-Verlag.

[StW75] Stephanopoulos, G., and A. W. Westerberg. 1975. The use of Hestenes' method of multipliers to resolve dual gaps in engineering system optimization. *JOTA*. 15:285–309.

[Sut83] Sutti, C. 1983. Nongradient minimization methods for parallel processing computers. *JOTA*. 39:465–488.

[Taj77] Tajibnapis, W. D. 1977. A correctness proof of a topology information maintenance protocol for a distributed computer network. *Commun. ACM*. 20:477–85.

[TaM85] Tanikawa, A., and H. Mukai. 1985. A new technique for nonconvex primal-dual decomposition of a large-scale separable optimization problem. *IEEE Trans. Auto. Contr.* AC-30:133–43.

[Tan71] Tanabe, K. 1971. Projection method for solving a singular system of linear equations and its applications. *Numer. Math.* 17:203–14.

[Tan81] Tanenbaum, A. S. 1981. *Computer Networks*. Englewood Cliffs, NJ: Prentice-Hall.

[Tar85] Tardos, E. 1985. A strongly polynomial minimum cost circulation algorithm. *Combinatorica*. 5:247–55.

[TBA86] Tsitsiklis, J. N., D. P. Bertsekas, and M. Athans. 1986. Distributed asynchronous deterministic and stochastic gradient optimization algorithms. *IEEE Trans. Auto. Contr.* AC-31:803–12.

[TBT88] Tseng, P., D. P. Bertsekas, and J. N. Tsitsiklis. 1988. Partially Asynchronous Parallel Algorithms for Network Flow and Other Problems. Laboratory for Information and Decision Systems Unpublished Report, Massachusetts Institute of Technology, Cambridge.

[Tho87] Thompson, K. M. 1987. A two-stage successive overrelaxation algorithm for solving the linear complementarity problem. Computer Sciences Dept., Technical Report 706, University of Wisconsin-Madison.

[Top85] Topkis, D. M. 1985. Concurrent broadcast for information dissemination. *IEEE Trans. Software Eng.* 13:207–31.

[Top87] Topkis, D. M. 1987. All-to-all broadcast by flooding in communications networks. Graduate School of Management, University of California-Davis. To appear in *IEEE Trans. Comput.*

[TsA84] Tsitsiklis, J. N., and M. Athans. 1984. Convergence and asymptotic agreement in distributed decision problems. *IEEE Trans. Auto. Contr.* AC-29:42–50.

[Tsa86] Tsai, W. K. 1986. Optimal quasi-static routing for virtual circuit networks subjected to stochastic inputs. PhD thesis. Dept. of Electrical Engineering and Computer Science, Massachusetts Institute of Technology, Cambridge.

[TsB86] Tsitsiklis, J. N., and D. P. Bertsekas. 1986. Distributed asynchronous optimal routing in data networks. *IEEE Trans. Auto. Contr.* AC-31:325–32.

[TsB87a] Tseng, P., and D. P. Bertsekas. 1987. Relaxation methods for problems with strictly convex separable costs and linear constraints. *Math. Prog.* 38:303–21.

[TsB87b] Tseng, P., and D. P. Bertsekas. 1987. Relaxation methods for linear programs. *Math. Oper. Res.* 12:569–96.

[TsB87c] Tseng, P., and D. P. Bertsekas. 1987. Relaxation methods for monotropic programs. Laboratory for Information and Decision Systems Report LIDS-P-1697, Massachusetts Institute of Technology, Cambridge. To appear in *Math. Prog.*

[Tse85] Tseng, P. 1985. The relaxation method for a special class of linear programming problems. Laboratory for Information and Decision Systems Report LIDS-P-1467, Massachusets Institute of Technology, Cambridge.

[Tse86] Tseng, P. 1986. Relaxation methods for monotropic programming problems. PhD thesis. Dept. of Electrical Eng. and Comp. Science, Massachusetts Institute of Technology, Cambridge.

[Tse87] Tseng, P. 1987. Private communication.

[Tse88] Tseng, P. 1988. Private communication.

[Tsi84] Tsitsiklis, J. N. 1984. Problems in decentralized decision making and computation. PhD thesis. Dept. of Electrical Engineering and Computer Science, Massachusetts Institute of Technology, Cambridge.

[Tsi87] Tsitsiklis, J. N. 1987. On the stability of asynchronous iterative processes. *Math. Sys. Theory.* 20:137–53.

[TTB86] Tsai, W. K., J. N. Tsitsiklis, and D. P. Bertsekas. 1986. Some issues in distributed asynchronous routing in virtual circuit data networks. *Proc. 25th Conf. Dec. & Contr.*, 1335–7.

[Ull84] Ullman, J. D. 1984. *Computational Aspects of VLSI.* Rockeville, MD: Computer Science Press.

[UrD86] Uresin, A., and M. Dubois. 1986. Generalized asynchronous iterations. *Proc. Conf. Algor. & Hardware Parallel Proc.*

[UrD88a] Uresin, A., and M. Dubois. 1988. Sufficient conditions for the convergence of asynchronous iterations. Computer Research Institute, Technical Report, University of Southern California-Los Angeles. To appear in *Parallel Comput.*

[UrD88b] Uresin, A., and M. Dubois. 1988. Parallel asynchronous algorithms for discrete data. Computer Research Institute, Technical Report CRI-88-05, University of Southern California-Los Angeles.

[VaB81] Valiant, L. G., and G. J. Brebner, 1981. Universal schemes for parallel communication. *Proc. 13th Annual ACM STOC.*, 263–77.

[Val82] Valiant, L. G. 1982. A scheme for fast parallel communication. *SiAM J. Comput.* Vol. 11:350–61.

[Var62] Varga, R. S. 1962. *Matrix Iterative Methods.* Englewood Cliffs, NJ: Prentice-Hall.

[VeP87] Verdu, S., and V. Poor. 1987. Abstract dynamic programming models under commutativity conditions. *SiAM J. Contr. & Optim.* 25:990–1006.

[Ver87] Verjus, J. P. 1987. On the proof of a distributed algorithm. *Inf. Proc. Lett.* 25:145–7.

[Vid78] Vidyasagar, M. 1978. *Nonlinear Systems Analysis.* Englewood Cliffs, NJ: Prentice-Hall.

[Whi82] Whittle, P. 1982. *Optimization Over Time*, Volume 1. New York: Wiley.

[Whi83] Whittle, P. 1983. *Optimization Over Time*, Volume 2. New York: Wiley.

[WiH80] Wing, O., and S. W. Huang. 1980. A computation model of parallel solution of linear equations. *IEEE Trans. Comput.* C-29:632–7.

[Wis71] Wismer, D. A., (ed.). 1971. *Optimization Methods for Large-Scale Systems with Applications*. New York: McGraw-Hill.

[WNM78] Watanabe, N., Y. Nishimura, and M. Matsubara. 1978. Decomposition in large system optimization using the method of multipliers. *JOTA.* 25:181–93.

[WoH85] Wong, E., and B. Hajek. 1985. *Stochastic Processes in Engineering Systems*. New York: Springer-Verlag.

[WuF84] Wu, C.-L., and T.-Y. Feng (eds.). 1984. *Interconnection Networks for Parallel and Distributed Processing*. New York: IEEE Computer Society Press.

[You71] Young, D. M. 1971. *Iterative Solution of Large Linear Systems*. New York: Academic Press.

[Zan69] Zangwill, W. I. 1969. *Nonlinear Programming: A Unified Approach*. Englewood Cliffs, NJ: Prentice-Hall.

[ZeL87] Zenios, S. A., and R. A. Lasken, 1987. Nonlinear network optimization on a massively parallel connection machine. Decision Sciences Dept., Report 87-08-03, The Wharton School, University of Pennsylvania, Philadelphia. To appear in *Ann. Oper. Res.*

[ZeM86] Zenios, S. A., and J. M. Mulvey. 1986. Relaxation techniques for strictly convex network problems. In C. L. Monma (ed.), *Algorithms and Software for Optimization, Annals of Operations Research*, Volume 5, Bazel, Switzerland: A. C. Baltzer.

[Zou76] Zoutendijk, G. 1976. *Mathematical Programming Methods*. Amsterdam: North-Holland.

Index